Beyond Our Borders

Linking the Law to . . .

Fourth Edition

Essentials of the Legal Environment

Roger LeRoy Miller
Institute for University Studies
Arlington, Texas

(John Elk III/Lonely Planet Images/Getty Images)

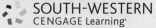

SOUTH-WESTERN
CENGAGE Learning

Australia • Brazil • Japan • Korea • Mexico • Singapore • Spain • United Kingdom • United States

SOUTH-WESTERN
CENGAGE Learning·

Essentials of the Legal Environment

FOURTH EDITION

Roger LeRoy Miller

Vice President and Editorial Director:
Jack Calhoun

Editor-in-Chief:
Rob Dewey

Senior Acquisitions Editor:
Vicky True-Baker

Senior Developmental Editor:
Jan Lamar

Director, Market Development Manager:
Lisa L. Lysne

Senior Brand Manager:
Kristen Hurd

Senior Marketing Communications Manager:
Sarah Greber

Production Manager:
Bill Stryker

Technology Project Manager:
Kristen Meere

Manufacturing Planner:
Kevin Kluck

Editorial Assistant:
Tristann Jones

Compositor:
Parkwood Composition Service

Senior Art Director:
Michelle Kunkler

Indexer:
Stephanie Reymann, Indexing Solutions

Internal Designer:
Bill Stryker

Cover Designer:
Rose Alcorn

Cover Images:
© Olaru Radian-Alexandru/Shutterstock.com
© DNK59/iStockphoto

For product information and technology assistance, contact us at
Cengage Learning Academic Resource Center
1-800-423-0563

For permission to use material from this text or product,
submit all requests online at
www.cengage.com/permissions.

Further permissions questions can be emailed to
permissionrequest@cengage.com.

ExamView® and ExamView Pro® are registered trademarks of FSCreations, Inc. Windows is a registered trademark of the Microsoft Corporation used herein under license. Macintosh and Power Macintosh are registered trademarks of Apple Computer, Inc., used herein under license.

Library of Congress Control Number: 2012949515

Instructor's Edition:
ISBN-13: 978-1-285-07905-9
ISBN-10: 1-285-07905-1

Student Edition:
ISBN-13: 978-1-133-58654-8
ISBN-10: 1-133-58654-6

South-Western, Cengage Learning
5191 Natorp Blvd.
Mason, OH 45040
USA

Cengage Learning products are represented in Canada by Nelson Education, Ltd.

For your course and learning solutions, visit **www.cengage.com.**

Purchase any of our products at your local college store or at our preferred online store at **www.cengagebrain.com.**

Printed in Canada
1 2 3 4 5 6 7 16 15 14 13 12

Contents in Brief

Contents

Unit Three

The Commercial
Environment 229

▶ Unit Four

The Employment Environment 399

Unit Five

The Regulatory Environment 459

▶ *Appendices*

Preface to the Instructor

It is no exaggeration to say that today's legal environment is changing at a pace never before experienced. In many instances, technology is both driving and facilitating this change. The expanded use of the Internet for both business and personal trans-actions has led to new ways of doing business and, consequently, to a changing legal environment for the twenty-first century. Other factors that have affected the legal environment include the recent economic recession and our nation's ongoing strug-gle to regain financial stability, combat joblessness, and reduce the national debt. In the midst of this evolving environment, however, one thing remains certain: for those entering the business world, an awareness of the legal and regulatory environment of business is critical.

The Fourth Edition of *Essentials of the Legal Environment* is designed to bring this awareness to your students. They will learn not only about the traditional legal envi-ronment but also about some of the most significant recent developments in the e-commerce environment. They will also be motivated to learn through our use of high-interest pedagogical features that explore real-life situations and legal challenges facing businesspersons and consumers. I believe that teaching the legal environment can be enjoyable and so, too, can learning about it.

▶ What's New in the Fourth Edition

Instructors have come to rely on the coverage, accuracy, and applicability of *Essentials of the Legal Environment*. To ensure that this text engages your students' interest, solidifies their understanding of the legal concepts presented, and provides the best teaching tools available, I have added several new elements to this edition. These new items are discussed in detail next.

In addition to the elements discussed on the following pages, you will find that every chapter in the Fourth Edition now includes the following exciting new changes:

- *A fresh four-color design* gives the text a dynamic feel and look.
- *New page cross-references "(See page 00.)"* have been inserted at the end of every *Issue Spotter* and every *Question and Case Problem* at the end of the chapters. This student-friendly study aid will help students easily locate the details needed to understand and answer the questions and problems.
- *Learning Objectives are now placed in the margins* next to the sections where the information to answer the *Learning Objectives* can be found.
- *New "Debate This" feature* that sparks in-class discussion or can be used as homework.
- *A new Key Terms section* for easy reference.
- *Condensed, easier-to-read margin definitions.*
- *Exhibits and margin quotations.*

New Chapter: *Mortgages and Foreclosures after the Recession*

For the Fourth Edition, I have included an entirely new chapter (Chapter 15) entitled ***Mortgages and Foreclosures after the Recession***. This chapter examines some of the mortgage-lending practices that contributed to the Great Recession and discusses the legal reforms enacted in response to it.

New *Spotlight Cases* and *Spotlight Case Problems*

For the Fourth Edition of *Essentials of the Legal Environment,* certain cases and case problems have been carefully chosen to spotlight as good teaching cases. **Spotlight Cases** and **Spotlight Case Problems** are labeled either by the name of one of the parties or by the subject involved. Some examples include *Spotlight on Amazon.com, Spotlight on Apple, Spotlight on the Seattle Mariners,* and *Spotlight on Commercial Speech.*

You will find these *Spotlight* decisions useful to illustrate the legal concepts under discussion, and students will enjoy studying these cases because they involve interesting and memorable facts.

New Highlighted and Numbered Case Examples

One of the more appreciated features of *Essentials of the Legal Environment* has always been the highlighted numbered examples in each chapter that clarify legal principles for students. Because many instructors use cases to illustrate how the law applies to business, for this edition, rather than presenting more excerpted cases in each chapter, I have expanded the in-text numbered examples to include **new Case Examples.**

These *Case Examples* are integrated appropriately throughout the text and present the facts, issues, and rulings from actual court cases. Students can quickly read through the *Case Examples* to see how courts apply the legal principles under discussion in the real world.

New Cases and Case Problems

The Fourth Edition of *Essentials of the Legal Environment* is filled with new cases and problems. I have included new cases from 2010, 2011, and 2012 in nearly every chapter. That means more than 85 percent of the cases are new to this edition. I have carefully selected the new cases using the following criteria:

1. They illustrate important points of law.
2. They are of high interest to students and instructors.
3. They are simple enough factually for legal environment students to understand.

I have also made it a point to find recent cases that enhance learning. As a result, I have also eliminated cases that are too difficult procedurally or factually.

New *Shifting Legal Priorities for Business* Features

This edition includes **a new feature entitled** *Shifting Legal Priorities for Business* that shows students how legal priorities are changing in the business world. Special emphasis is given to sustainability, ethical trends, and changing managerial responsibilities. Each discussion ends with a short section entitled **Managerial Implications** that points out why the changing priorities examined are significant to businesspersons.

Topics examined include the following:

- Sustainability and the Law (Chapter 1)
- Corporate Social Responsibility and "Out-Behaving" the Competition (Chapter 3)
- Prosecuting White-Collar Crime with the Honest-Services Fraud Law (Chapter 7)
- The National Export Initiative (Chapter 8)

New *Linking the Law to . . .* Features

Another **special new feature entitled** *Linking the Law to . . .* [**Accounting, Economics, Management, Marketing, or Taxation**] has been added to this edition. The ***Linking the Law to . . .*** feature appears in selected chapters to underscore how the law relates to various other disciplines in the typical business school curriculum. It not only enables instructors to meet AACSB teaching requirements but also provides vital and practical information to students on how the subjects they study are interconnected.

Some examples of the *Linking the Law to . . .* feature include:

- *Linking the Law to Management:* Dealing with Administrative Law (Chapter 5)
- *Linking the Law to Management:* Quality Control (Chapter 6)
- *Linking the Law to Marketing:* Trademarks and Service Marks (Chapter 8)
- *Linking the Law to Marketing:* Going Global (Chapter 9)
- *Linking the Law to Business Communications:* When E-Mails Become Enforceable Contracts (Chapter 12)

New Coverage of Contemporary Topics

To pique student interest from the outset, many chapters open with the latest news surrounding the legal topics under discussion. A section of text within that chapter further explores the topic.

For example, Chapter 8 discusses the patent infringement lawsuit filed by Apple, Inc., against Samsung for too closely imitating the iPhone and iPad. Chapter 15 discusses the settlement paid by Bank of America in 2011 for fraud relating to mortgage securities. The employment and labor law chapter (Chapter 16) includes a discussion of the recent NFL lockout, and Chapter 17 discusses the United States Supreme Court's 2011 decision in a gender-discrimination case against Walmart.

New Appendices

For quick and easy reference, and to help students study the legal concepts featured throughout this text, I have added five new appendices to this Fourth Edition of *Essentials of the Legal Environment.* They include:

- Appendix A—How to Brief Cases and Analyze Case Problems
- Appendix D—Answers to *Issue Spotters*
- Appendix E—Answers to the Even-Numbered *For Review* Questions
- Appendix F—Sample Answers to *Questions with Sample Answer*
- Appendix G—Sample Answers to *Case Problems with Sample Answer*

▶ Critical-Thinking Pedagogy

Today's business leaders are often required to think "outside the box" when making business decisions. For this reason, I have included a number of critical-thinking elements to the Fourth Edition that are designed to challenge students' understanding of the materials beyond simple retention. Your students' critical-thinking and legal-reasoning skills will increase as they work through the following pedagogical devices within the book:

- **Case-ending questions**—Many of the cases presented in the text conclude with a critical-thinking *Dimension Question* that raises a question about some aspect of the case for students to consider. Other cases conclude with a *What If the Facts Were Different?* question that requires students to analyze how the outcome of the case might be altered if the facts were different.

There is a special new item of case pedagogy for this edition. At the end of selected cases that have particular importance for business managers, I have included a new section entitled **Managerial Implications.** These sections point out the significance of the court's ruling in the case for business owners and managers.

- *Critical-Thinking Legal [Managerial or Technological] Questions*—These questions appear in nearly all of the chapters in the *Questions and Case Problems* section. They ask students to think critically about a specific hypothetical situation and how the law covered in the chapter should apply to that situation.
- **Feature-ending questions**—Concluding each of the features entitled *Linking the Law to . . .* , *Online Developments*, and *Beyond Our Borders* is a *For Critical Analysis* section that asks students to explore some of the implications or consequences of the court decision or topic discussed in the feature.
- *In Your Court* **case problems**—Several chapters provide this special case problem that challenges students to place themselves as the judge in the case described. Students must research the points of law relevant to the scenario and then reason why they came to their decision in the case.

Suggested answers to all critical-thinking questions can be found in both the *Instructor's Manual* and the *Answers Manual* that accompany this text on the IRCD.

▶ Additional Special Features in This Text

This edition of *Essentials of the Legal Environment* retains a number of pedagogical devices and special features from previous editions, including those discussed here.

Online Developments

The Fourth Edition contains many new *Online Developments* features, which examine cutting-edge cyberlaw issues coming before today's courts. Here are some examples:

- Raunchy Facebook Photos Receive First Amendment Protection (Chapter 4)
- Facebook Uses Privacy Concerns to Smear Google (Chapter 6)
- The Validity of E-Signatures and Online University Enrollment Agreements (Chapter 11)
- Live Chatting with Your State's Bankruptcy Court (Chapter 14)

Ethical Issues

This text also includes special features called **Ethical Issues.** These features, which are closely integrated with the text, open with a question addressing an ethical dimension of the topic being discussed. They are intended to make sure that students understand that ethics is a critical part of a business law course. **Nearly every *Ethical Issue* feature is new to this edition.**

Some of the timely topics addressed in these features include the following:

- Does the Threat of Terrorism Justify the U.S. Government's Use of Full-Body Scanners at Airports? (Chapter 4)
- Should the Police Be Able to Use High-Tech Tracking Devices at Will? (Chapter 7)
- Is It Appropriate to Use the Latest Global Economic Crisis as a Reason to Escape Contractual Obligations? (Chapter 13)

- Should Shareholders Have More Control over Corporate Officers' Compensation? (Chapter 20)

Beyond Our Borders

Beyond Our Borders features give students an awareness of the global legal environment by indicating how international laws or the laws of other nations deal with specific legal concepts or topics being discussed in the chapter.

For example, *Beyond Our Borders* features discuss Islamic law courts (Chapter 2), smartphone use and overtime pay requirements (Chapter 16), sexual harassment (Chapter 17), and corporate governance (Chapter 20).

Reviewing . . . Features

The Fourth Edition continues to offer a *Reviewing . . .* feature at the end of every chapter to help solidify students' understanding of the chapter materials. Each *Reviewing . . .* feature presents a hypothetical scenario and then asks a series of questions that require students to identify the issues and apply the legal concepts discussed in the chapter.

You can use these features as the basis for in-class discussion, or you can encourage students to use them for self-study prior to completing homework assignments.

▶ Essentials of the Legal Environment on the Web

The Web site for the Fourth Edition of *Essentials of the Legal Environment* can be found by going to **www.cengagebrain.com** and entering ISBN 9781133586548. The Web site offers an array of teaching/learning resources, including the following:

- *Practice quizzes* for every chapter in this text.
- *Appendix A: How to Brief Cases and Analyze Case Problems,* which is also available at the end of this text.
- *Legal reference materials,* including a "Statutes" page that offers links to the full text of selected statutes referenced in the text and a Spanish Glossary.
- *CourseMate,* which students can purchase, provides access to additional study tools—such as an e-book, additional quizzes, flashcards, *Key Terms,* and PowerPoint slides. For a demonstration of *CourseMate,* please visit **www.cengage.com/coursemate** or contact your sales representative.

CourseMate

▶ Supplemental Teaching Materials

This edition of *Essentials of the Legal Environment* is accompanied by a number of teaching and learning supplements, including those listed next. For further information on the items contained in the teaching/learning package, contact your local sales representative or visit the Web site that accompanies this text at **www.cengagebrain.com**.

Instructor's Resource CD-ROM (IRCD)

The IRDC includes the following:

- *Instructor's Manual*—Each chapter of the *Instructor's Manual* contains teaching suggestions, possible discussion questions, and additional information on key statutes or other legal sources that you may wish to use in your classroom. It also includes **additional cases on point** with at least one such case summary per chapter, answers to all *For Critical Analysis* questions in the features and all case-ending questions, and answers for the *Issue Spotters.*

In addition, the IRCD also contains the following teaching supplements:

- *ExamView.*
- *PowerPoint* slides.
- *Answers Manual*—Includes answers to the *Questions and Case Problems,* answers to the *For Critical Analysis* questions in the features and all case-ending questions, plus answers for the *Issue Spotters.*
- A comprehensive *Test Bank.*
- *Instructor's Manual* for the *Drama of the Law* video series.
- *Handbook of Landmark Cases and Statutes in Business Law and the Legal Environment.*
- *Handbook on Critical Thinking in Business Law and the Legal Environment.*
- *A Guide to Personal Law.*

Software, Video, and Multimedia Supplements

- *Business Law Digital Video Library*—Provides access to more than ninety videos that spark class discussion and clarify core legal concepts. Access is available as an optional package with each new text at no additional cost.
- **Westlaw®**—Ten free hours on Westlaw are available to qualified adopters.
- *CourseMate*—Brings business law concepts to life with interactive learning, study, and exam preparation tools that support this printed textbook. Built-in engagement tracking tools allow you to assess your students' study activities. Additionally, CourseMate includes an interactive e-book, which contains the entire contents of this printed textbook enhanced by the many advantages of a digital environment.

   For a demonstration of *CourseMate,* please visit **www.cengage.com/coursemate** or contact your sales representative.

▶ Acknowledgments

Numerous careful and conscientious users of *Essentials of the Legal Environment* were kind enough to help us revise the book. In addition, the staff at Cengage Learning went out of their way to make sure that this edition came out early and in accurate form. In particular, I wish to thank Rob Dewey and Vicky True-Baker for their countless new ideas, many of which have been incorporated into the Fourth Edition. Our production manager and designer, Bill Stryker, made sure of an error-free, visually attractive edition. I will always be in his debt. I also extend special thanks to Jan Lamar, my longtime developmental editor, for her many useful suggestions and for her efforts in coordinating reviews and ensuring the timely and accurate publication of all supplemental materials. I am particularly indebted to Kristen Hurd for her support and excellent marketing advice.

   I must especially thank Katherine Marie Silsbee, who provided expert research for this project, and Vickie Reierson, for her editing and proofreading services. I also wish to thank William Eric Hollowell, co-author of the *Instructor's Manual,* and *Test Bank,* for his excellent research efforts. The copyediting services of Susan Bradley and the proofreading services of Pat Lewis will not go unnoticed. I also thank Roxanna Lee for her assistance and Suzanne Jasin for her many special efforts on the project.

I am also indebted to the staff at Parkwood Composition, our compositor. Their ability to generate the pages for this text quickly and accurately made it possible to meet an ambitious printing schedule.

Finally, numerous thorough and meticulous users of previous editions have been gracious enough to offer their comments and suggestions on how to improve this text. I am particularly indebted to these reviewers, whom are listed below. With their help, I have been able to make this book even more useful for professors and students alike.

Acknowledgments for Previous Editions

Muhammad Abdullah
Pfeiffer University

Steven L. Arsenault
College of Charleston

Jane Bennett
Orange Coast College

Brent D. Clark
Davenport University

Richard L. Coffinberger
George Mason University

Teri Elkins
University of Houston

George Generas
University of Hartford

Teresa Gillespie
Seattle Pacific University

Gary Greene
Manatee Community College

Penelope L. Herickhoff
Mankato State University

Anne Keaty
University of Louisiana at Lafayette

James F. Kelley
Santa Clara University

Susan Key
University of Alabama at Birmingham

Karrin Klotz
University of Washington

Y. S. Lee
Oakland University

Susan J. Mitchell
Des Moines Area Community College

Tom Moore
Georgia College and State University

Michael J. O'Hara
University of Nebraska at Omaha

Mark Phelps
University of Oregon

G. Keith Roberts
University of Redlands

Gary Sambol
Rutgers, the State University of New Jersey–Camden Campus

Martha Wright Sartoris
North Hennepin Community College

Gwen Seaquist
Ithaca College

Craig R. Stilwell
Michigan State University

Dawn R. Swink
University of St. Thomas

Daphyne Thomas
James Madison University

Wayne Wells
St. Cloud State University

Daniel R. Wrentmore
Santa Barbara City College

Acknowledgments for the Fourth Edition

David G. Cohen
University of Massachusetts—Amherst

Gail D. Moore
Lander University

Robert Jon Routman
University of South Carolina—Upstate

I also wish to extend special thanks to the following individuals for their valuable input for the new Chapter 15:

Robert C. Bird
University of Connecticut

Thomas D. Cavenagh
North Central College—Illinois

Dean Bredeson
University of Texas at Austin

Joan Gabel
Florida State University

Corey Ciocchetti
University of Denver

Eric D. Yordy
Northern Arizona University

I know that I am not perfect. If you or your students find something you don't like or want changed, write or e-mail me your thoughts. That is how I can make *Essentials of the Legal Environment* an even better book in the future.

Roger LeRoy Miller

Dedication

To Ed Flood,

Whose positive attitude knows no bounds.
You truly inspire all of us.

R.L.M.

The Foundations

(John Elk III/Lonely Planet Images/Getty Images)

Chapter 1

Business and Its Legal Environment

> "Laws should be like clothes. They should be made to fit the people they are meant to serve."
>
> —Clarence Darrow, 1857–1938
> (American lawyer)

Learning Objectives

The five Learning Objectives below are designed to help improve your understanding of the chapter. After reading this chapter, you should be able to answer the following questions:

1. **What are four primary sources of law in the United States?**

2. **What is the common law tradition?**

3. **What is a precedent? When might a court depart from precedent?**

4. **What is the difference between remedies at law and remedies in equity?**

5. **What are some important differences between civil law and criminal law?**

(John Elk III/Lonely Planet Images/Getty Images)

Clarence Darrow asserts in the chapter-opening quotation above that laws should be created to serve the public. As part of the public, you have an interest in the law. When entering the world of business, you will find yourself subject to numerous laws and regulations. A basic knowledge of these laws and regulations is beneficial—if not essential—as you contemplate a successful career in today's business environment.

Law A body of enforceable rules governing relationships among individuals and between individuals and their society.

Although the law has various definitions, they all are based on the general observation that **law** consists of *enforceable rules governing relationships among individuals and between individuals and their society.* In some societies, these enforceable rules consist of unwritten principles of behavior, while in other societies they are set forth in ancient or contemporary law codes. In the United States, our rules consist of written laws and court decisions created by modern legislative and judicial bodies. Regardless of how such rules are created, they all have one feature in common: *they establish rights, duties, and privileges that are consistent with the values and beliefs of a society or its ruling group.*

In this introductory chapter, we first look at an important question: How does the legal environment affect business decision making? We next describe the basic sources of American law and the common law tradition. We conclude with a discussion of some general classifications of law.

▶ Business Activities and the Legal Environment

As those entering the business world will learn, laws and government regulations affect all business activities—hiring and firing decisions, workplace safety, the manufacturing and marketing of products, and business financing, to name just a few. To make good business decisions, a basic knowledge of the laws and regulations governing these activities is essential.

Moreover, in today's business setting, simply being aware of what conduct can lead to legal liability is not enough. Businesspersons are also under increasing pressure to make ethical decisions and to consider the consequences of their decisions for stockholders and employees (see Chapter 3).

Many Different Laws May Affect a Single Business Transaction

As you will note, each chapter in this text covers a specific area of the law and shows how the legal rules in that area affect business activities. Although compartmentalizing the law in this fashion facilitates learning, it does not indicate the extent to which many different laws may apply to just one transaction.

EXAMPLE 1.1 Suppose that you are the president of NetSys, Inc., a company that creates and maintains computer network systems for other business firms. NetSys also markets software for internal computer networks. One day, Janet Hernandez, an operations officer for Southwest Distribution Corporation (SDC), contacts you by e-mail about a possible contract involving SDC's computer network. In deciding whether to enter into a contract with SDC, you need to consider, among other things, the legal requirements for an enforceable contract. Are the requirements different for a contract for services and a contract for products? What are your options if SDC **breaches** (breaks, or fails to perform) the contract? The answers to these questions are part of contract law and sales law.

Other questions might concern payment under the contract. How can you guarantee that NetSys will be paid? For example, if SDC pays with a check that is returned for insufficient funds, what are your options? Answers to these questions can be found in the laws that relate to negotiable instruments (such as checks) and creditors' rights. Also, a dispute may arise over the rights to NetSys's software, or there may be a question of liability if the software is defective. There may even be an issue as to whether you and Hernandez had the authority to make the deal in the first place. Resolutions of these questions may be found in the laws that relate to intellectual property, e-commerce, torts, product liability, agency, business organizations, or professional liability. ●

Finally, if any dispute cannot be resolved amicably, then the laws and the rules concerning courts and court procedures spell out the steps of a lawsuit. Exhibit 1–1 on the following page illustrates the various areas of the law that may influence business decision making.

Linking the Law to Other Business School Disciplines

In all likelihood, you are taking a business law or legal environment course because you intend to enter the business world, though some of you may plan to become full-time practicing attorneys. You are most likely taking other business school courses—business communications, business statistics, economics, finance, management, marketing, and taxation, to name just a few possibilities. You will also take a course in accounting as well.

Breach The failure to perform a legal obligation.

● *Exhibit* 1–1 **Areas of the Law That May Affect Business Decision Making**

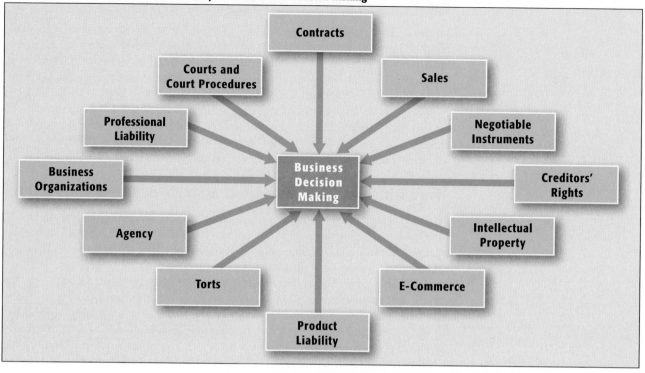

One of our goals in this text is to show how legal concepts can be useful for managers and businesspersons, whether their activities focus on finance, marketing, or some other business discipline. To that end, several chapters conclude with a special feature called *Linking the Law to* [a specific business course].

The Role of the Law in a Small Business

Some of you may end up working in a small business or even owning and running one yourself. The small-business owner is the most general of managers. When you seek additional financing, you become a finance manager. When you "go over the books" with your bookkeeper, you become an accountant. When you decide on a new advertising campaign, you are suddenly the marketing manager. When you consider the impact that a new tax provision will have on your business, you are a tax practitioner. When you hire employees and determine their salaries and benefits, you become a human resources manager.

Just as the various business school disciplines are linked to the law, so too are all of these different managerial roles that a small-business owner must perform. Exhibit 1–2 on the facing page shows some of the legal issues that may arise as part of the management of a small business. Large businesses face most of these issues, too.

▶ Sources of American Law

Primary Source of Law A document that establishes the law on a particular issue, such as a constitution, a statute, an administrative rule, or a court decision.

There are numerous sources of American law. **Primary sources of law,** or sources that establish the law, include the following:

1. The U.S. Constitution and the constitutions of the various states.
2. Statutes, or laws, passed by Congress and by state legislatures.

LEARNING OBJECTIVE 1 **What are four primary sources of law in the United States?**

Secondary Source of Law A publication that summarizes or interprets the law, such as a legal encyclopedia, a legal treatise, or an article in a law review.

3. Regulations created by administrative agencies.
4. Case law (court decisions).

We describe each of these important primary sources of law in the following pages. (See the appendix at the end of this chapter for a discussion of how to find statutes, regulations, and case law.)

Secondary sources of law are books and articles that summarize and clarify the primary sources of law. Legal encyclopedias, compilations (such as *Restatements of the Law*, which summarize court decisions on a particular topic), official comments to statutes, treatises, articles in law reviews published by law schools, and articles in other legal journals are examples of secondary sources of law. Courts often refer to secondary sources of law for guidance in interpreting and applying the primary sources of law discussed here.

• *Exhibit* 1–2 **Linking the Law to the Management of a Small Business**

Business Organization
What is the most appropriate business organizational form, and what type of personal liability does it entail?

Taxation
How will the small business be taxed, and are there ways to reduce those taxes?

Intellectual Property
Does the small business have any patents or other intellectual property that needs to be protected, and if so, what steps should the firm take?

Administrative Law
What types of government regulations apply to the business, and what must the firm do to comply with them?

Employment
Does the business need an employment manual, and does management have to explicitly inform employees of their rights?

Contracts, Sales, and Leases
Will the firm be regularly entering into contracts with others, and if so, should it hire an attorney to review those contracts?

Accounting
Do the financial statements created by an accountant need to be verified for accuracy?

Finance
What are appropriate and legal ways to raise additional capital so that the business can grow?

Constitutional Law

Constitutional Law   The body of law derived from the U.S. Constitution and the constitutions of the various states.

The federal government and the states have separate written constitutions that set forth the general organization, powers, and limits of their respective governments. **Constitutional law** is the law as expressed in these constitutions.

The U.S. Constitution is the supreme law of the land. As such, it is the basis of all law in the United States. A law in violation of the Constitution, if challenged, will be declared unconstitutional and will not be enforced no matter what its source. Because of its paramount importance in the American legal system, we discuss the U.S. Constitution at length in Chapter 4 and present the complete text of the Constitution in Appendix B.

The Tenth Amendment to the U.S. Constitution reserves to the states all powers not granted to the federal government. Each state in the union has its own constitution. Unless it conflicts with the U.S. Constitution or a federal law, a state constitution is supreme within the state's borders.

Statutory Law

Statutory Law   The body of law enacted by legislative bodies.

Citation   A reference to a publication in which a legal authority—such as a statute or a court decision—or other source can be found.

Ordinance   A regulation enacted by a city or county legislative body that becomes part of that state's statutory law.

Laws enacted by legislative bodies at any level of government, such as the statutes passed by Congress or by state legislatures, make up the body of law generally referred to as **statutory law.** When a legislature passes a statute, that statute ultimately is included in the federal code of laws or the relevant state code of laws. Whenever a particular statute is mentioned in this text, we usually provide a footnote showing its **citation** (a reference to a publication in which a legal authority—such as a statute or a court decision—or other source can be found). In the appendix following this chapter, we explain how you can use these citations to find statutory law.

Statutory law also includes local **ordinances**—statutes (laws, rules, or orders) passed by municipal or county governing units to administer matters not covered by federal or state law. Ordinances commonly have to do with city or county land use (zoning ordinances), building and safety codes, and other matters affecting only the local governing unit.

A federal statute, of course, applies to all states. A state statute, in contrast, applies only within the state's borders. State laws may vary from state to state. No federal statute may violate the U.S. Constitution, and no state statute or local ordinance may violate the U.S. Constitution or the relevant state constitution.

Uniform Law   A model law created by the National Conference of Commissioners on Uniform State Laws and/or the American Law Institute for the states to consider adopting.

UNIFORM LAWS   During the 1800s, the differences among state laws frequently created difficulties for businesspersons conducting trade and commerce among the states. To counter these problems, a group of legal scholars and lawyers formed the National Conference of Commissioners on Uniform State Laws (NCCUSL) in 1892 to draft **uniform laws** (model statutes) for the states to consider adopting. The NCCUSL still exists today and continues to issue uniform laws: it has issued more than two hundred uniform acts since its inception.

Each state has the option of adopting or rejecting a uniform law. *Only if a state legislature adopts a uniform law does that law become part of the statutory law of that state.* Note that a state legislature may adopt all or part of a uniform law as it is written, or the legislature may rewrite the law however the legislature wishes. Hence, even though many states may have adopted a uniform law, those states' laws may not be entirely "uniform."

THE UNIFORM COMMERCIAL CODE   One of the more important uniform acts is the Uniform Commercial Code (UCC), which was created through the joint efforts of the NCCUSL and the American Law Institute.[1] The UCC was first issued in 1952 and has been adopted in all fifty states,[2] the District of Columbia, and the Virgin Islands. The UCC facilitates commerce among the states by providing a uniform, yet flexible, set of rules governing commercial transactions. Because of its importance in the area of commercial law, we cite the UCC frequently in this text and will discuss it more fully in Chapter 13.

Administrative Law

Another important source of American law is *administrative law,* which consists of the rules, orders, and decisions of administrative agencies. An *administrative agency* is a federal, state, or local government agency established to perform a specific function. Administrative law and procedures, which will be examined in detail in Chapter 5, constitute a dominant element in the regulatory environment of business.

Rules issued by various administrative agencies affect almost every aspect of a business's operations, including its capital structure and financing, its hiring and firing procedures, its relations with employees and unions, and the way it markets its products. Regulations enacted to protect the environment often play a significant role in business operations. See this chapter's *Shifting Legal Priorities for Business* feature on the next page for a discussion of the concept of sustainability and how some environmental regulations encourage it.

Case Law and Common Law Doctrines

Case Law The rules of law announced in court decisions.

The rules of law announced in court decisions constitute another basic source of American law. These rules of law include interpretations of constitutional provisions, of statutes enacted by legislatures, and of regulations created by administrative agencies. Today, this body of judge-made law is referred to as **case law.** Case law—the doctrines and principles announced in cases—governs all areas not covered by statutory law or administrative law and is part of our common law tradition. We look at the origins and characteristics of the common law tradition in some detail in the pages that follow.

▶ The Common Law Tradition

Because of our colonial heritage, much of American law is based on the English legal system. A knowledge of this tradition is crucial to understanding our legal system today because judges in the United States still apply common law principles when deciding cases.

Early English Courts

LEARNING OBJECTIVE 2 **What is the common law tradition?**

Common Law The body of law developed from custom or judicial decisions in English and U.S. courts.

After the Normans conquered England in 1066, William the Conqueror and his successors began the process of unifying the country under their rule. One of the means they used to do this was the establishment of the king's courts, or *curiae regis*. Before the Norman Conquest, disputes had been settled according to the local legal customs and traditions in various regions of the country. The king's courts sought to establish a uniform set of rules for the country as a whole. What evolved in these courts was the beginning of the **common law**—a body of general rules that applied throughout

---

1. This institute was formed in the 1920s and consists of practicing attorneys, legal scholars, and judges.
2. Louisiana has adopted only Articles 1, 3, 4, 5, 7, 8, and 9.

SHIFTING LEGAL PRIORITIES FOR BUSINESS

Sustainability and the Law

Today, there are numerous statutes that deal with the environment (see Chapter 18). In the last few years, federal, state, and local statutes and administrative regulations have started to embrace the concept of sustainability. Although there is no one official definition, *sustainability* generally has been defined as economic development that meets the needs of the present while not compromising the ability of future generations to meet their own needs. For business managers, it means that they should engage in long-range planning rather than focusing only on short-run profitability.

Federal Law and Sustainability

Certain provisions of federal environmental laws directly address the topic of sustainability. For example, the Resource Conservation and Recovery Act[a] requires waste minimization as the preferred means of hazardous waste management. Facilities that generate or manage hazardous waste must certify that they have a waste minimization program that reduces the toxicity and quantity of the hazardous waste.

The Pollution Prevention Act (PPA)[b] requires that facilities minimize or

a. 42 U.S.C. Sections 6901 *et seq.* (1976).
b. 42 U.S.C. Sections 13101 *et seq.* (1990).

eliminate the release of pollutants into the environment whenever feasible. The PPA established a national policy to recycle any pollutants that cannot be prevented.

Finally, the Environmental Protection Agency (EPA) has undertaken a major effort to encourage sustainability. Its Web site devotes numerous pages to sustainability, sustainable development, and sustainable agriculture. The EPA also has a "sector strategies program" that seeks industry-wide environmental gains through innovative actions.

State Law and Sustainability

At least one state has legislatively committed itself to the concept of sustainable policies. More than a decade ago, the Oregon Sustainability Act was passed. This act officially defines *sustainability* as:

Using, developing, and protecting resources in a manner that enables people to meet current needs and provides that future generations can also meet future needs, from the joint perspective of environmental, economic, and community objectives.

Oregon's sustainability board recommends and proposes sustainability legislation and also develops related policies and programs.

A Chief Sustainability Officer

The giant chemical company DuPont has an official chief sustainability officer (CSO)—a position that did not exist a few years ago. This corporate officer is responsible not only for ensuring that the company complies with all federal, state, local, and international environmental regulations, but also for discovering so-called megatrends that can affect different markets.

DuPont, though best known as a chemical company, also sells agricultural seeds and crop-protection products. One megatrend that its CSO has identified is a growing world population that is going to require more production of corn, soybeans, and other crops from limited acreage. That is where sustainability comes in—producing more with less.

MANAGERIAL IMPLICATIONS

A company that adopts sustainable business practices today not only will promote desirable economic, social, and environmental results, but at the same time will enhance productivity, reduce costs, and thereby increase profitability. A company that has a clear understanding of sustainability will be more competitive as increasing consumer demand for "green" products and global concerns about the environment put pressure on all producers.

the entire English realm. Eventually, the common law tradition became part of the heritage of all nations that were once British colonies, including the United States.

Courts developed the common law rules from the principles underlying judges' decisions in actual legal controversies. Judges attempted to be consistent, and whenever possible, they based their decisions on the principles suggested by earlier cases. They sought to decide similar cases in a similar way and considered new cases with care, because they knew that their decisions would make new law. Each interpretation became part of the law on the subject and served as a legal **precedent**—that is, a court decision that furnished an example or authority for deciding subsequent cases involving identical or similar legal principles or facts.

Precedent A court decision that furnishes an example or authority for deciding subsequent cases involving identical or similar facts.

In the early years of the common law, there was no single place or publication where court opinions, or written decisions, could be found. Beginning in the late thirteenth and early fourteenth centuries, however, portions of significant decisions from each year were gathered together and recorded in *Year Books*. The *Year Books* were useful references for lawyers and judges. In the sixteenth century, the *Year Books* were discontinued, and other reports of cases became available. (See the appendix to this chapter for a discussion of how cases are reported, or published, in the United States today.)

Stare Decisis

The practice of deciding new cases with reference to former decisions, or precedents is called **stare decisis.**[3] This doctrine eventually became a cornerstone of the English and U.S. judicial systems.

Stare Decisis A common law doctrine under which judges are obligated to follow the precedents established in prior decisions.

THE IMPORTANCE OF PRECEDENTS IN JUDICIAL DECISION MAKING   Under the doctrine of *stare decisis,* once a court has set forth a principle of law as being applicable to a certain set of facts, that court and courts of lower rank must adhere to that principle and apply it in future cases involving similar fact patterns. *Stare decisis* has two aspects: first, decisions made by a higher court are binding on lower courts, and second, a court should not overturn its own precedents unless there is a strong reason to do so.

Binding Authority Any source of law that a court must follow when deciding a case.

Controlling precedents in a *jurisdiction* (the area in which a court has the power to apply the law—see Chapter 2) are referred to as *binding authorities.* A **binding authority** is any source of law that a court must follow when deciding a case. Binding authorities include constitutions, statutes, and regulations that govern the issue being decided, as well as court decisions that are controlling precedents within the jurisdiction. United States Supreme Court case decisions, no matter how old, remain controlling until they are overruled by a subsequent decision of the Supreme Court, by a constitutional amendment, or by congressional legislation.

STARE DECISIS AND LEGAL STABILITY   The doctrine of *stare decisis* helps the courts to be more efficient because if other courts have carefully reasoned through a similar case, their legal reasoning and opinions can serve as guides. *Stare decisis* also makes the law more stable and predictable. If the law on a given subject is well settled, someone bringing a case to court can usually rely on the court to make a decision based on what the law has been.

LEARNING OBJECTIVE 3   What is a precedent? When might a court depart from precedent?

DEPARTURES FROM PRECEDENT   Although courts are obligated to follow precedents, sometimes a court will depart from the rule of precedent if it decides that a given precedent should no longer be followed. If a court decides that a precedent is simply incorrect or that technological or social changes have rendered the precedent inapplicable, the court might rule contrary to the precedent. Cases that overturn precedent often receive a great deal of publicity.

CASE EXAMPLE 1.2   In *Brown v. Board of Education of Topeka,*[4] the United States Supreme Court expressly overturned precedent when it concluded that separate educational facilities for whites and blacks, which had been upheld as constitutional in numerous previous cases,[5] were inherently unequal. The Supreme Court's departure from

---

3. *Stare decisis* is pronounced *stahr*-ee dih-*si*-sis and means "to stand on decided cases."
4. 347 U.S. 483, 74 S.Ct. 686, 98 L.Ed. 873 (1954).
5. See *Plessy v. Ferguson,* 163 U.S. 537, 16 S.Ct. 1138, 41 L.Ed. 256 (1896).

precedent in the *Brown* decision received a tremendous amount of publicity as people began to realize the ramifications of this change in the law. ●

WHEN THERE IS NO PRECEDENT   At times, cases arise for which there are no precedents within the jurisdiction. When hearing such cases, called "cases of first impression," courts often look at precedents established in other jurisdictions for guidance. Precedents from other jurisdictions, because they are not binding on the court, are referred to as **persuasive authorities.** A court may also consider various other factors, including legal principles and policies underlying previous court decisions or existing statutes, fairness, social values and customs, public policy, and data and concepts drawn from the social sciences.

Persuasive Authority   Any legal authority or source of law that a court may look to for guidance but on which it need not rely in making its decision.

Equitable Remedies and Courts of Equity

A **remedy** is the means given to a party to enforce a right or to compensate for the violation of a right. **EXAMPLE 1.3**   Shem is injured because of Rowan's wrongdoing. If Shem files a lawsuit and is successful, a court can order Rowan to compensate Shem for the harm by paying Shem a certain amount. The compensation is Shem's remedy. ●

Remedy   The relief given to an innocent party to enforce a right or compensate for the violation of a right.

The kinds of remedies available in the early king's courts of England were severely restricted. If one person wronged another, the king's courts could award as compensation either money or property, including land. These courts became known as *courts of law,* and the remedies were called *remedies at law.* Even though this system introduced uniformity in the settlement of disputes, when plaintiffs wanted a remedy other than economic compensation, the courts of law could do nothing, so "no remedy, no right."

LEARNING OBJECTIVE 4   What is the difference between remedies at law and remedies in equity?

REMEDIES IN EQUITY   *Equity* is a branch of law, founded on what might be described as notions of justice and fair dealing, that seeks to supply a remedy when no adequate remedy at law is available. When individuals could not obtain an adequate remedy in a court of law, they petitioned the king for relief. Most of these petitions were decided by an adviser to the king, called a *chancellor,* who had the power to grant new and unique remedies. Eventually, formal chancery courts, or *courts of equity,* were established. The remedies granted by these courts were called *remedies in equity.*

Thus, two distinct court systems were created, each having its own set of judges and its own set of remedies. **Plaintiffs** (those bringing lawsuits) had to specify whether they were bringing an "action at law" or an "action in equity," and they chose their courts accordingly. **EXAMPLE 1.4**   A plaintiff might ask a court of equity to order the **defendant** (the person against whom a lawsuit is brought) to perform within the terms of a contract. A court of law could not issue such an order because its remedies were limited to payment of money or property as compensation for damages. A court of equity, however, could issue a decree for *specific performance*—an order to perform what was promised. A court of equity could also issue an **injunction,** directing a party to do or refrain from doing a particular act. In certain cases, a court of equity could allow for the *rescission* (cancellation) of the contract, thereby returning the parties to the positions that they held prior to the contract's formation. ● Equitable remedies will be discussed in Chapter 12.

Plaintiff   One who initiates a lawsuit.

Defendant   One against whom a lawsuit is brought.

Injunction   A court decree ordering a person to do or refrain from doing a certain act.

THE MERGING OF LAW AND EQUITY   Today, in most states, the courts of law and equity have merged, and thus the distinction between the two courts has largely disappeared. A plaintiff may now request both legal and equitable remedies in the same action, and the trial court judge may grant either form—or both forms—of relief. The

> *"Laws and institutions, like clocks, must occasionally be cleaned, wound up, and set to true time."*
>
> Henry Ward Beecher, 1813–1887
> (American clergyman and abolitionist)

Equitable Principles and Maxims
General propositions or principles of law that have to do with fairness (equity).

Statute of Limitations A federal or state statute setting the maximum time period during which a certain action can be brought or certain rights enforced.

Jurisprudence The science or philosophy of law.

Natural Law The belief that government and the legal system should reflect universal moral and ethical principles that are inherent in human nature.

distinction between remedies at law and equity remains significant, however, because a court normally will grant an equitable remedy only when the remedy at law (monetary damages) is inadequate. To request the proper remedy, a businessperson (or her or his attorney) must know what remedies are available for the specific kinds of harms suffered. Exhibit 1–3 below summarizes the procedural differences (applicable in most states) between an action at law and an action in equity.

EQUITABLE PRINCIPLES AND MAXIMS Over time, the courts have developed a number of **equitable principles and maxims** that provide guidance in deciding whether plaintiffs should be granted equitable relief. For example, one maxim has come to be known as the *equitable doctrine of laches*. The doctrine arose to encourage people to bring lawsuits while the evidence was fresh. If they failed to do so, they would not be allowed to bring a lawsuit. What constitutes a reasonable time, of course, varies according to the circumstances of the case. Time periods for different types of cases are now usually fixed by **statutes of limitations**. After the time allowed under a statute of limitations has expired, no action can be brought, no matter how strong the case was originally.

Schools of Legal Thought

How judges apply the law to specific cases, including disputes relating to the business world, depends in part on their philosophical approaches to law. Part of the study of law, often referred to as **jurisprudence**, involves learning about different schools of legal thought and discovering how each school's approach to law can affect judicial decision making.

THE NATURAL LAW SCHOOL Those who adhere to the **natural law** theory believe that a higher, or universal, law exists that applies to all human beings and that written laws should imitate these inherent principles. If a written law is unjust, then it is not a true (natural) law and need not be obeyed.

The natural law tradition is one of the oldest and more significant schools of jurisprudence. It dates back to the days of the Greek philosopher Aristotle (384–322 B.C.E.), who distinguished between natural law and the laws governing a particular nation. According to Aristotle, natural law applies universally to all humankind.

The notion that people have "natural rights" stems from the natural law tradition. Those who claim that a specific foreign government is depriving certain citizens of their human rights are implicitly appealing to a higher law that has universal applicability. The question of the universality of basic human rights also comes into play in the context of international business operations. For example, U.S. companies that have operations abroad often hire foreign workers as employees. Should the same

● *Exhibit* 1–3 **Procedural Differences between an Action at Law and an Action in Equity**

PROCEDURE	ACTION AT LAW	ACTION IN EQUITY
Initiation of lawsuit	By filing a complaint.	By filing a petition.
Decision	By jury or judge.	By judge (no jury).
Result	Judgment.	Decree.
Remedy	Monetary damages.	Injunction, specific performance, or rescission.

laws that protect U.S. employees apply to these foreign employees? This question is rooted implicitly in a concept of universal rights that has its origins in the natural law tradition.

LEGAL POSITIVISM   In contrast, *positive,* or national, law (the written law of a given society at a particular point in time) applies only to the citizens of that nation or society. Those who adhere to **legal positivism** believe that there can be no higher law than a nation's positive law. According to the positivist school, there is no such thing as "natural rights." Rather, human rights exist solely because of laws. If the laws are not enforced, anarchy will result. Thus, whether a law is "bad" or "good" is irrelevant. The law is the law and must be obeyed until it is changed—in an orderly manner through a legitimate lawmaking process. A judge with positivist leanings probably would be more inclined to defer to an existing law than would a judge who adheres to the natural law tradition.

Legal Positivism   A school of legal thought centered on the assumption that there is no law higher than the laws created by a national government.

THE HISTORICAL SCHOOL   The **historical school** of legal thought emphasizes the evolutionary process of law by concentrating on the origin and history of the legal system. This school looks to the past to discover what the principles of contemporary law should be. The legal doctrines that have withstood the passage of time—those that have worked in the past—are deemed best suited for shaping present laws. Hence, law derives its legitimacy and authority from adhering to the standards that historical development has shown to be workable. Followers of the historical school are more likely than those of other schools to adhere strictly to decisions made in past cases.

Historical School   A school of legal thought that emphasizes the evolutionary process of law and looks to the past to discover what the principles of contemporary law should be.

LEGAL REALISM   In the 1920s and 1930s, a number of jurists and scholars, known as *legal realists,* rebelled against the historical approach to law. **Legal realism** is based on the idea that law is just one of many institutions in society and that it is shaped by social forces and needs. This school holds that because the law is a human enterprise, judges should take social and economic realities into account when deciding cases. Legal realists also believe that the law can never be applied with total uniformity. Given that judges are human beings with unique experiences, value systems, and intellects, different judges will obviously bring different reasoning processes to the same case. For instance, female judges might be more inclined to give weight to the impact of a negative employment decision on women or minorities than male judges.

Legal Realism   A school of legal thought that generally advocates a less abstract and more realistic approach to the law, an approach that takes into account customary practices and the circumstances in which transactions take place.

Classifications of Law

The law may be broken down according to several classification systems. For example, one classification system divides law into **substantive law** (all laws that define, describe, regulate, and create legal rights and obligations) and **procedural law** (all laws that establish the methods of enforcing the rights established by substantive law).

Substantive Law   Law that defines, describes, regulates, and creates legal rights and obligations.

Procedural Law   Law that establishes the methods of enforcing the rights established by substantive law.

EXAMPLE 1.5   A state law that provides employees with the right to workers' compensation benefits for any on-the-job injuries they sustain is a substantive law because it creates legal rights (workers' compensation laws will be discussed in Chapter 16). Procedural laws, in contrast, establish the method by which an employee must notify the employer about an on-the-job injury, prove the injury, and periodically submit additional proof to continue receiving workers' compensation benefits. Note that a law regarding workers' compensation may contain both substantive and procedural provisions. •

Cyberlaw An informal term used to refer to all laws governing online communications and transactions.

Other classification systems divide law into federal law and state law or private law (dealing with relationships between persons) and public law (addressing the relationship between persons and their governments). Frequently, people use the term **cyberlaw** to refer to the emerging body of law that governs transactions conducted via the Internet. Cyberlaw is not really a classification of law, nor is it a new *type* of law. Rather, it is an informal term used to describe traditional legal principles that have been modified and adapted to fit situations that are unique to the online world. Of course, in some areas new statutes have been enacted, at both the federal and state levels, to cover specific types of problems stemming from online communications. Throughout this book, you will read about how the law is evolving to govern specific legal issues that arise in the online context.

Civil Law and Criminal Law

Civil Law The branch of law dealing with the definition and enforcement of all private or public rights, as opposed to criminal matters.

Civil law spells out the rights and duties that exist between persons and between persons and their governments, and the relief available when a person's rights are violated. Typically, in a civil case, a private party sues another private party (although the government can also sue a party for a civil law violation) to make sure that the other party complies with a duty or pays for the damage caused by the failure to comply with a duty. **EXAMPLE 1.6** If a seller fails to perform a contract with a buyer, the buyer may bring a lawsuit against the seller. The purpose of the lawsuit will be either to compel the seller to perform as promised or, more commonly, to obtain monetary damages for the seller's failure to perform. ● Much of the law that we discuss in this text is civil law. The whole body of tort law (see Chapter 6) is civil law.

LEARNING OBJECTIVE 5 What are some important differences between civil law and criminal law?

Criminal Law Law that has to do with wrongful actions committed against society for which society demands redress.

Criminal law has to do with wrongs committed against society for which society demands redress. Criminal acts are proscribed by local, state, or federal government statutes. Thus, criminal defendants are prosecuted by public officials, such as a district attorney (D.A.), on behalf of the state, not by their victims or other private parties. Whereas in a civil case the object is to obtain a remedy (such as monetary damages) to compensate the injured party, in a criminal case the object is to punish the wrongdoer in an attempt to deter others from similar actions. Penalties for violations of criminal statutes consist of fines and/or imprisonment—and, in some cases, death. We will discuss the differences between civil and criminal law in greater detail in Chapter 7.

National and International Law

Although the focus of this book is U.S. business law, increasingly businesspersons in this country engage in transactions that extend beyond our national borders. In these situations, the laws of other nations or the laws governing relationships among nations may come into play. For this reason, those who pursue a career in business today should have an understanding of the global legal environment.

National Law Law that pertains to a particular nation.

NATIONAL LAW The law of a particular nation, such as the United States or Sweden, is **national law.** National law, of course, varies from country to country because each country's law reflects the interests, customs, activities, and values that are unique to that nation's culture.

International Law The law that governs relations among nations.

INTERNATIONAL LAW In contrast to national law, international law applies to more than one nation. **International law** can be defined as a body of written and unwritten laws observed by independent nations and governing the acts of individuals as well as governments. International law is an intermingling of rules and constraints derived from a variety of sources, including the laws of individual nations, the customs that have evolved among nations in their relations with one another, and treaties and international organizations. In essence, international law is the result of centuries-old attempts to reconcile the traditional need of each nation to be the final authority over its own affairs with the desire of nations to benefit economically from trade and harmonious relations with one another.

The key difference between national law and international law is that government authorities can enforce national law. If a nation violates an international law, however, the most that other countries or international organizations can do (if persuasive tactics fail) is to take coercive actions against the violating nation. Coercive actions range from the severance of diplomatic relations and boycotts to, as a last resort, war. We will examine international law in Chapter 9.

 ## Reviewing . . . Business and Its Legal Environment

Suppose that the California legislature passes a law that severely restricts carbon dioxide emissions from automobiles in that state. A group of automobile manufacturers files a suit against the state of California to prevent the enforcement of the law. The automakers claim that a federal law already sets fuel economy standards nationwide and that these standards are essentially the same as carbon dioxide emission standards. According to the automobile manufacturers, it is unfair to allow California to impose more stringent regulations than those set by the federal law. Using the information presented in the chapter, answer the following questions.

1. Who are the parties (the plaintiffs and the defendant) in this lawsuit?
2. Are the plaintiffs seeking a legal remedy or an equitable remedy?
3. What is the primary source of the law that is at issue here?
4. Read through the appendix that follows this chapter, and then answer the following question: Where would you look to find the relevant California and federal laws?

 ## Debate This

Under the doctrine of *stare decisis,* courts are obligated to follow the precedents established in their jurisdiction unless there is a compelling reason not to. Should U.S. courts continue to adhere to this common law principle, given that our government now regulates so many areas by statute?

Key Terms

binding authority 9
breach 3
case law 7
citation 6
civil law 13
common law 7
constitutional law 6
criminal law 13
cyberlaw 13
defendant 10
equitable principles and maxims 11

historical school 12
injunction 10
international law 13
jurisprudence 11
law 2
legal positivism 12
legal realism 12
national law 13
natural law 11
ordinance 6
persuasive authority 10

plaintiff 10
precedent 8
primary source of law 4
procedural law 12
remedy 10
secondary source of law 5
stare decisis 9
statute of limitations 11
statutory law 6
substantive law 12
uniform law 6

Chapter Summary: Business and Its Legal Environment

Sources of American Law (See pages 4–7.)	1. *Constitutional law*—The law as expressed in the U.S. Constitution and the various state constitutions. The U.S. Constitution is the supreme law of the land. State constitutions are supreme within state borders to the extent that they do not violate the U.S. Constitution or a federal law. 2. *Statutory law*—Laws or ordinances created by federal, state, and local legislatures and governing bodies. None of these laws can violate the U.S. Constitution or the relevant state constitutions. Uniform laws, when adopted by a state legislature, become statutory law in that state. 3. *Administrative law*—The rules, orders, and decisions of federal or state government administrative agencies. 4. *Case law and common law doctrines*—Judge-made law, including interpretations of constitutional provisions, of statutes enacted by legislatures, and of regulations created by administrative agencies. The common law—the doctrines and principles embodied in case law—governs all areas not covered by statutory law (or agency regulations issued to implement various statutes).

The Common Law Tradition (See pages 7–12.)	1. *Common law*—Law that originated in medieval England with the creation of the king's courts, or *curiae regis,* and the development of a body of rules that were common to (or applied throughout) the land.
	 2. *Stare decisis*—A doctrine under which judges "stand on decided cases"—or follow the rule of precedent—in deciding cases. *Stare decisis* is the cornerstone of the common law tradition.
	 3. *Remedies*—A remedy is the means by which a court enforces a right or compensates for a violation of a right. Courts typically grant legal remedies (monetary damages) but may also grant equitable remedies (specific performance, injunction, or rescission) when the legal remedy is inadequate or unavailable.
	 4. *Schools of legal thought*—Judges' decision making is influenced by their philosophy of law. Four important schools of legal thought, or legal philosophies, are the following:
	    a. *Natural law tradition*—One of the oldest and more significant schools of legal thought. Those who believe in natural law hold that there is a universal law applicable to all human beings and that this law is of a higher order than positive, or conventional, law.
	    b. *Legal positivism*—A school of legal thought centered on the assumption that there is no law higher than the laws created by the government. Laws must be obeyed, even if they are unjust, to prevent anarchy.
	    c. *Historical school*—A school of legal thought that stresses the evolutionary nature of law and looks to doctrines that have withstood the passage of time for guidance in shaping present laws.
	    d. *Legal realism*—A school of legal thought that generally advocates a less abstract and more realistic approach to the law and takes into account customary practices and the circumstances surrounding the particular transaction.

Classifications of Law (See pages 12–14.)	The law may be broken down according to several classification systems, such as substantive or procedural law, federal or state law, and private or public law. Two broad classifications are civil and criminal law, and national and international law. Cyberlaw is not really a classification of law but a term that is used for the growing body of case law and statutory law that applies to Internet transactions.

ExamPrep

ISSUE SPOTTERS

—Check your answers to these questions against the answers provided in Appendix D at the end of this text.

1. The First Amendment to the U.S. Constitution provides protection for the free exercise of religion. A state legislature enacts a law that outlaws all religions that do not derive from the Judeo-Christian tradition. Is this law valid within that state? Why or why not? **(See page 6.)**
2. Under what circumstance might a judge rely on case law to determine the intent and purpose of a statute? **(See page 7.)**

BEFORE THE TEST

Go to **www.cengagebrain.com**, enter the ISBN 9781133586548, and click on "Find" to locate this textbook's Web site. Then, click on "Access Now" under "Study Tools," and select Chapter 1 at the top. There, you will find an Interactive Quiz that you can take to assess your mastery of the concepts in this chapter. Additionally, you will find Flashcards and a Glossary of important terms, as well as Video Questions (when assigned).

 For Review

Answers for the even-numbered questions in this **For Review** *section can be found in Appendix E at the end of this text.*

1. What are four primary sources of law in the United States?

2. What is the common law tradition?

3. What is a precedent? When might a court depart from precedent?

4. What is the difference between remedies at law and remedies in equity?

5. What are some important differences between civil law and criminal law?

Questions and Case Problems

1–1. Binding versus Persuasive Authority. A county court in Illinois is deciding a case involving an issue that has never been addressed before in that state's courts. The Iowa Supreme Court, however, recently decided a case involving a very similar fact pattern. Is the Illinois court obligated to follow the Iowa Supreme Court's decision on the issue? If the United States Supreme Court had decided a similar case, would that decision be binding on the Illinois court? Explain. **(See pages 9 and 10.)**

1–2. **Question with Sample Answer: Sources of Law.** This chapter discussed a number of sources of American law. Which source of law takes priority in each of the following situations, and why? **(See pages 4–7.)**

  1. A federal statute conflicts with the U.S. Constitution.

  2. A federal statute conflicts with a state constitution.

  3. A state statute conflicts with the common law of that state.

  4. A state constitutional amendment conflicts with the U.S. Constitution.

  5. A federal administrative regulation conflicts with a state constitution.

  —For a sample answer to Question 1–2, go to Appendix F at the end of this text.

1–3. Philosophy of Law. After World War II ended in 1945, an international tribunal of judges convened at Nuremberg, Germany. The judges convicted several Nazi war criminals of "crimes against humanity." Assuming that the Nazis who were convicted had not disobeyed any law of their country and had merely been following their government's (Hitler's) orders, what law had they violated? Explain. **(See page 11.)**

1–4. Reading Citations. Assume that you want to read the court's entire opinion in the case of *State v. Allen,* 268 P.3d 1198 (Kan. 2012). Read the section entitled "Finding Case Law" in the appendix that follows this chapter, and then explain specifically where you would find the court's opinion. **(See page 19.)**

1–5. *Stare Decisis.* In this chapter, we stated that the doctrine of *stare decisis* "became a cornerstone of the English and U.S. judicial systems." What does *stare decisis* mean, and why has this doctrine been so fundamental in the development of our legal tradition? **(See page 9.)**

1–6. Court Opinions. Read through the subsection entitled "Decisions and Opinions" in the appendix following this chapter. What is the difference between a concurring opinion and a majority opinion? Between a concurring opinion and a dissenting opinion? Why do judges and justices write concurring and dissenting opinions, given that these opinions will not affect the outcome of the case at hand, which has already been decided by majority vote? **(See page 25.)**

1–7. **In Your Court: Remedies.** Arthur Rabe is suing Xavier Sanchez for breaching a contract in which Sanchez promised to sell Rabe a Van Gogh painting for $150,000. **(See pages 10 and 11.)**

  1. In this lawsuit, who is the plaintiff, and who is the defendant?

  2. If Rabe wants Sanchez to perform the contract as promised, what remedy should Rabe seek?

  3. Suppose that Rabe wants to cancel the contract because Sanchez fraudulently misrepresented the painting as an original Van Gogh when in fact it is a copy. In this situation, what remedy should Rabe seek?

  4. Will the remedy Rabe seeks in either situation be a remedy at law or a remedy in equity?

  5. Suppose that the court finds in Rabe's favor and grants one of these remedies. Sanchez then appeals the decision to a higher court. Read through the subsection entitled "Parties to Lawsuits" in the appendix following this chapter. On appeal, which party in the *Rabe-*

Sanchez case will be the appellant (or petitioner), and which party will be the appellee (or respondent)? **(See page 25.)**

1–8. **A Question of Ethics: *Stare Decisis.*** On July 5, 1884, Dudley, Stephens, and Brooks—"all able-bodied English seamen"—and a teenage English boy were cast adrift in a lifeboat following a storm at sea. They had no water with them in the boat, and all they had for sustenance were two one-pound tins of turnips. On July 24, Dudley proposed that one of the four in the lifeboat be sacrificed to save the others. Stephens agreed with Dudley, but Brooks refused to consent—and the boy was never asked for his opinion. On July 25, Dudley killed the boy, and the three men then fed on the boy's body and blood. Four days later, the men were rescued by a passing vessel. They were taken to England and tried for the murder of the boy. If the men had not fed on the boy's body, they would probably have died of starvation within the four-day period. The boy, who was in a much weaker condition, would likely have died before the rest.

[Regina v. Dudley and Stephens, 14 Q.B.D. (Queen's Bench Division, England) 273 (1884)] **(See page 9.)**

1. The basic question in this case is whether the survivors should be subject to penalties under English criminal law, given the men's unusual circumstances. You be the judge and decide the issue. Give the reasons for your decision.

2. Should judges ever have the power to look beyond the written "letter of the law" in making their decisions? Why or why not?

1–9. **Critical-Thinking Legal Environment Question.** John's company is involved in a lawsuit with a customer, Beth. John argues that for fifty years higher courts in that state have decided cases involving circumstances similar to those of this case in a way that indicates that this case should be decided in favor of John's company. Is this a valid argument? If so, must the judge in this case rule as those other judges did? What argument could Beth use to counter John's reasoning? **(See pages 8 and 9.)**

The statutes, agency regulations, and case law referred to in this text establish the rights and duties of businesspersons engaged in various types of activities. The cases presented in the following chapters provide you with concise, real-life illustrations of how the courts interpret and apply these laws. Because of the importance of knowing how to find statutory, administrative, and case law, this appendix offers a brief introduction to how these laws are published and to the legal "shorthand" employed in referencing these legal sources.

▶ Finding Statutory and Administrative Law

When Congress passes laws, they are collected in a publication titled *United States Statutes at Large.* When state legislatures pass laws, they are collected in similar state publications. Most frequently, however, laws are referred to in their codified form—that is, the form in which they appear in the federal and state codes. In these codes, laws are compiled by subject.

United States Code

The *United States Code* (U.S.C.) arranges all existing federal laws of a public and permanent nature by subject. Each of the fifty subjects into which the U.S.C. arranges the laws is given a title and a title number. For example, laws relating to commerce and trade are collected in "Title 15, Commerce and Trade." Titles are subdivided by sections. A citation to the U.S.C. includes title and section numbers. Thus, a reference to "15 U.S.C. Section 1" means that the statute can be found in Section 1 of Title 15. ("Section" may also be designated by the symbol §, and "Sections" by §§.) In addition to the print publication of the U.S.C., the federal government also provides a searchable online database of the *United States Code* at **www.gpoaccess.gov/ uscode/index.html**.

Commercial publications of these laws and regulations are available and are widely used. For example, West Group publishes the *United States Code Annotated* (U.S.C.A.). The U.S.C.A. contains the complete text of laws included in the U.S.C., notes of court decisions that interpret and apply specific sections of the statutes, and the text of presidential proclamations and executive orders. The U.S.C.A. also includes research aids, such as cross-references to related statutes, historical notes, and other references. A citation to the U.S.C.A. is similar to a citation to the U.S.C.: "15 U.S.C.A. Section 1."

State Codes

State codes follow the U.S.C. pattern of arranging law by subject. The state codes may be called codes, revisions, compilations, consolidations, general statutes, or statutes, depending on the preferences of the state. In some codes, subjects are designated by number. In others, they are designated by name. For example, "13 Pennsylvania Consolidated Statutes Section 1101" means that the statute can be found in Title 13, Section 1101, of the Pennsylvania code. "California Commercial Code Section 1101" means the statute can be found in Section 1101 under the subject heading

"Commercial Code" of the California code. Abbreviations may be used. For example, "13 Pennsylvania Consolidated Statutes Section 1101" may be abbreviated "13 Pa. C.S. § 1101," and "California Commercial Code Section 1101" may be abbreviated "Cal. Com. Code § 1101."

Administrative Rules

Rules and regulations adopted by federal administrative agencies are compiled in the *Code of Federal Regulations* (C.F.R.). Like the U.S.C., the C.F.R. is divided into fifty titles. Rules within each title are assigned section numbers. A full citation to the C.F.R. includes title and section numbers. For example, a reference to "17 C.F.R. Section 230.504" means that the rule can be found in Section 230.504 of Title 17.

▶ Finding Case Law

Before discussing the case reporting system, we need to look briefly at the court system (which will be discussed in detail in Chapter 2). There are two types of courts in the United States: federal courts and state courts. Both the federal and state court systems consist of several levels, or tiers, of courts. *Trial courts,* in which evidence is presented and testimony is given, are on the bottom tier (which also includes lower courts handling specialized issues). Decisions from a trial court can be appealed to a higher court, which commonly would be an intermediate *court of appeals,* or an *appellate court.* Decisions from these intermediate courts of appeals may be appealed to an even higher court, such as a state supreme court or the United States Supreme Court.

State Court Decisions

Most state trial court decisions are not published. Except in New York and a few other states that publish selected opinions of their trial courts, decisions from state trial courts are merely filed in the office of the clerk of the court, where the decisions are available for public inspection. (Increasingly, they can be found online as well.) Written decisions of the appellate, or reviewing, courts, however, are published and distributed. As you will note, most of the state court cases presented in this book are from state appellate courts. The reported appellate decisions are published in volumes called *reports* or *reporters,* which are numbered consecutively. State appellate court decisions are found in the state reporters of that particular state.

REGIONAL REPORTERS State court opinions appear in regional units of the *National Reporter System,* published by West Group. Most lawyers and libraries have the West reporters because they report cases more quickly and are distributed more widely than the state-published reports. In fact, many states have eliminated their own reporters in favor of West's National Reporter System. The National Reporter System divides the states into the following geographic areas: *Atlantic* (A., A.2d, or A.3d), *North Eastern* (N.E. or N.E.2d), *North Western* (N.W. or N.W.2d), *Pacific* (P., P.2d, or P.3d), *South Eastern* (S.E. or S.E.2d), *South Western* (S.W., S.W.2d, or S.W.3d), and *Southern* (So., So.2d, or So.3d). (The *2d* and *3d* in the abbreviations refer to *Second Series* and *Third Series,* respectively.) The states included in each of these regional divisions are indicated in Exhibit 1A–1 on the following page, which illustrates West's National Reporter System.

• *Exhibit* 1A–1 **West's National Reporter System–Regional/Federal**

Regional Reporters	Coverage Beginning	Coverage
Atlantic Reporter (A., A.2d, or A.3d)	1885	Connecticut, Delaware, District of Columbia, Maine, Maryland, New Hampshire, New Jersey, Pennsylvania, Rhode Island, and Vermont.
North Eastern Reporter (N.E. or N.E.2d)	1885	Illinois, Indiana, Massachusetts, New York, and Ohio.
North Western Reporter (N.W. or N.W.2d)	1879	Iowa, Michigan, Minnesota, Nebraska, North Dakota, South Dakota, and Wisconsin.
Pacific Reporter (P., P.2d, or P.3d)	1883	Alaska, Arizona, California, Colorado, Hawaii, Idaho, Kansas, Montana, Nevada, New Mexico, Oklahoma, Oregon, Utah, Washington, and Wyoming.
South Eastern Reporter (S.E. or S.E.2d)	1887	Georgia, North Carolina, South Carolina, Virginia, and West Virginia.
South Western Reporter (S.W., S.W.2d, or S.W.3d)	1886	Arkansas, Kentucky, Missouri, Tennessee, and Texas.
Southern Reporter (So., So.2d, or So.3d)	1887	Alabama, Florida, Louisiana, and Mississippi.
Federal Reporters		
Federal Reporter (F., F.2d, or F.3d)	1880	U.S. Circuit Courts from 1880 to 1912; U.S. Commerce Court from 1911 to 1913; U.S. District Courts from 1880 to 1932; U.S. Court of Claims (now called U.S. Court of Federal Claims) from 1929 to 1932 and since 1960; U.S. Courts of Appeals since 1891; U.S. Court of Customs and Patent Appeals since 1929; U.S. Emergency Court of Appeals since 1943.
Federal Supplement (F.Supp. or F.Supp.2d)	1932	U.S. Court of Claims from 1932 to 1960; U.S. District Courts since 1932; U.S. Customs Court since 1956.
Federal Rules Decisions (F.R.D.)	1939	U.S. District Courts involving the Federal Rules of Civil Procedure since 1939 and Federal Rules of Criminal Procedure since 1946.
Supreme Court Reporter (S.Ct.)	1882	United States Supreme Court since the October term of 1882.
Bankruptcy Reporter (Bankr.)	1980	Bankruptcy decisions of U.S. Bankruptcy Courts, U.S. District Courts, U.S. Courts of Appeals, and the United States Supreme Court.
Military Justice Reporter (M.J.)	1978	U.S. Court of Military Appeals and Courts of Military Review for the Army, Navy, Air Force, and Coast Guard.

NATIONAL REPORTER SYSTEM MAP

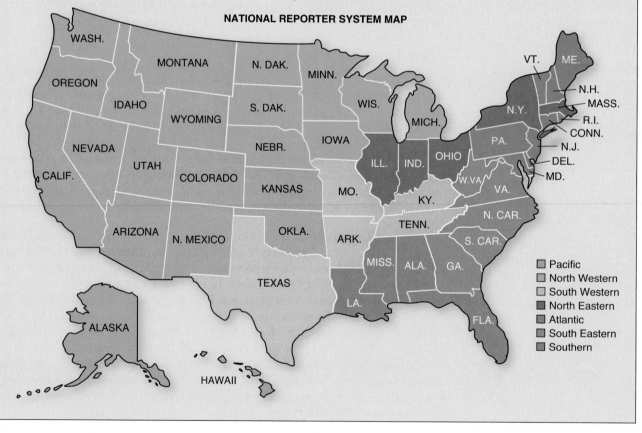

CASE CITATIONS   After appellate decisions have been published, they are normally referred to (cited) by the name of the case; the volume, name, and page number of the state's official reporter (if different from West's National Reporter System); the volume, name, and page number of the *National Reporter;* and the volume, name, and page number of any other selected reporter. This information is included in the *citation.* (Citing a reporter by volume number, name, and page number, in that order, is common to all citations.) When more than one reporter is cited for the same case, each reference is called a *parallel citation.*

Note that some states have adopted a "public domain citation system" that uses a somewhat different format for the citation. For example, in Wisconsin, a Wisconsin Supreme Court decision might be designated "2012 WI 23," meaning that the decision was the twenty-third issued by the Wisconsin Supreme Court in the year 2012. Parallel citations to the *Wisconsin Reports* and West's *North Western Reporter* are still included after the public domain citation.

Consider the following case citation: *Goldstein v. Lackard,* 81 Mass.App.Ct. 1112, 961 N.E.2d 163 (2012). We see that the opinion in this case can be found in Volume 81 of the official *Massachusetts Appeals Court Reports,* on page 1112. The parallel citation is to Volume 961 of the *North Eastern Reporter, Second Series,* page 163. In presenting appellate opinions in this text (starting in Chapter 2), in addition to the reporter, we give the name of the court hearing the case and the year of the court's decision. Sample citations to state court decisions are explained in Exhibit 1A–2 on pages 22–24.

Federal Court Decisions

Federal district (trial) court decisions are published unofficially in West's *Federal Supplement* (F.Supp. or F.Supp.2d), and opinions from the circuit courts of appeals (reviewing courts) are reported unofficially in West's *Federal Reporter* (F., F.2d, or F.3d). Cases concerning federal bankruptcy law are published unofficially in West's *Bankruptcy Reporter* (Bankr. or B.R.).

The official edition of the United States Supreme Court decisions is the *United States Reports* (U.S.), which is published by the federal government. Unofficial editions of Supreme Court cases include West's *Supreme Court Reporter* (S.Ct.) and the *Lawyers' Edition of the Supreme Court Reports* (L.Ed. or L.Ed.2d). Sample citations for federal court decisions are also listed and explained in Exhibit 1A–2.

Unpublished Opinions

Many court opinions that are not yet published or that are not intended for publication can be accessed through Westlaw® (abbreviated in citations as "WL"), an online legal database. When no citation to a published reporter is available for cases cited in this text, we give the WL citation (see Exhibit 1A–2 on page 24 for an example).

Old Case Law

On a few occasions, this text cites opinions from old, classic cases dating to the nineteenth century or earlier. Some of these are from the English courts. The citations to these cases may not conform to the descriptions given above because the reporters in which they were originally published were often known by the names of the persons who compiled the reporters.

● *Exhibit* 1A-2 **How to Read Citations**

STATE COURTS

282 Neb. 990, 808 N.W.2d 48 (2012)ᵃ

> *N.W.* is the abbreviation for West's publication of state court decisions rendered in the *North Western Reporter* of the National Reporter System. *2d* indicates that this case was included in the *Second Series* of that reporter. The number 808 refers to the volume number of the reporter; the number 48 refers to the page in that volume on which this case begins.

> *Neb.* is an abbreviation for *Nebraska Reports,* Nebraska's official reports of the decisions of its highest court, the Nebraska Supreme Court.

204 Cal.App.4th 112, 138 Cal.Rptr.3d 519 (2012)

> *Cal.Rptr.* is the abbreviation for West's unofficial reports—titled *California Reporter*—of the decisions of California courts.

93 A.D.3d 493, 940 N.Y.S.2d 75 (2012)

> *N.Y.S.* is the abbreviation for West's unofficial reports—titled *New York Supplement*—of the decisions of New York courts.

> *A.D.* is the abbreviation for *Appellate Division*, which hears appeals from the New York Supreme Court—the state's general trial court. The New York Court of Appeals is the state's highest court, analogous to other states' supreme courts.

313 Ga.App. 804, 723 S.E.2d 39 (2012)

> *Ga.App.* is the abbreviation for *Georgia Appeals Reports,* Georgia's official reports of the decisions of its court of appeals.

FEDERAL COURTS

___ U.S. ___, 132 S.Ct. 1201, 182 L.Ed.2d 42 (2012)

> *L.Ed.* is an abbreviation for *Lawyers' Edition of the Supreme Court Reports*, an unofficial edition of decisions of the United States Supreme Court.

> *S.Ct.* is the abbreviation for West's unofficial reports—titled *Supreme Court Reporter*—of decisions of the United States Supreme Court.

> *U.S.* is the abbreviation for *United States Reports*, the official edition of the decisions of the United States Supreme Court. The blank lines in this citation (or any other citation) indicate that the appropriate volume of the case reporter has not yet been published and no page number is available.

a. The case names have been deleted from these citations to emphasize the publications. It should be kept in mind, however, that the name of a case is as important as the specific page numbers in the volumes in which it is found. If a citation is incorrect, the correct citation may be found in a publication's index of case names. In addition to providing a check on errors in citations, the date of a case is important because the value of a recent case as an authority is likely to be greater than that of older cases from the same court.

▶ Reading and Understanding Case Law

The cases in this text have been condensed from the full text of the courts' opinions by the authors. For those wishing to review court cases for future research projects

• *Exhibit* 1A-2 **How to Read Citations—Continued**

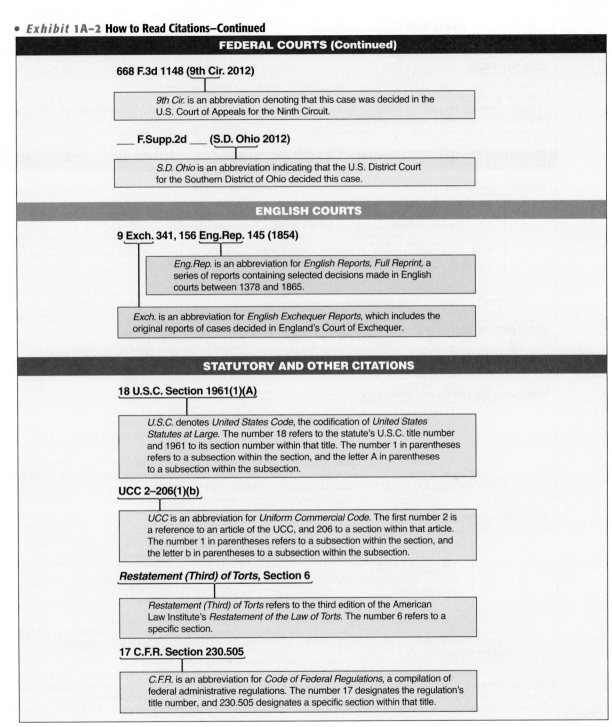

FEDERAL COURTS (Continued)

668 F.3d 1148 (9th Cir. 2012)

9th Cir. is an abbreviation denoting that this case was decided in the U.S. Court of Appeals for the Ninth Circuit.

___ F.Supp.2d ___ (S.D. Ohio 2012)

S.D. Ohio is an abbreviation indicating that the U.S. District Court for the Southern District of Ohio decided this case.

ENGLISH COURTS

9 Exch. 341, 156 Eng.Rep. 145 (1854)

Eng.Rep. is an abbreviation for *English Reports, Full Reprint,* a series of reports containing selected decisions made in English courts between 1378 and 1865.

Exch. is an abbreviation for *English Exchequer Reports,* which includes the original reports of cases decided in England's Court of Exchequer.

STATUTORY AND OTHER CITATIONS

18 U.S.C. Section 1961(1)(A)

U.S.C. denotes *United States Code,* the codification of *United States Statutes at Large.* The number 18 refers to the statute's U.S.C. title number and 1961 to its section number within that title. The number 1 in parentheses refers to a subsection within the section, and the letter A in parentheses to a subsection within the subsection.

UCC 2–206(1)(b)

UCC is an abbreviation for *Uniform Commercial Code.* The first number 2 is a reference to an article of the UCC, and 206 to a section within that article. The number 1 in parentheses refers to a subsection within the section, and the letter b in parentheses to a subsection within the subsection.

***Restatement (Third) of Torts,* Section 6**

Restatement (Third) of Torts refers to the third edition of the American Law Institute's *Restatement of the Law of Torts.* The number 6 refers to a specific section.

17 C.F.R. Section 230.505

C.F.R. is an abbreviation for *Code of Federal Regulations,* a compilation of federal administrative regulations. The number 17 designates the regulation's title number, and 230.505 designates a specific section within that title.

(Continued)

or to gain additional legal information, the following sections will provide useful insights into how to read and understand case law.

Case Titles and Terminology

The title of a case, such as *Adams v. Jones,* indicates the names of the parties to the lawsuit. The *v.* in the case title stands for *versus,* which means "against." In the trial

• *Exhibit* 1A–2 **How to Read Citations–Continued**

WESTLAW® CITATIONS[b]

2012 WL 164930

WL is an abbreviation for Westlaw. The number 2012 is the year of the document that can be found with this citation in the Westlaw database. The number 164930 is a number assigned to a specific document. A higher number indicates that a document was added to the Westlaw database later in the year.

UNIFORM RESOURCE LOCATORS (URLs)

http://www.westlaw.com[c]

The suffix *com* is the top level domain (TLD) for this Web site. The TLD *com* is an abbreviation for "commercial," which usually means that a for-profit entity hosts (maintains or supports) this Web site.

westlaw is the host name—the part of the domain name selected by the organization that registered the name. In this case, West registered the name. This Internet site is the Westlaw database on the Web.

www is an abbreviation for "World Wide Web." The Web is a system of Internet servers that support documents formatted in *HTML* (hypertext markup language) and other formats as well.

http://www.uscourts.gov

This is "The Federal Judiciary Home Page." The host is the Administrative Office of the U.S. Courts. The TLD *gov* is an abbreviation for "government." This Web site includes information and links from, and about, the federal courts.

http://www.law.cornell.edu/index.html

This part of a URL points to a Web page or file at a specific location within the host's domain. This page is a menu with links to documents within the domain and to other Internet resources.

This is the host name for a Web site that contains the Internet publications of the Legal Information Institute (LII), which is a part of Cornell Law School. The LII site includes a variety of legal materials and links to other legal resources on the Internet. The TLD *edu* is an abbreviation for "educational institution" (a school or a university).

http://www.ipl2.org/div/news

This part of the URL points to a static *news* page at this Web site, which provides links to online newspapers from around the world.

div is an abbreviation for "division," which is the way that ipl2 tags the content on its Web site as relating to a specific topic.

The site *ipl2* was formed from the merger of the Internet Public Library and the Librarians' Internet Index. It is an online service that provides reference resources and links to other information services on the Web. The site is supported chiefly by the *iSchool* at Drexel College of Information Science and Technology. The TLD *org* is an abbreviation for "organization" (normally nonprofit).

b. Many court decisions that are not yet published or that are not intended for publication can be accessed through Westlaw, an online legal database.

c. The basic form for a URL is "service://hostname/path." The Internet service for all of the URLs in this text is *http* (hypertext transfer protocol). Because most Web browsers add this prefix automatically when a user enters a host name or a hostname/path, we have generally omitted the *http://* from the URLs listed in this text.

court, Adams was the plaintiff—the person who filed the suit. Jones was the defendant. If the case is appealed, however, the appellate court will sometimes place the name of the party appealing the decision first, so the case may be called *Jones v. Adams.* Because some reviewing courts retain the trial court order of names, it is often impossible to distinguish the plaintiff from the defendant in the title of a reported appellate court decision. You must carefully read the facts of each case to identify the parties.

The following terms and phrases are frequently encountered in court opinions and legal publications. Because it is important to understand what these terms and phrases mean, we define and discuss them here.

PARTIES TO LAWSUITS As mentioned previously, the party initiating a lawsuit is referred to as the *plaintiff* or *petitioner,* depending on the nature of the action, and the party against whom a lawsuit is brought is the *defendant* or *respondent.* Lawsuits frequently involve more than one plaintiff and/or defendant.

When a case is appealed from the original court or jurisdiction to another court or jurisdiction, the party appealing the case is called the *appellant.* The *appellee* is the party against whom the appeal is taken. (In some appellate courts, the party appealing a case is referred to as the *petitioner,* and the party against whom the suit is brought or appealed is called the *respondent.*)

JUDGES AND JUSTICES The terms *judge* and *justice* are usually synonymous and represent two designations given to judges in various courts. All members of the United States Supreme Court, for example, are referred to as justices, and justice is the formal title often given to judges of appellate courts, although this is not always the case. In New York, a *justice* is a judge of the trial court (which is called the Supreme Court), and a member of the Court of Appeals (the state's highest court) is called a *judge.* The term *justice* is commonly abbreviated to J., and *justices,* to JJ. A Supreme Court case might refer to Justice Sotomayor as Sotomayor, J., or to Chief Justice Roberts as Roberts, C.J.

DECISIONS AND OPINIONS Most decisions reached by reviewing, or appellate, courts are explained in written *opinions.* The opinion contains the court's reasons for its decision, the rules of law that apply, and the judgment. When all judges or justices unanimously agree on an opinion, the opinion is written for the entire court and can be deemed a *unanimous opinion.* When there is not a unanimous agreement, a *majority opinion* is written. The majority opinion outlines the view supported by the majority of the judges or justices deciding the case. Sometimes, the majority agrees on the result, but not the reasoning. An opinion joined by the largest number of judges or justices, but less than a majority, is called a *plurality opinion.*

Often, a judge or justice who strongly wishes to make or emphasize a point that was not made or emphasized in the unanimous or majority opinion will write a *concurring opinion.* This means that the judge or justice agrees, or concurs, with the majority's decision, but for different reasons. When there is not a unanimous opinion, a *dissenting opinion* presents the views of one or more judges who disagree with the majority's decision. The dissenting opinion is important because it may form the basis of the arguments used years later in overruling the precedential majority opinion. Occasionally, a court issues a *per curiam* (Latin for "by the court") opinion, which does not indicate the judge or justice who authored the opinion.

A Sample Court Case

Knowing how to read and analyze a court opinion is an essential step in undertaking accurate legal research. A further step involves "briefing" the case. Legal researchers routinely brief cases by summarizing and reducing the texts of the opinions to their essential elements. (For instructions on how to brief a case, go to Appendix A at the end of this text.)

The cases contained within the chapters of this text have already been analyzed and partially briefed by the authors, and the essential aspects of each case are presented in a convenient format consisting of three basic sections: *Background and Facts, In the Words of the Court* (excerpts from the court's opinion), and *Decision and Remedy,* as shown in Exhibit 1A–3 on pages 27–29, which has also been annotated to illustrate the kind of information that is contained in each section. In the remaining chapters of this book, this basic case format is often expanded to include special introductory sections or special comments or considerations that follow the cases.

The sample court case we present and annotate in Exhibit 1A–3 is one that the United States Supreme Court decided in 2012. In 2004, the federal government attached a tracking device to Antoine Jones's car because he was suspected of dealing illegal drugs. The tracking device evidence was used at trial against Jones, who was convicted, but the U.S. Court of Appeals for the District of Columbia Circuit reversed the jury's decision. The Supreme Court had to decide whether the attachment of the tracking device constituted an unreasonable search under the Fourth Amendment to the U.S. Constitution (see Chapter 4).

You will note that triple asterisks (* * *) and quadruple asterisks (* * * *) frequently appear in the opinion. The triple asterisks indicate that we have deleted a few words or sentences from the opinion for the sake of readability or brevity. Quadruple asterisks mean that an entire paragraph (or more) has been omitted. Additionally, when the opinion cites another case or legal source, the citation to the case or other source has been omitted to save space and to improve the flow of the text. These editorial practices are continued in the other court opinions presented in this book. In addition, whenever we present a court opinion that includes a term or phrase that may not be readily understandable, a bracketed definition or paraphrase has been added.

THE SAMPLE COURT CASE STARTS ON THE FACING PAGE.

• *Exhibit* 1A–3 **A Sample Court Case**

UNITED STATES v. JONES

Supreme Court of the United States

__ U.S. __, 132 S.Ct. 945, 181 L.Ed.2d 911 (2012).

> This line identifies the opinion's author. Many decisions simply state a judge's name.

Justice *SCALIA* delivered the opinion of the Court.

We decide whether the attachment of a Global-Positioning-System (GPS) tracking device to an individual's vehicle, and subsequent use of that device to monitor the vehicle's movements on public streets, constitutes a search * * * within the meaning of the Fourth Amendment.

> The Court divided the opinion into parts. The first part of the opinion summarizes the case's factual background.

I

In 2004 **respondent** Antoine Jones * * * came under suspicion of

> A party who argues against an appeal. Many courts refer to such parties as appellees.

trafficking in narcotics and was made the target of an investigation * * * .

* * * In 2005 the Government applied to the United States District Court for the District of Columbia for a **warrant** authorizing the use of an

> An order authorizing certain conduct.

electronic tracking device on the Jeep Grand Cherokee registered to Jones's wife. A warrant issued, authorizing installation of the device in the District of Columbia and within 10 days.

On the 11th day, and not in the District of Columbia but in Maryland, agents installed a GPS tracking device on the undercarriage of the Jeep * * * . Over the next 28 days, the Government used the device to track the vehicle's movements * * * . * * * The device established the vehicle's location within 50 to 100 feet, and * * * it relayed more than 2,000 pages of data * * * .

The Government ultimately obtained a multiple-count **indictment**

> A grand jury's formal written accusation that a person has committed a crime.

charging Jones * * * with * * * **conspiracy** to distribute and possess with

> An agreement between two or more people to commit a criminal offense.

intent to distribute * * * cocaine * * * . Before trial, Jones filed **a motion to suppress** evidence obtained through the GPS device. The District Court * * *

> A motion to prevent the prosecution from introducing evidence of a crime because it was obtained illegally.

held [that most of the] data [was] **admissible,** because " '[a] person traveling

> Allowed to be introduced at trial.

in an automobile on public thoroughfares has no reasonable expectation of privacy in his movements from one place to another.' "

* * * [Following a **retrial**,] the jury returned a guilty verdict, and the

> A new trial of a case that has been tried before.

District Court sentenced Jones to life imprisonment.

The United States Court of Appeals for the District of Columbia Circuit

> Vacated, set aside, or voided.

reversed the conviction because of admission of the evidence obtained

(Continued)

• *Exhibit* 1A-3 **A Sample Court Case—Continued**

by warrantless use of the GPS device which, it said, violated the Fourth Amendment. * * * We granted *certiorari* * * * .

> A process by which the United States Supreme Court decides to hear a case.

* * * *

The Fourth Amendment provides in relevant part that "the right of the people to be secure in their persons, houses, papers, and **effects,** against unreasonable searches and seizures, shall not be violated." It is beyond dispute that a vehicle is an "effect" as that term is used in the Amendment. We hold that the Government's installation of a GPS device on a target's vehicle, and its use of that device to monitor the vehicle's movements, constitutes a "search."

> Property.

It is important to be clear about what occurred in this case: The Government physically occupied private property for the purpose of obtaining information. We have no doubt that such a physical intrusion would have been considered a "search" within the meaning of the Fourth Amendment when it was adopted.

The text of the Fourth Amendment reflects its close connection to property, since otherwise it would have referred simply to "the right of the people to be secure against unreasonable searches and seizures"; the phrase "in their persons, houses, papers, and effects" would have been **superfluous.**

> Unnecessary or redundant.

Consistent with this understanding, our Fourth Amendment jurisprudence was tied to **common-law trespass,** at least until the latter half of the 20th century. Thus, in *Olmstead v. United States,* we held that wiretaps attached to telephone wires on the public streets did not constitute a Fourth Amendment search because "there was no entry of the houses or offices of the defendants[.]"

> A body of legal principles and rules developed by courts, rather than by legislatures. In this context, the Court is referring to the common law of England.

> An unlawful intrusion on or interference with a person's property.

Our later cases, of course, have deviated from that exclusively property-based approach. In *Katz v. United States,* we said that "the Fourth Amendment protects people, not places," and found a violation in attachment of an eavesdropping device to a public telephone booth. Our later cases have applied the analysis of Justice Harlan's **concurrence** in that case, which said that a violation occurs when government officers violate a person's "reasonable expectation of privacy[.]"

> A separate opinion in which one or more judges agree with the majority's decision but give a different rationale.

The Government contends that * * * no search occurred here, since Jones had no "reasonable expectation of privacy" in the area of the Jeep accessed by Government agents (its underbody) and in the locations of the Jeep on the public roads, which were visible to all. But we need not address the

● *Exhibit* 1A–3 **A Sample Court Case—Continued**

Government's contentions, because Jones's Fourth Amendment rights do not rise or fall with the *Katz* formulation. At bottom, we must "assur[e] preservation of that degree of privacy against government that existed when the Fourth Amendment was adopted." As explained, for most of our history the Fourth Amendment was understood to embody a particular concern for government trespass upon the areas ("persons, houses, papers, and effects")

Lists or mentions explicitly.

it **enumerates.** *Katz* did not **repudiate** that understanding. * * * The *Katz*

Reject or renounce.

reasonable-expectation-of-privacy test has been *added to,* not *substituted for,* the common-law trespassory test.

* * * *

Upheld or declared valid as rendered.

The judgment of the Court of Appeals for the D.C. Circuit is **affirmed.**

Chapter 2

The Courts and Alternative Dispute Resolution

"An eye for an eye will make the whole world blind."

—Mahatma Gandhi, 1869–1948
(Indian political and spiritual leader)

(John Elk III/Lonely Planet Images/Getty Images)

Contents

Learning Objectives

The five Learning Objectives below are designed to help improve your understanding of the chapter. After reading this chapter, you should be able to answer the following questions:

1. **What is judicial review?**
2. **Before a court can hear a case, it must have jurisdiction. Over what must it have jurisdiction? How are the courts applying traditional jurisdictional concepts to cases involving Internet transactions?**
3. **What is the difference between a trial court and an appellate court?**
4. **What is discovery, and how does electronic discovery differ from traditional discovery?**
5. **What are three alternative methods of resolving disputes?**

Every society needs to have an established method for resolving disputes. Without one, as Mahatma Gandhi implied in the chapter-opening quotation, the biblical "eye for an eye" would lead to anarchy. This is particularly true in the business world—nearly every businessperson will face a lawsuit at some time in his or her career. For this reason, anyone involved in business needs to have an understanding of court systems in the United States, as well as the various methods of dispute resolution that can be pursued outside the courts.

In this chapter, after examining the judiciary's overall role in the American governmental scheme, we discuss some basic requirements that must be met before a party may bring a lawsuit before a particular court. We then look at the court systems of the United States in some detail and, to clarify judicial procedures, follow a hypothetical case through a state court system. Throughout this chapter, we indicate how court doctrines and procedures are being adapted to the needs of a cyber age. The chapter concludes with an overview of some alternative methods of settling disputes, including online dispute resolution.

▶ The Judiciary's Role in American Government

As you learned in Chapter 1, the body of American law includes the federal and state constitutions, statutes passed by legislative bodies, administrative law, and the case decisions and legal principles that form the common law. These laws would be meaningless, however, without the courts to interpret and apply them. This is the essential role of the judiciary—the courts—in the American governmental system: to interpret and to apply the law.

Judicial Review

Judicial Review The process by which a court decides on the constitutionality of legislative enactments and actions of the executive branch.

As the branch of government entrusted with interpreting the laws, the judiciary can decide, among other things, whether the laws or actions of the other two branches are constitutional. The process for making such a determination is known as **judicial review.** The power of judicial review enables the judicial branch to act as a check on the other two branches of government, in line with the checks-and-balances system established by the U.S. Constitution.

The Origins of Judicial Review in the United States

LEARNING OBJECTIVE 1 **What is judicial review?**

The power of judicial review was not mentioned in the Constitution, but the concept was not new at the time the nation was founded. Indeed, before 1789 state courts had already overturned state legislative acts that conflicted with state constitutions. Many of the founders expected the United States Supreme Court to assume a similar role with respect to the federal Constitution. Alexander Hamilton and James Madison both emphasized the importance of judicial review in their essays urging the adoption of the new Constitution.

▶ Basic Judicial Requirements

Before a court can hear a lawsuit, certain requirements must first be met. These requirements relate to *jurisdiction, venue,* and *standing to sue.* We examine each of these important concepts here.

Jurisdiction

Jurisdiction The authority of a court to hear and decide a specific case.

In Latin, *juris* means "law," and *diction* means "to speak." Thus, the term **jurisdiction** literally means "the power to speak the law." Before any court can hear a case, it must have jurisdiction over the person (or company) against whom the suit is brought (the defendant) or over the property involved in the suit. The court must also have jurisdiction over the subject matter of the dispute.

JURISDICTION OVER PERSONS OR PROPERTY Generally, a court can exercise personal jurisdiction (*in personam* jurisdiction) over any person or business that resides in a certain geographic area. A state trial court, for example, normally has jurisdictional authority over residents (including businesses) in a particular area of the state, such as a county or district. A state's highest court (often called the state supreme court)[1] has jurisdiction over all residents of that state.

A court can also exercise jurisdiction over property that is located within its boundaries. This kind of jurisdiction is known as *in rem* jurisdiction, or "jurisdiction over the thing." **EXAMPLE 2.1** A dispute arises over the ownership of a boat in dry dock in Fort Lauderdale, Florida. The boat is owned by an Ohio resident, over whom a Florida court normally cannot exercise personal jurisdiction. The other

---

1. As will be discussed shortly, a state's highest court is frequently referred to as the state supreme court, but there are exceptions. For example, in New York, the supreme court is a trial court.

party to the dispute is a resident of Nebraska. In this situation, a lawsuit concerning the boat could be brought in a Florida state court on the basis of the court's *in rem* jurisdiction. •

Long Arm Statute A state statute that permits a state to obtain personal jurisdiction over nonresident defendants.

Long Arm Statutes. Under the authority of a state **long arm statute**, a court can exercise personal jurisdiction over certain out-of-state defendants based on activities that took place within the state. Before exercising long arm jurisdiction over a nonresident, however, the court must be convinced that the defendant had sufficient contacts, or *minimum contacts,* with the state to justify the jurisdiction.[2] Generally, this means that the defendant must have enough of a connection to the state for the judge to conclude that it is fair for the state to exercise power over the defendant. If an out-of-state defendant caused an automobile accident or sold defective goods within the state, for instance, a court usually will find that minimum contacts exist to exercise jurisdiction over that defendant.

CASE EXAMPLE 2.2 An Xbox game system caught fire in Bonnie Broquet's home in Texas and caused substantial personal injuries. Broquet filed a lawsuit in a Texas court against Ji-Haw Industrial Company, a nonresident company that made the Xbox components. Broquet alleged that Ji-Haw's components had caused the fire. Ji-Haw argued that the Texas court lacked jurisdiction over it, but a state appellate court held that the Texas long arm statute authorized the exercise of jurisdiction over the out-of-state defendant.[3] • Similarly, a state may exercise personal jurisdiction over a nonresident defendant who is sued for breaching a contract that was formed within the state, even when that contract was negotiated over the phone or through online and offline correspondence.

Corporate Contacts. Because corporations are considered legal persons, courts use the same principles to determine whether it is fair to exercise jurisdiction over a corporation.[4] A corporation normally is subject to personal jurisdiction in the state in which it is incorporated, has its principal office, and is doing business. Courts apply the minimum-contacts test to determine if they can exercise jurisdiction over out-of-state corporations.

The minimum-contacts requirement usually is met if the corporation advertises or sells its products within the state, or places its goods into the "stream of commerce" with the intent that the goods be sold in the state. **EXAMPLE 2.3** A business is incorporated under the laws of Maine but has a branch office and manufacturing plant in Georgia. The corporation also advertises and sells its products in Georgia. These activities would likely constitute sufficient contacts with the state of Georgia to allow a Georgia court to exercise jurisdiction over the corporation. •

Some corporations, however, do not sell or advertise products or place any goods in the stream of commerce. Determining what constitutes minimum contacts in these situations can be more difficult. In the following case, the question before the court was whether a New Jersey firm had minimum contacts with North Carolina.

---

2. The minimum-contacts standard was established in *International Shoe Co. v. State of Washington,* 326 U.S. 310, 66 S.Ct. 154, 90 L.Ed. 95 (1945).

3. *Ji-Haw Industrial Co. v. Broquet,* 2008 WL 441822 (Tex.App.—San Antonio 2008).

4. In the eyes of the law, corporations are *legal persons*—entities that can sue and be sued. See Chapter 10.

Case 2.1 — Southern Prestige Industries, Inc. v. Independence Plating Corp.

Court of Appeals of North Carolina, 202 N.C.App. 372, 690 S.E.2d 768 (2010).

BACKGROUND AND FACTS Independence Plating Corporation (the defendant) is a New Jersey corporation that provides metal-coating services. Its only office and all of its personnel are located in New Jersey. It does not advertise out of state, but had a long-standing business relationship with Kidde Aerospace in North Carolina (filing under the name Southern Prestige Industries). For almost a year, Independence and Kidde engaged in frequent transactions. On November 18, 2008, Kidde initiated an action for breach of contract in a North Carolina state court, alleging defects in the metal-plating process carried out by Independence. Independence filed a motion to dismiss for lack of personal jurisdiction, which the trial court denied. Independence appealed, arguing that it had insufficient contacts with North Carolina for the state to exercise jurisdiction.

IN THE WORDS OF THE COURT . . .
CALABRIA, Judge.
    * * * *

In order to satisfy due process requirements, there must be "certain minimum contacts [between the nonresident defendant and the forum state—that is, the state in which the court is located] such that the maintenance of the suit does not offend 'traditional notions of fair play and substantial justice.' " In order to establish minimum contacts with North Carolina, the defendant must have purposefully availed itself of the privilege of conducting activities within the forum state and invoked the benefits and protections of the laws of North Carolina. The relationship between the defendant and the forum state must be such that the defendant should reasonably anticipate being haled into a North Carolina court.
    * * * *

* * * Our courts look at the following factors in determining whether minimum contacts exist: (1) the quantity of the contacts, (2) the nature and quality of the contacts, (3) the source and connection of the cause of action to the contacts, (4) the interest of the forum state, and (5) the convenience to the parties. [Emphasis added.]

In the instant case, the trial court found that the parties "had an ongoing business relationship characterized by frequent transactions between July 27, 2007, and April 25, 2008, as reflected by thirty-two purchase orders." Plaintiff would ship machined parts to defendant, who would then anodize the parts and return them to plaintiff in North Carolina. Defendant sent invoices totaling $21,018.70 to plaintiff in North Carolina, and these invoices were paid from plaintiff's corporate account at a North Carolina bank. Plaintiff filed a breach of contract action against defendant because the machined parts that were shipped to defendant from North Carolina and then anodized by defendant and shipped back to North Carolina were defective.
    * * * *

* * * After examining the ongoing relationship between the parties, the nature of their contacts, the interest of the forum state, the convenience of the parties, and the cause of action, we conclude defendant has "purposely availed" itself of the benefits of doing business in North Carolina and "should reasonably anticipate being haled" into a North Carolina court. We hold that defendant has sufficient minimum contacts with North Carolina to justify the exercise of personal jurisdiction over defendant without violating the due process clause.

DECISION AND REMEDY The North Carolina appellate court affirmed the trial court's decision. Independence had sufficient minimum contacts with North Carolina to justify the state's exercise of personal jurisdiction.

WHAT IF THE FACTS WERE DIFFERENT? *Suppose that the two parties had engaged in a single business transaction. Would the outcome of this case have been the same? Why or why not?*

JURISDICTION OVER SUBJECT MATTER Jurisdiction over subject matter is a limitation on the types of cases a court can hear. In both the federal and state court systems, there are courts of *general* (unlimited) *jurisdiction* and courts of *limited jurisdiction*. An example of a court of general jurisdiction is a state trial court or a federal district court.

Probate Court A state court of limited jurisdiction that conducts proceedings relating to the settlement of a deceased person's estate.

An example of a state court of limited jurisdiction is a probate court. **Probate courts** are state courts that handle only matters relating to the transfer of a person's assets and obligations after his or her death, including matters relating to the custody and guardianship of children.

Bankruptcy Court A federal court of limited jurisdiction that handles only bankruptcy proceedings.

An example of a federal court of limited subject-matter jurisdiction is a bankruptcy court. **Bankruptcy courts** handle only bankruptcy proceedings, which are governed by federal bankruptcy law (see Chapter 14).

ORIGINAL AND APPELLATE JURISDICTION   The distinction between courts of original jurisdiction and courts of appellate jurisdiction normally lies in whether the case is being heard for the first time. Courts having original jurisdiction are courts of the first instance, or trial courts—that is, courts in which lawsuits begin, trials take place, and evidence is presented. In the federal court system, the *district courts* are trial courts. In the various state court systems, the trial courts are known by various names, as will be discussed shortly.

The key point here is that any court having original jurisdiction is normally known as a trial court. Courts having appellate jurisdiction act as reviewing courts, or appellate courts. In general, cases can be brought before appellate courts only on appeal from an order or a judgment of a trial court or other lower court.

JURISDICTION OF THE FEDERAL COURTS   Because the federal government is a government of limited powers, the jurisdiction of the federal courts is limited. Federal courts have subject-matter jurisdiction in two situations: *federal questions* and *diversity of citizenship*.

Federal Questions.   Article III of the U.S. Constitution establishes the boundaries of federal judicial power. Section 2 of Article III states that "[t]he judicial Power shall extend to all Cases, in Law and Equity, arising under this Constitution, the Laws of the United States, and Treaties made, or which shall be made, under their Authority." This clause means that whenever a plaintiff's cause of action is based, at least in part, on the U.S. Constitution, a treaty, or a federal law, then a **federal question** arises, and the case comes under the judicial power of the federal courts. Any lawsuit involving a federal question, such as a person's rights under the U.S. Constitution, can originate in a federal court. Note that in a case based on a federal question, a federal court will apply federal law.

> **Federal Question**   A question that pertains to the U.S. Constitution, acts of Congress, or treaties. A federal question provides a basis for federal jurisdiction.

Diversity of Citizenship.   Federal district courts can also exercise original jurisdiction over cases involving **diversity of citizenship.** The most common type of diversity jurisdiction has two requirements:[5] (1) the plaintiff and defendant must be residents of different states, and (2) the dollar amount in controversy must exceed $75,000. For purposes of diversity jurisdiction, a corporation is a citizen of both the state in which it is incorporated and the state in which its principal place of business is located. A case involving diversity of citizenship can be filed in the appropriate federal district court. If the case starts in a state court, it can sometimes be transferred, or "removed," to a federal court. A large percentage of the cases filed in federal courts each year are based on diversity of citizenship.

> **Diversity of Citizenship**   A basis for federal court jurisdiction over a lawsuit between citizens of different states.

As noted, a federal court will apply federal law in cases involving federal questions. In a case based on diversity of citizenship, in contrast, a federal court will apply the relevant state law (which is often the law of the state in which the court sits).

EXCLUSIVE VERSUS CONCURRENT JURISDICTION   When both federal and state courts have the power to hear a case, as is true in lawsuits involving diversity of citizenship, **concurrent jurisdiction** exists. When cases can be tried only in federal courts or only in state courts, **exclusive jurisdiction** exists. Federal courts have exclusive jurisdiction in cases involving federal crimes, bankruptcy, patents, and copyrights; in suits against the United States; and in some areas of admiralty law (law

> **Concurrent Jurisdiction**   Jurisdiction that exists when two different courts have the power to hear a case.
>
> **Exclusive Jurisdiction**   Jurisdiction that exists when a case can be heard only in a particular court or type of court.

---

5. Diversity jurisdiction also exists in cases between (1) a foreign country and citizens of a state or of different states and (2) citizens of a state and citizens or subjects of a foreign country. These bases for diversity jurisdiction are less commonly used.

governing transportation on ocean waters). State courts also have exclusive jurisdiction over certain subject matter—for example, divorce and adoption.

When either a federal court or a state court can exercise jurisdiction, a party has a choice of courts in which to bring a suit. A number of factors can affect a party's decision to litigate in a federal or a state court, such as the availability of different remedies, the distance to the respective courthouses, or the experience or reputation of a particular judge. For example, if the dispute involves a trade secret, a party might conclude that a federal court—which has exclusive jurisdiction over copyrights, patents, and trademarks—would have more expertise in the matter.

A party might also choose a federal court over a state court if he or she is concerned about bias in a state court. In contrast, a plaintiff might choose to litigate in a state court if it has a reputation for awarding substantial amounts of damages or if the judge is perceived as being pro-plaintiff. The concepts of exclusive jurisdiction and concurrent jurisdiction are illustrated in Exhibit 2–1 below.

Jurisdiction in Cyberspace

The Internet's capacity to bypass political and geographic boundaries undercuts the traditional basis on which courts assert personal jurisdiction. As already discussed, for a court to compel a defendant to come before it, there must be at least minimum contacts—the presence of a salesperson within the state, for example. Are there sufficient minimum contacts if the defendant's only connection to a jurisdiction is an ad on a Web site originating from a remote location?

LEARNING OBJECTIVE 2 Before a court can hear a case, it must have jurisdiction. Over what must it have jurisdiction? How are the courts applying traditional jurisdictional concepts to cases involving Internet transactions?

THE "SLIDING-SCALE" STANDARD The courts have developed a standard—called a "sliding-scale" standard—for determining when the exercise of jurisdiction over an out-of-state defendant is proper. In developing this standard, the courts have identified three types of Internet business contacts: (1) substantial business conducted over the Internet (with contracts and sales, for example), (2) some interactivity through a Web site, and (3) passive advertising. Jurisdiction is proper for the first

• *Exhibit* 2–1 **Exclusive and Concurrent Jurisdiction**

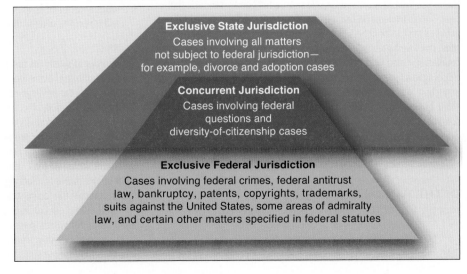

Exclusive State Jurisdiction
Cases involving all matters
not subject to federal jurisdiction—
for example, divorce and adoption cases

Concurrent Jurisdiction
Cases involving federal
questions and
diversity-of-citizenship cases

Exclusive Federal Jurisdiction
Cases involving federal crimes, federal antitrust
law, bankruptcy, patents, copyrights, trademarks,
suits against the United States, some areas of admiralty
law, and certain other matters specified in federal statutes

category, improper for the third, and may or may not be appropriate for the second.[6] An Internet communication is typically considered passive if people have to voluntarily access it to read the message, and active if it is sent to specific individuals.

INTERNATIONAL JURISDICTIONAL ISSUES   Because the Internet is global in scope, it obviously raises international jurisdictional issues. The world's courts seem to be developing a standard that echoes the minimum-contacts requirement applied by U.S. courts. Most courts are indicating that minimum contacts—doing business within the jurisdiction, for example—are enough to compel a defendant to appear and that a physical presence is not necessary. The effect of this standard is that a business firm has to comply with the laws in any jurisdiction in which it targets customers for its products. This situation is complicated by the fact that many countries' laws on particular issues—free speech, for example—are very different from U.S. laws.

The following *Spotlight Case* illustrates how federal courts apply a sliding-scale standard to determine if they can exercise jurisdiction over a foreign defendant whose only contact with the United States is through a Web site.

---

6. For a leading case on this issue, see *Zippo Manufacturing Co. v. Zippo Dot Com, Inc.*, 952 F.Supp. 1119 (W.D.Pa. 1997).

SPOTLIGHT ON GUCCI

Case 2.2   Gucci America, Inc. v. Wang Huoqing

United States District Court, Northern District of California, ___ F.Supp.2d ___ (2011).

BACKGROUND AND FACTS   Gucci America, Inc., is a New York corporation headquartered in New York City. Gucci manufactures and distributes high-quality luxury goods, including footwear, belts, sunglasses, handbags, and wallets, which are sold worldwide. In connection with its products, Gucci uses twenty-one federally registered trademarks (trademark law will be discussed in Chapter 8). Gucci also operates a number of boutiques, some of which are located in California. Wang Huoqing, a resident of the People's Republic of China, operates numerous Web sites. When Gucci discovered that Wang Huoqing's Web sites offered for sale counterfeit goods–products that bear Gucci's trademarks but are not genuine Gucci articles–it hired a private investigator in San Jose, California, to buy goods from the Web sites. The investigator purchased a wallet that was labeled Gucci but was counterfeit. Gucci filed a trademark infringement lawsuit against Wang Huoqing in a federal district court in California seeking damages and an injunction to prevent further infringement. Wang Huoqing was notified of the lawsuit via e-mail but did not appear in court. Gucci asked the court to enter a default judgment–that is, a judgment entered when the defendant fails to appear–but the court first had to determine whether it had personal jurisdiction over Wang Huoqing based on the Internet sales.

IN THE WORDS OF THE COURT . . .
Joseph C. *SPERO*, United States Magistrate Judge.
    * * * *
     * * * Under California's long-arm statute, federal courts in California may exercise jurisdiction to the extent permitted by the Due

Process Clause of the Constitution. The Due Process Clause allows federal courts to exercise jurisdiction where * * * the defendant has had sufficient minimum contacts with the forum to subject him or her to the specific jurisdiction of the court. The courts apply a three-part test to determine whether specific jurisdiction exists:

> (1) The nonresident defendant must do some act or consummate some transaction with the forum or perform some act by which he purposefully avails himself of the privilege of conducting activities in the forum, thereby invoking the benefits and protections of its laws; (2) the claim must be one which arises out of or results from the defendant's forum-related activities; and (3) exercise of jurisdiction must be reasonable.

* * * *

In order to satisfy the first prong of the test for specific jurisdiction, a defendant must have either purposefully availed itself of [taken advantage of] the privilege of conducting business activities within the forum or purposefully directed activities toward the forum. *Purposeful availment typically consists of action taking place in the forum that invokes the benefits and protections of the laws of the forum, such as executing or performing a contract within the forum.* To show purposeful availment, a plaintiff must show that the defendant "engage[d] in some form of affirmative conduct allowing or promoting the transaction of business within the forum state." [Emphasis added.]

"In the Internet context, the Ninth Circuit utilizes a sliding scale analysis under which 'passive' websites do not create sufficient contacts to establish purposeful availment, whereas interactive websites may create sufficient contacts, depending on how

Spotlight Case 2.2–Continued

interactive the website is." * * * *Personal jurisdiction is appropriate where an entity is conducting business over the Internet and has offered for sale and sold its products to forum [California] residents.* [Emphasis added.]

Here, the allegations and evidence presented by Plaintiffs in support of the Motion are sufficient to show purposeful availment on the part of Defendant Wang Huoqing. Plaintiffs have alleged that Defendant operates "fully interactive Internet websites operating under the Subject Domain Names" and have presented evidence in the form of copies of web pages showing that the websites are, in fact, interactive. * * * Additionally, Plaintiffs allege Defendant is conducting counterfeiting and infringing activities within this Judicial District and has advertised and sold his counterfeit goods in the State of California. * * * Plaintiffs have also presented evidence of one actual sale within this district, made by investigator Robert Holmes from the website bag2do.cn. * * * Finally, Plaintiffs have presented evidence that Defendant Wang

Huoqing owns or controls the twenty-eight websites listed in the Motion for Default Judgment. * * * Such commercial activity in the forum amounts to purposeful availment of the privilege of conducting activities within the forum, thus invoking the benefits and protections of its laws. Accordingly, the Court concludes that Defendant's contacts with California are sufficient to show purposeful availment.

DECISION AND REMEDY   The U.S. District Court for the Northern District of California held that it had personal jurisdiction over the foreign defendant, Wang Huoqing. The court entered a default judgment against Wang Huoqing and granted Gucci an injunction.

THE LEGAL ENVIRONMENT DIMENSION   *Is it relevant to the analysis of jurisdiction that Gucci America's principal place of business is in New York rather than California? Explain.*

Venue

Venue   The geographic district in which a legal action is tried and from which the jury is selected.

Jurisdiction has to do with whether a court has authority to hear a case involving specific persons, property, or subject matter. **Venue** (pronounced *ven-yoo*) is concerned with the most appropriate physical location for a trial. Two state courts (or two federal courts) may have the authority to exercise jurisdiction over a case, but it may be more appropriate or convenient to hear the case in one court than in the other.

Basically, the concept of venue reflects the policy that a court trying a suit should be in the geographic neighborhood (usually the county) where the incident leading to the lawsuit occurred or where the parties involved in the lawsuit reside. Venue in a civil case typically is where the defendant resides, whereas venue in a criminal case normally is where the crime occurred.

Pretrial publicity or other factors, though, may require a change of venue to another community, especially in criminal cases when the defendant's right to a fair and impartial jury has been impaired. **EXAMPLE 2.4**   Police raided a compound of religious polygamists in Texas and removed many children from the ranch. Authorities suspected that some of the girls were being sexually and physically abused. The raid received a great deal of media attention, and people living in the nearby towns would likely have been influenced by this publicity. In this situation, if the government filed criminal charges against a member of the religious sect, that individual might request—and would probably receive—a change of venue to another location. •

Standing to Sue

Standing to Sue   The requirement that an individual must have a sufficient stake in a controversy before he or she can bring a lawsuit.

Justiciable Controversy   A controversy that is not hypothetical or academic but real and substantial.

Before a person can bring a lawsuit before a court, the party must have **standing to sue,** or a sufficient stake in the matter to justify seeking relief through the court system. In other words, to have standing, a party must have a legally protected and tangible interest at stake in the litigation. The party bringing the lawsuit must have suffered a harm, or have been threatened by a harm, as a result of the action about which she or he has complained. Standing to sue also requires that the controversy at issue be a **justiciable[7] controversy**— a controversy that is real and substantial, as opposed to hypothetical or academic.

---

7. Pronounced jus-*tish*-uh-bul.

Note that in some situations a person may have standing to sue on behalf of another person, such as a minor or a mentally incompetent person. **EXAMPLE 2.5** Three-year-old Emma suffers serious injuries as a result of a defectively manufactured toy. Because Emma is a minor, her parent or legal guardian can bring a lawsuit on her behalf. •

▶ The State and Federal Court Systems

As mentioned earlier in this chapter, each state has its own court system. Additionally, there is a system of federal courts. Even though there are fifty-two court systems—one for each of the fifty states, one for the District of Columbia, plus a federal system—similarities abound. Exhibit 2–2 below illustrates the basic organizational structure characteristic of the court systems in many states. The exhibit also shows how the federal court system is structured.

Keep in mind that the federal courts are not superior to the state courts—they are simply an independent system of courts, which derives its authority from Article III, Sections 1 and 2, of the U.S. Constitution. We turn now to an examination of these court systems, beginning with the state courts.

The State Court Systems

Typically, a state court system will include several levels, or tiers, of courts. As indicated in Exhibit 2–2 below, state courts may include (1) trial courts of limited jurisdiction, (2) trial courts of general jurisdiction, (3) appellate courts, and (4) the state's highest court (often called the state supreme court). Generally, any person who is a party to a lawsuit has the opportunity to plead the case before a trial court and then, if he or she loses, before at least one level of appellate court. Only if the case involves a federal statute or a federal constitutional issue may the decision of a state supreme court on that issue be further appealed to the United States Supreme Court.

• *Exhibit* 2–2 **The State and Federal Court Systems**

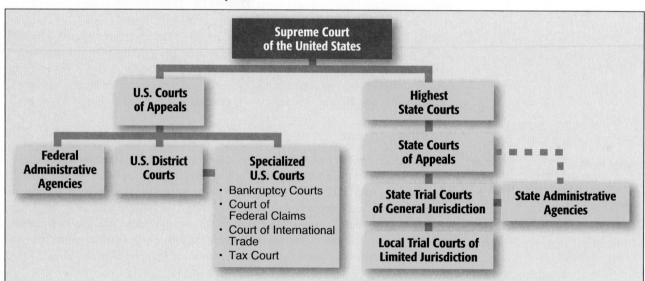

The states use various methods to select judges for their courts: in most states, judges are elected, but in some states, they are appointed. Usually, states specify the number of years that a judge will serve. In contrast, as you will read shortly, judges in the federal court system are appointed by the president of the United States and, if they are confirmed by the Senate, hold office for life—unless they engage in blatantly illegal conduct.

TRIAL COURTS   Trial courts are exactly what their name implies—courts in which trials are held and testimony taken. State trial courts have either general or limited jurisdiction. Trial courts that have general jurisdiction as to subject matter may be called county, district, superior, or circuit courts.[8] The jurisdiction of these courts is often determined by the size of the county in which the court sits. State trial courts of general jurisdiction have jurisdiction over a wide variety of subjects, including both civil disputes and criminal prosecutions. (In some states, trial courts of general jurisdiction may hear appeals from courts of limited jurisdiction.)

Some courts of limited jurisdiction are called special inferior trial courts or minor judiciary courts. **Small claims courts** are inferior trial courts that hear only civil cases involving claims of less than a certain amount, such as $5,000 (the amount varies from state to state). Suits brought in small claims courts are generally conducted informally, and lawyers are not required (in a few states, lawyers are not even allowed).

Another example of an inferior trial court is a local municipal court that hears mainly traffic cases. Decisions of small claims courts and municipal courts may sometimes be appealed to a state trial court of general jurisdiction. Other courts of limited jurisdiction as to subject matter include domestic relations or family courts, which handle primarily divorce actions and child-custody disputes, and probate courts.

A few states have even established Islamic law courts, which are courts of limited jurisdiction that serve the American Muslim community. This chapter's *Beyond Our Borders* feature discusses the rise of Islamic law courts.

Small Claims Court   A special court in which parties may litigate small claims (such as $5,000 or less) without an attorney.

Beyond Our Borders   Islamic Law Courts Abroad and at Home

Civil Law System   A system of law derived from the Roman Empire and based on a code rather than case law. Most European nations have this system.

Islamic law is one of the world's three most common legal systems, along with a **civil law system** and a common law system. In most Islamic countries, the law is based on *sharia*, a system of law derived from the Qur'an and the sayings and doings of Muhammad and his companions. Today, many non-Islamic countries are establishing Islamic courts for their Muslim citizens.

For example, Great Britain has councils that arbitrate disputes between British Muslims involving child custody, property, employment, and housing. These councils do not deal with criminal law or with any civil issues that would put *sharia* in direct conflict with British statutory law. Britain now has eighty-five officially recognized *sharia* courts that have the full power of their equivalent courts within the traditional British judicial system.

The use of Islamic courts in the United States has been somewhat controversial. The legality of arbitration clauses that require disputes to be settled in Islamic courts has been upheld by regular state courts in some states. For instance, in Texas, an American Muslim couple married and was issued an Islamic marriage certificate. Years later, a dispute arose over marital property. The parties involved had signed an arbitration agreement stating that all claims and disputes were to be submitted to arbitration in front of the Texas Islamic Court. A Texas appeals court ruled that the arbitration agreement was valid and enforceable.[9] In other states, however, there has been a public backlash against the use of Islamic courts. In 2010, Oklahoma voters approved an initiative that prevents *sharia* law from being used there. In early

Continued ➡

---

8. The name in Ohio is court of common pleas, and the name in New York is supreme court.
9. *Jabri v. Qaddura*, 108 S.W.3d 404 (Tex.App.–Fort Worth 2003).

2012, a federal appellate court struck down the law as being unconstitutional. Alabama's state government was contemplating a similar law as an amendment to its constitution.

• **For Critical Analysis**

One of the arguments against allowing sharia *courts in the United States is that we would no longer have a common legal framework within our society. Do you agree or disagree? Why?*

LEARNING OBJECTIVE 3 **What is the difference between a trial court and an appellate court?**

APPELLATE, OR REVIEWING, COURTS   Every state has at least one court of appeals (appellate court, or reviewing court), which may be an intermediate appellate court or the state's highest court. About three-fourths of the states have intermediate appellate courts. Generally, courts of appeals do not conduct new trials in which evidence is submitted and witnesses are examined. Rather, an appellate court panel of three or more judges reviews the record of the case on appeal, which includes a transcript of the trial proceedings, and determines whether the trial court committed an error.

Question of Fact In a lawsuit, an issue that involves only disputed facts and not what the law is on a given point.

Question of Law In a lawsuit, an issue involving the application or interpretation of a law.

Focus on Questions of Law.   Appellate courts generally focus on questions of law, not questions of fact. A **question of fact** deals with what really happened in regard to the dispute being tried—such as whether a party actually burned a flag. A **question of law** concerns the application or interpretation of the law—such as whether flag-burning is a form of speech protected by the First Amendment to the U.S. Constitution. Only a judge, not a jury, can rule on questions of law.

Defer to the Trial Court's Finding of Facts.   Appellate courts normally defer (or give weight) to a trial court's findings on questions of fact. This is because the trial court judge and jury were in a better position to evaluate testimony by directly observing witnesses' gestures, appearance, and nonverbal behavior during the trial. At the appellate level, the judges review the written transcript of the trial, which does not include these nonverbal elements.

An appellate court will challenge a trial court's finding of fact only when the finding is clearly erroneous—that is, when it is contrary to the evidence presented at trial—or when there is no evidence to support the finding. **EXAMPLE 2.6**   A jury concludes that a manufacturer's product harmed the plaintiff, but no evidence was submitted to the court to support that conclusion. In this situation, the appellate court will hold that the trial court's decision was erroneous. • The options exercised by appellate courts will be discussed later in this chapter.

BE CAREFUL The decisions of a state's highest court are final on questions of state law.

HIGHEST STATE COURTS   The highest appellate court in a state is usually called the supreme court but may be called by some other name. For example, in both New York and Maryland, the highest state court is called the court of appeals. The decisions of each state's highest court are final on all questions of state law. Only when issues of federal law are involved can a decision made by a state's highest court be overruled by the United States Supreme Court.

The Federal Court System

The federal court system is basically a three-tiered model consisting of (1) U.S. district courts (trial courts of general jurisdiction) and various courts of limited jurisdiction, (2) U.S. courts of appeals (intermediate courts of appeals), and (3) the United States Supreme Court.

Unlike state court judges, who are usually elected, federal court judges—including the justices of the Supreme Court—are appointed by the president of the United States and confirmed by the U.S. Senate. All federal judges receive lifetime appointments (because under Article III they "hold their offices during Good Behavior.") They do not receive regular salary increases, though. In fact, judicial pay—at both the federal and state levels—has fallen behind the private sector while judges' caseloads have steadily increased.

Ethical Issue ⚖

Can justice be served when courts are underfunded? The economic downturn that started a few years ago has led to massive budget cuts for many of this nation's court systems. In California, for example, which is experiencing unsustainable state government budget deficits, court funding has been reduced by hundreds of millions of dollars. As a consequence, a typical civil lawsuit may take several years to be heard by a court. Nationwide, the American Bar Association found that in the last several years most states have cut court funding by almost 15 percent. Twenty-six states have stopped filling judicial vacancies. Some have even forced judges to take a leave of absence without pay. One municipal court in Ohio stopped accepting new cases because it could not buy paper.

The end result is that the courts are limiting access to the justice system. According to Rebecca Love Kourlis of the Institute for the Advancement of the American Legal System, our traditional idea that everyone has an equal right to justice is being threatened. The American Bar Association reports that its members fear that "the underfunding of our judicial system threatens the fundamental nature of our tripartite system of government." That brings to mind the words of Judge Learned Hand, who said in 1951: "If we are to keep our democracy, there must be one commandment: Thou shalt not ration justice."

U.S. DISTRICT COURTS At the federal level, the district court is the equivalent of a state trial court of general jurisdiction. There is at least one federal district court in every state. The number of judicial districts can vary over time, primarily owing to population changes and corresponding caseloads. There are ninety-four federal judicial districts. U.S. district courts have original jurisdiction in federal matters. Federal cases typically originate in district courts. There are other courts with original, but special (or limited), jurisdiction, such as the federal bankruptcy courts and others shown in Exhibit 2–2 on page 38.

U.S. COURTS OF APPEALS In the federal court system, there are thirteen U.S. courts of appeals—also referred to as U.S. circuit courts of appeals. The federal courts of appeals for twelve of the circuits, including the U.S. Court of Appeals for the District of Columbia Circuit, hear appeals from the federal district courts located within their respective judicial circuits. The Court of Appeals for the Thirteenth Circuit, called the Federal Circuit, has national appellate jurisdiction over certain types of cases, such as cases involving patent law and cases in which the U.S. government is a defendant.

The decisions of the circuit courts of appeals are final in most cases, but appeal to the United States Supreme Court is possible. Exhibit 2–3 on the following page shows the geographic boundaries of the U.S. circuit courts of appeals and the boundaries of the U.S. district courts within each circuit.

THE UNITED STATES SUPREME COURT The highest level of the three-tiered model of the federal court system is the United States Supreme Court. According to the language of Article III of the U.S. Constitution, there is only one national Supreme Court.

• *Exhibit 2-3* **Boundaries of the U.S. Courts of Appeals and U.S. District Courts**

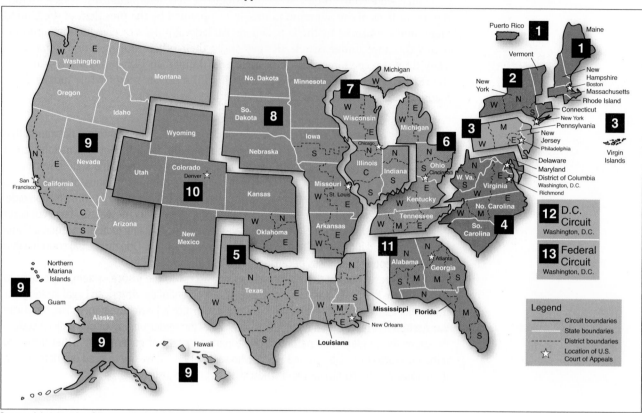

Source: Administrative Office of the United States Courts.

All other courts in the federal system are considered "inferior." Congress is empowered to create other inferior courts as it deems necessary. The inferior courts that Congress has created include the second tier in our model—the U.S. courts of appeals—as well as the district courts and any other courts of limited, or specialized, jurisdiction.

The United States Supreme Court consists of nine justices. Most of its work is as an appeals court. The Court can review any case decided by any of the federal courts of appeals, and it also has appellate authority over some cases decided in the state courts.

Appeals to the Court. To bring a case before the Supreme Court, a party requests that the Court issue a writ of *certiorari*. A **writ of *certiorari***[10] is an order issued by the Supreme Court to a lower court requiring the latter to send it the record of the case for review. The Court will not issue a writ unless at least four of the nine justices approve of it. This is called the **rule of four.** Whether the Court will issue a writ of *certiorari* is entirely within its discretion. The Court is not required to issue one, and most petitions for writs are denied. (Although thousands of cases are filed with the Supreme Court each year, it hears, on average, fewer than one hundred of these cases.)[11] A denial is not a decision on the merits of a case, nor does it indicate

Writ of *Certiorari*   A writ from a higher court asking a lower court for the record of a case.

Rule of Four   A rule of the United States Supreme Court under which the Court will not issue a writ of *certiorari* unless at least four justices approve.

---

10. Pronounced sur-shee-uh-*rah*-ree.

11. From the mid-1950s through the early 1990s, the United States Supreme Court reviewed more cases per year than it has in the last few years. In the Court's 1982–1983 term, for example, the Court issued opinions in 151 cases. In contrast, in its 2011–2012 term, the Court issued opinions in only **77** cases.

agreement with the lower court's opinion. Furthermore, a denial of the writ has no value as a precedent.

Petitions Granted by the Court. Typically, the Court grants petitions when cases raise important constitutional questions or when the lower courts are issuing conflicting decisions on a significant issue. The justices, however, never explain their reasons for hearing certain cases and not others, so it is difficult to predict which cases the Court will select.

▶ Following a State Court Case

To illustrate the procedures that would be followed in a civil lawsuit brought in a state court, we present a hypothetical case and follow it through the state court system. The case involves an automobile accident in which Kevin Anderson, driving a Lexus, struck Lisa Marconi, driving a Hyundai Genesis. The accident occurred at the intersection of Wilshire Boulevard and Rodeo Drive in Beverly Hills, California. Marconi suffered personal injuries, incurring medical and hospital expenses as well as lost wages for four months. Anderson and Marconi are unable to agree on a settlement, and Marconi sues Anderson. Marconi is the plaintiff, and Anderson is the defendant. Both are represented by lawyers.

During each phase of the **litigation** (the process of resolving a lawsuit through the court system), Marconi and Anderson will have to observe strict procedural requirements. A large body of law—procedural law—establishes the rules and standards for determining disputes in courts. Procedural rules are very complex, and they vary from court to court and from state to state. There is a set of federal rules of procedure as well as various sets of rules for state courts. Additionally, the applicable procedures will depend on whether the case is a civil or criminal proceeding. Generally, the Marconi-Anderson civil lawsuit will involve the procedures discussed in the following subsections. Keep in mind that attempts to settle the case may be ongoing throughout the trial.

The Pleadings

The complaint and answer (and the counterclaim and reply)—all of which are discussed below—taken together are called the **pleadings.** The pleadings inform each party of the other's claims and specify the issues (disputed questions) involved in the case. The style and form of the pleadings may be quite different in different states.

THE PLAINTIFF'S COMPLAINT   Marconi's suit against Anderson commences when her lawyer files a **complaint** with the appropriate court. The complaint contains a statement alleging (1) the facts necessary for the court to take jurisdiction, (2) a brief summary of the facts necessary to show that the plaintiff is entitled to a remedy,[12] and (3) a statement of the remedy the plaintiff is seeking. Complaints may be lengthy or brief, depending on the complexity of the case and the rules of the jurisdiction.

After the complaint has been filed, the sheriff, a deputy of the county, or another *process server* (one who delivers a complaint and summons) serves a **summons** and a copy of the complaint on defendant Anderson. The summons notifies Anderson

"Lawsuit: A machine which you go into as a pig and come out of as a sausage."
Ambrose Bierce, 1842–1914
(American journalist)

Litigation   The process of resolving a dispute through the court system.

Pleadings   Statements made by the plaintiff and the defendant in a lawsuit that detail the facts, charges, and defenses of a case.

Complaint   The pleading made by a plaintiff or a charge made by the state alleging wrongdoing on the part of the defendant.

Summons   A document informing a defendant that a legal action has been commenced against her or him and that the defendant must appear in court on a certain date to answer the plaintiff's complaint.

---

12. The factual allegations in a complaint must be enough to raise a right to relief above the speculative level. They must plausibly suggest that the plaintiff is entitled to a remedy. *Bell Atlantic Corp. v. Twombly,* 550 U.S. 544, 127 S.Ct. 1955, 167 L.Ed.2d 929 (2007).

that he must file an answer to the complaint with both the court and the plaintiff's attorney within a specified time period (usually twenty to thirty days).

The summons also informs Anderson that failure to answer may result in a **default judgment** for the plaintiff, meaning the plaintiff could be awarded the damages alleged in her complaint. Service of process is essential in our legal system. No case can proceed to a trial unless the plaintiff can prove that he or she has properly served the defendant.

Default Judgment   A judgment entered by a court against a defendant who has failed to appear in court to answer or defend against the plaintiff's claim.

THE DEFENDANT'S ANSWER   The defendant's **answer** either admits the statements or allegations set forth in the complaint or denies them and outlines any defenses that the defendant may have. If Anderson admits to all of Marconi's allegations in his answer, the court will enter a judgment for Marconi. If Anderson denies any of Marconi's allegations, the litigation will go forward.

Answer   Procedurally, a defendant's response to a complaint.

Anderson can deny Marconi's allegations and set forth his own claim that Marconi was in fact negligent and therefore owes him compensation for the damage to his Lexus. This is appropriately called a **counterclaim.** If Anderson files a counterclaim, Marconi will have to answer it with a pleading, normally called a **reply,** which has the same characteristics as an answer.

Counterclaim   A claim made by a defendant in a civil lawsuit against the plaintiff.

Reply   Procedurally, a plaintiff's response to a defendant's answer.

Anderson can also admit the truth of Marconi's complaint but raise new facts that may result in dismissal of the action. This is called raising an *affirmative defense.* For example, Anderson could assert the expiration of the time period under the relevant *statute of limitations* (a state or federal statute that sets the maximum time period during which a certain action can be brought or rights enforced) as an affirmative defense.

MOTION TO DISMISS   A **motion to dismiss** requests the court to dismiss the case for stated reasons. Grounds for dismissal of a case include improper delivery of the complaint and summons, improper venue, and the plaintiff's failure to state a claim for which a court could grant relief (a remedy). For instance, if Marconi had suffered no injuries or losses as a result of Anderson's negligence, Anderson could move to have the case dismissed because Marconi would not have stated a claim for which relief could be granted.

Motion to Dismiss   A pleading in which a defendant admits the facts as alleged by the plaintiff but asserts that the plaintiff's claim has no basis in law.

If the judge grants the motion to dismiss, the plaintiff generally is given time to file an amended complaint. If the judge denies the motion, the suit will go forward, and the defendant must then file an answer. Note that if Marconi wishes to discontinue the suit because, for example, an out-of-court settlement has been reached, she can likewise move for dismissal. The court can also dismiss the case on its own motion.

Pretrial Motions

Either party may attempt to get the case dismissed before trial through the use of various pretrial motions. We have already mentioned the motion to dismiss. Two other important pretrial motions are the motion for judgment on the pleadings and the motion for summary judgment.

At the close of the pleadings, either party may make a **motion for judgment on the pleadings,** or on the merits of the case. The judge will grant the motion only when there is no dispute over the facts of the case and the sole issue to be resolved is a question of law. In deciding on the motion, the judge may consider only the evidence contained in the pleadings.

Motion for Judgment on the Pleadings   A motion requesting the court to decide the issue solely on the pleadings without proceeding to trial.

Motion for Summary Judgment   A motion requesting the court to enter a judgment without proceeding to trial. The motion can be based on evidence outside the pleadings and will be granted only if no facts are in dispute.

In contrast, in a **motion for summary judgment,** the court may consider evidence outside the pleadings, such as sworn statements (affidavits) by parties or witnesses, or other documents relating to the case. Either party can make a motion for summary judgment. As with the motion for judgment on the pleadings, a motion for summary judgment will be granted only if there are no genuine questions of fact and the sole question is a question of law.

Discovery

Before a trial begins, each party can use a number of procedural devices to obtain information and gather evidence about the case from the other party or from third parties. The process of obtaining such information is known as **discovery.** Discovery includes gaining access to witnesses, documents, records, and other types of evidence.

The Federal Rules of Civil Procedure and similar rules in the states set forth the guidelines for discovery activity. Generally, discovery is allowed regarding any matter that is not privileged and is relevant to the claim or defense of any party. Discovery rules also attempt to protect witnesses and parties from undue harassment and to safeguard privileged or confidential material from being disclosed. If a discovery request involves privileged or confidential business information, a court can deny the request and can limit the scope of discovery in a number of ways. For instance, a court can require the party to submit the materials to the judge in a sealed envelope so that the judge can decide if they should be disclosed to the opposing party. A court may sanction parties who do not comply with discovery rules, such as submitting materials in a timely manner.

Discovery prevents surprises at trial by giving parties access to evidence that might otherwise be hidden. This allows both parties to learn as much as they can about what to expect at a trial before they reach the courtroom. It also serves to narrow the issues so that trial time is spent on the main questions in the case.

DEPOSITIONS AND INTERROGATORIES Discovery can involve the use of depositions or interrogatories, or both. A **deposition** is sworn testimony by a party to the lawsuit or any witness. The person being deposed (the deponent) answers questions asked by the attorneys, and the questions and answers are recorded by an authorized court official and sworn to and signed by the deponent. (Occasionally, written depositions are taken when witnesses are unable to appear in person.) The answers given to depositions will, of course, help the attorneys prepare their cases. They can also be used in court to impeach (challenge the credibility of) a party or a witness who changes her or his testimony at the trial. In addition, the answers given in a deposition can be used as testimony if the witness is not available at trial.

An **interrogatory** is a series of written questions for which written answers are prepared and then signed under oath. The main difference between interrogatories and written depositions is that interrogatories are directed to a party to the lawsuit (the plaintiff or the defendant), not to a witness, and the party can prepare answers with the aid of an attorney. The scope of interrogatories is broader because parties are obligated to answer the questions, even if that means disclosing information from their records and files.

REQUESTS FOR OTHER INFORMATION A party can serve a written request on the other party for an admission of the truth on matters relating to the trial. Any matter admitted under such a request is conclusively established for the trial. For example, Marconi can ask Anderson to admit that he was driving at a speed of forty-five miles an hour. A request for admission saves time at trial because the parties will not have to spend time proving facts on which they already agree.

Discovery A method by which the opposing parties obtain information from each other to prepare for trial.

Deposition The testimony of a party to a lawsuit or a witness taken under oath before a trial.

Interrogatory A series of written questions for which written answers are prepared and then signed under oath by the plaintiff or the defendant.

A party can also gain access to documents and other items not in her or his possession in order to inspect and examine them. Likewise, a party can gain "entry upon land" to inspect the premises. Anderson's attorney, for example, normally can gain permission to inspect and photocopy Marconi's car repair bills.

When the physical or mental condition of one party is in question, the opposing party can ask the court to order a physical or mental examination. If the court issues the order, which it will do only if the need for the information outweighs the right to privacy of the person to be examined, the opposing party can obtain the results of the examination.

ELECTRONIC DISCOVERY   Any relevant material, including information stored electronically, can be the object of a discovery request. The federal rules and most state rules now specifically allow all parties to obtain electronic "data compilations." Electronic evidence, or **e-evidence,** includes all types of computer-generated or electronically recorded information, such as e-mail, voice mail, tweets, blogs, spreadsheets, document preparation systems, and other data. E-evidence can reveal significant facts that are not discoverable by other means.

E-Evidence A type of evidence that consists of all computer-generated or electronically recorded information.

For example, computers automatically record certain information about files—such as who created the file and when, and who accessed, modified, or transmitted it—on their hard drives. This information can be obtained only from the file in its electronic format—not from printed-out versions.

LEARNING OBJECTIVE 4 **What is discovery, and how does electronic discovery differ from traditional discovery?**

E-Discovery Procedures.   The Federal Rules of Civil Procedure deal with the preservation, retrieval, and production of electronic data. Although traditional means, such as interrogatories and depositions, are still used to find out about the e-evidence, a party must usually hire an expert to retrieve evidence in its electronic format. The expert uses software to reconstruct e-mail (and sometimes social media) exchanges and establish who knew what and when they knew it. The expert can even recover files that the user thought had been deleted from a computer.

"The judicial system is the most expensive machine ever invented for finding out what happened and what to do about it."

Irving R. Kaufman, 1910–1992
(American jurist)

Advantages and Disadvantages.   Electronic discovery, or e-discovery, has significant advantages over paper discovery. Back-up copies of documents and e-mail can provide useful—and often quite damaging—information about how a particular matter progressed over several weeks or months. E-discovery can uncover the proverbial smoking gun that leads to litigation success, but it is also time consuming and expensive, especially when lawsuits involve large firms with multiple offices. Also, many firms are finding it difficult to fulfill their duty to preserve e-evidence from a vast number of sources.

For a discussion of some of the problems associated with preserving e-evidence for discovery, see this chapter's *Online Developments* feature on the facing page.

Pretrial Conference

Either party or the court can request a pretrial conference, or hearing. Usually, the hearing consists of an informal discussion between the judge and the opposing attorneys after discovery has taken place. The purpose of the hearing is to explore the possibility of a settlement without trial and, if this is not possible, to identify the matters that are in dispute and to plan the course of the trial.

Jury Selection

A trial can be held with or without a jury. The Seventh Amendment to the U.S. Constitution guarantees the right to a jury trial for cases in *federal* courts when the amount in controversy exceeds $20, but this guarantee does not apply to state courts.

ONLINE DEVELOPMENTS

The Duty to Preserve E-Evidence for Discovery

Today, less than 0.5 percent of new information is created on paper. Instead of sending letters and memos, people send e-mails and text messages, creating a massive amount of electronically stored information (ESI). The law requires parties to preserve ESI whenever there is a "reasonable anticipation of litigation."

Why Companies Fail to Preserve E-Evidence

Preserving e-evidence can be a challenge, though, particularly for large corporations that have electronic data scattered across multiple networks, servers, desktops, laptops, iPhones, iPads, and other smartphones and tablets. Although many companies have policies regarding back-up of office e-mail and computer systems, these may cover only a fraction of the e-evidence requested in a lawsuit.

Technological advances further complicate the situation. Users of BlackBerrys, for example, can configure them so that messages are transmitted with limited or no archiving rather than going through a company's servers and being recorded. How can a company preserve e-evidence that is never on its servers? In one case, the court held that a company had a duty to preserve transitory "server log data," which exist only temporarily on a computer's memory.[a]

Potential Sanctions and Malpractice Claims

A court may impose sanctions (such as fines) on a party that fails to preserve electronic evidence or to comply with e-discovery requests. A firm may be sanctioned if it provides e-mails without the attachments, does not produce all of the e-evidence requested, overwrites the contents of files, or fails to suspend its automatic e-mail deletion procedures. Sanctions for e-discovery violations

have become increasingly common in recent years.[b] Attorneys who fail to properly advise their clients concerning the duty to preserve e-evidence also often face sanctions and malpractice claims.[c]

Lessons from Intel

A party that fails to preserve e-evidence may even find itself at such a disadvantage that it will settle a dispute rather than continue litigation. For example, Advanced Micro Devices, Inc. (AMD), sued Intel Corporation, one of the world's largest microprocessor suppliers, for violating antitrust laws. Immediately after the lawsuit was filed, Intel began collecting and preserving the ESI on its servers. Although the company instructed its employees to retain documents and e-mails related to competition with AMD, many employees saved only copies of the e-mails that they had received and not e-mails that they had sent.

In addition, Intel did not stop its automatic e-mail deletion system, causing other information to be lost. In the end, although Intel produced data that were equivalent to "somewhere in the neighborhood of a pile [of paper] 137 miles high," its failure to preserve e-evidence led it to settle the dispute.[d]

FOR CRITICAL ANALYSIS

How might a large company protect itself from allegations that it intentionally failed to preserve electronic data?

---

b. See, for example, *Io Group, Inc. v. GLBT, Ltd.,* 2011; WL 4974337 (N.D.Cal. 2011); and *Genger v. TR Investors, LLC,* 26 A.3d 180 (Del.Supr. 2011).

c. See, for example, *Surowiec v. Capital Title Agency, Inc.,* 790 F.Supp.2d 997 (D.Ariz. 2011).

d. See *In re Intel Corp. Microprocessor Antitrust Litigation,* 2008 WL 2310288 (D.Del. 2008).

---

a. See *Columbia Pictures v. Brunell,* 2007 WL 2080419 (C.D.Cal. 2007).

Most states have similar guarantees in their own constitutions (although the threshold dollar amount is higher than $20). The right to a trial by jury does not have to be exercised, and many cases are tried without a jury. In most states and in federal courts, one of the parties must request a jury in a civil case, or the judge presumes the parties waive the right.

Before a jury trial commences, a jury must be selected. The jury selection process is known as **voir dire**.[13] During *voir dire* in most jurisdictions, attorneys for the plaintiff and the defendant ask prospective jurors oral questions to determine whether a potential jury member is biased or has any connection with a party to the action or with a prospective witness. In some jurisdictions, the judge may do all or part of the questioning based on written questions submitted by counsel for the parties.

Voir Dire The process in which the attorneys question prospective jurors to learn about their personal characteristics that may affect their ability to serve as impartial jurors.

---

13. Pronounced vwahr *deehr.*

During *voir dire,* a party may challenge a prospective juror *peremptorily*—that is, ask that an individual not be sworn in as a juror without providing any reason. Alternatively, a party may challenge a prospective juror *for cause*—that is, provide a reason why an individual should not be sworn in as a juror. If the judge grants the challenge, the individual is asked to step down. A prospective juror may not be excluded from the jury by the use of discriminatory challenges, however, such as those based on racial criteria or gender.

The Trial

At the beginning of the trial, the attorneys present their opening arguments, setting forth the facts that they expect to prove during the trial. Then the plaintiff's case is presented. In our hypothetical case, Marconi's lawyer would introduce evidence (relevant documents, exhibits, and the testimony of witnesses) to support Marconi's position. The defendant has the opportunity to challenge any evidence introduced and to cross-examine any of the plaintiff's witnesses.

DIRECTED VERDICTS   At the end of the plaintiff's case, the defendant's attorney has the opportunity to ask the judge to direct a verdict for the defendant on the ground that the plaintiff has presented no evidence that would justify the granting of the plaintiff's remedy. This is called a **motion for a directed verdict** (known in federal courts as a *motion for judgment as a matter of law*). If the motion is not granted (it seldom is granted), the defendant's attorney then presents the evidence and witnesses for the defendant's case. At the conclusion of the defendant's case, the defendant's attorney has another opportunity to make a motion for a directed verdict. The plaintiff's attorney can challenge any evidence introduced and cross-examine the defendant's witnesses.

CLOSING ARGUMENTS AND THE AWARD   After the defense concludes its presentation, the attorneys present their closing arguments, each urging a verdict in favor of her or his client. The judge instructs the jury in the law that applies to the case (these instructions are often called *charges*), and the jury retires to the jury room to deliberate on a verdict. In the Marconi-Anderson case, the jury will not only decide for the plaintiff or for the defendant but, if it finds for the plaintiff, will also decide on the amount of the **award** (the compensation to be paid to her).

Posttrial Motions

After the jury has rendered its verdict, either party may make a posttrial motion. If Marconi wins and Anderson's attorney has previously moved for a directed verdict, Anderson's attorney may make a **motion for judgment n.o.v.** (from the Latin *non obstante veredicto,* which means "notwithstanding the verdict"—called a *motion for judgment as a matter of law* in the federal courts). Such a motion will be granted only if the jury's verdict was unreasonable and erroneous. If the judge grants the motion, the jury's verdict will be set aside, and a judgment will be entered in favor of the opposite party (Anderson).

Alternatively, Anderson could make a **motion for a new trial,** asking the judge to set aside the adverse verdict and to hold a new trial. The motion will be granted if, after looking at all the evidence, the judge is convinced that the jury was in error but does not feel that it is appropriate to grant judgment for the other side. A judge can also grant a new trial on the basis of newly discovered evidence, misconduct by the participants or the jury during the trial (such as when an attorney or jury member has made prejudicial and inflammatory remarks), or error by the judge.

TAKE NOTE   A prospective juror cannot be excluded solely on the basis of his or her race or gender.

Motion for a Directed Verdict   A motion for the judge to direct a verdict for the party who filed the motion on the ground that the other party has not produced sufficient evidence to support her or his claim.

Award   The monetary compensation given to a party at the end of a trial or other proceeding.

Motion for Judgment *n.o.v.*   A motion requesting the court to grant judgment in favor of the party making the motion on the ground that the jury's verdict against him or her was unreasonable and erroneous.

Motion for a New Trial   A motion asserting that the trial was so fundamentally flawed that a new trial is necessary to prevent a miscarriage of justice.

The Appeal

Assume here that any posttrial motion is denied and that Anderson appeals the case. (If Marconi wins but receives a smaller monetary award than she sought, she can appeal also.) Keep in mind, though, that a party cannot appeal a trial court's decision simply because he or she is dissatisfied with the outcome of the trial.

A party must have legitimate grounds to file an appeal, meaning that he or she must be able to claim that the lower court committed an error. If Anderson has grounds to appeal the case, a notice of appeal must be filed with the clerk of the trial court within a prescribed time. Anderson now becomes the appellant, or petitioner, and Marconi becomes the appellee, or respondent.

FILING THE APPEAL   Anderson's attorney files the record on appeal with the appellate court. The record includes the pleadings, the trial transcript, the judge's rulings on motions made by the parties, and other trial-related documents. Anderson's attorney will also provide the reviewing court with a condensation of the record, known as an *abstract,* and a brief.

> **Brief**   A written summary or statement prepared by one side in a lawsuit to explain its case to the judge.

The **brief** is a formal legal document outlining the facts and issues of the case, the judge's rulings or jury's findings that should be reversed or modified, the applicable law, and arguments on Anderson's behalf (citing applicable statutes and relevant cases as precedents). Briefs can be filed electronically in many jurisdictions (see the discussion of electronic filing on the next page).

Marconi's attorney will file an answering brief. Anderson's attorney can file a reply to Marconi's brief, although it is not required. The reviewing court then considers the case.

APPELLATE REVIEW   As mentioned earlier, a court of appeals does not hear evidence. Rather, it reviews the record for errors of law. Its decision concerning a case is based on the record on appeal, the abstracts, and the attorneys' briefs. The attorneys can present oral arguments, after which the case is taken under advisement. In general, appellate courts do not reverse findings of fact unless the findings are unsupported or contradicted by the evidence.

An appellate court has the following options after reviewing a case:

1. The court can *affirm* the trial court's decision.
2. The court can *reverse* the trial court's judgment if it concludes that the trial court erred or that the jury did not receive proper instructions.
3. The appellate court can *remand* (send back) the case to the trial court for further proceedings consistent with its opinion on the matter.
4. The court might also affirm or reverse a decision *in part.* For example, the court might affirm the jury's finding that Anderson was negligent but remand the case for further proceedings on another issue (such as the extent of Marconi's damages).
5. An appellate court can also *modify* a lower court's decision. If the appellate court decides that the jury awarded an excessive amount in damages, for example, the court might reduce the award to a more appropriate, or fairer, amount.

APPEAL TO A HIGHER APPELLATE COURT   If the reviewing court is an intermediate appellate court, the losing party may decide to appeal to the state supreme court (the highest state court). Such a petition corresponds to a petition for a writ of *certiorari* from the United States Supreme Court. Although the losing party has a right to ask (petition) a higher court to review the case, the party does not have a right to have the case heard by the higher appellate court.

Appellate courts normally have discretionary power and can accept or reject an appeal. Like the United States Supreme Court, in general state supreme courts deny most appeals. If the appeal is granted, new briefs must be filed before the state supreme court, and the attorneys may be allowed or requested to present oral arguments. Like the intermediate appellate court, the supreme court may reverse or affirm the appellate court's decision or remand the case. At this point, the case typically has reached its end (unless a federal question is at issue and one of the parties has legitimate grounds to seek review by a federal appellate court).

Enforcing the Judgment

The uncertainties of the litigation process are compounded by the lack of guarantees that any judgment will be enforceable. Even if a plaintiff wins an award of damages in court, the defendant may not have sufficient assets or insurance to cover that amount. Usually, one of the factors considered before a lawsuit is initiated is whether the defendant has sufficient assets to cover the amount of damages sought, should the plaintiff win the case.

▶ The Courts Adapt to the Online World

We have already mentioned that the courts have attempted to adapt traditional jurisdictional concepts to the online world. Not surprisingly, the Internet has also brought about changes in court procedures and practices, including new methods for filing pleadings and other documents and issuing decisions and opinions. Some jurisdictions are exploring the possibility of cyber courts, in which legal proceedings could be conducted totally online.

Electronic Filing

The federal court system has now implemented its electronic filing system, Case Management/Electronic Case Files (CM/ECF), in nearly all of the federal courts. The system is available in federal district, appellate, and bankruptcy courts, as well as the Court of International Trade and the Court of Federal Claims. More than 33 million cases are on the CM/ECF system. Users can create a document using conventional software, save it as a PDF (portable digital file), then log on to a court's Web site and submit the PDF to the court via the Internet. Access to the electronic documents filed on CM/ECF is available through a system called PACER (Public Access to Court Electronic Records), which is a service of the U.S. Judiciary.

More than 60 percent of the states have some form of electronic filing. Some states, including Arizona, California, Colorado, Delaware, Mississippi, New Jersey, New York, and Nevada, offer statewide e-filing systems. Generally, when electronic filing is available, it is optional. Nonetheless, some state courts have now made e-filing mandatory in certain types of disputes, such as complex civil litigation.

Courts Online

Most courts today have sites on the Web. Of course, each court decides what to make available at its site. Some courts display only the names of court personnel and office phone numbers. Others add court rules and forms. Many appellate court sites include judicial decisions, although the decisions may remain online for only a limited time. In addition, in some states, such as California and Florida, court clerks offer information about the court's **docket** (the court's schedule of cases to be heard) and other searchable databases online.

Docket The list of cases entered on a court's calendar and thus scheduled to be heard by the court.

Appellate court decisions are often posted online immediately after they are rendered. Recent decisions of the U.S. courts of appeals, for example, are available online at their Web sites. The United States Supreme Court also has an official Web site and publishes its opinions there immediately after they are announced to the public.

Cyber Courts and Proceedings

Someday, litigants may be able to use cyber courts, in which judicial proceedings take place only on the Internet. The parties to a case could meet online to make their arguments and present their evidence. This might be done with e-mail submissions, through video cameras, in designated chat rooms, at closed sites, or through the use of other Internet facilities. These courtrooms could be efficient and economical. We might also see the use of virtual lawyers, judges, and juries—and possibly the replacement of court personnel with computer software.

Already the state of Michigan has passed legislation creating cyber courts that will hear cases involving technology issues and high-tech businesses. The state of Wisconsin recently enacted a rule authorizing the use of videoconferencing in both civil and criminal trials, at the discretion of the trial court.[14] In some situations, a Wisconsin judge can allow videoconferencing even over the objection of the parties, provided certain operational criteria are met.

The courts may also use the Internet in other ways. In a groundbreaking decision, for instance, a Florida county court granted "virtual" visitation rights in a couple's divorce proceeding. Each parent was ordered to set up a computerized videoconferencing system so that the child could visit with the parent who did not have custody via the Internet at any time. (Today, free Skype is readily available.)

▶ Alternative Dispute Resolution

Litigation is an expensive and time-consuming process. Because of the backlog of cases pending in many courts, several years may pass before a case is actually tried. For these and other reasons, more and more businesspersons are turning to **alternative dispute resolution (ADR)** as a means of settling their disputes.

Alternative Dispute Resolution (ADR) The resolution of disputes in ways other than those involved in the traditional judicial process, such as negotiation, mediation, and arbitration.

The great advantage of ADR is its flexibility. It ranges from the parties sitting down together to attempt to work out their differences to multinational corporations agreeing to resolve a dispute through a formal hearing before a panel of experts. Normally, the parties themselves can control how they will attempt to settle their dispute, what procedures will be used, whether a neutral third party will be present or make a decision, and whether that decision will be legally binding or nonbinding.

Today, more than 90 percent of cases are settled before trial through some form of ADR. Indeed, most states either require or encourage parties to undertake ADR prior to trial. Many federal courts have instituted ADR programs as well. In the following pages, we examine the basic forms of ADR. Keep in mind, though, that new methods of ADR—and new combinations of existing methods—are constantly being devised and employed.

Negotiation

Negotiation A process in which parties attempt to settle their dispute informally, with or without attorneys to represent them.

The simplest form of ADR is **negotiation,** in which the parties attempt to settle their dispute informally, with or without attorneys to represent them. Attorneys frequently advise their clients to negotiate a settlement voluntarily before they proceed

---

14. Wisconsin Statute Section 751.12.

to trial. Parties may even try to negotiate a settlement during a trial, or after the trial but before an appeal. Negotiation traditionally involves just the parties themselves and (typically) their attorneys. The attorneys, though, are advocates—they are obligated to put their clients' interests first.

Mediation

Mediation A method of settling disputes outside the courts by using a neutral third party who acts as a communicating agent between the parties and assists them in negotiating a settlement.

In **mediation,** a neutral third party acts as a mediator and works with both sides in the dispute to facilitate a resolution. The mediator talks with the parties separately as well as jointly and emphasizes their points of agreement in an attempt to help the parties evaluate their options. Although the mediator may propose a solution (called a *mediator's proposal*), he or she does not make a decision resolving the matter. States that require parties to undergo ADR before trial often offer mediation as one of the ADR options or (as in Florida) the only option.

One of the main advantages of mediation is that it is not as adversarial as litigation. In trials, the parties "do battle" with each other in the courtroom, trying to prove one another wrong, while the judge is usually a passive observer. In mediation, the mediator takes an active role and attempts to bring the parties together so that they can come to a mutually satisfactory resolution. The mediation process tends to reduce the hostility between the disputants, allowing them to resume their former relationship without bad feelings. For this reason, mediation is often the preferred form of ADR for disputes involving business partners, employers and employees, or other parties involved in long-term relationships.

LEARNING OBJECTIVE 5 What are three alternative methods of resolving disputes?

EXAMPLE 2.7 Two business partners, Mark Shalen and Charles Rowe, have a dispute over how the profits of their firm should be distributed. If the dispute is litigated, the parties will be adversaries, and their respective attorneys will emphasize how the parties' positions differ, not what they have in common. In contrast, when the dispute is mediated, the mediator emphasizes the common ground shared by Shalen and Rowe and helps them work toward agreement. The two men can work out the distribution of profits without damaging their continuing relationship as partners. •

Arbitration

Arbitration The settling of a dispute by submitting it to a disinterested third party who renders a decision that is often legally binding.

A more formal method of ADR is **arbitration,** in which an arbitrator (a neutral third party or a panel of experts) hears a dispute and imposes a resolution on the parties. Arbitration is unlike other forms of ADR because the third party hearing the dispute makes a decision for the parties. Exhibit 2–4 on the facing page outlines the basic differences among the three traditional forms of ADR. Usually, the parties in arbitration agree that the third party's decision will be *legally binding,* although the parties can also agree to *nonbinding* arbitration. (Arbitration that is mandated by the courts often is *nonbinding.*) In nonbinding arbitration, the parties can go forward with a lawsuit if they do not agree with the arbitrator's decision.

In some respects, formal arbitration resembles a trial, although usually the procedural rules are much less restrictive than those governing litigation. In the typical arbitration, the parties present opening arguments and ask for specific remedies. Evidence is then presented, and witnesses may be called and examined by both sides. The arbitrator then renders a decision.

THE ARBITRATOR'S DECISION The arbitrator's decision is called an *award.* It is usually the final word on the matter. Although the parties may appeal an arbitrator's decision, a court's review of the decision will be much more restricted in scope than an appellate court's review of a trial court's decision. The general view is that because

• *Exhibit* 2–4 **Basic Differences in the Traditional Forms of Alternative Dispute Resolution**

TYPE OF ADR	DESCRIPTION	NEUTRAL THIRD PARTY PRESENT	WHO DECIDES THE RESOLUTION
Negotiation	The parties meet informally with or without their attorneys and attempt to agree on a resolution.	No	The parties themselves reach a resolution.
Mediation	A neutral third party meets with the parties and emphasizes points of agreement to help them resolve their dispute.	Yes	The parties decide the resolution, but the mediator may suggest or propose a resolution.
Arbitration	The parties present their arguments and evidence before an arbitrator at a hearing, and the arbitrator renders a decision resolving the parties' dispute.	Yes	The arbitrator imposes a resolution on the parties that may be either binding or nonbinding.

the parties were free to frame the issues and set the powers of the arbitrator at the outset, they cannot complain about the results. A court will set aside an award only in the event of one of the following:

1. The arbitrator's conduct or "bad faith" substantially prejudiced the rights of one of the parties.
2. The award violates an established public policy.
3. The arbitrator exceeded her or his powers—that is, arbitrated issues that the parties did not agree to submit to arbitration.

Arbitration Clause A clause in a contract that provides that, in the event of a dispute, the parties will submit the dispute to arbitration rather than litigate the dispute in court.

ARBITRATION CLAUSES Just about any commercial matter can be submitted to arbitration. Frequently, parties include an **arbitration clause** in a contract (a written agreement—see Chapter 11), providing that any dispute that arises under the contract will be resolved through arbitration rather than through the court system. Parties can also agree to arbitrate a dispute after the dispute arises.

ARBITRATION STATUTES Most states have statutes under which arbitration clauses will be enforced. Some state statutes compel arbitration of certain types of disputes, such as those involving public employees. At the federal level, the Federal Arbitration Act (FAA), enacted in 1925, enforces arbitration clauses in contracts involving maritime activity and interstate commerce. Because of the breadth of the commerce clause (see Chapter 4), arbitration agreements involving transactions only slightly connected to the flow of interstate commerce may fall under the FAA.

In the following case, the parties had agreed to arbitrate disputes involving their contract, but a state law allowed one party to void a contractual provision that required arbitration outside the state. The court had to decide if the FAA preempted (see page 84 in Chapter 4) the state law.

Case 2.3 **Cleveland Construction, Inc. v. Levco Construction, Inc.**

Court of Appeals of Texas, First District, 359 S.W.3d 843 (2012).

BACKGROUND AND FACTS Cleveland Construction, Inc. (CCI), was the general contractor on a project to build a grocery store in Houston, Texas. CCI hired Levco Construction, Inc., as a subcontractor to perform excavation and grading. The contract included an arbitration provision stating that any disputes would be resolved by arbitration in Ohio. When a dispute arose between the parties, Levco filed a suit against CCI in a Texas state court. CCI sought

Case 2.3–Continues next page ➡

Case 2.3–Continued

to compel arbitration in Ohio under the Federal Arbitration Act (FAA), but a Texas statute allows a party to void a contractual provision that requires arbitration outside Texas. The Texas court granted an emergency motion preventing arbitration. CCI appealed.

IN THE WORDS OF THE COURT . . .
Evelyn N. *KEYES*, Justice.
* * * *

[Texas] Business and Commerce Code section 272.001 provides:

If a contract contains a provision making * * * any conflict arising under the contract subject to * * * arbitration in another state, that provision is voidable by the party obligated by the contract to perform the construction * * *.

Levco argues * * * that it "exercised its option to void the requirement in the Contract to arbitrate in Lake County, Ohio."

*The FAA preempts all otherwise applicable inconsistent state laws * * * under the Supremacy Clause of the United States Constitution. The FAA declares written provisions for arbitration "valid, irrevocable, and enforceable, save upon such grounds as exist at law or in equity for the revocation of any contract."* [Emphasis added.]

* * * Applying section 272.001 as Levco asks us to do here would prevent us from enforcing a term of the parties' arbitration agreement–the venue–on a ground that is not recognized by the FAA or by general state-law contract principles. We hold that the FAA preempts application of this provision under the facts of this case.

* * * By allowing a party to * * * declare void a previously bargained-for provision, application of section 272.001 would undermine the declared federal policy of rigorous enforcement of arbitration agreements.

DECISION AND REMEDY   The Texas appellate court reversed the trial court, holding that the FAA preempts the Texas statute. CCI could compel arbitration in Ohio.

THE LEGAL ENVIRONMENT DIMENSION   *How would business be affected if each state could pass a statute, like the one in Texas, allowing parties to void out-of-state arbitrations?*

THE ISSUE OF ARBITRABILITY   Actions in which one party files a motion to compel arbitration often occur when a dispute arises over an agreement that contains an arbitration clause. If a court finds that the subject matter in controversy is covered by the agreement to arbitrate—even when the claim involves the violation of a statute, such as an employment statute—then a party may be compelled to arbitrate the dispute. Usually, a court will allow the claim to be arbitrated if the court, in interpreting the statute, can find no legislative intent to the contrary.

KEEP IN MIND   Litigation–even of a dispute over whether a particular matter should be submitted to arbitration–can be time consuming and expensive.

No party, however, will be ordered to submit a particular dispute to arbitration unless the court is convinced that the party consented to do so.[15] Additionally, the courts will not compel arbitration if it is clear that the prescribed arbitration rules and procedures are inherently unfair to one of the parties.

The terms of an arbitration agreement can limit the types of disputes that the parties agree to arbitrate. When the parties do not specify limits, however, disputes can arise as to whether a particular matter is covered by the arbitration agreement, and then the court will have to resolve the issue of arbitrability.

MANDATORY ARBITRATION IN THE EMPLOYMENT CONTEXT   A significant question in the last several years has concerned mandatory arbitration clauses in employment contracts. Many claim that employees' rights are not sufficiently protected when workers are forced, as a condition of being hired, to agree to arbitrate all disputes and thus waive their rights under statutes specifically designed to protect employees. The United States Supreme Court, however, has generally held that mandatory arbitration clauses in employment contracts are enforceable.

The Gilmer Decision.   In a landmark decision, *Gilmer v. Interstate/Johnson Lane Corp.,*[16] the Supreme Court held that a claim brought under a federal statute prohibiting

---

15. See, for example, *Wright v. Universal Maritime Service Corp.,* 525 U.S. 70, 119 S.Ct. 391, 142 L.Ed.2d 361 (1998).
16. 500 U.S. 20, 111 S.Ct. 1647, 114 L.Ed.2d 26 (1991).

age discrimination (see Chapter 17) could be subject to arbitration. The Court concluded that the employee had waived his right to sue when he agreed, as part of a required registration application to be a securities representative with the New York Stock Exchange, to arbitrate "any dispute, claim, or controversy" relating to his employment.

One-Sided Clauses. Since the *Gilmer* decision, some courts have refused to enforce one-sided arbitration clauses on the ground that they are *unconscionable.* (An unconscionable clause is void because one party, as a result of disproportionate bargaining power, is forced to accept terms that are unfairly burdensome and that benefit the dominating party.) Thus, businesspersons considering using arbitration clauses in employment contracts should be careful that they are not too one sided—especially provisions on how the parties will split the costs of the arbitration procedure.

PRIVATE ARBITRATION PROCEEDINGS In 2011, the Delaware Chancery Court established a new confidential arbitration process, which allows parties to arbitrate their disputes in private. Because many companies are headquartered in Delaware, the court's caseload is heavy, and its influence on the business environment is significant. Delaware's decision to authorize secret arbitration proceedings has been controversial.

EXAMPLE 2.8 Two smartphone makers were the first to use Delaware's confidential arbitration procedures to reach a settlement of their dispute. Skyworks Solutions, Inc., makes technology that transmits signals from smartphones, and Advanced Analogic Technologies, Inc. (AATI), makes power management devices for smartphones. Skyworks had agreed to a merger deal with AATI for $262.5 million, but then backed out, claiming that AATI had not properly accounted for revenue. Both parties filed lawsuits and ended up arbitrating using Delaware's new process. The two reached a settlement to complete the merger for $256 million, without disclosing the details of their agreement. •

Providers of ADR Services

ADR services are provided by both government agencies and private organizations. A major provider of ADR services is the American Arbitration Association (AAA). Most of the largest U.S. law firms are members of this nonprofit association. Cases brought before the AAA are heard by an expert or a panel of experts in the area relating to the dispute and usually are settled quickly. The AAA has a special team devoted to resolving large, complex disputes across a wide range of industries.

Hundreds of for-profit firms around the country also provide various forms of dispute-resolution services. Typically, these firms hire retired judges to conduct arbitration hearings or otherwise assist parties in settling their disputes. The judges follow procedures similar to those of the federal courts and use similar rules. Generally, each party to the dispute pays a filing fee and a designated fee for a hearing session or conference.

Online Dispute Resolution

Online Dispute Resolution (ODR) The resolution of disputes with the assistance of organizations that offer dispute-resolution services via the Internet.

An increasing number of companies and organizations offer dispute-resolution services using the Internet. The settlement of disputes in these online forums is known as **online dispute resolution (ODR).** The disputes have most commonly involved disagreements over the rights to domain names (Web site addresses—see Chapter 8) or over the quality of goods sold via the Internet, including goods sold through Internet auction sites.

ODR may be best suited for resolving small- to medium-sized business liability claims, which may not be worth the expense of litigation or traditional ADR. Rules being developed in online forums, however, may ultimately become a code of conduct for everyone who does business in cyberspace. Most online forums do not automatically apply the law of any specific jurisdiction. Instead, results are often based on general, universal legal principles. As with most offline methods of dispute resolution, any party may appeal to a court at any time if the ADR is nonbinding arbitration.

Interestingly, some cities are using ODR as a means of resolving claims against them. **EXAMPLE 2.9**   New York City has used Cybersettle.com to resolve auto accident, sidewalk, and other personal-injury claims made against the city. Parties with complaints submit their claims, and the city submits its offers confidentially online. Whenever an offer exceeds the claim, a settlement is reached, and the plaintiff gets to keep half of the difference between his or her claim and the city's offer as a bonus. ●

▶ Reviewing . . . The Courts and Alternative Dispute Resolution

Stan Garner resides in Illinois and promotes boxing matches for SuperSports, Inc., an Illinois corporation. Garner created the promotional concept of the "Ages" fights—a series of three boxing matches pitting an older fighter (George Foreman) against a younger fighter. The concept included titles for each of the three fights ("Challenge of the Ages," "Battle of the Ages," and "Fight of the Ages"), as well as promotional epithets to characterize the two fighters ("the Foreman Factor"). Garner contacted Foreman and his manager, who both reside in Texas, to sell the idea, and they arranged a meeting at Caesar's Palace in Las Vegas, Nevada. At some point in the negotiations, Foreman's manager signed a nondisclosure agreement prohibiting him from disclosing Garner's promotional concepts unless they signed a contract. Nevertheless, after negotiations fell through, Foreman used Garner's "Battle of the Ages" concept to promote a subsequent fight. Garner filed a lawsuit against Foreman and his manager in a federal district court in Illinois, alleging breach of contract. Using the information presented in the chapter, answer the following questions.

1. On what basis might the federal district court in Illinois exercise jurisdiction in this case?
2. Does the federal district court have original or appellate jurisdiction?
3. Suppose that Garner had filed his action in an Illinois state court. Could an Illinois state court exercise personal jurisdiction over Foreman or his manager? Why or why not?
4. Assume that Garner had filed his action in a Nevada state court. Would that court have personal jurisdiction over Foreman or his manager? Explain.

▶ Debate This

In this age of the Internet, when people communicate via e-mail, tweets, Facebook, and Skype, is the concept of jurisdiction losing its meaning? Explain your answer.

▶ Key Terms

alternative dispute resolution (ADR) 51
answer 44
arbitration 52
arbitration clause 53
award 48
bankruptcy court 33
brief 49
civil law system 39

complaint 43
concurrent jurisdiction 34
counterclaim 44
default judgment 44
deposition 45
discovery 45
diversity of citizenship 34
docket 50

e-evidence 46
exclusive jurisdiction 34
federal question 34
interrogatory 45
judicial review 31
jurisdiction 31
justiciable controversy 37
litigation 43

long arm statute 32
mediation 52
motion for a directed verdict 48
motion for a new trial 48
motion for judgment *n.o.v.* 48
motion for judgment on the pleadings 44
motion for summary judgment 44
motion to dismiss 44

negotiation 51
online dispute resolution (ODR) 55
pleadings 43
probate court 33
question of fact 40
question of law 40
reply 44
rule of four 42

small claims court 39
standing to sue 37
summons 43
venue 37
voir dire 47
writ of *certiorari* 42

▶ Chapter Summary: The Courts and Alternative Dispute Resolution

The Judiciary's Role in American Government (See pages 30–31.)	The role of the judiciary—the courts—in the American governmental system is to interpret and apply the law. Through the process of judicial review—determining the constitutionality of laws—the judicial branch acts as a check on the executive and legislative branches of government.

Basic Judicial Requirements (See pages 31–38.)	1. *Jurisdiction*—Before a court can hear a case, it must have jurisdiction over the person against whom the suit is brought or the property involved in the suit, as well as jurisdiction over the subject matter.
	  a. *Limited versus general jurisdiction*—Limited jurisdiction exists when a court is limited to a specific subject matter, such as probate or divorce. General jurisdiction exists when a court can hear any kind of case.
	  b. *Original versus appellate jurisdiction*—Courts that have authority to hear a case for the first time (trial courts) have original jurisdiction. Courts of appeals, or reviewing courts, have appellate jurisdiction. Generally, appellate courts do not have original jurisdiction.
	  c. *Federal jurisdiction*—Arises (1) when a federal question is involved (when the plaintiff's cause of action is based, at least in part, on the U.S. Constitution, a treaty, or a federal law) or (2) when a case involves diversity of citizenship and the amount in controversy exceeds $75,000.
	  d. *Concurrent versus exclusive jurisdiction*—Concurrent jurisdiction exists when two different courts have authority to hear the same case. Exclusive jurisdiction exists when only state courts or only federal courts have authority to hear a case.
	2. *Jurisdiction in cyberspace*—Because the Internet does not have physical boundaries, traditional jurisdictional concepts have been difficult to apply in cases involving online activities. Courts are developing standards for determining when jurisdiction over a Web site owner or operator located in another state is proper.
	3. *Venue*—Venue has to do with the most appropriate location for a trial.
	4. *Standing to sue*—A requirement that a party must have a legally protected and tangible interest at stake sufficient to justify seeking relief through the court system. The controversy at issue must also be a justiciable controversy—one that is real and substantial, as opposed to hypothetical or academic.

The State and Federal Court Systems (See pages 38–43.)	1. *Trial courts*—Courts of original jurisdiction, in which legal actions are initiated.
	  a. *State*—Courts of general jurisdiction can hear any case. Courts of limited jurisdiction include domestic relations courts, probate courts, traffic courts, and small claims courts.
	  b. *Federal*—The federal district court is the equivalent of the state trial court. Federal courts of limited jurisdiction include the U.S. Tax Court, the U.S. Bankruptcy Court, and the U.S. Court of Federal Claims.
	2. *Intermediate appellate courts*—Courts of appeals, or reviewing courts; generally without original jurisdiction. Many states have an intermediate appellate court. In the federal court system, the U.S. circuit courts of appeals are the intermediate appellate courts.
	3. *Supreme (highest) courts*—Each state has a supreme court, although it may be called by some other name. Appeal from the state supreme court to the United States Supreme Court is possible only if the case involves a federal question. The United States Supreme Court is the highest court in the federal court system.

(Continued)

▶ Chapter Summary: The Courts and Alternative Dispute Resolution, Continued

Following a State Court Case (See pages 43–50.)	Rules of procedure prescribe the way in which disputes are handled in the courts. Rules differ from court to court, and separate sets of rules exist for federal and state courts, as well as for criminal and civil cases. A civil court case in a state court would involve the following procedures:
	
	1. *The pleadings—*
	  a. *Complaint—*Filed by the plaintiff with the court to initiate the lawsuit; served with a summons on the defendant.
	  b. *Answer—*A response to the complaint in which the defendant admits or denies the allegations made by the plaintiff; may assert a counterclaim or an affirmative defense.
	  c. *Motion to dismiss—*A request to the court to dismiss the case for stated reasons, such as the plaintiff's failure to state a claim for which relief can be granted.
	2. *Pretrial motions (in addition to the motion to dismiss)—*
	  a. *Motion for judgment on the pleadings—*May be made by either party; will be granted if the parties agree on the facts and the only question is how the law applies to the facts. The judge bases the decision solely on the pleadings.
	  b. *Motion for summary judgment—*May be made by either party; will be granted if the parties agree on the facts. The judge applies the law in rendering a judgment. The judge can consider evidence outside the pleadings when evaluating the motion.
	3. *Discovery—*The process of gathering evidence concerning the case. Discovery involves depositions, interrogatories, and various requests for information. Discovery may also involve electronically recorded information, such as e-mail, voice mail, word-processing documents, and other data compilations.
	4. *Pretrial conference—*Either party or the court can request a pretrial conference to identify the matters in dispute after discovery has taken place and to plan the course of the trial.
	5. *Trial—*Following jury selection (*voir dire*), the trial begins with opening statements from both parties' attorneys. The following events then occur:
	  a. The plaintiff's introduction of evidence (including the testimony of witnesses) supporting the plaintiff's position. The defendant's attorney can challenge evidence and cross-examine witnesses.
	  b. The defendant's introduction of evidence (including the testimony of witnesses) supporting the defendant's position. The plaintiff's attorney can challenge evidence and cross-examine witnesses.
	  c. Closing arguments by the attorneys in favor of their respective clients, the judge's instructions to the jury, and the jury's verdict.
	6. *Posttrial motions—*
	  a. *Motion for judgment n.o.v.* ("notwithstanding the verdict")—Will be granted if the judge is convinced that the jury was in error.
	  b. *Motion for a new trial—*Will be granted if the judge is convinced that the jury was in error; can also be granted on the grounds of newly discovered evidence, misconduct by the participants during the trial, or error by the judge.
	7. *Appeal—*Either party can appeal the trial court's judgment to an appropriate court of appeals. After reviewing the record on appeal, the appellate court holds a hearing and renders its opinion.

The Courts Adapt to the Online World (See pages 50–51.)	Nearly all of the federal appellate courts and bankruptcy courts and a majority of the federal district courts have implemented electronic filing systems.
Alternative Dispute Resolution (See pages 51–56.)	1. *Negotiation—*The parties come together, with or without attorneys to represent them, and try to reach a settlement without the involvement of a third party. 2. *Mediation—*The parties themselves reach an agreement with the help of a neutral third party, called a mediator. The mediator may propose a solution but does not make a decision resolving the matter. 3. *Arbitration—*A more formal method of ADR in which the parties submit their dispute to a neutral third party, the arbitrator, who renders a decision. The decision may or may not be legally binding. 4. *Providers of ADR services—*Both nonprofit and for-profit firms provide ADR services. 5. *Online dispute resolution—*A number of organizations now offer this service through online forums.

ExamPrep

ISSUE SPOTTERS

—Check your answers to these questions against the answers provided in Appendix D at the end of this text.

1. Sue contracts with Tom to deliver a quantity of computers to Sue's Computer Store. They disagree over the amount, the delivery date, the price, and the quality. Sue files a suit against Tom in a state court. Their state requires that their dispute be submitted to mediation or nonbinding arbitration. If the dispute is not resolved, or if either party disagrees with the decision of the mediator or arbitrator, will a court hear the case? Explain. **(See pages 52 and 53.)**
2. At the trial, after Sue calls her witnesses, offers her evidence, and otherwise presents her side of the case, Tom has at least two choices between courses of action. Tom can call his first witness, or what else might he do? **(See page 48.)**

BEFORE THE TEST

Go to **www.cengagebrain.com**, enter the ISBN 9781133586548, and click on "Find" to locate this textbook's Web site. Then, click on "Access Now" under "Study Tools," and select Chapter 2 at the top. There, you will find a Practice Quiz that you can take to assess your mastery of the concepts in this chapter. Additionally, you will find Flashcards and a Glossary of important terms, as well as Video Questions (when assigned).

For Review

Answers for the even-numbered questions in this **For Review** *section can be found in Appendix E at the end of this text.*

1. What is judicial review?
2. Before a court can hear a case, it must have jurisdiction. Over what must it have jurisdiction? How are the courts applying traditional jurisdictional concepts to cases involving Internet transactions?
3. What is the difference between a trial court and an appellate court?
4. What is discovery, and how does electronic discovery differ from traditional discovery?
5. What are three alternative methods of resolving disputes?

Questions and Case Problems

2–1. Standing to Sue. Jack and Maggie Turton bought a house in Jefferson County, Idaho, located directly across the street from a gravel pit. A few years later, the county converted the pit to a landfill. The landfill accepted many kinds of trash that cause harm to the environment, including major appliances, animal carcasses, containers with hazardous content warnings, leaking car batteries, and waste oil. The Turtons complained to the county, but the county did nothing. The Turtons then filed a lawsuit against the county alleging violations of federal environmental laws pertaining to groundwater contamination and other pollution. Do the Turtons have standing to sue? Why or why not? **(See page 37.)**

2–2. **Question with Sample Answer: Jurisdiction.** Marya Callais, a citizen of Florida, sustained numerous injuries when she was walking along a busy street in Tallahassee and a large crate flew off a passing truck and hit her. She experienced a great deal of pain and suffering, incurred significant medical expenses, and could not work for six months. She wishes to sue the trucking firm for

$300,000 in damages. The firm's headquarters are in Georgia, although the company does business in Florida. In what court may Callais bring suit—a Florida state court, a Georgia state court, or a federal court? What factors might influence her decision? **(See pages 31–35.)**

—For a sample answer to Question 2–2, go to Appendix F at the end of this text.

2–3. Discovery. Advance Technology Consultants, Inc. (ATC), contracted with RoadTrac, LLC, to provide software and client software systems for the products of global positioning satellite (GPS) technology being developed by RoadTrac. RoadTrac agreed to provide ATC with hardware with which ATC's software would interface. Problems soon arose, however, and RoadTrac filed a lawsuit against ATC alleging breach of contract. During discovery, RoadTrac requested ATC's customer lists and marketing procedures. ATC objected to providing this information because RoadTrac and ATC had become competitors in the GPS industry. Should a party to a lawsuit have to hand over its confidential business secrets as part of a discovery request? Why or why not? What limitations might a court consider imposing before requiring ATC to produce this material? **(See page 45.)**

2-4. Discovery. Rita Peatie filed a suit against Walmart, alleging injuries to her head, neck, and shoulder. Peatie claimed that she had been struck two years earlier by a metal cylinder falling from a store ceiling. Over the next two years, Peatie made three requests for delays to conduct discovery. The court granted the first request, but denied the others. On the day of the trial—four years after the alleged injury—the plaintiff again asked the court for more time to conduct discovery. Should the court allow it? Why or why not? [*Peatie v. Walmart Stores, Inc.,* 112 Conn.App. 8, 961 A.2d 1016 (2009)] **(See page 45.)**

2-5.   **Case Problem with Sample Answer: Venue.** Brandy Austin used powdered infant formula to feed her infant daughter shortly after her birth. Austin claimed that a can of Nestlé Good Start Supreme Powder Infant Formula was contaminated with *Enterobacter sakazakii* bacteria, which can cause infections of the bloodstream and central nervous system, in particular, meningitis (which is an inflammation of the tissue surrounding the brain or spinal cord). Austin filed an action against Nestlé in Hennepin County District Court in Minnesota. Nestlé argued for a change of venue because the alleged tortious action on the part of Nestlé occurred in South Carolina. Austin is a South Carolina resident and gave birth to her daughter in that state. Should the case be transferred to a South Carolina venue? Why or why not? [*Austin v. Nestle USA, Inc.,* 677 F.Supp.2d 1134 (D.Minn. 2009)] **(See page 37.)**

—**For a sample answer to Case Problem 2–5, go to Appendix G at the end of this text.**

2-6. Arbitration. PRM Energy Systems owned patents that were licensed to Primenergy to use in the United States. Their contract stated that "all disputes" would be settled by arbitration. Kobe Steel of Japan was interested in using the technology represented by PRM's patents. Primenergy agreed to let Kobe use the technology in Japan without telling PRM. When PRM learned about the secret deal, the firm filed a suit against Primenergy for fraud and theft. Does this dispute go to arbitration or to trial? Why? [*PRM Energy Systems v. Primenergy,* 592 F.3d 830 (8th Cir. 2010)] **(See page 52.)**

2-7.   **Spotlight on the National Football League: Arbitration.** Bruce Matthews played football for the National Football League on the Tennessee Titans. As part of his employment contract, he agreed to submit any dispute to arbitration. He also agreed that Tennessee law would determine all matters related to workers' compensation (see Chapter 16). After Matthews retired, he filed a workers' compensation claim in California. The arbitrator ruled that Matthews could pursue his claim in California but only under Tennessee law. Should this ruling be set aside? Explain. [*National Football League Players Association v. National Football League Management Council,* 2011 WL 1137334 (S.D.Cal. 2011)] **(See pages 52 and 53.)**

2-8. Minimum Contacts. Seal Polymer Industries sold two freight containers of latex gloves to Med-Express, Inc., a company based in North Carolina. When Med-Express failed to pay the $104,000 owed for the gloves, Seal Polymer sued in an Illinois court and obtained a judgment against Med-Express. Med-Express argued that it did not have minimum contacts with Illinois and therefore the Illinois judgment based on personal jurisdiction was invalid. Med-Express stated that it was incorporated under North Carolina law, had its principal place of business in North Carolina, and therefore had no minimum contacts with Illinois. Was this statement alone sufficient to prevent the Illinois judgment from being collected against Med-Express in North Carolina? Why or why not? [*Seal Polymer Industries v. Med-Express, Inc.,* 725 S.E.2d 5 (N.C.App. 2012)] **(See page 32.)**

2-9.   **A Question of Ethics: Agreement to Arbitrate.** *Nellie Lumpkin, who suffered from dementia, was admitted to the Picayune Convalescent Center, a nursing home. Because of her diminished mental condition, her daughter, Beverly McDaniel, signed the admissions agreement. It included a clause requiring the parties to submit any dispute to arbitration. After Lumpkin left the center two years later, she filed a suit against Picayune to recover damages for mistreatment and malpractice. Is it ethical for this dispute to go to arbitration? Explain.* [Covenant Health & Rehabilitation of Picayune, LP v. Lumpkin, 23 So.2d 1092 (Miss.App. 2009)] **(See page 55.)**

Ethics and Business Decision Making

Contents

Learning Objectives

The five Learning Objectives below are designed to help improve your understanding of the chapter. After reading this chapter, you should be able to answer the following questions:

1. **What is business ethics, and why is it important?**
2. **How can business leaders encourage their companies to act ethically?**
3. **How do duty-based ethical standards differ from outcome-based ethical standards?**
4. **What are six guidelines that an employee can use to evaluate whether his or her actions are ethical?**
5. **What types of ethical issues might arise in the context of international business transactions?**

(John Elk III/Lonely Planet Images/Getty Images)

Ethics scandals erupted throughout corporate America during the first decade of the 2000s. Heads of major corporations were tried for fraud, conspiracy, grand larceny, and obstruction of justice. In 2009, for example, Bernard Madoff was convicted of bilking investors out of more than $65 billion through a Ponzi scheme (an illegal pyramid operation) that he had perpetrated for decades. Ethical problems plagued many U.S. financial institutions as well. These ethical scandals contributed to the onset of the deepest recession since the Great Depression of the 1930s. In the economic crisis that began in 2008, not only did some $9 trillion in investment capital evaporate, but millions of workers lost their jobs.

In short, the scope and scale of corporate unethical behavior, especially in the financial sector, skyrocketed (with enormous repercussions worldwide). The ethics scandals of the last several years have taught everyone that business ethics cannot be taken lightly. How you should act in business—business ethics—is the focus of this chapter.

▶ Business Ethics

Ethics Moral principles and values applied to social behavior.

As you might imagine, business ethics is derived from the concept of ethics. **Ethics** can be defined as the study of what constitutes right or wrong behavior. It is the branch of philosophy that focuses on morality and the way in which moral principles

Business Ethics   A consensus as to what constitutes right or wrong behavior in the world of business and how moral principles are applied by businesspersons.

are derived and applied to one's conduct in daily life. Ethics has to do with questions relating to the fairness, justness, rightness, or wrongness of an action.

Business ethics focuses on what constitutes right or wrong behavior in the business world and on how businesspersons apply moral and ethical principles to situations that arise in the workplace. Because business decision makers often address more complex ethical dilemmas than they face in their personal lives, business ethics is more complicated than personal ethics.

Why Is Business Ethics Important?

LEARNING OBJECTIVE 1   **What is business ethics, and why is it important?**

To see why business ethics is so important, think about all the corporate executives who are sitting behind bars because of their unethical business decisions. As a result of their crimes, their companies suffered losses, and some were forced to enter bankruptcy, causing workers to lose their jobs and retirement funds.

If these executives had acted ethically, the corporations, shareholders, and employees of those companies would not have paid such a high price. Thus, an in-depth understanding of business ethics is important to the long-run viability of a corporation. It is also important to the well-being of individual officers and directors, and to the firm's employees. Finally, unethical corporate decision making can negatively affect suppliers, consumers, the community, and society as a whole.

The Moral Minimum

Moral Minimum   The minimum degree of ethical behavior expected of a business firm.

The minimum acceptable standard for ethical business behavior—known as the **moral minimum**—normally is considered to be compliance with the law. In many corporate scandals, had most of the businesspersons involved simply followed the law, they would not have gotten into trouble. Note, though, that in the interest of preserving personal freedom, as well as for practical reasons, the law does not—and cannot— codify all ethical requirements.

As they make business decisions, businesspersons must remember that just because an action is legal does not necessarily make it ethical. For instance, no law specifies the salaries that publicly held corporations can pay their officers. Nevertheless, if a corporation pays its officers an excessive amount relative to other employees, or to what officers at other corporations are paid, the executives' compensation might be challenged as unethical. (Executive bonuses can also present ethical problems—see page 67.)

In the following case, the court had to determine if a repair shop was entitled to receive full payment of an invoice or a lesser amount given its conduct in the matter.

Case 3.1   **Johnson Construction Co. v. Shaffer**

Court of Appeal of Louisiana, Second Circuit, 87 So.3d 203 (2012).

BACKGROUND AND FACTS   A truck owned by Johnson Construction Company needed repairs. John Robert Johnson, Jr., the company's president, took the truck with its attached fifteen-ton trailer to Bubba Shaffer, doing business as Shaffer's Auto and Diesel Repair. The truck was supposedly fixed, and Johnson paid the bill. The truck continued to leak oil and water. Johnson returned the truck to Shaffer who again claimed to have fixed the problem. Johnson paid

the second bill. The problems with the truck continued, however, so Johnson returned the truck and trailer a third time. Shaffer gave a verbal estimate of $1,000 for the repairs, but he ultimately sent an invoice for $5,863.49. Johnson offered to settle for $2,480, the amount of the initial estimate ($1,000), plus the costs of parts and shipping. Shaffer refused the offer and would not return Johnson's truck or trailer until full payment was made. Shaffer also charged Johnson a

Case 3.1—Continued

storage fee of $50 a day and 18 percent interest on the $5,863.49. Johnson Construction filed a suit against Shaffer alleging unfair trade practices. The trial court determined that Shaffer had acted deceptively and wrongfully in maintaining possession of the trailer on which it had performed no work. The trial court awarded Johnson $3,500 in general damages, plus $750 in attorneys' fees. Shaffer was awarded the initial estimate of $1,000 and appealed.

IN THE WORDS OF THE COURT . . .
LOLLEY, J. [Judge]
     * * * *

     * * * At the outset, we point out that Mr. Johnson maintained he had a verbal agreement with Bubba Shaffer, the owner of Shaffer's Auto Diesel and Repair, that the repairs to the truck would cost $1,000. Mr. Johnson also testified that he was not informed otherwise.

     The existence or nonexistence of a contract is a question of fact, and the finder of fact's determination may not be set aside unless it is clearly wrong.
     * * * *

     * * * At the trial of the matter, the trial court was presented with testimony from Mr. Johnson, Mr. Shaffer, and Michael Louton, a mechanic employed by Shaffer.* * * The trial court did not believe Mr. Johnson was informed of the cost for the additional work.

     * * * We cannot say that the trial court was clearly wrong in its determination. * * * The trial court viewed Mr. Shaffer's testimony

on the issue as "disingenuous" and we cannot see where that was an error.

     As for the amount that Shaffer contends is due for storage, had it invoiced Mr. Johnson the amount of the original estimate in the first place, there would have been no need to store the truck or trailer. * * * We cannot see how Shaffer would be entitled to any payment for storage when it failed to return the truck and trailer where an offer of payment for the agreed upon price had been conveyed.
     * * * *

     * * * So considering, we see no error in the trial court's characterization of Shaffer's actions with the trailer as holding "hostage in an effort to force payment for unauthorized repairs." * * * Shaffer had no legal right to retain possession of the trailer * * * . *Thus, the trial court did not err in its determination that Shaffer's retention of Johnson Construction's trailer [for four years!] was a deceptive conversion of the trailer.* [Emphasis added.]

DECISION AND REMEDY   The state appellate court affirmed the judgment of the trial court in favor of Johnson Construction Company. It affirmed the award of $3,500, plus $750 in attorneys' fees, as well as Shaffer's original award of $1,000.

WHAT IF THE FACTS WERE DIFFERENT?   *Suppose that Shaffer had invoiced Johnson for only $1,500. Would the outcome have been different?*

Short-Run Profit Maximization

Some people argue that a corporation's only goal should be profit maximization, which will be reflected in a higher market value. When all firms strictly adhere to the goal of profit maximization, resources tend to flow to where they are most highly valued by society. Thus, in theory, profit maximization ultimately leads to the most efficient allocation of scarce resources.

> "It's easy to make a buck. It's a lot tougher to make a difference."
>
> Tom Brokaw, 1940–present
> (American television journalist)

Corporate executives and employees have to distinguish, however, between *short-run* and *long-run* profit maximization. In the short run, a company may increase its profits by continuing to sell a product even though it knows that the product is defective. In the long run, though, because of lawsuits, large settlements, and bad publicity, such unethical conduct will cause profits to suffer. Thus, business ethics is consistent only with long-run profit maximization. An overemphasis on short-term profit maximization is the most common reason that ethical problems occur in business.

   CASE EXAMPLE 3.1   When the powerful narcotic painkiller OxyContin was first marketed, its manufacturer, Purdue Pharma, claimed that it was unlikely to lead to drug addiction or abuse. Internal company documents later showed that the company's executives knew that OxyContin could be addictive, but they kept this risk a secret to boost sales and maximize short-term profits. In 2007, Purdue Pharma and three former executives pleaded guilty to criminal charges that they misled regulators, patients, and physicians about OxyContin's risks of addiction. Purdue Pharma agreed to pay $600 million in fines and other payments. The three former executives agreed to pay $34.5 million in fines and were barred from federal health programs for a period of fifteen years—a ruling that was upheld by an administrative law judge in 2009. Thus, the company's focus on maximizing profits in the short run led to unethical conduct that hurt profits in the long run.[1] ●

"Gray Areas" in the Law

In many situations, business firms can predict with a fair amount of certainty whether a given action would be legal. For instance, firing an employee solely because of that person's race or gender would clearly violate federal laws prohibiting employment discrimination. In some situations, though, the legality of a particular action may be less clear. In part, this is because there are so many laws regulating business that it is increasingly possible to violate one of them without realizing it. The law also contains numerous "gray areas," making it difficult to predict with certainty how a court will apply a given law to a particular action.

In addition, many rules of law require a court to determine what is "foreseeable" or "reasonable" in a particular situation. Because a business has no way of predicting how a specific court will decide these issues, decision makers need to proceed with caution and evaluate an action and its consequences from an ethical perspective. The same problem often occurs in cases involving the Internet because it is often unclear how a court will apply existing laws in the context of cyberspace. Generally, if a company can demonstrate that it acted responsibly and in good faith in the circumstances, it has a better chance of successfully defending its action in court or before an administrative law judge.

The Importance of Ethical Leadership

LEARNING OBJECTIVE 2   **How can business leaders encourage their companies to act ethically?**

Talking about ethical business decision making is meaningless if management does not set standards. Furthermore, managers must apply the same standards to themselves as they do to the employees of the company.

If a company discovers that a manager has behaved unethically or engaged in misconduct, the company should take prompt remedial action. The following case illustrates what can happen when a manager fails to follow the standards that apply to other employees.

---

1. *United States v. Purdue Frederick Co.*, 495 F. Supp.2d 569 (W.D.Va. 2007).

Case 3.2   **Mathews v. B and K Foods, Inc.**

Missouri Court of Appeals, 332 S.W.3d 273 (2011).

BACKGROUND AND FACTS   Dianne Mathews was employed as a floral manager by B and K Foods, Inc. On July 15, 2010, her employment was terminated for submitting falsified time cards. On July 17, Mathews filed an application with the state for unemployment compensation (see Chapter 16). B and K objected, arguing that Mathews was not entitled to unemployment benefits because she had been discharged for misconduct at work. At a hearing held by the unemployment commission, the chief executive officer of B and K testified that it was company policy to deduct thirty minutes each day from the time sheets of employees, including managers, for a lunch break. When an individual was "not able to clock out for lunch" and worked straight through, that person could fill out a "no lunch sheet" for the day. Payroll would then add thirty minutes back to the person's work time. Mathews allegedly sometimes turned in "no lunch sheets" to cover time when she was running personal errands instead of working. Mathews admitted that she knew about the "no lunch sheet" policy and had used it on occasion but contended that her conduct was warranted. She claimed that a former employee who was a higher-level manager had told her that it was unnecessary to adjust her time card when she spent a few minutes on a personal errand. The unemployment commission concluded that Mathews was disqualified from seeking unemployment benefits due to misconduct. Mathews appealed.

Case 3.2–Continued

IN THE WORDS OF THE COURT . . .
William W. *FRANCIS*, Jr., Judge.

* * * *

"Misconduct" which would disqualify an employee from unemployment benefits is defined as:

> An act of wanton or willful disregard of the employer's interest, a deliberate violation of the employer's rules, a disregard of standards of behavior which the employer has the right to expect of his or her employee * * *.

Section 288.030.1(23).

"Work-related misconduct' must involve a willful violation of the rules or standards of the employer." * * * To willfully disregard Employer's interests, Claimant [Mathews] first had to be aware of the requirement, and then knowingly or consciously violate it. [Emphasis added.]

* * * *

Substantial evidence supported a finding that Claimant's conduct of falsifying her timecard record by turning in a "no lunch sheet" for time she had left the store to run a personal errand was a willful or deliberate violation of Employer's policy. First, Claimant herself testified she was familiar with the "no lunch sheet" and verified it was her practice during 2009 not to take a lunch break every day and to complete and turn in a "no lunch sheet" for each day. The "no lunch sheet" allowed managers to be compensated for *working* through their lunch breaks. Additionally, as a manager, Claimant was responsible for enforcing Employer's lunch policy with her subordinate employees. Mr. Gerard [the top corporate executive at B and K] testified they had no choice but to terminate Claimant because she was in a higher position and had a responsibility to enforce the lunch policy. Thus, Claimant was well aware of Employer's lunch policy when she made the affirmative choice to turn in a "no lunch sheet" for the time she spent running a personal errand.

* * * *

* * * Here, Claimant's knowledge of Employer's "no lunch sheet" policy is especially apparent because Claimant herself testified to her familiarity with it and she was responsible for enforcing the policy regularly with employees under her direct supervision.

Claimant's actions of turning in "no lunch sheets" and thereby claiming pay status for time she was out of the store conducting personal errands were a direct violation of Employer's policy. Claimant's conduct goes beyond a mere lack of judgment as evidence established she knew her behavior was inappropriate and against Employer's interest. * * * Accordingly, we affirm the decision of the Commission.

DECISION AND REMEDY A state intermediate appellate court affirmed the decision of the state unemployment commission. The court found that the employer had met its burden of proving that Matthews had engaged in work-related misconduct, which disqualified her from receiving unemployment benefits.

MANAGERIAL IMPLICATIONS *Any employer that discovers a manager is not following stated company policies should take immediate action to correct the situation. Although a company does not always need to terminate the manager for misconduct, as was done in this case, it must act decisively because its action will have a significant impact on workplace ethics. A company that allows managers to engage in unethical conduct without consequences sends a message to subordinate employees that such behavior is tolerated. Managers must live by the same rules as employees and face the same consequences when they fail to do so.*

ATTITUDE OF TOP MANAGEMENT One of the most important ways to create and maintain an ethical workplace is for top management to demonstrate its commitment to ethical decision making. A manager who is not totally committed to an ethical workplace rarely succeeds in creating one. Management's behavior, more than anything else, sets the ethical tone of a firm. Employees take their cues from management. **EXAMPLE 3.2** Devon, a BioTek employee, observes his manager cheating on her expense account. Later, when Devon is promoted to a managerial position, he "pads" his expense account as well, knowing that he is unlikely to face sanctions for doing so. •

Managers who set unrealistic production or sales goals increase the probability that employees will act unethically. If a sales quota can be met only through high-pressure, unethical sales tactics, employees will try to act "in the best interest of the company" and will continue to behave unethically.

A manager who looks the other way when she or he knows about an employee's unethical behavior also sets an example—one indicating that ethical transgressions will be accepted. Managers have found that discharging even one employee for ethical reasons has a tremendous impact as a deterrent to unethical behavior in the workplace.

BEHAVIOR OF OWNERS AND MANAGERS   Business owners and managers sometimes take more active roles in fostering unethical and illegal conduct. This may indicate to their co-owners, co-managers, employees, and others that unethical business behavior will be tolerated.

EXAMPLE 3.3   Attorney Samir Zia Chowman posted an ad on Craigslist seeking a woman for the position of a legal secretary. The ad stated that the position included secretarial and paralegal work, and *additional duties* for the firm's two lawyers. It requested applicants to send their picture and describe their physical features. One woman applied. Chowman e-mailed her stating that in addition to the legal work, she would be required to have sexual interaction with the lawyers. He also explained that she would need to perform sexual acts on them at the job interview. The woman filed a complaint with the Illinois bar association, which suspended Chowman's law license for one year. •

Creating Ethical Codes of Conduct

One of the most effective ways of setting a tone of ethical behavior within an organization is to create an ethical code of conduct. A well-written code of ethics explicitly states a company's ethical priorities and demonstrates the company's commitment to ethical behavior.

ETHICS TRAINING FOR EMPLOYEES   For an ethical code to be effective, its provisions must be clearly communicated to employees. Most large companies have implemented ethics training programs, in which managers discuss with employees on a face-to-face basis the firm's policies and the importance of ethical conduct. Smaller firms should also offer some form of ethics training to employees because if a firm is accused of an ethics violation, the court will consider the presence or absence of such training in evaluating the firm's conduct.

Some firms hold periodic ethics seminars during which employees can openly discuss any ethical problems that they may be experiencing and learn how the firm's ethical policies apply to those specific problems. Other companies require their managers to meet individually with employees and grade them on their ethical (or unethical) behavior.

THE SARBANES-OXLEY ACT AND WEB-BASED REPORTING SYSTEMS   The Sarbanes-Oxley Act[2] requires companies to set up confidential systems so that employees and others can "raise red flags" about suspected illegal or unethical auditing and accounting practices.

Some companies have implemented online reporting systems to accomplish this goal. In one such system, employees can click on an icon on their computers that anonymously links them with EthicsPoint, an organization based in Portland, Oregon. Through EthicsPoint, employees can report suspicious accounting practices, sexual harassment, and other possibly unethical behavior. EthicsPoint, in turn, alerts management personnel or the audit committee at the designated company to the possible problem. Those who have used the system say that it is less inhibiting than calling a company's toll-free number.

▶ Ethical Transgressions by Financial Institutions

One of the best ways to learn the ethical responsibilities inherent in operating a business is to look at the mistakes made by other companies. In the following subsections, we describe some of the worst ethical failures of financial institutions during

2. 15 U.S.C. Sections 7201 *et seq.*

the latter part of the first decade of the 2000s. Many of these ethical wrongdoings received wide publicity and raised public awareness of the need for ethical leadership throughout all businesses.

Corporate Stock Buybacks

In 2008 and 2009, many well-known financial companies in the United States either went bankrupt, were taken over by the federal government, or were bailed out by U.S. taxpayers. What most people do not know is that those same corporations were using their own cash funds to prop up the value of their stock in the years just before the economic crisis started in 2008.

Stock Buyback A company's purchase of shares of its own stock on the open market.

The theory behind a **stock buyback** is simple—the management of a corporation believes that the market price of its shares is "below their fair value." Therefore, instead of issuing dividends to shareholders or reinvesting profits, management uses the company's funds to buy its shares in the open market, thereby boosting the price of the stock. From 2005 to 2007, stock buybacks for the top five hundred U.S. corporations added up to $1.4 *trillion*.

Stock Option An agreement that grants the owner the option to buy a given number of shares of stock, usually within a set time period.

Who benefits from stock buybacks? The main individual beneficiaries are corporate executives who have been given **stock options,** which enable them to buy shares of the corporation's stock at a set price. When the market price rises above that level, the executives can profit by selling their shares. Although stock buybacks are legal and can serve legitimate purposes, they can easily be abused if managers use them just to increase the stock price in the short term so that they can profit from their options without considering the long-term needs of the company.

EXAMPLE 3.4 Goldman Sachs, an investment bank, bought back $15 billion of its stock in 2007. Yet by 2009, U.S. taxpayers had provided $10 billion in bailout funds to that same company. •

Executive Bonuses

Until the economic crisis began in 2008, the bonuses paid in the financial industry did not make headlines. After all, times were good. Why shouldn't those responsible for record company earnings be rewarded? When investment banks and commercial banks began to fail, however, or had to be bailed out or taken over by the federal government, executive bonuses became an important issue.

The financial industry had been profiting from the sale of risky assets to investors. Executives and others in the industry who had created and sold those risky assets suffered no liability—and even received bonuses. Of course, some of those firms that had enjoyed high short-run returns from their risky investments—and paid bonuses based on those profits—found themselves facing bankruptcy. **EXAMPLE 3.5** Lehman Brothers' chief executive officer earned almost $500 million between 2000 and the firm's demise in 2008. Even after Lehman Brothers entered bankruptcy, its new owners, Barclays and Nomura, legally owed $3.5 billion in bonuses to employees still on the payroll. In 2006, Goldman Sachs awarded its employees a total of $16.5 billion in bonuses. •

Public outrage mounted about the bonuses paid by firms receiving taxpayer funds. Congress subsequently included a provision in the American Recovery and Reinvestment Tax Act of 2009 to change the compensation system in the financial industry. The provision did not cap executive salaries but instead severely restricted the bonuses that can be paid by firms that receive federal bailout funds. Although cash bonuses to Wall Street executives fell, the total compensation for financial service firms came to a record $150 billion in 2010.

▶ Approaches to Ethical Reasoning

Ethical Reasoning A reasoning process in which an individual links his or her moral convictions or ethical standards to the particular situation at hand.

Each individual, when faced with a particular ethical dilemma, engages in **ethical reasoning**—that is, a reasoning process in which the individual examines the situation at hand in light of his or her moral convictions or ethical standards. Businesspersons do likewise when making decisions with ethical implications.

How do business decision makers decide whether a given action is the "right" one for their firms? What ethical standards should be applied? Broadly speaking, ethical reasoning relating to business traditionally has been characterized by two fundamental approaches. One approach defines ethical behavior in terms of duty, which also implies certain rights. The other approach determines what is ethical in terms of the consequences, or outcome, of any given action. We examine each of these approaches here.

In addition to the two basic ethical approaches, several theories have been developed that specifically address the social responsibility of corporations. Because these theories also influence today's business decision makers, we conclude this section with a short discussion of the different views of corporate social responsibility.

Duty-Based Ethics

Duty-based ethical standards often are derived from revealed truths, such as religious precepts. They can also be derived through philosophical reasoning.

RELIGIOUS ETHICAL STANDARDS In the Judeo-Christian tradition, the Ten Commandments of the Old Testament establish fundamental rules for moral action. Other religions have their own sources of revealed truth. Religious rules generally are absolute with respect to the behavior of their adherents. **EXAMPLE 3.6** The commandment "Thou shalt not steal" is an absolute mandate for a person who believes that the Ten Commandments reflect revealed truth. Even a benevolent motive for stealing (such as Robin Hood's) cannot justify the act because the act itself is inherently immoral and thus wrong. ●

KANTIAN ETHICS Duty-based ethical standards may also be derived solely from philosophical reasoning. The German philosopher Immanuel Kant (1724–1804), for example, identified some general guiding principles for moral behavior based on what he believed to be the fundamental nature of human beings. Kant believed that human beings are qualitatively different from other physical objects and are endowed with moral integrity and the capacity to reason and conduct their affairs rationally. Therefore, a person's thoughts and actions should be respected. When human beings are treated merely as a means to an end, they are being treated as the equivalent of objects and are being denied their basic humanity.

Categorical Imperative An ethical guideline according to which an action is evaluated in terms of what would happen if everyone else in the same situation (category) acted the same way.

A central theme in Kantian ethics is that individuals should evaluate their actions in light of the consequences that would follow if *everyone* in society acted in the same way. This **categorical imperative** can be applied to any action. **EXAMPLE 3.7** Suppose that you are deciding whether to cheat on an examination. If you have adopted Kant's categorical imperative, you will decide *not* to cheat because if everyone cheated, the examination (and the entire education system) would be meaningless. ●

THE PRINCIPLE OF RIGHTS Because a duty cannot exist without a corresponding right, duty-based ethical standards imply that human beings have basic rights. The principle that human beings have certain fundamental rights (to life, liberty, and the

Principle of Rights   The principle that human beings have certain fundamental rights. A key factor in determining whether a business decision is ethical is how it affects others' rights.

pursuit of happiness, for example) is deeply embedded in Western culture. As discussed in Chapter 1, the natural law tradition embraces the concept that certain actions (such as killing another person) are morally wrong because they are contrary to nature (the natural desire to continue living). Those who adhere to this **principle of rights,** or "rights theory," believe that a key factor in determining whether a business decision is ethical is how that decision affects the rights of others. These others include the firm's owners, its employees, the consumers of its products or services, its suppliers, the community in which it does business, and society as a whole.

Conflicting Rights.   A potential dilemma for those who support rights theory, however, is that there are often conflicting rights, and people may disagree on which rights are most important. When considering all those affected by a business decision to downsize a firm, for example, how much weight should be given to employees relative to shareholders? Which employees should be laid off first, those with the highest salaries or those who have worked there for less time (and have less seniority)? How should the firm weigh the rights of customers relative to the community, or employees relative to society as a whole?

LEARNING OBJECTIVE 3   How do duty-based ethical standards differ from outcome-based ethical standards?

Resolving Conflicts.   In general, rights theorists believe that whichever right is stronger in a particular circumstance takes precedence. **EXAMPLE 3.8**   A firm can either keep a manufacturing plant open, saving the jobs of twelve workers, or shut the plant down and avoid contaminating a river with pollutants that would endanger the health of tens of thousands of people. In this situation, a rights theorist can easily choose which group to favor. Not all choices are so clear-cut, however. ●

Outcome-Based Ethics: Utilitarianism

Utilitarianism   An approach to ethical reasoning in which an action is evaluated in terms of its consequences for those whom it will affect. A "good" action is one that results in the greatest good for the greatest number of people.

"The greatest good for the greatest number" is a paraphrase of the major premise of the utilitarian approach to ethics. **Utilitarianism** is a philosophical theory developed by Jeremy Bentham (1748–1832) and modified by John Stuart Mill (1806–1873)—both British philosophers. In contrast to duty-based ethics, utilitarianism is outcome oriented. It focuses on the consequences of an action, not on the nature of the action itself or on any set of preestablished moral values or religious beliefs.

Under a utilitarian model of ethics, an action is morally correct, or "right," when, among the people it affects, it produces the greatest amount of good for the greatest number. When an action affects the majority adversely, it is morally wrong. Applying the utilitarian theory thus requires (1) a determination of which individuals will be affected by the action in question; (2) a **cost-benefit analysis,** which involves an assessment of the negative and positive effects of alternative actions on these individuals; and (3) a choice among alternative actions that will produce maximum societal utility (the greatest positive net benefits for the greatest number of individuals).

Cost-Benefit Analysis   A decision-making technique that involves weighing the costs of a given action against the benefits of that action.

Corporate Social Responsibility

Corporate Social Responsibility   The idea that corporations can and should act ethically and be accountable to society for their actions.

For many years, groups concerned with civil rights, employee safety and welfare, consumer protection, environmental preservation, and other causes have pressured corporate America to behave in a responsible manner with respect to these causes. Thus was born the concept of **corporate social responsibility**—the idea that those who run corporations can and should act ethically and be accountable to society for their actions. Just what constitutes corporate social responsibility has been debated for some time, and there are a number of different theories today.

STAKEHOLDER APPROACH One view of corporate social responsibility stresses that corporations have a duty not just to shareholders, but also to other groups affected by corporate decisions (stakeholders), including employees, customers, creditors, suppliers, and the community. The reasoning behind this "stakeholder view" is that sometimes one or more of these other groups may have a greater stake in company decisions than do the shareholders. Although this may be true, as mentioned earlier in this chapter, it is often difficult to decide which group's interests should receive greater weight if the interests conflict.

During the last few years, layoffs numbered in the millions. Nonetheless, some corporations succeeded in reducing labor costs without layoffs. To avoid slashing their workforces, these employers turned to alternatives such as four-day workweeks, unpaid vacations and voluntary furloughs, wage freezes, pension cuts, and flexible work schedules. Some companies asked for and received from their workers wage cuts to prevent layoffs. Companies finding alternatives to layoffs included computer maker Dell (extended unpaid holidays), network router manufacturer Cisco Systems (four-day workweeks and end-of-year shutdowns), electronics giant Motorola (salary cuts), and automaker Honda (voluntary unpaid vacation time).

CORPORATE CITIZENSHIP Another theory of social responsibility argues that corporations should behave as good citizens by promoting goals that society deems worthwhile and by taking positive steps toward solving social problems. The idea is that because business controls so much of the wealth and power of this country, business, in turn, has a responsibility to society to use that wealth and power in socially beneficial ways.

Under a corporate citizenship view, companies are judged on how much they donate to social causes, as well as how they conduct their operations with respect to employment discrimination, human rights, environmental concerns, and similar issues. **EXAMPLE 3.9** Google, Inc., teamed up with investment firm Kohlberg Kravis Roberts & Company (KKR) to develop four solar energy farms that will serve the Sacramento Municipal Utility District in California. The four solar farms reportedly cost $95 million and will provide enough power for more than 13,000 average-sized U.S. homes. ●

A Way of Doing Business. A survey of U.S. executives undertaken by the Boston College Center for Corporate Citizenship found that more than 70 percent of those polled agreed that corporate citizenship must be treated as a priority. More than 60 percent said that good corporate citizenship added to their companies' profits. Strategist Michelle Bernhart has argued that corporate social responsibility cannot attain its maximum effectiveness unless it is treated as a way of doing business rather than as a special program.

Not all socially responsible activities can benefit a corporation, however. Corporate responsibility is most successful when a company undertakes activities that are relevant and significant to its stakeholders and related to its business operations. **EXAMPLE 3.10** The Brazilian firm Companhia Vale do Rio Doce is one of the world's largest diversified metals and mining companies. In 2008, it invested more than $150 million in social projects, including health care, infrastructure, and education. At the same time, it invested more than $300 million in environmental protection. One of its projects involves the rehabilitation of native species in the Amazon valley. To that end, it is planting almost 200 million trees in an attempt to restore 1,150 square miles of land where cattle breeding and farming have caused deforestation. ●

Globalization makes it increasingly difficult for major corporations to differentiate themselves from the competition based solely on their products and services. See this chapter's *Shifting Legal Priorities for Business* feature below on how corporate social responsibility may help corporations gain an edge over their competitors.

The Employee Recruiting and Retention Advantage. A key corporate stakeholder is a company's workforce, which may include potential employees—job seekers. Surveys of college students about to enter the job market confirm that young people are looking for socially responsible employers. Younger workers generally want to work for a company that allows them to participate in community projects.

▶ Ethical Business Guidelines and Solutions

Instilling ethical business decision making into the fabric of a business organization is no small task. The job is to encourage people to understand that they have to think more broadly about how their decisions will affect employees, shareholders, customers, and

SHIFTING LEGAL PRIORITIES FOR BUSINESS

Corporate Social Responsibility and "Outbehaving" the Competition

The worldwide explosion of information technology has made socially responsible behavior more important simply because it has become increasingly difficult to hide bad corporate behavior. In our transparent global economy, corporations that "outbehave" their competition ethically may also outperform them financially.

Managing a Company's Reputation

Before the advent of the Internet, a corporation that faced an ugly public relations situation simply hired consultants and then hid behind lawyers. Today, corporations can no longer manage their reputations the old-fashioned way. When customers are unhappy or employees are disgruntled, they let the entire world know by tweeting, blogging, or posting a video on YouTube.

In this online environment, corporations cannot control their stories. They can, however, control the way management operates. One strategy used to manage a corporation's reputation is to increase the amount and type of information made available to the public. To this end, more than 2,500 multinationals now release to

the public large quantities of managerial accounting information.

Internal Reports Designed for External Scrutiny

Some large companies refer to the managerial accounting information that they release to the public as their social responsibility reports. The antivirus software company Symantec Corporation issued its first corporate responsibility report in 2008. The report demonstrated the company's focus on critical environmental, social, and governance issues. Among other things, Symantec pointed out that it had adopted the Calvert Women's Principles, the first global code of corporate conduct designed to empower, advance, and invest in women worldwide.

A smaller number of multinationals provide what they call citizenship reports. For example, in 2011 General Electric (GE) released its Seventh Annual Citizenship Report, which it called "Sustainable Growth." GE's emphasis is on energy and climate change, demographics, growth markets, and financial markets.

Differentiation through "Doing Good"

In today's global economy, companies need to find ways other than through their products or services to differentiate themselves from their competitors. Companies must now compete in other areas, including how responsible their behavior is.

A key component of responsible behavior is the creation of trust between companies and their customers, employees, and suppliers. Companies that build trust also enjoy higher profits. Numerous studies have shown a strong correlation between the cost of obtaining supplies and the level of trust between the buyer of those raw materials and the seller.

MANAGERIAL IMPLICATIONS

Managers must recognize that everything they do can be instantaneously communicated around the world. Whenever a manager considers acting in a socially irresponsible way, he or she should envision a viral video exposing those actions to millions.

even the community. Ensuring that all employees get on the ethical business decision-making "bandwagon" is crucial in today's fast-paced world.

Guidelines to Making Ethical Business Decisions

The George S. May International Company has provided six basic guidelines to help corporate employees judge their actions. Each employee—no matter what her or his level in the organization—should evaluate her or his actions using the following six guidelines:

1. *The law.* Is the action you are considering legal? If you do not know the laws governing the action, then find out. Ignorance of the law is no excuse.
2. *Rules and procedures.* Are you following the internal rules and procedures that have already been laid out by your company? They have been developed to avoid problems. Is what you are planning to do consistent with your company's policies and procedures? If not, stop.
3. *Values.* Laws and internal company policies reinforce society's values. You might wish to ask yourself whether you are attempting to find a loophole in the law or in your company's policies. Next, you have to ask yourself whether you are following the "spirit" of the law as well as the letter of the law or the internal policy.
4. *Conscience.* If you feel any guilt, let your conscience be your guide. Alternatively, ask yourself whether you would be happy to be interviewed by the national news media about the actions you are going to take.
5. *Promises.* Every business organization is based on trust. Your customers believe that your company will do what it is supposed to do. The same is true for your suppliers and employees. Will your actions live up to the commitments you have made to others, both inside the business and outside?
6. *Heroes.* We all have heroes who are role models for us. Is what you are planning on doing an action that your "hero" would take? If not, how would your hero act? That is how you should be acting.

LEARNING OBJECTIVE 4   **What are six guidelines that an employee can use to evaluate whether his or her actions are ethical?**

Ethical Issue ⚖

Should you do the right thing even when it puts your job at risk? Dean Krehmeyer, executive director of the Business Roundtable's Institute for Corporate Ethics, once said, "Evidence strongly suggests being ethical—doing the right thing—pays." Sometimes, however, being ethical in the business world costs an employee his or her job.

For instance, Michael Woodford was chief executive officer for Olympus Corporation, a Tokyo-based camera maker. After thirty years with the company, he discovered that the company had been engaging in dubious accounting practices. After confronting management in 2011 about excessive spending on questionable acquisitions, Woodford was fired from the board of directors, and later, he resigned as chairman. Olympus initially denied any wrongdoing, but later acknowledged a $687 million payment for financial advice and expensive acquisitions to cover up investment losses. Many speculate that the company falsified a large amount of information in its financial reports over the years. Olympus's bookkeeping is under review. But Woodford, who did the right thing by encouraging the company to come clean about the cover-up, no longer works for the company. He plans to sue Olympus, but he may never be compensated for losing his job.

A Practical Solution to Ethics Questions

Corporate ethics officers and ethics committees require a practical method to investigate and solve specific ethics problems. Ethics consultant Leonard H. Bucklin of Corporate-Ethics.US has devised a procedure that he calls Business Process Pragmatism.™ It involves the following five steps:

1. *Inquiry.* Of course, an understanding of the facts must be the initial action. The parties involved might include the mass media, the public, employees, or customers. At this stage of the process, the ethical problem or problems are specified. A list of relevant ethical principles is created.
2. *Discussion.* Here, a list of action options is developed. Each option carries with it certain ethical principles. Finally, resolution goals should also be listed.
3. *Decision.* Working together, those participating in the process create a consensus decision, or a consensus plan of action for the corporation.
4. *Justification.* Does the consensus solution withstand moral scrutiny? At this point in the process, reasons should be attached to each proposed action or series of actions. Will the stakeholders involved accept these reasons?
5. *Evaluation.* Do the solutions to the corporate ethics issue satisfy corporate values, community values, and individual values? Ultimately, can the consensus resolution withstand moral scrutiny of the decisions made and the process used to reach those decisions?

"*Next to doing the right thing, the most important thing is to let people know you are doing the right thing.*"
John D. Rockefeller, 1839–1897
(American industrialist and philanthropist)

Business Ethics on a Global Level

Given the various cultures and religions throughout the world, it is not surprising that conflicts in ethics frequently arise between foreign and U.S. businesspersons. For example, in certain countries, the consumption of alcohol and specific foods is forbidden for religious reasons. Under such circumstances, it would be thoughtless and imprudent for a U.S. businessperson to invite a local business contact out for a drink.

The role played by women in other countries may also present some difficult ethical problems for firms doing business internationally. Equal employment opportunity is a fundamental public policy in the United States, and Title VII of the Civil Rights Act of 1964 prohibits discrimination against women in the employment context (see Chapter 17). Some other countries, however, offer little protection for women against gender discrimination in the workplace, including sexual harassment.

We look here at how laws governing workers in other countries, particularly developing countries, have created some especially difficult ethical problems for U.S. sellers of goods manufactured in foreign countries. We also examine some of the ethical ramifications of laws prohibiting U.S. businesspersons from bribing foreign officials to obtain favorable business contracts.

Monitoring the Employment Practices of Foreign Suppliers

LEARNING OBJECTIVE 5 What types of ethical issues might arise in the context of international business transactions?

Many U.S. businesses contract with companies in developing nations to produce goods, such as shoes and clothing, because the wage rates in those nations are significantly lower than wages in the United States. Yet what if a foreign company exploits its workers—by hiring women and children at below-minimum-wage rates, for example, or by requiring its employees to work long hours in a workplace full of health hazards? What if the company's supervisors routinely engage in workplace conduct that is offensive to women?

Given today's global communications network, few companies can assume that their actions in other nations will go unnoticed by "corporate watch" groups that discover and publicize unethical corporate behavior. As a result, U.S. businesses today usually take steps to avoid such adverse publicity—either by refusing to deal with certain suppliers or by arranging to monitor their suppliers' workplaces to make sure that the employees are not being mistreated.

Global companies are finding that they need to communicate ethics policies to their foreign suppliers as well. **EXAMPLE 3.11**   Apple, Inc., relies heavily on foreign component suppliers. Following a number of high-profile labor problems at its foreign suppliers and manufacturers, Apple started making significant efforts to evaluate practices at companies in its supply chain and to communicate its ethics policies to them. Although Apple has always kept its list of suppliers a secret, it decided to publicly release the list after its audits revealed numerous violations. Apple's Supplier Responsibility Report found that some of the facilities had docked worker pay as a disciplinary measure, had falsified pay records and forced workers to use machines without safeguards, and had engaged in unsafe environmental practices. Apple terminated its relationship with one of its suppliers and turned over its findings to the Fair Labor Association for further inquiry. ●

The Foreign Corrupt Practices Act

Another ethical problem in international business dealings has to do with the legitimacy of certain "side" payments to government officials. In the United States, most contracts are formed within the private sector. In many foreign countries, however, government officials make the decisions on most major construction and manufacturing contracts because of extensive government regulation and control over trade and industry. Side payments to government officials in exchange for favorable business contracts are not unusual in such countries, where they are not considered to be unethical. In the past, U.S. corporations doing business in these countries largely followed the dictum "When in Rome, do as the Romans do."

In the 1970s, however, the U.S. press, and government officials as well, uncovered a number of business scandals involving large side payments by U.S. corporations to foreign representatives for the purpose of securing advantageous international trade contracts. In response to this unethical behavior, in 1977 Congress passed the Foreign Corrupt Practices Act[3] (FCPA), which prohibits U.S. businesspersons from bribing foreign officials to secure advantageous contracts.

PROHIBITION AGAINST THE BRIBERY OF FOREIGN OFFICIALS   The first part of the FCPA applies to all U.S. companies and their directors, officers, shareholders, employees, and agents. It prohibits the bribery of officials of foreign governments if the purpose of the payment is to get the officials to act in their official capacity to provide business opportunities.

The FCPA does not prohibit payment of substantial sums to minor officials whose duties are ministerial. These payments are often referred to as "grease," or facilitating payments. They are meant to accelerate the performance of administrative services that might otherwise be carried out at a slow pace. Thus, for example, if a firm makes a payment to a minor official to speed up an import licensing process, the firm has not violated the FCPA.

Generally, the act, as amended, permits payments to foreign officials if such payments are lawful within the foreign country. The act also does not prohibit payments to private foreign companies or other third parties unless the U.S. firm knows that the payments will be passed on to a foreign government in violation of the FCPA. Business firms that violate the FCPA may be fined up to $2 million. Individual officers or directors who violate the act may be fined up to $100,000 (the fine cannot be paid by the company) and may be imprisoned for up to five years.

"Never doubt that a small group of committed citizens can change the world; indeed, it is the only thing that ever has."

Margaret Mead, 1901–1978
(American anthropologist)

---

3. 15 U.S.C. Sections 78dd-1 *et seq.*

ACCOUNTING REQUIREMENTS In the past, bribes were often concealed in corporate financial records. Thus, the second part of the FCPA is directed toward accountants. All companies must keep detailed records that "accurately and fairly" reflect the company's financial activities. In addition, all companies must have an accounting system that provides "reasonable assurance" that all transactions entered into by the company are accounted for and legal. These requirements assist in detecting illegal bribes. The FCPA further prohibits any person from making false statements to accountants or false entries in any record or account.

 Reviewing . . . Ethics and Business Decision Making

Isabel Arnett was promoted to CEO of Tamik, Inc., a pharmaceutical company that manufactures a vaccine called Kafluk, which supposedly provides some defense against bird flu. The company began marketing Kafluk throughout Asia. After numerous media reports that bird flu might soon become a worldwide epidemic, the demand for Kafluk increased, sales soared, and Tamik earned record profits. Tamik's CEO, Arnett, then began receiving disturbing reports from Southeast Asia that in some patients, Kafluk had caused psychiatric disturbances, including severe hallucinations, and heart and lung problems. Arnett was informed that six children in Japan had committed suicide by jumping out of windows after receiving the vaccine. To cover up the story and prevent negative publicity, Arnett instructed Tamik's partners in Asia to offer cash to the Japanese families whose children had died in exchange for their silence. Arnett also refused to authorize additional research within the company to study the potential side effects of Kafluk. Using the information presented in the chapter, answer the following questions.

1. This scenario illustrates one of the main reasons why ethical problems occur in business. What is that reason?
2. Would a person who adheres to the principle of rights consider it ethical for Arnett not to disclose potential safety concerns and to refuse to perform additional research on Kafluk? Why or why not?
3. If Kafluk prevented fifty Asian people who were exposed to bird flu from dying, would Arnett's conduct in this situation be ethical under a utilitarian cost-benefit analysis? Why or why not?
4. Did Tamik or Arnett violate the Foreign Corrupt Practices Act in this scenario? Why or why not?

Debate This

Executives in large corporations are ultimately rewarded if their companies do well, particularly as evidenced by rising stock prices. Consequently, shouldn't we just let those who run corporations decide what level of negative side effects of their goods or services is "acceptable"?

Key Terms

business ethics 62
categorical imperative 68
corporate social responsibility 69
cost-benefit analysis 69

ethical reasoning 68
ethics 61
moral minimum 62
principle of rights 69

stock buyback 67
stock option 67
utilitarianism 69

Chapter Summary: Ethics and Business Decision Making

| Business Ethics (See pages 61–66.) | 1. *Ethics*—Business ethics focuses on how moral and ethical principles are applied in the business context. |
| | 2. *The moral minimum*—Lawful behavior is the moral minimum. The law has its limits, though, and some actions may be legal but not ethical. |

(Continued)

▶ Chapter Summary: Ethics and Business Decision Making, Continued

Business Ethics—Continued	3. *Short-term profit maximization*—One of the more pervasive reasons why ethical breaches occur is the focus on short-term profit maximization. Executives should distinguish between short-run and long-run profit goals and focus on maximizing profits over the long run because only long-run profit maximization is consistent with business ethics. 4. *Legal uncertainties*—It may be difficult to predict with certainty whether particular actions are legal, given the numerous and frequent changes in the laws regulating business and the "gray areas" in the law. 5. *The importance of ethical leadership*—Management's commitment and behavior are essential in creating an ethical workplace. Management's behavior, more than anything else, sets the ethical tone of a firm and influences the behavior of employees. 6. *Ethical codes*—Most large firms have ethical codes or policies and training programs to help employees determine whether certain actions are ethical. In addition, the Sarbanes-Oxley Act requires firms to set up confidential systems so that employees and others can report suspected illegal or unethical auditing or accounting practices.
Ethical Transgressions by Financial Institutions (See pages 66–67.)	During the first decade of the 2000s, corporate wrongdoing among U.S. financial firms escalated. They sold increasingly risky assets to investors and invested in such assets themselves to increase short-term profits. Abusive use of stock buybacks and stock options also proliferated. When the economic crisis began, some investment banking firms such as Lehman Brothers were forced into bankruptcy, and others, including Goldman Sachs, had to accept bailout funds from the U.S. government. Nevertheless, the firms continued to pay exorbitant bonuses, which fueled public outrage, as the U.S. taxpayers had to pay the price through the federal bailouts and a deepening nationwide recession.
Approaches to Ethical Reasoning (See pages 68–71.)	1. *Duty-based ethics*—Ethics based on religious beliefs; philosophical reasoning, such as that of Immanuel Kant; and the basic rights of human beings (the principle of rights). A potential problem for those who support the latter approach is deciding which rights are more important in a given situation. Management constantly faces ethical conflicts and trade-offs when considering all those affected by a business decision. 2. *Outcome-based ethics (utilitarianism)*—Ethics based on philosophical reasoning, such as that of John Stuart Mill. Applying this theory requires a cost-benefit analysis, weighing the negative effects against the positive and deciding which course of action produces the best outcome. 3. *Corporate social responsibility*—A number of theories based on the idea that corporations can and should act ethically and be accountable to society for their actions. These include the stakeholder approach and corporate citizenship.
Ethical Business Guidelines and Solutions (See pages 71–73.)	1. Making ethical business decisions is crucial in today's legal environment. Doing the right thing pays off in the long run, both in terms of increasing profits and avoiding negative publicity and the potential for bankruptcy. We provide six guidelines for making ethical business decisions on page 72. 2. Corporate ethics officers and ethics committees require a practical method to investigate and solve specific ethics problems. For a pragmatic five-step procedure to solve ethical problems recommended by one expert, see page 73.
Business Ethics on a Global Level (See pages 73–75.)	Businesses must take account of the many cultural, religious, and legal differences among nations. Notable differences relate to the role of women in society, employment laws governing workplace conditions, and the practice of giving side payments to foreign officials to secure favorable contracts.

ExamPrep

ISSUE SPOTTERS

—Check your answers to these questions against the answers provided in Appendix D at the end of this text.

1. Delta Tools, Inc., markets a product that under some circumstances is capable of seriously injuring consumers. Does Delta have an ethical duty to remove this product from the market, even if the injuries occur only when the product is misused? Why or why not? **(See page 72.)**
2. Acme Corporation decides to respond to what it sees as a moral obligation to correct for past discrimination by adjusting pay differences among its employees. Does this raise an ethical conflict among Acme's employees? Between Acme and its employees? Between Acme and its shareholders? Explain your answers. **(See page 72.)**

BEFORE THE TEST

Go to **www.cengagebrain.com**, enter the ISBN 9781133586548, and click on "Find" to locate this textbook's Web site. Then, click on "Access Now" under "Study Tools," and select Chapter 3 at the top. There, you will find a Practice Quiz that you can take to assess your mastery of the concepts in this chapter. Additionally, you will find Flashcards and a Glossary of important terms, as well as Video Questions (when assigned).

For Review

Answers for the even-numbered questions in this **For Review** *section can be found in Appendix E at the end of this text.*

1. What is business ethics, and why is it important?
2. How can business leaders encourage their companies to act ethically?
3. How do duty-based ethical standards differ from outcome-based ethical standards?
4. What are six guidelines that an employee can use to evaluate whether his or her actions are ethical?
5. What types of ethical issues might arise in the context of international business transactions?

Questions and Case Problems

3–1. Business Ethics. Jason Trevor owns a commercial bakery in Blakely, Georgia, that produces a variety of goods sold in grocery stores. Trevor is required by law to perform internal tests on food produced at his plant to check for contamination. Three times in 2011, the tests of food products that contained peanut butter were positive for salmonella contamination. Trevor was not required to report the results to U.S. Food and Drug Administration officials, however, so he did not. Instead, Trevor instructed his employees to simply repeat the tests until the outcome was negative. Therefore, the products that had originally tested positive for salmonella were eventually shipped out to retailers. Five people who ate Trevor's baked goods in 2011 became seriously ill, and one person died from salmonella poisoning. Even though Trevor's conduct was legal, was it unethical for him to sell goods that had once tested positive for salmonella? If Trevor had followed the six basic guidelines for making ethical business decisions, would he still have sold the contaminated goods? Why or why not? **(See page 72.)**

3–2. Question with Sample Answer: Ethical Duties. Shokun Steel Co. owns many steel plants. One of its plants is much older than the others. Equipment at that plant is outdated and inefficient, and the costs of production are now two times higher than at any of Shokun's other plants. The company cannot raise the price of steel because of competition, both domestic and international. The plant employs more than a thousand workers and is located in Twin Firs, Pennsylvania, which has a population of about 45,000. Shokun is contemplating whether to close the plant. What factors should the firm consider in making its decision? Will the firm violate any ethical duties if it closes the plant? Analyze these questions from the two basic perspectives on ethical reasoning discussed in this chapter. **(See pages 68–70.)**
—For a sample answer to Question 3–2, go to Appendix F at the end of this text.

3–3. Ethical Leadership. David Krasner, who worked for HSH Nordbank AG, complained that his supervisor, Roland

Kiser, fostered an atmosphere of sexism that was demeaning to women. Among other things, Krasner claimed that career advancement was based on "sexual favoritism." He objected to Kiser's relationship with a female employee, Melissa Campfield, who was promoted before more qualified employees, including Krasner. How do a manager's attitudes and actions affect the workplace? [*Krasner v. HSH Nordbank AG,* 680 F.Supp.2d 502 (S.D.N.Y. 2010)] **(See page 65.)**

3–4. **Case Problem with Sample Answer: Ethics and the Law.** Prudential Insurance Co. of America has a policy not to change the amount of a salesperson's commission once a client has been quoted a price for insurance coverage. Despite this policy, Prudential used an insurance broker (who would receive a lower commission than Prudential's salesperson) who then offered a lower price to its client, York International Corp. A competing broker, Havensure, LLC, filed a suit against Prudential, arguing that the lower offer caused Havensure to lose York as a potential customer. Is a company's violation of its own policy unethical? Is it a basis for legal liability? Explain. [*Havensure, LLC v. Prudential Insurance Co. of America,* 595 F.3d 312 (6th Cir. 2010)] **(See pages 63 and 64.)**
—**For a sample answer to Case Problem 3–4, go to Appendix G at the end of this text.**

3–5. **Business Ethics.** While Jeffrey Skilling was chief executive officer of Enron Corp., he allegedly deceived investors about the company's finances by concealing losses, overstating profits, and lying to accountants and government agencies. At the time, the mood among Enron employees was upbeat because the company's prospects appeared "rosy." Among other things, many employees invested all their pension funds in Enron stock. What is unethical about this situation? Discuss. [*Skilling v. United States,* __ U.S. __, 130 S.Ct. 2896, 177 L.Ed.2d 619 (2010)] **(See page 63.)**

3–6. **Ethical Misconduct.** Frank Pasquale used his father's Social Security number to obtain a credit card. Later, pretending to act on behalf of his father's firm, Pasquale borrowed

$350,000. When he defaulted on the loan and his father confronted him, he produced forged documents that showed the loan had been paid. Adams Associates, LLC, which held the unpaid loan, filed a lawsuit against both Pasquales. Should the court issue a judgment against the father and the son? Discuss. [*Adams Associates, LLC v. Frank Pasquale Limited Partnership,* __ A.3d __ (N.J.Super A.D. 2011)] **(See pages 62 and 68.)**

3–7. **A Question of Ethics: Ethical Responsibility.** *The federal government spends time and money to find and destroy the labs in which methamphetamine (meth) is made, imprison its dealers and users, treat addicts, and provide services for affected families. Meth cannot be made without ingredients that are also used in cold and allergy medications. To recoup the costs of fighting the meth epidemic, twenty counties in Arkansas filed a suit against Pfizer, Inc., which makes and markets cold and allergy medications. [Ashley County, Arkansas v. Pfizer, Inc., 552 F.3d 659 (8th Cir. 2009)]* **(See pages 68–71.)**

1. What is Pfizer's ethical responsibility in this case?

2. To whom does Pfizer owe this responsibility? Why?

3–8. **Critical-Thinking Managerial Question.** Assume that you are a high-level manager for a shoe manufacturer. You know that your firm could increase its profit margin by producing shoes in Indonesia, where you could hire women for $100 a month to assemble them. You also know that human rights advocates recently accused a competing shoe manufacturer of engaging in exploitative labor practices because the manufacturer sold shoes made by Indonesian women for similarly low wages. You personally do not believe that paying $100 a month to Indonesian women is unethical because you know that in their country, $100 a month is a better-than-average wage rate. Assuming that the decision is yours to make, should you have the shoes manufactured in Indonesia and make higher profits for your company? Should you instead avoid the risk of negative publicity and the consequences of that publicity for the firm's reputation and subsequent profits? Are there other alternatives? Discuss fully. **(See pages 68–71.)**

Chapter 4

Constitutional Authority to Regulate Business

> "The United States Constitution has proved itself the most marvelously elastic compilation of rules of government ever written."
>
> —Franklin D. Roosevelt, 1882–1945
> (Thirty-second president of the United States, 1933–1945)

Learning Objectives

The five Learning Objectives below are designed to help improve your understanding of the chapter. After reading this chapter, you should be able to answer the following questions:

1. **What is the basic structure of the U.S. government?**
2. **What constitutional clause gives the federal government the power to regulate commercial activities among the various states?**
3. **What constitutional clause allows laws enacted by the federal government to take priority over conflicting state laws?**
4. **What is the Bill of Rights? What freedoms does the First Amendment guarantee?**
5. **Where in the Constitution can the due process clause be found?**

(John Elk III/Lonely Planet Images/Getty Images)

The U.S. Constitution is brief. It contains only about seven thousand words—less than one-third of the number of words in the average state constitution (see Appendix B). Perhaps its brevity explains why it has proved to be so "marvelously elastic," as Franklin Roosevelt pointed out in the chapter-opening quotation, and why it has survived for more than two hundred years—longer than any other written constitution in the world.

Laws that govern business have their origin in the lawmaking authority granted by this document, which is the supreme law in this country. As mentioned in Chapter 1, neither Congress nor any state can enact a law that is in conflict with the Constitution. In this chapter, we first look at some basic constitutional concepts and clauses and their significance for business. Then we examine how certain fundamental freedoms guaranteed by the Constitution affect businesspersons and the workplace.

We also examine privacy rights, which are protected by the Constitution and have come to the forefront in recent years. The Internet has significantly expanded the amount of information that the public can access about individuals. This is an area of growing concern, particularly as information concerning lawsuits and criminal records is widely available online.

▶ The Constitutional Powers of Government

Following the Revolutionary War, the states created a *confederal* form of government in which the states had the authority to govern themselves and the national government could exercise only limited powers. When problems arose because the nation was facing an economic crisis and state laws interfered with the free flow of commerce, a national convention was called, and the delegates drafted the U.S. Constitution. This document, after its ratification by the states in 1789, became the basis for an entirely new form of government.

A Federal Form of Government

Federal Form of Government   A system of government in which the states form a union and the sovereign power is divided between the central government and the member states.

The new government created by the U.S. Constitution reflected a series of compromises made by the convention delegates on various issues. Some delegates wanted sovereign power to remain with the states. Others wanted the national government alone to exercise sovereign power. The end result was a compromise—a **federal form of government** in which the national government and the states *share* sovereign power.

The Constitution sets forth specific powers that can be exercised by the national government and provides that the national government has the implied power to undertake actions necessary to carry out its expressly designated powers (or *enumerated powers*). All other powers are expressly "reserved" to the states or to the people under the Tenth Amendment to the Constitution.

Police Powers   Powers possessed by states as part of their inherent sovereignty.

In part because of this provision of the Tenth Amendment, state governments have the authority to regulate affairs within their borders as part of their inherent sovereignty. State regulatory powers are often referred to as **police powers.** The term does not relate solely to criminal law enforcement but rather refers to the broad right of state governments to regulate private activities to protect or promote the public order, health, safety, morals, and general welfare. Fire and building codes, antidiscrimination laws, parking regulations, zoning restrictions, licensing requirements, and thousands of other state statutes covering almost every aspect of life have been enacted pursuant to states' police powers. Local governments, including cities, also exercise police powers. Generally, state laws enacted pursuant to a state's police powers carry a strong presumption of validity.

The Separation of Powers

LEARNING OBJECTIVE 1 **What is the basic structure of the U.S. government?**

To make it difficult for the national government to use its power arbitrarily, the Constitution divided the national government's powers among the three branches of government. The legislative branch makes the laws, the executive branch enforces the laws, and the judicial branch interprets the laws. Each branch performs a separate function, and no branch may exercise the authority of another branch.

Checks and Balances   The system by which each of the three branches of the national government exercises a check on the actions of the others.

Additionally, a system of **checks and balances** allows each branch to limit the actions of the other two branches, thus preventing any one branch from exercising too much power. The following are examples of these checks and balances:

1. The legislative branch (Congress) can enact a law, but the executive branch (the president) has the constitutional authority to veto that law.
2. The executive branch is responsible for foreign affairs, but treaties with foreign governments require the advice and consent of the Senate.

3. Congress determines the jurisdiction of the federal courts, and the president appoints federal judges, with the advice and consent of the Senate, but the judicial branch has the power to hold actions of the other two branches unconstitutional.

The Commerce Clause

LEARNING OBJECTIVE 2 **What constitutional clause gives the federal government the power to regulate commercial activities among the various states?**

Commerce Clause The provision in Article I, Section 8, of the U.S. Constitution that gives Congress the power to regulate interstate commerce.

To prevent states from establishing laws and regulations that would interfere with trade and commerce among the states, the Constitution expressly delegated to the national government the power to regulate interstate commerce. Article I, Section 8, of the U.S. Constitution expressly permits Congress "[t]o regulate Commerce with foreign Nations, and among the several States, and with the Indian Tribes." This clause, referred to as the **commerce clause,** has had a greater impact on business than any other provision in the Constitution.

Initially, the commerce power was interpreted as being limited to *interstate* commerce (commerce among the states) and not applicable to *intrastate* commerce (commerce within a state). In 1824, however, in *Gibbons v. Ogden*[1] the United States Supreme Court held that commerce within a state could also be regulated by the national government as long as the commerce *substantially affected* commerce involving more than one state.

THE EXPANSION OF NATIONAL POWERS UNDER THE COMMERCE CLAUSE In the *Gibbons* case, the Supreme Court expanded the commerce clause to regulate activities that "substantially affect interstate commerce." As the nation grew and faced new kinds of problems, the commerce clause became a vehicle for the additional expansion of the national government's regulatory powers. Even activities that seemed purely local came under the regulatory reach of the national government if those activities were deemed to substantially affect interstate commerce.

CASE EXAMPLE 4.1 In 1942, in *Wickard v. Filburn,*[2] the Supreme Court held that wheat production by an individual farmer intended wholly for consumption on his own farm was subject to federal regulation. The Court reasoned that the home consumption of wheat reduced the market demand for wheat and thus could have a substantial effect on interstate commerce. •

The following *Classic Case* involved a challenge to the scope of the national government's constitutional authority to regulate local activities.

---

1. 22 U.S. (9 Wheat.) 1, 6 L.Ed. 23 (1824).
2. 317 U.S. 111, 63 S.Ct. 82, 87 L.Ed. 122 (1942).

Classic Case 4.1   **Heart of Atlanta Motel v. United States**

Supreme Court of the United States, 379 U.S. 241, 85 S.Ct. 348, 13 L.Ed.2d 258 (1964).

BACKGROUND AND FACTS The owner of the Heart of Atlanta Motel, in violation of the Civil Rights Act of 1964, refused to rent rooms to African Americans. The motel owner brought an action in a federal district court to have the Civil Rights Act declared unconstitutional, alleging that Congress had exceeded its constitutional authority to regulate commerce by enacting the act. The owner argued that his motel was not engaged in interstate commerce but was "of a purely local character." The motel, however, was accessible to state and interstate highways. The owner advertised nationally, maintained billboards throughout the state, and accepted convention trade from outside the state (75 percent of the guests were residents of other states). The court ruled that the act did not violate the Constitution and enjoined (prohibited) the owner from discriminating on the basis of race. The owner appealed. The case ultimately went to the United States Supreme Court.

Classic Case 4.1–Continues next page ➡

Classic Case 4.1–Continued

IN THE WORDS OF THE COURT . . .
Mr. Justice *CLARK* delivered the opinion of the Court.
* * * *

While the Act as adopted carried no congressional findings, the record of its passage through each house is replete [abounding] with evidence of the burdens that discrimination by race or color places upon interstate commerce * * * . This testimony included the fact that our people have become increasingly mobile with millions of all races traveling from State to State; that Negroes in particular have been the subject of discrimination in transient accommodations, having to travel great distances to secure the same; that often they have been unable to obtain accommodations and have had to call upon friends to put them up overnight. * * * These exclusionary practices were found to be nationwide, the Under Secretary of Commerce testifying that there is "no question that this discrimination in the North still exists to a large degree" and in the West and Midwest as well * * * . This testimony indicated a qualitative as well as quantitative effect on interstate travel by Negroes. The former was the obvious impairment of the Negro traveler's pleasure and convenience that resulted when he continually was uncertain of finding lodging. As for the latter, there was evidence that this uncertainty stemming from racial discrimination had the effect of discouraging travel on the part of a substantial portion of the Negro community * * * . We shall not burden this opinion with further details since the voluminous testimony presents overwhelming evidence that discrimination by hotels and motels impedes interstate travel.
* * * *

It is said that the operation of the motel here is of a purely local character. But, assuming this to be true, "if it is interstate commerce that feels the pinch, it does not matter how local the operation that applies the squeeze." * * * Thus *the power of Congress to promote interstate commerce also includes the power to regulate the local incidents thereof, including local activities in both the States of origin and destination, which might have a substantial and harmful effect upon that commerce.* [Emphasis added.]

DECISION AND REMEDY   The United States Supreme Court upheld the constitutionality of the Civil Rights Act of 1964. The power of Congress to regulate interstate commerce permitted the enactment of legislation that could halt local discriminatory practices.

THE LEGAL ENVIRONMENT DIMENSION   *Can you think of any businesses in today's economy that are "purely local in character"?*

IMPACT OF THIS CASE ON TODAY'S LEGAL ENVIRONMENT   *If the Supreme Court had invalidated the Civil Rights Act of 1964, the legal landscape of the United States would be much different today. The act prohibited discrimination based on race, color, national origin, religion, or gender in all "public accommodations" as well as discrimination in employment based on these criteria. Although state laws now prohibit many of these forms of discrimination as well, the protections available vary from state to state—and it is not certain when (and if) such laws would have been passed had the 1964 federal Civil Rights Act been deemed unconstitutional.*

THE COMMERCE CLAUSE TODAY   The national government continues to rely on the commerce clause for its constitutional authority to regulate business activities in the United States. The breadth of the commerce clause permits the national government to legislate in areas in which Congress has not explicitly been granted power.

In the last twenty years, however, the Supreme Court has begun to curb somewhat the national government's regulatory authority under the commerce clause. In 1995, the Court held—for the first time in sixty years—that Congress had exceeded its regulatory authority under the commerce clause. The Court struck down an act that banned the possession of guns within one thousand feet of any school because the act attempted to regulate an area that had "nothing to do with commerce."[3] Subsequently, the Court invalidated key portions of two other federal acts on the ground that they exceeded Congress's commerce clause authority.[4]

In one notable case, however, the Supreme Court did allow the federal government to regulate noncommercial activities taking place wholly within a state's borders. **CASE EXAMPLE 4.2**   About one dozen states have adopted laws that legalize

---

3. The United States Supreme Court held the Gun-Free School Zones Act of 1990 to be unconstitutional in *United States v. Lopez,* 514 U.S. 549, 115 S.Ct. 1624, 131 L.Ed.2d 626 (1995).
4. See *Printz v. United States,* 521 U.S. 898, 117 S.Ct. 2365, 138 L.Ed.2d 914 (1997), involving the Brady Handgun Violence Prevention Act of 1993; and *United States v. Morrison,* 529 U.S. 598, 120 S.Ct. 1740, 146 L.Ed.2d 658 (2000), concerning the federal Violence Against Women Act of 1994.

marijuana for medical purposes. Marijuana possession, however, is illegal under the federal Controlled Substances Act (CSA).[5] After the federal government seized the marijuana that two seriously ill California women were using on the advice of their physicians, the women filed a lawsuit. They argued that it was unconstitutional for the federal statute to prohibit them from using marijuana for medical purposes that were legal within the state. The Supreme Court, though, held that Congress has the authority to prohibit the *intra*state possession and noncommercial cultivation of marijuana as part of a larger regulatory scheme (the CSA).[6] In other words, state medical marijuana laws do not insulate the users from federal prosecution. •

THE "DORMANT" COMMERCE CLAUSE   The United States Supreme Court has interpreted the commerce clause to mean that the national government has the *exclusive* authority to regulate commerce that substantially affects trade and commerce among the states. This express grant of authority to the national government, which is often referred to as the "positive" aspect of the commerce clause, implies a negative aspect—that the states do not have the authority to regulate interstate commerce. This negative aspect of the commerce clause is often referred to as the "dormant" (implied) commerce clause.

The dormant commerce clause comes into play when state regulations affect interstate commerce. In this situation, the courts normally weigh the state's interest in regulating a certain matter against the burden that the state's regulation places on interstate commerce. Because courts balance the interests involved, it can be extremely difficult to predict the outcome in a particular case.

CASE EXAMPLE 4.3   Tri-M Group, LLC, a Pennsylvania electrical contractor, was hired to do work on a veteran's home in Delaware that was partially state funded. Delaware's regulations on state-funded projects allowed contractors to pay a lower wage rate to apprentices if the contractors had registered their apprenticeship programs in the state. Out-of-state contractors, however, were not eligible to pay the lower rate, unless they maintained a permanent office in Delaware. Tri-M filed a lawsuit in federal court claiming that Delaware's regulations discriminated against out-of-state contractors in violation of the dormant commerce clause. The state argued that the regulations were justified because it had a legitimate interest in safeguarding the welfare of all apprentices by requiring a permanent place of business in Delaware. The court, however, held that the state had not overcome the presumption of invalidity that applies to discriminatory regulations and that nondiscriminatory alternatives existed for ensuring the welfare of apprentices. Therefore, the regulations violated the dormant commerce clause.[7] •

The Supremacy Clause

Supremacy Clause The requirement in Article VI of the U.S. Constitution that provides that the Constitution, laws, and treaties of the United States are "the supreme Law of the Land."

Article VI of the Constitution provides that the Constitution, laws, and treaties of the United States are "the supreme Law of the Land." This article, commonly referred to as the **supremacy clause,** is important in the ordering of state and federal relationships. When there is a direct conflict between a federal law and a state law, the state law is rendered invalid. Because some powers are *concurrent* (shared by the federal government and the states), however, it is necessary to determine which law governs in a particular circumstance.

---

5. 21 U.S.C. Sections 801 *et seq.*

6. *Gonzales v. Raich,* 545 U.S. 1, 125 S.Ct. 2195, 162 L.Ed.2d 1 (2005).

7. *Tri-M Group, LLC v. Sharp,* 638 F.3d 406 (3d Cir. 2011). Sharp was the name of the secretary of the Delaware Department of Labor.

Preemption   A doctrine under which certain federal laws preempt, or take precedence over, conflicting state or local laws.

Preemption occurs when Congress chooses to act exclusively in a concurrent area. In this circumstance, a valid federal statute or regulation will take precedence over a conflicting state or local law or regulation on the same general subject. Often, it is not clear whether Congress, in passing a law, intended to preempt an entire subject area against state regulation. In these situations, the courts must determine whether Congress intended to exercise exclusive power over a given area. No single factor is decisive as to whether a court will find preemption. Generally, congressional intent to preempt will be found if a federal law regulating an activity is so pervasive, comprehensive, or detailed that the states have little or no room to regulate in that area. Also, when a federal statute creates an agency—such as the National Labor Relations Board—to enforce the law, the agency's rulings on matters that come within its jurisdiction will likely preempt state laws.

LEARNING OBJECTIVE 3   What constitutional clause allows laws enacted by the federal government to take priority over conflicting state laws?

CASE EXAMPLE 4.4   The United States Supreme Court heard a case involving a man who alleged that he had been injured by a faulty medical device (a balloon catheter that had been inserted into his artery following a heart attack). The Court found that the Medical Device Amendments of 1976 had included a preemption provision and that the device had passed the U.S. Food and Drug Administration's rigorous premarket approval process. Therefore, the Court ruled that the federal regulation of medical devices preempted the injured party's state common law claims for negligence, strict liability, and implied warranty (see Chapter 6).[8] ●

▶ Business and the Bill of Rights

The importance of having a written declaration of the rights of individuals eventually caused the first Congress of the United States to enact twelve amendments to the Constitution and submit them to the states for approval. The first ten of these amendments, commonly known as the **Bill of Rights,** were adopted in 1791 and embody a series of protections for the individual against various types of interference by the federal government.[9] Some constitutional protections apply to business entities as well. For example, corporations exist as separate legal entities, or legal persons, and enjoy many of the same rights and privileges as natural persons do. Summarized here are the protections guaranteed by these ten amendments (see Appendix B for the complete text of each amendment):

Bill of Rights   The first ten amendments to the U.S. Constitution.

LEARNING OBJECTIVE 4   What is the Bill of Rights? What freedoms does the First Amendment guarantee?

1. The First Amendment guarantees the freedoms of religion, speech, and the press and the rights to assemble peaceably and to petition the government.
2. The Second Amendment guarantees the right to keep and bear arms.
3. The Third Amendment prohibits, in peacetime, the lodging of soldiers in any house without the owner's consent.
4. The Fourth Amendment prohibits unreasonable searches and seizures of persons or property.
5. The Fifth Amendment guarantees the rights to indictment (formal accusation) by a grand jury, to due process of law, and to fair payment when private property is taken for public use. The Fifth Amendment also prohibits compulsory self-incrimination and double jeopardy (trial for the same crime twice).
6. The Sixth Amendment guarantees the accused in a criminal case the right to a speedy and public trial by an impartial jury and with counsel. The accused has

---

8. *Riegel v. Medtronic, Inc.,* 552 U.S. 312, 128 S.Ct. 999, 169 L.Ed.2d 892 (2008).

9. One of the proposed amendments was ratified more than two hundred years later (in 1992) and became the Twenty-seventh Amendment to the Constitution. See Appendix B.

the right to cross-examine witnesses against him or her and to solicit testimony from witnesses in his or her favor.

7. The Seventh Amendment guarantees the right to a trial by jury in a civil (non-criminal) case involving at least twenty dollars.[10]

8. The Eighth Amendment prohibits excessive bail and fines, as well as cruel and unusual punishment.

9. The Ninth Amendment establishes that the people have rights in addition to those specified in the Constitution.

10. The Tenth Amendment establishes that those powers neither delegated to the federal government nor denied to the states are reserved for the states.

We will look closely at several of these amendments in Chapter 7, in the context of criminal law and procedures. In this section, we examine two important guarantees of the First Amendment—freedom of speech and freedom of religion—after we discuss some limitations of certain governmental actions.

Limits on Federal and State Governmental Actions

As originally intended, the Bill of Rights limited only the powers of the national government. Over time, however, the United States Supreme Court "incorporated" most of these rights into the protections against state actions afforded by the Fourteenth Amendment to the Constitution. That amendment, passed in 1868 after the Civil War, provides, in part, that "[n]o State shall . . . deprive any person of life, liberty, or property, without due process of law." Starting in 1925, the Supreme Court began to define various rights and liberties guaranteed in the national Constitution as constituting "due process of law," which was required of state governments under the Fourteenth Amendment. Today, most of the rights and liberties set forth in the Bill of Rights apply to state governments as well as to the national government.

The rights secured by the Bill of Rights are not absolute. Many of the rights guaranteed by the first ten amendments are described in very general terms. For example, the Second Amendment states that people have a right to keep and bear arms, but it does not explain the extent of this right. As the Supreme Court noted in 2008, this does not mean that people can "keep and carry any weapon whatsoever in any manner whatsoever and for whatever purpose."[11] Legislatures can prohibit the carrying of concealed weapons or certain types of weapons, such as machine guns. Ultimately, it is the United States Supreme Court, as the final interpreter of the Constitution, that gives meaning to these rights and determines their boundaries.

BE CAREFUL Although most of the rights in the Bill of Rights apply to actions of the states, some of them apply only to actions of the federal government.

Beyond Our Borders — The Impact of Foreign Law on the United States Supreme Court

The United States Supreme Court interprets the rights provided in the U.S. Constitution. Changing public views on controversial topics, such as privacy in an era of terrorist threats or the rights of gay men and lesbians, may affect the way the Court decides a case. Should the Court also consider other nations' laws and world opinion when balancing individual rights in the United States?

Justices on the Court have increasingly considered foreign law when deciding issues of national importance. This trend started in 2003 when, for the first time ever, foreign law was cited in a majority opinion of the Court. The case was a controversial one in which the Court struck down laws that

Continued ➡️

10. Twenty dollars was forty days' pay for the average person when the Bill of Rights was written.
11. *District of Columbia v. Heller,* 554 U.S. 570, 128 S.Ct. 2783, 171 L.Ed.2d 637 (2008).

prohibited oral and anal sex between consenting adults of the same gender. In the majority opinion (an opinion that the majority of justices have signed), Justice Anthony Kennedy mentioned that the European Court of Human Rights and other foreign courts have consistently acknowledged that homosexuals have a right "to engage in intimate, consensual conduct."[12] The Court again looked at foreign law when deciding whether the death penalty was an appropriate punishment for persons who were juveniles when they committed their crimes.[13]

The practice of looking at foreign law has many critics, including Justice Antonin Scalia and other more conservative members of the Court, who believe that foreign views are irrelevant to rulings on U.S. law. Other Supreme Court justices, however, including Justice Stephen Breyer and Justice Ruth Bader Ginsburg, have publicly stated that in our increasingly global community we should not ignore the opinions of courts in the rest of the world.

● For Critical Analysis

Should U.S. courts, and particularly the United States Supreme Court, look to other nations' laws for guidance when deciding important issues—including those involving rights granted by the Constitution? If so, what impact might this have on their decisions? Explain.

The First Amendment—Freedom of Speech

A democratic form of government cannot survive unless people can freely voice their political opinions and criticize governmental actions or policies. Freedom of speech, particularly political speech, is thus a prized right, and traditionally the courts have protected this right to the fullest extent possible.

Symbolic Speech   Nonverbal expressions of beliefs.

Symbolic speech—gestures, movements, articles of clothing, and other forms of expressive conduct—is also given substantial protection by the courts. The Supreme Court held that the burning of the American flag to protest government policies is a constitutionally protected form of expression.[14] Similarly, wearing a T-shirt with a photo of a presidential candidate is a constitutionally protected form of expression. The test is whether a reasonable person would interpret the conduct as conveying some sort of message. **EXAMPLE 4.5**   As a form of expression, Bryan has gang signs tattooed on his torso, arms, neck, and legs. If a reasonable person would interpret this conduct as conveying a message, then it might be a protected form of symbolic speech. ●

REASONABLE RESTRICTIONS   Expression—oral, written, or symbolized by conduct—is subject to reasonable restrictions. A balance must be struck between a government's obligation to protect its citizens and those citizens' exercise of their rights. Reasonableness is analyzed on a case-by-case basis.

> *"If the freedom of speech is taken away, then dumb and silent we may be led like sheep to the slaughter."*
> George Washington, 1732–1799
> (First president of the United States, 1789–1797)

Content-Neutral Laws.   Laws that regulate the time, manner, and place, but not the content, of speech receive less scrutiny by the courts than do the laws that restrict the content of expression. If a restriction imposed by the government is content neutral, then a court may allow it. To be content neutral, the restriction must be aimed at combating some secondary societal problem, such as crime, and not at suppressing the expressive conduct or its message.

Courts have often protected nude dancing as a form of symbolic expression. Nevertheless, the courts typically allow content-neutral laws that ban *all* public nudity. **CASE EXAMPLE 4.6**   Ria Ora was charged with dancing nude at an annual

---

12. *Lawrence v. Texas,* 539 U.S. 558, 123 S.Ct. 2472, 156 L.Ed.2d 508 (2003).
13. *Roper v. Simmons,* 543 U.S. 551, 125 S.Ct. 1183, 161 L.Ed.2d 1 (2005).
14. See *Texas v. Johnson,* 491 U.S. 397, 109 S.Ct. 2533, 105 L.Ed.2d 342 (1989).

anti-Christmas protest in Harvard Square in Cambridge, Massachusetts, under a statute banning public displays of open and gross lewdness. Ora argued that the statute was overbroad and unconstitutional, and a trial court agreed. On appeal, however, a state appellate court upheld the statute as constitutional in situations in which there was an unsuspecting or unwilling audience.[15] ●

Compelling Government Interest
A test of constitutionality that requires the government to have convincing reasons for passing any law that restricts fundamental rights, such as free speech, or distinguishes between people based on a suspect trait.

Laws That Restrict the Content of Speech. If a law regulates the content of the expression, it must serve a compelling state interest and must be narrowly written to achieve that interest. Under the **compelling government interest** test, the government's interest is balanced against the individual's constitutional right to be free of law. For the statute to be valid, there must be a compelling governmental interest that can be furthered only by the law in question.

The United States Supreme Court has also held that schools may restrict students' free speech at school events. **CASE EXAMPLE 4.7** Some high school students held up a banner saying "Bong Hits 4 Jesus" at an off-campus but school-sanctioned event. The majority of the Court ruled that school officials did not violate the students' free speech rights when they confiscated the banner and suspended the students for ten days. Because the banner could reasonably be interpreted as promoting drugs, the Court concluded that the school officials' actions were justified.[16] ●

Can a high school suspend teenagers from extracurricular activities because they posted suggestive photos of themselves online at social networking sites? For a discussion of this issue, see this chapter's *Online Developments* feature on the following page.

CORPORATE POLITICAL SPEECH Political speech by corporations also falls within the protection of the First Amendment. **CASE EXAMPLE 4.8** Many years ago, the United States Supreme Court reviewed a Massachusetts statute that prohibited corporations from making political contributions or expenditures that individuals were permitted to make. The Court ruled that the Massachusetts law was unconstitutional because it violated the right of corporations to freedom of speech.[17] ● The Court has also held that a law prohibiting a corporation from using bill inserts to express its views on controversial issues violated the First Amendment.[18]

Corporate political speech continues to be given significant protection under the First Amendment. In 2010, the Court overturned a twenty-year-old precedent when it ruled that corporations can spend freely to support or oppose candidates for president and Congress.[19]

REMEMBER The First Amendment guarantee of freedom of speech applies only to *government* restrictions on speech.

COMMERCIAL SPEECH The courts also give substantial protection to *commercial speech,* which consists of communications—primarily advertising and marketing—made by business firms that involve only their commercial interests. The protection given to commercial speech under the First Amendment is not as extensive as that afforded to noncommercial speech, however. A state may restrict certain kinds of

---

15. *Commonwealth v. Ora,* 451 Mass. 125, 883 N.E.2d 1217 (2008).
16. *Morse v. Frederick,* 551 U.S. 393, 127 S.Ct. 2618, 168 L.Ed.2d 290 (2007).
17. *First National Bank of Boston v. Bellotti,* 435 U.S. 765, 98 S.Ct. 1407, 55 L.Ed.2d 707 (1978).
18. *Consolidated Edison Co. v. Public Service Commission,* 447 U.S. 530, 100 S.Ct. 2326, 65 L.Ed.2d 319 (1980).
19. *Citizens United v. Federal Election Commission,* 558 U.S. 50, 130 S.Ct. 876, 175 L.Ed.2d 753 (2010).

ONLINE DEVELOPMENTS

Raunchy Facebook Photos Receive First Amendment Protection

A federal judge in Indiana ruled that a high school did not have the right to punish students for posting raunchy photos of themselves on the Internet. According to the court, "The case poses timely questions about the limits school officials can place on out-of-school speech by students in the information age where Twitter, Facebook, MySpace, texts, and the like rule the day."[a]

High School Suspended the Teens from Extracurricular Activities

T.V. and M.K. were both entering the tenth grade at a public high school. During summer sleepovers, the girls took photos of each other pretending to suck on penis-shaped rainbow-colored lollipops and holding them in various suggestive positions. They later posted the photos on Facebook, MySpace, and Photo Bucket to be seen by persons granted "friend" status or given a password. The images did not identify the school that the girls attended.

When a parent complained to the school about the provocative online display, school officials suspended both girls from extracurricular activities for a portion of the upcoming school year. Both T.V. and M.K. were members of the high school's volleyball team, and M.K. was also a member of the cheerleading squad and the show choir. Through their parents, they filed a lawsuit claiming that the school had violated their First Amendment rights.

Can Online Photos Qualify as Symbolic Speech?

Expressive conduct is entitled to First Amendment protection if it meets a two-part, intent-plus-perception test. Conduct is symbolic speech if the "intent to convey a particularized message was

present" and if "the likelihood was great that the message would be understood by those who viewed it."[b]

Here, both girls testified that they were just trying to be funny when they took the photos and posted them online for their friends to see. Although the photos were suggestive, the girls were fully clothed, and the images were not pornographic or obscene. The court reasoned that the conduct depicted in the photos was intended to be humorous and would be understood as such by their teenage audience. Therefore, the photos were entitled to First Amendment protection as symbolic speech, even if they were "juvenile and silly."

Did the Off-Campus Speech Substantially Disrupt School Activities?

Although schools can restrict students' speech at times, this was not one of those times, according to the court. The conduct took place off campus and did not substantially disrupt the work and discipline of the high school. Schools generally can punish students only for off-campus speech that becomes an in-school problem, such as bullying, but here, the photos had only a minimal effect on the volleyball team. (Some of the other players and two parents had complained that the photos were inappropriate.) The court also struck down the provision in the student handbook banning out-of-school conduct that brings discredit or dishonor on the school, finding that it was impermissibly overbroad and vague.

FOR CRITICAL ANALYSIS

How might the outcome of this case have been different if the girls had posted the photos on the high school's public Web site for all to see?

---

a. *T.V. ex rel. B.V. v. Smith-Green Community School Corp.*, 807 F.Supp.2d 767 (N.D.Ind. 2011).

b. See *Texas v. Johnson*, 491 U.S. 397, 109 S.Ct. 2533, 105 L.Ed.2d 342 (1989).

---

advertising, for instance, in the interest of protecting consumers from being misled by the advertising practices. States also have a legitimate interest in the beautification of roadsides, and this interest allows states to place restraints on billboard advertising.

Generally, a restriction on commercial speech will be considered valid as long as it (1) seeks to implement a substantial government interest, (2) directly advances that interest, and (3) goes no further than necessary to accomplish its objective.

At issue in the following *Spotlight Case* was whether a government agency had unconstitutionally restricted commercial speech when it prohibited the inclusion of a certain illustration on beer labels.

SPOTLIGHT ON COMMERCIAL SPEECH

Case 4.2 **Bad Frog Brewery, Inc. v. New York State Liquor Authority**

United States Court of Appeals, Second Circuit, 134 F.3d 87 (1998).

BACKGROUND AND FACTS Bad Frog Brewery, Inc., makes and sells alcoholic beverages. Some of the beverages feature labels with a drawing of a frog making the gesture generally known as "giving the finger." Bad Frog's authorized New York distributor, Renaissance Beer Company, applied to the New York State Liquor Authority (NYSLA) for brand label approval, as required by state law before the beer could be sold in New York. The NYSLA denied the application, in part, because "the label could appear in grocery and convenience stores, with obvious exposure on the shelf to children of tender age." Bad Frog filed a suit in a federal district court against the NYSLA, asking for, among other things, an injunction against the denial of the application. The court granted summary judgment in favor of the NYSLA. Bad Frog appealed to the U.S. Court of Appeals for the Second Circuit.

IN THE WORDS OF THE COURT . . .
Jon O. *NEWMAN*, Circuit Judge.
* * * *

* * * To support its asserted power to ban Bad Frog's labels [NYSLA advances] * * * the State's interest in "protecting children from vulgar and profane advertising" * * * .

[This interest is] substantial * * * . *States have a compelling interest in protecting the physical and psychological well-being of minors* * * * . [Emphasis added.]
* * * *

* * * NYSLA endeavors to advance the state interest in preventing exposure of children to vulgar displays by taking only the limited step of barring such displays from the labels of alcoholic beverages. *In view of the wide currency of vulgar displays throughout contemporary society, including comic books targeted directly at children, barring such displays from labels for alcoholic beverages cannot realistically be expected to reduce children's exposure to such displays to any significant degree.* [Emphasis added.]

* * * If New York decides to make a substantial effort to insulate children from vulgar displays in some significant sphere of activity, at least with respect to materials likely to be seen by children, NYSLA's label prohibition might well be found to make a justifiable contribution to the material advancement of such an effort, but its currently isolated response to the perceived problem, applicable only to labels on a product that children cannot purchase, does not suffice. * * * A state must demonstrate that its commercial speech limitation is part of a substantial effort to advance a valid state interest, not merely the removal of a few grains of offensive sand from a beach of vulgarity.
* * * *

* * * Even if we were to assume that the state materially advances its asserted interest by shielding children from viewing the Bad Frog labels, it is plainly excessive to prohibit the labels from all use, including placement on bottles displayed in bars and taverns where parental supervision of children is to be expected. Moreover, to whatever extent NYSLA is concerned that children will be harmfully exposed to the Bad Frog labels when wandering without parental supervision around grocery and convenience stores where beer is sold, that concern could be less intrusively dealt with by placing restrictions on the permissible locations where the appellant's products may be displayed within such stores.

DECISION AND REMEDY The U.S. Court of Appeals for the Second Circuit reversed the judgment of the district court and remanded the case for the entry of a judgment in favor of Bad Frog. The NYSLA's ban on the use of the labels lacked a "reasonable fit" with the state's interest in shielding minors from vulgarity, and the NYSLA did not adequately consider alternatives to the ban.

WHAT IF THE FACTS WERE DIFFERENT? *If Bad Frog had sought to use the offensive label to market toys instead of beer, would the court's ruling likely have been the same? Explain your answer.*

UNPROTECTED SPEECH The United States Supreme Court has made it clear that certain types of speech will not be given any protection under the First Amendment. Speech that harms the good reputation of another, or defamatory speech (see Chapter 6), will not be protected. Speech that violates criminal laws (such as threatening speech) is not constitutionally protected. Other unprotected speech includes fighting words, or words that are likely to incite others to respond violently.

Obscene Speech. The First Amendment, as interpreted by the Supreme Court, also does not protect obscene speech. Establishing an objective definition of obscene speech has proved difficult, however, and the Court has grappled with this problem from time to time. In *Miller v. California,*[20] the Supreme Court created a test for legal obscenity, which involved a set of requirements that must be met for material to be legally obscene. Under this test, material is obscene if (1) the average person finds that it violates contemporary community standards; (2) the work taken as a whole appeals to a prurient (arousing or obsessive) interest in sex; (3) the work shows patently offensive sexual conduct; and (4) the work lacks serious redeeming literary, artistic, political, or scientific merit.

Because community standards vary widely, the *Miller* test has had inconsistent application, and obscenity remains a constitutionally unsettled issue. Numerous state and federal statutes make it a crime to disseminate and possess obscene materials, including child pornography.

Online Obscenity. Congress's first two attempts at protecting minors from pornographic materials on the Internet—the Communications Decency Act (CDA) of 1996[21] and the Child Online Protection Act (COPA) of 1998[22]—failed. Ultimately, the United States Supreme Court struck down both the CDA and COPA as unconstitutional restraints on speech, largely because the wording of these acts was overbroad and would restrict nonpornographic materials.[23]

In 2000, Congress enacted the Children's Internet Protection Act (CIPA),[24] which requires public schools and libraries to block adult content from access by children by installing **filtering software** on computers. Such software is designed to prevent persons from viewing certain Web sites by responding to a site's Internet address or its **meta tags,** or key words. CIPA was also challenged on constitutional grounds, but in 2003 the Supreme Court held that the act did not violate the First Amendment. The Court concluded that because libraries can disable the filters for any patrons who ask, the system is reasonably flexible and does not burden free speech to an unconstitutional extent.[25]

In 2003, Congress enacted the Prosecutorial Remedies and Other Tools to end the Exploitation of Children Today Act (Protect Act).[26] The act makes it a crime to knowingly advertise, present, distribute, or solicit "any material or purported material in a manner that reflects the belief, or that is intended to cause another to believe, that the material or purported material" is illegal child pornography. Thus, it is a crime to intentionally distribute virtual child pornography, which uses computer-generated images, not actual people.

In a case challenging the constitutionality of the Protect Act, the United States Supreme Court held that the statute was valid because it does not prohibit a substantial amount of protected speech.[27] Rather, the act generally prohibits offers to provide and requests to obtain child pornography—both of which are unprotected speech. Nevertheless, because of the difficulties of policing the Internet, as well as the constitutional complexities of prohibiting online obscenity through legislation, it remains a problem worldwide.

Filtering Software   A computer program that is designed to block access to certain Web sites based on their content.

Meta Tag   A key word in a document that can serve as an index reference to the document.

---

20. 413 U.S. 15, 93 S.Ct. 2607, 37 L.Ed.2d 419 (1973).

21. 47 U.S.C. Section 223(a)(1)(B)(ii).

22. 47 U.S.C. Section 231.

23. See *Reno v. American Civil Liberties Union,* 521 U.S. 844, 117 S.Ct. 2329, 138 L.Ed.2d 874 (1997); *Ashcroft v. American Civil Liberties Union,* 535 U.S. 564, 122 S.Ct. 1700, 152 L.Ed.2d 771 (2002); and *American Civil Liberties Union v. Ashcroft,* 322 F.3d 240 (3d Cir. 2003).

24. 17 U.S.C. Sections 1701–1741.

25. *United States v. American Library Association,* 539 U.S. 194, 123 S.Ct. 2297, 156 L.Ed.2d 221 (2003).

26. 18 U.S.C. Section 2252A(a)(5)(B).

27. *United States v. Williams,* 553 U.S. 285, 128 S.Ct. 1830, 170 L.Ed.2d 650 (2008).

The First Amendment—Freedom of Religion

The First Amendment states that the government may neither establish any religion nor prohibit the free exercise of religious practices. The first part of this constitutional provision is referred to as the *establishment clause,* and the second part is known as the *free exercise clause.* Government action, both federal and state, must be consistent with this constitutional mandate.

Establishment Clause   The provision in the First Amendment that prohibits the government from establishing any state-sponsored religion or enacting any law that promotes religion or favors one religion over another.

THE ESTABLISHMENT CLAUSE   The **establishment clause** prohibits the government from establishing a state-sponsored religion, as well as from passing laws that promote (aid or endorse) religion or show a preference for one religion over another. Although the establishment clause involves the separation of church and state, it does not require a complete separation. Rather, it requires the government to accommodate religions.

Establishment clause cases often involve such issues as the legality of allowing or requiring school prayers, using state-issued vouchers to pay tuition at religious schools, and teaching creation theories versus evolution. Federal or state laws that do not promote or place a significant burden on religion are constitutional even if they have some impact on religion. For a government law or policy to be constitutional, it must not have the primary effect of promoting or inhibiting religion.

Religious displays on public property have often been challenged as violating the establishment clause, and the United States Supreme Court has ruled on several such cases. Generally, the Court has focused on the proximity of the religious display to non-religious symbols, such as reindeer and candy canes, or to symbols from different religions, such as a menorah (a nine-branched candelabrum used in celebrating Hanukkah). The Court eventually took a slightly different approach when it held that public displays having historical, as well as religious, significance do not necessarily violate the establishment clause.[28] Other courts have ruled differently on this issue, however.

CASE EXAMPLE 4.9   Mount Soledad is a prominent hill near San Diego that has had a forty-foot cross on its top since 1913. In the 1990s, a war memorial was constructed next to the cross that included six walls listing the names of veterans. The site was privately owned until 2006, when Congress authorized the property's transfer to the federal government "to preserve a historically significant war memorial." Shortly thereafter, Steve Trunk and the Jewish War Veterans filed lawsuits claiming that the cross display violated the establishment clause because it endorsed the Christian religion. A federal appellate court agreed, finding that the primary effect of the memorial as a whole sent a strong message of endorsement and exclusion of non-Christian veterans. The court noted that although not all cross displays at war memorials violate the establishment clause, this cross physically dominated the site, was originally dedicated to religious purposes, had a long history of religious use, and was the only portion visible to drivers on the freeway below.[29] ●

Free Exercise Clause   The provision in the First Amendment that prohibits the government from interfering with people's religious practices or forms of worship.

THE FREE EXERCISE CLAUSE   The **free exercise clause** guarantees that a person can hold any religious belief that she or he wants, or a person can have no religious belief. The constitutional guarantee of personal religious freedom restricts only the actions of the government and not those of individuals or private businesses.

When religious *practices* work against public policy and the public welfare, however, the government can act. For instance, the government can require that a child

---

28. *Van Orden v. Perry,* 545 U.S. 677, 125 S.Ct. 2854, 162 L.Ed.2d 607 (2005).
29. *Trunk v. City of San Diego,* 629 F.3d 1099 (9th Cir. 2011).

receive certain types of vaccinations or medical treatment when the child's life is in danger—regardless of the child's or parent's religious beliefs. When public safety is an issue, an individual's religious beliefs often have to give way to the government's interests in protecting the public.

EXAMPLE 4.10 According to the Muslim faith, it is a religious violation for a woman to appear in public without a scarf over her head. Due to public safety concerns, many courts today do not allow the wearing of any headgear in courtrooms. In 2008, a Muslim woman was prevented from entering a courthouse in Georgia, because she refused to remove her scarf. As she left, she uttered an expletive at the court official and was arrested and brought before the judge, who ordered her to serve ten days in jail. ●

In the following case, the court had to decide whether a county ordinance that prohibited the use of steel cleats on tires was a violation of a church's right to freely exercise its religion.

BEWARE The free exercise clause applies only to the actions of the state and federal governments. Nevertheless, under federal employment laws (see Chapter 16), employers may be required to accommodate their employees' religious beliefs, at least to a reasonable extent.

Case 4.3 Mitchell County v. Zimmerman

Supreme Court of Iowa, 810 N.W.2d 1 (2012).

BACKGROUND AND FACTS Members of the Old Order Groffdale Conference Mennonite Church in Iowa generally use horses and buggies for transportation. About forty years ago, they started using tractors, particularly for hauling their agricultural products to market. To ensure that tractors are not used for pleasure purposes (thereby displacing the horse and buggy), their tires must be fitted with steel cleats that slow the tractors. Thus, it is a religious requirement of the Mennonites that any motorized tractor driven by a church member be equipped with steel cleats. To minimize road damage, over time the steel cleats have been made wider and are mounted on rubber belts to provide cushioning. Nevertheless, in 2009, finding that the Mennonites' steel cleats tended to damage newly resurfaced roads, Mitchell County adopted a road protection ordinance: "No tire on a vehicle moved on a highway is allowed to have any block, stud, flange, cleat, or spike, or any other protuberances of any material other than rubber." Eli Zimmerman, a Mennonite, received a citation for violating this ordinance. Zimmerman filed a motion to dismiss, which the trial court denied. Zimmerman appealed.

IN THE WORDS OF THE COURT . . .
MANSFIELD, J. [Judge]
* * * *

Zimmerman [for the Mennonites] contends [that] the district court erred in denying his motion to dismiss based on the First Amendment to the United States Constitution. * * * The Free Exercise Clause was part of the original Federal Bill of Rights and was made applicable to the states through the Fourteenth Amendment * * * .
* * * *

* * * The First Amendment's Free Exercise Clause does not prohibit a state from enforcing a neutral, generally applicable regulatory law, * * * . * * * Laws that are not neutral or of general applicability

require heightened scrutiny. They "must be justified by a compelling governmental interest and must be narrowly tailored to advance that interest."

We agree with the district court that religious practice is not being intentionally discriminated against. * * * The ordinance was passed by Mitchell County only after its engineers detected apparent damage caused to the roads by steel wheels. * * * This is not a case where new activity brushed up against a pre-existing ordinance, but where an ordinance was passed to deal with a long-standing religious practice.
* * * *

* * * Zimmerman contends that the Mitchell County ordinance is not generally applicable because it carries over exceptions that undermine the ordinance's purpose and demonstrate its underinclusivity.

Upon our review, we find [that] the county's ordinance lacks sufficient general applicability * * * . School buses are allowed to use ice grips and tire studs year round. * * * [Mitchell County] chose to prohibit only a particular source of harm to the roads that had a religious origin. [This] underinclusion of the ordinance undermines its general applicability.

Of course an ordinance can fail the general applicability test and still not amount to a free exercise violation. However, the ordinance must then undergo the most vigorous of scrutiny. That is, it must advance interests of the highest order and must be narrowly tailored in pursuit of those interests. *The County has the burden to show that the ordinance serves a compelling state interest and is the least restrictive means of attaining that interest. * * * We are not persuaded that the ordinance is narrowly tailored to achieve the stated objective of road preservation.* [Emphasis added.]

Given the lack of evidence of the degree to which the steel lugs harm the county's roads, the undisputed fact that other events cause road damage, and the undisputed fact that the County had tolerated

Case 4.3—Continued

steel lugs for many years before 2009, it is difficult to see that an outright ban on those lugs is necessary to serve a compelling state interest. The ordinance did not survive the strict scrutiny test because it was not the least restrictive means of serving what is claimed to be a compelling governmental interest in road protection.

DECISION AND REMEDY   The reviewing court reversed the trial court's decision and remanded the case for entry of an order of

dismissal. The ordinance was not clearly tailored to achieve the stated objective of road preservation.

WHAT IF THE FACTS WERE DIFFERENT?   *Suppose that Mitchell County had passed an ordinance that allowed the Mennonites to continue to use steel cleats on the newly resurfaced roads provided that the drivers paid a $5 fee each time they were on the road. Would the court have ruled differently? Why or why not?*

▶ Due Process and Equal Protection

LEARNING OBJECTIVE 5 **Where in the Constitution can the due process clause be found?**

Two other constitutional guarantees of great significance to Americans are mandated by the due process clauses of the Fifth and Fourteenth Amendments and the equal protection clause of the Fourteenth Amendment.

Due Process

Due Process Clause   The provisions in the Fifth and Fourteenth Amendments that guarantee that no person shall be deprived of life, liberty, or property without due process of law.

Both the Fifth and the Fourteenth Amendments provide that no person shall be deprived "of life, liberty, or property, without due process of law." The **due process clause** of each of these constitutional amendments has two aspects—procedural and substantive. Note that the due process clause applies to "legal persons," such as corporations, as well as to individuals.

PROCEDURAL DUE PROCESS   Procedural due process requires that any government decision to take life, liberty, or property must be made fairly—that is, the government must give a person proper notice and an opportunity to be heard. Fair procedures must be used in determining whether a person will be subjected to punishment or have some burden imposed on him or her. Fair procedure has been interpreted as requiring that the person have at least an opportunity to object to a proposed action before a fair, neutral decision maker (who need not be a judge).

   EXAMPLE 4.11   In most states, a driver's license is construed as a property interest. Therefore, the state must provide some sort of opportunity for a person to object before her or his license is suspended or terminated. ●

SUBSTANTIVE DUE PROCESS   Substantive due process protects an individual's life, liberty, or property against certain government actions regardless of the fairness of the procedures used to implement them. Substantive due process limits what the government may do in its legislative and executive capacities. Legislation must be fair and reasonable in content and must further a legitimate governmental objective. Only when state conduct is arbitrary or shocks the conscience, however, will it rise to the level of violating substantive due process.

   If a law or other governmental action limits a fundamental right, it will be held to violate substantive due process unless it promotes a compelling or overriding state interest. Fundamental rights include interstate travel, privacy, voting, marriage and family, and all First Amendment rights. Thus, a state must have a substantial reason for taking any action that infringes on a person's free speech rights. In situations not involving fundamental rights, a law or action does not violate substantive due process if it rationally relates to any legitimate governmental end. It is almost impossible for a law or action to fail the "rationality" test. Under this test, almost any government regulation of business will be upheld as reasonable.

Equal Protection

Under the Fourteenth Amendment, a state may not "deny to any person within its jurisdiction the equal protection of the laws." The United States Supreme Court has used the due process clause of the Fifth Amendment to make the **equal protection clause** applicable to the federal government as well. Equal protection means that the government must treat similarly situated individuals in a similar manner.

Both substantive due process and equal protection require review of the substance of the law or other governmental action rather than review of the procedures used. When a law or action limits the liberty of all persons to do something, it may violate substantive due process. When a law or action limits the liberty of some persons but not others, it may violate the equal protection clause. **EXAMPLE 4.12**   If a law prohibits all advertising on the sides of trucks, it raises a substantive due process question. If it makes an exception to allow truck owners to advertise their own businesses, it raises an equal protection issue. •

In an equal protection inquiry, when a law or action distinguishes between or among individuals, the basis for the distinction—that is, the classification—is examined. Depending on the classification, the courts apply different levels of scrutiny, or "tests," to determine whether the law or action violates the equal protection clause. The courts use one of three standards: *strict scrutiny, intermediate scrutiny,* or the *"rational basis" test.*

STRICT SCRUTINY   If a law or action prohibits or inhibits some persons from exercising a fundamental right, the law or action will be subject to "strict scrutiny" by the courts. Under this standard, the classification must be necessary to promote a *compelling state interest.* Also, if the classification is based on a *suspect trait*—such as race, national origin, or citizenship status—it must be necessary to promote a compelling government interest. Compelling state interests include remedying past unconstitutional or illegal discrimination, but do not include correcting the general effects of "society's discrimination." **EXAMPLE 4.13**   For a city to give preference to minority applicants in awarding construction contracts, it normally must identify past unconstitutional or illegal discrimination against minority construction firms. Because the policy is based on suspect traits (race and national origin), it will violate the equal protection clause *unless* it is necessary to promote a compelling state interest. • Generally, few laws or actions survive strict-scrutiny analysis by the courts.

INTERMEDIATE SCRUTINY   The standard of intermediate scrutiny is applied in cases involving gender discrimination or discrimination against illegitimate children (children born out of wedlock). Laws using gender or legitimacy classifications must be *substantially related to important government objectives.* **EXAMPLE 4.14** An important government objective is preventing illegitimate teenage pregnancies. Because males and females are not similarly situated in this regard—only females can become pregnant—a law that punishes men but not women for statutory rape will be upheld even though it treats men and women unequally. •

The state also has an important objective in establishing time limits (called *statutes of limitation*) for how long after an event a particular type of action can be brought. Nevertheless, the limitation period must be substantially related to the important objective of preventing fraudulent or outdated claims.

EXAMPLE 4.15   A state law requires illegitimate children to bring paternity suits within six years of their births in order to seek support from their fathers. A court will strike down this law if legitimate children are allowed to seek support from their parents at any time because distinguishing between support claims on the basis of legitimacy is not related to the important government objective of preventing fraudulent or outdated claims. •

THE "RATIONAL BASIS" TEST   In matters of economic and social welfare, a classification will be considered valid if there is any conceivable "rational basis" on which the classification might relate to a *legitimate government interest.* It is almost impossible for a law or action to fail the rational basis test.

EXAMPLE 4.16   A city ordinance that in effect prohibits all pushcart vendors, except a specific few, from operating in a particular area of the city will be upheld if the city offers a rational basis—such as reducing traffic in that area—for the ordinance. In contrast, a law that provides unemployment benefit payments only to people over six feet tall would clearly fail the rational basis test because it could not further any legitimate government interest. •

▶ Privacy Rights

The U.S. Constitution does not explicitly mention a general right to privacy. In a 1928 Supreme Court case, *Olmstead v. United States,*[30] Justice Louis Brandeis stated in his dissent that the right to privacy is "the most comprehensive of rights and the right most valued by civilized men." The majority of the justices at that time, however, did not agree with Brandeis.

It was not until the 1960s that the Supreme Court endorsed the view that the Constitution protects individual privacy rights. In a landmark 1965 case, *Griswold v. Connecticut,*[31] the Supreme Court held that a constitutional right to privacy was implied by the First, Third, Fourth, Fifth, and Ninth Amendments.

Today, privacy rights receive protection under various federal statutes as well the U.S. Constitution. In addition, state constitutions and statutes secure individuals' privacy rights, often to a significant degree. Privacy rights are also protected to an extent under tort law (see Chapter 6), consumer law, and employment law (see Chapter 16). In this section, after a brief look at some of the most important federal statutes protecting the privacy of individuals, we examine some current topics related to privacy rights.

Federal Statutes Protecting Privacy Rights

In the last several decades, Congress has enacted a number of statutes that protect the privacy of individuals in various areas of concern. Most of these statutes deal with personal information collected by governments or private businesses. Here, we look first at some of the most important federal statutes protecting individuals' privacy and then examine in more detail the protection given to the important area of medical information.

"There was, of course, no way of knowing whether you were being watched at any given moment."
George Orwell, 1903–1950
(Author, from his famous novel *1984*)

30. 277 U.S. 438, 48 S.Ct. 564, 72 L.Ed. 944 (1928).
31. 381 U.S. 479, 85 S.Ct. 1678, 14 L.Ed.2d 510 (1965).

FEDERAL PRIVACY LEGISLATION   In the 1960s, Americans were sufficiently alarmed by the accumulation of personal information in government files that they pressured Congress to pass laws permitting individuals to access their files. Congress responded in 1966 with the Freedom of Information Act, which allows any person to request copies of any information on her or him contained in federal government files. In 1974, Congress passed the Privacy Act, which also gives persons the right to access such information. These and other major federal laws protecting privacy rights are listed and described in Exhibit 4–1 below.

MEDICAL INFORMATION   Responding to the growing need to protect the privacy of individuals' health records—particularly computerized records—Congress passed the Health Insurance Portability and Accountability Act (HIPAA) of 1996.[32] This act defines and limits the circumstances in which an individual's "protected health information" may be used or disclosed.

HIPAA requires health-care providers and health-care plans, including certain employers who sponsor health plans, to inform patients of their privacy rights and of how their personal medical information may be used. The act also states that a person's medical records generally may not be used for purposes unrelated to health care—such as marketing, for example—or disclosed to others without the individual's permission.

---

32. HIPAA was enacted as Pub. L. No. 104-191 (1996) and is codified in 29 U.S.C.A. Sections 1181 *et seq.*

• *Exhibit* 4–1 **Federal Legislation Relating to Privacy**

TITLE OF ACT AND YEAR FORMED	PROVISIONS CONCERNING PRIVACY
Freedom of Information Act (1966)	Provides that individuals have a right to obtain access to information about them collected in government files.
Family and Educational Rights and Privacy Act (1974)	Limits access to computer-stored records of education-related evaluations and grades in private and public colleges and universities.
Privacy Act (1974)	Protects the privacy of individuals about whom the federal government has information. Under this act, agencies that use or disclose personal information must make sure that the information is reliable and guard against its misuse. Individuals must be able to find out what data concerning them the agency is compiling and how the data will be used. In addition, the agency must give individuals a means to correct inaccurate data and must obtain their consent before using the data for any other purpose.
Tax Reform Act (1976)	Preserves the privacy of personal financial information.
Right to Financial Privacy Act (1978)	Prohibits financial institutions from providing the federal government with access to a customer's records unless the customer authorizes the disclosure.
Electronic Communications Privacy Act (1986)	Prohibits the interception of information communicated by electronic means.
Driver's Privacy Protection Act (1994)	Prevents states from disclosing or selling a driver's personal information without the driver's consent.
Health Insurance Portability and Accountability Act (1996)	Prohibits the use of a consumer's medical information for any purpose other than that for which such information was provided, unless the consumer expressly consents to the use.
Financial Services Modernization Act (Gramm-Leach-Bliley Act) (1999)	Prohibits the disclosure of nonpublic personal information about a consumer to an unaffiliated third party unless strict disclosure and opt-out requirements are met.

Technological Advances and Privacy Rights

Although advances in technology offer many benefits, they may also raise privacy issues. For instance, many people have concerns about the personal data collected by social networking sites. Here, we look briefly at two other areas in which technological developments are raising privacy issues today—the online dissemination of court records and the U.S. government's efforts to combat terrorism.

COURT RECORDS   The online dissemination of information concerning civil and criminal cases raises new privacy issues. Although court proceedings have always been a matter of public record, previously persons had to go to a courthouse to examine the physical records. Now, technological improvements allow civil and criminal justice records to be shared, synthesized, sold, and analyzed electronically. From anywhere in the world, private individuals, businesses, and other organizations can instantly access court records either directly in a state database or from a private data firm.

The advent of electronically available court documents raises difficult questions about how to protect a person's privacy. Court records (and police reports) frequently disclose personal information, such as name, address, and date of birth. Criminals might use this information to perpetrate identity theft or intimidate a witness or victim. Employers and landlords may use the information to screen potential applicants. An employer might decide not to hire a person who was involved in a civil or criminal case, and a landlord might not rent property to that person.

THE USA PATRIOT ACT   The USA Patriot Act was passed by Congress in the wake of the terrorist attacks of September 11, 2001, and then reauthorized in 2006.[33] The Patriot Act has given government officials increased authority to monitor Internet activities and to gain access to personal financial information and student information.

Law enforcement officials may now track the telephone and e-mail communications of one party to find out the identity of the other party or parties. To gain access to these communications, the government must certify that the information likely to be obtained by such monitoring is relevant to an ongoing criminal investigation but does not need to provide proof of any wrongdoing.[34] Privacy advocates argue that this law adversely affects the constitutional rights of all Americans, and it has been widely criticized.

> *"The things most people want to know about are usually none of their business."*
> George Bernard Shaw, 1856–1950
> (Irish dramatist and socialist)

Ethical Issue

Does the threat of terrorism justify the U.S. government's use of full-body scanners at airports? The Transportation Security Administration (TSA) screens all persons seeking to board commercial airline flights for weapons, explosives, or other dangerous substances. In 2010, the TSA started using advanced imaging technology (AIT), or full-body scanners, as the primary screening device at many airports. Many travelers complained that they were being forced to undergo an electronic strip search because the scanners showed every part of one's body. Privacy advocates brought a lawsuit against the U.S. Department of Homeland Security, arguing that AIT was overly invasive and violated the Fourth Amendment's prohibition against unreasonable searches.

Ethical Issue Continues next page ➡

---

33. The Uniting and Strengthening America by Providing Appropriate Tools Required to Intercept and Obstruct Terrorism Act of 2001, also known as the USA Patriot Act, was enacted as Pub. L. No. 107-56 (2001) and reauthorized by Pub. L. No. 109-173 (2006).
34. See, for example, *American Civil Liberties Union v. National Security Agency,* 493 F.3d 644 (6th Cir. 2007).

In 2011, a federal appellate court held that the use of full-body scanners at airports was constitutional. The court balanced the intrusiveness of a full-body scan against a scan's ability to further a legitimate governmental interest. Here, the government had a critical need to ensure airline safety, and the full-body scanners, which can detect liquids and powders in addition to traditional weapons, furthered that interest. The court also found, however, that the TSA had violated the Administrative Procedure Act by changing its regulations to require AIT without following formal rulemaking procedures (see pages 110 and 111). Therefore, the court ordered the TSA to open itself up for public comments on the use of the scanners.[35]

35. *Electronic Privacy Information Center v. U.S. Department of Homeland Security,* 653 F.3d 1 (D.C.Cir. 2011).

▶ Reviewing . . . Constitutional Authority to Regulate Business

A state legislature enacted a statute that required any motorcycle operator or passenger on the state's highways to wear a protective helmet. Jim Alderman, a licensed motorcycle operator, sued the state to block enforcement of the law. Alderman asserted that the statute violated the equal protection clause because it placed requirements on motorcyclists that were not imposed on other motorists. Using the information presented in the chapter, answer the following questions.

1. Why does this statute raise equal protection issues instead of substantive due process concerns?
2. What are the three levels of scrutiny that the courts use in determining whether a law violates the equal protection clause?
3. Which standard, or test, of scrutiny would apply to this situation? Why?
4. Applying this standard, or test, is the helmet statute constitutional? Why or why not?

▶ Debate This

Legislation aimed at protecting people from themselves concerns the individual, as well as the public, in general. Protective helmet laws are just one example of such legislation. Should individuals be allowed to engage in unsafe activities if they choose to do so? Explain your answer.

▶ Key Terms

Bill of Rights 84	equal protection clause 94	meta tag 90
checks and balances 80	establishment clause 91	police powers 80
commerce clause 81	federal form of government 80	preemption 84
compelling government interest 87	filtering software 90	supremacy clause 83
due process clause 93	free exercise clause 91	symbolic speech 86

▶ Chapter Summary: Constitutional Authority to Regulate Business

The Constitutional Powers of Government (See pages 80–81.)	1. *A federal form of government*—The U.S. Constitution established a federal form of government, in which government powers are shared by the national government and the state governments. At the national level, government powers are divided among the legislative, executive, and judicial branches.
	2. *The regulatory powers of the states*—The Tenth Amendment reserves to the states all powers not expressly delegated to the national government. Under their police powers, state governments may regulate private activities in order to protect or promote the public order, health, safety, morals, and general welfare.

Chapter Summary: Constitutional Authority to Regulate Business—Continued

The Commerce Clause (See pages 81–83.)	1. *The expansion of national powers*—The commerce clause expressly permits Congress to regulate commerce. Over time, courts expansively interpreted this clause, thereby enabling the national government to wield extensive powers over the economic life of the nation. 2. *The commerce power today*—Today, the commerce power authorizes the national government, at least theoretically, to regulate every commercial enterprise in the United States. In recent years, the Supreme Court has reined in somewhat the national government's regulatory powers under the commerce clause. 3. *The "dormant" commerce clause*—If state regulations substantially interfere with interstate commerce, they will be held to violate the "dormant" commerce clause of the U.S. Constitution. The positive aspect of the commerce clause, which gives the national government the exclusive authority to regulate interstate commerce, implies a "dormant" aspect—that the states do *not* have this power.
The Supremacy Clause (See pages 83–84.)	The U.S. Constitution provides that the Constitution, laws, and treaties of the United States are "the supreme Law of the Land." Whenever a state law directly conflicts with a federal law, the state law is rendered invalid.
Business and the Bill of Rights (See pages 84–93.)	The Bill of Rights, which consists of the first ten amendments to the U.S. Constitution, was adopted in 1791 and embodies a series of protections for individuals—and, in some instances, business entities—against various types of interference by the federal government. Today, most of the protections apply against state governments as well. Freedoms guaranteed by the First Amendment that affect businesses include the following: 1. *Freedom of speech*—Speech, including symbolic speech, is given the fullest possible protection by the courts. Corporate political speech and commercial speech also receive substantial protection under the First Amendment. Certain types of speech, such as defamatory speech and lewd or obscene speech, are not protected under the First Amendment. Government attempts to regulate unprotected forms of speech in the online environment have, to date, met with numerous challenges. 2. *Freedom of religion*—Under the First Amendment, the government may neither establish any religion (the establishment clause) nor prohibit the free exercise of religion (the free exercise clause).
Due Process and Equal Protection (See pages 93–95.)	1. *Due process*—Both the Fifth and the Fourteenth Amendments provide that no person shall be deprived of "life, liberty, or property, without due process of law." Procedural due process requires that any government decision to take life, liberty, or property must be made fairly, using fair procedures. Substantive due process focuses on the content of legislation. Generally, a law that limits a fundamental right violates substantive due process unless the law promotes a compelling state interest, such as public safety. 2. *Equal protection*—Under the Fourteenth Amendment, a law or action that limits the liberty of some persons but not others may violate the equal protection clause. Such a law may be deemed valid, however, if there is a rational basis for the discriminatory treatment of a given group or if the law substantially relates to an important government objective.
Privacy Rights (See pages 95–98.)	Americans are increasingly concerned about privacy issues raised by Internet-related technology. The Constitution does not contain a specific guarantee of a right to privacy, but such a right has been derived from guarantees found in several constitutional amendments. A number of federal statutes protect privacy rights. Privacy rights are also protected by many state constitutions and statutes.

ExamPrep

ISSUE SPOTTERS

—Check your answers to these questions against the answers provided in Appendix D at the end of this text.

1. Can a state, in the interest of energy conservation, ban all advertising by power utilities if conservation could be accomplished by less restrictive means? Why or why not? (**See pages 87 and 88.**)

2. Would it be a violation of equal protection for a state to impose a higher tax on out-of-state companies doing business in the state than on in-state companies if the only reason for the tax is to protect the local firms from out-of-state competition? Explain. **(See page 94.)**

BEFORE THE TEST

Go to **www.cengagebrain.com**, enter the ISBN 9781133586548, and click on "Find" to locate this textbook's Web site. Then, click on "Access Now" under "Study Tools," and select Chapter 4 at the top. There, you will find a Practice Quiz that you can take to assess your mastery of the concepts in this chapter. Additionally, you will find Flashcards and a Glossary of important terms, as well as Video Questions (when assigned).

▶ For Review

Answers for the even-numbered questions in this **For Review** *section can be found in Appendix E at the end of this text.*

1. What is the basic structure of the U.S. government?
2. What constitutional clause gives the federal government the power to regulate commercial activities among the various states?
3. What constitutional clause allows laws enacted by the federal government to take priority over conflicting state laws?
4. What is the Bill of Rights? What freedoms does the First Amendment guarantee?
5. Where in the Constitution can the due process clause be found?

▶ Questions and Case Problems

4–1. Freedom of Speech. A mayoral election is about to be held in a large U.S. city. One of the candidates is Luis Delgado, and his campaign supporters wish to post campaign signs on lampposts and utility poles throughout the city. A city ordinance, however, prohibits the posting of any signs on public property. Delgado's supporters contend that the city ordinance is unconstitutional because it violates their rights to free speech. What factors might a court consider in determining the constitutionality of this ordinance? **(See pages 86–88.)**

4–2. **Question with Sample Answer: The Free Exercise Clause.** Thomas worked in the nonmilitary operations of a large firm that produced both military and nonmilitary goods. When the company discontinued the production of nonmilitary goods, Thomas was transferred to the plant producing military equipment. Thomas left his job, claiming that it violated his religious principles to participate in the manufacture of goods to be used in destroying life. In effect, he argued, the transfer to the military equipment plant forced him to quit his job. He was denied unemployment compensation by the state because he had not been effectively "discharged" by the employer but had voluntarily terminated his employment. Did the state's denial of unemployment benefits to Thomas violate the free exercise clause of the First Amendment? Explain. **(See page 91.)**
—**For a sample answer to Question 4–2, go to Appendix F at the end of this text.**

4–3. The Equal Protection Clause. With the objectives of preventing crime, maintaining property values, and preserving the quality of urban life, New York City enacted an ordinance to regulate the locations of commercial establishments that featured adult entertainment. The ordinance expressly applied to female, but not male, topless entertainment. Adele Buzzetti owned the Cozy Cabin, a New York City cabaret that featured female topless dancers. Buzzetti and an anonymous dancer filed a suit in a federal district court against the city, asking the court to block the enforcement of the ordinance. The plaintiffs argued, in part, that the ordinance violated the equal protection clause. Under the equal protection clause, what standard applies to the court's consideration of this ordinance? Under this test, how should the court rule? Why? **(See pages 94 and 95.)**

4–4. **Spotlight on Plagiarism: Due Process.** The Russ College of Engineering and Technology of Ohio University announced in a press conference that it had found "rampant and flagrant plagiarism" in the theses of mechanical engineering graduate students. Faculty singled out for "ignoring their ethical responsibilities" included Jay Gunasekera, chair of the department. Gunasekera was prohibited from advising students. He filed a suit against Dennis Irwin, the dean of Russ College, for violating his due process rights. What does due process require in these circumstances? Why? [*Gunasekera v. Irwin*, 551 F.3d 461 (6th Cir. 2009)] **(See pages 93–94.)**

4–5. The Commerce Clause. Under the federal Sex Offender Registration and Notification Act (SORNA), sex offenders must register and update their registration as sex offenders when they travel from one state to another. David Hall, a convicted sex offender in New York, moved to Virginia, where he did not update his registration. He was charged with violating SORNA. He claimed that the statute is unconstitutional, arguing that Congress cannot criminalize interstate travel if no commerce is involved. Is that reasonable? Why or why not? [*United States v. Guzman,* 591 F.3d 83 (2d Cir. 2010)] **(See pages 81–83.)**

4–6. 🔨 **Case Problem with Sample Answer: Establishment Clause.** Judge James DeWeese hung a poster in his courtroom showing the Ten Commandments. The American Civil Liberties Union filed a suit, alleging that the poster violated the establishment clause. DeWeese responded that his purpose was not to promote religion but to express his view about "warring" legal philosophies— moral relativism and moral absolutism. "Our legal system is based on moral absolutes from divine law handed down by God through the Ten Commandments." Does this poster violate the establishment clause? Why or why not? [*American Civil Liberties Union of Ohio Foundation, Inc. v. DeWeese,* 633 F.3d 424 (6th Cir. 2011)] **(See page 91.)**

—**For a sample answer to Case Problem 4–6, go to Appendix G at the end of this text.**

4–7. The Dormant Commerce Clause. In 2001, Puerto Rico enacted a law that requires specific labels on cement sold in Puerto Rico and imposes fines for any violations of these requirements. The law prohibits the sale or distribution of cement manufactured outside Puerto Rico that does not carry a required label warning that the cement may not be used in government-financed construction projects. Antilles Cement Corp., a Puerto Rican firm that imports foreign cement, filed a complaint in federal court, claiming that this law violated the dormant commerce clause. (The dormant commerce clause doctrine applies not only to commerce among the states and U.S. territories, but also to international commerce.) Did the 2001 Puerto Rican law violate the dormant commerce clause? Why or why not? [*Antilles Cement Corp. v. Fortuno,* 670 F.3d 310 (2012)] **(See page 83.)**

4–8. ⚖️ **A Question of Ethics: Freedom of Speech.** *Aric Toll owns and manages the Balboa Island Village Inn, a restaurant and bar in Newport Beach, California. Anne Lemen lives across from the Inn. Lemen complained to the authorities about the Inn's customers, whom she called "drunks" and "whores." Lemen told the Inn's bartender Ewa Cook that Cook "worked for Satan." She repeated her statements to potential customers, and the Inn's sales dropped more than 20 percent. The Inn filed a suit against Lemen. [Balboa Island Village Inn, Inc. v. Lemen, 40 Cal.4th 1141, 156 P.3d 339 (2007)]* **(See pages 86–88.)**

1. Are Lemen's statements about the Inn's owners and customers protected by the U.S. Constitution? In whose favor should the court rule? Why?

2. Did Lemen behave unethically in the circumstances of this case? Explain.

4–9. ✏️ **Critical-Thinking Legal Question.** Do you think that the threat of terrorism in the United States justifies the imposition of limits on the right to privacy? Generally, in the wake of the September 11, 2001, terrorist attacks, should Americans allow the federal government to listen to their phone calls and monitor their e-mails and Internet activity? Discuss. **(See page 97.)**

Unit Two

The Public Environment

(OlegAlbinsky/iStockphoto.com)

Chapter 5

Administrative Law

> "Perhaps more values today are affected by [administrative] decisions than by those of all the courts."
>
> —Robert H. Jackson, 1892–1954
> (Associate justice of the United States Supreme Court, 1941–1954)

Contents

Learning Objectives

The five Learning Objectives below are designed to help improve your understanding of the chapter. After reading this chapter, you should be able to answer the following questions:

1. **How are federal administrative agencies created?**
2. **How do the three branches of government limit the power of administrative agencies?**
3. **What are the three basic functions of most administrative agencies?**
4. **What sequence of events must normally occur before an agency rule becomes law?**
5. **How do administrative agencies enforce their rules?**

(©legAlbinsky/iStockphoto.com)

As the chapter-opening quotation above suggests, government agencies established to administer the law have a significant impact on the day-to-day operation of the government and the economy. In its early years, the United States had a simple, nonindustrial economy with little regulation. As the economy has grown and become more complex, the size of government has also increased, and so has the number of administrative agencies.

In some instances, new agencies have been created in response to a crisis. In the wake of the financial crisis that led to the Great Recession, for example, Congress enacted the Dodd-Frank Wall Street Reform and Consumer Protection Act of 2010. Among other things, this statute created the Financial Stability Oversight Council to identify and respond to emerging risks in the financial system. It also created the Consumer Financial Protection Bureau to protect consumers from alleged abusive practices by financial institutions, including banks and nonbanks offering consumer financial products, mortgage lenders, and credit-card companies.

As the number of agencies has multiplied, so have the rules, orders, and decisions that they issue. Today, there are rules covering almost every aspect of a business's operations (see this chapter's *Linking the Law to Management* feature on pages 120 and 121). The regulations that administrative agencies issue make up the body of **administrative law.** In this chapter, we explain the important principles of administrative law and their significant impact on businesses today.

Administrative Law The body of law created by administrative agencies in order to carry out their duties and responsibilities.

▶ The Practical Significance of Administrative Law

Administrative Agency A federal or state government agency established to perform a specific function.

Unlike statutory law, administrative law is created by administrative agencies, not by legislatures, but it is nevertheless of overriding significance for businesses. When Congress—or a state legislature—enacts legislation, it typically adopts a rather general statute and leaves the statute's implementation to an **administrative agency**, which then creates the detailed rules and regulations necessary to carry out the statute. The administrative agency, with its specialized personnel, has the time, resources, and expertise to make the detailed decisions required for regulation.

Administrative Agencies Exist at All Levels of Government

Administrative agencies are spread throughout the government. At the national level, numerous *executive agencies* exist within the cabinet departments of the executive branch. For example, the Food and Drug Administration is within the U.S. Department of Health and Human Services. Executive agencies are subject to the authority of the president, who has the power to appoint and remove officers of federal agencies. Exhibit 5–1 on the following page lists the cabinet departments and their most important subagencies.

There are also major *independent regulatory agencies* at the federal level, including the Federal Trade Commission, the Securities and Exchange Commission, and the Federal Communications Commission. The president's power is less pronounced in regard to independent agencies, whose officers serve for fixed terms and cannot be removed without just cause. Exhibit 5–2 on page 107 lists selected independent regulatory agencies and their principal functions.

There are administrative agencies at the state and local levels as well. Commonly, a state agency (such as a state pollution-control agency) is created as a parallel to a federal agency (such as the Environmental Protection Agency). Just as federal statutes take precedence over conflicting state statutes, so do federal agency regulations take precedence over conflicting state regulations. Because the rules of state and local agencies vary widely, we focus here exclusively on federal administrative law.

Agencies Provide a Comprehensive Regulatory Scheme

Often, administrative agencies at various levels of government work together and share the responsibility of creating and enforcing particular regulations.

EXAMPLE 5.1   When Congress enacted the Clean Air Act in 1963, it provided only general directions for the prevention of air pollution. The specific pollution-control requirements imposed on business are almost entirely the product of decisions made by the Environmental Protection Agency (EPA), which was created in 1970. Moreover, the EPA works with parallel environmental agencies at the state level to analyze existing data and determine the appropriate pollution-control standards. ●

Legislation and regulations have benefits—in Example 5.1 above, a cleaner environment than existed in decades past. At the same time, these benefits entail significant costs for business. The EPA has estimated the costs of compliance with the Clean Air Act at many tens of billions of dollars yearly. Although the agency has estimated (with a large margin of error) that the overall benefits of its regulations often exceed their costs, the burden on business is substantial.

● *Exhibit* 5–1 **Executive Departments and Important Subagencies**

DEPARTMENT NAME AND YEAR FORMED	SELECTED SUBAGENCIES
State–1789	Passport Office; Bureau of Diplomatic Security; Foreign Service; Bureau of Human Rights and Humanitarian Affairs; Bureau of Consular Affairs; Bureau of Intelligence and Research
Treasury–1789	Internal Revenue Service; U.S. Mint
Interior–1849	U.S. Fish and Wildlife Service; National Park Service; Bureau of Indian Affairs; Bureau of Land Management
Justice–1870[a]	Federal Bureau of Investigation; Drug Enforcement Administration; Bureau of Prisons; U.S. Marshals Service
Agriculture–1889	Soil Conservation Service; Agricultural Research Service; Food Safety and Inspection Service; Forest Service
Commerce–1913[b]	Bureau of the Census; Bureau of Economic Analysis; Minority Business Development Agency; U.S. Patent and Trademark Office; National Oceanic and Atmospheric Administration
Labor–1913[b]	Occupational Safety and Health Administration; Bureau of Labor Statistics; Employment Standards Administration; Office of Labor-Management Standards; Employment and Training Administration
Defense–1949[c]	National Security Agency; Joint Chiefs of Staff; Departments of the Air Force, Navy, Army; service academies
Housing and Urban Development–1965	Office of Community Planning and Development; Government National Mortgage Association; Office of Fair Housing and Equal Opportunity
Transportation–1967	Federal Aviation Administration; Federal Highway Administration; National Highway Traffic Safety Administration; Federal Transit Administration
Energy–1977	Office of Civilian Radioactive Waste Management; Office of Nuclear Energy; Energy Information Administration
Health and Human Services–1980[d]	Food and Drug Administration; Centers for Medicare and Medicaid Services; Centers for Disease Control and Prevention; National Institutes of Health
Education–1980[d]	Office of Special Education and Rehabilitation Services; Office of Elementary and Secondary Education; Office of Postsecondary Education; Office of Vocational and Adult Education
Veterans Affairs–1989	Veterans Health Administration; Veterans Benefits Administration; National Cemetery System
Homeland Security–2002	U.S. Citizenship and Immigration Services; Directorate of Border and Transportation Services; U.S. Coast Guard; Federal Emergency Management Agency

a. Formed from the Office of the Attorney General (created in 1789).
b. Formed from the Department of Commerce and Labor (created in 1903).
c. Formed from the Department of War (created in 1789) and the Department of the Navy (created in 1798).
d. Formed from the Department of Health, Education, and Welfare (created in 1953).

▶ Agency Creation and Powers

LEARNING OBJECTIVE 1   **How are federal administrative agencies created?**

Enabling Legislation   A statute enacted by Congress that authorizes the creation of an administrative agency and specifies the name, composition, and powers of the agency being created.

Congress creates federal administrative agencies. By delegating some of its authority to make and implement laws, Congress can monitor indirectly a particular area in which it has passed legislation without becoming bogged down in the details relating to enforcement—details that are often best left to specialists.

To create an administrative agency, Congress passes **enabling legislation**, which specifies the name, purposes, functions, and powers of the agency being created. Federal administrative agencies can exercise only those powers that Congress has delegated to them in enabling legislation. Through similar enabling acts, state legislatures create state administrative agencies.

● *Exhibit* **5-2 Selected Independent Regulatory Agencies**

NAME OF AGENCY AND YEAR FORMED	PRINCIPAL DUTIES
Federal Reserve System Board of Governors (the Fed)—1913	Determines policy with respect to interest rates, credit availability, and the money supply. Starting in 2008, the Federal Reserve became involved in various "bailouts" in the financial sector, including a "conservatorship" of two large mortgage institutions (Fannie Mae and Freddie Mac).
Federal Trade Commission (FTC)—1914	Prevents businesses from engaging in purported unfair trade practices; stops the formation of monopolies in the business sector; protects consumer rights.
Securities and Exchange Commission (SEC)—1934	Regulates the nation's stock exchanges, in which shares of stock are bought and sold; enforces the securities laws, which require full disclosure of the financial profiles of companies that wish to sell stock and bonds to the public.
Federal Communications Commission (FCC)—1934	Regulates all communications by telegraph, cable, telephone, radio, satellite, and television.
National Labor Relations Board (NLRB)—1935	Protects employees' rights to join unions and bargain collectively with employers; attempts to prevent unfair labor practices by both employers and unions.
Equal Employment Opportunity Commission (EEOC)—1964	Works to eliminate discrimination in employment based on religion, gender, race, color, disability, national origin, or age; investigates claims of discrimination.
Environmental Protection Agency (EPA)—1970	Undertakes programs aimed at reducing air and water pollution; works with state and local agencies to help fight environmental hazards. (It has recently been suggested that its status be elevated to that of a department.)
Nuclear Regulatory Commission (NRC)—1975	Ensures that electricity-generating nuclear reactors in the United States are built and operated safely; regularly inspects operations of such reactors.

Enabling Legislation—An Example

Congress created the Federal Trade Commission (FTC) in the Federal Trade Commission Act of 1914.[1] The act prohibits unfair and deceptive trade practices. It also describes the procedures that the agency must follow to charge persons or organizations with violations of the act, and it provides for judicial review of agency orders. The act grants the FTC the power to do the following:

1. Create "rules and regulations for the purpose of carrying out the Act."
2. Conduct investigations of business practices.
3. Obtain reports from interstate corporations concerning their business practices.
4. Investigate possible violations of federal antitrust statutes. (The FTC shares this task with the Antitrust Division of the U.S. Department of Justice.)
5. Publish findings of its investigations.
6. Recommend new legislation.
7. Hold trial-like hearings to resolve certain kinds of trade disputes that involve FTC regulations or federal antitrust laws.

The commission that heads the FTC is composed of five members, each of whom is appointed by the president, with the advice and consent of the Senate, for a term of seven years. The president designates one of the commissioners to be the chair.

1. 15 U.S.C. Sections 41–58.

Various offices and bureaus of the FTC undertake different administrative activities for the agency.

Agency Powers and the Constitution

Administrative agencies occupy an unusual niche in the U.S. governmental structure, because they exercise powers that are normally divided among the three branches of government. The constitutional principle of *checks and balances* allows each branch of government to act as a check on the actions of the other two branches. Furthermore, the U.S. Constitution authorizes only the legislative branch to create laws. Yet administrative agencies, to which the Constitution does not specifically refer, can make **legislative rules,** or *substantive rules,* that are as legally binding as laws that Congress passes.

Legislative Rule An administrative agency rule that carries the same weight as a congressionally enacted statute.

Interpretive Rule An administrative agency rule that is simply a statement or opinion issued by the agency explaining how it interprets and intends to apply the statutes it enforces.

Administrative agencies also issue **interpretive rules** that are not legally binding but simply indicate how an agency plans to interpret and enforce its statutory authority. **EXAMPLE 5.2** The Equal Employment Opportunity Commission periodically issues interpretive rules indicating how it plans to interpret the provisions of certain statutes, such as the Americans with Disabilities Act (see Chapter 17). These informal rules provide enforcement guidelines for agency officials. •

Courts generally hold that Article I of the U.S. Constitution is the basis for all administrative law. Section 1 of that article grants all legislative powers to Congress and requires Congress to oversee the implementation of all laws. Article I, Section 8, gives Congress the power to make all laws necessary for executing its specified powers. Under what is known as the **delegation doctrine,** the courts interpret these passages as granting Congress the power to establish administrative agencies and delegate to them the power to create rules for implementing those laws.

Delegation Doctrine A doctrine based on the U.S. Constitution, which has been construed to allow Congress to delegate some of its power to administrative agencies to make and implement laws.

The three branches of government exercise certain controls over agency powers and functions, as discussed next, but in many ways administrative agencies function independently. For this reason, administrative agencies, which constitute the **bureaucracy,** are sometimes referred to as the fourth branch of the U.S. government.

Bureaucracy The organizational structure, consisting of government bureaus and agencies, through which the government implements and enforces the laws.

EXECUTIVE CONTROLS The executive branch of government exercises control over agencies both through the president's power to appoint federal officers and through the president's veto power. The president may veto enabling legislation presented by Congress or congressional attempts to modify an existing agency's authority.

LEARNING OBJECTIVE 2 How do the three branches of government limit the power of administrative agencies?

LEGISLATIVE CONTROLS Congress exercises authority over agency powers through legislation. Congress gives power to an agency through enabling legislation and can take power away—or even abolish an agency altogether—through subsequent legislation. Legislative authority is required to fund an agency, and enabling legislation usually sets certain time and monetary limits on the funding of particular programs. Congress can always revise these limits.

In addition to its power to create and fund agencies, Congress has the authority to investigate the implementation of its laws and the agencies that it has created. Congress also has the power to "freeze" the enforcement of most federal regulations before the regulations take effect.

JUDICIAL CONTROLS The judicial branch exercises control over agency powers through the courts' review of agency actions. As you will read in the next subsection, the Administrative Procedure Act provides for judicial review of most agency decisions. Agency actions are not automatically subject to judicial review, however. The party seeking court review must first exhaust all administrative remedies under what is called the *exhaustion doctrine.* In other words, the complaining party normally must have gone through the administrative process (from complaint to hearing to final agency order—see Exhibit 5–3 on page 115) before seeking court review.

The Administrative Procedure Act. Sometimes, Congress specifies certain procedural requirements in an agency's enabling legislation. In the absence of any directives from Congress concerning a particular agency procedure, the Administrative Procedure Act (APA) of 1946[2] applies.

The Arbitrary and Capricious Test. One of Congress's goals in enacting the APA was to provide for more judicial control over administrative agencies. To that end, the APA provides that courts should "hold unlawful and set aside" agency actions found to be "arbitrary, capricious, an abuse of discretion, or otherwise not in accordance with law."[3] Under this standard, parties can challenge regulations as contrary to law or so irrational as to be arbitrary and capricious.

The arbitrary and capricious standard does not have a precise definition, but in applying it, courts typically consider whether the agency has done any of the following:

1. Failed to provide a rational explanation for its decision.
2. Changed its prior policy without justification.
3. Considered legally inappropriate factors.
4. Failed to consider a relevant factor.
5. Rendered a decision plainly contrary to the evidence.

Fair Notice. An administrative agency can change its policy to apply a new principle to future circumstances. Before the new principle can be applied, however, the agency must give fair notice of what conduct is expected or proscribed. This clarity is required by the due process clause of the Fifth Amendment (see page 93 in Chapter 4).

In the following *Spotlight Case,* a television network argued that an administrative agency applied a new principle without fair notice.

---

2. 5 U.S.C. Sections 551–706.
3. 5 U.S.C. Section 706(2)(A).

SPOTLIGHT ON FOX TELEVISION

Case 5.1 **Federal Communications Commission v. Fox Television Stations, Inc.**

Supreme Court of the United States, __ U.S. __, 132 S.Ct. 2307, 183 L.Ed.2d 234 (2012).

BACKGROUND AND FACTS The Communications Act of 1934 established a system of limited-term broadcast licenses subject to various conditions. One condition was the indecency ban, which prohibits the uttering of "any obscene, indecent, or profane language by means of radio communication." The Federal Communications Commission (FCC) first invoked this ban on indecent broadcasts in 1975. At that time, the FCC defined indecent speech as "language that describes, in terms patently offensive as measured by contemporary community standards for the broadcast medium, sexual or excretory activities or organs, at times of the day when there is a reasonable risk that children may be in the audience." Before 2004, one of the factors used by the FCC in determining whether a broadcaster had violated

the ban was whether the offensive language had been repeated, or "dwelled on," in the broadcast. If an offensive term was used just once in a broadcast, the FCC probably would not take any action. In 2004, however, the FCC changed this policy, declaring that an offensive term, such as the F-word, was actionably indecent even if it was used only once. In its 2004 ruling, the FCC specifically stated that previous FCC rulings allowing a "safe harbor" for a single utterance of an offensive term "were no longer good law." In 2006, the FCC applied this new rule to two Fox Television broadcasts, each of which contained a single use of the F-word, which had aired before the FCC's change in policy.

Spotlight Case 5.1–Continues next page ➡

Spotlight Case 5.1—Continued

After the FCC ruled that these broadcasts were actionably indecent, Fox appealed to the U.S. Court of Appeals for the Second Circuit for review. The appellate court reversed the agency's order. The FCC appealed to the United States Supreme Court.

IN THE WORDS OF THE COURT . . .
Justice *KENNEDY* delivered the opinion of the Court.
 * * * *

A fundamental principle in our legal system is that laws which regulate persons or entities must give fair notice of conduct that is forbidden or required. This requirement of clarity in regulation is essential to the protections provided by the Due Process Clause of the Fifth Amendment. It requires the invalidation of laws that are impermissibly vague. A conviction or punishment fails to comply with due process if the statute or regulation under which it is obtained fails to provide a person of ordinary intelligence fair notice of what is prohibited, or is so standardless that it authorizes or encourages seriously discriminatory enforcement. As this Court has explained, a regulation is not vague because it may at times be difficult to prove an incriminating fact but rather because it is unclear as to what fact must be proved. [Emphasis added.]

The void for vagueness doctrine addresses at least two connected but discrete due process concerns: first, that regulated parties should know what is required of them so they may act accordingly; second, precision and guidance are necessary so that those enforcing the law do not act in an arbitrary or discriminatory way. * * *

These concerns are implicated here because, at the outset, the broadcasters claim they did not have * * * fair notice of what was forbidden. Under the 2001 guidelines in force when the broadcasts occurred, a key consideration was whether the material dwelled on or repeated at length the offending description or depiction. In the 2004 order, issued after the broadcasts, the Commission changed course and held that fleeting expletives could be a statutory violation. In the

challenged orders now under review the Commission applied the new principle * * * and determined fleeting expletives were actionably indecent. * * * The Commission policy in place at the time of the broadcasts gave no notice to Fox that a fleeting expletive could be indecent. * * *
 * * * *

The Government raises two arguments in response, but neither is persuasive. * * * Though the Commission claims it will not consider the prior indecent broadcasts in any context, it has the statutory power to take into account any history of prior offenses when setting the level of a forfeiture penalty. * * * The Government's assurance it will elect not to do so is insufficient to remedy the constitutional violation.

In addition, * * * reputational injury provides further reason for granting relief to Fox. * * * The permanent Commission record describes in strongly disapproving terms the indecent material broadcast by Fox and Fox's efforts to protect children from being exposed to it. Commission sanctions on broadcasters for indecent material are widely publicized. The challenged orders could have an adverse impact on Fox's reputation that audiences and advertisers alike are entitled to take into account.

DECISION AND REMEDY   The United States Supreme Court vacated the judgment of the U.S. Court of Appeals for the Second Circuit, which had ruled the FCC's order unconstitutional on different grounds. The Court held that because the FCC failed to give Fox fair notice, fleeting expletives could be found indecent, The standards applied to the broadcasts at issue were vague. The Court ordered the FCC's administrative order to be set aside.

THE TECHNOLOGICAL DIMENSION   *Technological advances have made it easier for broadcasters to "bleep out" offending words in the programs that they air. Does this development support a more or less stringent enforcement policy by the FCC? Explain.*

The Administrative Process

LEARNING OBJECTIVE 3 **What are the three basic functions of most administrative agencies?**

Administrative Process The procedure used by administrative agencies in the administration of law.

Rulemaking The actions of administrative agencies when formally adopting new regulations or amending old ones.

All federal agencies must follow specific procedural requirements as they go about fulfilling their three basic functions: rulemaking, enforcement, and adjudication. These three functions make up what is known as the **administrative process.** As mentioned on page 109, the APA imposes requirements that all federal agencies must follow. This act is an integral part of the administrative process.

Rulemaking

The major function of an administrative agency is **rulemaking.** The APA defines a rule as "an agency statement of general or particular applicability and future effect designed to implement, interpret, or prescribe law and policy."[4] Regulations are sometimes said to be *legislative* because, like statutes, they have a binding effect. Thus, violators of agency rules may be punished. Because agency rules have such great legal force, the

---

4. 5 U.S.C. Section 551(4).

APA established procedures for agencies to follow in creating rules. Many rules must be adopted using the APA's *notice-and-comment rulemaking* procedure.

Notice-and-comment rulemaking involves three basic steps: (1) notice of the proposed rulemaking, (2) a comment period, and (3) the final rule. The APA recognizes some limited exceptions to these procedural requirements, but they are seldom invoked. If the required procedures are violated, the resulting rule may be invalid. The impetus for rulemaking may come from various sources, including Congress, the agency itself, or private parties who may petition an agency to begin a rulemaking (or repeal a rule). For instance, environmental groups have petitioned for stricter air-pollution controls to combat global warming.

LEARNING OBJECTIVE 4 **What sequence of events must normally occur before an agency rule becomes law?**

NOTICE OF THE PROPOSED RULEMAKING When a federal agency decides to create a new rule, the agency publishes a notice of the proposed rulemaking proceedings in the *Federal Register,* a daily publication of the executive branch that prints government orders, rules, and regulations. The notice states where and when the proceedings will be held, the agency's legal authority for making the rule (usually its enabling legislation), and the terms or subject matter of the proposed rule.

COMMENT PERIOD Following the publication of the notice of the proposed rulemaking proceedings, the agency must allow ample time for persons to comment on the proposed rule. The purpose of this comment period is to give interested parties the opportunity to express their views on the proposed rule in an effort to influence agency policy. The comments may be in writing or, if a hearing is held, may be given orally. The agency need not respond to all comments, but it must respond to any significant comments that bear directly on the proposed rule. The agency responds by either modifying its final rule or explaining, in a statement accompanying the final rule, why it did not make any changes. In some circumstances, particularly when the procedure being used in a specific instance is less formal, an agency may accept comments after the comment period is closed.

THE FINAL RULE After the agency reviews the comments, it drafts the final rule and publishes it in the *Federal Register.* Such a final rule must contain a "concise general statement of . . . basis and purpose" that describes the reasoning behind the rule.[5] The final rule may change the terms of the proposed rule, in light of the public comments, but cannot change the proposal too radically, or a new proposal and a new opportunity for comment are required. The final rule is later compiled along with the rules and regulations of other federal administrative agencies in the *Code of Federal Regulations.*

The Dodd-Frank Act mentioned on page 104 provides recent examples of the rulemaking process. Although the statute contains more than 1,700 pages, its provisions are expressed only in general terms. The Financial Oversight Council, for example, was charged with ensuring that no more bailouts will be required to rescue financial institutions that are "too big to fail." Thus, one of the council's first tasks was to propose a rule establishing criteria for identifying a "financial market utility" that "is or is likely to become systemically important."

When the rule becomes final, the council will be able to establish more stringent requirements for institutions that fall into that category. The council is also preparing proposed rules for increasing capital requirements for financial institutions and

---

5. 5 U.S.C. Section 555(c).

requiring complex financial institutions to prepare so-called living wills—plans for their orderly shutdown in the event that they fail.

Final rules have binding legal effect unless the courts later overturn them. Because they are as binding as legislation, they are often referred to as legislative rules, as mentioned previously. If an agency failed to follow proper rulemaking procedures when it issued the final rule, however, the rule may not be binding.

Indeed, a reviewing court will first examine whether the agency followed the procedures in the APA when a complaint reaches it. If an agency did so, then the court will most likely uphold the agency's rules. Ordinarily, courts will not require agencies to use procedures beyond those of the APA. If an agency has adopted a rule granting extra procedures, however, it must provide for those extra procedures.

Investigation

LEARNING OBJECTIVE 5 **How do administrative agencies enforce their rules?**

Although rulemaking is the most prominent agency activity, enforcement of the rules is also critical. Often, an agency itself enforces its rules. After final rules are issued, agencies conduct investigations to monitor compliance with those rules or the terms of the enabling statute. A typical agency investigation of this kind might begin when the agency receives a report of a possible violation.

Many agency rules also require considerable compliance reporting from regulated entities, and such a report may trigger an enforcement investigation. For example, environmental regulators often require reporting of emissions.

INSPECTIONS AND TESTS Many agencies gather information through on-site inspections. Sometimes, inspecting an office, a factory, or some other business facility is the only way to obtain the evidence needed to prove a regulatory violation. At other times, an inspection or test is used in place of a formal hearing to show the need to correct or prevent an undesirable condition. Administrative inspections and tests cover a wide range of activities, including safety inspections of underground coal mines, safety tests of commercial equipment and automobiles, and environmental monitoring of factory emissions. An agency may also ask a firm or individual to submit certain documents or records to the agency for examination.

Normally, business firms comply with agency requests to inspect facilities or business records because it is in any firm's interest to maintain a good relationship with regulatory bodies. In some instances, however, such as when a firm thinks an agency's request is unreasonable and may be detrimental to the firm's interest, the firm may refuse to comply with the request. In such situations, an agency may resort to the use of a subpoena or a search warrant.

SUBPOENAS There are two basic types of subpoenas. The subpoena *ad testificandum*[6] (to testify) is an ordinary subpoena. It is a writ, or order, compelling a witness to appear at an agency hearing. The subpoena *duces tecum*[7] (bring it with you) compels an individual or organization to hand over books, papers, records, or documents to the agency. An administrative agency may use either type of subpoena to obtain testimony or documents.

There are limits on what an agency can demand. To determine whether an agency is abusing its discretion in its pursuit of information as part of an investigation, a court may consider such factors as the following:

1. *The purpose of the investigation.* An investigation must have a legitimate purpose. Harassment is an example of an improper purpose. An agency may not issue an

---

6. Pronounced ad-tes-*tee-fee*-can-drum.

7. Pronounced *doo*-suhs *tee*-kum.

administrative subpoena to inspect business records if the motive is to harass or pressure the business into settling an unrelated matter.

2. *The relevance of the information being sought.* Information is relevant if it reveals that the law is being violated or if it assures the agency that the law is not being violated.

3. *The specificity of the demand for testimony or documents.* A subpoena must, for example, adequately describe the material being sought.

4. *The burden of the demand on the party from whom the information is sought.* In responding to a request for information, a party must bear the costs of, for example, copying the requested documents, but a business generally is protected from revealing information such as trade secrets.

SEARCH WARRANTS The Fourth Amendment protects against unreasonable searches and seizures by requiring that in most instances a physical search for evidence must be conducted under the authority of a search warrant. An agency's search warrant is an order directing law enforcement officials to search a specific place for a specific item and seize it for the agency. Although it was once thought that administrative inspections were exempt from the warrant requirement, the United States Supreme Court held in *Marshall v. Barlow's, Inc.,*[8] that the requirement does apply to the administrative process.

Agencies can conduct warrantless searches in several situations. Warrants are not required to conduct searches in highly regulated industries. Firms that sell firearms or liquor, for example, are automatically subject to inspections without warrants. Sometimes, a statute permits warrantless searches of certain types of hazardous operations, such as coal mines. Also, a warrantless inspection in an emergency situation is normally considered reasonable.

Adjudication

After conducting an investigation of a suspected rule violation, an agency may initiate an administrative action against an individual or organization. Most administrative actions are resolved through negotiated settlements at their initial stages, without the need for formal **adjudication** (the resolution of the dispute through a hearing conducted by the agency).

Adjudication The proceeding in which an administrative law judge hears and decides issues that arise when an administrative agency charges a person or a firm with an agency violation.

NEGOTIATED SETTLEMENTS Depending on the agency, negotiations may take the form of a simple conversation or a series of informal conferences. Whatever form the negotiations take, their purpose is to rectify the problem to the agency's satisfaction and eliminate the need for additional proceedings.

Settlement is an appealing option to firms for two reasons: to avoid appearing uncooperative and to avoid the expense involved in formal adjudication proceedings and in possible later appeals. Settlement is also an attractive option for agencies. To conserve their own resources and avoid formal actions, administrative agencies devote a great deal of effort to giving advice and negotiating solutions to problems.

FORMAL COMPLAINTS If a settlement cannot be reached, the agency may issue a formal complaint against the suspected violator. **EXAMPLE 5.3** The Environmental Protection Agency (EPA) finds that Acme Manufacturing, Inc., is polluting groundwater in violation of federal pollution laws. The EPA issues a complaint against the violator in an effort to bring the plant into compliance with federal regulations. ● This complaint is a public document, and a press release may accompany it. The party

---

8. 436 U.S. 307, 98 S.Ct. 1816, 56 L.Ed.2d 305 (1978).

Administrative Law Judge (ALJ) One who presides over an administrative agency hearing and has the power to administer oaths, take testimony, rule on questions of evidence, and make determinations of fact.

Ethical Issue ⚖

charged in the complaint responds by filing an answer to the allegations. If the charged party and the agency cannot agree on a settlement, the case will be adjudicated.

Agency adjudication involves a hearing before an **administrative law judge (ALJ).** Under the APA, before the hearing takes place, the agency must issue a notice that includes the facts and law on which the complaint is based, the legal authority for the hearing, and its time and place.

Do administrative agencies exercise too much authority? Administrative agencies, such as the Federal Trade Commission, combine in a single governmental entity functions normally divided among the three branches of government. They create rules, conduct investigations, and prosecute and pass judgment on violators. Yet administrative agencies' powers often go unchecked by the other branches, causing some businesspersons to suggest that it is unethical for agencies—which are not even mentioned in the U.S. Constitution—to wield so many powers.

Although agency rulemaking must comply with the requirements of the APA, the act applies only to legislative, not interpretive, rulemaking. In addition, the APA is largely procedural and aimed at preventing arbitrariness. It does little to ensure that the rules passed by agencies are fair or correct. Even on those rare occasions when an agency's ruling is challenged and later reviewed by a court, the court cannot reverse the agency's decision unless the agency exceeded its authority or acted arbitrarily. Courts typically are reluctant to second-guess an agency's rules, interpretations, and decisions. Moreover, once an agency has final regulations in place, it is difficult to revoke or alter them. President Barack Obama discovered this when he tried to change some of the rules that agencies had put into place in the last few months of the administration of his predecessor, President George W. Bush.

THE ROLE OF THE ADMINISTRATIVE LAW JUDGE The ALJ presides over the hearing and has the power to administer oaths, take testimony, rule on questions of evidence, and make determinations of fact. Although technically the ALJ is not an independent judge and works for the agency prosecuting the case (in our example, the EPA), the law requires an ALJ to be an unbiased adjudicator (judge).

Certain safeguards prevent bias on the part of the ALJ and promote fairness in the proceedings. For example, the APA requires that the ALJ be separate from an agency's investigative and prosecutorial staff. The APA also prohibits *ex parte* (private) communications between the ALJ and any party to an agency proceeding, such as the EPA or the factory. Finally, provisions of the APA protect the ALJ from agency disciplinary actions unless the agency can show good cause for such an action.

HEARING PROCEDURES Hearing procedures vary widely from agency to agency. Administrative agencies generally exercise substantial discretion over the type of procedure that will be used. Frequently, disputes are resolved through informal adjudication proceedings that resemble arbitration. **EXAMPLE 5.4** The Federal Trade Commission (FTC) charges Good Foods, Inc., with deceptive advertising. Representatives of Good Foods and of the FTC, their counsel, and the ALJ meet in a conference room to resolve the dispute informally. ●

A formal adjudicatory hearing, in contrast, resembles a trial in many respects. Prior to the hearing, the parties are permitted to undertake discovery—involving depositions, interrogatories, and requests for documents or other information, as described in Chapter 2—although the discovery process is not quite as extensive as it would be in a court proceeding. The hearing itself must comply with the procedural requirements of the APA and must also meet the constitutional standards of due process. During the hearing, the parties may give testimony, present other evidence, and cross-examine adverse witnesses. A significant difference between a trial and an administrative agency hearing, though, is that normally much more information, including hearsay (second-hand information), can be introduced as evidence during an administrative hearing. The burden of proof in an enforcement proceeding is placed on the agency.

AGENCY ORDERS   Following a hearing, the ALJ renders an **initial order,** or decision, on the case. Either party can appeal the ALJ's decision to the board or commission that governs the agency. If the factory in Example 5.3 on page 113 is dissatisfied with the ALJ's decision, it can appeal the decision to the EPA. If the factory is dissatisfied with the commission's decision, it can appeal the decision to a federal court of appeals.

If no party appeals the case, the ALJ's decision becomes the **final order** of the agency. The ALJ's decision also becomes final if a party appeals and the commission and the court decline to review the case. If a party appeals and the case is reviewed, the final order comes from the commission's decision or (if that decision is appealed to a federal appellate court) that of the reviewing court.

The administrative adjudication process is illustrated graphically in Exhibit 5–3 alongside on the left.

Initial Order   An agency's disposition in a matter other than a rulemaking. An administrative law judge's initial order becomes final unless it is appealed.

Final Order   The final decision of an administrative agency on an issue.

• *Exhibit* **5–3 The Process of Formal Administrative Adjudication**

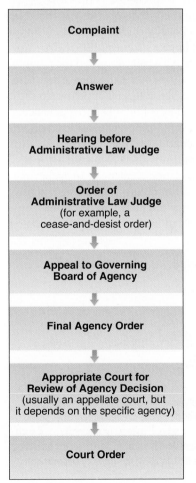

Judicial Deference to Agency Decisions

When asked to review agency decisions, courts historically granted some deference (significant weight) to the agency's judgment, often citing the agency's expertise in the subject area of the regulation. This deference seems especially appropriate when applied to an agency's analysis of factual questions, but should it also extend to an agency's interpretation of its own legal authority? In *Chevron U.S.A., Inc. v. Natural Resources Defense Council, Inc.,*[9] the United States Supreme Court held that it should, thereby creating a standard of broadened deference to agencies on questions of legal interpretation.

The Holding of the *Chevron* Case

At issue in the *Chevron* case was whether the courts should defer to an agency's interpretation of a statute giving it authority to act. The Environmental Protection Agency (EPA) had interpreted the phrase "stationary source" in the Clean Air Act as referring to an entire manufacturing plant, and not to each facility within a plant. The agency's interpretation enabled it to adopt the so-called bubble policy, which allowed companies to offset increases in emissions in part of a plant with decreases elsewhere in the plant—an interpretation that reduced the pollution-control compliance costs faced by manufacturers. An environmental group challenged the legality of the EPA's interpretation.

The United States Supreme Court held that the courts should defer to an agency's interpretation of *law* as well as fact. The Court found that the agency's interpretation of the statute was reasonable and upheld the bubble policy. The Court's decision in the *Chevron* case created a new standard for courts to use when reviewing agency interpretations of law. The standard involves the following two questions:

9. 467 U.S. 837, 104 S.Ct. 2778, 81 L.Ed.2d 694 (1984).

1. Did Congress directly address the issue in dispute in the statute? If so, the statutory language prevails.
2. If the statute is silent or ambiguous, is the agency's interpretation "reasonable"? If it is, a court should uphold the agency's interpretation even if the court would have interpreted the law differently.

When Courts Will Give *Chevron* Deference to Agency Interpretation

The notion that courts should defer to agencies on matters of law was controversial. Under the holding of the *Chevron* case, when the meaning of a particular statute's language is unclear and an agency interprets it, the court must follow the agency's interpretation as long as it is reasonable. This led to considerable discussion and litigation to test the boundaries of the *Chevron* holding. For instance, are courts required to give deference to all agency interpretations or only to those that result from adjudication or formal rulemaking procedures? The United States Supreme Court has held that in order for agency interpretations to be assured *Chevron* deference, they must meet the formal legal standards for notice-and-comment rulemaking. Nevertheless, there are still gray areas, and many agency interpretations are challenged in court.

CASE EXAMPLE 5.5   Citizens' Committee to Save Our Canyons brought an action challenging the U.S. Forest Service's decision to issue a special use permit to Wasatch Powerbird Guides (WPG), a helicopter-skiing business that operated within two national forests. Under the National Environmental Policy Act (NEPA), the U.S. Forest Service was required to complete an environmental impact statement (EIS) before issuing such a permit to WPG. Even though the Forest Service had completed the required EIS, Citizens' argued that the EIS had not sufficiently analyzed the increasing recreational pressures on the forests. When the case reached a federal appellate court, it agreed with the lower district court's ruling and upheld the Forest Service's issuance of the permit. The court noted that the Forest Service's EIS properly considered all relevant factors and allowed for public comment. The court found that the Forest Service's interpretation of the NEPA was reasonable and complied with its regulations.[10] ●

In the following case, a medical educational foundation challenged an agency regulation that required it to deduct Social Security contributions from the wages of physicians who were going through its hospital residency program. The Supreme Court had to decide if the "full-time employee" rule enacted by the Treasury Department was entitled to *Chevron* deference.

---

10. *Citizens' Committee to Save Our Canyons v. Krueger*, 513 F.3d 1169 (10th Cir. 2008).

Case 5.2   **Mayo Foundation for Medical Education and Research v. United States**

Supreme Court of the United States, ___ U.S. ___, 131 S.Ct. 704, 178 L.Ed.2d 588 (2011).

BACKGROUND AND FACTS   The Mayo Foundation for Medical Education and Research (Mayo) offers residency programs to physicians who have graduated from medical school and seek additional instruction in a chosen specialty. Although the resident physicians participate in some formal educational activities, they spend fifty to eighty hours a week caring for patients. As will be discussed in Chapter 16, the Federal Insurance Contributions Act (FICA) requires employees and

employers to pay Social Security taxes on all wages employees receive. FICA, however, excludes from its definition of *employment* any "service performed in the employ of . . . a school, college, or university . . . if such service is performed by a student who is enrolled and regularly attending classes at [the school]."[a] From 1951 to 2004, the Treasury Department

---

a. See U.S.C. Section 3121(b).

Case 5.2–Continued

construed the student exception as exempting students who work for their schools "as an incident to and for the purpose of pursuing a course of study." In late 2004, the department issued new regulations providing that the services of an employee who is normally scheduled to work forty or more hours per week "are not incident to and for the purpose of pursuing a course of study." As an example, the rule stated that a medical resident whose normal schedule requires him or her to perform services forty or more hours per week is not a student. Mayo filed a suit in a federal district court, asserting that this rule was invalid. The district court agreed, but the U.S. Court of Appeals for the Eighth Circuit reversed the trial court's ruling, concluding that the department's regulation was a permissible interpretation of an ambiguous statute. Mayo appealed to the United States Supreme Court.

IN THE WORDS OF THE COURT . . .
Chief Justice *ROBERTS* delivered the opinion of the Court.
* * * *

* * * Mayo's residency programs, which usually last three to five years, train doctors primarily through hands-on experience. * * * In 2005, Mayo paid its residents annual "stipends" ranging between $41,000 and $56,000 and provided them with health insurance, malpractice insurance, and paid vacation time.

Mayo residents also take part in "a formal and structured educational program." Residents are assigned textbooks and journal articles to read and are expected to attend weekly lectures and other conferences.
* * * *

On December 21, 2004, the [Treasury] Department adopted an amended rule prescribing that an employee's service is "incident" to his studies only when "[t]he educational aspect of the relationship between the employer and the employee, as compared to the service aspect of the relationship, [is] predominant." * * * The amended provision clarifies that the Department's analysis "is not affected by the fact that the services performed . . . may have an educational, instructional, or training aspect."
* * * *

We begin our analysis with the first step of the two-part framework announced in *Chevron,* and ask whether Congress has "directly addressed the precise question at issue." We agree with the Court of Appeals that Congress has not done so. The statute does not define the term "student," and does not otherwise attend to the precise question whether medical residents are subject to FICA.
* * * *

* * * Such an ambiguity would lead us inexorably [impossible to prevent] to *Chevron* step two, under which we may not disturb an agency rule unless it is " 'arbitrary or capricious in substance, or

manifestly contrary to the statute.' "
* * * *

* * * The Department issued the full-time employee rule pursuant to the explicit authorization to "prescribe all needful rules and regulations for the enforcement" of the Internal Revenue Code. *The Department issued the full-time employee rule only after notice-and-comment procedures, again a consideration identified in our precedents as a "significant" sign that a rule merits* Chevron *deference.* [Emphasis added.]
* * * *

The full-time employee rule easily satisfies the second step of Chevron, *which asks whether the Department's rule is a "reasonable interpretation" of the enacted text.* To begin, Mayo accepts that "the 'educational aspect of the relationship between the employer and the employee, as compared to the service aspect of the relationship, [must] be predominant' " in order for an individual to qualify for the exemption. Mayo objects, however, to the Department's conclusion that residents who work more than 40 hours per week categorically cannot satisfy that requirement. Because residents' employment is itself educational, Mayo argues, the hours a resident spends working make him "more of a student, not less of one." [Emphasis added.]

We disagree. Regulation, like legislation, often requires drawing lines. Mayo does not dispute that the Treasury Department reasonably sought a way to distinguish between workers who study and students who work. Focusing on the hours an individual works and the hours [she or] he spends in studies is a perfectly sensible way of accomplishing that goal.

* * * The Department reasonably determined that taxing residents under FICA would further the purpose of the Social Security Act. * * * Although Mayo contends that medical residents have not yet begun their "working lives" because they are not "fully trained," the Department certainly did not act irrationally in concluding that these doctors * * * are the kind of workers that Congress intended to both contribute to and benefit from the Social Security system.

DECISION AND REMEDY   The United States Supreme Court affirmed the decision of the appellate court, holding that the Treasury Department's full-time employee rule was valid. The Court found that the number of hours worked was a reasonable way to distinguish between workers who studied and students who worked. Therefore, the rule easily satisfied the *Chevron* standard.

THE LEGAL ENVIRONMENT DIMENSION   *Would the United States Supreme Court have deferred to the Treasury Department's full-time employee regulation even if it had disagreed with the rule? Why or why not?*

 Public Accountability

As a result of growing public concern over the powers exercised by administrative agencies, Congress passed several laws to make agencies more accountable through public scrutiny. We discuss here the most significant of these laws.

Freedom of Information Act

Enacted in 1966, the Freedom of Information Act (FOIA)[11] requires the federal government to disclose certain records to any person on request, even if no reason is given for the request. The FOIA exempts certain types of records. For other records, though, a request that complies with the FOIA procedures need only contain a reasonable description of the information sought. An agency's failure to comply with such a request can be challenged in a federal district court. The media, industry trade associations, public-interest groups, and even companies seeking information about competitors rely on these FOIA provisions to obtain information from government agencies.

At issue in the following case was whether certain documents requested by members of the media were exempt under the FOIA and thus not available for release to the public.

---

11. 5 U.S.C. Section 552.

Case 5.3 | United Technologies Corp. v. U.S. Department of Defense

United States Court of Appeals, District of Columbia Circuit, 601 F.3d 557 (2010).

BACKGROUND AND FACTS Sikorsky Aircraft Corporation makes helicopters, and Pratt and Whitney produces aircraft engines. United Technologies Corporation wholly owns both companies, which have various foreign and domestic military and civilian customers. Both companies also sell their products to the United States. The Defense Contract Management Agency (DCMA), an agency within the U.S. Department of Defense (DOD), monitors defense contractors, including Sikorsky and Pratt, to ensure that they satisfy their contractual obligations when providing services and supplies to the United States. If the DCMA discovers a problem, it notifies the contractor and may issue a corrective action request (CAR) or an audit report to the contractor to remedy the problem. In 2004, a reporter submitted a Freedom of Information Act (FOIA) request to the regional DCMA office for copies of all CARs that had been issued to Sikorsky during the previous year concerning Sikorsky's Black Hawk helicopter. Another reporter requested information, including a CAR and audit-related documents, concerning Pratt's airplane engine center at Middletown, Connecticut. Sikorsky and Pratt argued that the documents were exempt from FOIA disclosure. The DCMA disagreed and ruled that the documents could be disclosed. Sikorsky and Pratt filed separate suits against the DOD in a federal district court, arguing that the decision to release the documents was arbitrary, capricious, and contrary to law under the Administrative Procedure Act. They sought declaratory and injunctive relief preventing the documents' disclosure. The district court granted summary judgment to the DOD in both cases, and Sikorsky and Pratt appealed.

IN THE WORDS OF THE COURT . . .
Karen LeCraft HENDERSON, Circuit Judge.
  * * * *

Exemption 4 covers "trade secrets and commercial or financial information obtained from a person and privileged or confidential."

* * * *For the documents to be exempt from disclosure, their release must be likely to cause the contractors "substantial competitive harm" or "impair the Government's ability to obtain necessary information in the future." [Emphasis added.]

To qualify [as a "substantial competitive harm"], an identified harm must "flow from the affirmative use of proprietary information by competitors."
  * * * *

* * * Sikorsky and Pratt maintain that the documents contain sensitive proprietary information about their quality control processes. Pratt's Director of Quality Military Engines attested that "a competitor with similar expertise could and would use the information to gain insights into the strengths and weaknesses of [Pratt's] quality control system as well as manufacturing techniques and use those insights to revise and improve its own quality control and manufacturing systems." Similarly, Sikorsky asserted that "proprietary information regarding Sikorsky's manufacturing process and procedures" is "inextricably intertwined with the quality control information" included in the CARs and it asserted that "release of this proprietary information would substantially harm Sikorsky's competitive position because its competitors would use this information to their advantage * * * . In response, [the] DCMA simply stated that it had redacted [removed or obscured] all of the sensitive proprietary information and concluded that disclosure of the remaining information was not likely to cause the contractors substantial competitive harm.

We find [the] DCMA's response insufficient. The documents, even as redacted by [the] DCMA, appear to reveal details about Sikorsky's and Pratt's proprietary manufacturing and quality control processes. * * * The documents describe, in part, how the contractors build and inspect helicopters and/or engines. Once disclosed, competitors could, it appears, use the information to improve their own manufacturing and quality control systems, thus making "affirmative

Case 5.3–Continued

use of proprietary information" against which Exemption 4 is meant to guard.

DECISION AND REMEDY The federal appellate court concluded that the DCMA had failed to provide a reasoned basis for its conclusion. The court remanded the case to the DCMA to examine the relevant data and give a satisfactory explanation for its decision, if it could, "including a rational connection between the facts found and the choice made."

MANAGERIAL IMPLICATIONS *Businesses that c ontract with government agencies to provide goods or services can expect to have their processes and procedures monitored by these agencies. This means that proprietary information, including trade secrets, may find its way into various government reports or other documents. To protect this information from competitors, managers in such businesses would be wise to seek counsel as to what types of documents are exempt from disclosure under the FOIA.*

Government in the Sunshine Act

Congress passed the Government in the Sunshine Act,[12] or open meeting law, in 1976. It requires that "every portion of every meeting of an agency" be open to "public observation." The act also requires procedures to ensure that the public is provided with adequate advance notice of the agency's scheduled meeting and agenda. Like the FOIA, the Sunshine Act contains certain exceptions. Closed meetings are permitted when (1) the subject of the meeting concerns accusing any person of a crime, (2) open meetings would frustrate implementation of future agency actions, or (3) the subject of the meeting involves matters relating to future litigation or rule-making. Courts interpret these exceptions to allow open access whenever possible.

Regulatory Flexibility Act

> *"Law . . . is a human institution, created by human agents to serve human ends."*
> Harlan F. Stone, 1872–1946
> (Chief Justice of the United States Supreme Court, 1941–1946)

Concern over the effects of regulation on the efficiency of businesses, particularly smaller ones, led Congress to pass the Regulatory Flexibility Act.[13] Under this act, whenever a new regulation will have a "significant impact upon a substantial number of small entities," the agency must conduct a regulatory flexibility analysis. The analysis must measure the cost that the rule would impose on small businesses and must consider less burdensome alternatives. The act also contains provisions to alert small businesses about forthcoming regulations. The act relieved small businesses of some record-keeping burdens, especially with regard to hazardous waste management.

Small Business Regulatory Enforcement Fairness Act

The Small Business Regulatory Enforcement Fairness Act (SBREFA) of 1996[14] allows Congress to review new federal regulations for at least sixty days before they take effect. This period gives opponents of the rules time to present their arguments to Congress.

The SBREFA also authorizes the courts to enforce the Regulatory Flexibility Act. This helps to ensure that federal agencies, such as the Internal Revenue Service, consider ways to reduce the economic impact of new regulations on small businesses. Federal agencies are required to prepare guides that explain in plain English how small businesses can comply with federal regulations.

The SBREFA set up the National Enforcement Ombudsman to receive comments from small businesses about their dealings with federal agencies. Based on these

12. 5 U.S.C. Section 552b.
13. 5 U.S.C. Sections 601–612.
14. 5 U.S.C. Sections 801 *et seq.*

comments, Regional Small Business Fairness Boards rate the agencies and publicize their findings.

▶ Reviewing . . . Administrative Law

Assume that the Securities and Exchange Commission (SEC) has a rule under which it enforces statutory provisions prohibiting insider trading only when the insiders make monetary profits for themselves. Then the SEC makes a new rule, declaring that it has the statutory authority to bring enforcement actions against individuals even if they did not personally profit from the insider trading. The SEC simply announces the new rule without conducting a rulemaking proceeding. A stockbrokerage firm objects and says that the new rule was unlawfully developed without opportunity for public comment. The brokerage firm challenges the rule in an action that ultimately is reviewed by a federal appellate court. Using the information presented in the chapter, answer the following questions.

1. Is the SEC an executive agency or an independent regulatory agency? Does it matter to the outcome of this dispute? Explain.
2. Suppose that the SEC asserts that it has always had the statutory authority to pursue persons for insider trading regardless of whether they personally profited from the transaction. This is the only argument the SEC makes to justify changing its enforcement rules. Would a court be likely to find that the SEC's action was arbitrary and capricious under the Administrative Procedure Act (APA)? Why or why not?
3. Would a court be likely to give *Chevron* deference to the SEC's interpretation of the law on insider trading? Why or why not?
4. Now assume that a court finds that the new rule is merely "interpretive." What effect would this determination have on whether the SEC had to follow the APA's rulemaking procedures?

▶ Debate This

Because an administrative law judge (ALJ) acts as both judge and jury, there should always be at least three ALJs in each administrative hearing.

Linking the Law *to Management*
Dealing with Administrative Law

Whether you end up owning your own small business or working for a large corporation, you will be dealing with multiple aspects of administrative law. Recall that administrative law involves all of the rules, orders, and decisions of administrative agencies. At the federal level, these include the U.S. Food and Drug Administration, the Equal Employment Opportunity Commission, the National Labor Relations Board, and the U.S. Occupational Safety and Health Administration. All federal, state, and local government administrative agencies create rules that have the force of law. As a manager, you probably will have to pay more attention to administrative rules and regulations than to laws passed by local, state, and federal legislatures.

Federal versus State and Local Agency Regulations

The three levels of government create three levels of rules and regulations though their respective administrative agencies. Typically,

at least at the state level, there are agencies that govern business activities in a manner similar to federal agencies. You may face situations in which a state agency regulation and a federal agency regulation conflict. In general, federal agency regulations preempt, or take precedence over, conflicting state (or local) regulations.

As a manager, you will have to learn about agency regulations that pertain to your business activities. It will be up to you, as a manager or small-business owner, to ferret out those regulations that are most important and could potentially create the most liability if you violate them.

When Should You Participate in the Rulemaking Process?

All federal agencies and many state agencies invite public comments on proposed rules. For example, suppose that you manage a large construction company and your state occupational safety agency proposes a new rule requiring every employee on a construction site to wear hearing protection. You believe that the rule will lead to a less safe environment because your employees will not be able to communicate easily with one another.

Should you spend time offering comments to the agency? As an efficient manager, you make a trade-off calculation: First, you determine the value of the time that you would spend in attempting to prevent or at least alter the proposed rule. Then you compare this implicit cost with your estimate of the potential benefits your company would receive if the rule were not put into place.

Be Prepared for Investigations

All administrative agencies have investigatory powers. Agencies' investigators usually have the power to search business premises, although normally they first have to obtain a search warrant. As a manager, you have the choice of cooperating with agency investigators or providing the minimum amount of assistance. If you receive investigators regularly, you will often opt for cooperation. In contrast, if your business is rarely investigated, you may decide that the on-site proposed inspection is overreaching. Then you must

contact your company's attorney for advice on how to proceed.

If an administrative agency cites you for a regulatory violation, you will probably negotiate a settlement with the agency rather than take your case before an administrative law judge. You will have to weigh the cost of the negotiated settlement with the potential cost of fighting the enforcement action.

Management Involves Flexibility

Throughout your business career, you will face hundreds of administrative rules and regulations, investigations, and perhaps enforcement proceedings for rule violations. You may sometimes be frustrated by seemingly meaningless regulations. You must accept that these are part of the legal environment in which you will work. The rational manager looks at administrative law as just another parameter that he or she cannot easily alter.

FOR CRITICAL ANALYSIS

Why are owner/operators of small businesses at a disadvantage relative to large corporations when they attempt to decipher complex regulations that apply to their businesses?

Key Terms

adjudication 113
administrative agency 105
administrative law 104
administrative law judge (ALJ) 114
administrative process 110

bureaucracy 108
delegation doctrine 108
enabling legislation 106
final order 115
initial order 115

interpretive rule 108
legislative rule 108
notice-and-comment rulemaking 111
rulemaking 110

Chapter Summary: Administrative Law

Agency Creation and Powers (See pages 106–110.)	1. Under the U.S. Constitution, Congress can delegate the implementation of its laws to government agencies. Congress can thus indirectly monitor an area in which it has passed laws without becoming bogged down in details relating to enforcement.
	2. Administrative agencies are created by enabling legislation, which usually specifies the name, composition, and powers of the agency.
	3. Agencies can create legislative rules, which are as binding as formal acts of Congress.
	4. The three branches of government exercise controls over agency powers and functions.
	a. Executive controls—The president can control agencies through appointments of federal officers and through vetoes of bills affecting agency powers.
	b. Legislative controls—Congress can give power to an agency, take it away, increase or decrease the agency's funding, or abolish the agency.
	c. Judicial controls—Administrative agencies are subject to the judicial review of the courts. The Administrative Procedure Act of 1946 also limits agencies.

(Continued)

▶ Chapter Summary: Administrative Law, Continued

The Administrative Process
(See pages 110–115.)
	1. The administrative process consists of rulemaking, enforcement, and adjudicatory powers.
	2. Agencies are authorized to create new regulations—their rulemaking function. This power is conferred on an agency in the enabling legislation.
	3. Notice-and-comment rulemaking is the most common rulemaking procedure. It involves the publication of the proposed regulation in the *Federal Register,* followed by a comment period to allow private parties to comment on the proposed rule.
	4. Administrative agencies investigate the entities that they regulate, both during the rulemaking process to obtain data and after rules are issued to monitor compliance.
	5. The most important investigative tools available to an agency are the following:
	  a. Inspections and tests—Used to gather information and to correct or prevent undesirable conditions.
	  b. Subpoenas—Orders that direct individuals to appear at a hearing or to hand over specified documents.
	6. Limits on administrative investigations include the following:
	  a. The investigation must be for a legitimate purpose.
	  b. The information sought must be relevant, and the investigative demands must be specific and not unreasonably burdensome.
	  c. The Fourth Amendment protects companies and individuals from unreasonable searches and seizures by requiring search warrants in most instances.
	7. After a preliminary investigation, an agency may initiate an administrative action against an individual or organization by filing a complaint. Most such actions are resolved at this stage before they go through the formal adjudicatory process.
	8. If there is no settlement, the case is presented to an administrative law judge (ALJ) in a proceeding similar to a trial.
	9. After a case is concluded, the ALJ renders an initial order, which can be appealed by either party to the board or commission that governs the agency and ultimately to a federal appeals court. If no appeal is taken or the case is not reviewed, then the order becomes the final order of the agency. The charged party may be ordered to pay damages or to stop carrying on some specified activity.

Judicial Deference **to Agency Decisions** **(See pages 115–117.)**	1. When reviewing agency decisions, courts typically grant deference (significant weight or consideration) to an agency's findings of fact and interpretations of law. 2. If Congress directly addressed the issue in dispute when enacting the statute, courts must follow the statutory language. 3. If the statute is silent or ambiguous, a court will uphold an agency's decision if the agency's interpretation of the statute was reasonable, even if the court would have interpreted the law differently. (This is known as *Chevron* deference.) 4. An agency must follow notice-and-comment rulemaking procedures before it is entitled to judicial deference in its interpretation of the law.
Public Accountability **(See pages 117–120.)**	Congress has passed several laws to make agencies more accountable through public scrutiny. These laws include the Freedom of Information Act, the Government in the Sunshine Act, the Regulatory Flexibility Act, and the Small Business Regulatory Enforcement Fairness Act.

▶ ExamPrep

ISSUE SPOTTERS

—Check your answers to these questions against the answers provided in Appendix D at the end of this text.

1. The U.S. Department of Transportation (DOT) sometimes hears an appeal from a party whose contract with the DOT has been canceled. An administrative law judge (ALJ), who works for the DOT, hears this appeal. What safeguards promote the ALJ's fairness? **(See page 114.)**

2. Apples & Oranges Corporation learns that a federal administrative agency is considering a rule that will have a negative impact on the firm's ability to do business. Does the firm have any opportunity to express its opinion about the pending rule? Explain. **(See page 111.)**

BEFORE THE TEST

Go to **www.cengagebrain.com**, enter the ISBN 9781133586548, and click on "Find" to locate this textbook's Web site. Then click on "Access Now" under "Study Tools," and select Chapter 5 at the top. There, you will find a Practice Quiz that you can take to assess your mastery of the concepts in this chapter. Additionally, you will find Flashcards and a Glossary of important terms, as well as Video Questions (when assigned).

For Review

Answers for the even-numbered questions in this For Review *section can be found in Appendix E at the end of this text.*

1. How are federal administrative agencies created?
2. How do the three branches of government limit the power of administrative agencies?
3. What are the three basic functions of most administrative agencies?
4. What sequence of events must normally occur before an agency rule becomes law?
5. How do administrative agencies enforce their rules?

Questions and Case Problems

5–1. Rulemaking. For decades, the Federal Trade Commission (FTC) resolved fair trade and advertising disputes through individual adjudications. In the 1960s, the FTC began setting forth rules that defined fair and *unfair trade practices* (see Chapter 19). In cases involving violations of these rules, the due process rights of participants were more limited and did not include cross-examination. This was because, although anyone found violating a rule would receive a full adjudication, the legitimacy of the rule itself could not be challenged in the adjudication. Any party charged with violating a rule was almost certain to lose the adjudication. Affected parties complained to a court, arguing that their rights before the FTC were unduly limited by the new rules. What will the court examine to determine whether to uphold the new rules? **(See page 112.)**

5–2. **Question with Sample Answer: Rulemaking.** Assume that the Food and Drug Administration (FDA), using proper procedures, adopts a rule describing its future investigations. This new rule covers all future circumstances in which the FDA wants to regulate food additives. Under the new rule, the FDA is not to regulate food additives without giving food companies an opportunity to cross-examine witnesses. At a subsequent time, the FDA wants to regulate methylisocyanate, a food additive. The FDA undertakes an informal rulemaking procedure, without cross-examination, and regulates methylisocyanate. Producers protest, saying that the FDA promised them the opportunity for cross-examination. The FDA responds that the Administrative Procedure Act does not require such cross-examination and that it is free to withdraw the promise made in its new rule. If the producers challenge the FDA in court, on what basis would the court rule in their favor? **(See page 112.)**
—**For a sample answer to Question 5–2, go to Appendix F at the end of this text.**

5–3. Judicial Controls. Under federal law, when accepting bids on a contract, an agency must hold "discussions" with all offerors. An agency may ask a single offeror for "clarification" of its proposal, however, without holding "discussions" with the others. Regulations define clarifications as "limited exchanges." In 2001, the U.S. Air Force asked for bids on a contract. The winning contractor would examine, assess, and develop means of integrating national intelligence assets with the U.S. Department of Defense space systems, to enhance the capabilities of the Air Force's Space Warfare Center. Among the bidders were Information Technology & Applications Corp. (ITAC) and RS Information Systems, Inc. (RSIS). The Air Force asked the parties for more information on their subcontractors but did not allow them to change their proposals. Determining that there were weaknesses in ITAC's bid, the Air Force awarded the contract to RSIS. ITAC filed a suit against the government, contending that the postproposal requests to RSIS, and its responses, were improper "discussions." Should the court rule in ITAC's favor? Why or why not? [*Information Technology & Applications Corp. v. United States*, 316 F.3d 1312 (Fed.Cir. 2003)]. **(See pages 108 and 109.)**

5–4. Investigation. Riverdale Mills Corp. makes plastic-coated steel wire products in Massachusetts. Riverdale uses a water-based cleaning process that generates acidic and alkaline wastewater. To meet federal clean-water requirements, Riverdale has a system within its plant to treat the water. It then flows through a pipe that opens into a manhole-covered test pit outside the plant in full view of Riverdale's employees. Three hundred feet away, the pipe merges into the public sewer system. In October 1997, the U.S. Environmental Protection Agency (EPA) sent Justin Pimpare and Daniel Granz to inspect the plant. Without a search warrant and without Riverdale's express consent, the agents took samples from the test pit. Based on the samples,

Riverdale and James Knott, the company's owner, were charged with criminal violations of the federal Clean Water Act. The defendants sued the EPA agents in a federal district court, alleging violations of the Fourth Amendment. What right does the Fourth Amendment provide in this context? This right is based on a "reasonable expectation of privacy." Should the agents be held liable? Why or why not? [*Riverdale Mills Corp. v. Pimpare,* 392 F.3d 55 (1st Cir. 2004)] **(See page 113.)**

5–5. Rulemaking. The Investment Company Act prohibits a mutual fund from engaging in certain transactions in which there may be a conflict of interest between the manager of the fund and its shareholders. Under rules issued by the Securities and Exchange Commission (SEC), however, a fund that meets certain conditions may engage in an otherwise prohibited transaction. In 2004, the SEC added two new conditions. A year later, the SEC reconsidered the new conditions in terms of the costs that they would impose on the funds. Within eight days, and without asking for public input, the SEC readopted the conditions. The U.S. Chamber of Commerce—which is both a mutual fund shareholder and an association with mutual fund managers among its members—asked a federal appellate court to review the new rules. The Chamber charged that in readopting the rules, the SEC relied on materials not in the "rulemaking record" without providing an opportunity for public comment. The SEC countered that the information was otherwise "publicly available." In adopting a rule, should an agency consider information that is not part of the rulemaking record? Why or why not? [*Chamber of Commerce of the United States v. Securities and Exchange Commission,* 443 F.3d 890 (D.C.Cir. 2006)] **(See pages 110–112.)**

5–6. **Case Problem with Sample Answer: Powers of the Agency.** A well-documented rise in global temperatures has coincided with a significant increase in the concentration of carbon dioxide in the atmosphere. Many scientists believe that the two trends are related, because when carbon dioxide is released into the atmosphere, it produces a greenhouse effect, trapping solar heat. Under the Clean Air Act (CAA), the Environmental Protection Agency (EPA) is authorized to regulate "any" air pollutants "emitted into . . . the ambient air" that in its "judgment cause, or contribute to, air pollution." A group of private organizations asked the EPA to regulate carbon dioxide and other "greenhouse gas" emissions from new motor vehicles. The EPA refused, stating that Congress last amended the CAA in 1990 without authorizing new, binding auto-emissions limits. The petitioners—nineteen states, including Massachusetts—asked a district court to review the EPA's denial. Did the EPA have the authority to regulate greenhouse gas emissions from new motor vehicles? If so, was its stated reason for refusing to do so consistent with that authority? Discuss. [*Massachusetts v. Environmental Protection Agency,* 549 U.S. 497, 127 S.Ct. 1438, 167 L.Ed.2d 248 (2007)] **(See pages 106–109.)**

—For a sample answer to Case Problem 5–6, go to Appendix G at the end of this text.

5–7. Judicial Deference. Dave Conley, a longtime heavy smoker, was diagnosed with lung cancer and died two years later. His death certificate stated that the cause of death was cancer, but it also noted other significant conditions that had contributed to his death, including a history of cigarette smoking and coal mining. Conley's widow filed for benefits under the Black Lung Benefits Act, which provides for victims of black lung disease caused by coal mining. To qualify for benefits under the act, the exposure to coal dust must be a substantially contributing factor leading to the person's death. Under the statute, this meant to "hasten death." The U.S. Department of Labor collected Conley's work and medical records. An administrative law judge (ALJ) reviewed the record and took testimony from several physicians about the cause of Conley's death. Only one physician testified that the coal dust was a substantial factor in Conley's death, but he offered no evidence other than his testimony. Nevertheless, the ALJ ruled that the coal mining had been a substantial factor that had hastened Conley's death and awarded benefits to his widow. Conley's employer appealed to the Benefits Review Board (BRB), which reversed the ALJ's decision. The BRB found that there was insufficient evidence to hold that coal dust was a substantial factor in Conley's lung cancer. Conley's widow appealed. Should the court defer to the ALJ's decision on the cause of Conley's death? Which decision does the federal appellate court review, the ALJ's conclusions or the BRB's reversal? Explain your answers. [*Conley v. National Mines Corp.,* 595 F.3d 297 (6th Cir. 2010)] **(See pages 115 and 116.)**

5–8. Arbitrary and Capricious Test. Every year, Michael Manin, an airline pilot and flight instructor, had to renew his first-class airman medical certificate, which showed that he had met medical standards for aircraft operation. The application for renewal included questions regarding criminal history, including non-traffic misdemeanors. Manin had been convicted of disorderly conduct, a minor misdemeanor, in 1995 and again in 1997, but never disclosed these convictions on his yearly applications. The Federal Aviation Administration (FAA) discovered the two convictions in 2007 and issued an emergency order to revoke Manin's flight certificates in 2008. Manin filed an answer to this revocation order, as well as an administrative complaint. He claimed that he had not known he was required to report a conviction for a minor misdemeanor and also asserted that the complaint was stale (legally expired) under National Transportation Safety Board (NTSB) regulations. At the hearing on Manin's complaint, the administrative law judge affirmed the emergency revocation order. Manin appealed to the full NTSB, which also affirmed. Manin then appealed to a federal appellate court, claiming that the NTSB had departed from its precedent in prior cases without explanation. The FAA conceded that the NTSB's statement of the rules pertaining to staleness was inaccurate, but it urged the court to affirm anyway. How should the court rule? Does an agency's departure from precedent without explanation mean that its decision was arbitrary and capricious? Explain. [*Manin v. National Transportation Safety Board*, 627 F.3d 1239 (D.C.Cir. 2011)] **(See pages 109 and 114–115.)**

5–9. **A Question of Ethics: Rulemaking.** *To ensure highway safety and protect driver health, Congress charged federal agencies with regulating the hours of service of commercial motor vehicle operators. Between 1940 and 2003, the regulations that applied to long-haul truck drivers were mostly unchanged. In 2003, the Federal Motor Carrier Safety Administration (FMCSA) revised the regulations significantly, increasing the number of daily and weekly hours that drivers could work. The agency had not considered the impact of the changes on the health of the drivers, however, and the revisions were overturned. The FMCSA then issued a notice that it would reconsider the revisions and opened them up for public comment. The agency analyzed the costs to the industry and the crash risks due to driver fatigue under different options and concluded that the safety benefits of not increasing the hours did not outweigh the economic costs. In 2005, the agency issued a rule that was nearly identical to the 2003 version. Public Citizen,*

Inc., and others, including the Owner-Operator Independent Drivers Association, asked a district court to review the 2005 rule as it applied to long-haul drivers. [Owner-Operator Independent Drivers Association, Inc. v. Federal Motor Carrier Safety Administration, *494 F.3d 188 (D.C.Cir. 2007)]* **(See pages 110–112.)**

1. The agency's cost-benefit analysis included new methods that were not disclosed to the public in time for comments. Was this unethical? Should the agency have disclosed the new methodology sooner? Why or why not?

2. The agency created a graph to show the risk of a crash as a function of the time a driver spent on the job. The graph plotted the first twelve hours of a day individually, but the rest of the time was depicted with an aggregate figure at the seventeenth hour. This made the risk at those hours appear to be lower. Is it unethical for an agency to manipulate data? Explain.

5–10. **Critical-Thinking Legal Environment Question.** Does Congress delegate too much power to federal administrative agencies? Do the courts defer too much to Congress in its grant of power to those agencies? What are the alternatives to the agencies that we encounter in every facet of our lives? **(See page 114.)**

Chapter 6

Torts and Product Liability

> "Two wrongs do
> not make a right."
> —English Proverb

Contents

Learning Objectives

The five Learning Objectives below are designed to help improve your understanding of the chapter. After reading this chapter, you should be able to answer the following questions:

1. What is the purpose of tort law?
2. What are the four elements of negligence?
3. What is meant by strict liability? In what circumstances is strict liability applied?
4. What are the elements of a cause of action in strict product liability?
5. What defenses to liability can be raised in a product liability lawsuit?

(OlegAlbinsky/iStockphoto.com)

Tort A civil wrong not arising from a breach of contract.

Torts are wrongful actions. The word *tort* is French for wrong. Most of us agree with the chapter-opening quotation above—two wrongs do not make a right. Tort law is our nation's attempt to right a wrong. Through tort law, society tries to ensure that those who have suffered injuries as a result of the wrongful conduct of others receive compensation.

As you will see in later chapters, many of the lawsuits brought by or against business firms are based on the tort theories discussed in this chapter. Some of the torts examined here can occur in any context, including the business environment. Others, traditionally referred to as **business torts**, involve wrongful interference with the business rights of others. Business torts include such vague concepts as *unfair competition* and *wrongfully interfering with the business relations of another*.

Business Tort Wrongful interference with another's business rights.

As technological advances such as the Internet provide opportunities to commit new types of wrongs, the courts are extending tort law to cover these wrongs. For instance, not too long ago, Google announced that it was starting a competing service similar to Facebook's. The unveiling of Google+ was met with praise and some very damning criticisms that turned out to have been initiated by a public relations firm that Facebook regularly used. Was a *cyber tort* committed? You will decide later in this chapter.

Product liability encompasses the tort theories of negligence and strict liability. Because it is such an important part of doing business, we conclude this chapter with a comprehensive discussion of product liability.

▶ The Basis and Purpose of Tort Law

Two notions serve as the basis of all torts: wrongs and compensation. Tort law is designed to compensate those who have suffered a loss or injury due to another person's wrongful act. In a tort action, one person or group brings a personal suit against another person or group to obtain compensation or other relief for the harm suffered.

Generally, the purpose of tort law is to provide remedies for the invasion of various *protected interests*. Society recognizes an interest in personal physical safety, and tort law provides remedies for acts that cause physical injury or interfere with physical security and freedom of movement. Society recognizes an interest in protecting real and personal property, and tort law provides remedies for acts that cause destruction or damage to property.

LEARNING OBJECTIVE 1 **What is the purpose of tort law?**

Damages Available in Tort Actions

Because the purpose of tort law is to compensate the injured party for the harm suffered, it is important to have a basic understanding of the types of **damages** that plaintiffs seek in tort actions.

Damages Money sought as a remedy for a breach of contract or a tortious action.

COMPENSATORY DAMAGES **Compensatory damages** are intended to compensate or reimburse a plaintiff for actual losses—to make the plaintiff whole and put her or him in the same position that she or he would have been in had the tort not occurred. Compensatory damages awards are often broken down into *special damages* and *general damages*.

Compensatory Damages A monetary award equivalent to the actual value of injuries or damage sustained by the aggrieved party.

Special Damages. Special damages compensate the plaintiff for quantifiable monetary losses, such as medical expenses, lost wages and benefits, and the costs of repairing or replacing damaged property. **CASE EXAMPLE 6.1** Seaway Marine Transport operates the *Enterprise,* a large cargo ship made for storing coal. When the *Enterprise* positioned itself to receive a load of coal on the shores of Lake Erie, it struck a land-based coal-loading machine operated by Bessemer & Lake Erie Railroad Company. Seaway was found liable for negligence and had to pay $522,000 in special damages to compensate Bessemer for the cost of repairing the damage to the loading boom.[1] ●

General Damages. General damages compensate individuals (not companies) for the nonmonetary aspects of the harm suffered, such as pain and suffering. For instance, a court might award general damages for physical or emotional pain and suffering, loss of companionship, or loss (or impairment) of mental or physical capacity.

PUNITIVE DAMAGES Occasionally, **punitive damages** may also be awarded in tort cases to punish the wrongdoer and deter others from similar wrongdoing. Punitive damages are appropriate only when the defendant's conduct was particularly reprehensible (unacceptable). Usually, this means that punitive damages are available mainly in intentional tort actions (discussed next). More than thirty states have limited punitive damages, and some have imposed outright bans.

Punitive Damages Monetary damages that may be awarded to a plaintiff to punish the defendant and deter similar conduct in the future.

---

1. *Bessemer & Lake Erie Railroad Co. v. Seaway Marine Transport,* 596 F.3d 357 (6th Cir. 2010).

Classifications of Torts

There are two broad classifications of torts: *intentional torts* and *unintentional torts* (torts involving negligence). The classification of a particular tort depends largely on how the tort occurs (intentionally or negligently) and the surrounding circumstances. In the following pages, you will read about these two classifications of torts.

▶ Intentional Torts against Persons

Intentional Tort A wrongful act that is knowingly committed.

Tortfeasor One who commits a tort.

An **intentional tort,** as the term implies, requires *intent*. The **tortfeasor** (the one committing the tort) must intend to commit an act, the consequences of which interfere with the personal or business interests of another in a way not permitted by law. An evil or harmful motive is not required—in fact, the person committing the action may even have a beneficial motive for doing what turns out to be a tortious act.

In tort law, intent means only that the person committing the act intended the consequences of his or her act or knew with substantial certainty that certain consequences would result from the act. The law generally assumes that individuals intend the *normal* consequences of their actions. Thus, forcefully pushing another person—even if done in jest—is an intentional tort if injury results, because the object of a strong push can ordinarily be expected to fall down.

Assault and Battery

Assault Any word or action intended to make another person fearful of immediate physical harm.

An **assault** is any intentional and unexcused threat of immediate harmful or offensive contact, including words or acts that create in another person a reasonable apprehension of harmful contact. An assault can be completed even if there is no actual contact with the plaintiff, provided that the defendant's conduct creates a reasonable apprehension of imminent harm in the plaintiff. Tort law aims to protect individuals from having to expect harmful or offensive contact.

Battery The unexcused, harmful or offensive, intentional touching of another.

The *completion* of the act that caused the apprehension, if it results in harm to the plaintiff, is a **battery,** which is defined as an unexcused and harmful or offensive physical contact *intentionally* performed. **EXAMPLE 6.2** Ivan threatens Jean with a gun and then shoots her. The pointing of the gun at Jean is an assault. The firing of the gun (if the bullet hits Jean) is a battery. ● The contact can be harmful, or it can be merely offensive (such as an unwelcome kiss). Physical injury need not occur. The contact can involve any part of the body or anything attached to it—for example, a hat, a purse, or a jacket. The contact can be made by the defendant directly, or it can occur as a result of a force set in motion by the defendant, such as throwing a rock.

False Imprisonment

False imprisonment is the intentional confinement or restraint of another person's activities without justification. False imprisonment interferes with the freedom to move without restraint. The confinement can be accomplished through the use of physical barriers, physical restraint, or threats of physical force. Moral pressure or threats of future harm do not constitute false imprisonment. It is essential that the person under restraint does not wish to be restrained.

Businesspersons are often confronted with suits for false imprisonment after they have attempted to confine a suspected shoplifter for questioning. Under the "privilege to detain" granted to merchants in most states, a merchant can use *reasonable force* to detain or delay a person suspected of shoplifting the merchant's property. Although laws pertaining to this privilege vary from state to state, generally any detention must be conducted in a *reasonable* manner and for only a *reasonable* length of time. Undue force or unreasonable detention can lead to liability for the business.

Cities and counties may also face lawsuits for false imprisonment if they detain individuals without reason. In the following case, a man who was arrested and held in jail for several weeks because of clerical errors sued the county for false imprisonment.

Case 6.1   **Shoyoye v. County of Los Angeles**

Court of Appeal of California, Second District, 203 Cal.App. 4th 947, 137 Cal.Rptr.3d 839 (2012).

BACKGROUND AND FACTS   Adetokunbo Shoyoye was lawfully arrested in 2007 when he was at a police station reporting an unrelated incident. The police discovered that he had two outstanding warrants: one for an unpaid subway ticket and another for grand theft, which had been committed by someone who had stolen his identity. Shoyoye was incarcerated, but soon after, he was released on both warrants. A Los Angeles County employee, however, mistakenly attached information related to another person—who was scheduled to be sent to state prison—to Shoyoye's paperwork. This erroneous information was entered into the county sheriff's computer system under Shoyoye's name.

As a result, instead being released as ordered, Shoyoye was held in county jail for more than two weeks. During this time, he made numerous attempts to explain to various officials, including the prison's chaplain, that he was being detained for no reason. While in prison, he was subjected to strip searches and shackles. He was housed in a large dormitory with hundreds of inmates, many of whom were gang members. He feared that he might be sent to prison, put into "the hole" for further discipline, or become a victim of violence.

After his release, Shoyoye sued the county of Los Angeles for, among other things, false imprisonment. A jury awarded him $22,700 in economic damages (for past and future lost earnings and property loss) and $180,000 in noneconomic damages (for past and future pain and suffering). The county of Los Angeles appealed.

IN THE WORDS OF THE COURT . . .
SUZUKAWA, J. [Judge]
 * * * The County acknowledges that although its initial detention of Shoyoye was justified, it over-detained him by about 16 days as a result of an unintentional clerical error. The County contends on appeal that the evidence presented at trial was insufficient to support a verdict in favor of Shoyoye.

* * * *

* * * On August 22, 2007, Shoyoye was ordered released, subject to any other holds. He was transported back to Men's Central Jail, where he was processed and placed in a dormitory, expecting to be released at any time.

A County employee mistakenly attached to Shoyoye's paperwork information pertaining to a parolee scheduled to be sent to state prison for violating the terms of his parole. The other prisoner's name was Marquis Lance Parsee. A Department of Corrections ("DCL") hold intended for Parsee was entered into the County Sheriff's computer system regarding Shoyoye. A subsequent quality control check failed to detect the error. If a County employee had looked at the paper file on Shoyoye rather than the computer records, he or she would have realized that the DCL hold did not pertain to Shoyoye.

The elements of a tortious claim of false imprisonment are: (1) the non-consensual, intentional confinement of a person, (2) without lawful privilege, and (3) for an appreciable period of time, however brief. The evidence presented at trial was clearly sufficient to establish those elements. [Emphasis added.]

DECISION AND REMEDY   The state appellate court upheld the verdict of false imprisonment and affirmed the jury's award of $22,700 in economic damages and $180,000 in noneconomic damages to Shoyoye.

THE ETHICAL DIMENSION   *Shoyoye asked numerous county employees to verify that he had been wrongfully detained. What obligation did those employees have to attempt to discover "the truth"?*

Intentional Infliction of Emotional Distress

The tort of *intentional infliction of emotional distress* can be defined as an intentional act involving extreme and outrageous conduct that results in severe emotional distress to another. To be **actionable** (capable of serving as the ground for a lawsuit), the act must be so extreme and outrageous that it exceeds the bounds of decency

Actionable   Capable of serving as the basis of a lawsuit.

accepted by society. **EXAMPLE 6.3**   A father attacks a man who has had consensual sexual relations with the father's adult daughter. The father handcuffs the man to a pole and threatens to castrate and kill him unless he leaves town. This conduct may be sufficiently extreme to be actionable as an intentional infliction of emotional distress. ●

Courts in most jurisdictions are wary of emotional distress claims and confine them to truly outrageous behavior. Generally, repeated annoyances (such as those experienced by a person who is being stalked), coupled with threats, are sufficient to support a claim. Acts that cause indignity or annoyance alone usually are not enough.

Defamation

Defamation Anything published or publicly spoken that causes injury to another's good name, reputation, or character.

Libel Defamation in writing or other form having the quality of permanence (such as a digital recording).

Slander Defamation in oral form.

Defamation of character involves wrongfully hurting a person's good reputation. The law has imposed a general duty on all persons to refrain from making *false*, defamatory *statements of fact* about others. Breaching this duty in writing or other permanent form (such as a digital recording) involves the tort of **libel.** Breaching this duty orally involves the tort of **slander.** The tort of defamation can also arise when a false statement of fact is made about a person's product, business, or legal ownership rights to property.

STATEMENT OF FACT REQUIREMENT   Often at issue in defamation lawsuits is whether the defendant made a statement of fact or a *statement of opinion.* Statements of opinion normally are not actionable because they are protected under the First Amendment. In other words, making a negative statement about another person is not defamation unless the statement is false and represents something as a fact, as in "Lane cheats on his taxes," rather than a personal opinion, as in "Lane is a jerk."

THE PUBLICATION REQUIREMENT   The basis of the tort of defamation is the publication of a statement or statements that hold an individual up to contempt, ridicule, or hatred. *Publication* here means that the defamatory statements are communicated to persons other than the defamed party. **EXAMPLE 6.4**   If Thompson writes Andrews a private letter accusing him of embezzling funds, the action does not constitute libel. If Peters falsely states that Gordon is dishonest and incompetent when no one else is around, the action does not constitute slander. In neither situation was the message communicated to a third party. ●

The courts generally have held that even dictating a letter to a secretary constitutes publication, although the publication may be *privileged* (see page 131). Moreover, if a third party merely overhears defamatory statements by chance, the courts usually hold that this also constitutes publication. Defamatory statements made via the Internet are also actionable. Note further that any individual who republishes or repeats defamatory statements is liable even if that person reveals the source of such statements.

"My initial response was to sue her for defamation of character, but then I realized that I had no character."
Charles Barkley, 1963–present
(National Basketball Association player, 1984–2000)

DAMAGES FOR LIBEL   Once a defendant's liability for libel is established, general damages are presumed as a matter of law. General damages are designed to compensate the plaintiff for nonspecific harms such as disgrace or dishonor in the eyes of the community and emotional distress—harms that are difficult to measure. In other words, to recover damages in a libel case, the plaintiff need not prove that she or he was actually harmed in any way as a result of the libelous statement.

DAMAGES FOR SLANDER   In a case alleging slander, however, the plaintiff must prove *special damages* to establish the defendant's liability. In other words, the plaintiff must show that the slanderous statement caused the plaintiff to suffer actual economic or monetary losses. Unless this initial hurdle of proving special damages is overcome, a plaintiff alleging slander normally cannot go forward with the suit and recover any damages. This requirement is imposed in cases involving slander because slanderous statements have a temporary quality. In contrast, a libelous (written) statement has the quality of permanence, can be circulated widely (such as in tweets and blogs), and usually results from some degree of deliberation on the part of the author.

DEFENSES AGAINST DEFAMATION   Truth is normally an absolute defense against a defamation charge. In other words, if the defendant in a defamation suit can prove that his or her allegedly defamatory statements were true, normally no tort has been committed. Other defenses to defamation may exist if the statement is privileged or concerns a public figure.

Privilege   A legal right, exemption, or immunity granted to a person or a class of persons.

Privileged Communications.   In some circumstances, a person will not be liable for defamatory statements because she or he enjoys a **privilege**, or immunity. Privileged communications are of two types: absolute and qualified.[2] Only in judicial proceedings and certain government proceedings is an *absolute* privilege granted. Thus, statements made in a courtroom by attorneys and judges during a trial are absolutely privileged, as are statements made by government officials during legislative debate.

   In other situations, a person will not be liable for defamatory statements because he or she has a *qualified,* or conditional, privilege. Generally, if the statements are made in good faith and the publication is limited to those who have a legitimate interest in the communication, the statements fall within the area of qualified privilege. **EXAMPLE 6.5**   Jorge worked at Hewlett-Packard for five years and was being considered for a management position. His supervisor, Lydia, wrote a memo about Jorge's performance to those evaluating him for the management position. The memo contained certain negative statements. As long as Lydia honestly believed that what she wrote was true and limited her disclosure to company representatives, her statements would likely be protected by a qualified privilege. ●

Actual Malice   The deliberate intent to cause harm, which exists when a person makes a statement either knowing that it is false or showing a reckless disregard for whether it is true.

Public Figures.   Politicians, entertainers, professional athletes, and others in the public eye are considered *public figures*. In general, public figures are considered fair game, and false and defamatory statements about them that appear in the media will not constitute defamation unless the statements are made with **actual malice**.[3]

   To be made with actual malice, a statement must be made *with either knowledge of falsity or a reckless disregard of the truth*. Statements made about public figures, especially when the statements are made via a public medium, are usually related to matters of general interest. Furthermore, public figures generally have some access to a public medium for answering belittling falsehoods about themselves. For these reasons, public figures have a greater burden of proof because they must prove actual malice.

---

2. Note that the term *privileged communication* in this context is not the same as privileged communication between a professional, such as an attorney, and his or her client.
3. *New York Times Co. v. Sullivan,* 376 U.S. 254, 84 S.Ct. 710, 11 L.Ed.2d 686 (1964). See also *Tomblin v. WCHS-TV8,* 2011 WL 1789770 (4th Cir. 2011).

Invasion of the Right to Privacy

A person has a right to solitude and freedom from prying public eyes—in other words, to privacy. As discussed in Chapter 4, the Supreme Court has held that a fundamental right to privacy is implied by various amendments to the U.S. Constitution. Some state constitutions also explicitly provide for privacy rights. In addition, a number of federal and state statutes have been enacted to protect individual rights in specific areas. Tort law also safeguards these rights through the torts of *invasion of privacy*. The following four acts qualify as an invasion of privacy:

INTRUSION INTO AN INDIVIDUAL'S AFFAIRS OR SECLUSION　Invading someone's home or illegally searching someone's briefcase is an invasion of privacy. The tort has been held to extend to eavesdropping by wiretap, the unauthorized scanning of a bank account, compulsory blood testing, and peeping through windows. **EXAMPLE 6.6**　A female sports reporter for ESPN was digitally videoed through the peephole in her hotel room's door while naked. She won a lawsuit against the man who took the video and posted it on the Internet. ●

FALSE LIGHT　Publication of information that places a person in a false light is also an invasion of privacy. **EXAMPLE 6.7**　An Arkansas newspaper printed an article with the headline "Special Delivery: World's oldest newspaper carrier, 101, quits because she's pregnant!" Next to the article was a picture of a ninety-six-year-old woman who was not the subject of the article (and not pregnant). She sued the paper for false light and won. ●

PUBLIC DISCLOSURE OF PRIVATE FACTS　This type of invasion of privacy occurs when a person publicly discloses private facts about an individual that an ordinary person would find objectionable or embarrassing. A newspaper account of a private citizen's sex life or financial affairs could be an actionable invasion of privacy, even if the information revealed is true, because it should not be a matter of public concern.

Note, however, that news reports about public figures' personal lives are often not actionable because they *are* considered of legitimate public concern. For instance, when U.S. Congressman Anthony Weiner posted partially nude photos of himself on Twitter in 2011, it was of legitimate public concern. In contrast, the same inappropriate online communications by a neighbor might not be of legitimate public concern.

APPROPRIATION OF IDENTITY　In tort law, the use by one person of another person's name, likeness, or other identifying characteristics, without permission and for the benefit of the user, constitutes the tort of **appropriation.** Under the common law, using a person's name, picture, or other likeness for commercial purposes without permission is a tortious invasion of privacy.

Appropriation　In tort law, the use by one person of another person's name, likeness, or other identifying characteristic without permission and for the benefit of the user.

An individual's right to privacy normally includes the right to the exclusive use of her or his identity. **EXAMPLE 6.8**　An advertising agency asks a singer with a distinctive voice and stage presence to do a marketing campaign for a new automobile. The singer rejects the offer. If the agency then uses someone who imitates the singer's voice and dance moves in the ad, this would be actionable as an appropriation of identity. ●

Fraudulent Misrepresentation

A misrepresentation leads another to believe in a condition that is different from the condition that actually exists. This is often accomplished through a false or incorrect statement. Although persons sometimes make misrepresentations accidentally because

Fraudulent Misrepresentation Any misrepresentation, either by misstatement or by omission of a material fact, knowingly made with the intention of deceiving another and on which a reasonable person would and does rely to his or her detriment.

Puffery A salesperson's often exaggerated claims concerning the quality of property offered for sale.

they are unaware of the existing facts, the tort of **fraudulent misrepresentation,** or fraud, involves *intentional* deceit for personal gain. The tort includes several elements:

1. The misrepresentation of facts or conditions with knowledge that they are false or with reckless disregard for the truth.
2. An intent to induce another to rely on the misrepresentation.
3. Justifiable reliance by the deceived party.
4. Injuries suffered as a result of the reliance.
5. A causal connection between the misrepresentation and the injury suffered.

For fraud to occur, more than mere **puffery,** or *seller's talk,* must be involved. Fraud exists only when a person represents as a fact something she or he knows is untrue. For example, it is fraud to claim that a roof does not leak when you know it does. Facts are objectively ascertainable, whereas seller's talk is not. "I am the best accountant in town" is seller's talk. The speaker is not trying to represent something as fact because the term *best* is a subjective, not an objective, term.

Normally, the tort of misrepresentation or fraud occurs only when there is reliance on a *statement of fact.* Sometimes, however, reliance on a *statement of opinion* may involve the tort of misrepresentation if the individual making the statement of opinion has a superior knowledge of the subject matter. For instance, when a lawyer makes a statement of opinion about the law in a state in which the lawyer is licensed to practice, a court would construe reliance on such a statement to be equivalent to reliance on a statement of fact.

Wrongful Interference

Business torts involving wrongful interference are generally divided into two categories: wrongful interference with a contractual relationship and wrongful interference with a business relationship.

WRONGFUL INTERFERENCE WITH A CONTRACTUAL RELATIONSHIP Three elements are necessary for *wrongful interference with a contractual relationship* to occur:

1. A valid, enforceable contract must exist between two parties.
2. A third party must know that this contract exists.
3. The third party must *intentionally* induce a party to breach the contract.

CASE EXAMPLE 6.9 In the 1850s, opera singer Joanna Wagner was under contract to sing for a man named Lumley for a specified period of years. A man named Gye, who knew of this contract, nonetheless enticed Wagner to refuse to carry out the agreement. Wagner began to sing for Gye. Gye's action constituted a tort because it wrongfully interfered with the contractual relationship between Wagner and Lumley.[4] ●

WRONGFUL INTERFERENCE WITH A BUSINESS RELATIONSHIP Businesspersons devise countless schemes to attract customers. They are prohibited, however, from unreasonably interfering with another's business in their attempts to gain a share of the market.

There is a difference between competitive methods and predatory behavior—actions undertaken with the intention of unlawfully driving competitors completely out of the market. Attempting to attract customers in general is a legitimate business practice, whereas specifically targeting the customers of a competitor is more likely to be predatory.

---

4. *Lumley v. Gye,* 118 Eng.Rep. 749 (1853).

EXAMPLE 6.10 A shopping mall contains two athletic shoe stores: Joe's Athletics and Ultimate Sports. Joe's cannot station an employee at the entrance of Ultimate to divert customers by telling them that Joe's will beat Ultimate's prices. This type of activity constitutes the tort of wrongful interference with a business relationship, which is commonly considered to be an unfair trade practice. If this type of activity were permitted, Joe's would reap the benefits of Ultimate's advertising. ●

REMEMBER It is the intent to do an act that is important in tort law, not the motive behind the intent.

DEFENSES TO WRONGFUL INTERFERENCE A person can avoid liability for the tort of wrongful interference with a contractual or business relationship by showing that the interference was justified or permissible. Bona fide competitive behavior is a permissible interference even if it results in the breaking of a contract.

EXAMPLE 6.11 If Antonio's Meats advertises so effectively that it induces Sam's Restaurant to break its contract with DeBolt's Meat Company, Debolt's will be unable to recover against Antonio's on a wrongful interference theory. After all, the public policy that favors free competition through advertising outweighs any possible instability that such competitive activity might cause in contractual relations. ●

Although luring customers away from a competitor through aggressive marketing and advertising obviously interferes with the competitor's relationship with its customers, courts typically allow such activities in the spirit of competition. (For a discussion of Facebook's advertising campaign that alleged sweeping privacy violations by Google's social network, see this chapter's *Online Developments* feature on the facing page.)

▶ Intentional Torts against Property

Intentional torts against property include trespass to land, trespass to personal property, conversion, and disparagement of property. These torts are wrongful actions that interfere with individuals' legally recognized rights with regard to their land or personal property. The law distinguishes real property from personal property. *Real property* is land and things "permanently" attached to the land. *Personal property* consists of all other items, which are basically movable. Thus, a house and lot are real property, whereas the furniture inside a house is personal property. Cash and stocks and bonds are also personal property.

Trespass to Land

Trespass to Land The entry onto, above, or below the surface of land owned by another without the owner's permission.

A **trespass to land** occurs anytime a person, without permission, enters onto, above, or below the surface of land that is owned by another; causes anything to enter onto the land; or remains on the land or permits anything to remain on it. Actual harm to the land is not an essential element of this tort because the tort is designed to protect the right of an owner to exclusive possession of her or his property. Common types of trespass to land include walking or driving on someone else's land, shooting a gun over the land, and constructing a building so that part of it is on an adjoining landowner's property.

TRESPASS CRITERIA, RIGHTS, AND DUTIES Before a person can be a trespasser, the real property owner (or other person in actual and exclusive possession of the property) must establish that person as a trespasser. For example, "posted" trespass signs expressly establish as a trespasser a person who ignores these signs and enters onto the property. A guest in your home is not a trespasser—unless she or he has been asked to leave but refuses. Any person who enters onto your property to

ONLINE DEVELOPMENTS

Facebook Uses Privacy Concerns to "Smear" Google

With close to one billion users, Facebook is the largest social network in the world. Although Facebook has had various competitors, none has posed as much of a threat as Google. Several years ago, Google added a social networking feature called Social Circles that eventually became part of Google+. Today, Google+ has more than 100 million users and is growing faster than Facebook.

Privacy Policies Matter

For many users of social networks, privacy is a major concern. Facebook has faced a number of complaints about its privacy policy and has changed its policy several times to satisfy its critics and ward off potential government investigations. One of Google's main advertising points has been its social network's ability to keep "conversations" private and limited to as few individuals as users desire.

As the rivalry between Google and Facebook intensified, Facebook hired Burson-Marsteller, a public relations firm, to plant anonymous stories raising questions about Google's privacy policy. Although Facebook later claimed that Burson-Marsteller was only supposed to investigate how Social Circles collected and used data, several influential bloggers reported that they were approached by Burson-Marsteller and asked to publish negative stories about privacy concerns on Social Circles. In some instances, Burson-

Marsteller even offered to supply the stories—one would have claimed that Social Circles "enables people to trace their contacts' connections and profile information by crawling and scraping the sites you and your contacts use, such as Twitter, YouTube, and Facebook."

The Campaign Backfires

If Facebook's goal was to discredit Google, the plan failed dramatically. Bloggers across the Web responded with a mixture of derision and amazement. Some pointed out that planting anonymous stories violated Facebook's privacy policy for its own site, while others said that Facebook's effort to attack Google showed that the social networking giant was running scared. On *Wired*, Steven Levy concluded that "Facebook was running a smear campaign against itself."[a]

FOR CRITICAL ANALYSIS

If you were part of Google's legal team, on what basis might you think that you could sue Facebook and its public relations firm?

a. Steven Levy, "Facebook's Stealth Attack on Google Exposes Its Own Privacy Problem," *Wired*, May 12, 2011.

commit an illegal act (such as a thief entering a lumberyard at night to steal lumber) is established impliedly as a trespasser, without posted signs.

At common law, a trespasser is liable for damages caused to the property and generally cannot hold the owner liable for injuries sustained on the premises. This common law rule is being abandoned in many jurisdictions in favor of a *reasonable duty of care* rule that varies depending on the status of the parties. For instance, a landowner may have a duty to post a notice that guard dogs patrol the property. Also, under the *attractive nuisance* doctrine, children do not assume the risks of the premises if they are attracted to the property by some object, such as a swimming pool, an abandoned building, or a sand pile. Trespassers normally can be removed from the premises through the use of reasonable force without the owner's being liable for assault, battery, or false imprisonment.

DEFENSES AGAINST TRESPASS TO LAND One defense to a claim of trespass to land is to show that the trespass was warranted—for example, that the trespasser entered the property to assist someone in danger. Another defense is for the trespasser to show that he or she had a license to come onto the land. A *licensee* is one who is invited (or allowed to enter) onto the property of another for the licensee's benefit. A person who enters another's property to read an electric meter, for instance, is a licensee.

Trespass to Personal Property

Trespass to Personal Property The unlawful taking or harming of another's personal property or the interference with another's right to the exclusive possession of his or her personal property.

Whenever an individual wrongfully takes or harms the personal property of another or otherwise interferes with the lawful owner's possession of personal property, **trespass to personal property** occurs (also called *trespass to chattels* or *trespass to personalty*[5]). In this context, harm means not only destruction of the property, but also anything that diminishes its value, condition, or quality. Trespass to personal property involves intentional meddling with a possessory interest, including barring an owner's access to personal property.

EXAMPLE 6.12   Kelly takes Ryan's business law book as a practical joke and hides it so that Ryan is unable to find it for several days before the final examination. Here, Kelly has engaged in a trespass to personal property. (Kelly has also committed the tort of *conversion*.) ●

Conversion

Conversion Wrongfully taking or retaining possession of an individual's personal property and placing it in the service of another.

Whenever a person wrongfully possesses or uses the personal property of another without permission, the tort of **conversion** occurs. Any act that deprives an owner of personal property or the use of that property without that owner's permission and without just cause can be conversion.

CASE EXAMPLE 6.13   Jafar Vossoughi, an expert in applied mechanics and experimental biomechanics, taught at the University of the District of Columbia (UDC). Vossoughi set up a laboratory on campus to conduct research and continued working at the lab even after his employment contract expired. In 2000, without Vossoughi's knowledge, UDC threw away most of the lab's contents. Vossoughi sued UDC for conversion, seeking damages for the loss of his life's work. Vossoughi was awarded $1.65 million. On appeal, the court upheld this award as a reasonable estimate of the value of the property based on the time it would take Vossoughi to duplicate the work.[6] ●

THEFT AND TRESPASS   Often, when conversion occurs, a trespass to personal property also occurs. This is because the original taking of the personal property from the owner was a trespass and wrongfully retaining it is conversion. Conversion is the civil side of crimes related to theft, but it is not limited to theft. Even if the rightful owner consented to the initial taking of the property, so there was no theft or trespass, failure to return the personal property may still be conversion.

EXAMPLE 6.14   Chen borrows Mark's iPad to use while traveling home from school for the holidays. When Chen returns to school, Mark asks for his iPad back. Chen tells Mark that she gave it to her little brother for Christmas. In this situation, Mark can sue Chen for conversion, and Chen will have to either return the iPad or pay damages equal to its replacement value. ●

DEFENSES TO CONVERSION   Note that conversion can occur even if a person mistakenly believed that she or he was entitled to the goods. In other words, good intentions are not a defense against conversion. Someone who buys stolen goods, for example, can be liable for conversion even if he or she did not know that the goods were stolen. If the true owner brings a tort action against the buyer, the buyer must either return the property to the owner or pay the owner the full value of the property, despite having already paid the purchase price to the thief. A successful defense against the charge of conversion is that the purported owner does not, in fact, own the property or does not have a right to possess it that is superior to the right of the holder.

---

5. Pronounced *per*-sun-ul-tee.
6. *Trustees of University of District of Columbia v. Vossoughi*, 963 A.2d 1162 (D.C.App. 2009).

CHAPTER 6 | *Torts and Product Liability*   **137**

Disparagement of Property

Disparagement of Property
An economically injurious falsehood made about another's product or property.

Disparagement of property occurs when economically injurious falsehoods are made about another's product or property, not about another's reputation. Disparagement of property is a general term for torts specifically referred to as *slander of quality* or *slander of title*. Publication of false information about another's product, alleging that it is not what its seller claims, constitutes the tort of **slander of quality, or trade libel.** To establish trade libel, the plaintiff must prove that the improper publication caused a third party to refrain from dealing with the plaintiff and that the plaintiff sustained economic damages (such as lost profits) as a result.

Slander of Quality (Trade Libel) The publication of false information about another's product, alleging that it is not what its seller claims.

An improper publication may be both a slander of quality and defamation of character. For example, a statement that disparages the quality of a product may also, by implication, disparage the character of the person who would sell such a product.

Slander of Title The publication of a statement that denies or casts doubt on another's legal ownership of any property, causing financial loss to that property's owner.

When a publication denies or casts doubt on another's legal ownership of any property, and the property's owner suffers a financial loss as a result, the tort of **slander of title** may exist. Usually, this is an intentional tort in which someone knowingly publishes an untrue statement about property with the intent of discouraging a third party from dealing with the person slandered. For instance, a car dealer would have difficulty attracting customers after competitors published a notice that the dealer's stock consisted of stolen automobiles.

▶ Unintentional Torts (Negligence)

Negligence The failure to exercise the standard of care that a reasonable person would exercise in similar circumstances.

The tort of **negligence** occurs when someone suffers injury because of another's failure to live up to a required *duty of care*. In contrast to intentional torts, in torts involving negligence, the tortfeasor neither wishes to bring about the consequences of the act nor believes that they will occur. The actor's conduct merely creates a *risk* of such consequences. If no risk is created, there is no negligence. Moreover, the risk must be foreseeable—that is, it must be such that a reasonable person engaging in the same activity would anticipate the risk and guard against it. In determining what is reasonable conduct, courts consider the nature of the possible harm.

Many of the actions discussed earlier in the chapter in the section on intentional torts constitute negligence if the element of intent is missing. **EXAMPLE 6.15** Juan walks up to Maya and intentionally shoves her. Maya falls and breaks an arm as a result. In this situation, Juan has committed an intentional tort (assault and battery). If Juan carelessly bumps into Maya, however, and she falls and breaks an arm as a result, Juan's action will constitute negligence. In either situation, Juan has committed a tort. ●

To succeed in a negligence action, the plaintiff must prove each of the following:

LEARNING OBJECTIVE 2 **What are the four elements of negligence?**

1. *Duty*—That the defendant owed a duty of care to the plaintiff.
2. *Breach*—That the defendant breached that duty.
3. *Causation*—That the defendant's breach caused the plaintiff's injury.
4. *Damages*—That the plaintiff suffered a legally recognizable injury.

The Duty of Care and Its Breach

Duty of Care The duty of all persons, as established by tort law, to exercise a reasonable amount of care in their dealings with others.

Central to the tort of negligence is the concept of a **duty of care.** The basic principle underlying the duty of care is that people in society are free to act as they please so long as their actions do not infringe on the interests of others.

When someone fails to comply with the duty to exercise reasonable care, a potentially tortious act may have been committed. Failure to live up to a standard of care may be an act (accidentally setting fire to a building) or an omission (neglecting to put out a campfire). It may be a careless act or a carefully performed but nevertheless dangerous act that results in injury. Courts consider the nature of the act (whether it is outrageous or commonplace), the manner in which the act was performed (cautiously versus heedlessly), and the nature of the injury (whether it is serious or slight).

Reasonable Person Standard The standard of behavior expected of a hypothetical "reasonable person."

THE REASONABLE PERSON STANDARD

Tort law measures duty by the **reasonable person standard.** In determining whether a duty of care has been breached, the courts ask how a reasonable person would have acted in the same circumstances. The reasonable person standard is said to be "objective." It is not necessarily how a particular person would act. It is society's judgment on how people *should* act. If the so-called reasonable person existed, he or she would be careful, conscientious, even tempered, and honest. The courts frequently use this hypothetical reasonable person in decisions relating to other areas of law as well. That individuals are required to exercise a reasonable standard of care in their activities is a pervasive concept in business law. Many of the issues discussed in subsequent chapters have to do with this duty.

In negligence cases, the degree of care to be exercised varies, depending on the defendant's occupation or profession, her or his relationship with the plaintiff, and other factors. Generally, whether an action constitutes a breach of the duty of care is determined on a case-by-case basis. The outcome depends on how the judge (or jury, if it is a jury trial) decides a reasonable person in the position of the defendant would act in the particular circumstances of the case.

THE DUTY OF LANDOWNERS

Landowners are expected to exercise reasonable care to protect persons coming onto their property from harm. In some jurisdictions, landowners are held to owe a duty to protect even trespassers against certain risks. Landowners who rent or lease premises to tenants are expected to exercise reasonable care to ensure that the tenants and their guests are not harmed in common areas, such as stairways.

Business Invitee A person, such as a customer or a client, who is invited onto business premises by the owner of those premises.

Duty to Warn Business Invitees of Risks.

Retailers and other firms that explicitly or implicitly invite persons to come onto their premises are usually charged with a duty to exercise reasonable care to protect those persons, who are considered **business invitees. EXAMPLE 6.16** Liz enters a supermarket, slips on a wet floor, and sustains injuries as a result. The supermarket owner would be liable for damages if there was no sign warning that the floor was wet. A court would hold that the owner was negligent because he failed to exercise a reasonable degree of care in protecting the store's customers against foreseeable risks about which he knew or *should have known.* The owner should have warned Liz about the wet floor by posting a sign or setting orange cones around the wet surface. ●

The landowner also has a duty to discover and, within a reasonable amount of time, remove any hidden dangers that might injure a customer or other invitee. Store owners have a duty to protect customers from potentially slipping and injuring themselves on merchandise that has fallen off the shelves.

Obvious Risks Provide an Exception.

Some risks, of course, are so obvious that the owner need not warn of them. For instance, a business owner does not need to warn customers to open a door before attempting to walk through it. Other risks, however, may seem obvious to a business owner but may not be so in the eyes of another, such as a child. In addition, even if a risk is obvious, that does not necessarily excuse a business owner from the duty to protect its customers from foreseeable harm.

CASE EXAMPLE 6.17   Giorgio's Grill becomes a nightclub after hours. At those times, traditionally, as the manager of Giorgio's knew, the staff and customers threw paper napkins into the air as the music played. The napkins landed on the floor, but no one picked them up. One night, Jane Izquierdo went to Giorgio's. Although she had been to the club on other occasions and knew about the napkin-throwing tradition, she slipped and fell, breaking her leg. She sued Giorgio's for negligence but lost at trial because a jury found that the risk of slipping on the napkins was obvious. A state appellate court reversed, however, holding that the obviousness of a risk does not discharge a business owner's duty to its invitees to maintain the premises in a safe condition.[7] ●

> ### "A little neglect may breed great mischief."
> Benjamin Franklin, 1706–1790
> (American politician and inventor)

THE DUTY OF PROFESSIONALS   If an individual has knowledge or skill superior to that of an ordinary person, the individual's conduct must be consistent with that status. Because professionals—including physicians, dentists, architects, engineers, accountants, lawyers, and others—are required to have a certain level of knowledge and training, a higher standard of care applies. In determining whether professionals have exercised reasonable care, the law takes their training and expertise into account. Thus, an accountant's conduct is judged not by the reasonable person standard, but by the reasonable accountant standard.

If a professional violates her or his duty of care toward a client, the professional may be sued for **malpractice,** which is essentially professional negligence. For example, a patient might sue a physician for *medical malpractice.* A client might sue an attorney for *legal malpractice.*

Malpractice   Professional misconduct or the lack of the requisite degree of skill as a professional.

Causation

Another element necessary to a negligence action is *causation.* If a person fails in a duty of care and someone suffers an injury, the wrongful activity must have caused the harm for the activity to be considered a tort. In deciding whether there is causation, the court must address two questions: (1) Is there causation in fact? and (2) Was the act the proximate cause of injury?

IS THERE CAUSATION IN FACT?   Did the injury occur because of the defendant's act, or would it have occurred anyway? If an injury would not have occurred without the defendant's act, then there is causation in fact. **Causation in fact** can usually be determined by the *but for* test: "but for" the wrongful act, the injury would not have occurred. Theoretically, causation in fact is limitless. One could claim, for example, that "but for" the creation of the world, a particular injury would not have occurred. Thus, as a practical matter, the law has to establish limits, and it does so through the concept of proximate cause.

Causation in Fact   An act or omission without which an event would not have occurred.

WAS THE ACT THE PROXIMATE CAUSE OF THE INJURY?   Proximate cause, or legal cause, exists when the connection between an act and an injury is strong enough to justify imposing liability. Courts use proximate cause to limit the scope of the defendant's liability to a subset of the total number of potential plaintiffs that might have been harmed by the defendant's actions.

EXAMPLE 6.18   Ackerman carelessly leaves a campfire burning. The fire not only burns down the forest but also sets off an explosion in a nearby chemical plant that

Proximate Cause   Legal cause, which exists when the connection between an act and an injury is strong enough to justify imposing liability.

---

7. *Izquierdo v. Gyroscope, Inc.,* 946 So.2d 115 (Fla.App. 2007).

spills chemicals into a river, killing all the fish for a hundred miles downstream and ruining the economy of a tourist resort. Should Ackerman be liable to the resort owners? To the tourists whose vacations were ruined? These are questions of proximate cause that a court must decide. ●

The Injury Requirement and Damages

For a tort to have been committed, the injury the plaintiff suffered must be a *legally recognizable* injury. To recover damages (receive compensation), the plaintiff must have suffered some loss, harm, wrong, or invasion of a protected interest. Essentially, the purpose of tort law is to compensate for legally recognized injuries resulting from wrongful acts. If no legally recognizable harm or injury results from a given negligent action, there is nothing to compensate—and no tort exists.

EXAMPLE 6.19 If Mark carelessly bumps into a passerby, who stumbles and falls as a result, he may be liable in tort if the passerby is injured in the fall. If the person is unharmed, however, there normally cannot be a suit for damages because no injury was suffered. ●

Defenses to Negligence

Defendants often defend against negligence claims by asserting that the plaintiffs failed to prove the existence of one or more of the required elements for negligence. Additionally, there are three basic *affirmative* defenses in negligence cases (defenses that a defendant can use to avoid liability even if the facts are as the plaintiff state): *assumption of risk*, *superseding cause*, and *contributory and comparative negligence*.

Assumption of Risk   A plaintiff who voluntarily enters into a risky situation, knowing the risk involved, will not be allowed to recover. This is the defense of **assumption of risk.** The requirements of this defense are (1) knowledge of the risk and (2) voluntary assumption of the risk. The risk can be assumed by express agreement, or the assumption of risk can be implied by the plaintiff's knowledge of the risk and subsequent conduct. Courts do not apply the assumption of risk doctrine in emergency situations, however. Nor does this doctrine apply when a statute protects a class of people (such as employees) from harm and a member of the class is injured by the harm.

The assumption of risk defense frequently is asserted when the plaintiff is injured during recreational activities that involve known risk, such as skiing and skydiving. Note that assumption of risk can apply not only to participants in sporting events, but also to spectators and bystanders who are injured while attending those events.

In the following *Spotlight Case*, the issue was whether a spectator at a baseball game voluntarily assumed the risk of being hit by an errant ball thrown while the players were warming up before the game.

> **Assumption of Risk**   A doctrine under which a plaintiff may not recover for injuries or damage suffered from risks he or she knows of and has voluntarily assumed.

SPOTLIGHT ON THE SEATTLE MARINERS

Case 6.2   **Taylor v. Baseball Club of Seattle, LP**

Court of Appeals of Washington, 132 Wash.App. 32, 130 P.3d 835 (2006).

BACKGROUND AND FACTS   Delinda Taylor went to a Seattle Mariners baseball game at Safeco Field with her boyfriend and two minor sons. Their seats were four rows up from the field along the rightfield foul line. They arrived more than an hour before the game so they could see the players warm up and get their autographs.

When she walked in, Taylor saw that Mariners pitcher, Freddy Garcia, was throwing a ball back and forth with José Mesa right in front of their seats. As Taylor stood in front of her seat, she looked away from the field, and a ball thrown by Mesa got past Garcia and struck her in the face, causing serious injuries. Taylor sued the Mariners for the

Spotlight Case 6.2–Continued

allegedly negligent warm-up throw. The Mariners filed a motion for a summary judgment in which they argued that Taylor, a longtime Mariners fan, was familiar with baseball and the inherent risk of balls entering the stands, and therefore, she had assumed the risk of her injury. The trial court granted the motion and dismissed Taylor's case. Taylor appealed.

IN THE WORDS OF THE COURT . . .
DWYER, J. [Judge]

* * * *

* * * For many decades, courts have required baseball stadiums to screen some seats—generally those behind home plate—to provide protection to spectators who choose it.

A sport spectator's assumption of risk and a defendant sports team's duty of care are accordingly discerned under the doctrine of primary assumption of risk. * * * "Implied *primary* assumption of risk arises where a plaintiff has impliedly consented (often in advance of any negligence by defendant) to relieve defendant of a duty to plaintiff regarding specific *known* and appreciated risks." [Emphasis in original.]

* * * *

Under this implied primary assumption of risk, defendant must show that plaintiff had full subjective understanding of the specific risk, both its nature and presence, and that he or she voluntarily chose to encounter the risk.

* * * It is undisputed that the warm-up is part of the sport, that spectators such as Taylor purposely attend that portion of the event, and that the Mariners permit ticket-holders to view the warm-up.

* * * We find the fact that Taylor was injured during warm-up is not legally significant because that portion of the event is necessarily incident to the game.

* * * *

Here, there is no evidence that the circumstances leading to Taylor's injury constituted an unusual danger. It is undisputed that it is the normal, every-day practice at all levels of baseball for pitchers to warm up in the manner that led to this incident. *The risk of injuries such as Taylor's are within the normal comprehension of a spectator who is familiar with the game.* Indeed, the possibility of an errant ball entering the stands is part of the game's attraction for many spectators. [Emphasis added.]

* * * The record contains substantial evidence regarding Taylor's familiarity with the game. She attended many of her sons' baseball games, she witnessed balls entering the stands, she had watched Mariners' games both at the Kingdome and on television, and she knew that there was no screen protecting her seats, which were close to the field. In fact, as she walked to her seat she saw the players warming up and was excited about being in an unscreened area where her party might get autographs from the players and catch balls.

DECISION AND REMEDY The state intermediate appellate court affirmed the lower court's judgment. As a spectator who chose to sit in an unprotected area of seats, Taylor voluntarily undertook the risk associated with being hit by an errant baseball thrown during warm- ups before the start of the game.

WHAT IF THE FACTS WERE DIFFERENT? *Would the result in this case have been different if it had been Taylor's minor son, rather than Taylor herself, who had been struck by the ball? Should courts apply the doctrine of assumption of risk to children? Discuss.*

SUPERSEDING CAUSE An unforeseeable intervening event may break the connection between a wrongful act and an injury to another. If so, the event acts as a *superseding cause*—that is, it relieves a defendant of liability for injuries caused by the intervening event.

EXAMPLE 6.20 Derrick, while riding his bicycle, negligently hits Julie, who is walking on the sidewalk. As a result of the impact, Julie falls and hurts her hip. While she is waiting for help, a small aircraft crashes nearby and explodes, and some of the fiery debris hits her, causing her to sustain severe burns. Derrick will be liable for Julie's hip injury because the risk of hitting her with his bicycle was foreseeable. Normally, Derrick will not be liable for the burns caused by the plane crash—because the risk of a plane's crashing nearby and injuring Julie was not foreseeable. ●

CONTRIBUTORY AND COMPARATIVE NEGLIGENCE All individuals are expected to exercise a reasonable degree of care in looking out for themselves. In the past, under the common law doctrine of **contributory negligence,** a plaintiff who was also negligent (failed to exercise a reasonable degree of care) could not recover anything from the defendant. Under this rule, no matter how insignificant the plaintiff's negligence was relative to the defendant's negligence, the plaintiff was precluded from recovering any damages. Today, only a few jurisdictions still hold to this doctrine.

In most states, the doctrine of contributory negligence has been replaced by a **comparative negligence** standard. Under this standard, both the plaintiff's and the

Contributory Negligence A rule in tort law that completely bars the plaintiff from recovering any damages if the damage suffered is partly the plaintiff's own fault.

Comparative Negligence A rule in tort law that reduces the plaintiff's recovery in proportion to the plaintiff's degree of fault, rather than barring recovery completely.

defendant's negligence are computed, and the liability for damages is distributed accordingly. Some jurisdictions have adopted a "pure" form of comparative negligence that allows the plaintiff to recover, even if the extent of his or her fault is greater than that of the defendant. For example, if the plaintiff was 80 percent at fault and the defendant 20 percent at fault, the plaintiff may recover 20 percent of his or her damages.

Special Negligence Doctrines and Statutes

There are a number of special doctrines and statutes relating to negligence. We examine a few of them here.

Res Ipsa Loquitur — A doctrine under which negligence may be inferred simply because an event occurred, if it is the type of event that would not occur in the absence of negligence.

Res Ipsa Loquitur Generally, in lawsuits involving negligence, the plaintiff has the burden of proving that the defendant was negligent. In certain situations, however, under the doctrine of ***res ipsa loquitur***[8] (meaning "the facts speak for themselves"), the courts may infer that negligence has occurred. Then the burden of proof rests on the defendant—to prove she or he was *not* negligent. This doctrine is applied only when the event creating the damage or injury is one that ordinarily would occur only as a result of negligence.

CASE EXAMPLE 6.21 Mary Gubbins underwent abdominal surgery and suffered nerve damage in her spine near the area of the operation. She was unable to walk or stand for months, and even after regaining some use of her legs through physical therapy, her mobility was impaired. In her negligence lawsuit, Gubbins asserted *res ipsa loquitur,* because the injury never would have occurred in the absence of the surgeon's negligence.[9] ●

Negligence *Per Se* — An action or failure to act in violation of a statutory requirement.

Negligence Per Se Certain conduct, whether it consists of an action or a failure to act, may be treated as **negligence *per se*** (*per se* means "in or of itself"). Negligence *per se* may occur if an individual violates a statute or ordinance and thereby causes the kind of harm that the statute was intended to prevent. The statute must clearly set out what standard of conduct is expected, when and where it is expected, and of whom it is expected. The standard of conduct required by the statute is the duty that the defendant owes to the plaintiff, and a violation of the statute is the breach of that duty.

CASE EXAMPLE 6.22 A Delaware statute states that anyone "who operates a motor vehicle and who fails to give full time and attention to the operation of the vehicle" is guilty of inattentive driving. Michael Moore was cited for inattentive driving after he collided with Debra Wright's car when he backed a truck out of a parking space. Moore paid the ticket, which meant that he pleaded guilty to violating the statute. The day after the accident, Wright began having back pain, which eventually required surgery. She sued Moore for damages, alleging negligence *per se.* The Delaware Supreme Court ruled that the inattentive driving statute sets forth a sufficiently specific standard of conduct to warrant application of negligence *per se.*[10] ●

"Danger Invites Rescue" Doctrine Sometimes, a person who is trying to avoid harm—such as an individual who swerves to avoid a head-on collision with a drunk driver—ends up causing harm to another (such as a cyclist riding in the bike

8. Pronounced *rehz ihp*-suh *low*-kwuh-tuhr.
9. *Gubbins v. Hurson,* 885 A.2d 269 (D.C. 2005).
10. *Wright v. Moore,* 931 A.2d 405 (Del.Supr. 2007).

lane) as a result. In those situations, the original wrongdoer (the drunk driver in this scenario) is liable to anyone who is injured, even if the injury actually resulted from another person's attempt to escape harm. The "danger invites rescue" doctrine extends the same protection to a person who is trying to rescue another from harm—the original wrongdoer is liable for injuries to an individual attempting a rescue. The idea is that the rescuer should not be held liable for any damages because he or she did not cause the danger and because danger invites rescue.

EXAMPLE 6.23 Ludley, while driving down a street, fails to see a stop sign because he is trying to break up a squabble between his two young children in the car's back seat. Salter, on the curb near the stop sign, realizes that Ludley is about to hit a pedestrian and runs into the street to push the pedestrian out of the way. If Ludley's vehicle hits Salter instead, Ludley will be liable for Salter's injury, as well as for *any* injuries the other pedestrian sustained. • Whether rescuers injure themselves, the person rescued, or even a stranger, the original wrongdoer will still be liable.

SPECIAL NEGLIGENCE STATUTES A number of states have enacted statutes prescribing duties and responsibilities in certain circumstances. For example, most states now have what are called **Good Samaritan statutes.**[11] Under these statutes, someone who is aided voluntarily by another cannot turn around and sue the "Good Samaritan" for negligence. These laws were passed largely to protect physicians and medical personnel who voluntarily render medical services in emergency situations to those in need, such as individuals hurt in car accidents. Indeed, the California Supreme Court has interpreted the state's Good Samaritan statute to mean that a person who renders nonmedical aid is not immune from liability.[12] Thus, only medical personnel and persons rendering medical aid in emergencies are protected in California.

Many states have also passed **dram shop acts,**[13] under which a tavern owner or bartender may be held liable for injuries caused by a person who became intoxicated while drinking at the bar or who was already intoxicated when served by the bartender. Some states' statutes also impose liability on *social hosts* (persons hosting parties) for injuries caused by guests who became intoxicated at the hosts' homes. Under these statutes, it is unnecessary to prove that the tavern owner, bartender, or social host was negligent. **EXAMPLE 6.24** Jane hosts a Super Bowl party at which Raul, a minor, sneaks alcoholic drinks. Jane is potentially liable for damages resulting from Raul's drunk driving after the party. •

Strict Liability

Good Samaritan Statute A state statute stipulating that persons who provide emergency services to someone in peril cannot be sued for negligence.

Dram Shop Act A state statute that imposes liability on the owners of bars and taverns for injuries resulting from accidents caused by intoxicated persons when they contributed to the intoxication.

Strict Liability Liability regardless of fault.

LEARNING OBJECTIVE 3 What is meant by strict liability? In what circumstances is strict liability applied?

Another category of torts is called **strict liability,** or *liability without fault.* Intentional torts and torts of negligence involve acts that depart from a reasonable standard of care and cause injuries. Under the doctrine of strict liability, liability for injury is imposed for reasons other than fault. Strict liability for damages proximately caused by an abnormally dangerous or exceptional activity is one application of this doctrine. Courts apply the doctrine of strict liability in such cases because of the extreme risk of the activity. Even if blasting with dynamite is performed with all reasonable

11. These laws derive their name from the Good Samaritan story in the Bible. In the story, a traveler who had been robbed and beaten lay along the roadside, ignored by those passing by. Eventually, a man from the country of Samaria (the "Good Samaritan") stopped to render assistance to the injured person.
12. *Van Horn v. Watson,* 45 Cal.4th 322, 197 P.3d 164, 86 Cal.Rptr.3d 350 (2008).
13. Historically, a *dram* was a small unit of liquid, and distilled spirits (strong alcoholic liquor) were sold in drams. Thus, a dram shop was a place where liquor was sold in drams.

care, there is still a risk of injury. Balancing that risk against the potential for harm, it seems reasonable to ask the person engaged in the activity to pay for injuries caused by that activity. Although there is no fault, there is still responsibility because of the dangerous nature of the undertaking.

There are other applications of the strict liability principle. Persons who keep dangerous animals, for example, are strictly liable for any harm inflicted by the animals. A significant application of strict liability is in the area of *product liability* (see page 146).

▶ Cyber Torts

Torts can also be committed in the online environment. One of the most common types of **cyber torts** is online defamation, as we discuss next. We also discuss how the courts are attempting to address the problems associated with **spam**.

Online Defamation

An initial issue raised by online defamation was simply discovering who was committing it. In the real world, identifying the author of a defamatory remark generally is an easy matter, but suppose that a business firm has discovered that defamatory statements about its policies and products are being posted in an online forum. Such forums allow anyone to complain about a firm that they dislike while remaining anonymous.

IDENTIFYING THE AUTHORS   Therefore, a threshold barrier to anyone who seeks to bring an action for online defamation is discovering the identity of the person who posted the defamatory message. An Internet service provider (ISP)—a company that provides connections to the Internet—can disclose personal information about its customers only when ordered to do so by a court. Consequently, businesses and individuals are increasingly bringing lawsuits against "John Does" (fictitious names used in lawsuits when the identity of a party is not known). Then, using the authority of the courts, the plaintiffs can obtain from the ISPs the identity of the persons responsible for the defamatory messages.

LIABILITY OF INTERNET SERVICE PROVIDERS   Those who repeat or otherwise disseminate defamatory statements made by others can be held liable for defamation. Thus, newspapers, magazines, and radio and television stations can be subject to liability for defamatory content that they publish or broadcast, even though the content was prepared or created by others. Applying this rule to cyberspace, however, raises an important issue: Should ISPs be regarded as publishers and therefore be held liable for defamatory messages that are posted by their users in online forums or other arenas?

Before 1996, the courts grappled with this question. Then Congress passed the Communications Decency Act (CDA), which states that "no provider or user of an interactive computer service shall be treated as the publisher or speaker of any information provided by another information content provider."[14] Thus, under the CDA, ISPs generally are treated differently from publishers in other media and are not

Cyber Tort   A tort committed in cyberspace.

Spam   Bulk e-mails sent in large quantities without the consent of the recipients.

---
14. 47 U.S.C. Section 230.

liable for publishing defamatory statements that come from a third party.[15] Although the courts generally have construed the CDA as providing a broad shield to protect ISPs from liability for third-party content, recently some courts have started establishing some limits to CDA immunity.[16]

Spam

Businesses and individuals alike are targets of spam that floods virtual mailboxes with advertisements, solicitations, and other messages. Considered relatively harmless in the early days of the Internet, by 2013 spam accounted for roughly 75 percent of all e-mails.

STATE REGULATION OF SPAM   In an attempt to combat spam, thirty-six states have enacted laws that prohibit or regulate its use. Many state laws that regulate spam require the senders of e-mail ads to instruct the recipients on how they can "opt out" of further e-mail ads from the same sources. For instance, in some states an unsolicited e-mail ad must include a toll-free phone number or return e-mail address that the recipient can use to contact the sender to request that no more ads be e-mailed.

THE FEDERAL CAN-SPAM ACT   In 2003, Congress enacted the Controlling the Assault of Non-Solicited Pornography and Marketing (CAN-SPAM) Act. The legislation applies to any "commercial electronic mail messages" that are sent to promote a commercial product or service. Significantly, the statute preempts state antispam laws except for those provisions in state laws that prohibit false and deceptive e-mailing practices.

Generally, the act permits unsolicited commercial e-mail but prohibits certain spamming activities, including the use of a false return address and the inclusion of false, misleading, or deceptive information in e-mail. The statute also prohibits "dictionary attacks"—sending messages to randomly generated e-mail addresses—and the "harvesting" of e-mail addresses from Web sites with specialized software.

THE U.S. SAFE WEB ACT   After the CAN-SPAM Act prohibited false and deceptive e-mails originating in the United States, spamming from servers in other nations increased. These cross-border spammers generally were able to escape detection and legal sanctions because the Federal Trade Commission (FTC) lacked the authority to investigate foreign spamming.

Congress sought to rectify the situation by enacting the U.S. Safe Web Act of 2006. The act allows the FTC to cooperate and share information with foreign agencies in investigating and prosecuting those involved in Internet fraud and deception, including spamming. It also provides ISPs with a *safe harbor* (immunity from liability) for supplying information to the FTC concerning possible unfair or deceptive conduct in foreign jurisdictions.

There is some evidence that the U.S. Safe Web Act—in conjunction with the increased efforts of federal law enforcement and security experts—has been effective. The number

---

15. For a leading case on this issue, see *Zeran v. America Online, Inc.,* 129 F.3d 327 (4th Cir. 1997); *cert.* denied, 524 U.S. 937, 118 S.Ct. 2341, 141 L.Ed.2d 712 (1998). See also *Noah v. AOL Time Warner, Inc.,* 261 F.Supp.2d 532 (E.D.Va. 2003); and *Doe v. Bates,* 2006 WL 3813758 (E.D.Tex. 2006).

16. See, for example, *Fair Housing Council of San Fernando Valley v. Roommate.com, LLC,* 521 F.3d 1157 (9th Cir. 2008).

of spam messages sent appeared to have decreased somewhat between 2010 and 2011, although spam still flows at a rate of 70 billion messages per day. The Federal Bureau of Investigation has worked with dozens of ISPs to stop some of the automated spamming networks and has also been actively cooperating with other nations, leading to the arrest of several major spammers located in the Netherlands and Russia.

▶ Product Liability

Those who make, sell, or lease goods can be held liable for physical harm or property damage that those goods cause to a consumer, user, or bystander. This is called **product liability.** Product liability claims may be based on the theories of *negligence, misrepresentation,* and *strict liability.*

Negligence

If a manufacturer fails to exercise "due care" to make a product safe, a person who is injured by the product may sue the manufacturer for *negligence* (see page 137).

DUE CARE MUST BE EXERCISED   The manufacturer must exercise due care in designing the product, selecting the materials, using the appropriate production process, assembling the product, and placing adequate warnings on the label informing the user of dangers of which an ordinary person might not be aware. The duty of care also extends to the inspection and testing of any purchased products that are used in the final product sold by the manufacturer.

PRIVITY OF CONTRACT NOT REQUIRED   A product liability action based on negligence does not require *privity of contract* between the injured plaintiff and the defendant manufacturer. As will be discussed in Chapter 11, *privity of contract* refers to the relationship that exists between the promisor and the promisee of a contract. Privity is the reason that only the parties to a contract normally can enforce that contract. In the context of product liability law, privity is not required. This means that a person who was injured by a defective product need not be the one who actually purchased the product to maintain a negligence suit against the manufacturer or seller of the product.

Misrepresentation

When a user or consumer is injured as a result of a manufacturer's or seller's fraudulent misrepresentation, the basis of liability may be the tort of fraud. The intentional mislabeling of packaged cosmetics, for instance, or the intentional concealment of a product's defects would constitute fraudulent misrepresentation. The misrepresentation must concern a material fact, and the seller must have intended to induce the buyer's reliance on the misrepresentation. Misrepresentation on a label or advertisement is enough to show an intent to induce the reliance of anyone who may use the product. In addition, the buyer must have relied on the misrepresentation.

Strict Liability

Under the doctrine of strict liability (see page 143), people may be liable for the results of their acts regardless of their intentions or their exercise of reasonable care. In addition, liability does not depend on privity of contract. The law imposes strict product

Product Liability   The liability of manufacturers, sellers, and lessors of goods to consumers, users, and bystanders for injuries or damages that are caused by the goods.

RECALL   The elements of negligence include a duty of care, a breach of the duty, and an injury to the plaintiff proximately caused by the breach.

liability as a matter of public policy. This public policy rests on the following threefold assumption that:

1. Consumers should be protected against unsafe products.
2. Manufacturers and distributors should not escape liability for faulty products simply because they are not in privity of contract with the ultimate user of those products.
3. Manufacturers, sellers, and lessors of products generally are in a better position than consumers to bear the costs associated with injuries caused by their products—costs that they can ultimately pass on to all consumers in the form of higher prices.

California was the first state to impose strict product liability in tort on manufacturers. In a landmark decision, *Greenman v. Yuba Power Products, Inc.,*[17] the California Supreme Court set out the reason for applying tort law rather than contract law in cases involving consumers injured by defective products. According to the court, the "purpose of such liability is to ensure that the costs of injuries resulting from defective products are borne by the manufacturers . . . rather than by the injured persons who are powerless to protect themselves." Today, the majority of states recognize strict product liability, although some state courts limit its application to situations involving personal injuries (rather than property damage).

REQUIREMENTS FOR STRICT LIABILITY   After the *Restatement (Second) of Torts* was issued in 1964, Section 402A became a widely accepted statement of how the doctrine of strict liability should be applied to sellers of goods. The bases for an action in strict liability that are set forth in Section 402A of the *Restatement* can be summarized by the following six requirements. Depending on the jurisdiction, if these requirements are met, a manufacturer's liability to an injured party can be almost unlimited.

LEARNING OBJECTIVE 4 | **What are the elements of a cause of action in strict product liability?**

1. The product must be in a *defective condition* when the defendant sells it.
2. The defendant must normally be engaged in the *business of selling* (or otherwise distributing) that product.
3. The product must be *unreasonably dangerous* to the user or consumer because of its defective condition (in most states).
4. The plaintiff must incur *physical harm* to self or property by use or consumption of the product.
5. The defective condition must be the *proximate cause* of the injury or damage.
6. The *goods must not have been substantially changed* from the time the product was sold to the time the injury was sustained.

Proving a Defective Condition. Under these requirements, in any action against a manufacturer, seller, or lessor, the plaintiff does not have to show why or in what manner the product became defective. The plaintiff does, however, have to prove that the product was defective at the time it left the hands of the seller or lessor and that this defective condition made it "unreasonably dangerous" to the user or consumer. If the product was delivered in a safe condition and subsequent mishandling made it harmful to the user, the seller or lessor usually is not strictly liable.

Unreasonably Dangerous Products. The *Restatement* recognizes that many products cannot possibly be made entirely safe for all consumption, and thus holds sellers or lessors liable only for products that are *unreasonably* dangerous. A court may

---

17. 59 Cal.2d 57, 377 P.2d 897, 27 Cal.Rptr. 697 (1963).

Unreasonably Dangerous Product
A product that is defective to the point of threatening a consumer's health and safety.

consider a product so defective as to be an **unreasonably dangerous product** in either of the following situations:

1. The product is dangerous beyond the expectation of the ordinary consumer.
2. A less dangerous alternative was economically feasible for the manufacturer, but the manufacturer failed to produce it.

As will be discussed next, a product may be unreasonably dangerous for several reasons.

PRODUCT DEFECTS—RESTATEMENT (THIRD) OF TORTS   In 1997, the American Law Institute issued the *Restatement (Third) of Torts: Products Liability.* This *Restatement* defines the three types of product defects that have traditionally been recognized in product liability law—*manufacturing defects, design defects,* and *inadequate warnings.*

Manufacturing Defects.   According to Section 2(a) of the *Restatement (Third) of Torts: Products Liability,* a product "contains a manufacturing defect when the product departs from its intended design even though all possible care was exercised in the preparation and marketing of the product." Basically, a manufacturing defect is a departure from a product's design specifications that results in products that are physically flawed, damaged, or incorrectly assembled. A glass bottle that is made too thin and explodes in a consumer's face has a manufacturing defect.

Usually, such defects occur when a manufacturer fails to assemble, test, or adequately check the quality of a product. Liability is imposed on the manufacturer regardless of whether the manufacturer's quality control efforts were "reasonable." The idea behind holding defendants strictly liable for manufacturing defects is to encourage greater investment in product safety and stringent quality control standards. (For more information on how effective quality control procedures can help businesses reduce their potential legal liability for breached warranties and defective products, see the *Linking the Law to Management* feature on pages 152 and 153.)

Design Defects.   Unlike a product with a manufacturing defect, a product with a design defect is made in conformity with the manufacturer's design specifications, but nevertheless results in injury to the user because the design itself is flawed. The product's design creates an unreasonable risk to the user. A product "is defective in design when the foreseeable risks of harm posed by the product could have been reduced or avoided by the adoption of a reasonable alternative design by the seller or other distributor, or a predecessor in the commercial chain of distribution, and the omission of the alternative design renders the product not reasonably safe."[18]

To successfully assert a design defect, a plaintiff has to show that a reasonable alternative design was available and that the defendant's failure to adopt the alternative design rendered the product unreasonably dangerous. In other words, a manufacturer or other defendant is liable only when the harm was reasonably preventable.

Inadequate Warnings.   A product may also be deemed defective because of inadequate instructions or warnings. A product will be considered defective "when the foreseeable risks of harm posed by the product could have been reduced or avoided by the provision of reasonable instructions or warnings by the seller or other distributor, or a predecessor in the commercial chain of distribution, and the omission

---

18. *Restatement (Third) of Torts: Products Liability,* Section 2(b).

of the instructions or warnings renders the product not reasonably safe."[19] Generally, a seller must also warn consumers of the harm that can result from the *foreseeable misuse* of its product.

Important factors for a court to consider include the risks of a product, the "content and comprehensibility" and "intensity of expression" of warnings and instructions, and the "characteristics of expected user groups." Courts apply a "reasonableness" test to determine if the warnings adequately alert consumers to the product's risks. For example, children will likely respond more readily to bright, bold, simple warning labels, while educated adults might need more detailed information.

Ethical Issue

Should video game makers be required to attach labels to their games that warn parents of excessive violence? The video game industry uses a voluntary rating system that includes six age-specific labels. But California recently passed a law to make video game makers attach labels to their games that warned parents of excessive violence. When California legislated this requirement, video software dealers sued. The California act defined a violent video game as one in which "the range of options available to a player includes killing, maiming, dismembering, or sexually assaulting an image of a human being." While agreeing that some video games are unquestionably violent by everyday standards, the trial court pointed out that many video games are based on popular novels or motion pictures and have complex plot lines.

Accordingly, the court found that the definition of a violent video game was unconstitutionally vague and thus violated the First Amendment's guarantee of freedom of speech. The court also noted the existence of the voluntary rating system. The state appealed, but the U.S. Court of Appeals for the Ninth Circuit also found that the statute's definition of a violent video game was unconstitutionally broad.[20] The state appealed again.

In 2011, the United States Supreme Court affirmed the decision in favor of the video game and software industries. The Court noted that video games are entitled to First Amendment protection. Because California had failed to show that the statute was justified by a *compelling government interest* (see page 87) and that the law was narrowly tailored to serve that interest, the Court ruled that the statute was unconstitutional.[21]

In the following case, the court had to decide whether the plaintiff could pursue a theory of recovery alleging both a design defect and inadequate warnings.

---

19. *Restatement (Third) of Torts: Products Liability*, Section 2(c).
20. *Video Software Dealers Association v. Schwarzenegger*, 556 F.3d 950 (9th Cir. 2009).
21. *Brown v. Entertainment Merchants Association*, ___ U.S. ___, 131 S.Ct. 2729, 180 L.Ed.2d 708 (2011).

Case 6.3 **Johnson v. Medtronic, Inc.**

Missouri Court of Appeals, 365 S.W.3d 226 (2012).

BACKGROUND AND FACTS In 2005, Jeffrey Johnson was taken to the emergency room for an episode of atrial fibrillation, a heart rhythm disorder. Dr. David Hahn used a defibrillator manufactured by Medtronic, Inc., to deliver electric shocks to Johnson's heart. The defibrillator had synchronous and asynchronous modes, and it reverted to the asynchronous mode after each use. Dr. Hahn intended to deliver synchronized shocks, which required

him to select the synchronous mode for each shock. Unfortunately, Dr. Hahn did not read the device's instructions, which Medtronic provided both in a manual and on the device itself. As a result, he delivered a synchronized shock, followed by twelve asynchronous shocks that endangered Johnson's life. Johnson and his wife filed a product liability suit against Medtronic, asserting both that Medtronic

Case 6.3–Continues next page ➡

Case 6.3–Continued

had provided inadequate warnings about the defibrillator and that the device had a design defect. The trial court found for Medtronic under both product liability theories. Johnson appealed.

IN THE WORDS OF THE COURT . . .
James Edward WELSH, Judge.
* * * *

Jeffrey Johnson was not damaged as a result of the [defibrillator] being sold without an adequate warning, at least as described by the Johnsons. The undisputed facts established that Dr. Hahn failed to read or in any way follow the instructions * * * , and the Johnsons have not contended that the manner in which the instructions were provided failed to effectively communicate to users * * * .
* * * *

* * * We nevertheless conclude that [the Johnsons] have raised [enough evidence about] whether the [defibrillator] was * * * in a defective condition and unreasonably dangerous when put to a reasonably anticipated use and whether Dr. Hahn's actions constituted a "reasonably anticipated use" of the device.
* * * *

We recognize that Dr. Hahn's actions in this case were contrary to the instructions provided by Medtronic, both on a label on the defibrillator and in its instruction manual. However, *the fact that*

a particular use of a product is contrary to the manufacturer's instructions does not, per se, establish that the use could not be anticipated. [Emphasis added.]

The fact that we have rejected the Johnsons' failure to warn claim does not mandate a similar result as to the product defect claim. As the Missouri Supreme Court emphasized recently, "Design defect and failure to warn theories constitute distinct theories aimed at protecting consumers from dangers that arise in different ways."

In other words, in certain instances, a manufacturer may be held liable where it chooses to warn of the danger (even admittedly adequately warn) rather than preclude the danger by design.

DECISION AND REMEDY   The Missouri appellate court held that the Johnsons could not pursue a claim based on the inadequacy of Medtronic's warnings, but that they could pursue a claim alleging a design defect. The court therefore affirmed the trial court's decision in part and reversed it in part.

THE LEGAL ENVIRONMENT DIMENSION   *What could Medtronic have done to avoid possible liability to plaintiffs like the Johnsons? Was there a reasonable alternative design for the defibrillator?*

MARKET-SHARE LIABILITY   Ordinarily, in all product liability claims, a plaintiff must prove that the defective product that caused his or her injury was the product of a specific defendant. In a few situations, however, courts have dropped this requirement when plaintiffs could not prove which of many distributors of a harmful product supplied the particular product that caused the injuries.

EXAMPLE 6.25   Ken suffered from hemophilia. Because of his condition, he received injections of a blood protein known as antihemophiliac factor (AHF) concentrate. Ken later tested positive for the acquired immune deficiency syndrome (AIDS) virus. Because it was not known which manufacturer was responsible for the particular AHF he received, the court held that all of the manufacturers of AHF could be held liable under the theory of market-share liability. ●

Market-Share Liability   A theory under which liability is shared among all firms that manufactured and distributed a particular product during a certain period of time.

Under a theory of **market-share liability**, all firms that manufactured and distributed the product during the period in question are held liable for the plaintiff's injuries in proportion to the firms' respective shares of the market for that product during that period.

OTHER APPLICATIONS OF STRICT LIABILITY   Almost all courts extend the strict liability of manufacturers and other sellers to injured bystanders. **EXAMPLE 6.26**   A forklift that Trent is operating will not go into reverse, and as a result, it runs into a bystander. In this situation, the bystander can sue the manufacturer of the defective forklift under strict liability (and possibly bring a negligence action against the forklift operator as well). ●

Strict liability also applies to suppliers of component parts. **EXAMPLE 6.27**   Toyota buys brake pads from a subcontractor and puts them in Corollas without changing their composition. If those pads are defective, both the supplier of the brake pads and Toyota will be held strictly liable for the injuries caused by the defects. ●

Defenses to Product Liability

LEARNING OBJECTIVE 5 **What defenses to liability can be raised in a product liability lawsuit?**

Manufacturers, sellers, or lessors can raise several defenses to avoid liability for harms caused by their products. We look at some of these defenses in the following subsections.

ASSUMPTION OF RISK Assumption of risk can sometimes be used as a defense in a product liability action. To establish such a defense, the defendant must show that (1) the plaintiff knew and appreciated the risk created by the product defect and (2) the plaintiff voluntarily assumed the risk, even though it was unreasonable to do so.

PRODUCT MISUSE Similar to the defense of voluntary assumption of risk is that of product misuse, which occurs when a product is used for a purpose for which it was not intended. The courts have severely limited this defense, however, and it is now recognized as a defense only when the particular use was *not* reasonably foreseeable. If the misuse is foreseeable, the seller must take measures to guard against it.

COMPARATIVE NEGLIGENCE Developments in the area of comparative negligence, or fault (see page 141), have also affected the doctrine of strict liability. In the past, the plaintiff's conduct was not a defense to liability for a defective product. Today, courts in many jurisdictions consider the negligent or intentional actions of both the plaintiff and the defendant when apportioning liability and awarding damages.

Thus, a defendant may be able to limit at least some of its liability for injuries caused by its defective product if it can show that the plaintiff's misuse of the product contributed to the injuries. When proved, comparative negligence differs from other defenses in that it does not completely absolve the defendant of liability, but it can reduce the amount of damages that will be awarded to the plaintiff.

CASE EXAMPLE 6.28 Dan Smith was not wearing a hard hat at work when he was asked to start an air compressor. Because the compressor was old, he had to prop open a door to start it. When he got the engine started, the door fell from its position and hit his head, causing injury. Smith sued the manufacturer, claiming that the engine was defectively designed. The manufacturer argued that Smith had been negligent by failing to wear his hard hat and by propping the door open in an unsafe manner. Smith's attorney claimed that the plaintiff's ordinary negligence could not be used as a defense in product liability cases, but the Alaska Supreme Court disagreed. Alaska allows comparative negligence to be raised as a defense in product liability lawsuits.[22] ●

COMMONLY KNOWN DANGERS The dangers associated with certain products (such as sharp knives and guns) are so commonly known that manufacturers need not warn users of those dangers. If a defendant succeeds in convincing the court that a plaintiff's injury resulted from a commonly known danger, the defendant normally will not be liable.

CASE EXAMPLE 6.29 Marguerite Jamieson was injured when an elastic exercise rope that she had purchased slipped off her foot and struck her in the eye, causing injury. Jamieson claimed that the manufacturer, Woodward & Lothrop, should be liable because it had failed to warn users that the exercise rope might slip off a foot in such a manner. The court disagreed, stating, "Almost every physical object can be

---

22. *Smith v. Ingersoll-Rand Co.,* 14 P.3d 990 (Alaska 2000). See also *Winschel v. Brown,* 171 P.3d 142 (Alaska 2007).

inherently dangerous or potentially dangerous in a sense. . . . A manufacturer cannot manufacture a knife that will not cut . . . . The law does not require [manufacturers] to warn of such common dangers."[23] ●

———————
23. *Jamieson v. Woodward & Lothrop*, 247 F.2d 23, 101 D.C.App. 32 (1957).

▶ Reviewing . . . Torts and Product Liability

Two sisters, Darla and Irene, are partners in an import business located in a small town in Rhode Island. Irene is also campaigning to be the mayor of their town. Both sisters travel to other countries to purchase the goods they sell at their retail store. Irene buys Indonesian goods, and Darla buys goods from Africa. After a tsunami destroys many of the Indonesian towns where Irene usually purchases goods, she phones one of her contacts there and asks him to procure some items and ship them to her. He informs her that it will be impossible to buy these items now because the townspeople are being evacuated due to a water shortage. Irene is angry and tells her contact that if he cannot purchase the goods, he should just take them without paying for them after the town has been evacuated. Darla overhears her sister's instructions and is outraged. They have a falling-out, and Darla decides that she no longer wishes to be in business with her sister. Using the information presented in the chapter, answer the following questions.

1. Suppose that Darla tells several of her friends about Irene's instructing her contact to take goods without paying for them after the tsunami. If Irene files a tort action against Darla alleging slander, will her suit be successful? Why or why not?
2. Now suppose that Irene wins the election and becomes the city's mayor. Darla then writes a letter to the editor of the local newspaper disclosing Irene's misconduct. If Irene accuses Darla of committing libel, what defenses could Darla assert?
3. If Irene accepts goods shipped from Indonesia that were wrongfully obtained, has she committed an intentional tort against property? Explain.
4. Suppose now that Darla was in the store one day with an elderly customer, Betty Green, who was looking for a graduation gift for her granddaughter. When Darla went to the counter to answer the phone, Green continued to wander around the store and eventually went through an open door into the stockroom area, where she fell over some boxes on the floor and fractured her hip. Green files a negligence action against the store. Did Darla breach her duty of care? Why or why not?

▶ Debate This

Because of the often anonymous nature of the Internet, defamation has become an outdated legal concept. It is now too difficult to track down the person responsible for the defamatory statements.

Linking the Law *to Management*
Quality Control

In this chapter, you learned that manufacturing and design defects can give rise to product liability. Although it is possible to minimize liability through various defenses to product liability claims, all businesspersons know that such defenses do not necessarily fend off expensive lawsuits.

The legal issues surrounding product liability relate directly to quality control. Quality control is an important concern for every manager in all organizations. Companies that have cost-effective quality control systems produce products with fewer manufacturing and design defects. As a result, these companies incur fewer product liability lawsuits.

Three Types of Quality Control

Most management systems involve three types of quality control—(1) preventive, (2) concurrent, and (3) feedback. Preventive quality control occurs before the process begins, concurrent control takes place during the process, and feedback control occurs after it is finished.

In a typical manufacturing process, for example, preventive quality control might involve inspecting raw materials before they are put into the production process. Once the process begins, measuring and monitoring devices constantly assess quality standards as part of a concurrent quality control system. When the standards are not being met, employees correct the problem.

Once the manufacturing is completed, the products undergo a final quality inspection as part of the feedback quality control system. Of course, there are economic limits to how complete the final inspection will be. A refrigerator can be tested for an hour, a day, or a year. Management faces a trade-off. The less the refrigerator is tested, the sooner it gets to market and the faster the company receives its payment. The shorter the testing period, however, the higher the probability of a defect that will cost the manufacturer.

Total Quality Management (TQM)

Some managers attempt to reduce product liability costs by relying on a concurrent quality control system known as *total quality management* (TQM). This is an organizationwide effort to infuse quality into every activity in a company through continuous improvement. TQM techniques include the following:

- *Quality Circles*—These are groups of six to twelve employees who volunteer to meet regularly to discuss problems and how to solve them. In a continuous-stream manufacturing process, for example, a quality circle might consist of workers from different phases in the production process. Quality circles lead to changes in the production process that affect workers who are actually on the production line.
- *Benchmarking*—In benchmarking, a company continuously measures its products against those of its toughest competitors or the industry leaders in order to identify areas for improvement. In the automobile industry, benchmarking enabled several Japanese firms to overtake U.S. automakers in terms of quality. Some argue that Toyota gained worldwide market share by effectively using this type of quality control management system.
- *Six Sigma*—Motorola introduced the quality principles in the Six Sigma system in the 1980s, but Six Sigma has become a generic term for a quality control approach that takes nothing for granted. It is based on a five-step methodology: define, measure, analyze, improve, and control. Six Sigma controls emphasize discipline and a relentless attempt to achieve higher quality (and lower costs).

FOR CRITICAL ANALYSIS

Quality control leads to fewer defective products and fewer lawsuits—thus, it is important to a company's long-term financial health. At the same time, the more quality control imposed on an organization, the higher the average cost per unit that is produced and sold. How does a manager decide how much quality control to undertake?

 ## Key Terms

▶ Chapter Summary: Torts and Product Liability

TORTS AND CYBER TORTS

Intentional Torts against Persons (See pages 128–134.)	1. *Assault and battery*—An assault is an unexcused and intentional act that causes another person to be apprehensive of immediate harm. A battery is an assault that results in physical contact. 2. *False imprisonment*—The intentional confinement or restraint of another person's movement without justification. 3. *Intentional infliction of emotional distress*—An intentional act involving extreme and outrageous conduct that results in severe emotional distress to another. 4. *Defamation (libel or slander)*—A false statement of fact, not made under privilege, that is communicated to a third person and that causes damage to a person's reputation. For public figures, the plaintiff must also prove actual malice. 5. *Invasion of the right to privacy*—Wrongful intrusion into a person's private activities, publication of information that places a person in a false light, disclosure of private facts that an ordinary person would find objectionable, or the use of a person's name or likeness for commercial purposes without permission. 6. *Fraudulent misrepresentation*—A false representation made by one party, through misstatement of facts or through conduct, with the intention of deceiving another and on which the other reasonably relies to his or her detriment. 7. *Wrongful interference*—The knowing, intentional interference by a third party with an enforceable contractual relationship or an established business relationship between other parties for the purpose of advancing the economic interests of the third party.
Intentional Torts against Property (See pages 134–137.)	1. *Trespass to land*—The invasion of another's real property without consent or privilege. 2. *Trespass to personal property*—Unlawfully damaging or interfering with the owner's right to use, possess, or enjoy her or his personal property. 3. *Conversion*—Wrongfully taking personal property from its rightful owner or possessor and placing it in the service of another. 4. *Disparagement of property*—Any economically injurious falsehood that is made about another's product or property; an inclusive term for the torts of slander of quality and slander of title.
Unintentional Torts (Negligence) (See pages 137–143.)	1. *Negligence*—The careless performance of a legally required duty or the failure to perform a legally required act. Elements that must be proved are that a legal duty of care exists, that the defendant breached that duty, and that the breach caused a legally recognizable injury to another. 2. *Defenses to negligence*—The basic affirmative defenses in negligence cases are assumption of risk, superseding cause, and contributory or comparative negligence. 3. *Special negligence doctrines and statutes* include *res ipsa loquitur*, negligence *per se,* and special negligence statutes, such as Good Samaritan statutes.
Strict Liability (See pages 143–144.)	Under the doctrine of strict liability, a person may be held liable, regardless of the degree of care exercised, for damages or injuries caused by her or his product or activity.
Cyber Torts (See pages 144–146.)	General tort principles are being extended to cover cyber torts, or torts that occur in cyberspace, such as online defamation and spam.

PRODUCT LIABILITY

Liability Based on Negligence and Misrepresentation (See page 146.)	The manufacturer must use due care in designing the product, selecting materials, using the appropriate production process, assembling and testing the product, and placing adequate warnings on the label or product. Privity of contract is not required. A manufacturer is liable for failure to exercise due care to any person who sustains an injury proximately caused by a negligently made (defective) product.
Strict Product Liability Requirements (See pages 146–148.)	1. The defendant must sell the product in a defective condition. 2. The defendant must normally be engaged in the business of selling that product.

Chapter Summary: Torts and Product Liability, Continued

Strict Product Liability Requirements—Continued	3. The product must be unreasonably dangerous to the user or consumer because of its defective condition (in most states). 4. The plaintiff must incur physical harm to self or property by use or consumption of the product. 5. The defective condition must be the proximate cause of the injury or damage. 6. The goods must not have been substantially changed from the time the product was sold to the time the injury was sustained.
Product Defects (See pages 148–150.)	A product may be defective in its manufacture, its design, and in the instructions or warnings that come with it.
Other Applications of Strict Liability (See page 150.)	1. When plaintiffs cannot prove which of many distributors of a defective product supplied the particular product that caused the plaintiffs' injuries, some courts apply market-share liability. All firms that manufactured and distributed the harmful product during the period in question are then held liable for the plaintiffs' injuries in proportion to the firms' respective shares of the market. 2. Manufacturers and other sellers are liable for harms suffered by bystanders as a result of defective products. Suppliers of component parts are strictly liable for defective parts that, when incorporated into a product, cause injuries to users.
Defenses to Product Liability (See pages 151–152.)	1. *Assumption of risk*—The user or consumer knew of the risk of harm and voluntarily assumed it. 2. *Product misuse*—The user or consumer misused the product in a way unforeseeable by the manufacturer. 3. *Comparative negligence*—Liability may be distributed between the plaintiff and the defendant under the doctrine of comparative negligence if the plaintiff's misuse of the product contributed to the risk of injury. 4. *Commonly known dangers*—If a defendant succeeds in convincing the court that a plaintiff's injury resulted from a commonly known danger, such as the danger associated with using a sharp knife, the defendant will not be liable.

ExamPrep

ISSUE SPOTTERS

—Check your answers to these questions against the answers provided in Appendix D at the end of this text.

1. Jana leaves her truck's motor running while she enters a Kwik-Pik Store. The truck's transmission engages, and the vehicle crashes into a gas pump, starting a fire that spreads to a warehouse on the next block. The warehouse collapses, causing its billboard to fall and injure Lou, a bystander. Can Lou recover from Jana? Why or why not? (**See page 137.**)
2. Real Chocolate Company makes a box of candy, which it sells to Sweet Things, Inc., a distributor. Sweet sells the box to a Tasty Candy store, where Jill buys it. Jill gives it to Ken, who breaks a tooth on a stone the same size and color as a piece of the candy. If Real, Sweet, and Tasty were not negligent, can they be liable for the injury? Why or why not? (**See pages 143 and 144.**)

BEFORE THE TEST

Go to **www.cengagebrain.com**, enter the ISBN 9781133586548, and click on "Find" to locate this textbook's Web site. Then, click on "Access Now" under "Study Tools," and select Chapter 6 at the top. There, you will find a Practice Quiz that you can take to assess your mastery of the concepts in this chapter. Additionally, you will find Flashcards and a Glossary of important terms, as well as Video Questions (when assigned).

▶ For Review

Answers for the even-numbered questions in this For Review *section can be found in Appendix E at the end of this text.*

1. What is the purpose of tort law?

2. What are the four elements of negligence?

3. What is meant by strict liability? In what circumstances is strict liability applied?

4. What are the elements of a cause of action in strict product liability?

5. What defenses to liability can be raised in a product liability lawsuit?

▶ Questions and Case Problems

6–1. Liability to Business Invitees. Kim went to Ling's Market to pick up a few items for dinner. It was a stormy day, and the wind had blown water through the market's door each time it opened. As Kim entered through the door, she slipped and fell in the rainwater that had accumulated on the floor. The manager knew of the weather conditions but had not posted any sign to warn customers of the water hazard. Kim injured her back as a result of the fall and sued Ling's for damages. Can Ling's be held liable for negligence? Discuss. **(See page 138.)**

6–2. **Question with Sample Answer: Wrongful Interference.** Lothar owns a bakery. He has been trying to obtain a long-term contract with the owner of Martha's Tea Salons for some time. Lothar starts an intensive advertising campaign on radio and television and in the local newspaper. The advertising is so persuasive that Martha decides to break her contract with Harley's Bakery so that she can patronize Lothar's bakery. Is Lothar liable to Harley's Bakery for the tort of wrongful interference with a contractual relationship? Is Martha liable for this tort? Why or why not? **(See pages 133–134.)**

—**For a sample answer to Question 6–2, go to Appendix F at the end of this text.**

6–3. Product Liability. Carmen buys a television set manufactured by AKI Electronics. She is going on vacation, so she takes the set to her mother's house for her mother to use. Because the set is defective, it explodes, causing considerable damage to her mother's house. Carmen's mother sues AKI for the damage to her house. Discuss the theories under which Carmen's mother can recover from AKI. **(See page 148.)**

6–4. Defenses to Negligence. DeKeyser Express, Inc., dispatched its driver Lola Camp to transport three pallets of auto parts from Trelleborg YSH, Inc., to Mitsubishi Motors North America, Inc. Trelleborg loaded the pallets. Camp was concerned that they might shift during transport, but DeKeyser told her that she would not be liable for any damage. Camp drove to the delivery dock. When she opened the trailer door, the top pallet slipped. Trying to prevent its fall, Camp injured her shoulder and arm. She filed a suit against Trelleborg, claiming negligence. What is Trelleborg's

defense? Discuss. [*Camp v. TNT Logistics Corp.,* 553 F.3d 502 (7th Cir. 2009)] **(See pages 140–142.)**

6–5. Libel and Invasion of Privacy. *The Northwest Herald,* a newspaper, received regular e-mail reports from police departments about criminal arrests. When it received a report that Caroline Eubanks had been charged with theft, the Herald published the information. Later, the police sent an e-mail that retracted the report about Eubanks. The Herald published a correction. Eubanks filed a suit against the paper for libel and invasion of privacy. Does Eubanks have a good case for either tort? Why or why not? [*Eubanks v. Northwest Herald Newspapers,* 397 Ill.App.3d 746, 922 N.E.2d 1196 (2010)] **(See pages 130–132.)**

6–6. Business Torts of Wrongful Interference. Medtronic, Inc., is a medical technology company that competes for customers with St. Jude Medical S.C., Inc. James Hughes worked for Medtronic as a sales manager. His contract prohibited him from working for a competitor for one year after leaving Medtronic. Hughes sought a position as a sales director for St. Jude. St. Jude told Hughes that his contract with Medtronic was unenforceable and offered him a job. Hughes accepted. Medtronic filed a suit, alleging wrongful interference. Which type of interference was most likely the basis for this suit? Did it occur here? Explain. [*Medtronic, Inc. v. Hughes,* 2011 WL 134973 (Minn.App. 2011)] **(See pages 133–134.)**

6–7. 🔍 **Spotlight on AMTRAK: Proximate Cause.** Galen Stoller was killed at a railroad crossing when an AMTRAK train hit his car. The crossing was marked with a stop sign and a railroad-crossing symbol. The sign was not obstructed by vegetation, but there were no flashing lights. Galen's parents filed a lawsuit against the National Railroad Passenger Corp. (AMTRAK) and the Burlington Northern & Santa Fe Railroad Corp. The plaintiffs accused the defendants of negligence in the design and maintenance of the crossing. The defendants argued that Galen had not stopped at the stop sign. Was AMTRAK negligent? What was the proximate cause of the accident? Discuss. [*Henderson v. National Railroad Passenger Corp.,* 2011 WL 14458 (10th Cir. 2011)] **(See page 139.)**

6–8. **Case Problem with Sample Answer: Product Liability.** David Dobrovolny bought a new Ford F-350 pickup truck. A year later, the truck spontaneously caught fire in Dobrovolny's driveway. The truck was destroyed, but no other property was damaged, and no one was injured. Dobrovolny filed a suit in a Nebraska state court against Ford Motor Co. on a theory of strict product liability to recover the cost of the truck. Nebraska limits the application of strict product liability to situations involving personal injuries. Is Dobrovolny's claim likely to succeed? Why or why not? Is there another basis for liability on which he might recover? [*Dobrovolny v. Ford Motor Co.,* 281 Neb. 86, 793 N.W.2d 445 (2011)] **(See page 146.)**

—**For a sample answer to Case Problem 6–8, go to Appendix G at the end of this text.**

6–9. **In Your Court: Intentional Infliction of Emotional Distress.** While living in her home country of Egypt, Stephanie signed an employment contract with Anne, an Egyptian living in Washington, D.C. Stephanie traveled to the United States to work as a babysitter and maid in Anne's house. When Stephanie arrived, Anne confiscated her passport, held her in isolation, and forced her to work long hours under threat of having her deported. Stephanie worked seven days a week without breaks and was subjected to regular verbal and psychological abuse by Anne. Stephanie filed a complaint against Anne for intentional infliction of emotional distress. Anne argued that Stephanie's complaint should be dismissed because the allegations were insufficient to show outrageous intentional conduct that resulted in severe emotional distress. Assume that you are the judge and answer the following questions: **(See pages 129–130.)**

1. In most jurisdictions, what do courts generally use as the criteria for truly outrageous behavior.

2. In whose favor would you rule? Why?

6–10. **A Question of Ethics: Wrongful Interference.** *White Plains Coat & Apron Co. and Cintas Corp. are competitors. White Plains had five-year exclusive contracts with some of its customers. As a result of Cintas's soliciting of business, dozens of White Plains' customers breached their contracts and entered into rental agreements with Cintas. White Plains filed a suit against Cintas, alleging wrongful interference.* [White Plains Coat & Apron Co. v. Cintas Corp., 8 N.Y.3d 422, 867 N.E.2d 381 (2007)] **(See pages 133–134.)**

1. What are the two policies at odds in wrongful interference cases? When there is an existing contract, which of these interests should be accorded priority? Why?

2. Is a general interest in soliciting business for profit a sufficient defense to a claim of wrongful interference with a contractual relationship? What do you think? Why?

Chapter 7

Criminal Law and Cyber Crime

> "The crime problem is getting really serious. The other day, the Statue of Liberty had both hands up."
>
> —Jay Leno, 1950–present
> (American comedian and television host)

Contents

Learning Objectives

The five Learning Objectives below are designed to help improve your understanding of the chapter. After reading this chapter, you should be able to answer the following questions:

1. **What two elements must exist before a person can be held liable for a crime?**

2. **What are five broad categories of crimes?**

3. **What defenses can be raised to avoid liability for criminal acts?**

4. **What constitutional safeguards exist to protect persons accused of crimes?**

5. **How has the Internet expanded opportunities for identity theft?**

(OlegAlbinsky/iStockphoto.com)

Criminal law is an important part of the legal environment of business. Various sanctions—including damages for tortious conduct (see Chapter 6)—are used to bring about a society in which individuals engaging in business can compete and flourish. Additional sanctions are imposed under criminal law. Many statutes regulating business provide for criminal as well as civil sanctions.

As noted in the chapter-opening quotation above, crime is a serious problem in the United States, and some fear that the nation's economic difficulties will lead to even higher crime rates. Moreover, the government's ability to pay for prisons has declined due to the economic slowdown. Many prisons are at twice their capacity. Overcrowding became so severe in California prisons that in 2011 the United States Supreme Court ruled that conditions there violated the Eighth Amendment's prohibition against cruel and unusual punishment.[1] As a result, 46,000 inmates had to be released.

In this chapter, we look at how crimes are classified and what elements must be present for criminal liability to exist. We then examine various categories of crimes, the defenses that can be raised to avoid liability for criminal actions, and the rules of criminal procedure. Advances in technology now allow the authorities to track phone calls and vehicle movements with greater ease and precision. One such tech-

---

1. See *Brown v. Plata*, ___ U.S. ___, 131 S.Ct. 1910, 179 L.Ed.2d 969 (2011).

nique involves using GPS tracking devices to monitor certain suspects' movements, but is such use of GPS systems a violation of their constitutional rights? You will discover what the courts have to say later in this chapter. We conclude the chapter with a discussion of crimes that occur in cyberspace, often referred to as *cyber crime*.

▶ Civil Law and Criminal Law

Remember from Chapter 1 that *civil law* spells out the duties that exist between persons or between persons and their governments, excluding the duty not to commit crimes. Contract law, for example, is part of civil law. The whole body of tort law, which deals with the infringement by one person on the legally recognized rights of another, is also an area of civil law.

Criminal law, in contrast, has to do with crime. A **crime** can be defined as a wrong against society set forth in a statute and, if committed, punishable by society through fines and/or imprisonment—and, in some cases, death. Because crimes are *offenses against society as a whole,* criminals are prosecuted by a public official, such as a district attorney (D.A.), rather than by the crime victims.

Crime A wrong against society proclaimed in a statute and punishable by society through fines, imprisonment, or death.

Key Differences between Civil Law and Criminal Law

Because the state has extensive resources at its disposal when prosecuting criminal cases, there are procedural safeguards to protect the rights of defendants. We look here at one of these safeguards—the higher burden of proof that applies in a criminal case. Exhibit 7–1 below summarizes the key differences between civil law and criminal law.

In a civil case, the plaintiff usually must prove his or her case by a *preponderance of the evidence.* Under this standard, the plaintiff must convince the court that, based on the evidence presented by both parties, it is more likely than not that the plaintiff's allegation is true.

In a criminal case, in contrast, the state must prove its case **beyond a reasonable doubt.** If the jury views the evidence in the case as reasonably permitting either a guilty or a not guilty verdict, then the jury's verdict must be *not* guilty. In other words, the government (prosecutor) must prove beyond a reasonable doubt that the defendant committed every essential element of the offense with which she or he is

Beyond a Reasonable Doubt A standard of proof under which if there is any reasonable doubt that a criminal defendant committed the crime with which she or he has been charged, then the verdict must be "not guilty."

• *Exhibit 7–1* **Key Differences between Civil Law and Criminal Law**

ISSUE	CIVIL LAW	CRIMINAL LAW
Party who brings suit	The person who suffered harm.	The state.
Wrongful act	Causing harm to a person or to a person's property.	Violating a statute that prohibits some type of activity.
Burden of proof	Preponderance of the evidence.	Beyond a reasonable doubt.
Verdict	Three-fourths majority (typically).	Unanimous (almost always).
Remedy	Damages to compensate for the harm or a decree to achieve an equitable result.	Punishment (fine, imprisonment, or death).

charged. If the jurors are not convinced of the defendant's guilt beyond a reasonable doubt, they must find the defendant not guilty. Note also that in a criminal case, the jury's verdict normally must be unanimous—agreed to by all members of the jury—to convict the defendant. (In a civil trial by jury, in contrast, typically only three-fourths of the jurors need to agree.)

Civil Liability for Criminal Acts

Some torts, such as assault and battery, provide a basis for a criminal prosecution as well as a tort action. **EXAMPLE 7.1** Joe is walking down the street, minding his own business, when suddenly a passerby attacks him. In the ensuing struggle, the attacker stabs Joe several times, seriously injuring him. A police officer restrains and arrests the wrongdoer. In this situation, the attacker may be subject to both criminal prosecution by the state and a tort lawsuit brought by Joe. ●

Exhibit 7–2 below illustrates how the same act can result in both a tort action and a criminal action against the wrongdoer.

▶ Criminal Liability

LEARNING OBJECTIVE 1 **What two elements must exist before a person can be held liable for a crime?**

Two elements must exist simultaneously for a person to be convicted of a crime: (1) the performance of a prohibited act and (2) a specified state of mind or intent on the part of the actor. Additionally, to establish criminal liability, there must be a *concurrence* between the act and the intent. In other words, these two elements must occur together.

● *Exhibit 7–2* **Tort Lawsuit and Criminal Prosecution for the Same Act**

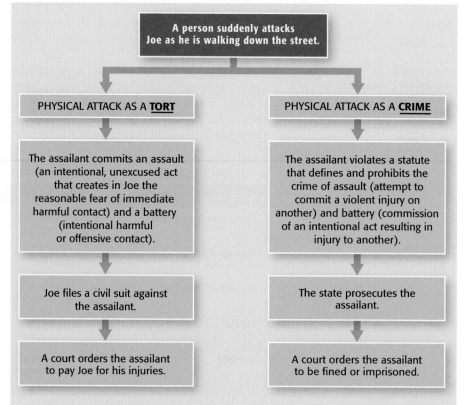

The Criminal Act and State of Mind

Every criminal statute prohibits certain behavior. Most crimes require an act of *commission,* meaning that a person must *do* something in order to be accused of a crime. In criminal law, a prohibited act is referred to as the ***actus reus,***[2] or guilty act. In some situations, an act of *omission* can be a crime, but only when a person has a legal duty to perform the omitted act, such as failing to file a tax return.

Actus Reus A guilty (prohibited) act. The commission of a prohibited act is one of the two essential elements required for criminal liability.

THE GUILTY ACT   The *guilty act* requirement is based on one of the premises of criminal law—that a person is punished for harm done to society. For a crime to exist, the guilty act must cause some harm to a person or to property. Thinking about killing someone or about stealing a car may be wrong, but the thoughts do no harm until they are translated into action. Of course, a person can be punished for attempting murder or robbery, but normally only if he or she took substantial steps toward the criminal objective.

Mens Rea Mental state, or intent. Normally, a wrongful mental state is as necessary as a wrongful act to establish criminal liability.

STATE OF MIND   A wrongful mental state, referred to as ***mens rea,***[3] generally is required to establish criminal liability. What constitutes such a mental state varies according to the wrongful action. For murder, the act is the taking of a life, and the mental state is the intent to take life. For theft, the guilty act is the taking of another person's property, and the mental state involves both the knowledge that the property belongs to another and the intent to deprive the owner of it.

Federal Laws and Overcriminalization

Criminal liability typically arises for actions that violate state criminal statutes. Federal criminal jurisdiction is normally limited to crimes that occur outside the jurisdiction of any state, crimes involving interstate commerce or communications, crimes that interfere with the operation of the federal government or its agents, and crimes directed at citizens or property located outside the United States. Federal jurisdiction also exists if a federal law or a federal government agency (such as the U.S. Environmental Protection Agency) defines a certain type of action as a crime. Today, businesspersons are subject to criminal penalties under numerous federal laws and regulations.

In recent years, an increasing number of laws and regulations have imposed criminal sanctions for strict liability crimes—that is, offenses that do not require a wrongful mental state to establish criminal liability. The federal criminal code now lists more than four thousand criminal offenses, many of which do not require a specific mental state. There are also at least ten thousand federal rules that can be enforced through criminal sanctions, and many of these rules do not require intent. Strict liability crimes are particularly common in environmental laws, laws aimed at combating illegal drugs, and other laws affecting public health, safety, and welfare.

Although proponents of such laws argue that they are necessary to protect the public and the environment, critics say the laws have led to *overcriminalization,* or the use of criminal law to solve social problems, such as illegal drug use. These critics argue that the removal of the requirement of intent, or malice, from criminal offenses increases the likelihood that people will commit crimes unknowingly—and perhaps even innocently. When an honest mistake can lead to a criminal conviction, the idea that a crime is a wrong against society is undermined.

---

2. Pronounced *ak*-tuhs *ray*-uhs.
3. Pronounced *mehns ray*-uh.

Corporate Criminal Liability

As will be discussed in Chapter 10, a *corporation* is a legal entity created under the laws of a state. At one time, it was thought that a corporation could not incur criminal liability because, although a corporation is a legal person, it can act only through its agents (corporate directors, officers, and employees). Therefore, the corporate entity itself could not "intend" to commit a crime. Over time, this view has changed. Obviously, corporations cannot be imprisoned, but they can be fined or denied certain legal privileges (such as a license).

LIABILITY OF THE CORPORATE ENTITY   Today, corporations normally are liable for the crimes committed by their agents and employees within the course and scope of their employment. For such criminal liability to be imposed, the prosecutor typically must show that the corporation could have prevented the act or that a corporate supervisor authorized or had knowledge of the act.

   CASE EXAMPLE 7.2   A prostitution ring, the Gold Club, was operating out of Economy Inn and Scottish Inn motels in West Virginia. A motel manager gave discounted rates to the prostitutes, and they paid him in cash. The corporation that owned the motels received a portion of the funds generated by the Gold Club's illegal operations. At trial, a jury found that the corporation was criminally liable because a supervisor within the corporation—the motel manager—knew of the prostitution, and the corporation allowed the practice to continue.[4] ●

LIABILITY OF CORPORATE DIRECTORS AND OFFICERS   Corporate directors and officers are personally liable for the crimes they commit, regardless of whether the crimes were committed for their personal benefit or on the corporation's behalf. Additionally, corporate directors and officers may be held liable for the actions of employees under their supervision. Under what has become known as the *responsible corporate officer doctrine,* a court may impose criminal liability on a corporate officer regardless of whether she or he participated in, directed, or even knew about a given criminal violation.

▶ Types of Crimes

LEARNING OBJECTIVE 2   **What are five broad categories of crimes?**

Federal, state, and local laws provide for the classification and punishment of hundreds of thousands of different criminal acts. Traditionally, though, crimes have been grouped into five broad categories, or types: violent crime, property crime, public order crime, white-collar crime, and organized crime.

   In addition, depending on their degree of seriousness, crimes typically are classified as felonies or misdemeanors. *Felonies* are serious crimes punishable by death or imprisonment for more than a year. Many states also define different degrees of felony offenses and vary the punishment according to the degree. *Misdemeanors* are less serious crimes, punishable by a fine or by confinement for up to a year. In most jurisdictions, *petty offenses* are considered to be a subset of misdemeanors. Petty offenses are minor violations, such as building code violations.

Violent Crime

Robbery   The act of forcefully and unlawfully taking personal property of any value from another.

Crimes against persons, because they cause others to suffer harm or death, are referred to as *violent crimes.* Murder is a violent crime. So, too, is sexual assault, or rape. **Robbery**—defined as the taking of cash, personal property, or any other article

---

4. The motel manager was sentenced to fifteen months in prison, and the corporation was ordered to forfeit the Scottish Inn property. *United States v. Singh,* 518 F.3d 236 (4th Cir. 2008).

of value from a person by means of force or fear—is another violent crime. Typically, states impose more severe penalties for *aggravated robbery*—robbery with the use of a deadly weapon.

Assault and battery, which were discussed in Chapter 6 in the context of tort law, are also classified as violent crimes. Remember that assault can involve an object or force put into motion by a person. **EXAMPLE 7.3** In 2009, on the anniversary of an abortion rights ruling, a man drove his vehicle into an abortion clinic building in Saint Paul, Minnesota. The police arrested him for aggravated assault, even though no one was injured. •

Each of these violent crimes is further classified by degree, depending on the circumstances surrounding the criminal act. These circumstances include the intent of the person who committed the crime, whether a weapon was used, and (in cases other than murder) the level of pain and suffering experienced by the victim.

Property Crime

The most common type of criminal activity is property crime—crimes in which the goal of the offender is to obtain some form of economic gain or to damage property. Robbery is a form of property crime, as well as a violent crime, because the offender seeks to gain the property of another. We look here at a number of other crimes that fall within the general category of property crime.

Burglary The unlawful entry or breaking into a building with the intent to commit a felony.

BURGLARY Traditionally, **burglary** was defined under the common law as breaking and entering the dwelling of another at night with the intent to commit a felony. Originally, the definition was aimed at protecting an individual's home and its occupants. Most state statutes have eliminated some of the requirements found in the common law definition. The time of day at which the breaking and entering occurs, for example, is usually immaterial. State statutes frequently omit the element of breaking, and some states do not require that the building be a dwelling. When a deadly weapon is used in a burglary, the person can be charged with *aggravated burglary* and punished more severely.

Larceny The wrongful taking and carrying away of another person's personal property with the intent to permanently deprive the owner of the property.

LARCENY Under the common law, the crime of **larceny** involved the unlawful taking and carrying away of someone else's personal property with the intent to permanently deprive the owner of possession. Put simply, larceny is stealing or theft. Whereas robbery involves force or fear, larceny does not. Therefore, picking pockets is larceny, not robbery. Similarly, taking company products and supplies home for personal use without authorization is larceny. (Note that a person who commits larceny generally can also be sued under tort law because the act of taking possession of another's property involves a trespass to personal property.)

Most states have expanded the definition of property that is subject to larceny statutes. Stealing computer programs may constitute larceny even though the "property" is not physical. So, too, can the theft of natural gas or Internet and television cable service.

OBTAINING GOODS BY FALSE PRETENSES It is a criminal act to obtain goods by means of false pretenses, such as buying groceries with a check knowing that you have insufficient funds to cover it or offering to sell someone the latest iPad knowing that you do not actually own the iPad. Statutes dealing with such illegal activities vary widely from state to state.

RECEIVING STOLEN GOODS   It is a crime to receive stolen goods. The recipient of such goods need not know the true identity of the owner or the thief. All that is necessary is that the recipient knows or should have known that the goods are stolen, which implies an intent to deprive the owner of those goods.

ARSON   The willful and malicious burning of a building (and, in some states, personal property) owned by another is the crime of **arson.** At common law, arson traditionally applied only to burning down another person's house. The law was designed to protect human life. Today, arson statutes have been extended to cover the destruction of any building, regardless of ownership, by fire or explosion.

Every state has a special statute that covers the act of burning a building for the purpose of collecting insurance. **EXAMPLE 7.4**   Benton owns an insured apartment building that is falling apart. If he sets fire to it himself or pays someone else to do so, he is guilty not only of arson but also of defrauding the insurer, which is attempted larceny. ● Of course, the insurer need not pay the claim when insurance fraud is proved.

FORGERY   The fraudulent making or altering of any writing (including electronic records) in a way that changes the legal rights and liabilities of another is **forgery.** **EXAMPLE 7.5**   Without authorization, Severson signs Bennett's name to the back of a check made out to Bennett and attempts to cash it. Severson has committed the crime of forgery. ● Forgery also includes changing trademarks, falsifying public records, counterfeiting, and altering a legal document.

Public Order Crime

Historically, societies have always outlawed activities that are considered to be contrary to public values and morals. Today, the most common public order crimes include public drunkenness, prostitution, gambling, and illegal drug use.

These crimes are sometimes referred to as victimless crimes because they normally harm only the offender. From a broader perspective, however, they are deemed detrimental to society as a whole because they may create an environment that gives rise to property and violent crimes. **EXAMPLE 7.6**   Clark is flying from Texas to California on a commercial airliner when he yells obscenities at a flight attendant after a beverage cart strikes his knee. Because Clark continues to be abusive and disorderly, the pilot diverts the plane and makes an unscheduled landing, and police arrest him. If Clark is subsequently found guilty of the public order crime of interfering with a flight crew, he may be sentenced to prison. ●

White-Collar Crime

Crimes that typically occur only in the business context are popularly referred to as **white-collar crimes.** Although there is no official definition of white-collar crime, the term is commonly used to mean an illegal act or series of acts committed by an individual or business entity using some nonviolent means. Usually, this kind of crime is committed in the course of a legitimate occupation. Corporate crimes fall into this category. In addition, certain property crimes, such as larceny and forgery, may also be white-collar crimes if they occur within the business context.

EMBEZZLEMENT   When a person who is entrusted with another person's funds or property fraudulently appropriates it, **embezzlement** occurs. Typically, embezzlement is carried out by an employee who steals funds. Banks are particularly prone to

Arson   The intentional burning of another's building.

Forgery   The fraudulent making or altering of any writing in a way that changes the legal rights and liabilities of another.

White-Collar Crime   Nonviolent crime committed by individuals or corporations to obtain a personal or business advantage.

Embezzlement   The fraudulent appropriation of funds or other property by a person to whom the funds or property has been entrusted.

> "It was beautiful and
> simple as all truly great
> swindles are."
>
> O. Henry, 1862–1910
> (American writer)

this problem, but embezzlement can occur in any firm. In a number of businesses, corporate officers or accountants have fraudulently converted funds for their own benefit and then "fixed" the books to cover up their crime. Embezzlement is not larceny, because the wrongdoer does not physically take the property from the possession of another, and it is not robbery, because force or fear is not used.

Embezzlement occurs whether the embezzler takes the funds directly from the victim or from a third person. If the financial officer of a large corporation pockets checks from third parties that were given to her to deposit into the corporate account, she is embezzling. Frequently, an embezzler takes a relatively small amount at one time but does so repeatedly over a long period. This might be done by underreporting income or deposits and embezzling the remaining amount, for example, or by creating fictitious persons or accounts and writing checks to them from the corporate account.

The intent to return embezzled property—or its actual return—is not a defense to the crime of embezzlement, as the following *Spotlight Case* illustrates.

SPOTLIGHT ON WHITE-COLLAR CRIME
Case 7.1 People v. Sisuphan

Court of Appeal of California, First District, 181 Cal.App.4th 800, 104 Cal.Rptr.3d 654 (2010).

BACKGROUND AND FACTS Lou Sisuphan was the director of finance at a Toyota dealership. His responsibilities included managing the financing contracts for vehicle sales and working with lenders to obtain payments. Sisuphan complained repeatedly to management about the performance and attitude of one of the finance managers, Ian McClelland. The general manager, Michael Christian, would not terminate McClelland "because he brought a lot of money into the dealership." One day, McClelland accepted $22,600 in cash and two checks totaling $7,275.51 from a customer in payment for a car. McClelland placed the cash, the checks, and a copy of the receipt in a large envelope. As he tried to drop the envelope into the safe through a mechanism at its top, the envelope became stuck. While McClelland went for assistance, Sisuphan wiggled the envelope free and kept it. On McClelland's return, Sisuphan told him that the envelope had dropped into the safe. When the payment turned up missing, Christian told all the managers he would not bring criminal charges if the payment was returned within twenty-four hours.

After the twenty-four-hour period had lapsed, Sisuphan told Christian that he had taken the envelope, and he returned the cash and checks to Christian. Sisuphan claimed that he had no intention of stealing the payment but had taken it to get McClelland fired. Christian fired Sisuphan the next day, and the district attorney later charged Sisuphan with embezzlement. After a jury trial, Sisuphan was found guilty. Sisuphan appealed, arguing that the trial court had erred by excluding evidence that he had returned the payment. The trial court had concluded that the evidence was not relevant because return of the property is not a defense to embezzlement.

IN THE WORDS OF THE COURT . . .
JENKINS, J. [Judge]
* * * *

Fraudulent intent is an essential element of embezzlement. Although restoration of the property is not a defense, evidence of repayment may

be relevant to the extent it shows that a defendant's intent at the time of the taking was not fraudulent. Such evidence is admissible "only when [a] defendant shows a relevant and probative [tending to prove] link in his subsequent actions from which it might be inferred his original intent was innocent." The question before us, therefore, is whether evidence that Sisuphan returned the money reasonably tends to prove he lacked the requisite intent at the time of the taking. [Emphasis added.]

Section 508 [of the California Penal Code], which sets out the offense of which Sisuphan was convicted, provides: "Every clerk, agent, or servant of any person who fraudulently appropriates to his own use, or secretes with a fraudulent intent to appropriate to his own use, any property of another which has come into his control or care by virtue of his employment * * * is guilty of embezzlement." Sisuphan denies he ever intended "to use the [money] to financially better himself, even temporarily" and contends the evidence he sought to introduce showed "he returned the [money] without having appropriated it to his own use in any way." He argues that this evidence negates fraudulent intent because it supports his claim that he took the money to get McClelland fired and acted "to help his company by drawing attention to the inadequacy and incompetency of an employee." We reject these contentions.

In determining whether Sisuphan's intent was fraudulent at the time of the taking, the issue is not whether he intended to spend the money, but whether he intended to use it for a purpose other than that for which the dealership entrusted it to him. *The offense of embezzlement contemplates a principal's entrustment of property to an agent for certain purposes and the agent's breach of that trust by acting outside his authority in his use of the property.* * * * Sisuphan's undisputed purpose—to get McClelland fired—was beyond the scope of his responsibility and therefore outside the trust afforded him by

Spotlight Case 7.1–Continues next page ➡

Spotlight Case 7.1—Continued

the dealership. Accordingly, even if the proffered [submitted] evidence shows he took the money for this purpose, it does not tend to prove he lacked fraudulent intent, and the trial court properly excluded this evidence. [Emphasis added.]

DECISION AND REMEDY   The California appellate court affirmed the trial court's decision. The fact that Sisuphan

had returned the payment was irrelevant. He was guilty of embezzlement.

THE LEGAL ENVIRONMENT DIMENSION   *Why was Sisuphan convicted of embezzlement instead of larceny? What is the difference between these two crimes?*

MAIL AND WIRE FRAUD   Among the most potent weapons against white-collar criminals are the federal laws that prohibit mail fraud[5] and wire fraud.[6] These laws make it a federal crime to devise any scheme that uses the U.S. mail, commercial carriers (such as FedEx), or wire (such as the telephone, television, or Internet) with the intent to defraud the public. These laws are often applied when persons send out advertisements or e-mails with the intent to obtain cash or property by false pretenses.

CASE EXAMPLE 7.7   Gabriel Sanchez and Timothy Lyons set up six charities and formed a fund-raising company, North American Acquisitions (NAA), to solicit donations on the charities' behalf through telemarketing. NAA raised more than $6 million, but the telemarketers kept 80 percent of the funds as commissions, the NAA took 10 percent, and most of the rest went to Sanchez. Lyons and Sanchez were both prosecuted for mail fraud and sentenced to fifteen years in prison.[7] •

Although most fraudulent schemes involve cheating the victim out of tangible property (funds), depriving a person of an intangible right to another's honest services can also be a crime. For a discussion of "honest-services fraud," see this chapter's *Shifting Legal Priorities for Business* feature on the facing page.

BRIBERY   The crime of bribery involves offering to give something of value to someone in an attempt to influence that person, who usually, but not always, is a public official, to act in a way that serves a private interest. Three types of bribery are considered crimes: bribery of public officials, commercial bribery, and bribery of foreign officials. As an element of the crime of bribery, intent must be present and proved. The bribe itself can be anything the recipient considers to be valuable. Realize that the *crime of bribery occurs when the bribe is offered*—it is not required that the bribe be accepted. *Accepting a bribe* is a separate crime.

Commercial bribery involves corrupt dealings between private persons or businesses. Typically, people make commercial bribes to obtain proprietary information, cover up an inferior product, or secure new business. Industrial espionage sometimes involves commercial bribes. **EXAMPLE 7.8**   Kent works at the firm of Jacoby & Meyers. He offers to pay Laurel, an employee in a competing firm, in exchange for that firm's trade secrets and price schedules. Kent has committed commercial bribery. • So-called kickbacks, or payoffs for special favors or services, are a form of commercial bribery in some situations.

THE THEFT OF TRADE SECRETS   Trade secrets constitute a form of intellectual property that can be extremely valuable for many businesses (see Chapter 8). The

---

5. The Mail Fraud Act of 1990, 18 U.S.C. Sections 1341–1342.
6. 18 U.S.C. Section 1343.
7. *United States v. Lyons,* 569 F.3d 995 (9th Cir. 2009).

SHIFTING LEGAL PRIORITIES FOR BUSINESS

Prosecuting White-Collar Crime with the Honest-Services Fraud Law

The honest-services fraud law dates back to 1988 and consists of only twenty-eight words in the *United States Code*. The law is broad enough to encompass just about every conceivable white-collar criminal act. Consequently, it has allowed federal prosecutors to impose criminal penalties on a broad swath of misconduct by private and public officials.

The key to the law is that it requires individuals to provide the "intangible right of honest services" to their employers. Critics point out that the law is used when the purported crime committed is "fuzzy." When a businessperson is charged with honest-services fraud, there is often a nagging question as to whether the actions involved were truly a crime or just aggressive business behavior.

Interestingly, criminal fraud requires that a victim be cheated out of tangible property, such as money. Honest-services fraud changes that concept. It involves depriving the victim of an intangible right to another's honest services.

How Congress Got Involved

Under the U.S. Constitution, the federal government does not have the power to punish fraud directly, but it does have the power to regulate the U.S. mails and interstate commerce. In the 1970s, federal prosecutors started using the federal laws against mail and wire fraud whenever such actions deprived someone of funds or property.

Then, a federal prosecutor used the legal theory that a fraudulent action to deprive the public of "honest services" is equivalent to a theft of intangible rights. In 1987, however, the United States Supreme Court rejected this concept of honest services.[a] Congress subsequently created a law stating that any scheme to deprive another of honest services will be considered a scheme to defraud.

The United States Supreme Court Decides

In 2010, the United States Supreme Court issued a ruling that could have a major impact on future white-collar crime and political fraud cases. The Court ruled that the honest-services fraud law could not be used against Jeffrey Skilling, who had been convicted for his role in the collapse of Enron.[b] According to the Court, honest-

a. *McNally v. United States,* 483 U.S. 350, 107 S.Ct. 2875, 97 L.Ed.2d 292 (1987).
b. *Skilling v. United States,* ___ U.S. ___, 130 S.Ct. 2896, 177 L.Ed.2d 619 (2010).

services fraud can only be applied in cases that involve bribes and kickbacks. Because there was no evidence that Skilling had solicited or accepted side payments in exchange for making misrepresentations about the company, he did not commit honest-services fraud.

The Court did not overturn Skilling's conviction, however. Instead, the Court left it up to the lower court to determine whether Skilling's conviction could be upheld on other grounds. In fact, the Court remanded numerous honest-services fraud cases for reconsideration in light of its decision.

MANAGERIAL IMPLICATIONS

Although the Court did not strike down the entire honest-services fraud law, the justices significantly narrowed its scope to prevent it from being unconstitutionally vague. Federal prosecutors can still prosecute businesspersons and owners who solicit or accept bribes or kickbacks for honest-services fraud, though. There are also many other federal and state laws that criminalize fraud and certain wrongful business conduct.

Economic Espionage Act of 1996[8] made the theft of trade secrets a federal crime. The act also made it a federal crime to buy or possess trade secrets of another person, knowing that the trade secrets were stolen or otherwise acquired without the owner's authorization.

Violations of the act can result in steep penalties. An individual who violates the act can be imprisoned for up to ten years and fined up to $500,000. If a corporation or other organization violates the act, it can be fined up to $5 million. Additionally, the law provides that any property acquired as a result of the violation is subject to criminal *forfeiture*—meaning that the government can take the property. A theft of trade secrets conducted via the Internet, for example, could result in the forfeiture of every computer or other device used to commit or facilitate the crime.

---

8. 18 U.S.C. Sections 1831–1839.

Organized Crime

As mentioned, white-collar crime takes place within the confines of the legitimate business world. *Organized crime,* in contrast, operates *illegitimately* by, among other things, providing illegal goods and services. For organized crime, the traditional preferred markets are gambling, prostitution, illegal narcotics, and loan sharking (lending at higher than legal interest rates), along with counterfeiting and credit-card scams.

MONEY LAUNDERING   The profits from organized crime and illegal activities amount to billions of dollars a year, particularly the profits from illegal drug transactions and, to a lesser extent, from racketeering, prostitution, and gambling. Under federal law, banks, savings and loan associations, and other financial institutions are required to report currency transactions involving more than $10,000. Consequently, those who engage in illegal activities face difficulties in depositing their cash profits from illegal transactions.

   As an alternative to simply storing cash from illegal transactions in a safe-deposit box, wrongdoers and racketeers have invented ways to launder "dirty" money through legitimate businesses to make it "clean." **Money laundering** is engaging in financial transactions to conceal the identity, source, or destination of illegally gained funds.

   EXAMPLE 7.9   Harris, a successful drug dealer, becomes a partner with a restaurateur. Little by little, the restaurant shows increasing profits. As a partner in the restaurant, Harris is able to report the "profits" of the restaurant as legitimate income on which he pays federal and state taxes. He can then spend those funds without worrying that his lifestyle may exceed the level possible with his reported income. •

THE RACKETEER INFLUENCED AND CORRUPT ORGANIZATIONS ACT   In 1970, in an effort to curb the apparently increasing entry of organized crime into the legitimate business world, Congress passed the Racketeer Influenced and Corrupt Organizations (RICO) Act.[9] The statute, which was enacted as part of the Organized Crime Control Act, makes it a federal crime to do the following:

1. Use income obtained from racketeering activity to purchase any interest in an enterprise.
2. Acquire or maintain an interest in an enterprise through racketeering activity.
3. Conduct or participate in the affairs of an enterprise through racketeering activity.
4. Conspire to do any of the preceding activities.

Broad Application of RICO.   The broad language of RICO has allowed it to be applied in cases that have little or nothing to do with organized crime. RICO incorporates by reference twenty-six separate types of federal crimes and nine types of state felonies and declares that if a person commits two of these offenses, he or she is guilty of "racketeering activity." Under the criminal provisions of RICO, any individual found guilty is subject to a fine of up to $25,000 per violation, imprisonment for up to twenty years, or both. Additionally, the statute provides that those who violate RICO may be required to forfeit (give up) any assets, in the form of property or cash, that were acquired as a result of the illegal activity or that were "involved in" or an "instrumentality of" the activity.

Penalties.   In the event of a RICO violation, the government can seek civil penalties, such as the divestiture of a defendant's interest in a business (called forfeiture)

Money Laundering   Engaging in financial transactions to conceal the identity, source, or destination of illegally gained funds.

---

9. 18 U.S.C. Sections 1961–1968.

or the dissolution of the business. Moreover, in some cases, the statute allows private individuals to sue violators and potentially to recover three times their actual losses (treble damages), plus attorneys' fees, for business injuries caused by a violation of the statute. This is perhaps the most controversial aspect of RICO and one that continues to cause debate in the nation's federal courts. The prospect of receiving treble damages in civil RICO lawsuits has given plaintiffs a financial incentive to pursue businesses and employers for violations.

▶ Defenses to Criminal Liability

Persons charged with crimes may be relieved of criminal liability if they can show that their criminal actions were justified under the circumstances. In certain circumstances, the law may also allow a person to be excused from criminal liability because she or he lacks the required mental state. We look at several of the defenses to criminal liability here.

Note that procedural violations, such as obtaining evidence without a valid search warrant, may also operate as defenses. As you will read later in this chapter, evidence obtained in violation of a defendant's constitutional rights normally may not be admitted in court. If the evidence is suppressed, then there may be no basis for prosecuting the defendant.

LEARNING OBJECTIVE 3 **What defenses can be raised to avoid liability for criminal acts?**

Justifiable Use of Force

Self-Defense The legally recognized privilege to protect oneself or one's property against injury by another.

Probably the best-known defense to criminal liability is **self-defense.** Other situations, however, also justify the use of force: the defense of one's dwelling, the defense of other property, and the prevention of a crime. In all of these situations, it is important to distinguish between deadly and nondeadly force. *Deadly force* is likely to result in death or serious bodily harm. *Nondeadly force* is force that reasonably appears necessary to prevent the imminent use of criminal force.

Generally speaking, people can use the amount of nondeadly force that seems necessary to protect themselves, their dwellings, or other property or to prevent the commission of a crime. Deadly force can be used in self-defense if the defender *reasonably believes* that imminent death or grievous bodily harm will otherwise result, if the attacker is using unlawful force (an example of lawful force is that exerted by a police officer), and if the defender has not initiated or provoked the attack. Deadly force normally can be used to defend a dwelling only if the unlawful entry is violent and the person believes deadly force is necessary to prevent imminent death or great bodily harm. In some jurisdictions, however, deadly force can also be used if the person believes it is necessary to prevent the commission of a felony in the dwelling.

Necessity

Sometimes, criminal defendants can be relieved of liability by showing that a criminal act was necessary to prevent an even greater harm. **EXAMPLE 7.10** Trevor is a convicted felon and, as such, is legally prohibited from possessing a firearm. While he and his wife are in a convenience store, a man draws a gun, points it at the cashier, and asks for all the cash. Afraid that the man will start shooting, Trevor grabs the gun and holds onto it until police arrive. In this situation, if Trevor is charged with possession of a firearm, he can assert the defense of necessity. ●

Insanity

A person who suffers from a mental illness may be incapable of the state of mind required to commit a crime. Thus, insanity can be a defense to a criminal charge. Note that an insanity defense does not allow a person to avoid prison. It simply means that if the defendant successfully proves insanity, she or he will be placed in a mental institution.

The courts have had difficulty deciding what the test for legal insanity should be, and psychiatrists as well as lawyers are critical of the tests used. Almost all federal courts and some states use the relatively liberal substantial capacity test set forth in the Model Penal Code:

> A person is not responsible for criminal conduct if at the time of such conduct as a result of mental disease or defect he or she lacks substantial capacity either to appreciate the wrongfulness of his [or her] conduct or to conform his [or her] conduct to the requirements of the law.

Some states use the *M'Naghten* test,[10] under which a criminal defendant is not responsible if, at the time of the offense, he or she did not know the nature and quality of the act or did not know that the act was wrong. Other states use the irresistible-impulse test. A person operating under an irresistible impulse may know an act is wrong but cannot refrain from doing it. Under any of these tests, proving insanity is extremely difficult. For this reason, the insanity defense is rarely used and usually is not successful.

Mistake

Everyone has heard the saying "Ignorance of the law is no excuse." Ordinarily, ignorance of the law or a mistaken idea about what the law requires is not a valid defense. A *mistake of fact,* as opposed to a *mistake of law,* can excuse criminal responsibility if it negates the mental state necessary to commit a crime. **EXAMPLE 7.11** If Oliver Wheaton mistakenly walks off with Julie Tyson's briefcase because he thinks it is his, there is no crime. Theft requires knowledge that the property belongs to another. (If Wheaton's act causes Tyson to incur damages, however, she may sue him in a civil action for trespass to personal property or conversion—torts that were discussed in Chapter 6.) •

Duress

Duress Unlawful pressure brought to bear on a person, causing the person to perform an act that she or he would not otherwise have performed.

Duress exists when the *wrongful threat* of one person induces another person to perform an act that she or he would not otherwise have performed. In such a situation, duress is said to negate the mental state necessary to commit a crime because the defendant was forced or compelled to commit the act.

Duress can be used as a defense to most crimes except murder. The states vary in how duress is defined and what types of crimes it can excuse, however. Generally, to successfully assert duress as a defense, the defendant must reasonably believe in the immediate danger, and the jury (or judge) must conclude that the defendant's belief was reasonable.

Entrapment

Entrapment A defense in which the defendant claims that he or she was induced by a public official—usually undercover—to commit a crime that he or she would not otherwise have committed.

Entrapment is a defense designed to prevent police officers or other government agents from enticing persons to commit crimes in order to later prosecute them for those crimes. In the typical entrapment case, an undercover agent *suggests* that a

---

10. A rule derived from *M'Naghten's Case,* 8 Eng.Rep. 718 (1843).

crime be committed and somehow pressures or induces an individual to commit it. The agent then arrests the individual for the crime.

For entrapment to succeed as a defense, both the suggestion and the inducement must take place. The defense is intended not to prevent law enforcement agents from setting a trap for an unwary criminal but rather to prevent them from pushing the individual into it. The crucial issue is whether the person who committed a crime was predisposed to commit the illegal act or did so because the agent induced it.

Statute of Limitations

With some exceptions, such as for the crime of murder, statutes of limitations apply to crimes just as they do to civil wrongs. In other words, the state must initiate criminal prosecution within a certain number of years. If a criminal action is brought after the statutory time period has expired, the accused person can raise the statute of limitations as a defense.

Immunity

Accused persons are understandably reluctant to give information if it will be used to prosecute them, and they cannot be forced to do so. The privilege against *self-incrimination* is guaranteed by the Fifth Amendment to the U.S. Constitution, which reads, in part, "nor shall [any person] be compelled in any criminal case to be a witness against himself." When the state wishes to obtain information from a person accused of a crime, the state can grant *immunity* from prosecution or agree to prosecute for a less serious offense in exchange for the information. Once immunity is given, the person can no longer refuse to testify on Fifth Amendment grounds because he or she now has an absolute privilege against self-incrimination.

Often, a grant of immunity from prosecution for a serious crime is part of the **plea bargaining** between the defendant and the prosecuting attorney. The defendant may be convicted of a lesser offense, while the state uses the defendant's testimony to prosecute accomplices for serious crimes carrying heavy penalties.

Plea Bargaining The process by which a defendant and the prosecutor in a criminal case work out a mutually satisfactory disposition, subject to court approval.

▶ Constitutional Safeguards and Criminal Procedures

Criminal law brings the power of the state, with all its resources, to bear against the individual. Criminal procedures are designed to protect the constitutional rights of individuals and to prevent the arbitrary use of power on the part of the government.

The U.S. Constitution provides specific safeguards for those accused of crimes, as mentioned in Chapter 4. Most of these safeguards protect individuals against state government actions, as well as federal government actions, by virtue of the due process clause of the Fourteenth Amendment. These protections are set forth in the Fourth, Fifth, Sixth, and Eighth Amendments.

LEARNING OBJECTIVE 4 What constitutional safeguards exist to protect persons accused of crimes?

Fourth Amendment Protections

The Fourth Amendment protects the "right of the people to be secure in their persons, houses, papers, and effects." Before searching or seizing private property, law enforcement officers must obtain a **search warrant**—an order from a judge or other public official authorizing the search or seizure.

Search Warrant An order granted by a public authority, such as a judge, that authorizes law enforcement personnel to search particular premises or property.

Ethical Issue ⚖️

Should the police be able to use high-tech tracking devices at will? New and emerging technologies are available for surveillance. In particular, a Global Positioning System (GPS) tracker can easily be attached to a suspect's car that is parked in a public location. Does such an action constitute an unreasonable search in violation of the Fourth Amendment? According to the United States Supreme Court, it does. In *United States v. Jones,*[11] a unanimous Court pointed out the real issue is that the government "physically occupied private property [the car] for the purpose of obtaining information. We have no doubt that such physical intrusion would have been considered a 'search' within the meaning of the Fourth Amendment when it was adopted." Attaching a GPS tracker to a car is no different than entering a person's home to make a search. Both require search warrants.

Undoubtedly, there will be continued debate about how much technology can legally be used to track people's movements. How much surveillance should society accept? Should the most recent Supreme Court decision also apply to cell phones, e-mail, and other digital documents? For instance, the Federal Bureau of Investigation and local police departments routinely engage in secret cell phone tracking by using devices known as Stingrays. Using the reasoning in the *Jones* case, this technology will probably be subject to the Court's ruling.

Probable Cause   Reasonable grounds for believing that a person should be arrested or searched.

To obtain a search warrant, law enforcement officers must convince a judge that they have reasonable grounds, or **probable cause**, to believe a search will reveal a specific illegality. Probable cause requires the officers to have trustworthy evidence that would convince a reasonable person that the proposed search or seizure is more likely justified than not. Furthermore, the Fourth Amendment prohibits general warrants. It requires a particular description of what is to be searched or seized. General searches through a person's belongings are impermissible. The search cannot extend beyond what is described in the warrant. Although search warrants require specificity, if a search warrant is issued for a person's residence, items that are in that residence may be searched even if they do not belong to that individual.

In the following case, police officers obtained a search warrant and conducted a search for weapons in the home of a suspect's foster mother. A judge later ruled that the warrant was not supported by probable cause, and the homeowners sued individual police officers for executing an illegal search warrant.

---

11. ___ U.S. ___, 132 S.Ct. 945, 181 LEd.2d 911 (2012). This case was presented in Exhibit 1A–3 on pages 27–29.

Case 7.2   **Messerschmidt v. Millender**

Supreme Court of the United States, ___ U.S. ___, 132 S.Ct. 1235, 182 L.Ed.2d 47 (2012).

BACKGROUND AND FACTS   The Los Angeles County Sheriff's Department was protecting a woman from a man named Jerry Ray Bowen, when he tried to kill her with a sawed-off shotgun. The woman told the police that she and Bowen used to date, that Bowen was a gang member, and that she thought Bowen was staying at the home of Augusta Millender, his foster mother. After investigating the incident further, the police, including Curt Messerschmidt, prepared a warrant to search the home for all guns and gang-related material, and a magistrate approved it. When

the police served the search warrant, they discovered that Bowen was not at the home but searched it anyway. Millender and others sued individual police officers in federal court for subjecting them to an illegal search. A federal appellate court held that the police had lacked probable cause for such a broad search and that they could be held personally liable. Messerschmidt and the other police officers appealed. The United States Supreme Court granted *certiorari* to determine whether the police officers were immune from personal liability.

Case 7.2–Continued

IN THE WORDS OF THE COURT . . .
Chief Justice ROBERTS delivered the opinion of the Court.
* * * *

The validity of the warrant is not before us. The question instead is whether Messerschmidt and [the other officers] are entitled to immunity from damages, even assuming that the warrant should not have been issued.

"The doctrine of qualified immunity protects government officials 'from liability for civil damages insofar as their conduct does not violate clearly established statutory or constitutional rights of which a reasonable person would have known.'" * * * "Whether an official protected by qualified immunity may be held personally liable for an allegedly unlawful official action generally turns on the 'objective legal reasonableness' of the action * * *."

Where the alleged Fourth Amendment violation involves a search or seizure pursuant to a warrant, the fact that a neutral magistrate has issued a warrant is the clearest indication that the officers acted in an objectively reasonable manner * * *. "Nonetheless, * * * we have recognized an exception allowing suit when 'it is obvious that no

reasonably competent officer would have concluded that a warrant should issue.'" [Emphasis added.]

Our precedents make clear, however, that the threshold for establishing this exception is a high one, and it should be. * * * As we explained in [another case], "in the ordinary case, an officer cannot be expected to question the magistrate's probable-cause determination" because "it is the magistrate's responsibility to determine whether the officer's allegations establish probable cause and, if so, to issue a warrant comporting in form with the requirements of the Fourth Amendment."

DECISION AND REMEDY   The United States Supreme Court reversed the decision of the federal appellate court. It held that Messerschmidt and the other police officers were immune from personal liability.

THE LEGAL ENVIRONMENT DIMENSION   *How would police officers behave if they could always be held personally liable for executing unconstitutional warrants? Would they be more or less inclined to apply for and execute search warrants? Explain.*

Fifth Amendment Protections

The Fifth Amendment offers significant protections for accused persons. One is the guarantee that no one can be deprived of "life, liberty, or property without due process of law." Two other important Fifth Amendment provisions protect persons against double jeopardy and self-incrimination.

DUE PROCESS OF LAW   *Due process of law* has both procedural and substantive aspects. Procedural due process requirements underlie criminal procedures. The law must be carried out in a fair and orderly way. In criminal cases, due process means that defendants should have an opportunity to object to the charges against them before a fair, neutral decision maker, such as a judge. Defendants must also be given the opportunity to confront and cross-examine witnesses and accusers and to present their own witnesses.

Double Jeopardy   A situation occurring when a person is tried twice for the same criminal offense.

DOUBLE JEOPARDY   The Fifth Amendment also protects persons from **double jeopardy**—that is, being tried twice for the same criminal offense. The prohibition against double jeopardy means that once a criminal defendant is acquitted (found not guilty) of a particular crime, the government may not retry him or her for the same crime.

The prohibition against double jeopardy does not preclude the crime victim from bringing a civil suit against that same defendant to recover damages, however. In other words, a person found "not guilty" of assault and battery in a state criminal case can be sued for damages by the victim in a civil tort case.

Additionally, a state's prosecution of a crime will not prevent a separate federal prosecution relating to the same activity (and vice versa), provided the activity can be classified as a different crime. **CASE EXAMPLE 7.12**   Professional football player Michael Vick was convicted in federal court for operating a dogfighting ring and sentenced to serve twenty-three months in federal prison. A year later, the state where the crime took place, Virginia, filed its own charges against Vick for dogfighting. He pleaded guilty to those charges and received a *suspended sentence* (meaning that the judge reserved the option of imposing a sentence later if circumstances, such as future violations, warranted it).[12] ●

SELF-INCRIMINATION   As explained earlier, the Fifth Amendment grants a privilege against **self-incrimination**. Thus, in any criminal proceeding, an accused person cannot be compelled to give testimony that might subject her or him to any criminal prosecution.

The Fifth Amendment's guarantee against self-incrimination extends only to natural persons. Because a corporation is a legal entity and not a natural person, the privilege against self-incrimination does not apply to it. Similarly, the business records of a partnership do not receive Fifth Amendment protection. When a partnership is required to produce these records, it must do so even if the information incriminates the persons who constitute the business entity. Normally, sole proprietors—those who fully own their businesses and are unincorporated—cannot be compelled to produce their business records. These individuals have full protection against self-incrimination because there is no separate business entity (see Chapter 10 for more on the different types of business formation).

Protections under the Sixth and Eighth Amendments

The Sixth Amendment guarantees several important rights for criminal defendants: the right to a speedy trial, the right to a jury trial, the right to a public trial, the right to confront witnesses, and the right to counsel. The Sixth Amendment right to counsel is one of the rights of which a suspect must be advised when he or she is arrested. In many cases, a statement that a criminal suspect makes in the absence of counsel is not admissible at trial unless the suspect has knowingly and voluntarily waived this right.

The Eighth Amendment prohibits excessive bail and fines, as well as cruel and unusual punishment. Under this amendment, prison officials are required to provide humane conditions of confinement, including adequate food, clothing, shelter, and medical care. If a prisoner has a serious medical problem, for instance, and a correctional officer is deliberately indifferent to it, a court could find that the prisoner's Eighth Amendment rights were violated. Critics of the death penalty claim that it constitutes cruel and unusual punishment.[13]

The Exclusionary Rule and the *Miranda* Rule

Two other procedural protections for criminal defendants are the exclusionary rule and the *Miranda* rule.

THE EXCLUSIONARY RULE   Under what is known as the **exclusionary rule**, all evidence obtained in violation of the constitutional rights spelled out in the Fourth, Fifth, and Sixth Amendments, as well as all evidence derived from illegally obtained evidence, normally must be excluded from the trial. Evidence derived from illegally obtained evidence is known as the "fruit of the poisonous tree." For example, if a confession is obtained after an illegal arrest, the arrest is "the poisonous tree," and the confession, if "tainted" by the arrest, is the "fruit."

Self-Incrimination   The giving of testimony that may subject the testifier to criminal prosecution.

Exclusionary Rule   In criminal procedure, a rule under which any evidence that is obtained in violation of the accused's rights guaranteed by the Fourth, Fifth, and Sixth Amendments to the U.S. Constitution, as well as any evidence derived from illegally obtained evidence, will not be admissible in court.

---

12. See *United States v. Kizeart*, 2010 WL 3768023 (S.D.Ill. 2010).
13. For an example of a case challenging the constitutionality of the death penalty, see *Baze v. Rees*, 553 U.S. 35, 128 S.Ct. 1520, 170 L.Ed.2d 420 (2008).

The purpose of the exclusionary rule is to deter police from conducting warrant-less searches and engaging in other misconduct. The rule is sometimes criticized because it can lead to injustice. Many a defendant has "gotten off on a technicality" because law enforcement personnel failed to observe procedural requirements. Even though a defendant may be obviously guilty, if the evidence of that guilt was obtained improperly (without a valid search warrant, for example), it normally cannot be used against the defendant in court.

> **REMEMBER** Once a suspect has been informed of his or her rights, anything that person says can be used as evidence in a trial.

THE *MIRANDA* RULE   In *Miranda v. Arizona*,[14] a case decided in 1966, the United States Supreme Court established the rule that individuals who are arrested must be informed of certain constitutional rights, including their Fifth Amendment right to remain silent and their Sixth Amendment right to counsel. If the arresting officers fail to inform a criminal suspect of these constitutional rights, any statements the suspect makes normally will not be admissible in court.

Over time, as part of a continuing attempt to balance the rights of accused persons against the rights of society, the United States Supreme Court has carved out numerous exceptions to the *Miranda* rule. For example, the Court has recognized a "public safety" exception, holding that certain statements—such as statements concerning the location of a weapon—are admissible even if the defendant was not given *Miranda* warnings. Additionally, a suspect must unequivocally and assertively request to exercise his or her right to counsel in order to stop police questioning. Saying "Maybe I should talk to a lawyer" during an interrogation after being taken into custody is not enough. Police officers are not required to decipher the suspect's intentions in such situations.

▶ The Criminal Process

As mentioned, a criminal prosecution differs significantly from a civil case in several respects. These differences reflect the desire to safeguard the rights of the individual against the state. Here, we discuss three phases of the criminal process—arrest, indictment or information, and trial—in more detail. We conclude with a discussion of sentencing guidelines.

The Arrest

Before a warrant for arrest can be issued, there must be probable cause to believe that the individual in question has committed a crime. As discussed earlier, *probable cause* can be defined as a substantial likelihood that the person has committed or is about to commit a crime. Note that probable cause involves a likelihood, not just a possibility. Arrests can be made without a warrant if there is no time to get one, but the action of the arresting officer is still judged by the standard of probable cause.

The Indictment or Information

> **Indictment** A charge by a grand jury that a named person has committed a crime.
>
> **Grand Jury** A group of citizens called to decide, after hearing the state's evidence, whether a reasonable basis exists for believing that a crime has been committed and that a trial ought to be held.

Individuals must be formally charged with having committed specific crimes before they can be brought to trial. If issued by a grand jury, this charge is called an **indictment**.[15] A **grand jury** usually consists of more jurors than the ordinary trial jury. A grand jury does not determine the guilt or innocence of an accused party. Rather, its function is to hear the state's evidence and to determine whether a

---

14. 384 U.S. 436, 86 S.Ct. 1602, 16 L.Ed.2d 694 (1966).

15. Pronounced in-*dyte*-ment.

reasonable basis (probable cause) exists for believing that a crime has been committed and that a trial ought to be held.

Usually, grand juries are used in cases involving serious crimes, such as murder. For lesser crimes, an individual may be formally charged with a crime by what is called an **information,** or criminal complaint. An information will be issued by a government prosecutor if the prosecutor determines that there is sufficient evidence to justify bringing the individual to trial.

The Trial

At a criminal trial, the accused person does not have to prove anything. The entire burden of proof is on the prosecutor (the state). As mentioned earlier, the prosecution must show that, based on all the evidence presented, the defendant's guilt is established *beyond a reasonable doubt.* If there is a reasonable doubt as to whether a criminal defendant committed the crime with which she or he has been charged, then the verdict must be "not guilty."

Note that giving a verdict of "not guilty" is not the same as stating that the defendant is innocent. It merely means that not enough evidence was properly presented to the court to prove guilt beyond a reasonable doubt. Courts have complex rules about what types of evidence may be presented and how the evidence may be brought out in criminal cases. These rules are designed to ensure that evidence in trials is relevant, reliable, and not prejudicial toward the defendant.

Sentencing Guidelines

In 1984, Congress passed the Sentencing Reform Act. This act created the U.S. Sentencing Commission, which was charged with the task of standardizing sentences for federal crimes. The commission's guidelines establish a range of possible penalties for each federal crime and require the judge to select a sentence from within that range.

In other words, the guidelines originally established a mandatory system because judges were not allowed to deviate from the specified sentencing range. Some federal judges felt uneasy about imposing long prison sentences on certain criminal defendants, particularly first-time offenders and those convicted of offenses involving small quantities of illegal drugs.[16]

PROBLEMS WITH CONSTITUTIONALITY   In 2005, the United States Supreme Court held that certain provisions of the federal sentencing guidelines were unconstitutional. **CASE EXAMPLE 7.13** Freddie Booker was arrested with 92.5 grams of crack cocaine in his possession. Booker admitted to police that he had sold an additional 566 grams of crack cocaine, but he was never charged with, or tried for, possessing this additional quantity. Nevertheless, under the federal sentencing guidelines the judge was required to sentence Booker to twenty-two years in prison. The Court ruled that this sentence was unconstitutional because a jury did not find beyond a reasonable doubt that Booker had possessed the additional 566 grams of crack.[17] ●

CURRENT USES   Essentially, the Court's ruling changed the federal sentencing guidelines from mandatory to advisory. Depending on the circumstances of the case,

Information A formal accusation or complaint (without an indictment) issued in certain types of actions (usually criminal actions involving lesser crimes) by a government prosecutor.

"In school, every period ends with a bell. Every sentence ends with a period. Every crime ends with a sentence."
Steven Wright, 1955–present
(American comedian)

---
16. See, for example, *United States v. Angelos,* 345 F.Supp.2d 1227 (D. Utah 2004).
17. *United States v. Booker,* 543 U.S. 220, 125 S.Ct. 738, 160 L.Ed.2d 621 (2005).

a federal trial judge may now depart from the guidelines if he or she believes that it is reasonable to do so. Sentencing guidelines still exist and provide for enhanced punishment for certain types of crimes, including white-collar crimes, violations of the Sarbanes-Oxley Act (see Chapter 3), and violations of securities laws.[18] The United States Supreme Court has also held that a sentencing judge cannot presume that a sentence within the applicable guidelines is reasonable.[19]

The sentencing judge must take into account the various sentencing factors that apply to an individual defendant. When the defendant is a business firm, these factors include the company's history of past violations, management's cooperation with federal investigators, and the extent to which the firm has undertaken specific programs and procedures to prevent criminal activities by its employees.

▶ Cyber Crime

The U.S. Department of Justice broadly defines *computer crime* as any violation of criminal law that involves knowledge of computer technology for its perpetration, investigation, or prosecution. Many computer crimes fall under the broad label of **cyber crime,** which describes any criminal activity occurring via a computer in the virtual community of the Internet.

> **Cyber Crime** A crime that occurs online, in the virtual community of the Internet, as opposed to the physical world.

Most cyber crimes are simply existing crimes, such as fraud and theft of intellectual property, in which the Internet is the instrument of wrongdoing. **EXAMPLE 7.14** Richard O'Dwyer ran TVShack, which was a Web site with links directing users to copyrighted TV shows and movies. In 2010, U.S. authorities seized his .net domain name. O'Dwyer simply moved the site to a .cc domain over which the United States apparently has no authority. U.S. authorities claimed that his site was nothing more than a search-engine for pirated content. ●

Here, we look at several types of activity that constitute cyber crimes against persons or property.

Cyber Fraud

As pointed out in Chapter 6, fraud is any misrepresentation knowingly made with the intention of deceiving another and on which a reasonable person would and does rely to her or his detriment. **Cyber fraud,** then, is fraud committed over the Internet. Frauds that were once conducted solely by mail or phone can now be found online, and new technology has led to increasingly creative ways to commit fraud.

> **Cyber Fraud** Any misrepresentation knowingly made over the Internet with the intention of deceiving another and on which a reasonable person would and does rely to his or her detriment.

ONLINE AUCTION FRAUD Online auction fraud, in its most basic form, is a simple process. A person puts up an expensive item for auction, on either a legitimate or a fake auction site, and then refuses to send the product after receiving payment. Or, as a variation, the wrongdoer may provide the purchaser with an item that is worth less than the one offered in the auction.

ONLINE RETAIL FRAUD Somewhat similar to online auction fraud is online retail fraud, in which consumers pay directly (without bidding) for items that are never delivered. As with other forms of online fraud, it is difficult to determine the actual extent of online sales fraud, but anecdotal evidence suggests that it is a substantial problem.

---

18. The sentencing guidelines were amended in 2003, as required under the Sarbanes-Oxley Act of 2002, to impose stiffer penalties for corporate securities fraud.

19. *Nelson v. United States,* 555 U.S. 350, 129 S.Ct. 890, 172 L.Ed.2d 719 (2009).

CASE EXAMPLE 7.15   Jeremy Jaynes grossed more than $750,000 per week selling nonexistent or worthless products such as "penny stock pickers" and "Internet history erasers." By the time he was arrested, he had amassed an estimated $24 million from his various fraudulent schemes.[20] ●

Cyber Theft

In cyberspace, thieves are not subject to the physical limitations of the "real" world. A thief can steal data stored in a networked computer with Internet access from anywhere on the globe. Only the speed of the connection and the thief's computer equipment limit the quantity of data that can be stolen.

Identity Theft   The theft of personal information, such as a person's name, driver's license number, or Social Security number, to access the victim's financial resources.

IDENTITY THEFT   Not surprisingly, there has been a marked increase in identity theft in recent years. **Identity theft** occurs when the wrongdoer steals a form of identification—such as a name, date of birth, or Social Security number—and uses the information to access the victim's financial resources.

The Internet has provided even easier access to private data as users surrender a wealth of information about themselves without knowing it. Most Web sites collect data on those who visit their sites. The data may include the areas of the site the user visits and the links on which the user clicks. Furthermore, Web browsers often store information such as the consumer's name and e-mail address. Finally, every time a purchase is made online, the item is linked to the purchaser's name, allowing Web retailers to amass a database of who is buying what.

LEARNING OBJECTIVE 5   How has the Internet expanded opportunities for identity theft?

In the following case, the court had to decide whether to suppress evidence of an identity theft crime that officers found at the defendant's girlfriend's house.

---

20. *Jaynes v. Commonwealth of Virginia*, 276 Va.App. 443, 666 S.E.2d 303 (2008).

Case 7.3   **United States v. Oliver**

United States Court of Appeals, Fifth Circuit, 630 F.3d 397 (2011).

BACKGROUND AND FACTS   Lonnie Oliver, Jr., was arrested by officers investigating an identity theft scheme to file fraudulent claims for unemployment benefits. Oliver and others were suspected of gaining access to people's names, Social Security numbers, and other identifiers, and stealing this data to file for and receive unemployment benefits. After he was read his *Miranda* rights, Oliver confessed to his role in the scheme. Oliver also consented to a search of his car, but he refused to consent to a search of his home. Oliver's co-defendant then told the police that Oliver had stored a laptop computer and a cardboard box containing items related to the scheme at the apartment of Oliver's girlfriend, Erica Armstrong.

Acting on this information, several agents went to Armstrong's apartment, and she gave them the box and the laptop computer. Inside the box, officers found hundreds of personal identifiers. They also found a notebook labeled "business ideas" with Oliver's notes for the scheme. After the laptop was seized, officers obtained a warrant to search its contents and found evidence that Oliver had used it to submit fraudulent unemployment claims. Oliver filed a motion to

suppress the evidence in the cardboard box on the ground that it had been obtained unconstitutionally because he had not consented to the search. Further, he claimed that the evidence found on the laptop should also be excluded as "fruit of the poisonous tree" because the warrant to search the laptop was issued on the basis of an affidavit that relied, in part, on the evidence in the box. The district court denied the motion. Oliver appealed.

IN THE WORDS OF THE COURT . . .
CRONE, District Judge:

At the suppression hearing, Armstrong stated she observed Oliver—who told her he worked from home—using a laptop and a notebook. According to Armstrong, she first became aware of Oliver's cardboard box when, before traveling out of town, he informed her that he had left it in her apartment under her bed. * * * After Oliver had not been in contact with Armstrong for several days, she looked through the box for information to contact him. In the box, Armstrong

Case 7.3—Continued

found a notebook, a ziplock bag containing credit cards, a white envelope containing identification cards, and other loose paperwork resembling tax documents. Later that day, Agent McReynolds arrived at her apartment inquiring about Oliver. Armstrong did not reveal, and federal authorities were unaware, that Armstrong had already searched the box when she handed it over to McReynolds and agents subsequently examined its contents.

* * * *

* * * *Where a private individual examines the contents of a closed container, a subsequent search of the container by government officials does not constitute an unlawful search for purposes of the Fourth Amendment as long as the government search does not exceed the scope of the private search.* [Emphasis added.]

* * * *

In the present case, * * * Armstrong readily and willingly gave Agent McReynolds the box, which she had already searched, as it was not locked or otherwise safeguarded and was left in her dining room. *Oliver's decision to leave his unsecured cardboard box in an easily accessible and common area of the apartment for several days without notifying or otherwise communicating his whereabouts to Armstrong made it reasonably foreseeable that she would examine his belongings, including the box, to look for a way to contact him.* Given these circumstances, the court finds that the initial private search, which was reasonably foreseeable, and the searcher's act, later that day, of voluntarily giving authorities the box, in which no

reasonable expectation of privacy remained, rendered the subsequent police search permissible under the Fourth Amendment. [Emphasis added.]

* * * *

Oliver also objects to the district court's ruling that the contents of the laptop computer were admissible under the independent source doctrine. Evidence not obtained as a result of police illegality, but rather through a legal, independent source, need not be suppressed. Oliver contends that Agent McReynolds's affidavit in support of the warrant relied on evidence that was illegally obtained. * * * In this circumstance, the affidavit contained sufficient independent information to make the resulting warrant a distinct, untainted source that permitted the agents to reseize and search the laptop lawfully.

DECISION AND REMEDY   The federal appellate court affirmed the lower court's decision that the searches of the box and the laptop computer were legal and that the evidence found therefore was admissible. Because there was sufficient (admissible) evidence to support aggravated identity theft, Oliver pleaded guilty.

WHAT IF THE FACTS WERE DIFFERENT?   *Suppose that Armstrong had not looked through the cardboard box before the police searched it. Would the box's contents have been admissible? Why or why not?*

Phishing   The attempt to acquire financial or other personal information from consumers by sending e-mail messages that purport to be from a legitimate business.

Phishing.   A distinct form of identity theft known as **phishing** has added a different wrinkle to the practice. In a phishing attack, the perpetrators "fish" for financial data and passwords from consumers by posing as a legitimate business such as a bank or credit-card company. The phisher sends an e-mail asking the recipient to "update" or "confirm" vital information, often with the threat that an account or some other service will be discontinued if the information is not provided. Once the unsuspecting individual enters the information, the phisher can use it to masquerade as that person or to drain his or her bank or credit account.

Vishing   A variation of phishing that involves some form of voice communication.

Vishing.   When phishing involves some form of voice communication, the scam is known as **vishing.** In one variation, the consumer receives an e-mail saying there is a problem with an account and that she or he should call a certain telephone number to resolve the problem. Sometimes, the e-mail even says that a telephone call is being requested so that the recipient will know that this is not a phishing attempt. Of course, the goal is to get the consumer to divulge passwords and account information during the call.

EMPLOYMENT FRAUD   Cyber criminals also look for victims at online job-posting sites. Claiming to be an employment officer in a well-known company, the criminal sends bogus e-mail messages to job seekers. The message asks the unsuspecting job seeker to reveal enough information to allow for identity theft. **CASE EXAMPLE 7.16**   The job site Monster.com had to ask all of its users to change their passwords because cyber thieves had broken into its databases to steal user identities, passwords, and other data. The theft of 4.5 million users' personal information from Monster.com was one of Britain's largest cyber theft cases.[21] ●

Hacking and Cyberterrorism

Hacker A person who uses one computer to break into another.

A **hacker** is someone who uses one computer to break into another. The danger posed by hackers has increased significantly because of *botnets,* or networks of computers that have been appropriated by hackers without the knowledge of their owners. A hacker will secretly install a program on thousands, if not millions, of personal computer "robots," or "bots," that allows him or her to forward transmissions to an even larger number of systems.

EXAMPLE 7.17   In 2011, someone hacked into Sony Corporation's PlayStation 3 video gaming and entertainment networks. The incident forced the company to temporarily shut down its online gaming services and affected more than 100 million online accounts that provide gaming, chat, and music streaming services. ●

Hackers who break into computers without authorization often commit cyber theft, but sometimes their principal aim is to prove how smart they are by gaining access to others' password-protected computers. **Cyberterrorists** are hackers who, rather than trying to gain attention, strive to remain undetected so that they can exploit computers for a serious impact.

Cyberterrorist A hacker whose purpose is to exploit a target computer to create a serious impact, such as sabotage.

Cyberterrorists, as well as hackers, may target businesses. The goals of a hacking operation might include a wholesale theft of data, such as a merchant's customer files, or the monitoring of a computer to discover a business firm's plans and transactions. A cyberterrorist might also want to insert false codes or data. For example, the processing control system of a food manufacturer could be changed to alter the levels of ingredients so that consumers of the food would become ill.

A cyberterrorist attack on a major financial institution, such as the New York Stock Exchange or a large bank, could leave securities or money markets in flux and seriously affect the daily lives of millions of citizens. Similarly, any prolonged disruption of computer, cable, satellite, or telecommunications systems due to the actions of expert hackers would have serious repercussions on business operations—and national security—on a global level.

Prosecution of Cyber Crime

Cyber crime has raised new issues in the investigation of crimes and the prosecution of offenders. Determining the "location" of a cyber crime and identifying a criminal in cyberspace are two significant challenges for law enforcement.

JURISDICTION AND IDENTIFICATION CHALLENGES   A threshold issue is, of course, jurisdiction (see page 31). Jurisdiction is normally based on physical geography, and each state and nation has jurisdiction over crimes committed within its boundaries. But geographic boundaries simply do not apply in cyberspace. A person who commits an act against a business in California, where the act is a cyber crime, might never have set foot in California but might instead reside in New York, or even in Canada, where the act may not be a crime.

Identifying the wrongdoer can also be difficult. Cyber criminals do not leave physical traces, such as fingerprints or DNA samples, as evidence of their crimes. Even electronic "footprints" (digital evidence) can be hard to find and follow. For

---

21. John Bingham, "Monster.com Hacking Follows Tradition of Cyber Theft," *Telegraph.co.uk.,* January 28, 2009.

example, e-mail may be sent through a remailer, an online service that guarantees that a message cannot be traced to its source.

For these reasons, laws written to protect physical property are often difficult to apply in cyberspace. Nonetheless, governments at the state and federal level have taken significant steps toward controlling cyber crime. For example, they are applying existing criminal statutes and enacting new laws that specifically address wrongs committed in cyberspace. California, for instance, which has the highest identity theft rate in the nation, established a new eCrime unit in 2011 to investigate and prosecute cyber crimes. Other states, including Florida, Louisiana, and Texas, also have special law enforcement units that focus solely on Internet crimes.

THE COMPUTER FRAUD AND ABUSE ACT   Perhaps the most significant federal statute specifically addressing cyber crime is the Counterfeit Access Device and Computer Fraud and Abuse Act of 1984.[21] This act is commonly known as the Computer Fraud and Abuse Act, or CFAA.

Among other things, the CFAA provides that a person who accesses a computer online, without authority, to obtain classified, restricted, or protected data (or attempts to do so) is subject to criminal prosecution. Such data could include financial and consumer credit records, medical records, legal files, military and national security files, and other confidential information in government or private computers. The crime has two elements: accessing a computer without authority and taking the data.

This theft is a felony if it is committed for a commercial purpose or for private financial gain, or if the value of the stolen information exceeds $5,000. Penalties include fines and imprisonment for up to twenty years. For a discussion of whether it should be a violation of the CFAA to post fake pictures on the Internet's social media sites, see this chapter's *Online Developments* feature below.

---

21. 18 U.S.C. Section 1030.

ONLINE DEVELOPMENTS

Prosecuting Those Who Post False Information on the Internet

The Computer Fraud and Abuse Act (CFAA) was enacted nearly thirty years ago. At that time, the new law was aimed at computer hacking. Since then, Congress has greatly expanded the act's reach. Today, the CFAA criminalizes any computer use that "exceeds authorized access" to any computer.

Posting Fake Photos Can Be a Crime

Just a few years ago, the Justice Department prosecuted a woman for supposedly violating the "terms of service" of MySpace.com. The woman had set up a MySpace account pretending to be a sixteen-year-old boy and had used the account to harass a thirteen-year-old girl (who subsequently committed suicide). Because the woman's profile did not use her actual photo, she was charged with conspiracy to violate the CFAA because MySpace's terms of service

require that all profile information be truthful.[a] Another defendant was prosecuted for posing as someone else and posting sexually inappropriate messages on Facebook that purported to be from her.[b] In both instances, many suggested that the prosecutors were attempting to criminalize actions that, however blameworthy they may have been, were hardly crimes under the law.

Civil Suits Filed by Private Parties

In addition to potential criminal penalties, the CFAA also allows private parties to bring civil suits against other private parties. An employer can sue a former employee for excessive Internet

---

a. *United States v. Drew,* 259 F.R.D. 449 (C.D.Cal. 2009).
b. *In re Rolando S.,* 197 Cal.App.4th 936, 129 Cal.Rptr.3d 49 (2011).

(Continued)

usage while at work. In other words, if the employer can prove (through keystroke monitoring, for example) that the employee visited Facebook and sent too many personal e-mails from work, the employer has grounds to sue. In one case, the terms of service on a company's Web site stated that no competitors could visit it. When one of them did, the company sued that competitor.

Have We Gone Too Far?

Agreements are breached every day. Employees routinely ignore their bosses' instructions. If such actions involve a computer or the Internet, however, they become federal crimes. In other words, the law today gives computer owners the power to criminalize any computer use with which they disagree.

FOR CRITICAL ANALYSIS

Is the expansion of the 1984 Computer Fraud and Abuse Act part of the overcriminalization trend in this country? Why or why not?

 ## Reviewing . . . Criminal Law and Cyber Crime

Edward Hanousek worked for Pacific & Arctic Railway and Navigation Company (P&A) as a roadmaster of the White Pass & Yukon Railroad in Alaska. As an officer of the corporation, Hanousek was responsible "for every detail of the safe and efficient maintenance and construction of track, structures, and marine facilities of the entire railroad," including special projects. One project was a rock quarry, known as "6-mile," above the Skagway River. Next to the quarry, and just beneath the surface, ran a high-pressure oil pipeline owned by Pacific & Arctic Pipeline, Inc., P&A's sister company. When the quarry's backhoe operator punctured the pipeline, an estimated 1,000 to 5,000 gallons of oil were discharged into the river. Hanousek was charged with negligently discharging a harmful quantity of oil into a navigable water of the United States in violation of the criminal provisions of the Clean Water Act (CWA). Using the information presented in the chapter, answer the following questions.

1. Did Hanousek have the required mental state (*mens rea*) to be convicted of a crime? Why or why not?
2. Which theory discussed in the chapter would enable a court to hold Hanousek criminally liable for violating the statute regardless of whether he participated in, directed, or even knew about the specific violation?
3. Could the quarry's backhoe operator who punctured the pipeline also be charged with a crime in this situation? Explain.
4. Suppose that at trial, Hanousek argued that he could not be convicted because he was not aware of the requirements of the CWA. Would this defense be successful? Why or why not?

 ## Debate This

Because of overcriminalization, particularly by the federal government, Americans may be breaking the law regularly without knowing it. Should Congress rescind many of the more than four thousand federal crimes now on the books? Discuss fully.

Key Terms

actus reus 161	entrapment 170	phishing 179
arson 164	exclusionary rule 174	plea bargaining 171
beyond a reasonable doubt 159	forgery 164	probable cause 172
burglary 163	grand jury 175	robbery 162
crime 159	hacker 180	search warrant 171
cyber crime 177	identity theft 178	self-defense 169
cyber fraud 177	indictment 175	self-incrimination 174
cyberterrorist 180	information 176	vishing 179
double jeopardy 173	larceny 163	white-collar crime 164
duress 170	*mens rea* 161	
embezzlement 164	money laundering 168	

▶ Chapter Summary: Criminal Law and Cyber Crime

Civil Law and Criminal Law (See pages 159–160.)	1. *Civil law*—Spells out the duties that exist between persons or between citizens and their governments, excluding the duty not to commit crimes. 2. *Criminal law*—Has to do with crimes, which are wrongs against society defined in statutes and, if committed, punishable by society through fines and/or imprisonment—and, in some cases, death. Because crimes are *offenses against society as a whole,* they are prosecuted by a public official, not by victims. 3. *Key differences*—An important difference between civil and criminal law is that the standard of proof is higher in criminal cases. 4. *Civil liability for criminal acts*—A criminal act may give rise to both criminal liability and tort liability.
Criminal Liability (See pages 160–162.)	1. *Guilty act and state of mind*—In general, some form of harmful act must be committed for a crime to exist. An intent to commit a crime, or a wrongful mental state, is generally required for a crime to exist. 2. *Liability of corporations*—Corporations normally are liable for the crimes committed by their agents within the course and scope of their employment. Corporate directors and officers are personally liable for the crimes they commit and may be held liable for the actions of employees under their supervision.
Types of Crimes (See pages 162–169.)	1. *Violent crimes*—Cause others to suffer harm or death. Violent crimes include murder, assault and battery, sexual assault (rape), and robbery. 2. *Property crimes*—The most common form of crime. The offender's goal is to obtain some economic gain or to damage property. This category includes burglary, larceny, obtaining goods by false pretenses, receiving stolen property, arson, and forgery. 3. *Public order crimes*—Acts, such as public drunkenness, prostitution, and illegal drug use, that a statute has established are contrary to public values and morals. 4. *White-collar crimes*—Illegal acts committed by a person or business using nonviolent means to obtain a personal or business advantage. Embezzlement, mail and wire fraud, bribery, and the theft of trade secrets are examples. 5. *Organized crime*—A form of crime conducted by groups operating illegitimately to satisfy the public's demand for illegal goods and services. This category also includes money laundering and RICO violations.
Defenses to Criminal Liability (See pages 169–171.)	Defenses to criminal liability include justifiable use of force, necessity, insanity, mistake, duress, entrapment, and the statute of limitations. Also, in some cases defendants may be relieved of criminal liability, at least in part, if they are given immunity.
Constitutional Safeguards and Criminal Procedures (See pages 171–175.)	1. *Fourth Amendment*—Provides protection against unreasonable searches and seizures and requires that probable cause exist before a warrant for a search or an arrest can be issued. 2. *Fifth Amendment*—Requires due process of law, prohibits double jeopardy, and protects against self-incrimination. 3. *Sixth Amendment*—Provides guarantees of a speedy trial, a trial by jury, a public trial, the right to confront witnesses, and the right to counsel. 4. *Eighth Amendment*—Prohibits excessive bail and fines, and cruel and unusual punishment. 5. *Exclusionary rule and Miranda rule*—The exclusionary rule is a criminal procedural rule that prohibits the introduction at trial of any evidence obtained in violation of constitutional rights, as well as any evidence derived from the illegally obtained evidence. The *Miranda* set forth by the Supreme Court in *Miranda v. Arizona* holding that individuals who are arrested must be informed of certain constitutional rights, including their right to counsel.
The Criminal Process (See pages 175–177.)	Procedures governing arrest, indictment, and trial for a crime are designed to safeguard the rights of the individual. The federal government has established sentencing laws or guidelines, which are no longer mandatory but provide a range of penalties for each federal crime.

(Continued)

Chapter Summary: Criminal Law and Cyber Crime, *Continued*

Cyber Crime (See pages 177–182.)	Cyber crimes occur in cyberspace. Examples include cyber fraud, cyber theft, hacking, and cyberterrorism. A significant federal statute addressing cyber crime is the Computer Fraud and Abuse Act of 1984.

ExamPrep

ISSUE SPOTTERS

—Check your answers to these questions against the answers provided in Appendix D at the end of this text.

1. Daisy takes her roommate's credit card, intending to charge expenses that she incurs on a vacation. Her first stop is a gas station, where she uses the card to pay for gas. With respect to the gas station, has she committed a crime? If so, what is it? **(See page 163.)**
2. Without permission, Ben downloads consumer credit files from a computer belonging to Consumer Credit Agency. He then sells the data to Dawn. Has Ben committed a crime? If so, what is it? **(See page 181.)**

BEFORE THE TEST

Go to **www.cengagebrain.com**, enter the ISBN 9781133586548, and click on "Find" to locate this textbook's Web site. Then click on "Access Now" under "Study Tools," and select Chapter 7 at the top. There, you will find a Practice Quiz that you can take to assess your mastery of the concepts in this chapter. Additionally, you will find Flashcards and a Glossary of important terms, as well as Video Questions (when assigned).

For Review

Answers for the even-numbered questions in this For Review *section can be found in Appendix E at the end of this text.*

1. What two elements must exist before a person can be held liable for a crime?
2. What are five broad categories of crimes?
3. What defenses can be raised to avoid liability for criminal acts?
4. What constitutional safeguards exist to protect persons accused of crimes?
5. How has the Internet expanded opportunities for identity theft?

Questions and Case Problems

7–1. Types of Cyber Crimes. The following situations are similar, but each represents a variation of a particular crime. Identify the crime and point out the differences in the variations. (See pages 179–180.)

1. Chen, posing fraudulently as Diamond Credit Card Co., sends an e-mail to Emily, stating that the company has observed suspicious activity in her account and has frozen the account. The e-mail asks her to reregister her credit-card number and password to reopen the account.
2. Claiming falsely to be Big Buy Retail Finance Co., Conner sends an e-mail to Dino, asking him to confirm or update his personal security information to prevent his Big Buy account from being discontinued.

3. Felicia posts her résumé on GotWork.com, an online job-posting site, seeking a position in business and managerial finance and accounting. Hayden, who misrepresents himself as an employment officer with International Bank & Commerce Corp., sends her an e-mail asking for more personal information.

7–2. **Question with Sample Answer: Cyber Scam.** Kayla, a student at Learnwell University, owes $20,000 in unpaid tuition. If Kayla does not pay the tuition, Learnwell will not allow her to graduate. To obtain the funds to pay the debt, she sends e-mail letters to people that she does not personally know asking for financial help to send Milo, her disabled child, to a special school. In reality, Kayla has no children. Is this a crime? If so, which one? (See page 177.)

—For a sample answer to Question 7–2, go to Appendix F at the end of this text.

7–3. Identity Theft. Oleksiy Sharapka ordered merchandise online using stolen credit cards. He had the items sent to outlets of Mail Boxes, Etc., and then arranged for someone to deliver the items to his house. He subsequently shipped the goods overseas, primarily to Russia. Sharapka was indicted in a federal district court. At the time of his arrest, government agents found in his possession, among other things, more than three hundred stolen credit-card numbers, including numbers issued by American Express. There was evidence that he had used more than ten of the American Express numbers to buy goods worth between $400,000 and $1 million from at least fourteen vendors. Did Sharapka commit any crimes? If so, who were his victims? Explain. [*United States v. Sharapka*, 526 F.3d 58 (1st Cir. 2008)] (See page 178.)

7–4. Cyber Crime. Jiri Klimecek was a member of a group that overrode copyright protection in movies and music to make them available for download online. Klimecek bought and installed a server and paid to connect it to the Internet. He knew that users could access the server to upload and download copyrighted works. He obtained access to movies and music to make them available. When charged with copyright infringement, he claimed that he had not understood the full scope of the operation. Did Klimecek commit a crime? Explain. [*United States v. Klimecek*, __ F.3d __ (7th Cir. 2009)] (See page 177.)

7–5. Case Problem with Sample Answer: Search and Seizure. Three police officers, including Maria Trevizo, pulled over a car with a suspended registration. One of the occupants, Lemon Johnson, wore clothing consistent with membership in the Crips gang. Trevizo searched him "for officer safety" and found a gun. Johnson was charged with illegal possession of a weapon. What standard should apply to an officer's search of a passenger during a traffic stop? Should a warrant be required? Could a search proceed solely on the basis of probable cause? Would a reasonable suspicion short of probable cause be enough? Discuss. [*Arizona v. Johnson*, 555 U.S. 323, 129 S.Ct. 781, 172 L.Ed.2d 694 (2009)] (See pages 171–172.)

—For a sample answer to Case Problem 7–5, go to Appendix G at the end of this text.

7–6. Sentencing Guidelines. Paul Wilkinson worked for a company that sold fuel to various military bases. He paid an employee of a competitor to provide him with information about bids for contracts for which both companies were bidding. The information enabled Wilkinson to rig the bids and win contracts. When the scam was uncovered, he was indicted for conspiracy to defraud the government, to commit wire fraud, and to steal trade secrets. He pleaded guilty to the charges under a plea arrangement. Given the nature

of the offenses, the federal sentencing guidelines provide for a prison term of fifty-one to sixty-three months with no possibility of probation. Due to Wilkinson's cooperation, the prosecution recommended fifty-one months. His attorney argued for a term of ten to sixteen months. The judge sentenced Wilkinson to three years' probation and eight hundred hours of community service, but no prison term. The government appealed, arguing that the sentence was too light and thus violated the sentencing guidelines. Can a trial judge give such a light sentence under the sentencing guidelines? Explain your answer. [*United States v. Wilkinson*, 590 F.3d 259 (4th Cir. 2010)] (See pages 176–177.)

7–7. Searches. Charles Byrd was in a minimum-security jail awaiting trial. A team of sheriff's deputies took several inmates into a room for a strip search without any apparent justification. Byrd was ordered to remove all of his clothing except his boxer shorts. A female deputy searched Byrd while several male deputies watched. One of the male deputies videotaped the search. Byrd filed a suit against the sheriff's department. Did the search violate Byrd's rights? Discuss. [*Byrd v. Maricopa County Sheriff's Department*, 629 F.3d 1135 (9th Cir. 2011)] (See pages 171–172.)

7–8. Credit-Card Theft. Jacqueline Barden was shopping for school clothes with her children when her purse and automobile were taken. In Barden's purse were her car keys, credit and debit cards for herself and her children, as well as the children's Social Security cards and birth certificates needed for enrollment at school. Immediately after the purse and car were stolen, Rebecca Mary Turner attempted to use Barden's credit card at a local Exxon gas station, but the card was declined. The gas station attendant recognized Turner because she had previously written bad checks and used credit cards that did not belong to her. Turner was later arrested while attempting to use one of Barden's checks to pay for merchandise at a Walmart—where the clerk also recognized Turner from prior criminal activity. Turner claimed that she had not stolen Barden's purse or car, and that a friend had told her he had some checks and credit cards and asked her to try using them at Walmart. Turner was convicted at trial. She appealed, claiming that there was insufficient evidence that she committed credit- and debit-card theft. Was the evidence sufficient to uphold her conviction? Why or why not? [*Turner v. State of Arkansas*, 2012 Ark.App. 150 (2012)] (See page 163.)

7–9. A Question of Ethics: Identity Theft. *Twenty-year-old Davis Omole worked at a cell phone store. He stole customers' personal information and used the stolen identities to create a hundred different accounts on eBay. Omole held more than three hundred auctions on eBay listing for sale items that he did not own. From these auctions, he collected $90,000. Charged with identity theft, Omole displayed contempt for the court and ridiculed his victims, calling them stupid for having been cheated. [United States v. Omole, 523 F.3d 691 (7th Cir. 2008)]* (See pages 177–178.)

1. Before and during his trial, Omole displayed contempt for the court and the victims. What do these factors show about Omole's ethics?

2. Under the federal sentencing guidelines, Omole could have been imprisoned for more than eight years, but he received a sentence of only three years, two of which were the mandatory sentence for identity theft. Was this sentence too lenient? Explain.

7–10. In Your Court: Criminal Liability and Sentencing. Gavin, a fifteen-year-old student, was eating lunch on the grounds of a school. He threw a half-eaten apple toward the outside wall of a classroom some distance away. The apple sailed through a slowly closing door and struck a teacher who was in the room. The teacher was knocked to the floor and lost consciousness for a few minutes. Gavin was charged with assault by "any means of force likely to produce great bodily injury." Gavin stated that he did not intend to hit the teacher but only intended to see the apple splatter against the outside wall. Assume that you are one of the judges on the appellate court panel reviewing this case and answer the following questions.

1. What are the two elements of criminal liability? Are both elements present in this case? **(See page 160.)**

2. The trial court convicted Gavin, among other things, to send a message to his classmates that his actions were wrong. Is this a sufficient reason, in itself, to convict a defendant such as Gavin? Why or why not? **(See page 176.)**

Chapter 8

Intellectual Property and Internet Law

Contents

Learning Objectives

The five Learning Objectives below are designed to help improve your understanding of the chapter. After reading this chapter, you should be able to answer the following questions:

1. What is intellectual property?

2. Why is the protection of trademarks important?

3. How does the law protect patents?

4. What laws protect authors' rights in the works they generate?

5. What are trade secrets, and what laws offer protection for this form of intellectual property?

(OlegAlbinsky/iStockphoto.com)

Intellectual Property Property resulting from intellectual, creative processes.

LEARNING OBJECTIVE 1 What is intellectual property?

Intellectual property is any property resulting from intellectual, creative processes—the products of an individual's mind. Although it is an abstract term for an abstract concept, intellectual property is nonetheless familiar to almost everyone. The information contained in books and computer files is intellectual property. The apps in your iPhone or iPad, the movies you see, and the music you listen to are all forms of intellectual property.

A significant concern for many businesspersons is the need to protect their rights in intellectual property, which may be more valuable than their physical property, such as machinery and buildings. For instance, technology companies, such as Apple, Inc., the maker of the iPhone and iPad, derive most of their profits from their intellectual property rights. Apple sued rival Samsung Electronics Company in 2011, claiming that Samsung's Galaxy line of mobile phones and tablets—those that run Google's Android software—unlawfully copied the look, design, and user interface of Apple's iPhone and iPad. In 2012, a jury found that Samsung had willfully infringed Apple's patents and had "diluted" Apple's iPhone *trade dress* (see page 191). The jury awarded more than $1 billion in damages to Apple in the case.[1]

The need to protect creative works was first recognized in Article I, Section 8, of the U.S. Constitution (see Appendix B), and statutory protection of these rights

---

1. *Apple, Inc. v. Samsung Electronics Co.*, Case Nos. CV 11-1846 and CV 12-0630 (N.D. Cal. August 24, 2012).

began in the 1940s. Laws protecting patents, trademarks, and copyrights are explicitly designed to protect and reward inventive and artistic creativity. These laws continue to evolve to meet the challenges of modern society.

Laws providing for trademarks, patents, copyrights, and trade secrets are designed to protect creative and inventive works. *Trademarks, patents, copyrights,* and *trade secrets* are all forms of intellectual property. The study of intellectual property law is important because intellectual property has taken on an increasing significance not only within the United States but globally as well.

▶ Trademarks and Related Property

Trademark   A word, symbol, sound, or design that has become sufficiently associated with a good or has been registered with a government agency.

A **trademark** is a distinctive word, symbol, sound, or design that identifies the manufacturer as the source of particular goods and distinguishes its products from those made or sold by others. At common law, the person who used a symbol or mark to identify a business or product was protected in the use of that trademark. Clearly, by using another's trademark, a business could lead consumers to believe that its goods were made by the other business. The law seeks to avoid this kind of confusion.

In the following *Classic Case* concerning Coca-Cola, the defendants argued that the Coca-Cola trademark was entitled to no protection under the law because the term did not accurately represent the product.

Classic Case 8.1   **Coca-Cola Co. v. Koke Co. of America**

Supreme Court of the United States, 254 U.S. 143, 41 S.Ct. 113, 65 L.Ed. 189 (1920).

BACKGROUND AND FACTS   The Coca-Cola Company brought an action in a federal district court to prevent other beverage companies from using the words *Koke* and *Dope* for their products. The defendants contended that the Coca-Cola trademark was a fraudulent representation and that Coca-Cola was therefore not entitled to any help from the courts. By use of the Coca-Cola name, the defendants alleged, the Coca-Cola Company represented that the beverage contained cocaine (from coca leaves). The district court granted the *injunction* (see page 10), but the federal appellate court reversed. The Coca-Cola Company appealed to the United States Supreme Court.

IN THE WORDS OF THE COURT . . .
Mr. Justice *HOLMES* delivered the opinion of the Court.
    * * * *

    * * * Before 1900 the beginning of [Coca-Cola's] good will was more or less helped by the presence of cocaine, a drug that, like alcohol or opium, may be described as a deadly poison or as a valuable item of the pharmacopœa [collection of pharmaceuticals] according to the [purposes of the speaker]. * * * After the Food and Drug Act of June 30, 1906, if not earlier, long before this suit was brought, it was eliminated from the plaintiff's compound.

    * * * Since 1900 the sales have increased at a very great rate corresponding to a like increase in advertising. The name now characterizes a beverage to be had at almost any soda fountain. It means a single thing coming from a single source, and well known to the community. It hardly would be too much to say that the drink characterizes the name as much as the name the drink. In other words Coca-Cola probably means to most persons the plaintiff's familiar product to be had everywhere rather than a compound of particular substances. * * * Before this suit was brought the plaintiff had advertised to the public that it must not expect and would not find cocaine, and had eliminated everything tending to suggest cocaine effects except the name and the picture of the leaves and nuts, which probably conveyed little or nothing to most who saw it. It appears to us that it would be going too far to deny the plaintiff relief against a palpable fraud because possibly here and there an ignorant person might call for the drink with the hope for incipient cocaine intoxication. The plaintiff's position must be judged by the facts as they were when the suit was begun, not by the facts of a different condition and an earlier time.

DECISION AND REMEDY   The United States Supreme Court upheld the district court's injunction. The competing beverage companies were prevented from calling their products *Koke.* The Court did not prevent them from calling their products *Dope,* however.

Classic Case 8.1–Continued

WHAT IF THE FACTS WERE DIFFERENT?　*Suppose that Coca-Cola had been trying to make the public believe that its product contained cocaine. Would the result in the case likely have been different? Explain your answer.*

IMPACT OF THIS CASE ON TODAY'S LEGAL ENVIRONMENT　*In this early case, the United States Supreme*

Court made it clear that trademarks and trade names (and nicknames for those marks and names, such as the nickname "Coke" for "Coca-Cola") that are in common use receive protection under the common law. This holding is significant historically because it is the predecessor to the Lanham Act of 1946, which was passed later to protect trademark rights.

Trademark Protection and Trademark Dilution

LEARNING OBJECTIVE 2　Why is the protection of trademarks important?

Statutory protection of trademarks and related property is provided at the federal level by the Lanham Act of 1946.[2] The Lanham Act was enacted, in part, to protect manufacturers from losing business to rival companies that used confusingly similar trademarks. The act incorporates the common law of trademarks and provides remedies for owners of trademarks who wish to enforce their claims in federal court. Many states also have trademark statutes.

Before 1995, federal trademark law prohibited only the unauthorized use of the same (identical) mark on competing—or on noncompeting but "related"—goods or services. Protection was given only when the unauthorized use would likely confuse consumers as to the origin of those goods and services. In 1995, Congress amended the Lanham Act by passing the Federal Trademark Dilution Act,[3] which allowed trademark owners to bring a suit in federal court for *trademark dilution.*

Trademark dilution laws protect distinctive or famous trademarks (such as McDonald's or Apple) from certain unauthorized uses even when the use is on noncompeting goods or is unlikely to confuse. More than half of the states have also enacted trademark dilution laws.

Trademark Registration

Trademarks may be registered with the state or with the federal government. To register for protection under federal trademark law, a person must file an application with the U.S. Patent and Trademark Office in Washington, D.C. A mark can be registered (1) if it is currently in commerce or (2) if the applicant intends to put the mark into commerce within six months.

Registration of a trademark with the U.S. Patent and Trademark Office gives notice on a nationwide basis that the trademark belongs exclusively to the registrant. The registrant is also allowed to use the symbol ® to indicate that the mark has been registered. Registration is renewable between the fifth and sixth years after the initial registration and every ten years thereafter.

Trademark Infringement

Once a trademark is established—either under the common law or through registration—the owner has exclusive use of it and has the right to bring a legal action against anyone who infringes on the trademark. The tort of *trademark infringement* occurs when a party who does not own a trademark copies it to a substantial degree or uses it in its entirety—whether intentionally or not.

---

2. 15 U.S.C. Sections 1051–1128.
3. 15 U.S.C. Section 1125.

When a trademark has been *infringed* (used without authorization), the owner has a cause of action against the infringer. To succeed in a trademark infringement action, the owner must show that the defendant's use of the mark created a likelihood of confusion about the origin of the defendant's goods or services. **EXAMPLE 8.1** An independent athletic clothing manufacturer uses the check-mark "swoosh" that is the trademark of Nike. Consumers would believe that this manufacturer's products were Nike-brand clothing, even though they were not. •

The owner need not prove that the infringer acted intentionally or that the trademark was registered (although registration does provide proof of the date of inception of the trademark's use).

The most commonly granted remedy for trademark infringement is an injunction to prevent further infringement. Under the Lanham Act, a trademark owner that successfully proves infringement can recover actual damages, plus the profits that the infringer wrongfully received from the unauthorized use of the mark. A court can also order the destruction of any goods bearing the unauthorized trademark. In some situations, the trademark owner may also be able to recover attorneys' fees.

Distinctiveness of the Mark

A central objective of the Lanham Act is to reduce the likelihood that consumers will be confused by similar marks. For that reason, only those trademarks that are deemed sufficiently distinctive from all competing trademarks will be protected.

STRONG MARKS   Fanciful, arbitrary, or suggestive trademarks are generally considered to be the most distinctive (strongest) trademarks because they are normally taken from outside the context of the particular product and thus provide the best means of distinguishing one product from another.

Fanciful Trademarks. Fanciful trademarks include invented words, such as Xerox for one manufacturer's copiers and Zynga for a creator of online video games used worldwide.

Arbitrary Trademarks. Arbitrary trademarks use common words that ordinarily would not be associated with the product, such as *Dutch Boy* as a name for paint. A single letter used in a particular style can be an arbitrary trademark.
CASE EXAMPLE 8.2   ESPN sued Quiksilver, Inc., a maker of surfer clothing, alleging trademark infringement. ESPN claimed that Quiksilver had used the stylized "X" mark on its clothing that ESPN uses in connection with the "X Games," a competition focusing on extreme action sports. Quiksilver filed counterclaims for trademark infringement and dilution, arguing that it had a long history of using the stylized X on its products. A federal district court held that the X on Quiksilver's clothing was clearly an arbitrary mark, noting that "the two Xs are similar enough that a consumer might well confuse them."[4] •

Suggestive Trademarks. Suggestive trademarks bring to mind something about a product without describing the product directly. For instance, "blu-ray" is a suggestive mark that is associated with the high-quality, high-definition video contained on a particular optical data storage disc. Although blue-violet lasers are used to read blu-ray discs, the term *blu-ray* does not directly describe the disc.

SECONDARY MEANING   Descriptive terms, geographic terms, and personal names are not inherently distinctive and do not receive protection under the law *until* they acquire a secondary meaning. A secondary meaning arises when customers begin to

---

4. *ESPN, Inc. v. Quiksilver, Inc.*, 586 F.Supp.2d 219 (S.D.N.Y. 2008).

associate a specific term or phrase, such as *London Fog*, with specific trademarked items (coats with "London Fog" labels) made by a particular company. Whether a secondary meaning becomes attached to a term or name usually depends on how extensively the product is advertised, the market for the product, the number of sales, and other factors. Once a secondary meaning is attached to a term or name, a trademark is considered distinctive and is protected.

GENERIC TERMS   Generic terms are terms that refer to an entire class of products, such as *bicycle* and *computer*. Generic terms receive no protection, even if they acquire secondary meanings. A particularly thorny problem for a business arises when its trademark acquires generic use. For instance, *aspirin* and *thermos* were originally trademarked products, but today the words are used generically.

Service, Certification, and Collective Marks

Service Mark   A mark used in the sale or advertising of services to distinguish the services of one person from those of others.

A **service mark** is essentially a trademark that is used to distinguish the *services* (rather than the products) of one person or company from those of another. For instance, each airline has a particular mark or symbol associated with its name. Titles and character names used in radio and television are frequently registered as service marks. (For information on how companies use trademarks and service marks, see this chapter's *Linking the Law to Marketing* feature on pages 204 and 205.)

Certification Mark   A mark used by one or more persons, other than the owner, to certify the region, materials, mode of manufacture, quality, or other characteristic of specific goods or services.

Other marks protected by law include certification marks and collective marks. A **certification mark** is used by one or more persons, other than the owner, to certify the region, materials, mode of manufacture, quality, or other characteristic of specific goods or services. Certification marks include such marks as "Good Housekeeping Seal of Approval" and "UL Tested."

Collective Mark   A mark used by members of a cooperative, association, labor union, or other organization to certify the region, materials, mode of manufacture, quality, or other characteristic of specific goods or services.

When used by members of a cooperative, association, labor union, or other organization, a certification mark is referred to as a **collective mark**. **EXAMPLE 8.3** Collective marks appear at the ends of movie credits to indicate the various associations and organizations that participated in making the movie. The union marks found on the tags of certain products are also collective marks. •

Trade Dress and Trade Names

Trade Dress   The image and overall appearance of a product.

The term **trade dress** refers to the image and overall appearance of a product. Trade dress is a broad concept and can include all or part of the total image or overall impression created by a product or its packaging. **EXAMPLE 8.4**   The distinctive decor, menu, and style of service of a particular restaurant may be regarded as the restaurant's trade dress. Similarly, trade dress can include the layout and appearance of a mail-order catalogue, the use of a lighthouse as part of a golf hole's design, the fish shape of a cracker, or the G-shaped design of a Gucci watch. • Basically, trade dress is subject to the same protection as trademarks.

Trade Name   A name used in commercial activity to designate a particular business.

The term **trade name** is used to indicate part or all of a business's name, whether the business is a sole proprietorship, a partnership, or a corporation. Generally, a trade name is directly related to a business and its goodwill. A trade name may be protected as a trademark if it is the same as the company's trademarked product—for example, Coca-Cola.

Unless it is also used as a trademark or service mark, a trade name cannot be registered with the federal government. Trade names are protected under the common law, however. As with trademarks, words must be unusual or fancifully used if they are to be protected as trade names. For instance, the courts held that the word *Safeway* was sufficiently fanciful to obtain protection as a trade name for a grocery chain.

Counterfeit Goods

Counterfeit goods copy or otherwise imitate trademarked goods, but they are not the genuine trademarked goods. The importation of goods bearing counterfeit (fake) trademarks poses a growing problem for U.S. businesses, consumers, and law enforcement. In addition to having negative financial effects on legitimate businesses, sales of certain counterfeit goods, such as pharmaceuticals and nutritional supplements, can present serious public health risks. It is estimated that nearly 7 percent of the goods imported into the United States are counterfeit.

Congress enacted the Stop Counterfeiting in Manufactured Goods Act[5] (SCMGA) to combat counterfeit goods. The act made it a crime to intentionally traffic in, or attempt to traffic in, counterfeit goods or services, or to knowingly use a counterfeit mark on or in connection with goods or services. This act also prohibits the creation or shipment of counterfeit labels that are not attached to a product. Persons found guilty of violating the SCMGA may be fined up to $2 million or imprisoned for up to ten years (or more if they are repeat offenders).

▶ Cyber Marks

Cyber Mark   A trademark in cyberspace.

In cyberspace, trademarks are sometimes referred to as **cyber marks.** We turn now to a discussion of how new laws and the courts are addressing trademark-related issues in cyberspace.

Domain Names

Domain Name   An Internet address consisting of a series of letters and symbols used to identify site operators on the Web.

As e-commerce expanded worldwide, one issue that emerged involved the rights of a trademark owner to use the mark as part of a domain name. A **domain name** is part of an Internet address, such as "westlaw.com." Every domain name ends with a top-level domain (TLD), which is the part to the right of the period that indicates the type of entity that operates the site (for example, *com* is an abbreviation for "commercial").

The second-level domain (SLD)—the part of the name to the left of the period—is chosen by the business entity or individual registering the domain name. Competition for SLDs among firms with similar names and products has led to numerous disputes. By using the same, or a similar, domain name, parties have attempted to profit from a competitor's goodwill, sell pornography, offer for sale another party's domain name, or otherwise infringe on others' trademarks.

The Internet Corporation for Assigned Names and Numbers (ICANN), a non-profit corporation, oversees the distribution of domain names and operates an online arbitration system. Due to numerous complaints, ICANN completely overhauled the domain name distribution system. In 2012, ICANN started selling new generic top-level domain names (gTLDs) for an initial price of $185,000, plus an annual fee of $25,000. Whereas TLDs were limited to only a few terms—such as *com, net,* and *org*—gTLDs can take any form. ICANN anticipates that many companies and corporations will want gTLDs based on their brands. For example, Apple, Inc., might want to use *ipad* or *imac* as a gTLD.

Even after a domain name is officially assigned by ICANN, other disputes can arise as the *Online Developments* feature on the facing page illustrates.

---

5. Pub. L. No. 109-181 (2006), which amended 18 U.S.C. Sections 2318–2320.

ONLINE DEVELOPMENTS

Can a Person Change His or Her Name to That of a Domain Name?

Often, the name of a Web site can determine the degree of commercial success of that online site. Not surprisingly, there are unending legal disputes over who owns domain names. There are also disputes about the assignability of domain names. Once the Internet Corporation for Assigned Names and Numbers (ICANN) assigns a domain name to its owner, can that owner then change his own name to that of his domain name?

Introducing Mr. NJweedman.com. . .

As absurd as this may sound, Robert Edward Forchion, Jr., applied to the courts to change his name to that of his Web site, *NJweedman.com*. Forchion has devoted his entire adult life to promoting the legalization of marijuana. In fact, while living in New Jersey—where he legally owns the Web site name, *NJweedman. com*—he became known as NJweedman. Not surprisingly, the Web site discusses his efforts to legalize marijuana. In 2009, Forchion left New Jersey, claiming that he was fleeing political persecution for his support of the legalization of marijuana. He moved to Los Angeles, California, where he has managed a Rastafarian Temple, as well as a medical marijuana dispensary. (California is one of nearly twenty states that allows the legal distribution of medical marijuana.)

Court Rulings on the Name Change Petition

In 2001, while a resident of New Jersey, Forchion petitioned a New Jersey Superior Court, Law Division, to legally change his name to *NJweedman.com*. The Law Division denied his request, and he appealed. In 2004, the New Jersey Superior Court, Appellate Division, ultimately accepted the trial court's decision: "In rejecting

this request, the [lower court] judge concluded that 'in his zeal to legalize marijuana . . . [Forchion seeks] to glamorize, persuade others to use marijuana, and to violate the law . . . .'" The court went on to state that the requested name change "implied glamorization by name of a substance that is illegal and prohibited to possess or to use."[a]

After Forchion moved to Los Angeles, he again petitioned another court to change his name to *NJweedman.com*. The Superior Court of Los Angeles County denied the petition. Forchion appealed, but to no avail. The appellate court confirmed that even if Forchion spelled out his new name as "NJweedman DOT COM," such a name could cause confusion if Forchion ever lost control over his current domain name to somebody else. Additionally, this type of personal name might be so similar to another Web site name or a trademark that its multiple uses would create confusion. In any event, granting Forchion a new personal name that is the same as a Web site advocating that individuals violate the law should not be permitted, even in California.[b]

FOR CRITICAL ANALYSIS

If the courts had allowed Forchion to change his name to NJweedman.com, what, if any, complications would this present to the ICANN system of assigning domain names? Discuss.

---

a. *State v. Forchion,* 182 N.J. 150, 862 A.2d 58 (2004).
b. *In re Forchion,* 198 Cal.App.4th 1284, 130 Cal.Rptr.3d 690 (2011).

Cybersquatting and Meta Tags

Cybersquatting The act of registering a domain name that is the same as, or confusingly similar to, the trademark of another and then offering to sell that domain name back to the trademark owner.

One of the goals of the new ICANN system is to alleviate the problem of *cybersquatting.* **Cybersquatting** occurs when a person registers a domain name that is the same as, or confusingly similar to, the trademark of another and then offers to sell the domain name back to the trademark owner. During the 1990s, cybersquatting led to so much litigation that Congress passed the Anticybersquatting Consumer Protection Act (ACPA) of 1999, which amended the Lanham Act—the federal law protecting trademarks discussed earlier. The ACPA makes it illegal to "register, traffic in, or use" a domain name (1) if the name is identical or confusingly similar to the trademark of another and (2) if the person registering, trafficking in, or using the domain name has a "bad faith intent" to profit from that trademark.

Despite the ACPA, cybersquatting continues to present a problem for businesses, largely because more TLDs and gTLDS are now available and many more companies are registering domain names. Indeed, domain name registrars have proliferated.

These companies charge a fee to businesses and individuals to register new names and to renew annual registrations (often through automated software). Many of these companies also buy and sell expired domain names. Although all registrars are supposed to relay information about these transactions to ICANN and the other companies that keep a master list of domain names, this does not always occur. The speed at which domain names change hands and the difficulty in tracking mass automated registrations have created an environment in which cybersquatting can flourish.

Cybersquatting is costly for businesses, which must attempt to register all variations of a name to protect their domain name rights from would-be cybersquatters. Large corporations may have to register thousands of domain names across the globe just to protect their basic brands and trademarks.

Search engines compile their results by looking through a Web site's key-word field. *Meta tags,* or key words, may be inserted into this field to increase the likelihood that a site will be included in search engine results. Using another's trademark in a meta tag without the owner's permission normally also constitutes trademark infringement.

Trademark Dilution in the Online World

As discussed on page 189, trademark dilution occurs when a trademark is used, without authorization, in a way that diminishes the distinctive quality of the mark. Unlike trademark infringement, a claim of dilution does not require proof that consumers are likely to be confused by a connection between the unauthorized use and the mark. For this reason, the products involved do not have to be similar, as illustrated in the following *Spotlight Case.*

SPOTLIGHT ON HASBRO, INC.

Case 8.2   **Hasbro, Inc. v. Internet Entertainment Group, Ltd.**

United States District Court, Western District of Washington, ____ F.Supp.2d ____ (1996).

BACKGROUND AND FACTS   In 1949, Hasbro, Inc.–then known as the Milton Bradley Company–first published the children's board game, Candy Land. Hasbro is the owner of the trademark "Candy Land," which has been registered with the U.S. Patent and Trademark Office since 1951. Over the years, Hasbro has produced several versions of the game, including Candy Land puzzles, a travel version, a PC game, and a handheld electronic version. In the mid-1990s, Brian Cartmell and his employer, the Internet Entertainment Group, Ltd., used the term *candyland.com* as a domain name for a sexually explicit Internet site. Anyone who performed an online search using the word *candyland* was directed to this adult Web site. Hasbro filed a trademark dilution claim in a federal court, seeking a permanent injunction to prevent the defendants from using the Candy Land trademark.

IN THE WORDS OF THE COURT. . .
DWYER, U.S. District Judge
* * * *

2. Hasbro has demonstrated a probability of proving that defendants Internet Entertainment Group, Ltd., Brian Cartmell

and Internet Entertainment Group, Inc. (collectively referred to as "defendants") have been diluting the value of Hasbro's CANDY LAND mark by using the name CANDYLAND to identify a sexually explicit Internet site, and by using the name string "candyland.com" as an Internet domain name which, when typed into an Internet-connected computer, provides Internet users with access to that site.
* * * *

4. Hasbro has shown that defendants' use of the CANDY LAND name and the domain name candyland.com in connection with their Internet site is causing irreparable injury to Hasbro.

5. *The probable harm to Hasbro from defendants' conduct outweighs any inconvenience that defendants will experience if they are required to stop using the CANDYLAND name.* [Emphasis added.]
* * * *

THEREFORE, IT IS HEREBY ORDERED that Hasbro's motion for preliminary injunction is granted.

DECISION AND REMEDY   The federal district court granted Hasbro an injunction against the defendants, agreeing that

Spotlight Case 8.2–Continued

the domain name, *candyland,* was "causing irreparable injury to Hasbro." The judge ordered the defendants to immediately remove all content from the *candyland.com* Web site and to stop using the Candy Land mark.

THE ECONOMIC DIMENSION *How can companies protect themselves from others who create Web sites that have similar domain names, and what limits each company's ability to be fully protected?*

Licensing

License In the context of intellectual property law, an agreement permitting the use of a trademark, copyright, patent, or trade secret for certain limited purposes.

One way to make use of another's trademark or other form of intellectual property, while avoiding litigation, is to obtain a license to do so. A **license** in this context is an agreement permitting the use of a trademark, copyright, patent, or trade secret for certain limited purposes. The party that owns the intellectual property rights and issues the license is the *licensor,* and the party obtaining the license is the *licensee.*

A license grants only the rights expressly described in the license agreement. A licensor might, for example, allow the licensee to use the trademark as part of its company name, or as part of its domain name, but not otherwise use the mark on any products or services. Disputes frequently arise over licensing agreements, particularly when the license involves uses on the Internet or in different nations.

CASE EXAMPLE 8.5   George V Restauration S.A. and others owned and operated the Buddha Bar Paris. One of the owners allowed Little Rest Twelve, Inc., to use the Buddha Bar trademark in New York City. When a dispute arose, the owners of Buddha Bar Paris withdrew their permission for Buddha Bar NYC's use of their mark, but Little Rest continued to use it. The owners of the mark filed a suit against Little Rest, and ultimately a state appellate court granted an injunction preventing Little Rest from using the mark.[6] ●

▶ Patents

Patent A government grant that gives an inventor the exclusive right or privilege to make, use, or sell his or her invention for a limited time period.

A **patent** is a grant from the government that gives an inventor the exclusive right to make, use, and sell an invention for a period of twenty years. Patents for designs, as opposed to inventions, are given for a fourteen-year period. For either a regular patent or a design patent, the applicant must demonstrate to the satisfaction of the U.S. Patent and Trademark Office that the invention, discovery, process, or design is *novel, useful,* and *not obvious* in light of current technology.

LEARNING OBJECTIVE 3 **How does the law protect patents?**

Until 2011, patent law in the United States differed from many other countries because the first person to invent a product or process obtained the patent rights rather than the first person to file for a patent. It was often difficult to prove who invented an item first, however, which prompted Congress to change the system in 2011 by passing the America Invents Act. Now, the first person to file an application for a patent on the product or process receives patent protection. In addition, under the new law there is a nine-month limit for challenging a patent on any ground.

The period of patent protection begins on the date when the patent application is filed, rather than when the patent is issued, which can sometimes be years later. After the patent period ends (either fourteen or twenty years later), the product or process enters the *public domain* (see page 202), and anyone can make, sell, or use the invention without paying the patent holder.

---

6. *George V Restauration S.A. v. Little Rest Twelve, Inc.,* 58 A.D.3d 428, 871 N.Y.S.2d 65 (2009).

What Is Patentable?

Under federal law, "[w]hoever invents or discovers any new and useful process, machine, manufacture, or composition of matter, or any new and useful improvement thereof, may obtain a patent therefor, subject to the conditions and requirements of this title."[7] As mentioned, to be patentable, the item must be novel, useful, and not obvious.

Almost anything is patentable, except the laws of nature, natural phenomena, and abstract ideas (including algorithms). Even artistic methods, certain works of art, and the structures of storylines are patentable, provided that they are novel and not obvious.

Plants that are reproduced asexually (by means other than from seed), such as hybrid or genetically engineered plants, are patentable in the United States, as are genetically engineered (or cloned) microorganisms and animals. **CASE EXAMPLE 8.6**   Monsanto, Inc., sells its patented genetically modified (GM) seeds to farmers as a way to achieve higher yields using fewer pesticides. Monsanto requires farmers who buy GM seeds to sign licensing agreements promising to plant the seeds for only one crop cycle and to pay a technology fee. To ensure compliance, Monsanto has investigated and prosecuted farmers who use the GM seeds illegally. Monsanto has filed more than 90 lawsuits against nearly 150 U.S. farmers and has been awarded more than $15 million in damages.[8] ●

Patent Infringement

> *"To invent, you need a good imagination and a pile of junk."*
>
> Thomas Edison, 1847–1931
> (American inventor)

If a firm makes, uses, or sells another's patented design, product, or process without the patent owner's permission, it commits the tort of patent infringement. Patent infringement may occur even though the patent owner has not put the patented product in commerce. Patent infringement may also occur even though not all features or parts of an invention are copied. (With respect to a patented process, however, all steps or their equivalent must be copied for infringement to exist.)

Often, litigation for patent infringement is so costly that the patent owner will instead offer to sell to the infringer a license to use the patented design, product, or process. Indeed, in many cases the costs of detection, prosecution, and monitoring are so high that patents are valueless to their owners, because the owners cannot justify the costs of protecting them.

If a patent is infringed, the patent holder may sue for relief in federal court. The patent holder can seek an injunction against the infringer and can also request damages for royalties and lost profits.

In the past, permanent injunctions were routinely granted to prevent future infringement. After a United States Supreme Court ruling, however, patent holders today are not automatically entitled to a permanent injunction against future infringing activities. According to the Court, a patent holder must prove that it has suffered irreparable injury and that the public interest would not be *disserved* by a permanent injunction.[9] This decision gives courts discretion to decide what is equitable in the circumstances and allows them to consider what is in the public interest rather than just the interests of the parties.

▶ Copyrights

Copyright   The exclusive right of an author to publish, print, or sell an intellectual production for a statutory period of time.

A **copyright** is an intangible property right granted by federal statute to the author or originator of certain literary or artistic productions. The Copyright Act of 1976,[10] as amended, governs copyrights. Works created after January 1, 1978, are automatically

---

7. 35 U.S.C. Section 101.
8. *Monsanto Co. v. Scruggs,* 459 F.3d 1328 (2006).
9. *eBay, Inc. v. MercExchange, LLC,* 547 U.S. 388, 126 S.Ct. 1837, 164 L.Ed.2d 641 (2006).
10. 17 U.S.C. Sections 101 *et seq.*

given statutory copyright protection for the life of the author, plus 70 years. For copyrights owned by publishing houses, the copyright expires 95 years from the date of publication or 120 years from the date of creation, whichever is first. For works by more than one author, the copyright expires 70 years after the death of the last surviving author.

Copyrights can be registered with the U.S. Copyright Office (www.copyright.gov) in Washington, D.C. A copyright owner no longer needs to place a © or *Copr.* or *Copyright* on the work, however, to have the work protected against infringement. Chances are that if somebody created it, somebody owns it.

CASE EXAMPLE 8.7   Rusty Carroll operated an online term paper business, R2C2 Inc., which offered up to 300,000 research papers for sale. Some individuals whose work had been posted on the site, without their permission, sued Carroll for copyright infringement. The court prohibited Carroll and his online business from selling any term paper without proof that the paper's author had given his or her permission.[11] ●

What Is Protected Expression?

LEARNING OBJECTIVE 4   What laws protect authors' rights in the works they generate?

Works that are copyrightable include books, records, films, artworks, architectural plans, menus, music videos, product packaging, and computer software. To be protected, a work must be "fixed in a durable medium" from which it can be perceived, reproduced, or communicated. Protection is automatic. Registration is not required.

To obtain protection under the Copyright Act, a work must be original and fall into one of the following categories:

BE CAREFUL   If a creative work does not fall into a certain category, it might not be copyrighted, but it may be protected by other intellectual property law.

- Literary and musical works.
- Dramatic works as well as pantomimes and choreographic works.
- Pictorial, graphic, and sculptural works.
- Motion pictures and other audiovisual works.
- Sound recordings, architectural works, and computer software.

The Copyright Act excludes copyright protection for any "idea, procedure, process, system, method of operation, concept, principle or discovery, regardless of the form in which it is described, explained, illustrated, or embodied." Note that it is not possible to copyright an idea. The underlying ideas embodied in a work may be freely used by others. What is copyrightable is the particular way in which an idea is expressed. Whenever an idea and an expression are inseparable, the expression cannot be copyrighted. A standard calendar, for instance, cannot be copyrighted.

Ethical Issue ⚖

Should the federal Copyright Act preempt plaintiffs from bringing "idea-submission" claims under state law? In the past, federal courts generally held that the Copyright Act preempted (superseded) claims in state courts alleging the theft of ideas. In 2011, however, a federal appellate court's decision in the case, *Montz v. Pilgrim Films,*[12] opened the door to such claims. The plaintiff, Larry Montz, had presented representatives from NBC Universal with a concept for a reality-style television program that would follow two paranormal investigators who search for evidence of ghosts. A number of meetings and discussions took place during which Montz provided scripts, videos, and other materials for the proposed show. Ultimately, the studio decided that it was not interested. Three years later, however, NBC partnered with Pilgrim Films to produce *Ghost Hunters,* a series on the Syfy Channel

Ethical Issue **Continues next page** ➡

---

11. *Weidner v. Carroll*, No. 06-782-DRH, U.S. District Court for the Southern District of Illinois, January 21, 2010.
12. 649 F.3d 975 (9th Cir. 2011).

that depicts a team of investigators who travel around the country looking for paranormal activity. Montz sued the producers for copyright infringement, breach of contract, and breach of confidence. He claimed that he had expressly conditioned the disclosure of his idea on an expectation that he would be a partner with NBC on the production and would receive a share of any profits.

The lower court dismissed his case, but the appellate court reversed, finding that the Copyright Act did not preempt Montz's two state law claims (breach of an implied contract and breach of confidence). The court reasoned that the state claims asserted rights that are qualitatively different from the rights protected by copyright. The contract claim survived preemption because it required proof of an extra element—the implied agreement of payment for use of a concept—which is a personal right that is different from copyright law. Similarly, the breach of confidence claim required the extra element of a confidential relationship between the parties.

Unlike ideas, compilations of facts are copyrightable. A *compilation* is a work formed by the collection and assembling of preexisting materials or of data that are selected, coordinated, or arranged in such a way that the resulting work as a whole constitutes an original work of authorship. The key requirement for the copyrightability of a compilation is originality.

Copyright Infringement

Whenever the form or expression of an idea is copied, an infringement of copyright occurs. The reproduction does not have to be exactly the same as the original, nor does it have to reproduce the original in its entirety. If a substantial part of the original is reproduced, copyright infringement has occurred.

REMEDIES FOR COPYRIGHT INFRINGEMENT   Those who infringe copyrights may be liable for damages or criminal penalties. These range from actual damages or statutory damages, imposed at the court's discretion, to criminal proceedings for willful violations. Actual damages are based on the harm caused to the copyright holder by the infringement, while statutory damages, not to exceed $150,000, are provided for under the Copyright Act. Criminal proceedings may result in fines and/or imprisonment. A court can also issue a permanent injunction against a defendant when the court deems it necessary to prevent future copyright infringement.

THE "FAIR USE" EXCEPTION   An exception to liability for copyright infringement is made under the *"fair use" doctrine*. A person or organization can reproduce copyrighted material without paying *royalties* for purposes such as criticism, comment, news reporting, teaching (including multiple copies for classroom use), scholarship, and research. (*Royalties* are fees paid to the copyright holder for the privilege of reproducing the copyrighted material.) In determining whether the use made of a work in a particular case is a fair use, a court considers the following:

1. The purpose of the use.
2. The nature of the copyrighted work.
3. How much of the original is copied.
4. The effect of the use on the market for the copyrighted work.

Under the *"first sale" doctrine*, once a copyright owner sells or gives away a copy of a work, the copyright owner no longer has the right to control the distribution of that copy. **EXAMPLE 8.8**   Miranda buys a copyrighted book, such as *The Hunger Games* by Suzanne Collins. She can legally sell it to another person. ●

Copyrights in Digital Information

Copyright law is probably the most important form of intellectual property protection on the Internet, largely because much of the material on the Web (software, for example) is copyrighted and in order to be transferred online, it must be "copied." Generally, anytime a party downloads software or music into a computer's random access memory, or RAM, without authorization, a copyright is infringed. Technology has vastly increased the potential for copyright infringement.

CASE EXAMPLE 8.9 In one case, a rap song that was included in the sound track of a movie had used only a few seconds from the guitar solo of another's copyrighted sound recording without permission. Nevertheless, a federal appellate court held that digitally sampling a copyrighted sound recording of any length constitutes copyright infringement.[13] •

In 1998, Congress implemented the provisions of the World Intellectual Property Organization (WIPO) treaty by updating U.S. copyright law. The law—the Digital Millennium Copyright Act of 1998—is a landmark step in the protection of copyright owners and, because of the leading position of the United States in the creative industries, serves as a model for other nations. Among other things, the act established civil and criminal penalties for anyone who circumvents (gets around) encryption software or other technological antipiracy protection. Also prohibited are the manufacture, import, sale, and distribution of devices or services for circumvention.

MP3 and File-Sharing Technology

Soon after the Internet became popular, a few enterprising programmers created software to compress large data files, particularly those associated with music, so that they could more easily be transmitted online. The best-known compression and decompression system is MP3, which enables music fans to download songs or entire CDs onto their computers or onto portable listening devices, such as iPods. The MP3 system also made it possible for music fans to access other fans' files by engaging in file-sharing via the Internet.

Peer-to-Peer (P2P) Networking The sharing of resources (such as files, hard drives, and processing styles) among multiple computers without the need for a central network server.

Distributed Network A network that can be used by persons located (distributed) around the country or the globe to share computer files.

Cloud Computing A subscription-based or pay-per-use service that, in real time over the Internet, extends a computer's software or storage capabilities.

File-sharing is accomplished through **peer-to-peer (P2P) networking.** The concept is simple. Rather than going through a central Web server, P2P involves numerous personal computers (PCs) that are connected to the Internet. Individuals on the same network can access files stored on a single PC through a **distributed network,** which has parts dispersed in many locations. Persons scattered throughout the country or the world can work together on the same project by using file-sharing programs.

A newer method of sharing files via the Internet is **cloud computing,** which is essentially a subscription-based or pay-per-use service that extends a computer's software or storage capabilities. Cloud computing can deliver a single application through a browser to multiple users, or it may be a utility program to pool resources and provide data storage and virtual servers that can be accessed on demand. Apple, Amazon, Facebook, Google, IBM, and Sun Microsystems are using and developing cloud-computing services. By using the services of large companies with excess storage and computing capacity, a company can increase its information technology capabilities without investing in new infrastructure, training new personnel, or licensing new software.

---

13. *Bridgeport Music, Inc. v. Dimension Films,* 410 F.3d 792 (6th Cir. 2005).

SHARING STORED MUSIC FILES   When file-sharing is used to download others' stored music files, copyright issues arise. Recording artists and their labels have lost large amounts of royalties and revenues because relatively few CDs are purchased and then made available on distributed networks, from which everyone can get them for free.

    CASE EXAMPLE 8.10   Napster, Inc., operated a Web site with free software that enabled users to copy and transfer MP3 files via the Internet. When firms in the recording industry sued Napster, the court held that Napster was liable for copyright infringement because it had assisted others in obtaining unauthorized copies of copyrighted music.[14] •

THE EVOLUTION OF FILE-SHARING TECHNOLOGIES   After the *Napster* decision, the recording industry filed and won numerous lawsuits against companies that distribute online file-sharing software. Other companies then developed technologies that allow P2P network users to share stored music files, without paying a fee, more quickly and efficiently than ever. Software such as Morpheus, KaZaA, and LimeWire, for example, provides users with an interface that is similar to a Web browser. When a user performs a search, the software locates a list of peers that have the file available for downloading. Because of the automated procedures, the companies do not maintain a central index and are unable to supervise whether users are exchanging copyrighted files.

    In 2005, the United States Supreme Court clarified that companies that distribute file-sharing software intending that it be used to violate copyright laws can be liable for users' copyright infringement. **CASE EXAMPLE 8.11**   Music and film industry organizations sued Grokster, Ltd., for copyright infringement. The United States Supreme Court held that anyone who distributes file-sharing software "with the object of promoting its use to infringe copyright, as shown by clear expression or other affirmative steps taken to foster infringement, . . . is liable for the resulting acts of infringement by third parties." Although the music and film industries won the case, they have not been able to prevent new technology from enabling copyright infringement.[15] •

▶ Trade Secrets

The law of trade secrets protects some business processes and information that are not or cannot be patented, copyrighted, or trademarked against appropriation by a competitor. A **trade secret** is basically information of commercial value. This may include customer lists, plans, research and development, pricing information, marketing techniques, and production methods—anything that makes an individual company unique and that would have value to a competitor.

    Unlike copyright and trademark protection, protection of trade secrets extends both to ideas and to their expression. (For this reason, and because there are no registration or filing requirements for trade secrets, trade secret protection may be well suited for software.) Of course, the secret formula, method, or other information must be disclosed to some persons, particularly to key employees. Businesses generally attempt to protect their trade secrets by having all employees who use the process or information agree in their contracts, or in confidentiality agreements, never to divulge it.

Trade Secret   Information or a process that gives a business an advantage over competitors that do not know the information or process.

---

14. *A&M Records, Inc. v. Napster, Inc.,* 239 F.3d 1004 (9th Cir. 2001).

15. *Metro-Goldwyn-Mayer Studios, Inc. v. Grokster, Ltd.,* 545 U.S. 913, 125 S.Ct. 2764, 162 L.Ed.2d 781 (2005). Grokster, Ltd., later settled this dispute out of court and stopped distributing its software.

State and Federal Law on Trade Secrets

Under Section 757 of the *Restatement of Torts,* those who disclose or use another's trade secret, without authorization, are liable to that other party if (1) they discovered the secret by improper means or (2) their disclosure or use constitutes a breach of a duty owed to the other party. The theft of confidential business data by industrial espionage, as when a business taps into a competitor's computer, is a theft of trade secrets without any contractual violation and is actionable in itself.

Although trade secrets have long been protected under the common law, today most states' laws are based on the Uniform Trade Secrets Act, which has been adopted in forty-seven states. Additionally, in 1996 Congress passed the Economic Espionage Act, which made the theft of trade secrets a federal crime.

LEARNING OBJECTIVE 5 What are trade secrets, and what laws offer protection for this form of intellectual property?

Trade Secrets in Cyberspace

Today's computer technology undercuts a business firm's ability to protect its confidential information, including trade secrets. For instance, a former employee's continued use of a Twitter account after leaving the company may be the grounds for a lawsuit alleging misappropriation of trade secrets.

CASE EXAMPLE 8.12 Noah Kravitz worked for a company called PhoneDog as a product reviewer and video blogger. PhoneDog provided him with the Twitter account "@PhoneDog_Noah." Kravitz's popularity grew, and he had approximately 17,000 followers by the time he quit. PhoneDog requested that Kravitz stop using the Twitter account. Although Kravitz changed his handle to "@noahkravitz," he continued to use the account. Subsequently, PhoneDog sued Kravitz for misappropriation of trade secrets. Kravitz moved for a dismissal, but the court found that the complaint adequately stated a cause of action for misappropriation of trade secrets and allowed the suit to continue.[16] ●

For a summary of trade secrets and other forms of intellectual property, see Exhibit 8–1 on the following page.

● International Protection for Intellectual Property

For many years, the United States has been a party to various international agreements relating to intellectual property rights. For example, the Paris Convention of 1883, to which 173 countries are signatory, allows parties in one country to file for patent and trademark protection in any of the other member countries. Other international agreements include the Berne Convention, the Agreement on Trade-Related Aspects of Intellectual Property Rights (or more simply, the TRIPS agreement), and the Madrid Protocol.

The Berne Convention

Under the Berne Convention of 1886 (an international copyright agreement), if a U.S. citizen writes a book, every country that has signed the convention must recognize the U.S. author's copyright in the book. Also, if a citizen of a country that has not signed the convention first publishes a book in one of the 165 countries that have signed, all other countries that have signed the convention must recognize that author's copyright. Copyright notice is not needed to gain protection under the Berne Convention for works published after March 1, 1989.

---

16. *PhoneDog v. Kravitz,* 2011 WL 5415612 (N.D.Cal. 2011).

• *Exhibit* 8–1 **Forms of Intellectual Property**

	DEFINITION	HOW ACQUIRED	DURATION	REMEDY FOR INFRINGEMENT
Patent	A grant from the government that gives an inventor exclusive rights to an invention.	By filing a patent application with the U.S. Patent and Trademark Office and receiving its approval.	Twenty years from the date of the application; for design patents, fourteen years.	Monetary damages, including royalties and lost profits, *plus* attorneys' fees. Damages may be tripled for intentional infringements.
Copyright	The right of an author or originator of a literary or artistic work, or other production that falls within a specified category, to have the exclusive use of that work for a given period of time.	Automatic (once the work or creation is put in tangible form). Only the *expression* of an idea (and not the idea itself) can be protected by copyright.	For authors: the life of the author, plus 70 years. For publishers: 95 years after the date of publication or 120 years after creation.	Actual damages plus profits received by the party who infringed *or* statutory damages under the Copyright Act, *plus* costs and attorneys' fees in either situation.
Trademark (service mark and trade dress)	Any distinctive word, name, symbol, or device (image or appearance), or combination thereof, that an entity uses to distinguish its goods or services from those of others. The owner has the exclusive right to use that mark or trade dress.	1. At common law, ownership created by use of the mark. 2. Registration with the appropriate federal or state office gives notice and is permitted if the mark is currently in use or will be within the next six months.	Unlimited, as long as it is in use. To continue notice by registration, the owner must renew by filing between the fifth and sixth years, and thereafter, every ten years.	1. Injunction prohibiting the future use of the mark. 2. Actual damages plus profits received by the party who infringed (can be increased under the Lanham Act). 3. Destruction of articles that infringed. 4. *Plus* costs and attorneys' fees.
Trade Secret	Any information that a business possesses and that gives the business an advantage over competitors (including formulas, lists, patterns, plans, processes, and programs).	Through the originality and development of the information and processes that constitute the business secret and are unknown to others.	Unlimited, so long as not revealed to others. Once revealed to others, it is no longer a trade secret.	Monetary damages for misappropriation (the Uniform Trade Secrets Act also permits punitive damages if willful), *plus* costs and attorneys' fees.

In 2011, the European Union agreed to extend the period of royalty protection for musicians from fifty years to seventy years. This decision aids major record labels—as well as performers and musicians—who previously faced losing royalties from sales of their older recordings. The profits of musicians and record companies have been shrinking in recent years because of the sharp decline in sales of compact discs and the rise in digital downloads (both legal and illegal).

In the following case, the United States Supreme Court had to decide if Congress had exceeded its authority under the U.S. Constitution when it enacted a law that restored copyright protection to many foreign works that were already in the public domain. (*Public domain* means that rights to certain intellectual property, such as songs and other published works, belong to everyone and are not protected by copyright or patent laws.)

Case 8.3 **Golan v. Holder**

Supreme Court of the United States, ___ U.S. ___, 132 S.Ct. 873, 181 L.Ed.2d 835 (2012).

BACKGROUND AND FACTS The United States joined the Berne Convention—an international treaty on intellectual property right protection—in 1989, but it failed to give foreign copyright holders the same protections enjoyed by U.S. authors. Contrary to the Berne Convention, the United States did not protect any foreign work that had already entered the public domain. In 1994, Congress enacted the Uruguay Round Agreements Act (URAA), which "restored" copyright protection for many foreign works that were already in the public domain. The URAA put foreign and domestic works on the same footing, allowing their copyrights to extend for the same terms. Lawrence Golan, along with a group of musicians, conductors, and publishers, filed a suit against Eric Holder, in his capacity as the U.S. attorney general, challenging the URAA and claiming that it violated the copyright clause of the U.S. Constitution.

These individuals had enjoyed free access to foreign works in the public domain before the URAA's enactment, and they argued that Congress had exceeded its constitutional authority in passing the URAA. A federal appellate court held that Congress did not violate the copyright clause by passing the URAA. The petitioners appealed. The United States Supreme Court granted certiorari to resolve the matter.

IN THE WORDS OF THE COURT . . .
Justice *GINSBURG* delivered the opinion of the Court.
* * * *

* * * The Constitution states that "Congress shall have Power . . . to promote the Progress of Science . . . by securing for limited Times to Authors . . . the exclusive Right to their . . . Writings." Petitioners [Golan and others] find in this grant of authority an impenetrable [impassable] barrier to the extension of copyright protection to authors whose writings, for whatever reason, are in the public domain. We see no such barrier in the text of the Copyright Clause * * * .
* * * *

The text of the Copyright Clause does not exclude application of copyright protection to works in the public domain. * * * Petitioners' contrary argument relies primarily on the Constitution's confinement of a copyright's lifespan to a "limited Tim[e]." "Removing works

from the public domain," they contend, "violates the 'limited times' restriction by turning a fixed and predictable period into one that can be reset or resurrected at any time, even after it expires."

Our decision in [a prior case] is largely dispositive [capable of settling a dispute] of petitioners' limited-time argument.[a] There we addressed the question of whether Congress violated the Copyright Clause when it extended, by 20 years, the terms of existing copyrights. Ruling that Congress acted within constitutional bounds, we declined to infer from the text of the Copyright Clause "the command that a time prescription, once set, becomes forever 'fixed' or 'inalterable.'" *"The word 'limited,' we observed, "does not convey a meaning so constricted." Rather, the term is best understood to mean "confine[d] within certain bounds," "restrain[ed]," or "circumscribed."* The construction petitioners tender closely resembles the definition rejected in *Eldred* [the prior case] and is similarly infirm [weak]. [Emphasis added.]
* * * *

* * * In aligning the United States with other nations bound by the Berne Convention, and thereby according equitable treatment to once disfavored foreign authors, Congress can hardly be charged with a design to move stealthily toward a regime of perpetual copyrights.

DECISION AND REMEDY The United States Supreme Court affirmed the judgment of the federal appellate court that ruled the URAA does not violate the U.S. Constitution's copyright clause. Thus, Golan and the others could no longer use, without permission, any of the previous public domain foreign works, which are indeed protected by the URAA. By passing the URAA in the United States, Congress, in effect, took the foreign works that Golan and others had been using out of the public domain. Henceforth, U.S. copyright and patent laws cover all such foreign intellectual property.

THE GLOBAL DIMENSION *What does the Court's decision in this case mean for copyright holders in the United States who want copyright protection in other countries? Will other nations be more or less inclined to protect U.S. authors? Explain.*

---

a. See *Eldred v. Ashcroft,* 537 U.S. 186, 123 S.Ct. 769, 154 L.Ed.2d 683 (2003).

The TRIPS Agreement

Representatives from more than one hundred nations signed the TRIPS agreement in 1994. The agreement established, for the first time, standards for the international protection of intellectual property rights, including patents, trademarks, and copyrights for movies, computer programs, books, and music. The TRIPS agreement provides that each member country must include in its domestic laws broad intellectual property rights and effective remedies (including civil and criminal penalties) for violations of those rights.

Generally, the TRIPS agreement forbids member nations from discriminating against foreign owners of intellectual property rights in the administration, regulation, or adjudication of those rights. In other words, a member nation cannot give its own nationals (citizens) favorable treatment without offering the same treatment to nationals of all member countries. **EXAMPLE 8.13** A U.S. software manufacturer brings a suit for the infringement of intellectual property rights under Germany's national laws. Because Germany is a member nation, the U.S. manufacturer is entitled to receive the same treatment as a German manufacturer. ●

Each member nation must also ensure that legal procedures are available for parties who wish to bring actions for infringement of intellectual property rights. Additionally, a related document established a mechanism for settling disputes among member nations.

▶ Reviewing . . . Intellectual Property and Internet Law

Two computer science majors, Trent and Xavier, have an idea for a new video game, which they propose to call "Hallowed." They form a business and begin developing their idea. Several months later, Trent and Xavier run into a problem with their design and consult with a friend, Brad, who is an expert in creating computer source codes. After the software is completed but before Hallowed is marketed, a video game called Halo 2 is released for both the Xbox and PlayStation 3 systems. Halo 2 uses source codes similar to those of Hallowed and imitates Hallowed's overall look and feel, although not all the features are alike. Using the information presented in the chapter, answer the following questions.

1. Would the name *Hallowed* receive protection as a trademark or as trade dress?
2. If Trent and Xavier had obtained a patent on Hallowed, would the release of Halo 2 infringe on their patent? Why or why not?
3. Based only on the facts described above, could Trent and Xavier sue the makers of Halo 2 for copyright infringement? Why or why not?
4. Suppose that Trent and Xavier discover that Brad took the idea of Hallowed and sold it to the company that produced Halo 2. Which type of intellectual property issue does this raise?

▶ Debate This

Congress has amended the Copyright Act several times. Copyright holders now have protection for many decades. Was Congress justified in extending the copyright time periods? Why or why not?

Linking the Law *to Marketing*
Trademarks and Service Marks

In your marketing courses, you will learn about the importance of trademarks. As a marketing manager, you will be involved with creating trademarks or service marks for your firm, protecting existing marks, and ensuring that you do not infringe on anyone else's marks.

The Broad Range of Trademarks and Service Marks

The courts have held that trademarks and service marks consist of much more than well-known brand names, such as Sony and Apple.

As a marketing manager, you will need to be aware that parts of a brand or other product identification often qualify for trademark protection.

- **Catchy phrases**—Marketers have developed certain phrases that have become associated with their brands, such as Nike's "Just Do It!" Take care not to use another brand's catchy phrase in your own marketing program. Note, too, that not all phrases can become part of a trademark or service mark. When a phrase is extremely common, the courts normally will not grant trademark or service mark protection to it. America Online, Inc., for example, was unable to protect its phrases "You have mail" and "You've got mail."

- **Abbreviations**—The public sometimes abbreviates a well-known trademark. For instance, Budweiser beer became known as Bud and Coca-Cola as Coke. Do not use any name for a product or service that closely resembles a well-known abbreviation, such as Koke for a cola drink.
- **Shapes**—The shape of a brand name, a service mark, or a container can take on exclusivity if the shape clearly aids in product or service identification. For example, just about everyone recognizes the shape of a Coca-Cola bottle.
- **Ornamental colors**—Sometimes, color combinations can become part of a service mark or trademark. For example, the combination of bright orange and purple is associated with FedEx's unique identity. The courts have protected this color combination. The same holds for the black-and-copper color combination of Duracell batteries.
- **Ornamental designs**—Symbols and designs associated with a particular mark normally are protected, so do not attempt to copy them. For instance, Levi's places a small red tag on the left side of the rear pocket of its jeans.
- **Sounds**—Sounds can also be protected. For example, the familiar roar of the Metro-Goldwyn-Mayer lion is protected.

When to Protect Your Trademarks and Service Marks

Once your company has established a trademark or a service mark, as a manager, you will have to decide how aggressively you wish to protect those marks. If you fail to protect them, your company faces the possibility that they will become generic. Remember that *aspirin, thermos, shredded wheat,* and many other familiar terms were once legally protected trademarks.

Protecting exclusive rights to a mark can be expensive, so you will have to determine how much it is worth to your company to protect your rights. Coca-Cola and Rolls-Royce run newspaper and magazine ads stating that their names are protected trademarks and cannot be used as generic terms. Occasionally, such ads threaten lawsuits against any competitors that infringe the trademarks. If you work in a small company, making such major expenditures to protect your trademarks and service marks will not be cost-effective.

FOR CRITICAL ANALYSIS

The U.S. Patent and Trademark Office requires that a registered trademark or service mark be put into commercial use within three years after the application has been approved. Why do you think the federal government put this requirement into place?

 Key Terms

certification mark 191	distributed network 199	service mark 191
cloud computing 199	domain name 192	trade dress 191
collective mark 191	intellectual property 187	trade name 191
copyright 196	license 195	trade secret 200
cyber mark 192	patent 195	trademark 188
cybersquatting 193	peer-to-peer (P2P) networking 199	

Chapter Summary: Intellectual Property and Internet Law

Trademarks and Related Property (See pages 188–192.)	1. A *trademark* is a distinctive word, symbol, sound, or design that has become sufficiently associated with a good or has been registered with a government agency. 2. The major federal statutes protecting trademarks and related property are the Lanham Act of 1946 and the Federal Trademark Dilution Act of 1995. Generally, to be protected, a trademark must be sufficiently distinctive from all competing trademarks. 3. *Trademark infringement* occurs when a party who does not own a trademark copies it to a substantial degree or uses it in its entirety.
Cyber Marks (See pages 192–195.)	A *cyber mark* is a trademark in cyberspace. Trademark infringement in cyberspace occurs when one person uses, in a domain name or in meta tags, a name that is the same as, or confusingly similar to, the protected mark of another.

(Continued)

Chapter Summary: Intellectual Property and Internet Law, Continued

Patents (See pages 195–196.)	1. A *patent* is a grant from the government that gives an inventor the exclusive right to make, use, and sell an invention for a period of twenty years (fourteen years for a design patent) from the date when the application for a patent is filed. To be patentable, an invention (or a discovery, process, or design) must be novel, useful, and not obvious in light of current technology. Computer software may be patented. 2. Almost anything is patentable, except the laws of nature, natural phenomena, and abstract ideas (including algorithms). 3. *Patent infringement* occurs when a person uses or sells another's patented design, product, or process without the patent owner's permission. The patent holder can sue the infringer in federal court and request an injunction, but must prove irreparable injury to obtain a permanent injunction against the infringer.
Copyrights (See pages 196–200.)	1. A *copyright* is an intangible property right granted by federal statute to the author or originator of certain literary or artistic productions. The Copyright Act of 1976 governs copyrights. 2. *Copyright infringement* occurs whenever the form or expression of an idea is copied without the permission of the copyright holder. An exception applies if the copying is deemed a "fair use." 3. To protect copyrights in digital information, Congress passed the Digital Millennium Copyright Act of 1998. 4. Technology that allows users to share files online often raises copyright infringement issues. 5. The United States Supreme Court has ruled that companies that provide file-sharing software to users can be held liable for copyright infringement if they take affirmative steps to promote unauthorized copying of copyrighted material.
Trade Secrets (See pages 200–201.)	*Trade secrets* include customer lists, plans, research and development, and pricing information, for example. Trade secrets are protected under the common law and, in some states, under statutory law against misappropriation by competitors.
International Protection for Intellectual Property (See pages 201–204.)	Various international agreements provide international protection for intellectual property. A landmark agreement is the 1994 Agreement on Trade-Related Aspects of Intellectual Property Rights (TRIPS), which provides for enforcement procedures in all countries signatory to the agreement.

ExamPrep

ISSUE SPOTTERS

—Check your answers to these questions against the answers provided in Appendix D at the end of this text.

1. Global Products develops, patents, and markets software. World Copies, Inc., sells Global's software without the maker's permission. Is this patent infringement? If so, how might Global save the cost of suing World for infringement and at the same time profit from World's sales? **(See pages 195 and 196.)**
2. In 2000, Eagle Corporation began marketing software under the mark "Eagle." In 2011, Eagle.com, Inc., a different company selling different products, begins to use *eagle* as part of its URL and registers it as a domain name. Can Eagle Corporation stop this use of *eagle*? If so, what must the company show? **(See pages 189 and 193.)**

BEFORE THE TEST

Go to **www.cengagebrain.com**, enter the ISBN 9781133586548, and click on "Find" to locate this textbook's Web site. Then click on "Access Now" under "Study Tools," and select Chapter 8 at the top. There, you will find a Practice Quiz that you can take to assess your mastery of the concepts in this chapter. Additionally, you will find Flashcards and a Glossary of important terms, as well as Video Questions (when assigned).

For Review

Answers for the even-numbered questions in this For Review *section can be found in Appendix E at the end of this text.*

1. What is intellectual property?

2. Why is the protection of trademarks important?

3. How does the law protect patents?

4. What laws protect authors' rights in the works they generate?

5. What are trade secrets, and what laws offer protection for this form of intellectual property?

Questions and Case Problems

8–1. Patent Infringement. John and Andrew Doney invented a hard-bearing device for balancing rotors. Although they registered their invention with the U.S. Patent and Trademark Office, it was never used as an automobile wheel balancer. Some time later, Exetron Corp. produced an automobile wheel balancer that used a hard-bearing device with a support plate similar to that of the Doneys' device. Given that the Doneys had not used their device for automobile wheel balancing, does Exetron's use of a similar device infringe on the Doneys' patent? Why or why not? **(See page 196.)**

8–2. **Question with Sample Answer: Fair Use.** Professor Littrell is teaching a summer seminar in business torts at State University. Several times during the course, he makes copies of relevant sections from business law texts and distributes them to his students. Littrell does not realize that the daughter of one of the textbook authors is a member of his seminar. She tells her father about Littrell's copying activities, which have taken place without her father's or his publisher's permission. Her father sues Littrell for copyright infringement. Littrell claims protection under the fair use doctrine. Who will prevail? Explain. **(See page 198.)**

—For a sample answer to Question 8–2, go to Appendix F at the end of this text.

8–3. Licensing. Redwin Wilchcombe composed, performed, and recorded a song titled *Tha Weedman* at the request of Lil Jon, a member of Lil Jon & the East Side Boyz (LJESB), for LJESB's album "Kings of Crunk." Wilchcombe was not paid, but was given credit on the album as a producer. After the album had sold 2 million copies, Wilchcombe filed a suit against LJESB, alleging copyright infringement. The defendants claimed that they had a license to use the song. Do the facts support this claim? Explain. [*Wilchcombe v. TeeVee Toons, Inc.,* 555 F.3d 949 (11th Cir. 2009)] **(See page 195.)**

8–4. Trade Secrets. Jesse Edwards was an employee of Carbon Processing and Reclamation, LLC (CPR). In his car were unmarked boxes of company records. Edwards's wife, Channon, who suspected him of hiding financial information from her, gained access to the documents. William

Jones, the owner of CPR, filed a suit, contending that Channon's unauthorized access to the files was a theft of trade secrets. Could the information in the documents be trade secrets? Should liability be imposed? Why or why not? [*Jones v. Hamilton,* 55 So.3d 134 (Ala.Civ.App. 2010)] **(See page 200.)**

8–5. **Spotlight on Macy's: Copyright Infringement.** United Fabrics International, Inc., bought a fabric design from an Italian designer and registered a copyright to it with the U.S. Copyright Office. When Macy's, Inc., began selling garments with a similar design, United filed a copyright infringement suit against Macy's. Macy's argued that United did not own a valid copyright to the design and so could not claim infringement. Does United have to prove that the copyright is valid to establish infringement? Explain. [*United Fabrics International, Inc. v. C & J Wear, Inc.,* 630 F.3d 1255 (9th Cir. 2011)] **(See page 198.)**

8–6. **Case Problem with Sample Answer: Copyright Infringement.** Universal Music Group (UMG) regularly ships free, unsolicited promotional CDs to music critics and others. The labels state that they are "the property of the record company" and for "Promotional Use Only—Not for Sale." When Troy Augusto sold some of the CDs through online auction sites, UMG filed a complaint in a federal district court, alleging copyright infringement. UMG argued that it had only licensed the CDs to the recipients and that ownership had not transferred to Augusto. Could Augusto sell, or otherwise dispose of, the CDs? Explain. [*UMG Recordings, Inc. v. Augusto,* 628 F.3d 1175 (9th Cir. 2011)] **(See page 198.)**

—For a sample answer to Case Problem 8–6, go to Appendix G at the end of this text.

8–7. Trade Secrets. In 1988, Hanjuan Jin, a citizen of the People's Republic of China, began working at Motorola as a software engineer in a division that created proprietary standards for cellular communications. In 2004 and 2005, in contradiction to Motorola's policies, Jin also began working as a consultant for Lemko Corp. Lemko introduced Jin to Sun Kaisens, a Chinese software company. During 2005, Jin returned to Beijing on several occasions and began working with Sun

Kaisens and with the Chinese military. The following year, she started corresponding with Sun Kaisens's management about a possible full-time job in China. In 2007, after one of several medical leaves, she returned to Motorola, where she accessed and downloaded thousands of documents on her personal mobile devices. The next day, she tried to board a flight to China but was randomly searched by U.S. Customs and Border Protection officials at a U.S. airport. Ultimately, U.S. officials discovered the thousands of downloaded Motorola documents. Are there any circumstances under which Jin could avoid being prosecuted for theft of trade secrets? If so, what are these circumstances? Discuss fully. [*United States v. Hanjuan Jin*, 833 F.Supp.2d 977, (N.D.Ill. 2012)] **(See pages 200–201.)**

8–8. **A Question of Ethics: Copyright Infringement.** *Custom Copies, Inc., in Gainesville, Florida, is a copy shop that reproduces and distributes, for profit, on request, material published and owned by others. One of the copy shop's primary activities is the preparation and sale of coursepacks, which contain compilations of readings for college courses. For a particular coursepack, a teacher selects the readings and delivers a syllabus to the copy shop, which obtains the materials from a library, copies them, and then binds and sells the copies. Blackwell Publishing, Inc., in Malden, Massachusetts, publishes books and journals in medicine and other fields and owns the copyrights to these publications. Blackwell and others filed a suit in a federal district court against Custom Copies, alleging copyright infringement for its "routine and systematic reproduction of materials from plaintiffs' publications, without seeking permission," to compile coursepacks for classes at the University of Florida. The plaintiffs asked the court to issue an injunction and award them damages, as well as the profit from the infringement. The defendant filed a motion to dismiss the complaint. [Blackwell Publishing, Inc. v. Custom Copies, Inc., __ F.Supp.2d __ (N.D.Fla. 2007)]* **(See pages 198–200.)**

1. Custom Copies argued, in part, that it did not "distribute" the coursepacks. Does a copy shop violate copyright law if it only copies materials for coursepacks? Does the copying fall under the "fair use" exception? Should the court grant the defendants' motion? Why or why not?

2. What is the potential impact if copies of a book or journal are created and sold without the permission of, and the payment of royalties or a fee to, the copyright owner? Explain.

8–9. **In Your Court: Copyright Infringement.** Over an approximately forty-year time span, several well-known authors gave Random House, Inc., an exclusive license to "print, publish, and sell" their specific works "in book form." The authors later individually contracted with Rosetta Books, giving Rosetta Books a license to print exactly the same text as e-books. The e-books would have different online covers, title pages, and forewords, along with various other features unique to the electronic format. When the e-books came out in 2001, Random House filed a lawsuit against Rosetta Books, alleging copyright infringement and asking for an injunction to prohibit Rosetta from offering these works in digital form. Assume that you are the judge in the federal court hearing this case and answer the following questions: **(See pages 198–200.)**

1. A central issue in this case has to do with how to interpret the language of the contract (license) between the parties, particularly with respect to the phrase "in book form." Should the phrase be interpreted to include e-books? Why or why not?

2. What will your ruling be in this case? How will your interpretation of the phrase "in book form" affect your ruling?

3. Some of the contracts were signed long before e-books became an option for publishers. Should this fact affect your interpretation of the phrase "in book form"?

8–10. **Critical-Thinking Managerial Question.** Sync Computers, Inc., makes computer-related products under the brand name "Sync," which the company registers as a trademark. Without Sync's permission, E-Product Corp. embeds the Sync mark in E-Product's Web site, in black type on a blue background. This tag causes the E-Product site to be returned at the top of the list of results on a search engine query for "Sync." Does E-Product's use of the Sync mark as a meta tag without Sync's permission constitute trademark infringement? Explain. **(See pages 189 and 194.)**

Chapter 9

International Law in a Global Economy

> "The merchant
> has no country."
>
> —Thomas Jefferson, 1743–1826
> (Third president of the United States,
> 1801–1809)

Contents

Learning Objectives

The five Learning Objectives below are designed to help improve your understanding of the chapter. After reading this chapter, you should be able to answer the following questions:

1. **What is the principle of comity?**

2. **What is the act of state doctrine? In what circumstances is this doctrine applied?**

3. **Under the Foreign Sovereign Immunities Act, in which situations is a foreign state subject to the jurisdiction of U.S. courts?**

4. **What are three clauses commonly included in international business contracts?**

5. **What federal law allows U.S. citizens, as well as citizens of foreign nations, to file civil actions in U.S. courts for torts that were committed overseas?**

(OlegAlbinsky/iStockphoto.com)

International business transactions are not unique to the modern world. Indeed, commerce has always crossed national borders, as President Thomas Jefferson noted in the chapter-opening quotation above. What is new in our day is the dramatic growth in world trade and the emergence of a global business community. Because exchanges of goods, services, and ideas on a global level are now routine, students of business law and the legal environment should be familiar with the laws pertaining to international business transactions.

Future businesspersons should also be aware that in response to the latest economic recession, the U.S. government has undertaken an initiative to encourage exports of goods and services to foreign markets by U.S. companies. Accordingly, we examine this recent initiative in this chapter's *Shifting Legal Priorities for Business* feature on page 213.

In this chapter, we also examine how both international law and national law frame business operations in the global context. We also look at some selected areas relating to business activities in a global context, including international sales contracts, civil dispute resolution, letters of credit, and investment protection. We conclude the chapter with a discussion of the application of certain U.S. laws in a transnational setting.

▶ International Principles and Doctrines

Treaty   A formal written agreement negotiated between two or more nations.

Recall from our discussion in Chapter 1 that *international law* (see page 13) can be defined as a body of law—formed as a result of international customs, **treaties**, and organizations (such as the United Nations)—that governs relations among or between nations. *National law*, in contrast, is the law of a particular nation, such as Brazil or Japan.

Here, we look at some legal principles and doctrines of international law that have evolved over time and that the courts of various nations have employed—to a greater or lesser extent—to resolve or reduce conflicts that involve a foreign element. The three important legal principles and doctrines discussed in the following subsections are based primarily on courtesy and respect and are applied in the interests of maintaining harmonious relations among nations.

The Principle of Comity

Comity   The principle by which one nation defers to and gives effect to the laws and judicial decrees of another nation. This recognition is based primarily on respect.

Under the principle of **comity**, one nation will defer to and give effect to the laws and judicial decrees of another country, as long as they are consistent with the law and public policy of the accommodating nation.

LEARNING OBJECTIVE 1   **What is the principle of comity?**

CASE EXAMPLE 9.1   Karen Goldberg's husband was killed in a terrorist bombing in Israel. She filed a lawsuit in a federal court in New York against UBS AG, a Switzerland-based company with offices in the United States. Goldberg claimed that UBS was liable under the U.S. Anti-Terrorism Act for aiding and abetting the murder of her husband because it provided financial services to the international terrorist organizations responsible for his murder. UBS argued that the case should be transferred to a court in Israel, which would offer a remedy "substantially the same" as the one available in the United States. The court refused to transfer the case, however, because that would require an Israeli court to take evidence and judge the emotional damage suffered by Goldberg, "raising distinct concerns of comity and enforceability." U.S. courts hesitate to impose U.S. law on foreign courts when such law is "an unwarranted intrusion" on the policies governing a foreign nation's judicial system.[1] ●

The Act of State Doctrine

Act of State Doctrine   A doctrine providing that the judicial branch of one country will not examine the validity of public acts committed by a recognized foreign government within its own territory.

The **act of state doctrine** provides that the judicial branch of one country will not examine the validity of public acts committed by a recognized foreign government within its own territory.

A government controls the natural resources, such as oil reserves, within its territory. It can decide to exploit the resources or preserve them, or to establish a balance between exploitation and preservation. Does the act of state doctrine apply to such decisions even though they may affect market prices in other countries? That was the question in the following case.

---

1. *Goldberg v. UBS AG*, 690 F.Supp.2d 92 (E.D.N.Y. 2010).

Case 9.1   **Spectrum Stores, Inc. v. Citgo Petroleum Corp.**

United States Court of Appeals, Fifth District, 632 F.3d 938 (2011).

BACKGROUND AND FACTS   Spectrum Stores, Inc., and other U.S. gasoline retailers (the plaintiffs) filed a suit against Citgo Petroleum Corporation and other oil production companies in a federal district court. The plaintiffs alleged that the defendants had conspired to fix the prices of crude oil and refined petroleum products in the United States, primarily by limiting the production of crude oil. Citgo is owned by the national oil company of Venezuela, and most of the other defendants are owned entirely or in part by Venezuela or Saudi Arabia. Both nations are members of the Organization of Petroleum Exporting Countries (OPEC), which was formed by several oil-rich

Case 9.1—Continued

nations "to ensure the stabilization of oil markets in order to secure an efficient, economic and regular supply of petroleum." Spectrum sought damages, an injunction, and other relief. The court dismissed the suit, and Spectrum appealed.

IN THE WORDS OF THE COURT . . .
E. Grady *JOLLY*, Circuit Judge:

* * * *

Under the act of state doctrine, the courts of one country will not sit in judgment on the acts of the government of another, done within its own territory. The doctrine is grounded in the principle that juridical review of acts of state of a foreign power could embarrass the conduct of foreign relations by the political branches of the government.

* * * *

* * * Adjudication of this suit would necessarily call into question the acts of foreign governments with respect to exploitation of their natural resources. * * * Exploitation of natural resources is an inherently sovereign function.

* * * The availability of oil has become a significant factor in international relations * * *. The United States has a grave interest in the petro-politics of the Middle East and * * * the foreign policy arms of the executive and legislative branches are intimately involved in this sensitive area.

* * * The granting of any relief to Appellants would effectively order foreign governments to dismantle their chosen means of exploiting the valuable natural resources within their sovereign territories. *Recognizing that the judiciary is neither competent nor*

authorized to frustrate the longstanding foreign policy of the political branches by wading so brazenly into the sphere of foreign relations, we decline to sit in judgment of the acts of the foreign states that comprise OPEC. [Emphasis added.]

* * * *

We sum up: Appellants, retailers of gasoline products in the United States, have asked [this court] to adjudicate the merits of their * * * claims against oil production companies that have allegedly participated in a conspiracy to fix prices. Reducing their claims to basics, Appellants allege a conspiracy that is orchestrated by the sovereign member nations of OPEC. * * * Any ruling on the merits of this case would, by its core essence, impermissibly interfere with the Executive Branch's longstanding policy of engaging with OPEC nations regarding the global supply of oil through diplomacy instead of private litigation. * * * Adjudication of Appellants' claims is precluded by the act of state doctrine.

DECISION AND REMEDY The U.S. Court of Appeals for the Fifth Circuit affirmed the lower court's judgment. Granting relief to the plaintiffs would effectively order foreign governments to dismantle their chosen means of exploiting the resources within their own territories. Under the act of state doctrine, a U.S. court will not rule on the validity of a foreign government's acts within its own territory.

THE GLOBAL DIMENSION *Suppose that a U.S. court declared that a foreign nation's act was illegal. Would such a declaration encroach on foreign policy matters falling under the authority of other branches of government? Why or why not?*

LEARNING OBJECTIVE 2 **What is the act of state doctrine? In what circumstances is this doctrine applied?**

Expropriation The seizure by a government of a privately owned business or personal property for a proper public purpose and with just compensation.

Confiscation A government's taking of a privately owned business or personal property without a proper public purpose or an award of just compensation.

The act of state doctrine can have important consequences for individuals and firms doing business with, and investing in, other countries. This doctrine is frequently employed in cases involving **expropriation,** which occurs when a government seizes a privately owned business or privately owned goods for a proper public purpose and awards just compensation. When a government seizes private property for an illegal purpose and without just compensation, the taking is referred to as a **confiscation.** The line between these two forms of taking is sometimes blurred because of differing interpretations of what is illegal and what constitutes just compensation.

EXAMPLE 9.2 Flaherty, Inc., a U.S. company, owns a mine in Brazil. The government of Brazil seizes the mine for public use and claims that the profits Flaherty has already realized from the mine constitute just compensation. Flaherty disagrees, but the act of state doctrine may prevent that company's recovery in a U.S. court. •

When applicable, both the act of state doctrine and the doctrine of *sovereign immunity,* which we discuss next, tend to shield foreign nations from the jurisdiction of U.S. courts. As a result, firms or individuals who own property overseas generally have little legal protection against government actions in the countries where they operate.

Sovereign Immunity A doctrine that immunizes foreign nations from the jurisdiction of U.S. courts when certain conditions are satisfied.

The Doctrine of Sovereign Immunity

When certain conditions are satisfied, the doctrine of **sovereign immunity** protects foreign nations from the jurisdiction of U.S. courts. In 1976, Congress codified this rule in the Foreign Sovereign Immunities Act (FSIA).[2] The FSIA exclusively governs the circumstances in which an action may be brought in the United States against a foreign nation, including attempts to attach (take legal action against, see Chapter 14) a foreign nation's property. Because the law is jurisdictional in nature, a plaintiff has the burden of showing that a defendant is not entitled to sovereign immunity.

Section 1605 of the FSIA sets forth the major exceptions to the jurisdictional immunity of a foreign state. A foreign state is not immune from the jurisdiction of U.S. courts in the following situations:

LEARNING OBJECTIVE 3   **Under the Foreign Sovereign Immunities Act, in which situations is a foreign state subject to the jurisdiction of U.S. courts?**

1. When the foreign state has waived its immunity either explicitly or by implication.
2. When the foreign state has engaged in commercial activity within the United States or in commercial activity outside the United States that has "a direct effect in the United States."[3]
3. When the foreign state has committed a tort in the United States or has violated certain international laws.

In applying the FSIA, questions frequently arise as to whether an entity is a "foreign state" and what constitutes a "commercial activity." Under Section 1603 of the FSIA, a *foreign state* includes both a political subdivision of a foreign state and an instrumentality of a foreign state. Section 1603 broadly defines a *commercial activity* as a regular course of commercial conduct, transaction, or act that is carried out by a foreign state within the United States. Section 1603, however, does not describe the particulars of what constitutes a commercial activity. Thus, the courts are left to decide whether a particular activity is governmental or commercial in nature.

▶ Doing Business Internationally

Export   The sale of goods and services by domestic firms to buyers located in other countries.

A U.S. domestic firm can engage in international business transactions in a number of ways. The simplest way is for U.S. firms to **export** their goods and services to markets abroad. Alternatively, a U.S. firm can establish foreign production facilities so as to be closer to the foreign market or markets in which its products are sold. The advantages may include lower labor costs, fewer government regulations, and lower taxes and trade barriers. A domestic firm can also obtain revenues by licensing its technology to an existing foreign company or by selling franchises to overseas entities.

Exporting

Exporting can take two forms: direct exporting and indirect exporting. In *direct exporting,* a U.S. company signs a sales contract with a foreign purchaser that provides for the conditions of shipment and payment for the goods. (How payments are made in international transactions will be discussed later in this chapter.) If sufficient business develops in a foreign country, a U.S. corporation may set up a specialized marketing organization in that foreign market by appointing a foreign agent or a foreign distributor. This is called *indirect exporting.*

When a U.S. firm desires to limit its involvement in an international market, it will typically establish an *agency relationship* (see Chapter 16) with a foreign firm. The foreign firm then acts as the U.S. firm's agent and can enter into contracts in the foreign location on behalf of the principal (the U.S. company).

---

2. 28 U.S.C. Sections 1602–1611.
3. See, for example, *O'Bryan v. Holy See,* 556 F.3d 361 (6th Cir. 2009).

Distribution Agreement A contract between a seller and a distributor of the seller's products setting out the terms and conditions of the distributorship.

When a foreign country represents a substantial market, a U.S. firm may wish to appoint a distributor located in that country. The U.S. firm and the distributor enter into a **distribution agreement,** which is a contract between the seller and the distributor setting out the terms and conditions of the distributorship. These terms and conditions—for example, price, currency of payment, availability of supplies, and method of payment—primarily involve contract law. Disputes concerning distribution agreements may involve jurisdictional or other issues, as well as contract law.

In response to the latest economic recession, the U.S. government has taken a greater interest in the export of goods and services to foreign markets by U.S. companies. For a discussion of a recent federal initiative to encourage exports, see this chapter's *Shifting Legal Priorities for Business* feature below.

Manufacturing Abroad

An alternative to direct or indirect exporting is the establishment of foreign manufacturing facilities. Typically, U.S. firms establish manufacturing plants abroad if they believe that doing so will reduce their costs—particularly for labor, shipping, and raw

SHIFTING LEGAL PRIORITIES FOR BUSINESS

The National Export Initiative

Although the United States is one of the world's major exporters, exports make up a much smaller share of annual output in the United States than they do in our most important trading partners. In an effort to increase this nation's exports, in 2010 the Obama administration created the National Export Initiative (NEI) with a goal of doubling U.S. exports by 2015.

Some commentators believe that another goal of the NEI is to reduce outsourcing—the practice of having manufacturing or other activities performed in lower-wage countries such as China and India. Especially in view of the higher unemployment rate, there is increasing concern that U.S. jobs are being shipped overseas.

The Export Promotion Cabinet

An important component of the NEI is the Export Promotion Cabinet, which reports directly to the president. The cabinet's members include officials from the Departments of Agriculture, Commerce, and State, as well as from the Small Business Administration, the U.S. Export-Import

Bank, and the Office of the U.S. Trade Representative. All members must submit detailed plans to the president that outline the steps they will take to increase U.S. exports.

Increased Efforts to Promote Exports

The U.S. Commerce Department will play a leading role in the NEI and is receiving increased funding to do so. More than three hundred trade experts from the department will serve as advocates for U.S. companies and will help some twenty thousand "client companies" increase their export sales.

In addition, the Commerce Department's International Trade Administration will play a more active role in promoting U.S. exports in the emerging high-growth markets of Brazil, China, and India. Finally, the department will identify market opportunities in fast-growing sectors, such as environmental goods and services, biotechnology, and renewable energy.

Increased Export Financing

Under the NEI, the U.S. Export-Import Bank is increasing by 50 percent the

financing that it makes available to small and medium-sized businesses. In the initial phase of the NEI, the bank added hundreds of new small-business clients that sell a wide variety of products, from sophisticated polymers to date palm trees and nanotechnology-based cosmetics.

In addition, the administration has proposed that $30 billion be used to boost lending to small businesses, especially for export purposes.

MANAGERIAL IMPLICATIONS
Managers in companies that are now outsourcing or are thinking of doing so may wish to reconsider. Increasingly, the federal government is taking a stance against outsourcing. As long as unemployment remains high in the United States, the emphasis will be on the creation of jobs at home. These efforts will often be backed by subsidies and access to federally supported borrowing initiatives.

materials—and enable them to compete more effectively in foreign markets. Foreign firms have done the same in the United States. Sony and other Japanese manufacturers have established U.S. plants to avoid import duties that the U.S. Congress may impose on Japanese products entering this country.

A U.S. firm can manufacture goods in other countries in several ways. Two of these ways are through licensing and franchising.

LICENSING   A U.S. firm can obtain revenues from abroad by licensing a foreign manufacturing company to use its copyrighted, patented, or trademarked intellectual property or trade secrets. Like any other licensing agreement (see Chapter 8), a licensing agreement with a foreign-based firm calls for a payment of royalties on some basis—such as so many cents per unit produced or a certain percentage of profits from units sold in a particular geographic territory.

FRANCHISING   Franchising is a well-known form of licensing. As you will read in Chapter 10, in a franchise arrangement the owner of a trademark, trade name, or copyright (the franchisor) licenses another (the franchisee) to use the trademark, trade name, or copyright under certain conditions or limitations in the selling of goods or services. In return, the franchisee pays a fee, which is usually based on a percentage of gross or net sales.

EXAMPLE 9.3   The Coca-Cola Bottling Company licenses firms worldwide to employ (and keep confidential) its secret formula for the syrup used in its soft drink. In return, the foreign firms licensed to make the syrup pay Coca-Cola a percentage of the income earned from the sale of the soft drink. •

▶ Regulation of Specific Business Activities

Doing business abroad can affect the economies, foreign policies, domestic policies, and other national interests of the countries involved. For this reason, nations impose laws to restrict or facilitate international business. Controls may also be imposed by international agreements. Here, we discuss how different types of international activities are regulated.

Investment Protections

Firms that invest in foreign nations face the risk that the foreign government may take possession of the investment property. Expropriation, as already mentioned, occurs when property is taken and the owner is paid just compensation for what is taken. Expropriation generally does not violate observed principles of international law. Such principles are usually violated, however, when a government confiscates property without compensation (or without adequate compensation). Few remedies are available for confiscation of property by a foreign government. Claims are often resolved by lump-sum settlements after negotiations between the United States and the taking nation.

To counter the deterrent effect that the possibility of confiscation may have on potential investors, many countries guarantee that foreign investors will be compensated if their property is taken. A guaranty can take the form of statutory laws or provisions in international treaties. As further protection for foreign investments, some countries provide insurance for their citizens' investments abroad.

Export Controls

The U.S. Constitution provides in Article I, Section 9, that "No Tax or Duty shall be laid on Articles exported from any State." Thus, Congress cannot impose any export taxes. Congress can, however, use a variety of other devices to control exports. Congress may set export quotas on various items, such as grain being sold abroad. Under the Export Administration Act of 1979,[4] the flow of technologically advanced products and technical data can be restricted.

While restricting certain exports, the United States (and other nations) also uses devices such as export incentives and subsidies to stimulate other exports and thereby aid domestic businesses. Under the Export Trading Company Act of 1982,[5] U.S. banks are encouraged to invest in export trading companies, which are formed when exporting firms join together to export a line of goods. The U.S. Export-Import Bank provides financial assistance, consisting primarily of credit guaranties given to commercial banks that in turn lend funds to U.S. exporting companies.

Import Controls

"The notion dies hard that in some sort of way exports are patriotic but imports are immoral."

Lord Harlech, 1918–1985
(English writer)

Import restrictions include strict prohibitions, quotas, and tariffs. Under the Trading with the Enemy Act of 1917,[6] for instance, no goods may be imported from nations that have been designated enemies of the United States. Other laws prohibit the importation of illegal drugs, books that urge insurrection against the United States, and agricultural products that pose dangers to domestic crops or animals. The import of goods that infringe U.S. patents is also prohibited. The International Trade Commission investigates allegations that imported goods infringe U.S. patents and imposes penalties if necessary.

Quota A set limit on the amount of goods that can be imported.

Tariff A tax on imported goods.

QUOTAS AND TARIFFS   Limits on the amounts of goods that can be imported are known as **quotas.** At one time, the United States had legal quotas on the number of automobiles that could be imported from Japan. Today, Japan "voluntarily" restricts the number of automobiles exported to the United States. **Tariffs** are taxes on imports. A tariff usually is a percentage of the value of the import, but it can be a flat rate per unit (for example, per barrel of oil). Tariffs raise the prices of goods, causing some consumers to purchase more domestically manufactured goods and fewer imported goods. (For a discussion of tariffs and other considerations for businesses going global, see this chapter's *Linking the Law to Marketing* feature on pages 224–225.)

ANTIDUMPING DUTIES   The United States has laws specifically directed at what it sees as unfair international trade practices. **Dumping,** for example, is the sale of imported goods at "less than fair value." *Fair value* is usually determined by the price of those goods in the exporting country. Foreign firms that engage in dumping in the United States hope to undersell U.S. businesses to obtain a larger share of the U.S. market. To prevent this, an extra tariff—known as an *antidumping duty*—may be assessed on the imports.

Dumping The selling of goods in a foreign country at a price below the price charged for the same goods in the domestic market.

MINIMIZING TRADE BARRIERS   Restrictions on imports are also known as *trade barriers.* The elimination of trade barriers is sometimes seen as essential to the world's economic well-being. Most of the world's leading trading nations are members of

---

4. 50 U.S.C. Sections 2401–2420.
5. 15 U.S.C. Sections 4001, 4003.
6. 12 U.S.C. Section 95a.

the World Trade Organization (WTO), which was established in 1995. To minimize trade barriers among nations, each member country of the WTO is required to grant **normal trade relations (NTR) status** to other member countries. This means each member is obligated to treat other members at least as well as it treats the country that receives its most favorable treatment with regard to imports or exports. Various regional trade agreements and associations also help to minimize trade barriers between nations. Here is a brief description of some of these agreements:

1. *The European Union (EU)*—The EU is a single integrated trading unit made up of twenty-seven European nations. The EU has gone a long way toward creating a new body of law to govern all of the member nations—although some of its efforts to create uniform laws have been confounded by nationalism. The council and the commission issue regulations, or directives, that define EU law in various areas, such as environmental law. The directives normally are binding on all member countries.

2. *The North American Free Trade Agreement (NAFTA)*—NAFTA created a regional trading unit consisting of Canada, Mexico, and the United States. The goal of NAFTA is to eliminate tariffs among these three countries on substantially all goods by reducing the tariffs incrementally over a period of time.

3. *The Central America–Dominican Republic–United States Free Trade Agreement (CAFTA-DR)*—CAFTA-DR was formed by Costa Rica, the Dominican Republic, El Salvador, Guatemala, Honduras, Nicaragua, and the United States. Its purpose is to reduce tariffs and improve market access among all of the signatory nations. Legislatures from all seven countries have approved the CAFTA-DR, despite significant opposition in certain nations.

4. *The Republic of Korea–United States Free Trade Agreement (KORUS FTA)*—KORUS, which was ratified by Congress in 2011, is the United States' first free trade agreement with South Korea. The treaty's provisions will eliminate 95 percent of each nation's tariffs on industrial and consumer exports within five years. KORUS is the largest free trade agreement the United States has entered into since NAFTA, and it may boost U.S. exports by more than $10 billion a year. It will benefit U.S. automakers, farmers, ranchers, and manufacturers by enabling them to compete in new markets.

▶ Commercial Contracts in an International Setting

An international contract should be in writing. There are several important points that should be addressed in an international contract.

Contract Clauses

Language and legal differences among nations can create special problems for parties to international contracts when disputes arise. To avoid these problems, parties should include special provisions in the contract that designate the language of the contract, where any disputes will be resolved, and the substantive law that will be applied in settling any disputes. Parties to international contracts should also indicate in their contracts what acts or events will excuse the parties from performance under the contract and whether disputes under the contract will be arbitrated or litigated.

CHOICE-OF-LANGUAGE CLAUSE   A deal struck between a U.S. company and a company in another country normally involves two languages. Typically, many phrases in one language are not readily translatable into another. Consequently, the complex contractual terms involved may not be understood by one party in the other party's language. To make sure that no disputes arise out of this language problem, an international sales contract should have a **choice-of-language clause** designating the official language by which the contract will be interpreted in the event of disagreement.

Choice-of-Language Clause A clause in a contract designating the official language by which the contract will be interpreted in the event of a future disagreement over the contract's terms.

FORUM-SELECTION CLAUSE When a dispute arises, litigation may be pursued in courts of different nations. There are no universally accepted rules as to which court has jurisdiction over a particular subject matter or parties to a dispute. Consequently, parties to an international transaction should always include in the contract a **forum-selection clause** indicating what court, jurisdiction, or tribunal will decide any disputes arising under the contract. It is especially important to indicate the specific court that will have jurisdiction. The forum does not necessarily have to be within the geographic boundaries of the home nation of either party.

Forum-Selection Clause A provision in a contract designating the court, jurisdiction, or tribunal that will decide any disputes arising under the contract.

CASE EXAMPLE 9.4 Garware Polyester, Ltd., based in Mumbai, India, developed and made plastics and high-tech polyester film. Intermax Trading Corporation, based in New York, acted as Garware's North American sales agent and sold its products on a commission basis. Garware and Intermax had executed a series of agency agreements under which the courts of Mumbai, India, would have exclusive jurisdiction over any disputes relating to their agreement. When Intermax fell behind in its payments to Garware, Garware filed a lawsuit in a U.S. court to collect the balance due, claiming that the forum-selection clause did not apply to sales of warehoused goods. The court, however, sided with Intermax. Because the forum-selection clause was valid and enforceable, Garware had to bring its complaints against Intermax in a court in India.[7] •

CHOICE-OF-LAW CLAUSE A contractual provision designating the applicable law—such as the law of Germany or California—is called a **choice-of-law clause.** Every international contract typically includes a choice-of-law clause. At common law (and in European civil law systems), parties are allowed to choose the law that will govern their contractual relationship, provided that the law chosen is the law of a jurisdiction that has a substantial relationship to the parties and to the international business transaction.

Choice-of-Law Clause A clause in a contract designating the law (such as the law of a particular state or nation) that will govern the contract.

Under Section 1–105 of the Uniform Commercial Code (see Chapter 13), parties may choose the law that will govern the contract as long as the choice is "reasonable." Article 6 of the United Nations Convention on Contracts for the International Sale of Goods, however, imposes no limitation on the parties' choice of what law will govern the contract. The 1986 Hague Convention on the Law Applicable to Contracts for the International Sale of Goods—often referred to as the Choice-of-Law Convention—allows unlimited autonomy in the choice of law. The Hague Convention indicates that whenever a contract does not specify a choice of law, the governing law is that of the country in which the *seller's* place of business is located.

Force Majeure Clause A provision in a contract stipulating that certain unforeseen events—such as war, political upheavals, or acts of God—will excuse a party from liability for nonperformance of contractual obligations.

FORCE MAJEURE CLAUSE Every contract, particularly those involving international transactions, should have a *force majeure* **clause.** *Force majeure* is a French term meaning "impossible or irresistible force"—sometimes loosely identified as "an act of God." In international business contracts, *force majeure* clauses commonly

---

7. *Garware Polyester, Ltd. v. Intermax Trading Corp.,* ___ F.Supp.2d ___ (S.D.N.Y. 2001); see also *Laasko v. Xerox Corp.,* 566 F.Supp.2d 1018 (C.D.Cal. 2008).

stipulate that in addition to acts of God, a number of other eventualities (such as government orders or embargoes) may excuse a party from liability for nonperformance.

Civil Dispute Resolution

International contracts frequently include arbitration clauses. By means of such clauses, the parties agree in advance to be bound by the decision of a specified third party in the event of a dispute, as discussed in Chapter 2. The United Nations Convention on the Recognition and Enforcement of Foreign Arbitral Awards (often referred to as the New York Convention) assists in the enforcement of arbitration clauses, as do provisions in specific treaties among nations. The New York Convention has been implemented in nearly one hundred countries, including the United States.

If a sales contract does not include an arbitration clause, litigation may occur. If the contract contains forum-selection and choice-of-law clauses, the lawsuit will be heard by a court in the specified forum and decided according to that forum's law. If no forum and choice of law have been specified, however, legal proceedings will be more complex and attended by much more uncertainty. For instance, litigation may take place in two or more countries, with each country applying its own choice-of-law rules to determine the substantive law that will be applied to the particular transactions. Even if a plaintiff wins a favorable judgment in a lawsuit litigated in the plaintiff's country, there is no way to predict whether courts in the defendant's country will enforce the judgment.

Beyond Our Borders   Arbitration versus Litigation

Businesspersons often find it advantageous to include arbitration clauses in their international contracts because arbitration awards are usually easier to enforce than court judgments. A problem in collecting court judgments is that the application of the principle of comity varies from one nation to another. Many nations have not signed bilateral agreements with the United States agreeing to enforce judgments rendered in U.S. courts.

Even when the United States has an agreement with another nation, a judgment by a court in that nation may not be enforced in the United States if it conflicts with U.S. laws or policies, especially if the case involves important constitutional rights, such as freedom of the press or religion. For instance, a U.S. federal appellate court refused to enforce a French default judgment against a U.S. firm, Viewfinder, Inc., on constitutional grounds. Viewfinder operated a Web site that posted photographs from fashion shows and fashion industry information. Several French clothing designers filed an action in a French court alleging that the Web site showed photos of their clothing designs. Because Viewfinder defaulted and did not appear in the French court to contest the allegations, the French court awarded the designers more than $175,000. When the designers came to the United States to enforce the judgment, Viewfinder convinced the U.S. court that its conduct on the Web site was protected expression under the First Amendment.[8]

Sometimes, arbitration can also be used to prevent a judgment from being collected. Consider a dispute between Chevron Corporation and Ecuador. After years of litigation, a group of Amazon Indians and farmers won an $18.2 billion verdict in an Ecuadoran court against Chevron for allegedly dumping toxic waste into their rivers and rain forests. But Chevron did not own any property in Ecuador that the government could seize to collect the debt. Chevron filed an action in a New York federal court and convinced the judge that the Ecuadoran trial was tainted by fraud and corruption. Meanwhile, Chevron also took its case to an arbitration panel for the United Nations Commission on International Trade Law (UNCITRAL), which blocked the

---

8. *Sarl Louis Feraud International v. Viewfinder, Inc.*, 489 F.3d 474 (2d Cir. 2007).

plaintiffs from collecting on the Ecuadoran judgment. UNCITRAL issued an order that bans enforcement of the Ecuadoran judgment in the United States or anywhere else in the world.[9]

• For Critical Analysis
What might be some advantages of arbitrating disputes involving international transactions? Are there any disadvantages? Explain your answer.

In the following case, the parties had agreed to arbitrate any disputes in Guernsey, which is a British Crown dependency in the English Channel. The court had to decide whether the agreement was enforceable even though one party was a U.S. citizen and the other may have had its principal place of business in the United States.

---

9. *In re Chevron Corp.*, 650 F.3d 276 (3d Cir. 2011).

Case 9.2   S&T Oil Equipment & Machinery, Ltd. v. Juridica Investments, Ltd.

United States Court of Appeals, Fifth Circuit, ___ F.3d ___ (2012).

BACKGROUND AND FACTS   Juridica Investments, Ltd. (JIL), entered into a financing contract with S&T Oil Equipment & Machinery, Ltd., a U.S. company. The contract included an arbitration provision stating that any disputes would be arbitrated "in St. Peter Port, Guernsey, Channel Islands." The contract also stated that it was executed in Guernsey and would be fully performed there. When a dispute arose between the parties, JIL initiated arbitration in Guernsey. Nevertheless, S&T filed a suit in federal district court in the United States. When JIL filed a motion to dismiss in favor of arbitration, the court granted the motion and compelled arbitration under the Convention on the Recognition and Enforcement of Foreign Arbitral Awards. S&T appealed.

IN THE WORDS OF THE COURT . . .
PER CURIAM: [By the Whole Court]
      * * * *

      * * * "A court should compel arbitration if (1) there is a written agreement to arbitrate the matter; (2) the agreement provides for arbitration in a Convention signatory nation; (3) the agreement arises out of a commercial legal relationship; and (4) a party to the agreement is not an American citizen."

      The parties dispute whether the fourth * * * factor is satisfied in this case. In considering this fourth factor, courts must ask the following: Is a party to the agreement not an American citizen or does the commercial relationship have some reasonable relation with one or more foreign states? If either question is answered in the affirmative, then the fourth * * * factor is satisfied.
      * * * *

      Although it is not absolutely clear where JIL has its principal place of business, it is evident that the commercial relationship between S&T and JIL has some reasonable relation with one or

*more foreign states. Even if JIL's principal place of business is in the United States, the * * * agreement's arbitral clause can still be enforceable under the Convention if the legal relationship between JIL and S&T involved "property abroad, envisages performance or enforcement abroad, or has some other reasonable relation with on or more foreign states." As we stated in [another case], this reasonable relation with a foreign state must be "independent of the arbitral clause itself."* [Emphasis added.]

      Here, it is evident that the legal relationship between JIL and S&T envisaged performance abroad. The * * * agreement specifically states that it was executed in Guernsey and would be performed by JIL "exclusively and wholly in and from Guernsey." Indeed, pursuant to the terms of the * * * agreement, JIL performed part of the agreement abroad when it wired funds from Guernsey to cover * * * legal fees and costs * * *.

      Given these facts, it is evident that the commercial relationship between S&T and JIL has some reasonable relation with one or more foreign states that is independent of the arbitral clause itself. As such, the fourth * * * factor is satisfied in this case. The district court therefore did not err in compelling arbitration.

DECISION AND REMEDY   The U.S. Court of Appeals for the Fifth Circuit held that arbitration was required under the Convention on the Recognition and Enforcement of Foreign Arbitral Awards. It therefore affirmed the district court's judgment compelling arbitration.

THE GLOBAL DIMENSION   *What would happen if Congress did not require a reasonable relationship with a foreign state for arbitration agreements between U.S. citizens? Would there be more or fewer agreements to arbitrate disputes abroad?*

▶ Payment Methods for International Transactions

Currency differences between nations and the geographic distance between parties to international sales contracts add a degree of complexity to international sales that does not exist in the domestic market. Because international contracts involve greater financial risks, special care should be taken in drafting these contracts to specify both the currency in which payment is to be made and the method of payment.

Monetary Systems

Although our national currency, the U.S. dollar, is one of the primary forms of international currency, any U.S. firm undertaking business transactions abroad must be prepared to deal with one or more other currencies. After all, a Japanese firm may want to be paid in Japanese yen for goods and services sold outside Japan. Both firms therefore must rely on the convertibility of currencies.

Foreign Exchange Market A worldwide system in which foreign currencies are bought and sold.

Currencies are convertible when they can be freely exchanged one for the other at some specified market rate in a **foreign exchange market.** Foreign exchange markets make up a worldwide system for the buying and selling of foreign currencies. The foreign exchange rate is simply the price of a unit of one country's currency in terms of another country's currency. For example, if today's exchange rate is one hundred Japanese yen for one dollar, that means that anybody with one hundred yen can obtain one dollar, and vice versa. Like other prices, the exchange rate is set by the forces of supply and demand.

Correspondent Bank A bank in which another bank has an account (and vice versa) for the purpose of facilitating fund transfers.

Frequently, a U.S. company can rely on its domestic bank to take care of all international transfers of funds. Commercial banks often transfer funds internationally through their **correspondent banks** in other countries. **EXAMPLE 9.5** A customer of Citibank wishes to pay a bill in euros to a company in Paris. Citibank can draw a bank check payable in euros on its account in Crédit Agricole, a Paris correspondent bank, and then send the check to the French company to which its customer owes the funds. Alternatively, Citibank's customer can request a wire transfer of the funds to the French company. Citibank instructs Crédit Agricole by wire to pay the necessary amount in euros. ●

Letters of Credit

Because buyers and sellers engaged in international business transactions are frequently separated by thousands of miles, special precautions are often taken to ensure performance under the contract. Sellers want to avoid delivering goods for which they might not be paid. Buyers desire the assurance that sellers will not be paid until there is evidence that the goods have been shipped. Thus, **letters of credit** are frequently used to facilitate international business transactions.

Letter of Credit A written instrument, usually issued by a bank on behalf of a customer or other person, in which the issuer promises to honor drafts or other demands for payment by third parties in accordance with the terms of the instrument.

PARTIES TO A LETTER OF CREDIT In a simple letter-of-credit transaction, the *issuer* (a bank) agrees to issue a letter of credit and to ascertain whether the *beneficiary* (seller) performs certain acts. In return, the *account party* (buyer) promises to reimburse the issuer for the amount paid to the beneficiary. The transaction may also involve an *advising bank* that transmits information and a *paying bank* that expedites payment under the letter of credit. See Exhibit 9–1 on the facing page for an illustration of a letter-of-credit transaction.

Under a letter of credit, the issuer is bound to pay the beneficiary (seller) when the beneficiary has complied with the terms and conditions of the letter of credit. The beneficiary looks to the issuer, not to the account party (buyer), when it presents the documents required by the letter of credit. Typically, the letter of credit will require

● *Exhibit* 9–1 **A Letter-of-Credit Transaction**

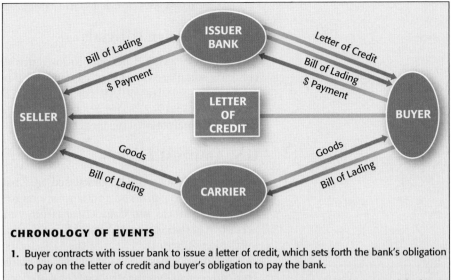

CHRONOLOGY OF EVENTS

1. Buyer contracts with issuer bank to issue a letter of credit, which sets forth the bank's obligation to pay on the letter of credit and buyer's obligation to pay the bank.

2. Letter of credit is sent to seller informing seller that on compliance with the terms of the letter of credit (such as presentment of necessary documents—in this example, a bill of lading), the bank will issue payment for the goods.

3. Seller delivers goods to carrier and receives a bill of lading.

4. Seller delivers the bill of lading to issuer bank and, if the document is proper, receives payment.

5. Issuer bank delivers the bill of lading to buyer.

6. Buyer delivers the bill of lading to carrier.

7. Carrier delivers the goods to buyer.

8. Buyer settles with issuer bank.

that the beneficiary deliver a *bill of lading* to the issuing bank to prove that shipment has been made. A letter of credit assures the beneficiary (seller) of payment and at the same time assures the account party (buyer) that payment will not be made until the beneficiary has complied with the terms and conditions of the letter of credit.

THE VALUE OF A LETTER OF CREDIT The basic principle behind letters of credit is that payment is made against the documents presented by the beneficiary and not against the facts that the documents purport to reflect. Thus, in a letter-of-credit transaction, the issuer does not police the underlying contract. A letter of credit is independent of the underlying contract between the buyer and the seller. Eliminating the need for banks (issuers) to inquire into whether actual contractual conditions have been satisfied greatly reduces the costs of letters of credit. Moreover, the use of a letter of credit protects both buyers and sellers.

DON'T FORGET A letter of credit is independent of the underlying contract between the buyer and the seller.

▶ U.S. Laws in a Global Context

The internationalization of business raises questions about the extraterritorial application of a nation's laws—that is, the effect of the country's laws outside its boundaries. To what extent do U.S. domestic laws apply to other nations' businesses? To what extent do U.S. domestic laws apply to U.S. firms doing business abroad? Here, we discuss the extraterritorial application of certain U.S. laws, including bribing of foreign officials, antitrust laws, tort laws, and laws prohibiting employment discrimination.

Bribing Foreign Officials

Giving cash or in-kind benefits to foreign government officials to obtain business contracts and other favors is often considered normal practice. To reduce such bribery by representatives of U.S. corporations, Congress enacted the Foreign Corrupt Practices Act in 1977.[10] This act and its implications for American businesspersons engaged in international business transactions were discussed in Chapter 7.

U.S. Antitrust Laws

U.S. antitrust laws (to be discussed in Chapter 19) have a wide application. They may *subject* firms in foreign nations to their provisions, as well as *protect* foreign consumers and competitors from violations committed by U.S. citizens. Section 1 of the Sherman Act—the most important U.S. antitrust law—provides for the extraterritorial effect of the U.S. antitrust laws.

The United States is a major proponent of free competition in the global economy. Thus, any conspiracy that has a *substantial effect* on U.S. commerce is within the reach of the Sherman Act. The law applies even if the violation occurs outside the United States, and foreign governments as well as businesses can be sued for violations.

International Tort Claims

LEARNING OBJECTIVE 5 **What federal law allows U.S. citizens, as well as citizens of foreign nations, to file civil actions in U.S. courts for torts that were committed overseas?**

The international application of tort liability is growing in significance and controversy. An increasing number of U.S. plaintiffs are suing foreign (or U.S.) entities for torts that these entities have allegedly committed overseas. Often, these cases involve human rights violations by foreign governments. The Alien Tort Claims Act (ATCA),[11] adopted in 1789, allows even foreign citizens to bring civil suits in U.S. courts for injuries caused by violations of international law or a treaty of the United States.

Since 1980, plaintiffs have increasingly used the ATCA to bring actions against companies operating in other countries. ATCA actions have been brought against companies doing business in nations such as Colombia, Ecuador, Egypt, Guatemala, India, Indonesia, Nigeria, and Saudi Arabia. Some of these cases have involved alleged environmental destruction. In addition, mineral companies in Southeast Asia have been sued for collaborating with oppressive government regimes.

The following *Spotlight Case* involved claims against hundreds of corporations that allegedly "aided and abetted" the government of South Africa in maintaining its apartheid (racially discriminatory) regime.

---

10. 15 U.S.C. Sections 78m–78ff.
11. 28 U.S.C. Section 1350.

SPOTLIGHT ON INTERNATIONAL TORTS CLAIMS

Case 9.3   **Khulumani v. Barclay National Bank, Ltd.**

United States Court of Appeals, Second Circuit, 504 F.3d 254 (2007).

BACKGROUND AND FACTS   The Khulumani plaintiffs, along with other plaintiff groups, filed class-action claims on behalf of victims of apartheid-related atrocities, human rights violations, crimes against humanity, and unfair and discriminatory forced-labor practices. The plaintiffs brought this action in federal district court under the Alien Tort Claims Act (ATCA) against a number of

Spotlight Case 9.3—Continued

corporations, including Bank of America, Barclay National Bank, Citigroup, Credit Suisse Group, General Electric, and IBM. The district court dismissed the plaintiffs' complaints in their entirety. The court held that the plaintiffs had failed to establish subject-matter jurisdiction under the ATCA. The plaintiffs appealed to the U.S. Court of Appeals for the Second Circuit.

IN THE WORDS OF THE COURT . . .
PER CURIAM. [By the Whole Court]
* * * *

* * * [This court] vacate[s] the district court's dismissal of the plaintiffs' ATCA claims because the district court erred in holding that aiding and abetting violations of customary international law cannot provide a basis for ATCA jurisdiction. *We hold that* * * * *a plaintiff may plead a theory of aiding and abetting liability under the ATCA.* * * * [The majority of the judges on the panel that heard this case agreed on the result but differed on the reasons, which were presented in two concurring opinions. One judge believed that liability on these facts is "well established in international law," citing such examples as the Rome Statute of the International Criminal Court. Another judge stated that according to Section 876(b) of the *Restatement (Second) of Torts,* liability could be assessed in part for "facilitating the commission of human rights violations by providing the principal tortfeasor with the tools, instrumentalities, or services to commit those violations."] [Emphasis added.]
* * * *

* * * We decline to affirm the dismissal of plaintiffs' ATCA claims on the basis of the prudential concerns[a] raised by the defendants. * * * The Supreme Court [has] identified two different respects in which courts should consider prudential concerns [exercise great caution and carefully evaluate international norms and potential adverse foreign policy consequences] in deciding whether to hear claims brought under the ATCA.[b] First, * * * courts should consider prudential concerns in the context of determining whether to recognize a cause of action under the ATCA. Specifically, * * * the determination whether a norm is sufficiently definite to support a cause of action should (and, indeed, inevitably must) involve an element of judgment about the practical consequences of making that cause available to litigants in the federal courts. Second, * * * in certain cases, other prudential principles might operate to limit the availability of relief in the federal courts for violations of customary international law.
* * * *

One such principle * * * [is] a policy of case-specific deference to the political branches [of the U.S. government]. *This policy of judicial deference to the Executive Branch on questions of foreign policy has long been established under the prudential justiciability [appropriate for a court to resolve] doctrine known as the political question doctrine. Another prudential doctrine that the defendants raise in this case is international comity.* This doctrine * * * asks whether adjudication of the case by a United States court would offend amicable working relationships with a foreign country. [Emphasis added.]

DECISION AND REMEDY The U.S. Court of Appeals for the Second Circuit vacated the district court's dismissal of the plaintiffs' claims and remanded the case for further proceedings. According to the reviewing court, a plaintiff may plead a theory of aiding and abetting liability under the Alien Tort Claims Act.

THE LEGAL ENVIRONMENT DIMENSION *What are the ramifications of the ruling for the defendants?*

---

a. The term *prudential concerns* refers to the defendants' arguments that the plaintiffs do not have standing to pursue their case in a U.S. court. Here, *prudential* means that the arguments are based on judicially (or legislatively) created principles rather than on the constitutionally based requirements set forth in the U.S. Constitution.

b. The court is referring to the decision of the United States Supreme Court in *Sosa v. Alvarez-Machain,* 542 U.S. 692, 124 S.Ct. 2739, 159 L.Ed.2d 718 (2004).

 Ethical Issue

Should U.S. courts allow "forum-shopping" plaintiffs to sue companies for aiding and abetting global terrorism? Some plaintiffs are bringing actions in U.S. courts alleging that certain banks and other companies in foreign countries have aided and abetted terrorist activities. Foreign plaintiffs may assert claims for aiding and abetting under the ATCA, while U.S. nationals may also bring claims under the Anti-Terrorism Act (ATA).

In 2009, some 1,600 plaintiffs, including both U.S. and foreign nationals, brought claims against Arab Bank, alleging that the bank knowingly provided financial services to terrorist organizations that attacked Israel. A U.S. district court held that it had jurisdiction to hear the claims.[12] Similarly, in 2010, a federal court held that it had jurisdiction to hear a case brought by a U.S. citizen against an international Switzerland-based financial institution for helping fund the terrorists that killed her husband, a Canadian citizen, in Israel.[13]

Ethical Issue **Continues next page** ➡

---

12. *Almog v. Arab Bank,* 471 F.Supp.2d 257 (E.D.N.Y. 2007).
13. *Goldberg v. UBS AG,* 690 F.Supp.2d 92 (E.D.N.Y. 2010). See *Case Example 9.1* on page 210 for further discussion of this case.

> Although punishing those who aid terrorists is certainly desirable, some have suggested that such rulings may encourage international "forum shopping." Victims of global terrorism may bring lawsuits in U.S. courts against foreign defendants that have little or no contact with the United States because of the potential for large damages awards—and treble damages if the victims are U.S. nationals.

Antidiscrimination Laws

Laws in the United States prohibit discrimination on the basis of race, color, national origin, religion, gender, age, and disability, as will be discussed in Chapter 17. These laws, as they affect employment relationships, generally apply extraterritorially. U.S. employees working abroad for U.S. employers are protected under the Age Discrimination in Employment Act of 1967. The Americans with Disabilities Act of 1990, which requires employers to accommodate the needs of workers with disabilities, also applies to U.S. nationals working abroad for U.S. firms.

In addition, the major law regulating employment discrimination—Title VII of the Civil Rights Act of 1964—applies extraterritorially to all U.S. employees working for U.S. employers abroad. U.S. employers must abide by U.S. discrimination laws unless to do so would violate the laws of the country where their workplaces are located. This "foreign laws exception" prevents employers from being subjected to conflicting laws.

▶ Reviewing . . . International Law in a Global Economy

Robco, Inc., was a Florida arms dealer. The armed forces of Honduras contracted to purchase weapons from Robco over a six-year period. After the government was replaced and a democracy installed, the Honduran government sought to reduce the size of its military, and its relationship with Robco deteriorated. Honduras refused to honor the contract by purchasing the inventory of arms, which Robco could sell only at a much lower price. Robco filed a suit in a federal district court in the United States to recover damages for this breach of contract by the government of Honduras. Using the information provided in the chapter, answer the following questions.

1. Should the Foreign Sovereign Immunities Act preclude this lawsuit? Why or why not?
2. Does the act of state doctrine bar Robco from seeking to enforce the contract? Explain.
3. Suppose that before this lawsuit, the new government of Honduras had enacted a law making it illegal to purchase weapons from foreign arms dealers. What doctrine might lead a U.S. court to dismiss Robco's case in that situation?
4. Now suppose that the U.S. court hears the case and awards damages to Robco, but the government of Honduras has no assets in the United States that can be used to satisfy the judgment. Under which doctrine might Robco be able to collect the damages by asking another nation's court to enforce the U.S. judgment?

▶ Debate This

The U.S. federal courts are accepting too many lawsuits initiated by foreigners that concern matters not relevant to this country.

Linking the Law *to Marketing*
Going Global

Today, U.S. exports amount to more than 14 percent of the U.S. gross domestic product. In your marketing classes in business school, you will learn about domestic marketing. If you work for many U.S. firms, though, you will also need to know about marketing on a global basis.

Legal and Economic Constraints on Going Global

If you are the global marketing manager for your company, you will need to be aware of the following legal considerations that we outlined in this chapter:

- **Tariffs**—Determine what tariffs may be imposed on your company's products. If your company must pay relatively high tariffs and compete against domestic producers who face no tariffs, you may be wasting your time.
- **Quotas**—The United States has strict quotas on imports of textiles, sugar, and many dairy products. Other countries have quotas, too. If those quotas are highly restrictive, there is no point in trying to sell your company's products in those countries.
- **Exchange controls**—When your company exports to another country, that country has to pay for those U.S.-made goods in dollars. Sometimes, governments impose restrictions on the amount of dollars that may be purchased in the foreign exchange market to pay for goods from the United States.
- **Trade agreements**—Some countries may have signed bilateral or international trade agreements that make it particularly attractive for you to attempt to market your company's products in those countries. Consult a specialist in international trade agreements to find out precisely how those agreements can help your company.

Global Marketing Standardization

According to former Harvard professor Ted Levitt, "global marketing" is today's trend for marketers. Levitt, who devised the notion of global marketing standardization, or a global vision, contends that advances in communication and technology have created a "small" world. By this he means that consumers everywhere want the same items that they have seen in popular movies exported from the United States, for example, or featured on the Internet.

Consider Each Culture Separately

No matter how "small" the world has become, countries still have different sets of shared values that affect their citizens' preferences. Therefore, as a global marketing manager, you will have to become intimately acquainted with the cultures of the countries where you conduct marketing campaigns.

For example, Samsonite used an advertising campaign with an image of its luggage being carried on a magic flying carpet. Afterwards, it learned that most Middle Eastern consumers thought that Samsonite was selling carpets.

Similarly, the translation of names and slogans into other languages is fraught with pitfalls. Toyota had to drop the "2" from its model MR2 in France because the combination of sounds sounded like a French swear word.

FOR CRITICAL ANALYSIS
Why should a global marketing manager consult local attorneys in other countries before creating a marketing campaign abroad?

Key Terms

act of state doctrine 210
choice-of-language clause 217
choice-of-law clause 217
comity 210
confiscation 211
correspondent bank 220
distribution agreement 213

dumping 215
export 212
expropriation 211
force majeure clause 217
foreign exchange market 220
forum-selection clause 217
letter of credit 220

normal trade relations (NTR) status 216
quota 215
sovereign immunity 211
tariff 215
treaty 210

Chapter Summary: International Law in a Global Economy

International Principles and Doctrines (See pages 210–212.)	1. *The principle of comity*—Under this principle, nations give effect to the laws and judicial decrees of other nations for reasons of courtesy and international harmony. 2. *The act of state doctrine*—A doctrine under which U.S. courts avoid passing judgment on the validity of public acts committed by a recognized foreign government within its own territory. 3. *The doctrine of sovereign immunity*—When certain conditions are satisfied, foreign nations are immune from U.S. jurisdiction under the Foreign Sovereign Immunities Act of 1976.

(Continued)

▶ Chapter Summary: International Law in a Global Economy, Continued

Doing Business Internationally (See pages 212–214.)	U.S. domestic firms may engage in international business transactions in several ways. These include (1) exporting, which may involve foreign agents or distributors, and (2) manufacturing abroad through licensing arrangements and franchising operations.
Regulation of Specific Business Activities (See pages 214–216.)	In the interests of their economies, foreign policies, domestic policies, or other national priorities, nations impose laws that restrict or facilitate international business. Such laws regulate foreign investments, exporting, and importing. The World Trade Organization attempts to minimize trade barriers among nations, as do regional trade agreements and associations.
Commercial Contracts in an International Setting (See pages 216–219.)	International business contracts often include choice-of-language, forum-selection, and choice-of-law clauses to reduce the uncertainties associated with interpreting the language of the agreement and dealing with legal differences. Most domestic and international contracts include *force majeure* clauses. They commonly stipulate that acts of God and certain other events may excuse a party from liability for nonperformance of the contract. Arbitration clauses are also frequently found in international contracts.
Payment Methods for International Transactions (See pages 220–221.)	1. *Currency conversion*—Because nations have different monetary systems, payment on international contracts requires currency conversion at a rate specified in a foreign exchange market. 2. *Correspondent banking*—Correspondent banks facilitate the transfer of funds from a buyer in one country to a seller in another. 3. *Letters of credit*—Letters of credit facilitate international transactions by ensuring payment to sellers and assuring buyers that payment will not be made until the sellers have complied with the terms of the letters of credit. Typically, compliance occurs when a bill of lading is delivered to the issuing bank.
U.S. Laws in a Global Context (See pages 221–224.)	1. *Bribing of foreign officials*—To reduce bribery of foreign officials by representatives of U.S. corporations, Congress enacted the Foreign Corrupt Practices Act in 1977. 2. *Antitrust laws*—U.S. antitrust laws may be applied beyond the borders of the United States. Any conspiracy that has a substantial effect on commerce within the United States may be subject to the Sherman Act, even if the violation occurs outside the United States. 3. *International tort claims*—The Alien Tort Claims Act allows foreign citizens to bring civil suits in U.S. courts for injuries caused by violations of international law or a U.S. treaty. 4. *Antidiscrimination laws*—The major U.S. laws prohibiting employment discrimination, including Title VII of the Civil Rights Act of 1964, the Age Discrimination in Employment Act of 1967, and the Americans with Disabilities Act of 1990, cover U.S. employees working abroad for U.S. firms—*unless* to apply the U.S. laws would violate the laws of the host country.

▶ ExamPrep

ISSUE SPOTTERS

—Check your answers to these questions against the answers provided in Appendix D at the end of this text.

1. Café Rojo, Ltd., an Ecuadoran firm, agrees to sell coffee beans to Dark Roast Coffee Company, a U.S. firm. Dark Roast accepts the beans but refuses to pay. Café Rojo sues Dark Roast in an Ecuadoran court and is awarded damages, but Dark Roast's assets are in the United States. Under what circumstances would a U.S. court enforce the judgment of the Ecuadoran court? **(See page 210.)**
2. Gems International, Ltd., is a foreign firm that has a 12 percent share of the U.S. market for diamonds. To capture a larger share, Gems offers its products at a below-cost discount to U.S. buyers (and inflates the prices in its own country to make up the difference). How can this attempt to undersell U.S. businesses be defeated? **(See page 215.)**

BEFORE THE TEST

Go to **www.cengagebrain.com**, enter the ISBN 9781133586548, and click on "Find" to locate this textbook's Web site. Then click on "Access Now" under "Study Tools," and select Chapter 9 at the top. There, you will find a Practice Quiz that you can take to assess your mastery of the concepts in this chapter. Additionally, you will find Flashcards and a Glossary of important terms, as well as Video Questions (when assigned).

▶ For Review

Answers for the even-numbered questions in this **For Review** *section can be found in Appendix E at the end of this text.*

1. What is the principle of comity?

2. What is the act of state doctrine? In what circumstances is this doctrine applied?

3. Under the Foreign Sovereign Immunities Act in which situations is a foreign state subject to the jurisdiction of U.S. courts?

4. What are three clauses commonly included in international business contracts?

5. What federal law allows U.S. citizens, as well as citizens of foreign nations, to file civil actions in U.S. courts for torts that were committed overseas?

▶ Questions and Case Problems

9–1. Letters of Credit. The Swiss Credit Bank issued a letter of credit in favor of Antex Industries to cover the sale of 92,000 electronic integrated circuits manufactured by Electronic Arrays. The letter of credit specified that the chips would be transported to Tokyo by ship. Antex shipped the circuits by air. Payment on the letter of credit was dishonored because the shipment by air did not fulfill the precise terms of the letter of credit. Should a court compel payment? Explain. **(See page 220.)**

9–2. **Question with Sample Answer: Dumping.** The U.S. pineapple industry alleged that producers of canned pineapple from the Philippines were selling their canned pineapple in the United States for less than its fair market value (dumping). The Philippine producers also exported other products, such as pineapple juice and juice concentrate, that used separate parts of the same fresh pineapple, so they shared raw material costs, according to the producers' own financial records. To determine fair value and antidumping duties, the plaintiffs argued that a court should calculate the Philippine producers' cost of production and allocate a portion of the shared fruit costs to the canned fruit. The result of this allocation showed that more than 90 percent of the canned fruit sales were below the cost of production. Is this a reasonable approach to determining the production costs and fair market value of canned pineapple in the United States? Why or why not? **(See page 215.)**

—For a sample answer to Question 9–2, go to Appendix F at the end of this text.

9–3. Comity. Jan Voda, M.D., a resident of Oklahoma, owns three U.S. patents related to guiding catheters for use in interventional cardiology, as well as corresponding foreign patents issued by the European Patent Office, Canada, France, Germany, and Great Britain. Voda filed a suit in a federal district court against Cordis Corp., a U.S. firm, alleging infringement of the U.S. patents under U.S. patent law and of the corresponding foreign patents under the patent laws of the various foreign countries. Cordis admitted, "The XB catheters have been sold domestically and internationally since 1994. The XB catheters were manufactured in Miami Lakes, Florida, from 1993 to 2001 and have been manufactured in Juarez, Mexico, since 2001." Cordis argued, however, that Voda could not assert infringement claims under foreign patent law because the court did not have jurisdiction over such claims. Which of the important international legal principles discussed in this chapter would be most likely to apply in this case? How should the court apply it? Explain. [*Voda v. Cordis Corp.,* 476 F.3d 887 (Fed.Cir. 2007)] **(See page 210.)**

9–4. **Case Problem with Sample Answer: Sovereign Immunity.** When Ferdinand Marcos was president of the Republic of the Philippines, he put assets into a company called Arelma. Its holdings are in New York. A group of plaintiffs, referred to as the Pimentel class, brought a class-action suit in a U.S. district court for human rights violations by Marcos. They won a judgment of $2 billion and sought to attach (take legal action against) Arelma's assets to help pay the judgment. At the same time, the Republic of the Philippines established a commission to recover property wrongfully taken by Marcos. A court in the Philippines was determining whether Marcos's property, including Arelma, should be forfeited to the Republic or to other parties. The Philippine government, in opposition to the Pimentel judgment, moved to dismiss the U.S. court proceedings. The district court refused, and the U.S. Court of Appeals for the Ninth Circuit agreed that the Pimentel class should take the assets. The Republic of the Philippines appealed. What are the key international legal issues?

[*Republic of the Philippines v. Pimentel*, 553 U.S. 851, 128 S. Ct. 2180, 171 L.Ed.2d 131 (2008)] **(See pages 211–212.)** —**For a sample answer to Case Problem 9–4, go to Appendix G at the end of this text.**

9–5. Dumping. The fuel for nuclear power plants is low-enriched uranium (LEU). LEU consists of feed uranium enriched by energy to a certain assay—the percentage of the isotope necessary for a nuclear reaction. The amount of energy is described by an industry standard as a "separative work unit" (SWU). A nuclear utility may buy LEU from an enricher, or the utility may provide an enricher with feed uranium and pay for the SWUs necessary to produce LEU. Under an SWU contract, the LEU returned to the utility may not be exactly the uranium the utility provided. This is because feed uranium is fungible and trades like a commodity (such as wheat or corn), and profitable enrichment requires the constant processing of undifferentiated stock. LEU imported from foreign enrichers, including Eurodif, S.A., was purportedly being sold in the United States for "less than fair value." Does this constitute dumping? Explain. If so, what could be done to prevent it? [*United States v. Eurodif, S.A.*, 555 U.S. 305, 129 S.Ct. 878, 172 L.Ed.2d 679 (2009)] **(See page 215.)**

9–6. International Agreements and Jurisdiction. The plaintiffs in this case were descendants of Holocaust victims who had lived in various countries in Europe. Before the Holocaust, the plaintiffs' ancestors had purchased insurance policies from Assicurazioni Generali, S.P.A., an Italian insurance company. When Generali refused to pay benefits under the policies, the plaintiffs, who were U.S. citizens and the beneficiaries of these policies, sued for breach of the insurance contracts. Due to certain agreements among nations after World War II, such lawsuits could not be filed for many years. In 2000, however, the United States agreed that Germany could establish a foundation—the International Commission on Holocaust-Era Insurance Claims, or ICHEIC—that would compensate victims who had suffered losses at the hands of the Germans during the war. Whenever a German company was sued in a U.S. court based on a Holocaust-era claim, the U.S. government would inform the court that the matter should be referred to the ICHEIC as the exclusive forum and remedy for the resolution. There was no such agreement with Italy, however. The plaintiffs sued the Italy-based Generali in a U.S. district court. The court dismissed the suit, and the plaintiffs appealed. Did the plaintiffs have to take their claim to the ICHEIC rather than sue in a U.S. court? Why or why not? [*In re Assicurazioni Generali, S.P.A.*, 592 F.3d 113 (2d Cir. 2010)] **(See page 222.)**

9–7. Sovereign Immunity. Bell Helicopter Textron, Inc., designs, makes, and sells helicopters with distinctive and famous trade dress that identifies them as Bell aircraft. Bell also owns the helicopters' design patents. Bell's Model 206 Series includes the Jet Ranger. Thirty-six years after Bell developed the Jet Ranger, the Islamic Republic of Iran began to make and sell counterfeit Model 206 Series helicopters and parts. Iran's counterfeit versions—the Shahed 278 and the Shahed 285—use Bell's *trade dress* (see Chapter 8). The Shahed aircraft was promoted at an international air show in Iran to aircraft customers. Bell filed a suit in a federal district court against Iran, alleging violations of trademark and patent laws. Is Iran—a foreign nation—exempt in these circumstances from the jurisdiction of U.S. courts? Explain. [*Bell Helicopter Textron, Inc. v. Islamic Republic of Iran*, 764 F.Supp.2d 122 (D.D.C. 2011)] **(See pages 211–212.)**

9–8. Sovereign Immunity. Technology Incubation and Entrepreneurship Training Society (TIETS) entered into a joint-venture agreement with Mandana Farhang and M.A. Mobile to develop and market certain technology for commercial purposes. Farhang and M.A. Mobile filed suit in a federal district court in California, where they both were based, alleging claims under the joint-venture agreement and a related nondisclosure agreement. The parties agreed that TIETS was a "foreign state" covered by the Foreign Sovereign Immunities Act (FSIA) because it was a part of the Indian government. Nevertheless, Farhang and M.A. Mobile argued that TIETS did not enjoy sovereign immunity because it had engaged in a commercial activity that had a direct effect in the United States. Could TIETS still be subject to the jurisdiction of U.S. courts under the commercial activities exception even though the joint venture was to take place outside the United States? If so, how? [*Farhang v. Indian Institute of Technology*, 2012 WL 113739 (N.D.Cal. Jan. 12, 2012)] **(See page 212.)**

9–9. In Your Court: Foreign Sovereign Immunities Act. Texas Trading & Milling Corp. and other companies brought an action for breach of contract against the Republic of Nigeria and its central bank. Nigeria had contracted to purchase more cement from Texas Trading than it could use. Unable to accept delivery of the cement, Nigeria repudiated the contract, claiming immunity under the Foreign Sovereign Immunities Act (FSIA) of 1976 because the buyer of the cement was the Nigerian government. Assume that you are the judge in the trial court hearing this case and answer the following questions: **(See page 212.)**

1. What section of the FSIA is particularly applicable to this dispute?

2. Given the provisions of that section, should the doctrine of sovereign immunity remove the dispute from the jurisdiction of U.S. courts? Explain your reasoning.

9–10. Critical-Thinking Legal Environment Question. Business cartels and monopolies that are legal in some countries may engage in practices that violate U.S. antitrust laws. In view of this fact, what are some of the implications of applying U.S. antitrust laws extraterritorially? **(See page 222.)**

The Commercial Environment

(.shock/iStockphoto.com)

Chapter 10

Business Organizations

"Why not go out on a limb?
Isn't that where the fruit is?"

—Frank Scully, 1892–1964
(American author)

Contents

Learning Objectives

The five Learning Objectives below are designed to help improve your understanding of the chapter. After reading this chapter, you should be able to answer the following questions:

1. **What advantages and disadvantages are associated with sole proprietorships?**

2. **What is meant by joint and several liability? Why is this often considered to be a disadvantage of doing business as a general partnership?**

3. **What are the two options for managing a limited liability company?**

4. **What is cumulative voting?**

5. **What are the rights and duties of the directors and officers of a corporation?**

(iShock/iStockphoto.com)

Many Americans would agree with Frank Scully's suggestion in the chapter-opening quotation that most people need to "go out on a limb" to reap the benefits of creating a business. Certainly, an entrepreneur's primary motive for undertaking a business enterprise is to make profits. An *entrepreneur* is by definition one who initiates and assumes the financial risks of a new enterprise and undertakes to provide or control its management.

One question faced by any entrepreneur who wishes to start up a business is what form of business organization to choose for the business endeavor. Traditionally, entrepreneurs have used three major forms to structure their business enterprises: the sole proprietorship, the partnership, and the corporation. In this chapter, we first examine sole proprietorships and franchises. Next, we discuss another common form of business organizations—partnerships, as well as variations on partnerships, including limited liability partnerships and limited liability companies. In the latter half of this chapter, we discuss the corporation, including its formation and taxation, as well as the duties and rights of its shareholders and directors.

For a summary of the advantages and disadvantages of each of the business forms discussed in this chapter, see Exhibit 10–2 on pages 253 and 254.

▶ Sole Proprietorships and Franchises

Sole Proprietorship The simplest form of business organization, in which the owner is the business.

Many entrepreneurs choose to start their business as a **sole proprietorship,** which is the simplest form of business organization. In a sole proprietorship, the owner *is* the business. Thus, anyone who does business without creating a separate business organization, such as a partnership or corporation, has a sole proprietorship.

In addition, instead of setting up a business through which to market their own products or services, many entrepreneurs opt to purchase a *franchise*. We discuss both of these forms of doing business next.

Sole Proprietorships

More than two-thirds of all U.S. businesses are sole proprietorships. They are usually small enterprises with revenues of less than $1 million per year. Sole proprietors can own and manage any type of business, ranging from a home office undertaking to a large construction firm. Today, a number of online businesses that sell goods and services on a nationwide basis are organized as sole proprietorships.

ADVANTAGES OF THE SOLE PROPRIETORSHIP A major advantage of the sole proprietorship is that the proprietor owns the entire business and has a right to receive all of the profits (because he or she assumes all of the risk). In addition, it is often easier and less costly to start a sole proprietorship than to start any other kind of business, as few legal formalities are involved.

This type of business organization also offers more flexibility than does a partnership or a corporation. The sole proprietor is free to make any decision she or he wishes concerning the business—including whom to hire and when to take a vacation. A sole proprietor pays only personal income taxes (including Social Security and Medicare taxes) on the business's profits, which are reported as personal income on his or her personal income tax return. Sole proprietors are also allowed to establish certain retirement accounts that are tax-exempt until the funds are withdrawn.

LEARNING OBJECTIVE 1 What advantages and disadvantages are associated with sole proprietorships?

DISADVANTAGES OF THE SOLE PROPRIETORSHIP The major disadvantage of the sole proprietorship is that the proprietor alone bears the burden of any losses or liabilities incurred by the business enterprise. In other words, the sole proprietor has unlimited liability, or legal responsibility, for all obligations incurred in doing business. This unlimited liability is a major factor to be considered in choosing a business form.

EXAMPLE 10.1 Sheila operates a golf shop as a sole proprietorship. One day, Dean, a customer, is seriously injured when a display of golf clubs—which Sheila had failed to secure—falls on him. If Dean sues Sheila's business and wins, her personal liability could easily exceed the limits of her insurance policy. In that situation, Sheila could lose her business, and perhaps her house and any other personal assets that could be used to pay the judgment to Dean. ●

The sole proprietorship also has the disadvantage of lacking continuity on the death of the proprietor. When the owner dies, so does the business—it is automatically dissolved. Another disadvantage is that the proprietor's opportunity to raise capital is limited to personal funds and the funds of those who are willing to make loans.

Franchises

Franchise Any arrangement in which the owner of a trademark, trade name, or copyright licenses another to use that trademark, trade name, or copyright in the selling of goods or services.

Franchisee One receiving a license to use another's (the franchisor's) trademark, trade name, or copyright in the sale of goods and services.

A **franchise** is defined as any arrangement in which the owner of a trademark, a trade name, or a copyright licenses others to use the trademark, trade name, or copyright in the selling of goods or services. A **franchisee** (a purchaser of a

Franchisor   One licensing another (the franchisee) to use the owner's trademark, trade name, or copyright in the selling of goods or services.

franchise) is generally legally independent of the **franchisor** (the seller of the franchise). At the same time, the franchisee is economically dependent on the franchisor's integrated business system. In other words, a franchisee can operate as an independent businessperson but still obtain the advantages of a regional or national organization.

Today, franchising companies and their franchisees account for a significant portion of all U.S. retail sales. Well-known franchises include 7-Eleven, Holiday Inn, and McDonald's.

TYPES OF FRANCHISES   Generally, the majority of franchises fall into one of three classifications: distributorships, chain-style business operations, or manufacturing or processing-plant arrangements. We briefly describe these types of franchises here.

1. *Distributorship*—A *distributorship* arises when a manufacturing concern (franchisor) licenses a dealer (franchisee) to sell its product. Often, a distributorship covers an exclusive territory, as in a car dealership, for example.
2. *Chain-style business operation*—In a *chain-style business operation,* such as a Burger King restaurant or Hilton hotel, a franchise operates under a franchisor's trade name and is identified as a member of a select group of dealers that engage in the franchisor's business. The franchisee generally is required to follow standardized or prescribed methods of operation. Often, the franchisor requires that the franchisee maintain certain standards of operation. Sometimes, the franchisee is obligated to obtain materials and supplies exclusively from the franchisor.
3. *Manufacturing or processing-plant arrangement*—In a *manufacturing or processing-plant arrangement,* the franchisor transmits to the franchisee the essential ingredients or formula to make a particular product. The franchisee then markets the product either at wholesale or at retail in accordance with the franchisor's standards. Examples of this type of franchise are Pepsi-Cola and other soft-drink bottling companies.

"Business opportunities are like buses, there's always another one coming."
Richard Branson, 1950–present
(British entrepreneur)

LAWS GOVERNING FRANCHISING   Because a franchise relationship is primarily a contractual relationship, it is governed by contract law. If the franchise exists primarily for the sale of products manufactured by the franchisor, the law governing sales contracts as expressed in Article 2 of the Uniform Commercial Code applies (see Chapter 13). Additionally, the federal government (and most states) has enacted laws governing certain aspects of franchising. Generally, these laws are designed to protect prospective franchisees from dishonest franchisors and to prohibit franchisors from terminating franchises without good cause.

The federal government has enacted laws that protect franchisees in certain industries, such as automobile dealerships and service stations. These laws protect the franchisee from unreasonable demands and bad faith terminations of the franchise by the franchisor. Additionally, the Franchise Rule of the Federal Trade Commission (FTC) requires franchisors to disclose material facts that a prospective franchisee needs to make an informed decision concerning the purchase of a franchise. The rule was designed to enable potential franchisees to weigh the risks and benefits of an investment. The rule requires the franchisor to make numerous written disclosures to prospective franchisees.

For example, a franchisor is required to disclose whether projected earnings figures are based on actual data or hypothetical scenarios. All representations made to a prospective franchisee must have a reasonable basis. Franchisors are also required to explain termination, cancellation, and renewal provisions of the franchise contract before the agreement is signed.

THE FRANCHISE CONTRACT   The franchise contract specifies the terms and conditions of the franchise and spells out the rights and duties of the franchisor and the franchisee. If either party fails to perform the contractual duties, that party may be subject to a lawsuit for breach of contract. Generally, statutes and case law governing franchising tend to emphasize the importance of good faith and fair dealing in franchise relationships. Here, we look at some of the major issues that typically are addressed in a franchise contract.

Payment for the Franchise.   The franchisee ordinarily pays an initial fee or lump-sum price for the franchise license (the privilege of being granted a franchise). This fee is separate from the various products that the franchisee purchases from or through the franchisor. In some industries, the franchisor relies heavily on the initial sale of the franchise for realizing a profit. In other industries, the continued dealing between the parties brings profit to both. In most situations, the franchisor will receive a stated percentage of the annual sales or annual volume of business done by the franchisee.

Business Premises.   The franchise agreement may specify whether the premises for the business must be leased or purchased outright. In some cases, a building must be constructed or remodeled to meet the terms of the agreement. The agreement usually will specify whether the franchisor supplies equipment and furnishings for the premises or whether this is the responsibility of the franchisee.

Location of the Franchise.   Typically, the franchisor will determine the territory to be served. Some franchise contracts give the franchisee exclusive rights, or "territorial rights," to a certain geographic area. Other franchise contracts, though they define the territory allotted to a particular franchise, either specifically state that the franchise is nonexclusive or are silent on the issue of territorial rights. Many franchise cases involve disputes over territorial rights, and the implied covenant of good faith and fair dealing often comes into play in this area of franchising.

   EXAMPLE 10.2   Dundee Ice Cream Company offers franchising opportunities nationwide. Suppose that Dundee's franchise contract does not give Mike Jovanovic, a franchisee, exclusive territorial rights or is silent on the issue. If Dundee allows a competing franchise to be established nearby, Jovanovic may suffer a significant loss in profits. In this situation, a court may hold that Dundee's actions breached an implied covenant of good faith and fair dealing. ●

Quality Control by the Franchisor.   Although the day-to-day operation of the franchise business is normally left to the franchisee, the franchise agreement may provide for the amount of supervision and control agreed on by the parties. When the franchisee prepares a product or provides a service, the contract often provides that the franchisor will establish certain standards for the facility. As a general rule, the validity of a provision permitting the franchisor to establish and enforce certain quality standards is unquestioned.

TERMINATION OF THE FRANCHISE   Usually, the franchise agreement will specify that termination must be "for cause," such as death or disability of the franchisee, insolvency of the franchisee, or breach of the franchise agreement. Most franchise contracts provide that notice of termination must be given. If no set time for termination is specified, then a reasonable time, with notice, will be implied.

Wrongful Termination.   Because a franchisor's termination of a franchise often has adverse consequences for the franchisee, much franchise litigation involves claims of wrongful termination. Generally, the termination provisions of contracts are more favorable to the franchisor. This means that the franchisee, who normally invests a substantial amount of time and funds to make the franchise operation successful, may receive little or nothing for the business on termination. The franchisor owns the trademark and hence the business.

Good Faith and Fair Dealing. Federal and state laws protect franchisees from the arbitrary or unfair termination of their franchises by the franchisors. Generally, both statutory and case law emphasize the importance of good faith and fair dealing in terminating a franchise relationship. If a court perceives that a franchisor has unfairly terminated a franchise, the franchisee will be provided with a remedy for wrongful termination. If a franchisor's decision to terminate a franchise was made in the normal course of the franchisor's business operations, however, and reasonable notice of termination was given to the franchisee, generally a court will not consider the termination wrongful.

The importance of good faith and fair dealing in a franchise relationship is underscored by the consequences of the franchisor's acts in the following *Spotlight Case.*

SPOTLIGHT ON HOLIDAY INNS

Case 10.1   Holiday Inn Franchising, Inc. v. Hotel Associates, Inc.

Court of Appeals of Arkansas, 2011 Ark.App. 147 (2011).

BACKGROUND AND FACTS   Buddy House was in the construction business in Arkansas and Texas. For decades, he collaborated on projects with Holiday Inns Franchising, Inc. Their relationship was characterized by good faith—many projects were undertaken without written contracts. At Holiday Inn's request, House inspected a hotel in Wichita Falls, Texas, to estimate the cost of getting it into shape. Holiday Inn wanted House to renovate the hotel and operate it as a Holiday Inn. House estimated that recovering the cost of renovation would take him more than ten years, so he asked for a franchise term longer than Holiday Inn's usual ten years. Holiday Inn refused, but said that if the hotel were run "appropriately," the term would be extended at the end of ten years. House bought the hotel, renovated it, and operated it as Hotel Associates, Inc. (HAI), generating substantial profits. He refused offers to sell it for as much as $15 million.

Before the ten years had passed, Greg Aden, a Holiday Inn executive, developed a plan to license a different local hotel as a Holiday Inn instead of renewing House's franchise license. Aden stood to earn a commission from licensing the other hotel. No one informed House of Aden's plan. When the time came, HAI applied for an extension of its franchise, and Holiday Inn asked for major renovations. HAI spent $3 million to comply with this request. Holiday Inn did not renew HAI's license, however, but instead granted a franchise to the other hotel. HAI sold its hotel for $5 million and filed a suit in an Arkansas state court against Holiday Inn, asserting fraud. The court awarded HAI compensatory and punitive damages. Holiday Inn appealed.

IN THE WORDS OF THE COURT . . .
Raymond R. *ABRAMSON*, Judge.
    * * * *

Generally, a mere failure to volunteer information does not constitute fraud. But *silence can amount to actionable fraud in some circumstances where the parties have a relation of trust or confidence, where there is inequality of condition and knowledge, or where there are other attendant circumstances.* [Emphasis added.]

In this case, substantial evidence supports the existence of a duty on Holiday Inn's part to disclose the Aden [plan] to HAI. Buddy House had a long-term relationship with Holiday Inn characterized by honesty, trust, and the free flow of pertinent information. He testified that [Holiday Inn's] assurances at the onset of licensure [the granting of the license] led him to believe that he would be relicensed after ten years if the hotel was operated appropriately. Yet, despite Holiday Inn's having provided such an assurance to House, it failed to apprise House of an internal business plan * * * that advocated licensure of another facility instead of the renewal of his license. *A duty of disclosure may exist where information is peculiarly within the knowledge of one party and is of such a nature that the other party is justified in assuming its nonexistence.* Given House's history with Holiday Inn and the assurance he received, we are convinced he was justified in assuming that no obstacles had arisen that jeopardized his relicensure. [Emphasis added.]

Holiday Inn asserts that it would have provided Buddy House with the Aden [plan] if he had asked for it. But, Holiday Inn cannot satisfactorily explain why House should have been charged with the responsibility of inquiring about a plan that he did not know existed. Moreover, several Holiday Inn personnel testified that Buddy House in fact should have been provided with the Aden plan. Aden himself stated that * * * House should have been given the plan. * * * In light of these circumstances, we see no ground for reversal on this aspect of HAI's cause of action for fraud.

DECISION AND REMEDY   The state intermediate appellate court affirmed the lower court's judgment and its award of compensatory damages. The appellate court increased the amount of punitive damages, however, citing Holiday Inn's "degree of reprehensibility."

THE LEGAL ENVIRONMENT DIMENSION   *Why should House and HAI have been advised of Holiday Inn's plan to grant a franchise to a different hotel in their territory?*

▶ Partnerships

Traditionally, partnerships have been classified as either *general partnerships* or *limited partnerships*. The two forms of partnership differ considerably in regard to legal requirements and the rights and liabilities of partners. Additionally, the *limited liability partnership* is designed for professionals who normally do business as partners in a partnership. We look next at the basic characteristics of each of these forms.

General Partnerships

Partnership An agreement by two or more persons to carry on, as co-owners, a business for profit.

A general partnership, or **partnership**, arises from an agreement, express or implied, between two or more persons to carry on a business for profit. There are three essential elements to a partnership:

1. A sharing of profits and losses.
2. A joint ownership of the business.
3. An equal right in the management of the business.

Joint ownership of property does not in and of itself create a partnership. In fact, the sharing of income and even profits from such ownership is usually not enough to create a partnership. Note, though, that while the sharing of profits from ownership of property does not prove the existence of a partnership, sharing *both profits and losses* usually does.

EXAMPLE 10.3 Zoe and Cienna buy a restaurant together, open a joint bank account, and share the net profits or losses from the restaurant. Zoe manages the restaurant, and Cienna handles the bookkeeping. After eight years, Cienna quits and does no more work for the business. Zoe no longer wants to share the profits with Cienna and claims that she and Cienna did not establish a partnership. A court will likely find that a partnership existed, however, because Zoe and Cienna shared management responsibilities, had a joint bank account, and shared the profits and losses equally. ●

No particular form of partnership agreement is necessary for the creation of a partnership, but for practical reasons, the partnership agreement should be in writing. Basically, the partners may agree to almost any terms when establishing the partnership so long as they are not illegal or contrary to public policy.

Articles of Partnership A written agreement that sets forth each partner's rights in, and obligations to, the partnership.

The partnership agreement is called the **articles of partnership.** The articles usually specify the name and location of the business, the duration of the partnership, the purpose of the business, each partner's share of the profits, how the partnership will be managed, and how assets will be distributed on dissolution, among other things.

ADVANTAGES AND DISADVANTAGES OF A PARTNERSHIP A partnership is a legal entity only for limited purposes, such as the partnership name and title of ownership and property. A key advantage of the partnership is that the firm itself does not pay federal income taxes, although the firm must file an information return with the Internal Revenue Service. Profit from the partnership (whether distributed or not) is "passed through" the partnership to be taxed as an individual partner's personal income.

LEARNING OBJECTIVE 2 What is meant by joint and several liability? Why is this often considered to be a disadvantage of doing business as a general partnership?

The main disadvantage of the partnership is that the partners are subject to *personal* liability for partnership obligations. Partners are jointly and severally liable for partnership obligations, including contracts, torts, and breaches of trust. The term *severally* means separately, or individually. In other words, **joint and several liability** means that a third party may sue, at his or her option, any one or more of the partners without suing all of them or the partnership. This is true even if the partner did not participate in, ratify, or know about whatever it was that gave rise to the cause of action.

Joint and Several Liability A doctrine under which a plaintiff may sue, and collect a judgment from, any of several jointly liable defendants.

If the third party is successful, he or she may collect on the judgment only against the assets of those partners named as defendants. A judgment against only some of the partners does not extinguish the others' joint liability, however.

EXAMPLE 10.4   Brian and Julie are partners. If Tom sues Brian for a debt on a partnership contract and wins, Tom can collect the amount of the judgment against Brian only. If Tom cannot collect enough from Brian, however, Tom can later sue Julie for the difference. ● Additionally, a partner who commits a tort that results in a judgment against the partnership may be required to repay the firm for any damages it pays.

Fiduciary Relationship   A relationship founded on trust and confidence.

FIDUCIARY DUTIES   Partners stand in a **fiduciary relationship.** A fiduciary relationship is one of extraordinary trust and loyalty. Each partner must act in good faith for the benefit of the partnership. Fiduciary duties include a *duty of loyalty* and a *duty of care.*

1. A partner's duty of loyalty has two aspects. A partner must account to the partnership for any profit or benefit from the firm's business or the use of its property. A partner must also refrain from dealing with the firm as an adverse party or competing with it.
2. A partner's duty of care is limited to refraining from negligent or reckless conduct, intentional misconduct, and violations of the law.

Dissociation   The severance of the relationship between a partner and a partnership.

DISSOCIATION OF A PARTNERSHIP   Dissociation occurs when a partner ceases to be associated in the carrying on of the partnership business. Although a partner always has the *power* to dissociate from the firm, he or she may not have the *right* to dissociate. When a partner's dissociation is in breach of the partnership agreement, for instance, it is wrongful. **EXAMPLE 10.5**   Jenson & Burke's partnership agreement states that it is a breach of the agreement for any partner to assign partnership property to a creditor without the consent of the others. If a partner, Janis, makes such an assignment, she has not only breached the agreement but has also wrongfully dissociated from the partnership. ●

Dissociation normally entitles the partner to have his or her interest purchased by the partnership and terminates his or her actual authority to act for the partnership and to participate in running the business. Otherwise, the partnership continues to do business without the dissociating partner.

Limited Partnerships

Limited Partnership (LP)   A partnership consisting of one or more general partners and one or more limited partners.
General Partner   A partner who assumes responsibility for the management of the partnership and liability for its debts.
Limited Partner   A partner who contributes capital to the partnership but has no right to participate in the management or operation of the business and assumes no liability for partnership debts beyond the capital contributed.

A special and quite popular form of partnership is the **limited partnership (LP),** which consists of at least one general partner and one or more limited partners. A limited partnership is a creature of statute, because it does not come into existence until a *certificate of limited partnership* is filed with the appropriate state office.

A **general partner** assumes responsibility for the management of the partnership and liability for all partnership debts. A **limited partner** has no right to participate in the general management or operation of the partnership and assumes no liability for partnership debts beyond the amount of capital he or she has contributed. Thus, one of the major benefits of becoming a limited partner is this limitation on liability, both with respect to lawsuits brought against the partnership and the amount of funds placed at risk.

Limited Liability Partnership (LLP)   A form of partnership that allows professionals to enjoy tax benefits of a partnership while limiting their personal liability for the malpractice of other partners.

Limited Liability Partnerships

The **limited liability partnership (LLP)** is a hybrid form of business designed mostly for professionals, such as attorneys and accountants, who normally do business as partners in a partnership. In fact, nearly all of the large accounting firms are LLPs.

LLP Formation and Operation   LLPs must be formed and operated in compliance with state statutes, which often include provisions of the Uniform Partnership Act (UPA). The appropriate form must be filed with a state agency, and the business's name must include either "Limited Liability Partnership" or "LLP." In addition, an LLP must file an annual report with the state to remain qualified as an LLP in that state.

In most states, it is relatively easy to convert a traditional partnership into an LLP because the firm's basic organizational structure remains the same. Additionally, all of the statutory and common law rules governing partnerships still apply (apart from those modified by the state's LLP statute).

Advantages and Disadvantages of an LLP   Many professionals work together using the partnership business form. Family members often do business together as partners also. The major advantage of the LLP is that it allows a partnership to continue as a *pass-through entity* for tax purposes, but limits the personal liability of the partners. As discussed previously, a major disadvantage of the general partnership is the unlimited personal liability of its owner-partners. Partners in a general partnership are also subject to joint and several (individual) liability for partnership obligations, which exposes each partner to potential liability for the malpractice of another partner.

The LLP allows professionals to avoid personal liability for the malpractice of other partners. A partner in an LLP is still liable for her or his own wrongful acts, such as negligence, however. Also liable is the partner who supervised the party who committed a wrongful act. (This is generally true for all types of partners and partnerships, not just LLPs.)

EXAMPLE 10.6   A group of five lawyers operates as an LLP. One of the attorneys, Dan Kolcher, is sued for malpractice and loses. If the firm had been organized as a general partnership—and the firm did not have sufficient malpractice insurance to pay the judgment—the other attorneys' personal assets could be used to satisfy Kolcher's obligation. Because the firm is organized as an LLP, however, no other partner at the law firm can be held personally liable for Kolcher's malpractice, unless she or he acted as Kolcher's supervisor. In the absence of a supervisor, only Kolcher's personal assets can be used to satisfy the judgment (to the extent that it exceeds the liability insurance coverage). •

Although LLP statutes vary from state to state, generally each state statute limits the liability of partners in some way. For example, Delaware law protects each innocent partner from the "debts and obligations of the partnership arising from negligence, wrongful acts, or misconduct." The UPA more broadly exempts partners from personal liability for any partnership obligation, "whether arising in contract, tort, or otherwise."

▶ Limited Liability Companies

The **limited liability company (LLC)** is a hybrid form of business enterprise that offers the limited liability of the corporation but the tax advantages of a partnership. This business form is governed by state LLC statutes.

Formation of an LLC

Like a corporation, LLP, or LP, an LLC must be formed and operated in compliance with state law. About one-fourth of the states specifically require LLCs to have at least two owners, called **members.** In the rest of the states, although some LLC statutes are silent on this issue, one-member LLCs are usually permitted.

"Surround yourself with partners who are better than you are."
David Ogilvy, 1911–1999
(Scottish advertising executive)

Limited Liability Company (LLC)
A hybrid form of business enterprise that offers the limited liability of the corporation but the tax advantages of a partnership.

Member   A person who has an ownership interest in a limited liability company.

Articles of Organization   The document filed with a designated state official by which a limited liability company is formed.

To form an LLC, **articles of organization** must be filed with a state agency—usually the secretary of state's office. Typically, the articles are required to set forth such information as the name of the business, its principal address, the name and address of a registered agent, the names of the owners, and information on how the LLC will be managed. The business's name must include the words "Limited Liability Company" or the initials "LLC."

Advantages and Disadvantages of the LLC

A key advantage of the LLC is that the liability of members is limited to the amount of their investments. Another advantage is the flexibility of the LLC in regard to taxation. An LLC that has *two or more members* can choose to be taxed either as a partnership or as a corporation. Unless an LLC indicates that it wishes to be taxed as a corporation, the IRS automatically taxes it as a partnership. This means that the LLC as an entity pays no taxes. Rather, as in a partnership, profits are "passed through" the LLC to the members, who then personally pay taxes on the profits.

If an LLC's members want to reinvest the profits in the business, however, rather than distribute the profits to members, they may prefer that the LLC be taxed as a corporation. Corporate income tax rates may be lower than personal tax rates. For federal income tax purposes, one-member LLCs are automatically taxed as sole proprietorships unless they indicate that they wish to be taxed as corporations. With respect to state taxes, most states follow the IRS rules. Still another advantage of the LLC is the flexibility it offers in terms of business operations and management—as will be discussed shortly.

The disadvantages of the LLC are relatively few. Although initially there was uncertainty over how LLCs would be taxed, that disadvantage no longer exists. The main disadvantage is that state LLC statutes are not yet uniform. An LLC in one state therefore has to check the rules in the other states in which the firm does business to ensure that it retains its limited liability.

REMEMBER   A uniform law is a "model" law. It does not become the law of any state until the state legislature adopts it, either in part or in its entirety.

The LLC Operating Agreement

Operating Agreement   In a limited liability company, an agreement in which the members set forth the details of how the business will be managed and operated.

The members of an LLC can decide how to operate the various aspects of the business by forming an **operating agreement.** Operating agreements typically contain provisions relating to management, how profits will be divided, the transfer of membership interests, whether the LLC will be dissolved on the death or departure of a member, and other important issues.

An operating agreement need not be in writing and indeed need not even be formed for an LLC to exist. Generally, though, LLC members should protect their interests by forming a written operating agreement. As with any business arrangement, disputes may arise over any number of issues. If there is no agreement covering the topic under dispute, such as how profits will be divided, the state LLC statute will govern the outcome. For example, most LLC statutes provide that if the members have not specified how profits will be divided, they will be divided equally among the members. Generally, when an issue is not covered by an operating agreement or by an LLC statute, the courts apply the principles of partnership law.

CASE EXAMPLE 10.7   Clifford Kuhn, Jr., and Joseph Tumminelli formed Touch of Class Limousine Service as an LLC. They did not create a written operating agreement but orally agreed that Kuhn would provide the financial backing and bring in customers, and that Tumminelli would manage the company's day-to-day operations. Tumminelli embezzled $283,000 from the company after cashing customers' checks at Quick Cash, Inc. Kuhn filed a lawsuit against Tumminelli, the banks, and others in a New Jersey state court to recover the embezzled funds. He argued that Quick Cash and the banks were liable because Tumminelli did not have the authority to cash the company's checks. The court, however, held that without a written operating agreement to the contrary, a member of an LLC, like a partner in a partnership, *does* have the authority to cash the firm's checks.[1] ●

The members of an LLC can also set forth in their operating agreement provisions governing decision-making procedures. For instance, the agreement can include procedures for choosing or removing managers. Members may also specify in their agreement how voting rights will be apportioned.

Management of an LLC

Basically, there are two options for managing an LLC. The members may decide in their operating agreement to be either a "member-managed" LLC or a "manager-managed" LLC. Most LLC statutes and the Uniform Limited Liability Company Act (ULLCA) provide that unless the articles of organization specify otherwise, an LLC is assumed to be member managed.

LEARNING OBJECTIVE 3 **What are the two options for managing a limited liability company?**

In a *member-managed* LLC, all of the members participate in management, and decisions are made by majority vote. In a *manager-managed* LLC, the members designate a group of persons to manage the firm. The management group may consist of only members, both members and nonmembers, or only nonmembers.

Managers in a manager-managed LLC owe fiduciary duties to the LLC and its members, including the *duty of loyalty* and the *duty of care,* just as corporate directors and officers owe fiduciary duties to the corporation and its shareholders (as will be discussed later in this chapter).

In Alabama, where the following case arose, managers owe fiduciary duties to the LLC and its members.

---

1. *Kuhn v. Tumminelli,* 366 N.J.Super. 431, 841 A.2d 496 (2004).

Case 10.2 **Polk v. Polk**

Court of Civil Appeals of Alabama, 70 So.3d 363 (2011).

BACKGROUND AND FACTS Leslie Polk and his children, Yurii and Dusty Polk and Lezanne Proctor, formed Polk Plumbing, LLC, in Alabama. Leslie, Dusty, and Yurii performed commercial plumbing work, and Lezanne, an accountant, maintained the financial records and served as the office manager. After a couple of years, Yurii quit the firm. Eighteen months later, Leslie "fired" Dusty and Lezanne. He denied them access to the LLC's books and offices but continued to operate the business. Dusty and Lezanne filed a suit in an Alabama state court against Leslie, claiming breach of fiduciary duty. The court submitted the claim to a jury with the instruction that in Alabama employment relationships are "at will" (see Chapter 16). The court also told the jury that it could not consider the plaintiffs' "firing" as part of their claim. The jury awarded Dusty and Lezanne one dollar each in damages. They appealed, arguing that the judge's instructions to the jury were prejudicial—that is, that the instructions had substantially affected the outcome of the trial.

IN THE WORDS OF THE COURT . . .
MOORE, Judge.
* * * *

In this case, Dusty and Lezanne served as managers of the LLC. The LLC's Operating Agreement * * * provided that

> the Members may elect one or more of the Members to serve as Managers of the Company for the purpose of handling the day to day details of the Company. * * * The Managers shall serve for a period of one year or until their replacement or recall is voted by a majority of the Members.

Based on the evidence presented at trial showing that the parties continued to act as managers of the LLC after the first year of operation, the foregoing contractual provision guaranteed that Dusty and Lezanne would remain managers until replaced or recalled by a vote of the majority of the members. Hence, their employment as managers of the

Case 10.2—Continues next page ➡

Case 10.2–Continued

LLC was not at will and the trial court erred in instructing the jury that it was. [Emphasis added.]

The trial court further erred in not allowing the jury to consider the circumstances of Dusty and Lezanne's "firing" as part of their breach-of-fiduciary-duty claim. * * * The record contains no evidence indicating that a vote was ever held to recall or replace Dusty and Lezanne. Rather, as Leslie testified, he simply acted in disregard of the terms of the Operating Agreement and instead rested on his right as the patriarch of the family to "fire" Dusty and Lezanne for, in his opinion, not working enough. Hence, * * * Leslie did not have the authority under the Operating Agreement to terminate the management positions of Dusty and Lezanne in the manner in which he did.

* * * *

By failing to instruct the jury that it also could consider Leslie's "firing" of Dusty and Lezanne as evidence in support of their breach-of-fiduciary-duty claim, we conclude that the trial court probably injuriously affected substantial rights of Dusty and Lezanne.

* * * *

Had the jury properly considered all the evidence supporting their breach-of-fiduciary-duty claim, it might have concluded that a higher amount of compensatory damages and possibly even punitive damages should have been awarded to Dusty and Lezanne.

DECISION AND REMEDY   A state intermediate appellate court reversed the lower court's judgment on the claim for breach of fiduciary duty and remanded the case for a new trial. The lower court committed reversible error by instructing the jury that Dusty and Lezanne's employment as managers was at will and by failing to instruct the jury that it could consider their "firing" as evidence in support of their claim.

WHAT IF THE FACTS WERE DIFFERENT?   *Suppose that Leslie owned a majority of the shares in Polk Plumbing. Could his "firing" of Dusty and Lezanne still be considered as evidence of a breach of fiduciary duty? Explain.*

Dissociation and Dissolution of an LLC

An LLC member has the *power* to dissociate from the LLC at any time, but he or she may not have the *right* to dissociate. Under the ULLCA, the events that trigger a member's dissociation include voluntary withdrawal, expulsion by other members or by court order, bankruptcy, incompetence, and death. Generally, even if a member dies or otherwise dissociates from an LLC, the other members may continue to carry on LLC business, unless the operating agreement has contrary provisions.

 ## Corporations

Corporation   A legal business form that complies with statutory requirements.

A third and very widely used type of business organizational form is the **corporation.** Corporations are owned by *shareholders*—those who have purchased ownership shares in the business. A *board of directors,* elected by the shareholders, manages the business. The board of directors normally employs *officers* to oversee day-to-day operations.

The corporation, like the limited partnership, is a creature of statute. The corporation's existence as a legal entity, which can be perpetual, depends generally on state law. One of the key advantages of the corporate form of business is that the liability of its owners (shareholders) is limited to their investments. The shareholders usually are not personally liable for the obligations of the corporation.

Another advantage is that a corporation can raise capital by selling shares of corporate stock to investors. A key disadvantage of the corporate form is that any distributed corporate income is taxed twice. The corporate entity pays taxes on the firm's income, and when income is distributed to shareholders, the shareholders again pay taxes on that income.

S Corporation   A business corporation that qualifies for special income tax treatment.

Some small corporations are able to avoid this double-taxation feature of the corporation by electing to be treated, for tax purposes, as an **S corporation.** Subchapter S of the Internal Revenue Code allows qualifying corporations to be taxed in a way similar to the way a partnership is taxed. In other words, an S corporation is not taxed at the corporate level. As in a partnership, the income is taxed only once—when it is distributed to the shareholder-owners, who pay personal income taxes on their respective shares of the profits.

The Nature of the Corporation

The corporation's existence depends generally on state law. Each state has its own body of corporate law, and these laws are not entirely uniform. The Model Business Corporation Act is a codification of modern corporation law that has been influential in the drafting and revision of state corporation statutes. Today, the majority of state statutes are guided by the revised version of the MBCA, known as the Revised Model Business Corporation Act.

A corporation can consist of one or more *natural* persons (as opposed to the artificial "person" of the corporation) identified under a common name. The primary document needed to incorporate—that is, form the corporation according to state law—is the **articles of incorporation.** These articles include such information about the corporation as its functions and the structure of its organization. As soon as a corporation is formed, an organizational meeting is held to adopt **bylaws** (rules for managing the firm) and to elect a board of directors.

The corporation substitutes itself for its shareholders in conducting corporate business and in incurring liability, yet its authority to act and the liability for its actions are separate and apart from the individuals who own it. In certain limited situations, however, the "corporate veil" can be pierced—that is, liability for the corporation's obligations can be extended to shareholders (see pages 247 and 248).

Corporate Personnel and Taxation

Responsibility for the overall management of the corporation is entrusted to a *board of directors,* which is elected by the shareholders. The board of directors hires *corporate officers* and other employees to run the daily business operations of the corporation. When an individual purchases a share of stock in a corporation, that person becomes a *shareholder* and an owner of the corporation. Unlike the members in a partnership, the body of shareholders can change constantly without affecting the continued existence of the corporation.

DIVIDENDS   Corporate profits are taxed by state and federal governments. Corporations can do one of two things with corporate profits—retain them or pass them on to shareholders in the form of **dividends.**

Whether a corporation retains its profits or passes them on to the shareholders as dividends, those profits are subject to income tax by various levels of government. Failure to pay taxes can lead to severe consequences. For instance, a state can suspend the entity's corporate status until the taxes are paid or even dissolve the corporation for failing to pay taxes.

DOUBLE TAXATION   Another important aspect of corporate taxation is that corporate profits can be subject to *double taxation.* The company pays tax on its profits, and then if the profits are passed on to the shareholders as dividends, the shareholders must also pay income tax on them (unless the dividends represent distributions of capital). The corporation normally does not receive a tax deduction for dividends it distributes. This double-taxation feature is one of the major disadvantages of the corporate form.

Profits not distributed are retained by the corporation. These **retained earnings,** if invested properly, will yield higher corporate profits in the future and thus normally cause the price of the company's stock to rise. Individual shareholders can then reap the benefits of these retained earnings in the capital gains they receive when they sell their shares.

Articles of Incorporation   The document filed with the appropriate governmental agency, usually the secretary of state, when a business is incorporated.

Bylaws   A set of governing rules adopted by a corporation or other association.

Dividend   A distribution to corporate shareholders of corporate profits or income, disbursed in proportion to the number of shares held.

Retained Earnings   The portion of a corporation's profits that has not been paid out as dividends to shareholders.

Constitutional Rights of Corporations

A corporation is recognized under state and federal law as a "person," and it enjoys many of the same rights and privileges that U.S. citizens enjoy. The Bill of Rights guarantees a person, as a citizen, certain protections, and corporations are considered persons in most instances. Accordingly, a corporation has the same right as a natural person to equal protection of the laws under the Fourteenth Amendment. It has the right of access to the courts as an entity that can sue or be sued. It also has the right of due process before denial of life, liberty, or property, as well as freedom from unreasonable searches and seizures and from double jeopardy.

Under the First Amendment, corporations are entitled to freedom of speech. As discussed in Chapter 4, however, commercial speech (such as advertising) receives significantly less protection than noncommercial speech. Generally, a corporation is not entitled to claim the Fifth Amendment privilege against self-incrimination. Agents or officers of the corporation therefore cannot refuse to produce corporate records on the ground that it might incriminate them. Additionally, the privileges and immunities clause of the U.S. Constitution (Article IV, Section 2) does not protect corporations.

Classification of Corporations

Domestic Corporation   A corporation that does business in, and is organized under the law of, a given state.

Foreign Corporation   In a given state, a corporation that does business in the state without being incorporated therein.

Alien Corporation   A designation in the United States for a corporation formed in another country but doing business in the United States.

Close Corporation   A corporation whose shareholders are limited to a small group of persons.

The classification of a corporation depends on its purpose, ownership characteristics, and location. A corporation is referred to as a **domestic corporation** by its home state (the state in which it incorporates). A corporation formed in one state but doing business in another is referred to in that other state as a **foreign corporation.** A corporation formed in another country—say, Mexico—but doing business in the United States is referred to in the United States as an **alien corporation.**

Many corporate enterprises in the United States fall into the category of close corporations. A **close corporation** is one whose shares are held by a single person, members of a family, or relatively few nonrelated persons. Usually, the members of the small group constituting a close corporation are personally known to one another.

Close corporations are often managed by their shareholders, who may hold the positions of directors and officers. Management of a close corporation often resembles that of a sole proprietorship or a partnership. As a corporation, the firm must meet all specific legal requirements set forth in state statutes. Still, close corporations have a substantial amount of flexibility in determining the rules by which they will operate.

Torts and Criminal Acts

"Did you expect a corporation to have a conscience, when it has no soul to be damned and no body to be kicked?"

Edward Thurlow, 1731–1806
(English jurist)

A corporation is liable for the torts committed by its agents or officers within the course and scope of their employment. This principle applies to a corporation exactly as it applies to the ordinary agency relationships (see Chapter 16).

Under modern criminal law, a corporation may be held liable for the criminal acts of its agents and employees, provided the punishment is one that can be applied to the corporation. Although corporations cannot be imprisoned, they can be fined. (Of course, corporate directors and officers can be imprisoned, and many have been in recent years.) In addition, under sentencing guidelines for crimes committed by corporate employees (white-collar crimes), corporate lawbreakers can face fines amounting to hundreds of millions of dollars, though the guidelines allow judges to impose less severe penalties in certain circumstances.

CASE EXAMPLE 10.8   Brian Gauthier worked as a dump truck driver for Angelo Todesca Corporation. Although the truck was missing its back-up alarm that automatically sounded when the truck was put into reverse, Angelo allowed Gauthier to continue driving the truck. At a worksite, when Gauthier backed up to dump the truck's load, he struck and killed a police officer who was facing away from the truck. The state charged Angelo and Gauthier with the crime of vehicular homicide. Angelo argued that a corporation could not be guilty of vehicular homicide because it cannot operate a vehicle. The court ruled that if an employee commits a crime "while engaged in corporate business that the employee has been authorized to conduct," the corporation can be held liable for the crime. Hence, the court held that Angelo was liable for Gauthier's negligent operation of its truck, which resulted in a person's death.[2] ●

▶ Corporate Ownership—Shareholders

The acquisition of a share of stock makes a person an owner and shareholder in a corporation. Shareholders thus own the corporation. Although they have no legal title to corporate property, such as buildings and equipment, they do have an *equitable* (ownership) interest in the firm.

As a general rule, shareholders have no responsibility for the daily management of the corporation, although they are ultimately responsible for choosing the board of directors, which does have such control. Ordinarily, corporate officers and other employees owe no direct duty to individual shareholders. Their duty is to the corporation as a whole. A director, however, is in a fiduciary relationship to the corporation and therefore serves the interests of the shareholders. Generally, there is no legal relationship between shareholders and creditors of the corporation. Shareholders can, in fact, be creditors of the corporation and thus have the same rights of recovery against the corporation as any other creditor.

In this section, we look at shareholders' powers, meetings, and voting, which generally are established in the articles of incorporation and under the state's general incorporation law. In addition, we examine the rights and liabilities of shareholders.

Shareholders' Powers

Shareholders must approve fundamental corporate changes before the changes can be effected. Hence, shareholders are empowered to amend the articles of incorporation and bylaws, approve a merger or the dissolution of the corporation, and approve the sale of all or substantially all of the corporation's assets. Some of these powers are subject to prior board approval. Shareholder approval may also be requested (though it is not required) for certain other actions.

Shareholders elect directors to the board of directors by a vote, and they have the inherent power to remove a director from office *for cause* (breach of duty or misconduct, for example) by a majority vote.[3] Some state statutes (and some corporate charters) even permit removal of directors *without cause* by the vote of a majority of the holders of outstanding shares entitled to vote.

Shareholders' Meetings

Shareholders' meetings must occur at least annually, and additional, special meetings can be called as needed to take care of urgent matters. Because it is usually not practical for owners of only a few shares of stock of publicly traded corporations to attend shareholders' meetings, such stockholders normally give third parties written authorization to vote their shares at the meeting. This authorization is called a **proxy**

2. *Commonwealth v. Angelo Todesca Corp.*, 446 Mass. 128, 842 N.E.2d 930 (2006).
3. A director can often demand court review of removal for cause.

(from the Latin *procurare,* "to manage, take care of"). Proxies are often solicited by management, but any person can solicit proxies to concentrate voting power.

When shareholders want to change a company policy, they can put their idea up for a shareholder vote. They can do this by submitting a shareholder proposal to the board of directors and asking the board to include the proposal in the proxy materials that are sent to all shareholders before meetings. The Securities and Exchange Commission (SEC), which regulates the purchase and sale of securities (see Chapter 20), has special provisions relating to proxies and shareholder proposals.

An SEC rule provides that all shareholders who own stock worth at least $1,000 are eligible to submit proposals for inclusion in corporate proxy materials. The corporation is required to include information on whatever proposals will be considered at the shareholders' meeting along with proxy materials. Only those proposals that relate to significant policy considerations rather than ordinary business operations must be included.

Shareholder Voting

Quorum   The number of members of a decision-making body that must be present before business may be transacted.

BE CAREFUL   Once a quorum is present, a vote can be taken even if some shareholders leave without casting their votes.

For shareholders to conduct business during a meeting, a *quorum* must be present. (A **quorum** is the minimum number of members of a body of officials or other group that must be present in order for business to be validly transacted.) Generally, a quorum exists when shareholders holding more than 50 percent of the outstanding shares are present. Corporate business matters are presented in the form of *resolutions,* which shareholders vote to approve or disapprove. Some state statutes have set forth specific voting requirements, and corporations' articles or bylaws must abide by these statutory requirements. Some states provide that the unanimous written consent of shareholders is a permissible alternative to holding a shareholders' meeting.

Once a quorum is present, voting can proceed. A majority vote of the shares represented at the meeting is usually required to pass resolutions. At times, more than a simple majority vote will be required either by a statute or by the corporate charter.

CUMULATIVE VOTING   Most states permit or even require shareholders to elect directors by *cumulative voting,* a method of voting designed to allow minority shareholders to be represented on the board of directors. When cumulative voting is allowed or required, the number of members of the board to be elected is multiplied by the total number of voting shares. The result equals the number of votes a shareholder has, and this total can be cast for one or more nominees for director. All nominees stand for election at the same time. When cumulative voting is not required either by statute or under the articles, the entire board can be elected by a simple majority of shares at a shareholders' meeting.

LEARNING OBJECTIVE 4   **What is cumulative voting?**

EXAMPLE 10.9   A corporation has 10,000 shares issued and outstanding. One group of shareholders (the minority shareholders) holds only 3,000 shares, and the other group of shareholders (the majority shareholders) holds the other 7,000 shares. Three members of the board are to be elected. The majority shareholders' nominees are Acevedo, Barkley, and Craycik. The minority shareholders' nominee is Drake. Can Drake be elected by the minority shareholders?

If cumulative voting is allowed, the answer is yes. The minority shareholders have 9,000 votes among them (the number of directors to be elected times the number of shares held by the minority shareholders equals 3 times 3,000, which equals 9,000 votes). All of these votes can be cast to elect Drake. The majority shareholders have 21,000 votes (3 times 7,000 equals 21,000 votes), but these votes have to be distributed among their three nominees. The principle of cumulative voting is that no matter how the majority shareholders cast their 21,000 votes, they will not be able to elect all three directors if the minority shareholders cast all of their 9,000 votes for Drake, as illustrated in Exhibit 10–1 below. •

OTHER VOTING TECHNIQUES Before a shareholders' meeting, a group of shareholders can agree in writing, in a *shareholder voting agreement,* to vote their shares together in a specified manner. Such agreements usually are held to be valid and enforceable. A shareholder can also appoint a voting agent and vote by proxy, as mentioned previously.

Rights and Liabilities of Shareholders

As mentioned earlier, shareholders have the right to participate in elections of the board of directors and in shareholders' annual meetings. In this section, we examine additional rights of shareholders, their potential liabilities, and the duties that majority shareholders may owe to minority shareholders.

RIGHTS OF SHAREHOLDERS Shareholders possess numerous rights. A significant right—the right to vote their shares—has already been discussed. We now look at some additional rights of shareholders.

Stock Certificate A certificate issued by a corporation evidencing the ownership of a specified number of shares in the corporation.

Stock Certificates. A **stock certificate** is a certificate issued by a corporation that evidences ownership of a specified number of shares in the corporation. In jurisdictions that require the issuance of stock certificates, shareholders have the right to demand that the corporation issue certificates. In most states, boards of directors may provide that shares of stock will be uncertificated—that is, no actual, physical stock certificates will be issued. When shares are uncertificated, the corporation may be required to send each shareholder a letter or some other form of notice that contains the same information that would normally appear on the face of stock certificates.

Preemptive Rights Rights held by shareholders that entitle them to purchase newly issued shares of a corporation's stock, equal in percentage to shares already held, before the stock is offered to any outside buyers.

Preemptive Rights. With **preemptive rights,** which are based on a common law concept, a shareholder receives a preference over all other purchasers to subscribe to or purchase a prorated share of a new issue of stock. In other words, a shareholder who is given preemptive rights can purchase the same percentage of the new shares being issued as she or he already holds in the company. This allows each shareholder to maintain her or his proportionate control, voting power, or financial interest in the corporation.

EXAMPLE 10.10 A shareholder who owns 10 percent of a company and who has preemptive rights can buy 10 percent of any new issue (to maintain his or her 10 percent position). Thus, if the shareholder owns 100 shares of 1,000 outstanding shares, and the corporation issues 1,000 more shares, the shareholder can buy 100 of the new shares. •

• *Exhibit* **10–1 Results of Cumulative Voting**
Cumulative voting gives minority shareholders a greater chance of electing a director of their choice. By casting all of their 9,000 votes for one candidate (Drake), the minority shareholders will succeed in electing Drake to the board.

BALLOT	MAJORITY SHAREHOLDERS' VOTES			MINORITY SHAREHOLDERS' VOTES	DIRECTORS ELECTED
	Acevedo	**Barkley**	**Craycik**	**Drake**	
1	10,000	10,000	1,000	9,000	Acevedo/Barkley/Drake
2	9,001	9,000	2,999	9,000	Acevedo/Barkley/Drake
3	6,000	7,000	8,000	9,000	Barkley/Craycik/Drake

Most statutes either (1) grant preemptive rights but allow them to be negated in the corporation's articles or (2) deny preemptive rights except to the extent that they are granted in the articles. The result is that the articles of incorporation determine the existence and scope of preemptive rights. Generally, preemptive rights apply only to additional, newly issued stock sold for cash and must be exercised within a specified time period, usually thirty days.

Dividends.   As mentioned on page 241, a *dividend* is a distribution of corporate profits or income *ordered by the directors* and paid to the shareholders in proportion to their respective shares in the corporation. Dividends can be paid in cash, property, stock of the corporation that is paying the dividends, or stock of other corporations.[4]

State laws vary, but each state determines the general circumstances and legal requirements under which dividends are paid. State laws also control the sources of revenue to be used. Only certain funds are legally available for paying dividends. Depending on state law, dividends may be paid from the following sources:

1. *Retained earnings*—All states allow dividends to be paid from retained earnings— the undistributed net profits earned by the corporation, including capital gains from the sale of fixed assets.
2. *Net profits*—A few states allow dividends to be issued from current net profits without regard to deficits in prior years.
3. *Surplus*—A number of states allow dividends to be paid out of any kind of surplus.

Illegal Dividends.   Sometimes, dividends are improperly paid from an unauthorized account, or their payment causes the corporation to become insolvent. Generally, in such situations, shareholders must return illegal dividends only if they knew that the dividends were illegal when the payment was received. A dividend paid while the corporation is insolvent is automatically an illegal dividend, and shareholders may be required to return the payment to the corporation or its creditors. Whenever dividends are illegal or improper, the board of directors can be held personally liable for the amount of the payment.

When directors fail to declare a dividend, shareholders can ask a court to compel the directors to meet and to declare a dividend. To succeed, the shareholders must show that the directors have acted so unreasonably in withholding the dividend that their conduct is an abuse of their discretion.

Inspection Rights.   Shareholders in a corporation enjoy both common law and statutory inspection rights. The shareholder's right of inspection is limited, however, to the inspection and copying of corporate books and records for a *proper purpose,* provided the request is made in advance. The shareholder can inspect in person, or an attorney, accountant, or other type of assistant can do so.

Transfer of Shares.   Corporate stock represents an ownership right in intangible personal property. The law generally recognizes the right to transfer stock to another person unless there are valid restrictions on its transferability. Although stock certificates are negotiable and freely transferable by indorsement and delivery, transfer of stock in close corporations usually is restricted. These restrictions must be reasonable and may be set out in the bylaws or in a shareholder agreement. The existence of any restrictions on transferability must always be indicated on the face of the stock certificate.

---

4. On one occasion, a distillery declared and paid a "dividend" in bonded whiskey.

When shares are transferred, a new entry is made in the corporate stock book to indicate the new owner. Until the corporation is notified and the entry is complete, all rights—including voting rights, the right to notice of shareholders' meetings, and the right to dividend distributions—remain with the current record owner.

The Shareholder's Derivative Suit. When those in control of a corporation—the corporate directors—fail to sue in the corporate name to redress a wrong suffered by the corporation, shareholders are permitted to do so in what is known as a **shareholder's derivative suit.** Before a derivative suit can be brought, some wrong must have been done to the corporation, and the shareholders must have presented their complaint to the board of directors. Only if the directors fail to solve the problem or to take appropriate action can the derivative suit go forward.

The right of shareholders to bring a derivative action is especially important when the wrong suffered by the corporation results from the actions of corporate directors or officers. This is because the directors and officers would probably want to prevent any action against themselves. When shareholders bring a derivative suit, they are not pursuing rights or benefits for themselves personally but are acting as guardians of the corporate entity. Therefore, if the suit is successful, any damages recovered normally go into the corporation's treasury, not to the shareholders personally.

Derivative actions are less common in other countries than in the United States, as this chapter's *Beyond Our Borders* feature below explains.

Shareholder's Derivative Suit A suit brought by a shareholder to enforce a corporate cause of action against a third person.

Beyond Our Borders — Derivative Actions in Other Nations

Today, most of the claims brought against directors and officers in the United States are those alleged in shareholders' derivative suits. Other nations, however, put more restrictions on the use of such suits.

German law, for example, does not provide for derivative litigation, and a corporation's duty to its employees is just as significant as its duty to its shareholder-owners. The United Kingdom has no statute authorizing derivative actions, which are permitted only to challenge directors' actions that the shareholders could not legally ratify. Japan authorizes derivative actions but also permits a company to sue the plaintiff-shareholder for damages if the action is unsuccessful.

For Critical Analysis
Do corporations benefit from shareholders' derivative suits? If so, how?

LIABILITIES OF SHAREHOLDERS One of the hallmarks of the corporate organization is that shareholders are not personally liable for the debts of the corporation. If the corporation fails, shareholders can lose their investments, but that is generally the limit of their liability. Certain instances can arise in which a shareholder can be personally liable. One relates to illegal dividends, which were discussed previously. Three others relate to disregarding the corporate veil, watered stock, and breaching a fiduciary duty.

Piercing the Corporate Veil. In some unusual situations, owners use a corporate entity to perpetrate a fraud, circumvent the law, or in some other way accomplish an illegitimate objective. In these cases, the court will ignore the corporate structure and **pierce the corporate veil,** thus exposing the shareholders to personal liability.

In other words, when the facts show that great injustice would result from the use of a corporation to avoid individual responsibility, a court will look beyond the corporate structure to the individual stockholder.

Pierce the Corporate Veil To disregard the corporate entity and hold the shareholders personally liable for a corporate obligation.

The following are some of the factors that cause the courts to pierce the corporate veil:

1. A party is tricked or misled into dealing with the corporation rather than the individual.
2. The corporation is set up never to make a profit or always to be insolvent, or it is too "thinly" capitalized—that is, it has insufficient capital at the time of formation to meet its prospective debts or other potential liabilities.
3. Statutory corporate formalities, such as holding required corporate meetings, are not followed.
4. Personal and corporate interests are **commingled** (mixed together) to such an extent that the corporation has no separate identity.

Commingle To put funds or goods together into one mass so that the funds or goods no longer have separate identities.

In the following case, when a close corporation failed to pay its legal fees, its attorneys sought to hold the shareholders personally liable. The court had to decide whether to pierce the corporate veil.

Case 10.3 | Brennan's, Inc. v. Colbert

Court of Appeal of Louisiana, Fourth Circuit, 85 So.3d 787 (2012).

BACKGROUND AND FACTS Pip, Jimmy, and Theodore Brennan are brothers, as well as shareholders of Brennan's, Inc., which owns and operates the famous Brennan's Restaurant in New Orleans. In 1998, the Brennan brothers retained attorney Edward Colbert and his firm, Kenyon & Kenyon, LLP, to represent Brennan's, Inc., in a dispute. All bills were sent to Brennan's, Inc., and the payments came from the company's checking accounts. As a close corporation, Brennan's, Inc., did not hold formal corporate meetings with agendas and minutes, but it did maintain corporate books, hold corporate bank accounts, and file corporate tax returns. In 2005, Brennan's, Inc., sued Colbert and his law firm for legal malpractice. In its answer, Kenyon & Kenyon demanded unpaid legal fees both from Brennan's, Inc., and from the Brennan brothers personally. The trial court found that the brothers could not be held personally liable. On appeal, Kenyon & Kenyon argued that it should be allowed to pierce the corporate veil because Brennan's, Inc., did not observe corporate formalities and because the Brennan brothers did not honor their promises to pay their legal bills.

IN THE WORDS OF THE COURT . . .
Daniel L. **DYSART**, Judge.
     * * * *
As a general rule, a corporation is a distinct legal entity, separate from the individuals who compose it, thus insulating the shareholders from personal liability.

There are limited exceptions where the court may ignore the corporate fiction and find the shareholders personally liable for the debts of a corporation. One of those exceptions is where the corporation is found to be the "alter ego" of the shareholder. It usually involves situations where fraud or deceit has been practiced by the shareholder through the corporation. Another basis is where the

shareholders disregard the corporate formalities to the extent that the corporation and the shareholders are no longer distinct entities.
     * * * *
Absent fraud, malfeasance or criminal wrongdoing, courts have been reluctant to hold a shareholder personally liable for corporate obligations. When a party seeks to pierce the corporate veil, the totality of the circumstances is determinative. [Emphasis added.]
     * * * *
The Kenyon firm was aware of the nature of the operation of Brennan's, Inc., * * * prior to being retained. The client was Brennan's, Inc., bills were sent to Brennan's, Inc., and payments were paid with checks from the Brennan's, Inc., bank accounts. * * * Brennan's, Inc., maintained its own accounting records and filed its own tax returns. * * * The Kenyon firm acknowledged that Brennan's, Inc., *acting through its shareholders,* promised to make good on the debt. [Emphasis in original.]

There is no evidence that the Brennan brothers ever agreed to bind themselves personally for any debt incurred in connection with the legal services provided by the Kenyon firm. There is no written retention agreement between the corporation and the Kenyon firm, nor is there a written guaranty from any of the brothers.

The Kenyon firm admits that there is no requirement for small, [close] corporations to operate with the formality usually expected of larger corporation. The Kenyon firm has failed to establish that the lack of corporate formalities, particularly, meetings, agendas and minutes, is sufficient to pierce the corporation veil. Brennan's, Inc., at all times since its inception has maintained corporate books, corporate bank accounts, and has filed corporate tax returns.
     * * * *
The Kenyon firm has not proven that any of the Brennan brothers made promises to pay the firm's bills without the intent to pay them. * * * *If a broken promise to pay was sufficient to establish fraud, then*

Case 10.3–Continued

every lawsuit against a corporation for a debt would automatically allow for the piercing of the corporate veil. Clearly, a juridical entity such as a corporation can only speak through its shareholders. [Emphasis added.]

DECISION AND REMEDY   The Louisiana appellate court held that Kenyon & Kenyon could not hold the Brennan brothers

personally liable by piercing the corporate veil. It therefore affirmed the trial court's judgment for the Brennan brothers.

THE ETHICAL DIMENSION   *Should the Brennan brothers be held personally liable because they misled their attorneys? Why or why not?*

Watered Stock   Shares of stock issued by a corporation for which the corporation receives, as payment, less than the stated value of the shares.

Watered Stock.   When a corporation issues shares for less than their fair market value, the shares are referred to as **watered stock**.[5] Usually, the shareholder who receives watered stock must pay the difference to the corporation (the shareholder is personally liable). In some states, the shareholder who receives watered stock may be liable to creditors of the corporation for unpaid corporate debts.

Duties of a Majority Shareholder.   In some instances, a majority shareholder is regarded as having a fiduciary duty to the corporation and to the minority shareholders. This occurs when a single shareholder (or a few shareholders acting in concert) owns a sufficient number of shares to exercise *de facto* (actual) control over the corporation. In these situations, majority shareholders owe a fiduciary duty to the minority shareholders.

When a majority shareholder breaches her or his fiduciary duty to a minority shareholder, the minority shareholder can sue for damages. A breach of fiduciary duties by those who control a close corporation normally constitutes what is known as *oppressive conduct.* A common example of a breach of fiduciary duty occurs when the majority shareholders "freeze out" the minority shareholders and exclude them from the benefits of participating in the firm.

CASE EXAMPLE 10.11   Four brothers—Iraj, Ahmad, Mannoch, and Aboli Mazloom— formed a close corporation to operate a liquor store. Each owned one-quarter of the company, and all four were directors. After disagreements arose, Iraj asked the company to purchase his shares, but his requests were refused. The brothers also refused to perform a valuation of the company, denied Iraj access to the corporate information he requested, and did not declare any dividends. Iraj sued his brothers in a South Carolina court, alleging breach of fiduciary duty. The court awarded Iraj punitive damages. Ahmad, Mannoch, and Aboli, the majority shareholders, had violated their fiduciary duty to Iraj, the minority shareholder.[6] ●

▶ Corporate Management—Directors and Officers

LEARNING OBJECTIVE 5   What are the rights and duties of the directors and officers of a corporation?

The board of directors is the ultimate authority in every corporation. A director occupies a position of responsibility unlike that of other corporate personnel. Directors have responsibility for all policymaking decisions necessary to the management of all corporate affairs. Just like shareholders, directors cannot act individually to bind the corporation but must act *as a body* in carrying out routine corporate business. The board selects and removes the corporate officers, determines the capital structure of the corporation, and declares dividends. Each director has one vote, and customarily the majority rules.

---

5. The phrase *watered stock* was originally used to describe cattle that were kept thirsty during a long drive and then were allowed to drink large quantities of water just before their sale. The increased weight of the "watered stock" allowed the seller to reap a higher profit.

6. *Mazloom v. Mazloom,* 382 S.C. 307, 675 S.E.2d 746 (2009).

Election of Directors

Normally, the incorporators appoint the first board of directors at the time the corporation is created, or the corporation itself names the directors in the articles. The initial board serves until the first annual shareholders' meeting. Subsequent directors are elected by a majority vote of the shareholders. A director usually serves for a term of one year—from annual meeting to annual meeting. Longer and staggered terms are permissible under most state statutes. A common practice is to elect one-third of the board members each year for a three-year term. In this way, there is greater management continuity.

Compensation of Directors

In the past, corporate directors rarely were compensated, but today they are often paid at least nominal sums and may receive more substantial compensation in large corporations because of the time, work, effort, and especially risk involved. Most states permit the corporate articles or bylaws to authorize compensation for directors.

Directors also gain through indirect benefits, such as business contacts and prestige, and other rewards, such as stock options. In many corporations, directors are also chief corporate officers (president or chief executive officer, for example) and receive compensation in their managerial positions.

Board of Directors' Meetings

The board of directors conducts business by holding formal meetings with recorded minutes. The dates of regular meetings are usually established in the articles or bylaws or by board resolution, and no further notice is customarily required. Special meetings can be called, with notice sent to all directors. Today, most states allow directors to participate in board of directors' meetings from remote locations via telephone or Web conferencing, provided that all the directors can simultaneously hear each other during the meeting.

Unless the articles of incorporation or bylaws specify a greater number, a majority of the board of directors normally constitutes a quorum. Once a quorum is present, the directors transact business and vote on issues affecting the corporation. Each director present at the meeting has one vote.[7] Ordinary matters generally require a simple majority vote, but certain extraordinary issues may require a greater-than-majority vote.

Rights of Directors

A corporate director must have certain rights to function properly in that position. The *right to participation* means that directors are entitled to participate in all board of directors' meetings and have a right to be notified of these meetings.

A director also has a *right of inspection,* which means that each director can access the corporation's books and records, facilities, and premises. Inspection rights are essential for directors to make informed decisions and to exercise the necessary supervision over corporate officers and employees.

When a director becomes involved in litigation by virtue of her or his position or actions, the director may also have a *right to indemnification* (reimbursement) for the legal costs, fees, and damages incurred.

---

7. Except in Louisiana, which allows a director to vote by proxy under certain circumstances.

Corporate Officers and Executives

The board of directors hire officers and other executive employees. At a minimum, most corporations have a president, one or more vice presidents, a secretary, and a treasurer. In most states, an individual can hold more than one office, such as president and secretary, and can be both an officer and a director of the corporation. Corporate officers and other high-level managers are employees of the company, so their rights are defined by employment contracts. Regardless of the terms of an employment contract, however, the board of directors normally can remove a corporate officer at any time with or without cause.

Duties and Liabilities of Directors and Officers

Directors and officers are deemed to be fiduciaries of the corporation because their relationship with the corporation and its shareholders is one of trust and confidence. As fiduciaries, directors and officers owe ethical—and legal—duties to the corporation and the shareholders as a whole. These fiduciary duties include the duty of care and the duty of loyalty.

DUTY OF CARE   Directors and officers must exercise *due care* in performing their duties. Generally, directors and officers are required to act in good faith, to exercise the care that an ordinarily prudent person would exercise in similar circumstances, and to do what they believe is in the best interests of the corporation. Directors and officers whose failure to exercise due care results in harm to the corporation or its shareholders can be held liable for negligence.

Duties for Reasonable Decisions and Supervision.   Directors and officers are expected to be informed on corporate matters and to conduct a reasonable investigation of the situation before making a decision. They cannot decide on the spur of the moment without adequate research. Directors are also expected to exercise a reasonable amount of supervision when they delegate work to corporate officers and employees.

EXAMPLE 10.12   Morgan, a corporate director at a mortgage company, fails to attend any board meetings for four years. In addition, he never inspects any of the corporate books and generally fails to supervise the efforts of the company's president and loan managers. Meanwhile, Denise, a corporate officer, makes improper loans and permits many late-payment fees. In this situation, Morgan can be held liable to the corporation for losses resulting from the unsupervised actions of Denise. ●

The Business Judgment Rule.   Directors and officers are expected to exercise due care and to use their best judgment in guiding corporate management, but they are not insurers of business success. Under the **business judgment rule,** a corporate director or officer will not be liable to the corporation or to its shareholders for honest mistakes of judgment and bad business decisions. Courts give significant deference to the decisions of corporate directors and officers, and consider the reasonableness of a decision at the time it was made, without the benefit of hindsight. Thus, corporate decision makers are not subjected to second-guessing by shareholders or others in the corporation.

The business judgment rule will apply as long as the director or officer:

1. Took reasonable steps to become informed about the matter.
2. Had a rational basis for his or her decision.

> *"If it is not in the interest of the public, it is not in the interest of the business."*
> Joseph H. Defrees, 1812–1885
> (U.S. congressman)

Business Judgment Rule   A rule that immunizes corporate management from liability for actions that are undertaken in good faith and are within both the power of the corporation and the authority of management to make.

3. Did not have a conflict of interest between his or her personal interest and that of the corporation.

In fact, unless there is evidence of bad faith, fraud, or a clear breach of fiduciary duties, most courts will apply the rule and protect directors and officers who make bad business decisions from liability for those choices. Consequently, if there is a reasonable basis for a business decision, a court is unlikely to interfere with that decision, even if the corporation suffers as a result.

EXAMPLE 10.13   If the directors of the American Cola Corporation decide, with due care, to change the taste of American Cola (the principal product of the company) and the public rejects the new product, the directors are not liable for the lost sales. ●

Ethical Issue

Does the business judgment rule go too far in protecting directors and officers from liability? The business judgment rule generally insulates corporate decision makers from liability for bad decisions even though this may seem to contradict the goal of greater corporate accountability. Is the rule fair to shareholders?

In one case, a Delaware court ruled against shareholders of Citigroup, Inc., who claimed that the bank's directors had breached their fiduciary duties. The shareholders alleged that the directors caused Citigroup to engage in subprime lending (discussed in Chapter 15) even in the face of "red flags" that should have warned the bank to change its practices. Those red flags included the steady decline of the housing market, the dramatic increase in foreclosures, and the collapse of other subprime lenders. The shareholders claimed that the directors' failure to adequately protect the corporation's exposure to risk given those warning signs was a breach of their duties and resulted in significant losses to Citigroup. The court, however, found "the warning signs alleged by plaintiffs are not evidence that the directors consciously disregarded their duties or otherwise acted in bad faith; at most they evidence that the directors made bad business decisions." Thus, under the business judgment rule, the court dismissed the shareholders' claims of breach of fiduciary duty.[8]

Another case also involved the business judgment rule. Early in 2007, a foreign firm had announced its intention to acquire Lyondell Chemical Company. Over the next several months, Lyondell's directors did nothing to prepare for a possible merger. They failed to research Lyondell's market value and made no attempt to seek out other potential buyers. The $13 billion cash merger was negotiated and finalized in less than one week in July 2007, during which time the directors met for a total of only seven hours to discuss it. Shortly afterward, shareholders filed a lawsuit alleging that the directors had breached their fiduciary duties by failing to maximize the sale price of the corporation. The Delaware Supreme Court ruled that the directors were protected by the business judgment rule.[9]

Duty of Loyalty   *Loyalty* can be defined as faithfulness to one's obligations and duties. In the corporate context, the duty of loyalty requires directors and officers to subordinate their personal interests to the welfare of the corporation. For instance, directors may not use corporate funds or confidential corporate information for personal advantage. Similarly, they must refrain from putting their personal interests above those of the corporation.

The duty of loyalty also requires officers and directors to *fully disclose* to the board of directors any potential conflict of interest that might arise in any corporate transaction. State statutes contain different standards, but a contract between a corporation and one of its officers or directors generally will *not* be voidable if all of the following

---

8. *In re Citigroup, Inc., Shareholder Derivative Litigation,* 964 A.2d 106 (Del.Ch. 2009). The court did allow the shareholders to maintain a claim for waste based on the directors' approval of a chief executive officer compensation package, however.

9. *Lyondell Chemical Co. v. Ryan,* 970 A.2d 235 (Del.Sup. 2009).

are true: if the contract was fair and reasonable to the corporation at the time it was made, if there was a full disclosure of the interest of the officers or directors involved in the transaction, and if the contract was approved by a majority of the disinterested directors or shareholders.

▶ Major Business Forms Compared

When deciding which form of business organization would be most appropriate, businesspersons normally take into account several factors, including the liability of the owners, tax considerations, and the need for capital. Each major form of business organization offers advantages and disadvantages with respect to these and other factors.

Exhibit 10–2 below and on the next page summarizes the essential advantages and disadvantages of each form of business organization discussed in this chapter.

• *Exhibit* 10–2 **Major Business Forms Compared**

CHARACTERISTIC	SOLE PROPRIETORSHIP	PARTNERSHIP	CORPORATION
Method of creation	Created at will by owner.	Created by agreement of the parties.	Authorized by the state under the state's corporation law.
Legal position	Not a separate entity; owner is the business.	A general partnership is a separate legal entity in most states.	Always a legal entity separate and distinct from its owners—a legal fiction for the purposes of owning property and being a party to litigation.
Liability	Unlimited liability.	Unlimited liability.	Limited liability of shareholders—shareholders are not liable for the debts of the corporation.
Duration	Determined by owner; automatically dissolved on owner's death.	Terminated by agreement of the partners, but can continue to do business even when a partner dissociates from the partnership.	Can have perpetual existence.
Transferability of interest	Interest can be transferred, but individual's proprietorship then ends.	Although partnership interest can be assigned, assignee does not have full rights of a partner.	Shares of stock can be transferred.
Management	Completely at owner's discretion.	Each partner has a direct and equal voice in management unless expressly agreed otherwise in the partnership agreement.	Shareholders elect directors, who set policy and appoint officers.
Taxation	Owner pays personal taxes on business income.	Each partner pays pro rata share of income taxes on net profits, whether or not they are distributed.	Double taxation—corporation pays income tax on net profits, with no deduction for dividends, and shareholders pay income tax on disbursed dividends they receive.
Organizational fees, annual license fees, and annual reports	None or minimal.	None or minimal.	All required.
Transaction of business in other states	Generally no limitation.	Generally no limitation.[a]	Normally must qualify to do business and obtain certificate of authority.

a. A few states have enacted statutes requiring that foreign partnerships qualify to do business there.

Exhibit 10–2 Continued ➡

• *Exhibit* 10–2 **Major Business Forms Compared–Continued**

CHARACTERISTIC	LIMITED PARTNERSHIP	LIMITED LIABILITY COMPANY	LIMITED LIABILITY PARTNERSHIP
Method of creation	Created by agreement to carry on a business for a profit. At least one party must be a general partner and the other(s) limited partner(s). Certificate of limited partnership is filed. Charter must be issued by the state.	Created by an agreement of the member-owners of the company. Articles of organization are filed. Charter must be issued by the state.	Created by agreement of the partners. A statement of qualification for the limited liability partnership is filed.
Legal position	Treated as a legal entity.	Treated as a legal entity.	Generally, treated same as a general partnership.
Liability	Unlimited liability of all general partners; limited partners are liable only to the extent of capital contributions.	Member-owners' liability is limited to the amount of capital contributions or investments.	Varies, but under the Uniform Partnership Act, liability of a partner for acts committed by other partners is limited.
Duration	By agreement in certificate, or by termination of the last general partner (retirement, death, and the like) or last limited partner.	Unless a single-member LLC, can have perpetual existence (same as a corporation).	Remains in existence until cancellation or revocation.
Transferability of interest	Interest can be assigned (same as in a general partnership), but if assignee becomes a member with consent of other partners, certificate must be amended.	Member interests are freely transferable.	Interest can be assigned same as in a general partnership.
Management	General partners have equal voice or by agreement. Limited partners may not retain limited liability if they actively participate in management.	Member-owners can fully participate in management, or can designate a group of persons to manage on behalf of the members.	Same as a general partnership.
Taxation	Generally taxed as a partnership.	LLC is not taxed, and members are taxed personally on profits "passed through" the LLC.	Same as a general partnership.
Organizational fees, annual license fees, and annual reports	Organizational fee required; usually not others.	Organizational fee required; others vary with states.	Fees are set by each state for filing statements of qualification, foreign qualification, and annual reports.
Transaction of business in other states	Generally no limitation.	Generally no limitation, but may vary depending on state.	Must file a statement of foreign qualification before doing business in another state.

▶ Reviewing . . . Business Organizations

David Brock is on the board of directors of Firm Body Fitness, Inc., which owns a string of fitness clubs in New Mexico. Brock owns 15 percent of the Firm Body stock, and he is also employed as a tanning technician at one of the fitness clubs. After the January financial report showed that Firm Body's tanning division was operating at a substantial net loss, the board of directors, led by Marty Levinson, discussed the possibility of terminating the tanning operations. Brock successfully convinced a majority of the board that the tanning division was necessary to market the clubs' overall fitness package. By April, the tanning division's financial losses had risen. The board hired a business analyst, who conducted surveys and determined that the tanning operations did not significantly increase membership. A shareholder, Diego Peñada, discovered that Brock owned stock in Sunglow, Inc., the company from which Firm Body purchased its tanning equipment, and he had not informed the other directors of this interest. Peñada notified Levinson, who privately reprimanded Brock. Using the information presented in the chapter, answer the following questions.

1. What duties did Brock, as a director, owe to Firm Body?
2. Does the fact that Brock owned shares in Sunglow establish a conflict of interest? Why or why not?
3. Suppose that Firm Body brought an action against Brock claiming that he had breached the duty of loyalty by not disclosing his interest in Sunglow to the other directors. Can Brock use the business judgment rule as a defense? Explain.
4. Now suppose that Firm Body did not file an action against Brock. What type of a lawsuit might Peñada be able to bring based on these facts?

Debate This

Because most shareholders never bother to vote for directors, shareholders have no real control over corporations.

Key Terms

alien corporation 242	fiduciary relationship 236	operating agreement 238
articles of incorporation 241	foreign corporation 242	partnership 235
articles of organization 238	franchise 231	pierce the corporate veil 247
articles of partnership 235	franchisee 231	preemptive rights 245
business judgment rule 251	franchisor 232	proxy 243
bylaws 241	general partner 236	quorum 244
close corporation 242	joint and several liability 235	retained earnings 241
commingle 248	limited liability company (LLC) 237	S corporation 240
corporation 240	limited liability partnership (LLP) 236	shareholder's derivative suit 247
dissociation 236	limited partner 236	sole proprietorship 231
dividend 241	limited partnership (LP) 236	stock certificate 245
domestic corporation 242	member 237	watered stock 249

Chapter Summary: Business Organizations

Sole Proprietorships and Franchises (See pages 231–234.)	1. *Sole proprietorships*—The simplest form of business; used by anyone who does business without creating an organization. The owner is the business. The owner pays personal income taxes on all profits and is personally liable for all business debts. 2. *Franchise*—Distributorships, chain-style operations, and manufacturing/processing-plant arrangements are three types of franchises. Franchises are governed by contract law and by federal and state statutory and regulatory laws. The franchise contract defines the relationship between the franchisor and the franchisee. Usually, the contract provides for the date and/or conditions of termination of the franchise arrangement. Both federal and state statutes attempt to protect franchisees from franchisors that unfairly or arbitrarily terminate franchises.
Partnerships (See pages 235–237.)	1. *General partnership*—Created by agreement of the parties; not treated as an entity except for limited purposes. Partners have unlimited liability for partnership debts, and each partner normally has an equal voice in management. Income is "passed through" the partnership to the individual partners. 2. *Limited partnership (LP)*—Must be formed in compliance with statutory requirements; consists of one or more general partners, who have unlimited liability for partnership losses, and one or more limited partners, who are liable only to the extent of their contributions. Only general partners can participate in management.

(Continued)

▶ Chapter Summary: Business Organizations, Continued

Partnerships–Continued	3. *Limited liability partnership (LLP)*–Articles must be filed with the appropriate state agency. Typically, an LLP is formed by professionals who work together as partners. LLP statutes vary, but generally they allow professionals to avoid personal liability for the malpractice of other partners. LLP partners continue to be liable for their own wrongful acts and for the wrongful acts of those whom they supervise.
Limited Liability Companies (LLCs) (See pages 237–240.)	Articles of organization must be filed with the appropriate state office setting forth the name of the business, its principal address, and the names of the owners (called *members*). Advantages of the LLC include limited liability and the option to be taxed as a partnership or as a corporation. Members have the power to disassociate from the LLC, but may not have the right. The members decide, in an operating agreement, how the business will be managed and what rules will apply to the organization.
Corporations (See pages 240–243.)	1. *Corporation*–Formed in compliance with statutory requirements. It is a separate legal entity and can have perpetual existence. The shareholder-owners elect directors, who set policy and hire officers to run the day-to-day business. The corporation pays income tax on net profits; shareholders pay income tax on disbursed dividends (double taxation). 2. *Classification of corporations*–A corporation is referred to as a *domestic corporation* within its home state. A corporation is referred to as a *foreign corporation* by any state that is not its home state. A corporation is referred to as an *alien corporation* if it originates in another country but does business in the United States. A *close corporation* is one whose shares are held by a single person, family members, or a few nonrelated persons. 3. *Torts and criminal acts*–The corporation is liable for the torts committed by its agents or officers within the course and scope of their employment. In some circumstances, a corporation can be held liable (and be fined) for the criminal acts of its agents and employees.
Corporate Ownership– Shareholders (See pages 243–249.)	1. *Shareholders' powers*–Shareholders are empowered to amend articles of incorporation and bylaws; approve corporate mergers, dissolutions, and sales; and elect or remove directors from the board. 2. *Shareholders' meetings and voting*–Meetings must be held annually or can be called in special instances. Shareholders may vote by proxy and may submit proposals to be included in the proxy materials. For business to be conducted, a quorum must be present. Most resolutions are passed by a majority vote, but cumulative voting and shareholder voting agreements can influence a board of directors' voting results. 3. *Shareholders' rights and liabilities*–In addition to voting rights, other rights include the right to a stock certificate and preemptive rights, dividends, corporate record inspections, the transfer of shares, and shareholders' derivative suits. Shareholders rarely are held liable for a corporation's debts; however, they can be held liable for keeping illegal dividends, disregarding the corporate veil, receiving watered stock, and breaching a fiduciary duty to minority shareholders.

Corporate Management– Directors and Officers (See pages 249–253.)	1. *Directors*–The first board of directors is usually appointed by the incorporators; thereafter, directors are elected by the shareholders. Directors usually serve a one-year term, although longer and staggered terms are permitted under most state statutes. The board of directors conducts business by holding formal meetings with recorded minutes. Often, a quorum is the majority of the corporate directors. Directors' rights include the rights of participation, inspection, and indemnification.
	2. *Corporate officers and executives*–Directors usually hire corporate officers and other executive employees. As employees, corporate officers and executives have the rights defined by their employment contracts. The following are other aspects of corporate management:
	  a. *Duty of care*–Directors and officers are obligated to act in good faith, to use prudent business judgment in the conduct of corporate affairs, and to act in the corporation's best interests.
	  b. *The business judgment rule*–This rule immunizes officers (and directors) from liability when they acted in good faith, acted in the best interests of the corporation, and exercised due care.
	  c. *Duty of loyalty*–Officers (and directors) have a fiduciary duty to subordinate their own interests to those of the corporation in matters relating to the corporation.

ExamPrep

ISSUE SPOTTERS

—Check your answers to these questions against the answers provided in Appendix D at the end of this text.

1. Hal and Gretchen are partners in a delivery business. When business is slow, without Gretchen's knowledge, Hal leases out the delivery vehicles as moving vans. The vehicles would otherwise be sitting idle in a parking lot. Can Hal keep the lease money, or does he have to account to Gretchen? **(See page 236.)**
2. Wonder Corporation has an opportunity to buy stock in XL, Inc. The directors decide that instead of Wonder buying the stock, the directors will buy it. Yvon, a Wonder shareholder, learns of the purchase and wants to sue the directors on the corporation's behalf. Can she do it? If so, why? If not, explain. **(See page 247.)**

BEFORE THE TEST

Go to **www.cengagebrain.com**, enter the ISBN 9781133586548, and click on "Find" to locate this textbook's Web site. Then click on "Access Now" under "Study Tools," and select Chapter 10 at the top. There, you will find a Practice Quiz that you can take to assess your mastery of the concepts in this chapter. Additionally, you will find Flashcards and a Glossary of important terms, as well as Video Questions (when assigned).

For Review

Answers for the even-numbered questions in this For Review *section can be found in Appendix E at the end of this text.*

1. What advantages and disadvantages are associated with sole proprietorships?
2. What is meant by joint and several liability? Why is this often considered to be a disadvantage of doing business as a general partnership?
3. What are the two options for managing a limited liability company?
4. What is cumulative voting?
5. What are the rights and duties of the directors and officers of a corporation?

Questions and Case Problems

10–1. Franchising. Maria, Pablo, and Vicky are recent college graduates who would like to go into business for themselves. They are considering purchasing a franchise. If they enter into a franchising arrangement, they would have the support of a large company that could answer any questions they might have. Also, a firm that has been in business for many years would be experienced in dealing with some of the problems that novice businesspersons might encounter. These and other attributes of franchises can lessen some of the risks of the marketplace. What other aspects of franchising—positive and negative—should Maria, Pablo, and Vicky consider before committing themselves to a particular franchise? **(See pages 233 and 234.)**

10–2. **Question with Sample Answer: Franchises.** Omega Computers, Inc., is a franchisor that grants exclusive physical territories to its franchisees with retail locations, including Pete's Digital Products. Omega sells more than two hundred of the franchises before establishing an interactive Web site. On the site, a customer can order Omega's products directly from the franchisor. When Pete's sets up a Web site through which a customer can also order Omega's products, Omega and Pete's file suits against each other, alleging that each is in violation of the franchise relationship. To decide this issue, what factors should the court consider? How might these parties have avoided this conflict? Discuss. **(See page 233.)**

—For a sample answer to Question 10–2, go to Appendix F at the end of this text.

10–3. Forms of Business Organization. In each of the following situations, determine whether Georgio's Fashions is a sole proprietorship, a partnership, or a limited partnership. **(See pages 235 and 236.)**

1. Georgio's defaults on a payment to supplier Dee Creations. Dee sues Georgio's and each of the owners of Georgio's personally for payment of the debt.

2. Georgio's is owned by three persons, two of whom are not allowed to participate in the firm's management.

10–4. Limited Liability Companies. To share the expenses and profits of a venture to develop oil and gas deposits, ORX Resources, Inc., partnered with MBW Exploration, LLC. Mark Washauer signed the agreement with ORX on behalf of MBW, which had not yet been formed. MBW did not have a bank account. Initially, Washauer paid for its participation in the partnership with personal checks. Later, MBW's share of unpaid partnership expenses amounted to more than $84,220. Could Washauer be held personally liable? Explain. [*ORX Resources, Inc. v. MBW Exploration, LLC,* 32 So.3d 931 (La.App. 2010)] **(See page 238.)**

10–5. Fiduciary Duties of Partners. Karl Horvath, Hein Rüsen, and Carl Thomas formed a partnership, HRT Enterprises, to buy a manufacturing plant. Rüsen and Thomas leased the plant to their own company, Merkur Steel. Merkur then sublet the premises to other companies owned by Rüsen and Thomas. The rent that these companies paid to Merkur was higher than the rent Merkur paid to HRT, which meant that Merkur profited from the arrangement. Rüsen and Thomas did not tell Horvath about the subleases. Did Rüsen and Thomas breach their fiduciary duties to HRT and Horvath? Discuss. [*Horvath v. HRT Enterprises,* 489 Mich.App. 992, 800 N.W.2d 595 (2011)] **(See page 236.)**

10–6. **Case Problem with Sample Answer: Management of an LLC.** James Williford, Patricia Mosser, Marquetta Smith, and Michael Floyd formed two member-managed limited liability companies—Bluewater Bay, LLC, and Bluewater Logistics, LLC (collectively Bluewater)—in Mississippi to bid on contracts related to the aftermath of Hurricane Katrina. Under Mississippi law, every member of a member-managed LLC is entitled to participate in managing the business. Under Bluewater's operating agreements, "a 75% Super Majority Vote of the members" could redeem any member's interest if the "member has either committed a felony or under any other circumstances that would jeopardize the company status" as a contractor. Bluewater had completed more than $5 million in contracts when Smith told Williford that he was "fired" and that she, Mosser, and Floyd were exercising their "super majority" right to buy him out. No reason was provided. Williford filed a suit in a Mississippi state court against Bluewater and the other members, who then told Williford that they had changed their minds about buying him out but that he was still fired. Did Smith, Mosser, and Floyd breach the state LLC statute, their fiduciary duties, or the Bluewater operating agreements? Discuss. [*Bluewater Logistics, LLC v. Williford,* 55 So.3d 148 (Miss. 2011)] **(See page 239.)**

—**For a sample answer to Case Problem 10–6, go to Appendix G at the end of this text.**

10–7. Duty of Loyalty. Kids International Corp. produced children's wear for Walmart and other retailers. Gila Dweck was a Kids director and its chief executive officer. Because she felt that she was not paid enough for the company's success, she started Success Apparel to compete with the firm. Success operated out of Kids' premises, used its employees, borrowed on its credit, took advantage of its business opportunities, and capitalized on its customer relationships. As an "administrative fee," Dweck paid Kids 1 percent of Success's total sales. Did Dweck breach any fiduciary duties? Explain. [*Dweck v. Nasser,* 2012 WL 161590 (Del. Ch. 2012)] **(See page 252.)**

10–8. Duties of Majority Shareholders. Bill McCann was the president and chief executive officer of McCann Ranch & Livestock Co. He and his brother Ron each owned 36.7 percent of the stock, but Ron had been removed from the board of directors on their father's death and was not authorized to work for the firm. Their mother, Gertrude, owned the rest of the stock, which was to pass to Bill on her death. The corporation paid Gertrude's personal expenses in an amount that represented about 75 percent of the net corporate income. Bill received regular salary increases. The corporation did not issue a dividend. Was Ron the victim of a freeze-out? Discuss. [*McCann v. McCann,* 152 Idaho 809, 275 P.3d 824 (2012)] **(See page 249.)**

10–9. Piercing the Corporate Veil. In 1997, Leon Greenblatt, Andrew Jahelka, and Richard Nichols incorporated Loop Corp. with only $1,000 of capital. Three years later, Banco Panamericano, Inc., which was run entirely by Greenblatt and owned by a Greenblatt family trust, extended a large line of credit to Loop. Loop's subsidiaries then participated in the credit, giving $3 million to Loop while acquiring a security interest in Loop itself. Loop then opened an account with Wachovia Securities, LLC, to buy stock shares using credit provided by Wachovia. When the stock values plummeted, Loop owed Wachovia $1.89 million. Loop also defaulted on its loan from Banco, but Banco agreed to lend Loop millions of dollars more. Rather than repay Wachovia with the influx of funds, Loop gave the funds to closely related entities and "compensated" Nichols and Jahelka without issuing any W-2 forms (forms reporting compensation to the Internal Revenue Service). The evidence also showed that Loop made loans to other related entities and shared office space, equipment, and telephone and fax numbers with related entities. Loop also moved employees among related entities, failed to file its tax returns on time (or sometimes at all), and failed to follow its own bylaws. In a lawsuit brought by Wachovia, can the court hold Greenblatt, Jahelka, and Nichols personally liable by piercing the corporate veil? Why or why not? [*Wachovia Securities, LLC v. Banco Panamericano, Inc.,* 674 F.3d 743 (9th Cir. 2012)] **(See pages 247–248.)**

10–10. **In Your Court: Franchises.** Excell Lodge entered into a contract with Host Inn, Inc., to operate a Host Inn franchise west of a major city's airport. Because another Host Inn, named "Host East," already served the market near the airport, the franchisor (Host Inn, Inc.)

named Excell's facility "Host West." Three years later, the franchisor bought a Hyatt hotel in the vicinity of the same airport and called it "Host Gateway." The presence of three Host properties in the same market caused some customer confusion. Also, Host West and the new Host Gateway competed for the same customers, which caused Host West to suffer a decrease in the growth of its business. Host West sued the franchisor, alleging that by establishing Host Gateway, the franchisor had denied Host West the fruits of its contract in breach of the implied covenant of good faith and fair dealing. Assume that you are the judge in the trial court hearing this case, and answer the following questions: (**See page 233.**)

1. Assume that the franchisor has made a motion for summary judgment in its favor, claiming that its actions were perfectly legal because the franchise contract itself was silent as to whether, and where, the franchisor could authorize a franchise to compete with Host West. Would you grant this motion? Why or why not?

2. Does a franchisor violate the implied covenant of good faith and fair dealing if it competes against one of its franchises in the same geographic market, as Host West alleged? How would you rule on this issue, and why?

3. Suppose that instead of purchasing a hotel in the area and operating it itself in direct competition with its franchise, the franchisor instead contracted with another company to serve as a franchisee in the same area. Would this change in the factual situation affect your decision as to whether the franchisor had violated the implied covenant of good faith and fair dealing?

10–11. **Critical-Thinking Legal Environment Question.** Do corporations benefit from shareholders' derivative suits? If so, how? (**See page 247.**)

Chapter 11

Formation of Traditional and E-Contracts

> "All sensible people are selfish, and nature is tugging at every contract to make the terms of it fair."
>
> —Ralph Waldo Emerson, 1803–1882
> (American essayist and poet)

Contents

Learning Objectives

The five Learning Objectives below are designed to help improve your understanding of the chapter. After reading this chapter, you should be able to answer the following questions:

1. **What are the four basic requirements for the formation of a valid contract?**
2. **What elements are necessary for an effective acceptance?**
3. **What is consideration?**
4. **What is a covenant not to compete? When will such a covenant be enforceable?**
5. **What is the Uniform Electronic Transactions Act? What are some of the major provisions of this act?**

(.shock/iStockphoto.com)

Promise An assertion that something either will or will not happen in the future.

As Ralph Waldo Emerson observed in the chapter-opening quotation above, people act in their own self-interest by nature, and this influences the terms they seek in their contracts. Contract law must therefore provide rules to determine which contract terms will be enforced and which promises must be kept. A **promise** is an assertion that something either will or will not happen in the future.

Like other types of law, contract law reflects our social values, interests, and expectations at a given point in time. It shows, for example, what kinds of promises our society thinks should be legally binding. It distinguishes between promises that create only *moral* obligations (such as a promise to take a friend to lunch) and promises that are legally binding (such as a promise to pay for merchandise purchased).

Contract law also demonstrates what excuses our society accepts for breaking certain types of promises. In addition, it shows what promises are considered to be contrary to public policy—that is, against the interests of society as a whole—and therefore legally invalid. Increasingly, contracts are formed online. While some believe that we need a new body of law to cover *e-contracts* (see page 278), others point out that we can apply existing contract law quite easily.

The common law governs all contracts except when it has been modified or replaced by statutory law, such as the Uniform Commercial Code (UCC), or by administrative agency regulations. Contracts relating to services, real estate, employment, and insurance, for example, generally are governed by the common law of contracts. Contracts for the sale and lease of goods, however, are governed by the UCC. The relationship between general contract law and the law governing sales and leases of goods will be explored in Chapter 13. In this chapter and Chapter 12, covering the common law of contracts, we sometimes indicate briefly in footnotes the areas in which the UCC has significantly altered common law contract principles.

▶ An Overview of Contract Law

Before we look at the numerous rules that courts use to determine whether a particular promise will be enforced, it is necessary to understand some fundamental concepts of contract law. In this section, we describe the general function of contract law, provide the definition of a contract, and introduce the objective theory of contracts.

The Function and Definition of a Contract

No aspect of modern life is entirely free of contractual relationships. You acquire rights and obligations, for example, when you borrow funds or buy or lease a house. Contract law is designed to provide stability and predictability for both buyers and sellers in the marketplace. Contract law assures the parties to private agreements that the promises they make will be enforceable.

By supplying procedures for enforcing private agreements, contract law provides an essential condition for the existence of a market economy. Without a legal framework of reasonably ensured expectations within which to plan and venture, businesspersons would be able to rely only on others' good faith. Contract law is necessary to ensure compliance with a promise or to entitle the innocent party to some form of relief.

Contract An agreement that can be enforced in court; formed by two or more competent parties who agree, for consideration, to perform or to refrain from performing some legal act now or in the future.

THE DEFINITION OF A CONTRACT A **contract** is a legally binding agreement between two or more parties who agree to perform or to refrain from performing some act now or in the future. Generally, contract disputes arise when there is a promise of future performance. A party who fails to fulfill a contractual promise is subject to the sanctions of a court (see Chapter 12) and may be required to pay monetary damages or, in limited instances, to perform the promised act.

THE OBJECTIVE THEORY OF CONTRACT In determining whether a contract has been formed, the element of intent is of prime importance. In contract law, intent is determined by the *objective theory of contracts.* This theory is that a party's intention to enter into a contract is judged by outward, objective facts as interpreted by a *reasonable person,* rather than by the party's own secret, subjective intentions. Objective facts include (1) what the party said when entering into the contract, (2) how the party acted or appeared, and (3) the circumstances surrounding the transaction.

Requirements of a Valid Contract

The following four requirements must be met for a valid contract to exist. If any of these elements is lacking, no contract will have been formed. (Each requirement will be explained more fully later in this chapter.)

LEARNING OBJECTIVE 1 What are the four basic requirements for the formation of a valid contract?

1. *Agreement*—An agreement to form a contract includes an *offer* and an *acceptance.* One party must offer to enter into a legal agreement, and another party must accept the terms of the offer.

2. *Consideration*—Any promises made by the parties must be supported by legally sufficient and bargained-for consideration (something of value received or promised to convince a person to make a deal).

3. *Contractual capacity*—Both parties entering into the contract must have the contractual capacity to do so. The law must recognize them as possessing characteristics that qualify them as competent parties.

4. *Legality*—The contract's purpose must be to accomplish some goal that is legal and not against public policy.

Even if all of the elements of a valid contract are present, a contract may be unenforceable if the following requirements are not met:

1. *Voluntary consent*—The apparent consent of both parties must be voluntary. For example, if a contract was formed as a result of fraud, a mistake, or duress, the contract may not be enforceable.

2. *Form*—The contract must be in whatever form the law requires—for example, some contracts must be in writing to be enforceable.

The failure to fulfill either requirement may be raised as a *defense* to the enforceability of an otherwise valid contract, as will be discussed in Chapter 12.

▶ Types of Contracts

There are numerous types of contracts. They are categorized based on legal distinctions as to their formation, performance, and enforceability. Exhibit 11–1 below illustrates three classifications, or categories, of contracts based on their mode of formation.

Contract Formation

These three classifications of contracts are based on how and when a contract is formed. The best way to explain each type of contract is to compare the various types, as we do in the following pages.

Offeror   A person who makes an offer.

Offeree   A person to whom an offer is made.

BILATERAL VERSUS UNILATERAL CONTRACTS   Every contract involves at least two parties. The **offeror** is the party making the offer. The **offeree** is the party to whom the offer is made. The offeror always promises to do or not to do something and thus is also a promisor. Whether the contract is classified as *bilateral* or *unilateral* depends on what the offeree must do to accept the offer and bind the offeror to a contract.

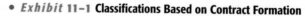

• *Exhibit* 11–1 **Classifications Based on Contract Formation**

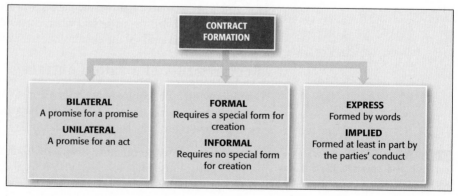

CONTRACT FORMATION

BILATERAL
A promise for a promise
UNILATERAL
A promise for an act

FORMAL
Requires a special form for creation
INFORMAL
Requires no special form for creation

EXPRESS
Formed by words
IMPLIED
Formed at least in part by the parties' conduct

Bilateral Contract A type of contract that arises when a promise is given in exchange for a return promise.

Bilateral Contracts. If the offeree can accept simply by promising to perform, the contract is a **bilateral contract.** Hence, a bilateral contract is a "promise for a promise." For example, a contract in which one person agrees to buy another person's automobile for a specified price is a bilateral contract. No performance, such as the payment of funds or delivery of goods, need take place for a bilateral contract to be formed. The contract comes into existence at the moment the promises are exchanged.

EXAMPLE 11.1 Javier offers to buy Ann's e-reader for $200. Javier tells Ann that he will give her the cash for the e-reader on the following Friday, when he gets paid. Ann accepts Javier's offer and promises to give him the e-reader when he pays her on Friday. Javier and Ann have formed a bilateral contract. •

Unilateral Contract A contract that results when an offer can be accepted only by the offeree's performance.

Unilateral Contracts. If the offer is phrased so that the offeree can accept only by completing the contract performance, the contract is a **unilateral contract.** Hence, a unilateral contract is a "promise for an act." In other words, the contract is formed not at the moment when promises are exchanged but rather when the contract is *performed.*

Contests, lotteries, and other competitions involving prizes are examples of offers to form unilateral contracts. If a person complies with the rules of the contest—such as by submitting the right lottery number at the right place and time—a unilateral contract is formed, binding the organization offering the prize to a contract to perform as promised in the offer.

In the following case, the court was asked to determine if an employer owed a bonus to a former employee. One issue for the court was whether the parties' employment contract was bilateral or unilateral.

Case 11.1 | **Schwarzrock v. Remote Technologies, Inc.**

Court of Appeals of Minnesota, 2011 WL 68262 (2011).

BACKGROUND AND FACTS Remote Technologies, Inc., is a Minnesota-based manufacturer of home-theater and home-automation controls. Remote employs product trainers to conduct training sessions for its dealers. Nick Schwarzrock contacted Remote to apply for employment. Remote offered Schwarzrock a position as a trainer and sent him a letter, stating that the compensation was "$60,000 per year salary, plus bonus." The day after starting work, Schwarzrock signed an employment agreement (EA) that expressly "superseded all previous correspondence." The EA stated, in part, that the salary "constitutes the full and exclusive . . . compensation for . . . the performance of all Employee's promises." Less than three months later, Baker fired Schwarzrock for "lots of reasons." Schwarzrock filed a lawsuit in a Minnesota state court against Remote, claiming that he was owed a bonus and alleging breach of contract, among other things. On this claim, the court held that there was no breach of contract and that the bonus was discretionary. Schwarzrock appealed.

IN THE WORDS OF THE COURT . . .
CONNOLLY, Judge.
* * * *
* * * The [lower] court held that there can be no breach of contract where respondent [Remote] abided by the terms of the parties'

agreement and that appellant [Schwarzrock] "cannot ignore the blatant terms of the EA to which he clearly assented."
* * * *
An offer of employment on particular terms for an unspecified duration generally creates a binding unilateral contract once it is accepted by the employee. Here, respondent offered appellant a position as a national product trainer on particular terms, which included compensation, for an unspecified amount of time. Although appellant alleges that his "compensation package was an essential term of a bilateral negotiated contract," he provides no support for the alleged bilateral nature of the contract. [Emphasis added.]

The EA presented appellant with another unilateral offer of employment, which explained that the * * * "bonus" was discretionary: "Employee understands and agrees that any additional compensation to Employee (whether a bonus or other form of additional compensation) shall rest in the sole discretion of [the employer] * * * ." Appellant signed the EA and continued working for respondent.

In the case of unilateral contracts for employment, where an * * * employee retains employment with knowledge of new or changed conditions, the new or changed conditions may become a contractual obligation. In this manner, an original employment contract may

Case 11.1—Continues next page ➡

Case 11.1–Continued

be modified or replaced by a subsequent unilateral contract. *The employee's retention of employment constitutes acceptance of the offer of a unilateral contract; by continuing to stay on the job, although free to leave, the employee supplies the necessary consideration for the offer.* [Emphasis added.]

* * * *

It is well established that where contracts relating to the same transaction are put into several instruments they will be read together and each will be construed with reference to the other. * * * Respondent intended to offer appellant both a specified salary and a bonus program; the offer letter and the EA do not contradict each other on these terms. Reading them together, we conclude that the plain terms of the parties' agreement stated that payment of the bonus was within respondent's discretion.

DECISION AND REMEDY   The state intermediate appellate court affirmed the lower court's judgment. Remote's letter may have implied that a bonus was not discretionary, but the EA clarified or modified the offer by clearly stating that it was. Schwarzrock accepted this unilateral offer when he signed the EA and continued working.

WHAT IF THE FACTS WERE DIFFERENT?   *Suppose that the court had ruled that Schwarzrock was employed under a bilateral contract, as he alleged. Would the result have been different? Explain.*

FORMAL VERSUS INFORMAL CONTRACTS   Another classification system divides contracts into formal contracts and informal contracts. **Formal contracts** require a special form or method of formation to be enforceable. For example, letters of credit, which frequently are used in international sales contracts (see Chapter 9), are a type of formal contract because a special form and language are required to create them.

Formal Contract   A contract that by law requires a specific form for its validity.

Informal contracts (also called *simple contracts*) include all other contracts. No special form is required (except for certain types of contracts that must be in writing), as the contracts usually are based on their substance rather than their form. Typically, businesspersons put their contracts in writing to ensure that there is some proof of a contract's existence should problems arise.

Informal Contract   A contract that does not require a specified form or formality to be valid.

EXPRESS VERSUS IMPLIED CONTRACTS   Contracts may also be categorized as express or implied by the conduct of the parties. In an **express contract,** the terms of the agreement are fully and explicitly stated in words, oral or written. A signed lease for an apartment or a house is an express written contract. If a classmate accepts your offer to sell your textbooks from last semester for $300, an express oral contract has been made.

Express Contract   A contract in which the terms of the agreement are stated in words, oral or written.

A contract that is implied from the conduct of the parties is called an **implied contract.** This type of contract differs from an express contract in that the *conduct* of the parties, rather than their words, creates and defines at least some of the terms of the contract. Normally, if the following requirements are met, a court will hold that an implied contract was formed:

Implied Contract   A contract formed in whole or in part from the conduct of the parties (as opposed to an express contract).

1. The plaintiff furnished some service or property.
2. The plaintiff expected to be paid for that service or property, and the defendant knew or should have known that payment was expected (by using the objective-theory-of-contracts test discussed on page 261).
3. The defendant had a chance to reject the services or property and did not.

EXAMPLE 11.2   Martin, a business owner, needs a certified public accountant (CPA) to complete his tax return. He notices the firm of McDonnell & Lyman, CPAs, in his neighborhood. He drops by the firm's office, explains his problem to Mary, a CPA, and learns what fees will be charged. The next day, Martin returns and gives the firm's receptionist all of the necessary information and documents, such as W-2 forms. Then he walks out the door without saying anything expressly to Mary. In this situation, Martin has entered into an implied contract to pay Mary the usual and reasonable fees for her services. The contract is implied by Martin's conduct and by Mary's. She expects to be paid for completing the tax return. By bringing in the records Mary will need to do the work, Martin has implied an intent to pay her. ●

Contract Performance

Executed Contract   A contract that has been completely performed by both parties.

Executory Contract   A contract that has not yet been fully performed.

Contracts are also classified according to their state of performance. A contract that has been fully performed on both sides is called an **executed contract.** A contract that has not been fully performed on either side is called an **executory contract.** If one party has fully performed but the other has not, the contract is said to be executed on the one side and executory on the other, but the contract is still classified as executory.

EXAMPLE 11.3   You agreed to buy ten tons of coal from Western Coal Company. Western has delivered the coal to your steel mill, where it is now being burned. At this point, the contract is an executory contract—it is executed on the part of Western and executory on your part. After you pay Western for the coal, the contract will be executed on both sides. ●

Contract Enforceability

As noted earlier, a *valid contract* has the four elements necessary for contract formation. Valid contracts may be enforceable, voidable, or unenforceable. Additionally, a contract may be referred to as a *void contract,* as described next.

- *Voidable contracts*—A *voidable contract* is a valid contract but one that can be avoided at the option of one or both of the parties. The party having the option can elect either to avoid any duty to perform or to *ratify* (make valid) the contract. If the contract is avoided, both parties are released from it. If it is ratified, both parties must fully perform their respective legal obligations. For example, contracts entered into under fraudulent conditions are voidable at the option of the defrauded party.
- *Unenforceable contracts*—An *unenforceable contract* is one that cannot be enforced because of certain legal defenses against it. Such a contract is valid in that it satisfies the legal requirements of a contract, but it has been rendered unenforceable by some statute or law. For example, some contracts must be in writing. If they are not, they will not be enforceable except in certain exceptional circumstances.
- *Void contracts*—A *void contract* is no contract at all. The terms *void* and *contract* are contradictory. None of the parties has any legal obligations if a contract is void. A contract can be void because, for example, one of the parties was previously determined by a court to be legally insane (and thus lacked the legal capacity to enter into a contract) or because the purpose of the contract was illegal.

▶ Agreement

Agreement   A meeting of two or more minds in regard to the terms of a contract, usually broken down into two events: an offer and an acceptance.

Regardless of whether a contract is formed in the traditional way by exchanging paper documents or online by exchanging electronic messages or documents, an essential element for contract formation is **agreement.** The parties must agree on the terms of the contract. Ordinarily, agreement is evidenced by two events: an *offer* and an *acceptance.* One party offers a certain bargain to another party, who then accepts that bargain.

The Offer

Offer A promise or commitment to do or refrain from doing some specified act in the future.

An **offer** is a promise or commitment to perform or refrain from performing some specified act in the future. Recall that the party making an offer is called the *offeror*, and the party to whom the offer is made is called the *offeree*. Three elements are necessary for an offer to be effective:

1. There must be a serious, objective intention by the offeror.
2. The terms of the offer must be reasonably certain, or definite, so that the parties and the court can ascertain the terms of the contract.
3. The offer must be communicated to the offeree.

Once an effective offer has been made, the offeree's acceptance of that offer creates a legally binding contract (providing the other essential elements for a valid and enforceable contract are present).

INTENTION   The first requirement for an effective offer is a serious, objective intention on the part of the offeror. Intent is not determined by the *subjective* intentions, beliefs, or assumptions of the offeror. Rather, it is determined by what a reasonable person in the offeree's position would conclude the offeror's words and actions meant. Offers made in obvious anger, jest, or undue excitement do not meet the serious-and-objective-intent test. Because these offers are not effective, an offeree's acceptance does not create an agreement.

In the *Classic Case* presented next, the court considered whether an offer made "after a few drinks" met the serious-intent requirement.

Classic Case 11.2   Lucy v. Zehmer

Supreme Court of Appeals of Virginia, 196 Va. 493, 84 S.E.2d 516 (1954).

BACKGROUND AND FACTS   W. O. Lucy and A. H. Zehmer had known each other for fifteen to twenty years. For some time, Lucy had been wanting to buy Zehmer's farm. Zehmer had always told Lucy that he was not interested in selling. One night, Lucy stopped in to visit with the Zehmers at a restaurant they operated. Lucy said to Zehmer, "I bet you wouldn't take $50,000 for that place." Zehmer replied, "Yes, I would, too; you wouldn't give fifty." Throughout the evening, the conversation returned to the sale of the farm. At the same time, the parties were drinking whiskey. Eventually, Zehmer wrote up an agreement, on the back of a restaurant check, for the sale of the farm, and he asked his wife, Ida, to sign it—which she did. When Lucy brought an action in a Virginia state court to enforce the agreement, Zehmer argued that he had been "high as a Georgia pine" at the time and that the offer had been made in jest: "two doggoned drunks bluffing to see who could talk the biggest and say the most." Lucy claimed that he had not been intoxicated and did not think Zehmer had been, either, given the way Zehmer handled the transaction. The trial court ruled in favor of the Zehmers, and Lucy appealed.

IN THE WORDS OF THE COURT . . .
BUCHANAN, J. [Justice] delivered the opinion of the court.
    * * * *

In his testimony, Zehmer claimed that he "was high as a Georgia pine," and that the transaction "was just a bunch of two doggoned drunks bluffing to see who could talk the biggest and say the most." That claim is inconsistent with his attempt to testify in great detail as to what was said and what was done.
    * * * *

The appearance of the contract, the fact that it was under discussion for forty minutes or more before it was signed; Lucy's objection to the first draft because it was written in the singular, and he wanted Mrs. Zehmer to sign it also; the rewriting to meet that objection and the signing by Mrs. Zehmer; the discussion of what was to be included in the sale, the provision for the examination of the title, the completeness of the instrument that was executed, the taking possession of it by Lucy with no request or suggestion by either of the defendants that he give it back, are facts which furnish persuasive evidence that the execution

Classic Case 11.2–Continued

of the contract was a serious business transaction rather than a casual, jesting matter as defendants now contend.

* * * *

In the field of contracts, as generally elsewhere, *we must look to the outward expression of a person as manifesting his intention rather than to his secret and unexpressed intention.* The law imputes to a person an intention corresponding to the reasonable meaning of his words and acts. [Emphasis added.]

* * * *

Whether the writing signed by the defendants and now sought to be enforced by the complainants was the result of a serious offer by Lucy and a serious acceptance by the defendants, or was a serious offer by Lucy and an acceptance in secret jest by the defendants, in either event it constituted a binding contract of sale between the parties.

DECISION AND REMEDY The Supreme Court of Virginia determined that the writing was an enforceable contract and reversed

the ruling of the lower court. The Zehmers were required by court order to follow through with the sale of the Ferguson Farm to the Lucys.

WHAT IF THE FACTS WERE DIFFERENT? *Suppose that the day after Lucy signed the agreement, he decided that he did not want the farm after all, and Zehmer sued Lucy to perform the contract. Would this change in the facts alter the court's decision that Lucy and Zehmer had created an enforceable contract? Why or why not?*

IMPACT OF THIS CASE ON TODAY'S LEGAL ENVIRONMENT *This is a classic case in contract law because it so clearly illustrates the objective theory of contracts with respect to determining whether an offer was intended. Today, the objective theory of contracts continues to be applied by the courts, and the* Lucy v. Zehmer *decision is routinely cited as a significant precedent in this area.*

Expressions of Opinion. An expression of opinion is not an offer. It does not demonstrate an intention to enter into a binding agreement. **CASE EXAMPLE 11.4** Hawkins took his son to McGee, a physician, and asked McGee to operate on the son's hand. McGee said that the boy would be in the hospital three or four days and that the hand would *probably* heal a few days later. The son's hand did not heal for a month, but nonetheless the father did not win a suit for breach of contract. The court held that McGee did not make an offer to heal the son's hand in three or four days. He merely expressed an opinion as to when the hand would heal.[1] ●

BE CAREFUL An opinion is not an offer and not a contract term. Goods or services can be "perfect" in one party's opinion and "poor" in another's.

Statements of Future Intent. A statement of an *intention* to do something in the future is not an offer. **EXAMPLE 11.5** If Samir says, "I *plan* to sell my stock in Novation, Inc., for $150 per share," no contract is created if John "accepts" and tenders $150 per share for the stock. Samir has merely expressed his intention to enter into a future contract for the sale of the stock. If John accepts and tenders the $150 per share, no contract is formed, because a reasonable person would conclude that Samir was only *thinking about* selling his stock, not *promising* to sell it. ●

Preliminary Negotiations. A request or invitation to negotiate is not an offer but only an expression of a willingness to discuss the possibility of entering into a contract. Examples are statements such as "Will you sell Forest Acres?" and "I wouldn't sell my car for less than $8,000." A reasonable person would not conclude that such statements indicated an intention to enter into binding obligations.

Likewise, when the government and private firms need to have construction work done, they invite contractors to submit bids. The *invitation* to submit bids is not an offer, and a contractor does not bind the government or private firm by submitting a bid. (The bids that the contractors submit are offers, however, and the government or private firm can bind the contractor by accepting the bid.)

---

1. *Hawkins v. McGee*, 84 N.H. 114, 146 A. 641 (1929).

DEFINITENESS OF TERMS   The second requirement for an effective offer involves the definiteness of its terms. An offer must have reasonably definite terms so that a court can determine if a breach has occurred and give an appropriate remedy. The specific terms required depend, of course, on the type of contract. Generally, a contract must include the following terms, either expressed in the contract or capable of being reasonably inferred from it:

1. The identification of the parties.
2. The identification of the object or subject matter of the contract (also the quantity, when appropriate), including the work to be performed, with specific identification of such items as goods, services, and land.
3. The consideration to be paid.
4. The time of payment, delivery, or performance.

An offer may invite an acceptance to be worded in such specific terms that the contract is made definite. **EXAMPLE 11.6**   Marcus Business Machines contacts your corporation and offers to sell "from one to ten MacCool copying machines for $1,600 each; state number desired in acceptance." Your corporation agrees to buy two copiers. Because the quantity is specified in the acceptance, the terms are definite, and the contract is enforceable. •

COMMUNICATION   The third requirement for an effective offer is communication—the offer must be communicated to the offeree. **EXAMPLE 11.7**   Tolson advertises a reward for the return of her lost cat. Dirk, not knowing of the reward, finds the cat and returns it to Tolson. Ordinarily, Dirk cannot recover the reward because an essential element of a reward contract is that the one who claims the reward must have known it was offered. A few states would allow recovery of the reward, but not on contract principles—Dirk would be allowed to recover on the basis that it would be unfair to deny him the reward just because he did not know about it. •

Termination of the Offer

The communication of an effective offer to an offeree gives the offeree the power to transform the offer into a binding, legal obligation (a contract) by an acceptance. This power of acceptance does not continue forever, though. It can be terminated either by the *action of the parties* or by *operation of law.*

Revocation   In contract law, the withdrawal of an offer by the offeror. Unless the offer is irrevocable, it can be revoked at any time prior to acceptance without liability.

TERMINATION BY ACTION OF THE OFFEROR   The offeror's act of withdrawing an offer is referred to as **revocation**. Unless an offer is irrevocable, the offeror usually can revoke the offer (even if he or she has promised to keep the offer open), as long as the revocation is communicated to the offeree before the offeree accepts. Revocation may be accomplished by an express repudiation of the offer (for example, with a statement such as "I withdraw my previous offer of October 17") or by the performance of acts that are inconsistent with the existence of the offer and that are made known to the offeree.

EXAMPLE 11.8   Michelle offers to sell some land to Gary. A month passes, and Gary, who has not accepted the offer, learns that Michelle has sold the property to Liam. Because Michelle's sale of the land to Liam is inconsistent with the continued existence of the offer to Gary, the offer to Gary is effectively revoked. •

The general rule followed by most states is that a revocation becomes effective when the offeree or the offeree's *agent* (see page 401 in Chapter 16) actually receives it. Therefore, a letter of revocation mailed on April 1 and delivered at the offeree's residence or place of business on April 3 becomes effective on April 3.

TERMINATION BY ACTION OF THE OFFEREE If the offeree rejects the offer—by words or by conduct—the offer is terminated. Any subsequent attempt by the offeree to accept will be construed as a new offer, giving the original offeror (now the offeree) the power of acceptance. Like a revocation, a rejection of an offer is effective only when it is actually received by the offeror or the offeror's agent. **EXAMPLE 11.9** Goldfinch Farms offers to sell specialty Maitake mushrooms to a Japanese buyer, Kinoko Foods. If Kinoko rejects the offer by sending a letter via U.S. mail, the rejection will not be effective (and the offer will not be terminated) until Goldfinch receives the letter. ● Merely inquiring about an offer does not constitute rejection.

A **counteroffer** is a rejection of the original offer and the simultaneous making of a new offer. **EXAMPLE 11.10** Burke offers to sell his home to Lang for $270,000. Lang responds, "Your price is too high. I'll offer to purchase your house for $250,000." Lang's response is called a counteroffer because it rejects Burke's offer to sell at $270,000 and creates a new offer by Lang to purchase the home at a price of $250,000. ●

At common law, the **mirror image rule** requires that the offeree's acceptance match the offeror's offer exactly. In other words, the terms of the acceptance must "mirror" those of the offer. If the acceptance materially changes or adds to the terms of the original offer, it will be considered not an acceptance but a counteroffer—which, of course, need not be accepted. The original offeror can, however, accept the terms of the counteroffer and create a valid contract.[2]

TERMINATION BY OPERATION OF LAW The power of the offeree to transform the offer into a binding, legal obligation can be terminated by operation of law through the occurrence of any of the following events:

1. Lapse of time.
2. Destruction of the specific subject matter of the offer.
3. Death or incompetence of the offeror or the offeree.
4. Supervening illegality of the proposed contract. (A statute or court decision that makes an offer illegal automatically terminates the offer.)

An offer terminates automatically by law when the period of time *specified in the offer* has passed. If the offer states that it will be left open until a particular date, then the offer will terminate at midnight on that day. If the offer states that it will be left open for a number of days, such as ten days, this time period normally begins to run when the offer is actually received by the offeree, not when it is formed or sent.

If the offer does not specify a time for acceptance, the offer terminates at the end of a *reasonable* period of time, which is determined by the subject matter of the contract, business and market conditions, and other relevant circumstances. An offer to sell farm produce, for example, will terminate sooner than an offer to sell farm equipment because farm produce is perishable and subject to greater fluctuations in market value.

The Acceptance

An **acceptance** is a voluntary act by the offeree that shows consent, or agreement, to the terms of an offer. The offeree's act may consist of words or conduct. The acceptance must be unequivocal and must be communicated to the offeror. Generally, only

Counteroffer An offeree's response to an offer in which the offeree rejects the original offer and at the same time makes a new offer.

Mirror Image Rule A common law rule that requires that the terms of the offeree's acceptance adhere exactly to the terms of the offeror's offer for a valid contract to be formed.

Acceptance A voluntary act by the offeree that shows consent, or agreement, to the terms of an offer.

---

2. The mirror image rule has been greatly modified in regard to sales contracts. Section 2–207 of the UCC provides that a contract is formed if the offeree makes a definite expression of acceptance (such as signing the form in the appropriate location), even though the terms of the acceptance modify or add to the terms of the original offer.

the person to whom the offer is made or that person's agent can accept the offer and create a binding contract.

LEARNING OBJECTIVE 2 **What elements are necessary for an effective acceptance?**

UNEQUIVOCAL ACCEPTANCE   To exercise the power of acceptance effectively, the offeree must accept unequivocally. This is the mirror image rule. If the acceptance is subject to new conditions or if its terms materially change the original offer, the acceptance may be deemed a counteroffer that implicitly rejects the original offer.

Certain terms, when included in an acceptance, will not change the offer sufficiently to constitute rejection. **EXAMPLE 11.11**   In response to an art dealer's offer to sell a painting, the offeree, Ashton Gibbs, replies, "I accept. Please send a written contract." Gibbs is requesting a written contract but is not making it a condition for acceptance. Therefore, the acceptance is effective without the written contract. In contrast, if Gibbs replies, "I accept *if* you send a written contract," the acceptance is expressly conditioned on the request for a writing, and the statement is not an acceptance but a counteroffer. (Notice how important each word is!)[3] ●

Ordinarily, silence cannot constitute acceptance, even if the offeror states, "By your silence and inaction, you will be deemed to have accepted this offer." This general rule applies because an offeree should not be put under a burden of liability to act affirmatively in order to reject an offer. No consideration—that is, nothing of value—has passed to the offeree to impose such a liability.

COMMUNICATION OF ACCEPTANCE   Whether the offeror must be notified of the acceptance depends on the nature of the contract. In a unilateral contract, the full performance of some act is called for. Acceptance is usually evident, and notification is therefore unnecessary (unless the law requires it or the offeror asks for it). In a bilateral contract, in contrast, communication of acceptance is necessary, because acceptance is in the form of a promise. The bilateral contract is formed when the promise is made rather than when the act is performed.

CASE EXAMPLE 11.12   Powerhouse Custom Homes, Inc., entered into a credit agreement with 84 Lumber Company. When Powerhouse failed to pay, 84 Lumber filed a suit to collect. During mediation, the parties agreed to a deadline for objections to whatever agreement they might reach. If there were no objections, the agreement would be binding. Powerhouse then offered to pay less than the amount owed, and 84 Lumber did not respond. Powerhouse argued that 84 Lumber accepted the offer by not objecting to it within the deadline. Nonetheless, the court ruled in 84 Lumber's favor for the entire amount of the debt. To form a contract, an offer must be accepted unequivocally. Powerhouse made an offer, but 84 Lumber did not communicate acceptance.[4] ●

MODE AND TIMELINESS OF ACCEPTANCE   Acceptance in bilateral contracts must be timely. The general rule is that acceptance in a bilateral contract is timely if it is made before the offer is terminated. Problems may arise, though, when the parties involved are not dealing face to face. In such situations, the offeree should use an authorized mode of communication.

The Mailbox Rule.   Acceptance takes effect, thus completing formation of the contract, at the time the offeree sends or delivers the communication via the mode expressly or impliedly authorized by the offeror. This is the so-called **mailbox rule,**

Mailbox Rule   A rule providing that an acceptance of an offer becomes effective on dispatch.

---

3. For sales contracts, the UCC provides that an acceptance may still be effective even if some terms are added. The new terms are simply treated as proposals for additions to the contract.
4. *Powerhouse Custom Homes, Inc. v. 84 Lumber Co.,* 307 Ga.App. 605, 705 S.E2d 704 (2011).

also called the *deposited acceptance rule,* which the majority of courts follow. Under this rule, if the authorized mode of communication is the mail, then an acceptance becomes valid when it is dispatched (placed in the control of the U.S. Postal Service)—*not* when it is received by the offeror.

The mailbox rule does not apply to instantaneous forms of communication, such as face to face, telephone, or fax. There is still some uncertainty in the courts as to whether e-mail should be considered an instantaneous form of communication to which the mailbox rule does not apply. If the parties have agreed to conduct transactions electronically and if the Uniform Electronic Transactions Act (UETA—see pages 282 and 283) applies, then e-mail is considered sent when it either leaves the sender's control or is received by the recipient. This rule, which takes the place of the mailbox rule when the UETA applies, essentially allows an e-mail acceptance to become effective when sent (as it would if sent by U.S. mail).

Authorized Means of Communication. When an offeror specifies how acceptance should be made, such as by overnight delivery, the contract is not formed unless the offeree uses that mode of acceptance. Both the offeror and the offeree are bound in contract the moment the specified means of acceptance is employed.

EXAMPLE 11.13 Motorola Mobility offers to sell 144 Atrix 4G smartphones and 72 Lapdocks to Call-Me-Plus phone stores. The offer states that Call-Me-Plus must accept the offer via FedEx overnight delivery. The acceptance is effective (and a binding contract is formed) the moment that Call-Me-Plus gives the overnight envelope containing the acceptance to the FedEx driver. •

If the offeror does not expressly specify a certain mode of acceptance, then acceptance can be made by any reasonable means. The prevailing business usages and the surrounding circumstances determine whether a mode of acceptance is reasonable. Usually, the offeror's choice of a particular means in making the offer implies that the offeree can use the same or a faster means for acceptance. **EXAMPLE 11.14** If the offer is made via Priority U.S. Mail, it would be reasonable to accept the offer via Priority Mail or a faster method, such as a fax or FedEx overnight delivery. •

Substitute Method of Acceptance. If the offeror authorizes a particular method of acceptance, but the offeree accepts by a different means, the acceptance may still be effective if the substituted method serves the same purpose as the authorized means. The use of a substitute method of acceptance is not effective on dispatch, though. No contract will be formed until the acceptance is received by the offeror.

EXAMPLE 11.15 If an offer specifies FedEx overnight delivery but the offeree accepts by overnight delivery from another carrier, such as UPS, the acceptance will still be effective, but not until the offeror receives it. •

▶ Consideration

The second requirement for the formation of a valid contract is *consideration.* **Consideration** usually is defined as the value (such as cash) given in return for a promise (in a bilateral contract) or in return for a performance (in a unilateral contract).

Elements of Consideration

Often, consideration is broken down into two parts: (1) something of *legally sufficient value* must be given in exchange for the promise, and (2) usually, there must be a *bargained-for exchange.*

Consideration The value given in return for a promise or a performance in a contractual agreement.

LEARNING OBJECTIVE 3 **What is consideration?**

LEGALLY SUFFICIENT VALUE   The "something of legally sufficient value" may consist of (1) a promise to do something that one has no prior legal duty to do, (2) the performance of an action that one is otherwise not obligated to undertake, or (3) the refraining from an action that one has a legal right to undertake (called a *forbearance*).

Consideration in bilateral contracts normally consists of a promise in return for a promise, as explained earlier. In contrast, unilateral contracts involve a promise in return for a performance. **EXAMPLE 11.16** Anita says to her neighbor, "When you finish painting the garage, I will pay you $100." Anita's neighbor paints the garage. The act of painting the garage is the consideration that creates Anita's contractual obligation to pay her neighbor $100. ●

BARGAINED-FOR EXCHANGE   The second element of consideration is that it must provide the basis for the bargain struck between the contracting parties. The item of value must be given or promised by the promisor (offeror) in return for the promisee's promise, performance, or promise of performance.

This element of bargained-for exchange distinguishes contracts from gifts. **EXAMPLE 11.17** Roberto says to his son, "In consideration of the fact that you are not as wealthy as your brothers, I will pay you $5,000." The fact that the word *consideration* is used does not, by itself, mean that consideration has been given. Indeed, this is not an enforceable promise because the son does not have to do anything in order to receive the promised $5,000. Because the son does not need to give Roberto something of legal value in return for his promise, there is no bargained-for exchange. Rather, Roberto has simply stated his motive for giving his son a gift. ●

Adequacy of Consideration

Legal sufficiency of consideration involves the requirement that consideration be something of legally sufficient value in the eyes of the law. Adequacy of consideration involves how much consideration is given. Essentially, adequacy of consideration concerns the fairness of the bargain. On the surface, fairness would appear to be an issue when the items exchanged are of unequal value. In general, however, a court will not question the adequacy of consideration if the consideration is legally sufficient. Under the doctrine of freedom of contract, parties are normally free to bargain as they wish. If people could sue merely because they had entered into an unwise contract, the courts would be overloaded with frivolous suits.

In extreme cases, a court may consider the adequacy of consideration in terms of its amount or worth because inadequate consideration may indicate that fraud, duress, or undue influence was involved or that the element of bargained-for exchange was lacking. It may also reflect a party's incompetence. For instance, an individual might have been too intoxicated or too young to make a contract. (Defenses to enforceability of a contract will be discussed in Chapter 12.)

Agreements That Lack Consideration

Sometimes, one of the parties (or both parties) to an agreement may think that consideration has been exchanged when in fact it has not. Here, we look at some situations in which the parties' promises or actions do not qualify as contractual consideration.

PREEXISTING DUTY   Under most circumstances, a promise to do what one already has a legal duty to do does not constitute legally sufficient consideration. The preexisting legal duty may be imposed by law or may arise out of a previous contract.

A sheriff, for example, cannot collect a reward for providing information leading to the capture of a criminal if the sheriff already has a legal duty to capture the criminal.

Likewise, if a party is already bound by contract to perform a certain duty, that duty cannot serve as consideration for a second contract. **EXAMPLE 11.18** Bauman-Bache, Inc., begins construction on a seven-story office building and after three months demands an extra $75,000 on its contract. If the extra $75,000 is not paid, the contractor will stop working. The owner of the land, finding no one else to complete the construction, agrees to pay the extra $75,000. The agreement is unenforceable because it is not supported by legally sufficient consideration. Bauman-Bache had a preexisting contractual duty to complete the building. ●

The rule regarding preexisting duty is meant to prevent extortion and the so-called holdup game. What happens, though, when an honest contractor who has contracted with a landowner to construct a building runs into extraordinary difficulties that were totally unforeseen at the time the contract was formed? In the interests of fairness and equity, the courts sometimes allow exceptions to the preexisting duty rule.

PAST CONSIDERATION Promises made in return for actions or events that have already taken place are unenforceable. These promises lack consideration in that the element of bargained-for exchange is missing. In short, a person can bargain for something to take place now or in the future but not for something that has already taken place. Therefore, *past consideration* is no consideration.

EXAMPLE 11.19 Elsie, a real estate agent, does her friend, Judy, a favor by selling Judy's house and not charging a commission. Later, Judy says to Elsie, "In return for your generous act, I will pay you $3,000." This promise involves past consideration. Consequently, a court would not enforce it. Judy is simply creating a situation in which she presents a gift to Elsie. ●

Promissory Estoppel

Sometimes, individuals rely on promises, and such reliance may form a basis for contract rights and duties. Under the doctrine of **promissory estoppel** (also called detrimental reliance), a person who has reasonably relied on the promise of another can often obtain some measure of recovery.

When this doctrine is applied, the promisor is **estopped,** or barred, from revoking the promise. For the doctrine of promissory estoppel to be applied, a number of elements are required:

1. There must be a promise.
2. The promisee must justifiably rely on the promise.
3. The reliance normally must be of a substantial and definite character.
4. Justice will be better served by the enforcement of the promise.

CASE EXAMPLE 11.20 Jeffrey and Kathryn Dow often said that one day they would give their land to their daughter, Teresa. When Teresa married Jarrod Harvey, the Dows agreed to finance the construction of a house on the land. But when Jarrod died, Teresa financed the house with the life insurance proceeds. Jeffrey did much of the work on the house. Teresa then asked her parents for a deed to the property so that she could obtain a *mortgage* (see Chapter 15). They refused. She filed a suit against her parents. The court ruled in Teresa's favor. The Dows' actions demonstrated their intent to give Teresa the land. Thus, Teresa had detrimentally relied on her parents' promise to give her the land when she built the house.[5] ●

Promissory Estoppel A doctrine that can be used to enforce a promise when the promisee has justifiably relied on it, and justice will be better served by enforcing it.

Estop Bar, impede, or preclude.

---

5. *Harvey v. Dow,* 11 A.3d 303 (2011).

Contractual Capacity

Contractual Capacity The capacity required by the law for a party who enters into a contract to be bound by that contract.

In addition to agreement and consideration, for a contract to be deemed valid, the parties to the contract must have **contractual capacity**—the legal ability to enter into a contractual relationship. Courts generally presume the existence of contractual capacity. In some situations, however, when a person is young, intoxicated, or mentally incompetent, capacity is lacking or may be questionable.

Minors

Today, in almost all states, the *age of majority* (when a person is no longer a minor) for contractual purposes is eighteen years.[6] In addition, some states provide for the termination of minority on marriage. Minority status may also be terminated by a minor's *emancipation,* which occurs when a child's parent or legal guardian relinquishes the legal right to exercise control over the child. Normally, minors who leave home to support themselves are considered emancipated. Several jurisdictions permit minors themselves to petition a court for emancipation. For business purposes, a minor may petition a court to be treated as an adult.

The general rule is that a minor can enter into any contract that an adult can, provided that the contract is not one prohibited by law for minors (for example, the sale of tobacco or alcoholic beverages). A contract entered into by a minor, however, is voidable at the option of that minor, subject to certain exceptions.

The legal avoidance, or setting aside, of a contractual obligation is referred to as *disaffirmance.* To disaffirm, a minor must express his or her intent, through words or conduct, not to be bound to the contract.

CASE EXAMPLE 11.21 Fifteen-year-old Morgan Kelly was a cadet in her high school's Navy Junior Reserve Officer Training Corps. As part of the program, she visited Camp Lejeune, North Carolina, which is a U.S. Marine Corps training facility. To enter the camp, she was required to sign a waiver that exempted the Marines from all liability for any injuries arising from her visit. While participating in activities on the camp's confidence-building course, Kelly fell from the "Slide for Life" and suffered serious injuries. She filed a suit to recover her medical costs. The Marines asserted that she had signed their waiver of liability. The court ruled in Kelly's favor. Liability waivers are generally enforceable contracts, but a minor can avoid a contract by disaffirming it. Disaffirmance can occur at any time during minority. In this case, Kelly disaffirmed the waiver when she filed her suit to recover for the cost of her injuries.[7] •

Intoxication

Intoxication is a condition in which a person's normal capacity to act or think is inhibited by alcohol or some other drug. A contract entered into by an intoxicated person can be either voidable or valid (and thus enforceable). If the person was sufficiently intoxicated to lack mental capacity, then the agreement may be voidable even if the intoxication was purely voluntary.

If, despite intoxication, the person understood the legal consequences of the agreement, the contract will be enforceable. For the contract to be voidable, the person must prove that the intoxication impaired her or his reason and judgment so severely that she or he did not comprehend the legal consequences of entering into the contract.

---

6. The age of majority may still be twenty-one for other purposes, such as the purchase and consumption of alcohol.

7. *Kelly v. United States,* 809 F.Supp.2d 429 (2011).

Mental Incompetence

If a court has previously determined that a person is mentally incompetent and has appointed a guardian to represent the individual, any contract made by the mentally incompetent person is *void*—no contract exists. Only the guardian can enter into binding legal obligations on behalf of the mentally incompetent person.

▶ Legality

Legality is the fourth requirement for a valid contract to exist. For a contract to be valid and enforceable, it must be formed for a legal purpose. A contract to do something that is prohibited by federal or state statutory law is illegal and, as such, void from the outset and thus unenforceable. Here, we examine contracts that are contrary to statute or contrary to public policy.

Contracts Contrary to Statute

Any contract to commit a crime is a contract in violation of a statute. Thus, a contract to sell illegal drugs in violation of criminal laws is unenforceable, as is a contract to loan funds to a person at an interest rate above the lawful maximum interest rate allowed by state law.

GAMBLING   Gambling is the creation of risk for the purpose of assuming it. Traditionally, the states have deemed gambling contracts illegal and thus void. All states have statutes that regulate gambling, and many states allow certain forms of gambling, such as horse racing, poker machines, and charity-sponsored bingo. In addition, nearly all states allow state-operated lotteries and gambling on Native American reservations. Even in states that permit certain types of gambling, though, courts often find that gambling contracts are illegal.
   CASE EXAMPLE 11.22 Video poker machines are legal in Louisiana, but their use requires the approval of the state video gaming commission. Gaming Venture, Inc., did not obtain this approval before agreeing with Tastee Restaurant Corporation to install poker machines in some of its restaurants. Later, Tastee allegedly backed out of the deal. Because of the failure to obtain approval, the state held that the agreement between Tastee and Gaming Venture was an illegal gambling contract and therefore void.[8] ●

LICENSING STATUTES   All states require members of certain professions—including physicians, lawyers, real estate brokers, accountants, architects, electricians, and stockbrokers—to have licenses. If a statute's purpose is to protect the public from unauthorized practitioners, then a contract involving an unlicensed practitioner is generally illegal and unenforceable.

Contracts Contrary to Public Policy

Although contracts involve private parties, some are not enforceable because of the negative impact they would have on society. These contracts are said to be *contrary to public policy*. Examples include a contract to commit an immoral act, such as selling a child, and a contract to prohibit marriage.

---

8. *Gaming Venture, Inc. v. Tastee Restaurant Corp.*, 996 So.2d 515 (La.App. 5 Cir. 2008).

CONTRACTS IN RESTRAINT OF TRADE Restraint of trade involves interfering with free competition. Contracts in restraint of trade usually adversely affect the public (which favors competition in the economy) and typically violate one or more federal or state statutes.

An exception is recognized when the restraint is reasonable and an integral part of a contract. Many such exceptions involve a type of restraint called a **covenant not to compete.**

Covenant Not to Compete
A contractual promise of one party to refrain from competing with another party for a certain period of time and within a certain geographic area.

Covenants Not to Compete and the Sale of an Ongoing Business. Covenants not to compete are often contained in contracts concerning the sale of an ongoing business. In this situation, a covenant not to compete is created when a seller agrees not to open a new store in a certain geographic area surrounding the old store. Such agreements enable the seller to sell, and the purchaser to buy, the "goodwill" and "reputation" of an ongoing business.

EXAMPLE 11.23 If a well-known merchant sold his store and opened a competing business a block away, many of the merchant's customers would likely do business at his new store. Hence, the good name and reputation sold to the new merchant for a price would then be less valuable. ●

LEARNING OBJECTIVE 4 What is a covenant not to compete? When will such a covenant be enforceable?

Covenants Not to Compete in Employment Contracts. Sometimes, agreements not to compete are included in employment contracts. People in middle- or upper-level management positions commonly agree not to work for competitors or start competing businesses for a specified period of time after termination of employment.

Such agreements are legal in most states so long as the specified period of time is not excessive and the geographic restriction is reasonable. What constitutes a reasonable time period may be shorter in the online environment than in conventional employment contracts because the restrictions apply worldwide. To be reasonable, a restriction on competition must protect a legitimate business interest and must not be any greater than necessary to protect that interest.

In the following case, a physician claimed that the covenant not to compete he signed was unreasonable and should be declared illegal.

Case 11.3 **Emerick v. Cardiac Study Center, Inc.**

Court of Appeals of Washington, Division 2, 166 Wash.App. 1039 (2012).

BACKGROUND AND FACTS Cardiac Study Center, Inc., is a medical practice group of approximately fifteen cardiologists. In 2002, Cardiac hired Dr. Robert Emerick as an employee. In 2004, Emerick became a shareholder of Cardiac and signed a shareholder employment agreement. The agreement included a covenant not to compete, which required any doctor who left the group to promise not to practice competitively in the surrounding area for a period of five years. In 2005, patients and other medical providers began to complain to Cardiac about Emerick's conduct. Some physicians stopped referring patients to Cardiac as a result. Finally, Cardiac terminated Emerick's employment in late 2009. Emerick sued Cardiac, seeking a declaration that the covenant not to compete was unenforceable. The trial court issued a summary judgment in favor of Emerick, and Cardiac appealed.

IN THE WORDS OF THE COURT . . .
ARMSTRONG, P.J. [Presiding Judge]
* * * *

* * * *Courts will enforce a covenant not to compete if it is reasonable and lawful.* We test reasonableness by asking (1) whether the restraint is necessary to protect the employer's business or goodwill, (2) whether it imposes on the employee any greater restraint than is reasonably necessary to secure the employer's business or goodwill, and (3) whether enforcing the covenant would injure the public through loss of the employee's service and skill to the extent that the court should not enforce the covenant [that is,] whether it violates public policy. [Emphasis added.]

* * * Specifically, an employer has a "legitimate interest in protecting its existing client base" and in prohibiting the employee from taking its clients.

Case 11.3–Continued

* * * Cardiac provided Emerick with an immediate client base and established referral sources when he moved to the area. Moreover, Emerick had access to Cardiac's business model and goodwill. These are all protectable business interests that the trial court should have considered in assessing the covenant's enforceability.

DECISION AND REMEDY   The state intermediate appellate court reversed the trial court's order granting summary judgment for Emerick. The case was remanded for further proceedings.

MANAGERIAL IMPLICATIONS   *Many covenants not to compete are considered unenforceable. Nonetheless, business managers can create restrictive covenants that are indeed reasonable, that do not cover a very large geographic area, and that do not last for decades. Business managers who make such covenants not to complete will often find that courts will deem them enforceable.*

Reformation.   Occasionally, depending on the jurisdiction, courts will *reform* covenants not to compete to make the terms more reasonable and then enforce the reformed covenant. Courts usually resort to contract *reformation* only when necessary to prevent undue burdens or hardships.

UNCONSCIONABLE CONTRACTS OR CLAUSES   Ordinarily, a court does not look at the fairness, or equity, of a contract. In other words, it does not inquire into the adequacy of consideration. Persons are assumed to be reasonably intelligent, and the court does not come to their aid just because they have made an unwise or foolish bargain.

In certain circumstances, however, bargains are so oppressive that the courts relieve innocent parties of part or all of their duties. Such a bargain may be evidenced by an **unconscionable contract or clause.** (*Unconscionable*[9] means grossly unethical or unfair.) An unconscionable contract is one in which the terms of the agreement are so unfair as to "shock the conscience" of the court. Court decisions have distinguished between *procedural* and *substantive unconscionability*.

Procedural Unconscionability.   Procedural unconscionability has to do with how a term becomes part of a contract. It relates to factors bearing on a party's lack of knowledge or understanding of the contract terms because of inconspicuous print, unintelligible language (legalese), lack of opportunity to read the contract, lack of opportunity to ask questions about the contract's meaning, and other factors.

Substantive Unconscionability.   Substantive unconscionability describes contracts, or portions of contracts, that are oppressive or overly harsh. Courts generally focus on provisions that deprive one party of the benefits of the agreement or leave that party without a remedy for nonperformance by the other.

Contracts entered into because of one party's vastly superior bargaining power may be deemed unconscionable. These situations usually involve an **adhesion contract,** which is a contract drafted by one party (such as a dishonest retail dealer) and then presented to another (such as an uneducated consumer) on a take-it-or-leave-it basis.

EXAMPLE 11.24   Smith, a welfare recipient with a fourth-grade education, agrees to purchase a fifty-five-inch LCD flat-screen TV from A-Plus Appliances for $3,000, signing a two-year contract. The same type of TV usually sells for $1,500. After paying $900, Smith refuses to pay more, and A-Plus sues to collect the balance. A court will hold this type of contract to be unconscionable. Courts look at factors such as the buyer's lack of education, the disparity of bargaining power between the parties, and the price of the goods. ●

Unconscionable Contract or Clause
A contract or clause that is void on the basis of public policy because one party is forced to accept terms that are unfairly burdensome and that unfairly benefit the other party.

Adhesion Contract   A standard-form contract in which the stronger party dictates the terms.

---

9. Pronounced un-*kon*-shun-uh-bul.

▶ E-Contracts

E-Contract A contract that is formed electronically.

Numerous contracts are formed online. Electronic contracts, or **e-contracts**, must meet the same basic requirements—agreement, consideration, contractual capacity, and legality—as traditional paper contracts. Disputes concerning e-contracts, however, tend to center on contract terms and whether the parties voluntarily agreed to those terms.

Online contracts may be formed not only for the sale of goods and services but also for *licensing*. The "sale" of software generally involves a license, or a right to use the software, rather than the passage of title (ownership rights) from the seller to the buyer. **EXAMPLE 11.25** Galynn wants to obtain software that will allow her to work on spreadsheets on her iPad. She goes online and purchases GridMagic. During the transaction, she has to click on several on-screen "I agree" boxes to indicate that she understands that she is purchasing only the right to use the software and will not obtain any ownership rights. After she agrees to these terms (the licensing agreement), she can download the software. ●

As you read through the following subsections, keep in mind that although we typically refer to the offeror and the offeree as a *seller* and a *buyer,* in many online transactions these parties would be more accurately described as a *licensor* and a *licensee.*

Online Offers

"If two men agree on everything, you can be sure one of them is doing the thinking."

Lyndon Baines Johnson, 1908–1973
(Thirty-sixth president of the United States, 1963–1969)

Sellers doing business via the Internet can protect themselves against contract disputes and legal liability by creating offers that clearly spell out the terms that will govern their transactions if the offers are accepted. All important terms should be conspicuous and easy to view.

The seller's Web site should include a hypertext link to a page containing the full contract so that potential buyers are made aware of the terms to which they are assenting. The contract generally must be displayed online in a readable format, such as a twelve-point typeface. All provisions should be reasonably clear. **EXAMPLE 11.26** Netquip sells heavy equipment, such as trucks and trailers, on its Web site. Because Netquip's pricing schedule is very complex, the full schedule must be provided and explained on the Web site. In addition, the terms of the sale (such as any warranties and the refund policy) must be fully disclosed. ●

PROVISIONS TO INCLUDE   An important rule to keep in mind is that the offeror controls the offer and thus the resulting contract. The seller should therefore determine the terms she or he wants to include in a contract and provide for them in the offer. In some instances, a standardized contract form may suffice. At a minimum, an online offer should include the following provisions:

1. A clause that clearly indicates what constitutes the buyer's agreement to the terms of the offer, such as a box containing the words "I accept" that the buyer can click on to indicate acceptance. (Mechanisms for accepting online offers will be discussed further on the facing page.)
2. A provision specifying how payment for the goods (including any applicable taxes) must be made.
3. A statement of the seller's refund and return policies.
4. Disclaimers of liability for certain uses of the goods. For example, an online seller of business forms may add a disclaimer that the seller does not accept responsibil-

ity for the buyer's reliance on the forms rather than on an attorney's advice.

5. A provision specifying the remedies available to the buyer if the goods are found to be defective or if the contract is otherwise breached. Any limitation of remedies should be clearly spelled out.

6. A statement indicating how the seller will use the information gathered about the buyer.

7. Provisions relating to dispute settlement, such as an arbitration clause or a *forum-selection clause* (discussed below).

DISPUTE-SETTLEMENT PROVISIONS   Online offers frequently include provisions relating to dispute settlement. For example, the offer might include an arbitration clause specifying that any dispute arising under the contract will be arbitrated in a designated forum.

Many online contracts also contain a *forum-selection clause* indicating the forum, or location (such as a court or jurisdiction), for the resolution of any dispute arising under the contract. As discussed in Chapter 2, significant jurisdictional issues may occur when parties are at a great distance, as they often are when they form contracts via the Internet. A forum-selection clause will help to avert future jurisdictional problems and also help to ensure that the seller will not be required to appear in court in a distant state.

CASE EXAMPLE 11.27   Facebook, Inc. (FB), is headquartered in California. The "Terms of Use" that govern FB users' accounts include a forum-selection clause that provides for the resolution of all disputes in a California court. Potential FB users cannot become actual users unless they click on an acknowledgment that they have agreed to this term. Mustafa Fteja was an active user of facebook.com when his account was disabled. He sued FB in a federal court in New York, claiming that it had disabled his FB page without justification and for discriminatory reasons. FB filed a motion to transfer the case to California under the forum-selection clause. The court found that the forum-selection clause in FB's e-contract was binding and transferred the case. Fteja had been informed of the consequences of his click—he would be bound to the forum-selection clause. When he clicked on the button and became an FB user, he agreed to resolve all disputes with FB in California.[10] ●

Some online contracts may also include a *choice-of-law* clause specifying that any dispute arising out of the contract will be settled in accordance with the law of a particular jurisdiction, such as a state or country. Choice-of-law clauses are particularly common in international contracts, but they may also appear in e-contracts to specify which state's laws will govern in the United States.

Online Acceptances

The *Restatement (Second) of Contracts* states that parties may agree to a contract "by written or spoken words or by other action or by failure to act."[11] The UCC, which governs sales contracts, has a similar provision. Section 2–204 of the UCC states that any contract for the sale of goods "may be made in any manner sufficient to show agreement, including conduct by both parties which recognizes the existence of such a contract."

CLICK-ON AGREEMENTS   The courts have used these provisions to conclude that a binding contract can be created by conduct, including the act of clicking on a box

---

10. *Fteja v. Facebook, Inc.*, 841 F.Supp.2d 829 (S.D.N.Y. 2012).
11. *Restatement (Second) of Contracts*, Section 19.

Click-on Agreement An agreement that arises when a buyer, engaging in a transaction on a computer, indicates assent to be bound by the terms of an offer by clicking on a button that says, for example, "I agree."

indicating "I accept" or "I agree" to accept an online offer. The agreement resulting from such an acceptance is often called a **click-on agreement** (also referred to as a *click-on license* or *click-wrap agreement*).

Generally, the law does not require that the parties have read all of the terms in a contract for it to be effective. Therefore, clicking on a box that states "I agree" to certain terms can be enough. The terms may be contained on a Web site through which the buyer is obtaining goods or services, or they may appear on a computer screen when software is loaded from a CD-ROM or DVD or downloaded from the Internet.

Shrink-Wrap Agreement An agreement whose terms are expressed in a document located inside a box in which goods (usually software) are packaged.

SHRINK-WRAP AGREEMENTS   A **shrink-wrap agreement** (or *shrink-wrap license*) is an agreement whose terms are expressed inside a box in which the goods are packaged. (The term *shrink-wrap* refers to the plastic that covers the box.) Usually, the party who opens the box is told that she or he agrees to the terms by keeping whatever is in the box. Similarly, when the purchaser opens a software package, he or she agrees to abide by the terms of the limited license agreement.

EXAMPLE 11.28 John orders a new iMac from Big Dog Electronics, which ships it to him. Along with the iMac, the box contains an agreement setting forth the terms of the sale, including what remedies are available. The document also states that John's retention of the computer for longer than thirty days will be construed as an acceptance of the terms. ●

In some cases, courts have enforced the terms of shrink-wrap agreements in the same way as the terms of other contracts. These courts have reasoned that by including the terms with the product, the seller proposed a contract that the buyer could accept by using the product after having an opportunity to read the terms. Sometimes, however, courts have refused to enforce certain terms in shrink-wrap agreements because the buyer did not expressly consent to them. An important factor is when the parties form their contract.

Ethical Issue ⚖

Is it fair to enforce shrink-wrap and click-wrap terms that buyers were not aware of at the time they agreed to a purchase? Most people realize that if they sign a written contract without reading it, they can be held to its terms. But are most people aware that they nonetheless can be legally bound by a whole host of conditions included in the packaging of electronics or software, not to mention the music, movies, and software they download from the Web? Simply by buying and keeping the latest electronic gadgets, we enter into binding contracts with the manufacturers that include rather one-sided terms. The terms may be unfair, but the law says we are bound. For instance, just by installing or downloading certain software today, users routinely agree to allow the companies to install tracking software on their computers.

Moreover, many software programs automatically delete files from the users' hard drives. Consumers and businesspersons are often unaware of these consequences, and yet by buying and installing the software, they have agreed that they will not hold the manufacturer liable.

E-Signatures

E-Signature An electronic sound, symbol, or process attached to or logically associated with a record and executed or adopted by a person with the intent to sign the record.

To be enforced, a contract generally requires the signature of the party against whom enforcement is sought. In the days when many people could not write, they signed documents with an "X." Then came the handwritten signature, followed by typed signatures, printed signatures, and, most recently, electronic signatures, or **e-signatures**.

Throughout the evolution of signature technology, debates over what constitutes a valid signature have occurred, and with good reason: without some agreement on what constitutes a valid signature, little business or legal work could be accomplished. A significant issue in the context of e-commerce is the legal effect of e-signatures. For more on the validity of e-signatures in the online setting, see this chapter's *Online Developments* feature on the following page.

STATE LAWS GOVERNING E-SIGNATURES Most states have laws governing e-signatures. The problem is that the state e-signature laws are not uniform. In an attempt to create more uniformity among the states, in 1999, the National Conference of Commissioners on Uniform State Laws and the American Law Institute issued the Uniform Electronic Transactions Act (UETA—see the next page). The UETA states, among other things, that a signature may not be denied legal effect or enforceability solely because it is in electronic form.

FEDERAL LAW ON E-SIGNATURES AND E-DOCUMENTS In 2000, Congress enacted the Electronic Signatures in Global and National Commerce Act (E-SIGN Act) to provide that no contract, record, or signature may be "denied legal effect" solely because it is in an electronic form. In other words, under this law, an e-signature is as valid as a signature on paper, and an e-document can be as enforceable as a paper document.

For an e-signature to be enforceable, the contracting parties must have agreed to use e-signatures. For an e-document to be valid, it must be in a form that can be retained and accurately reproduced.

Contracts and documents that are exempt include court papers, divorce decrees, evictions, foreclosures, health-insurance terminations, prenuptial agreements, and wills. Also, the only agreements governed by the Uniform Commercial Code (UCC) that fall under this law are those covered by Articles 2 and 2A, as well as UCC 1–107 and 1–206.

Despite its limitations, the E-SIGN Act enormously expanded the possibilities for contracting online. **EXAMPLE 11.29** A businessperson can open an account with a financial institution, obtain a mortgage or other loan, buy insurance, and purchase real estate over the Internet. Payments and transfers of funds can be done entirely online. • This can avoid the time and costs associated with producing, delivering, signing, and returning paper documents.

Partnering Agreements

Partnering Agreement An agreement between a seller and a buyer who frequently do business with each other concerning the terms and conditions that will apply to all subsequently formed electronic contracts.

One way that online sellers and buyers can prevent disputes over signatures in their e-contracts, as well as disputes over the terms and conditions of those contracts, is to form partnering agreements. In a **partnering agreement,** a seller and a buyer who frequently do business with each other agree in advance on the terms and conditions that will apply to all transactions subsequently conducted electronically. The partnering agreement can also establish special access and identification codes to be used by the parties when transacting business electronically.

A partnering agreement reduces the likelihood that disputes will arise under the contract because the buyer and the seller have agreed in advance to the terms and conditions that will accompany each sale. Furthermore, if a dispute does arise, a court or arbitration forum will be able to refer to the partnering agreement when determining the parties' intent.

ONLINE DEVELOPMENTS

The Validity of E-Signatures and Online University Enrollment Agreements

The number of online institutions offering bachelor's, master's, and even doctorate degrees has grown dramatically over the past decade. Like the classes, the enrollment procedures for these colleges and universities are carried out online. Most, if not all, of these schools ask enrolling students to agree that any disputes will be solved by arbitration. How valid are these enrollment agreements when the students simply indicate their assent via what the online universities call e-signatures?

Online Students Claim Their E-Signatures Were Invalid

Scott Rosendahl alleged that online Ashford University's enrollment adviser misleadingly claimed that Ashford offered one of the cheapest undergraduate degree programs in the country when in fact it did not. Veronica Clarke enrolled in the doctor of psychology program at the online University of the Rockies. She alleged that its enrollment adviser told her that the doctor of psychology program would qualify her to become a clinical psychologist in the U.S. military, but that statement was false.

Rosendahl and Clarke sued their respective universities for violation of unfair competition laws and false advertising laws, fraud, and negligent misrepresentation.

Online Universities Argue for Arbitration

The universities pointed out that each student electronically agreed to the enrollment provision that clearly contained a requirement that all disputes be arbitrated. Each agreement stated, "Such arbitration shall be the sole remedy for the resolution of any dispute or controversies between the parties to this agreement."

One issue was whether the e-signatures on the agreement were valid. Each application form had an "acknowledgment and signature" paragraph that stated "my signature on this application certifies that I have read, understood, and agreed to my rights and responsibilities as set forth in this application."

Both students had to click on an electronic box, acknowledging that they had read the agreement and had consented to it. When they clicked on the box, the phrase "Signed by E-Signature" appeared on the signature line.

The Court Rules in Favor of the Online Universities

The universities submitted copies of Rosendahl's and Clarke's online application forms to the court. Both forms contained the arbitration agreement and were signed with e-signatures. Rosendahl and Clarke provided no proof that they did not consent to the enrollment agreements. Thus, the court held that the universities had proved the existence of valid arbitration agreements.[a]

FOR CRITICAL ANALYSIS

Did the fact that the arbitration agreements were valid prevent Rosendahl and Clarke from pursuing their claims for negligent misrepresentation and fraud ? Why or why not ?

---

a. *Rosendahl v. Bridgepoint Education, Inc.,* 2012 WL 667049 (S.D.Cal. 2012).

The Uniform Electronic Transactions Act

LEARNING OBJECTIVE 5 What is the Uniform Electronic Transactions Act? What are some of the major provisions of this act?

As noted, the UETA represents one of the first comprehensive efforts to create uniformity and introduce certainty in state laws pertaining to e-commerce. The primary purpose of the UETA is to remove barriers to e-commerce by giving the same legal effect to electronic records (e-records) and signatures as is given to paper documents and signatures.

The UETA broadly defines an *e-signature* as "an electronic sound, symbol, or process attached to or logically associated with a record and executed or adopted by a person with the intent to sign the record."[12] A *record* is defined as "information that is inscribed on a tangible medium or that is stored in an electronic or other medium and is retrievable in perceivable [visual] form."[13]

---

12. UETA 102(8).
13. UETA 102(15).

The UETA does not apply to all writings and signatures but only to electronic records and electronic signatures *relating to a transaction*. A *transaction* is defined as an interaction between two or more people relating to business, commercial, or governmental activities.[14]

Some highlights of the UETA include the following:

1. *The UETA will not apply to a transaction unless each of the parties has previously agreed to conduct transactions by electronic means.* The agreement need not be explicit, however, and it may be implied by the conduct of the parties and the surrounding circumstances. **EXAMPLE 11.30** Austin gives out a business card with an e-mail address on it. Thus, it can be inferred that Austin has consented to transact business electronically. ●

2. *If an electronic record or signature is the act of a particular person, the record or signature may be attributed to that person.* **EXAMPLE 11.31** Trey types his name at the bottom of an e-mail purchase order. That typed name will qualify as a "signature" and be attributed to Trey. ●

3. *The effect of a record is to be determined from the context and surrounding circumstances.* In other words, a record may have legal effect even if no one has signed it. **EXAMPLE 11.32** Darby sends a fax to Corina. The fax contains a letterhead identifying Darby as the sender, but Darby's signature does not appear on the faxed document. Depending on the circumstances, the fax may be attributed to Darby. ●

---

14. UETA 2(12) and 3.

Reviewing . . . Formation of Traditional and E-Contracts

Ted and Betty Hyatt live in California, a state that provides extensive statutory protection for consumers. The Hyatts decided to buy a computer so that they could use e-mail to stay in touch with their grandchildren, who live in another state. Over the phone, they ordered a computer from CompuEdge, Inc. When the box arrived, it was sealed with a brightly colored sticker warning that the terms enclosed within the box would govern the sale unless the customer returned the computer within thirty days. Among those terms was a clause that required any disputes to be resolved in Tennessee state courts. The Hyatts then signed up for Internet service through CyberTool, an Internet service provider. They downloaded CyberTool's software and clicked on the "quick install" box that allowed them to bypass CyberTool's "Terms of Service" page. It was possible to read this page by scrolling to the next screen, but the Hyatts did not realize this. The terms included a clause that stated all disputes were to be submitted to a Virginia state court. As soon as the Hyatts attempted to e-mail their grandchildren, they experienced problems using CyberTool's e-mail service, which continually stated that the network was busy. They also were unable to receive the photos sent by their grandchildren. Using the information presented in the chapter, answer the following questions.

1. Did the Hyatts accept the list of contract terms included in the computer box? Why or why not? What is the name used for this type of e-contract?
2. What type of agreement did the Hyatts form with CyberTool?
3. Suppose that the Hyatts experienced trouble with the computer's components after they had used the computer for two months. What factors will a court consider in deciding whether to enforce the forum-selection clause? Would a court be likely to enforce the clause in this contract? Why or why not?
4. Are the Hyatts bound by the contract terms specified on CyberTool's "Terms of Service" page that they did not read? Which of the required elements for contract formation might the Hyatts claim were lacking? How might a court rule on this issue?

Debate This

The terms and conditions in click-on agreements are so long and detailed that no one ever reads the agreements. Therefore, the act of clicking on "Yes, I agree" is not really an acceptance.

Linking the Law *to Marketing*

Customer Relationship Management

Increasingly, the contracting process is moving online. Online offers for millions of goods and services populate large and small Web sites. The vast amount of data collected from online shoppers has pushed *customer relationship management* (CRM) to the forefront. CRM is a marketing strategy that allows companies to acquire information about customers' wants, needs, and behaviors. They can then use that information to build customer relationships and loyalty. The focus of CRM is understanding customers as individuals rather than simply as a group of consumers. As Exhibit 11–2 to the right shows, CRM is a closed system that uses feedback from customers to build relationships.

Two Examples—Netflix and Amazon

If you use Netflix.com, you choose movies based on your individual preferences. Netflix asks you to rate movies you have rented on a scale of one to five. Using a computer algorithm, Netflix then creates an individualized rating system that predicts how you will rate thousands of different movies. By applying your individual rating system to movies you have not seen, Netflix is able to suggest movies that you might like. Amazon.com uses similar technology to recommend books and music that you might wish to buy. Amazon sends out numerous "personalized" e-mails with suggestions based on its customers' individualized-buying habits. For both Netflix and Amazon, CRM allows for a focused marketing effort, rather than the typical shotgun approach used by spam advertising on the Internet.

CRM in Online versus Traditional Companies

For online companies, all customer information has some value because the cost of obtaining it, analyzing it, and utilizing it is so small. In contrast, for traditional companies obtaining data to be used for CRM requires a different process that is much more costly. An automobile company, for example, obtains customer information from a variety of sources, including customer surveys

• *Exhibit* 11–2 **A Customer Relationship Management Cycle**

Understand interactions with current customers.

Create a customer database with customer-buying habits.

Use information technology to store all customer data.

Identify customer wants and needs.

Determine how to leverage customer information.

and online inquiries. Integrating, storing, and managing such information makes CRM much more expensive for traditional companies than for online companies.

FOR CRITICAL ANALYSIS

Online companies not only target individual customers, but they also utilize each customer's buying habits to create generalized marketing campaigns. Might any privacy issues arise as an online company creates a database to be used for generalized marketing campaigns? Explain.

Key Terms

acceptance 269	agreement 265	click-on agreement 280
adhesion contract 277	bilateral contract 263	consideration 271

▶ Chapter Summary: Formation of Traditional and E-Contracts

An Overview of Contract Law (See pages 261–262.)	Contract law establishes what kinds of promises will be legally binding and supplies procedures for enforcing legally binding promises, or agreements. A contract is a legally binding agreement between two or more parties who agree to perform or to refrain from performing some act now or in the future. Requirements of a valid contract are (1) agreement, (2) consideration, (3) contractual capacity, and (4) legality.
Types of Contracts (See pages 262–265.)	1. *Bilateral*—A promise for a promise. 2. *Unilateral*—A promise for an act (acceptance is the completed—or substantial—performance of the contract by the offeree). 3. *Formal*—Requires a special form for contract formation. 4. *Informal*—Requires no special form for contract formation. 5. *Express*—Formed by words (oral, written, or a combination). 6. *Implied*—Formed at least in part by the conduct of the parties. 7. *Executed*—A fully performed contract. 8. *Executory*—A contract not yet fully performed. 9. *Valid*—A contract that results when the elements necessary for contract formation exist. 10. *Voidable*—A contract that may be legally canceled at the option of one or both of the parties. 11. *Unenforceable*—A valid contract rendered unenforceable by some statute or legal defense. 12. V*oid*—A contract that has no legal force or binding effect; treated as if the contract never existed.

Agreement (See pages 265–271.)	1. *Requirements of the offer:*
	   a. *Intent*—The offeror must have a serious, objective by the offer. Offers made in anger, jest, or undue excitement do not qualify.
	   b. *Definiteness*—The terms of the offer must be sufficiently definite to be ascertainable by the parties or by a court.
	   c. *Communication*—The offer must be communicated to the offeree.
	2. *Termination of the offer:*
	   a. *By action of the parties*—An offer can be revoked or withdrawn at any time before acceptance without liability. A counteroffer is a rejection of the original offer and the making of a new offer.
	   b. *By operation of law*—An offer can terminate by (a) lapse of time, (b) destruction of the subject matter, (c) death or incompetence of the parties, or (d) supervening illegality.
	3. *Acceptance*—Acceptance can be made only by the offeree or the offeree's agent, and it must be unequivocal. Under the common law (mirror image rule), if new terms or conditions are added to the acceptance, it will be considered a counteroffer.

Consideration (See pages 271–273.)	1. *Elements of consideration*—Consideration is the value given in exchange for a promise. A contract cannot be formed without sufficient consideration. Consideration is often broken down into two parts: (a) something of *legally sufficient value* must be given in exchange for the promise, and (b) there must be a *bargained-for exchange.* 2. *Adequacy of consideration*—Adequacy of consideration relates to "how much" consideration is given and whether a fair bargain was reached.

(Continued)

▶ Chapter Summary: Formation of Traditional and E-Contracts, Continued

Consideration—Continued	3. *Agreements that lack consideration*—Consideration is lacking when a *preexisting duty* or *past consideration exists.*
	4. *Promissory estoppel*—When injustice can be avoided only by enforcing a promise that would otherwise be unenforceable, this doctrine might allow a contract to be enforced.
Contractual Capacity **(See pages 274–275.)**	Contractual capacity is the legal ability to enter into a contractual relationship. Situations in which capacity is lacking include being a minor, intoxicated, or mentally incompetent.
Legality **(See pages 275–277.)**	For a contract to be valid and enforceable, it must be formed for a legal purpose. *Contracts contrary to statute* and *contracts contrary to public policy* are two examples of contracts that are not enforceable on the ground of illegality. Contracts contrary to statute include those to commit crimes as well as contracts that violate other laws, such as state gambling and licensing laws. Contracts contrary to public policy include those that restrain competition, are unconscionable, or release a party from liability no matter who is at fault.
E-Contracts **(See pages 278–283.)**	E-contracts must meet the same basic requirements—agreement, consideration, capacity, and legality—as traditional paper contracts.
	1. *Online offers*—The terms of contract offers presented via the Internet should be as inclusive as the terms in an offer made in a written (paper) document. The offer should be displayed in an easily readable format and should include some mechanism, such as an "I agree" or "I accept" box, by which the customer can accept the offer. Because jurisdictional issues frequently arise with online transactions, the offer should include dispute-settlement provisions and a forum-selection clause.
	2. *Online acceptances*:
	a. *Click-on agreement*—An agreement created when a buyer, completing a transaction on a computer, is required to indicate her or his assent to be bound by the terms of an offer by clicking on a box that says, for example, "I agree."
	b. *Shrink-wrap agreement*—An agreement whose terms are expressed inside a box in which the goods are packaged. The party who opens the box is informed that, by keeping the goods that are in the box, he or she agrees to the terms of the shrink-wrap agreement.
	3. *E-signatures*—The Electronic Signatures in Global and National Commerce Act (E-SIGN Act) of 2000 gave validity to e-signatures by providing that no contract, record, or signature may be "denied legal effect" solely because it is in an electronic form. To reduce the likelihood that disputes will arise under their e-contracts, parties who frequently do business with each other online may form a *partnering agreement,* setting out the terms and conditions that will apply to all their subsequent electronic transactions.
	4. *The Uniform Electronic Transactions Act (UETA)*—The Uniform Electronic Transactions Act (UETA) defines an e-signature as "an electronic sound, symbol, or process attached to or logically associated with a record and executed or adopted by a person with the intent to sign the record." This act has been adopted by most states to create rules to support the enforcement of e-contracts. The UETA provides for the validity of e-signatures and may ultimately create more uniformity among the states in this respect. Under the UETA, contracts entered into online, as well as other documents, are presumed to be valid.

▶ ExamPrep

ISSUE SPOTTERS

—Check your answers to these questions against the answers provided in Appendix D at the end of this text.

1. Before Maria starts her first year of college, Fred promises to give her $5,000 when she graduates. She goes to college, borrowing and spending far more than $5,000. At the beginning of the spring semester of her senior year, she reminds Fred of the promise. Fred sends her a note that says, "I revoke the promise." Is Fred's promise binding? Explain. **(See page 273.)**

2. Applied Products, Inc., does business with Beltway Distributors, Inc., online. Under the Uniform Electronic Transactions Act, what determines the effect of the electronic documents evidencing the parties' deal? Is a party's "signature" necessary? Explain. **(See pages 281–283.)**

BEFORE THE TEST

Go to **www.cengagebrain.com**, enter the ISBN 9781133586548, and click on "Find" to locate this textbook's Web site. Then click on "Access Now" under "Study Tools," and select Chapter 11 at the top. There, you will find a Practice Quiz that you can take to assess your mastery of the concepts in this chapter. Additionally, you will find Flashcards and a Glossary of important terms, as well as Video Questions (when assigned).

▶ For Review

Answers for the even-numbered questions in this **For Review** *section can be found in Appendix E at the end of this text.*

1. What are the four basic requirements for the formation of a valid contract?
2. What elements are necessary for an effective acceptance?
3. What is consideration?
4 What is a covenant not to compete? When will such a covenant be enforceable?
5. What is the Uniform Electronic Transactions Act? What are some of the major provisions of this act?

▶ Questions and Case Problems

11–1. Intention. Ball writes to Sullivan and inquires how much Sullivan is asking for a specific forty-acre tract of land Sullivan owns. Sullivan replies to Ball with a letter stating, "I will not take less than $60,000 for the forty-acre tract as specified." Ball immediately sends Sullivan a fax stating, "I accept your offer for $60,000 for the forty-acre tract as specified." Discuss whether Ball can hold Sullivan to a contract for sale of the land. **(See pages 266–267.)**

11–2. Offer and Acceptance. Carrie offered to sell a set of legal encyclopedias to Antonio for $300. Antonio said that he would think about her offer and let her know his decision the next day. Norvel, who had overheard the conversation between Carrie and Antonio, said to Carrie, "I accept your offer" and gave her $300. Carrie gave Norvel the books. The next day, Antonio, who had no idea that Carrie had already sold the books to Norvel, told Carrie that he accepted her offer. Has Carrie breached a valid contract with Antonio? Explain. **(See pages 265–271.)**

11–3. **Question with Sample Answer: Preexisting Duty.** Ben hired Lewis to drive his racing car in a race. Tuan, a friend of Lewis, promised to pay Lewis $3,000 if he won the race. Lewis won the race, but Tuan refused to pay the $3,000. Tuan contended that no legally binding contract had been formed because he had received no consideration from Lewis for his promise to pay the $3,000. Lewis sued Tuan for breach of contract, arguing that winning the race was the consideration given in exchange for Tuan's promise to pay the $3,000. What rule of law discussed in this chapter supports Tuan's claim? Explain. **(See pages 272–273.)**

—For a sample answer to Question 11–3, go to Appendix F at the end of this text.

11–4. Covenants Not to Compete. Joseph, who owns the only pizza parlor in Middletown, learns that Giovanni is about to open a competing pizza parlor in the same small town, just a few blocks from Joseph's restaurant. Joseph offers Giovanni $10,000 in return for Giovanni's promise not to open a pizza parlor in the Middletown area. Giovanni accepts the $10,000 but goes ahead with his plans, in spite of the agreement. When Giovanni opens his restaurant for business, Joseph sues to prevent Giovanni's continued operation of his restaurant or to recover the $10,000. The court denies recovery. On what basis? **(See page 276.)**

11–5. **Spotlight on Taco Bell: Implied Contract.** Thomas Rinks and Joseph Shields developed Psycho Chihuahua, a caricature of a Chihuahua dog with a "do-not-back-down" attitude. They promoted and marketed the character through their company, Wrench, L.L.C. Ed Alfaro and Rudy Pollak, representatives of Taco Bell Corp., learned of Psycho Chihuahua and met with Rinks and Shields to talk about using the character as a Taco Bell "icon." Wrench sent artwork, merchandise, and marketing ideas to Alfaro, who promoted the character within Taco Bell. Alfaro asked Wrench to propose terms for Taco Bell's use of Psycho Chihuahua. Taco Bell did not accept Wrench's terms, but Alfaro continued to promote the character within the company. Meanwhile, Taco Bell hired a new advertising agency, which proposed an advertising campaign involving a Chihuahua. When Alfaro learned of this proposal, he sent the

Psycho Chihuahua materials to the agency. Taco Bell made a Chihuahua the focus of its marketing but paid nothing to Wrench. Wrench filed a suit against Taco Bell in a federal court claiming that it had an implied contract with Taco Bell and that Taco Bell breached that contract. Do these facts satisfy the requirements for an implied contract? Why or why not? [*Wrench, LLC v. Taco Bell Corp.,* 256 F.3d 446 (6th Cir. 2001), *cert.* denied, 534 U.S. 1114, 122 S.Ct. 921, 151 L.Ed.2d 805 (2002)] **(See page 264.)**

11–6. Unconscionable Contracts or Clauses. Erica Bishop's apartment lease listed her and her children as members of the household and required her to notify the landlord if any of them moved out. The lease also held her responsible for the acts of all members. Any criminal act was a ground for eviction. When Bishop's son, Derek, was convicted of the robbery of a nearby store, she was given thirty days to vacate the apartment. Bishop responded that Derek had moved out, but she had forgotten to tell the landlord. Besides, she contended, the lease was unconscionable. Is she correct? Discuss. [*Bishop v. Housing Authority of South Bend,* 920 N.E.2d 772 (Ind.App. 2010)] **(See page 277.)**

11–7. Disaffirmance. J.T., a minor, is a motocross competitor. At Monster Mountain MX Park, he signed a waiver of liability to "hold harmless the park for any loss due to negligence." Riding around the Monster Mountain track, J.T. rode over a blind jump, became airborne, and crashed into a tractor that he had not seen until he was in the air. To recover for his injuries, J.T. filed a suit against Monster Mountain, alleging negligence for its failure to remove the tractor from the track. Does the liability waiver bar this claim? Explain. [*J.T. v. Monster Mountain, LLC,* 754 F.Supp.2d 1323 (M.D.Ala. 2010)] **(See page 274.)**

11–8. Case Problem with Sample Answer: Contract Types. Kim Panenka asked to borrow $4,750 from her sister, Kris, so that Kim could make her mortgage payment. Kris deposited a check for that amount into Kim's bank account. Hours later, Kim asked to borrow another $1,100. Kris took a cash advance on her credit card and deposited this amount into Kim's account. About a week later, Kim asked Kris for $845.40 to pay a dental bill. Kris paid the bill by credit card. After Kris asked for repayment several times and did not receive payment, she filed a suit against her sister in a Wisconsin state court. At the trial, Kim admitted that she had asked for the various amounts

and that the funds had not been a gift, but she testified that the sisters had a long history of paying for things for each other without expecting repayment. Kris countered that she had "loaned" Kim these amounts. Can the court impose a contract between the sisters? Explain. [*Panenka v. Panenka,* 331 Wis.2d 731, 795 N.W.2d 493 (2011)] **(See pages 262–265.)**

—For a sample answer to Case Problem 11–8, go to Appendix G at the end of this text.

11–9. Consideration. In March 1997, Leonard Kranzler loaned Lewis Saltzman $100,000. Saltzman signed a written memo that stated, "Loaned to Lewis Saltzman $100,000 to be paid back with interest." Saltzman made fifteen payments on the loan, but these payments did not cover the entire amount. The last payment was made in July 2005. In June 2007—more than ten years after the date of the loan but less than two years after the date of the last payment—Kranzler filed a suit in an Illinois state court against Saltzman, seeking to recover the outstanding principal and interest. Saltzman admitted that he had borrowed the funds and had made payments on the loan, but he claimed that Kranzler's complaint was barred by a ten-year statute of limitations. Does Kranzler need to prove a new promise with new consideration to collect the unpaid debt? Explain. [*Kranzler v. Saltzman,* 347 Ill.Dec. 519, 942 N.E.2d 722 (1 Dist. 2011)] **(See pages 271–273.)**

11–10. Online Acceptances. Heather Reasonover opted to try Internet service from Clearwire Corp. Clearwire sent her a confirmation e-mail that included a link to its Web site. Clearwire also sent her a modem. In the enclosed written materials, at the bottom of a page, in small type was the Web site's URL. When Reasonover plugged in the modem, an "I accept terms" box appeared. Without clicking on the box, Reasonover quit the page but continued to use Clearwire's service. A clause in Clearwire's "Terms of Service," accessible only through its Web site, required its subscribers to submit any dispute to arbitration. Is Reasonover bound to this clause? Why or why not? [*Kwan v. Clearwire Corp.,* 2012 WL 32380 (W.D.Wash. 2012)] **(See pages 279–280.)**

11–11. Critical-Thinking Ethical Question. Should the goal of protecting minors from the consequences of unwise contracts ever outweigh the goal of encouraging minors to behave in a responsible manner? **(See page 274.)**

Chapter 12

Contract Performance, Breach, and Remedies

> "Men keep their engagements when it is to the advantage of both not to break them."
>
> —Solon, Sixth century B.C.E.
> (Athenian legal reformer)

Learning Objectives

The five Learning Objectives below are designed to help improve your understanding of the chapter. After reading this chapter, you should be able to answer the following questions:

1. **In what types of situations might voluntary consent to a contract's terms be lacking?**

2. **What are the elements of fraudulent misrepresentation?**

3. **What is substantial performance?**

4. **What is the standard measure of compensatory damages when a contract is breached?**

5. **What equitable remedies can a court grant, and in what circumstances will a court consider granting them?**

(iStockphoto.com)

As pointed out in the chapter-opening quotation above, a contract will not be broken so long as "it is to the advantage of both" parties not to break it. In a perfect world, every party who signed a contract would perform his or her duties completely and in a timely fashion, thereby discharging (terminating) the contract. In the real world, however, things frequently become complicated. Certainly, events often occur that may affect our performance or our ability to perform contractual duties. Just as rules are necessary to determine when a legally enforceable contract exists, so also are they required to determine when one of the parties can justifiably say, "I have fully performed, so I am now discharged from my obligations under this contract."

When it is no longer advantageous for a party to fulfill his or her contractual obligations, breach of contract may result. A *breach of contract* occurs when a party fails to perform part or all of the required duties under a contract. Once this occurs, the other party—the nonbreaching party—can choose one or more of several remedies. A *remedy* is the relief provided for an innocent party when the other party has breached the contract. It is the means employed to enforce a right or to redress an injury. Some of the most common remedies available to a nonbreaching party will be examined later in this chapter.

▶ Voluntary Consent

Voluntary Consent Knowledge of, and genuine assent to, the terms of a contract.

Two parties, each with full legal capacity and for a legal purpose, have entered into a contract that is supported by consideration. The contract thus meets the four requirements for a valid contract that were specified in Chapter 11. Nonetheless, the contract may be unenforceable if the parties have not voluntarily consented to its terms.

Lack of **voluntary consent** (assent) can be used as a defense to the contract's enforceability. Voluntary consent may be lacking because of a mistake, fraudulent misrepresentation, undue influence, or duress—in other words, because there is no true "meeting of the minds." In this section, we examine problems relating to voluntary consent.

Mistakes

LEARNING OBJECTIVE 1   **In what types of situations might voluntary consent to a contract's terms be lacking?**

We all make mistakes, so it is not surprising that mistakes are made when contracts are formed. It is important to distinguish between *mistakes of value or quality* and *mistakes of fact.* Only a mistake of fact makes a contract voidable.

If a mistake concerns the future market value or quality of the object of the contract, the mistake is one of value, and either party can normally enforce the contract. **EXAMPLE 12.1**   Chi buys a violin from Bev for $250. Although the violin is very old, neither party believes that it is extremely valuable. Later, however, an antiques dealer informs the parties that the violin is rare and worth thousands of dollars. Although both parties were mistaken, the mistake is not a mistake of fact that warrants canceling the contract. ●

Mistakes of fact occur in two forms—*unilateral* and *bilateral.* We look next at these two types of mistakes and illustrate them graphically in Exhibit 12–1 below.

Unilateral Mistake A mistake that occurs when one party to a contract is mistaken as to a material fact.

UNILATERAL MISTAKES   A **unilateral mistake** is made by only one of the parties. In general, a unilateral mistake does not give the mistaken party any right to relief from the contract. In other words, the contract normally is enforceable against the mistaken party.

EXAMPLE 12.2   Elena intends to sell her personal jet ski for $6,500. When she learns that Chin is interested in buying a used personal jet ski, she sends him an e-mail offering to sell the jet ski to him. When typing the e-mail, however, she mistakenly keys in the price of $5,600. Chin immediately sends Elena an e-mail reply accepting

● *Exhibit* 12–1 **Mistakes of Fact**

her offer. Even though Elena intended to sell her personal jet ski for $6,500, she has made a unilateral mistake and is bound by the contract to sell it to Chin for $5,600. ●

There are at least two exceptions to this rule. The contract may not be enforceable if:

1. The other party to the contract knows or should have known that a mistake was made.
2. The error was due to a substantial mathematical mistake in addition, subtraction, division, or multiplication and was made inadvertently and without gross negligence—that is, the intentional failure to perform a duty in reckless disregard of the consequences.

Of course, the mistake must still involve some *material fact*—that is, a fact that a reasonable person would attach importance to when determining his or her course of action.

BILATERAL (MUTUAL) MISTAKES When both parties are mistaken about the same fact, a **bilateral mistake** has occurred, and the contract can be rescinded by either party. Normally, the contract is voidable by the adversely affected party. Note that, as with a unilateral mistake, the mistake must be about a material fact. One type of bilateral mistake can occur when a word or term in a contract is subject to more than one reasonable interpretation. In that situation, if the parties to the contract attach materially different meanings to the term, their mutual misunderstanding may allow the contract to be rescinded or cancelled.

Bilateral Mistake A mistake that occurs when both parties to a contract are mistaken about the same material fact.

CASE EXAMPLE 12.3 L&H Construction Company contracted with Circle Redmont, Inc., to make a staircase and flooring system. Circle Redmont's original proposal was to "engineer, fabricate, and install" the system. Installation was later eliminated as part of the deal. In the final agreement, payment was due on Circle Redmont's "supervision" instead of "completion" of installation. But the final agreement still included the wording, "engineer, fabricate, and install." Once the project was under way, Circle Redmont claimed that this wording was a mistake. L&H insisted that installation was included. L&H filed a suit against Circle Redmont, claiming a mutual mistake. The court held that the contract was unclear. Circle Redmont's witnesses stated that the final agreement embodied the parties' understanding—Circle Redmont would only supervise the installation, not perform it. The court determined that the witnesses were credible.[1] ●

Fraudulent Misrepresentation

In the context of contract law, fraud affects the authenticity of the innocent party's consent to the contract. When an innocent party consents to a contract with fraudulent terms, the contract usually can be avoided because the innocent party has not *voluntarily* consented to the terms. Normally, the innocent party can either cancel the contract and be restored to the original position or enforce the contract and seek damages for any harms resulting from the fraud.

Typically, fraudulent misrepresentation consists of the following elements:

LEARNING OBJECTIVE 2 What are the elements of fraudulent misrepresentation?

1. A misrepresentation of a material fact.
2. An intent to deceive.
3. The justifiable reliance of the innocent party on the misrepresentation.

To collect damages, a party must have been harmed as a result of the misrepresentation.

MISREPRESENTATION HAS OCCURRED The first element of proving fraud is to show that misrepresentation of a material fact has occurred. This misrepresentation can occur by words or actions. For instance, an art gallery owner's statement

---

1. *L&H Construction Co. v. Circle Redmont, Inc.,* 55 So.3d 630 (2011).

"This painting is a Picasso" is a misrepresentation of fact if the painting was done by another artist. Similarly, if a customer asks to see only Jasper Johns paintings and the owner immediately leads the customer over to paintings that were not done by Johns, the owner's actions can be a misrepresentation.

Misrepresentation by Conduct. Misrepresentation also occurs when a party takes specific action to conceal a fact that is material to the contract. For instance, if a seller, by her or his actions, prevents a buyer from learning of some fact that is material to the contract, the seller's behavior constitutes misrepresentation by conduct.

CASE EXAMPLE 12.4 Actor Tom Selleck contracted to purchase a horse named Zorro for his daughter from Dolores Cuenca. Cuenca acted as though Zorro was fit to ride in competitions, when in reality the horse suffered from a medical condition. Selleck filed a lawsuit against Cuenca for wrongfully concealing the horse's condition, and a jury awarded Selleck more than $187,000 for Cuenca's misrepresentation by conduct.[2] ●

Another example of misrepresentation by conduct is the untruthful denial of knowledge or information concerning facts that are material to the contract when such knowledge or information is requested.

Misrepresentation of Law. Misrepresentation of law *ordinarily* does not entitle a party to be relieved of a contract. **EXAMPLE 12.5** Tanya has a parcel of property that she is trying to sell to Levi. Tanya knows that a local building ordinance prohibits constructing a structure higher than three stories on the property. Nonetheless, she tells Levi, "You can build a condominium one hundred stories high if you want." Levi buys the land and later discovers that Tanya's statement is false. Normally, Levi cannot avoid the contract because under the common law, people are assumed to know state and local laws. ●

Misrepresentation by Silence. Ordinarily, neither party to a contract has a duty to come forward and disclose facts, and a contract normally will not be set aside because certain pertinent information has not been volunteered. **EXAMPLE 12.6** Jude is selling a car that has been in an accident and has been repaired. He does not need to volunteer this information to a potential buyer. If, however, the buyer asks him if the car has had extensive bodywork and he lies, Jude has committed fraudulent misrepresentation. ●
In general, if the seller knows of a serious defect or a serious potential problem that the buyer cannot reasonably be expected to discover, the seller may have a duty to speak.

In the following case, the issue of misrepresentation by silence was at the heart of the dispute. A real estate investor sued for fraud after a seller failed to disclose material facts about the property's value.

---

2. *Selleck v. Cuenca*, Case No. GIN056909, North County of San Diego, California, decided September 9, 2009.

Case 12.1   Fazio v. Cypress/GR Houston I, LP

Court of Appeals of Texas, First District, ___ S.W.3d ___ (2012).

BACKGROUND AND FACTS Peter Fazio began talks with Cypress/GR Houston I, LP, to buy retail property whose main tenant was a Garden Ridge store. In performing a background investigation, Fazio and his agents became concerned about Garden Ridge's financial health. Nevertheless, after being assured that Garden Ridge had a positive financial outlook, Fazio sent Cypress a letter of intent to buy the property for $7.67 million "based on the currently reported absolute net income of $805,040." Cypress then agreed

Case 12.1–Continued

to provide all information in its possession, but it failed to disclose that (1) a consultant for Garden Ridge had recently requested a $240,000 reduction in the annual rent as part of a restructuring of the company's real estate leases and (2) Cypress's bank was so concerned about Garden Ridge's financial health that it had required a personal guaranty of the property's loan. The parties entered into a purchase agreement, but Garden Ridge went into bankruptcy shortly after the deal closed. Fazio sued Cypress for fraud after he was forced to sell the property for only $3.75 million. A jury found in Fazio's favor, but the trial court awarded judgment *n.o.v.* ("notwithstanding the verdict"–see page 48) to Cypress. Fazio appealed.

IN THE WORDS OF THE COURT . . .
Evelyn V. *KEYES*, Justice.
  * * * *

  *We * * * hold that Fazio's claims clearly fall within the category of claims for which an action for fraudulent inducement lies.* [Emphasis added.]

  Cypress knew from the express representation in the LOI [letter of intent] that Fazio was willing to pay the requested purchase price of $7,667,000 for the Property "based on the currently reported absolute net income of $805,040." It further knew that this income was generated by rental income received from Garden Ridge. Fazio agreed in the LOI to conduct due diligence [background investigation], and, in accepting the LOI, Cypress agreed to "provide Buyer with all information in [its] possession * * * ." Fazio, an experienced real estate investor, and his experienced agents conducted reasonable due diligence before Fazio signed the Purchase Agreement, including requesting and reviewing all economic information about the Property in Cypress's possession. When Fazio discovered disturbing information about Garden Ridge in the financial statements provided to him, he conducted further investigations with both Garden Ridge and Cypress.

He was repeatedly assured that all was well and that Garden Ridge anticipated strong sales * * * .

  A reasonable person in Fazio's position would clearly have attached importance to the facts that approximately eight months before he purchased the Property in September 2003, Garden Ridge had retained [a consultant] to assist it in restructuring and renegotiating Garden Ridge's real estate leases; [the consultant] had prepared a letter for Garden Ridge to send to landlords; a copy of that letter, stating that Garden Ridge was restructuring and that as part of its restructuring it needed to reduce its occupancy costs at certain stores, including the Garden Ridge store on the Property, was sent to Cypress's President, Maguire, on March 5, 2003; and [the consultant] had contacted Cypress's Director of Finance and others at Cypress on at least three other occasions to discuss the proposed rent relief, seeking an annual rent reduction of 30% for the Property, or $241,512.

  A reasonable real estate investor who had signed an LOI to purchase the Property for $7,667,000 on September 2, 2003 would also attach importance to and be induced to act on the information that, on August 14, 2003, Cypress's lender, Guaranty Bank, had requested that Cypress's President execute a personal guaranty of the balance of $4,500,000 on the $5,704,000 loan secured by the Property because the bank was concerned about Garden Ridge's financial condition.

  * * * We * * * hold that Cypress's active concealment of this material information, which it was under a duty to disclose as financial information material to the real estate transaction in its possession, was fraudulent as a matter of law.

DECISION AND REMEDY   The Texas appellate court reversed the trial court and held that Cypress was liable to Fazio for fraud.

THE ETHICAL DIMENSION   *Was Cypress's conduct unethical? Why or why not?*

Scienter Knowledge by the misrepresenting party that material facts have been falsely represented or omitted with an intent to deceive.

INTENT TO DECEIVE   The second element of fraud is knowledge on the part of the misrepresenting party that facts have been misrepresented. This element, usually called *scienter*,[3] or "guilty knowledge," generally signifies that there was an intent to deceive. *Scienter* clearly exists if a party knows that a fact is not as stated. *Scienter* also exists if a party makes a statement that he or she believes not to be true or makes a statement recklessly, without regard to whether it is true or false. Finally, this element is met if a party says or implies that a statement is made on some basis, such as personal knowledge or personal investigation, when it is not.

CASE EXAMPLE 12.7   Robert Sarvis applied for a position as a business law professor two weeks after his release from prison. On his résumé, he said that he had been a corporate president for fourteen years and had taught business law at another college. After he was hired, his probation officer alerted the college to Sarvis's criminal history. The college immediately fired him, and Sarvis sued for breach of his employment contract. The court concluded that by not disclosing his history, Sarvis clearly exhibited an intent to deceive and that the college had justifiably relied on

---

3. Pronounced sy-*en*-ter.

his misrepresentations. Therefore, the college could rescind Sarvis's employment contract.[4] •

RELIANCE ON THE MISREPRESENTATION   The third element of fraud is *justifiable reliance* on the misrepresentation of fact. The deceived party must have a justifiable reason for relying on the misrepresentation, and the misrepresentation must be an important factor (but not necessarily the sole factor) in inducing the party to enter into the contract.

Reliance is not justified if the innocent party knows the true facts or relies on obviously extravagant statements. **EXAMPLE 12.8** If a used-car dealer tells you, "This old Cadillac will get over sixty miles to the gallon," you normally would not be justified in relying on this statement. Suppose, however, that Merkel, a bank director, induces O'Connell, a co-director, to sign a statement that the bank has sufficient assets to meet its liabilities by telling O'Connell, "We have plenty of assets to satisfy our creditors." This statement is false. If O'Connell knows the true facts or, as a bank director, should know the true facts, he is not justified in relying on Merkel's statement. If O'Connell does not know the true facts, however, *and has no way of finding them out,* he may be justified in relying on the statement. •

Undue Influence

Undue influence arises from special kinds of relationships in which one party can greatly influence another party, thus overcoming that party's free will. A contract entered into under excessive or undue influence lacks voluntary assent and is therefore voidable.

In various types of relationships, one party may have an opportunity to dominate and unfairly influence another party. Minors and elderly people, for example, are often under the influence of guardians (persons who are legally responsible for others). If a guardian induces a young or elderly ward (the person whom the guardian looks after) to enter into a contract that benefits the guardian, undue influence may have been exerted. Undue influence can arise from a number of confidential or fiduciary relationships: attorney-client, physician-patient, parent-child, husband-wife, or trustee-beneficiary.

The essential feature of undue influence is that the party being taken advantage of does not exercise free will in entering into a contract. It is not enough that a person is elderly or suffers from some mental or physical impairment. There must be clear and convincing evidence that the person did not act of her or his free will.

Duress

Agreement to the terms of a contract is not voluntary if one of the parties is forced into the agreement. The use of threats to force a party to enter into a contract is referred to as *duress*. In addition, blackmail or extortion to induce consent to a contract constitutes duress. Duress is both a defense to the enforcement of a contract and a ground for the rescission of a contract.

To establish duress, there must be proof of a threat to do something that the threatening party has no right to do. Generally, for duress to occur, the threatened act must be wrongful or illegal and must render the person incapable of exercising free will. A threat to exercise a legal right, such as the right to sue someone, ordinarily does not constitute duress.

---

4. *Sarvis v. Vermont State Colleges,* 172 Vt. 76, 772 A.2d 494 (2001).

▶ The Statute of Frauds—Writing Requirement

Another defense to the enforceability of a contract is *form*—that is, some contracts need to be in writing. Every state has a statute, modeled after an old English act, that stipulates what types of contracts must be in writing. Although the statutes vary slightly from state to state, all states require certain types of contracts to be in writing or evidenced by a written (or electronic) memorandum signed by the party against whom enforcement is sought, unless certain exceptions apply. In this text, we refer to these statutes collectively as the **Statute of Frauds.**

Statute of Frauds A state statute under which certain types of contracts must be in writing to be enforceable.

The actual name of the Statute of Frauds is misleading because it neither applies to fraud nor invalidates any type of contract. Rather, it denies *enforceability* to certain contracts that do not comply with its requirements. (Note that in some states, an oral contract that would otherwise be unenforceable under the Statute of Frauds may be enforced under the doctrine of *promissory estoppel*—see page 273 in Chapter 11.)

The following types of contracts are said to fall "within" or "under" the Statute of Frauds and therefore require a writing:

1. Contracts involving interests in land.
2. Contracts that cannot by their terms be performed within one year from the day after the date of formation.
3. Collateral, or secondary, contracts, such as promises to answer for the debt or duty of another and promises by the administrator or executor of an estate to pay a debt of the estate personally—that is, out of his or her own pocket.
4. Promises made in consideration of marriage.
5. Under the Uniform Commercial Code (UCC—see Chapter 13), contracts for the sale of goods priced at $500 or more.

"The pen is mightier than the sword, and considerably easier to write with."

Marty Feldman, 1934–1982
(English actor and comedian)

(See this chapter's *Beyond Our Borders* feature below to learn whether other countries have requirements similar to those in the Statute of Frauds.)

Beyond Our Borders | The Statute of Frauds and International Sales Contracts

The Convention on Contracts for the International Sale of Goods (CISG) provides rules that govern international sales contracts between citizens of countries that have ratified the convention (agreement). Article 11 of the CISG does not incorporate any Statute of Frauds provisions. Rather, it states that a "contract for sale need not be concluded in or evidenced by writing and is not subject to any other requirements as to form."

Article 11 accords with the legal customs of most nations, which no longer require contracts to meet certain formal or writing requirements to be enforceable. Ironically, even England, the nation that enacted the original Statute of Frauds in 1677, has repealed all of it except the provisions relating to collateral promises and to transfers of interests in land. Many other countries that once had such statutes have also repealed all or parts of them. Civil law countries, such as France, have never required certain types of contracts to be in writing. Obviously, without a writing requirement, contracts can take on any form.

• For Critical Analysis

If a country does not have a Statute of Frauds and a dispute arises over an oral agreement, how can the parties substantiate their positions?

A writing can consist of any confirmation, invoice, sales slip, check, fax, or e-mail—or such items in combination. The written contract need not consist of a single document to constitute an enforceable contract. One document may incorporate another document by expressly referring to it. Several documents may form a single contract if they are physically attached—such as by staple, paper clip, or glue—or even if they are only placed in the same envelope. To be legally sufficient, the writing need only contain the essential terms of the contract, not every term. (See this chapter's *Linking the Law to Business Communication* feature on pages 314 and 315.)

▶ Third Party Rights

Once it has been determined that a valid and legally enforceable contract exists, attention can turn to the rights and duties of the parties to the contract. A contract is a private agreement between the parties who have entered into it, and traditionally these parties alone have rights and liabilities under the contract. This principle is referred to as *privity of contract.* A *third party*—one who is not a direct party to a particular contract—normally does not have rights under that contract.

There are exceptions to the rule of privity of contract. One exception allows a party to a contract to transfer the rights or duties arising from the contract to another person through an *assignment* (of rights) or a *delegation* (of duties). Another exception involves a *third party beneficiary contract*—a contract in which the parties to the contract intend that the contract benefit a third party.

Assignments

In a bilateral contract, the two parties have corresponding rights and duties. One party has a *right* to require the other to perform some task, and the other has a *duty* to perform it. The transfer of contractual *rights* to a third party is known as an **assignment.**

Assignment   The act of transferring to another all or part of one's rights arising under a contract.

THE EFFECT OF AN ASSIGNMENT   When rights under a contract are assigned unconditionally, the rights of the *assignor*[5] (the party making the assignment) are extinguished. The third party (the *assignee,*[6] or party receiving the assignment) has a right to demand performance from the other original party to the contract (the *obligor*). The assignee takes only those rights that the assignor originally had. As a general rule, all rights can be assigned. Exceptions are made, however, in some circumstances. We discuss these exceptions next.

When a Contract Is Personal in Nature.   When a contract is for personal services, such as piano lessons, or personal in nature, the rights under the contract normally cannot be assigned. **CASE EXAMPLE 12.9**   Leo and Grace Flattery sold their farm to Stanek Cattle Company but kept an acre of the land for their home. A contract provision gave Stanek "a right of first refusal to acquire the acre." A year later, Stanek sold the farm to William and Sharon Malone. Seven years later, the Flatterys transferred their interest in the acre to Timothy and Deann Crall. The Malones filed a suit against the Flatterys to cancel the transfer to the Cralls and to exercise the "right of first refusal" from the original contract between the Flatterys and Stanek. The court held that "a right of first refusal" clause was personal in nature and therefore *not* assignable, unless expressly noted in the contract. The original contract made no such assignment (to the Malones), so the Flatterys could transfer the acre of land to the Cralls.[7] ●

---

5. Pronounced uh-*sye*-nore.
6. Pronounced uh-*sye*-nee.
7. *Malone v. Flattery,* 797 N.W.2d 624 (Iowa App. 2011).

When an Assignment Will Significantly Change the Risk or Duties of the Obligor. A right cannot be assigned if assignment will significantly increase or alter the risks or the duties of the *obligor* (the party owing performance under the contract).

EXAMPLE 12.10 Alex owns a hotel. He takes out a policy with North Insurance, Inc., to insure against fire, theft, floods, and vandalism. Alex attempts to assign the insurance policy to Carmen who also owns a hotel. This assignment is ineffective because it may substantially alter the insurance company's duty of performance and the risk that it undertakes. •

When the Contract Prohibits Assignment. If a contract stipulates that the right cannot be assigned, then *ordinarily* it cannot be assigned. This rule has several exceptions:

1. A contract cannot prevent an assignment of the right to receive funds. This exception exists to encourage the free flow of funds and credit in modern business settings.
2. The assignment of rights in real estate often cannot be prohibited because such a prohibition is contrary to public policy. Prohibitions of this kind are called restraints against *alienation* (transfer of land ownership).
3. The assignment of *negotiable instruments* (which include checks and promissory notes) cannot be prohibited.
4. In a contract for the sale of goods, the right to receive damages for breach of contract or for payment of an account owed may be assigned even though the sales contract prohibits such assignment.

NOTICE OF ASSIGNMENT   Once a valid assignment of rights has been made to a third party, the third party should notify the obligor of the assignment. Giving notice is not legally necessary to establish the validity of the assignment because an assignment is effective immediately, whether or not notice is given.

In the following *Spotlight Case,* the issue was whether the right to buy advertising space in certain publications at a steep discount was validly assigned from the original owner to companies that he later formed.

SPOTLIGHT ON *PC MAGAZINE*

Case 12.2 **Gold v. Ziff Communications Co.**

Appellate Court of Illinois, First District, 322 Ill.App.3d 32, 748 N.E.2d 198, 254 Ill.Dec. 752 (2001).

BACKGROUND AND FACTS   In 1982, Ziff Communications Company, a publisher of specialty magazines, bought *PC Magazine* from its founder, Anthony Gold, for more than $10 million. As part of the deal, Ziff gave Gold or a company that he owned and controlled "ad/list rights"–rights to advertise at an 80 percent discount on a limited number of pages in Ziff publications and free use of Ziff's subscriber lists. In 1983, Gold formed Software Communications, Inc. (SCI), a mail-order software business that he wholly owned, to use the ad/list rights. In 1987 and 1988, he formed two new mail-order companies, Hanson & Connors, Inc., and PC Brand, Inc. Gold told Ziff that he was allocating his ad/list rights to Hanson & Connors, which took over most of SCI's business, and to PC Brand, of which Gold

owned 90 percent. Ziff's other advertisers complained about this "allocation." Ziff refused to run large ads for Hanson & Connors or to release its subscriber lists to the company. Ziff also declared PC Brand ineligible for the ad discount because it "was not controlled by Gold." Gold and his companies filed a suit in an Illinois state court against Ziff, alleging breach of contract. The court ordered Ziff to pay the plaintiffs more than $88 million in damages and interest. Ziff appealed to an intermediate state appellate court, arguing, in part, that Gold had not properly assigned the ad/list rights to Hanson & Connors and PC Brand.

Spotlight Case **12.2–Continues next page** ➡

IN THE WORDS OF THE COURT . . .
Justice *COUSINS*, delivered the opinion of the court.
* * * *

Ziff * * * argues that Gold never properly reassigned his rights under the amended ad/list agreement from SCI to PC Brand and Hanson. We agree with plaintiffs that assignments can be implied from circumstances. *No particular mode or form * * * is necessary to effect a valid assignment, and any acts or words are sufficient which show an intention of transferring or appropriating the owner's interest.* [Emphasis added.]

In the instant case, it is undisputed that gold owned 100% of SCI. In a letter dated May 13, 1988, Gold, as president of SCI, instructed Ziff that he was allocating the ad/list rights to Hanson and PC Brand. Additionally, SCI stopped using the ad/list rights when PC Brand and

Hanson were formed. * * * Gold's behavior toward his companies and his conduct toward the obligor, Ziff, implied that the ad/list rights were assigned to PC Brand and Hanson.

DECISION AND REMEDY   The state intermediate appellate court affirmed the lower court's decision on this issue. The appellate court remanded the case, however, for a new trial on the amount of the damages, reasoning that some parts of the award "were not within the reasonable contemplation of the parties."

THE SOCIAL DIMENSION   *Would the assignments in this case have been valid if Gold had not notified Ziff?*

Delegations

Delegation   The transfer of a contractual duty to a third party.

Just as a party can transfer rights through an assignment, a party can also transfer duties. The transfer of contractual *duties* to a third party is known as a **delegation.** Normally, a delegation of duties does not relieve the party making the delegation (the *delegator*) of the obligation to perform in the event that the party to whom the duty has been delegated (the *delegatee*) fails to perform. No special form is required to create a valid delegation of duties. As long as the delegator expresses an intention to make the delegation, it is effective—the delegator need not even use the word *delegate.*

As a general rule, any duty can be delegated. Delegation is prohibited, however, in the following circumstances:

1. When special trust has been placed in the obligor (the person contractually obligated to perform).
2. When performance depends on the personal skill or talents of the obligor.
3. When performance by a third party will vary materially from that expected by the *obligee* (the one to whom performance is owed) under the contract.
4. When the contract expressly prohibits delegation.

If a delegation of duties is enforceable, the obligee must accept performance from the delegatee. The obligee can legally refuse performance from the delegatee only if the duty is one that cannot be delegated.

As mentioned, a valid delegation of duties does not relieve the delegator of obligations under the contract. Thus, if the delegatee fails to perform, the delegator is still liable to the obligee.

Third Party Beneficiaries

Third Party Beneficiary   One for whose benefit a promise is made in a contract but who is not a party to the contract.

Intended Beneficiary   A third party for whose benefit a contract is formed and who can sue the promisor if the contract is breached.

Incidental Beneficiary   A third party who incidentally benefits from a contract but whose benefit was not the reason the contract was formed.

Another exception to the doctrine of privity of contract occurs when the original parties to the contract intend at the time of contracting that the contract performance directly benefit a third person. In this situation, the third person becomes a **third party beneficiary** of the contract. As an **intended beneficiary** of the contract, the third party has legal rights and can sue the promisor directly for breach of the contract.

The benefit that an **incidental beneficiary** receives from a contract between two parties is unintentional. Because the benefit is unintentional, an incidental beneficiary cannot sue to enforce the contract. **CASE EXAMPLE 12.11** In 2000, spectators at the infamous boxing match in which Mike Tyson was disqualified for biting his opponent's ear sued Tyson and the fight's promoters for a refund on the basis of breach of contract. The spectators claimed that they were third party beneficiaries of the contract between Tyson and the fight's promoters. The court, however, held that the spectators could not sue because they were not in contractual privity with the defendants. Any benefits they received from the contract were incidental to the contract, and according to the court, the spectators got what they paid for: "the right to view whatever event transpired."[8] ●

▶ Performance and Discharge

Discharge The termination of one's obligation under a contract.

Performance The fulfillment of one's duties arising under a contract.

The most common way to **discharge,** or terminate, one's contractual duties is by the **performance** of those duties. For example, a buyer and seller have a contract for the sale of a 2012 Lexus for $42,000. This contract will be discharged on the performance by the parties of their obligations under the contract—the buyer's payment of $42,000 to the seller and the seller's transfer of possession of the Lexus to the buyer.

The duty to perform under a contract may be *conditioned* on the occurrence or nonoccurrence of a certain event, or the duty may be *absolute*. In this section, we look at conditions of performance and the degree of performance required. We then examine some other ways in which a contract can be discharged, including discharge by agreement of the parties and discharge by operation of law.

Conditions of Performance

In most contracts, promises of performance are not expressly conditioned or qualified. Instead, they are *absolute promises*. They must be performed, or the parties promising the acts will be in breach of contract. **EXAMPLE 12.12** JoAnne contracts to sell Alfonso a painting for $10,000. The parties' promises are unconditional: JoAnne's transfer of the painting to Alfonso and Alfonso's payment of $10,000 to JoAnne. The payment does not have to be made if the painting is not transferred. ●

Condition A qualification, provision, or clause in a contractual agreement. The occurrence or nonoccurrence of the condition creates, suspends, or terminates the obligations of the contracting parties.

In some situations, however, contractual promises are conditioned. A **condition** is a possible future event, the occurrence or nonoccurrence of which will trigger the performance of a legal obligation or terminate an existing obligation under a contract. If the condition is not satisfied, the obligations of the parties are discharged. **EXAMPLE 12.13** Restoration Motors offers to buy Charlie's 1960 Cadillac limousine only if an expert appraiser estimates that it can be restored for less than a certain price. Thus, the parties' obligations are conditioned on the outcome of the appraisal. If the condition is not satisfied—that is, if the appraiser deems the cost to be above that price—their obligations are discharged. ●

Discharge by Performance

Tender A timely offer or expression of willingness to pay a debt or perform an obligation.

The great majority of contracts are discharged by performance. The contract comes to an end when both parties fulfill their respective duties by performing the acts they have promised. Performance can also be accomplished by tender. **Tender** is an unconditional offer to perform by a person who is ready, willing, and able to do so. Therefore, a seller who places goods at the disposal of a buyer has tendered delivery and can demand payment. A buyer who offers to pay for goods has tendered payment and can demand delivery of the goods. Once performance has been tendered,

---

8. *Castillo v. Tyson,* 268 A.D.2d 336, 701 N.Y.S.2d 423 (Sup.Ct.App.Div. 2000).

the party making the tender has done everything possible to carry out the terms of the contract. If the other party then refuses to perform, the party making the tender can sue for breach of contract.

There are two basic types of performance—*complete performance* and *substantial performance*. In addition, a contract may stipulate that performance must meet the personal satisfaction of either the contracting party or a third party. Such a provision must be considered in determining whether the performance rendered satisfies the contract.

COMPLETE PERFORMANCE

When a party performs exactly as agreed, there is no question as to whether the contract has been performed. When a party's performance is perfect, it is said to be complete.

Normally, conditions expressly stated in a contract must be fully satisfied for complete performance to take place. For example, most construction contracts require the builder to meet certain specifications. If the specifications are conditions, complete performance is required to avoid *material breach* (see the facing page). If the conditions are met, the other party to the contract must then fulfill her or his obligation to pay the builder. If the specifications are not conditions and if the builder, without the other party's permission, fails to comply with the specifications, performance is not complete. What effect does such a failure have on the other party's obligation to pay? The answer is part of the doctrine of substantial performance.

SUBSTANTIAL PERFORMANCE

A party who in good faith performs substantially all of the terms of a contract can enforce the contract against the other party under the doctrine of substantial performance. Note that good faith is required. Intentionally failing to comply with the terms is a breach of the contract.

To qualify as substantial performance, the performance must not vary greatly from the performance promised in the contract, and it must create substantially the same benefits as those promised in the contract. If the omission, variance, or defect in performance is unimportant and can easily be compensated for by awarding damages, a court is likely to hold that the contract has been substantially performed.

EXAMPLE 12.14   A couple contracts with a construction company to build a house. The contract specifies that Brand X plasterboard be used for the walls. The builder cannot obtain Brand X plasterboard, and the buyers are on holiday in the mountains of Peru and unreachable. The builder decides to install Brand Y instead, which he knows is identical in quality and durability to Brand X plasterboard. All other aspects of construction conform to the contract. In this situation, a court will likely hold that the builder has substantially performed his end of the bargain, and therefore the couple will be obligated to pay the builder. The court might award the couple damages for the use of a different brand of plasterboard, but the couple would still have to pay the contractor the contract price, less the amount of damages. ●

Courts decide whether the performance was substantial on a case-by-case basis, examining all of the facts of the particular situation. If performance is substantial, the other party's duty to perform remains absolute (except that the party can sue for damages due to the minor deviation).

CASE EXAMPLE 12.15   Wisconsin Electric Power Company (WEPCO) contracted with Union Pacific Railroad to transport coal to WEPCO from mines in Colorado. The contract required WEPCO to notify Union Pacific monthly of how many tons of coal (below a certain maximum) it wanted to have shipped the next month. Union Pacific was to make "good faith reasonable efforts" to meet the schedule. The contract also required WEPCO to supply the railcars. When WEPCO did not supply the railcars,

LEARNING OBJECTIVE 3   **What is substantial performance?**

Union Pacific used its own railcars and delivered 84 percent of the requested coal. A federal appellate court held that in this situation, the delivery of 84 percent of the contracted amount constituted substantial performance.[9] ●

PERFORMANCE TO THE SATISFACTION OF ANOTHER   Contracts often state that completed work must personally satisfy one of the parties or a third person. The question is whether this satisfaction becomes a **condition precedent**, requiring actual personal satisfaction or approval for discharge, or whether the test of satisfaction is performance that would satisfy a *reasonable person* (substantial performance).

When the subject matter of the contract is personal, a contract to be performed to the satisfaction of one of the parties is conditioned, and performance must actually satisfy that party. For example, contracts for portraits, works of art, and tailoring are considered personal. Therefore, only the personal satisfaction of the party fulfills the condition—unless a court finds the party is expressing dissatisfaction just to avoid payment or otherwise is not acting in good faith.

Most other contracts need to be performed only to the satisfaction of a reasonable person unless they *expressly state otherwise.* When such contracts require performance to the satisfaction of a third party (for example, "to the satisfaction of Robert Ames, the supervising engineer"), the courts are divided. A majority of courts require the work to be satisfactory to a reasonable person, but some courts hold that the personal satisfaction of the third party designated in the contract (Robert Ames, in this example) must be met. Again, the personal judgment must be made honestly, or the condition will be excused.

MATERIAL BREACH OF CONTRACT   A **breach of contract** is the nonperformance of a contractual duty. The breach is *material* when performance is not at least substantial. If there is a material breach, then the nonbreaching party is excused from the performance of contractual duties and has a cause of action to sue for damages resulting from the breach. If the breach is *minor* (not material), the nonbreaching party's duty to perform can sometimes be suspended until the breach has been remedied, but the duty to perform is not entirely excused. Once the minor breach has been corrected, the nonbreaching party must resume performance of the contractual obligations undertaken.

Any breach entitles the nonbreaching party to sue for damages, but only a material breach discharges the nonbreaching party from the contract. The policy underlying these rules allows contracts to go forward when only minor problems occur but allows them to be terminated if major difficulties arise.

Condition Precedent   In a contractual agreement, a condition that must be met before a party's promise becomes absolute.

Breach of Contract   The failure, without legal excuse, of a promisor to perform the obligations of a contract.

Ethical Issue ⚖

Is it a material breach for a hospital to accept a donation and then refuse to honor a part of its commitment under the contract? Country singer Garth Brooks was born in Yukon, Oklahoma. Since becoming famous, he has made generous contributions to charities in that town. When his mother, Colleen Brooks, died, he donated $500,000 to Integris Rural Health, Inc. The intention of the donation was that it would be used to build a new women's health center in Yukon, which would be named in memory of his mother. Several years passed after Brooks had made the donation, but the health center was not built. Integris claimed that it intended to do something to honor Colleen Brooks but insisted that it had never promised to build a new health center. When Integris refused to return the $500,000, Garth Brooks sued for breach of contract.

Ethical Issue **Continues next page** ➡

9. *Wisconsin Electric Power Co. v. Union Pacific Railroad Co.,* 557 F.3d 504 (7th Cir. 2009).

Was the hospital's failure to build a women's health center and name it after Brooks's mother a material breach of the contract? A jury thought so. In January 2012, a jury in Rogers County, Oklahoma, awarded Brooks $500,000 in actual damages for material breach of contract. The jury also awarded Brooks another $500,000 because it found the hospital guilty of reckless disregard and intentionally acting with malice toward others.

ANTICIPATORY REPUDIATION OF A CONTRACT   Before either party to a contract has a duty to perform, one of the parties may refuse to perform her or his contractual obligations. This is called **anticipatory repudiation.** When anticipatory repudiation occurs, it is treated as a material breach of contract, and the nonbreaching party is permitted to bring an action for damages immediately, even though the scheduled time for performance under the contract may still be in the future. Until the non-breaching party treats this early repudiation as a breach, however, the breaching party can retract the anticipatory repudiation by proper notice and restore the parties to their original obligations.

An anticipatory repudiation is treated as a present, material breach for two reasons. First, the nonbreaching party should not be required to remain ready and willing to perform when the other party has already repudiated the contract. Second, the nonbreaching party should have the opportunity to seek a similar contract elsewhere and may have the duty to do so to minimize his or her loss.

Quite often, an anticipatory repudiation occurs when market prices change significantly, making performance of the contract extremely unfavorable to one of the parties.

EXAMPLE 12.16   Shasta Manufacturing Company contracts to manufacture and sell 100,000 personal computers to New Age, Inc., a computer retailer with one hundred outlet stores. Delivery is to be made two months from the date of the contract. One month later, three suppliers of computer parts raise their prices to Shasta. Because of these higher prices, Shasta stands to lose $500,000 if it sells the computers to New Age at the contract price. Shasta writes to New Age, stating that it cannot deliver the 100,000 computers at the agreed-on contract price. Even though you might sympathize with Shasta, its letter is an anticipatory repudiation of the contract, allowing New Age the option of treating the repudiation as a material breach and proceeding immediately to pursue remedies, even though the contract delivery date is still a month away. ●

Discharge by Agreement of the Parties

Any contract can be discharged by agreement of the parties. The agreement can be contained in the original contract, or the parties can form a new contract for the express purpose of discharging the original contract.

DISCHARGE BY MUTUAL RESCISSION   *Rescission* is the process by which a contract is canceled or terminated and the parties are returned to the positions they occupied before forming it. For **mutual rescission** to take place, the parties must make another agreement that also satisfies the legal requirements for a contract: an offer, an acceptance, and consideration. Ordinarily, if the parties agree to rescind the original contract, their promises not to perform the acts stipulated in the original contract will be legal consideration for the second contract (the rescission).

Oral agreements to rescind *executory contracts* (in which neither party has performed) generally are enforceable, even if the original agreement was in writing. Under the Uniform Commercial Code, however, an agreement rescinding a contract for the sale of goods, regardless of price, must be in writing if the contract requires a

Anticipatory Repudiation   An assertion or action by a party indicating that he or she will not perform an obligation that the party is contractually obligated to perform at a future time.

REMEMBER   The risks that prices will fluctuate and values will change are ordinary business risks for which the law normally does not provide relief.

Mutual Rescission   An agreement between the parties to cancel their contract, releasing the parties from further obligations under the contract.

written rescission. Also, agreements to rescind contracts involving transfers of realty must be in writing.

When one party has fully performed, an agreement to cancel the original contract normally will not be enforceable. Because the performing party has received no consideration for the promise to call off the original bargain, additional consideration is necessary.

DISCHARGE BY NOVATION   A contractual obligation may also be discharged through novation. A **novation** occurs when both of the parties to a contract agree to substitute a third party for one of the original parties. The requirements of a novation are as follows:

Novation The substitution, by agreement, of a new contract for an old one, with the rights under the old one being terminated.

1. A previous valid obligation.
2. An agreement by all the parties to a new contract.
3. The extinguishing of the old obligation (discharge of the prior party).
4. A new, valid contract.

EXAMPLE 12.17   Union Corporation contracts to sell its pharmaceutical division to British Pharmaceuticals, Ltd. Before the transfer is completed, Union, British Pharmaceuticals, and a third company, Otis Chemicals, execute a new agreement to transfer all of British Pharmaceuticals' rights and duties in the transaction to Otis Chemicals. As long as the new contract is supported by consideration, the novation will discharge the original contract (between Union and British Pharmaceuticals) and replace it with the new contract (between Union and Otis Chemicals). ●

A novation expressly or impliedly revokes and discharges a prior contract. The parties involved may expressly state in the new contract that the old contract is now discharged. If the parties do not expressly discharge the old contract, it will be impliedly discharged if the new contract's terms are inconsistent with the old contract's terms.

DISCHARGE BY ACCORD AND SATISFACTION   For a contract to be discharged by **accord and satisfaction,** the parties must agree to accept performance that is different from the performance originally promised. An *accord* is a contract to perform some act to satisfy an existing contractual duty. The duty has not yet been discharged. A *satisfaction* is the performance of the accord agreement. An accord and its satisfaction discharge the original contractual obligation.

Accord and Satisfaction An agreement and payment (or other performance) between two parties, one of whom has a right of action against the other.

Once the accord has been made, the original obligation is merely suspended. The obligor (the one owing the obligation) can discharge the obligation by performing either the obligation agreed to in the accord or the original obligation. If the obligor refuses to perform the accord, the obligee (the one to whom performance is owed) can bring action on the original obligation or seek a decree compelling specific performance on the accord.

EXAMPLE 12.18   Frazer obtains a judgment against Ling for $8,000. Later, both parties agree that the judgment can be satisfied by Ling's transfer of his automobile to Frazer. This agreement to accept the auto in lieu of $8,000 is the accord. If Ling transfers the car to Frazer, the accord is fully performed, and the debt is discharged. If Ling refuses to transfer the car, the accord is breached. Because the original obligation is merely suspended, Frazer can sue Ling to enforce the original judgment for $8,000 or bring an action for breach of the accord. ●

Discharge by Operation of Law

Under certain circumstances, contractual duties may be discharged by operation of law. These circumstances include material alteration of the contract, the running of the statute of limitations, bankruptcy, and the impossibility or impracticability of performance.

MATERIAL ALTERATION   To discourage parties from altering written contracts, the law operates to allow an innocent party to be discharged when the other party has materially altered a written contract without consent. For example, contract terms such as quantity or price might be changed without the knowledge or consent of all parties. If so, the party who was not involved in the alteration can treat the contract as discharged or terminated.

STATUTES OF LIMITATIONS   Statutes of limitations restrict the period during which a party can sue on a particular cause of action. After the applicable limitations period has passed, a suit can no longer be brought. For instance, the limitations period for bringing suits for breach of oral contracts is usually two to three years. For written contracts, it is four to five years, and for recovery of amounts awarded in judgments, ten to twenty years, depending on state law. Suits for breach of a contract for the sale of goods generally must be brought within four years after the cause of action has accrued. By their original agreement, the parties can reduce this four-year period to not less than one year, but they cannot agree to extend it.

BANKRUPTCY   A proceeding in bankruptcy attempts to allocate the assets a debtor owns to creditors in a fair and equitable fashion. Once the assets have been allocated, the debtor receives a *discharge in bankruptcy*. A discharge in bankruptcy will ordinarily bar creditors from enforcing most of their contracts with the debtor. Partial payment of a debt *after* discharge in bankruptcy will not revive the debt. (Bankruptcy will be discussed in detail in Chapter 14.)

IMPOSSIBILITY OR IMPRACTICABILITY OF PERFORMANCE   After a contract has been made, performance may become impossible in an objective sense. This is known as **impossibility of performance** and may discharge a contract.

Objective Impossibility of Performance. *Objective impossibility* ("It can't be done") must be distinguished from *subjective impossibility* ("I'm sorry, I simply can't do it"). Two examples of subjective impossibility are the inability to deliver goods on time because of a freight car shortage and the inability to make payment on time because the bank is closed. In effect, the party in each of these situations is saying, "It is impossible for me to perform," not "It is impossible for anyone to perform." Accordingly, such excuses do not discharge a contract, and the nonperforming party is normally held in breach of contract. Three basic types of situations, however, generally qualify as grounds for the discharge of contractual obligations based on impossibility of performance:[10]

1. *When one of the parties to a personal contract dies or becomes incapacitated before performance.* **EXAMPLE 12.19**   Fred, a famous dancer, contracts with Ethereal Dancing Guild to play a leading role in its new ballet. Before the ballet can be performed, Fred becomes ill and dies. His personal performance was essential to the completion of the contract. Thus, his death discharges the contract and his estate's liability for his nonperformance. ●

2. *When the specific subject matter of the contract is destroyed.* **EXAMPLE 12.20**   A-1 Farm Equipment agrees to sell Gudgel the green tractor on its lot and promises to have it ready for Gudgel to pick up on Saturday. On Friday night, however, a truck veers off the nearby highway and smashes into the tractor, destroying it beyond

"Law is a practical matter."

Roscoe Pound, 1870–1964
(American jurist)

Impossibility of Performance   A doctrine under which a party to a contract is relieved of his or her duty to perform when performance becomes objectively impossible or totally impracticable (through no fault of either party).

---

10. *Restatement (Second) of Contracts*, Sections 262–266; and UCC 2–615.

repair. Because the contract was for this specific tractor, A-1's performance is rendered impossible owing to the accident. •

3. *When a change in law renders performance illegal.* **EXAMPLE 12.21**   A contract to build an apartment building becomes impossible to perform when the zoning laws are changed to prohibit the construction of residential rental property at the planned location. •

Temporary Impossibility. An occurrence or event that makes performance temporarily impossible operates to suspend performance until the impossibility ceases. Then, ordinarily, the parties must perform the contract as originally planned. If, however, the lapse of time and the change in circumstances surrounding the contract make it substantially more burdensome for the parties to perform the promised acts, the contract is discharged.

For instance, actor Gene Autry was drafted into the U.S. Army in 1942. Being drafted rendered his contract with a movie production company temporarily impossible to perform, and it was suspended until the end of World War II. When Autry got out of the army, the purchasing power of the dollar had declined so much that performance of the contract would have been substantially burdensome to him. Therefore, the contract was discharged.[11]

CASE EXAMPLE 12.22 On August 22, 2005, Keefe Hurwitz contracted to sell his home in Madisonville, Louisiana, to Wesley and Gwendolyn Payne for a price of $241,500. On August 26—just four days after the parties signed the contract— Hurricane Katrina made landfall and caused extensive property damage to the house. The cost of repairs was estimated at $60,000 and Hurwitz would have to make the repairs before the *closing date* (see Chapter 15). Hurwitz did not have the funds and refused to pay $60,000 for the repairs only to sell the property to the Paynes for the previously agreed-on price of $241,500. The Paynes filed a lawsuit to enforce the contract. Hurwitz claimed that Hurricane Katrina had made it impossible for him to perform and had discharged his duties under the contract. The court, however, ruled that Hurricane Katrina had caused only a temporary impossibility. Hurwitz was required to pay for the necessary repairs and to perform the contract as written. In other words, he could not obtain a higher purchase price to offset the cost of the repairs.[12] •

Commercial Impracticability. When a supervening event does not render performance objectively impossible, but does make it much more difficult or expensive to perform, the courts may excuse the parties' obligations under the contract. For someone to invoke the doctrine of **commercial impracticability** successfully, however, the anticipated performance must become significantly more difficult or costly than originally contemplated at the time the contract was formed.[13]

In addition, the reason for the added burden of performing must not have been foreseeable. **CASE EXAMPLE 12.23** In one case, the court allowed a party to rescind a contract for the sale of land because of a potential problem with contaminated groundwater under the land. The court found that "the potential for substantial and unbargained-for" liability made contract performance economically impracticable.[14] •

Commercial Impracticability   A doctrine under which a court may excuse the parties from performing a contract when the performance becomes much more difficult or costly due to an event that the parties did not foresee or anticipate at the time the contract was made.

---

11. See *Autry v. Republic Productions,* 30 Cal.2d 144, 180 P.2d 888 (1947).
12. *Payne v. Hurwitz,* 978 So.2d 1000 (La.App. 1st Cir., 2008).
13. *Restatement (Second) of Contracts,* Section 264.
14. *Cape-France Enterprises v. Estate of Peed,* 305 Mont. 513, 29 P.3d 1011 (2001).

See Exhibit 12–2 below for a summary of the ways in which a contract can be discharged.

▶ Damages for Breach of Contract

A breach of contract entitles the nonbreaching party to sue for monetary damages. Damages are designed to compensate a party for harm suffered as a result of another's wrongful act.

In the context of contract law, damages compensate the nonbreaching party for the loss of the bargain, including lost profits. Often, courts say that innocent parties are to be placed in the position they would have occupied had the contract been fully performed. (See this chapter's *Online Developments* feature on the facing page for a discussion of the effect of breaching the terms of use in an online testing service contract.)

Types of Damages

There are basically four broad categories of damages:

1. Compensatory (to cover direct losses and costs).
2. Consequential (to cover indirect and foreseeable losses).
3. Punitive (to punish and deter wrongdoing).
4. Nominal (to recognize wrongdoing when no monetary loss is shown).

LEARNING OBJECTIVE 4 **What is the standard measure of compensatory damages when a contract is breached?**

COMPENSATORY DAMAGES   Damages that compensate the nonbreaching party for the *loss of the bargain* are known as *compensatory damages* (see page 127). These damages compensate the injured party only for damages actually sustained and proved to have arisen directly from the loss of the bargain caused by the breach of contract. They simply replace what was lost because of the wrong or damage. The standard measure of compensatory damages is the difference between the value of the breaching party's promised performance under the contract and the value of her

● *Exhibit* 12–2 **Contract Discharge**

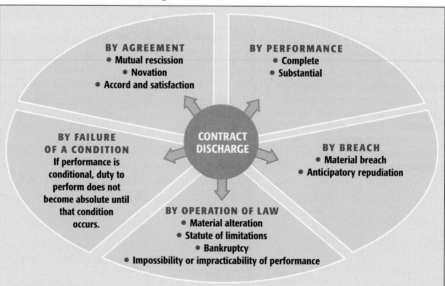

ONLINE DEVELOPMENTS

The Effect of Breaching an Online Testing Service's Terms of Use

Increasingly, online testing services are available for almost any subject. Employers, for example, use online behavioral testing to evaluate the employability of applicants. Schools and counseling services can administer an online test to assess the probability that an adolescent is chemically dependent.

Additionally, California uses an online test to establish a driver-impairment index for those who have been arrested for drunk driving.

Typical Terms and Conditions of Use

Most online testing services have a relatively short list of terms and conditions for using their tests. For instance, most testing services require that fees be paid for each test and for its scoring. Also, the school, employer, or other entity that is using the online test usually must agree that the persons who administer the test are qualified.

In addition, the test user must agree that no decision or diagnosis can be made solely on the basis of the online test results.

Violation of the Online Terms

If the test user violates any of the terms and conditions, the implied contract with the testing service has been breached. The following is a typical provision from an online testing service:

When You Breach This Agreement:

- Each time you administer a test, the agreement granted herein will automatically terminate once the scoring has been provided to you.
- The Company has the right to terminate the authorization granted to you if you breach the terms and conditions of use for any test or if you violate the terms and conditions and obligations under this agreement.
- Once you breach your duties under this agreement, the Company will suffer immediate and irreparable damages.
- You therefore acknowledge that injunctive relief will be appropriate.

FOR CRITICAL ANALYSIS

What possible "immediate and irreparable" damages might an online testing service experience if the test user breaches the contract?

"The duty to keep a contract at common law means a prediction that you must pay damages if you do not keep it—and nothing else."

Oliver Wendell Holmes, Jr., 1841–1935
(Associate justice of the United States Supreme Court, 1902–1932)

or his actual performance. This amount is reduced by any loss that the injured party has avoided, however.

EXAMPLE 12.24 Wilcox contracts to perform certain services exclusively for Hernandez during the month of March for $4,000. Hernandez cancels the contract and is in breach. Wilcox is able to find another job during the month of March but can earn only $3,000. He can sue Hernandez for breach and recover $1,000 as compensatory damages. Wilcox can also recover from Hernandez the amount that he spent to find the other job. ● Expenses that are caused directly by a breach of contract—such as those incurred to obtain performance from another source—are known as *incidental damages.*

The measurement of compensatory damages varies by type of contract. Certain types of contracts deserve special mention. They are contracts for the sale of goods, the sale of land, and construction.

The Sale of Goods. In a contract for the sale of goods, the usual measure of compensatory damages is an amount equal to the difference between the contract price and the market price at the time and place at which the goods were to be delivered or tendered.[15] **EXAMPLE 12.25** Chrylon Corporation contracts to buy ten model UTS network servers from an XEXO Corporation dealer for $8,000 each. The dealer, however, fails to deliver the ten servers to Chrylon. The market price of the servers

---

15. See UCC 2–708 and 2–713.

at the time the buyer learns of the breach is $8,150. Chrylon's measure of damages is therefore $1,500 (10 × $150) plus any incidental damages (expenses) caused by the breach. ● In a situation in which the buyer breaches and the seller has not yet produced the goods, compensatory damages normally equal lost profits on the sale, not the difference between the contract price and the market price.

The Sale of Land. Ordinarily, because each parcel of land is unique, the remedy for a seller's breach of a contract for a sale of real estate is specific performance—that is, the buyer is awarded the parcel of property for which she or he bargained. When this remedy is unavailable (for example, when the seller has sold the property to someone else), or when the buyer is the breaching party, the measure of damages is ordinarily the same as in contracts for the sale of goods—that is, the difference between the contract price and the market price of the land. The majority of states follow this rule.

Construction Contracts. The measure of damages in a building or construction contract varies depending on which party breaches and when the breach occurs. If the owner breaches *before performance has begun,* the contractor can recover only the profits that would have been made on the contract—that is, the total contract price less the cost of materials and labor. If the owner breaches *during performance,* the contractor can recover the profits, plus the costs incurred in partially constructing the building. If the owner breaches *after the construction has been completed,* the contractor can recover the entire contract price, plus interest.

When the construction contractor breaches the contract—either by failing to undertake construction or by stopping work partway through the project—the measure of damages is the cost of completion, which includes reasonable compensation for any delay in performance. If the contractor finishes late, the measure of damages is the loss of use.

How should a court rule when the performance of both parties—the construction contractor and the owner—falls short of what their contract required? That was the issue in the following case.

Case 12.3 **Jamison Well Drilling, Inc. v. Pfeifer**

Court of Appeals of Ohio, Third District, 2011 Ohio 521 (2011).

BACKGROUND AND FACTS   Jamison Well Drilling, Inc., contracted to drill a water well for Ed Pfeifer in Crawford County, Ohio. Pfeifer agreed to pay Jamison $4,130 for the labor and supplies. Jamison drilled the well and installed a storage tank. The Ohio Department of Health requires that a well be lined with a minimum of twenty-five vertical feet of casing, but Jamison installed only eleven feet of casing in the drilled well. The county health department later tested the water in the well for bacteria and repeatedly found that the levels were too high. The state health department investigated and discovered that the well's casing did not comply with its requirements. The department ordered that the well be abandoned and sealed. Pfeifer used the storage tank but paid Jamison nothing. Jamison filed a suit in an Ohio state court against Pfeifer to recover the contract price

and other costs. The court entered a judgment for Jamison for $970 for the storage tank. Jamison appealed.

IN THE WORDS OF THE COURT . . .
WILLAMOWSKI, J. [Judge]
           * * * *

The parties in this case entered into a contract * * * in which the Plaintiff was to drill a well for the Defendant for Four Thousand One Hundred Thirty and 00/100 Dollars ($4,130.00). There were additional charges and discounts applied to this figure which resulted in the Plaintiff seeking Four Thousand Nine Hundred Thirty-three and 00/100 Dollars ($4,933.00).

Evidence presented at the hearing indicated that the Ohio Department of Health determined that the well was not in compliance

Case 12.3–Continued

with the State law and must be sealed. Due to this fact, there is sufficient evidence to indicate that the Plaintiff is not entitled to the full contract price.

Despite not being entitled to a full contract price, the Plaintiff installed certain material on the Defendant's property. A review of "Exhibit B" (an invoice provided to the Defendant by the Plaintiff) reveals that a 400-gallon tank was installed by the Plaintiff. The cost of this tank was Nine Hundred Seventy and 00/100 Dollars ($970.00). * * * *While the Plaintiff was not entitled to his full contract price, it would be unfair to allow the Defendant to keep the tank without paying for it* * * *.* [Emphasis added.]

Since Jamison's actions caused the well to be in noncompliance * * *, Jamison is responsible for the well having to be abandoned and sealed. Although Pfeifer assumed the risk that the well would be unusable due to low production of water, he contracted for a well that would comply with all statutory and administrative requirements. This well had to be abandoned because it did not comply with Ohio law. There was no evidence presented that Pfeifer assumed the risk that the well would have to be abandoned due to noncompliance. Thus,

Jamison is not entitled to recover for the labor and materials as set forth in the contract as the contract was not completed as intended. [Emphasis added.]

However, * * * Jamison should be permitted to recover the cost of the storage tank which Pfeifer was able to use. The value of the tank was set forth in Exhibit B which was admitted into evidence. Pfeifer testified that he was using the tank. * * * Therefore, the trial court did not abuse its discretion in reaching its decision.

DECISION AND REMEDY A state intermediate appellate court affirmed the lower court's decision. The judgment struck a balance that recognized the completed project had value and the storage tank was functional, but the well was not usable.

WHAT IF THE FACTS WERE DIFFERENT? *Suppose that Pfeifer had paid Jamison for the work before the well was ordered sealed and had later filed a suit to recover for breach of contract. What would have been the measure of damages?*

Consequential Damages Special damages that compensate for a loss that is not direct or immediate.

CONSEQUENTIAL DAMAGES Foreseeable damages that result from a party's breach of contract are referred to as **consequential damages,** or *special damages.* Consequential damages differ from compensatory damages in that they are caused by special circumstances beyond the contract itself. They flow from the consequences, or results, of a breach. When a seller fails to deliver goods, knowing that the buyer is planning to use or resell those goods immediately, consequential damages are awarded for the loss of profits from the planned resale.

EXAMPLE 12.26 Gilmore contracts to have a specific item shipped to her—one that she desperately needs to repair her printing press. In her contract with the shipper, Gilmore states that she must receive the item by Monday or she will not be able to print her paper and will lose $950. If the shipper is late, Gilmore normally can recover the consequential damages caused by the delay (that is, the $950 in losses). •

To recover consequential damages, the breaching party must know (or have reason to know) that special circumstances will cause the nonbreaching party to suffer an additional loss.

NOTE A seller who does not wish to take on the risk of consequential damages can limit the buyer's remedies via contract.

PUNITIVE DAMAGES *Punitive damages* generally are not awarded in an action for breach of contract. Such damages have no legitimate place in contract law because they are, in essence, penalties, and a breach of contract is not unlawful in a criminal sense. A contract is simply a civil relationship between the parties. The law may compensate one party for the loss of the bargain—no more and no less. When a person's actions cause both a breach of contract and a tort, punitive damages may be available. Overall, though, punitive damages are almost never available in contract disputes.

NOMINAL DAMAGES When no actual damage or financial loss results from a breach of contract and only a technical injury is involved, the court may award *nominal damages* to the innocent party. Nominal damages awards are often small, such as one dollar, but they do establish that the defendant acted wrongfully.

Mitigation of Damages

In most situations, when a breach of contract occurs, the innocent injured party is held to a duty to mitigate, or reduce, the damages that he or she suffers. Under this doctrine of **mitigation of damages**, the duty owed depends on the nature of the contract.

In the majority of states, a person whose employment has been wrongfully terminated has a duty to mitigate damages incurred because of the employer's breach of the employment contract. In other words, a wrongfully terminated employee has a duty to take a similar job if it is available. If the employee fails to do this, the damages received will be equivalent to the employee's salary less the income she or he would have received in a similar job obtained by reasonable means. Normally, the employee is under no duty to take a job that is not of the same type and rank.

CASE EXAMPLE 12.27 Harry De La Concha was employed by Fordham University. De La Concha claimed that he had been injured in an altercation with Fordham's director of human resources and filed for workers' compensation benefits. (These benefits are available for on-the-job injuries regardless of fault, as you will read in Chapter 16.) Fordham then fired De La Concha, who sought to be reinstated by arguing that he had been terminated in retaliation for filing a workers' compensation claim. The New York state workers' compensation board held that De La Concha had failed to mitigate his damages because he had not even looked for another job, and a state court affirmed the decision. Because De La Concha had failed to mitigate his damages, any compensation he received would be reduced by the amount he could have obtained from other employment.[16] ●

Some states require a landlord to use reasonable means to find a new tenant if a tenant abandons the premises and fails to pay rent. If an acceptable tenant becomes available, the landlord is required to lease the premises to him or her to mitigate the damages recoverable from the former tenant. The former tenant is still liable for the difference between the amount of the rent under the original lease and the rent received from the new tenant. If the landlord has not taken reasonable steps to find a new tenant, a court will likely reduce any award by the amount of rent the landlord could have received had he or she done so.

Liquidated Damages versus Penalties

A **liquidated damages** provision in a contract specifies that a certain dollar amount is to be paid in the event of a future default or breach of contract. (*Liquidated* means determined, settled, or fixed.) Liquidated damages differ from penalties. A **penalty** specifies a certain amount to be paid in the event of a default or breach of contract and is designed to penalize the breaching party. Liquidated damages provisions normally are enforceable. In contrast, if a court finds that a provision calls for a penalty, the agreement as to the amount will not be enforced, and recovery will be limited to actual damages.[17]

To determine whether a particular provision is for liquidated damages or for a penalty, the court must answer two questions:

1. At the time the contract was formed, was it apparent that damages would be difficult to estimate in the event of a breach?
2. Was the amount set as damages a reasonable estimate and not excessive?

---

16. *De La Concha v. Fordham University,* 814 N.Y.S.2d 320, 28 A.3d 963 (2006).
17. This is also the rule under the UCC. See UCC 2–718(1).

If the answers to both questions are yes, the provision normally will be enforced. If either answer is no, the provision usually will not be enforced. Liquidated damages provisions are frequently used in construction contracts because it is difficult to estimate the amount of damages that would be caused by a delay in completing the work.

EXAMPLE 12.28 Ray Curl is a construction contractor. He enters into a contract with a developer to build a home in a new subdivision. The contract includes a clause that requires Curl to pay $300 for every day he is late in completing the project. This is a liquidated damages provision because it specifies a reasonable amount that Curl must pay to the developer if his performance is late. •

▶ Equitable Remedies

LEARNING OBJECTIVE 5 **What equitable remedies can a court grant, and in what circumstances will a court consider granting them?**

In some situations, damages are an inadequate remedy for a breach of contract. In these cases, the nonbreaching party may ask the court for an equitable remedy. Equitable remedies include rescission and restitution, specific performance, and reformation. Additionally, a court acting in the interests of equity may sometimes step in and impose contractual obligations in an effort to prevent the unjust enrichment of one party at the expense of another (quasi contract).

Rescission and Restitution

As discussed earlier in this chapter, *rescission* is essentially an action to undo, or cancel, a contract—to return nonbreaching parties to the positions that they occupied before the transaction. When fraud, mistake, duress, or failure of consideration is present, rescission is available. Rescission may also be available by statute. The failure of one party to perform under a contract entitles the other party to rescind the contract. The rescinding party must give prompt notice to the breaching party.

Restitution An equitable remedy under which a person is restored to his or her original position before formation of a contract.

To rescind a contract, both parties generally must make **restitution** to each other by returning goods, property, or funds previously conveyed. If the physical property or goods can be returned, they must be. If the property or goods have been consumed, restitution must be made in an equivalent dollar amount.

Essentially, restitution involves the recapture of a benefit conferred on the defendant that has unjustly enriched her or him. **EXAMPLE 12.29** Andrea pays $32,000 to Myles in return for his promise to design a house for her. The next day, Myles calls Andrea and tells her that he has taken a position with a large architectural firm in another state and cannot design the house. Andrea decides to hire another architect that afternoon. Andrea can obtain restitution of $32,000 because Myles has received an unjust benefit of $32,000. •

Restitution may be appropriate when a contract is rescinded, but the right to restitution is not limited to rescission cases. For example, restitution might be available when there has been misconduct by a party in a confidential or other special relationship and sometimes even in criminal cases.

Specific Performance

Specific Performance An equitable remedy requiring exactly the performance that was specified in a contract. Usually, it is granted only when money damages would be an inadequate remedy and the subject matter of the contract is unique (for example, real property).

The equitable remedy of **specific performance** calls for the performance of the act promised in the contract. This remedy is attractive to a nonbreaching party because it provides the exact bargain promised in the contract. It also avoids some of the problems inherent in a suit for damages, such as collecting a judgment and arranging another contract. In addition, the actual performance may be more valuable (to the promisee) than the monetary damages.

Normally, however, specific performance will not be granted unless the party's legal remedy (monetary damages) is inadequate. For this reason, contracts for the sale of goods rarely qualify for specific performance. The legal remedy—monetary damages—is ordinarily adequate in such situations because substantially identical goods can be bought or sold in the market. Only if the goods are unique will a court grant specific performance. For example, paintings, sculptures, or rare books or coins are so unique that monetary damages will not enable a buyer to obtain substantially identical substitutes in the market.

THE SALE OF LAND   A court may grant specific performance to a buyer in an action for a breach of contract involving the sale of land. In this situation, the legal remedy of monetary damages may not compensate the buyer adequately because every parcel of land is unique: the same land in the same location obviously cannot be obtained elsewhere. Only when specific performance is unavailable (such as when the seller has sold the property to someone else) will monetary damages be awarded instead.

CASE EXAMPLE 12.30 Howard Stainbrook entered into a contract to sell Trent Low forty acres of mostly timbered land for $45,000. Low agreed to pay for a survey of the property and other costs in addition to the price. He gave Stainbrook a check for $1,000 to show his intent to fulfill the contract. One month later, Stainbrook died. His son David became the executor of the estate. After he discovered that the timber on the property was worth more than $100,000, David asked Low to withdraw his offer to buy the forty acres. Low refused and filed a suit against David seeking specific performance of the contract. The court found that because Low had substantially performed his obligations under the contract and offered to perform the rest, he was entitled to specific performance.[18] ●

CONTRACTS FOR PERSONAL SERVICES   Personal-service contracts require one party to work personally for another party. Courts normally refuse to grant specific performance of contracts for personal services. This is because to order a party to perform personal services against his or her will amounts to a type of involuntary servitude (slavery), which is contrary to the public policy expressed in the Thirteenth Amendment to the Constitution. Moreover, the courts do not want to monitor contracts for personal services.

EXAMPLE 12.31 If you contract with a brain surgeon to perform brain surgery on you and the surgeon refuses to perform, the court will not compel (and you certainly would not want) the surgeon to perform under these circumstances. There is no way the court can ensure meaningful performance in such a situation. ●

Reformation

Reformation A court-ordered correction of a written contract so that it reflects the true intentions of the parties.

Reformation is an equitable remedy used when the parties have *imperfectly* expressed their agreement in writing. Reformation enables a court to modify, or rewrite, the contract to reflect the parties' true intentions. Courts order reformation most often when fraud or mutual mistake is present. **EXAMPLE 12.32** Carson contracts to buy a forklift from Shelley, but the written contract refers to a crane. Thus, a mutual mistake has occurred, and a court could reform the contract so that the writing conforms to the parties' original intention as to the piece of equipment being sold. ●

Courts frequently reform contracts in two other situations. The first occurs when two parties who have made a binding oral contract agree to put the oral contract in writing but, in doing so, make an error in stating the terms. Usually, the courts allow into evidence the correct terms of the oral contract, thereby reforming the written contract.

---

18. *Stainbrook v. Low,* 842 N.E.2d 386 (Ind.App. 2006).

The second situation occurs when the parties have executed a written covenant not to compete (see Chapter 11). If the covenant not to compete is for a valid and legitimate purpose (such as the sale of a business) but the area or time restraints are unreasonable, some courts will reform the restraints by making them reasonable and will enforce the entire contract as reformed. Other courts, however, will throw out the entire restrictive covenant as illegal.

Exhibit 12–3 below graphically presents the remedies, including reformation, that are available to the nonbreaching party.

Recovery Based on Quasi Contract

Quasi Contract A fictional contract imposed on parties by a court in the interests of fairness and justice.

In some situations, when no actual contract exists, a court may step in to prevent one party from being unjustly enriched at the expense of another party. **Quasi contract** is a legal theory under which an obligation is imposed in the absence of an agreement. It allows the courts to act as if a contract exists when there is no actual contract or agreement between the parties. The courts can also use this theory when the parties entered a contract that is unenforceable for some reason.

Quasi-contractual recovery is often granted when one party has partially performed under a contract that is unenforceable. It provides an alternative to suing for damages and allows the party to recover the reasonable value of the partial performance. **EXAMPLE 12.33** Ericson contracts to build two oil derricks for Petro Industries. The derricks are to be built over a period of three years, but the parties do not create a written contract. Therefore, the Statute of Frauds will bar the enforcement of the contract. After Ericson completes one derrick, Petro Industries informs him that it will not pay for the derrick. Ericson can sue Petro Industries under the theory of quasi contract. ●

To recover on quasi contract, the party seeking recovery must show the following:

1. The party conferred a benefit on the other party.
2. The party conferred the benefit with the reasonable expectation of being paid.
3. The party did not act as a volunteer in conferring the benefit.
4. The party receiving the benefit would be unjustly enriched by retaining the benefit without paying for it.

▶ Contract Provisions Limiting Remedies

A contract may include provisions stating that no damages can be recovered for certain types of breaches or that damages must be limited to a maximum amount. The contract may also provide that the only remedy for breach is replacement, repair, or

● *Exhibit* **12-3 Remedies for Breach of Contract**

refund of the purchase price. Provisions stating that no damages can be recovered are called *exculpatory clauses*. Provisions that affect the availability of certain remedies are called *limitation-of-liability clauses*.

Whether these contract provisions and clauses will be enforced depends on the type of breach that is excused by the provision. Normally, a provision excluding liability for fraudulent or intentional injury will not be enforced. Likewise, a clause excluding liability for illegal acts or violations of law will not be enforced. A clause excluding liability for negligence may be enforced in certain cases, however. When an exculpatory clause for negligence is contained in a contract made between parties who have roughly equal bargaining positions, the clause usually will be enforced.

Reviewing . . . Contract Performance, Breach, and Remedies

Val's Foods signs a contract to buy 1,500 pounds of basil from Sun Farms, a small organic herb grower, as long as an independent organization inspects and certifies that the crop contains no pesticide or herbicide residue. Val's has a number of contracts with different restaurant chains to supply pesto and intends to use Sun Farms' basil in its pesto to fulfill these contracts. While Sun Farms is preparing to harvest the basil, an unexpected hailstorm destroys half the crop. Sun Farms attempts to purchase additional basil from other farms, but it is late in the season and the price is twice the normal market price. Sun Farms is too small to absorb this cost and immediately notifies Val's that it will not fulfill the contract. Using the information presented in the chapter, answer the following questions.

1. Suppose that the basil does not pass the chemical-residue inspection. Which concept discussed in the chapter might allow Val's to refuse to perform the contract in this situation?
2. Under which legal theory or theories might Sun Farms claim that its obligation under the contract has been discharged by operation of law? Discuss fully.
3. Suppose that Sun Farms contacts every basil grower in the country and buys the last remaining chemical-free basil anywhere. Nevertheless, Sun Farms is able to ship only 1,475 pounds to Val's. Would this fulfill Sun Farms' obligations to Val's? Why or why not?
4. Now suppose that Sun Farms sells its operations to Happy Valley Farms. As a part of the sale, all three parties agree that Happy Valley will provide the basil as stated under the original contract. What is this type of agreement called? Does it discharge the obligations of any of the parties? Explain.

Debate This

The doctrine of commercial impracticability should be abolished.

Linking the Law *to Business Communication*
When E-Mails Become Enforceable Contracts

Most business students must take a course in business communication. These courses cover the planning and preparation of oral and written communications, including electronic messages.

Indeed, e-mails have become so pervasive that an increasing number of contracts are created via e-mail.

Voluntary Consent and Mistakes

One defense to contract enforceability is a lack of voluntary consent, sometimes due to mistakes. Often, when a mistake is unilateral, the courts will still enforce the contract. Consequently, your e-mail communications can result in an enforceable contract even if you make a typographic error in, say, a dollar amount. If you are making an offer or an acceptance via e-mail, you should treat that communication as carefully as if you were writing or typing it on a sheet of paper. Today, unfortunately, many individuals in the business world treat e-mails somewhat casually. Remember that you are creating an enforceable contract if you make an offer or an acceptance via e-mail, and reread your e-mails several times before you hit the send button.

The Sufficiency of the Writing

In this chapter, you also learned about the Statute of Frauds. The legal definitions of written memoranda and signatures have changed in our electronic age. Today, an e-mail definitely constitutes a writing. A writing can also be a series of e-mail exchanges between two parties. In other words, five e-mail exchanges taken together may form a single contract. (In the past, before e-mails and faxes, this applied to written communications on pieces of paper that were stapled or clipped together.) If one or more e-mails name the parties, identify the subject matter, and lay out the consideration, a court normally will accept those e-mails as constituting a writing sufficient to satisfy the Statute of Frauds.

The Importance of Clear, Precise E-Mail Language

In addition to typographic errors, casually written e-mails may contain ambiguities and miscommunications. Nevertheless, those e-mails may create an enforceable contract, whether you intended it or not. Therefore, all of your business e-mails should be carefully written.

At a minimum, when you are e-mailing business contacts, you should:

1. **Create a precise and informative subject line.** Rather than saying "we should discuss" or "important information," be specific in the subject line of the e-mail, such as "change delivery date for portable generators."
2. **Repeat the subject within the body of the e-mail message.** In the actual e-mail message, avoid phrases with indefinite antecedents such as "This is . . . ." Good business e-mail communication involves a repetition of most of the subject line. That way, if your recipient skips the subject line, the message will still be clear.
3. **Focus on a limited number of subjects, usually one.** Do not ramble and discuss a variety of topics in your e-mail. If necessary, send e-mails on different topics.
4. **Create e-mails that are just as attractive as if they were written on letterhead.** Obviously, e-mails that have no particular format, no paragraphs, bad grammar, misspellings, and incorrect punctuation create a negative impression. More important, if your language is not precise, you may find that you have created an enforceable contract when you did not intend to do so. At a minimum, use the spelling and grammar checker in your word-processing program.
5. **Proofread your work.** This aspect of e-mail communications is so important that it is worth repeating. Proofreading your e-mails before you hit the send button is the most important step that you can take to avoid contract misinterpretations.

FOR CRITICAL ANALYSIS

Sometimes, in contract disputes, one party produces a printout of an e-mail that supposedly was sent, but the other party contends that it was never received. How can the sender avoid this problem?

Key Terms

▶ Chapter Summary: Contract Performance, Breach, and Remedies

Voluntary Consent (See pages 290–294.)	Lack of voluntary consent can be used as a defense to contract enforceability. Voluntary consent can be lacking in the following four ways:
	 1. *Mistakes*–
	    a. *Unilateral mistakes*–Generally, the party making the mistake is bound by the contract *unless* the other party knows or should have known of the mistake or the mistake is an inadvertent mathematical error–such as an error in addition or subtraction–committed without gross negligence.
	    b. *Bilateral (mutual) mistakes*–When both parties are mistaken about the same material fact, such as identity, either party can avoid the contract. If the mistake concerns value or quality, either party can enforce the contract.
	 2. *Fraudulent misrepresentation*–When fraud occurs, usually the innocent party can enforce or avoid the contract. To obtain damages, the innocent party must have suffered an injury.
	 3. *Undue influence*–Undue influence arises from special relationships in which one party can greatly influence another party, thus overcoming that party's free will. Usually, the contract is voidable.
	 4. *Duress*–Duress is the use of a threat, such as the threat of violence or serious economic loss, to force a party to enter a contract. The party forced to enter the contract can rescind the contract.

The Statute of Frauds– Writing Requirement (See pages 295–296.)	The Statute of Frauds is another defense to the enforceability of a contract. The following types of contracts fall under the Statute of Frauds and must be in writing to be enforceable: 1. Contracts involving interests in land. 2. Contracts that cannot by their terms be performed within one year from the day after the date of formation. 3. Collateral, or secondary, contracts, such as promises to answer for the debt or duty of another. 4. Promises made in consideration of marriage. 5. Under the UCC, contracts for the sale of goods priced at $500 or more.
Third Party Rights (See pages 296–299.)	1. *Assignments*–An assignment is the transfer of rights under a contract to a third party. The third party to whom the rights are assigned has a right to demand performance from the other original party to the contract. Generally, all rights can be assigned, but there are a few exceptions, such as when a statute prohibits assignment or when the contract calls for personal services. 2. *Delegations*–A delegation is the transfer of duties under a contract to a third party, who then assumes the obligation of performing the contractual duties previously held by the one making the delegation. As a general rule, any duty can be delegated, except in a few situations, such as when the contract expressly prohibits delegation or when performance depends on the personal skills of the original party. 3. *Third party beneficiaries*–A third party beneficiary is one who benefits from a contract between two other parties. If the party was an intended beneficiary, then the third party has legal rights and can sue the promisor directly to enforce the contract. If the contract benefits the third party unintentionally, then the third party cannot sue to enforce the contract.

Performance and Discharge (See pages 299–306.)	1. *Conditions of performance*–Contract obligations are sometimes subject to conditions. A condition is a possible future event, the occurrence or nonoccurrence of which will trigger the performance of a contract obligation or terminate an existing obligation.
	 2. *Discharge by performance*–A contract may be discharged by complete performance or by substantial performance. In some instances, performance must be to the satisfaction of another. Totally inadequate performance constitutes a material breach of contract. An anticipatory repudiation of a contract allows the other party to sue immediately for breach of contract. A condition that must be fulfilled before a party's promise becomes absolute is called a *condition precedent*.
	 3. *Discharge by agreement*–Parties may agree to discharge their contractual obligations in several ways:
	    a. *By mutual rescission*–The parties mutually agree to rescind (cancel) the contract.
	    b. *By novation*–A new party is substituted for one of the primary parties to a contract.
	    c. *By accord and satisfaction*–The parties agree to render and accept performance different from that on which they originally agreed.

Chapter Summary: Contract Performance, Breach, and Remedies, Continued

Performance and Discharge—Continued	4. *Discharge by operation of law*—Parties' obligations under contracts may be discharged by operation of law owing to one of the following: a. Material alteration. b. Statutes of limitations. c. Bankruptcy. d. Impossibility or impracticability of performance.
Damages for Breach of Contract (See pages 306–311.)	Damages are the legal remedy designed to compensate the nonbreaching party for the loss of the bargain. By awarding monetary damages, the court tries to place the parties in the positions that they would have occupied had the contract been fully performed. 1. *Compensatory damages*—Damages that compensate the nonbreaching party for injuries actually sustained and proved to have arisen directly from the loss of the bargain resulting from the breach of contract. a. In breached contracts for the sale of goods, the usual measure of compensatory damages is the difference between the contract price and the market price. b. In breached contracts for the sale of land, the measure of damages is ordinarily the same as in contracts for the sale of goods. 2. *Consequential damages*—Damages resulting from special circumstances beyond the contract itself—the damages flow only from the consequences of a breach. For a party to recover consequential damages, the damages must be the foreseeable result of a breach of contract, and the breaching party must have known at the time the contract was formed that special circumstances existed that would cause the nonbreaching party to incur additional loss on breach of the contract. Also called *special damages.* 3. *Punitive damages*—Damages awarded to punish the breaching party. These damages are rare. 4. *Nominal damages*—Damages small in amount (such as one dollar) that are awarded when a breach has occurred but no actual injury has been suffered. 5. *Mitigation of damages*—The nonbreaching party frequently has a duty to *mitigate* (lessen or reduce) the damages incurred as a result of the contract's breach. 6. *Liquidated damages*—Damages that may be specified in a contract as the amount to be paid to the nonbreaching party in the event the contract is breached in the future. Clauses providing for liquidated damages are enforced if the damages were difficult to estimate at the time the contract was formed and if the amount stipulated is reasonable. If the amount is construed to be a penalty, the clause will not be enforced.
Equitable Remedies (See pages 311–313.)	1. *Rescission*—A remedy whereby a contract is canceled and the parties are restored to the positions that they occupied prior to the transaction. Available when fraud, a mistake, duress, or failure of consideration is present. The rescinding party must give prompt notice of the rescission to the breaching party. 2. *Restitution*—When a contract is rescinded, both parties must make restitution to each other by returning the goods, property, or funds previously conveyed. Restitution prevents the unjust enrichment of the parties. 3. *Specific performance*—An equitable remedy calling for the performance of the act promised in the contract. This remedy is available only in special situations—such as those involving contracts for the sale of unique goods or land—in which monetary damages would be an inadequate remedy. Specific performance is not available as a remedy in breached contracts for personal services. 4. *Reformation*—An equitable remedy allowing a contract to be "reformed," or rewritten, to reflect the parties' true intentions. Available when an agreement is imperfectly expressed in writing. 5. *Recovery based on quasi contract*—An equitable theory imposed by the courts to prevent unjust enrichment in a situation in which no enforceable contract exists. The party seeking recovery must show the following: a. A benefit was conferred on the other party.

(Continued)

Chapter Summary: Contract Performance, Breach, and Remedies, *Continued*

Equitable Remedies— Continued	b. The party conferring the benefit did so with the expectation of being paid. c. The benefit was not volunteered. d. Retaining the benefit without paying for it would result in the unjust enrichment of the party receiving the benefit.
Contract Provisions Limiting Remedies (See pages 313–314.)	A contract may provide that no damages (or only a limited amount of damages) can be recovered in the event the contract is breached. Clauses excluding liability for fraudulent or intentional injury or for illegal acts cannot be enforced. Clauses excluding liability for negligence may be enforced if both parties hold roughly equal bargaining power.

ExamPrep

ISSUE SPOTTERS

—Check your answers to these questions against the answers provided in Appendix D at the end of this text.

1. Ira, a famous and wealthy musician, dies. Jen, his widow, sells their farm to Kris, who asks what should be done with all the "junk" on the property. Jen says that Kris can do whatever he wants with it. Unknown to Jen or Kris, in a cabinet in the house are the master tapes for an unreleased album. Can Kris keep the tapes? Why or why not? **(See page 291.)**

2. Ready Foods contracts to buy two hundred carloads of frozen pizzas from Speedy Distributors. Before Ready or Speedy starts performing, can either party call off the deal? What if Speedy has already shipped the pizzas? Explain your answers. **(See page 302.)**

BEFORE THE TEST

Go to **www.cengagebrain.com**, enter the ISBN 9781133586548, and click on "Find" to locate this textbook's Web site. Then click on "Access Now" under "Study Tools," and select Chapter 12 at the top. There, you will find a Practice Quiz that you can take to assess your mastery of the concepts in this chapter. Additionally, you will find Flashcards and a Glossary of important terms, as well as Video Questions (when assigned).

For Review

Answers for the even-numbered questions in this For Review *section can be found in Appendix E at the end of this text.*

1. In what types of situations might voluntary consent to a contract's terms be lacking?
2. What are the elements of fraudulent misrepresentation?
3. What is substantial performance?
4. What is the standard measure of compensatory damages when a contract is breached?
5. What equitable remedies can a court grant, and in what circumstances will a court consider granting them?

Questions and Case Problems

12–1. Substantial Performance. The Caplans own a real estate lot, and they contract with Faithful Construction, Inc., to build a house on it for $360,000. The specifications list "all plumbing bowls and fixtures . . . to be Crane brand." The Caplans leave on vacation, and during their absence Faithful is unable to buy and install Crane plumbing fixtures. Instead, Faithful installs Kohler brand fixtures, an equivalent in the industry. On completion of the building contract, the Caplans inspect the work, discover the substitution, and refuse to accept the house, claiming Faithful has breached the conditions set forth in the specifications. Discuss fully the Caplans' claim.

12–2. Compensatory Damages. Ken owns and operates a famous candy store and makes most of the candy sold in the store. Business is particularly heavy during the Christmas season. Ken contracts with Sweet, Inc., to purchase ten thousand pounds of sugar to be delivered on or before November 15. Ken has informed Sweet that this particular order is to be used for the Christmas season. Because of problems at the refinery, the sugar is not tendered to Ken until December 10. Ken refuses to accept the sugar, saying it is too late. Ken has been unable to purchase the quantity of sugar needed to meet his Christmas orders and has had to turn down numerous regular customers, some of whom have indicated that they will purchase candy elsewhere in the future. What sugar Ken has been able to purchase has cost him 10 cents per pound more than the price contracted for with Sweet. Ken sues Sweet for breach of contract, claiming as damages the higher price paid for sugar from others, lost profits from this year's lost Christmas sales, future lost profits from customers who said that they will stop doing business with him, and punitive damages for failure to meet the contracted delivery date. Sweet claims Ken is limited to compensatory damages only. Discuss who is correct, and why. **(See pages 306–307, and 309.)**

12–3. Question with Sample Answer: Objective Impossibility of Performance. Millie contracted to sell Frank 1,000 bushels of corn to be grown on her farm. Owing to drought conditions during the growing season, Millie's yield was much less than anticipated, and she could deliver only 250 bushels to Frank. Frank accepted the lesser amount but sued Millie for breach of contract. Can Millie defend successfully on the basis of objective impossibility of performance? Explain. **(See page 304.)**

—**For a sample answer to Question 12–3, go to Appendix F at the end of this text.**

12–4. Quasi Contract. Middleton Motors, Inc., a struggling Ford dealership in Madison, Wisconsin, sought managerial and financial assistance from Lindquist Ford, Inc., a successful Ford dealership in Bettendorf, Iowa. While the two dealerships negotiated the terms for the services and a cash infusion, Lindquist sent Craig Miller, its general manager, to assume control of Middleton. After about a year, the parties had not agreed on the terms, Lindquist had not invested any money, Middleton had not made a profit, and Miller was fired without being paid. Lindquist and Miller filed a suit in a federal district court against Middleton based on quasi contract, seeking to recover Miller's pay for his time. What are the requirements to recover on a theory of quasi contract? Which of these requirements is most likely to be disputed in this case? Why? [*Lindquist Ford, Inc. v. Middleton Motors, Inc.,* 557 F.3d 469 (7th Cir. 2009)] **(See page 313.)**

12–5. Mistake. When Steven Simkin divorced Laura Blank, they agreed to split their assets equally. They owned an account with Bernard L. Madoff Investment Securities estimated to be worth $5.4 million. Simkin kept the account and paid Blank more than $6.5 million—including $2.7 million to offset the amount of the funds that they believed were in the account. Later, they learned that the account actually contained no funds due to its manager's fraud. Could their agreement be rescinded on the basis of a mistake? Discuss. [*Simkin v. Blank,* 80 A.D.3d 401, 915 N.Y.S.2d 47 (1 Dept. 2011)] **(See page 291.)**

12–6. Case Problem with Sample Answer: Notice of Assignment. Arnold Kazery was the owner of a hotel leased to George Wilkinson. The lease included renewal options of ten years each. When Arnold transferred his interest in the property to his son, Sam, no one notified Wilkinson. For the next twenty years, Wilkinson paid the rent to Arnold and renewed the lease by notice to Arnold. When Wilkinson wrote to Arnold that he was exercising another option to renew, Sam filed a suit against him, claiming that the lease was void. Did Wilkinson give proper notice to renew? Discuss. [*Kazery v. Wilkinson,* 52 So.3d 1270 (Miss.App. 2011)] **(See page 297.)**

—**For a sample answer to Case Problem 12–6, go to Appendix G at the end of this text.**

12–7. Consequential Damages. After submitting the high bid at a foreclosure sale, David Simard entered a contract to purchase real property in Maryland for $192,000. Simard defaulted (failed to pay) on the contract, so a state court ordered the property to be resold at Simard's expense, as required by state law. The property was then resold for $163,000, but the second purchaser also defaulted on his contract. The court then ordered a second resale, resulting in a final price of $130,000. Assuming that Simard is liable for consequential damages, what is the extent of his liability? Is he liable for losses and expenses related to the first resale? If so, is he also liable for losses and expenses related to the second resale? Why or why not? [*Burson v. Simard,* 35 A.3d 1154 (Md. 2012)] **(See page 309.)**

12–8. In Your Court: Damages. Charles Kloss had worked for Honeywell, Inc., for over fifteen years when Honeywell decided to transfer the employees at its Ballard facility to its Harbour Pointe facility. Honeywell planned to hire a medical person at the Harbour Pointe facility and promised Kloss that if he completed a nursing program and became a registered nurse (RN), the company would hire him for the medical position. When Kloss graduated from his RN program, however, Honeywell did not assign him to a medical position, but instead gave him a job in its maintenance department. Shortly thereafter, Kloss left the company and eventually sued Honeywell for damages (lost wages) resulting from Honeywell's breach of the employment contract. Assume that you are the judge in the trial court hearing this case and answer the following questions: **(See pages 310 and 313.)**

1. One of the issues you will need to decide in this case is whether Kloss, by voluntarily leaving the maintenance job at Honeywell, had failed to mitigate his damages. How will you rule on this issue? Explain your reasoning.

2. Assume that Honeywell's promise to hire Kloss after he completed his nursing program was made orally. Is there any legal theory under which you can enforce the promise?

12–9. **A Question of Ethics: Assignment and Delegation.** *Premier Building & Development, Inc., entered a listing agreement giving Sunset Gold Realty, LLC, the exclusive right to find a tenant for some commercial property. The terms of the listing agreement stated that it was binding on both parties and "their . . . assigns." Premier Building did not own the property at the time, but had the option to purchase it. To secure financing for the project, Premier Building established a new company called Cobblestone Associates. Premier Building then bought the property and conveyed it to Cobblestone the same day. Meanwhile, Sunset Gold found a tenant for the property, and Cobblestone became the landlord Cobblestone acknowl-*

edged its obligation to pay Sunset Gold for finding a tenant, but it later refused to pay Sunset Gold's commission. Sunset Gold then sued Premier Building and Cobblestone for breach of the listing agreement. [Sunset Gold Realty, LLC v. Premier Building & Development, Inc., 36 A.3d 243 (Conn.App.Ct. 2012)] **(See page 296.)**

1. Is Premier Building relieved of its contractual duties if it assigned the contract to Cobblestone? Why or why not?

2. Given that Sunset Gold performed its obligations under the listing agreement, did Cobblestone behave unethically in refusing to pay Sunset Gold's commission? Why or why not?

12–10. **Critical-Thinking Legal Question.** Describe the types of individuals who might be capable of exerting undue influence on others. **(See page 294.)**

Chapter 13

Sales and Leases

> "I am for free commerce with all nations."
>
> —George Washington, 1732–1799
> (First president of the United States, 1789–1797)

Contents

- **The Scope of Articles 2 (Sales) and 2A (Leases)**
- **The Formation of Sales and Lease Contracts**
- **The Performance of Sales and Lease Contracts**
- **Remedies for Breach of Sales and Lease Contracts**
- **Sales and Lease Warranties**

Learning Objectives

The five Learning Objectives below are designed to help improve your understanding of the chapter. After reading this chapter, you should be able to answer the following questions:

1. How do Article 2 and Article 2A of the UCC differ?

2. Under the UCC, if an offeree includes additional or different terms in an acceptance, will a contract result? If so, what happens to these terms?

3. What remedies are available to a seller or lessor when the buyer or lessee breaches the contract?

4. What remedies are available to a buyer or lessee if the seller or lessor breaches the contract?

5. What implied warranties arise under the UCC?

(shock/iStockphoto.com)

The chapter-opening quotation above echoes a sentiment that most Americans believe—free commerce will benefit our nation. This is particularly true with respect to the Uniform Commercial Code (UCC). The UCC facilitates commercial transactions by making the laws governing sales and lease contracts uniform, clearer, simpler, and more readily applicable to the numerous difficulties that can arise during such transactions.

Recall from Chapter 1 that the UCC is one of many uniform (model) acts drafted by the National Conference of Commissioners on Uniform State Laws and submitted to the states for adoption. Once a state legislature has adopted a uniform act, the act becomes statutory law in that state. Thus, when we turn to sales and lease contracts, we move away from common law principles and into the area of statutory law.

This chapter opens with a look at the broad scope of the UCC's Articles 2 and 2A. After examining the formation of sales and lease contracts, we look at the performance required in such contracts and the remedies available if a contract is breached. We also examine the warranties, both express and implied, that can arise in contracts to sell or lease goods.

▶ The Scope of Articles 2 (Sales) and 2A (Leases)

Of all the attempts to produce a uniform body of laws relating to commercial transactions in the United States, none has been as comprehensive or successful as the UCC. The UCC has been adopted in whole or in part by all of the states. (Note, however, that Louisiana has not adopted Articles 2 and 2A.)

Article 2 of the UCC sets forth the requirements for *sales contracts,* as well as the duties and obligations of the parties involved in the sales contract—although the parties can agree to terms different from those stated in the UCC. Article 2A covers similar issues for *lease contracts.* Because of their importance to commercial sales or lease transactions, respectively, we take a closer look at the UCC's Articles 2 and 2A next.

LEARNING OBJECTIVE 1 **How do Article 2 and Article 2A of the UCC differ?**

Article 2—The Sale of Goods

Sales Contract A contract for the sale of goods under which the ownership of goods is transferred from a seller to a buyer for a price.

Article 2 of the UCC governs **sales contracts,** or contracts for the sale of goods. To facilitate commercial transactions, Article 2 modifies some of the common law contract requirements that were discussed in the previous chapters. To the extent that it has not been modified by the UCC, however, the common law of contracts—including the requirements for agreement, consideration, capacity, and legality—also applies to sales contracts.

In general, the rule is that whenever a conflict arises between a common law contract rule and the state statutory law based on the UCC, the UCC controls. In other words, when a UCC provision addresses a certain issue, the UCC rule governs, but when the UCC is silent, the common law governs. The relationship between general contract law and the law governing sales of goods is illustrated in Exhibit 13–1 below. (For a discussion of an issue involving state taxation of sales that occur online, see this chapter's *Online Developments* feature on the facing page.)

● *Exhibit* **13–1** **The Law Governing Contracts**

This exhibit graphically illustrates the relationship between general contract law and statutory law (UCC Articles 2 and 2A) governing contracts for the sale and lease of goods. Sales contracts are not governed exclusively by Article 2 of the UCC but are also governed by general contract law whenever it is relevant and has not been modified by the UCC.

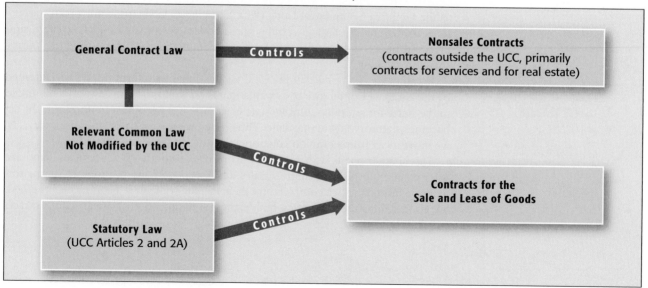

ONLINE DEVELOPMENTS

Local Governments Attempt to Tax Online Travel Companies

A battle is raging across the United States between state and local governments and online retailers. The online retailers claim that because they do not have a physical presence in a state, they should not have to collect state and local taxes for the goods and services they sell. Although most states have laws that require their residents to report online purchases and pay taxes on them (so-called use taxes), few U.S. consumers comply with these laws.

Local Governments Sue Online Travel Companies

Travelocity, Priceline.com, Hotels.com, and Orbitz.com are online travel companies (OTCs) that offer, among other things, hotel booking services. By 2013, more than twenty cities—including Atlanta, Charleston, Philadelphia, and San Antonio—had filed suits claiming that the OTCs owed taxes on hotel reservations that they had booked. All of the cities involved in the suits impose a hotel occupancy tax, which is essentially a sales tax.

The issue is not whether the OTCs should pay the tax but rather how it should be assessed and collected. OTCs typically purchase blocks of hotel rooms at a wholesale rate and then resell the rooms to customers at a marked-up resale rate, keeping the difference as profit. The OTCs forward to the hotels an amount intended to cover the hotel occupancy tax (sales tax) based on the wholesale prices of the rooms sold. The hotels then remit the tax on the rooms sold by the OTCs to the city taxing authority.

The cities claim, however, that the OTCs should assess the occupancy tax rates on the retail prices that they charge, rather than on the wholesale prices of the rooms. Of course, the retail prices are higher, so the cities would collect more tax if the retail price is used as the base. The cities also want the OTCs to register with the local jurisdictions and to collect and remit the required taxes directly.

The Cities Are Losing in Court

When these lawsuits were first brought a few years ago, city governments generally obtained favorable rulings, both in federal district courts[a] and in state courts.[b] In contrast, when some of these suits were retried or reviewed by higher courts, the OTCs prevailed. In 2012, for example, the city of Goodlettsville, Tennessee, lost its continuing case against Priceline.com and nine other OTCs. In siding with the OTCs, the court said, "If the Tennessee legislature intends to permit its political subdivisions to tax the retail rate paid by the consumers to the OTCs for hotel bookings, the legislature may do so through appropriate statutory language."[c]

In contrast, when the South Carolina Department of Revenue sued Travelscape, LLC, another OTC, the Supreme Court of South Carolina held that the OTC had to remit taxes based on the retail price of the hotel rooms sold.[d] The South Carolina decision reflected a minority opinion, however. As of early 2012, the OTCs had prevailed in fifteen of nineteen cases nationwide.

FOR CRITICAL ANALYSIS

What are possible benefits if cities and states do not *impose a sales tax on the difference between the wholesale price of rooms and the retail price of rooms sold by OTCs?*

---

a. See, for example, *City of Goodlettsville v. Priceline.com, Inc.,* 605 F.Supp.2d 982 (M.D.Tenn. 2009).

b. See *City of Atlanta v. Hotels.com, LP,* 285 Ga. 231, 674 S.E.2d 898 (2009).

c. *City of Goodlettsville v. Priceline.com, Inc.,* 844 F.Supp.2d 897 (M.D.Tenn. 2012).

d. *Travelscape, LLC v. South Carolina Department of Revenue,* 391 S.C. 89, 705 S.E.2d 28 (2011).

In regard to Article 2, keep two points in mind:

1. Article 2 deals with the sale of *goods* and does not cover items such as real property (real estate) and services. Thus, if the subject matter of a dispute is goods, the UCC governs. If it is real estate or services, the common law applies.
2. In some situations, the rules may vary, depending on whether the buyer or the seller is a *merchant.*

We look now at how the UCC defines a *sale, goods,* and *merchant status.*

What Is a Sale?

Sale The passing of title to property from the seller to the buyer for a price.

The UCC defines a **sale** as "the passing of title [evidence of ownership rights] from the seller to the buyer for a price". The price may be payable in cash (or its equivalent, such as a check or credit card) or in other goods or services.

What Are Goods?

Tangible Property Property that has physical existence and can be distinguished by the senses of touch and sight.

To be characterized as a *good,* an item of property must be *tangible,* and it must be *movable.* **Tangible property** has physical existence—it can be touched or seen. *Intangible property*—such as corporate stocks and bonds or patents—has only conceptual existence and thus does not come under Article 2. A *movable* item can be carried from place to place. Hence, real estate is excluded from Article 2.

Who Is a Merchant?

Merchant A person who is engaged in the purchase and sale of goods.

Article 2 governs the sale of goods in general. It applies to sales transactions between all buyers and sellers. In addition, the UCC imposes certain special business standards on **merchants** because of their commercial expertise. Such standards do not apply to the casual or inexperienced seller or buyer (consumer).

In general, a merchant is a person who deals in goods of the kind involved in the sales contract or who, by occupation, holds himself or herself out as having knowledge and skill unique to the practices or goods involved in the transaction.

Article 2A—Leases

Lease Under Article 2A of the UCC, a transfer of the right to possess and use goods for a period of time in exchange for payment.

Leases of personal property (goods) have become increasingly common. Consumers and business firms lease automobiles, industrial equipment, items for use in the home (such as floor polishers), and many other types of goods. Article 2A of the UCC was created to fill the need for uniform guidelines in this area.

Article 2A covers any transaction that creates a **lease** of goods or a sublease of goods. Article 2A is essentially a repetition of Article 2, except that it applies to leases of goods rather than sales of goods and thus varies to reflect differences between sales and lease transactions. (Note that Article 2A is not concerned with leases of real property, such as land or buildings.)

Lessor A person who transfers the right to the possession and use of goods to another in exchange for rental payments.

Lessee A person who acquires the right to the possession and use of another's goods in exchange for rental payments.

Article 2A defines a *lease agreement* as a lessor and lessee's bargain with respect to the lease of goods, as found in their language and as implied by other circumstances. A **lessor** is one who transfers the right to the possession and use of goods under a lease. A **lessee** is one who acquires the right to the possession and use of goods under a lease. In other words, the lessee is the party who is leasing the goods from the lessor. Article 2A applies to all types of leases of goods. Special rules apply to certain types of leases, however, including consumer leases and finance leases.

▶ The Formation of Sales and Lease Contracts

Article 2 and Article 2A of the UCC modify common law rules for the formation of sales and lease contracts in several ways. Remember, though, that parties to sales contracts are basically free to establish whatever terms they wish. The UCC comes into play only when the parties have failed to provide in their contract for a contingency that later gives rise to a dispute. The UCC makes this clear time and again by using such phrases as "unless the parties otherwise agree" or "absent a contrary agreement by the parties."

Offer

In general contract law, the moment a definite offer is met by an unqualified acceptance, a binding contract is formed. In commercial sales transactions, the verbal exchanges, correspondence, and actions of the parties may not reveal exactly when a binding contractual obligation arises. The UCC states that an agreement sufficient to constitute a contract can exist even if the moment of its making is undetermined.

OPEN TERMS   Remember from Chapter 11 that under the common law of contracts, an offer must be definite enough for the parties (and the courts) to ascertain its essential terms when it is accepted. In contrast, the UCC states that a sales or lease contract will not fail for indefiniteness even if one or more terms are left open as long as (1) the parties intended to make a contract and (2) there is a reasonably certain basis for the court to grant an appropriate remedy. Normally, under Article 2 the only term that must be specified is the quantity—because there is almost no way to determine objectively what is a reasonable quantity of goods for someone to buy.

In contrast, a court can objectively determine a reasonable price for particular goods by looking at the market. Thus, if the parties have not agreed on a price, the court will determine a "reasonable price at the time for delivery." If the parties do not specify payment terms, payment is due at the time and place at which the buyer is to receive the goods. When no delivery terms are specified, the buyer normally takes delivery at the seller's place of business.

MERCHANT'S FIRM OFFER   Under common law contract principles, an offer can be revoked at any time before acceptance. The UCC has an exception that applies only to **firm offers** for the sale or lease of goods made by a merchant (regardless of whether or not the offeree is a merchant). A firm offer arises when a merchant gives assurances *in a signed writing* that the offer will remain open. A firm offer is irrevocable without the necessity of consideration for the stated period or, if no definite period is stated, a reasonable period (neither to exceed three months).

EXAMPLE 13.1   Osaka, a used-car dealer, e-mails Bennett on January 1, stating, "I have a used 2013 Mazda CX-5 on the lot that I'll sell you for $19,000 any time between now and January 31." This e-mail creates a firm offer, and Osaka will be liable for breach if he sells that Mazda to someone other than Bennett before January 31. •

Acceptance

Acceptance of an offer to buy, sell, or lease goods generally may be made in any reasonable manner and by any reasonable means. The UCC permits acceptance of an offer to buy goods "either by a prompt *promise* to ship or by the prompt or current shipment of conforming or nonconforming goods." *Conforming goods* (see page 329) accord with the contract's terms, whereas *nonconforming goods* do not.

The prompt shipment of nonconforming goods constitutes both an acceptance, which creates a contract, and a breach of that contract. This rule does not apply if the seller **seasonably** (within a reasonable amount of time) notifies the buyer that the nonconforming shipment is offered only as an *accommodation,* or as a favor. The notice of accommodation must clearly indicate to the buyer that the shipment does not constitute an acceptance and, thus, that no contract has been formed.

EXAMPLE 13.2   McFarrell Pharmacy orders five cases of Johnson & Johnson 3-by-5-inch gauze pads from H.T. Medical Supply, Inc. If H.T. ships five cases of Xeroform 3-by-5-inch gauze pads instead, the shipment acts as both an acceptance of McFarrell's offer and a *breach* of the resulting contract. McFarrell may sue H.T. for any appropriate damages. If, however, H.T. notifies McFarrell that the Xeroform gauze pads are being shipped *as an accommodation*—because H.T. has only Xeroform pads in stock—the shipment will constitute a counteroffer, not an acceptance. A contract will be formed only if McFarrell accepts the Xeroform gauze pads. •

CONTRAST   The common law requires that the parties make their terms definite before they have a contract. The UCC applies general commercial standards to make the terms of a contract definite.

Firm Offer   An offer (by a merchant) that is irrevocable without the necessity of consideration for a stated period of time (not to exceed three months). A firm offer by a merchant must be in writing and must be signed by the offeror.

BE AWARE   The UCC provides that acceptance can be made by any means of communication that is reasonable under the circumstances.

Seasonably   Within a specified time period or, if no period is specified, within a reasonable time.

COMMUNICATION OF ACCEPTANCE   Under the common law, because a unilateral offer invites acceptance by a performance, the offeree need not notify the offeror of performance unless the offeror would not otherwise know about it. In other words, a unilateral offer can be accepted by beginning performance. The UCC is more stringent than the common law in this regard because it requires notification. Under the UCC, if the offeror is not notified within a reasonable time that the offeree has accepted the contract by beginning performance, then the offeror can treat the offer as having lapsed before acceptance.

LEARNING OBJECTIVE 2   Under the UCC, if an offeree includes additional or different terms in an acceptance, will a contract result? If so, what happens to these terms?

ADDITIONAL TERMS   Under the common law, variations in terms between the offer and the offeree's acceptance violate the *mirror image rule* (see page 269 in Chapter 11), which requires that the terms of an acceptance exactly mirror the offer. This rule causes considerable problems in commercial transactions, however, particularly when different standardized purchase order forms are used.

To avoid these problems, the UCC dispenses with the mirror image rule. Under the UCC, a contract is formed if the offeree makes a *definite* expression of acceptance (such as signing the form in the appropriate location), even though the terms of the acceptance modify or add to the terms of the original offer.

What happens to these new terms? The answer depends on whether the parties are nonmerchants or merchants.

When One or Both Parties Are Nonmerchants.   If one (or both) of the parties is a nonmerchant, the contract is formed according to the terms of the original offer submitted by the original offeror and *not* according to the additional terms of the acceptance.

CASE EXAMPLE 13.3   OfficeSupplyStore.com is the Web site of Office Supply Store, Inc., based in Washington State. Employees of the Kansas City School District in Missouri allegedly bought $17,642.54 worth of office supplies—without the authority or approval of their employer—at OfficeSupplyStore.com. The invoices accompanying the goods contained a *forum-selection clause* (see page 217) that stated all disputes would be resolved in California. When the goods were not paid for, Office Supply filed a suit against the school board and the district's employees in a California court.

The school board objected to the forum-selection clause, claiming that it was not binding. The court held that additional terms—such as a forum-selection clause—included in an invoice delivered by a seller to a nonmerchant buyer with the purchased goods do not become part of the contract unless the buyer expressly agrees. The school board was not a merchant, so the forum-selection clause could be construed only *as a proposal* for an addition to the contract.[1] ●

Rules When Both Parties Are Merchants. The drafters of the UCC created a special rule for merchants to avoid the "battle of the forms," which occurs when two merchants exchange separate standard forms containing different contract terms. Under the UCC, in contracts *between merchants*, the additional terms *automatically* become part of the contract unless one of the following conditions exists:

1. The original offer expressly limited acceptance to its terms.
2. The new or changed terms materially alter the contract.
3. The offeror objects to the new or changed terms within a reasonable period of time.

---

1. *OfficeSupplyStore.com v. Kansas City School Board,* 334 S.W.3d 574 (2011).

In the following case, a party conditioned its acceptance of an offer on the other parties' agreement to additional terms by a specific date. When the parties agreed to the most important terms after the deadline, the court had to decide if there was an enforceable contract.

Case 13.1 **WPS, Inc. v. Expro Americas, LLC**

Court of Appeals of Texas, First District, 369 S.W.3d 384 (2012).

BACKGROUND AND FACTS In April 2006, WPS, Inc., submitted a formal proposal to manufacture equipment for Expro Americas, LLC, and Surface Production Systems, Inc. (SPS). Expro and SPS then submitted two purchase orders. WPS accepted the first purchase order, in part, and the second order conditionally. Among other things, WPS required that, by April 28, 2006, Expro and SPS give their "full release to proceed" and agree to "pay all valid costs associated with any order cancellation." The parties' negotiations continued, and Expro and SPS eventually submitted a third purchase order on May 9, 2006. The third purchase order did not comply with all of WPS's requirements, but it did give WPS full permission to proceed and agreed that Expro and SPS would pay all cancellation costs. With Expro and SPS's knowledge, WPS then began work under the third purchase order. Expro and SPS soon canceled the order, however, so WPS sent them an invoice for the cancellation costs. At trial, the jury and court concluded that there was a contract and found in WPS's favor. Expro and SPS appealed.

IN THE WORDS OF THE COURT . . .
Terry *JENNINGS*, Justice.
* * * *

* * * WPS replied with a conditional acceptance of the second purchase order. WPS also stated that its conditional acceptance depended upon the receipt of a revised purchase order by April 28, 2006. Although it is undisputed that Expro * * * and SPS did not issue a revised purchase order by this date, the evidence * * * reveals that the parties continued their discussions and negotiations over those matters that had yet to be resolved. * * * *The parties operated as if they had additional time to resolve the outstanding differences.* [Emphasis added.]

Expro * * * and SPS submitted their revised third purchase order on May 9, 2006, agreeing in writing to virtually all the matters that had remained unresolved to that date. * * * Most importantly, Expro * * * and SPS provided * * * a "full release to proceed" and agreed to "pay all valid costs associated with any order cancellation." In his testimony, [SPS's vice president] conceded that *the term "Release to Proceed" "basically means that one party is in agreement,"* authorizing the other party to go forward. * * * WPS had previously sought the release to proceed so that it could "diligently" perform its obligations under the contract. The jury could have reasonably concluded that WPS, having now obtained the release * * * and * * * [the] promise to pay cancellation charges * * *, was contractually obligated to perform and meet the delivery date. [Emphasis added.]

DECISION AND REMEDY The Texas appellate court found that WPS had a contract with Expro and SPS. It affirmed the judgment for WPS.

THE LEGAL ENVIRONMENT DIMENSION *By allowing a party to condition its acceptance on additional terms, does contract law make negotiations more or less efficient? Explain your answer.*

Consideration

The common law rule that a contract requires consideration also applies to sales and lease contracts. Unlike the common law, however, the UCC does not require a contract modification to be supported by new consideration. An agreement modifying a contract for the sale or lease of goods needs no consideration to be binding.

The Statute of Frauds

The UCC contains Statute of Frauds provisions covering sales and lease contracts. Under these provisions, sales contracts for goods priced at $500 or more and lease contracts requiring payments of $1,000 or more must be in writing to be enforceable. (These low threshold amounts may eventually be raised.)

SUFFICIENCY OF THE WRITING   To satisfy the UCC's Statute of Frauds provisions, a writing or a memorandum need only indicate that the parties intended to form a contract and be signed by the party against whom enforcement is sought. The contract normally will not be enforceable beyond the quantity of goods shown in the writing, however. All other terms can be proved in court by oral testimony. For leases, the writing must reasonably identify and describe the goods leased and the lease term.

SPECIAL RULES FOR CONTRACTS BETWEEN MERCHANTS   Once again, the UCC provides a special rule for merchants in sales transactions (there is no corresponding rule for leases under Article 2A). Merchants can satisfy the Statute of Frauds if, after the parties have agreed orally, one of the merchants sends a signed written confirmation of the terms to the other merchant within a reasonable time. Unless the merchant who receives the confirmation objects in writing to its contents within ten days after receipt, the contract is enforceable, even though the receiving merchant has not signed anything. Generally, courts hold that an e-mail confirmation is sufficient.

EXAMPLE 13.4   Alfonso, a merchant-buyer in Cleveland, contracts over the telephone to purchase $4,000 worth of spare aircraft parts from Goldstein, a merchant-seller in New York City. Two days later, Goldstein sends a written, signed confirmation detailing the terms of the oral contract, and Alfonso subsequently receives it. If Alfonso does not notify Goldstein in writing of his objection to the contents of the confirmation within ten days of receipt, Alfonso cannot raise the Statute of Frauds as a defense against the enforcement of the oral contract. ●

EXCEPTIONS   The UCC defines three exceptions to the writing requirements of the Statute of Frauds:

1. *Specially manufactured goods.* An oral contract will still be enforceable if it is for goods that are specially manufactured for a particular buyer and the seller has substantially started manufacturing the goods.
2. *Partial performance.* An oral contract that has been partially performed (such as when some of the contracted goods have been paid for and accepted) will be enforceable to the extent that it has been performed.
3. *Admissions.* When the party against whom enforcement is sought admits to making an oral contract, the contract is enforceable, but only as to the quantity of goods that the party admitted. **CASE EXAMPLE 13.5**   Gerald Lindgren, a farmer, agreed by phone to sell his crops to Glacial Plains Cooperative. The parties reached four oral agreements: two for the delivery of soybeans and two for the delivery of corn. Lindgren made the soybean deliveries and part of the first corn delivery, but he sold the rest of his corn to another dealer. Glacial Plains bought corn elsewhere, paying a higher price, and then sued Lindgren for breach of contract. In papers filed with the court, Lindgren acknowledged his oral agreements with Glacial Plains and admitted that he did not fully perform. The court applied the admissions exception and held that the four agreements were enforceable.[2] ●

These three exceptions and other ways in which sales law differs from general contract law are summarized in Exhibit 13–2 on the facing page.

---

2. *Glacial Plains Cooperative v. Lindgren,* 759 N.W.2d 661 (Minn.App. 2009).

• *Exhibit* 13-2 **Major Differences between Contract Law and Sales Law**

	CONTRACT LAW	SALES LAW
Contract Terms	Contract must contain all material terms.	Open terms are acceptable, if parties intended to form a contract, but the contract is not enforceable beyond quantity term.
Acceptance	Mirror image rule applies. If additional terms are added in acceptance, counteroffer is created.	Additional terms will not negate acceptance unless acceptance is made expressly conditional on assent to the additional terms.
Contract Modification	Modification requires consideration.	Modification does not require consideration.
Irrevocable Offers	Option contracts (with consideration).	Merchants' firm offers (without consideration).
Statute of Frauds Requirements	All material terms must be included in the writing.	Writing is required only for the sale of goods of $500 or more, but contract is not enforceable beyond quantity specified. Merchants can satisfy the requirement by a confirmatory memorandum evidencing their agreement. *Exceptions:* 1. Specially manufactured goods. 2. Partial performance. 3. Admissions by party against whom enforcement is sought.

The Performance of Sales and Lease Contracts

To understand the obligations of the parties under a sales or lease contract, it is necessary to know the duties and obligations each party has assumed under the terms of the contract. Keep in mind that "duties and obligations" under the contract terms include those specified by the agreement, by custom, and by the UCC.

In the performance of a sales or lease contract, the basic obligation of the seller or lessor is to *transfer and deliver conforming goods*. The basic obligation of the buyer or lessee is to *accept and pay for conforming goods* in accordance with the contract. Overall performance of a sales or lease contract is controlled by the agreement between the parties. When the contract is unclear and disputes arise, the courts look to the UCC and impose standards of good faith and commercial reasonableness.

The Good Faith Requirement

The obligations of *good faith* and *commercial reasonableness* underlie every sales and lease contract. The UCC's good faith provision, which can never be disclaimed, says that every contract or duty within the act imposes an obligation of good faith in its performance or enforcement." *Good faith* means honesty in fact. For a merchant, it means honesty in fact and the observance of reasonable commercial standards of fair dealing in the trade. In other words, merchants are held to a higher standard of performance or duty than are nonmerchants.

Obligations of the Seller or Lessor

The basic duty of the seller or lessor is to deliver the goods called for under the contract to the buyer or lessee. Goods that conform to the contract description in every way are called **conforming goods**. To fulfill the contract, the seller or

Conforming Goods   Goods that conform to contract specifications.

Tender of Delivery A seller's or lessor's act of placing conforming goods at the disposal of the buyer or lessee and giving the buyer or lessee whatever notification is reasonably necessary to enable the buyer or lessee to take delivery.

lessor must either deliver or tender delivery of conforming goods to the buyer or lessee. **Tender of delivery** occurs when the seller or lessor makes conforming goods available to the buyer or lessee and gives the buyer or lessee whatever notification is reasonably necessary to enable the buyer or lessee to take delivery.

Tender must occur at a *reasonable hour* and in a *reasonable manner.* For example, a seller cannot call the buyer at 2:00 A.M. and say, "The goods are ready. I'll give you twenty minutes to get them." Unless the parties have agreed otherwise, the goods must be tendered for delivery at a reasonable hour and kept available for a reasonable period of time to enable the buyer to take possession of them. Normally, all goods called for by a contract must be tendered in a single delivery—unless the parties have agreed that the goods may be delivered in several lots or *installments.*

PLACE OF DELIVERY The buyer and seller (or lessor and lessee) may agree that the goods will be delivered to a particular destination where the buyer or lessee will take possession. If the contract does not designate the place of delivery, then the goods must be made available to the buyer at the *seller's place of business* or, if the seller has none, the *seller's residence.* If, at the time of contracting, the parties know that the goods identified to the contract are located somewhere other than the seller's business, then the *location of the goods* is the place for their delivery.

Perfect Tender Rule A rule under which a seller or lessor is required to deliver goods that conform perfectly to the requirements of the contract.

THE PERFECT TENDER RULE Under the **perfect tender rule**, the seller or lessor is required to deliver goods that conform to the terms of the contract in every detail. If the goods or tender of delivery fail in *any respect* to conform to the contract, the buyer or lessee has the right to accept the goods, reject the entire shipment, or accept part and reject part.

It should be noted, though, that if the goods conform in every respect, the buyer or lessee does not have a right to reject the goods, as the following case illustrates.

Case 13.2   Wilson Sporting Goods Co. v. U.S. Golf & Tennis Centers, Inc.

Court of Appeals of Tennessee, 2012 WL 601804 (2012).

BACKGROUND AND FACTS U.S. Golf & Tennis Centers, Inc., operates two retail sporting goods stores that specialize in golf and tennis equipment. U.S. Golf agreed to buy 96,000 golf balls from Wilson Sporting Goods Company for a total price of $20,000. The parties negotiated the agreement via fax, and Wilson affirmed that U.S. Golf was receiving the lowest price (five dollars per two-dozen unit) "that Wilson offered to any one in the market." Wilson shipped golf balls to U.S. Golf that conformed to the contract in quantity and quality, but Wilson did not receive payment. U.S. Golf claimed that it had learned that Wilson had sold the product for two dollars per unit to another buyer and asked Wilson to reduce the contract price of the balls to four dollars per unit (for a total of $16,000). Wilson refused and filed a lawsuit to collect the $20,000. The trial court entered a judgment in favor of Wilson for $33,099.28 (which included the contract price, plus interest, attorneys' fees, and certain allowable expenses). U.S. Golf appealed.

IN THE WORDS OF THE COURT . . .
SUSANO, Jr. J. [Judge]
    * * * *

When Wilson filed suit in September 2007, the $20,000 balance on the contract was past due and owing. The record reflects a series of fax communications between Mr. Bell [owner of U.S. Golf & Tennis] and Wilson * * * in which Mr. Bell repeatedly sought written confirmation that the Company [U.S. Golf & Tennis] had received the "lowest price" for the golf balls. In its faxes, Wilson confirmed that the Company received the lowest price "that Wilson offered to any one in the market."
    * * * *

    * * * [Tennessee's version of the Uniform Commercial Code provides] that "if the goods or the tender of delivery fail in any respect to conform to the contract," the buyer may, among other options, "reject the whole . . . The defendants assert that when Mr. Bell

Case 13.2–Continued

"learned [that] Wilson charged him more than he had agreed to pay, [he] asked repeatedly to [be able to] return the disputed product," but Wilson refused.

The defendants essentially conclude that the parties' contract became unenforceable after Mr. Bell cancelled the contract by "rejecting the delivery once he learned of the price dispute . . . ." Wilson responds that the goods in no way failed to conform to the contract, and that there was no rejection or justifiable revocation of acceptance of the goods by the Company. Accordingly, Wilson concludes that the Code sections relied upon by the defendants do not apply to permit the defendants to cancel the contract. In a word, Wilson is *correct.* [Emphasis in original.]

Nothing in the evidence before us shows or even suggests that the defendants ever rejected delivery of the shipment of the golf balls or that [they] ever had the right to do so. The defendants do not dispute that the product received by the Company conformed to the contract with respect to quantity and quality. Their sole contention at trial was that the price charged was not the lowest available price, as contemplated by the contract. The trial court, however, found that the parties had a contract for an agreed total purchase price of $20,000, and that "the lowest price for the specific goods ordered and received

was confirmed." The evidence was that "both [Wilson's] witness and defendant Arthur H. Bell testified that the price agreed upon for the golf balls was $20,000.00." In addition to the fact that the contract's terms regarding price are clear, there is *nothing in the record* to contradict Wilson's confirmations to Mr. Bell that the defendants did receive the lowest price offered to anyone for the goods received. [Emphasis in original.]

DECISION AND REMEDY   The state appellate court affirmed the lower court's judgment in favor of Wilson for $33,099.28 in damages. Because it was undisputed that the shipment of golf balls conformed to the contract, U.S. Golf was obligated to accept the goods and pay the agreed-on price.

WHAT IF THE FACTS WERE DIFFERENT?   *Suppose that U.S. Golf had presented as evidence a contract between Wilson and another buyer a week after this shipment was delivered to U.S. Golf. In that contract, Wilson agreed to sell the same golf balls for four dollars per unit to a different buyer. Would the court have ruled differently? Why or why not?*

A tender of nonconforming goods automatically constitutes a breach of contract. Because of the rigidity of the perfect tender rule, several exceptions to the rule have been created. Some of these exceptions are discussed next.

Cure The right of a party who tenders nonconforming performance to correct that performance within the contract period.

Cure.   The UCC does not specifically define the term **cure,** but it refers to the right of the seller or lessor to repair, adjust, or replace defective or nonconforming goods. When any delivery is rejected because of nonconforming goods and the time for performance has not yet expired, the seller or lessor can attempt to "cure" the defect *within the contract time for performance.* To do so, the seller or lessor must seasonably notify the buyer or lessee of the intention to cure. Once the time for performance under the contract has expired, the seller or lessor can still exercise the right to cure if he or she has *reasonable grounds to believe that the nonconforming tender will be acceptable to the buyer or lessee.*

EXAMPLE 13.6 In the past, Reddy Electronics frequently allowed the Topps Company to substitute certain electronic supplies when the goods Reddy ordered were not available. Under a new contract for the same type of goods, Reddy rejects the substitute supplies on the last day Topps can perform the contract. Topps had reasonable grounds to believe Reddy would accept a substitute. Therefore, Topps can cure within a reasonable time, even though conforming delivery will occur after the actual time limit for performance allowed under the contract. ●

The right to cure substantially restricts the right of the buyer or lessee to reject goods. For example, if a lessee refuses a tender of goods as nonconforming but does not disclose the nature of the defect to the lessor, the lessee cannot later assert the defect as a defense if the defect is one that the lessor could have cured. Generally, buyers and lessees must act in good faith and state specific reasons for refusing to accept goods.

Commercial Impracticability.   As discussed in Chapter 12 on page 305, events unforeseen by either party when a contract was made may make performance commercially impracticable. When this occurs, the perfect tender rule no longer applies. According to the UCC, a delay in delivery or nondelivery in whole or in part is not a breach if performance has been made impracticable "by the occurrence of a contingency the nonoccurrence of which was a basic assumption on which the contract was made." The seller or lessor must, however, notify the buyer or lessee as soon as practicable that there will be a delay or nondelivery.

EXAMPLE 13.7 Houston Oil Company receives its supplies from the Middle East and has a contract to supply Northwest Fuels with one hundred thousand barrels of oil. Because of an oil embargo by the Organization of Petroleum Exporting Countries, Houston is unable to secure oil supplies to meet the terms of the contract with Northwest. Because of the same embargo, Houston also cannot secure oil from any other source. This situation comes under the commercial impracticability exception to the perfect tender doctrine. ●

Ethical Issue ⚖

Is it appropriate to use the latest global economic crisis as a reason to escape contractual obligations? Starting as early as 2007 and lasting through at least 2012, many companies were hit hard by the global economic crisis. When economic conditions make it difficult (or even impossible) for parties to perform, should the courts void agreements because of commercial impracticability? Many companies have argued that the latest economic crisis was the equivalent of a natural disaster (an act of God), but in general, financial difficulties do not excuse a defaulting party's breach.

In 1999, Chrysler entered into an agreement with the city of Twinsburg, Ohio, and the county in which it is located. Chrysler received a 50 percent tax exemption on certain property for a ten-year period. In exchange, the company was to invest about $125 million in a stamping plant—a facility that manufactures sheetmetal "stampings" for automotive assembly plants—in Twinsburg. This plant was to maintain almost three hundred full-time employment positions. When the auto industry crashed during the financial crisis, Chrysler filed for bankruptcy in 2009.

As part of its restructuring, Chrysler planned to close the Twinsburg plant. Under its agreement with the city, Chrysler could do so if its changed circumstances were due to altered economic conditions beyond its reasonable control. When the city challenged the closing, the bankruptcy court determined that the plant's closing was in fact caused by a change in economic conditions that were beyond Chrysler's control.[3] Thus, the global economic slowdown was equivalent to an act of God, at least in terms of commercial impracticability.

Substitution of Carriers.   When an agreed-on manner of delivery (such as the carrier to be used to transport the goods) becomes impracticable or unavailable through no fault of either party, but a commercially reasonable substitute is available, the seller must use this substitute performance, which is sufficient tender to the buyer.

EXAMPLE 13.8 A sales contract calls for a large generator to be delivered via Roadway Trucking Corporation on or before June 1. The contract terms clearly state the importance of the delivery date. The employees of Roadway Trucking go on strike. The seller is required to make a reasonable substitute tender, perhaps by rail if that is available. Note that the seller normally will be responsible for any additional shipping costs, unless other arrangements have been made in the sales contract. ●

Installment Contract   A contract in which payments due are made periodically.

Installment Contracts.   An **installment contract** is a single contract that requires or authorizes delivery in two or more separate lots to be accepted and paid for sepa-

---

3. *In re Old Carco, LLC,* 452 Bankr. 100 (2011). The court used the name *Old Carco* to designate the pre-bankrupt Chrysler Company.

rately. With an installment contract, a buyer or lessee can reject an installment *only if the nonconformity substantially impairs the value* of the installment and cannot be cured. If the buyer or lessee subsequently accepts a nonconforming installment and fails to notify the seller or lessor of cancellation, however, the contract is reinstated.

Unless the contract provides otherwise, the entire installment contract is breached only when one or more nonconforming installments *substantially* impair the value of the *whole contract.* **EXAMPLE 13.9** A contract calls for the parts of a machine to be delivered in installments. The first part is necessary for the operation of the machine, but when it is delivered, it is irreparably defective. The failure of this first installment will be a breach of the whole contract because the machine will not operate without the first part. The situation would likely be different, however, if the contract had called for twenty carloads of plywood and only 6 percent of one carload had deviated from the thickness specifications in the contract. It is unlikely that a court would find that a defect in 6 percent of one installment substantially impaired the value of the whole contract. •

The point to remember is that the UCC significantly alters the right of the buyer or lessee to reject the entire contract if the contract requires delivery to be made in several installments. The UCC strictly limits rejection to cases of *substantial* nonconformity.

Destruction of Identified Goods. Sometimes, an unexpected event, such as a fire, totally destroys goods through no fault of either party and before risk passes to the buyer or lessee. In such a situation, *if the goods were identified at the time the contract was formed,* the parties are excused from performance. If the goods are only partially destroyed, however, the buyer or lessee can inspect them and either treat the contract as void or accept the damaged goods with a reduction in the contract price.

Assurance and Cooperation. The UCC provides that if one of the parties to a contract has "reasonable grounds" to believe that the other party will not perform as contracted, she or he may *in writing* "demand adequate assurance of due performance" from the other party. Until such assurance is received, she or he may "suspend" further performance without liability. What constitutes "reasonable grounds" is determined by commercial standards. If such assurances are not forthcoming within a reasonable time (not to exceed thirty days), the failure to respond may be treated as a *repudiation* of the contract.

Sometimes, the performance of one party depends on the cooperation of the other. The UCC provides that when such cooperation is not forthcoming, the other party can suspend his or her own performance without liability and hold the uncooperative party in breach or proceed to perform the contract in any reasonable manner.

Obligations of the Buyer or Lessee

Once the seller or lessor has adequately tendered delivery, the buyer or lessee is obligated to accept the goods and pay for them according to the terms of the contract.

PAYMENT In the absence of any specific agreements, the buyer or lessee must make payment at the time and place the goods are *received.* When a sale is made on credit, the buyer is obligated to pay according to the specified credit terms (for example, 60, 90, or 120 days), not when the goods are received. The credit period usually begins on the *date of shipment.* Under a lease contract, a lessee must make the lease payment that was specified in the contract.

Payment can be made by any means agreed on between the parties—cash or any other method generally acceptable in the commercial world. If the seller demands

"Obstacles are those frightful things you see when you take your eyes off your goal."
Henry Ford, 1863–1947
(Founder of Ford Motor Company)

cash when the buyer offers a check, credit card, or the like, the seller must allow the buyer reasonable time to obtain legal tender.

RIGHT OF INSPECTION   Unless the parties otherwise agree, or for collect-on-delivery transactions, the buyer or lessee has an absolute right to inspect the goods before making payment. This right allows the buyer or lessee to verify that the goods tendered or delivered conform to the contract. Inspection can take place at any reasonable place and time and in any reasonable manner. If the goods are not as ordered, the buyer or lessee has no duty to pay. An opportunity for inspection is therefore a condition precedent to the right of the seller or lessor to enforce payment.

CASE EXAMPLE 13.10   Jessie Romero wanted to buy a new Silverado pickup from Scoggin-Dickey Chevrolet-Buick, Inc. In their contract, Romero agreed, among other things, that he would supply two trade-in vehicles. Romero did not have the vehicles with him when he signed the contract but said that their combined value was $15,000. Romero took possession of the truck, but when he brought in the trade-in vehicles, the dealership inspected them and determined that they had very little commercial value. The dealership then refused to go through with the deal, took back the pickup, and offered to partially refund Romero's down payment.

Romero rejected the offer and filed a lawsuit to enforce the contract. The court found that the dealership had a right to inspect the goods (trade-in vehicles) identified in the contract at any reasonable place and time prior to payment or acceptance. In this case, the dealership had inspected the vehicles on their delivery and had determined that they did not conform to the description in the contract. The contract was conditioned on the acceptance of the trade-in vehicles, and the dealership was entitled to reject nonconforming goods and thereby cancel the contract.[4] ●

ACCEPTANCE   A buyer or lessee demonstrates acceptance of the delivered goods by doing any of the following:

1. If, after having had a reasonable opportunity to inspect the goods, the buyer or lessee signifies to the seller or lessor that the goods either are conforming or are acceptable in spite of their nonconformity.
2. If the buyer or lessee has had a reasonable opportunity to inspect the goods and has *failed to reject* them within a reasonable period of time, then acceptance is presumed.
3. In sales contracts, if the buyer *performs any act inconsistent with the seller's ownership,* then the buyer will be deemed to have accepted the goods. For example, any use or resale of the goods—except for the limited purpose of testing or inspecting the goods—generally constitutes an acceptance.

PARTIAL ACCEPTANCE   If some of the goods delivered do not conform to the contract and the seller or lessor has failed to cure, the buyer or lessee can make a *partial* acceptance. The same is true if the nonconformity was not reasonably discoverable before acceptance. (In the latter situation, the buyer or lessee may be able to revoke the acceptance, see page 339.)

A buyer or lessee cannot accept less than a single commercial unit, however. The UCC defines a *commercial unit* as a unit of goods that, by commercial usage, is viewed as a "single whole" for purposes of sale, and its division would materially impair the character of the unit, its market value, or its use. A commercial unit can be a single article (such as a machine), a set of articles (such as a suite of furniture or an

"Resolve to perform what you ought; perform without fail what you resolve."
Benjamin Franklin, 1706–1790
(American politician and inventor)

---

4. *Romero v. Scoggin-Dickey Chevrolet-Buick, Inc.,* __ S.W.3d __ (Tex.App. 2010).

assortment of sizes), a quantity (such as a bale, a gross, or a carload), or any other unit treated in the trade as a single whole.

Anticipatory Repudiation

What if, before the time for contract performance, one party clearly communicates to the other the intention not to perform? Such an action is a breach of the contract by *anticipatory repudiation*. When anticipatory repudiation occurs, the nonbreaching party can do the following:

1. Treat the repudiation as a final breach by pursuing a remedy.
2. Wait to see if the repudiating party will decide to honor the contract despite the avowed intention to renege.
3. In either situation, the nonbreaching party may *suspend* performance.

The UCC permits the breaching party to "retract" his or her repudiation (subject to some limitations). This can be done by any method that clearly indicates the party's intent to perform. Once retraction is made, the rights of the repudiating party under the contract are reinstated. There can be no retraction, however, if since the time of the repudiation the other party has canceled or materially changed position or otherwise indicated that the repudiation is final.

▶ Remedies for Breach of Sales and Lease Contracts

When one party fails to carry out the performance promised in a contract, a breach occurs, and the aggrieved party looks for remedies. These remedies range from retaining the goods to requiring the breaching party's performance under the contract. The general purpose of these remedies is to put the aggrieved party "in as good a position as if the other party had fully performed."

Remedies under the UCC are *cumulative* in nature. In other words, an innocent party to a breached sales or lease contract is not limited to one exclusive remedy. (Of course, a party still may not recover twice for the same harm.)

<table>
<tr><td>**LEARNING OBJECTIVE 3** What remedies are available to a seller or lessor when the buyer or lessee breaches the contract?</td></tr>
</table>

Remedies of the Seller or Lessor

When the buyer or lessee is in breach, the remedies available to the seller or lessor depend on the circumstances at the time of the breach, such as which party has possession of the goods. If the goods are in the buyer's or lessee's possession, the seller or lessor can sue to recover the purchase price of the goods or the lease payments due.

If the breach occurs before the goods have been delivered to the buyer or lessee, the seller or lessor has the right to pursue the remedies discussed next.

THE RIGHT TO WITHHOLD DELIVERY In general, sellers and lessors can withhold or stop performance of their obligations under a contract when buyers or lessees are in breach. If a buyer or lessee has wrongfully rejected or revoked acceptance, failed to make proper and timely payment, or repudiated a part of the contract, the seller or lessor can withhold delivery of the goods. If a breach results from the buyer's or lessee's *insolvency*—that is, the inability to pay debts as they become due—the seller or lessor can refuse to deliver the goods unless the buyer or lessee pays in cash.

THE RIGHT TO RECLAIM THE GOODS Under a sales contract, if a seller discovers that the buyer has received goods on credit and is insolvent, the seller can demand return of the goods. The demand generally must be made within ten days of the buyer's receipt of the goods. The seller can demand and reclaim the goods at any time if the buyer misrepresented his or her solvency in writing within three months before the delivery.

In regard to lease contracts, if the lessee is in default (fails to make payments that are due, for example), the lessor may reclaim the leased goods that are in the possession of the lessee.

THE RIGHT TO RESELL THE GOODS Sometimes, a buyer or lessee breaches or repudiates a contract when the seller or lessor is still in possession of the goods (or when the goods have been delivered to a carrier or bailee, but the buyer or lessee has not yet received them). In this event, the seller or lessor can resell or dispose of the goods.

When the goods contracted for are unfinished at the time of breach, the seller or lessor can do one of two things: (1) cease manufacturing the goods and resell them for scrap or salvage value, or (2) complete the manufacture of the goods and resell or dispose of them. In any case, the seller or lessor can recover any deficiency between the resale price and the contract price, along with *incidental damages* (costs to the seller or lessor resulting from the breach).

THE RIGHT TO RECOVER THE PURCHASE PRICE An unpaid seller or lessor can bring an action to recover the purchase price or payments due under the contract (and incidental damages), only under one of the following circumstances:

1. When the buyer or lessee has accepted the goods and has not revoked acceptance.
2. When conforming goods have been lost or damaged after the risk of loss has passed to the buyer or lessee.
3. When the buyer or lessee has breached the contract after the contract goods have been identified and the seller or lessor is unable to resell the goods.

If a seller or lessor sues for the contract price of goods that he or she has been unable to resell or dispose of, the goods must be held for the buyer or lessee. The seller or lessor can resell at any time before collection of the judgment from the buyer or lessee, but the net proceeds from the sale must be credited to the buyer or lessee.

EXAMPLE 13.11 Southern Realty contracts with Gem Point to purchase one thousand pens with Southern Realty's name inscribed on them. Gem Point delivers the pens, but Southern Realty refuses to accept them. In this situation, Gem Point can bring an action for the purchase price because it delivered conforming goods, and Southern Realty refused to accept or pay for the goods. Gem Point obviously cannot resell to anyone else because the pens have Southern Realty's business name inscribed on them. •

THE RIGHT TO RECOVER DAMAGES If a buyer or lessee repudiates a contract or wrongfully refuses to accept the goods, a seller or lessor can bring an action to recover the damages that were sustained. Ordinarily, the amount of damages equals the difference between the contract price or lease payments and the market price (at the time and place of tender of the goods), plus incidental damages.

Sometimes, the difference between the contract price or lease payments and the market price is too small to place the seller or lessor in the position that he or she would have been in if the buyer or lessee had fully performed. In these situations, the proper measure of damages is the seller's or lessor's lost profits, including a reasonable allowance for overhead and other incidental expenses.

Remedies of the Buyer or Lessee

The UCC makes numerous remedies available to the buyer or lessee in the event of a breach. Of course, the buyer or lessee can recover as much of the price as has been paid. Here, we discuss four additional remedies: the rights to reject the goods, to obtain specific performance, to obtain cover, and to recover damages.

THE RIGHT OF REJECTION　If either the goods or the tender of the goods by the seller or lessor fails to conform to the contract in *any respect,* the buyer or lessee normally can reject the goods. If some of the goods conform to the contract, the buyer or lessee can keep the conforming goods and reject the rest.

Timeliness and Reason for Rejection Required.　The buyer or lessee must reject the goods within a reasonable amount of time and must notify the seller or lessor *seasonably* (in a timely fashion). Failure to do so precludes the buyer or lessee from using those defects to justify rejection or to establish breach when the seller or lessor could have cured the defects if they had been stated seasonably.

Duties of Merchant Buyers and Lessees When Goods Are Rejected.　If a *merchant buyer* or *lessee* rightfully rejects goods, he or she is required to follow any reasonable instructions received from the seller or lessor with respect to the goods controlled by the buyer or lessee.

For instance, the seller or lessor might ask the buyer or lessee to store the goods in the buyer's or lessee's warehouse until the next day, when the seller or lessor can retrieve them. If there are no instructions, the buyer or lessee may store the goods or reship them to the seller or lessor. In any of these situations, the buyer or lessee is entitled to reimbursement for the costs involved.

THE RIGHT TO OBTAIN SPECIFIC PERFORMANCE　A buyer or lessee can obtain specific performance—that is, exactly what was contracted for—when the goods are unique or when the buyer's or lessee's remedy at law (monetary damages) is inadequate. Specific performance may be appropriate, for example, when the contract is for the purchase of a particular work of art, a copyright, or a similarly unique item. Monetary damages may not be sufficient in these circumstances.

EXAMPLE 13.12　Sutherlin contracts to sell his antique car to Fenwick for $30,000, with delivery and payment due on June 14. Fenwick tenders payment on June 14, but Sutherlin refuses to deliver. Because the antique car is unique, Fenwick can probably obtain specific performance of the contract from Sutherlin. ●

Cover　A remedy that allows the buyer or lessee, on the seller's or lessor's breach, to purchase or lease the goods from another seller or lessor and substitute them for the goods due under the contract.

THE RIGHT OF COVER　In certain situations, buyers and lessees can protect themselves by obtaining **cover**—that is, by substituting goods for those that were due under the contract. This option is available to a buyer or lessee who has rightfully rejected goods or revoked acceptance. The option is also available when the seller or lessor repudiates the contract or fails to deliver the goods. After purchasing substitute goods, the buyer or lessee can recover from the seller or lessor the difference between the cost of cover and the contract price, plus incidental and consequential damages, less the expenses (such as delivery costs) that were saved as a result of the breach.

Consequential damages include any loss suffered by the buyer or lessee that the seller or lessor could have foreseen (had reason to know about) at the time of the contract. **EXAMPLE 13.13**　Murdock Contractors tells a heavy equipment manufacturer that it needs a certain piece of equipment by July 1 to close a $50,000 deal. The manufacturer can foresee that if the equipment is not delivered by that date, Murdock will suffer consequential damages. ●

THE RIGHT TO RECOVER DAMAGES If a seller or lessor repudiates the contract or fails to deliver the goods, the buyer or lessee can sue for damages. The measure of recovery is the difference between the contract price and the market price of the goods (at the place the seller or lessor was supposed to deliver) at the time the buyer or lessee *learned* of the breach. The buyer or lessee can also recover incidental and consequential damages less expenses that were saved as a result of the seller's or lessor's breach.

When the seller or lessor breaches a warranty, the measure of damages equals the difference between the value of the goods as accepted and their value if they had been delivered as warranted. For this and other types of breaches in which the buyer or lessee has accepted the goods, the buyer or lessee is entitled to recover for any loss resulting in the ordinary course of events.

CASE EXAMPLE 13.14 Les Entreprises Jacques Defour & Fils, Inc., contracted to buy a thirty-thousand-gallon industrial tank from Dinsick Equipment Corporation for $70,000. Les Entreprises hired Xaak Transport, Inc., to pick up the tank, but when Xaak arrived at the pickup location, there was no tank. Les Entreprises paid Xaak $7,459 for its services and filed a suit against Dinsick. The court awarded compensatory damages of $70,000 for the tank and incidental damages of $7,459 for the transport. To establish a breach of contract requires an enforceable contract, substantial performance by the nonbreaching party, a breach by the other party, and damages. In this case, Les Entreprises agreed to buy a tank and paid the price. Dinsick failed to tender or deliver the tank, or to refund the price. The shipping costs were a necessary part of performance, so this was a reasonable expense.[5] ●

When the Seller or Lessor Delivers Nonconforming Goods

When the seller or lessor delivers nonconforming goods, the buyer or lessee has several remedies available under the UCC.

THE RIGHT TO REJECT THE GOODS If either the goods or the tender of the goods by the seller or lessor fails to conform to the contract *in any respect,* the buyer or lessee can reject the goods in whole or in part. If the buyer or lessee rejects the goods, she or he may then obtain cover, cancel the contract, or sue for damages for breach of contract, just as if the seller or lessor had refused to deliver the goods.

CASE EXAMPLE 13.15 Jorge Jauregui contracted to buy a Kawai RX5 piano from Bobb's Piano Sales. Bobb's represented that the piano was in new condition and qualified for the manufacturer's warranty. Jauregui paid the contract price, but the piano was delivered with "unacceptable damage," according to Jauregui, who videotaped its condition. Jauregui rejected the piano and filed a lawsuit for breach of contract. The court ruled that Bobb's had breached the contract by delivering nonconforming goods. Jauregui was entitled to damages equal to the contract price with interest, plus the sales tax, delivery charge, and attorneys' fees.[6] ●

The buyer or lessee must reject the goods within a reasonable amount of time after delivery and must seasonably notify the seller or lessor. When rejecting goods,

---

5. *Les Entreprises Jacques Defour & Fils, Inc., v. Dinsick Equipment Corp.* __ F.Supp.2d __ N.D.Ill. (2011).
6. *Jauregui v. Bobb's Piano Sales & Service, Inc.,* 922 So.2d 303 (Fla.App. 2006).

the buyer or lessee must also designate defects that would have been apparent to the seller or lessor on reasonable inspection. Failure to do so precludes the buyer or lessee from using such defects to justify rejection or to establish breach when the seller could have cured the defects if they had been disclosed in a timely fashion.

REVOCATION OF ACCEPTANCE   Acceptance of the goods precludes the buyer or lessee from exercising the right of rejection, but it does not necessarily prevent the buyer or lessee from pursuing other remedies. In certain circumstances, a buyer or lessee is permitted to *revoke* her or his acceptance of the goods. Acceptance of a lot or a commercial unit can be revoked if the nonconformity *substantially* impairs the value of the lot or unit and if one of the following factors is present:

1. Acceptance was predicated on the reasonable assumption that the nonconformity would be cured, and it has not been cured within a reasonable time.
2. The buyer or lessee did not discover the nonconformity before acceptance, either because it was difficult to discover before acceptance or because assurances made by the seller or lessor that the goods were conforming kept the buyer or lessee from inspecting the goods.

Revocation of acceptance is not effective until notice is given to the seller or lessor. Notice must occur within a reasonable time after the buyer or lessee either discovers or *should have discovered* the grounds for revocation. Additionally, revocation must occur before the goods have undergone any substantial change (such as spoilage) not caused by their own defects. Once acceptance is revoked, the buyer or lessee can pursue remedies, just as if the goods had been rejected. (See this chapter's *Beyond Our Borders* below for a glimpse at how international sales law deals with revocation of acceptance.)

Beyond Our Borders   An International Approach to Revocation of Acceptance

Under the UCC, a buyer or lessee who has accepted goods may be able to revoke acceptance under the circumstances mentioned above. The United Nations Convention on Contracts for the International Sale of Goods (CISG) also allows buyers to rescind their contracts after they have accepted the goods.

   The CISG, however, takes a somewhat different—and more direct—approach to the problem than the UCC does. In the same circumstances that permit a buyer to revoke acceptance under the UCC, under the CISG the buyer can simply declare that the seller has *fundamentally* breached the contract and proceed to sue the seller for the breach.

   Article 25 of the CISG states that a "breach of contract committed by one of the parties is fundamental if it results in such detriment to the other party as substantially to deprive him [or her] of what he [or she] is entitled to expect under the contract." For example, to revoke acceptance of a shipment under the CISG, a buyer need not prove that the nonconformity of one shipment substantially impaired the value of the whole lot. The buyer can simply file a lawsuit alleging that the seller is in breach.

- **For Critical Analysis**
What is the essential difference between revoking acceptance and bringing a suit for breach of contract?

Additional Provisions Affecting Remedies

The parties to a sales or lease contract can vary their respective rights and obligations by contractual agreement. For example, a seller and buyer can expressly provide for remedies in addition to those provided in the UCC. The parties can also specify remedies in lieu of those provided in the UCC, or they can change the measure of damages. As under the common law of contracts, they may also include clauses providing for liquidated damages in the event of a breach or a delay in performance.

Additionally, a seller can stipulate that the buyer's only remedy on the seller's breach will be repair or replacement of the item, or the seller can limit the buyer's remedy to return of the goods and refund of the purchase price. In sales and lease contracts, an agreed-on remedy is in addition to those provided in the UCC unless the parties expressly agree that the remedy is exclusive of all others.

▶ Sales and Lease Warranties

Warranty is an age-old concept. In sales and lease law, a warranty is an assurance or guarantee by the seller or lessor of certain facts concerning the goods being sold or leased. The UCC has numerous rules governing product warranties as they occur in sales and lease contracts.

Because a warranty imposes a duty on the seller or lessor, a breach of warranty is a breach of the seller's or lessor's promise. Assuming that the parties have not agreed to limit or modify the remedies available, if the seller or lessor breaches a warranty, the buyer or lessee can sue to recover damages from the seller or lessor. Under some circumstances, a breach of warranty can allow the buyer or lessee to cancel the agreement.

Title Warranties

Title warranty arises automatically in most sales contracts. There are three types of warranties of title: *good title, no liens,* and *no infringements.*

GOOD TITLE   In most cases, sellers warrant that they have valid title to the goods sold and that transfer of the title is rightful. If the buyer subsequently learns that the seller did not have good title to the goods that were purchased, the buyer can sue the seller for breach of this warranty.

EXAMPLE 13.16 Alexis steals a diamond ring from Calvin and sells it to Emma, who does not know that the ring is stolen. If Calvin discovers that Emma has the ring, then he has the right to reclaim it from Emma. When Alexis sold Emma the ring, Alexis automatically warranted to Emma that the title conveyed was valid and that its transfer was rightful. Because a thief has no title to stolen goods, Alexis breached the warranty of title imposed by the UCC and became liable to Emma for appropriate damages. ●

NO LIENS   A second warranty of title provided by the UCC protects buyers who are unaware of any *liens*[7]—that is, encumbrances on a property to satisfy or protect a claim for payment of a debt—against goods at the time the contract was made. This protects buyers who, for instance, unknowingly buy goods that are subject to a creditor's *security interest*—that is, an interest in the goods that secures payment or performance. If a creditor repossesses the goods from a buyer who *had no knowledge of the security interest,* the buyer can recover from the seller for breach of warranty.

The buyer who has *actual knowledge* of a security interest has no recourse against a seller. If the seller is a merchant and the buyer is a "buyer in the ordinary course of business," however, the buyer is free of the security interest even if he or she knows

---

7. Pronounced *leens.*

of it. An exception occurs if the buyer knows the sale is in violation of the security interest. Then, he or she is subject to it.

NO INFRINGEMENTS   A third type of title warranty is a warranty against infringement of any patent, trademark, or copyright. In other words, a merchant is deemed to warrant that the goods delivered are free from any patent, trademark, or copyright claims of a third person. If this warranty is breached and the buyer is sued by the claim holder, the buyer *must notify the seller* of the lawsuit within a reasonable time to enable the seller to decide whether to participate in the defense against it.

Express Warranties

A seller or lessor can create an **express warranty** by making representations concerning the quality, condition, description, or performance potential of the goods. Under Article 2 of the UCC, express warranties arise when a seller or lessor indicates any of the following:

1. That the goods conform to any *affirmation* (a declaration that something is true) *of fact* or *promise* that the seller or lessor makes to the buyer or lessee about the goods. Such affirmations or promises are usually made during the bargaining process. Statements such as "these drill bits will *easily* penetrate stainless steel—and without dulling" are express warranties.
2. That the goods conform to any *description* of them. For example, a label that reads "Crate contains one 150-horsepower diesel engine" or a contract that calls for the delivery of a "wool coat" creates an express warranty that the content of the goods sold conforms to the description.
3. That the goods conform to any *sample or model* of the goods shown to the buyer or lessee.

Express warranties can be found in a seller's or lessor's advertisement, brochure, or promotional materials, in addition to being made orally or in an express warranty provision in a sales or lease contract.

BASIS OF THE BARGAIN   To create an express warranty, a seller or lessor does not have to use formal words such as *warrant* or *guarantee*. It is only necessary that a reasonable buyer or lessee would regard the representation as being part of the basis of the bargain. The UCC does not define "basis of the bargain," however, and it is a question of fact in each case whether a representation was made at such a time and in such a way that it induced the buyer or lessee to enter into the contract. Therefore, if an express warranty is not intended, the marketing agent or salesperson should not promise too much.

STATEMENTS OF OPINION AND VALUE   Only statements of fact create express warranties. A seller or lessor who makes a statement that merely relates to the value or worth of the goods, or states an opinion about or recommends the goods, does not create an express warranty. **EXAMPLE 13.17**   Jesse, an electronics salesperson, may claim that the quality of his 3D televisions is "excellent and unsurpassed." Jesse's statement is known as *puffery* (see page 133 in Chapter 6) and creates no warranty. ● It is not always easy to determine whether a statement constitutes an express warranty or puffery. The reasonableness of the buyer's or lessee's reliance appears to be the controlling criterion in many cases.

Express Warranty   A seller's or lessor's oral or written promise, ancillary to an underlying sales or lease agreement, as to the quality, description, or performance of the goods being sold or leased.

Implied Warranties

Implied Warranty   A warranty that the law derives from either the situation of the parties or the nature of the transaction.

An **implied warranty** is one that *the law derives* by inference from the nature of the transaction or the relative situations or circumstances of the parties. Under the UCC, merchants impliedly warrant that the goods they sell or lease are merchantable and, in certain circumstances, fit for a particular purpose.

In addition, an implied warranty may arise from a *course of dealing, course of performance,* or *usage of trade.*

Implied Warranty of Merchantability   A warranty by a merchant seller or lessor of goods that the goods are reasonably fit for the general purpose for which they are sold or leased.

IMPLIED WARRANTY OF MERCHANTABILITY   Every sale or lease of goods made *by a merchant* who deals in goods of the kind sold or leased automatically gives rise to an **implied warranty of merchantability.** **EXAMPLE 13.18**   A merchant who is in the business of selling ski equipment makes an implied warranty of merchantability every time he sells a pair of skis. A neighbor selling her skis at a garage sale does not (because she is not in the business of selling goods of this type). •

Merchantable Goods.   Goods that are *merchantable* are "reasonably fit for the ordinary purposes for which such goods are used." They must be of at least average, fair, or medium-grade quality. The quality must be comparable to a level that will pass without objection in the trade or market for goods of the same description. To be merchantable, the goods must also be adequately packaged and labeled, and they must conform to the promises or affirmations of fact made on the container or label, if any.

The warranty of merchantability may be breached even though the merchant did not know or could not have discovered that a product was defective and thus not merchantable. Of course, merchants are not absolute insurers against all accidents occurring in connection with their goods. For instance, a bar of soap is not unmerchantable merely because a user could slip and fall by stepping on it.

Merchantable Food.   The UCC recognizes the serving of food or drink to be consumed on or off the premises as a sale of goods subject to the implied warranty of merchantability. Merchantable food means food that is fit to eat. Courts generally determine whether food is fit to eat on the basis of consumer expectations. The courts assume that consumers should reasonably expect on occasion to find cherry pits in cherry pie, for example, because such substances are natural incidents of the food. In contrast, consumers would not reasonably expect to find a piece of glass in a soft drink—because this substance is not natural to the food product.

In the following *Classic Case,* the court had to determine whether a fish bone was a substance that one should reasonably expect to find in fish chowder.

Classic Case 13.3   **Webster v. Blue Ship Tea Room, Inc.**

Supreme Judicial Court of Massachusetts, 347 Mass. 421, 198 N.E.2d 309 (1964).

BACKGROUND AND FACTS   Blue Ship Tea Room, Inc., was located in Boston in an old building overlooking the ocean. Priscilla Webster, who had been born and raised in New England, went to the restaurant and ordered fish chowder. The chowder was milky in color. After three or four spoonfuls, she felt something lodged in her throat. As a result, she underwent two esophagoscopies. In the second esophagoscopy, a fish bone was found and removed. Webster filed a lawsuit against the restaurant in a Massachusetts state court for breach

of the implied warranty of merchantability. The jury rendered a verdict for Webster, and the restaurant appealed to the state's highest court.

IN THE WORDS OF THE COURT . . .
REARDON, Justice.
   [The plaintiff] ordered a cup of fish chowder. Presently, there was set before her "a small bowl of fish chowder." * * * After 3 or 4 [spoonfuls] she was aware that something had lodged in her throat

Classic Case 13.3–Continued

because she "couldn't swallow and couldn't clear her throat by gulping and she could feel it." This misadventure led to two esophagoscopies [procedures in which a telescope-like instrument is used to look into the throat] at the Massachusetts General Hospital, in the second of which, on April 27, 1959, a fish bone was found and removed. The sequence of events produced injury to the plaintiff which was not insubstantial.

*We must decide whether a fish bone lurking in a fish chowder, about the ingredients of which there is no other complaint, constitutes a breach of implied warranty under applicable provisions of the Uniform Commercial Code * * * .* As the judge put it in his charge [jury instruction], "Was the fish chowder fit to be eaten and wholesome? * * * Nobody is claiming that the fish itself wasn't wholesome. * * * But the bone of contention here—I don't mean that for a pun—but was this fish bone a foreign substance that made the fish chowder unwholesome or not fit to be eaten?" [Emphasis added.]

* * * *

[We think that it] is not too much to say that a person sitting down in New England to consume a good New England fish chowder embarks on a gustatory [taste-related] adventure which may entail the removal of some fish bones from his bowl as he proceeds. We are not inclined to tamper with age-old recipes by any amendment reflecting the plaintiff's view of the effect of the Uniform Commercial Code upon them. We are aware of the heavy body of case law involving foreign substances in food, but we sense a strong distinction between them

and those relative to unwholesomeness of the food itself, [such as] tainted mackerel, and a fish bone in a fish chowder. * * * We consider that the joys of life in New England include the ready availability of fresh fish chowder. We should be prepared to cope with the hazards of fish bones, the occasional presence of which in chowders is, it seems to us, to be anticipated, and which, in the light of a hallowed tradition, do not impair their fitness or merchantability.

DECISION AND REMEDY The Supreme Judicial Court of Massachusetts "sympathized with a plaintiff who has suffered a peculiarly New England injury" but entered a judgment for the defendant, Blue Ship Tea Room. A fish bone in fish chowder is not a breach of the implied warranty of merchantability.

THE E-COMMERCE DIMENSION *If Webster had made the chowder herself from a recipe that she had found on the Internet, could she have successfully brought an action against its author for a breach of the implied warranty of merchantability? Explain your answer.*

IMPACT OF THIS CASE ON TODAY'S LEGAL ENVIRONMENT *This classic case, phrased in memorable language, was an early application of the UCC's implied warranty of merchantability to food products. The case established the rule that consumers should expect to find, on occasion, elements of food products that are natural to the product (such as fish bones in fish chowder). Courts today still apply this rule.*

Implied Warranty of Fitness for a Particular Purpose A warranty that arises when a seller knows the particular purpose for which a buyer will use the goods and knows that the buyer is relying on his or her skill and judgment to select suitable goods.

LEARNING OBJECTIVE 5 What implied warranties arise under the UCC?

IMPLIED WARRANTY OF FITNESS FOR A PARTICULAR PURPOSE The **implied warranty of fitness for a particular purpose** arises when any seller or lessor (merchant or nonmerchant) knows the particular purpose for which a buyer or lessee will use the goods *and* knows that the buyer or lessee is relying on the skill and judgment of the seller or lessor to select suitable goods.

A "particular purpose" of the buyer or lessee differs from the "ordinary purpose for which goods are used" (merchantability). Goods can be merchantable but unfit for a particular purpose. **EXAMPLE 13.19** Denzel needs a gallon of paint to match the color of his living room walls—a light shade somewhere between coral and peach. He takes a sample to the local hardware store and requests a gallon of paint of that color. Instead, he is given a gallon of bright blue paint. Here, Gail, the salesperson, has not breached any warranty of implied merchantability—the bright blue paint is of high quality and suitable for interior walls—but she has breached an implied warranty of fitness for a particular purpose. ●

A seller or lessor is not required to have actual knowledge of the buyer's or lessee's particular purpose, so long as the seller or lessor "has reason to know" the purpose. For an implied warranty to be created, however, the buyer or lessee must have *relied* on the skill or judgment of the seller or lessor in selecting or furnishing suitable goods.

OTHER IMPLIED WARRANTIES The UCC recognizes that implied warranties can arise (or be excluded or modified) from course of dealing, course of performance, or usage of trade.

- The *course of dealing* is a sequence of conduct between the parties to a transaction that establishes a common basis for their understanding.

- *Course of performance* is the conduct that occurs under an agreement, indicating what the parties to the agreement intended for it to mean.
- *Usage of trade* is a practice or method of dealing so regularly observed as to justify an expectation that it will be observed in a particular transaction.

Thus, in the absence of evidence to the contrary, when both parties to a contract have knowledge of a well-recognized trade custom, the courts will infer that they both intended for that custom to apply to their contract. **EXAMPLE 13.20** If an industrywide custom is to lubricate a new car before it is delivered, and a dealer fails to do so, the dealer can be liable to a buyer for breach of implied warranty. •

Warranty Disclaimers

Because each type of warranty is created in a different way, the manner in which each one can be disclaimed or limited by the seller varies.

EXPRESS WARRANTIES   A seller or lessor can disclaim all oral express warranties by including in the contract a written (or an electronically recorded) disclaimer that is expressed in clear language, and conspicuous, and called to the buyer's or lessee's attention. This allows the seller or lessor to avoid false allegations that oral warranties were made, and it ensures that only representations made by properly authorized individuals are included in the bargain.

Note, however, that a buyer or lessee must be made aware of any warranty disclaimers or modifications *at the time the contract is formed.* In other words, any oral or written warranties—or disclaimers—made during the bargaining process as part of a contract's formation cannot be modified at a later time by the seller or lessor.

IMPLIED WARRANTIES   Generally, unless circumstances indicate otherwise, the implied warranties of merchantability and fitness are disclaimed by the expressions "as is" or "with all faults" or other similar phrases. The phrase must be one that in common understanding calls the buyer's or lessee's attention to the fact that there are no implied warranties. (Note, however, that some states have laws that forbid "as is" sales. Other states do not allow disclaimers of warranties of merchantability for consumer goods.)

CASE EXAMPLE 13.21 Mandy Morningstar advertised a "lovely, eleven-year-old mare" with extensive jumping ability for sale. After examining the mare twice, Sue Hallett contracted to buy the horse. The contract she signed described the horse as an eleven-year-old mare, but indicated that the horse was being sold "as is." Shortly after the purchase, a veterinarian determined that the horse was actually sixteen years old and in no condition for jumping. Hallett stopped payment and tried to return the horse and cancel the contract. Morningstar sued for breach of contract. The court held that the statement in the contract describing the horse as eleven years old constituted an express warranty, which Morningstar had breached. Although the "as is" clause effectively disclaimed any implied warranties (of merchantability and fitness for a particular purpose, such as jumping), the court ruled that it did not disclaim the express warranty concerning the horse's age.[8] •

KNOW THIS Courts generally view warranty disclaimers unfavorably, especially when consumers are involved.

Disclaimer of the Implied Warranty of Merchantability.   To specifically disclaim an implied warranty of merchantability, a seller or lessor must mention the word *merchantability.* The disclaimer need not be written, but if it is, the writing (or record) must be conspicuous. Under the UCC, a term or clause is conspicuous when it is

---

8. *Morningstar v. Hallett,* 858 A.2d 125 (Pa.Super.Ct. 2004).

written or displayed in such a way that a reasonable person would notice it. Words are conspicuous when they are in capital letters, in a larger font size, or in a different color than the surrounding text.

Disclaimer of the Implied Warranty of Fitness. To specifically disclaim an implied warranty of fitness for a particular purpose, the disclaimer must be in a writing (or record) and must be conspicuous. The word *fitness* does not have to be mentioned. It is sufficient if, for example, the disclaimer states, "There are no warranties that extend beyond the description on the face hereof."

Reviewing . . . Sales and Leases

Guy Holcomb owns and operates Oasis Goodtime Emporium, an adult entertainment establishment. Holcomb wanted to create an adult Internet system for Oasis that would offer customers adult theme videos and "live" chat room programs using performers at the club. On May 10, Holcomb signed a work order authorizing Crossroads Consulting Group "to deliver a working prototype of a customer chat system, demonstrating the integration of live video and chatting in a Web browser." In exchange for creating the prototype, Holcomb agreed to pay Crossroads $64,697. On May 20, Holcomb signed an additional work order in the amount of $12,943 for Crossroads to install a customized firewall system. The work orders stated that Holcomb would make monthly installment payments to Crossroads, and both parties expected the work would be finished by September. Due to unforeseen problems largely attributable to system configuration and software incompatibility, the project required more time than anticipated. By the end of the summer, the Web site was still not ready, and Holcomb had fallen behind in the payments to Crossroads. Crossroads was threatening to cease work and file suit for breach of contract unless the bill was paid. Rather than make further payments, Holcomb wanted to abandon the Web site project. Using the information presented in the chapter, answer the following questions.

1. Would a court be likely to decide that the transaction between Holcomb and Crossroads was covered by the Uniform Commercial Code (UCC)? Why or why not?
2. Would a court be likely to consider Holcomb a merchant under the UCC? Why or why not?
3. Did the parties have a valid contract under the UCC? Explain.
4. Suppose that Holcomb and Crossroads meet in October in an attempt to resolve their problems. At that time, the parties reach an oral agreement that Crossroads will continue to work without demanding full payment of the past-due amounts and Holcomb will pay Crossroads $5,000 per week. Assuming that the contract falls under the UCC, is the oral agreement enforceable? Why or why not?

Debate This

No express warranties should be created by the oral statements made by salespersons about a product.

Key Terms

conforming goods 329	implied warranty	sale 323
cover 337	of merchantability 342	sales contract 322
cure 331	installment contract 332	seasonably 325
express warranty 341	lease 324	tangible property 324
firm offer 325	lessee 324	tender of delivery 330
implied warranty 342	lessor 324	
implied warranty of fitness	merchant 324	
for a particular purpose 343	perfect tender rule 330	

Chapter Summary: Sales and Leases

The Scope of Articles 2 (Sales) and 2A (Leases) (See pages 322–324.)	1. *Article 2 (sales)*—Article 2 of the UCC governs contracts for the sale of goods (tangible, movable personal property). The common law of contracts also applies to sales contracts to the extent that the common law has not been modified by the UCC. If there is a conflict between a common law rule and the UCC, the UCC controls. Special rules apply to merchants. 2. *Article 2A (leases)*—Article 2A governs contracts for the lease of goods. Except that it applies to leases, instead of sales, of goods, Article 2A is essentially a repetition of Article 2 and varies only to reflect differences between sales and lease transactions.
The Formation of Sales and Lease Contracts (See pages 324–329.)	1. *Offer*—Not all terms have to be included for a contract to be formed (only the subject matter and quantity term must be specified). A written and signed offer by a *merchant,* covering a period of three months or less, is irrevocable without payment of consideration. 2. *Acceptance*—Acceptance may be made by any reasonable means of communication. The acceptance of a unilateral offer can be made by a promise to ship or by prompt shipment of conforming goods. Acceptance by performance requires notice within a reasonable time. 3. *Consideration*—A modification of a contract for the sale of goods does not require consideration. 4. *The Statute of Frauds*—All contracts for the sale of goods priced at $500 or more must be in writing. A writing is sufficient as long as it indicates a contract between the parties and is signed by the party against whom enforcement is sought. When written confirmation of an oral contract *between merchants* is not objected to in writing by the receiver within ten days, the contract is enforceable. Exceptions to the requirement of a writing exist (see Exhibit 13–2 on page 329).
The Performance of Sales and Lease Contracts (See pages 329–335.)	1. *Obligations of the seller or lessor*—The seller or lessor must tender *conforming goods* to the buyer. Tender must take place at a *reasonable hour* and in a *reasonable manner.* Under the perfect tender doctrine, the seller or lessor must tender goods that conform exactly to the terms of the contract. Exceptions to the perfect tender doctrine include cure, commercial impracticability, and destruction of identified goods. 2. *Obligations of the buyer or lessee*—On tender of delivery by the seller or lessor, the buyer or lessee must pay for the goods at the time and place the buyer or lessee receives the goods, even if the place of shipment is the place of delivery, unless the sale is made on credit. The buyer or lessee can accept delivered goods expressly in words or by conduct or by failing to reject the goods after a reasonable period of time following inspection or after having had a reasonable opportunity to inspect them. A buyer will be deemed to have accepted goods if he or she performs any act inconsistent with the seller's ownership. 3. *Anticipatory repudiation*—If, before the time for performance, either party clearly indicates to the other an intention not to perform, this is called anticipatory repudiation.
Remedies for Breach of Sales and Lease Contracts (See pages 335–340.)	1. *Remedies of the seller or lessor*—Under the UCC, when a buyer or lessee breaches the contract, a seller or lessor can withhold or discontinue performance. If the seller or lessor is still in possession of the goods, the seller or lessor can resell or dispose of the goods and hold the buyer or lessee liable for any loss. If the goods cannot be resold or disposed of, an unpaid seller or lessor can bring an action to recover the purchase price or payments due under the contract. If the buyer or lessee repudiates the contract or wrongfully refuses to accept goods, the seller or lessor can recover the damages that were sustained. 2. *Remedies of the buyer or lessee*—When the seller or lessor breaches, the buyer or lessee can choose from a number of remedies. Remedies include obtaining cover or specific performance, suing to recover damages, rejecting the goods, accepting the goods and recovering damages, or revoking acceptance. The parties can agree to vary their respective rights and remedies in their agreement.
Sales and Lease Warranties (See pages 340–345.)	1. *Title warranties*—The seller or lessor automatically warrants that he or she has good title, and that there are no liens or infringements on the property being sold or leased. 2. *Express warranties*—An express warranty arises under the UCC when a seller or lessor indicates, as part of the basis of the bargain, that the goods conform to any of the following: (a) an affirmation or promise of fact, (b) a description of the goods, and (c) a sample shown to the buyer or lessee.

Chapter Summary: Sales and Leases, Continued

Sales and Lease Warranties—Continued	3. *Implied warranties—* a. The implied warranty of merchantability automatically arises when the seller or lessor is a merchant who deals in the kind of goods sold or leased. The seller or lessor warrants that the goods sold or leased are of proper quality, are properly labeled, and are reasonably fit for the ordinary purposes for which such goods are used. b. The implied warranty of fitness for a particular purpose arises when the buyer's or lessee's purpose or use is expressly known by the seller or lessor and the buyer or lessee purchases or leases the goods in reliance on the seller's or lessor's selection. 4. *Warranty disclaimers*—Warranties can be disclaimed or qualified by a seller or lessor, but disclaimers generally must be specific and unambiguous, and often, in writing.

ExamPrep

ISSUE SPOTTERS

—Check your answers to these questions against the answers provided in Appendix D at the end of this text.

1. E-Design, Inc., orders 150 computer desks. Fav-O-Rite Supplies, Inc., ships 150 printer stands. Is this an acceptance of the offer or a counteroffer? If it is an acceptance, is it a breach of the contract? What if Fav-O-Rite told E-Design it was sending the printer stands as "an accommodation"? **(See page 325.)**
2. Pic Post-Stars agrees to sell Ace Novelty five thousand posters of celebrities, to be delivered on April 1. On March 1, Pic tells Ace, "The deal's off." Ace says, "I expect you to deliver. I'll be waiting." Can Ace sue Pic without waiting until April 1? Why or why not? **(See page 335.)**

BEFORE THE TEST

Go to **www.cengagebrain.com**, enter the ISBN 9781133586548, and click on "Find" to locate this textbook's Web site. Then click on "Access Now" under "Study Tools," and select Chapter 13 at the top. There, you will find a Practice Quiz that you can take to assess your mastery of the concepts in this chapter. Additionally, you will find Flashcards and a Glossary of important terms, as well as Video Questions (when assigned).

For Review

Answers for the even-numbered questions in this For Review *section can be found in Appendix E at the end of this text.*

1. How do Article 2 and Article 2A of the UCC differ?
2. Under the UCC, if an offeree includes additional or different terms in an acceptance, will a contract result? If so, what happens to these terms?
3. What remedies are available to a seller or lessor when the buyer or lessee breaches the contract?
4. What remedies are available to a buyer or lessee if the seller or lessor breaches the contract?
5. What implied warranties arise under the UCC?

Questions and Case Problems

13–1. Anticipatory Repudiation and Remedies. Topken has contracted to sell Lorwin five hundred washing machines of a certain model at list price. Topken is to ship the goods on or before December 1. Topken produces one thousand washing machines of this model but has not yet prepared Lorwin's shipment. On November 1, Lorwin repudiates the contract. Discuss the remedies available to Topken. **(See page 335.)**

13–2. The Perfect Tender Rule. Ames contracts to ship one hundred Model Z TVs to Curley. The terms of delivery are Ames's city, by Green Truck Lines, with delivery on or before April 30. On April 15, Ames discovers that because of an error in inventory control, all Model Z sets have been sold. Ames has Model X, a similar but slightly more expensive unit, in stock. On April 16, Ames ships one hundred Model X sets, with notice that Curley will be charged the Model Z price. Curley (in a proper manner) rejects the Model X sets when they are tendered on April 18. Ames does not wish to be held in breach of contract, even though he has tendered nonconforming goods. Discuss Ames's options. **(See page 300.)**

13–3. **Question with Sample Answer: Merchant's Firm Offer.** On September 1, Jennings, a used-car dealer, wrote a letter to Wheeler, stating, "I have a 1955 Thunderbird convertible in mint condition that I will sell you for $13,500 at any time before October 9. [signed] Peter Jennings." By September 15, having heard nothing from Wheeler, Jennings sold the Thunderbird to another party. On September 29, Wheeler accepted Jennings's offer and tendered the $13,500. When Jennings told Wheeler he had sold the car to another party, Wheeler claimed Jennings had breached their contract. Is Jennings in breach? Explain. **(See page 325.)**

—For a sample answer to Question 13–3, go to Appendix F at the end of this text.

13–4. The Statute of Frauds. Fallsview Glatt Kosher Caterers ran a business that provided travel packages, including food, entertainment, and lectures on religious subjects, to customers during the Passover holiday at a New York resort. Willie Rosenfeld verbally agreed to pay Fallsview $24,050 for the Passover package for himself and his family. Rosenfeld did not appear at the resort and never paid the money owed. Fallsview sued Rosenfeld for breach of contract. Rosenfeld claimed that the contract was unenforceable because it was not in writing and violated the UCC's Statute of Frauds. Is the contract valid? Explain. [*Fallsview Glatt Kosher Caterers, Inc. v. Rosenfeld,* 794 N.Y.S.2d 790 (N.Y. Super. 2005)] **(See pages 327–328.)**

13–5. Breach and Damages. Utility Systems of America, Inc., was doing roadwork when Chad DeRosier, a nearby landowner, asked Utility to dump 1,500 cubic yards of fill onto his property. Utility agreed but exceeded DeRosier's request by dumping 6,500 cubic yards. Utility offered to remove the extra fill for $9,500. DeRosier paid a different contractor $46,629 to remove the fill and do certain other work, and filed a suit against Utility. Because Utility charged nothing for the fill, was there a breach of contract? If so, would the damages be greater than $9,500? Discuss. [*DeRosier v. Utility Systems of America, Inc.,* 780 N.W.2d 1 (Minn.App. 2010)] **(See page 338.)**

13–6. Additional Terms. B.S. International, Ltd. (BSI), makes costume jewelry. JMAM, LLC, is a wholesaler of costume jewelry. JMAM sent BSI a letter with the terms for orders, including the necessary procedure for obtaining credit for items that customers rejected. The letter stated, "By signing below, you agree to the terms." Steven Baracsi, BSI's owner, signed the letter and returned it. For six years, BSI made jewelry for JMAM, which resold it. Items rejected by customers were sent back to JMAM, but were never returned to BSI. BSI filed a suit against JMAM, claiming $41,294.21 for the unreturned items. BSI showed the court a copy of JMAM's terms. Across the bottom had been typed a "PS" requiring the return of rejected merchandise. Was this "PS" part of the contract? Discuss. [*B.S. International, Ltd. v. JMAM, LLC,* 13 A.3d 1057 (R.I. 2011)] **(See pages 326–340.)**

13–7. **Case Problem with Sample Answer: Remedies of the Buyer.** Woodridge USA Properties, LP, bought eighty-seven commercial truck trailers under a contract with southeast Trailer Mart (STM), Inc. Southeastern Freight Lines, Inc., owned the lot in Atlanta, Georgia, where the trailers were stored. Gerald McCarty, an independent sales agent who arranged the deal, showed Woodridge the documents of title. They did not indicate that Woodridge was the buyer. Woodridge asked McCarty to hold the documents and sell the trailers for Woodridge. Within three months, all of the trailers had been sold, but McCarty had not given the proceeds to Woodridge. Woodridge—without mentioning the title documents—asked STM to refund the contract price. STM refused. Later, Woodridge filed a suit in a federal district court against STM, claiming that the title documents had been defective and seeking damages. Does Woodridge have a right to recover damages for accepted goods? What would be the measure of the damages? Explain. [*Woodridge USA Properties, L.P. v. Southeast Trailer Mart, Inc.,* ___ F.3d ___ (11th Cir. 2011)] **(See pages 337–338.)**

—For a sample answer to Case Problem 13–7, go to Appendix G at the end of this text.

13–8. Partial Performance and the Statute of Frauds. After a series of e-mails, Jorge Bonilla, the sole proprietor of a printing company in Uruguay, agreed to buy a used printer from Crystal Graphics Equipment, Inc., in New York. Crystal Graphics, through its agent, told Bonilla that the printing press was fully operational, contained all of its parts, and was in excellent condition except for some damage to one of the printing towers. Bonilla paid $95,000. Crystal Graphics sent him a signed, stamped invoice reflecting this payment. The invoice was dated six days after Bonilla's conversation with the agent. When the printing press arrived, Bonilla discovered that it was missing parts and was damaged. Crystal Graphics sent replacement parts, but they did not work. Ultimately, Crystal Graphics was never able to make the printer operational. Bonilla sued, alleging breach of contract, breach of the implied covenant of good faith and fair dealing, breach of express warranty, and breach of implied warranty. Crystal Graphics claimed that the contract was not enforceable because it did not satisfy the Statute of Frauds. Can Crystal Graphics prevail on this basis? Why or why not? [*Bonilla v. Crystal Graphics Equipment, Inc.,* 2012 WL 360145 (S.D.Fla. 2012)] **(See page 328.)**

13–9. **Spotlight on Apple: Implied Warranties.** Alan Vitt purchased an iBook G4 Laptop Computer from Apple, Inc. Shortly after the one-year warranty expired, the laptop failed to work due to a weakness in the product manufacture. Vitt sued Apple, arguing that the laptop did not last "at least a couple of years," which Vitt believed is what a reasonable consumer should expect from a laptop. Vitt claimed that Apple's descriptions of the laptop as "durable," "rugged," "reliable," and "high performance" were affirmative statements concerning the quality and performance of the laptop, which Apple did not meet. How should the court rule? Discuss your answer. [*Vitt v. Apple Computer, Inc.,* 2012 WL 627702 (9th Cir. 2012)] **(See page 342.)**

13–10. **In Your Court: Remedies of the Buyer.** PopCo, Inc., which bottles and distributes soft drinks, purchased bottle-labeling equipment from Gemini Industries Co. The contract stated that in the event of a breach of contract, PopCo's remedy was limited to repair, replacement, or refund. When the equipment was installed in PopCo's plant, problems arose immediately. Gemini attempted to repair the equipment, but when it still did not work properly several months later, Gemini refunded the purchase price, and PopCo returned the equipment. PopCo then asked Gemini to pay PopCo for the losses it had incurred due to the equipment's failure and the delay in obtaining alternative machinery. Gemini claimed that it owed nothing to PopCo because its remedy for breach was limited to repair, replacement, or refund. PopCo asserted that the limited remedy had failed of its essential purpose. In the lawsuit that followed, the court granted summary judgment in Gemini's favor, and PopCo appealed. Assume that you are a judge on the appellate court reviewing the case, and answer the following questions: **(See pages 337–340.)**

1. PopCo argued that Gemini had eliminated the remedy of "refund" by electing to pursue repair or replacement. Thus, the remedy had failed in its essential purpose. Do you find PopCo's argument persuasive?

2. In whose favor will you rule in this case, and why?

Chapter 14

Creditors' Rights and Bankruptcy

> "Capitalism without bankruptcy is like Christianity without hell."
>
> —Frank Borman, 1928–present
> (U.S. astronaut and businessman)

Contents

Learning Objectives

The four Learning Objectives below are designed to help improve your understanding of the chapter. After reading this chapter, you should be able to answer the following questions:

1. **What is a prejudgment attachment? What is a writ of execution? How does a creditor use these remedies?**

2. **In a bankruptcy proceeding, what constitutes the debtor's estate in property? What property is exempt from the estate under federal bankruptcy law?**

3. **What is the difference between an exception to discharge and an objection to discharge?**

4. **In a Chapter 11 reorganization, what is the role of the debtor in possession?**

(.shock/iStockphoto.com)

Many people often struggle to pay their monthly debts. Although in the old days debtors were punished and sometimes even sent to jail for failing to pay their debts, today, people in debt rarely go to jail. They have many other options. In this chapter, we discuss some basic laws that assist the debtor and creditor in resolving disputes.

We then turn to the topic of bankruptcy—a last resort in resolving debtor-creditor problems. As implied by the chapter-opening quotation, bankruptcy may be a necessary evil in our capitalistic society. Hence, every businessperson should have some understanding of the bankruptcy process. In this chapter, we first focus on some basic laws that assist creditors and debtors in resolving disputes. We then examine the process of bankruptcy as a last resort in resolving creditor-debtor problems.

▶ Laws Assisting Creditors

Both the common law and statutory laws other than Article 9 of the Uniform Commercial Code (UCC) create various rights and remedies for creditors. Here, we discuss some of these rights and remedies.

Liens

Lien A claim against specific property to satisfy a debt.

A **lien** is an encumbrance on (claim against) property to satisfy a debt or protect a claim for the payment of a debt. Creditors' liens may arise under the common law or under statutory law. Statutory liens include *mechanic's liens,* whereas *artisan's liens* were recognized by common law. *Judicial liens* arise when a creditor attempts to collect on a debt before or after a judgment is entered by a court.

Mechanic's and artisan's liens can be an important tool for creditors because these liens normally take priority over perfected security interests—unless a statute provides otherwise. Other types of liens can also be useful because a lien creditor generally has priority over an unperfected secured party. In other words, if a creditor obtains a lien *before* another party perfects a security interest in the same property, the lienholder has priority. If the lien is not obtained until *after* another's security interest in the property is perfected, the perfected security interest has priority.

Mechanic's Lien A statutory lien on the real property of another created to ensure priority of payment for work performed.

MECHANIC'S LIEN If a person contracts for labor, services, or materials to be furnished for making improvements on real property and does not immediately pay for the improvements, the creditor can file a **mechanic's lien** on the property. This creates a special type of debtor-creditor relationship in which the real estate itself becomes security for the debt.

EXAMPLE 14.1 Jason paints a house for Gladys, a homeowner, for an agreed-on price to cover labor and materials. If Gladys refuses to pay for the work or pays only a portion of the charges, a mechanic's lien against the property can be created. Jason is the lienholder, and the real property is encumbered (burdened) with a mechanic's lien for the amount owed. If Gladys does not pay the lien, the property can be sold to satisfy the debt. •

State law governs the procedures that must be followed to create a mechanic's lien. Generally, the lienholder must file a written notice of lien within a specific time period (usually 60 to 120 days) from the last date labor or materials were provided. Notice of the foreclosure and sale must be given to the debtor in advance, however. (*Foreclosure* here means the process by which the creditor deprives the debtor of the property.)

In the following case, a contractor attempted to foreclose on a piece of property under a mechanic's lien. The property owner claimed to be unaware of any work done by the contractor. Could this prevent the foreclosure?

Case 14.1　　**BHP Land Services, Inc. v. Seymour**

Superior Court of Connecticut, 137 Conn.App. 165, 47 A.3d 950 (2011).

BACKGROUND AND FACTS　Jean Seymour lived in Barkhamsted, Connecticut, but she also owned a house, a horse barn, and several acres of land in Enfield. Jean's daughter, Jennifer, lived on the Enfield property, which she called the RoundTuit Ranch. Jennifer boarded, trained, and sold horses on the ranch. Jean paid the property taxes and the mortgage but did not participate in the RoundTuit business. Jennifer did not pay rent, but she paid the costs of the business, including snow plowing and house repairs. Jennifer hired

BHP Land Services, Inc., to remove tree stumps and grade two acres for $2,450 per acre. When the work was done, Jennifer paid the bill. The next year, she hired BHP to do similar work on another nine acres at the same price per acre. When Jennifer did not pay the bill, BHP filed a suit in a Connecticut state court against Jean, who responded that she had never authorized the work.

Case 14.1–Continues next page ➡

Case 14.1—Continued

IN THE WORDS OF THE COURT . . .
KLACZAK, Lawrence C., J.T.R. [Judge Trial Referee[a]]
* * * *

In this case the plaintiff in its [complaint] seeks to foreclose a mechanic's lien on a parcel of property known as 100 Fletcher Road, Enfield, Connecticut.
* * * *

A mechanic's lien is available to one who has a claim for services rendered for the improvement of a plot of land. The owner of the land upon which improvement is made, or someone having authority, must have consented to the services having been rendered. [Emphasis added.]
* * * *

Jean Seymour had given her daughter apparent carte blanche authority to operate the ranch as she saw fit * * * when this clearing work was done. Any improvements to the property inured [came in effect] to Jean's benefit as the record owner. Jennifer also acted as her mother's agent when they appeared at [the Enfield] Inland Wetland Agency regarding the grading, clearing and seeding project on the property.

a. A judge trial referee is a judge who has been designated by the chief justice of the Connecticut Supreme Court to hear a certain case.

Clearly, on that occasion, Jean represented that Jennifer could act as her agent and, further, she (Jean), was obviously aware that work was expected to be done which would enhance the property. The Court concludes that Jean permitted Jennifer to act as the agent of the property owner. Jennifer had the authority to do work on the property without any authorization from Jean and she had unfettered authority to act as the agent of the owner.

The complaint sufficiently alleges * * * facts to substantiate an order to foreclose the mechanic's lien, and the evidence as discussed herein supports the Court's finding.
* * * *

Judgment shall enter against the defendant in the amount of $26,250, which was the * * * price for the work done.

DECISION AND REMEDY The court found that Jennifer Seymour had the authority to act as her mother's agent (see Chapter 16) and have work done on the property. Therefore, the court issued a judgment in BHP's favor and ordered a hearing to determine the terms of the foreclosure, as well as its fees and costs.

THE LEGAL ENVIRONMENT DIMENSION *When no actual contract exists, under what theory may a court step in to prevent a property owner from being unjustly enriched by the work, labor, or services of a contractor?*

Artisan's Lien A possessory lien on personal property of another person to ensure payment to a person who has made improvements on and added value to that property.

ARTISAN'S LIEN When a debtor fails to pay for labor and materials furnished for the repair or improvement of personal property, a creditor can recover payment through an **artisan's lien.** In contrast to a mechanic's lien, an artisan's lien is *possessory.* The lienholder ordinarily must have retained possession of the property and have expressly or impliedly agreed to provide the services on a cash, not a credit, basis. The lien remains in existence as long as the lienholder maintains possession of the property, and the lien is terminated once possession is voluntarily surrendered—unless the surrender is only temporary.

EXAMPLE 14.2 Selena leaves her diamond ring at the jeweler's to be repaired and to have her initials engraved on the band. In the absence of an agreement, the jeweler can keep the ring until Selena pays for the services. Should Selena fail to pay, the jeweler has a lien on Selena's ring for the amount of the bill and normally can sell the ring in satisfaction of the lien. ●

Modern statutes permit the holder of an artisan's lien to foreclose and sell the property subject to the lien to satisfy payment of the debt. As with a mechanic's lien, the holder of an artisan's lien must give notice to the owner of the property prior to foreclosure and sale. The sale proceeds are used to pay the debt and the costs of the legal proceedings, and the surplus, if any, is paid to the former owner.

JUDICIAL LIENS A creditor can bring a legal action against a debtor to collect a past-due debt. If the creditor is successful, the court awards the creditor a judgment against the debtor (usually for the amount of the debt plus any interest and legal costs incurred). Frequently, however, the creditor is unable to collect the awarded amount.

To ensure that a judgment will be collectible, the creditor can request that certain nonexempt property of the debtor be seized to satisfy the debt. A court's order to seize the debtor's property is known as a *writ of attachment* if it is issued before a judgment. If the court's order is issued after a judgment, it is referred to as a *writ of execution.*

Writ of Attachment.   In the context of judicial liens, **attachment** is a court-ordered seizure of property before a judgment is secured for a past-due debt. Attachment rights are created by state statutes. Normally, attachment is a *prejudgment* remedy occurring either at the time a lawsuit is filed or immediately afterwards. The due process clause of the Fourteenth Amendment to the U.S. Constitution requires that the debtor be given notice and an opportunity to be heard (see Chapter 4).

To attach before judgment, a creditor must comply with the specific state's statutory requirements. The creditor must have an enforceable right to payment of the debt under law and must follow certain procedures or risk liability for wrongful attachment. Typically, the creditor must file an **affidavit** with the court and post a bond. The affidavit states that the debtor is in default and indicates the statutory grounds under which attachment is sought. The bond covers at least the court costs, the value of the debtor's loss of use of the goods, and the value of the property attached.

When the court is satisfied that all of the requirements have been met, it issues a **writ of attachment,** which directs the sheriff or other public officer to seize nonexempt property. If the creditor prevails at trial, the seized property can be sold to satisfy the judgment.

Writ of Execution.   If the creditor wins at trial and the debtor will not or cannot pay the judgment, the creditor is entitled to go back to the court and request a **writ of execution.** This writ is a court order directing the sheriff to seize and sell any of the debtor's nonexempt real or personal property that is within the court's geographic jurisdiction (usually the county in which the courthouse is located).

The proceeds of the sale are used to pay off the judgment, accrued interest, and the costs of the sale. Any excess is paid to the debtor. The debtor can pay the judgment and redeem the nonexempt property any time before the sale takes place. (Because of exemption laws and bankruptcy laws, however, many judgments are uncollectible.)

Garnishment

Garnishment occurs when a creditor is permitted to collect a debt by seizing property of the debtor (such as wages or funds in a bank account) that is being held by a third party. As a result of a garnishment proceeding, the debtor's employer may be ordered by the court to turn over a portion of the debtor's wages to pay the debt.

CASE EXAMPLE 14.3   Helen Griffin failed to pay a debt she owed to Indiana Surgical Specialists. When Indiana Surgical filed a lawsuit to collect, the court issued a judgment in favor of Indiana Surgical and a garnishment order to withhold the appropriate amount from Griffin's earnings until her debt was paid. At the time, Griffin was working as an independent contractor (see Chapter 16 for a discussion of independent-contractor status) driving for a courier service. She claimed that her wages could not be garnished because she was not an employee. The court held that payments for the services of an independent contractor fall within the definition of earnings and can be garnished.[1] •

Attachment The legal process of seizing another's property under a court order to secure satisfaction of a judgment yet to be rendered.

LEARNING OBJECTIVE 1 **What is a prejudgment attachment? What is a writ of execution? How does a creditor use these remedies?**

Affidavit A statement of facts confirmed by the oath or affirmation of the party making it and made before a person having the authority to administer the oath or affirmation.

Writ of Attachment A writ used to enforce obedience to an order or judgment of the court.

Writ of Execution A writ that puts in force a court's decree or judgment.

Garnishment A legal process whereby a creditor appropriates a debtor's property or wages that are in the hands of a third party.

---

1. *Indiana Surgical Specialists v. Griffin,* 867 N.E.2d 260 (Ind.App. 2007).

PROCEDURES Garnishment can be a prejudgment remedy, requiring a hearing before a court, but it is most often a postjudgment remedy. State law governs garnishment, so the procedure varies. In some states, the creditor needs to obtain only one order of garnishment, which will then apply continuously to the debtor's wages until the entire debt is paid. In other states, the judgment creditor must go back to court for a separate order of garnishment for each pay period.

LIMITATIONS Both federal and state laws limit the amount that can be taken from a debtor's weekly take-home pay through garnishment proceedings.[2] Federal law provides a framework to protect debtors from suffering unduly when paying judgment debts.[3] State laws also provide dollar exemptions, and these amounts are often larger than those provided by federal law.

Under federal law, an employer cannot dismiss an employee because his or her wages are being garnished.

Creditors' Composition Agreements

Creditors may contract with the debtor for discharge of the debtor's liquidated debts (debts that are definite, or fixed, in amount) on payment of a sum less than that owed. These agreements are called **creditors' composition agreements,** or simply composition agreements, and usually are held to be enforceable.

Suretyship and Guaranty

When a third person promises to pay a debt owed by another in the event the debtor does not pay, either a *suretyship* or a *guaranty* relationship is created. The third person's income and assets become the security for the debt owed. Exhibit 14–1 on the facing page illustrates these relationships.

Suretyship and guaranty provide creditors with the right to seek payment from the third party if the primary debtor defaults on her or his obligations. At common law, there were significant differences in the liability of a surety and a guarantor, as discussed in the following subsections. Today, however, the distinctions outlined here have been abolished in some states.

SURETY A contract of strict **suretyship** is a promise made by a third person to be responsible for the debtor's obligation. It is an express contract between the **surety** (the third party) and the creditor. The surety in the strictest sense is primarily liable for the debt of the principal. The creditor need not exhaust all legal remedies against the principal debtor before holding the surety responsible for payment. The creditor can demand payment from the surety from the moment the debt is due.

EXAMPLE 14.4 Roberto Delmar wants to borrow from the bank to buy a used car. Because Roberto is still in college, the bank will not lend him the funds unless his father, José Delmar, who has dealt with the bank before, will cosign the note (add his signature to the note, thereby becoming a surety and thus jointly liable for payment of the debt). When José cosigns the note, he becomes primarily liable to the bank. On the note's due date, the bank can seek payment from either Roberto or José, or both jointly. ●

Creditors' Composition Agreement An agreement formed between a debtor and his or her creditors in which the creditors agree to accept a lesser sum than that owed by the debtor in full satisfaction of the debt.

Suretyship An express contract in which a third party (the surety) promises to be primarily responsible for a debtor's obligation to a creditor.

Surety A third party who agrees to be primarily responsible for the debt of another.

---

2. Some states (for example, Texas) do not permit garnishment of wages by private parties except under a child-support order.

3. For example, the federal Consumer Credit Protection Act of 1968, 15 U.S.C. Sections 1601–1693r, provides that a debtor can retain either 75 percent of disposable earnings per week or a sum equivalent to thirty hours of work paid at federal minimum-wage rates, whichever is greater.

• *Exhibit* **14–1 Suretyship and Guaranty Parties**
In a suretyship or guaranty arrangement, a third party promises to be responsible for a debtor's obligations. A third party who agrees to be responsible for the debt even if the primary debtor does not default is known as a surety. A third party who agrees to be *secondarily* responsible for the debt—that is, responsible only if the primary debtor defaults—is known as a guarantor.

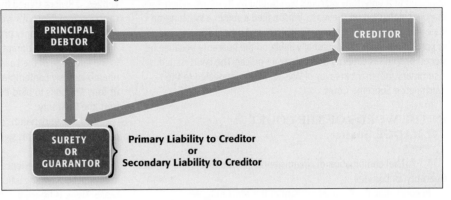

GUARANTY With a suretyship arrangement, the surety is *primarily* liable for the debtor's obligation. With a guaranty arrangement, the **guarantor**—the third person making the guaranty—is *secondarily* liable. The guarantor can be required to pay the obligation *only after the principal debtor defaults,* and default usually takes place only after the creditor has made an attempt to collect from the debtor.

Guarantor A person who agrees to satisfy the debt of another (the debtor) only if and when the debtor fails to pay the debt.

EXAMPLE 14.5 BX Enterprises, a small corporation, needs to borrow funds to meet its payroll. The bank is skeptical about the creditworthiness of BX and requires Dawson, its president, who is a wealthy businessperson and the owner of 70 percent of BX Enterprises, to sign an agreement making himself personally liable for payment if BX does not pay off the loan. As a guarantor of the loan, Dawson cannot be held liable until BX Enterprises is in default. •

Under the Statute of Frauds, a guaranty contract between the guarantor and the creditor must be in writing to be enforceable. Under common law, a suretyship agreement did not need to be in writing to be enforceable, and oral surety agreements were sufficient. Today, however, some states require a writing (record) to enforce a suretyship.

In the following *Spotlight Case,* the issue was whether a guaranty of a lease signed by the president of a corporation was enforceable against the officer personally, although he claimed to have signed the guaranty only as a representative of the corporation.

SPOTLIGHT ON PERSONAL GUARANTIES

Case 14.2 **Wilson Court Limited Partnership v. Tony Maroni's, Inc.**

Supreme Court of Washington, 134 Wash.2d 692, 952 P.2d 590 (1998).

BACKGROUND AND FACTS Tony Riviera founded Tony Maroni's, Inc., to sell Tony Maroni's Famous Gourmet Pizza in Seattle, Washington. Tony Maroni's, Inc., agreed to lease retail space owned by Wilson Court Limited Partnership. Tony Riviera, Tony Maroni's president, signed the lease for 1,676 square feet of space for a sixty-month term. When he signed the lease, Riviera also signed a guaranty agreement that was incorporated by reference in the lease.

Spotlight Case **14.2**–Continues next page ➡

Spotlight Case 14.2–Continued

On the signature line of the guaranty, Riviera wrote "President" after his name. The guaranty did not specifically identify who was bound, referring only to "the undersigned" or "Guarantor." Riviera also signed the lease in a representative capacity, but the lease clearly indicated that only Tony Maroni's was bound by its terms. When Tony Maroni's defaulted on the lease, Wilson filed a suit in a Washington state court against Tony Maroni's, Riviera, and others. Riviera asserted, in part, that he was not personally liable on the guaranty because he signed only in his capacity as a corporate officer. The court issued a summary judgment in favor of Wilson. Riviera appealed to the Washington Supreme Court.

IN THE WORDS OF THE COURT . . .
TALMADGE, Justice.
* * * *

* * * [The] combination of circumstances [in this case] renders the Guaranty ambiguous.

In construing the Guaranty in light of this ambiguity, we acknowledge contracts to answer for the debt of another must be explicit and are strictly construed, but we must also recognize the commercial context in which this Guaranty was signed. Where two commercial entities sign a commercial agreement, we will give such an agreement a commercially reasonable construction. In this case, such a construction leads us to the conclusion Riviera is personally liable on the Guaranty as a matter of law.

First, any ambiguity in the Guaranty was created by Riviera himself in adding the descriptive language to his signature. *Such ambiguity will be construed against Riviera as the party who drafted this language.* [Emphasis added.]

Second, the language of the Guaranty itself compels the view Riviera is personally liable. We must interpret the Lease and Guaranty as a whole, giving reasonable effect to each of its parts. The plain language of the Guaranty clearly contemplates three separate entities, the Landlord, the Tenant and the Guarantor, and so designates them. It identifies Wilson as the Landlord, Tony Maroni's as the Tenant,

and addresses the obligations of a separate third party, referred to interchangeably as the undersigned or Guarantor. * * * The only reasonable interpretation of these provisions is that the Landlord, Tenant and undersigned/Guarantor are three separate and distinct entities. If Riviera signed the Guaranty only in his representative capacity, Tony Maroni's would be both Tenant and Guarantor, rendering the Guaranty provisions absurd.

Moreover, the Guaranty language stands in stark contrast to the language of the Lease where a corporate obligation was unambiguously contemplated. Riviera signed the Lease as president of Tony Maroni's to bind the company. No such intent can be gleaned from the Guaranty.

Third, the very nature of a guaranty is such that Riviera created personal liability by his signature.
* * * *

Riviera is an experienced businessperson with prior experience in commercial leasing who dealt directly with Wilson in securing the Lease. There is no evidence or assertion of any improper conduct by Wilson. Given the commercial sophistication of the parties, the circumstances under which the Guaranty was entered into, and the nature of the Guaranty, a commercially reasonable approach to this case requires us * * * to hold Riviera personally liable under the Guaranty.

DECISION AND REMEDY   The Washington Supreme Court affirmed the judgment of the lower court. The president was personally liable because otherwise the corporation would be the guarantor of its own lease. This would be commercially unreasonable because, as a matter of law, a party cannot be the guarantor of its own contract.

WHAT IF THE FACTS WERE DIFFERENT?   *Suppose that the parties had carefully read the contract before they signed it. If they had been sure that the agreement stated what they intended and if everything discussed was in writing, how might the outcome of this case have been different?*

ACTIONS THAT RELEASE THE SURETY AND GUARANTOR   Basically, the same actions will release a surety or a guarantor from an obligation. In general, the same rules apply to both sureties and guarantors. So, for simplicity, this subsection and the following subsections will refer just to sureties.

If a material modification is made in the terms of the original contract between the principal debtor and the creditor—without the surety's consent—the surety's obligation will be discharged. (The extent to which the surety is discharged depends on whether he or she was compensated and the amount of the loss suffered a result of the modification.) Similarly, if a debt is secured by collateral and the creditor surrenders the collateral to the debtor or impairs the collateral without the surety's consent, these acts can reduce the surety's obligation.

Naturally, any payment of the principal obligation by the debtor or by another person on the debtor's behalf will discharge the surety from the obligation. Even if the creditor refused to accept payment of the principal debt when it was tendered, the surety's obligation can be discharged.

DEFENSES OF THE SURETY AND THE GUARANTOR Generally, the surety (or guarantor) can also assert any of the defenses available to a principal debtor to avoid liability on the obligation to the creditor. A few exceptions do exist, however. The surety cannot assert the principal debtor's incapacity or bankruptcy as a defense, nor can the surety assert the statute of limitations as a defense.

Obviously, a surety may also have her or his own defenses—for example, her or his own incapacity or bankruptcy. If the creditor fraudulently induced the surety to guarantee the debt of the debtor, the surety can assert fraud as a defense. In most states, the creditor has a legal duty to inform the surety, before the formation of the suretyship contract, of material facts known by the creditor that would substantially increase the surety's risk. Failure to so inform may constitute fraud and renders the suretyship obligation voidable.

RIGHTS OF THE SURETY AND THE GUARANTOR Usually, when the surety (or guarantor) pays the debt owed to the creditor, the surety (or guarantor) is entitled to certain rights.

> **Right of Subrogation** The right of a person to stand in the place of (be substituted for) another, giving the substituted party the same legal rights against the debtor that the creditor had.

The Right of Subrogation. The surety has the legal **right of subrogation,** which means that any right the creditor had against the debtor now becomes the right of the surety. Included are creditor rights in bankruptcy, rights to collateral possessed by the creditor, and rights to judgments secured by the creditor. In short, the surety stands in the shoes of the creditor and may pursue any remedies that were available to the creditor against the debtor.

> **Right of Reimbursement** The legal right of a person to be repaid or indemnified for costs, expenses, or losses incurred or expended on behalf of another.

The Right of Reimbursement. The surety has a **right of reimbursement** from the debtor. Basically, the surety is entitled to receive from the debtor all outlays made on behalf of the suretyship arrangement. Such outlays can include expenses incurred as well as the actual amount of the debt paid to the creditor.

> **Co-Surety** One who assumes liability jointly with another surety for the payment of an obligation.
>
> **Right of Contribution** The right of a co-surety who pays more than her or his proportionate share on a debtor's default to recover the excess paid from other co-sureties.

The Right of Contribution. Two or more sureties are called **co-sureties.** When one co-surety pays more than her or his proportionate share on a debtor's default, she or he is entitled to recover from the other co-sureties the amount paid above that surety's obligation. This is the **right of contribution.** Generally, a co-surety's liability either is determined by agreement between the co-sureties or, in the absence of an agreement, is specified in the suretyship contract itself.

EXAMPLE 14.6 Two co-sureties—Yasser and Itzhak—are obligated under a suretyship contract to guarantee the debt of Jules. Itzhak's maximum liability is $15,000, and Yasser's is $10,000. Jules owes $10,000 and is in default. Itzhak pays the creditor the entire $10,000. In the absence of an agreement to the contrary, Itzhak can recover $4,000 from Yasser. The amount of the debt that Yasser agreed to cover is divided by the total amount that Itzhak and Yasser together agreed to cover. The result is multiplied by the amount of the default, yielding the amount that Yasser owes—($10,000 ÷ $25,000) × $10,000 = $4,000. •

▶ Laws Assisting Debtors

The law assists and protects debtors as well as creditors. Certain property of the debtor, for example, is exempt from creditors' actions. Of course, bankruptcy laws, which will be discussed on the next page, are designed specifically to assist debtors.

In most states, certain types of real and personal property are exempt from execution or attachment. State exemption statutes usually include both real and personal property.

Exempted Real Property

Probably the most familiar real property exemption is the **homestead exemption.** Each state permits the debtor to retain the family home, either in its entirety or up to a specified dollar amount, free from the claims of unsecured creditors or trustees in bankruptcy (see page 364).

The purpose of the homestead exemption is to ensure that the debtor will retain some form of shelter. **EXAMPLE 14.7** Van Cleave owes Acosta $40,000. The debt is the subject of a lawsuit, and the court awards Acosta a judgment of $40,000 against Van Cleave. Van Cleave's homestead is valued at around $50,000. There are no outstanding mortgages or other liens. To satisfy the judgment debt, Van Cleave's family home is sold at public auction for $45,000. Assume that the homestead exemption is $25,000. First, Van Cleave is given $25,000 as his homestead exemption. Second, Acosta is paid $20,000 toward the judgment debt, leaving a $20,000 deficiency that can be paid from any other nonexempt property that Van Cleave has, if permitted by state law. ●

Exempted Personal Property

Personal property that is most often exempt under state law includes the following:

1. Household furniture up to a specified dollar amount.
2. Clothing and certain personal possessions, such as family pictures or a religious text.
3. A vehicle (or vehicles) for transportation (at least up to a specified dollar amount).
4. Certain classified animals, usually livestock but including pets.
5. Equipment that the debtor uses in a business or trade, such as tools or professional instruments, up to a specified dollar amount.

▶ Bankruptcy Law

Bankruptcy law in the United States has two goals:

1. To protect a debtor by giving him or her a fresh start, free from creditors' claims.
2. To ensure equitable treatment to creditors who are competing for the debtor's assets.

Bankruptcy law is federal law, but state laws on secured transactions, liens, judgments, and exemptions also play a role in federal bankruptcy proceedings. (For a discussion of how bankruptcy law affects consumers and businesses, see this chapter's *Linking the Law to Economics* feature on page 376.)

Bankruptcy law before 2005 was based on the Bankruptcy Reform Act of 1978, as amended (called the Bankruptcy Code or, simply, the Code). In 2005, Congress enacted bankruptcy reform legislation that significantly overhauled certain provisions of the Code for the first time in twenty-five years.

Bankruptcy Courts

Bankruptcy proceedings are held in federal bankruptcy courts, which are under the authority of U.S. district courts. Rulings by bankruptcy courts can be appealed to the district courts. The bankruptcy court holds proceedings dealing with the procedures required to administer the debtor's estate in bankruptcy. For a discussion of how bankruptcy courts are adapting to the use of social media, see this chapter's *Online Developments* feature on the facing page.

ONLINE DEVELOPMENTS

Live Chatting with Your State's Bankruptcy Court

Chatting on social media has become a way of life for most people in this country and elsewhere. Online chats preceded social media and are still used at thousands of retail Web sites. Today, some tech-savvy employees at bankruptcy courts are using the retail online chat model to answer questions about bankruptcy.

Arizona Was First to Use Live Chats

The U.S. Bankruptcy Court for the District of Arizona started live chatting several years ago. It added live chat to its Web site as part of a strategic initiative to educate the public about bankruptcy. Rather than leaving voice messages, people who access the court's Web site can send and receive text messages via an easy-to-use chat box. The court's goal is to respond to a chat request within thirty seconds.

In 2011, New Mexico became the second state to add online chatting to its bankruptcy court's Web site. Nevada followed with its live chat in 2012. The courts that have adopted online chatting average about ten chats a day. Most chats last less than ten minutes.

Who Uses Bankruptcy Court Chat Rooms?

At first, only individuals interested in filing for bankruptcy without an attorney used the live chat services. When paralegals learned that they could get quick answers to their questions online, they also began to use the services.

Then, during the real estate meltdown of the last few years, many real estate lawyers expanded into the area of bankruptcy law, often as a way to help their clients avoid foreclosure through bankruptcy filings. Many of these lawyers have also used live chat to expand their knowledge of bankruptcy law.

FOR CRITICAL ANALYSIS

Are there any downsides to live chats with bankruptcy courts? If so, what are they?

Types of Bankruptcy Relief

The Code is contained in Title 11 of the *United States Code* (U.S.C.) and has eight "chapters." Chapters 1, 3, and 5 of the Code include general definitional provisions and provisions governing case administration and procedures, creditors, the debtor, and the estate. These three chapters of the Code normally apply to all types of bankruptcies.

Four chapters of the Code set forth the most important types of relief that debtors can seek.

1. *Chapter 7*—Provides for *liquidation* proceedings—that is, the selling of all nonexempt assets and the distribution of the proceeds to the debtor's creditors.
2. *Chapter 11*—Governs *reorganizations* and is used mostly by corporate debtors.
3. *Chapter 12 (for family farmers and family fishermen)*—Provides for adjustment of the debts of parties with regular income.
4. *Chapter 13 (for individuals)*—Provides for adjustment of the debts of parties with regular income.

Note that a debtor need not be *insolvent* (unable to pay debts when due) to file for bankruptcy relief under the Code. Anyone obligated to a creditor can declare bankruptcy.

The Code requires the clerk of the court to give all debtors written notice of the general purpose, benefits, and costs of each chapter of bankruptcy under which they may proceed. In some instances, to avoid bankruptcy proceedings, creditors may prefer private, negotiated adjustments of creditor-debtor relations, also known as **workouts.** Often, these out-of-court workouts are more flexible, faster, and less costly.

Workout An out-of-court agreement between a debtor and creditors that establishes a payment plan for discharging the debtor's debts.

Chapter 7—Liquidation

Liquidation under Chapter 7 is the most familiar type of bankruptcy proceeding and is often referred to as an *ordinary,* or *straight, bankruptcy.* Put simply, a debtor in a liquidation bankruptcy turns all assets over to a trustee. The trustee sells the non-exempt assets and distributes the proceeds to creditors. With certain exceptions, the remaining debts are then **discharged** (extinguished), and the debtor is relieved of the obligation to pay the debts.

Any "person"—defined as including individuals, partnerships, and corporations—may be a debtor under Chapter 7. Railroads, insurance companies, banks, savings and loan associations, investment companies licensed by the U.S. Small Business Administration, and credit unions *cannot* be Chapter 7 debtors, however. Other chapters of the Code or other federal or state statutes apply to them. A husband and wife may file jointly for bankruptcy under a single petition.

A straight bankruptcy may be commenced by the filing of either a voluntary or an involuntary **petition in bankruptcy**—the document that is filed with a bankruptcy court to initiate bankruptcy proceedings. If a debtor files the petition, then it is a *voluntary bankruptcy.* If one or more creditors file a petition to force the debtor into bankruptcy, then it is called an *involuntary bankruptcy.*

We discuss both voluntary and involuntary bankruptcy proceedings under Chapter 7 in the following subsections.

Voluntary Bankruptcy

To bring a voluntary petition in bankruptcy, the debtor files official forms designated for that purpose in the bankruptcy court. The law now requires that *before* debtors can file a petition, they must receive credit counseling from an approved nonprofit agency within the 180-day period preceding the date of filing. Debtors filing a Chapter 7 petition must include a certificate proving that they have received individual or group counseling from an approved agency within the last 180 days (roughly six months).

A **consumer-debtor** who is filing a liquidation bankruptcy must confirm the accuracy of the petition's contents. The debtor must also state in the petition, at the time of filing, that he or she understands the relief available under other chapters of the Code and has chosen to proceed under Chapter 7. Attorneys representing consumer-debtors must file an affidavit stating that they have informed the debtors of the relief available under each chapter of the Code.

In addition, the attorneys must reasonably attempt to verify the accuracy of the consumer-debtors' petitions and schedules (described below). Failure to do so is considered perjury.

CHAPTER 7 SCHEDULES The voluntary petition contains the following schedules:

1. A list of both **secured creditors** and **unsecured creditors,** their addresses, and the amount of debt owed to each.
2. A statement of the financial affairs of the debtor.
3. A list of all property owned by the debtor, including property claimed by the debtor to be exempt.
4. A list of current income and expenses.
5. A certificate of credit counseling (as discussed previously).
6. Proof of payments received from employers within sixty days prior to the filing of the petition.

Liquidation The sale of the assets of a business or an individual for cash and the distribution of the cash received to creditors, with the balance going to the owner(s).

Discharge The termination of a debtor's obligation.

Petition in Bankruptcy The document that is filed with a bankruptcy court to initiate bankruptcy proceedings.

Consumer-Debtor One whose debts result primarily from the purchases of goods for personal, family, or household use.

Secured Creditor A lender or seller who has a security interest in collateral that secures a debt.

Unsecured Creditor A creditor whose debt is not backed by any collateral.

7. A statement of the amount of monthly income, itemized to show how the amount is calculated.

8. A copy of the debtor's federal income tax return for the most recent year ending immediately before the filing of the petition.

The official forms must be completed accurately, sworn to under oath, and signed by the debtor. To conceal assets or knowingly supply false information on these schedules is a crime under the bankruptcy laws.

With the exception of tax returns, failure to file the required schedules within forty-five days after the filing of the petition (unless an extension is granted) will result in an automatic dismissal of the petition. The debtor has up to seven days before the date of the first creditors' meeting to provide a copy of the most recent tax returns to the trustee.

TAX RETURNS DURING BANKRUPTCY In addition, a debtor may be required to file a tax return at the end of each tax year while the case is pending and to provide a copy to the court. This may be done at the request of the court or of the **U.S. trustee**—a government official who performs administrative tasks that a bankruptcy judge would otherwise have to perform, including supervising the work of the bankruptcy trustee.

Any *party in interest* (a party, such as a creditor, who has a valid interest in the outcome of the proceedings) may make this request as well. Debtors may also be required to file tax returns during Chapter 11 and 13 bankruptcies.

SUBSTANTIAL ABUSE AND THE MEANS TEST In the past, a bankruptcy court could dismiss a Chapter 7 petition for relief (discharge of debts) if the use of Chapter 7 would constitute a "substantial abuse" of bankruptcy law. Today, the law provides a *means test* to determine a debtor's eligibility for Chapter 7. The purpose of the test is to keep upper-income people from abusing the bankruptcy process by filing for Chapter 7, as was thought to have happened in the past. The test forces more people to file for Chapter 13 bankruptcy rather than have their debts discharged under Chapter 7.

The Basic Formula. A debtor wishing to file for bankruptcy must complete the means test to determine whether she or he qualifies for Chapter 7. The debtor's average monthly income in recent months is compared with the median income in the geographic area in which the person lives. (The U.S. Trustee Program provides these data at its Web site.) If the debtor's income is below the median income, the debtor usually is allowed to file for Chapter 7 bankruptcy, as there is no presumption of bankruptcy abuse.

Applying the Means Test to Future Disposable Income. If the debtor's income is above the median income, then further calculations must be made to determine whether the person will have sufficient disposable income in the future to repay at least some of his or her unsecured debts. *Disposable income* is calculated by subtracting living expenses and interest payments on secured debt, such as mortgage payments, from monthly income.

In making this calculation, the debtor's recent monthly income is presumed to continue for the next sixty months. Living expenses are the amounts allowed under formulas used by the Internal Revenue Service (IRS). The IRS allowances include modest allocations for food, clothing, housing, utilities, transportation (including car payments), health care, and other necessities. (The U.S. Trustee Program's Web site

U.S. Trustee A government official who performs certain administrative tasks that a bankruptcy judge would otherwise have to perform.

also provides these amounts.) The allowances do not include expenditures for items such as cell phones and cable television service.

Can the Debtor Afford to Pay Unsecured Debts?   Once future disposable income has been estimated, that amount is used to determine whether the debtor will have income that could be applied to unsecured debts. The court may also consider the debtor's bad faith or other circumstances indicating abuse.

CASE EXAMPLE 14.8   At thirty-three years old, Lisa Hebbring owned a home and a car, but had $11,124 in credit-card debt. Hebbring was earning $49,000 per year when she filed for Chapter 7 bankruptcy. Her petition listed monthly net income of $2,813 and expenditures of $2,897, for a deficit of $84. In calculating her income, Hebbring excluded a $313 monthly deduction for contributions to retirement plans. The U.S. trustee filed a motion to dismiss Hebbring's petition due to substantial abuse, claiming that the retirement contributions should be disallowed. The court agreed and dismissed the Chapter 7 petition. Because Hebbring's retirement contributions were not reasonably necessary based on her age and financial circumstances, the court found that she was capable of paying her unsecured debts.[4] ●

ADDITIONAL GROUNDS FOR DISMISSAL   As noted, a debtor's voluntary petition for Chapter 7 relief may be dismissed for substantial abuse or for failing to provide the necessary documents (such as schedules and tax returns) within the specified time.

In addition, a motion to dismiss a Chapter 7 filing may be granted in two other situations. First, if the debtor has been convicted of a violent crime or a drug-trafficking offense, the victim can file a motion to dismiss the voluntary petition.[5] Second, if the debtor fails to pay postpetition domestic-support obligations (which include child and spousal support), the court may dismiss the debtor's Chapter 7 petition.

Order for Relief A court's grant of assistance to a complainant. In bankruptcy proceedings, the order relieves the debtor of the immediate obligation to pay the debts listed in the bankruptcy petition.

ORDER FOR RELIEF   If the voluntary petition for bankruptcy is found to be proper, the filing of the petition will itself constitute an order for relief. (An **order for relief** is the court's grant of assistance to a debtor.) Once a consumer-debtor's voluntary petition has been filed, the clerk of the court (or other appointee) must give the trustee and creditors notice of the order for relief by mail not more than twenty days after the entry of the order.

Involuntary Bankruptcy

An involuntary bankruptcy occurs when the debtor's creditors force the debtor into bankruptcy proceedings. An involuntary case cannot be filed against a farmer[6] or a charitable institution. For an involuntary action to be filed against other debtors, the following requirements must be met: If the debtor has twelve or more creditors, three or more of those creditors having unsecured claims totaling at least $14,425 must join in the petition. If a debtor has fewer than twelve creditors, one or more creditors having a claim of $14,425 or more may file.

If the debtor challenges the involuntary petition, a hearing will be held, and the debtor's challenge will fail if the bankruptcy court finds either of the following:

---

4. *Hebbring v. U.S. Trustee,* 463 F.3d 902 (9th Cir. 2006).

5. Note that the court may not dismiss a case on this ground if the debtor's bankruptcy is necessary to satisfy a claim for a domestic-support obligation.

6. The definition of *farmer* includes persons who receive more than 50 percent of their gross income from farming operations, such as tilling the soil; dairy farming; ranching; or the production or raising of crops, poultry, or livestock. Corporations and partnerships, as well as individuals, can be farmers.

1. The debtor generally is not paying debts as they become due.
2. A general receiver, assignee, or custodian took possession of, or was appointed to take charge of, substantially all of the debtor's property within 120 days before the filing of the involuntary petition.

If the court allows the bankruptcy to proceed, the debtor will be required to supply the same information in the bankruptcy schedules as in a voluntary bankruptcy.

An involuntary petition should not be used as an everyday debt-collection device, and the Code provides penalties for the filing of frivolous (unjustified) petitions against debtors. If the court dismisses an involuntary petition, the petitioning creditors may be required to pay the costs and attorneys' fees incurred by the debtor in defending against the petition. If the petition was filed in bad faith, damages can be awarded for injury to the debtor's reputation. Punitive damages may also be awarded.

Automatic Stay

The filing of a petition, either voluntary or involuntary, operates as an **automatic stay** on (suspension of) almost all litigation and other action by creditors against the debtor or the debtor's property. Basically, once a petition is filed, creditors cannot start or continue most legal actions against the debtor to recover claims. Additionally, they cannot take any action to collect, assess, or recover a claim against the debtor that arose before the bankruptcy filing.

CASE EXAMPLE 14.9 Stefanie Kuehn filed for bankruptcy. When she requested a transcript from the university at which she obtained her master's degree, the university refused because she owed more than $6,000 in tuition. Kuehn complained, and the court ruled that the university had violated the automatic stay when it refused to provide a transcript because it was attempting to collect an unpaid tuition debt.[7] ●

The Code provides several exceptions to the automatic stay. For example, collection efforts can continue for domestic-support obligations, which include any debt owed to or recoverable by a spouse, former spouse, child of the debtor, a child's parent or guardian, or a governmental unit. In addition, proceedings against the debtor related to divorce, child custody or visitation, domestic violence, and support enforcement are not stayed.

Property of the Estate

On the commencement of a liquidation proceeding under Chapter 7, an **estate in property** is created. The estate consists of all the debtor's interests in property currently held, wherever located, together with *community property* (property jointly owned by a husband and wife in certain states), property transferred in a transaction voidable by the trustee, proceeds and profits from the property of the estate, and certain after-acquired property.

Interests in certain property—such as gifts, inheritances, property settlements (from divorce), and life insurance death proceeds—to which the debtor becomes entitled *within 180 days after filing* may also become part of the estate. Withholdings for employee benefit plan contributions are excluded from the estate.

Generally, though, the filing of a bankruptcy petition fixes a dividing line: property acquired before the filing of the petition becomes property of the estate, and property acquired after the filing of the petition, except as just noted, remains the debtor's.

---

7. *In re Kuehn,* 563 F.3d 289 (7th Cir. 2009).

Exemptions

An individual debtor is entitled to exempt certain property from the bankruptcy. The Code exempts the following property:[8]

LEARNING OBJECTIVE 2 **In a bankruptcy proceeding, what constitutes the debtor's estate in property? What property is exempt from the estate under federal bankruptcy law?**

1. Up to $21,625 in equity in the debtor's residence and burial plot (the homestead exemption).
2. Interest in a motor vehicle up to $3,450.
3. Interest, up to $550 for a particular item, in household goods and furnishings, wearing apparel, appliances, books, animals, crops, and musical instruments (the aggregate total of all items is limited to $11,525).
4. Interest in jewelry up to $1,450.
5. Interest in any other property up to $1,150, plus any unused part of the $21,625 homestead exemption up to $10,825.
6. Interest in any tools of the debtor's trade up to $2,175.
7. A life insurance contract owned by the debtor (other than a credit life insurance contract).
8. Certain interests in accrued dividends and interest under life insurance contracts owned by the debtor, not to exceed $11,525.
9. Professionally prescribed health aids.
10. The right to receive Social Security and certain welfare benefits, alimony and support, certain retirement funds and pensions, and education savings accounts held for specific periods of time.
11. The right to receive certain personal-injury and other awards up to $21,625.

STATE VERSUS FEDERAL EXEMPTIONS Individual states have the power to pass legislation precluding debtors from using the federal exemptions within the state. A majority of the states have done this. In those states, debtors may use only state, not federal, exemptions. In the rest of the states, an individual debtor (or a husband and wife filing jointly) may choose either the exemptions provided under state law or the federal exemptions.

THE HOMESTEAD EXEMPTION As noted earlier in this chapter, the Code limits the amount that can be claimed under the homestead exemption in bankruptcy. In general, if the debtor acquired the home within three and one-half years preceding the date of filing, the maximum equity exempted is $146,450 even if state law would permit a higher amount.

In addition, the state homestead exemption is available only if the debtor has lived in the state for two years before filing the petition. Furthermore, a debtor who has violated securities law, been convicted of a felony, or engaged in certain other intentional misconduct may not be permitted to claim the homestead exemption at all.

The Bankruptcy Trustee

Promptly after the order for relief has been entered, a bankruptcy trustee is appointed. The basic duty of the trustee is to collect the debtor's available estate and reduce it to cash for distribution, preserving the interests of both the debtor and the unsecured creditors. This requires that the trustee be accountable for administering the debtor's estate.

---

8. The dollar amounts stated in the Bankruptcy Code are adjusted automatically every three years on April 1 based on changes in the Consumer Price Index. The adjusted amounts are rounded to the nearest $25. The amounts stated in this chapter are in accordance with those computed on April 1, 2010.

To enable the trustee to accomplish this duty, the Code gives the trustee certain powers, stated in both general and specific terms. These powers must be exercised within two years of the order for relief.

CREDITORS' MEETING AND CLAIMS   Not more than forty days after the order of relief has been granted, the trustee must call a meeting of the creditors listed in the schedules filed by the debtor. The debtor must attend this meeting and submit to an examination under oath. At the meeting, the trustee ensures that the debtor is aware of the potential consequences of bankruptcy and the possibility of filing under a different chapter of the Code.

To be entitled to receive a portion of the debtor's estate, each creditor normally files a *proof of claim* with the bankruptcy court clerk within ninety days of the creditors' meeting. The proof of claim lists the creditor's name and address, as well as the amount that the creditor asserts is owed to the creditor by the debtor.

DUTIES FOR MEANS TESTING   The trustee is required to review promptly all materials filed by the debtor to determine if there is substantial abuse. Within ten days after the first meeting of the creditors, the trustee must file a statement as to whether the case is presumed to be an abuse under the means test. The trustee must provide all creditors with a copy of this statement.

When there is a presumption of abuse, the trustee must either file a motion to dismiss the petition (or convert it to a Chapter 13 case) or file a statement setting forth the reasons why the motion would not be appropriate.

TRUSTEE'S POWERS   The trustee has the power to require persons holding the debtor's property at the time the petition is filed to deliver the property to the trustee.[9] To enable the trustee to implement this power, the Code provides that the trustee has rights *equivalent* to those of certain other parties, such as a creditor who has a judicial lien. This power of a trustee, which is equivalent to that of a lien creditor, is known as the *strong-arm power.*

In addition, the trustee also has specific *powers of avoidance*—that is, the trustee can set aside a sale or other transfer of the debtor's property, taking it back as a part of the debtor's estate. These powers of avoidance extend to any voidable rights available to the debtor, preferences, and fraudulent transfers by the debtor (discussed next). A trustee can also avoid certain statutory liens.

The debtor shares most of the trustee's avoidance powers. Thus, if the trustee does not take action to enforce one of these rights, the debtor in a liquidation bankruptcy can enforce it.

VOIDABLE RIGHTS   A trustee steps into the shoes of the debtor. Thus, any reason that a debtor can use to obtain the return of his or her property can be used by the trustee as well. The grounds for recovery include fraud, duress, incapacity, and mutual mistake.

EXAMPLE 14.10 Blane sells his boat to Inga. Inga gives Blane a check, knowing that she has insufficient funds in her bank account to cover the check. Inga has committed fraud. Blane has the right to avoid that transfer and recover the boat from Inga. If Blane files for Chapter 7 bankruptcy, the trustee can exercise the same right to recover the boat from Inga, and the boat becomes part of the debtor's estate. •

---

9. Usually, though, the trustee takes constructive, rather than actual, possession of the debtor's property. For instance, a trustee might change the locks on the doors and hire a security guard to constructively take possession of a business's inventory.

Preference In bankruptcy proceedings, a property transfer or payment made by the debtor that favors one creditor over others.

Preferred Creditor A creditor who has received a preferential transfer from a debtor.

PREFERENCES   A debtor is not permitted to make a property transfer or a payment that favors—or gives a **preference** to—one creditor over others. The trustee is allowed to recover payments made both voluntarily and involuntarily to one creditor in preference over another.

To have made a preferential payment that can be recovered, an *insolvent* debtor generally must have transferred property, for a *preexisting* debt, during the *ninety days* prior to the filing of the petition in bankruptcy. The transfer must have given the creditor more than the creditor would have received as a result of the bankruptcy proceedings. The Code presumes that the debtor is insolvent during the ninety-day period before filing a petition.

If a **preferred creditor** (one who has received a preferential transfer from the debtor) has sold the property to an innocent third party, the trustee cannot recover the property from the innocent party. The trustee can generally force the preferred creditor to pay the value of the property, however.

Preferences to Insiders.   Sometimes, the creditor receiving the preference is an *insider.* An insider is any individual, partner, partnership, or officer or director of a corporation (or a relative of one of these) who has a close relationship with the debtor. In this situation, the avoidance power of the trustee is extended to transfers made within one year before filing. (If the transfer was fraudulent, as will be discussed shortly, the trustee can avoid transfers made within *two years* before filing.)

Note, however, that if the transfer occurred before the ninety-day period, the trustee is required to prove that the debtor was insolvent at the time it occurred or that the transfer was made to or for the benefit of an insider.

Transfers That Do Not Constitute Preferences.   Not all transfers are preferences. To be a preference, the transfer must be made in exchange for something other than current consideration.

Most courts do not consider a debtor's payment for services rendered within fifteen days prior to the payment to be a preference. If a creditor receives payment in the ordinary course of business, such as payment of last month's cell phone bill, the trustee in bankruptcy cannot recover the payment.

To be recoverable, a preference must be a transfer for an antecedent (preexisting) debt, such as a year-old landscaping bill. In addition, the Code permits a consumer-debtor to transfer any property to a creditor up to a total value of $5,850, without the transfer's constituting a preference. Payments of domestic-support debts do not constitute a preference. Neither do payments required under a plan created by an approved credit counseling agency.

FRAUDULENT TRANSFERS   A trustee can set aside fraudulent transfers or obligations if (1) they were made within two years of the filing of the petition or (2) they were made with actual intent to hinder, delay, or defraud a creditor.

EXAMPLE 14.11   April is planning to petition for bankruptcy, so she sells her gold jewelry, worth $10,000, to a friend for $500. The friend agrees that in the future he will "sell" the jewelry back to April for the same amount. This is a fraudulent transfer that the trustee can undo. •

Distribution of Property

The Code provides specific rules for the distribution of the debtor's property to secured and unsecured creditors. If any amount remains after the priority classes of creditors have been satisfied, it is turned over to the debtor. Exhibit 14–2 below illustrates the collection and distribution of property in most voluntary bankruptcies.

DISTRIBUTION TO SECURED CREDITORS   The Code requires that consumer-debtors file a statement of intention with respect to the secured collateral. They can choose to pay off the debt and redeem the collateral, claim it is exempt, reaffirm the debt and continue making payments, or surrender the property to the secured party. If the collateral is surrendered to the secured party, the secured creditor can enforce the security interest either by accepting the property in full satisfaction of the debt or by selling the collateral and using the proceeds to pay off the debt.

Thus, the secured party has priority over unsecured parties as to the proceeds from the disposition of the collateral. Should the collateral be insufficient to cover the secured debt owed, the secured creditor becomes an unsecured creditor for the difference.

DISTRIBUTION TO UNSECURED CREDITORS   Bankruptcy law establishes an order of priority for classes of debts owed to unsecured creditors, and they are paid in the order of their priority. Each class must be fully paid before the next class is entitled to any of the remaining proceeds.

If there are insufficient proceeds to pay the full amount to all the creditors in a class, the proceeds are distributed *proportionately* to the creditors in that class, and classes lower in priority receive nothing. If there is any balance remaining after all the creditors are paid, it is returned to the debtor.

In almost all Chapter 7 bankruptcies, the funds will be insufficient to pay all creditors. Note that claims for domestic-support obligations, such as child support and alimony, have the highest priority among unsecured claims, so these debts must be paid first. If any amount remains after the priority classes of creditors have been satisfied, it is turned over to the debtor.

● *Exhibit* 14–2 **Collection and Distribution of Property in Most Voluntary Bankruptcies**
This exhibit illustrates the property that might be collected in a debtor's voluntary bankruptcy and how it might be distributed to creditors. Involuntary bankruptcies and some voluntary bankruptcies could include additional types of property and other creditors.

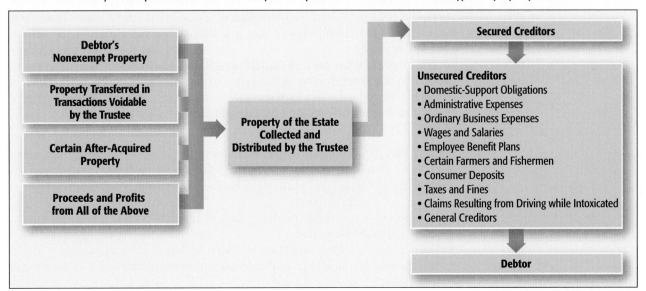

Discharge

From the debtor's point of view, the primary purpose of liquidation is to obtain a fresh start through the discharge of debts. A discharge voids, or sets aside, any judgment on a discharged debt and prevents any action to collect it. Certain debts, however, are not dischargeable in bankruptcy. Also, certain debtors may not qualify to have all debts discharged in bankruptcy. These situations are discussed next.

LEARNING OBJECTIVE 3 **What is the difference between an exception to discharge and an objection to discharge?**

EXCEPTIONS TO DISCHARGE   The most important claims that are not dischargeable under Chapter 7 include the following:

1. Claims for back taxes accruing within two years prior to bankruptcy.
2. Claims for amounts borrowed by the debtor to pay federal taxes or any nondischargeable taxes.
3. Claims against property or funds obtained by the debtor under false pretenses or by false misrepresentations.
4. Claims based on fraud or misuse of funds by the debtor or claims involving the debtor's embezzlement or larceny (see Chapter 7).
5. Domestic-support obligations and property settlements.
6. Claims for amounts due on a retirement loan account.
7. Claims based on willful or malicious conduct by the debtor toward another or the property of another.
8. Certain government fines and penalties.
9. Certain student loans, unless payment of the loans causes an undue hardship for the debtor and the debtor's dependents.

Ethical Issue

Are the consequences of student loan defaults too onerous? In the United States today, the amount of student loans outstanding exceeds $1 trillion, and more than 20 percent of these loans are in default. A borrower is considered in default if he or she has not made regular payments on a student loan for nine months. If you go into default on your student loans, the U.S. Department of Education can do the following to collect the debt: (1) keep your tax refund, if you have one; (2) garnish your paycheck without obtaining a court judgment; and (3) take your federal benefits, such as Social Security retirement payments or disability payments. In addition, in some states any professional license that you have can be revoked. Last but not least, the Department of Education can bring a lawsuit against you. If it wins, it can collect the judgment from your bank accounts or place a lien on any real property that you own.

Furthermore, whether you owe the debt to the federal government or to a private lender, student loan debt generally is *not* dischargeable in bankruptcy. You may be able to have your payments deferred but for only three years. Under certain circumstances, student loan debts may be canceled, but the rules limit this option to only a very few borrowers.

OBJECTIONS TO DISCHARGE   In addition to the exceptions to discharge previously listed, a bankruptcy court may deny a discharge to the debtor for reasons relating to his or her *conduct* and not to the debt. The situations in which a court can deny discharge include the following:

1. The debtor's concealment or destruction of property with the intent to hinder, delay, or defraud a creditor.
2. The debtor's fraudulent concealment or destruction of financial records.
3. The granting of a discharge to the debtor within eight years prior to the filing of the petition.

4. The debtor's failure to complete the required consumer education course (unless such a course was not available).

5. Proceedings in which the debtor could be found guilty of a felony. (Basically, a court may not discharge any debt until the completion of the felony proceedings against the debtor.)

When a discharge is denied under these circumstances, the debtor's assets are still distributed to the creditors. After the bankruptcy proceeding, however, the debtor remains liable for the unpaid portions of all claims.

Reaffirmation Agreement An agreement between a debtor and a creditor in which the debtor voluntarily agrees to pay a debt dischargeable in bankruptcy.

REAFFIRMATION OF DEBT   An agreement to pay a debt dischargeable in bankruptcy is called a **reaffirmation agreement.** A debtor may wish to pay a debt—for example, a debt owed to a family member, physician, bank, or some other creditor—even though the debt could be discharged in bankruptcy. Also, as noted previously, a debtor cannot retain secured property while continuing to pay without entering into a reaffirmation agreement.

Procedures.   To be enforceable, reaffirmation agreements must be made before the debtor is granted a discharge. The agreement must be signed and filed with the court (along with the original disclosure documents, as you will read shortly). Court approval is required unless the debtor is represented by an attorney during the negotiation of the reaffirmation agreement and submits the proper documents and certifications. Even when the debtor is represented by an attorney, court approval may be required if it appears that the reaffirmation will result in undue hardship to the debtor.

When court approval is required, a separate hearing will take place. The court will approve the reaffirmation only if it finds that the agreement will not result in undue hardship to the debtor and that the reaffirmation is consistent with the debtor's best interests.

Required Disclosures.   To discourage creditors from engaging in abusive reaffirmation practices, the law provides specific language for disclosures that must be given to debtors entering reaffirmation agreements. Among other things, these disclosures explain that the debtor is not required to reaffirm any debt, but that liens on secured property, such as mortgages and cars, will remain in effect even if the debt is not reaffirmed.

The reaffirmation agreement must disclose the amount of the debt reaffirmed, the rate of interest, the date payments begin, and the right to rescind. The disclosures also caution the debtor: "Only agree to reaffirm a debt if it is in your best interest. Be sure you can afford the payments you agree to make."

The original disclosure documents must be signed by the debtor, certified by the debtor's attorney, and filed with the court at the same time as the reaffirmation agreement. A reaffirmation agreement that is not accompanied by the original signed disclosures will not be effective.

Chapter 11—Reorganization

Reorganization A plan for the readjustment of a corporation and its debts, the submission of the plan to a bankruptcy court, and the court's approval or rejection of the plan.

The type of bankruptcy proceeding used most commonly by corporate debtors is the Chapter 11 **reorganization.** In a reorganization, the creditors and the debtor formulate a plan under which the debtor pays a portion of its debts and the rest of the debts are discharged. The debtor is allowed to continue in business. Although this type of bankruptcy is generally a corporate reorganization, any debtor who is eligible for Chapter 7 relief is eligible for Chapter 11 relief. (Note that railroads, which are not eligible under Chapter 7, are eligible under Chapter 11.)

The same principles that govern the filing of a liquidation (Chapter 7) petition apply to reorganization (Chapter 11) proceedings. The case may be brought either voluntarily or involuntarily. The automatic-stay provision and its exceptions apply in reorganizations as well, as do the provisions regarding substantial abuse and additional grounds for dismissal of bankruptcy petitions.

Once a petition for Chapter 11 has been filed, a bankruptcy court, after notice and a hearing, can dismiss or suspend all proceedings in a case at any time if dismissal or suspension would better serve the interests of the creditors. The Bankruptcy Code also allows a court, after notice and a hearing, to dismiss a case under reorganization "for cause." Cause includes the absence of a reasonable likelihood of rehabilitation, the inability to effect a plan, and an unreasonable delay by the debtor that is prejudicial to (may harm the interests of) creditors.

Debtor in Possession

Debtor in Possession (DIP) In Chapter 11 bankruptcy proceedings, a debtor who is allowed to continue in possession of the estate in property (the business) and to continue business operations.

On entry of the order for relief, the debtor in Chapter 11 generally continues to operate the business as a **debtor in possession (DIP).** The court, however, may appoint a trustee (often referred to as a *receiver*) to operate the debtor's business if gross mismanagement of the business is shown or if appointing a trustee is in the best interests of the estate.

The DIP's role is similar to that of a trustee in a liquidation. The DIP is entitled to avoid preferential payments made to creditors and fraudulent transfers of assets. The DIP has the power to decide whether to cancel or assume prepetition *executory contracts* (see page 265 in Chapter 11) or unexpired leases. Cancellation of executory contracts or unexpired leases can be a substantial benefit to a Chapter 11 debtor.

LEARNING OBJECTIVE 4 **In a Chapter 11 reorganization, what is the role of the debtor in possession?**

EXAMPLE 14.12 APT Corporation leases an office building for a twenty-year term. After five years, APT can no longer pay the rent due under the lease and has filed for Chapter 11 reorganization. In this situation, the debtor in possession could cancel the lease so that APT will not be required to continue paying the substantial rent due for fifteen more years. ●

Creditors' Committees

As soon as practicable after the entry of the order for relief, a committee of unsecured creditors is appointed. If the debtor has filed a plan accepted by the creditors, however, the trustee may decide not to call a meeting of the creditors. The committee may consult with the trustee or the debtor concerning the administration of the case or the formulation of the plan. Additional creditors' committees may be appointed to represent special interest creditors, and a court may order the trustee to change a committee's membership as needed to ensure adequate representation of the creditors.

Generally, no orders affecting the estate will be entered without the consent of the committee or a hearing in which the judge is informed of the position of the committee. Businesses with debts of less than $2.19 million that do not own or manage real estate can avoid creditors' committees. In these fast-track proceedings, orders can be entered without a committee's consent.

The Reorganization Plan

A reorganization plan is established to conserve and administer the debtor's assets in the hope of an eventual return to successful operation and solvency. The plan must be fair and equitable and must do the following:

1. Designate classes of claims and interests.
2. Specify the treatment to be afforded the classes. (The plan must provide the same treatment for all claims in a particular class.)
3. Provide an adequate means for execution. (Individual debtors must utilize post-petition assets as necessary to execute the plan.)
4. Provide for payment of tax claims over a five-year period.

FILING THE PLAN　　Only the debtor may file a plan within the first 120 days after the date of the order for relief. This period may be extended up to eighteen months from the date of the order for relief. If the debtor does not meet the 120-day deadline or obtain an extension, or if the debtor fails to obtain the required creditor consent (discussed below) within 180 days, any party may propose a plan. If a small-business debtor chooses to avoid a creditors' committee, the time for the debtor's filing is 180 days.

ACCEPTANCE AND CONFIRMATION OF THE PLAN　　Once the plan has been developed, it is submitted to each class of creditors for acceptance. Each class must accept the plan unless the class is adversely affected by it. The plan need not provide for full repayment to unsecured creditors. Instead, creditors receive a percentage of each dollar owed to them by the debtor.

A class has accepted the plan when a majority of the creditors, representing two-thirds of the amount of the total claim, vote to approve it. Confirmation is conditioned on the debtor's certifying that all postpetition domestic-support obligations have been paid in full. For small-business debtors, if the plan meets the listed requirements, the court must confirm the plan within forty-five days (unless this period is extended).

Even when all classes of creditors accept the plan, the court may refuse to confirm it if it is not "in the best interests of the creditors." The plan can also be modified upon the request of the debtor, trustee, U.S. trustee, or holder of an unsecured claim. If an unsecured creditor objects to the plan, specific rules apply to the value of property to be distributed under the plan. Tax claims must be paid over a five-year period.

Even if only one class of creditors has accepted the plan, the court may still confirm the plan under the Code's so-called **cram-down provision.** In other words, the court may confirm the plan over the objections of a class of creditors. Before the court can exercise this right of cram-down confirmation, it must be demonstrated that the plan is fair and equitable, and does not discriminate unfairly against any creditors.

Cram-Down Provision A provision of the Bankruptcy Code that allows a court to confirm a debtor's Chapter 11 reorganization plan even though only one class of creditors has accepted it.

DISCHARGE　　The plan is binding on confirmation. The law provides, however, that confirmation of a plan does not discharge an individual debtor. *For individual debtors, the plan must be completed before discharge will be granted,* unless the court orders otherwise. For all other debtors, the court may order discharge at any time after the plan is confirmed. The debtor is given a reorganization discharge from all claims not protected under the plan. This discharge does not apply to any claims that would be denied discharge under liquidation.

▶ Bankruptcy Relief under Chapter 12 and Chapter 13

In addition to bankruptcy relief through liquidation (Chapter 7) and reorganization (Chapter 11), the Code also provides for family-farmer and family-fisherman debt adjustments (Chapter 12) and individuals' repayment plans (Chapter 13).

Chapter 12—Family Farmers and Fishermen

Chapter 12 bankruptcy relief is for small farmers and family fishermen. For purposes of Chapter 12, a *family farmer* is one whose gross income is at least 50 percent farm dependent and whose debts are at least 50 percent farm related.[10] The total debt must not exceed $3,792,650. A partnership or a close corporation (see Chapter 10) that is at least 50 percent owned by the farm family can also qualify as a family farmer.[11]

A *family fisherman* is one whose gross income is at least 50 percent dependent on commercial fishing operations and whose debts are at least 80 percent related to commercial fishing. The total debt for a family fisherman must not exceed $1,757,475. As with family farmers, a partnership or close corporation can also qualify.

FILING THE PETITION   The procedure for filing a family-farmer or family-fisherman bankruptcy plan is similar to the procedure for filing a repayment plan under Chapter 13, which will be discussed below. The debtor must file a plan not later than ninety days after the order for relief. The filing of the petition acts as an automatic stay against creditors' and co-obligors' actions against the estate.

A farmer or fisherman who has already filed a reorganization or repayment plan may convert the plan to a Chapter 12 plan. The debtor may also convert a Chapter 12 plan to a liquidation plan.

CONTENT AND CONFIRMATION OF THE PLAN   The content of a plan under Chapter 12 is basically the same as that of a Chapter 13 repayment plan (described below). The plan can be modified by the debtor but, except for cause, must be confirmed or denied within forty-five days of the filing of the plan.

The plan must provide for payment of secured debts at the value of the collateral. If the secured debt exceeds the value of the collateral, the remaining debt is unsecured. For unsecured debtors, the plan must be confirmed if either the value of the property to be distributed under the plan equals the amount of the claim or the plan provides that all of the debtor's disposable income to be received in a three-year period (or longer, by court approval) will be applied to making payments. Completion of payments under the plan discharges all debts provided for by the plan.

Chapter 13—Individuals' Repayment Plan

Chapter 13 of the Bankruptcy Code provides for the "Adjustment of Debts of an Individual with Regular Income." Individuals (not partnerships or corporations) with regular income who owe fixed unsecured debts of less than $360,475 or fixed secured debts of less than $1,081,400 may take advantage of bankruptcy repayment plans.

Many small-business debtors have a choice of filing under either Chapter 11 or Chapter 13. Repayment plans offer some advantages because they are typically less expensive and less complicated than reorganization or liquidation proceedings.

FILING THE PETITION   A Chapter 13 repayment plan case can be initiated only by the filing of a voluntary petition by the debtor or by the conversion of a Chapter 7 petition (because of a finding of substantial abuse under the means test, for instance).

---

10. Note that the Bankruptcy Code defines a *family farmer* and a *farmer* differently. To be a farmer, a person or business must receive 50 percent of gross income from a farming operation that the person or business owns or operates.

11. Note that for a corporation or partnership to qualify under Chapter 12, at least 80 percent of the value of the firm's assets must consist of assets related to the farming operation.

Certain liquidation and reorganization cases may be converted to Chapter 13 with the consent of the debtor.[12] A trustee, who will make payments under the plan, must be appointed. On the filing of a repayment plan petition, the automatic stay previously discussed takes effect. Although the stay applies to all or part of the debtor's consumer debt, it does not apply to any business debt incurred by the debtor or to any domestic-support obligations.

GOOD FAITH REQUIREMENT   The Bankruptcy Code imposes the requirement of good faith on a debtor in both the filing of the petition and the filing of the plan. The Code does not define good faith, but if the circumstances as a whole indicate bad faith, a court can dismiss a debtor's Chapter 13 petition.

CASE EXAMPLE 14.13   Roger and Pauline Buis formed an air show business, called Otto Airshows that included a helicopter decorated as "Otto the Clown." After a competitor won a defamation lawsuit against the Buises and Otto Airshows, the Buises stopped doing business as Otto Airshows and formed a new firm, Prop and Rotor Aviation, Inc., to which they leased the Otto equipment. Within a month, they filed a bankruptcy petition under Chapter 13. The plan and the schedules did not mention the lawsuit, the equipment lease, and several other items. The court therefore dismissed the Buises' petition due to bad faith. The debtors had not included all of their assets and liabilities on their initial petition, and they had timed its filing to avoid payment on the defamation judgment.[13] ●

THE REPAYMENT PLAN   A plan of rehabilitation by repayment must provide for the following:

1. The turning over to the trustee of future earnings or income of the debtor as necessary for execution of the plan.
2. Full payment through deferred cash payments of all claims entitled to priority, such as taxes.[14]
3. Identical treatment of all claims within a particular class. (The Code permits the debtor to list co-debtors, such as guarantors or sureties, as a separate class.)

Timely Payments.   The repayment plan may provide for payment of all obligations in full or for payment of a lesser amount. The debtor must begin making payments under the proposed plan within thirty days after the plan has been filed and must continue to make "timely" payments from her or his disposable income. If the debtor fails to make timely payments or does not commence payments within the thirty-day period, the court can convert the case to a liquidation bankruptcy or dismiss the petition.

The Length of the Plan.   The length of the payment plan can be three or five years, depending on the debtor's family income. If the debtor's family income is less than the median family income in the relevant geographic area under the means test, the term of the proposed plan must be three years. The term may not exceed five years.

In putting together a repayment plan, a debtor must apply the means test to identify the amount of disposable income that will be available to repay creditors. The

---

12. A Chapter 13 repayment plan may be converted to a Chapter 7 liquidation either at the request of the debtor or, under certain circumstances, "for cause" by a creditor. A Chapter 13 case may be converted to a Chapter 11 case after a hearing.
13. *In re Buis,* 337 Bankr. 243 (N.D.Fla. 2006).
14. As with a Chapter 11 reorganization plan, full repayment of all claims is not always required.

debtor is allowed to deduct certain expenses from monthly income to arrive at this amount. Which expenses are allowed, however, is sometimes left up to the courts.

CASE EXAMPLE 14.14 Jason Ransom filed a Chapter 13 bankruptcy petition. Among his assets, he listed a Toyota Camry that he owned free of any debt. In his monthly expenses, however, he claimed a car-ownership deduction of $471 and a separate $388 deduction for costs to operate the car. He proposed a five-year plan that would repay about 25 percent of his unsecured debt. FIA Card Services, N.A., an unsecured creditor, objected to the plan, arguing against the car-ownership allowance. The United States Supreme Court ruled in FIA's favor. The Bankruptcy Code limits a debtor's expenses to those that are applicable or appropriate. A deduction is appropriate only if the debtor will incur that expense during the life of the Chapter 13 plan. A debtor who does not make loan or lease payments may not take a car-ownership deduction. Thus, Ransom, who owned the car free and clear, could not claim the car-ownership deduction.[15] ●

Confirmation of the Plan.   After the plan is filed, the court holds a confirmation hearing, at which interested parties (such as creditors) may object to the plan. The hearing must be held at least twenty days, but no more than forty-five days, after the meeting of the creditors. The debtor must have filed all prepetition tax returns and paid all postpetition domestic-support obligations before a court will confirm any plan. The court will confirm a plan with respect to each claim of a secured creditor under any of the following circumstances:

1. If the secured creditors have accepted the plan.
2. If the plan provides that secured creditors retain their liens until there is payment in full or until the debtor receives a discharge.
3. If the debtor surrenders the property securing the claims to the creditors.

DISCHARGE   After the completion of all payments, the court grants a discharge of all debts provided for by the repayment plan. Except for allowed claims not provided for by the plan, certain long-term debts provided for by the plan, certain tax claims, payments on retirement accounts, and claims for domestic-support obligations, all other debts are dischargeable. Under current law, debts related to injury or property damage caused while driving under the influence of alcohol or drugs are nondischargeable.

Certain student loan debts can be discharged under Chapter 13, but only if the court finds that payment of the debt would constitute an "undue hardship" for the debtor. In the following case, a debtor had proposed to discharge some of his student loan debt in a Chapter 13 repayment plan. The United States Supreme Court had to decide whether some oversights by the creditor and lower court rendered the discharge of the debt void.

---

15. *Ransom v. FIA Card Services, N.A.,* __ U.S. __ , 131 S.Ct. 716, 178 L.Ed.2d 603 (2011).

Case 14.3   **United Student Aid Funds, Inc. v. Espinosa**

Supreme Court of the United States, ___ U.S. ___, 130 S.Ct. 1367, 176 L.Ed.2d 158 (2010).

BACKGROUND AND FACTS   Francisco Espinosa filed a petition for an individual repayment plan under Chapter 13 of the Bankruptcy Code. The plan proposed that Espinosa would repay only the principal of his student loan debt and that the interest on the loan would be discharged once the principal was repaid. Under Chapter 13, a student loan cannot be discharged unless the bankruptcy court finds that payment of the debt would constitute an undue hardship for the debtor. Notwithstanding this requirement, no undue hardship hearing was requested by the debtor, by the court, or by the creditor, United Student Aid Funds (United). The creditor received notice of the plan but did not object to it—nor did the

Case 14.3–Continued

creditor file an appeal after the bankruptcy court subsequently confirmed the plan. Years later, however, United filed a motion under Federal Rule of Civil Procedure 60(b)(4) asking the bankruptcy court to rule that its order confirming the plan was void because the order was issued in violation of the laws and rules governing bankruptcy. The court denied United's petition and ordered the creditor to cease its collection efforts. The creditor appealed to the U.S. District Court for the District of Arizona, and the district court reversed the bankruptcy court's ruling. On further appeal, the U.S. Court of Appeals for the Ninth Circuit reversed the district court's judgment. United appealed to the United States Supreme Court.

IN THE WORDS OF THE COURT . . .
Justice *THOMAS* delivered the opinion of the Court.
  * * * *

A discharge under Chapter 13 "is broader than the discharge received in any other chapter." Chapter 13 nevertheless restricts or prohibits entirely the discharge of certain types of debts. As relevant here, [Section] 1328(a) [of the Bankruptcy Code] provides that when a debtor has completed the repayments required by a confirmed plan, a bankruptcy court "shall grant the debtor a discharge of all debts provided for by the plan or disallowed under Section 502 of this title, except," *inter alia* [among others], "any debt * * * of the kind specified in [Section] 523(a)(8). [That section], in turn, specifies certain student loan debts "unless excepting such debt from discharge * * * would impose an undue hardship on the debtor and the debtor's dependents." * * * *[The] Bankruptcy Rules require a party seeking to determine the dischargeability of a student loan debt to commence an adversary proceeding by serving a summons and complaint on affected creditors.* We must decide whether the Bankruptcy Court's order confirming Espinosa's plan is "void" under Federal Rule of Civil Procedure 60(b)(4) because the Bankruptcy Court confirmed the plan without complying with these requirements. [Emphasis added.]

The Bankruptcy Court's order confirming Espinosa's proposed plan was a final judgment, from which United [Student Aid Funds] did not appeal. * * * Rule 60(b)(4)–the provision under which United brought this motion–authorizes the court to relieve a party from a final judgment if "the judgment is void."
  * * * *

"A judgment is not void" * * * "simply because it is or may have been erroneous." Similarly, a motion under Rule 60(b)(4) is not a substitute for a timely appeal. Instead, Rule 60(b)(4) applies only in the rare instance where a judgment is premised either on a certain

type of jurisdictional error or on a violation of due process that deprives a party of notice or the opportunity to be heard.
  * * * *

Unable to demonstrate a jurisdictional error or a due process violation, United and the Government, as *amicus* [friend of the court], urge us to expand the universe of judgment defects that support Rule 60(b)(4) relief. Specifically, they contend that the Bankruptcy Court's confirmation order is void because the court lacked statutory authority to confirm Espinosa's plan absent a finding of undue hardship.
  * * * *

*Given the Code's clear * * * requirement for an undue hardship determination, the Bankruptcy Court's failure to find undue hardship before confirming Espinosa's plan was a legal error. But the order remains enforceable and binding on United because United had notice of the error and failed to object or timely appeal.* [Emphasis added.]

United's response–that it had no obligation to object to Espinosa's plan until Espinosa served it with the summons and complaint the Bankruptcy Rules require–is unavailing [ineffective]. Rule 60(b)(4) does not provide a license for litigants to sleep on their rights. United had actual notice of the filing of Espinosa's plan, its contents, and the Bankruptcy Court's subsequent confirmation of the plan. In addition, United filed a proof of claim regarding Espinosa's student loan debt, thereby submitting itself to the Bankruptcy Court's jurisdiction with respect to that claim. United therefore forfeited its arguments regarding the validity of service or the adequacy of the Bankruptcy Court's procedures by failing to raise a timely objection in that court.

DECISION AND REMEDY   The United States Supreme Court affirmed the judgment of the U.S. Court of Appeals for the Ninth Circuit. The bankruptcy court's confirmation order concerning Espinosa's Chapter 13 repayment plan was not void, and the student loan debt was thus discharged.

MANAGERIAL IMPLICATIONS   *Business owners and managers should be aware that courts generally have little sympathy for those who "sleep on their rights." In this case, the creditor could have objected to the plan, but it did not. The creditor also could have appealed the confirmation order, but it did not. Only years later did the creditor seek to have the confirmation order declared void. If a client or other debtor petitions for bankruptcy relief, businesspersons should protect their rights by responding promptly to any notices from the debtor or the bankruptcy court.*

▶ **Reviewing. . . Creditors' Rights and Bankruptcy**

Three months ago, Janet Hart's husband of twenty years died of cancer. Although he had medical insurance, he left Janet with outstanding medical bills of more than $50,000. Janet has worked at the local library for the past ten years, earning $1,500 per month. Since her husband's death, Janet also has received $1,500 in Social Security benefits and $1,100 in life insurance proceeds every month, giving her a monthly income of $4,100. After she pays the mortgage payment of $1,500 and the amounts due on other debts each month, Janet barely has enough left over to buy groceries for her family (she has two teenage daughters at home). She decides to file for Chapter 7 bankruptcy, hoping for a fresh start. Using the information provided in the chapter, answer the following questions.

(Continued)

1. Under the Bankruptcy Code after the reform act, what must Janet do before filing a petition for relief under Chapter 7?
2. How much time does Janet have after filing the bankruptcy petition to submit the required schedules? What happens if Janet does not meet the deadline?
3. Assume that Janet files a petition under Chapter 7. Further assume that the median family income in the state in which Janet lives is $49,300. What steps would a court take to determine whether Janet's petition is presumed to be "substantial abuse" under the means test?
4. Suppose that the court determines that no presumption of substantial abuse applies in Janet's case. Nevertheless, the court finds that Janet does have the ability to pay at least a portion of the medical bills out of her disposable income. What would the court likely order in that situation?

▶ Debate This

Rather than being allowed to file Chapter 7 bankruptcy petitions, individuals and couples should always be forced to make an effort to pay off their debts through Chapter 13.

Linking the Law *to Economics*

The Effects of Bankruptcy Law on Consumers and Businesses

The economic crisis that started in late 2007 led to a significant increase in bankruptcy filings by U.S. consumers and businesses. In 2008, bankruptcy filings by consumers were up by more than 30 percent. In the same year, 136 publicly traded U.S. companies filed for bankruptcy, an increase of 74 percent from a year earlier. In a typical month in 2009, about 100,000 consumers filed for bankruptcy protection.

Bankruptcy in the United States is permitted under Article I, Section 8, of the U.S. Constitution, which authorizes Congress to enact "uniform Laws on the subject of Bankruptcies throughout the United States." In your business law or legal environment course, you learn about the types of bankruptcy and their procedures. In your economics courses, you learn about how bankruptcy law affects the behavior of individuals and businesses.

Bankruptcy Law Can Change the Incentives Facing Consumers

Before the framing of the U.S. Constitution, there were debtors' prisons in the United States, and debtors who could not pay their debts were sometimes sent to prison. The threat of going to prison certainly caused consumers to borrow less and to make a great effort to repay what they owed. Today, of course, we no longer have debtors' prisons, so consumers who are unable to pay their debts know that although they may be ruined financially if they have to file for bankruptcy, they will not go to prison.

It goes without saying that the easier and less costly it is for consumers to declare bankruptcy and effectively "start over with a clean slate," the more debt they will demand and the less they will worry about repaying their creditors. Indeed, one of the reasons that the bankruptcy reform law was enacted in 2005 was to prevent abuse of the bankruptcy process. According to some, it had become too easy for consumers to avoid paying their debts in full.

Bankruptcy Law Also Affects the Incentives of Businesses That Lend

Consumers typically obtain credit from banks, credit-card companies, auto loan companies, finance companies, and major retailers. These lending entities end up charging a competitive interest rate because the market for consumer credit is highly competitive. That competitive interest rate includes a risk premium to cover the consumer debt that is never repaid.

Consequently, the easier it is for consumers to file for bankruptcy and wipe out their debts, the higher the risk to the lenders. In other words, the more forgiving the bankruptcy laws are, the more the lending entities will charge consumers for credit. As you learn in your economics courses, all government actions that change incentives lead to other changes in the economy. In this situation, laws that are more favorable to borrowers are by definition less favorable to lenders. The result is higher market interest rates for loans.

FOR CRITICAL ANALYSIS
In what ways do bankruptcy laws benefit the economy as a whole?

Key Terms

affidavit 353
artisan's lien 352
attachment 353
automatic stay 363
consumer-debtor 360
co-surety 357
cram-down provision 371
creditors' composition agreement 354
debtor in possession (DIP) 370
discharge 360
estate in property 363
garnishment 353

guarantor 355
homestead exemption 358
lien 351
liquidation 360
mechanic's lien 351
order for relief 362
petition in bankruptcy 360
preference 366
preferred creditor 366
reaffirmation agreement 369
reorganization 369
right of contribution 357

right of reimbursement 357
right of subrogation 357
secured creditor 360
surety 354
suretyship 354
unsecured creditor 360
U.S. trustee 361
workout 359
writ of attachment 353
writ of execution 353

Chapter Summary: Creditors' Rights and Bankruptcy

	LAWS ASSISTING CREDITORS

Liens (See pages 351–353.)	1. *Mechanic's lien*—A nonpossessory, filed lien on an owner's real estate for labor, services, or materials furnished to or used to make improvements on the realty.
	 2. *Artisan's lien*—A possessory lien on an owner's personal property for labor performed or value added.
	 3. *Judicial liens*—
	   a. *Writ of attachment*—A court-ordered seizure of property prior to a court's final determination of the creditor's rights to the property. Attachment is available only on the creditor's posting of a bond and strict compliance with the applicable state statutes.
	   b. *Writ of execution*—A court order directing the sheriff to seize (levy) and sell a debtor's nonexempt real or personal property to satisfy a court's judgment in the creditor's favor.

Garnishment (See pages 353–354.)	A collection remedy that allows the creditor to attach a debtor's funds (such as wages owed or bank accounts) and property that are held by a third person.
Creditors' Composition Agreements (See page 354.)	A contract between a debtor and his or her creditors by which the debtor's debts are discharged by payment of a sum less than the amount that is actually owed.
Suretyship and Guaranty (See pages 354–357.)	Under contract, a third person agrees to be primarily or secondarily liable for the debt owed by the principal debtor. A creditor can turn to this third person for satisfaction of the debt.
	LAWS ASSISTING DEBTORS
Exemptions (See page 358.)	Certain property of a debtor is exempt from creditors' actions under state laws. Each state permits a debtor to retain the family home, either in its entirety or up to a specified dollar amount, free from the claims of unsecured creditors or trustees in bankruptcy (homestead exemption).

(Continued)

Chapter Summary: Creditors' Rights and Bankruptcy, Continued

BANKRUPTCY—A COMPARISON OF CHAPTERS 7, 11, 12, AND 13

Issue	Chapter 7	Chapter 11	Chapters 12 and 13
Purpose	Liquidation.	Reorganization.	Adjustment.
Who Can Petition	Debtor (voluntary) or creditors (involuntary).	Debtor (voluntary) or creditors (involuntary).	Debtor (voluntary) only.
Who Can Be a Debtor	Any "person" (including partnerships and corporations) except railroads, insurance companies, banks, savings and loan institutions, investment companies licensed by the U.S. Small Business Administration, and credit unions. Farmers and charitable institutions cannot be involuntarily petitioned.	Any debtor eligible for Chapter 7 relief; railroads are also eligible.	*Chapter 12*—Any family farmer (one whose gross income is at least 50 percent farm dependent and whose debts are at least 50 percent farm related) or family fisherman (one whose gross income is at least 50 percent dependent on and whose debts are at least 80 percent related to commercial fishing) or any partnership or close corporation at least 50 percent owned by a family farmer or fisherman, when total debt does not exceed $3,792,650 for a family farmer and $1,757,475 for a family fisherman. *Chapter 13*—Any individual (not partnerships or corporations) with regular income who owes fixed (liquidated) unsecured debts of less than $360,475 or fixed secured debts of less than $1,081,400.
Procedure Leading to Discharge	Nonexempt property is sold with proceeds to be distributed (in order) to priority groups. Dischargeable debts are terminated.	Plan is submitted. If it is approved and followed, debts are discharged.	Plan is submitted and must be approved if the value of the property to be distributed equals the amount of the claims or if the debtor turns over disposable income for a three- or five-year period. If the plan is followed, debts are discharged.
Advantages	On liquidation and distribution, most debts are discharged, and the debtor has an opportunity for a fresh start.	Debtor continues in business. Creditors can either accept the plan, or it can be "crammed down" on them. The plan allows for the reorganization and liquidation of debts over the plan period.	Debtor continues in business or possession of assets. If the plan is approved, most debts are discharged after a three-year period.

ExamPrep

ISSUE SPOTTERS

—Check your answers to these questions against the answers provided in Appendix D at the end of this text.

1. Joe contracts with Larry of Midwest Roofing to fix Joe's roof. Joe pays half of the contract price in advance. Larry and Midwest complete the job, but Joe refuses to pay the rest of the price. What can Larry and Midwest do? **(See page 351.)**
2. Ogden is a vice president of Plumbing Service, Inc. (PSI). On May 1, Ogden loans PSI $10,000. On June 1, the firm repays the loan. On July 1, PSI files for bankruptcy. Quentin is appointed trustee. Can Quentin recover the $10,000 paid to Ogden on June 1? Why or why not? **(See page 366.)**

BEFORE THE TEST

Go to **www.cengagebrain.com**, enter the ISBN 9781133586548, and click on "Find" to locate this textbook's Web site. Then click on "Access Now" under "Study Tools," and select Chapter 14 at the top. There, you will find a Practice Quiz that you can take to assess your mastery of the concepts in this chapter. Additionally, you will find Flashcards and a Glossary of important terms, as well as Video Questions (when assigned).

For Review

Answers for the even-numbered questions in this **For Review** *section can be found in Appendix E at the end of this text.*

1. What is a prejudgment attachment? What is a writ of execution? How does a creditor use these remedies?
2. In a bankruptcy proceeding, what constitutes the debtor's estate in property? What property is exempt from the estate under federal bankruptcy law?
3. What is the difference between an exception to discharge and an objection to discharge?
4. In a Chapter 11 reorganization, what is the role of the debtor in possession?

Questions and Case Problems

14–1. Artisan's Lien. Air Ruidoso, Ltd., operated a commuter airline and air charter service between Ruidoso, New Mexico, and airports in Albuquerque and El Paso. Executive Aviation Center, Inc., provided services for airlines at the Albuquerque International Airport. When Air Ruidoso failed to pay more than $10,000 that it owed for fuel, oil, and oxygen, Executive Aviation took possession of Air Ruidoso's plane. Executive Aviation claimed that it had a lien on the plane and filed a suit in a New Mexico state court to foreclose. Do supplies such as fuel, oil, and oxygen qualify as "materials" for the purpose of creating an artisan's lien? Why or why not? **(See page 352.)**

14–2. **Question with Sample Answer: Voluntary versus Involuntary Bankruptcy.** Burke has been a rancher all her life, raising cattle and crops. Her ranch is valued at $500,000, almost all of which is exempt under state law. Burke has eight creditors and a total indebtedness of $70,000. Two of her largest creditors are Oman ($30,000 owed) and Sneed ($25,000 owed). The other six creditors have claims of less than $5,000 each. A drought has ruined all of Burke's crops and forced her to sell many

of her cattle at a loss. She cannot pay off her creditors. **(See pages 360–363.)**

1. Under the Bankruptcy Code, can Burke, with a $500,000 ranch, voluntarily petition herself into bankruptcy? Explain.
2. Could either Oman or Sneed force Burke into involuntary bankruptcy? Explain.

—For a sample answer to Question 14–2, go to Appendix F at the end of this text.

14–3. Discharge in Bankruptcy. Cathy Coleman took out loans to complete her college education. After graduation, Coleman worked as a teacher before she filed a Chapter 13 bankruptcy petition. The court confirmed a five-year plan that required Coleman to commit all of her disposable income to paying the student loans. Less than a year later, she was laid off. Still owing more than $100,000 in student loans, Coleman asked the court to discharge the debt on the ground that paying it would be an undue hardship for her. Under Chapter 13, are student loans dischargeable? Should the court grant her request? What argument could be made in support of Coleman's request? [*In re Coleman,* 560 F.3d 1000 (9th Cir. 2009)] **(See page 374.)**

14–4. Discharge. Caroline McAfee loaned $400,000 to Carter Oaks Crossing. Joseph Harman, Carter's president, signed a personal guaranty for the loan. Later, Harman obtained a discharge in bankruptcy under Chapter 7 for his personal debts. His petition did not list the guaranty among the debts. When Carter defaulted on the loan, McAfee sought to collect the unpaid amount from Harman based on the guaranty. Harman argued that the guaranty had been discharged in his bankruptcy. Is Harman correct? Why or why not? [*Harman v. McAfee*, 302 Ga.App. 698, 691 S.E.2d 586 (2010)] **(See pages 368–369.)**

14–5. Guaranty. Majestic Group Korea, Ltd., borrowed $1.5 million from Overseas Private Investment Corp. (OPIC) to finance a Ruby Tuesday's restaurant. Nam Koo Kim, the sole owner of Majestic, and his spouse Hee Sun Kim signed personal guaranties for full payment of the loan. Majestic defaulted. OPIC filed a suit against the Kims to recover. Hee claimed that she did not understand the extent of her liability when she signed the guaranty. Was Hee liable for the debt? Explain. [*Overseas Private Investment Corp. v. Kim*, 69 A.D.3d 1185, 895 N.Y.S.2d 217 (2010)] **(See page 355.)**

14–6. Protection for Debtors. Bill and Betty Ma owned half of a two-unit residential building. Betty lived in the unit, but Bill did not. To collect a judgment against them, Mei-Fang Zhang obtained a writ of execution directing the sheriff to seize and sell the building. State law allowed a $100,000 homestead exemption if the debtor lived in the home and $175,000 if the debtor was also disabled and "unable to engage in gainful employment." Bill argued that he could not work because of "gout and dizziness." How much of an exemption was the couple allowed? Why? [*Zhang v. Tse*, __ F.Supp.2d __ (N.D.Cal. 2011)] **(See pages 353–364.)**

14–7. **Case Problem with Sample Answer: Automatic Stay.** Michelle Gholston leased a Chevy Impala from EZ Auto Van Rentals. In November 2011, Gholston filed for bankruptcy. Around November 21, the bankruptcy court notified EZ Auto of Gholston's bankruptcy and the imposition of an automatic stay. Nevertheless, because Gholston had fallen behind on her payments, EZ Auto repossessed the vehicle on November 28. Gholston's attorney then reminded EZ Auto about the automatic stay, but the company failed to return the car. As a result of the car's repossession, Gholston suffered damages that included emotional distress, lost wages, attorneys' fees, and car rental expenses. Can Gholston recover from EZ Auto? Why or why not? [*In re Gholston*, 2012 WL 639288 (M.D.Fla. 2012)] **(See page 363.)**

—**For a sample answer to Case Problem 14–7, go to Appendix G at the end of this text.**

14–8. **A Question of Ethics: Guaranty Contracts.** *73-75 Main Avenue, LLC, agreed to lease commercial property to PP Door Enterprise, Inc. if its principal officers executed personal guaranties and provided credit information. Nan Zhang signed the lease as manager of PP Door. The principals of PP Door signed the lease and guaranty agreements. When PP Door failed to make monthly payments, the lessor sued PP Door and its owner, Ping Ying Li. Li testified that she was the sole owner of PP Door but denied that Zhang was its manager. She also denied signing the guaranty agreement. She claimed that she had signed the credit authorization form because Zhang had told her he was too young to have good credit. Li claimed to have no knowledge of the lease agreement. She did admit, however, that she had paid the rent because Zhang had been in a car accident and had asked her to help pay his bills, including the rent.* [*73-75 Main Avenue, LLC v. PP Door Enterprise, Inc.*, 120 Conn.App. 150, 991 A.2d 650 (2010)] **(See page 355.)**

1. Li argued that she was not liable on the lease agreement because Zhang was not authorized to bind her to the lease. Do the facts support Li? Why or why not?

2. Li claimed that the guaranty for rent was not enforceable against her. Why might the court agree?

Chapter 15

Mortgages and Foreclosures after the Recession

> "People are living longer than ever before, a phenomenon undoubtedly made necessary by the 30-year mortgage."
>
> —Doug Larson, 1926–present
> (U.S. columnist)

Contents

Learning Objectives

The five Learning Objectives below are designed to help improve your understanding of the chapter. After reading this chapter, you should be able to answer the following questions:

1. **What is a subprime mortgage, and how does it differ from a standard fixed-rate mortgage?**

2. **When is private mortgage insurance required? Which party does it protect?**

3. **How do the TILA provisions protect borrowers and curb abusive practices by mortgage lenders?**

4. **What is a short sale, and what advantages over mortgage foreclosure might it offer borrowers?**

5. **In a mortgage foreclosure, what legal rights do mortgage holders have if the sale proceeds are insufficient to pay the underlying debt?**

(shock/iStockphoto.com)

During the first decade of the 2000s, the United States experienced one of the biggest real estate bubbles in its history as housing prices in many areas increased at unprecedented rates. The bubble started to shrink in 2006 and was still deflating in 2013. As a result of the collapse of the housing market and the financial crisis that accompanied it, the United States and much of the rest of the world suffered through what is now called the Great Recession.

Today, the real estate market is still in turmoil. Many people have lost their homes to foreclosure because they could not make the payments on their *mortgages*—the loans that borrowers obtain to purchase homes. Others can afford the payments but choose not to pay because they owe more on the properties than those properties are worth. The ongoing flood of foreclosures led the Obama administration in 2012 to propose an extension of the laws that were aimed at temporarily modifying mortgages.

It has become apparent that some of the mortgage process during the bubble years was fraught with fraud. Bank of America, for instance, paid nearly $20 billion in 2011 to settle claims involving mortgage-backed securities that it had designated as safe investments. In reality, many of the securities were based on mortgages granted to borrowers who could not afford to repay them. Other major mortgage companies, including Citigroup, JPMorgan Chase, and Wells Fargo, faced similar fraud claims.

In this chapter, we examine the rights and obligations of homeowners and lenders. We begin with a discussion of the different types of mortgages. Next, we examine protections of lenders and borrowers. Finally, we discuss the options that lenders and homeowners have when the homeowners cannot make their mortgage payments.

▶ Types of Mortgages and Loans

When individuals purchase real property, they typically borrow funds from a financial institution for part or all of the purchase price. A **mortgage** is a written instrument that gives a creditor (the *mortgagee*) an interest in, or lien on, the debtor's (the *mortgagor's*) real property as security for the payment of a debt.

Mortgage loans are contracts and, as such, come in a variety of forms. Next, we address a few of the most common types of mortgages and mortgage-related loans.

Fixed-Rate Mortgages

Fixed-rate mortgages are the simplest mortgage loans. A **fixed-rate mortgage** is a standard mortgage with a fixed, or unchanging, rate of interest. Payments on the loan remain the same for the duration of the mortgage, which ranges from fifteen to forty years.

Lenders determine the interest rate based on a variety of factors, including the borrower's credit history, credit score, income, and debts. Today, for a borrower to qualify for a standard fixed-rate mortgage loan, lenders typically require that the monthly mortgage payment (including principal, interest, taxes, and insurance) not exceed 28 percent of the person's gross income.

Adjustable-Rate Mortgages

The rate of interest paid by the borrower changes periodically with an **adjustable-rate mortgage (ARM).** Typically, the initial interest rate is set relatively low and is fixed for a specified period, such as a year or three years. After that, the interest rate adjusts periodically, often annually. ARMs generally are described in terms of the initial fixed period and the adjustment period. For example, if the interest rate is fixed for three years and then adjusts annually, the mortgage is called a 3/1 ARM. If the rate adjusts annually after five years, the mortgage is a 5/1 ARM.

The lender calculates the interest rate adjustment by adding together two numbers—an index rate and a margin—which are specified in the mortgage loan documents. The index rate is generally a government-determined rate that changes periodically, such as the interest rate on U.S. Treasury securities. Thus, the interest rate can be adjusted downward as well as upward, depending on movements of the index rate.

Most ARMs have interest rate caps that limit how much the rate can rise over the duration of the loan. In addition, some ARMs have caps that stipulate the maximum increase that can occur in any particular adjustment period.

EXAMPLE 15.1 Greta and Marcus obtain a 3/1 ARM from Neighbors Bank to purchase a home. The mortgage's initial interest rate is 4 percent. The loan documents stipulate that the rate can rise no more than 3 percentage points in one adjustment period. The margin is fixed at 2 percentage points. After three years, when the first adjustment is to be made, the relevant index rate is 6 percent. This means that the adjusted interest rate would rise to 8 percent (the index rate of 6 percent plus the margin of 2 percent). Since the interest rate can rise no more than 3 percentage points in any one period, and the initial rate was 4 percent, the new adjusted rate cannot be higher than 7 percent. ● (Note that some ARMs also limit the amount the rate can fall.)

Mortgage A written document that gives a creditor (the mortgagee) an interest in, or lien on, the debtor's (mortgagor's) real property as security for a debt.

Fixed-Rate Mortgage A standard mortgage with a fixed, or unchanging, rate of interest.

Adjustable-Rate Mortgage (ARM) A mortgage in which the rate of interest paid by the borrower changes periodically.

"Mortgage: a house with a guilty conscience."
Anonymous

Interest-Only (IO) Mortgages

Interest-Only (IO) Mortgage A mortgage that allows the borrower to pay only the interest portion of the monthly payment for a specified period of time.

With an **interest-only (IO) mortgage,** the borrower can choose to pay only the interest portion of the monthly payments and forgo paying any of the principal for a specified period of time, such as three to ten years. After the IO payment option is exhausted, the borrower's payment increases to include payments on the principal.

Subprime Mortgages

LEARNING OBJECTIVE 1 What is a subprime mortgage, and how does it differ from a standard fixed-rate mortgage?

Subprime Mortgage A high-risk loan made to a borrower who does not qualify for a standard mortgage because of a poor credit rating or high debt-to-income ratio.

During the late 1990s and the first decade of the 2000s, *subprime lending* increased significantly. A **subprime mortgage** is a loan made to a borrower who does not qualify for a standard mortgage. Often, such borrowers have poor credit scores or a high current *debt-to-income ratio*—that is, the total amount owed as a percentage of current after-tax income. Subprime mortgages are riskier than traditional mortgages and have a higher default rate.

Consequently, lenders charge a higher interest rate for subprime loans. Subprime mortgages can be fixed-rate, adjustable-rate, or IO loans. Subprime lending allows many people who could not otherwise purchase real property to do so, but at a higher risk to the lender.

Home Equity Loans

Home Equity Loan A loan for which the borrower's home equity—the portion of the home's value that is paid off—is the collateral.

Home equity refers to the portion of a home's value that is "paid off." **EXAMPLE 15.2** If Susanna has a home valued at $200,000 and owes the bank $120,000 on her mortgage, she has 40 percent equity in her house ($80,000/$200,000 = 40 percent). With a **home equity loan,** a bank accepts the borrower's equity as *collateral,* which can be seized if the loan is not repaid on time. If Susanna takes out a $30,000 home equity loan, the amount is added to the amount of her mortgage ($30,000 + $120,000 = $150,000), so she now has only $50,000 (25 percent) equity in her $200,000 home. ●

Borrowers often take out home equity loans to obtain funds to renovate the property itself. Others obtain home equity loans to pay off debt, such as credit-card debt, that carries a higher interest rate than they will pay on the home equity loan. This strategy can lead to problems, however, if the borrower cannot keep up the payments. Many Americans who lost their homes during the latest major recession were able to pay their original mortgage loans, but not their home equity loans.

From the lender's perspective, a home equity loan is riskier than a mortgage loan because home equity loans are *subordinated,* which means that they take a lower priority in any proceeding that occurs if the homeowner fails to make the payments on the primary mortgage.

▶ Lender and Borrower Protections

When lenders (creditors) grant mortgages, they are lending large amounts for long periods. Consequently, they take steps to protect their interest. Borrowers, too, have protections. We discuss some of the protections for lenders and borrowers next.

Lender Protections

LEARNING OBJECTIVE 2 When is private mortgage insurance required? Which party does it protect?

One precaution that lenders can take to protect their interest in a mortgage is to require borrowers to obtain mortgage insurance. In addition, lenders will ensure that the mortgage is recorded appropriately and contains the necessary provisions.

MORTGAGE INSURANCE   Most creditors require a borrower to purchase mortgage insurance if the borrower does not make a down payment of at least 20 percent of the purchase price. (The *down payment* is the part of the purchase price paid up front.)

EXAMPLE 15.3   Frank and Joy apply for a mortgage loan with Sterling Silver Bank to purchase a house for $100,000. They make a down payment of only $10,000 (10 percent of the purchase price). Sterling Silver Bank requires them to purchase insurance to cover the remaining 10 percent of the 20 percent down payment. If Frank and Joy stop making payments on the loan, the bank can repossess the house and also receive reimbursement from the insurer for the covered portion of the loan. •

RECORDING THE MORTGAGE   Lenders protect their interests in a mortgage by recording the mortgage with the appropriate office in the county where the property is located. Recording ensures that the creditor is officially on record as holding an interest in the property. A lender that fails to record a mortgage could find itself in the position of an *unsecured creditor* (see page 360).

IMPORTANT MORTGAGE PROVISIONS   To further protect their interests, lenders ensure that mortgage documents comply with applicable statutes. Because a mortgage involves a transfer of real property, for instance, it must be in writing (see page 295 in Chapter 12). Lenders also make sure that mortgage documents contain the following important provisions:

1. *The terms of the underlying loan.* These include the loan amount, the interest rate, the period of repayment, and other important financial terms, such as the margin and index rate for an ARM. Many lenders include a **prepayment penalty clause,** which requires the borrower to pay a penalty if the mortgage is repaid in full within a certain period. A prepayment penalty helps to protect the lender should the borrower refinance within a short time after obtaining a mortgage.

2. *Provisions relating to the maintenance of the property.* Because the mortgage conveys an interest in the property to the lender, the lender will require the borrower to maintain the property in such a way that the lender's investment is protected.

3. *A statement obligating the borrower to maintain homeowners' insurance on the property.* This type of insurance protects the lender's interest in the event of a loss due to certain hazards, such as fire or storm damage.

4. *A list of the nonloan financial obligations to be paid by the borrower.* For example, the borrower typically is required to pay all property taxes, assessments, and other claims against the property.

Although a record number of homeowners have failed to keep up with their mortgage payments in recent years, courts have continued to enforce the terms of plainly written financing documents. Even in today's more protective environment, borrowers cannot avoid the clear meaning of terms in financing documents, although the effect may be harsh.

Borrower Protections

During the real estate boom in the first years of the 2000s, some lenders were less than honest with borrowers about the loan terms that they were signing. As a result, many individuals failed to understand how much the monthly payments on ARMs, interest-only mortgages, and other exotic types of loans might increase. In addition, fees and penalties were not always properly disclosed.

Prepayment Penalty Clause A clause in a mortgage loan contract that requires the borrower to pay a penalty if the mortgage is repaid in full within a certain period.

Who should benefit when a mortgage-participating bank fails? During the heyday of mortgage lending in the early 2000s, many banks wanted a "piece of the action." A bank could do this by becoming a *participating* bank when another bank contemplated making a multimillion-dollar mortgage and wanted to share the risk. In this way, Silverton Bank participated in half of a $4 million loan that Renasant Bank made to Eric and Tricia Ericson for the construction of a house in Tennessee.

By the time the construction was completed, however, the housing market had started to collapse, and ultimately the Ericsons defaulted on the $4 million loan. In the meantime, Silverton Bank, the participating bank, had failed and been taken over by the Federal Deposit Insurance Corporation. The principal lender, Renasant Bank, orally promised the Ericsons that if it could purchase Silverton's participating loan at a discount, it would credit the Ericsons with the full discount. When Renasant acquired the loan at a $475,000 discount, however, it refused to grant the Ericsons the credit.

Renasant argued that it did not have to apply the discount to the Ericsons' loan balance until they had repaid the entire balance, but the court ruled in favor of the Ericsons. Renasant had breached the oral agreement by refusing to give the Ericsons the $475,000 discount that it had obtained when it repurchased Silverton's participating loan.[1]

In an effort to provide more protection for borrowers, Congress and the Federal Reserve Board have instituted a number of new requirements, mostly in the form of required disclosures. Here, we examine the most important statutes that provide protection for borrowers. First, though, we look at some of the practices that led to the enactment of these statutes.

Predatory Lending Loan terms or lending procedures that are excessive, deceptive, or not properly disclosed.

PREDATORY LENDING AND OTHER IMPROPER PRACTICES The general term **predatory lending** is often used to describe situations in which borrowers are the victims of loan terms or lending procedures that are excessive, deceptive, or not properly disclosed. Predatory lending typically occurs during the loan origination process. It includes a number of practices ranging from failure to disclose terms to providing misleading information to outright dishonesty.

Two specific types of improper practices are often at the core of a violation.

1. *Steering and targeting* occurs when the lender manipulates a borrower into accepting a loan product that benefits the lender but is not the best loan for the borrower. For instance, a lender may steer a borrower toward an ARM, even though the buyer qualifies for a fixed-rate mortgage.
2. *Loan flipping* occurs when a lender convinces a homeowner to refinance soon after obtaining a mortgage. Such early refinancing rarely benefits the homeowner and may, in fact, result in prepayment penalties.

LEARNING OBJECTIVE 3 How do the TILA provisions protect borrowers and curb abusive practices by mortgage lenders?

THE TRUTH-IN-LENDING ACT The Truth-in-Lending Act (TILA) of 1968[2] requires lenders to disclose the terms of a loan in clear, readily understandable language so that borrowers can make rational choices. With respect to real estate transactions, the TILA applies only to residential loans.

Annual Percentage Rate (APR) The cost of credit on a yearly basis, typically expressed as an annual percentage.

Required Disclosures. The major terms that must be disclosed under the TILA include the loan principal, the interest rate at which the loan is made, the **annual percentage rate,** or **APR** (the actual cost of the loan on a yearly basis), and all fees and costs associated with the loan. The TILA requires that these disclosures be made on standardized forms and based on uniform calculation formulas.

---

1. *Renasant Bank v. Ericson,* 2012 WL 6400659 (M.D.Tenn. 2012).
2. 15 U.S.C. Sections 1601–1693r.

Certain types of loans—including ARMs, open-ended home equity loans, and high-interest loans—have specially tailored disclosure requirements. The Mortgage Disclosure Improvement Act of 2008[3] amended the TILA to strengthen the disclosures required for ARMs, which, as mentioned earlier, played a leading role in the recent real estate meltdown.

Prohibitions and Requirements.　The TILA prohibits certain lender abuses and creates certain borrower rights. Among the prohibited practices is the charging of prepayment penalties on most subprime mortgages and home equity loans.

The TILA also addresses other unfair, abusive, or deceptive home mortgage–lending practices. It provides that lenders may not coerce an **appraiser** into misstating the value of a property on which a loan is to be issued. Also, a loan cannot be advertised as a fixed-rate loan if, in fact, its rate or payment amounts will change.

Right to Rescind.　A mortgage cannot be finalized until at least seven days after a borrower has received the TILA paperwork. Even if all required disclosures are provided, the TILA gives the borrower the right to rescind (cancel) a mortgage *within three business days.* Sunday is the only day of the week that is not a business day. If the lender fails to provide material TILA disclosures, including the three-day right to rescind, the rescission period lasts up to three years.

Written Representations.　The TILA requirements apply to the written materials the lender provides, not to any oral representations. If a lender provides the required TILA disclosures, a borrower who fails to read the relevant documents cannot claim fraud, even if the lender orally misrepresented the terms of the loan.

CASE EXAMPLE 15.4　Patricia Ostolaza and José Diaz owned a home on which they had two mortgage loans provided by Bank of America. Anthony Falcone told them that he could refinance their mortgages in a manner that would reduce their monthly payments. Falcone said that he represented Bank of America when in fact he represented Countrywide Home Loans, Inc. At the closing of the new loan, the homeowners were given all of the relevant documents, including the TILA disclosure statement. The documents accurately stated the monthly payment under the new loan, which was higher than the couple's original payments. The homeowners later sued Falcone and Countrywide Bank, alleging fraud, but the court dismissed the suit because the homeowners had been given the opportunity to read all of the relevant disclosure documents, but had not done so.[4] ●

THE HOME OWNERSHIP AND EQUITY PROTECTION ACT　The Home Ownership and Equity Protection Act (HOEPA) of 1994[5] amended the TILA to create a new category for certain high-cost and high-fee mortgage loans. A loan can qualify for protection under HOEPA either because it carries a high rate of interest or because it imposes high fees on the borrower. In general, HOEPA applies if:

- The APR for the loan exceeds an identified index rate by 8 percentage points for a first mortgage or 10 percentage points for a second mortgage.
- The fees exceed 8 percent of the loan amount or an identified dollar amount, whichever is larger.

---

3. This act was contained in Sections 2501 through 2503 of the Housing and Economic Recovery Act of 2008, Pub. L. No. 110-289, enacted on July 30, 2008. Congress then amended its provisions as part of the Emergency Economic Stabilization Act of 2008 (also known as the Bailout Bill), Pub. L. No. 110-343, enacted on October 3, 2008.

4. *Ostolaza-Diaz v. Countrywide Bank, N.A.,* 2010 WL 95145 (4th Cir. 2010).

5. 15 U.S.C. Sections 1637 and 1647.

Appraiser　An individual who specializes in determining the value of specified real or personal property.

Special Consumer Protections. If a loan qualifies for HOEPA protection, the consumer must receive several disclosures in addition to those required by the TILA. The lender must disclose the APR, the regular payment amount, and any required *balloon payments* (large payments that usually pay off the entire balance of the loan). For loans with a variable rate of interest, the lender must disclose that the rate and monthly payments may increase and state the potential maximum monthly payment. These disclosures must be provided at least three business days before the loan is finalized.

In addition, the lender must provide a written notice stating that the consumer is not required to complete the loan process simply because he or she received the disclosures or signed the loan application. Borrowers must also be informed that they could lose their home if they default on the loan.

HOEPA also prohibits lenders from engaging in certain practices, such as loans that result in negative amortization. **Negative amortization** occurs when the monthly payments are insufficient to cover the interest due on the loan. The difference is then added to the principal, so the balance owed on the loan increases over time.

Negative Amortization The condition when the payment made by the borrower is less than the interest due on the loan and the difference is added to the principal, thereby increasing the balance owed on the loan over time.

Remedies and Liabilities. For HOEPA violations, consumers can obtain damages in an amount equal to all finance charges and fees paid if the lender's failure to disclose is deemed material. Any failure to comply with HOEPA provisions also extends the borrower's right to rescind the loan for up to three years.

Whether a particular loan is covered by HOEPA and thus is entitled to the statute's significant protections can have important ramifications because it can determine whether a borrower can recover on a lender's failure to comply with HOEPA's provisions and the amount of the recovery.

In the following case, a consumer attempted to recover from a lender for alleged violations of the TILA and HOEPA.

Case 15.1 ***In re* Kitts**

United States Bankruptcy Court, District of Utah, 447 Bankr. 330 (2011).

BACKGROUND AND FACTS Facing the loss of his family's home in Park City, Utah, to creditors, Brian Kitts sought to refinance the debt. He entered into two mortgage loan agreements for $1.35 million and $39,603.47, respectively, with Winterfox, LLC. As part of the deal, Kitts paid $87,500 in "loan origination fees." Kitts defaulted on the loans and filed a petition in a federal bankruptcy court to declare bankruptcy. He also filed a complaint against Winterfox to recover damages for alleged violations of the federal Truth-in-Lending Act (TILA). The court dismissed the action, but on appeal, a federal district court ruled that Winterfox had failed to make certain required disclosures. The district court remanded the case for "further fact finding concerning damages" for violation of the TILA, as well as for Kitts's request for attorneys' fees.

IN THE WORDS OF THE COURT . . .
Joel T. *MARKER,* **Bankruptcy Judge.**
* * * *
* * * Both loans qualify as high-cost mortgages [covered by HOEPA] from an interest-rate standpoint based on evidence regarding the APRs of those loans.

* * * *
* * * Based on the facts that Winterfox made two loans to the Debtor, provided no disclosures at all, and attempted in this litigation to cover up its failure to disclose with fabricated documents, the Court concludes that the maximum statutory damages of $2,000 for each violation are appropriate for total statutory damages of $4,000.
* * * *

On the issue of finance charges in connection with the Winterfox loans, the parties do not dispute the fact that Winterfox charged $87,500 in "loan origination fees" to the Debtor * * * . The parties also do not dispute that the $87,500 was paid from the Winterfox loan proceeds rather than being paid out of pocket by the Debtor. *The major dispute is over the purely legal question of whether finance charges that are paid from the loan proceeds, rather than finance charges paid out of pocket by the Debtor, qualify as "finance charges paid by the consumer" under [the TILA].* Winterfox also argues in the alternative that finance charges should not be awarded as damages

Case 15.1–Continues next page ➡

Case 15.1–Continued

because its "failure to comply [with HOEPA] is not material." [Emphasis added.]

Finance charges qualify as compensable damages under [HOEPA]. * * * This view comports with both the formal nature of the underlying financial transaction as well as the remedial nature of TILA and the equity protection purpose of HOEPA. [Emphasis added.]

Winterfox's failure to provide any of the required disclosures constitutes a material failure to comply with [HOEPA]. Accordingly, the Court awards the [plaintiff] damages of $87,500 for the Debtor's finance charges.

     * * * *

The Court's task in determining a "reasonable" [attorneys'] fee is a difficult one. * * * Based on the underlying administration of the main bankruptcy case, the relative complexity of the issues in this adversary proceeding, the contributions of both parties to the length and expense of this adversary proceeding, the [plaintiff's] ultimate degree of success on the merits before the Court and the District Court, and the relative billing rates of the [plaintiff's] counsel, the Court finds that 750 hours is a reasonable number of hours spent in prosecution of this adversary proceeding at $200/hour for a total fee and cost award of $150,000.

DECISION AND REMEDY   The court concluded that HOEPA covered the Winterfox loans. The plaintiff was awarded statutory TILA damages of $4,000, $87,500 for the finance charges paid in connection with the loans, and $150,000 for attorneys' fees.

THE ECONOMIC DIMENSION   *Why would a borrower, who is relatively sophisticated (as the court found Kitts) and can afford to buy a million-dollar home, agree to pay such high loan origination fees?*

HIGHER-PRICED MORTGAGE LOANS   Another category of expensive loans for which buyers are offered protection is called Higher-Priced Mortgage Loans (HPMLs). To be an HPML, a mortgage must have an APR that exceeds the average prime offer rate for a comparable transaction by 1.5 percentage points for a first mortgage or 3.5 percentage points (or more) for a second mortgage. (The *average prime offer rate* is the rate offered to the best-qualified borrowers.)

As with a HOEPA loan, consumers receiving an HPML receive additional protections. First, lenders cannot make an HPML without verifying the consumer's ability to repay the loan. Second, prepayment penalties are severely restricted. Additionally, lenders must establish escrow accounts for borrowers' payments for homeowners' insurance and property taxes for first mortgages. (An *escrow account* holds funds to be paid to a third party.) Finally, lenders cannot structure a loan to evade the HPML protections.

▶ Foreclosures

> **Foreclosure** A proceeding in which a creditor either takes title to, or forces the sale of, the debtor's property in satisfaction of a debt.

If a homeowner *defaults*, or fails to make mortgage payments, the lender has the right to foreclose on the mortgaged property. **Foreclosure** is a process that allows a lender to legally repossess and auction off the property that is securing a loan.

Foreclosure is expensive and time consuming, however, and generally benefits neither the borrower, who loses his or her home, nor the lender, which faces the prospect of a loss on its loans. Therefore, various methods to avoid foreclosure have been developed. We look first at some of these methods and then turn to the foreclosure process itself.

How to Avoid Foreclosure

In the past, especially during the Great Depression of the 1930s, a number of alternatives to foreclosure were developed. More recently, as foreclosures have become more common than at any time since the Great Depression, Congress has intervened to aid in the modification of mortgage loans.

> **Forbearance** An agreement between a lender and a borrower in which the lender agrees to temporarily cease requiring mortgage payments, to delay foreclosure, or to accept smaller payments than previously scheduled.

FORBEARANCE AND WORKOUT AGREEMENTS   The first preforeclosure option a borrower has is called a forbearance. A **forbearance** is the postponement, for a limited time, of part or all of the payments on a loan in jeopardy of foreclosure. A lender grants forbearance when it expects that, during the forbearance period, the borrower can solve the problem by securing a new job, selling the property, or finding another acceptable solution.

Workout Agreement A formal contract between a debtor and his or her creditors in which the parties agree to negotiate a payment plan for the amount due on the loan instead of proceeding to foreclosure.

When a borrower fails to make payments as required, the lender may attempt to negotiate a **workout agreement**—a written document that describes the rights and responsibilities of the parties as they try to resolve the default without proceeding to foreclosure. In such an agreement, the lender will likely agree to delay seeking foreclosure or other legal rights. In exchange, the borrower may agree to provide the lender with financial information on which a workout might be constructed.

Whether a workout agreement is possible or preferable to foreclosure depends on many factors, including the value of the property, the amount of the unpaid principal, the market in which the property will be sold, the relationship of the lender and the borrower, and the financial condition of the borrower.

HOUSING AND URBAN DEVELOPMENT ASSISTANCE A lender may be able to work with the borrower to obtain an interest-free loan from the U.S. Department of Housing and Urban Development (HUD) to bring the mortgage current. HUD assistance may be available if the loan is at least four months (but not more than twelve months) delinquent, if the property is not in foreclosure, and if the borrower is able to make full mortgage payments. When the lender files a claim, HUD pays the lender the amount necessary to make the mortgage current. The borrower executes a note to HUD, and a lien for the second loan is placed on the property. The promissory note is interest free and comes due if the property is sold.

Short Sale A sale of real property for an amount that is less than the balance owed on the mortgage loan.

SHORT SALES When a borrower is unable to make mortgage payments, the lender may agree to a **short sale**—that is, a sale of the property for less than the balance due on the mortgage loan. The borrower must obtain the lender's permission for the short sale and typically has to show some hardship, such as the loss of a job, a decline in the value of the home, a divorce, or a death in the household. The lender receives the proceeds of the sale, and the borrower still owes the balance of the debt to the lender, unless the lender specifically agrees to forgive the remaining debt.

LEARNING OBJECTIVE 4 What is a short sale, and what advantages over mortgage foreclosure might it offer borrowers?

A short sale can offer several advantages. Although the borrower's credit rating is affected, the negative impact is less than it would be with a foreclosure, which generally remains on the borrower's credit report for seven years. The short sale process also avoids the expense of foreclosure for the lender and the trauma of being evicted from the home for the homeowner. But because the lender often has approval rights in a short sale, the sale process can take much longer than a standard real estate transaction. In addition, although the parties' losses are mitigated, the borrower still loses her or his home.

SALE AND LEASEBACK In some situations, the homeowner may be able to sell the property to an investor who is looking for an income property. The owner sells the property to the investor and then leases it back at an amount that is less than the monthly mortgage payment. The owner-seller uses the proceeds of the sale to pay off the mortgage and still has the use and possession of the property. In some circumstances, this strategy can also be used to raise capital when there is no risk of loss of the property.

HOME AFFORDABLE MODIFICATION PROGRAM In 2009, the U.S. Treasury Department launched the Home Affordable Modification Program (HAMP) to encourage private lenders to modify mortgages so as to lower the monthly payments of borrowers who are in default. The purpose of HAMP is not to force lenders to forgive all high-risk mortgages, but rather to reduce monthly mortgage payments to a level that the homeowner can reasonably pay. The program may share in the costs of modifying the loan and provides incentives to lenders based on successful loan modification.

Qualifications.   HAMP modifications are not available for every mortgage. To qualify for a HAMP modification, all of the following must be true:

1. The loan must have originated on or before January 1, 2009.
2. The home must be occupied by the owner and must be the homeowner's primary residence.[6]
3. The unpaid balance may not exceed $729,750 for a single-unit property.[7]
4. The homeowner must be facing financial hardship and either be more than sixty days late on mortgage payments or be at risk of imminent default. Homeowners are required to verify their hardship through appropriate documentation.

Restructuring the Mortgage.   The goal is to reduce the debtor's mortgage payment to 31 percent of his or her gross monthly income. The loan is restructured by adding any delinquencies (such as accrued interest, past-due taxes, or unpaid insurance premiums) to the principal amount. This increases the number of payments but eliminates the delinquencies by spreading them over the life of the loan.

Once the loan is restructured, lenders try to incrementally lower the mortgage interest rate to a level at which the payments are less than 31 percent of the debtor's income. If the lender cannot reach the 31 percent target by lowering the interest rate to 2 percent, then the lender can **reamortize** the loan (change the way the payments are configured), extending the schedule of payments for up to forty years.

The borrower then begins a ninety-day trial period to determine his or her ability to make three modified monthly payments. If the borrower succeeds, the lender offers permanent modifications.

Reamortize Change the way mortgage payments are configured, extending the term over which payments will be made.

VOLUNTARY CONVEYANCE   Under some circumstances, the parties may benefit from a **deed in lieu of foreclosure,** by which the property is voluntarily conveyed (transferred) to the lender in satisfaction of the mortgage. A property that has a current market value close to the outstanding loan principal and on which no other loans have been taken might be the subject of such a conveyance.

Although the lender faces the risk that it may ultimately sell the property for less than the loan amount, the lender avoids the time, risk, and expense of foreclosure litigation. The borrower who gives the property to the lender without a fight also avoids the foreclosure process and may preserve a better credit rating than if he or she had been forced to give up the property involuntarily.

Deed in Lieu of Foreclosure An alternative to foreclosure in which the mortgagor voluntarily conveys the property to the lender in satisfaction of the mortgage.

FRIENDLY FORECLOSURE   Another way for the parties to avoid a contested foreclosure is to engage in a friendly foreclosure. In such a transaction, the borrower in default agrees to submit to the court's jurisdiction, to waive any defenses as well as the right to appeal, and to cooperate with the lender. This process takes longer than a voluntary conveyance, but all of the parties have greater certainty as to the finality

6. Investor-owned homes, vacant homes, and condemned properties are not eligible under the program.
7. Higher limits are allowed for properties with two to four units.

of the transaction with respect to others who might have a financial interest in the property.

The Foreclosure Procedure

If all efforts to find another solution fail, the lender will proceed to foreclosure—a process that dates back to English law. A formal foreclosure is necessary to extinguish the borrower's equitable *right of redemption* (see page 394).

To bring a foreclosure action, a creditor must have *standing to sue* (see page 37 in Chapter 2). In the following *Spotlight Case*, the court had to decide whether a bank could foreclose on a mortgage even though it could not prove when it became the owner of the debtor's promissory note.

SPOTLIGHT ON CHASE BANK

Case 15.2 McLean v. JPMorgan Chase Bank, N.A.

District Court of Appeal of Florida, 79 So.3d 170 (2012).

BACKGROUND AND FACTS On May 11, 2009, JPMorgan Chase Bank (Chase) filed a foreclosure action against Robert McLean. The complaint alleged that Chase was entitled to enforce the mortgage and note on which McLean had defaulted. Nevertheless, the attached mortgage identified a different mortgagee and lender, and Chase claimed that the note had been "lost, stolen, or destroyed." When McLean filed a motion to dismiss, Chase produced a mortgage assignment dated May 14, 2009, which was three days *after* it had filed the lawsuit. Eventually, Chase also filed the original note. Although the indorsement to Chase was undated, Chase then filed a motion for summary judgment. The trial court granted Chase's motion even though the accompanying affidavit failed to show that Chase owned the mortgage or note when it filed the complaint. McLean appealed.

IN THE WORDS OF THE COURT . . .
PER CURIAM. [By the Whole Court]
* * * *

A crucial element in any mortgage foreclosure proceeding is that the party seeking foreclosure must demonstrate that it has standing to foreclose.
* * * *

* * * A party's standing is determined at the time the lawsuit was filed. Stated another way, *"the plaintiff's lack of standing at the inception of the case is not a defect that may be cured by the acquisition of standing after the case is filed." Thus, a party is not permitted to establish the right to maintain an action retroactively by acquiring standing to file a lawsuit after the fact.* [Emphasis added.]
* * * *

In the present case, as is common in recent foreclosure cases, Chase did not attach a copy of the original note to its complaint, but instead [filed a claim] to re-establish a lost note. Later, however,

Chase filed * * * the original promissory note, which bore a special endorsement in favor of Chase. [Thus,] * * * it obtained standing to foreclose, at least at some point.

Nonetheless, the record evidence is insufficient to demonstrate that Chase had standing to foreclose *at the time the lawsuit was filed.* [Emphasis in original.] The mortgage was assigned to Chase three days after Chase filed the instant foreclosure complaint. While the original note contained an undated special endorsement in Chase's favor, the affidavit filed in support of summary judgment did not state when the endorsement was made to Chase. Furthermore, the affidavit, which was dated after the lawsuit was filed, did not specifically state when Chase became the owner of the note, nor did the affidavit indicate that Chase was the owner of the note before suit was filed.

We therefore reverse the summary judgment and corresponding final judgment of foreclosure. On remand, in order for Chase to be entitled to summary judgment, it must show * * * that it was the holder of the note on the date the complaint was filed ([meaning] that the note was endorsed to Chase on or before the date the lawsuit was filed). By contrast, if the evidence shows that the note was endorsed to Chase after the lawsuit was filed, then Chase had no standing at the time the complaint was filed, in which case the trial court should dismiss the instant lawsuit and Chase must file a new complaint.

DECISION AND REMEDY The Florida appellate court held that Chase did not prove it had standing to foreclose against McLean. The court therefore reversed the trial court's grant of summary judgment.

THE LEGAL ENVIRONMENT DIMENSION *If Chase cannot prove that it owned the note at the time of its complaint, what will happen next? Will Chase prevail? Why or why not?*

Judicial Foreclosure A court-supervised foreclosure proceeding in which the court determines the validity of the debt and, if the borrower is in default, issues a judgment for the lender.

Power of Sale Foreclosure A foreclosure procedure that is not court supervised and is available only in some states.

TYPES OF FORECLOSURES   Two common types of foreclosure used in the United States are **judicial foreclosure** and **power of sale foreclosure.** In a judicial foreclosure, which is available in all states, a court supervises the process. In a power of sale foreclosure, the lender is allowed to foreclose on and sell the property without judicial supervision. If the sale proceeds cover the mortgage debt and foreclosure costs, the debtor receives any surplus. If the proceeds do not cover the debt and costs, the mortgage (creditor) can seek to recover the difference through a *deficiency judgment* (see page 393).

Only a few states permit power of sale foreclosures because borrowers have less protection when a court does not supervise the process. In these states, lenders must strictly comply with the terms of the state statute governing power of sale foreclosures. Failure to follow the statutory requirements can lead to the foreclosure being invalidated.

CASE EXAMPLE 15.5   Antonio Ibanez obtained a home loan, as did Mark and Tammy LaRace. Each of the loans subsequently changed hands several times through various banks, as is common in the mortgage-lending industry. Both Ibanez and the LaRaces defaulted on their mortgages. U.S. Bank foreclosed on the Ibanez mortgage, and Wells Fargo foreclosed on the LaRace mortgage. Both banks published the required notices, and then bought the homes at the foreclosure auctions. Both banks purchased the properties for significantly less than the purported market value. At the time of the foreclosures, each bank represented that it was the "owner (assignee) and holder" of the mortgage. When the banks later filed for a court declaration stating that they owned the properties, however, the court ruled against them. The court found that the banks had failed to show that they were holders of the mortgages at the time of the foreclosures. Therefore, they did not have the authority to foreclose, and the foreclosure sales were invalid.[8] ●

Acceleration Clause A clause that makes the entire loan balance become due if the borrower misses or is late making the monthly payments.

ACCELERATION CLAUSES   In a strict foreclosure, the lender may seek only the amount of the missed payments, not the entire loan amount. Therefore, lenders often include an *acceleration clause* in their loan documents. An **acceleration clause** allows the lender to call the entire loan due—even if only one payment is late or missed. Thus, with an acceleration clause, the lender can foreclose only once on the entire amount of the loan rather than having to foreclose on smaller amounts over a period of time as each payment is missed.

Notice of Default A formal notice to a borrower who is behind in making mortgage payments that the borrower is in default and may face foreclosure.

Notice of Sale A formal notice to a borrower who is in default on a mortgage that the mortgaged property will be sold in a foreclosure proceeding.

NOTICE OF DEFAULT AND NOTICE OF SALE   To initiate a foreclosure, a lender must record a **notice of default** with the appropriate county office. The borrower is then on notice of a possible foreclosure and can take steps to pay the loan and cure the default. If the loan is not paid within a reasonable time (usually three months), the borrower will receive a **notice of sale.** In addition, the notice of sale usually is posted on the property, recorded with the county, and published in a newspaper.

The property is then sold in an auction on the courthouse steps at the time and location indicated in the notice of sale. The buyer generally has to pay cash within twenty-four hours for the property. If the procedures are not followed precisely, the parties may have to resort to litigation to establish clear ownership of the property.

The following case illustrates how the notice requirements work.

---

8. These two foreclosure cases were consolidated on appeal and ruled on jointly by the Massachusetts Supreme Court in *U.S. Bank, N.A. v. Ibanez,* 458 Mass. 637, 941 N.E.2d 40 (2011).

Case 15.3 Mitchell v. Valteau

Court of Appeal of Louisiana, Fourth Circuit, 30 So.3d 1108 (2010).

BACKGROUND AND FACTS In 2001, Dr. Pamela Mitchell borrowed $143,724 to purchase a house and lot. The loan was secured by a mortgage on the property. The mortgage provided for the sale of the property in the event of a default. In 2006, Mitchell defaulted on her mortgage payments. The lending bank commenced a foreclosure proceeding, and the trial court ordered the issuance of a writ of seizure and sale. On January 23, 2007, Mitchell was served personally with a notice of seizure and the date of the sheriff's sale. Subsequently, the lending bank and Mitchell entered into a repayment agreement that postponed the seizure and sale. Mitchell made two payments and then was unable to comply with the payment terms of the new agreement. The trial court ordered that the original petition be amended and that an amended writ of seizure be issued, which the sheriff completed. The sheriff was unable to serve Mitchell at her residence on seven occasions, however. Therefore, the court appointed a receiver who accepted the service of process on Mitchell's behalf. On January 3, 2008, the property was sold at a sheriff's sale. Several months later, Mitchell filed a petition to annul the judicial sale and to ask for damages for wrongful seizure against the sheriff, Paul Valteau, as well as the lending bank and others. The bank filed a motion for summary judgment, which the trial court granted. Mitchell appealed.

IN THE WORDS OF THE COURT . . .
Patricia Rivet MURRAY, Judge.
        * * * *

A creditor seeking to enforce a mortgage or privilege on property by executory process must file a petition praying for the seizure and sale of the property affected by the mortgage or privilege. * * * In this case, [the bank] filed a petition for executor process and attached thereto authentic evidence satisfying all three requirements for obtaining an order of seizure and sale: a copy of the note, mortgage agreement, and a certified copy of the assignment of the mortgage note to it. * * * It is undisputed that

Dr. Mitchell was served with the initial notice of seizure. Dr. Mitchell, however, contends that the sheriff also was required to serve her with the amended notice of seizure from which her property was seized and sold. [Emphasis added.]

Resolution of the issue of whether service of the amended notice of seizure was required turns on construction of several * * * statutory provisions. La. C.C.P. Art. [Louisiana Code of Civil Procedure Article] 2721 provides that the sheriff must serve upon the defendant "a written notice of the seizure of the property. ["] La. C.C.P. Art. 2293(B) also provides that the sheriff shall serve "a notice of seizure."
        * * * *

Construing La. R.S. [Louisiana Revised Statutes] 13:3852 and La. C.C.P. Art. 2293(B) * * * [a prior court] rejected a debtor's argument that she was entitled to a second notice of seizure when the first sale was delayed.
        * * * *

The situation in this case is analogous to the situation presented in the [referenced] case. Dr. Mitchell defaulted on her loan agreement and [the bank] established its right to proceed by executory process to seize and sell the Property. Dr. Mitchell was served with a notice of seizure. Thereafter, she entered into the repayment agreement, [which] expressly provided that the executor proceeding would be placed on hold for the time the repayment agreement was in place. The agreement also provided for the resumption of the foreclosure in the event of a default in its terms, which Dr. Mitchell acknowledged occurred. When the executory proceeding was resumed, there was no obligation to serve Dr. Mitchell with another notice of seizure.

DECISION AND REMEDY The Louisiana appellate court upheld the trial court's decision. There was no obligation to serve Mitchell with another notice of seizure.

THE LEGAL ENVIRONMENT DIMENSION *How might the lender have avoided the dispute in this case?*

DEFICIENCY JUDGMENTS If any equity remains after the foreclosed property is sold, the borrower is often able to keep the difference between the sale price and the mortgage amount. If the sale amount is not enough to cover the loan amount, the lender (in the majority of states) can ask a court for a *deficiency judgment*—that is, a judgment against the borrower for the amount of debt remaining unpaid after the collateral is sold. A deficiency judgment requires the borrower to make up the difference to the lender over time.

LEARNING OBJECTIVE 5 In a mortgage foreclosure, what legal rights do mortgage holders have if the sale proceeds are insufficient to pay the underlying debt?

A lender who successfully bids on property at a foreclosure sale is considered to have received repayment of the loan in the amount of the bid. The lender can recover the difference between that amount and the amount of the unpaid debt in a deficiency action against the debtor.

EXAMPLE 15.6 Tristan Lee obtains a loan from Springwater Finance Company to buy a home. The loan is secured by a mortgage on the house. Lee defaults on the loan, and Springwater forecloses on the property. At the time, Lee owes $175,000 on the loan. The lender successfully bids $150,000 for the property at the sale. Immediately afterward, Springwater obtains an appraisal that determines the fair market value of the property to be $135,000. It later sells the property for $125,000. Springwater can recover $25,000 in a deficiency action against Lee. ●

Redemption Rights

Equitable Right of Redemption The right of a mortgagor who is in default to redeem or purchase the property before foreclosure proceedings by paying the full amount of the debt, plus any interest and costs.

Statutory Right of Redemption A right provided by statute in some states under which mortgagors can buy back their property after a judicial foreclosure for a limited period of time.

Every state allows a homeowner to buy the property *after default and before the foreclosure sale* by paying the full amount of the debt, plus any interest and costs that have accrued. This **equitable right of redemption** allows a defaulting borrower to gain title and regain possession of a property, but it ends when the property is sold at a foreclosure auction.

The **statutory right of redemption,** in contrast, entitles the borrower to repurchase property even *after a judicial foreclosure.* In other words, in states that provide for statutory redemption, the homeowner has a right to buy the property back from a third party who bought it at a foreclosure sale. Generally, the borrower may exercise this right for up to one year from the time the house is sold at a foreclosure sale.[9]

The borrower[10] must pay the price at which the house was sold at the foreclosure sale (the redemption price), plus taxes, interest, and assessments, as opposed to the balance owed on the foreclosed loan. Some states allow the borrower to retain possession of the property after the foreclosure sale and up until the statutory redemption period ends. If the borrower does not exercise the right of redemption, the new buyer receives title to and possession of the property.

---

9. Some states do not allow a borrower to waive the statutory right of redemption. This means that a buyer at auction must wait one year to obtain title to, and possession of, a foreclosed property.

10. Some states also allow spouses of a defaulting borrower or creditors holding liens on the property to purchase the property under the statutory right of redemption.

▶ Reviewing. . . Mortgages and Foreclosures after the Recession

Al and Betty Smith own their home, which is valued at $200,000, completely—they have 100 percent home equity. They lost most of their savings in the stock market during the Great Recession. Needing funds to start a new business, they decide to take out a home equity loan. They borrow $150,000 for ten years at an interest rate of 12 percent. On the date they take out the loan, a ten-year Treasury bond is yielding 3 percent. The Smiths pay a total of $10,000 in "points and fees" to Alpha Bank. The Smiths are not given any notices that they can lose their home if they do not meet their obligations under the loan. Two weeks after consummating the loan, the Smiths change their minds and want to rescind the loan. Using the information presented in the chapter, answer the following questions.

1. Is the Smiths' loan covered by the Truth-in-Lending Act as amended by the Home Ownership and Equity Protection Act? Why or why not?

2. Do the Smiths have a right to rescind the loan two weeks after the fact, or is it too late? Explain.

3. Assume now that Alpha Bank had given the Smiths all of the required notices before the loan was consummated. If all other facts remain the same, would the Smiths have a right to rescind? Why or why not?

4. Suppose now that the Smiths never rescind the loan and that they default four years later while still owing Alpha Bank $120,000. The bank forecloses and raises only $110,000 when the house is sold at auction. In the majority of states, what options does Alpha Bank have to recover the difference? Explain.

Debate This

Federal legislation enacted in the past few years has unfairly benefited those who should not have bought such expensive houses and taken on so much debt.

Key Terms

acceleration clause 392	foreclosure 388	power of sale foreclosure 392
adjustable-rate mortgage (ARM) 382	home equity loan 383	predatory lending 385
annual percentage rate (APR) 385	interest-only (IO) mortgage 383	prepayment penalty clause 384
appraiser 386	judicial foreclosure 392	reamortize 390
deed in lieu of foreclosure 390	mortgage 382	short sale 389
equitable right of redemption 394	negative amortization 387	statutory right of redemption 394
fixed-rate mortgage 382	notice of default 392	subprime mortgage 393
forbearance 388	notice of sale 392	workout agreement 389

Chapter Summary: Mortgages and Foreclosures after the Recession

Types of Mortgages and Loans (See pages 382–383.)	A mortgage loan is a contract between a creditor (mortgagee) and a borrower (mortgagor). There are many types of mortgages, including: 1. *Fixed-rate mortgages*—Standard mortgages with a fixed rate of interest and payments that stay the same for the duration of the loan. 2. *Adjustable-rate mortgages (ARMs)*—Mortgages in which the interest rate changes periodically, usually starting low and increasing over time. 3. *Interest-only mortgages*—Mortgages that allow borrowers to pay only the interest portion of the monthly payments for a limited time, after which the size of the payment increases. 4. *Subprime mortgages*—Mortgages that carry higher rates of interest because they are made to borrowers who do not qualify for standard mortgages. 5. *Home equity loans*—Loans for which a bank accepts the borrower's equity in the home as collateral. If the loan is not repaid on time, the home can be seized.

Lender and Borrower Protections (See pages 383–388.)	1. *Lender protections*—To protect its interests, a creditor may (a) require private mortgage insurance if the down payment is less than 20 percent of the purchase price, (b) perfect its security interest by recording the mortgage in the appropriate office, and (c) include a prepayment penalty clause and a clause requiring the borrower to maintain homeowners' insurance in the mortgage contract.
	2. *Borrower protections*—Congress has implemented legislation to protect borrowers from predatory lending practices.
	   a. *Truth-in-Lending Act (TILA)*—This federal statute requires mortgage lenders to disclose the terms of a loan in clear, readily understandable language on standardized forms.
	   b. *The Home Ownership and Equity Protection Act (HOEPA) of 1994*—This federal statute creates special rules for high-cost and high-fee mortgage products.
	   c. *Higher-priced mortgage loans (HPMLs)*—To qualify as an HPML, a mortgage must have an APR that exceeds the average prime offer rate by a certain amount for a comparable transaction.

Foreclosures (See pages 388–394.)	If the borrower defaults, the lender can foreclose on the mortgaged property. The foreclosure process allows a lender to repossess and auction the property. 1. *Ways to avoid foreclosure proceedings*—Foreclosures can sometimes be avoided through a forbearance or a workout agreement, an interest-free loan from the U.S. Department of Housing and Urban Development, a short sale, a sale and leaseback, a modification under the Home Affordable Modification Program, a deed in lieu of foreclosure, or a friendly foreclosure.

(Continued)

Chapter Summary: Mortgages and Foreclosures after the Recession, Continued

Foreclosures–Continued	2. *Foreclosure procedures*–In a judicial foreclosure, which is available in all states, a court supervises the process. In a power of sale foreclosure, which is permitted in only a few states, the lender can foreclose on and sell the property without judicial supervision.
	   a. To initiate a foreclosure, the lender records a notice of default with the county. If the loan is not paid, the borrower receives a notice of sale, and the property is sold at auction.
	   b. In most states, if the sale proceeds do not cover the loan amount, the lender can obtain a deficiency judgment for the amount due.
	3. *Redemption rights*–
	   a. *Equitable right of redemption*–In all states, the borrower has the right to purchase the property after default by paying the full amount of the debt, plus interest and costs, before the foreclosure sale.
	   b. *Statutory right of redemption*–In some states, the borrower has the right to repurchase the property even after a judicial foreclosure.

ExamPrep

ISSUE SPOTTERS

—**Check your answers to these questions against the answers provided in Appendix D at the end of this text.**

1. Ruth Ann borrows $175,000 from Sunny Valley Bank to buy a home. What are the major terms of the mortgage that must be disclosed in the writing under the Truth-in-Lending Act? (**See page 385.**)

2. Tanner borrows $150,000 from Southeast Credit Union to buy a home, which secures the loan. Two years into the term, Tanner stops making payments on the mortgage. After six months without payments, Southeast informs Tanner that he is in default and that it will proceed to foreclosure. What is foreclosure, and what is the usual procedure? (**See page 392.**)

BEFORE THE TEST

Go to **www.cengagebrain.com**, enter the ISBN 9781133586548, and click on "Find" to locate this textbook's Web site. Then click on "Access Now" under "Study Tools," and select Chapter 15 at the top. There, you will find a Practice Quiz that you can take to assess your mastery of the concepts in this chapter. Additionally, you will find Flashcards and a Glossary of important terms, as well as Video Questions (when assigned).

For Review

Answers for the even-numbered questions in this For Review *section can be found in Appendix E at the end of this text.*

1. What is a subprime mortgage, and how does it differ from a standard fixed-rate mortgage?

2. When is private mortgage insurance required? Which party does it protect?

3. How do the TILA provisions protect borrowers and curb abusive practices by mortgage lenders?

4. What is a short sale, and what advantages over mortgage foreclosure might it offer borrowers?

5. In a mortgage foreclosure, what legal rights do mortgage holders have if the sale proceeds are insufficient to pay the underlying debt?

▶ Questions and Case Problems

15–1. Disclosure Requirements. Rancho Mortgage, Inc., wants to launch a new advertising campaign designed to attract homebuyers in a difficult economic environment. Rancho plans to promote its new loan product, which offers a fixed interest rate for the first five years and then switches to a variable interest rate. Rancho believes that Spanish-speaking homebuyers have been underserved in recent years, and it wants to advertise particularly to that market. What must Rancho say (and not say) in its advertising campaigns about the structure or terms of the loan product? Why? **(See pages 385–386.)**

15–2. ❓ **Question with Sample Answer: Real Estate Financing.** Jane Lane refinanced her mortgage with Central Equity, Inc. Central Equity split the transaction into two separate loan documents with separate Truth-in-Lending disclosure statements and settlement statements. Two years later, Lane tried to exercise her right to rescission under the Home Ownership and Equity Protection Act (HOEPA), but Central Equity refused. Central Equity said that the loans were two separate loan transactions and because neither loan imposed sufficient fees and costs to trigger HOEPA, its protections did not apply. Lane claimed that the costs and fees combined into a single transaction (which Lane expected the loan to be) would surpass the HOEPA threshold and trigger its protections. Because Central Equity did not provide the necessary disclosures under HOEPA, Lane argues that she can properly rescind under its provisions. Is Lane correct? Does loan splitting allow the lender to count each loan transaction with a borrower separately for purposes of HOEPA? Why or why not? **(See page 386.)**

—For a sample answer to Question 15–2, go to Appendix F at the end of this text.

15–3. Lender's Options. In 2011, Frank relocates and purchases a five-year-old house for $450,000. He pays $90,000 as a down payment and finances the remaining $360,000 of the purchase price with a loan from Bank of Town. Frank signs mortgage paperwork, giving Bank of Town a mortgage interest in the home. Frank pays on the loan for three years. At that point, the housing market has declined significantly. Frank's home is now valued at $265,000. The balance due on his loan is $354,000. In addition, the economy has slowed, and the booming business that Frank started when he bought the home has seen a decrease in revenues. It seems inevitable that Frank will not be able to make his payments. Discuss Bank of Town's options in this situation. **(See pages 388–393.)**

15–4. Right of Rescission. George and Mona Antanuos obtained a mortgage loan secured with rental property from the First National Bank of Arizona. At the closing, First National provided the Antanuoses with a "Notice of Right to Cancel," informing them about their TILA three-day rescission period. The following day, according to the Antanuoses, they informed the bank via fax that they wished to exercise their right to rescind. When First National refused to rescind the agreement, the Antanuoses sued the bank. The Antanuoses did not dispute that a consumer's right to rescind under the TILA applies only to the consumer's original dwelling and that they used their commercial property as a security interest. Instead, the Antanuoses argued that the bank was prohibited from denying them the rescission right because they relied on the bank's disclosure, which would have been required under the TILA, to their detriment. Would the court be convinced? Explain. [*Antanuos v. First National Bank of Arizona,* 508 F.Supp.2d 466 (E.D.Va. 2007)] **(See pages 385–386.)**

15–5. Mortgage Foreclosure. In January 2003, Gary Ryder and Washington Mutual Bank, F.A., executed a note in which Ryder promised to pay $2,450,000, plus interest at a rate that could vary from month to month. The amount of the first payment was $10,933. The note was to be paid in full by February 1, 2033. A mortgage on Ryder's real property at 345 Round Hill Road in Greenwich, Connecticut, in favor of the bank secured his obligations under the note. The note and mortgage required Ryder to pay the taxes on the property, which he did not do in 2004 and 2005. The bank notified him that he was in default and, when he failed to act, paid $50,095.92 in taxes, penalties, interest, and fees. Other disputes arose between the parties, and Ryder filed a suit against the bank, alleging, in part, breach of contract. He charged, among other things, that some of his timely payments were not processed and were subjected to incorrect late fees, forcing him to make excessive payments and ultimately resulting in "non-payment by Ryder." The bank filed a counterclaim, seeking to foreclose on the mortgage. What should a creditor be required to prove to foreclose on mortgaged property? What would be a debtor's most effective defense? Which party in this case is likely to prevail on the bank's counterclaim? Why? [*Ryder v. Washington Mutual Bank, F.A.,* 501 F.Supp.2d 311 (D.Conn. 2007)] **(See pages 391–392.)**

15–6. Foreclosures. Roderick and Linda Sharpe borrowed $51,300 secured by a mortgage on their home. About six years later, with more than $68,000 needed to pay off the mortgage, the Sharpes defaulted. The mortgage holder, Wells Fargo Home Mortgage, foreclosed on the property. Immediately before and after the foreclosure sale, Wells Fargo obtained two separate real estate brokers' opinions as to the property's fair market value. Each opinion was based on the prices of three comparable houses then on the market and three comparable houses that had sold within the previous six months. Both opinions set the value at $33,500.

This was the price at the sale. The Sharpes objected, arguing that the value of the property was $65,000 based on an appraisal that they could not provide. Was the sale price fair? Explain. [In re Sharpe, 425 Bankr. 620 (N.D.Ala. 2010)] **(See pages 393–394.)**

15–7. **Case Problem with Sample Answer: Deficiency Judgments.** First Brownsville Co. executed a promissory note secured by a mortgage so that it could build and operate a mini-warehouse storage business. When First Brownsville defaulted on the loan, Beach Community Bank sought to foreclose on the property in Florida state court. The court determined that First Brownsville owed $1,224,475, entered judgment for Beach Community, and scheduled a foreclosure sale. Beach Community was the only interested bidder at the foreclosure sale, so it bought the property for a mere $1,300. Pursuant to Florida law, Beach Community then sought a deficiency judgment. At the hearing, expert testimony established that the property's fair market value had been $1,480,000 a year earlier, but that the property was worth only $770,000 at the time of the sale. What should be the amount of Beach Community's deficiency judgment? Why? [*Beach Community Bank v. First Brownsville Co.*, 85 So.3d 1119 (Fla.App. 1st Dist. 2012)] **(See page 393.)**

—For a sample answer to Case Problem 15–7, go to Appendix G at the end of this text.

15–8. **A Question of Ethics: Predatory Lending.** *Peter Sutton's home was subject to two mortgages with payments of more than $1,400 per month, but his only source of income was $1,080 monthly from Social Security. Hoping to reduce the size of the payments, Sutton contacted Apex Mortgage Services. According to Sutton, the broker led him to believe that he could refinance with Countrywide Home Loans, Inc., for payments of $428 per month. In the end, the broker arranged an adjustable-rate loan from Countrywide with initial payments of about $1,000 per month subject to future increases. The loan included a prepayment penalty. Sutton paid the broker a fee and signed the agreement, but later claimed that he did not understand the terms. The payments proved too much for Sutton to afford, and he defaulted on the loan. Sutton sued the broker and lender claiming violations of federal law.* [*Sutton v. Countrywide Home Loans, Inc.*, ___ F.3d ___ (11th Cir. 2009)] **(See page 385.)**

1. Who is ethically responsible for Sutton's predicament? To what extent did Sutton have a duty to read and understand what he signed? Discuss.

2. Sutton argued that he should not have to pay the broker's fee because the broker did not provide any services that were of value. Do you agree? Why or why not?

3. Did Countrywide, the lender, have any ethical obligation to monitor the activities of the broker? Would the result have been different if Countrywide had intervened before the documents were signed? Explain.

Unit Four

The Employment Environment

Chapter 16

"The employer generally gets
the employees he deserves."

—Sir Walter Gilbey, 1831–1914
(English merchant)

Employment, Immigration, and Labor Law

Contents

Learning Objectives

The five Learning Objectives below are designed to help improve your understanding of the chapter. After reading this chapter, you should be able to answer the following questions:

1. **What are the duties of parties to an agency relationship?**

2. **What federal statute governs working hours and wages?**

3. **Under the Family and Medical Leave Act, in what circumstances may an employee take family or medical leave?**

4. **What are the two most important federal statutes governing immigration and employment today?**

5. **What federal statute gave employees the right to organize unions and engage in collective bargaining?**

(©Svetlana Larina, 2009. Used under license from Shutterstock.com)

Employment at Will A common law doctrine under which either party may terminate an employment relationship at any time for any reason.

Until the early 1900s, most employer-employee relationships were governed by the common law. Even today, as we will see, private employers have considerable freedom to hire and fire workers under the common law doctrine of **employment at will.** (This is one reason why employers generally get the employees they deserve, as the chapter-opening quotation above observed.)

In addition, however, numerous statutes and administrative agency regulations now govern the workplace. In this chapter and the next, we look at the most significant laws regulating employment relationships and at how these laws are changing to adapt to new technologies and new problems such as the influx of illegal immigrants. We also consider some current controversies, such as the degree to which employers can regulate their employees' use of social media and whether the states can enact their own laws to regulate immigration.

Of course, an important aspect of the employment relationship is the right to strike, and labor laws authorize both strikes by employees and lockouts by employers. In 2011, for instance, the owners of the teams in both the National Football League and the National Basketball Association imposed lockouts against the players during disputes over salaries and other issues (discussed on page 429).

In this chapter, we look at the most significant laws regulating employment relationships. As part of our discussion of employment relationships, we also explore agency relationships. Note that we will deal with important employment discrimination laws in the next chapter.

Agency Relationships

Agency A relationship between two parties in which one party (the agent) agrees to represent or act for the other (the principal).

Agent A person authorized by another to act for or in place of him or her.

Principal A person who, by agreement or otherwise, authorizes an agent to act on his or her behalf in such a way that the acts of the agent become binding on the principal.

One of the most common, important, and pervasive legal relationships is that of **agency.** In an agency relationship between two parties, one of the parties, called the **agent,** agrees to represent or act for the other, called the **principal.** The principal has the right to control the agent's conduct in matters entrusted to the agent. By using agents, a principal can conduct multiple business operations simultaneously in various locations. A familiar example of an agent is a corporate officer who serves in a representative capacity for the owners of a corporation. In this capacity, the officer has the authority to bind the principal (the corporation) to a contract.

The term *fiduciary* is at the heart of agency law. The term can be used both as a noun and as an adjective. When used as a noun, it refers to a person having a duty created by her or his undertaking to act primarily for another's benefit in matters connected with the undertaking. When used as an adjective, as in *fiduciary relationship,* it means that the relationship involves trust and confidence.

In a principal-agent relationship, the parties agree that the agent will act *on behalf and instead of* the principal in negotiating and transacting business with third persons. An agent is empowered to perform legal acts that are binding on the principal and can bind the principal in a contract with a third person.

Agency relationships commonly exist between employers and employees. Agency relationships also may sometimes exist between employers and independent contractors who are hired to perform special tasks or services.

Employer-Employee Relationships

An employee is one whose physical conduct is *controlled,* or subject to control, by the employer. Normally, all employees who deal with third parties are deemed to be agents. **EXAMPLE 16.1** Kayla, a salesperson in a department store, is an agent of the store (the principal) and acts on the store's behalf. Any sale of goods Kayla makes to a customer is binding on the store. Similarly, most representations of fact made by Kayla with respect to the goods sold are binding on the store. ●

Employment laws, which we will discuss later in this chapter, apply only to the employer-employee relationship. Statutes governing Social Security, withholding taxes, workers' compensation, unemployment compensation, workplace safety, and the like are applicable only if there is employer-employee status. *These laws do not apply to independent contractors.*

Employer–Independent Contractor Relationships

Independent Contractor One who works for, and receives payment from, an employer but whose working conditions and methods are not controlled by the employer. An independent contractor is *not* an employee but may be an agent.

Independent contractors are not employees because, by definition, those who hire them have no control over the details of their physical performance. Section 2 of the *Restatement (Third) of Agency* defines an **independent contractor** as follows:

> [An independent contractor is] a person who contracts with another to do something for him [or her] but who is not controlled by the other nor subject to the other's right to control with respect to his [or her] physical conduct in the performance of the undertaking. *He [or she] may or may not be an agent.* [Emphasis added.]

Building contractors and subcontractors are independent contractors—a property owner does not control the acts of either of these professionals. Truck drivers who own their equipment and hire themselves out on a per-job basis are independent contractors, but truck drivers who drive company trucks on a regular basis are usually employees.

The relationship between a person or firm and an independent contractor may or may not involve an agency relationship. **EXAMPLE 16.2** Brooke, an owner of real estate, hires Tom, a real estate broker, to negotiate a sale of property. Brooke has contracted with Tom (an independent contractor) and has established an agency relationship for the specific purpose of assisting in the sale of the property. In contrast, Henry, an owner of real estate, hires Millie, an appraiser, to estimate the value of his property. Henry does not control the conduct of Millie's work. Henry has contracted with Millie, an independent contractor, but he has not established an agency relationship. Millie has no power to transact any business for Henry and is not subject to his control with respect to the conduct of her work. •

Determining Employee Status

The courts are frequently asked to determine whether a particular worker is an employee or an independent contractor. How a court decides this issue can have a significant effect on the rights and liabilities of the parties.

CRITERIA USED BY THE COURTS   In determining whether a worker has the status of an employee or an independent contractor, the courts often consider the following questions:

1. How much control can the employer exercise over the details of the work? (If an employer can exercise considerable control over the details of the work, this would indicate employee status. This is perhaps the most important factor weighed by the courts in determining employee status.)
2. Is the worker engaged in an occupation or business distinct from that of the employer? (If so, this points to independent-contractor status, not employee status.)
3. Is the work usually done under the employer's direction or by a specialist without supervision? (If the work is usually done under the employer's direction, this would indicate employee status.)
4. Does the employer supply the tools at the place of work? (If so, this would indicate employee status.)
5. For how long is the person employed? (If the person is employed for a long period of time, this would indicate employee status.)
6. What is the method of payment—by time period or at the completion of the job? (Payment by time period, such as once every two weeks or once a month, would indicate employee status.)
7. What degree of skill is required of the worker? (If little skill is required, this may indicate employee status.)

CRITERIA USED BY THE INTERNAL REVENUE SERVICE   The Internal Revenue Service (IRS) has established its own criteria for determining whether a worker is an independent contractor or an employee. The most important factor in this determination is the degree of control the business exercises over the worker.

The IRS tends to closely scrutinize a firm's classification of its workers because employers can avoid certain tax liabilities by hiring independent contractors instead of employees. Even when a firm classifies a worker as an independent contractor, the IRS may decide that the worker is actually an employee. In that situation, the employer will be responsible for paying any applicable Social Security, withholding, and unemployment taxes.

Ethical Issue ⚖️

Should small businesses be allowed to hire "permalancers"? Freelancers, of course, are independent contractors. Today, small businesses across the country are turning increasingly to *permalancers*—that is, freelancers who stay on a business's payroll for years. From the business's perspective, the advantages are obvious. The cost savings from using freelancers rather than employees can be as much as 30 percent because the business does not have to pay payroll and unemployment taxes or workers' compensation premiums. Additionally, freelancers do not receive health-care and other benefits offered to employees. Finally, during an economic downturn, the business has more flexibility because it can let freelancers go quickly and usually without cost.

The IRS and state tax authorities, however, view permalancers differently. In early 2010, the IRS launched an ongoing program to examine six thousand companies to make sure that permanent workers have not been misclassified as independent contractors. The Obama administration also revised some regulations to make it harder for businesses to classify workers as independent contractors. The IRS is targeting small businesses not only because they hire many freelancers but also because, unlike larger companies, they usually do not have on-staff attorneys to defend them and thus are likely to acquiesce when the IRS clamps down.

These efforts raise some ethical issues, however. Certainly, the tax authorities will gain some revenues but at the cost of reducing the flexibility of small businesses. If the businesses hire fewer workers as a result, are the taxes collected worth the possible increase in unemployment? Another trade-off to consider is between the advantages that a business obtains from hiring permalancers, such as tax savings, and the disadvantages to those workers, such as no employee benefits.

Agency Formation

Agency relationships normally are *consensual*—that is, they come about by voluntary consent and agreement between the parties. Generally, the agreement need not be in writing, and consideration is not required.

A person must have *contractual capacity* (see Chapter 11) to be a principal. Those who cannot legally enter into contracts directly should not be allowed to do so indirectly through an agent. Any person can be an agent, though, regardless of whether he or she has the capacity to enter a contract.

An agency relationship can be created for any legal purpose. An agency relationship that is created for an illegal purpose or that is contrary to public policy is unenforceable. **EXAMPLE 16.3** Sharp (as principal) contracts with McKenzie (as agent) to sell illegal narcotics. This agency relationship is unenforceable because selling illegal narcotics is a felony and is contrary to public policy. ●

Generally, an agency relationship can arise in four ways: by agreement of the parties, by ratification, by estoppel, or by operation of law.

AGENCY BY AGREEMENT OF THE PARTIES Most agency relationships are based on an express or implied agreement that the agent will act for the principal and that the principal agrees to have the agent so act. An agency agreement can take the form of an express written contract or be created by an oral agreement. **EXAMPLE 16.4** Reese asks Cary, a gardener, to contract with others for the care of his lawn on a regular basis. Cary agrees. An agency relationship is established between Reese and Cary for the lawn care. ●

An agency agreement can also be implied by conduct. **EXAMPLE 16.5** A hotel expressly allows only Boris Koontz to park cars, but Boris has no employment contract there. The hotel's manager tells Boris when to work, as well as where and how to park the cars. The hotel's conduct amounts to a manifestation of its willingness to have

Boris park its customers' cars, and Boris can infer from the hotel's conduct that he has authority to act as a parking valet. It can be inferred that Boris is an agent-employee of the hotel, his purpose being to provide valet parking services for hotel guests. ●

In the following case, the court had to decide whether an agency relationship arose when a man who was being hospitalized asked his wife to sign the admissions papers for him.

Case 16.1   Laurel Creek Health Care Center v. Bishop

Court of Appeals of Kentucky, 2010 WL 985299 (2010).

BACKGROUND AND FACTS   Gilbert Bishop was admitted to Laurel Creek Health Care Center suffering from various physical ailments. During an examination, Bishop told Laurel Creek staff that he could not use his hands well enough to write or hold a pencil, but he was otherwise found to be mentally competent. Bishop's sister, Rachel Combs, testified that when she arrived at the facility she offered to sign the admissions forms, but Laurel Creek employees told her that it was their policy to have a patient's spouse sign the admissions papers if the patient was unable to do so. Combs also testified that Bishop asked her to get his wife, Anna, so that she could sign his admissions papers. Combs then brought Anna to the hospital, and Anna signed the admissions paperwork, which contained a provision for mandatory arbitration. Subsequently, Bishop went into cardiopulmonary arrest and died. Following his death, Bishop's family brought an action in a Kentucky state court against Laurel Creek for negligence. Laurel Creek requested that the trial court order the parties to proceed to arbitration in accordance with the mandatory arbitration provision contained in the admissions paperwork signed by Anna. The trial court denied the request on the ground that Anna was not Bishop's agent and had no legal authority to make decisions for him. Laurel Creek appealed.

IN THE WORDS OF THE COURT . . .
LAMBERT, Judge.

* * * *

Laurel Creek first argues that this is a case of actual agency and that Anna Bishop had actual authority as Gilbert's agent to sign the admissions paperwork and is therefore bound by the arbitration agreement therein.

* * * *

We agree with Laurel Creek that Gilbert created an actual agency relationship between him and his wife. According to his sister, Rachel,

Gilbert specifically asked that his wife be brought to the nursing home so that she could sign the admissions documents for him, and Anna acted upon that delegation of authority and signed the admissions papers. This is consistent with the creation of actual authority as described in the *Restatement (Third) of Agency,* [Section] 2.01, Comment c (2006). The *Restatement* explains the rationale for the creation of actual agency in three steps. *First,* "*the principal manifests assent to be affected by the agent's action.*" In the instant case, Gilbert asked that Anna come to the hospital to sign the papers for him. *Second,* "*the agent's actions establish the agent's consent to act on the principal's behalf.*" Here, Anna signed all the admissions papers per her husband's request and therefore consented to act on Gilbert's behalf. *Third, by acting within such authority, the agent affects the principal's legal relations with third parties.* Clearly here, Anna's actions affected Gilbert's relations with Laurel Creek, a third party. [Emphasis added.]

* * * *

* * * The evidence indicates that Gilbert indicated to Laurel Creek that he was physically incapable of signing the documents but was of sound mental capacity and wanted his wife to sign the documents on his behalf. When Gilbert communicated this to his sister, and the sister brought Anna in to sign the documents, Gilbert created an agency relationship upon which Laurel Creek relied.

DECISION AND REMEDY   The Kentucky Court of Appeals reversed the trial court's judgment and remanded the case for further proceedings consistent with its opinion. An actual agency relationship between Bishop and his wife had been formed, and the trial court had erred when it found otherwise.

THE ECONOMIC DIMENSION   *Which party benefited from the court's ruling? Why?*

Ratification The act of accepting and giving legal force to an obligation that previously was not enforceable.

AGENCY BY RATIFICATION   On occasion, a person who is in fact not an agent (or who is an agent acting outside the scope of her or his authority) may make a contract on behalf of another (a principal). If the principal affirms that contract by word or by action, an agency relationship is created by **ratification**. Ratification involves a question of intent, and intent can be expressed by either words or conduct. The basic requirements for ratification will be discussed later in this chapter.

AGENCY BY ESTOPPEL   When a principal causes a third person to believe that another person is his or her agent, and the third person deals with the supposed agent, the principal is "estopped to deny" the agency relationship. In such a situation, the principal's actions create the *appearance* of an agency that does not in fact exist. The third person must prove that she or he *reasonably* believed that an agency relationship existed, though.[1] Facts and circumstances must show that an ordinary, prudent person familiar with business practice and custom would have been justified in concluding that the agent had authority.

CASE EXAMPLE 16.6   Marsha and Jerry Wiedmaier owned Wiedmaier, Inc., a corporation that operated a truck stop. Their son, Michael, did not own any interest in the corporation but had worked at the truck stop as a fuel operator. Michael decided to form his own business called Extreme Diecast, LLC. To obtain a line of credit with Motorsport Marketing, Inc., a company that sells racing memorabilia, Michael asked his mother to sign the credit application form. After Marsha had signed as "Secretary-Owner" of Wiedmaier, Inc., Michael added his name to the list of corporate owners and faxed it to Motorsport. Later, when Michael stopped making payments on the merchandise he had ordered, Motorsport sued Wiedmaier, Inc., for the unpaid balance. The court ruled that Michael was an apparent agent of Wiedmaier, Inc., because the credit application had caused Motorsport to reasonably believe that Michael was acting as Wiedmaier's agent in ordering merchandise.[2] ●

Note that the acts or declarations of a purported *agent* in and of themselves do not create an agency by estoppel. Rather, it is the deeds or statements *of the principal* that create an agency by estoppel. In other words, in Case Example 16.6 above, if Marsha Wiedmaier had not signed the credit application on behalf of the principal-corporation, then Motorsport would not have been reasonable in believing that Michael was Wiedmaier's agent.

AGENCY BY OPERATION OF LAW   The courts may find an agency relationship in the absence of a formal agreement in other situations as well. This can occur in family relationships, such as when one spouse purchases certain basic necessaries and charges them to the other spouse's charge account. The courts will often rule that a spouse is liable to pay for the necessaries, either because of a social policy of promoting the general welfare of the spouse or because of a legal duty to supply necessaries to family members.

Agency by operation of law may also occur in emergency situations, when the agent's failure to act outside the scope of his or her authority would cause the principal substantial loss. If the agent is unable to contact the principal, the courts will often grant this emergency power. **EXAMPLE 16.7**   Linda's car is struck by a train, and she is injured. Jake, a railroad engineer, may contract (on the behalf of his employer) for medical care for Linda. ●

Duties of Agents and Principals

Once the principal-agent relationship has been created, both parties have duties that govern their conduct. As discussed previously, an agency relationship is *fiduciary*—one of trust. In a fiduciary relationship, each party owes the other the

---

1. These concepts also apply when a person who is in fact an agent undertakes an action that is beyond the scope of her or his authority, as will be discussed on pages 409 and 410.

2. *Motorsport Marketing, Inc. v. Wiedmaier, Inc.,* 195 S.W.3d 492 (Mo.App. 2006).

duty to act with the utmost good faith. We now examine the various duties of agents and principals.

AGENT'S DUTIES TO THE PRINCIPAL The duties that an agent owes to a principal are set forth in the agency agreement or arise by operation of law. The duties are implied from the agency relationship *whether or not the identity of the principal is disclosed to a third party.* Generally, the agent owes the principal the five duties described below.

Performance. An agent must use reasonable diligence and skill in performing the work. The degree of skill or care required of an agent is usually that expected of a reasonable person under similar circumstances. If an agent has represented himself or herself as possessing special skills (such as those that an accountant or attorney possesses), the agent is expected to use them.

Notification. An agent must notify the principal of all matters that come to his or her attention concerning the subject matter of the agency. Under the law of agency, notice to the agent is notice to the principal. **EXAMPLE 16.8** Annette, the manager (the agent) of a grocery store, is notified of a spilled gallon of milk in one of the aisles. If she fails to take steps to clean up the spill and a customer is injured, the store's owner (the principal) is liable for the injury. •

Loyalty. The duty of loyalty means that the agent must act solely for the benefit of his or her principal and not in the interest of himself or herself, or a third party. It also means that any information (such as a customer list) acquired through the agency relationship is confidential. It would be a breach of loyalty to disclose such information either during the agency relationship or after its termination.

Furthermore, an agent employed by a principal to buy cannot buy from himself or herself. **EXAMPLE 16.9** If Verona asks Bob to buy an acre of land in a certain area of the city for her, Bob cannot take advantage of the relationship to secretly sell his own acre in that area to her. • Similarly, an agent employed to sell cannot become the purchaser without the principal's consent. **EXAMPLE 16.10** If Gail asks Kurt to sell her Kindle e-reader, Kurt cannot buy the e-reader without Gail's consent. •

Obedience. When an agent is acting on behalf of the principal, the agent must follow all lawful and clearly stated instructions of the principal. During emergency situations, however, when the principal cannot be consulted, the agent may deviate from the instructions if the circumstances warrant it (such as when the principal would suffer a financial loss if the agent failed to act).

Accounting. The agent must keep and make available to the principal an account of all property and funds received and paid out on behalf of the principal. This includes gifts from third persons in connection with the agency. **EXAMPLE 16.11** A gift from June, a customer, to Jeremy, a salesperson, for prompt deliveries made by Jeremy's firm belongs to the firm. • Additionally, the agent must maintain separate accounts for the principal's funds and for the agent's personal funds, and the agent must not intermingle these accounts.

PRINCIPAL'S DUTIES TO THE AGENT The principal also has certain duties to the agent, either expressed or implied by law. Three such duties are discussed here.

Compensation. The principal has a duty to pay the agent for services rendered. If the parties have agreed on the amount of compensation, the principal must pay that

LEARNING OBJECTIVE 1 What are the duties of parties to an agency relationship?

amount on completion of the agent's activities. If no amount is expressly agreed on, then the principal owes the agent the customary compensation for the agent's services.

Reimbursement and Indemnification. When an agent disburses funds at the request of the principal or to pay for necessary expenses in the course of reasonable performance of his or her agency duties, the principal must reimburse the agent. Agents cannot recover for expenses incurred by their own misconduct, however.

A principal must also *indemnify* (compensate) an agent for liabilities incurred because of authorized acts, as well as for losses suffered by the agent or others because of the principal's failure to perform his or her duties. **EXAMPLE 16.12** If an agent orders supplies on the principal's behalf and the agent is held liable for the payment, the principal must indemnify the agent for the liability. •

Cooperation. A principal must cooperate with the agent and assist the agent in performing his or her duties. The principal must do nothing to prevent that performance. **EXAMPLE 16.13** Peggy (the principal) creates an exclusive agency by granting Don (the agent) an exclusive territory within which Don may sell Peggy's products. If Peggy starts to sell the products herself within Don's territory—or permits another agent to do so—Peggy has not cooperated with the agent. By violating the exclusive agency, Peggy can be held liable for Don's lost sales or profits. •

Agent's Authority

The liability of a principal to third parties with whom an agent contracts depends on whether the agent had the authority to enter into legally binding contracts on the principal's behalf. An agent's authority to act can be either *actual* (express or implied) or *apparent*. If an agent contracts outside the scope of his or her authority, the principal may still become liable by ratifying the contract.

ACTUAL AUTHORITY (EXPRESS OR IMPLIED) *Express authority* of an agent is embodied in that which the principal has engaged the agent to do. It can be given orally or in writing. The *equal dignity rule* in most states requires that if the contract being executed is or must be in writing, then the agent's authority must also be in writing. **EXAMPLE 16.14** Zorba orally asks Parkinson to sell a ranch that Zorba owns. Parkinson finds a buyer and signs a sales contract on behalf of Zorba to sell the ranch. A contract for an interest in land must be in writing. The buyer cannot enforce the contract unless Zorba subsequently ratifies Parkinson's agency status *in writing*. Once the contract is ratified, either party can enforce rights under it. •

Implied authority of an agent can be (1) conferred by custom, (2) inferred from the position the agent occupies, or (3) inferred as being reasonably necessary to carry out express authority. Authority to manage a business, for example, implies authority to do what is reasonably required to operate the business. Such actions include forming contracts to hire employees, buy merchandise and equipment, and advertise the products sold in a store.

APPARENT AUTHORITY Actual authority (express or implied) arises from what the principal makes clear to the agent. *Apparent authority,* in contrast, arises when the principal, by either word or action, causes a *third party* reasonably to believe that an agent has authority to act, even though the agent has no express or implied authority.

If the third party changes his or her position in reliance on the principal's representations, the principal may be *estopped* (barred) from denying that the agent had authority. **EXAMPLE 16.15** Emily Anderson, a salesperson for Gold Products, has no authority to collect payments for orders solicited from customers. A customer, Martin Huerta, pays Anderson for an order. Anderson takes the payment to Gold's accountant, who accepts the payment and sends Huerta a receipt. This procedure is followed for other orders by Huerta. Finally, however, Anderson disappears with one of Huerta's payments. Because of Gold's repeated acts of accepting Huerta's payment, Huerta reasonably expected that Anderson had authority to receive payments. Although Anderson did not have authority, Gold's conduct gave her apparent authority. ●

Liability in Agency Relationships

Frequently, a question arises as to which party, the principal or the agent, should be held liable for contracts formed by the agent or for torts or crimes committed by the agent. We look here at these aspects of agency law.

LIABILITY FOR CONTRACTS Liability for contracts formed by an agent depends on how the principal is classified and on whether the actions of the agent were authorized or unauthorized. Principals are classified as disclosed, partially disclosed, or undisclosed.

A **disclosed principal** is a principal whose identity is known by the third party at the time the contract is made by the agent. A **partially disclosed principal** is a principal whose identity is not known by the third party, but the third party knows that the agent is or may be acting for a principal at the time the contract is made. **EXAMPLE 16.16** Sarah has contracted with a real estate agent to sell certain property. She wishes to keep her identity a secret, but the agent makes it perfectly clear to potential buyers of the property that the agent is acting in an agency capacity. In this situation, Sarah is a partially disclosed principal. ●

An **undisclosed principal** is a principal whose identity is totally unknown by the third party, and the third party has no knowledge that the agent is acting in an agency capacity at the time the contract is made.

AUTHORIZED ACTS If an agent acts within the scope of her or his authority, normally the principal is obligated to perform the contract regardless of whether the principal was disclosed, partially disclosed, or undisclosed. Whether the agent may also be held liable under the contract, however, depends on the disclosed, partially disclosed, or undisclosed status of the principal.

Disclosed or Partially Disclosed Principal. A disclosed or partially disclosed principal is liable to a third party for a contract made by an agent who is acting within the scope of her or his authority. If the principal is disclosed, an agent has no contractual liability for the nonperformance of the principal or the third party. If the principal is partially disclosed, in most states the agent is also treated as a party to the contract, and the third party can hold the agent liable for contractual nonperformance.[3]

Undisclosed Principal. When neither the fact of agency nor the identity of the principal is disclosed, the undisclosed principal is bound to perform just as if the

Disclosed Principal A principal whose identity is known to a third party at the time the agent makes a contract with the third party.

Partially Disclosed Principal A principal whose identity is unknown by a third party, but the third party knows that the agent is or may be acting for a principal at the time the agent and the third party form a contract.

Undisclosed Principal A principal whose identity is unknown by a third person, and the third person has no knowledge that the agent is acting for a principal at the time the agent and the third person form a contract.

3. *Restatement (Third) of Agency,* Section 6.02.

principal had been fully disclosed at the time the contract was made. The agent is also liable as a party to the contract.

When a principal's identity is undisclosed and the agent is forced to pay the third party, the agent is entitled to be indemnified (compensated) by the principal. The principal had a duty to perform, even though his or her identity was undisclosed, and failure to do so will make the principal ultimately liable. Once the undisclosed principal's identity is revealed, the third party generally can elect to hold either the principal or the agent liable on the contract.

Conversely, the undisclosed principal can require the third party to fulfill the contract, *unless* (1) the undisclosed principal was expressly excluded as a party in the contract; (2) the contract is a check (or other negotiable instrument) signed by the agent with no indication of signing in a representative capacity; or (3) the performance of the agent is personal to the contract, allowing the third party to refuse the principal's performance.

CASE EXAMPLE 16.17 Bobby Williams bought a car at Sherman Henderson's auto repair business in Monroe, Louisiana, for $3,000. Henderson negotiated and made the sale for the car's owner, Joe Pike, whose name was not disclosed. Williams drove the car to Memphis, Tennessee, where his daughter was a student. Three days after the sale, the car erupted in flames. Williams extinguished the blaze and contacted Henderson. The vehicle was soon stolen, which prevented Williams from returning it to Henderson. Williams later filed suits against both Pike and Henderson. The court noted that the state had issued Pike a permit to sell the car. The car was displayed for sale at Henderson's business, and Henderson actually sold it. This made Pike the principal and Henderson his agent. The fact that their agency relationship was not made clear to Williams made Pike an undisclosed principal. Williams could thus hold both Pike and Henderson liable for the condition of the car.[4] ●

UNAUTHORIZED ACTS If an agent has no authority but nevertheless contracts with a third party, the principal cannot be held liable on the contract. It does not matter whether the principal was disclosed, partially disclosed, or undisclosed. The *agent* is liable, however.

EXAMPLE 16.18 Scranton signs a contract for the purchase of a truck, purportedly acting as an agent under authority granted by Johnson. In fact, Johnson has not given Scranton any such authority. Johnson refuses to pay for the truck, claiming that Scranton had no authority to purchase it. The seller of the truck is entitled to hold Scranton liable for payment. ●

LIABILITY FOR TORTS AND CRIMES Obviously, any person, including an agent, is liable for her or his own torts and crimes. Whether a principal can also be held liable for an agent's torts and crimes depends on several factors. A principal may also be liable for harm an agent caused to a third party under the doctrine of ***respondeat superior,***[5] a Latin term meaning "let the master respond." It imposes **vicarious liability,** or indirect liability, on the employer—that is, liability without regard to the personal fault of the employer—for torts committed by an employee in the course or scope of employment.

Determining the Scope of Employment. The key to determining whether a principal may be liable for the torts of an agent under the doctrine of *respondeat superior* is whether the torts are committed within the scope of the agency or employment. The

Respondeat Superior A principle of law whereby a principal or an employer is held liable for the wrongful acts committed by agents or employees acting within the scope of their agency or employment.

Vicarious Liability Legal responsibility placed on one person for the acts of another.

---

4. *Williams v. Pike,* 58 So.3d 525 (2011).
5. Pronounced ree-*spahn*-dee-uht soo-*peer*-ee-your.

factors that courts consider in determining whether a particular act occurred within the course and scope of employment are as follows:

1. Whether the employee's act was authorized by the employer.
2. The time, place, and purpose of the act.
3. Whether the act was one commonly performed by employees on behalf of their employers.
4. The extent to which the employer's interest was advanced by the act.
5. The extent to which the private interests of the employee were involved.
6. Whether the employer furnished the means or instrumentality (for example, a truck or a machine) by which the injury was inflicted.
7. Whether the employer had reason to know that the employee would do the act in question and whether the employee had ever done it before.
8. Whether the act involved the commission of a serious crime.

A useful insight into the "scope of employment" concept may be gained from the judge's classic distinction between a "detour" and a "frolic" in the case of *Joel v. Morison.*[6] In this case, an English court held that if a servant merely took a detour from his master's business, the master will be responsible. If, however, the servant was on a "frolic of his own" and not in any way "on his master's business," the master will not be liable.

For instance, an employee going to and from work or to and from meals is usually considered outside the scope of employment. If travel is part of a person's position, however, such as a traveling salesperson or a regional representative of a company, then travel time is normally considered within the scope of employment. Thus, the duration of the business trip, including the return trip home, is within the scope of employment unless there is a significant departure from the employer's business.

Liability for an Agent's Intentional Torts.   Most intentional torts that employees commit have no relation to their employment. Thus, their employers will not be held liable. Nevertheless, under the doctrine of *respondeat superior,* the employer can be liable for intentional torts of the employee that are committed within the course and scope of employment, just as the employer is liable for negligence. For instance, an employer is liable when an employee (such as a "bouncer" at a nightclub or a security guard at a department store) commits the tort of assault and battery or false imprisonment while acting within the scope of employment.

In addition, an employer who knows or should know that an employee has a propensity for committing tortious acts is liable for the employee's acts even if they would not ordinarily be considered within the scope of employment. For example, if the employer hires a bouncer knowing that he has a history of arrests for assault and battery, the employer may be liable if the employee viciously attacks a patron in the parking lot after hours.

An employer may also be liable for permitting an employee to engage in reckless actions that can injure others. **EXAMPLE 16.19**   An employer observes an employee smoking while filling containerized trucks with highly flammable liquids. Failure to stop the employee will cause the employer to be liable for any injuries that result if a truck explodes. ●

Liability for an Independent Contractor's Torts.   Generally, an employer is not liable for physical harm caused to a third person by the negligent act of an independent contractor in the performance of the contract. This is because the employer does not have the right to control the details of an independent contractor's perfor-

---

6. 6 Car. & P. 501, 172 Eng. Reprint 1338 (1834).

mance. Exceptions to this rule are made in certain situations, though, such as when unusually hazardous activities are involved.

Typical examples of such activities include blasting operations, the transportation of highly volatile chemicals, or the use of poisonous gases. In these situations, an employer cannot be shielded from liability merely by using an independent contractor. Strict liability is imposed on the employer-principal as a matter of law. Also, in some states, strict liability may be imposed by statute.

Liability for an Agent's Crimes. An agent is liable for his or her own crimes. A principal or employer is not liable for an agent's crime even if the crime was committed within the scope of authority or employment—unless the principal participated by conspiracy or other action. In some jurisdictions, under specific statutes, a principal may be liable for an agent's violation, in the course and scope of employment, of regulations, such as those governing sanitation, prices, weights, and the sale of liquor.

▶ Wage and Hour Laws

Unlike agent-principal relationships, employment relationships are between employers and employees. When an employer hires an employee, it must comply with many employment laws designed to define that relationship, as well as protect workers. These laws do not apply to agency relationships. One important area of employment law, for example, regulates how many hours employees can work, as well as the minimum wage that they can be paid. These laws are known as wage and hour laws.

In the 1930s, Congress enacted several laws regulating the wages and working hours of employees. In 1931, Congress passed the Davis-Bacon Act,[7] which requires contractors and subcontractors working on federal government construction projects to pay "prevailing wages" to their employees. In 1936, the Walsh-Healey Act[8] was passed. This act requires that a minimum wage, as well as overtime pay at 1.5 times regular pay rates, be paid to employees of manufacturers or suppliers entering into contracts with agencies of the federal government.

LEARNING OBJECTIVE 2 **What federal statute governs working hours and wages?**

In 1938, Congress passed the Fair Labor Standards Act (FLSA).[9] This act extended wage and hour requirements to cover all employers engaged in interstate commerce or in the production of goods for interstate commerce, plus selected types of other businesses. More than 130 million American workers are protected (or covered) by the FLSA, which is enforced by the Wage and Hour Division of the U.S. Department of Labor.

Here, we examine the FLSA's provisions in regard to child labor, minimum wages, and overtime pay.

Child Labor

The FLSA sets many restrictions on the use of child labor. Examples include:

- Children under fourteen years of age are allowed to do only certain types of work, such as deliver newspapers, work for their parents, and work in the entertainment and (with some exceptions) agricultural areas.
- Children who are fourteen or fifteen years of age are allowed to work, but not in hazardous occupations. There are also numerous restrictions on the number of hours per day (particularly on school days) and per week that they can work.

---

7. 40 U.S.C. Sections 276a–276a-5.
8. 41 U.S.C. Sections 35–45.
9. 29 U.S.C. Sections 201–260.

- Working times and hours are not restricted for persons sixteen to eighteen, but they cannot be employed in hazardous jobs or jobs detrimental to their health or well-being.

Minimum Wages

Minimum Wage The lowest hourly wage that an employer may pay a worker.

The FLSA provides that a **minimum wage** of $7.25 per hour must be paid to employees in covered industries. Congress periodically revises this federal minimum wage. Additionally, many states have minimum wage laws. When the state minimum wage is greater than the federal minimum wage, the employee is entitled to the higher wage.

Overtime Provisions

Under the FLSA, employees who work more than forty hours per week normally must be paid 1.5 times their regular pay for all hours over forty. Note that the FLSA overtime provisions apply only after an employee has worked more than forty hours per *week*. Thus, employees who work for ten hours a day, four days per week, are not entitled to overtime pay because they do not work more than forty hours per week.

Certain employees—usually executive, administrative, and professional employees, as well as outside salespersons and computer programmers—are exempt from the FLSA's overtime provisions. Employers are not required to pay overtime wages to exempt employees. Employers can voluntarily pay overtime to ineligible employees but cannot waive or reduce the overtime requirements of the FLSA. (Smartphones and other technology have raised new issues concerning overtime wages, as discussed in this chapter's *Beyond Our Borders* feature below.)

Beyond Our Borders   Brazil Workers Get Overtime Pay for Smartphone Use after Work

Workers in the United States are increasingly arguing that they should receive overtime pay for the time they spend staying connected to work through their iPads, smartphones, or other electronic devices. Indeed, many employers require their employees to carry a mobile device, such as a BlackBerry, iPhone, or tablet, to keep in contact.

Checking e-mail, responding to text messages, tweeting, and using LinkedIn or other employment-related apps can be considered work. If employees who are not exempt under the overtime regulations are required to use mobile devices after office hours, the workers may have a valid claim to overtime wages. The Federal Labor Standards Act is not clear about what constitutes work, however, so workers have difficulty showing they are entitled to overtime wages.

In Brazil, however, employees who answer work-related e-mails on their smartphones or other electronic devices after hours are now entitled to receive overtime wages. Under legislation enacted in 2012, e-mail from an employer is considered the equivalent of instructions given directly to an employee. Thus, time spent responding to these communications constitutes work. A few other nations also require payment to workers for staying connected through smartphones and other devices after they have gone home.

• For Critical Analysis
What are the pros and cons of paying overtime wages to workers who check e-mail and perform other work-related tasks electronically after hours?

To qualify under the administrative employee exemption, an employee must be paid a salary, not hourly wages, and that employee's primary duty must be directly related to the management or general business operations of the employer. In addition, the employee's primary duty must include the exercise of discretion and independent judgment with respect to matters of significance.

In the following case, the issue before the court was whether an employee of a pharmaceutical company was exempt from the overtime requirements of the FLSA as an administrative employee.

Case 16.2 Smith v. Johnson & Johnson

United States Court of Appeals, Third Circuit, 593 F.3d 280 (2010).

BACKGROUND AND FACTS Patty Lee Smith was a senior professional sales representative for McNeil Pediatrics, a wholly owned subsidiary of Johnson & Johnson (J&J). Smith's position required her to visit prescribing doctors to describe the benefits of J&J's pharmaceutical drug Concerta. Smith, however, did not sell Concerta (a controlled substance) directly to the doctors, as such sales are prohibited by law. J&J gave Smith a list of target doctors and told her to complete an average of ten visits per day, visiting every doctor on her target list at least once each quarter. To schedule visits with reluctant doctors, Smith had to be inventive and cultivate relationships with each doctor's staff—an endeavor in which she found that coffee and doughnuts were useful tools. J&J left the itinerary and order of Smith's visits to her discretion. J&J gave her a budget, and she could use the funds to take the doctors to lunch or to sponsor seminars. In Smith's deposition, she stated that she was unsupervised about 95 percent of the time. According to Smith, "It was really up to me to run the territory the way I wanted to." Smith earned a base salary of $66,000 but was not paid overtime. Smith filed a suit in a federal district court under the Fair Labor Standards Act (FLSA), seeking overtime pay. J&J moved for summary judgment in its favor, arguing that Smith was exempt from the FLSA's overtime requirements because she was an administrative employee. The court granted the motion, and Smith appealed.

IN THE WORDS OF THE COURT . . .
GREENBERG, Circuit Judge.
  * * * *
Under the administrative employee exemption, anyone employed in a bona fide administrative capacity is exempt from the FLSA's overtime requirements. The Secretary [of Labor] has defined an administrative employee as someone:

  *(1) Compensated on a salary or fee basis at a rate of not less than $455 per week * * * exclusive of board, lodging or other facilities;*

  (2) Whose primary duty is the performance of office or non-manual work directly related to the management or general business operations of the employer or the employer's customers; and
  (3) Whose primary duty includes the exercise of discretion and independent judgment with respect to matters of significance. [Emphasis added.]

The parties agree that Smith's salary qualifies her for the administrative employee exemption, but dispute her qualification for that exemption under the remaining two sections.

We find that the administrative employee exemption applies to Smith. While testifying at her deposition Smith elaborated on the independent and managerial qualities that her position required. Her non-manual position required her to form a strategic plan designed to maximize sales in her territory. We think that this requirement satisfied the "directly related to the management or general business operations of the employer" provision of the administrative employee exemption because it involved a high level of planning and foresight, and the strategic plan that Smith developed guided the execution of her remaining duties.

When we turn to the "exercise of discretion and independent judgment with respect to matters of significance" requirement, we note that Smith executed nearly all of her duties without direct oversight. In fact, she described herself as the manager of her own business who could run her own territory as she saw fit. Given these descriptions, we conclude that Smith was subject to the administrative employee exemption.

DECISION AND REMEDY The U.S. Court of Appeals for the Third Circuit affirmed the judgment of the district court. Smith qualified as an administrative employee and was thus exempt from the overtime requirements of the FLSA.

THE ETHICAL DIMENSION *Is it unfair to exempt certain employees to deprive them of overtime wages? Why or why not?*

▶ Family and Medical Leave

In 1993, Congress passed the Family and Medical Leave Act (FMLA)[10] to allow employees to take time off from work for family or medical reasons. A majority of the states also have legislation allowing for a leave from employment for family or medical

---

10. 29 U.S.C. Sections 2601, 2611–2619, 2651–2654.

reasons, and many employers maintain private family-leave plans for their workers. FMLA regulations recently created new categories of leave for military caregivers and for qualifying emergencies that arise due to military service.

Coverage and Application

The FMLA requires employers that have fifty or more employees to provide employees with up to twelve weeks of unpaid family or medical leave during any twelve-month period. The FMLA expressly covers private and public (government) employees who have worked for their employers for at least a year.[11] An employee may take *family leave* to care for a newborn baby or a child recently placed for adoption or foster care.[12] An employee can take *medical leave* when the employee or the employee's spouse, child, or parent has a "serious health condition" requiring care.

LEARNING OBJECTIVE 3   **Under the Family and Medical Leave Act, in what circumstances may an employee take family or medical leave?**

In addition, an employee caring for a family member with a serious injury or illness incurred as a result of military duty can now take up to *twenty-six weeks of military caregiver leave* within a twelve-month period.[13] Also, an employee can take up to twelve weeks of *qualifying exigency* (emergency) *leave* to handle specified *nonmedical* emergencies when a spouse, parent, or child is on, or called to, active military duty.[14] For instance, when a spouse is deployed overseas, an employee may take exigency leave to arrange for child care or to deal with financial or legal matters.

When an employee takes FMLA leave, the employer must continue the worker's health-care coverage on the same terms as if the employee had continued to work. On returning from FMLA leave, most employees must be restored to their original position or to a comparable position (with nearly equivalent pay and benefits, for example). An important exception allows the employer to avoid reinstating a *key employee*—defined as an employee whose pay falls within the top 10 percent of the firm's workforce.

Violations

An employer that violates the FMLA can be required to provide various remedies, including the following:

1. Damages to compensate an employee for lost benefits, denied compensation, and actual monetary losses (such as the cost of providing for care of the family member) up to an amount equivalent to the employee's wages for twelve weeks (twenty-six weeks for military caregiver leave);
2. Job reinstatement; and
3. Promotion, if a promotion has been denied.

A successful plaintiff is entitled to court costs and attorneys' fees, and, if bad faith on the part of the employer is shown, can recover two times the amount of damages awarded by a judge or jury. Supervisors can also be held personally liable, as employers, for violations of the act. Employers generally are required to notify employees when an absence will be counted against leave authorized under the act. If

---

11. Note that changes to the FMLA rules allow employees who have taken a break from their employment to qualify for FMLA leave if they worked a total of twelve months during the previous seven years. See 29 C.F.R. Section 825.110(b)(1-2).
12. The foster care must be state sanctioned before such an arrangement falls within the coverage of the FMLA.
13. 29 C.F.R. Section 825.200.
14. 29 C.F.R. Section 825.126.

an employer fails to provide such notice, and the employee consequently is damaged because he or she did not receive notice, the employer may be sanctioned.

▶ Worker Health and Safety

Under the common law, employees who were injured on the job had to file lawsuits against their employers to obtain recovery. Today, numerous state and federal statutes protect employees and their families from the risk of accidental injury, death, or disease resulting from their employment. This section discusses the primary federal statute governing health and safety in the workplace, along with state workers' compensation laws.

The Occupational Safety and Health Act

At the federal level, the primary legislation protecting employees' health and safety is the Occupational Safety and Health Act of 1970,[15] which is administered by the Occupational Safety and Health Administration (OSHA). The act imposes on employers a general duty to keep workplaces safe. To this end, OSHA has established specific safety standards that employers must follow depending on the industry. For instance, OSHA regulations require the use of safety guards on certain mechanical equipment and set maximum levels of exposure to substances in the workplace that may be harmful to a worker's health.

REQUIREMENTS The act also requires that employers post certain notices in the workplace, perform prescribed record keeping, and submit specific reports. For instance, employers with eleven or more employees are required to keep occupational injury and illness records for each employee. Each record must be made available for inspection when requested by an OSHA compliance officer. Whenever a work-related injury or disease occurs, employers must make reports directly to OSHA. If an employee dies or three or more employees are hospitalized because of a work-related incident, the employer must notify OSHA within eight hours. A company that fails to do so will be fined and may also be prosecuted under state law. Following the incident, a complete inspection of the premises is mandatory.

ENFORCEMENT OSHA compliance officers may enter and inspect the facilities of any establishment covered by the Occupational Safety and Health Act. Employees may also file complaints of violations. Under the act, an employer cannot discharge an employee who files a complaint or who, in good faith, refuses to work in a high-risk area if bodily harm or death might result.

State Workers' Compensation Laws

Workers' Compensation Laws State statutes establishing an administrative procedure for compensating workers for injuries that arise out of—or in the course of—their employment, regardless of fault.

State **workers' compensation laws** establish an administrative procedure for compensating workers injured on the job. Instead of suing, an injured worker files a claim with the administrative agency or board that administers local workers' compensation claims.

Most workers' compensation statutes are similar. No state covers all employees. Typically, domestic workers, agricultural workers, temporary employees, and employees of common carriers (companies that provide transportation services to the public) are excluded, but minors are covered. Usually, the statutes allow employers to purchase insurance from a private insurer or a state fund to pay workers' compensation

15. 29 U.S.C. Sections 553, 651–678.

benefits in the event of a claim. Most states also allow employers to be *self-insured*—that is, employers that show an ability to pay claims do not need to buy insurance.

In general, the only requirements to recover benefits under state workers' compensation laws are:

1. The existence of an employment relationship; and
2. An *accidental* injury that *occurred on the job or in the course of employment,* regardless of fault. (If an injury occurs while an employee is commuting to or from work, it usually will not be considered to have occurred on the job or in the course of employment and hence will not be covered.)

An injured employee must notify her or his employer promptly (usually within thirty days of the accident). Generally, an employee must also file a workers' compensation claim with the appropriate state agency or board within a certain period (sixty days to two years) from the time the injury is first noticed, rather than from the time of the accident.

An employee's acceptance of workers' compensation benefits bars the employee from suing for injuries caused by the employer's negligence. By barring lawsuits for negligence, workers' compensation laws also prevent employers from raising common law defenses to negligence, such as contributory negligence, or assumption of risk. A worker may sue an employer who *intentionally* injures the worker, however.

▶ Income Security

Federal and state governments participate in insurance programs designed to protect employees and their families by covering the financial impact of retirement, disability, death, hospitalization, and unemployment. The key federal law on this subject is the Social Security Act of 1935.[16]

Social Security

The Social Security Act provides for old-age (retirement), survivors', and disability insurance. The act is therefore often referred to as OASDI. Both employers and employees must "contribute" under the Federal Insurance Contributions Act (FICA)[17] to help pay for benefits that will partially make up for the employees' loss of income on retirement.

The basis for the employee's and the employer's contributions is the employee's annual wage base—the maximum amount of the employee's wages that are subject to the tax. The employer withholds the employee's FICA contribution from the employee's wages and then matches this contribution. Retired workers are then eligible to receive monthly payments from the Social Security Administration, which administers the Social Security Act. Social Security benefits are fixed by statute but increase automatically with increases in the cost of living.

Medicare

Medicare, a federal government health-insurance program, is administered by the Social Security Administration for people sixty-five years of age and older and for some under the age of sixty-five who are disabled. It originally had two parts, one pertaining to hospital costs and the other to nonhospital medical costs, such as

---

16. 42 U.S.C. Sections 301–1397e.
17. 26 U.S.C. Sections 3101–3125.

visits to physicians' offices. Medicare now offers additional coverage options and a prescription-drug plan. People who have Medicare hospital insurance can also obtain additional federal medical insurance if they pay small monthly premiums, which increase as the cost of medical care increases. As with Social Security contributions, both the employer and the employee "contribute" to Medicare, but unlike Social Security, there is no cap on the amount of wages subject to the Medicare tax.

Private Pension Plans

The major federal act regulating employee retirement plans is the Employee Retirement Income Security Act (ERISA) of 1974.[18] This act empowers a branch of the U.S. Department of Labor to enforce its provisions governing employers that have private pension funds for their employees.

ERISA created the Pension Benefit Guaranty Corporation (PBGC), an independent federal agency, to provide timely and uninterrupted payment of voluntary private pension benefits. The pension plans pay annual insurance premiums (at set rates adjusted for inflation) to the PBGC, which then pays benefits to participants in the event that a plan is unable to do so.

ERISA does not require an employer to establish a pension plan. When a plan exists, however, ERISA specifies standards for its management. A key provision of ERISA concerns vesting. **Vesting** gives an employee a legal right to receive pension benefits at some future date when he or she stops working. Before ERISA was enacted, some employees who had worked for companies for as long as thirty years received no pension benefits when their employment terminated, because those benefits had not vested. ERISA establishes complex vesting rules. Generally, however, all employee contributions to pension plans vest immediately, and employee rights to employer contributions to a plan vest after five years of employment.

Vesting The creation of an absolute or unconditional right or power.

Unemployment Compensation

To ease the financial impact of unemployment, the United States has a system of unemployment insurance. The Federal Unemployment Tax Act (FUTA) of 1935[19] created a state-administered system that provides unemployment compensation to eligible individuals. Under this system, employers pay into a fund, and the proceeds are paid out to qualified unemployed workers. The FUTA and state laws require employers that fall under the provisions of the act to pay unemployment taxes at regular intervals.

To be eligible for unemployment compensation, a worker must be willing and able to work. Workers who have been fired for misconduct or who have voluntarily left their jobs are not eligible for benefits. In the past, workers had to be actively seeking employment to continue receiving benefits. Due to the high unemployment rates after the Great Recession, however, President Barack Obama announced measures that allow jobless persons to retain their unemployment benefits while pursuing additional education and training (rather than seeking employment).

The Consolidated Omnibus Budget Reconciliation Act

For workers whose jobs have been terminated—and who are thus no longer eligible for group health-insurance plans—federal law also provides a right to continue their health-care coverage. The Consolidated Omnibus Budget Reconciliation Act (COBRA)

---

18. 29 U.S.C. Sections 1001 *et seq.*
19. 26 U.S.C. Sections 3301–3310.

of 1985[20] prohibits an employer from eliminating a worker's medical, optical, or dental insurance on the voluntary or involuntary termination of the worker's employment.

Employers, with some exceptions, must provide information about COBRA's provisions to an employee who faces termination or a reduction of hours that would affect his or her eligibility for coverage under the plan. Only workers fired for gross misconduct are excluded from protection. An employer that does not comply with COBRA risks substantial penalties, such as a tax of up to 10 percent of the annual cost of the group plan or $500,000, whichever is less.

Employer-Sponsored Group Health Plans

The Health Insurance Portability and Accountability Act (HIPAA),[21] which was discussed in Chapter 4 in the context of privacy protections, contains provisions that affect employer-sponsored group health plans. HIPAA does not require employers to provide health insurance, but it does establish requirements for those that do provide such coverage. For instance, HIPAA strictly limits an employer's ability to exclude coverage for *preexisting conditions*, except pregnancy.

In addition, HIPAA restricts the manner in which covered employers collect, use, and disclose the health information of employees and their families. Employers must train employees, designate privacy officials, and distribute privacy notices to ensure that employees' health information is not disclosed to unauthorized parties. Failure to comply with HIPAA regulations can result in civil penalties of up to $100 per person per violation (with a cap of $25,000 per year). The employer is also subject to criminal prosecution for certain types of HIPAA violations and can face up to $250,000 in criminal fines and imprisonment for up to ten years if convicted.

▶ Employee Privacy Rights

In the last thirty years, concerns about the privacy rights of employees have arisen in response to the sometimes invasive tactics used by employers to monitor and screen workers. Perhaps the greatest privacy concern in today's employment arena has to do with electronic performance monitoring.

Electronic Monitoring in the Workplace

According to a survey by the American Management Association, more than half of employers engage in some form of surveillance of their employees. Types of monitoring include reviewing employees' e-mail, blogs, instant messages, tweets, Internet use, and computer files; video recording of employee job performance; and recording and reviewing telephone conversations, voice mail, and text messages.

Various specially designed software products have made it easier for employers to track employees' Internet use, including the specific Web sites visited and the time spent surfing the Web. Indeed, inappropriate Web surfing seems to be a primary concern for employers. More than 75 percent of them are monitoring workers' Web connections.

EMPLOYEE PRIVACY RIGHTS UNDER CONSTITUTIONAL AND TORT LAW   Recall from Chapter 4 that the U.S. Constitution does not explicitly guarantee a right to privacy. A personal right to privacy, however, has been inferred from other constitutional

---

20. 29 U.S.C. Sections 1161–1169.
21. 29 U.S.C.A. Sections 1181 *et seq.*

guarantees provided by the First, Third, Fourth, Fifth, and Ninth Amendments to the Constitution. Tort law (see Chapter 6), state constitutions, and a number of state and federal statutes also provide for privacy rights.

When determining whether an employer should be held liable for violating an employee's privacy rights, the courts generally weigh the employer's interests against the employee's reasonable expectation of privacy. Normally, if employees have been informed that their communications are being monitored, they cannot reasonably expect those interactions to be private. If employees are not informed that certain communications are being monitored, however, the employer may be held liable for invading their privacy. For this reason, most employers notify their employees about electronic monitoring.

THE ELECTRONIC COMMUNICATIONS PRIVACY ACT   Employers must comply with the Electronic Communications Privacy Act (ECPA) of 1986.[22] This act amended existing federal wiretapping law to cover electronic forms of communications, such as communications via cell phones or e-mail. The ECPA prohibits the intentional interception of any wire or electronic communication and the intentional disclosure or use of the information obtained by the interception. Excluded from coverage, however, are any electronic communications through devices that are "furnished to the subscriber or user by a provider of wire or electronic communication service" and that are being used by the subscriber or user, or by the provider of the service, "in the ordinary course of its business."

This "business-extension exception" to the ECPA permits employers to monitor employees' electronic communications made in the ordinary course of business. It does not, however, permit employers to monitor employees' personal communications.

THE STORED COMMUNICATIONS ACT   Part of the ECPA is known as the Stored Communications Act (SCA).[23] The SCA prohibits intentional and unauthorized access to *stored* electronic communications and sets forth criminal and civil sanctions for violators. A person can violate the SCA by intentionally accessing a stored electronic communication or by intentionally exceeding the authorization given to access the communication. The SCA also prevents "providers" of communication services (such as cell phone companies and social media networks) from divulging private communications to certain entities and individuals.

For a discussion of how some employers are creating their own social media networks, see this chapter's *Online Developments* feature on the following page.

Other Types of Monitoring

In addition to monitoring their employees' online activities, employers also engage in other types of employee screening and monitoring. These practices, which have included lie-detector tests, drug tests, genetic testing, and employment screening, have often been subject to challenge as violations of employee privacy rights.

LIE-DETECTOR TESTS   At one time, many employers required employees or job applicants to take lie-detector (polygraph) tests in connection with their employment. In 1988, Congress passed the Employee Polygraph Protection Act,[24] which generally prohibits employers from requiring or causing employees or job applicants

22. 18 U.S.C. Sections 2510–2521.
23. 18 U.S.C. Sections 2701–2711.
24. 29 U.S.C. Sections 2001 *et seq.*

Social Media in the Workplace Come of Age

What do corporate giant Dell, Inc., and relatively small Nikon Instruments have in common? They—and many other companies— have created internal social media networks using enterprise social networking software and systems, such as Salesforce.com, Chatter, Yammer, and Socialcast.

A glance at the posts on these internal networks reveals that they are quite different from typical posts on Facebook, LinkedIn, and Twitter. Rather than being personal, the tone is businesslike. The posts deal with workplace concerns such as how a team is solving a problem or how to sell a new product.

Benefits and Pitfalls of Internal Social Media Networks

Internal social media networks offer businesses several advantages. Perhaps the most important is that employees can obtain real-time information about important issues, such as production glitches. They can also exchange tips about how to deal with problems, such as difficult customers. News about the company's new products or those of a competitor is available immediately.

Furthermore, employees spend much less time sorting through e-mail. Rather than wasting their fellow employees' time by sending mass e-mailings, workers can post messages or collaborate on presentations via the company's internal network.

Of course, the downside is that these networks may become polluted with annoying "white noise." If employees start posting comments about what they ate for lunch, for example, the system will lose much of its utility. Companies can prevent this from happening, though, by establishing explicit guidelines on what can be posted.

Keeping the Data Safe

Another concern is how to keep all that data and those corporate secrets safe. When a company sets up a social media network, it usually decides which employees can see which files and which employees will belong to each specific "social" group within the company. Often, the data created through a social media network are kept on the company's own servers in secure "clouds."

FOR CRITICAL ANALYSIS

What problems might arise if data from an internal social media system are stored on third party servers?

to take lie-detector tests or suggesting or requesting that they do so. The act also restricts employers' ability to use or ask about the results of any lie-detector test or to take any negative employment action based on the results.

Employers excepted from these prohibitions include federal, state, and local government employers; certain security service firms; and companies manufacturing and distributing controlled substances. Other employers may use lie-detector tests when investigating losses attributable to theft, including embezzlement and the theft of trade secrets.

DRUG TESTING   In the interests of public safety, many employers, including government employers, require their employees to submit to drug testing.

Public Employers.   Government (public) employers are constrained in drug testing by the Fourth Amendment to the U.S. Constitution, which prohibits unreasonable searches and seizures (see Chapter 4). Drug testing of public employees is allowed by statute for transportation workers and is normally upheld by the courts when drug use in a particular job may threaten public safety. Also, when there is a reasonable basis for suspecting government employees of using drugs, courts often find that drug testing does not violate the Fourth Amendment.

Private Employers.   The Fourth Amendment does not apply to drug testing conducted by private employers. Hence, the privacy rights and drug testing of private-sector employees are governed by state law, which varies widely. Many states have statutes that allow drug testing by private employers but place restrictions on when and how the testing may be performed. A collective bargaining agreement may also provide protection against drug testing (or authorize drug testing under certain conditions).

Whether a private employer's drug tests are permissible typically depends on whether the tests are reasonable. Random drug tests and even "zero-tolerance" policies (that deny a "second chance" to employees who test positive for drugs) have been held to be reasonable.

In addition to drug tests, federal government employees have long been required to submit to background checks as a condition of employment. Many workers who work at U.S. government facilities are employees of private contractors, not of the government. They generally have not been subject to drug testing and background checks. Recent standards, however, now require background checks for all federal workers—including contract employees.

In the following case, several federal contract workers asserted that their privacy rights had been violated.

Case 16.3 National Aeronautics and Space Administration v. Nelson

Supreme Court of the United States, __ U.S. __, 131 S.Ct. 746, 178 L.Ed.2d 667 (2011).

BACKGROUND AND FACTS In 2007, contract employees with long-term access to federal facilities were ordered to complete a standard background check—the National Agency Check with Inquiries (NACI). The NACI is designed to obtain information on such issues as counseling and treatment, as well as mental and financial stability. The National Aeronautics and Space Administration (NASA) is an independent federal agency charged with planning and conducting "space activities." One of NASA's facilities is the Jet Propulsion Laboratory (JPL) in Pasadena, California, which is NASA's primary center for deep-space robotics and communications. Robert Nelson and other JPL employees filed a lawsuit in a federal district court against NASA, claiming that the NACI violated their privacy rights. The court denied the plaintiffs' request to prohibit use of the NACI, but the U.S. Court of Appeals for the Ninth Circuit reversed this decision. NASA appealed to the United States Supreme Court, arguing that the Privacy Act of 1974 provides sufficient protection for employees' privacy. This act allows the government to retain information only for "relevant and necessary" purposes, requires written consent before the information may be disclosed, and imposes criminal liability for violations.

IN THE WORDS OF THE COURT . . .
Justice *ALITO* delivered the opinion of the Court.
Respondents in this case, federal contract employees at a Government laboratory, claim that two parts of a standard employment background investigation violate their rights * * * . Respondents challenge a section of a form questionnaire that asks employees about treatment or counseling for recent illegal-drug use. They also object to certain open-ended questions on a form sent to employees' designated references.
* * * *
We will assume for present purposes that the Government's challenged inquiries implicate a privacy interest of constitutional significance. We hold, however, that, whatever the scope of this interest,

it does not prevent the Government from asking reasonable questions *** in an employment background investigation that is subject to the Privacy Act's safeguards against public disclosure.* [Emphasis added.]
* * * *

* * * The questions challenged by respondents are part of a standard employment background check of the sort used by millions of private employers. The Government itself has been conducting employment investigations since the earliest days of the Republic. Since 1871, the President has enjoyed statutory authority to ascertain the fitness of applicants for the civil service as to age, health, character, knowledge and ability for the employment sought and that [statute] appears to have been regarded as a codification of established practice. Standard background investigations similar to those at issue here became mandatory for all candidates for the federal civil service in 1953. And the particular investigations challenged in this case arose from a decision to extend that requirement to federal contract employees requiring long-term access to federal facilities.

As this long history suggests, the Government has an interest in conducting basic employment background checks. Reasonable investigations of applicants and employees aid the Government in ensuring the security of its facilities and in employing a competent, reliable workforce.

DECISION AND REMEDY The United States Supreme Court reversed the judgment of the lower court and remanded the case. The NACI does not violate an individual's right to privacy because its inquiries are reasonable and the Privacy Act protects against the disclosure of private information.

WHAT IF THE FACTS WERE DIFFERENT? *Suppose that after the decision in this case, a JPL employee refused to cooperate in an NACI background check. What would be the most likely consequences?*

GENETIC TESTING   A serious privacy issue arose when some employers began conducting genetic testing of employees or prospective employees in an effort to identify individuals who might develop significant health problems in the future. To date, however, only a few cases involving this issue have come before the courts.

To prevent the improper use of genetic information in employment and health insurance, in 2008 Congress passed the Genetic Information Nondiscrimination Act (GINA).[25] Under GINA, employers cannot make decisions about hiring, firing, job placement, or promotion based on the results of genetic testing. GINA also prohibits group health plans and insurers from denying coverage or charging higher premiums based solely on a genetic predisposition to developing a specific disease in the future.

Immigration Law

LEARNING OBJECTIVE 4   **What are the two most important federal statutes governing immigration and employment today?**

The United States had no laws restricting immigration until the late nineteenth century. Today, the most important laws governing immigration and employment are the Immigration Reform and Control Act (IRCA) of 1986[26] and the Immigration Act of 1990.[27] In recent years, immigration law has become an area of increasing concern for businesses as the number of immigrants—especially illegal immigrants—to the United States has grown.

An estimated 12 million illegal immigrants now live in the United States. The great majority came to find jobs, but U.S. employers face serious penalties if they hire illegal immigrants. Thus, an understanding of immigration laws has become increasingly important for businesses.

Immigration Reform and Control Act

When the Immigration Reform and Control Act (IRCA) was enacted in 1986, it provided amnesty to certain groups of illegal aliens living in the United States at the time. It also established a system that sanctions employers that hire illegal immigrants who lack work authorization.

The IRCA makes it illegal to hire, recruit, or refer for a fee someone not authorized to work in this country. Through Immigration and Customs Enforcement officers, the federal government conducts random compliance audits and engages in enforcement actions against employers that hire illegal immigrants.

I-9 Verification The process of verifying the employment eligibility and identity of a new worker.

I-9 EMPLOYMENT VERIFICATION   To comply with current law (based on the 1986 act), an employer must perform **I-9 verifications** for new hires, including those hired as "contractors" or "day workers" if they work under the employer's direct supervision. Form I-9, Employment Eligibility Verification, which is available from U.S. Citizenship and Immigration Services,[28] must be completed within three days of a worker's commencement of employment. The three-day period is to allow the employer to check the form's accuracy and to review and verify documents establishing the prospective worker's identity and eligibility for employment in the United States.

The employer must attest, under penalty of perjury, that an employee produced documents establishing his or her identity and legal employability. Acceptable docu-

---

25. 26 U.S.C. Section 9834; 42 U.S.C. Sections 300gg-53, 1320d-9, 2000ff-1 to 2000ff-11.
26. 29 U.S.C. Section 1802.
27. This act amended various provisions of the Immigration and Nationality Act of 1952, 8 U.S.C. Sections 1101 *et seq.*
28. U.S. Citizenship and Immigration Services is a federal agency that is part of the U.S. Department of Homeland Security.

ments include a U.S. passport establishing the person's citizenship or a document authorizing a foreign citizen to work in the United States, such as a Permanent Resident Card or an Alien Registration Receipt.

Note that most legal actions alleging violations of I-9 rules are brought against employees. An employee must state that she or he is a U.S. citizen or otherwise authorized to work in the United States. If the employee enters false information on an I-9 form or presents false documentation, the employer can fire the worker, who then may be subject to deportation.

The IRCA prohibits "knowing" violations, including situations in which an employer "should have known" that the worker was unauthorized. Good faith is a defense under the statute, and employers are legally entitled to rely on a document authorizing a person to work that reasonably appears on its face to be genuine, even if it is later established to be counterfeit.

ENFORCEMENT   U.S. Immigration and Customs Enforcement (ICE) is the largest investigative arm of the U.S. Department of Homeland Security. ICE has a general inspection program that conducts random compliance audits. Other audits may occur if the agency receives a written complaint alleging an employer's violations. Government inspections include a review of an employer's file of I-9 forms. The government does not need a subpoena or a warrant to conduct such an inspection.

PENALTIES   An employer who violates the law by hiring an unauthorized alien is subject to substantial penalties. The employer may be fined up to $2,200 for each unauthorized employee for a first offense, $5,000 per employee for a second offense, and up to $11,000 for subsequent offenses. Criminal penalties, including additional fines and imprisonment for up to ten years, apply to employers who have engaged in a "pattern or practice of violations."

The Immigration Act

Often, U.S. businesses find that they cannot hire sufficient domestic workers with specialized skills. For this reason, U.S. immigration laws have long made provisions for businesses to hire foreign workers with special qualification. The Immigration Act of 1990 placed caps on the number of visas (entry permits) that can be issued to immigrants each year.

Most temporary visas are set aside for workers who can be characterized as "persons of extraordinary ability," members of the professions holding advanced degrees, or other skilled workers and professionals. To hire these individuals, employers must submit a petition to U.S. Citizenship and Immigration Services, which determines whether the job candidate meets the legal standards. Each visa is for a specific job, and the law limits the employee's ability to change jobs once in the United States.

I-551 ALIEN REGISTRATION RECEIPTS   A company seeking to hire a noncitizen worker may do so if the worker is self-authorized. This means that the worker either is a lawful permanent resident or has a valid temporary Employment Authorization Document. A lawful permanent resident can prove his or her status to an employer by presenting an **I-551 Alien Registration Receipt**, known as a "green card," or a properly stamped foreign passport.

Many immigrant workers are not already self-authorized, and employers may attempt to obtain labor certification, or green cards, for the immigrants they wish to hire. Approximately fifty thousand new green cards are issued each year. A green

"Immigration is the sincerest form of flattery."
Jack Paar, 1918–2004
(American entertainer)

I-551 Alien Registration Receipt
A document, commonly known as a "green card," that shows that a foreign-born individual has been lawfully admitted for permanent residency in the United States.

card can be obtained only for a person who is being hired for a permanent, full-time position.

THE H-1B VISA PROGRAM

The most common and controversial visa program today is the H-1B visa system. To obtain an H-1B visa, the potential employee must be qualified in a "specialty occupation," meaning that the individual has highly specialized knowledge and has attained a bachelor's or higher degree or its equivalent. Individuals with H-1B visas can stay in the United States for three to six years and can work only for the sponsoring employer.

The recipients of these visas include many high-tech workers, such as computer programmers and electronics specialists. A maximum of sixty-five thousand H-1B visas is set aside each year for new immigrants, and that limit is typically reached within the first few weeks of the year.

LABOR CERTIFICATION

A common criticism of the H-1B visa system is that it depresses the wages of U.S. workers because H-1B workers may be willing to work for less. The law addresses this complaint by requiring employers to pay H-1B workers the prevailing wage. Before an employer can submit an H-1B application, it must file a Labor Certification application on Form ETA 9035.

The employer must agree to provide a wage level at least equal to the wages offered to other individuals with similar experience and qualifications and attest that the hiring will not adversely affect other workers similarly employed. The employer must also inform U.S. workers of the intent to hire a foreign worker by posting the form.

H-2, O, L, AND E VISAS

Other specialty temporary visas are available for other categories of employees. H-2 visas provide for workers performing agricultural labor of a seasonal nature. O visas provide entry for persons who have "extraordinary ability in the sciences, arts, education, business or athletics which has been demonstrated by sustained national or international acclaim." L visas allow a company's foreign managers or executives to work inside the United States. E visas permit the entry of certain foreign investors or entrepreneurs.

Ethical Issue

Should Arizona and other states be allowed to engage in cooperative immigration law enforcement? As the unemployment rate has remained stubbornly high since the Great Recession, public resentment toward illegal immigrants has been growing, especially because some believe that illegal immigrants have taken job opportunities that otherwise would have gone to U.S. citizens. With state budgets under increasing pressure, there is also concern about the cost of providing education and other services for illegal immigrants.

Until recently, federal laws have governed immigration and the treatment of illegal immigrants. In 2010, however, the governor of Arizona signed that state's Support Our Law Enforcement and Safe Neighborhoods Act, which required Arizona law enforcement officials to identify, charge, and potentially deport immigrants who are in the state illegally. The law required immigrants to carry their immigration documents at all times. Under the state law, police could verify the status of individuals during any law enforcement action and whenever there was a "reasonable suspicion that someone was an illegal alien." In addition, Arizona citizens could also sue police officers for not enforcing the law.

The federal government, however, insisted that federal immigration laws preempt any state legislation and that, therefore, Arizona and other states were prohibited from carrying out their own policing of illegal immigrants. The federal government appealed the case to the United States Supreme Court, which granted *certiorari*.

In 2012, the Court struck down nearly every provision of the Arizona law, ruling that federal law preempts state law.[29] The Court, however, upheld the controversial "show-me-your-papers" provision that required police to check the immigration status of persons stopped for any violation. Additionally, the Court ruled that states could not pass laws that make it a crime for immigrants not to carry their registration documents or make it a crime for those without work permits to seek employment. States also cannot authorize law enforcement to arrest people based solely on a reasonable suspicion that they are in the country illegally.

▶ Labor Laws and Unions

In the 1930s, in addition to wage-hour laws, the government also enacted the first of several labor laws. These laws protect employees' rights to join labor unions, to bargain with management over the terms and conditions of employment, and to conduct strikes.

Federal Labor Laws

Federal labor laws governing union-employer relations have developed considerably since the first law was enacted in 1932. Initially, the laws were concerned with protecting the rights and interests of workers. Subsequent legislation placed some restraints on unions and granted rights to employers. Coverage of federal labor laws is broad and extends to all employers whose business activity either involves or affects interstate commerce.

NORRIS-LAGUARDIA ACT   In 1932, Congress protected peaceful strikes, picketing, and boycotts in the Norris-LaGuardia Act.[30] The statute restricted the power of federal courts to issue injunctions against unions engaged in peaceful strikes. In effect, this act established a national policy permitting employees to organize.

LEARNING OBJECTIVE 5 **What federal statute gave employees the right to organize unions and engage in collective bargaining?**

NATIONAL LABOR RELATIONS ACT   One of the foremost statutes regulating labor is the National Labor Relations Act (NLRA) of 1935.[31] This act established the rights of employees to organize unions, engage in collective bargaining, and to call a strike. The act also specifically defined a number of employer practices as unfair to labor:

1. Interference with the efforts of employees to form, join, or assist labor organizations or with the efforts of employees to engage in concerted activities for their mutual aid or protection.
2. An employer's domination of a labor organization or contribution of financial or other support to it.
3. Discrimination in the hiring or awarding of tenure to employees based on union affiliation.
4. Discrimination against employees for filing charges under the act or giving testimony under the act.
5. Refusal to bargain collectively with the duly designated representative of the employees.

The NLRA also created the National Labor Relations Board (NLRB) to oversee union elections and to prevent employers from engaging in unfair and illegal union activities

---

29. *Arizona v. United States,* 2012 WL 2368661 (2012).
30. 29 U.S.C. Sections 101–110, 113–115.
31. 20 U.S.C. Section 151.

and unfair labor practices. When a union or employee believes that an employer has violated federal labor law (or vice versa), a charge is filed with a regional office of the NLRB. The NLRB has the authority to investigate employees' charges of unfair labor practices and to file complaints against employers in response to these charges.

When violations are found, the NLRB may issue a *cease-and-desist order* compelling the employer to stop engaging in the unfair practices. Cease-and-desist orders can be enforced by a federal appellate court if necessary.

LABOR-MANAGEMENT RELATIONS ACT   The Labor-Management Relations Act (LMRA) of 1947[32] was passed to proscribe certain unfair union practices, such as the *closed shop*. A **closed shop** requires union membership by its workers as a condition of employment. Although the act made the closed shop illegal, it preserved the legality of the union shop. A **union shop** does not require membership as a prerequisite for employment but can, and usually does, require that workers join the union after a specified amount of time on the job.

The LMRA also prohibited unions from refusing to bargain with employers, engaging in certain types of picketing, and *featherbedding*—causing employers to hire more employees than necessary. The act also allowed individual states to pass their own **right-to-work laws,** which make it illegal for union membership to be required for *continued* employment in any establishment. Thus, union shops are technically illegal in the twenty-three states that have right-to-work laws.

LABOR-MANAGEMENT REPORTING AND DISCLOSURE ACT   In 1959, Congress enacted the Labor-Management Reporting and Disclosure Act (LMRDA).[33] The act established an employee bill of rights and reporting requirements for union activities. The act strictly regulates unions' internal business procedures, including union elections.

Union Organization

Typically, the first step in organizing a union at a particular firm is to have the workers sign authorization cards. An **authorization card** usually states that the worker desires to have a certain union, such as the United Auto Workers, represent the workforce. If a majority of the workers sign authorization cards, the union organizers (unionizers) present the cards to the employer and ask for formal recognition of the union. The employer is not required to recognize the union at this point in the process, but it may do so voluntarily on a showing of majority support.

UNION ELECTIONS   If the employer refuses to voluntarily recognize the union after a majority of the workers sign authorization cards—or if fewer than 50 percent of the workers sign authorization cards—the union organizers present the cards to the NLRB with a petition for an election. For an election to be held, the unionizers must demonstrate that at least 30 percent of the workers to be represented support a union or an election on unionization.

The proposed union must also represent an *appropriate bargaining unit.* Not every group of workers can form a single union. One key requirement of an appropriate bargaining unit is a *mutuality of interest* among all the workers to be represented by the union. Factors considered in determining whether there is a mutuality of interest include the *similarity of the jobs* of all the workers to be unionized and their physical location.

Closed Shop A firm that requires union membership by its workers as a condition of employment. The closed shop was made illegal by the Labor-Management Relations Act of 1947.

Union Shop A firm that requires all workers, once employed, to become union members within a specified period of time as a condition of their continued employment.

Right-to-Work Law A state law providing that employees may not be required to join a union as a condition of retaining employment.

Authorization Card A card signed by an employee that gives a union permission to act on his or her behalf in negotiations with management.

---

32. 29 U.S.C. Sections 141 *et seq.*
33. 29 U.S.C. Sections 401 *et seq.*

If all of these requirements are met, an election is held. The NLRB supervises the election and ensures secret voting and voter eligibility. If the proposed union receives majority support in a fair election, the NLRB certifies the union as the bargaining representative for the employees.

UNION ELECTION CAMPAIGNS   Many disputes between labor and management arise during union election campaigns. Generally, the employer has control over unionizing activities that take place on company property during working hours. Thus, an employer may limit the campaign activities of union supporters as long as the employer has a legitimate business reason for doing so. The employer may also reasonably limit the times and places that union solicitation occurs so long as the employer is not discriminating against the union.

EXAMPLE 16.20 A union is seeking to organize clerks at a department store owned by Amanti Enterprises. Amanti can prohibit all union solicitation in areas of the store open to the public because that activity could seriously interfere with the store's business. If Amanti allows solicitation for charitable causes in the workplace, however, it may not prohibit union solicitation. •

An employer may campaign among its workers against the union, but the NLRB carefully monitors and regulates the tactics used by management. Otherwise, management might use its economic power to coerce the workers into voting against unionization. If the employer issued threats or engaged in other unfair labor practices, the NLRB may certify the union even though it lost the election. Alternatively, the NLRB may ask a court to order a new election.

Collective Bargaining

Collective Bargaining The process by which labor and management negotiate the terms and conditions of employment.

After the NLRB certifies the union, the union's local office will be authorized to negotiate with management on behalf of the workers in the bargaining unit. **Collective bargaining**—the process by which labor and management negotiate the terms and conditions of employment—is at the heart of the federal labor laws.

NEGOTIATING TERMS AND CONDITIONS   Wages, hours of work, and certain other conditions of employment may be discussed during collective bargaining sessions. For instance, subjects for negotiation may include workplace safety, employee discounts, health-care plans, pension funds, and apprentice programs. Other subjects that may be raised include the establishment of college scholarship programs for the children of workers and the adoption of new technologies on the factory floor.

Some demands are illegal in collective bargaining. Management need not bargain over a provision that would be illegal if it were included in a contract. For example, if a union presents a demand for featherbedding, management need not respond to the demand because, as mentioned earlier, featherbedding is illegal under the Labor-Management Relations Act.

Management need not bargain over a decision to shut down certain facilities. It must bargain, however, over the economic consequences of this decision. Thus, issues such as *severance pay* (pay given to an employee on his or her termination) in the event of plant shutdown or rights of transfer to other plants are considered mandatory subjects of collective bargaining.

GOOD FAITH   Once an employer and a union sit down at the conference table, they must negotiate in good faith and make a reasonable effort to come to an agreement. They are not obligated to reach an agreement. They must, however, approach the negotiations with the idea that an agreement is possible. Both parties may engage in hard bargaining, but the bargaining process itself must be geared to reaching a compromise—not avoiding a compromise.

Although good faith is a matter of subjective intent, a party's actions can be used to evaluate the party's good or bad faith. Excessive delaying tactics may be proof of bad faith, as is insistence on obviously unreasonable contract terms. The following additional actions constitute bad faith in bargaining:

- Rejecting a proposal without offering a counterproposal.
- Engaging in a campaign among workers to undermine the union.
- Unilaterally changing wages or terms and conditions of employment during the bargaining process.
- Constantly shifting positions on disputed contract terms.
- Sending bargainers who lack authority to commit the company to a contract.

Strikes

Strike An action undertaken by unionized workers when collective bargaining fails. The workers leave their jobs, refuse to work, and (typically) picket the employer's workplace.

Even when labor and management have bargained in good faith, they may be unable to reach a final agreement. When extensive collective bargaining has been conducted and an impasse results, the union may call a strike against the employer to pressure it into making concessions. In a **strike,** the unionized workers leave their jobs and refuse to work. The workers also typically picket the workplace, walking or standing outside the facility with signs stating their complaints.

A strike is an extreme action. Striking workers lose their rights to be paid, and management loses production and may lose customers when orders cannot be filled. Labor law regulates the circumstances and conduct of strikes. Most strikes take the form of "economic strikes," which are initiated because the union wants a better contract. **EXAMPLE 16.21** In 2010, the union representing workers at the Disneyland Hotel organized a hunger strike to draw attention to the prolonged contract dispute over health-care benefits and workloads. After two years of negotiations with the hotel, the workers still did not have a signed contract with health-care benefits. ●

THE RIGHT TO STRIKE   The right to strike is guaranteed by the NLRA, within limits, and strike activities, such as picketing, are protected by the free speech guarantee of the First Amendment to the U.S. Constitution. Persons who are not employees have a right to participate in picketing an employer. The NLRA also gives workers the right to refuse to cross a picket line of fellow workers who are engaged in a lawful strike. Employers are permitted to hire replacement workers (often called "scabs" by union supporters) to substitute for the workers who are on strike.

ILLEGAL STRIKES   An otherwise lawful strike may become illegal because of the conduct of the strikers. Violent strikes (including the threat of violence) are illegal. The use of violence against management employees or substitute workers is illegal. Certain forms of "massed picketing" are also illegal. If the strikers form a barrier and deny management or other nonunion workers access to the plant, the strike is illegal. Similarly, "sit-down" strikes, in which employees simply stay in the plant without working, are illegal.

A *secondary boycott* is another type of illegal strike. It is a strike directed against someone other than the strikers' employer, such as the companies that sell materials to the employer.

Lockouts

Lockout An employer's act of shutting down the business to prevent employees from working.

Lockouts are the employer's counterpart to the worker's right to strike. A **lockout** occurs when the employer shuts down to prevent employees from working. Lockouts usually are used when the employer believes that a strike is imminent. Lockouts may be a legal employer response.

Some lockouts are illegal, however. An employer may not use a lockout as a tool to break the union and pressure employees into decertification. Consequently, an employer must show some economic justification for instituting a lockout.

EXAMPLE 16.22 In 2011, the owners of the National Football League (NFL) teams imposed a lockout on the National Football League Players Association, the players' union, after negotiations on a new collective bargaining agreement broke down. At issue was the owners' proposal to decrease players' salaries and extend the season by two games. The owners claimed that the salary decrease was necessary because their profits from ticket sales had declined due to the struggling economy. When the lockout was imposed, the union requested decertification, which cleared the way for a group of players to file an antitrust lawsuit (see Chapter 19). Meanwhile, retired NFL players filed a complaint against the league seeking more medical benefits and better pensions. A settlement was reached before the start of the 2011 football season. The players accepted 3 percent less of the revenue generated (47 percent rather than 50 percent) in exchange for better working conditions and more retirement benefits. The owners agreed to keep the same number of games per season. ●

Unfair Labor Practices

The preceding sections have discussed unfair labor practices involved in the significant acts of union elections, collective bargaining, and strikes. Many unfair labor practices may occur within the normal working relationship as well. The most important unfair practices are listed in Exhibit 16–1 below.

● *Exhibit* 16–1 **Basic Unfair Labor Practices**

IT IS UNFAIR FOR EMPLOYERS TO . . .	IT IS UNFAIR FOR UNIONS TO . . .
1. Refuse to recognize a union and refuse to bargain in good faith. 2. Interfere with, restrain, or coerce employees in their efforts to form a union and bargain collectively. 3. Dominate a union. 4. Discriminate against union workers. 5. Punish employees for engaging in concerted activity.	1. Refuse to bargain in good faith. 2. Picket to coerce unionization without the support of a majority of the employees. 3. Demand the hiring of unnecessary workers. 4. Discriminate against nonunion workers. 5. Agree to participate in a secondary boycott. 6. Engage in an illegal strike.

▶ Reviewing . . . Employment, Immigration, and Labor Law

Rick Saldona began working as a traveling salesperson for Aimer Winery in 2007. Sales constituted 90 percent of Saldona's work time. Saldona worked an average of fifty hours per week but received no overtime pay. In June 2011, Saldona's new supervisor, Caesar Braxton, claimed that Saldona had been inflating his reported sales calls and required Saldona to submit to a lie-detector test. Saldona reported Braxton to the U.S. Department of Labor, which prohibited Aimer from requiring Saldona to take a lie-detector test for this purpose. In August 2011, Saldona's wife, Venita, fell from a ladder and sustained a head injury while employed as a full-time agricultural harvester. Saldona delivered to Aimer's human resources department a letter from his wife's physician indicating that she would need daily care for several months, and Saldona took leave until

(Continued)

December 2011. Aimer had sixty-three employees at that time. When Saldona returned to Aimer, he was informed that his position had been eliminated because his sales territory had been combined with an adjacent territory. Using the information presented in the chapter, answer the following questions.

1. Would Saldona have been legally entitled to receive overtime pay at a higher rate? Why or why not?
2. What is the maximum length of time Saldona would have been allowed to take leave to care for his injured spouse?
3. Under what circumstances would Aimer have been allowed to require an employee to take a lie-detector test?
4. Would Aimer likely be able to avoid reinstating Saldona under the key employee exception? Why or why not?

Debate This

The doctrine of *respondeat superior* should be modified to make agents solely liable for some of their tortious acts.

Key Terms

agency 401
agent 401
authorization card 426
closed shop 426
collective bargaining 427
disclosed principal 408
employment at will 400
I-9 verification 422

I-551 Alien Registration Receipt 423
independent contractor 401
lockout 429
minimum wage 412
partially disclosed principal 408
principal 401
ratification 404
respondent superior 409

right-to-work law 426
strike 428
undisclosed principal 408
union shop 426
vesting 417
vicarious liability 409
workers' compensation laws 415

Chapter Summary: Employment, Immigration, and Labor Law

Agency Relationships (See pages 401–403.)	In a *principal-agent* relationship, an agent acts on behalf of and instead of the principal in dealing with third parties. An employee who deals with third parties is normally an agent. An independent contractor is not an employee, and the employer has no control over the details of physical performance. An independent contractor may or may not be an agent.
Agency Formation (See pages 403–405.)	Agency relationships may be formed by agreement of the parties, by ratification, by estoppel, and by operation of law.
Duties of Agents and Principals (See pages 405–407.)	1. *Agent's duties*—An agent must (a) use reasonable diligence and skill in performing his or her duties, (b) notify the principal of all matters concerning the subject matter of the agency, (c) act solely for the principal's benefit and no one else's, (d) follow all of the principal's lawful and clearly stated instructions, and (e) make available to the principal an accounting of all funds or property received and paid out on the principal's behalf. 2. *Principal's duties*—The principal must (a) pay for the agreed-on value of the agent's services, (b) reimburse the agent for all expenses relating to the agency, and (c) cooperate with and assist the agent in performing his or her duties.
Agent's Authority (See pages 407–408.)	1. *Actual authority*—Can be either express or implied. *Express authority* can be oral or in writing. Authorization must be in writing if the agent is to execute a contract that must be in writing. *Implied authority* is customarily associated with the position of the agent or authority and is deemed necessary for the agent to carry out expressly authorized tasks. 2. *Apparent authority*—Exists when the principal, by word or action, causes a third party reasonably to believe that an agent has authority to act, even though the agent has no express or implied authority.

▶ Chapter Summary: Employment, Immigration, and Labor Law, Continued

Liability in Agency Relationships (See pages 408–411.)	1. *Liability for contracts*—If the principal's identity is disclosed or partially disclosed at the time the agent forms a contract with a third party, the principal is liable to the third party under the contract if the agent acted within the scope of his or her authority. If the principal's identity is undisclosed at the time of contract formation, the agent is personally liable to the third party, but if the agent acted within the scope of his or her authority, the principal is also bound by the contract. 2. *Liability for agent's torts*—Under the doctrine of *respondeat superior,* the principal is liable for any harm caused to another through the agent's torts if the agent was acting within the scope of her or his employment at the time the harmful act occurred. 3. *Liability for independent contractor's torts*—A principal is not liable for harm caused by an independent contractor's negligence, unless hazardous activities are involved (in this situation, the principal is strictly liable for any resulting harm) or other exceptions apply. 4. *Liability for agent's crimes*—An agent is responsible for his or her own crimes, even if the crimes were committed while the agent was acting within the scope of authority or employment.
Wage and Hour Laws (See pages 411–413.)	1. *Davis-Bacon Act (1931)*—Requires contractors and subcontractors working on federal government construction projects to pay their employees "prevailing wages." 2. *Walsh-Healey Act (1936)*—Requires firms that contract with federal agencies to pay their employees a minimum wage and overtime pay. 3. *Fair Labor Standards Act (1938)*—Extended wage and hour requirements to cover all employers whose activities affect interstate commerce plus certain other businesses. The act has specific requirements in regard to child labor, minimum wages, and overtime pay.
Family and Medical Leave (See pages 413–415.)	The Family and Medical Leave Act (FMLA) requires employers with fifty or more employees to provide their employees with up to twelve weeks of unpaid leave (twenty-six weeks for military caregiver leave) during any twelve-month period.
Worker Health and Safety (See pages 415–416.)	1. *Occupational Safety and Health Act (1970)*—Requires employers to meet specific safety and health standards that are established and enforced by the Occupational Safety and Health Administration (OSHA). 2. *State workers' compensation laws*—Establish an administrative procedure for compensating workers who are injured in accidents that occur on the job, regardless of fault.
Income Security (See pages 416–418.)	1. *Social Security and Medicare*—Provide for old-age (retirement), survivors', and health insurance. Both employers and employees must make contributions to help pay for these benefits. 2. *The Employee Retirement Income Security Act (ERISA) of 1974*—Establishes standards for the management of employer-provided pension plans. 3. *The Federal Unemployment Tax Act (FUTA) of 1935*—Creates a system that provides unemployment compensation to eligible individuals. 4. *The Consolidated Omnibus Budget Reconciliation Act (COBRA) of 1985*—Requires employers to give employees, on termination of employment, the option of continuing their medical, optical, or dental insurance coverage for a certain period. 5. *The Health Insurance Portability and Accountability Act (HIPAA)*—Establishes certain requirements for employer-sponsored health insurance. Employers must comply with a number of administrative, technical, and procedural safeguards to ensure the privacy of employees' health information.
Employee Privacy Rights (See pages 418–422.)	A right to privacy has been inferred from guarantees provided by the First, Third, Fourth, Fifth, and Ninth Amendments to the U.S. Constitution. State laws may also provide for privacy rights. Employer practices that are often challenged by employees as invasive of their privacy rights include electronic performance monitoring, lie-detector tests, drug testing, and genetic testing.
Immigration Law (See pages 422–425.)	1. *Immigration Reform and Control Act (1986)*—Prohibits employers from hiring illegal immigrants; administered by U.S. Citizenship and Immigration Services. Compliance audits and enforcement actions are conducted by U.S. Immigration and Customs Enforcement. 2. *Immigration Act (1990)*—Limits the number of legal immigrants entering the United States by capping the number of visas (entry permits) that are issued each year.

(Continued)

Chapter Summary: Employment, Immigration, and Labor Law, Continued

Labor Laws and Unions (See pages 425–429.)	1. *Federal labor laws*— a. *Norris-LaGuardia Act* (1932)—Protects peaceful strikes, picketing, and primary boycotts. b. *National Labor Relations Act* (1935)—Established the rights of employees to engage in collective bargaining and to strike; also defined specific employer practices as unfair to labor. The National Labor Relations Board (NLRB) was created to administer and enforce the act. c. *Labor-Management Relations Act* (1947)—Proscribes certain unfair union practices, such as the closed shop. d. *Labor-Management Reporting and Disclosure Act* (1959)—Established an employee bill of rights and reporting requirements for union activities. 2. *Union organization*—Union campaign activities and elections must comply with the requirements established by federal labor laws and the NLRB. 3. *Collective bargaining*—The process by which labor and management negotiate the terms and conditions of employment (such as wages, benefits, and working conditions). The central legal right of a labor union is to engage in collective bargaining on the members' behalf. 4. *Strikes*—When collective bargaining reaches an impasse, union members may use their ultimate weapon in labor-management struggles—the strike. A strike occurs when unionized workers leave their jobs and refuse to work.

ExamPrep

ISSUE SPOTTERS

—Check your answers to these questions against the answers provided in Appendix D at the end of this text.

1. Erin, an employee of Fine Print Shop, is injured on the job. For Erin to obtain workers' compensation, does her injury have to have been caused by Fine Print's negligence? Does it matter whether the action causing the injury was intentional? Explain. **(See pages 415–416.)**

2. Onyx applies for work with Precision Design Company, which tells her that it requires union membership as a condition of employment. She applies for work with Quality Engineering, Inc., which does not require union membership as a condition of employment but requires employees to join a union after six months on the job. Are these conditions legal? Why or why not? **(See page 426.)**

BEFORE THE TEST

Go to **www.cengagebrain.com**, enter the ISBN 9781133586548, and click on "Find" to locate this textbook's Web site. Then click on "Access Now" under "Study Tools," and select Chapter 16 at the top. There, you will find a Practice Quiz that you can take to assess your mastery of the concepts in this chapter. Additionally, you will find Flashcards and a Glossary of important terms, as well as Video Questions (when assigned).

For Review

Answers for the even-numbered questions in this For Review *section can be found in Appendix E at the end of this text.*

1. What are the duties of parties to an agency relationship?

2. What federal statute governs working hours and wages?

3. Under the Family and Medical Leave Act, in what circumstances may an employee take family or medical leave?

4. What are the two most important federal statutes governing immigration and employment today?

5. What federal statute gave employees the right to organize unions and engage in collective bargaining?

Questions and Case Problems

16–1. Wages and Hours. Calzoni Boating Co. is an interstate business engaged in manufacturing and selling boats. The company has five hundred nonunion employees. Representatives of these employees are requesting a four-day, ten-hours-per-day workweek, and Calzoni is concerned that this would require paying time and a half after eight hours per day. Which federal act is Calzoni thinking of that might require this? Will the act in fact require paying time and a half for all hours worked over eight hours per day if the employees' proposal is accepted? Explain. **(See page 412.)**

16–2. **Question with Sample Answer: Agent's Duties to the Principal.** Iliana is a traveling sales agent. Iliana not only solicits orders but also delivers the goods and collects payments from her customers. Iliana places all payments in her private checking account and at the end of each month draws sufficient cash from her bank to cover the payments made. Giberson Corp., Iliana's employer, is totally unaware of this procedure. Because of a slowdown in the economy, Giberson tells all its sales personnel to offer 20 percent discounts on orders. Iliana solicits orders, but she offers only 15 percent discounts, pocketing the extra 5 percent paid by customers. Iliana has not lost any orders, and she is rated as one of Giberson's top salespersons. Giberson now learns of Iliana's actions. Discuss fully Giberson's rights in this matter. **(See pages 406 and 409.)**

—For a sample answer to Question 16–2, go to Appendix F at the end of this text.

16–3. Unfair Labor Practices. Consolidated Stores is undergoing a unionization campaign. Before the union election, management states that the union is unnecessary to protect workers. Management also provides bonuses and wage increases to the workers during this period. The employees reject the union. Union organizers protest that the wage increases during the election campaign unfairly prejudiced the vote. Should these wage increases be regarded as an unfair labor practice? Discuss. **(See pages 427–429.)**

16–4. Illegal Aliens. Nicole Tipton and Sadik Seferi owned and operated a restaurant in Iowa. Acting on a tip from the local police, agents of Immigration and Customs Enforcement executed search warrants at the restaurant and at an apartment where some restaurant workers lived. The agents discovered six undocumented aliens working at the restaurant and living together. When the I-9 forms for the restaurant's employees were reviewed, none were found for the six aliens. They were paid in cash while other employees were paid by check. The jury found Tipton and Seferi guilty of hiring and harboring illegal aliens. Both were given prison terms. The defendants challenged the conviction, contending that they did not violate the law because they did not know that the workers were unauthorized aliens. Was that argument credible? Why or why not? [*United States v. Tipton,* 518 F.3d 591 (8th Cir. 2008)] **(See pages 422–423.)**

16–5. Liability Based on Actual or Apparent Authority. Summerall Electric Co. and other subcontractors were hired by National Church Services, Inc. (NCS), which was the general contractor on a construction project for the Church of God at Southaven. As work progressed, payments from NCS to the subcontractors were late and eventually stopped altogether. The church had paid NCS in full for the entire project beforehand, but apparently NCS had mismanaged the project. When payments from NCS stopped, the subcontractors filed *mechanic's liens* (see page 351 in Chapter 14) for the value of the work they had performed but for which they had not been paid. The subcontractors sued the church, contending that it was liable for the payments because NCS was its agent on the basis of either actual or apparent authority. Was NCS an agent for the church, thereby making the church liable to the subcontractors? Explain your reasoning. [*Summerall Electric Co. v. Church of God at Southaven,* 25 So.3d 1090 (App.Miss. 2010)] **(See pages 407–408.)**

16–6. **Case Problem with Sample Answer: Independent Contractors.** William Moore owned Moore Enterprises, a wholesale tire business. William's son, Jonathan, worked as a Moore Enterprises employee while he was in high school. Later, Jonathan started his own business, called Morecedes Tire. Morecedes regrooved tires and sold them to businesses, including Moore Enterprises. A decade after Jonathan started Morecedes, William offered him work with Moore Enterprises. On the first day, William told Jonathan to load certain tires on a trailer but did not tell him how to do it. Was Jonathan an independent contractor? Discuss. [*Moore v. Moore,* __ P.3d __ (Idaho 2011)] **(See page 402.)**

—For a sample answer to Case Problem 16–6, go to Appendix G at the end of this text.

16–7. Unfair Labor Practices. The Laborers' International Union of North America and Shaw Stone & Webster Construction, Inc., agreed on a provision that required all employees to pay dues to the union. Sebedeo Lopez went to work for Shaw Stone without paying the union dues. When the union pressed the company to fire him, Lopez agreed to pay. The union continued to demand his discharge, however, and Shaw Stone fired him. Was the union guilty of unfair labor practices? Why or why not? [*Laborers' International Union of North America, Local 578 v. National Labor Relations Board,* 594 F.3d 732 (10th Cir. 2010)] **(See pages 426 and 429.)**

16–8. Workers' Compensation. As a safety measure, Dynea USA, Inc., required an employee, Tony Fairbanks, to wear steel-toed boots. One of the boots caused a sore on Fairbanks's leg. The skin over the sore broke, and within a week, Fairbanks was hospitalized with a methicillin-resistant staphylococcus aureus (MRSA) infection. He filed a workers' compensation claim. Dynea argued that the MRSA bacteria that caused the infection had been on Fairbanks's skin before he came to work. What are the requirements to recover workers' compensation benefits? Does this claim qualify? Explain. [*Dynea USA, Inc. v. Fairbanks,* 241 Or.App. 311, 250 P.3d 389 (2011)] **(See pages 415–416.)**

16–9. **A Question of Ethics: Workers' Compensation.** *Beverly Tull had worked for Atchison Leather Products, Inc., in Kansas for ten years when, in 1999, she began to complain of hand, wrist, and shoulder pain. Atchison recommended that she contact a certain physician, who in April 2000 diagnosed the condition as carpal tunnel syndrome "severe enough" for surgery. In August, Tull filed a claim with the state workers' compensation board. Because Atchison changed workers' compensation insurance companies every year, a dispute arose as to which company should pay Tull's claim. Fearing liability, no insurer would authorize treatment, and Tull was forced to delay surgery until December. The board granted her temporary total disability benefits for the subsequent six weeks that she missed work. On April 23, 2002, Berger Co. bought Atchison. The new employer adjusted Tull's work to be less demanding and stressful, but she continued to suffer pain. In July, a physician diagnosed her condition as permanent. The board granted her permanent partial disability benefits. By May 2005, the bickering over the financial responsibility for Tull's claim involved five insurers—four of which had each covered Atchison for a single year and one of which covered Berger. [Tull v. Atchison Leather Products, Inc., 37 Kan.App.2d 87, 150 P.3d 316 (2007)]* **(See pages 415–416.)**

1. When an injured employee files a claim for workers' compensation, there is a proceeding to assess the injury and determine the amount of compensation. Should a dispute between insurers over the payment of the claim be resolved in the same proceeding? Why or why not?

2. The board designated April 23, 2002, as the date of Tull's injury. What is the reason for determining the date of a worker's injury? Should the board in this case have selected this date or a different date? Why?

3. How should the board assess liability for the payment of Tull's medical expenses and disability benefits? Would it be appropriate to impose joint and several liability on the insurers, or should the individual liability of each of them be determined? Explain.

Chapter 17

Employment Discrimination

> "Equal rights for all, special privileges for none."
>
> —Thomas Jefferson, 1743–1826
> (Third president of the United States, 1801–1809)

Contents

- **Title VII of the Civil Rights Act of 1964**
- **Discrimination Based on Age**
- **Discrimination Based on Disability**
- **Defenses to Employment Discrimination**
- **Affirmative Action**

Learning Objectives

The four Learning Objectives below are designed to help improve your understanding of the chapter. After reading this chapter, you should be able to answer the following questions:

1. **Generally, what kind of conduct is prohibited by Title VII of the Civil Rights Act of 1964, as amended?**

2. **What is the difference between disparate-treatment discrimination and disparate-impact discrimination?**

3. **What federal act prohibits discrimination based on age?**

4. **What are three defenses to claims of employment discrimination?**

(©Svetlana Larina, 2009. Used under license from Shutterstock.com)

Protected Class A group of persons with defining characteristics—such as race, color, religion, national origin, gender, age, and disability—who historically have been discriminated against.

Out of the 1960s civil rights movement to end racial and other forms of discrimination grew a body of law protecting employees against discrimination in the workplace. This protective legislation further eroded the employment-at-will doctrine, which was discussed in the previous chapter. In the past several decades, judicial decisions, administrative agency actions, and legislation have restricted the ability of both employers and unions to discriminate against workers on the basis of race, color, religion, national origin, gender, age, or disability. A class of persons defined by one or more of these criteria is known as a **protected class.** The laws designed to protect these individuals embody the sentiment expressed by Thomas Jefferson in the chapter-opening quotation.

One of the most talked-about cases in 2011 was the Walmart gender discrimination case. A group of female employees sued Walmart, the nation's largest private employer, alleging that store managers who had discretion over pay and promotions were biased against women and disproportionately favored men. The United States Supreme Court ruled in favor of Walmart, effectively blocking the *class action*—a lawsuit in which a small group of plaintiffs sues on behalf of a larger group. The Court held that the women could not maintain a class action because they had failed to prove a companywide policy of discrimination that had a common effect on all

Employment Discrimination Treating employees or job applicants unequally on the basis of race, color, national origin, religion, gender, age, or disability.

women covered by the class action.[1] This important decision may limit the rights of employees to sue their employers for job discrimination in a class action, but it does not change the rights of individuals to sue for employment discrimination.

Several federal statutes prohibit **employment discrimination** against members of protected classes. The most important statute is Title VII of the Civil Rights Act of 1964.[2] Title VII prohibits discrimination on the basis of race, color, religion, national origin, or gender at any stage of employment. The Age Discrimination in Employment Act of 1967[3] and the Americans with Disabilities Act of 1990[4] prohibit discrimination on the basis of age and disability, respectively.

This chapter focuses on the kinds of discrimination prohibited by these federal statutes. Note, though, that discrimination against employees on the basis of any of these criteria may also violate state human rights statutes or other state laws or public policies prohibiting discrimination.

▶ Title VII of the Civil Rights Act of 1964

LEARNING OBJECTIVE 1 Generally, what kind of conduct is prohibited by Title VII of the Civil Rights Act of 1964, as amended?

Title VII of the Civil Rights Act of 1964 and its amendments prohibit job discrimination against employees, applicants, and union members on the basis of race, color, national origin, religion, or gender at any stage of employment. Title VII applies to employers with fifteen or more employees, labor unions with fifteen or more members, labor unions that operate hiring halls (to which members go regularly to be rationed jobs as they become available), employment agencies, and state and local governing units or agencies. A special section of the act prohibits discrimination in most federal government employment.

The Equal Employment Opportunity Commission

Compliance with Title VII is monitored by the Equal Employment Opportunity Commission (EEOC). A victim of alleged discrimination must file a claim with the EEOC before bringing a suit against the employer. The EEOC may investigate the dispute and attempt to obtain the parties' voluntary consent to an out-of-court settlement. If a voluntary agreement cannot be reached, the EEOC may then file a suit against the employer on the employee's behalf. If the EEOC decides not to investigate the claim, the victim may bring her or his own lawsuit against the employer.

The EEOC does not investigate every claim of employment discrimination, regardless of the merits of the claim. Generally, it investigates only "priority cases," such as cases involving retaliatory discharge (firing an employee in retaliation for submitting a claim to the EEOC) and cases involving types of discrimination that are of particular concern to the EEOC.

Intentional and Unintentional Discrimination

Title VII prohibits both intentional and unintentional discrimination.

Disparate-Treatment Discrimination Intentional discrimination against individuals on the basis of color, gender, national origin, race, or religion.

INTENTIONAL DISCRIMINATION Intentional discrimination by an employer against an employee is known as **disparate-treatment discrimination**. Because intent may sometimes be difficult to prove, courts have established certain procedures

---

1. *Wal-Mart Stores, Inc. v. Dukes,* ___ U.S. ___, 131 S.Ct. 2541, 180 L.Ed.2d 374 (2011).
2. 42 U.S.C. Sections 2000e–2000e-17.
3. 29 U.S.C. Sections 621–634.
4. 42 U.S.C. Sections 12102–12118.

for resolving disparate-treatment cases. **EXAMPLE 17.1** Barbara applies for employment with a construction firm and is rejected. If she sues on the basis of disparate-treatment discrimination in hiring, she must show that (1) she is a member of a protected class, (2) she applied and was qualified for the job in question, (3) she was rejected by the employer, and (4) the employer continued to seek applicants for the position or filled the position with a person not in a protected class. ●

If Barbara in Example 17.1 above can meet these relatively easy requirements, she has made out a ***prima facie* case** of illegal discrimination. *Prima facie* is Latin for "at first sight." Legally, it refers to a fact that is presumed to be true unless contradicted by evidence. Making out a *prima facie* case of discrimination means that the plaintiff has met her initial burden of proof and will win in the absence of a legally acceptable employer defense. (Defenses will be discussed later in this chapter.) The burden then shifts to the employer-defendant, who must articulate a legal reason for not hiring the plaintiff. To prevail, the plaintiff must then show that the employer's reason is a *pretext* (not the true reason) and that discriminatory intent actually motivated the employer's decision.

UNINTENTIONAL DISCRIMINATION Employers often use interviews and testing procedures to choose from among a large number of applicants for job openings. Minimum educational requirements are also common. These practices and procedures may have an unintended discriminatory impact on a protected class. (For tips on how human resources managers can prevent these types of discrimination claims, see the *Linking the Law to Management* feature on page 455.)

Disparate-impact discrimination occurs when a protected group of people is adversely affected by an employer's practices, procedures, or tests, even though they do not appear to be discriminatory. In a disparate-impact discrimination case, the complaining party must first show statistically that the employer's practices, procedures, or tests are discriminatory in effect. Once the plaintiff has made out a *prima facie* case, the burden of proof shifts to the employer to show that the practices or procedures in question were justified. There are two ways of proving that disparate-impact discrimination exists, as discussed next.

Pool of Applicants. A plaintiff can prove a disparate impact by comparing the employer's workforce with the pool of qualified individuals available in the local labor market. The plaintiff must show that as a result of educational or other job requirements or hiring procedures, the percentage of nonwhites, women, or members of other protected classes in the employer's workforce does not reflect the percentage of that group in the pool of qualified applicants. If a person challenging an employment practice can show a connection between the practice and the disparity, he or she has made out a *prima facie* case and need not provide evidence of discriminatory intent.

Rate of Hiring. A plaintiff can prove disparate-impact discrimination by comparing the selection rates of whites and nonwhites (or members of another protected class), regardless of the racial balance in the employer's workforce. When an educational or other job requirement or hiring procedure excludes members of a protected class from an employer's workforce at a substantially higher rate than nonmembers, discrimination exists.

The EEOC has devised a test, called the "four-fifths rule," to determine whether an employment examination is discriminatory on its face. Under this rule, a selection rate for protected classes that is less than four-fifths, or 80 percent, of the rate for the group with the highest rate will generally be regarded as evidence of disparate

Prima Facie **Case** A case in which the plaintiff has produced sufficient evidence to prove his or her conclusion if the defendant produces no evidence to rebut it.

Disparate-Impact Discrimination Discrimination that results from certain employer practices or procedures that, although not discriminatory on their face, have a discriminatory effect.

LEARNING OBJECTIVE 2 **What is the difference between disparate-treatment discrimination and disparate-impact discrimination?**

impact. **EXAMPLE 17.2**   One hundred white applicants take an employment test, and fifty pass the test and are hired. One hundred minority applicants take the test, and twenty pass the test and are hired. Because twenty is less than four-fifths (80 percent) of fifty, the test would be considered discriminatory under the EEOC guidelines. ●

Ethical Issue

Is there an implicit bias against job applicants who have been unemployed long term? Even though the recession that started in December 2007 has officially ended, the national unemployment rate has remained above 8 percent. As a result, many individuals have been unable to find work for several years. Today, the long-term unemployed are facing apparent discrimination when they apply for jobs. Some employers have indicated that they will not consider an applicant who has been unemployed longer than six months, especially if he or she has not pursued additional training or education during the period of unemployment.

Because the long-term unemployed do not form a protected class, they cannot sue for discrimination under federal law. They may soon get help from the states, however. At least thirteen states are considering legislation to prohibit discrimination against the unemployed in help-wanted ads. The New York–based National Employment Law Project is urging legislation that would explicitly prohibit employers and employment agencies from eliminating long-term unemployed applicants from consideration for jobs.

Discrimination Based on Race, Color, and National Origin

Title VII prohibits employers from discriminating against employees or job applicants on the basis of race, color, or national origin. If an employer's standards or policies for selecting or promoting employees have a discriminatory effect on employees or job applicants in these protected classes, then a presumption of illegal discrimination arises. To avoid liability, the employer must then show that its standards or policies have a substantial, demonstrable relationship to realistic qualifications for the job in question.

CASE EXAMPLE 17.3   Jiann Min Chang was an instructor at Alabama Agricultural and Mechanical University (AAMU). When AAMU terminated his employment, Chang filed a lawsuit claiming discrimination based on national origin. Chang established a *prima facie* case because he (1) was a member of a protected class, (2) was qualified for the job, (3) suffered an adverse employment action, and (4) was replaced by someone outside his protected class (a non-Asian instructor). When the burden of proof shifted to the employer, however, AAMU showed that Chang had argued with a university vice president and refused to comply with her instructions. The court ruled that the university had not renewed Chang's contract for a legitimate reason—insubordination—and therefore was not liable for unlawful discrimination.[5] ●

REVERSE DISCRIMINATION   Note that discrimination based on race can also take the form of *reverse discrimination*, or discrimination against "majority" individuals, such as white males. **CASE EXAMPLE 17.4**   An African American woman fired four white men from their management positions at a school district. The men filed a lawsuit for racial discrimination, alleging that the woman was trying to eliminate white males from the department. The woman claimed that the terminations were part of a reorganization plan to cut costs in the department. The jury sided with the men and awarded them nearly $3 million in damages. The verdict was upheld on appeal (though the damages award was reduced slightly).[6] ●

---

5. *Jiann Min Chang v. Alabama Agricultural and Mechanical University,* 2009 WL 3403180 (11th Cir. 2009).
6. *Johnston v. School District of Philadelphia,* 2006 WL 999966 (E.D.Pa. 2006).

In 2009, the United States Supreme Court issued a decision that will affect future disparate-impact and reverse discrimination litigation. **CASE EXAMPLE 17.5** The fire department in New Haven, Connecticut, administered a test to determine which firefighters were eligible for promotions. No African Americans and only two Hispanic firefighters passed the test. Fearing that it would be sued for racial discrimination if it used the test results for promotions, the city basically discarded the results. The white firefighters (and one Hispanic) who had passed the test then sued the city, claiming reverse discrimination.

The lower courts found in favor of the city, but the United States Supreme Court held that an employer can engage in intentional discrimination to remedy an unintentional disparate impact only if the employer has "a strong basis in evidence" to believe that it will be successfully sued for disparate-impact discrimination "if it fails to take the race-conscious, discriminatory action." Mere fear of litigation was not a sufficient reason for the city to discard its test results.[7] •

POTENTIAL "SECTION 1981" CLAIMS   Victims of racial or ethnic discrimination may also have a cause of action under 42 U.S.C. Section 1981. This section, which was enacted as part of the Civil Rights Act of 1866 to protect the rights of freed slaves, prohibits discrimination on the basis of race or ethnicity in the formation or enforcement of contracts. Because employment is often a contractual relationship, Section 1981 can provide an alternative basis for a plaintiff's action and is potentially advantageous because it does not place a cap on damages.

Discrimination Based on Religion

Title VII of the Civil Rights Act of 1964 also prohibits government employers, private employers, and unions from discriminating against persons because of their religion. Employers cannot treat their employees more or less favorably based on their religious beliefs or practices and cannot require employees to participate in any religious activity (or forbid them from participating in one).

EXAMPLE 17.6   Jason Sewell claimed that his employer, a car dealership, fired him for not attending the weekly prayer meetings of dealership employees. If the dealership did require its employees to attend prayer gatherings and fired Sewell for not attending, he has a valid claim of religious discrimination. •

REASONABLE ACCOMMODATION   An employer must "reasonably accommodate" the religious practices of its employees, unless to do so would cause undue hardship to the employer's business. If an employee's religion prohibits him or her from working on a certain day of the week or at a certain type of job, for instance, the employer must make a reasonable attempt to accommodate these religious requirements.

Employers must reasonably accommodate an employee's religious belief even if the belief is not based on the doctrines of a traditionally recognized religion, such as Christianity or Judaism, or a denomination, such as Baptist. The only requirement is that the belief be sincerely held by the employee.

UNDUE HARDSHIP   A reasonable attempt to accommodate does not necessarily require the employer to permanently make a change on an employee's behalf, especially if to do so would cause the employer undue hardship.

---

7. *Ricci v. DeStefano*, 557 U.S. 557, 129 S.Ct. 2658, 174 L.Ed.2d 490 (2009).

CASE EXAMPLE 17.7 Miguel Sánchez-Rodríguez sold cell phones in shopping malls for AT&T in Puerto Rico. After six years, Sánchez informed his supervisors that he had become a Seventh Day Adventist and could no longer work on Saturdays for religious reasons. AT&T responded that his inability to work on Saturdays would cause it hardship.

As a reasonable accommodation, the company suggested that Sánchez swap schedules with others and offered him two other positions that did not require work on Saturdays. Sánchez could not find workers to swap shifts with him, however, and declined the other jobs because they would result in less income. He began missing work on Saturdays. After a time, AT&T indicated that it would discipline him for any additional Saturdays that he missed. Eventually, he was placed on active disciplinary status. Sánchez resigned and filed a religious discrimination lawsuit against AT&T. The court found in favor of AT&T, and a federal appellate court affirmed. The company had made adequate efforts at accommodation by allowing Sánchez to swap shifts and offering him other positions that did not require work on Saturdays.[8] ●

Discrimination Based on Gender

Under Title VII, as well as other federal acts (including the Equal Pay Act of 1963, which we also discuss here), employers are forbidden from discriminating against employees on the basis of gender. Employers are prohibited from classifying jobs as male or female and from advertising in help-wanted columns that are designated male or female unless the employer can prove that the gender of the applicant is essential to the job. Employers also cannot have separate male and female seniority lists or refuse to promote employees based on gender.

GENDER MUST BE A DETERMINING FACTOR Generally, to succeed in a suit for gender discrimination, a plaintiff must demonstrate that gender was a determining factor in the employer's decision to fire or refuse to hire or promote her or him. Typically, this involves looking at all of the surrounding circumstances.

CASE EXAMPLE 17.8 Wanda Collier worked for Turner Industries Group, LLC, in the maintenance department. She complained to her supervisor that Jack Daniell, the department head, treated her unfairly. Her supervisor told her that Daniell had a problem with her gender and was harder on women. The supervisor talked to Daniell but did not take any disciplinary action. A month later, Daniell confronted Collier, pushing her up against a wall and berating her. After this incident, Collier filed a formal complaint and kept a male co-worker with her at all times. A month later, she was fired. She subsequently filed a lawsuit alleging gender discrimination. The court concluded that there was enough evidence that gender was a determining factor in Daniell's conduct to allow Collier's claims to go to a jury.[9] ●

PREGNANCY DISCRIMINATION The Pregnancy Discrimination Act of 1978,[10] which amended Title VII, expanded the definition of gender discrimination to include discrimination based on pregnancy. Women affected by pregnancy, childbirth, or related medical conditions must be treated—for all employment-related purposes, including the receipt of benefits under employee benefit programs—the same as other persons not so affected but similar in ability to work.

> *"A sign that says 'men only' looks very different on a bathroom door than a courthouse door."*
>
> Thurgood Marshall, 1908–1993
> (Associate justice of the United States Supreme Court, 1967–1991)

---

8. *Sánchez-Rodríguez v. AT&T Mobility Puerto Rico, Inc.,* 673 F.3d 1 (1st Cir. 2012).
9. *Collier v. Turner Industries Group, LLC,* 797 F.Supp.2d 1029 (D. Idaho 2011).
10. 42 U.S.C. Section 2000e(k).

WAGE DISCRIMINATION   Several laws prohibit employers from gender-based wage discrimination. The Equal Pay Act of 1963 requires equal pay for male and female employees doing similar work at the same establishment (a barber and a hair stylist, for example). To determine whether the Equal Pay Act has been violated, a court will look to the primary duties of the two jobs—the job content rather than the job description controls. If the wage differential is due to "any factor other than gender," such as a seniority or merit system, then it does not violate the Equal Pay Act.

The continuing disparity between the wages of men and women prompted Congress to pass the Paycheck Fairness Act of 2009, which closed some of the loopholes in the Equal Pay Act. The Paycheck Fairness Act clarified employers' defenses and prohibited the use of gender-based differentials in assessing an employee's education, training, or experience. It also provided additional remedies for wage discrimination similar to those available for discrimination based on race and national origin.

Congress also enacted the Lilly Ledbetter Fair Pay Act of 2009, which made discriminatory wages actionable under federal law regardless of when the discrimination began.[11] This act overturned a previous decision by the United States Supreme Court that had limited plaintiffs' time period to file a wage discrimination complaint to 180 days after the employer's decision.[12] Today, if a plaintiff continues to work for the employer while receiving discriminatory wages, the time period for filing a complaint is basically unlimited.

Constructive Discharge

The majority of Title VII complaints involve unlawful discrimination in decisions to hire or fire employees. In some situations, however, employees who leave their jobs voluntarily can claim that they were "constructively discharged" by the employer. **Constructive discharge** occurs when the employer causes the employee's working conditions to be so intolerable that a reasonable person in the employee's position would feel compelled to quit.

Constructive Discharge A termination of employment brought about by making the employee's working conditions so intolerable that the employee reasonably feels compelled to leave.

PROVING CONSTRUCTIVE DISCHARGE   The plaintiff must present objective proof of intolerable working conditions, which the employer knew or had reason to know about yet failed to correct within a reasonable time period. Courts generally also require the employee to show causation—that the employer's unlawful discrimination caused the working conditions to be intolerable. Put a different way, the employee's resignation must be a foreseeable result of the employer's discriminatory action.

EXAMPLE 17.9   Khalil's employer humiliates him in front of his co-workers by informing him that he is being demoted to an inferior position. Khalil's co-workers then continually insult and harass him about his national origin (he is from Iran). The employer is aware of this discriminatory treatment but does nothing to remedy the situation, despite repeated complaints from Khalil. After several months, Khalil quits his job and files a Title VII claim. In this situation, Khalil would likely have sufficient evidence to maintain an action for constructive discharge in violation of Title VII. ●

APPLIES TO ALL TITLE VII DISCRIMINATION   Note that constructive discharge is a theory that plaintiffs can use to establish any type of discrimination claims under Title VII, including race, color, national origin, religion, gender, pregnancy, and sexual

---

11. Pub. L. No. 111-2, 123 Stat. 5 (January 5, 2009), amending 42 U.S.C. Section 2000e-5[e].
12. *Ledbetter v. Goodyear Tire Co.,* 550 U.S. 618, 127 S.Ct. 2162, 167 L.Ed.2d 982 (2007).

harassment. Constructive discharge has also been successfully used in situations that involve discrimination based on age or disability (both of which will be discussed later in this chapter). Constructive discharge is most commonly asserted in cases involving sexual harassment, however.

When constructive discharge is claimed, the employee can pursue damages for loss of income, including back pay. These damages ordinarily are not available to an employee who left a job voluntarily.

Sexual Harassment

Sexual Harassment The demanding of sexual favors in return for job promotions or other benefits, or language or conduct that is so sexually offensive that it creates a hostile working environment.

Title VII also protects employees against **sexual harassment** in the workplace. Sexual harassment can take two forms: *quid pro quo* harassment and hostile-environment harassment. *Quid pro quo* is a Latin phrase that is often translated to mean "something in exchange for something else." *Quid pro quo* harassment occurs when sexual favors are demanded in return for job opportunities, promotions, salary increases, and the like. According to the United States Supreme Court, hostile-environment harassment occurs when "the workplace is permeated with discriminatory intimidation, ridicule, and insult, that is sufficiently severe or pervasive to alter the conditions of the victim's employment and create an abusive working environment."[13]

The courts determine whether the sexually offensive conduct was sufficiently severe or pervasive as to create a hostile environment on a case-by-case basis. Typically, a single incident of sexually offensive conduct is not enough to create a hostile environment (although there have been exceptions when the conduct was particularly objectionable). Note also that if the employee who is alleging sexual harassment has signed an *arbitration clause* (see Chapter 2 on page 53), she or he will most likely be required to arbitrate the claim.[14]

HARASSMENT BY SUPERVISORS   For an employer to be held liable for a supervisor's sexual harassment, the supervisor normally must have taken a *tangible employment action* against the employee. A **tangible employment action** is a significant change in employment status or benefits, such as when an employee is fired, refused a promotion, demoted, or reassigned to a position with significantly different responsibilities. Only a supervisor, or another person acting with the authority of the employer, can cause this sort of injury. A constructive discharge also qualifies as a tangible employment action.[15]

Tangible Employment Action A significant change in employment status, such as a change brought about by firing or failing to promote an employee.

THE *ELLERTH/FARAGHER* AFFIRMATIVE DEFENSE   In 1998, the United States Supreme Court issued several important rulings that have had a lasting impact on cases alleging sexual harassment by supervisors.[16] The Court held that an employer (a city) was liable for a supervisor's harassment of employees even though the employer was unaware of the behavior. Although the city had a written policy against sexual harassment, it had not distributed the policy to its employees and had not established any complaint procedures for employees who felt that they had been sexually harassed. In another case, the Court held that an employer can be liable for

---

13. *Harris v. Forklift Systems,* 510 U.S. 17, 114 S.Ct. 367, 126 L.Ed.2d 295 (1993). See also *Billings v. Town of Grafton,* 515 F.3d 39 (1st Cir. 2008).
14. See, for example, *EEOC v. Cheesecake Factory, Inc.,* 2009 WL 1259359 (D.Ariz. 2009).
15. See, for example, *Pennsylvania State Police v. Suders,* 542 U.S. 129, 124 S.Ct. 2342, 159 L.Ed.2d 204 (2004).
16. *Burlington Industries, Inc. v. Ellerth,* 524 U.S. 742, 118 S.Ct. 2257, 141 L.Ed.2d 633 (1998); and *Faragher v. City of Boca Raton,* 524 U.S. 775, 118 S.Ct. 2275, 141 L.Ed.2d 662 (1998).

a supervisor's sexual harassment even though the employee does not suffer adverse job consequences.

The Court's decisions in these cases established what has become known as the "*Ellerth/Faragher* affirmative defense" to charges of sexual harassment. The defense has two elements:

1. That the employer has taken reasonable care to prevent and promptly correct any sexually harassing behavior (by establishing effective antiharassment policies and complaint procedures, for example).
2. That the plaintiff-employee unreasonably failed to take advantage of any preventive or corrective opportunities provided by the employer to avoid harm.

An employer that can prove both elements will not be liable for a supervisor's harassment.

RETALIATION BY EMPLOYERS Employers sometimes retaliate against employees who complain about sexual harassment or other Title VII violations. Retaliation can take many forms. An employer might demote or fire the person, or otherwise change the terms, conditions, and benefits of his or her employment. Title VII prohibits retaliation, and employees can sue their employers. In a *retaliation claim,* an individual asserts that she or he has suffered a harm as a result of making a charge, testifying, or participating in a Title VII investigation or proceeding.

Plaintiffs do not have to prove that the challenged action adversely affected their workplace or employment.[17] Instead, to prove retaliation, plaintiffs must show that the challenged action was one that would likely have dissuaded a reasonable worker from making or supporting a charge of discrimination.

In the following case, the court had to decide whether a female law professor had been retaliated against for engaging in protected conduct.

---

17. *Burlington Northern and Santa Fe Railroad Co. v. White,* 548 U.S. 53, 126 S.Ct. 2405, 165 L.Ed.2d 345 (2006).

Case 17.1 **Morales-Cruz v. University of Puerto Rico**

United States Court of Appeals, First Circuit, 676 F.3d 220 (2012).

BACKGROUND AND FACTS In 2003, Myrta Morales-Cruz began a tenure-track teaching position at the University of Puerto Rico School of Law. During Morales-Cruz's probationary period, one of her co-teachers in a law school clinic had an affair with one of their students, and it resulted in a pregnancy. In 2008, Morales-Cruz wanted the university's administrative committee to approve a one-year extension for her tenure review. The law school's dean asked Morales-Cruz about her co-teacher's affair and criticized her for failing to report it. He later recommended granting the extension but called Morales-Cruz insecure, immature, and fragile. Similarly, a law school committee recommended granting the extension, but a dissenting professor commented that Morales-Cruz had shown poor judgment, in regard to the co-teacher's affair, had personality flaws, and had trouble with complex and sensitive situations. Morales-Cruz learned about these comments and complained in writing to the university's

chancellor. As a result, the dean then recommended denying the one-year extension, and the administrative committee ultimately did just that. When her employment was terminated, Morales-Cruz sued the university under Title VII. Among other things, she asserted that the dean had retaliated against her for complaining to the chancellor. The district court found that Morales-Cruz had not stated a proper retaliation claim under Title VII.

IN THE WORDS OF THE COURT . . .
SELYA, Circuit Judge.
* * * *

The amended complaint alleges that various officials described the plaintiff as "fragile," "immature," "unable to handle complex and sensitive

Case 17.1–Continues next page ➡

Case 17.1—Continued

issues," * * * and exhibiting "lack of judgment." These descriptors are admittedly unflattering—but they are without exception gender-neutral. All of them apply equally to persons of either gender * * * .

* * * *

* * * Title VII makes it unlawful for an employer to take materially adverse action against an employee "because he has opposed any practice made an unlawful employment practice by this subchapter." *To state a cause of action under this portion of the statute, the pleading must contain plausible allegations indicating that the plaintiff opposed a practice prohibited by Title VII and suffered an adverse employment action as a result of that opposition.* [Emphasis added.]

The plaintiff alleges that she was retaliated against for writing to the Chancellor to complain about the "discriminatory" comments made in the course of her request for an extension. In support of this allegation, she points out that after she sent her letter the Dean reversed his position on her extension. This construct suffers from

a fatal flaw: her factual allegations do not support a reasonable inference that she was engaging in protected conduct when she opposed the remarks made.

* * * The facts alleged * * * provide no reasonable basis for inferring that the comments cited reflected gender-based discrimination. Those comments were unarguably gender-neutral and do not afford an objectively reasonable foundation for a retaliation action.

DECISION AND REMEDY   The U.S. Court of Appeals for the First Circuit held that Morales-Cruz could not bring a retaliation claim under Title VII. It therefore affirmed the district court's judgment for the University of Puerto Rico.

THE ETHICAL DIMENSION   *Could Morales-Cruz's dean have had legitimate reasons for changing his mind about the one-year extension? If so, what were they?*

HARASSMENT BY CO-WORKERS AND NONEMPLOYEES   When harassment by co-workers, rather than supervisors, creates a hostile working environment, an employee may still have a cause of action against the employer. Normally, though, the employer will be held liable only if the employer knew, or should have known, about the harassment and failed to take immediate remedial action.

Occasionally, a court may also hold an employer liable for harassment by *nonemployees* if the employer knew about the harassment and failed to take corrective action. **EXAMPLE 17.10**   Gordon, who owns and manages a Great Bites restaurant, knows that one of his regular customers, Dean, repeatedly harasses Sharon, a waitress. If Gordon does nothing and permits the harassment to continue, he may be liable under Title VII even though Dean is not an employee of the restaurant. •

SAME-GENDER HARASSMENT   In *Oncale v. Sundowner Offshore Services, Inc.,*[18] the United States Supreme Court held that Title VII protection extends to situations in which individuals are sexually harassed by members of the same gender. Proving that the harassment in same-gender cases is "based on sex" can be difficult, though. It is easier to establish a case of same-gender harassment when the harasser is homosexual.

CASE EXAMPLE 17.11   James Tepperwien was a security officer at a nuclear power plant owned by Entergy Nuclear Operations. Tepperwien twice reported to his superiors that Vito Messina, another security officer who allegedly was gay, had sexually harassed him. After the first incident, Entergy made all the security officers read and sign its no-tolerance antiharassment policy. After the second incident, Messina was placed on administrative leave for ten weeks. After Messina returned to work, Tepperwien was disciplined for failing to report some missing equipment. He then filed another harassment complaint and quit his job, claiming that he had been constructively discharged and that Entergy had not taken sufficient steps to prevent further harassment.

The court noted that a male victim of same-gender harassment must show that he was harassed because he was male. The court found that Tepperwien had presented credible

---

18. 523 U.S. 75, 118 S.Ct. 998, 140 L.Ed.2d 207 (1998).

evidence that Messina was a homosexual and had made sexual advances toward other security officers. This evidence was sufficient to establish a *prima facie* case of hostile-environment sexual harassment, allowing the case to go to trial, but it was not enough to show the intolerable conditions required for a finding of constructive discharge.[19] ●

SEXUAL ORIENTATION HARASSMENT   Although federal law (Title VII) does not prohibit discrimination or harassment based on a person's sexual orientation, a growing number of states have enacted laws that prohibit sexual orientation discrimination in private employment. Some states, such as Michigan, specifically prohibit discrimination based on a person's gender identity or expression.

Also, many companies have voluntarily established nondiscrimination policies that include sexual orientation. (Workers in the United States often have more protection against sexual harassment in the workplace than workers in other countries, as this chapter's *Beyond Our Borders* feature below explains.)

Beyond Our Borders   Sexual Harassment in Other Nations

The problem of sexual harassment in the workplace is not confined to the United States. Indeed, it is a worldwide problem for female workers. In Argentina, Brazil, Egypt, Turkey, and many other countries, there is no legal protection against any form of employment discrimination.

Even in those countries that do have laws prohibiting discriminatory employment practices, including gender-based discrimination, those laws often do not specifically include sexual harassment as a discriminatory practice. Several countries have attempted to remedy this omission by passing new laws or amending others to specifically prohibit sexual harassment in the workplace. Japan, for example, has amended its Equal Employment Opportunity Law to include a provision making sexual harassment illegal. Thailand has also passed its first sexual-harassment law.

The European Union has adopted a directive that specifically identifies sexual harassment as a form of discrimination. Nevertheless, women's groups throughout Europe contend that corporations in European countries tend to view sexual harassment with "quiet tolerance." They contrast this attitude with that of most U.S. corporations, which have implemented specific procedures to deal with harassment claims.

Sexual harassment continues to be a persistent problem, in part, because some people do not consider unwanted sexual advances toward women in the workplace to be sexual harassment. In addition, women who have been subjected to sexual advances by men in positions of power may be reluctant to come forward with their claims.

For example, in 2011 U.S. authorities arrested Dominique Strauss-Kahn, then the head of the International Monetary Fund and a prominent French politician, for allegedly assaulting an immigrant hotel maid in New York. Only after his arrest in New York did reports that Strauss-Kahn had been making unwanted sexual advances to female employees for years appear in France. Two French women who had worked for Strauss-Kahn between 2007 and 2010 filed sexual-harassment claims against him.

● For Critical Analysis
Why do you think U.S. corporations are more aggressive than European companies in taking steps to prevent sexual harassment in the workplace?

Online Harassment

Employees' online activities can create a hostile working environment in many ways. Racial jokes, ethnic slurs, or other comments contained in e-mail, text or instant messages, and blog posts can become the basis for a claim of hostile-environment

---

19. *Tepperwien v. Entergy Nuclear Operations, Inc.,* 606 F.Supp.2d 427 (S.D.N.Y. 2009).

harassment or other forms of discrimination. A worker who sees sexually explicit images on a co-worker's computer screen may find the images offensive and claim that they create a hostile working environment. Nevertheless, employers may be able to avoid liability for online harassment by taking prompt remedial action.

Remedies under Title VII

Employer liability under Title VII may be extensive. If the plaintiff successfully proves that unlawful discrimination occurred, he or she may be awarded reinstatement, back pay, retroactive promotions, and damages. Compensatory damages are available only in cases of intentional discrimination. Punitive damages may be recovered against a private employer only if the employer acted with malice or reckless indifference to an individual's rights.

The statute limits the total amount of compensatory and punitive damages that the plaintiff can recover from specific employers—ranging from $50,000 against employers with one hundred or fewer employees to $300,000 against employers with more than five hundred employees.

▶ Discrimination Based on Age

LEARNING OBJECTIVE 3 | **What federal act prohibits discrimination based on age?**

Age discrimination is potentially the most widespread form of discrimination, because anyone—regardless of race, color, national origin, or gender—could be a victim at some point in life. The Age Discrimination in Employment Act (ADEA) of 1967, as amended, prohibits employment discrimination on the basis of age against individuals forty years of age or older. The act also prohibits mandatory retirement for nonmanagerial workers. For the act to apply, an employer must have twenty or more employees, and the employer's business activities must affect interstate commerce. The EEOC administers the ADEA, but the act also permits private causes of action against employers for age discrimination.

The ADEA includes a provision that extends protections against age discrimination to federal government employees.[20] In 2008, the United States Supreme Court ruled that this provision encompasses not only claims of age discrimination, but also claims of retaliation for complaining about age discrimination, which are not specifically mentioned in the statute.[21] Thus, the ADEA protects federal and private-sector employees from retaliation based on age-related complaints.

Procedures under the ADEA

> *"Growing old is like being increasingly penalized for a crime you have not committed."*
>
> Anthony Powell, 1905–2000
> (English novelist)

The burden-shifting procedure under the ADEA differs from the procedure under Title VII as a result of a United States Supreme Court decision in 2009 that dramatically changed the burden of proof in age discrimination cases.[22] As explained earlier, if the plaintiff in a Title VII case can show that the employer was motivated, at least in part, by unlawful discrimination, the burden of proof shifts to the employer to articulate a legitimate nondiscriminatory reason. Thus, in cases in which the employer has a "mixed motive" for discharging an employee, the employer has the burden of proving its reason was legitimate.

Under the ADEA, in contrast, a plaintiff must show that the unlawful discrimination was not just a reason but *the* reason for the adverse employment action. In

---

20. See 29 U.S.C. Section 632(a) (2000 ed., Supp. V).
21. *Gomez-Perez v. Potter,* 553 U.S. 474, 128 S.Ct. 1931, 170 L.Ed.2d 887 (2008).
22. *Gross v. FBL Financial Services,* 553 U.S. 474, 129 S.Ct. 2343, 174 L.Ed.2d 119 (2009).

other words, the employee has the burden of establishing "but for" causation—that is, that age discrimination was the reason for the adverse decision.

Thus, to establish a *prima facie* case, the plaintiff must show that he or she (1) was a member of the protected age group, (2) was qualified for the position from which he or she was discharged, and (3) was discharged because of age discrimination. Then the burden shifts to the employer. If the employer offers a legitimate reason for its action, then the plaintiff must show that the stated reason is only a pretext and that the plaintiff's age was the real reason for the employer's decision.

The following case illustrates the procedure for establishing an age discrimination claim under the ADEA.

Case 17.2   **Mora v. Jackson Memorial Foundation, Inc.**

United States Court of Appeals, Eleventh Circuit, 597 F.3d 1201 (2010).

BACKGROUND AND FACTS   Josephine Mora was sixty-two years old when she was fired from her job as a fund-raiser for Jackson Memorial Foundation, Inc. Mora's supervisor became dissatisfied with her work and recommended that she be fired. The foundation's chief executive officer, Mr. Rodriguez, agreed. Later, however, Rodriguez decided to give Mora a different position in his office. Mora worked with Rodriguez for a month, and more errors and issues with professionalism supposedly arose. Mora contended that when Rodriguez fired her, he told her, "I need someone younger I can pay less." A former employee stated that she had heard this conversation, adding that she heard Rodriguez say to Mora, "You are very old; you are very inept. I need somebody younger that I can pay less and I can control." Another former employee stated that Rodriguez told her and another employee that Mora was "too old to be working here anyway." Rodriguez denied that he made these statements, and one of the employees substantiated Rodriguez's version of events. Mora sued the foundation in a federal district court for wrongful termination under the Age Discrimination in Employment Act (ADEA). The foundation moved for summary judgment, arguing that regardless of the discrimination issue, Mora still would have been terminated for poor job performance. The district court granted the motion, and Mora appealed.

IN THE WORDS OF THE COURT . . .
PER CURIAM [By the Whole Court].
    * * * *

After Plaintiff [Mora] appealed, the Supreme Court, in *Gross v. FBL Financial Services,* clarified the nature of ADEA claims. The Supreme Court concluded that ADEA claims are not subject to the burden-shifting protocol set forth for Title VII suits in *Price Waterhouse v. Hopkins.*[a] The ADEA requires that "age [be] the reason that the employer decided to act." *Because an ADEA plaintiff must establish "but for" causality, no "same decision" affirmative defense [the argument that the same decision—to fire someone, for example— would have been made regardless of alleged discrimination] can*

exist: the employer either acted "because of" the plaintiff's age or it did not. [Emphasis added.]

Because the Supreme Court has excluded the whole idea of a "mixed motive" ADEA claim—and the corresponding "same decision" defense— we need not consider the district court's analysis of Defendant's [the foundation's] affirmative defense. Instead, * * * we look to determine whether a material factual question exists on this record about whether Defendant discriminated against her. We say "Yes."
    * * * *

A plaintiff in an ADEA claim may "establish a claim of illegal age discrimination through either direct evidence or circumstantial evidence." Plaintiff's testimony that Rodriguez fired her because she was "too old" was substantiated by the affidavits of two other employees of Defendant. Rodriguez and [another employee] testified that no such comments were made * * * .

The resolution of this case depends on whose account of the pertinent conversations a jury would credit. We conclude that a reasonable juror could accept that Rodriguez made the discriminatory-sounding remarks and that the remarks are sufficient evidence of a discriminatory motive which was the "but for" cause of Plaintiff's dismissal. Summary judgment for Defendant was therefore incorrect.

We have considered cases factually similar to Plaintiff's. In [one case], we concluded that statements from a county official who "didn't want to hire any old pilots" were direct evidence of discrimination * * * . In [another case], we likewise concluded that an employer's statement that he wanted "aggressive, young men like himself to be promoted" was circumstantial evidence of discrimination.

While these cases were litigated under the now-defunct ADEA mixed motive theory, they remain instructive. Plaintiff's situation is similar. A reasonable juror could find that Rodriguez's statements should be taken at face value and that he fired Plaintiff because of her age.

DECISION AND REMEDY   The U.S. Court of Appeals for the Eleventh Circuit vacated (set aside) the decision of the trial court and

---

a. 490 U.S. 228, 109 S.Ct. 1775, 104 L.Ed.2d 268 (1989).

Case 17.2–Continues next page ➡

Case 17.2–Continued

remanded the case for further proceedings. Because there was a "disputed question of material fact" as to whether Mora had been fired because of her age, Jackson Memorial was not entitled to summary judgment.

MANAGERIAL IMPLICATIONS   *Business owners and supervisory personnel should be careful to avoid statements*

regarding an employee's age that may sound discriminatory. If the employee later has to be dismissed due to poor performance, comments about his or her age may become the basis for an age discrimination lawsuit.

State Employees Not Covered by the ADEA

Generally, the states are immune from lawsuits brought by private individuals in federal court—unless a state consents to the suit. This immunity stems from the United States Supreme Court's interpretation of the Eleventh Amendment (the text of this amendment is included in Appendix B).

In two Florida cases, professors and librarians contended that their employers—two Florida state universities—denied them salary increases and other benefits because they were getting old and their successors could be hired at lower cost. The universities claimed that as agencies of a sovereign state, they could not be sued in federal court without the state's consent. The cases ultimately reached the United States Supreme Court, which held that the Eleventh Amendment bars private parties from suing state employers for violations of the ADEA.[23]

State immunity under the Eleventh Amendment is not absolute, however, as the Supreme Court explained in 2004. In some situations, such as when fundamental rights are at stake, Congress has the power to abolish state immunity to private suits through legislation that unequivocally shows Congress's intent to subject states to private suits.[24] As a general rule, though, the Court has found that state employers are immune from private suits brought by employees under the ADEA (for age discrimination, as noted above), the Americans with Disabilities Act[25] (for disability discrimination), and the Fair Labor Standards Act[26] (which relates to wages and hours). In contrast, states are not immune from the requirements of the Family and Medical Leave Act.[27]

▶ Discrimination Based on Disability

The Americans with Disabilities Act (ADA) of 1990 was designed to eliminate discriminatory employment practices that prevent otherwise qualified workers with disabilities from fully participating in the national labor force. The ADA prohibits disability-based discrimination in workplaces with fifteen or more workers (with the exception of state government employers, who are generally immune under the Eleventh Amendment, as just discussed).

Basically, the ADA requires that employers "reasonably accommodate" the needs of persons with disabilities unless to do so would cause the employer to suffer an "undue hardship." In 2008, Congress enacted the ADA Amendments Act,[28] which broadened the coverage of the ADA's protections, as will be discussed shortly.

---

23. *Kimel v. Florida Board of Regents,* 528 U.S. 62, 120 S.Ct. 631, 145 L.Ed.2d 522 (2000).
24. *Tennessee v. Lane,* 541 U.S. 509, 124 S.Ct. 1978, 158 L.Ed.2d 820 (2004).
25. *Board of Trustees of the University of Alabama v. Garrett,* 531 U.S. 356, 121 S.Ct. 955, 148 L.Ed.2d 866 (2001).
26. *Alden v. Maine,* 527 U.S. 706, 119 S.Ct. 2240, 144 L.Ed.2d 636 (1999).
27. *Nevada Department of Human Resources v. Hibbs,* 538 U.S. 721, 123 S.Ct. 1972, 155 L.Ed.2d 953 (2003).
28. 42 U.S.C. Sections 12103 and 12205a.

Procedures under the ADA

To prevail on a claim under the ADA, a plaintiff must show that he or she (1) has a disability, (2) is otherwise qualified for the employment in question, and (3) was excluded from the employment solely because of the disability. As in Title VII cases, a plaintiff must pursue her or his claim through the EEOC before filing an action in court for a violation of the ADA. The EEOC may decide to investigate and perhaps even sue the employer on behalf of the employee. If the EEOC decides not to sue, then the employee is entitled to sue in court.

Significantly, the United States Supreme Court held in 2002 that the EEOC could bring a suit against an employer for disability-based discrimination even though the employee had agreed to submit any job-related disputes to arbitration (see Chapter 2). The Court reasoned that because the EEOC was not a party to the arbitration agreement, the agreement was not binding on the EEOC.[29]

Plaintiffs in lawsuits brought under the ADA may obtain many of the same remedies available under Title VII. These include reinstatement, back pay, a limited amount of compensatory and punitive damages (for intentional discrimination), and certain other forms of relief. Repeat violators may be ordered to pay fines of up to $100,000.

What Is a Disability?

The ADA is broadly drafted to cover persons with a wide range of disabilities. Specifically, the ADA defines *disability* to include any of the following:

1. A physical or mental impairment that substantially limits one or more of an individual's major life activities.
2. A record of such impairment.
3. Being regarded as having such an impairment.

Health conditions that have been considered disabilities under the federal law include blindness, alcoholism, heart disease, cancer, muscular dystrophy, cerebral palsy, paraplegia, diabetes, acquired immune deficiency syndrome (AIDS), testing positive for the human immunodeficiency virus (HIV), and morbid obesity (defined as existing when an individual's weight is two times the normal weight for his or her height).

A separate provision in the ADA prevents employers from taking adverse employment actions based on stereotypes or assumptions about individuals who associate with people who have disabilities.[30]

At one time, the courts focused on whether a person was disabled *after* the use of corrective devices or medication. With this approach, a person with severe myopia, or nearsightedness, which can be corrected with lenses, for instance, would not qualify as disabled because that individual's major life activities were not substantially impaired. In 2008, Congress amended the ADA to strengthen its protections and prohibit employers from considering mitigating measures or medications when determining if an individual has a disability. Disability is now determined on a case-by-case basis.

A condition may fit the definition of disability in one set of circumstances, but not in another. What makes the difference in an individual situation? The court in the following case answered that question.

"Jobs are physically easier, but the worker now takes home worries instead of an aching back."

Homer Bigart, 1907–1991
(American journalist)

---

29. *EEOC v. Waffle House, Inc.,* 534 U.S. 279, 122 S.Ct. 754, 151 L.Ed.2d 755 (2002).
30. 42 U.S.C. Section 12112(b)(4). Under this provision, an employer cannot, for instance, refuse to hire the parent of a child with a disability based on the assumption that the parent will miss work too often or be unreliable.

Case 17.3   **Rohr v. Salt River Project Agricultural Improvement and Power District**

United States Court of Appeals, Ninth Circuit, 555 F.3d 850 (2009).

BACKGROUND AND FACTS   Larry Rohr has type 2 diabetes. Type 2 results from the body's failure to properly use insulin. If left untreated, type 2 can cause seizures and a coma. Rohr tires quickly and suffers from high blood pressure, deteriorating vision, and loss of feeling in his hands and feet. Insulin injections, other medicine, blood tests, and a strict diet are fixtures of his daily life. If he fails to follow this regimen, his blood sugar rises to a level that aggravates his disease. At the time of his diagnosis, he was a welding metallurgy specialist for the Salt River Project Agricultural Improvement and Power District, which provides utility services to homes in Arizona. Due to the effort required to manage his diabetes, particularly his strict diet schedule, Rohr's physician forbade his assignment to tasks involving overnight, out-of-town travel. Salt River told Rohr that this would prevent him from performing the essential functions of his job, such as responding to power outages. Rohr was asked to transfer, apply for disability benefits, or take early retirement. He filed a suit in a federal district court against Salt River, alleging discrimination. The court issued a summary judgment in the employer's favor. Rohr appealed.

IN THE WORDS OF THE COURT . . .
BAER, Senior District Judge:
* * * *

The ADA defines "disability," in pertinent part, as "a physical or mental impairment that substantially limits one or more of the major life activities of such individual." Diabetes is a "physical impairment" because it affects the digestive, hemic [blood] and endocrine systems, and eating is a "major life activity." Whether Rohr's diabetes substantially limits his eating is an individualized inquiry. *Once an impairment is found, the issue is whether Rohr's diabetes substantially limits his activity of eating.* [Emphasis added.]
* * * *

To determine whether an insulin-dependent type 2 diabetic like Rohr is substantially limited in his eating, we must compare the condition, manner or duration under which he can eat as compared to the condition, manner or duration under which the average person in the general population can eat.

* * * *

Finally, we must consider not only whether the symptoms of Rohr's diabetes substantially limit one of his major life activities, but also whether his efforts to mitigate [diminish] the disease constitute a substantial limitation.
* * * *

* * * For people like Rohr, who must treat their diabetes with insulin, the failure to take insulin will result in severe problems and eventually death. Insulin injections themselves can be dangerous. * * * It is difficult to determine how much insulin to take, as the necessary amount varies depending on the food and activity level. * * * To obtain the appropriate balance, Rohr must test his blood glucose levels * * * numerous times a day.

If daily insulin injections alone more or less stabilized Rohr's blood sugar levels, such that any limitation imposed on his diet would be minor, then Rohr's major life activity of eating might not be substantially limited. However, [there are] substantial limitations on his eating in spite of his medicine and insulin. He must snack regularly, plan his daily schedule around his diet, avoid skipping meals and eat immediately when he feels dizzy or light-headed. * * * Straying from a diet for more than one or two meals is not a cause for medical concern for most people, and skipping a meal, or eating a large one, does not expose them to the risk of fainting. * * * For Rohr, the effort required to control his diet is itself substantially limiting.

DECISION AND REMEDY   The U.S. Court of Appeals for the Ninth Circuit vacated the lower court's judgment and remanded the case for trial. Diabetes satisfies the ADA's definition of *disability* if it significantly restricts an individual's eating habits.

THE E-COMMERCE DIMENSION   *If Rohr could have monitored his condition and regimen through a cell phone or other portable Internet connection, would the result in this case likely have been affected? Explain.*

Reasonable Accommodation

The ADA does not require that employers accommodate the needs of job applicants or employees with disabilities who are not otherwise qualified for the work. If a job applicant or an employee with a disability, with reasonable accommodation, can perform essential job functions, however, the employer must make the accommodation.

Required modifications may include installing ramps for a wheelchair, establishing more flexible working hours, creating or modifying job assignments, and creating or improving training materials and procedures. Generally, employers should give primary consideration to employees' preferences in deciding what accommodations should be made.

UNDUE HARDSHIP   Employers who do not accommodate the needs of persons with disabilities must demonstrate that the accommodations would cause "undue hardship" in terms of being significantly difficult or expensive for the employer. Usually, the courts decide whether an accommodation constitutes an undue hardship on a case-by-case basis by looking at the employer's resources in relation to the specific accommodation.

EXAMPLE 17.12   Bryan Lockhart, who uses a wheelchair, works for a cell phone company that provides parking for its employees. Lockhart informs the company supervisors that the parking spaces are so narrow that he is unable to extend the ramp on his van that allows him to get in and out of the vehicle. Lockhart therefore requests that the company reasonably accommodate his needs by paying a monthly fee for him to use a larger parking space in an adjacent lot. In this situation, a court would likely find that it would not be an undue hardship for the employer to pay for additional parking for Lockhart. ●

JOB APPLICATIONS AND PREEMPLOYMENT PHYSICAL EXAMS   Employers must modify their job-application process so that those with disabilities can compete for jobs with those who do not have disabilities. For instance, a job announcement might be modified to allow job applicants to respond by e-mail or letter, as well as by telephone, so that it does not discriminate against potential applicants with hearing impairments.

Employers are restricted in the kinds of questions they may ask on job-application forms and during preemployment interviews. Furthermore, they cannot require persons with disabilities to submit to preemployment physicals unless such exams are required of all other applicants. An employer can condition an offer of employment on the applicant's successfully passing a medical examination, but can disqualify the applicant only if the exam reveals medical problems that would render the applicant unable to perform the job.

EXAMPLE 17.13   Jennings Transportation, Inc., needs to hire a truck driver. When filling this position, Jennings cannot screen out all of the applicants who are unable to meet the U.S. Department of Transportation's hearing standard. Jennings would have to first prove that (1) drivers who are deaf are not qualified to perform the essential job function of driving safely and (2) these drivers pose a higher risk of accidents than drivers who can hear. ●

SUBSTANCE ABUSERS   Drug addiction is a disability under the ADA because drug addiction is a substantially limiting impairment. Those who are actually using illegal drugs are not protected by the act, however. The ADA protects only persons with *former* drug addictions—those who have completed or are now in a supervised drug-rehabilitation program. Individuals who have used drugs casually in the past are not protected under the act. They are not considered addicts and therefore do not have a disability (addiction).

People suffering from alcoholism are protected by the ADA. Employers cannot legally discriminate against employees simply because they are suffering from alcoholism. Of course, employers have the right to prohibit the use of alcohol in the workplace and can require that employees not be under the influence of alcohol while working. Employers can also fire or refuse to hire a person who is an alcoholic if he or she poses a substantial risk of harm either to himself or herself or to others and the risk cannot be reduced by reasonable accommodation.

HEALTH-INSURANCE PLANS   Workers with disabilities must be given equal access to any health insurance provided to other employees. Under 2010 health-care reforms, employers cannot exclude preexisting health conditions from coverage. An employer can put a limit, or cap, on health-care payments under its group health policy—as long as such caps are "applied equally to all insured employees" and do not "discriminate on the basis of disability." Whenever a group health-care plan makes a disability-based distinction in its benefits, the plan violates the ADA (unless the employer can justify its actions under the *business necessity* defense, which will be discussed next).

Defenses to Employment Discrimination

LEARNING OBJECTIVE 4 **What are three defenses to claims of employment discrimination?**

The first line of defense for an employer charged with employment discrimination is, of course, to assert that the plaintiff has failed to meet his or her initial burden of proving that discrimination occurred. Once a plaintiff succeeds in proving that discrimination occurred, the burden shifts to the employer to justify the discriminatory practice.

Often, employers attempt to justify the discrimination by claiming that it was the result of a business necessity, a bona fide occupational qualification, or a seniority system. In some cases, as noted earlier, an effective antiharassment policy and prompt remedial action when harassment occurs may shield employers from liability for sexual harassment under Title VII.

Business Necessity

Business Necessity An employment practice that discriminates against members of a protected class but is necessary for job performance.

An employer may defend against a claim of disparate-impact (unintentional) discrimination by asserting that a practice that has a discriminatory effect is a **business necessity.** For instance, if requiring a high school diploma is shown to have a discriminatory effect, an employer might argue that a high school education is necessary for workers to perform the job at a required level of competence. If the employer can demonstrate to the court's satisfaction that a definite connection exists between a high school education and job performance, the employer normally will succeed in this business necessity defense.

Bona Fide Occupational Qualification

Bona Fide Occupational Qualification (BFOQ) An identifiable characteristic reasonably necessary to the normal operation of a particular business.

Another defense applies when discrimination against a protected class is essential to a job—that is, when a particular trait is a **bona fide occupational qualification (BFOQ).** Race, however, can never be a BFOQ. Generally, courts have restricted the BFOQ defense to instances in which the employee's gender is essential to the job. **EXAMPLE 17.14** Urban Minxx, a women's clothing store, might legitimately hire only female sales attendants if part of an attendant's job involves assisting clients in the store's dressing rooms. ●

Seniority Systems

Seniority System A system in which those who have worked longest for the employer are first in line for promotions, salary increases, and other benefits.

An employer with a history of discrimination might have no members of protected classes in upper-level positions. Even if the employer now seeks to be unbiased, it may face a lawsuit in which the plaintiff asks a court to order that minorities be promoted ahead of schedule to compensate for past discrimination. If no present intent to discriminate is shown, however, and if promotions or other job benefits are distributed according to a fair **seniority system** (in which workers with more years of service are promoted first or laid off last), the employer normally has a good defense against the suit.

According to the United States Supreme Court, this defense may also apply to alleged discrimination under the ADA. The case involved a baggage handler who had injured his back and requested an assignment to a different position at U.S. Airways, Inc. The airline refused to give the employee the position because another employee had seniority. The Court sided with U.S. Airways. If an employee with a disability requests an accommodation that conflicts with an employer's seniority system, the accommodation generally will not be considered "reasonable" under the act.[31]

After-Acquired Evidence of Employee Misconduct

In some situations, employers have attempted to avoid liability for employment discrimination on the basis of *after-acquired evidence*—that is, evidence that the employer discovers after a lawsuit is filed—of an employee's misconduct.

EXAMPLE 17.15   Baylor Industrial, Inc., fires Eileen, who then sues Baylor for employment discrimination. During pretrial investigation, Baylor learns that Eileen made material misrepresentations on her employment application—misrepresentations that, had Baylor known about them, would have served as grounds to fire Eileen. •

According to the United States Supreme Court, after-acquired evidence of wrongdoing cannot be used to shield an employer entirely from liability for employment discrimination. It may, however, be used to limit the amount of damages for which the employer is liable.[32]

▶ Affirmative Action

Affirmative Action Job-hiring policies that give special consideration to members of protected classes in an effort to overcome present effects of past discrimination.

Federal statutes and regulations providing for equal opportunity in the workplace were designed to reduce or eliminate discriminatory practices with respect to hiring, retaining, and promoting employees. **Affirmative action** programs go a step further and attempt to "make up" for past patterns of discrimination by giving members of protected classes preferential treatment in hiring or promotion. During the 1960s, all federal and state government agencies, private companies that contracted to do business with the federal government, and institutions that received federal funding were required to implement affirmative action policies.

Title VII of the Civil Rights Act of 1964 neither requires nor prohibits affirmative action. Thus, most private firms have not been required to implement affirmative action policies, though many have voluntarily done so. Affirmative action programs have been controversial, however, particularly when they have resulted in reverse discrimination (discussed on page 438).

Constitutionality of Affirmative Action Programs

Because of their inherently discriminatory nature, affirmative action programs may violate the equal protection clause of the Fourteenth Amendment to the U.S. Constitution. The United States Supreme Court has held that any federal, state, or local affirmative action program that uses racial or ethnic classifications as the basis for making decisions is subject to strict scrutiny by the courts.[33] Recall from Chapter 4 that strict scrutiny is the highest standard, which means that most programs do not survive a court's analysis under this test.

Today, an affirmative action program normally is constitutional only if it attempts to remedy past discrimination and does not make use of quotas or preferences. Furthermore, once such a program has succeeded in the goal of remedying past discrimination, it must be changed or dropped.

---

31. *U.S. Airways, Inc. v. Barnett,* 535 U.S. 391, 122 S.Ct. 1516, 152 L.Ed.2d 589 (2002).

32. *McKennon v. Nashville Banner Publishing Co.,* 513 U.S. 352, 115 S.Ct. 879, 130 L.Ed.2d 852 (1995).

33. See the landmark decision in *Adarand Constructors, Inc. v. Peña,* 515 U.S. 200, 115 S.Ct. 2097, 132 L.Ed.2d 158 (1995).

Affirmative Action in Schools

Most of the affirmative action cases that have reached the United States Supreme Court in the last twenty years have been in the context of university admissions programs and schools, rather than employment. Generally, the Court has found that a school admissions policy that *automatically* awards minority applicants a specified number of points needed to guarantee admission violates the equal protection clause.[34]

A school can, however, "consider race or ethnicity more flexibly as a 'plus' factor in the context of individualized consideration of each and every applicant."[35] In other words, it is unconstitutional for schools to apply a mechanical formula that gives "diversity bonuses" based on race or ethnicity.

CASE EXAMPLE 17.16   In 2007, the United States Supreme Court ruled on two cases involving the use of racial classifications in assigning students to schools in Seattle, Washington, and Jefferson County, Kentucky. Both school districts had adopted student assignment plans that relied on race to determine which schools certain children would attend. The Seattle school district plan classified children as "white" or "nonwhite" and used the racial classifications as a "tiebreaker" to determine which high school the students would attend. The school district in Jefferson County classified students as "black" or "other" to assign children to elementary schools. Parent groups from the relevant public schools filed lawsuits claiming that the racial preferences violated the equal protection clause. The Court held that the school districts failed to show that the use of racial classifications in their student assignment plans was necessary to achieve their stated goal of racial diversity. Hence, the Court found that the affirmative action programs of both school districts were unconstitutional.[36] ●

---

34. *Gratz v. Bollinger,* 539 U.S. 244, 123 S.Ct. 2411, 156 L.Ed.2d 257 (2003).
35. *Grutter v. Bollinger,* 539 U.S. 306, 123 S.Ct. 2325, 156 L.Ed.2d 304 (2003).
36. The Court consolidated the two cases and issued one opinion for both. *See Parents Involved in Community Schools v. Seattle School District No. 1,* 551 U.S. 701, 127 S.Ct. 2738, 168 L.Ed.2d 508 (2007).

 Reviewing . . . Employment Discrimination

Amaani Lyle, an African American woman, took a job as a scriptwriters' assistant at Warner Television Productions. She worked for the writers of *Weeds,* a popular, adult-oriented television series. One of her essential job duties was to type detailed notes for the scriptwriters during brainstorming sessions in which they discussed jokes, dialogue, and story lines. The writers then combed through Lyle's notes after the meetings for script material. During these meetings, the three male scriptwriters told lewd and vulgar jokes and made sexually explicit comments and gestures. They often talked about their personal sexual experiences and fantasies, and some of these conversations were then used in episodes of *Weeds.*

During the meetings, Lyle never complained that she found the writers' conduct offensive. After four months, she was fired because she could not type fast enough to keep up with the writers' conversations during the meetings. She filed a suit against Warner alleging sexual harassment and claiming that her termination was based on racial discrimination. Using the information presented in the chapter, answer the following questions.

1. Would Lyle's claim of racial discrimination be for intentional (disparate treatment) or unintentional (disparate impact) discrimination? Explain.
2. Can Lyle establish a *prima facie* case of racial discrimination? Why or why not?
3. Lyle was told when she was hired that typing speed was extremely important to her position. At the time, she maintained that she could type eighty words per minute, so she was not given a typing test. It later turned out that Lyle could type only fifty words per minute. What impact might typing speed have on Lyle's lawsuit?
4. Lyle's sexual-harassment claim is based on the hostile work environment created by the writers' sexually offensive conduct at meetings that she was required to attend. The writers, however, argue that their behavior was essential to the "creative process" of writing *Weeds,* a show that routinely contained sexual innuendos and adult humor. Which defense discussed in the chapter might Warner assert using this argument?

Debate This

Members of minority groups and women have made enough economic progress in the last several decades that they no longer need special legislation to protect them.

Linking the Law *to Management*

Human Resource Management

Your career may lead to running a small business, managing a small part of a larger business, or making decisions for the operations of a big business. In any context, you may be responsible for employment decisions. As this chapter has suggested, an ill-conceived hiring or firing process can lead to a lawsuit. As a manager, you must also ensure that employees do not practice discrimination on the job. Enter the human resource management specialist.

What Is Human Resource Management?

Human resource management (HRM) is the acquisition, maintenance, and development of an organization's employees. HRM involves the design and application of formal systems in an organization to ensure the effective and efficient use of human talent to accomplish organizational goals.

All managers need to be skilled in HRM. Some firms require managers to play an active role in recruiting and selecting personnel, as well as in developing training programs. Those who work in a human resources department should be especially aware of the issues outlined in this chapter (and in Chapter 16).

The Acquisition Phase of HRM

Acquiring talented employees is the first step in an HRM system. All recruitment must be done without violating any of the laws and regulations outlined in this chapter. Obviously, recruitment must be colorblind, as well as indifferent to gender, religion, national origin, and age. Devise recruitment methods that do not have even the slightest hint of discriminatory basis. Recruitment methods must also give an equal chance to people with disabilities. Only the applicant's qualifications can be considered, not his or her disability.

If a candidate with a disability is rejected, make sure to document that the rejection is based solely on the applicant's lack of training or ability.

On-the-Job HRM Issues

In addition, the HRM professional must also monitor the working environment. Sexual harassment is a major concern. You may need to work closely with an employment law specialist to develop antiharassment rules and policies. You also need to publish them and provide training to ensure that all employees are familiar with the firm's policy. In addition, you should create and supervise a grievance system so that any harassment can be stopped before it becomes actionable.

HRM Issues concerning Employee Termination

Even in employment-at-will jurisdictions, lawsuits can arise for improper termination. Develop a system to protect your company from lawsuits, such as procedures for documenting an employee's misconduct and the employer's warnings or other disciplinary actions. The company should also have an established policy for dealing with improper or incompetent behavior, and should be clear about the amount of severance pay that terminated employees will receive. Sometimes, it is better to err on the side of generosity to maintain the goodwill of terminated employees.

FOR CRITICAL ANALYSIS
What are some types of actions that an HRM professional can take to reduce the probability of harassment lawsuits against her or his company?

Key Terms

affirmative action 453
bona fide occupational
    qualification (BFOQ) 452
business necessity 452
constructive discharge 441

disparate-impact discrimination 437
disparate-treatment discrimination 436
employment discrimination 436
prima facie case 437
protected class 435

seniority system 452
sexual harassment 442
tangible employment action 442

Chapter Summary: Employment Discrimination

Title VII of the Civil Rights Act of 1964 (See pages 436–446.)	Title VII prohibits employment discrimination based on race, color, national origin, religion, or gender. 1. *Procedures*—Employees must file a claim with the Equal Employment Opportunity Commission (EEOC). The EEOC may sue the employer on the employee's behalf. If it does not, the employee may sue the employer directly. 2. *Types of discrimination*—Title VII prohibits both intentional (disparate-treatment) and unintentional (disparate-impact) discrimination. Disparate-impact discrimination occurs when an employer's practice, such as hiring only persons with a certain level of education, has the effect of discriminating against a class of persons protected by Title VII. Title VII also extends to discriminatory practices, such as various forms of harassment, in the online environment. 3. *Remedies for discrimination under Title VII*—If a plaintiff proves that unlawful discrimination occurred, he or she may be awarded reinstatement, back pay, and retroactive promotions. Damages (both compensatory and punitive) may be awarded for intentional discrimination.
Discrimination Based on Age (See pages 446–448.)	The Age Discrimination in Employment Act (ADEA) of 1967 prohibits employment discrimination on the basis of age against individuals forty years of age or older. Procedures for bringing a case under the ADEA are similar to those for bringing a case under Title VII.
Discrimination Based on Disability (See pages 448–452.)	The Americans with Disabilities Act (ADA) of 1990 prohibits employment discrimination against persons with disabilities who are otherwise qualified to perform the essential functions of the jobs for which they apply. 1. *Procedures and remedies*—To prevail on a claim under the ADA, the plaintiff must show that she or he has a disability, is otherwise qualified for the employment in question, and was excluded from the employment solely because of the disability. Procedures under the ADA are similar to those required in Title VII cases. Remedies are also similar to those under Title VII. 2. *Definition of disability*—The ADA defines *disability* as a physical or mental impairment that substantially limits one or more major life activities, a record of such impairment, or being regarded as having such an impairment. 3. *Reasonable accommodation*—Employers are required to reasonably accommodate the needs of persons with disabilities. Reasonable accommodations may include altering job-application procedures, modifying the physical work environment, and permitting more flexible work schedules. Employers are not required to accommodate the needs of all workers with disabilities.
Defenses to Employment Discrimination (See pages 452–453.)	If a plaintiff proves that employment discrimination occurred, employers may avoid liability by successfully asserting certain defenses. Employers may assert that the discrimination was required for reasons of business necessity, to meet a bona fide occupational qualification, or to maintain a legitimate seniority system. Evidence of prior employee misconduct acquired after the employee has been fired is not a defense to discrimination.
Affirmative Action (See pages 453–454.)	Affirmative action programs attempt to "make up" for past patterns of discrimination by giving members of protected classes preferential treatment in hiring or promotion.

ExamPrep

ISSUE SPOTTERS

—Check your answers to these questions against the answers provided in Appendix D at the end of this text.

1. Ruth is a supervisor for Subs & Suds, a restaurant. Tim is a Subs & Suds employee. The owner announces that some employees will be discharged. Ruth tells Tim that if he has sex with her, he can keep his job. Is this sexual harassment? Why or why not? **(See page 442.)**

2. Koko, a person with a disability, applies for a job at Lively Sales Corporation for which she is well qualified, but she is rejected. Lively continues to seek applicants and eventually fills the position with a person who does not have a disability. Could Koko succeed in a suit against Lively for discrimination? Explain. **(See page 449.)**

BEFORE THE TEST

Go to **www.cengagebrain.com**, enter the ISBN 9781133586548, and click on "Find" to locate this textbook's Web site. Then click on "Access Now" under "Study Tools," and select Chapter 17 at the top. There, you will find a Practice Quiz that you can take to assess your mastery of the concepts in this chapter. Additionally, you will find Flashcards and a Glossary of important terms, as well as Video Questions (when assigned).

 For Review

Answers for the even-numbered questions in this **For Review** *section can be found in Appendix E at the end of this text.*

1. Generally, what kind of conduct is prohibited by Title VII of the Civil Rights Act of 1964, as amended?
2. What is the difference between disparate-treatment discrimination and disparate-impact discrimination?
3. What federal act prohibits discrimination based on age?
4. What are three defenses to claims of employment discrimination?

 Questions and Case Problems

17–1. Title VII Violations. Discuss fully whether either of the following actions would constitute a violation of Title VII of the 1964 Civil Rights Act, as amended. **(See pages 436–438, 452.)**

1. Tennington, Inc., is a consulting firm and has ten employees. These employees travel on consulting jobs in seven states. Tennington has an employment record of hiring only white males.

2. Novo Films, Inc., is making a film about Africa and needs to employ approximately one hundred extras for this picture. To hire these extras, Novo advertises in all major newspapers in Southern California. The ad states that only African Americans need apply.

17–2. Question with Sample Answer: Discrimination Based on Religion. When Kayla Caldwell got a job as a cashier at a Costco store, she wore multiple pierced earrings and had four tattoos, but she had no facial piercings. Over the next two years, Caldwell engaged in various forms of body modification, including facial piercing and cutting. Then Costco revised its dress code to prohibit all facial jewelry, except earrings. Caldwell was told that she would have to remove her facial jewelry. She asked for a complete exemption from the code, asserting that she was a member of the Church of Body Modification and that eyebrow piercing was part of her religion. She was told to remove the jewelry, cover it, or go home. She went home and was later discharged for her absence. Based on these facts, will Caldwell be successful in a lawsuit against Costco for religious discrimination in violation of Title VII? Does an employer have an obligation to accommodate its employees' religious practices? If so, to what extent? **(See page 439.)**

—For a sample answer to Question 17–2, go to Appendix F at the end of this text.

17–3. Spotlight on the Civil Rights Act: Discrimination Based on Gender. Burlington Coat Factory Warehouse, Inc., had a dress code that required male salesclerks to wear business attire consisting of slacks, shirt, and a necktie. Female salesclerks, by contrast, were required to wear a smock so that customers could readily identify them. Karen O'Donnell and other female employees refused to wear the smock. Instead they reported to work in business attire and were suspended. After numerous suspensions, the female employees were fired for violating Burlington's dress code policy. All other conditions of employment, including salary, hours, and benefits, were the same for female and male employees. Was the dress code policy discriminatory? Why or why not? [*O'Donnell v. Burlington Coat Factory Warehouse, Inc.,* 656 F.Supp. 263 (S.D. Ohio 1987)] **(See page 440.)**

17–4. Defenses to Employment Discrimination. The Milwaukee County Juvenile Detention Center established a new policy that required each unit of the facility to be staffed at all times by at least one officer of the same gender as the detainees housed at a unit. The purpose of the policy, administrators said, was to reduce the likelihood of sexual abuse of juveniles by officers of the other gender. Because there were many more male units in the center than female units, the policy had the effect of reducing the number of shifts available for women officers and increasing the number of shifts for men. Two female officers sued for gender discrimination. The district court held for the county, finding that the policy of assignment was based on a bona fide occupational qualification (BFOQ) and so was not illegal gender discrimination. The officers appealed. What would be evidence that the county had a valid BFOQ? [*Henry v. Milwaukee County,* 539 F.3d 573 (7th Cir. 2008)] **(See page 452.)**

17–5. Discrimination Based on Gender. Brenda Lewis worked for two years at Heartland Inns of America, LLC, and gradually worked her way up the management ladder. Lewis, who described herself as a tomboy, was commended for her good work. When she moved to a different Heartland hotel, the director of operations, Barbara Cullinan, told one of the owners that Lewis was not a "good fit" for the front desk because she was not feminine enough. Cullinan told various people that the hotel wanted "pretty" girls at the front desk. Explaining to Lewis that her hiring had not been done properly, Cullinan said Lewis would need to perform another interview. Cullinan fired Lewis soon after the interview. The reason given in a letter was that Lewis was hostile during the interview process. Lewis sued Heartland for discrimination based on unlawful gender stereotyping. The district court dismissed the suit. Lewis appealed. Does her claim fall under Title VII's restriction on discrimination based on gender? Why or why not? [*Lewis v. Heartland Inns of America, LLC,* 591 F.3d 1033 (8th Cir. 2010)] **(See page 440.)**

17–6. **Case Problem with Sample Answer: Retaliation.** Entek International, an Oregon-based company, hired Shane Dawson, a male homosexual, as a temporary production-line worker. Dawson worked with twenty-four other employees, all male. Certain individuals at work began making derogatory comments about Dawson's sexual orientation, calling him a "fag," a "homo," and a "worthless queer." Oregon law prohibits discrimination based on sexual orientation. Dawson asked his supervisor, Troy Guzon, to do something about the treatment he was receiving, but Guzon did not. In fact, Guzon also made derogatory comments about Dawson's sexual orientation. Dawson began to experience stress, and his work deteriorated. As a result of this situation, he went to the human resources department and filed a complaint. Two days later, he was fired. Dawson initiated a lawsuit, claiming that he had been fired in retaliation for filing a complaint, but the district court granted Entek a summary judgment. Dawson appealed. How should the federal appellate court rule? Has Dawson established a claim for retaliatory discharge? Should his case be allowed to go forward to a trial? Explain. [*Dawson v. Entek International,* 630 F.3d 928 (9th Cir. 2011)] **(See pages 443–445.)**

—**For a sample answer to Case Problem 17–6, go to Appendix G at the end of this text.**

17–7. **Sexual Harassment.** Billie Bradford worked for the Kentucky Department of Community Based Services (DCBS). One of Bradford's co-workers, Lisa Stander, routinely engaged in extreme sexual behavior (such as touching herself and making crude comments) in Bradford's presence. Bradford and others regularly complained about Stander's conduct to their supervisor, Angie Taylor. Rather than resolve the problem, Taylor nonchalantly told Stander to stop, encouraged Bradford to talk to Stander, and suggested that Stander was just having fun. Assuming that Bradford was subjected to a hostile work environment, could DCBS be liable? Why or why not? [*Bradford v. Department of Community Based Services,* 2012 WL 360032 (E.D.Ky. 2012)] **(See pages 442–445.)**

17–8. **In Your Court: Age Discrimination.** Ted Rhodes sold oil-field equipment for Anson Oil Tools. When he was discharged in 2008 at age fifty-six, he was told that the discharge was part of a reduction in the workforce and that he would be considered for reemployment. Within six weeks, Anson hired a forty-two-year-old person to do the

same job. Rhodes brought a suit against Anson in a federal district court, claiming that the real reason he was discharged was age discrimination. At the trial, Anson offered as a defense Rhodes's "poor work performance" but did not present any company sales records or goals. Rhodes countered with customers' testimony about his expertise and diligence. The jury found that Rhodes was discharged because of his age. Anson appealed the decision. Assume that you are a judge on the federal appellate court reviewing this case and answer the following questions: **(See pages 446–447.)**

1. Remember that as an appellate court judge, you should defer to the trial court's findings of fact—unless you conclude that there is no justification for the trial court's findings. Thus, the question you need to decide is whether a reasonable jury could have found that Rhodes was a victim of age discrimination in violation of the Age Discrimination in Employment Act (ADEA). How will you answer this question? Why?

2. Does it matter that Rhodes's replacement was also a member of the class of persons protected by the ADEA? Will your answer to this question affect your answer to Question 1?

17–9. **A Question of Ethics: Discrimination Based on Disability.** *Titan Distribution, Inc., employed Quintak, Inc., to run its tire mounting and distribution operation in Des Moines, Iowa. Robert Chalfant worked for Quintak as a second-shift supervisor at Titan. He suffered a heart attack in 1992 and underwent heart bypass surgery in 1997. He also had arthritis. In July 2002, Titan decided to terminate Quintak. Chalfant applied to work at Titan. On his application, he described himself as having a disability. After a physical exam, Titan's doctor concluded that Chalfant could work in his current capacity, and he was notified that he would be hired. Despite the notice, Nadis Barucic, a Titan employee, wrote "not pass px" at the top of Chalfant's application, and he was not hired. He took a job with AMPCO Systems, a parking ramp management company. This work involved walking up to five miles a day and lifting more weight than he had at Titan. In September, Titan eliminated its second shift. Chalfant filed a suit in a federal district court against Titan, in part, under the Americans with Disabilities Act (ADA). Titan argued that the reason it had not hired Chalfant was not that he did not pass the physical, but no one—including Barucic—could explain why she had written "not pass px" on his application. Later, Titan claimed that Chalfant was not hired because the entire second shift was going to be eliminated.* [*Chalfant v. Titan Distribution, Inc., 475 F.3d 982 (8th Cir. 2007)*] **(See pages 448–451.)**

1. What must Chalfant establish to make his case under the ADA? Can he meet these requirements? Explain.

2. In employment-discrimination cases, punitive damages can be appropriate when an employer acts with malice or reckless indifference to an employee's protected rights. Would an award of punitive damages to Chalfant be appropriate in this case? Discuss.

The Regulatory Environment

(spxChrome)

Chapter 18

Environmental Law

> "Man, however, much he may like to pretend the contrary, is part of nature."
>
> —Rachel Carson, 1907–1964
> (American writer and conservationist)

Contents

Learning Objectives

The five Learning Objectives below are designed to help improve your understanding of the chapter. After reading this chapter, you should be able to answer the following questions:

1. **Under what common law theories can polluters be held liable?**
2. **What does the Environmental Protection Agency do?**
3. **What is an environmental impact statement, and who must file one?**
4. **What major federal statutes regulate air and water pollution?**
5. **What is Superfund? What categories of persons are liable under Superfund?**

(spxChrome)

As the chapter-opening quotation above observes, we are all "part of nature." Consequently, concern over the degradation of the environment has increased over time in response to the environmental effects of population growth, urbanization, and industrialization. Environmental protection is not without a price, however. For many businesses, the costs of complying with environmental regulations are high, and for some they may seem too high. A constant tension exists between the desirability of increasing profits and productivity and the need to protect the environment.

To a great extent, environmental law consists of statutes passed by federal, state, or local governments and regulations issued by administrative agencies. Before examining statutory and regulatory environmental laws, however, we look at the remedies against environmental pollution that are available under the common law.

▶ Common Law Actions

LEARNING OBJECTIVE 1 Under what common law theories can polluters be held liable?

Common law remedies against environmental pollution originated centuries ago in England. Those responsible for operations that created dirt, smoke, noxious odors, noise, or toxic substances were sometimes held liable under common law theories of nuisance or negligence. Today, injured individuals continue to rely on the common law to obtain damages and injunctions against business polluters.

Nuisance

Nuisance A common law doctrine under which persons may be held liable for using their property in a manner that unreasonably interferes with others' rights to use or enjoy their own property.

Under the common law doctrine of **nuisance,** persons may be held liable if they use their property in a manner that unreasonably interferes with others' rights to use or enjoy their own property. In these situations, the courts commonly balance the harm caused by the pollution against the costs of stopping it.

Courts have often refused to issue an injunction prohibiting the pollution altogether on the ground that the hardships that would be imposed on the polluter and on the community are relatively greater than the hardships suffered by the plaintiff.

EXAMPLE 18.1 Hewitt's Factory causes neighboring landowners to suffer from smoke, soot, and vibrations. The factory, however, may be left in operation if it is the core of the local economy. The injured parties may be awarded only monetary damages, which may include compensation for the decrease in the value of their property caused by Hewitt's operation. ●

Under the common law, individuals were denied *standing* (access to the courts—see Chapter 2) unless they suffered a harm distinct from the harm suffered by the public at large. In some states, a property owner still may not bring a nuisance action unless she or he can identify a "private nuisance"—a distinct harm separate from that affecting the general public. A public authority (such as a state's attorney general), though, can sue to abate a "public" nuisance.

Negligence and Strict Liability

An injured party may sue a business polluter in tort under the negligence and strict liability theories discussed in Chapter 6. The basis for a negligence action is the business's alleged failure to use reasonable care toward the party whose injury was foreseeable and was caused by the lack of reasonable care. For instance, employees might sue an employer whose failure to use proper pollution controls contaminated the air and caused the employees to suffer respiratory illnesses. Lawsuits for personal injuries caused by exposure to a toxic substance, such as asbestos, radiation, or hazardous waste, have given rise to a growing body of tort law known as **toxic torts.**

Toxic Tort A civil wrong arising from exposure to a toxic substance, such as asbestos, radiation, or hazardous waste.

Businesses that engage in ultrahazardous activities—such as the transportation of radioactive materials—are strictly liable for any injuries the activities cause. In a strict liability action, the injured party does not need to prove that the business failed to exercise reasonable care.

▶ Federal, State, and Local Regulations

All levels of government in the United States regulate some aspect of the environment. In this section, we look at some of the ways in which the federal, state, and local governments control business activities and land use in the interests of environmental preservation and protection.

Federal Regulations

Congress has enacted a number of statutes to control the impact of human activities on the environment. Exhibit 18–1 on the next page lists and summarizes some major federal environmental statutes. Some of these laws have been passed in an attempt to improve the quality of air and water. Other laws specifically regulate toxic chemicals, including pesticides, herbicides, and hazardous wastes.

LEARNING OBJECTIVE 2 | What does the Environmental Protection Agency do?

ENVIRONMENTAL REGULATORY AGENCIES The primary agency regulating environmental law is, of course, the Environmental Protection Agency (EPA). Other

• *Exhibit* 18–1 **Major Federal Environmental Statutes**

POPULAR NAME	PURPOSE	STATUTE REFERENCE
Rivers and Harbors Appropriations Act (1899)	To prohibit ships and manufacturers from discharging and depositing refuse in navigable waterways.	33 U.S.C. Sections 401–418.
Federal Insecticide, Fungicide, and Rodenticide Act (1947)	To control the use of pesticides and herbicides.	7 U.S.C. Sections 136–136y.
Federal Water Pollution Control Act (1948)	To eliminate the discharge of pollutants from major sources into navigable waters.	33 U.S.C. Sections 1251–1387.
Clean Air Act (1963, 1970)	To control air pollution from mobile and stationary sources.	42 U.S.C. Sections 7401–7671q.
National Environmental Policy Act (1969)	To limit environmental harm from federal government activities.	42 U.S.C. Sections 4321–4370d.
Ocean Dumping Act (1972)	To prohibit the dumping of radiological, chemical, and biological warfare agents and high-level radioactive waste into the ocean.	16 U.S.C. Sections 1401–1445.
Endangered Species Act (1973)	To protect species that are threatened with extinction.	16 U.S.C. Sections 1531–1544.
Safe Drinking Water Act (1974)	To regulate pollutants in public drinking water systems.	42 U.S.C. Sections 300f–300j-25.
Resource Conservation and Recovery Act (1976)	To establish standards for hazardous waste disposal.	42 U.S.C. Sections 6901–6986.
Toxic Substances Control Act (1976)	To regulate toxic chemicals and chemical compounds.	15 U.S.C. Sections 2601–2692.
Comprehensive Environmental Response, Compensation, and Liability Act (1980)	To regulate the clean-up of hazardous waste–disposal sites.	42 U.S.C. Sections 9601–9675.
Oil Pollution Act (1990)	To establish liability for the clean-up of navigable waters after oil spills.	33 U.S.C. Sections 2701–2761.
Small Business Liability Relief and Brownfields Revitalization Act (2002)	To allow developers who comply with state voluntary clean-up programs to avoid federal liability for the properties that they decontaminate and develop.	42 U.S.C. Section 9628.

Environmental Impact Statement (EIS)
A statement required by the National Environmental Policy Act for any major federal action that will significantly affect the quality of the environment.

federal agencies with authority to regulate specific environmental matters include the Department of the Interior, the Department of Defense, the Department of Labor, the Food and Drug Administration, and the Nuclear Regulatory Commission.

All agencies of the federal government must take environmental factors into consideration when making significant decisions. In addition, as mentioned, state and local agencies play an important role in enforcing federal environmental legislation.

Most federal environmental laws provide that private parties can sue to enforce environmental regulations if government agencies fail to do so—or if agencies go too far in their enforcement actions. Typically, a threshold hurdle in such suits is meeting the requirements for standing to sue.

ENVIRONMENTAL IMPACT STATEMENTS   The National Environmental Policy Act (NEPA)[1] requires that an **environmental impact statement (EIS)** be prepared for every major federal action that significantly affects the quality of the environment.

---

1. 42 U.S.C. Sections 4321–4370d.

An EIS must analyze the following:

1. The impact on the environment that the action will have.
2. Any adverse effects on the environment and alternative actions that might be taken.
3. Irreversible effects the action might generate.

LEARNING OBJECTIVE 3 **What is an environmental impact statement, and who must file one?**

An action qualifies as "major" if it involves a substantial commitment of resources (monetary or otherwise). An action is "federal" if a federal agency has the power to control it. If a private developer wishes to construct a ski resort on federal land, for example, an EIS may be needed. The construction or operation of a nuclear plant, which requires a federal permit, requires an EIS. If an agency decides that an EIS is unnecessary, it must issue a statement supporting this conclusion.

Private individuals, consumer interest groups, businesses, and others who believe that a federal agency's actions threaten the environment often use EISs as a means of challenging those actions.

State and Local Regulations

In addition to the federal regulations, many states have enacted laws to protect the environment. State laws may restrict a business's discharge of chemicals into the air or water or regulate its disposal of toxic wastes. States may also regulate the disposal or recycling of other wastes, including glass, metal, plastic containers, and paper. Additionally, states may restrict emissions from motor vehicles.

City, county, and other local governments also regulate some aspects of the environment. For instance, local zoning laws may be designed to inhibit or regulate the growth of cities and suburbs or to protect the natural environment. In the interest of safeguarding the environment, such laws may prohibit certain land uses. Even when zoning laws permit a business's proposed development, the proposal may have to be altered to lessen the development's impact on the environment. In addition, cities and counties may impose rules regulating methods of waste removal, the appearance of buildings, the maximum noise level, and other aspects of the local environment.

State and local regulatory agencies also play a significant role in implementing federal environmental legislation. Typically, the federal government relies on state and local governments to enforce federal environmental statutes and regulations such as those regulating air quality.

▶ Air Pollution

Congress first authorized funds for air-pollution research and enacted the Clean Air Act to address multistate air pollution back in the 1950s and 1960s.[2] The Clean Air Act provides the basis for issuing regulations to control pollution coming both from mobile sources (such as automobiles and other vehicles) and from stationary sources (such as electric utilities and industrial plants).

LEARNING OBJECTIVE 4 **What major federal statutes regulate air and water pollution?**

Mobile Sources of Air Pollution

Regulations governing air pollution from automobiles and other mobile sources specify pollution standards and establish time schedules for meeting the standards. The EPA periodically updates the pollution standards in light of new developments and data, reducing the amount of emissions allowed.

REDUCING EMISSIONS OVER THE LONG TERM   The Obama administration has announced a long-term goal of reducing emissions, including those from cars

---

2. 42 U.S.C. Sections 7401–7671.

and SUVs, by 80 percent by 2050. In 2010, the administration ordered the EPA to develop national standards regulating fuel economy and emissions for medium- and heavy-duty trucks starting with 2014 models.

GREENHOUSE GASES A growing concern among many scientists and others around the world is that greenhouse gases, such as carbon dioxide (CO_2), are contributing to global warming. The Clean Air Act, as amended, however, does not specifically mention CO_2 emissions. Therefore, until 2009, the EPA did not regulate CO_2 emissions from motor vehicles.

CASE EXAMPLE 18.2 Environmental groups and several states sued the EPA in an effort to force the agency to regulate CO_2 emissions. When the case reached the United States Supreme Court, the EPA argued that the plaintiffs lacked standing because global warming has widespread effects and thus an individual plaintiff could not show the particularized harm required for standing. Furthermore, the agency maintained, it did not have authority under the Clean Air Act to address global climate change and regulate CO_2.

The Court, however, ruled that Massachusetts had standing because its coastline, including state-owned lands, faced an imminent threat from rising sea levels caused by global warming. The Court also held that the Clean Air Act's broad definition of air pollutant gives the EPA authority to regulate CO_2 and requires the EPA to regulate any air pollutants that might "endanger public health or welfare." Accordingly, the Court ordered the EPA to determine whether CO_2 was a pollutant that endangered public health.[3] ● The EPA later concluded that greenhouse gases, including CO_2 emissions, do constitute a public danger.

Stationary Sources of Air Pollution

The Clean Air Act authorizes the EPA to establish air-quality standards for stationary sources (such as manufacturing plants) but recognizes that the primary responsibility for preventing and controlling air pollution rests with state and local governments.

The EPA sets primary and secondary levels of ambient standards—that is, the maximum permissible levels of certain pollutants—and the states formulate plans to achieve those standards. Different standards apply depending on whether the sources of pollution are located in clean areas or polluted areas and whether they are existing sources or major new sources.

HAZARDOUS AIR POLLUTANTS The standards are aimed at controlling hazardous air pollutants—those likely to cause death or serious irreversible or incapacitating illness such as cancer or neurological and reproductive damage. The Clean Air Act requires the EPA to list all regulated hazardous air pollutants on a prioritized schedule. In all, nearly two hundred substances, including asbestos, benzene, beryllium, cadmium, and vinyl chloride, have been classified as hazardous. They are emitted from stationary sources by a variety of business activities, including smelting (melting ore to produce metal), dry cleaning, house painting, and commercial baking.

MAXIMUM ACHIEVABLE CONTROL TECHNOLOGY Instead of establishing specific emissions standards for each hazardous air pollutant, the 1990 amendments to the Clean Air Act require major sources of pollutants to use pollution-control

"There's so much pollution in the air now that if it weren't for our lungs, there'd be no place to put it all."

Robert Orben, 1927–present
(American comedian)

---

3. *Massachusetts v. Environmental Protection Agency,* 549 U.S. 497, 127 S.Ct. 1438, 167 L.Ed.2d 248 (2007).

equipment that represents the *maximum achievable control technology,* or MACT, to reduce emissions. The EPA issues guidelines as to what equipment meets these standards.[4]

Mercury is one of the listed hazardous substances. The EPA attempted nonetheless to remove mercury from its list of hazardous substances emitted from electric utility steam-generating units. In the following case, New Jersey and others challenged this delisting.

---

4. The EPA has also issued rules to regulate hazardous air pollutants emitted by landfills. See 40 C.F.R. Sections 60.750–60.759.

Case 18.1   New Jersey v. Environmental Protection Agency

United States Court of Appeals, District of Columbia Circuit, 517 F.3d 574 (2008).

BACKGROUND AND FACTS The Environmental Protection Agency (EPA) published a rule—the Delisting Rule—that had the effect of removing from its regulation the emissions of mercury from steam-generating electricity plants that used coal or oil as their energy sources. This Delisting Rule ran counter to the EPA's own conclusions at the end of 2000 that it was "appropriate and necessary" to regulate mercury emissions. At that time, it placed mercury on its list of hazardous air pollutants (HAPs) to be monitored at electricity-generating sites. New Jersey and fourteen additional states, as well as various state agencies, challenged the EPA's action.

IN THE WORDS OF THE COURT . . .
ROGERS, Circuit Judge.
* * * *

First, Congress required EPA to regulate more than one hundred specific HAPs, including mercury and nickel compounds. Further, EPA was required to list and to regulate, on a prioritized schedule, "all categories and subcategories of major sources and areas sources" that emit one or more HAPs. *In seeking to ensure that regulation of HAPs reflects the "maximum reduction in emissions which can be achieved by application of [the] best available control technology," Congress imposed specific, strict pollution control requirements on both new and existing sources of HAPs.* [Emphasis added.]

Second, Congress restricted the opportunities for EPA and others to intervene in the regulation of HAP sources. For HAPs that result in health effects other than cancer, as is true of mercury, Congress directed that the Administrator "may delete any source category" from

the section 112(c)(1) list only after determining that "emissions from no source in the category or subcategory concerned . . . exceed a level which is adequate to protect public health with an ample margin of safety and no adverse environmental effect will result from emissions from any source."
* * * *

EPA maintains that it possesses authority to remove EGUs [electrical generating units] from * * * [the] list under the "fundamental principle of administrative law that an agency has inherent authority to reverse an earlier administrative determination or ruling where an agency has a principled basis for doing so."

EPA states in its brief that it has previously removed sources listed * * * without satisfying the requirements of [the statute]. But previous statutory violations cannot excuse the one now before the court. "We do not see how merely applying an unreasonable statutory interpretation for several years can transform it into a reasonable interpretation."

DECISION AND REMEDY The U.S. Court of Appeals for the District of Columbia Circuit ruled in favor of New Jersey and the other plaintiffs. The EPA was required to rescind its delisting of mercury.

WHAT IF THE FACTS WERE DIFFERENT? *Suppose that the EPA had carried out scientific tests that showed mercury was relatively harmless as a by-product of electricity generation. How might this have affected the court's ruling?*

Violations of the Clean Air Act

For violations of emission limits under the Clean Air Act, the EPA can assess civil penalties of up to $25,000 per day. Additional fines of up to $5,000 per day can be assessed for other violations, such as failing to maintain the required records. To penalize those who find it more cost-effective to violate the act than to comply with it, the EPA is authorized to obtain a penalty equal to the violator's economic benefits from noncompliance. Persons who provide information about violators may be paid up to $10,000. Private individuals can also sue violators.

Those who knowingly violate the act may be subject to criminal penalties, including fines of up to $1 million and imprisonment for up to two years (for false statements or failures to report violations). Corporate officers are among those who may be subject to these penalties.

▶ Water Pollution

Water pollution stems mostly from industrial, municipal, and agricultural sources. Pollutants entering streams, lakes, and oceans include organic wastes, heated water, sediments from soil runoff, nutrients (including fertilizers and human and animal wastes), and toxic chemicals and other hazardous substances. We look here at laws and regulations governing water pollution.

Federal regulations governing the pollution of water can be traced back to the Rivers and Harbors Appropriations Act of 1899.[5] These regulations prohibited ships and manufacturers from discharging or depositing refuse in navigable waterways without a permit. In 1948, Congress passed the Federal Water Pollution Control Act (FWPCA),[6] but its regulatory system and enforcement powers proved to be inadequate.

The Clean Water Act

In 1972, amendments to the FWPCA—known as the Clean Water Act (CWA)—established the following goals:

1. To make waters safe for swimming.
2. To protect fish and wildlife.
3. To eliminate the discharge of pollutants into the water.

The amendments set specific time schedules, which were extended by amendment and by the Water Quality Act.[7] Under these schedules, the EPA limits the discharge of various types of pollutants based on the technology available for controlling them.

FOCUS ON POINT-SOURCE EMISSIONS   The CWA established a permit system, called the National Pollutant Discharge Elimination System (NPDES), for regulating discharges from "point sources" of pollution that include industrial, municipal (such as pipes and sewage treatment plants), and agricultural facilities.[8] Under this system, any point source emitting pollutants into water must have a permit. Pollution not from point sources, such as runoff from small farms, is not subject to much regulation.

NPDES permits can be issued by the EPA and authorized state agencies and Indian tribes, but only if the discharge will not violate water-quality standards. NPDES permits must be reissued every five years. Although initially the NPDES system focused mainly on industrial wastewater, it was later expanded to cover storm water discharges.

In practice, the permit system under the CWA includes the following elements:

1. National effluent (pollution) standards set by the EPA for each industry.
2. Water-quality standards set by the states under EPA supervision.

"Among the treasures of our land is water—fast becoming our most valuable, most prized, most critical resource."

Dwight D. Eisenhower, 1890–1969
(Thirty-fourth president of the United States, 1953–1961)

---

5. 33 U.S.C. Sections 401–418.
6. 33 U.S.C. Sections 1251–1387.
7. This act amended 33 U.S.C. Section 1251.
8. 33 U.S.C. Section 1342.

3. A *discharge permit* program that sets water-quality standards to limit pollution.
4. Special provisions for toxic chemicals and for oil spills.
5. Construction grants and loans from the federal government for *publicly owned treatment works*, primarily sewage treatment plants.

When water from rainstorms flows over streets, parking lots, commercial sites, and other developed areas, the water collects sediments, trash, used motor oil, raw sewage, pesticides, and other toxic contaminants. This polluted runoff flows into urban storm sewers, which often empty into rivers or oceans.

In the following case, the plaintiffs claimed that Los Angeles County, California, was responsible for heavily polluted stormwater runoff flowing into navigable rivers in the surrounding area.

Case 18.2   Natural Resources Defense Council, Inc. v. County of Los Angeles

United States Court of Appeals, Ninth Circuit, 673 F.3d 880 (2011).

BACKGROUND AND FACTS   Two environmental organizations—the Natural Resources Defense Council (NRDC) and the Santa Monica Baykeeper—brought a lawsuit against the county of Los Angeles and the Los Angeles County Flood Control District, which included eighty-four cities and some unincorporated areas. The NRDC and Santa Monica alleged that the county and the district were discharging urban stormwater runoff into navigable waters in violation of the Clean Water Act. The levels of pollutants detected in four rivers—the Santa Clara River, the Los Angeles River, the San Gabriel River, and Malibu Creek—exceeded the limits allowed in the National Pollutant Discharge Elimination System (NPDES) permit that governs municipal stormwater discharges in Los Angeles County.

All parties agreed that the rivers did not meet water-quality standards. The issue was whether the NRDC and Santa Monica had proved that the county and the district were responsible. The defendants claimed that there was no evidence establishing their responsibility for discharging stormwater carrying pollutants into the rivers. The federal district court held in favor of the defendants (the county and district agencies), and the NRDC and Santa Monica appealed.

IN THE WORDS OF THE COURT . . .
M. *SMITH*, Circuit Judge:
* * * *

This case concerns high levels of pollutants, particularly heavy metals and fecal bacteria, identified by mass-emissions monitoring stations for the four Watershed Rivers (the Monitoring Stations). * * * The purpose of mass-emissions monitoring is to * * * estimate the mass emissions from the MS4 [the main municipal storm sewer system in Los Angeles County], * * * [and] determine if the MS4 is contributing to exceedances of Water Quality Standards. The [NPDES] Permit requires that mass-emission readings be taken five times per year for the Watershed Rivers.

The Los Angeles River and San Gabriel River Monitoring Stations are located in a channelized portion of the MS4 [where the water

flows through a concrete-lined structure] that is owned and operated by the District.

The Malibu Creek Monitoring Station is not located within a channelized portion of the MS4 but at an "existing stream gage station" near Malibu Canyon Road. * * * The Santa Clara River Monitoring Station is located in the City of Santa Clara and [is also not in the channelized portion of the MS4].
* * * *

"The Clean Water Act regulates the discharge of pollutants into navigable waters, prohibiting their discharge unless certain statutory exceptions apply." One such exception is for discharges by entities or individuals who hold NPDES permits. The NPDES permitting program is the "centerpiece" of the Clean Water Act and the primary method for enforcing the effluent and water-quality standards established by the EPA and state governments.

* * * Since the inception of the NPDES, Congress has expanded NPDES permitting to bring municipal dischargers within the Clean Water Act's coverage.
* * * *

Section 402(p)(3)(iii) of the CWA [Clean Water Act] mandates that permits for discharges from municipal separate storm sewers *shall require controls to reduce the discharge of pollutants* to the maximum extent practicable (MEP), including management practices, control techniques and systems, design and engineering methods, and such other provisions as the Director determines appropriate for the control of such pollutants. [Emphasis in original.]
* * * *

Our prior case law emphasizes that NPDES permit enforcement is not scattershot—each permit term is simply enforced as written.
* * * *

[This] Permit's provisions plainly specify that the mass-emissions monitoring is intended to measure compliance and that "[a]ny violation of this Order" is a Clean Water Act violation. The Permit

Case 18.2–Continues next page ➡

Case 18.2–Continued

is available for public inspection to aid this purpose. Accordingly, we agree with the district court's determination that an exceedance detected through mass-emissions monitoring is a Permit violation that gives rise to liability for contributing dischargers.

* * * *

* * * There is evidence in the record showing that polluted stormwater from the MS4 was added to two of the Watershed Rivers: the Los Angeles River and San Gabriel River. Because the mass-emissions stations, as the appropriate locations to measure compliance, for these two rivers are located in a section of the MS4 owned and operated by the District, when pollutants were detected, they had not yet exited the point source into navigable waters. As such, there is no question over who controlled the polluted stormwater at the time it was measured or who caused or contributed to the exceedances when that water was again discharged to the rivers—in both cases, the District. As a matter

of law and fact, the MS4 is distinct from the two navigable rivers; the MS4 is an intra-state man-made construction—not a naturally occurring Watershed River.

DECISION AND REMEDY   The federal appellate court concluded that the plaintiffs were entitled to summary judgment on the district's liability for discharges into the Los Angeles River and San Gabriel River. Accordingly, the court reversed the lower court's decision on these claims but affirmed it as to the Santa Clara River and Malibu Creek, because those monitoring stations were not located within the channelized portion of the MS4.

THE ETHICAL DIMENSION   *The court rejected the district's argument that it should not be held liable for merely channeling pollutants that were generated by others. Under the Clean Water Act, does it matter who created the pollution? If so, should it matter? Explain.*

STANDARDS FOR EQUIPMENT   Regulations generally specify that the *best available control technology*, or BACT, be installed. The EPA issues guidelines as to what equipment meets this standard. Essentially, the guidelines require the most effective pollution-control equipment available.

New sources must install BACT equipment before beginning operations. Existing sources are subject to timetables for the installation of BACT equipment and must immediately install equipment that utilizes the *best practical control technology*, or BPCT. The EPA also issues guidelines as to what equipment meets this standard.

Wetlands Water-saturated areas of land that are designated by a government agency as protected areas that support wildlife and therefore cannot be filled in or dredged by private contractors or parties without a permit.

WETLANDS   The CWA prohibits the filling or dredging of **wetlands** unless a permit is obtained from the Army Corps of Engineers. The EPA defines *wetlands* as "those areas that are inundated or saturated by surface or ground water at a frequency and duration sufficient to support . . . vegetation typically adapted for life in saturated soil conditions."

Wetlands are thought to be vital to the ecosystem because they filter streams and rivers and provide habitat for wildlife. Although in the past the EPA's broad interpretation of what constitutes a wetland generated substantial controversy, the courts have considerably scaled back the CWA's protection of wetlands in recent years.[9]

VIOLATIONS OF THE CLEAN WATER ACT   Under the CWA, violators are subject to a variety of civil and criminal penalties. Depending on the violation, civil penalties range from $10,000 per day to $25,000 per day, but not more than $25,000 per violation. Criminal penalties, which apply only if a violation was intentional, range from a fine of $2,500 per day and imprisonment for up to one year to a fine of $1 million and fifteen years' imprisonment. An injunction and damages can also be imposed. The polluting party can be required to clean up the pollution or pay for the cost of doing so.

In the following case, landowners filed a federal lawsuit challenging an EPA order finding that they had violated the CWA. The United States Supreme Court had to decide whether the federal courts could review the EPA's decision.

9. See, for example, *Rapanos v. United States*, 547 U.S. 715, 126 S.Ct. 2208, 165 L.Ed.2d 159 (2006).

Case 18.3 | Sackett v. Environmental Protection Agency

Supreme Court of the United States, ___ U.S. ___, 132 S. Ct. 1367, 182 L.Ed.2d 367 (2012).

BACKGROUND AND FACTS To build a home in Idaho, Michael and Chantell Sackett filled part of their residential lot with dirt and rock. A few months later, they received a compliance order from the Environmental Protection Agency (EPA). The order asserted that, because their property was near a major lake, the Sacketts had polluted wetlands in violation of the Clean Water Act. The order required the Sacketts to restore their property immediately, and they faced heavy fines of $75,000 a day. The Sacketts requested a hearing with the EPA. When a hearing was denied, they sued the EPA in federal district court, asserting, among other things, that the compliance order was "arbitrary and capricious" under the Administrative Procedure Act (APA). The district court found that it could not review the EPA's compliance order. On appeal, a federal appellate court affirmed, concluding that the Sacketts had to wait for the EPA to bring an enforcement action against them. The United States Supreme Court granted *certiorari* to resolve the matter.

IN THE WORDS OF THE COURT . . .
Justice *SCALIA* delivered the opinion of the Court.
 * * * *

 * * * The APA * * * provides for judicial review of "final agency action for which there is no other adequate remedy in a court." We consider first whether the compliance order is final agency action. There is no doubt it is agency action, which the APA defines as including even a "failure to act." But is it *final?* It has all of the hallmarks of APA finality that our opinions establish. Through the order, the EPA " 'determined' " " 'rights or obligations.' " By reason of the order, the Sacketts have the legal obligation to "restore" their property according to an agency-approved Restoration Work Plan, and must give the EPA access to their property and to "records and documentation related to the conditions at the Site." Also, " 'legal consequences . . . flow' " from issuance of the order. * * * The order exposes the Sacketts to double penalties in a future enforcement proceeding.

The issuance of the compliance order also marks the " 'consummation' " of the agency's decision-making process. As the Sacketts learned when they unsuccessfully sought a hearing, * * * [the] compliance order * * * [was] not subject to further agency review. * * *

The APA's judicial review provision also requires that the person seeking APA review of final agency action have "no other adequate remedy in a court[.]" In Clean Water Act enforcement cases, judicial review ordinarily comes by way of a civil action brought by the EPA * * * . But the Sacketts cannot initiate that process, and each day they wait for the agency to drop the hammer, they accrue * * * an additional $75,000 in potential liability.
 * * * *

 * * * Compliance orders * * * can obtain quick remediation through voluntary compliance. The Government warns that the EPA is less likely to use the orders if they are subject to judicial review. That may be true—but it will be true for all agency actions subjected to judicial review. * * * *There is no reason to think that the Clean Water Act was uniquely designed to enable the strong-arming of regulated parties into "voluntary compliance" without the opportunity for judicial review* * * * . Compliance orders will remain an effective means of securing prompt voluntary compliance in those many cases where there is no substantial basis to question their validity. [Emphasis added.]

DECISION AND REMEDY The United States Supreme Court held that the Sacketts could challenge the EPA's compliance order in federal court. The Court reversed the judgment of the federal appellate court.

THE LEGAL ENVIRONMENT DIMENSION *What does the Court's decision in this case mean for people and businesses that face compliance orders? Are they more or less likely to acquiesce to orders they find objectionable?*

Drinking Water

The Safe Drinking Water Act[10] requires the EPA to set maximum levels for pollutants in public water systems. Public water system operators must come as close as possible to meeting the EPA's standards by using the best available technology that is economically and technologically feasible.

Under the act, each supplier of drinking water is required to send every household that it supplies with water an annual statement describing the source of its water. Suppliers must also disclose the level of any contaminants contained in the water and any possible health concerns associated with the contaminants.

The EPA is particularly concerned about contamination from underground sources, such as pesticides and wastes leaked from landfills or disposed of in underground

---

10. 42 U.S.C. Sections 300f to 300j-25.

injection wells. Many of these substances are associated with cancer and may cause damage to the central nervous system, liver, and kidneys. Although some evidence suggests that trace amounts of pharmaceuticals may be entering the nation's drinking water, the law does not yet require suppliers to test for or report these substances. The drugs come from prescription medications taken by humans and antibiotics and other medications given to livestock.

Ethical Issue ⚖

Should the government begin regulating the presence of pharmaceuticals in drinking water? The amount of pharmaceuticals used by the American public and in agriculture (antibiotics and hormones given to livestock) has grown substantially in recent years. Now trace amounts of many drugs have been detected in our nation's water supply.

In 2008, for example, the drinking water of at least 41 million Americans in twenty-four regions across the country was found to contain small amounts of prescription drugs. Some of these trace amounts came from unmetabolized drugs that had passed through the humans and animals that ingested them, but the rest had been flushed down the toilet. For years, pharmacists, physicians, and the federal government have recommended that people dispose of unused medications by flushing them away. This prevents children from accidentally ingesting the drugs and keeps controlled substances, such as the painkillers oxycodone and morphine, from falling into the hands of people who might abuse them. In making these recommendations, however, no one considered the long-term effect on the environment of adding pharmaceuticals to the water supply.

Clearly, the quantities present in water now are far below medicinal doses, but no one knows how long-term exposure to random combinations of drugs will affect humans or wildlife. As yet there is little scientific evidence about the long-term effects. The federal government does not require drinking water to be tested for drugs, so Americans do not know whether their drinking water is contaminated. Requiring that water be tested and that all traces of drugs be filtered from it would be enormously expensive. In a time of economic recession, should the government wait until there is scientific proof of the harmful effects on humans and wildlife before regulating? Or, should the government enact legislation to address the problem before it becomes worse?

Ocean Dumping

The Marine Protection, Research, and Sanctuaries Act of 1972[11] (popularly known as the Ocean Dumping Act), as amended in 1983, regulates the transportation and dumping of material into ocean waters. It prohibits entirely the ocean dumping of radiological, chemical, and biological warfare agents and high-level radioactive waste.

The act also established a permit program for transporting and dumping other materials, and designated certain areas as marine sanctuaries. Each violation of any provision in the Ocean Dumping Act may result in a civil penalty of up to $50,000. A knowing violation is a criminal offense that may result in a $50,000 fine, imprisonment for not more than a year, or both. A court may also grant an injunction to prevent an imminent or continuing violation of the Ocean Dumping Act.

Oil Pollution

After more than 10 million gallons of oil leaked into Alaska's Prince William Sound from the *Exxon Valdez* supertanker in 1989, Congress responded by passing the Oil Pollution Act.[12] (At that time, the *Exxon Valdez* disaster was the worst oil spill in U.S.

---

11. 16 U.S.C. Sections 1401–1445.
12. 33 U.S.C. Sections 2701–2761.

history, but the BP oil spill in the Gulf of Mexico in 2010 surpassed it.) Under this act, any onshore or offshore oil facility, oil shipper, vessel owner, or vessel operator that discharges oil into navigable waters or onto an adjoining shore can be liable for clean-up costs, as well as damages.

Under the act, damage to natural resources, private property, and the local economy, including the increased cost of providing public services, is compensable. The penalties range from $2 million to $350 million, depending on the size of the vessel and on whether the oil spill came from a vessel or an offshore facility. The party held responsible for the clean-up costs can bring a civil suit for contribution from other potentially liable parties. Oil tankers using U.S. ports must now be double hulled to limit the severity of accidental spills.

▶ Toxic Chemicals

Originally, most environmental clean-up efforts were directed toward reducing smog and making water safe for fishing and swimming. Today, the control of toxic chemicals used in agriculture and in industry has become increasingly important.

Pesticides and Herbicides

Under the Federal Insecticide, Fungicide, and Rodenticide Act (FIFRA),[13] pesticides and herbicides must be:

1. Registered before they can be sold.
2. Certified and used only for approved applications.
3. Used in limited quantities when applied to food crops.

The EPA can cancel or suspend registration of substances that are identified as harmful and may also inspect factories where the chemicals are made. Under 1996 amendments to FIFRA, there must be no more than a one-in-a-million risk to people of developing cancer from any kind of exposure to the substance, including eating food that contains pesticide residues.[14]

It is a violation of FIFRA to sell a pesticide or herbicide that is either unregistered or has had its registration canceled or suspended. It is also a violation to sell a pesticide or herbicide with a false or misleading label or to destroy or deface any labeling required under the act. Penalties for commercial dealers include imprisonment for up to one year and a fine of no more than $25,000. Farmers and other private users of pesticides or herbicides who violate the act are subject to a $1,000 fine and incarceration for up to thirty days.

Note that a state can also regulate the sale and use of federally registered pesticides. **CASE EXAMPLE 18.3** After the EPA conditionally registered Strongarm, a weed-killing pesticide, Dow Agrosciences, LLC, sold Strongarm to Texas peanut farmers. When the farmers applied it, however, Strongarm damaged their crops and failed to control the growth of weeds. The farmers sued Dow, but the lower courts ruled that FIFRA preempted their claims. The farmers appealed to the United States Supreme Court. The Supreme Court held that under a specific provision of FIFRA, a state can regulate the sale and use of federally registered pesticides so long as the regulation does not permit anything that FIFRA prohibits.[15] ●

---

13. 7 U.S.C. Sections 135–136y.
14. 21 U.S.C. Section 346a.
15. *Bates v. Dow Agrosciences, LLC,* 544 U.S. 431, 125 S.Ct. 1788, 161 L.Ed.2d 687 (2005).

Toxic Substances

The Toxic Substances Control Act[16] was passed:

1. To regulate chemicals and chemical compounds that are known to be toxic—such as asbestos and polychlorinated biphenyls, popularly known as PCBs.
2. To institute investigation of any possible harmful effects from new chemical compounds.

The regulations authorize the EPA to require that manufacturers, processors, and other organizations planning to use chemicals first determine their effects on human health and the environment. The EPA can regulate substances that potentially pose an imminent hazard or an unreasonable risk of injury to health or the environment. The EPA may require special labeling, limit the use of a substance, set production quotas, or prohibit the use of a substance altogether.

▶ Hazardous Waste Disposal

Some industrial, agricultural, and household wastes pose more serious threats than others. If not properly disposed of, these toxic chemicals may present a substantial danger to human health and the environment. If released into the environment, they may contaminate public drinking water resources.

Resource Conservation and Recovery Act

In 1976, Congress passed the Resource Conservation and Recovery Act (RCRA)[17] in reaction to concern over the effects of hazardous waste materials on the environment. The RCRA required the EPA to determine which forms of solid waste should be considered hazardous and to establish regulations to monitor and control hazardous waste disposal. The act also requires all producers of hazardous waste materials to label and package properly any hazardous waste to be transported. The RCRA was amended in 1984 and 1986 to decrease the use of land containment in the disposal of hazardous waste and to require smaller generators of hazardous waste to comply with the act.

Under the RCRA, a company may be assessed a civil penalty of up to $25,000 for each violation. Penalties are based on the seriousness of the violation, the probability of harm, and the extent to which the violation deviates from RCRA requirements. Criminal penalties include fines of up to $50,000 for each day of violation, imprisonment for up to two years (in most instances), or both. Criminal fines and the period of imprisonment can be doubled for certain repeat offenders.

Superfund

LEARNING OBJECTIVE 5 **What is Superfund? What categories of persons are liable under Superfund?**

In 1980, Congress passed the Comprehensive Environmental Response, Compensation, and Liability Act (CERCLA),[18] commonly known as Superfund, to regulate the clean-up of leaking hazardous waste–disposal sites. A special federal fund was created for that purpose.

CERCLA, as amended, has four primary elements:

1. It established an information-gathering and analysis system that enables the government to identify chemical dump sites and determine the appropriate action.

---

16. 15 U.S.C. Sections 2601–2692.
17. 42 U.S.C. Sections 6901–6986.
18. 42 U.S.C. Sections 9601–9675.

2. It authorized the EPA to respond to hazardous substance emergencies and to arrange for the clean-up of a leaking site directly if the persons responsible for the problem fail to clean up the site.

3. It created a Hazardous Substance Response Trust Fund (also known as Superfund) to pay for the clean-up of hazardous sites using funds obtained through taxes on certain businesses.

4. It allowed the government to recover the cost of clean-up from the persons who were (even remotely) responsible for hazardous substance releases.

POTENTIALLY RESPONSIBLE PARTIES   Superfund provides that when a release or a threatened release of hazardous chemicals from a site occurs, the EPA can clean up the site and recover the cost of the clean-up from the following persons:

1. The person who generated the wastes disposed of at the site.
2. The person who transported the wastes to the site.
3. The person who owned or operated the site at the time of the disposal.
4. The current owner or operator.

Potentially Responsible Party (PRP)
A party liable for the costs of cleaning up a hazardous waste–disposal site. Any person who generated the hazardous waste, transported it, owned or operated the waste site at the time of disposal, or owns or operates the site at the present time may be responsible for some or all of the clean-up costs.

A person falling within one of these categories is referred to as a **potentially responsible party (PRP).** If the PRPs do not clean up the site, the EPA can clean up the site and recover the clean-up costs from the PRPs.

JOINT AND SEVERAL LIABILITY   Liability under Superfund is usually *joint and several*—that is, a person who generated *only a fraction of the hazardous waste* disposed of at the site may nevertheless be liable for *all* of the clean-up costs. CERCLA authorizes a party who has incurred clean-up costs to bring a "contribution action" against any other person who is liable or potentially liable for a percentage of the costs.

MINIMIZING LIABILITY   One way for a business to minimize its potential liability under Superfund is to conduct environmental compliance audits of its own operations regularly. A business can perform internal investigations of its own operations and lands to determine whether any environmental hazards exist.

The EPA encourages companies to conduct self-audits and promptly detect, disclose, and correct wrongdoing. Companies that do so are subject to lighter penalties (fines may be reduced as much as 75 percent) for violations of environmental laws. Under EPA guidelines, the EPA will waive all fines if a small company corrects environmental violations within 180 days after being notified of the violations (or 360 days if pollution-prevention techniques are involved). The policy does not apply to criminal violations of environmental laws, though, or to actions that pose a significant threat to public health, safety, or the environment.

DEFENSES   There are a few defenses to liability under CERCLA. The most important is the innocent landowner defense.[19] Under this defense, an innocent property owner may be able to avoid liability by showing that he or she had no contractual or employment relationship with the person who released the hazardous substance on the land. Thus, if the property was transferred by contract from the third party who disposed of the substances to the current owner, the defense normally will not be available.

To assert the defense, the landowner must be able to show that at the time the property was acquired, she or he had no reason to know that hazardous substances

---

19. 42 U.S.C. Section 9601(35)(B).

had been disposed of on it. The landowner must also show that at the time of the purchase, she or he undertook all appropriate investigation into the previous ownership and uses of the property to determine whether there was reason to be concerned about hazardous substances. In effect, this defense protects only property owners who took precautions and investigated the possibility of environmental hazards at the time they bought the property.

▶ Reviewing . . . Environmental Law

Early in the 2000s, residents of Lake Caliopa, Minnesota, began noticing an unusually high number of lung ailments among their population. A group of concerned local citizens pooled their resources and commissioned a study of the frequency of these health conditions per capita compared to national averages. The study concluded that residents of Lake Caliopa experienced four to seven times the frequency of asthma, bronchitis, and emphysema as the population nationwide. During the study period, citizens began expressing concerns about the large volume of smog emitted by the Cotton Design apparel manufacturing plant on the outskirts of town. The plant had opened its production facility two miles east of town beside the Tawakoni River in 1999 and employed seventy full-time workers by 2011.

Just downstream on the Tawakoni River, the city of Lake Caliopa operated a public waterworks facility, which supplied all city residents with water. In August 2012, the Minnesota Pollution Control Agency required Cotton Design to install new equipment to control air and water pollution. In May 2013, citizens brought a class-action lawsuit in a Minnesota state court against Cotton Design for various respiratory ailments allegedly caused or compounded by smog from Cotton Design's factory. Using the information presented in the chapter, answer the following questions.

1. Under the common law, what would each plaintiff be required to identify in order to be given relief by the court?
2. Are air-quality regulations typically overseen by the federal, state, or local government?
3. What standard for limiting emissions into the air does Cotton Design's pollution-control equipment have to meet?
4. What information must Lake Caliopa send to every household that the city supplies with water?

▶ Debate This

The courts should reject all cases in which the wetlands in question do not consist of actual bodies of water that exist during the entire year.

▶ Key Terms

environmental impact statement (EIS) 462   potentially responsible party (PRP) 473   wetlands 468
nuisance 461   toxic tort 461

▶ Chapter Summary: Environmental Law

Common Law Actions (See pages 460–461.)	1. *Nuisance*—A common law doctrine under which actions against pollution-causing activities may be brought. In some states, an action is permissible only if an individual suffers a harm separate and distinct from that of the general public. 2. *Negligence and strict liability*—Parties may recover damages for injuries sustained as a result of a firm's pollution-causing activities if they can demonstrate that the harm was a foreseeable result of the firm's failure to exercise reasonable care (negligence). Businesses engaging in ultrahazardous activities are liable for whatever injuries the activities cause, regardless of whether the firms exercise reasonable care.

Chapter Summary: Environmental Law, Continued

Federal, State, and Local Regulations (See pages 461–463.)	1. *Federal regulations*—See Exhibit 18-1 on page 462 for a list of major federal environmental legislation.
	    a. *Environmental protection agencies*—The primary agency regulating environmental law is the federal Environmental Protection Agency (EPA). The EPA administers most federal environmental policies and statutes.
	    b. *Assessing environmental impact*—The National Environmental Policy Act of 1969 imposes environmental responsibilities on all federal agencies and requires the preparation of an environmental impact statement (EIS) for every major federal action. An EIS must analyze the action's impact on the environment, its adverse effects and possible alternatives, and its irreversible effects on environmental quality.
	 2. *State and local regulations*—Activities affecting the environment are controlled at the local and state levels through regulations relating to land use, the disposal and recycling of garbage and waste, and pollution-causing activities in general.

Air Pollution (See pages 463–466.)	1. *Mobile sources*—Automobiles and other vehicles are mobile sources of air pollution, and the EPA establishes pollution-control standards and time schedules for meeting these standards. 2. *Stationary sources*—The Clean Air Act requires the EPA to list all regulated hazardous air pollutants that are emitted from stationary sources on a prioritized schedule. These include substances such as asbestos, mercury, and vinyl chloride that are known to cause harm to humans. Major sources of air pollution are required to use the *maximum achievable control technology* to reduce emissions.
Water Pollution (See pages 466–471.)	1. *Clean Water Act*—This 1972 act amended an earlier federal law by setting specific time schedules to improve water quality. The act also requires cities and businesses to obtain a permit before discharging waste into navigable waters. The EPA limits discharges of various pollutants based on the technology available for controlling them. Certain water-saturated areas are designated wetlands and protected from dredging or filling without a permit. This is intended to provide natural habitat to support wildlife, such as migratory birds. 2. *Drinking water*—Federal law requires the EPA to set maximum levels for pollutants in public water systems and requires public systems to use the best available technology to prevent contamination from underground sources. Each supplier of public water must send to every household it supplies with water an annual statement describing the water's source, the level of any contaminants, and any possible health concerns associated with these contaminants. 3. *Ocean dumping*—Federal law prohibits the dumping of radiological, chemical, and biological warfare agents and high-level radioactive waste into the ocean. 4. *Oil pollution*—Federal law provides that any offshore or onshore oil facility, oil shipper, vessel owner, or vessel operator that discharges oil into navigable waters or onto a shoreline is liable for clean-up costs and damages.
Toxic Chemicals (See pages 471–472.)	The federal government regulates the pesticides and herbicides that can be used in agriculture, as well as the use and transportation of chemical compounds known to be toxic.
Hazardous Waste Disposal (See pages 472–474.)	Federal laws regulate the disposal of certain types of industrial, agricultural, and household wastes that present serious dangers to human health and the environment. These hazardous wastes must be properly labeled and packaged before they can be transported. Moreover, under Superfund, when a hazardous substance is released into the environment, the EPA can clean up the site and recover the costs from a broad array of potentially responsible parties.

ExamPrep

ISSUE SPOTTERS

—Check your answers to these questions against the answers provided in Appendix D at the end of this text.

1. ChemCorp generates hazardous wastes from its operations. Disposal Trucking Company transports those wastes to Eliminators, Inc., which owns a hazardous waste–disposal site. Eliminators sells the property on which the disposal

site is located to Fluid Properties, Inc. If the Environmental Protection Agency cleans up the site, from whom can it recover the cost? **(See pages 472–474.)**

2. Resource Refining Company's plant emits smoke and fumes. Resource's operation includes a short railway system, and trucks enter and exit the grounds continuously. Constant vibrations from the trains and trucks rattle nearby residential neighborhoods. The residents sue Resource. Are there any reasons why the court might refuse to issue an injunction against Resource's operation? Explain. **(See page 461.)**

BEFORE THE TEST

Go to **www.cengagebrain.com**, enter the ISBN 9781133586548, and click on "Find" to locate this textbook's Web site. Then click on "Access Now" under "Study Tools," and select Chapter 18 at the top. There, you will find a Practice Quiz that you can take to assess your mastery of the concepts in this chapter. Additionally, you will find Flashcards and a Glossary of important terms, as well as Video Questions (when assigned).

▶ For Review

Answers for the even-numbered questions in this For Review *section can be found in Appendix E at the end of this text.*

1. Under what common law theories can polluters be held liable?
2. What does the Environmental Protection Agency do?
3. What is an environmental impact statement, and who must file one?
4. What major federal statutes regulate air and water pollution?
5. What is Superfund? What categories of persons are liable under Superfund?

▶ Questions and Case Problems

18–1. Clean Air Act. Current scientific knowledge indicates that there is no safe level of exposure to a cancer-causing agent. In theory, even one molecule of such a substance has the potential for causing cancer. Section 112 of the Clean Air Act requires that all cancer-causing substances be regulated to ensure a margin of safety. Some environmental groups have argued that all emissions of such substances must be eliminated if a margin of safety is to be reached. Such total elimination would likely shut down many major U.S. industries. Should the Environmental Protection Agency totally eliminate all emissions of cancer-causing chemicals? Discuss. **(See pages 463–466.)**

18–2. **Question with Sample Answer: Environmental Laws.** Fruitade, Inc., is a processor of a soft drink called Freshen Up. Fruitade uses returnable bottles, which it cleans with a special acid to allow for further beverage processing. The acid is diluted with water and then allowed to pass into a navigable stream. Fruitade crushes its broken bottles and throws the crushed glass into the stream. Discuss fully any environmental laws that Fruitade has violated. **(See pages 466–467.)**

—For a sample answer to Question 18–2, go to Appendix F at the end of this text.

18–3. Clean Water Act. The Anacostia River, which flows through Washington, D.C., is one of the ten most polluted rivers in the country. For bodies of water such as the Anacostia, the Clean Water Act requires states (which, under the act, include the District of Columbia) to set a "total maximum daily load" (TMDL) for pollutants. A TMDL is to be set "at a level necessary to implement the applicable water-quality standards with seasonal variations." The Anacostia contains biochemical pollutants that consume oxygen, putting the river's aquatic life at risk for suffocation. In addition, the river is murky, stunting the growth of plants that rely on sunlight and impairing recreational use. The Environmental Protection Agency (EPA) approved one TMDL limiting the *annual* discharge of oxygen-depleting pollutants and a second limiting the *seasonal* discharge of pollutants contributing to turbidity. Neither TMDL limited daily discharges. Friends of the Earth, Inc. (FoE), asked a federal district court to review the TMDLs. What is FoE's best argument in this dispute? What is the EPA's likely response? What should the court rule, and why? [*Friends of the Earth, Inc. v. Environmental Protection Agency,* 446 F.3d 140 (D.C.Cir. 2006)] **(See pages 466–467.)**

18–4. Environmental Impact Statement. The fourth largest crop in the United States is alfalfa, of which 5 percent is exported to Japan. RoundUp Ready alfalfa is genetically engineered to resist glyphosate, the active ingredient in the herbicide RoundUp. The U.S. Department of Agriculture (USDA) regulates genetically engineered agricultural products through the Animal and Plant Health Inspection Service (APHIS). APHIS concluded that RoundUp Ready alfalfa does not have any harmful effects on the health of humans or livestock and deregulated it. Geertson Seed Farms and others filed a suit in a federal district court against Mike Johanns (the secretary of the USDA) and others, asserting that APHIS's decision required the preparation of an environmental impact statement (EIS). The plaintiffs argued, among other things, that the introduction of RoundUp Ready alfalfa might significantly decrease the availability of, or even eliminate, all nongenetically engineered varieties. The plaintiffs were concerned that the RoundUp Ready alfalfa might contaminate standard alfalfa because alfalfa is pollinated by bees, which can travel as far as two miles from a pollen source. If contamination occurred, farmers would not be able to market "contaminated" varieties as "organic," which would affect the sales of "organic" livestock and exports to Japan, which does not allow the import of glyphosate-resistant alfalfa. Should an EIS be prepared in this case? Why or why not? [*Geertson Seed Farms v. Johanns*, __ F.Supp.2d __ (N.D.Cal. 2007)] **(See pages 462–463.)**

18–5. **Case Problem with Sample Answer: Environmental Impact Statement.** The U.S. National Park Service (NPS) manages the Grand Canyon National Park in Arizona under a management plan that is subject to periodic review. In 2006, after nine years of background work and the completion of a comprehensive environmental impact statement, the NPS issued a new management plan for the park. One part of the plan allowed for the continued use of rafts on the Colorado River, which runs through the Grand Canyon. The number of the rafts was limited, however. Several environmental groups criticized the plan because they felt that it still allowed too many rafts on the river. The groups requested that a federal appellate court overturn the plan, claiming that it violated the wilderness status of the national park. When can a federal court overturn a determination by an agency such as the NPS? Explain. [*River Runners for Wilderness v. Martin*, 593 F.3d 1064 (9th Cir. 2010)] **(See pages 462–463.)**

—For a sample answer to Case Problem 18–5, go to Appendix G at the end of this text.

18–6. **A Question of Ethics: Regulations.** *In the Clean Air Act, Congress allowed California, which has particular problems with clean air, to adopt its own standard for emissions from cars and trucks, subject to the approval of the Environmental Protection Agency (EPA) according to certain criteria. Congress also allowed other states to adopt California's standard after the EPA's approval. In 2004, in an effort to address global warming, the California Air Resources Board amended the state's standard to attain "the maximum feasible and cost-effective reduction of GHG [greenhouse gas] emissions from motor vehicles." The regulation, which applies to new passenger vehicles and light-duty trucks for 2009 and later, imposes decreasing limits on emissions of carbon dioxide through 2016. While EPA approval was pending, Vermont and other states adopted similar standards. Green Mountain Chrysler Plymouth Dodge Jeep and other auto dealers, automakers, and associations of automakers filed a suit in a federal district court against George Crombie (secretary of the Vermont Agency of Natural Resources) and others, seeking relief from the state regulations. [Green Mountain Chrysler Plymouth Dodge Jeep v. Crombie, __ F.Supp.2d __ (D.Vt. 2007)]* **(See pages 463–464.)**

1. Under the Environmental Policy and Conservation Act (EPCA), the National Highway Traffic Safety Administration sets fuel economy standards for new cars. The plaintiffs argued, among other things, that the EPCA, which prohibits states from adopting fuel economy standards, preempts Vermont's GHG regulation. Do the GHG rules equate to the fuel economy standards? Discuss.

2. Do Vermont's rules tread on the efforts of the federal government to address global warming internationally? Who should regulate GHG emissions? The federal government? The state governments? Both? Neither? Why?

3. The plaintiffs claimed that they would go bankrupt if they were forced to adhere to the state's GHG standards. Should they be granted relief on this basis? Does history support their claim? Explain.

18–7. **Critical-Thinking Legal Question.** It has been estimated that for every dollar spent cleaning up hazardous waste sites, administrative agencies spend seven dollars in overhead. Can you think of any way to trim these administrative costs? Explain. **(See pages 472–474.)**

Chapter 19

Antitrust Law and Promoting Competition

> "Competition is not only the basis of protection to the consumer but is the incentive to progress."
>
> —Herbert Hoover, 1874–1964
> (Thirty-first president of the United States, 1929–1933)

Contents

Learning Objectives

The four Learning Objectives below are designed to help improve your understanding of the chapter. After reading this chapter, you should be able to answer the following questions:

1. **What is a monopoly? What is market power? How do these concepts relate to each other?**

2. **What type of activity is prohibited by Section 2 of the Sherman Act?**

3. **What are the four major provisions of the Clayton Act, and what types of activities do these provisions prohibit?**

4. **What agencies of the federal government enforce the federal antitrust laws?**

(spxChrome)

Antitrust Law Laws protecting commerce from unlawful restraints.

The laws regulating economic competition in the United States are referred to as **antitrust laws.** They include the Sherman Antitrust Act of 1890,[1] and the Clayton Act[2] and the Federal Trade Commission Act,[3] which were both passed in 1914 to further curb alleged anticompetitive or unfair business practices. In addition, Congress later amended the 1914 acts to broaden and strengthen their coverage. We examine these major federal antitrust statutes in this chapter.

The basis of antitrust legislation is the desire to foster competition. Antitrust legislation was initially created—and continues to be enforced—because of our society's belief that competition leads to lower prices and generates more product information. As President Herbert Hoover indicated in the chapter-opening quotation above, competition not only protects the consumer but also provides "the incentive to progress."

Consumers and society as a whole benefit when producers strive to develop better products that they can sell at lower prices to beat the competition. This is still true today, which is why the government is concerned about the pricing of e-books, as you will read later in this chapter.

---

1. 15 U.S.C. Sections 1–7.
2. 15 U.S.C. Sections 12–27.
3. 15 U.S.C. Sections 41–58.

The Sherman Antitrust Act

In 1890, Congress passed "An Act to Protect Trade and Commerce against Unlawful Restraints and Monopolies"—commonly known as the Sherman Antitrust Act or, more simply, as the Sherman Act. The Sherman Act was and remains one of the government's more powerful weapons in the effort to maintain a competitive economy.

Sections 1 and 2 contain the main provisions of the Sherman Act. They are as follows:

1. Every contract, combination in the form of trust or otherwise, or conspiracy, in restraint of trade or commerce among the several States, or with foreign nations, is hereby declared to be illegal [and is a felony punishable by a fine and/or imprisonment].

2. Every person who shall monopolize, or attempt to monopolize, or combine or conspire with any other person or persons, to monopolize any part of the trade or commerce among the several States, or with foreign nations, shall be deemed guilty of a felony [and is similarly punishable].

> *"I don't know what a monopoly is until somebody tells me."*
> Steve Ballmer, 1956–present
> (Chief executive officer of Microsoft Corporation)

Differences between Section 1 and Section 2

LEARNING OBJECTIVE 1 What is a monopoly? What is market power? How do these concepts relate to each other?

These two sections of the Sherman Act are quite different. Violation of Section 1 requires two or more persons, as a person cannot contract or combine or conspire alone. Thus, the essence of the illegal activity is *the act of joining together.* In contrast, Section 2 can apply either to one person or to two or more persons because it refers to "every person." Thus, unilateral conduct can result in a violation of Section 2.

The cases brought to court under Section 1 of the Sherman Act differ from those brought under Section 2. Section 1 cases are often concerned with finding an agreement (written or oral) that leads to a restraint of trade. Section 2 cases deal with the structure of a monopoly that already exists in the marketplace. The term **monopoly** generally is used to describe a market in which there is a single seller or a very limited number of sellers. Whereas Section 1 focuses on agreements that are restrictive—that is, agreements that have a wrongful purpose—Section 2 looks at the so-called misuse of **monopoly power** in the marketplace.

Monopoly A term generally used to describe a market in which there is a single seller or a very limited number of sellers.

Monopoly Power The ability of a monopoly to dictate what takes place in a given market.

Market Power The power of a firm to control the market price of its product. A monopoly has the greatest degree of market power.

Monopoly power exists when a firm has an extreme amount of **market power**—the power to affect the market price of its product. Both Section 1 and Section 2 seek to curtail market practices that result in undesired monopoly pricing and output behavior. For a case to be brought under Section 2, however, the "threshold" or "necessary" amount of monopoly power must already exist. We will return to a discussion of these two sections of the Sherman Act after we look at the act's jurisdictional requirements.

Jurisdictional Requirements

The Sherman Act applies only to restraints that have a substantial impact on interstate commerce. Courts generally have held that any activity that substantially affects interstate commerce falls within the scope of the Sherman Act. As will be discussed later in this chapter, the Sherman Act also extends to U.S. nationals abroad that are engaged in activities that have an effect on U.S. foreign commerce. State laws regulate local restraints on competition.

Section 1 of the Sherman Act

The underlying assumption of Section 1 of the Sherman Act is that society's welfare is harmed if rival firms are permitted to join in an agreement that consolidates their market power or otherwise restrains competition. The types of trade restraints that Section 1 of the Sherman Act prohibits generally fall into two broad categories: *horizontal restraints* and *vertical restraints,* both of which will be discussed shortly. First, though, we look at the rules that the courts may apply when assessing the anticompetitive impact of alleged restraints on trade.

Per Se Violations versus the Rule of Reason

Per Se Violation   A type of anticompetitive agreement that is considered to be so injurious to the public that there is no need to determine whether it actually injures market competition.

Rule of Reason   A test by which a court balances the positive effects (such as economic efficiency) of an agreement against its potentially anticompetitive effects.

Some restraints are so blatantly and substantially anticompetitive that they are deemed *per se* **violations**—illegal *per se* (on their face, or inherently)—under Section 1. Other agreements, however, even though they result in enhanced market power, do not *unreasonably* restrain trade. Using what is called the **rule of reason,** the courts analyze anticompetitive agreements that allegedly violate Section 1 of the Sherman Act to determine whether they may, in fact, constitute reasonable restraints on trade.

WHY THE RULE OF REASON WAS DEVELOPED   The need for a rule-of-reason analysis of some agreements in restraint of trade is obvious—if the rule of reason had not been developed, almost any business agreement could conceivably be held to violate the Sherman Act. Justice Louis Brandeis effectively expressed this sentiment in a 1918 Supreme Court decision:

> Every agreement concerning trade, every regulation of trade, restrains. To bind, to restrain, is of their very essence. The true test of legality is whether the restraint imposed is such as merely regulates and perhaps thereby promotes competition or whether it is such as may suppress or even destroy competition.[4]

FACTORS TO CONSIDER UNDER THE RULE OF REASON   When analyzing an alleged Section 1 violation under the rule of reason, a court will consider several factors. These factors include the purpose of the agreement, the parties' market ability to implement the agreement to achieve that purpose, and the effect or potential effect of the agreement on competition. A court might also consider whether the parties could have achieved their purpose by less restrictive means.

CASE EXAMPLE 19.1   The National Football League (NFL) includes thirty-two separately owned professional teams. Each team has its own name, colors, and logo, as well as related intellectual property that it markets through National Football League Properties (NFLP). Until 2000, the NFLP granted nonexclusive licenses to a number of vendors, permitting them to manufacture and sell apparel bearing NFL team insignias. American Needle, Inc., was one of those licensees.

In late 2000, the teams authorized the NFLP to grant exclusive licenses, and the NFLP granted Reebok International an exclusive ten-year license to manufacture and sell trademarked headwear for all thirty-two NFL teams. It then declined to renew American Needle's nonexclusive license. American Needle sued, claiming that the NFL teams, the NFLP, and Reebok had violated Section 1 of the Sherman Act. The United States Supreme Court agreed. The Court concluded that the agreement among the NFL teams to license their intellectual property exclusively through the NFLP to Reebok constituted concerted activity.[5] ●

Ethical Issue ⚖

Should TV programmers and distributors be held in violation of the Sherman Act? When consumers want cable or satellite television programming, they can choose among various cable and satellite providers, or distributors. Each distributor, however, will offer multichannel packages. In other words, a consumer cannot order just the channels that she or he watches regularly. All of the multichannel packages include some very popular

4. *Chicago Board of Trade v. United States,* 246 U.S. 231, 38 S.Ct. 242, 62 L.Ed. 683 (1918).
5. *American Needle, Inc. v. National Football League,* ___ U.S. ___, 130 S.Ct. 2201, 176 L.Ed.2d 947 (2010).

channels and other channels that have very low viewership. Thus, consumers are forced to pay for some unwanted channels to get the ones they do want.

Feeling that this situation was unfair, a group of consumers sued NBC Universal, the Walt Disney Company, and other programmers, as well as cable and satellite distributors, under the Sherman Act. The consumers claimed that these companies—because of their full or partial ownership of broadcast channels and their ownership or control of multiple cable or satellite channels—had a high degree of market power vis-à-vis all distributors. They also claimed that the programmers had exploited this power by requiring the "bundling" of numerous channels in each multichannel package offered to consumers.

The U.S. Court of Appeals for the Ninth Circuit disagreed. The court pointed out that the Sherman Act applies to actions that diminish competition. In this instance, though, there was still competition among programmers and distributors.[6]

Horizontal Restraints

Horizontal Restraint Any agreement that in some way restrains competition between rival firms competing in the same market.

The term **horizontal restraint** is encountered frequently in antitrust law. A horizontal restraint is any agreement that in some way restrains competition between rival firms competing in the same market.

Price-Fixing Agreement An agreement between competitors to fix the prices of products or services at a certain level.

PRICE FIXING   Any **price-fixing agreement**—an agreement among competitors to fix prices—constitutes a *per se* violation of Section 1. The agreement on price need not be explicit. As long as it restricts output or artificially fixes price, the agreement violates the law. See this chapter's *Online Developments* feature on the following page for a discussion of the U.S. government's claims that price fixing is occurring in the e-book industry.

Price Fixing Is Never Reasonable.   Perhaps the definitive case involving price-fixing agreements is still the 1940 case of *United States v. Socony-Vacuum Oil Co.*[7] In that case, a group of independent oil producers in Texas and Louisiana were caught between falling demand due to the Great Depression of the 1930s and increasing supply from newly discovered oil fields in the region. In response to these conditions, a group of major refining companies agreed to buy "distress" gasoline (excess supplies) from the independents so as to dispose of it in an "orderly manner." Although there was no explicit agreement as to price, it was clear that the purpose of the agreement was to limit the supply of gasoline on the market and thereby raise prices.

The United States Supreme Court recognized the effects that such an agreement could have on open and free competition. The Court held that the reasonableness of a price-fixing agreement is never a defense. Any agreement that restricts output or artificially fixes price is a *per se* violation of Section 1. The rationale of the *per se* rule was best stated in what is now the most famous portion of the Court's opinion—footnote 59. In that footnote, Justice William O. Douglas compared a freely functioning price system to a body's central nervous system, condemning price-fixing agreements as threats to "the central nervous system of the economy."

Price Fixing Today.   Price-fixing cartels (groups) are still commonplace in today's business world, particularly among global companies (see page 493 for a discussion of the extraterritorial application of the Sherman Act). For instance, in 2011, Samsung Electronics, Sharp Corporation, and five other makers of liquid crystal displays (LCDs) for notebook computers and other devices agreed to pay more than

---

6. *Brantley v. NBC Universal, Inc.,* 675 F.3d 1192 (9th Cir. 2012).
7. 310 U.S. 150, 60 S.Ct. 811, 84 L.Ed. 1129 (1940).

ONLINE DEVELOPMENTS

The Justice Department Goes after E-Book Pricing

In 2012, the U.S. Department of Justice filed a lawsuit against five major book publishers and Apple, Inc., charging that they had conspired to fix the prices of e-books. According to the complaint, publishing executives met "in private rooms for dinner in upscale Manhattan restaurants" to discuss ways to limit e-book price competition. As a result, claims the Justice Department, consumers paid "tens of millions of dollar more for e-books than they otherwise would have paid."

The E-Book Market Explodes

E-books were only a niche product until a few years ago when Amazon.com released its first Kindle e-book reader. To sell more Kindles, Amazon offered thousands of popular books for downloading at $9.99 per e-book. Amazon kept 50 percent and gave 50 percent to the publishers, who had to agree to Amazon's pricing. Although Amazon suffered losses on its e-book sales, it made up the losses by selling more Kindles.

Enter Apple's iPad

When the iPad entered the scene, Apple and the book publishers agreed to use Apple's "agency" model, which allowed the publishers to set their own prices while Apple kept 30 percent as a commission. Apple was already using this model for games and apps for its iPhones and iPads.

The Justice Department, however, decided that because the publishers chose prices that were relatively similar, price fixing was evident. Nowhere in the Justice Department's complaint did it acknowledge that the agency model is the standard approach for many types of sales. Indeed, the Justice Department claimed that

the agency model is *per se* illegal and "would not have occurred without the conspiracy among the defendants." Yet the model is used in many industries and has been upheld by federal courts for years.

Amazon Still Leads, but Not by Much

When the Kindle was king, Amazon had 90 percent of the e-book market. Since the advent of the iPad, Barnes & Noble's Nook, and other e-book readers, Kindle's market share has fallen to 60 percent because of increased competition. E-books now cost anywhere from zero to $14.99.

It's *Gone with the Wind* All Over Again

During the Great Depression, the federal government brought a similar antitrust lawsuit. At the time, Macy's, the department store chain, sold books at a steep discount. It was selling the novel *Gone with the Wind* for the equivalent of $15 in today's dollars, whereas smaller stores charged double or triple that price. Publishers and booksellers lobbied for protection from what they called predatory pricing. Ultimately, the federal government did not prevail, but for a while, retail book prices stayed high.

FOR CRITICAL ANALYSIS

The publishing business is in dire straits today with retail bookstores going bankrupt and publishers laying off hundreds of employees. Why do you think the declining book business was worthy of so much attention from the Justice Department?

$553 million to settle price-fixing claims against them. Price-fixing accusations are also frequently made against drug manufacturers.

CASE EXAMPLE 19.2 The manufacturer of the prescription drug Cardizem CD, which can help prevent heart attacks, was about to lose its patent on the drug. Another company developed a generic version in anticipation of the patent's expiration. After the two firms became involved in litigation over the patent, the first company agreed to pay the second company $40 million per year not to market the generic version until their dispute was resolved. This agreement was held to be a *per se* violation of the Sherman Act because it restrained competition between rival firms and delayed the entry of generic versions of Cardizem into the market.[8] ●

Group Boycott The refusal of a group of competitors to deal with a particular person or firm.

GROUP BOYCOTTS A **group boycott** is an agreement by two or more sellers to refuse to deal with (boycott) a particular person or firm. Such group boycotts have been held to constitute *per se* violations of Section 1 of the Sherman Act. Section 1 has been violated if it can be demonstrated that the boycott or joint refusal to deal

---

8. *In re Cardizem CD Antitrust Litigation*, 332 F.3d 896 (6th Cir. 2003).

was undertaken with the intention of eliminating competition or preventing entry into a given market. Some boycotts, such as group boycotts against a supplier for political reasons, may be protected under the First Amendment right to freedom of expression, however.

HORIZONTAL MARKET DIVISION   It is a *per se* violation of Section 1 of the Sherman Act for competitors to divide up territories or customers. **EXAMPLE 19.3** Alred Office Supply, Belmont Business, and Carlson's, Inc., compete against one another in the states of Iowa, Kansas, and Nebraska. By agreement, Alred sells products only in Iowa, Belmont sells only in Kansas, and Carlson's sells only in Nebraska. This concerted action reduces costs and allows all three businesses—assuming there is no other competition—to raise the price of the goods sold in their respective states. The same violation would take place if the three companies agreed that Alred would sell only to institutional purchasers (such as governments and schools) in all three states, Belmont only to wholesalers, and Carlson's only to retailers. •

TRADE ASSOCIATIONS   Businesses in the same general industry or profession frequently organize trade associations to pursue common interests. A trade association may engage in various joint activities such as exchanging information, representing the members' business interests before governmental bodies, conducting advertising campaigns, and setting regulatory standards to govern the industry or profession.

Generally, the rule of reason is applied to many of these horizontal actions. If a court finds that a trade association practice or agreement that restrains trade is sufficiently beneficial both to the association and to the public, it may deem the restraint reasonable.

A **concentrated industry** is one in which either a single firm or a small number of firms control a large percentage of market sales. In concentrated industries, trade associations can be, and have been, used to facilitate anticompetitive actions, such as fixing prices or allocating markets. When trade association agreements have substantially anticompetitive effects, a court will find that they violate Section 1 of the Sherman Act.

Vertical Restraints

A **vertical restraint** of trade results from an agreement between firms at different levels in the manufacturing and distribution process. In contrast to horizontal relationships, which occur at the same level of operation, vertical relationships encompass the entire chain of production. The chain of production normally includes the purchase of inventory, basic manufacturing, distribution to wholesalers, and eventual sale of a product at the retail level. When a single firm carries out two or more of the separate functional phases, it is considered to be a **vertically integrated firm.**

Even though firms operating at different functional levels are not in direct competition with one another, they are in competition with other firms. Thus, agreements between firms standing in a vertical relationship may affect competition. Some vertical restraints are *per se* violations of Section 1. Others are judged under the rule of reason.

TERRITORIAL OR CUSTOMER RESTRICTIONS   In arranging for the distribution of its products, a manufacturing firm often wishes to insulate dealers from direct competition with other dealers selling the product. To this end, it may institute territorial restrictions or attempt to prohibit wholesalers or retailers from reselling the product to certain classes of buyers, such as competing retailers.

"The idea of imposing restrictions on a free economy to assure freedom of competition is like breaking a man's leg to make him run faster."

Morris R. Sayre, 1946–present
(American politician)

Concentrated Industry An industry in which a large percentage of market sales is controlled by either a single firm or a small number of firms.

Vertical Restraint Any restraint of trade created by agreements between firms at different levels in the manufacturing and distribution process.

Vertically Integrated Firm A firm that carries out two or more functional phases (manufacture, distribution, and retailing, for example) of the chain of production.

Territorial and customer restrictions were once considered *per se* violations of Section 1 of the Sherman Act.[9] In 1977, however, the United States Supreme Court reconsidered the treatment accorded to such vertical restrictions and held that they should be judged under the rule of reason.

RESALE PRICE MAINTENANCE AGREEMENTS   An agreement between a manufacturer and a distributor or retailer in which the manufacturer specifies what the retail prices of its products must be is referred to as a **resale price maintenance agreement.**

Such agreements were once considered to be *per se* violations of Section 1, but in 1997 the United States Supreme Court ruled that *maximum* resale price maintenance agreements should be judged under the rule of reason.[10] The setting of a maximum price that retailers and distributors can charge for a manufacturer's products may sometimes increase competition and benefit consumers.

> **Resale Price Maintenance Agreement** An agreement between a manufacturer and a retailer in which the manufacturer specifies what the retail prices of its products must be.

▶ Section 2 of the Sherman Act

> **LEARNING OBJECTIVE 2**   **What type of activity is prohibited by Section 2 of the Sherman Act?**

Section 1 of the Sherman Act prohibits certain concerted, or joint, activities that restrain trade. In contrast, Section 2 condemns "every person who shall monopolize, or attempt to monopolize." Thus, two distinct types of behavior are subject to sanction under Section 2: *monopolization* and *attempts to monopolize*.

One tactic that may be involved in either offense is **predatory pricing.** Predatory pricing occurs when one firm attempts to drive its competitors from the market by selling its product at prices substantially *below* the normal costs of production. Once the competitors are eliminated, the firm (predator) presumably will attempt to recapture its losses and go on to earn higher profits by driving prices up far above their competitive levels.

> **Predatory Pricing** The pricing of a product below cost with the intent to drive competitors out of the market.

Monopolization

The United States Supreme Court has defined the offense of **monopolization** as involving two elements: "(1) the possession of monopoly power in the relevant market and (2) the willful acquisition or maintenance of [that] power as distinguished from growth or development as a consequence of a superior product, business acumen, or historic accident."[11] A violation of Section 2 requires that both these elements—monopoly power and an intent to monopolize—be established.

> **Monopolization** The possession of monopoly power in the relevant market and the willful acquisition or maintenance of that power, as distinguished from growth or development as a consequence of a superior product, business acumen, or historic accident.

MONOPOLY POWER   The Sherman Act does not define *monopoly*. In economic theory, monopoly refers to control of a single market by a single entity. It is well established in antitrust law, however, that a firm may be deemed a monopolist even though it is not the sole seller in a market. Additionally, size alone does not determine whether a firm is a monopoly.

EXAMPLE 19.4   Stage Stop Store, a "mom and pop" grocery business located in the isolated town of Happy Camp, Colorado, is the only grocery store serving that market. Thus, Stage Stop Store is a monopolist. Size in relation to the market is what matters because monopoly involves the power to affect prices. ●

Monopoly power may be proved by direct evidence that the firm used its power to control prices and restrict output.[12] Usually, however, there is not enough evidence

---

9. See *United States v. Arnold, Schwinn & Co.,* 388 U.S. 365, 87 S.Ct. 1856, 18 L.Ed.2d 1249 (1967).
10. *State Oil Co. v. Khan,* 522 U.S. 3, 118 S.Ct. 275, 139 L.Ed.2d 199 (1997).
11. *United States v. Grinnell Corp.,* 384 U.S. 563, 86 S.Ct. 1698, 16 L.Ed.2d 778 (1966).
12. See, for example, *Broadcom Corp. v. Qualcomm, Inc.,* 501 F.3d 297 (3d Cir. 2007).

to show that the firm was intentionally controlling prices, so the plaintiff has to offer indirect, or circumstantial, evidence of monopoly power. To prove monopoly power indirectly, the plaintiff must show that the firm has a dominant share of the relevant market and that there are significant barriers for new competitors entering that market.

In the following case, the court had to decide whether there was sufficient evidence to show that a company possessed monopoly power in the relevant market.

Case 19.1 E. I. DuPont de Nemours and Co. v. Kolon Industries, Inc.

United States Court of Appeals, Fourth Circuit, 637 F.3d 435 (2011).

BACKGROUND AND FACTS   DuPont manufactures and sells para-aramid fiber, which is a complex synthetic fiber used to make body armor, fiber-optic cables, and tires, among other things. Although several companies around the world manufacture this fiber, only three sell into the U.S. market—DuPont (based in the United States), Teijin (based in the Netherlands), and Kolon Industries, Inc. (based in Korea). DuPont is the industry leader, producing more than 70 percent of all para-aramid fibers purchased in the United States. In February 2009, DuPont brought a lawsuit against Kolon for misappropriation of trade secrets. Kolon counterclaimed that DuPont had monopolized and attempted to monopolize the para-aramid market in violation of Section 2 of the Sherman Act. Kolon claimed that DuPont had illegally used multiyear supply agreements for all of its high-volume para-aramid fiber customers. Under the agreements, the customers were required to purchase between 80 and 100 percent of their para-aramid needs from DuPont.

Kolon alleged that those agreements removed substantial commercial opportunities from competition and limited other para-aramid fiber producers' ability to compete. DuPont moved to dismiss the counterclaim, arguing that Kolon had failed to sufficiently plead (demonstrate) unlawful exclusionary conduct, among other things. A federal district court agreed and dismissed Kolon's counterclaim. Kolon appealed to the U.S. Court of Appeals for the Fourth Circuit.

IN THE WORDS OF THE COURT . . .
James WYNN, United States Circuit Judge.
  * * * *

  * * * To prove a Section 2 monopolization offense, a plaintiff must establish two elements: (1) the possession of monopoly power; and (2) willful acquisition or maintenance of that power—as opposed to simply superior products or historic accidents. An attempted monopolization offense consists of: (1) the use of anticompetitive conduct; (2) with specific intent to monopolize; and (3) a dangerous probability of success. [Emphasis added.]
  * * * *

  * * * To run afoul of Section 2, a defendant must be guilty of illegal conduct "to foreclose competition, to gain a competitive advantage, or to destroy a competitor." Conduct that might otherwise be lawful may be impermissibly exclusionary under antitrust law when practiced by a monopolist. Indeed, "a monopolist is not free to take certain actions

that a company in a competitive * * * market may take, because there is no market constraint on a monopolist's behavior." And although not per se illegal, exclusive dealing arrangements can constitute an improper means of acquiring or maintaining a monopoly.
  * * * *

Here, the district court assumed that Kolon adequately pled possession of monopoly power. That assumption was correct, given that Kolon pled, among other things, that: numerous barriers to entry into the U.S. para-aramid fiber market exist and supply is low; DuPont has long dominated the U.S. para-aramid fiber market; and DuPont currently controls over 70 percent of that market, i.e., that "DuPont's market share remains greater than 70% of all sales by purchase volume of para-aramid fiber in the United States."
  * * * *

  * * * Kolon complained that "because DuPont's supply contracts severely restricted access to customers and preclude effective competition, DuPont's conduct has had a direct, substantial, and adverse effect on competition. And DuPont's anticompetitive conduct has allowed it to control output and increase prices for para-aramid fiber in the United States." And "[b]y precluding Kolon from competition for these customers when demand for para-aramid fibers has significantly increased and supply is low, DuPont's conduct has constrained the only potential entrant to the United States in decades from effectively entering the market, reducing if not practically eliminating additional competition, as well as preserving and growing DuPont's monopoly position." These allegations are sufficient to withstand a motion to dismiss.

DECISION AND REMEDY   The federal appellate court reversed the district court's decision, finding that Kolon had alleged sufficient facts to show that DuPont's behavior violated the prohibition against monopolization and attempted monopolization in Section 2 of the Sherman Act.

MANAGERIAL IMPLICATIONS   *Kolon's success in raising antitrust issues against a major supplier of a particular product in the United States can give some hope to other companies that are attempting to expand their market share against a dominant competitor. In other words, managers who see competitive opportunities, even though their companies have only a very small market share, may be able to resort to the courts to prevent the dominant company or companies from acting in anticompetitive ways.*

RELEVANT MARKET   Before a court can determine whether a firm has a dominant market share, it must define the relevant market. The relevant market consists of two elements: a relevant product market and a relevant geographic market.

Relevant Product Market.   The relevant product market includes all products that, although produced by different firms, have identical attributes, such as sugar. It also includes products that are reasonably interchangeable for the purpose for which they are produced. Products will be considered reasonably interchangeable if consumers treat them as acceptable substitutes.[13]

What should the relevant product market include? This is often a key issue in monopolization cases because the way the market is defined may determine whether a firm has monopoly power. In defining the relevant product market, the key issue is the degree of interchangeability between products. By defining the product market narrowly, the degree of a firm's market power is enhanced.

CASE EXAMPLE 19.5   Whole Foods Market, Inc., wished to acquire Wild Oats Markets, Inc., its main competitor in nationwide high-end organic food supermarkets. The Federal Trade Commission (FTC) filed a Section 2 claim against Whole Foods to prevent the merger. The FTC argued that the relevant product market consisted of only "premium natural and organic supermarkets" rather than all supermarkets, as Whole Foods maintained. An appellate court accepted the FTC's narrow definition of the relevant market and remanded the case to the lower court to decide what remedies were appropriate, as the merger had already taken place. Whole Foods later entered into a settlement with the FTC under which it was required to divest (sell or give up control over) thirteen stores, most of which were formerly Wild Oats outlets.[14] •

Relevant Geographic Market.   The second component of the relevant market is the geographic boundaries of the market. For products that are sold nationwide, the geographic boundaries of the market encompass the entire United States. If transportation costs are significant or a producer and its competitors sell in only a limited area (one in which customers have no access to other sources of the product), the geographic market is limited to that area. A national firm may thus compete in several distinct areas and have monopoly power in one area but not in another.

Generally, the geographic market is that section of the country within which a firm can increase its price a bit without attracting new sellers or without losing many customers to alternative suppliers outside that area. Of course, the Internet and e-commerce are changing the notion of the size and limits of a geographic market. It may become difficult to perceive any geographic market as local, except for products that are not easily transported, such as concrete.

THE INTENT REQUIREMENT   Monopoly power, in and of itself, does not constitute the offense of monopolization under Section 2 of the Sherman Act. The offense also requires an *intent* to monopolize.

Why Intent Is Required.   A dominant market share may be the result of business acumen or the development of a superior product. It may simply be the result of a historic accident. In these situations, the acquisition of monopoly power is not an antitrust violation. Indeed, it would be contrary to society's interest to condemn every firm that acquired a position of power because it was well managed and efficient and marketed a product desired by consumers.

KEEP IN MIND   Section 2 of the Sherman Act essentially condemns the act of monopolizing, not the possession of monopoly power.

---

13. See, for example, *HDC Medical, Inc. v. Minntech Corp.,* 474 F.3d 543 (8th Cir. 2007).
14. *FTC v. Whole Foods Market, Inc.,* 548 F.3d 1028 (D.C.Cir. 2008); and 592 F.Supp.2d 107 (D.D.C. 2009).

Intent May Be Inferred. If a firm possesses market power as a result of carrying out some purposeful act to acquire or maintain that power through anticompetitive means, then it is in violation of Section 2. In most monopolization cases, intent may be inferred from evidence that the firm had monopoly power and engaged in anticompetitive behavior.

UNILATERAL REFUSALS TO DEAL As discussed previously, joint refusals to deal (group boycotts) are subject to close scrutiny under Section 1 of the Sherman Act. A single manufacturer acting unilaterally, though, normally is free to deal, or not to deal, with whomever it wishes.[15]

Nevertheless, in limited circumstances, a unilateral refusal to deal will violate antitrust laws. These instances involve offenses proscribed under Section 2 of the Sherman Act and occur only if (1) the firm refusing to deal has—or is likely to acquire—monopoly power and (2) the refusal is likely to have an anticompetitive effect on a particular market.

EXAMPLE 19.6 Clark Industries, the owner of three of the four major downhill ski areas in Blue Hills, Idaho, refuses to continue participating in a jointly offered six-day "all Blue Hills" lift ticket. Clark's refusal to cooperate with its smaller competitor is a violation of Section 2 of the Sherman Act. Because Clark owns three-fourths of the local ski areas, it has monopoly power, and thus its unilateral refusal has an anticompetitive effect on the market. •

Attempts to Monopolize

Section 2 also prohibits **attempted monopolization** of a market, which requires proof of the following three elements:

Attempted Monopolization Any action by a firm to eliminate competition and gain monopoly power.

1. Anticompetitive conduct.
2. The specific intent to exclude competitors and garner monopoly power.
3. A "dangerous" probability of success in achieving monopoly power. The probability cannot be dangerous unless the alleged offender possesses some degree of market power.

Only *serious* threats of monopolization are condemned as violations.

EXAMPLE 19.7 Big Deal, Inc., owns five rock-format radio stations in Cincinnati, Ohio, and is a major concert promoter in the area. Big Deal's share of the ad revenue in the relevant market is about 90 percent. Big Deal's stations refuse to accept ads for performers who do not contract with Big Deal to promote their concerts. Consequently, many artists are intimidated into contracting exclusively with Big Deal. Big Deal's activities represent an attempt to monopolize the market in violation of Section 2 of the Sherman Act. Although exclusive or favored arrangements between firms are common and generally are lawful, they may be unlawful when used by a monopolist. Big Deal is a monopolist in its relevant market. How the firm uses its monopoly power and how its actions affect competition make its practices illegal. The effects may include an increase in ticket prices and a decreasing market share for the firm's competitors, for instance. •

As mentioned earlier, predatory pricing is a form of anticompetitive conduct that, in theory, could be used by firms that are attempting to monopolize. (Predatory pricing may also lead to claims of price discrimination, to be discussed shortly.) Predatory bidding involves the acquisition and use of *monopsony power,* which is

---

15. See, for example, *Pacific Bell Telephone Co. v. Linkline Communications, Inc.,* 555 U.S. 438, 129 S.Ct. 1109, 172 L.Ed.2d 836 (2009).

market power on the *buy* side of a market. This may occur when a buyer bids up the price of an input too high for its competitors to pay, causing them to leave the market. The predatory bidder may then attempt to drive down input prices to reap above-competitive profits and recoup any losses it suffered in bidding up the prices.

The question in the following *Spotlight Case* was whether a claim of predatory bidding is sufficiently similar to a claim of predatory pricing that the same test should apply to both.

SPOTLIGHT ON WEYERHAEUSER
Case 19.2   Weyerhaeuser Co. v. Ross-Simmons Hardwood Lumber Co.

Supreme Court of the United States, 549 U.S. 312, 127 S.Ct. 1069, 166 L.Ed.2d 911 (2007).

BACKGROUND AND FACTS   Weyerhaeuser Company entered the Pacific Northwest's hardwood lumber market in 1980. By 2000, Weyerhaeuser owned six mills processing 65 percent of the red alder logs in the region. Meanwhile, Ross-Simmons Hardwood Lumber Company operated a single competing mill. When the prices of logs rose and those for lumber fell, Ross-Simmons suffered heavy losses. Several million dollars in debt, the mill closed in 2001. Ross-Simmons filed a suit in a federal district court against Weyerhaeuser, alleging attempted monopolization under Section 2 of the Sherman Act. Ross-Simmons claimed that Weyerhaeuser used its dominant position in the market to bid up the prices of logs and prevent its competitors from being profitable. Weyerhaeuser argued that the antitrust test for predatory pricing applies to a claim of predatory bidding and that Ross-Simmons had not met this standard. The district court ruled in favor of the plaintiff, a federal appellate court affirmed, and Weyerhaeuser appealed.

IN THE WORDS OF THE COURT . . .
Justice THOMAS delivered the opinion of the Court.
    * * * *

    Predatory-pricing and predatory-bidding claims are analytically similar. This similarity results from the close theoretical connection between monopoly and monopsony. The kinship between monopoly and monopsony suggests that similar legal standards should apply to claims of monopolization and to claims of monopsonization.
    * * * Both claims involve the deliberate use of unilateral pricing measures for anticompetitive purposes. And both claims logically require firms to incur short-term losses on the chance that they might reap supracompetitive [above-competitive] profits in the future.
    * * * *
    * * * *"Predatory pricing schemes are rarely tried, and even more rarely successful." Predatory pricing requires a firm to suffer certain losses in the short term on the chance of reaping supracompetitive profits in the future. A rational business will rarely make this sacrifice. The same reasoning applies to predatory bidding. [Emphasis added.]
    * * * *
    * * * A failed predatory-pricing scheme may benefit consumers. * * * Failed predatory-bidding schemes can also * * * benefit consumers.

In addition, predatory bidding presents less of a direct threat of consumer harm than predatory pricing. A predatory-pricing scheme ultimately achieves success by charging higher prices to consumers. By contrast, a predatory-bidding scheme could succeed with little or no effect on consumer prices because a predatory bidder does not necessarily rely on raising prices in the output market to recoup its losses.
    * * * *
    * * * [Thus] our two-pronged [predatory pricing] test should apply to predatory-bidding claims.
    * * * A plaintiff must prove that the alleged predatory bidding led to below-cost pricing of the predator's outputs. That is, the predator's bidding on the buy side must have caused the cost of the relevant output to rise above the revenues generated in the sale of those outputs. * * * Given the multitude of procompetitive ends served by higher bidding for inputs, the risk of chilling procompetitive behavior with too lax a liability standard is * * * serious * * *. Consequently, only higher bidding that leads to below-cost pricing in the relevant output market will suffice as a basis for liability for predatory bidding.

    A predatory-bidding plaintiff also must prove that the defendant has a dangerous probability of recouping the losses incurred in bidding up input prices through the exercise of monopsony power. Absent proof of likely recoupment, a strategy of predatory bidding makes no economic sense because it would involve short-term losses with no likelihood of offsetting long-term gains.

    Ross-Simmons has conceded that it has not satisfied [this] standard. Therefore, its predatory-bidding theory of liability cannot support the jury's verdict.

DECISION AND REMEDY   The United States Supreme Court held that the antitrust test that applies to claims of predatory pricing also applies to claims of predatory bidding. Because Ross-Simmons conceded that it had not met this standard, the Court vacated the lower court's judgment and remanded the case.

THE ECONOMIC DIMENSION   *Why does a plaintiff alleging predatory bidding have to prove that the defendant's "bidding on the buy side caused the cost of the relevant output to rise above the revenues generated in the sale of those outputs"?*

The Clayton Act

LEARNING OBJECTIVE 3 What are the four major provisions of the Clayton Act, and what types of activities do these provisions prohibit?

In 1914, Congress attempted to strengthen federal antitrust laws by enacting the Clayton Act. The Clayton Act was aimed at specific anticompetitive or monopolistic practices that the Sherman Act did not cover. The substantive provisions of the act deal with four distinct forms of business behavior, which are declared illegal but not criminal. In each instance, the act states that the behavior is illegal only if it tends to substantially lessen competition or to create monopoly power.

The major offenses under the Clayton Act are set out in Sections 2, 3, 7, and 8 of the act.

Section 2—Price Discrimination

Price Discrimination Setting prices in such a way that two competing buyers pay two different prices for an identical product or service.

Section 2 of the Clayton Act prohibits **price discrimination,** which occurs when a seller charges different prices to competing buyers for identical goods or services. Congress strengthened this section by amending it with the passage of the Robinson-Patman Act in 1936.

As amended, Section 2 prohibits price discrimination that cannot be justified by differences in production costs, transportation costs, or cost differences due to other reasons. In short, a seller is prohibited from charging a lower price to one buyer than is charged to that buyer's competitor.

REQUIREMENTS   To violate Section 2, the seller must be engaged in interstate commerce, the goods must be of like grade and quality, and goods must have been sold to two or more purchasers. In addition, the effect of the price discrimination must be to substantially lessen competition, tend to create a monopoly, or otherwise injure competition. Without proof of an actual injury resulting from the price discrimination, the plaintiff cannot recover damages.

Note that price discrimination claims can arise from discounts, offsets, rebates, or allowances given to one buyer over another. Moreover, giving favorable credit terms, delivery, or freight charges to some buyers but not others can also lead to allegations of price discrimination. For example, offering goods to different customers at the same price but including free delivery for certain buyers may violate Section 2 in some circumstances.

"Becoming number one is easier than remaining number one."
Bill Bradley, 1943–present
(American politician and athlete)

DEFENSES   There are several statutory defenses to liability for price discrimination. We discuss some of the common defenses next.

Cost Justification.   If the seller can justify the price reduction by demonstrating that a particular buyer's purchases saved the seller costs in producing and selling the goods, the seller will not be liable for price discrimination.

Meeting the Price of Competition.   If the seller charged the lower price in a good faith attempt to meet an equally low price of a competitor, the seller will not be liable for price discrimination.

Changing Market Conditions.   A seller may lower its price on an item in response to changing conditions affecting the market for or the marketability of the goods concerned. Thus, if an advance in technology makes a particular product less marketable than it was previously, a seller can lower the product's price.

Section 3—Exclusionary Practices

Under Section 3 of the Clayton Act, sellers or lessors cannot sell or lease goods "on the condition, agreement or understanding that the . . . purchaser or lessee thereof shall not use or deal in the goods . . . of a competitor or competitors of the seller." In effect, this section prohibits two types of vertical agreements involving exclusionary practices—exclusive-dealing contracts and tying arrangements.

Exclusive-Dealing Contract
An agreement under which a seller forbids a buyer to purchase products from the seller's competitors.

EXCLUSIVE-DEALING CONTRACTS   A contract under which a seller forbids a buyer to purchase products from the seller's competitors is called an **exclusive-dealing contract.** A seller is prohibited from making an exclusive-dealing contract under Section 3 if the effect of the contract is "to substantially lessen competition or tend to create a monopoly."

CASE EXAMPLE 19.8   Standard Oil Company, the largest gasoline seller in the nation in the late 1940s, made exclusive-dealing contracts with independent stations in seven western states. The contracts involved 16 percent of all retail outlets, with sales amounting to approximately 7 percent of all retail sales in that market. In a case decided in 1949, the United States Supreme Court said that the market was substantially concentrated because the seven largest gasoline suppliers all used exclusive-dealing contracts with their independent retailers. Together, these suppliers controlled 65 percent of the market. Looking at market conditions after the arrangements were instituted, the Court found that market shares were extremely stable and that entry into the market was apparently restricted. The Court held that Section 3 of the Clayton Act had been violated because competition was "foreclosed in a substantial share" of the relevant market.[16] ●

Note that since the Supreme Court's 1949 decision, a number of subsequent decisions have called the holding in this case into doubt. Today, it is clear that to violate antitrust law, an exclusive-dealing agreement (or *tying arrangement,* discussed next) must qualitatively and substantially harm competition. To prevail, a plaintiff must present affirmative evidence that the performance of the agreement will foreclose competition and harm consumers.

Tying Arrangement   An agreement between a buyer and a seller in which the buyer of a specific product or service becomes obligated to purchase additional products or services from the seller.

TYING ARRANGEMENTS   When a seller conditions the sale of a product (the tying product) on the buyer's agreement to purchase another product (the tied product) produced or distributed by the same seller, a **tying arrangement** results. The legality of such an agreement depends on many factors, particularly the purpose of the agreement and the agreement's likely effect on competition in the relevant markets.

EXAMPLE 19.9   Morshigi Precision, Inc., manufactures computer hardware and provides repair service for the hardware. Morshigi also makes and markets software and provides support for those who use the software, but the company refuses to provide software support to those who do not buy its hardware service. Morshigi's practice is a tying arrangement. When a seller conditions the sale of one of its products on the purchase of another of its products, a tying arrangement results. Depending on the purpose of the agreement and the effect of the agreement on competition in the market for the two products, the agreement may be illegal. ●

Section 3 of the Clayton Act has been held to apply only to commodities, not to services. Some tying arrangements, however, can also be considered agreements that restrain trade in violation of Section 1 of the Sherman Act. Thus, cases involving

---

16. *Standard Oil Co. of California v. United States,* 337 U.S. 293, 69 S.Ct. 1051, 93 L.Ed. 1371 (1949).

tying arrangements of services have been brought under Section 1 of the Sherman Act. Although earlier cases condemned tying arrangements as illegal *per se,* courts now evaluate tying agreements under the rule of reason.

Section 7—Mergers

Under Section 7 of the Clayton Act, a person or business organization cannot hold stock and/or assets in another entity "where the effect . . . may be to substantially lessen competition." Section 7 is the statutory authority for preventing mergers or acquisitions that could result in monopoly power or a substantial lessening of competition in the marketplace. Section 7 applies to horizontal mergers and vertical mergers, both of which we discuss in the following subsections.

A crucial consideration in most merger cases is the **market concentration** of a product or business. Determining market concentration involves allocating percentage market shares among the various companies in the relevant market. When a small number of companies control a large share of the market, the market is concentrated. If the four largest grocery stores in Chicago accounted for 80 percent of all retail food sales, for example, the market clearly would be concentrated in those four firms.

Competition, however, is not necessarily diminished solely as a result of market concentration, and courts will consider other factors in determining whether a merger will violate Section 7. One factor of particular importance in evaluating the effects of a merger is whether the merger will make it more difficult for *potential* competitors to enter the relevant market.

Market Concentration The degree to which a small number of firms control a large percentage share of a relevant market; determined by calculating the percentages held by the largest firms in that market.

HORIZONTAL MERGERS Mergers between firms that compete with each other in the same market are called **horizontal mergers.** If a horizontal merger creates an entity with a significant market share, the merger will be presumed illegal because it increases market concentration.

When analyzing the legality of a horizontal merger, the courts also consider three other factors: the overall concentration of the relevant product market, the relevant market's history of tending toward concentration, and whether the apparent design of the merger is to establish market power or to restrict competition.

Horizontal Merger A merger between two firms that are competing in the same marketplace.

VERTICAL MERGERS A **vertical merger** occurs when a company at one stage of production acquires a company at a higher or lower stage of production. An example of a vertical merger is a company merging with one of its suppliers or retailers. Whether a vertical merger will be deemed illegal generally depends on several factors, such as whether the merger would produce a firm controlling an undue percentage share of the relevant market.

The courts also analyze whether the merger would result in a significant increase in the concentration of firms in that market, the barriers to entry into the market, and the apparent intent of the merging parties. Mergers that do not prevent competitors of either merging firm from competing in a segment of the market will not be condemned as "foreclosing" competition and are legal.

Vertical Merger The acquisition by a company at one level in a marketing chain of a company at a higher or lower level in the chain (such as a company merging with one of its suppliers or retailers).

Section 8—Interlocking Directorates

The Clayton Act also deals with *interlocking directorates,* which exist when individuals serve as directors on the boards of two or more competing companies. No person may be a director or officer in two or more competing corporations at the same time if either of the competitors has capital, surplus, or undivided profits adding up to more than $27,784,000. An exception to this rule is made if the competitive sales of either corporation are less than $2,778,400. The Federal Trade Commission (FTC) adjusts these threshold amounts each year. (The amounts given here are those announced by the FTC in 2012.)

The reasoning behind the FTC's prohibition of interlocking directorates is that if two competing businesses share the same officers and directors, it is very likely that the organizations will not compete with one another, or will not compete aggressively. If directors or officers do not comply with this prohibition, they may be liable under the Clayton Act.

▶ Enforcement and Exemptions

LEARNING OBJECTIVE 4 What agencies of the federal government enforce the federal antitrust laws?

The federal agencies that enforce the federal antitrust laws are the U.S. Department of Justice (DOJ) and the Federal Trade Commission (FTC). The FTC was established by the Federal Trade Commission Act of 1914. Section 5 of that act condemns all forms of anticompetitive behavior that are not covered under other federal antitrust laws.

Agency Actions

Divestiture The act of selling one or more of a company's divisions or parts, such as a subsidiary or plant.

Only the DOJ can prosecute violations of the Sherman Act, which can be either criminal or civil offenses. Either the DOJ or the FTC can enforce the Clayton Act, but violations of that statute are not crimes and can be pursued only through civil proceedings. The DOJ or the FTC may ask the courts to impose various remedies, including **divestiture** (making a company give up one or more of its operating functions) and dissolution. A meatpacking firm, for example, might be forced to divest itself of control or ownership of butcher shops.

The FTC has the sole authority to enforce violations of Section 5 of the Federal Trade Commission Act. FTC actions are effected through administrative orders, but if a firm violates an FTC order, the FTC can seek court sanctions for the violation.

The president, of course, plays a role in establishing enforcement policies at the agencies. The Obama administration has taken a more active antitrust stance than the George W. Bush administration did. The Obama administration is vigorously enforcing antitrust regulations—similar to the approach that the European Union has taken in recent years.

Private Actions

CONTRAST Section 5 of the Federal Trade Commission Act is broader than the other antitrust laws. It covers nearly all anticompetitive behavior, including conduct that does not violate either the Sherman Act or the Clayton Act.

A private party who has been injured as a result of a violation of the Sherman Act or the Clayton Act can sue for damages and attorneys' fees. In some instances, private parties may also seek injunctive relief to prevent antitrust violations. The courts have determined that the ability to sue depends on the directness of the injury suffered by the would-be plaintiff.

Thus, a person wishing to sue under the Sherman Act must prove the following:

1. The antitrust violation either caused or was a substantial factor in causing the injury that was suffered.
2. The unlawful actions of the accused party affected business activities of the plaintiff that were protected by the antitrust laws.

In 2007, the United States Supreme Court limited the ability of private parties to pursue antitrust lawsuits without presenting some evidence of facts that suggest that an illegal agreement was made.

CASE EXAMPLE 19.10 A group of subscribers to local telephone and high-speed Internet services filed a class-action lawsuit against several regional telecommunication companies (including Bell Atlantic). The plaintiffs claimed that the companies had conspired with one another and engaged in *parallel conduct*—offering similar services and pricing—over a period of years to prevent other companies from entering the market and competing. The Supreme Court dismissed the case, finding that "without more, parallel conduct does not suggest conspiracy." A bare assertion of conspiracy is not enough to allow an antitrust lawsuit to go forward. The Court noted that more specificity is necessary to avoid potentially "massive" discovery costs, which are especially likely to occur when the suit is brought by a large class of plaintiffs.[17] ●

Treble Damages

Treble Damages Damages that, by statute, are three times the amount that the fact finder determines is owed.

In recent years, more than 90 percent of all antitrust actions have been brought by private plaintiffs. One reason for this is that successful plaintiffs may recover **treble damages**—three times the damages that they have suffered as a result of the violation. In a situation involving a price-fixing agreement, normally each competitor is jointly and severally liable for the total amount of any damages, including treble damages if they are imposed.

Exemptions from Antitrust Laws

There are many legislative and constitutional limitations on antitrust enforcement. Most of the statutory or judicially created exemptions to antitrust laws apply in such areas as labor, insurance, and foreign trade (see Exhibit 19–1 on the next page). One of the most significant exemptions covers joint efforts by businesspersons to obtain legislative, judicial, or executive action. Under this exemption, for example, Blu-ray producers can jointly lobby Congress to change the copyright laws without being held liable for attempting to restrain trade. Another exemption covers professional baseball teams.

▶ U.S. Antitrust Laws in the Global Context

U.S. antitrust laws have a broad application. Not only may persons in foreign nations be subject to their provisions, but the laws may also be applied to protect foreign consumers and competitors from violations committed by U.S. business firms. Consequently, *foreign persons,* a term that by definition includes foreign governments, may sue under U.S. antitrust laws in U.S. courts.

The Extraterritorial Application of U.S. Antitrust Laws

Section 1 of the Sherman Act provides for the extraterritorial effect of the U.S. antitrust laws. The United States is a major proponent of free competition in the global economy, and thus any conspiracy that has a *substantial effect* on U.S. commerce is within the reach of the Sherman Act. The violation may even occur outside the

---

17. *Bell Atlantic Corp. v. Twombly,* 550 U.S. 544, 127 S.Ct. 1955, 167 L.Ed.2d 929 (2007).

• *Exhibit* 19–1 **Exemptions to Antitrust Enforcement**

EXEMPTION	SOURCE AND SCOPE
Labor	Clayton Act—Permits unions to organize and bargain without violating antitrust laws and specifies that strikes and other labor activities normally do not violate any federal law.
Agricultural associations	Clayton Act and Capper-Volstead Act of 1922—Allow agricultural cooperatives to set prices.
Fisheries	Fisheries Cooperative Marketing Act of 1976—Allows the fishing industry to set prices.
Insurance companies	McCarran-Ferguson Act of 1945—Exempts the insurance business in states in which the industry is regulated.
Exporters	Webb-Pomerene Act of 1918—Allows U.S. exporters to engage in cooperative activity to compete with similar foreign associations. Export Trading Company Act of 1982—Permits the U.S. Department of Justice to exempt certain exporters.
Professional baseball	The United States Supreme Court has held that professional baseball is exempt because it is not "interstate commerce."[a]
Oil marketing	Interstate Oil Compact of 1935—Allows states to set quotas on oil to be marketed in interstate commerce.
Defense activities	Defense Production Act of 1950—Allows the president to approve, and thereby exempt, certain activities to further the military defense of the United States.
Small businesses' cooperative research	Small Business Administration Act of 1958—Allows small firms to undertake cooperative research.
State actions	The United States Supreme Court has held that actions by a state are exempt if the state clearly articulates and actively supervises the policy behind its action.[b]
Regulated industries	Industries (such as airlines) are exempt when a federal administrative agency (such as the Federal Aviation Administration) has primary regulatory authority.
Businesspersons' joint efforts to seek government action	Cooperative efforts by businesspersons to obtain legislative, judicial, or executive action are exempt unless it is clear that an effort is "objectively baseless" and is an attempt to make anticompetitive use of government processes.[c]

a. *Federal Baseball Club of Baltimore, Inc. v. National League of Professional Baseball Clubs,* 259 U.S. 200, 42 S.Ct. 465, 66 L.Ed. 898 (1922). A federal district court has held that this exemption applies only to the game's reserve system. (Under the reserve system, teams hold players' contracts for the players' entire careers. The reserve system generally is being replaced by the free agency system.) See *Piazza v. Major League Baseball,* 831 F.Supp. 420 (E.D.Pa. 1993).

b. See *Parker v. Brown,* 317 U.S. 341, 63 S.Ct. 307, 87 L.Ed. 315 (1943).

c. *Eastern Railroad Presidents Conference v. Noerr Motor Freight, Inc.,* 365 U.S. 127, 81 S.Ct. 523, 5 L.Ed.2d 464 (1961); and *United Mine Workers of America v. Pennington,* 381 U.S. 657, 89 S.Ct. 1585, 14 L.Ed.2d 626 (1965). These two cases established the exception often referred to as the *Noerr-Pennington* doctrine.

United States, and foreign governments as well as persons can be sued for violation of U.S. antitrust laws. Before U.S. courts will exercise jurisdiction and apply antitrust laws, it must be shown that the alleged violation had a substantial effect on U.S. commerce. U.S. jurisdiction is automatically invoked, however, when a *per se* violation occurs.

If a domestic firm, for example, joins a foreign cartel to control the production, price, or distribution of goods, and this cartel has a *substantial effect* on U.S. commerce, a *per se* violation may exist. Hence, both the domestic firm and the foreign cartel could be sued for violation of the U.S. antitrust laws. Likewise, if a foreign firm doing business in the United States enters into a price-fixing or other anticompetitive agreement to control a portion of U.S. markets, a *per se* violation may exist.

In the following case, the court had to decide whether an alleged anticompetitive conspiracy had a substantial effect on U.S. commerce.

Case 19.3 | Carrier Corp. v. Outokumpu Oyj

United States Court of Appeals, Sixth Circuit, 673 F.3d 430 (2012).

BACKGROUND AND FACTS   Carrier Corporation is a U.S. firm that manufactures air-conditioning and refrigeration (ACR) equipment. To make these products, Carrier uses ACR copper tubing bought from Outokumpu Oyj, a Finnish company. Carrier is one of the world's largest purchasers of ACR copper tubing. The Commission of the European Communities (EC) found that Outokumpu had conspired with other companies to fix ACR tubing prices in Europe. Carrier then filed a lawsuit in a U.S. court, alleging that the cartel had also conspired to fix prices in the United States by agreeing that only Outokumpu would sell ACR tubing in the U.S. market. The district court dismissed Carrier's claim for lack of jurisdiction. Carrier appealed.

IN THE WORDS OF THE COURT . . .
Karen Nelson *MOORE*, Circuit Judge.
* * * *

Carrier's complaint describes, in some detail, an elaborate worldwide conspiracy in which the U.S. market for ACR copper tubing was assigned to Outokumpu. Furthermore, *Carrier alleges that this conspiracy caused the price of goods purchased within the United States to increase, which in turn caused a direct antitrust injury.* In support of these allegations, the complaint references numerous specific dates during which the * * * cartel met and the various agreements its members entered into. *Assuming that these allegations are true, as we must, we conclude that Carrier has met any applicable requirement that it allege a [substantial] effect on U.S. commerce.* [Emphasis added.]

Outokumpu, which attached the full EC decision to its motion to dismiss, counters that many of the details contained in the complaint are drawn from [an] EC * * * decision that found no evidence that the cartel's focus extended beyond Europe. * * *   As a consequence,

Outokumpu argues that any details regarding specific meetings and agreements occurring during the [cartel] meetings are of no assistance to Carrier because they relate only to a European conspiracy.

We are [not] persuaded by this argument. * * * The EC * * * decision clearly states that "insofar as the activities of the cartel relate to sales in countries that are not members of the Community * * * they lie outside the scope of this Decision." Thus, any silence on the part of the EC decision as to U.S. markets may simply reflect the limited scope of the decision.
* * * *

Furthermore, Carrier offers additional circumstantial allegations that corroborate its claim that the market-allocation scheme extended to the United States. Although Carrier's complaint provides numerous circumstantial allegations, of particular interest is its claim that [Outokumpu's competitors] initially refrained from aggressively competing for Carrier's U.S. business until 2003, and then suddenly began doing so at that time. It is true that the mere fact that competitors do not intrude upon one another's markets does not necessarily mean that an illegal market-allocation scheme is taking place. When two companies refrain from entering a market and then suddenly do so after a cartel dissolves, however, there are good grounds for suspicion.

DECISION AND REMEDY   The federal appellate court found that the district court had jurisdiction over Carrier's Sherman Act claims. It therefore reversed the district court's judgment for the defendants.

THE LEGAL ENVIRONMENT DIMENSION   *When this case proceeds, should the district court apply the rule of reason? Why or why not?*

The Application of Foreign Antitrust Laws

Large U.S. companies increasingly need to worry about the application of foreign antitrust laws as well. The European Union, in particular, has stepped up its enforcement actions against antitrust violators, as discussed in this chapter's *Beyond Our Borders* feature below.

Beyond Our Borders | The European Union's Expanding Role in Antitrust Litigation

The European Union (EU) has laws promoting competition that are stricter in many respects than those of the United States. Although the EU's laws provide only for civil, rather than criminal, penalties, the rules exhibit a different philosophy and define more conduct as anticompetitive than U.S. laws do.

Continued ➠

The EU actively pursues antitrust violators, especially individual companies and cartels that engage in monopolistic conduct. For example, in 2009 the EU fined Intel, Inc., $1.44 billion in an antitrust case. According to European regulators, Intel offered computer manufacturers and retailers price discounts and marketing subsidies if they agreed to buy Intel's semiconductor chips rather than the chips produced by Intel's main competitor in Europe. The EU has also fined Microsoft Corporation more than $2 billion in the last ten years for anticompetitive conduct.

The EU is investigating Google, Inc., for potentially violating European antitrust laws by thwarting competition in Internet search engines. Ironically, in 2011, Microsoft—which has paid substantial fines to the EU for its own anticompetitive conduct—filed its own complaint with the EU against Google. Among other things, Microsoft claims that Google has unlawfully restricted competing search engines from accessing YouTube, content from book publishers, advertiser data, and more. (A similar case brought against Google in the United States for monopolizing or attempting to monopolize Internet search engines was dismissed in 2011.[18])

• For Critical Analysis

Some commentators argue that EU regulators are too focused on reining in powerful U.S. technology companies, such as Microsoft and Intel. How might the large fines imposed by the EU on successful U.S. technology firms affect competition in the United States?

Many other nations also have laws that promote competition and prohibit trade restraints. For instance, Japanese antitrust laws forbid unfair trade practices, monopolization, and restrictions that unreasonably restrain trade. China's antitrust rules restrict monopolization and price fixing (although China has claimed that the government may set prices on exported goods without violating these rules). Indonesia, Malaysia, South Korea, and Vietnam all have statutes protecting competition. Argentina, Brazil, Chile, Peru, and several other Latin American countries have adopted modern antitrust laws as well.

Most of these antitrust laws apply extraterritorially, as U.S. antitrust laws do. This means that a U.S. company may be subject to another nation's antitrust laws if the company's conduct has a substantial effect on that nation's commerce. For instance, South Korea fined Intel, Inc., the world's largest semiconductor chip maker, $25 million for antitrust violations in 2008.

---

18. *TradeComet.com, LLC v. Google, Inc.*, 647 F.3d 472 (2d Cir. 2011).

▶ Reviewing . . . Antitrust Law and Promoting Competition

The Internet Corporation for Assigned Names and Numbers (ICANN) is a nonprofit entity that organizes Internet domain names. It is governed by a board of directors elected by various groups with commercial interests in the Internet. One of ICANN's functions is to authorize an entity to serve as a registrar for certain "top-level domains" (TLDs). ICANN entered into an agreement with VeriSign to provide registry services for the ".com" TLD in accordance with ICANN's specifications. VeriSign complained that ICANN was restricting the services that it could make available as a registrar and was blocking new services, imposing unnecessary conditions on those services, and setting prices at which the services were offered. VeriSign claimed that ICANN's control of the registry services for domain names violated Section 1 of the Sherman Act. Using the information presented in the chapter, answer the following questions.

1. Should ICANN's actions be judged under the rule of reason or be deemed a *per se* violation of Section 1 of the Sherman Act? Explain.
2. Should ICANN's action be viewed as a horizontal or a vertical restraint of trade? Discuss.
3. Does it matter that ICANN's directors are chosen by groups with a commercial interest in the Internet? Why or why not?
4. If the dispute is judged under the rule of reason, what might be ICANN's defense for having a standardized set of registry services that must be used?

Debate This

The Internet and the rise of e-commerce have rendered our antitrust concepts and laws obsolete.

Key Terms

antitrust law 478
attempted monopolization 487
concentrated industry 483
divestiture 492
exclusive-dealing contract 490
group boycott 482
horizontal merger 491
horizontal restraint 481

market concentration 491
market power 479
monopolization 484
monopoly 479
monopoly power 479
per se violation 480
predatory pricing 484
price discrimination 489

price-fixing agreement 481
resale price maintenance agreement 484
rule of reason 480
treble damages 493
tying arrangement 490
vertical merger 491
vertical restraint 483
vertically integrated firm 483

Chapter Summary: Antitrust Law and Promoting Competition

The Sherman Antitrust Act—Section 1 and Section 2 (See pages 479–488.)	1. *Major provisions*—
	   a. *Section 1*—Prohibits contracts, combinations, and conspiracies in restraint of trade.
	     (1) Horizontal restraints subject to Section 1 include price-fixing agreements, group boycotts (joint refusals to deal), horizontal market divisions, and trade association agreements.
	     (2) Vertical restraints subject to Section 1 include territorial or customer restrictions and resale price maintenance agreements.
	   b. *Section 2*—Prohibits monopolies and attempts to monopolize.
	 2. *Jurisdictional requirements*—The Sherman Act applies only to activities that have a significant impact on interstate commerce.
	 3. *Interpretive rules*—
	   a. *Per se rule*—Applied to restraints on trade that are so inherently anticompetitive that they cannot be justified and are deemed illegal as a matter of law.
	   b. *Rule of reason*—Applied when an anticompetitive agreement may be justified by legitimate benefits. Under the rule of reason, the lawfulness of a trade restraint will be determined by the purpose and effects of the restraint.

The Clayton Act (1914) (See pages 489–492.)	The major provisions are as follows:
	 1. *Section 2*—As amended in 1936 by the Robinson-Patman Act, prohibits price discrimination that substantially lessens competition and prohibits a seller engaged in interstate commerce from selling to two or more buyers goods of similar grade and quality at different prices when the result is a substantial lessening of competition or the creation of a competitive injury.
	 2. *Section 3*—Prohibits exclusionary practices, such as exclusive-dealing contracts and tying arrangements, when the effect may be to substantially lessen competition.
	 3. *Section 7*—Prohibits mergers when the effect may be to substantially lessen competition or to tend to create a monopoly.
	   a. *Horizontal merger*—The acquisition by merger or consolidation of a competing firm engaged in the same relevant market. Will be presumed unlawful if the entity created by the merger will have more than a small percentage market share.
	   b. *Vertical merger*—The acquisition by a seller of one of its suppliers or retailers or vice versa. Will be unlawful if the merger prevents competitors of either merging firm from competing in a segment of the market that otherwise would be open to them, resulting in a substantial lessening of competition.
	 4. *Section 8*—Prohibits interlocking directorates.

(Continued)

▶ Chapter Summary: Antitrust Law and Promoting Competition, Continued

Enforcement and Exemptions (See pages 492–493.)	1. *Enforcement*—Federal agencies that enforce antitrust laws are the U.S. Department of Justice and the Federal Trade Commission. The latter was established by the Federal Trade Commission Act of 1914. Private parties who have been injured as a result of violations of the Sherman Act or Clayton Act may also bring civil suits. In recent years, many private parties have filed such suits largely because, if successful, they may be awarded treble damages and attorneys' fees. 2. *Exemptions*—Numerous exemptions from antitrust enforcement have been created. See Exhibit 19–1 on page 494 for a list of significant exemptions.
U.S. Antitrust Laws in the Global Context (See pages 493–496.)	1. *Application of U.S. laws*—U.S. antitrust laws are broad and can be applied in foreign nations to protect foreign consumers and competitors. Foreign governments and persons can also bring actions under U.S. antitrust laws. Section 1 of the Sherman Act applies to any conspiracy that has a substantial effect on U.S. commerce. 2. *Application of foreign laws*—Many other nations also have laws that promote competition and prohibit trade restraints, and some are more restrictive than U.S. laws. These foreign antitrust laws are increasingly being applied to U.S. firms.

▶ ExamPrep

ISSUE SPOTTERS

—Check your answers to these questions against the answers provided in Appendix D at the end of the text.

1. Under what circumstances would Pop's Market, a small store in a small, isolated town, be considered a monopolist? If Pop's is a monopolist, is it in violation of Section 2 of the Sherman Act? Why or why not? **(See page 484.)**
2. Maple Corporation conditions the sale of its syrup on the buyer's agreement to buy Maple's pancake mix. What factors would a court consider in deciding whether this arrangement violates the Clayton Act? **(See page 490.)**

BEFORE THE TEST

Go to **www.cengagebrain.com**, enter the ISBN 9781133586548, and click on "Find" to locate this textbook's Web site. Then click on "Access Now" under "Study Tools," and select Chapter 19 at the top. There, you will find a Practice Quiz that you can take to assess your mastery of the concepts in this chapter. Additionally, you will find Flashcards and a Glossary of important terms, as well as Video Questions (when assigned).

▶ For Review

Answers for the even-numbered questions in this For Review *section can be found in Appendix E at the end of this text.*

1. What is a monopoly? What is market power? How do these concepts relate to each other?
2. What type of activity is prohibited by Section 2 of the Sherman Act?
3. What are the four major provisions of the Clayton Act, and what types of activities do these provisions prohibit?
4. What agencies of the federal government enforce the federal antitrust laws?

▶ Questions and Case Problems

19–1. Section 1 of the Sherman Act. An agreement that is blatantly and substantially anticompetitive is deemed a *per se* violation of Section 1 of the Sherman Act. Under what rule is an agreement analyzed if it appears to be anticompetitive but is not a *per se* violation? In making this analysis, what factors will a court consider? **(See page 480.)**

19–2. Section 1 of the Sherman Act. Allitron, Inc., and Donovan, Ltd., are interstate competitors selling similar appliances, principally in the states of Illinois, Indiana, Kentucky, and Ohio. Allitron and Donovan agree that Allitron will no longer sell in Indiana and Ohio and that Donovan will no longer sell in Illinois and Kentucky. Have Allitron and Donovan violated any antitrust laws? If so, which law? Explain. **(See page 483.)**

19–3. **Question with Sample Answer: Group Boycott.** Jorge's Appliance Corp. was a new retail seller of appliances in Sunrise City. Because of its innovative sales techniques and financing, Jorge's caused the appliance department of No-Glow Department Store, a large chain store with a great deal of buying power, to lose a substantial amount of sales. No-Glow told a number of appliance manufacturers from whom it made large-volume purchases that if they continued to sell to Jorge's, No-Glow would stop buying from them. The manufacturers immediately stopped selling appliances to Jorge's. Jorge's filed a suit against No-Glow and the manufacturers, claiming that their actions constituted an antitrust violation. No-Glow and the manufacturers were able to prove that Jorge's was a small retailer with a small market share. They claimed that because the relevant market was not substantially affected, they were not guilty of restraint of trade. Discuss fully whether there was an antitrust violation. **(See pages 482–483.)**

—For a sample answer to Question 19–3, go to Appendix F at the end of this text.

19–4. Restraint of Trade. In 1999, residents of the city of Madison, Wisconsin, became concerned that excessive consumption of liquor seemed to be increasing near the campus of the University of Wisconsin–Madison (UW), leading to more frequent use of detoxification facilities and calls for police services in the campus area. Under pressure from UW, which shared these concerns, the city initiated a new policy, imposing conditions on area taverns to discourage price reduction "specials" believed to encourage high-volume and dangerous drinking. In 2002, the city began to draft an ordinance to ban all drink specials. Tavern owners responded by announcing that they had "voluntarily" agreed to discontinue drink specials on Friday and Saturday nights after 8 P.M. The city put its ordinance on hold. UW student Nic Eichenseer and others filed a suit in a Wisconsin state court against the Madison–Dane County Tavern League, Inc. (an association of local tavern owners), and others, alleging violations of antitrust law. On what might the plaintiffs base a claim for relief? Are the defendants in this case exempt from the antitrust laws? What should the court rule? Why? [*Eichenseer v. Madison–Dane County Tavern League, Inc.*, 2006 WI App. 226, 725 N.W.2d 274 (2006)] **(See pages 482–483.)**

19–5. Tying Arrangement. John Sheridan owned a Marathon gas station franchise. He sued Marathon Petroleum Co. under Section 1 of the Sherman Act and Section 3 of the Clayton Act, charging it with illegally tying the processing of credit-card sales to the gas station. As a condition of obtaining a Marathon dealership, dealers had to agree to let the franchisor process credit cards. They could not shop around to see if credit-card processing could be obtained at a lower price from another source. The district court dismissed the case for failure to state a claim. Sheridan appealed. Is there a tying arrangement? If so, does it violate the law? Explain. [*Sheridan v. Marathon Petroleum Co.*, 530 F.3d 590 (7th Cir. 2008)] **(See page 490.)**

19–6. **Case Problem with Sample Answer: Section 2 of the Sherman Act.** When Deer Valley Resort Co. (DVRC) was developing its ski resort in the Wasatch Mountains near Park City, Utah, it sold parcels of land in the resort village to third parties. Each sales contract reserved the right of approval over the conduct of certain businesses on the property, including ski rentals. For fifteen years, DVRC permitted Christy Sports, LLC, to rent skis in competition with DVRC's ski rental outlet. When DVRC opened a new mid-mountain ski rental outlet, it revoked Christy's permission to rent skis. This meant that most skiers who flew into Salt Lake City and shuttled to Deer Valley had few choices: they could carry their ski equipment onto their flights, take a shuttle into Park City and look for cheaper ski rentals there, or rent from DVRC. Christy filed a suit in a federal district court against DVRC. Was DVRC's action an attempt to monopolize in violation of Section 2 of the Sherman Act? Why or why not? [*Christy Sports, LLC v. Deer Valley Resort Co.*, 555 F.3d 1188 (10th Cir. 2009)] **(See page 487.)**

—For a sample answer to Case Problem 19–6, go to Appendix G at the end of this text.

19–7. **Spotlight on Sony: Price Fixing.** A group of consumers, including Keven Starr, sued several companies that produce, license, and distribute music sold as digital files over the Internet or on CDs. These companies controlled 80 percent of the digital music sold in the United States. They formed joint ventures called MusicNet and Duet to sell music to consumers. Through these ventures, the music sellers could communicate about pricing, terms, and use restrictions. Because the prices were so high, most consumers avoided them. Instead, song-by-song distribution over the Internet became more common. As a result, the music companies were forced to lower prices, but most sales were still done through MusicNet as the distributor. Eventually, the music companies agreed to a price of 70 cents wholesale for songs distributed on the Internet, but they refused to sell through another distributor, eMusic, which charged 25 cents per song. Consumers alleged that the music companies engaged in a conspiracy to restrain the distribution of Internet music and to fix and maintain artificially high prices. Do the consumers have a credible antitrust case to pursue in this situation? Discuss. [*Starr v. Sony BMG Music Entertainment*, 592 F.3d 314 (2d Cir. 2010)] **(See page 481.)**

19–8. Price Discrimination. Dayton Superior Corp. made and distributed commercial concrete construction products. Dayton's customers, including Spa Steel Products, Inc., competed with each other to sell Dayton's products. Spa Steel's customers began to buy Dayton's products from competitors whose prices for the same products were 10 to 15 percent lower than Spa Steel's prices. Consequently, Spa Steel lost sales. Could Spa Steel successfully allege price discrimination under the Clayton Act? Why or why not? [*Dayton Superior Corp. v. Spa Steel Products, Inc.,* 2012 WL 113663 (N.D.N.Y. 2012)] **(See page 489.)**

19–9. **A Question of Ethics: Section 1 of the Sherman Act.** *In the 1990s, DuCoa, LP, made choline chloride, a B-complex vitamin essential for the growth and development of animals. The U.S. market for choline chloride was divided into thirds among DuCoa, Bioproducts, Inc., and Chinook Group, Ltd. To stabilize the market and keep the price of the vitamin higher than it would otherwise be, the companies agreed to fix the price and allocate market share by deciding which of them would offer the lowest price to each customer. At times, however, the companies disregarded the agreement. During an increase in competitive activity in August 1997, Daniel Rose became president of DuCoa. The next month, a subordinate advised him of the conspiracy. By February 1998, Rose had begun to implement a strategy to persuade DuCoa's competitors to rejoin the conspiracy. By April, the three companies had reallocated their* market shares and increased their prices. In June, the U.S. Department of Justice began to investigate allegations of price fixing in the vitamin market. Ultimately, a federal district court convicted Rose of conspiracy to violate Section 1 of the Sherman Act. *[United States v. Rose, 449 F.3d 627 (5th Cir. 2006)]* **(See page 481.)**

1. The court "enhanced" Rose's sentence to thirty months' imprisonment, one year of supervised release, and a $20,000 fine based on, among other things, his role as "a manager or supervisor" in the conspiracy. Rose appealed this enhancement to the U.S. Court of Appeals for the Fifth Circuit. Was it fair to increase Rose's sentence on this ground? Why or why not?

2. Was Rose's participation in the conspiracy unethical? If so, how might Rose have behaved ethically instead? If not, could any of the participants' conduct be considered unethical? Explain.

19–10. **Critical-Thinking Legal Question.** Critics of antitrust law claim that in the long run, competitive market forces will eliminate private monopolies unless they are fostered by government regulation. Can you think of any examples of monopolies that continue to be fostered by government in the United States? **(See page 479.)**

Chapter 20

Investor Protection and Corporate Governance

> "You are remembered for the rules you break."
>
> —Douglas MacArthur, 1880–1964
> (U.S. Army general)

Contents

Learning Objectives

The five Learning Objectives below are designed to help improve your understanding of the chapter. After reading this chapter, you should be able to answer the following questions:

1. What is meant by the term *securities*?
2. What are the two major statutes regulating the securities industry?
3. What is insider trading? Why is it prohibited?
4. What are some of the features of state securities laws?
5. What certification requirements does the Sarbanes-Oxley Act impose on corporate executives?

(spxChrome)

Security Generally, a stock certificate, bond, note, or other document or record evidencing an ownership interest in a corporation or a promise of repayment of debt by a corporation.

LEARNING OBJECTIVE 1 What is meant by the term *securities?*

After the stock market crash of 1929, Congress enacted legislation to regulate securities markets. **Securities** generally are defined as any instruments representing corporate ownership (stock) or debts (bonds). The goal of regulation was to provide investors with more information to help them make buying and selling decisions about securities and to prohibit deceptive, unfair, and manipulative practices.

Today, the sale and transfer of securities are heavily regulated by federal and state statutes and by government agencies, and even more regulations have been enacted since the Great Recession. For example, the Dodd-Frank Wall Street Reform and Consumer Protection Act,[1] which Congress passed in 2010, required significant changes to the financial regulatory environment to reform Wall Street. Despite such efforts to regulate the securities markets, people continue to break the rules—and are remembered for it—as the chapter-opening quotation above indicates.

Violations are not always clear, though. Consider what happened when Facebook went public and issued stock in 2012. Facebook and its underwriters at Morgan Stanley determined that there was enough interest by investors to justify an opening price of $38 per share. Within a few weeks, however, the value of a share was $25.75—30 percent below the original price. A rash of lawsuits were filed, and government regulators began an investigation. Many suspected that rather than making information available to all investors, Facebook had provided it only to underwriters

---

1. Pub. L. No. 111-203, July 21, 2010, 124 Stat. 1376; 12 U.S.C. Sections 5301 *et seq.*

and certain (institutional) investors, which is a violation of the securities laws, as you will read in this chapter.

▶ The Securities and Exchange Commission

LEARNING OBJECTIVE 2 **What are the two major statutes regulating the securities industry?**

In 1931, in the wake of the stock market crash of 1929, the U.S. Senate passed a resolution calling for an extensive investigation of securities trading. The investigation led, ultimately, to the enactment of the Securities Act of 1933, which is also known as the *truth-in-securities* bill. In the following year, Congress passed the Securities Exchange Act. This 1934 act created the Securities and Exchange Commission (SEC) as an independent regulatory agency.

The SEC administers the Securities Act of 1933 and the 1934 act. The SEC also plays a key role in interpreting the provisions of these acts (and their amendments) and in creating regulations governing the purchase and sale of securities. The basic functions of the SEC are as follows:

1. Interprets federal securities laws and investigates securities law violations.
2. Issues new rules and amends existing rules.
3. Oversees the inspection of securities firms, brokers, investment advisers, and ratings agencies.
4. Oversees private regulatory organizations in the securities, accounting, and auditing fields.
5. Coordinates U.S. securities regulation with federal, state, and foreign authorities.

Updating the Regulatory Process

The SEC is working to make the regulatory process more efficient and more relevant to today's securities trading practices. To this end, the SEC has embraced modern technology and communications methods, especially the Internet, more completely than many other federal agencies have. For example, the agency now requires companies to file certain information electronically so that it can be posted on the SEC's EDGAR (Electronic Data Gathering, Analysis, and Retrieval) database.

The SEC now requires companies to make disclosures regarding climate change, as discussed in this chapter's *Shifting Legal Priorities for Business* feature on the facing page.

The SEC's Expanding Regulatory Powers

Since its creation, the SEC's regulatory functions have gradually been increased by legislation granting it authority in different areas. For example, to further curb securities fraud, Congress enacted the Securities Enforcement Remedies and Penny Stock Reform Act of 1990.[2] This act expanded the SEC's enforcement options and allowed SEC administrative law judges to hear cases involving more types of alleged securities law violations, such as fraudulent financial reporting and financial fraud. The Securities Acts Amendments of 1990 authorized the SEC to seek sanctions against those who violate foreign securities laws.[3]

The National Securities Markets Improvement Act of 1996 expanded the power of the SEC to exempt persons, securities, and transactions from the requirements of the securities laws.[4]

---

2. 15 U.S.C. Section 77g.
3. 15 U.S.C. Section 78a.
4. 15 U.S.C. Sections 77z-3, 78mm.

SHIFTING LEGAL PRIORITIES FOR BUSINESS

Securities and Exchange Commission Disclosures and Climate Change

The Securities and Exchange Commission (SEC) requires companies to reveal the potential financial impacts of future events such as increased competition, changes in regulatory rules, and pending lawsuits. In short, publicly traded corporations must disclose material information about future developments that might affect their earnings so that investors can make sound investment decisions.

Should that information include the potential impact of climate change related to global warming?

The Risks and Opportunities of Climate Change

For several years, environmental groups, large institutional investors such as state pension funds, and other groups petitioned the SEC, asking the commission to require that publicly held companies disclose climate-related information that could materially affect their operations.

The groups cited a number of potential costs related to climate change, such as property losses in flooded coastal areas that would affect the property owners and their insurers, increased costs for food producers due to crop losses, and increased costs for pollution-control equipment to curb greenhouse gas emissions. At the same time, climate change could also present

opportunities for companies that produce goods and services that can mitigate the effects of global warming or supply energy without generating emissions.

The SEC Responds

In 2010, the SEC decided that climate change had become a sufficiently important issue that publicly held companies should disclose their exposure to it. Accordingly, the SEC issued a guidance to aid companies in deciding when and whether to disclose the potential impacts of climate change on their future profitability.[a]

In announcing the decision, Mary Schapiro, the SEC chair, pointed out that "we are not opining on whether the world's climate is changing, at what pace it might be changing, or due to what causes. Nothing that the commission does today should be construed as weighing in on these topics."

The SEC's guidance suggests that companies note in their quarterly and annual reports to shareholders any significant developments in federal and state legislation and regulations regarding climate change. For example, companies should disclose estimates for any material capital expenditures for pollution-control facilities. Risk factors related to existing

or pending environmental legislation or regulations should be disclosed. In particular, companies should be "sensitive to greenhouse gas legislation or regulation."

The material impact of treaties or international conventions related to climate change should also be considered and disclosed. Companies whose businesses are "reasonably likely to be affected by such agreements should monitor the progress of any potential agreements and consider the possible impact."

Finally, the SEC suggested that companies consider changes in demand for their products or services, both existing and proposed, that might occur as a consequence of climate change or environmental legislation and regulations. For example, there might be a decrease in demand for services related to carbon-based energy, such as drilling or equipment maintenance services.

MANAGERIAL IMPLICATIONS
For the moment, only managers working in publicly held companies must worry about the SEC's guidelines with respect to climate change. Nonetheless, nonpublic companies sometimes "go public." Thus, managers in those companies should also monitor pending legislation, national and international, that might affect their businesses.

a. 17 C.F.R. Parts 211, 231, and 241 (Release Nos. 33-9106 and 34-61469; FR-82).

▶ The Securities Act of 1933

The Securities Act of 1933[5] governs initial sales of stock by businesses. The act was designed to prohibit various forms of fraud and to stabilize the securities industry by requiring that all essential information concerning the issuance of securities be made available to the investing public. Basically, the purpose of this act is to require disclosure. The 1933 act provides that all securities transactions must be registered with the SEC, unless they are exempt from registration requirements.

5. 15 U.S.C. Sections 77–77aa.

What Is a Security?

Section 2(1) of the Securities Act of 1933 contains a broad definition of securities, which generally include the following:[6]

1. Instruments and interests commonly known as securities, such as preferred and common stocks, treasury stocks, bonds, debentures, and stock warrants.
2. Any interests in securities, such as stock options, puts, calls, or other types of privilege on a security or on the right to purchase a security or a group of securities in a national security exchange.
3. Notes, instruments, or other evidence of indebtedness, including certificates of interest in a profit-sharing agreement and certificates of deposit.
4. Any fractional undivided interest in oil, gas, or other mineral rights.
5. Investment contracts, which include interests in limited partnerships and other investment schemes.

Investment Contract In securities law, a transaction in which a person invests in a common enterprise reasonably expecting profits that are derived primarily from the efforts of others.

THE *HOWEY* TEST   In interpreting the act, the United States Supreme Court has held that an **investment contract** is any transaction in which a person (1) invests (2) in a common enterprise (3) reasonably expecting profits (4) derived *primarily* or *substantially* from others' managerial or entrepreneurial efforts. Known as the *Howey* test, this definition continues to guide the determination of what types of contracts can be considered securities.[7]

    CASE EXAMPLE 20.1   Alpha Telcom sold, installed, and maintained pay-phone systems. As part of its pay-phone program, Alpha guaranteed buyers a 14 percent return on the amount of their purchase. Alpha was operating at a net loss, however, and continually borrowed funds to pay investors the fixed rate of return it had promised. Eventually, the company filed for bankruptcy, and the SEC brought an action alleging that Alpha had violated the Securities Act of 1933. In this situation, a federal court concluded that the pay-phone program was a security because it involved an investment contract.[8] ●

TYPES OF SECURITIES   For our purposes, it is probably convenient to think of securities in their most common forms—stocks and bonds issued by corporations. Bear in mind, though, that securities can take many forms, including interests in whiskey, cosmetics, worms, beavers, boats, vacuum cleaners, muskrats, and cemetery lots. Almost any stake in the ownership or debt of a company can be considered a security. Investment contracts in condominiums, franchises, limited partnerships in real estate, and oil or gas or other mineral rights have qualified as securities.

Registration Statement

Prospectus A written document, required by securities laws, that describes the security being sold, the financial operations of the issuing corporation, and the investment or risk attaching to the security.

Section 5 of the Securities Act of 1933 broadly provides that a security must be *registered* before being offered to the public unless it qualifies for an exemption. The issuing corporation must file a *registration statement* with the SEC and must provide all investors with a *prospectus*. A **prospectus** is a written disclosure document that describes the security being sold, the financial operations of the issuing corporation, and the investment or risk attaching to the security. The prospectus also serves as a selling tool for the issuing corporation.

---

6. 15 U.S.C. Section 77b(1). Amendments in 1982 added stock options.
7. *SEC v. W. J. Howey Co.,* 328 U.S. 293, 66 S.Ct. 1100, 90 L.Ed. 1244 (1946).
8. *SEC v. Alpha Telcom, Inc.,* 187 F.Supp.2d 1250 (2002).

The SEC now allows an issuer to deliver its prospectus to investors electronically via the Internet.[9] In principle, the registration statement and the prospectus supply sufficient information to enable unsophisticated investors to evaluate the financial risk involved.

CONTENTS OF THE REGISTRATION STATEMENT The registration statement must be written in plain English and fully describe the following:

1. The securities being offered for sale, including their relationship to the registrant's other capital securities.
2. The corporation's properties and business (including a financial statement certified by an independent public accounting firm).
3. The management of the corporation, including managerial compensation, stock options, pensions, and other benefits. Any interests of directors or officers in any material transactions with the corporation must be disclosed.
4. How the corporation intends to use the proceeds of the sale.
5. Any pending lawsuits or special risk factors.

All companies, both domestic and foreign, must file their registration statements electronically so that they can be posted on the SEC's EDGAR database. The EDGAR database includes material on initial public offerings, proxy statements, corporations' annual reports, registration statements, and other documents that have been filed with the SEC. Investors can access the database via the Internet to obtain information that can be used to make investment decisions.

REGISTRATION PROCESS The registration statement does not become effective until it has been reviewed and approved by the SEC (unless it is filed by a *well-known seasoned issuer,* as discussed below). The 1933 act restricted the types of activities that an issuer can engage in at each stage in the registration process.

Prefiling Period. During the *prefiling period* (before the registration statement is filed), the issuer normally cannot sell or offer to sell the securities. Once the registration statement has been filed, a waiting period begins while the SEC reviews the registration statement for completeness.[10]

Waiting Period. During the *waiting period,* the securities can be offered for sale but cannot be sold by the issuing corporation. Only certain types of offers are allowed. All issuers can distribute a *preliminary prospectus,* which contains most of the information that will be included in the final prospectus but often does not include a price.

Most issuers can also use a *free-writing prospectus* during this period (although some inexperienced issuers will need to file a preliminary prospectus first).[11] A **free-writing prospectus** is any type of written, electronic, or graphic offer that describes the issuer or its securities and includes a legend indicating that the investor may obtain the prospectus at the SEC's Web site.

DON'T FORGET The purpose of the Securities Act of 1933 is disclosure—the SEC does not consider whether a security is worth the investment price.

Free-Writing Prospectus Any type of written, electronic, or graphic offer that describes the issuing corporation or its securities and includes a legend indicating that the investor may obtain the prospectus at the Securities and Exchange Commission's Web site.

---

9. Basically, an electronic prospectus must meet the same requirements as a printed prospectus. The SEC has special rules that address situations in which the graphics, images, or audio files in a printed prospectus cannot be reproduced in an electronic form. 17 C.F.R. Section 232.304.
10. The waiting period must last at least twenty days but always extends much longer because the SEC inevitably requires numerous changes and additions to the registration statement.
11. See SEC Rules 164 and 433.

Posteffective Period.   Once the SEC has reviewed and approved the registration statement and the waiting period is over, the registration is effective, and the *posteffective period* begins. The issuer can now offer and sell the securities without restrictions. If the company issued a preliminary or free-writing prospectus to investors, it must provide those investors with a final prospectus either before or at the time they purchase the securities. The issuer can require investors to download the final prospectus from a Web site if it notifies them of the appropriate Internet address.

WELL-KNOWN SEASONED ISSUERS   A *well-known seasoned issuer* (WKSI) is a firm that has issued at least $1 billion in securities in the previous three years or has at least $700 million of value of outstanding stock in the hands of the public. WKSIs can file registration statements the day they announce a new offering and are not required to wait for SEC review and approval. They can also use a free-writing prospectus at any time, even during the prefiling period.

Exempt Securities and Transactions

Certain types of securities are exempt from the registration requirements of the Securities Act of 1933. These securities—which generally can also be resold without being registered—are summarized in Exhibit 20–1 on the facing page under the "Exempt Securities" heading.[12] The exhibit also lists and describes certain transactions that are exempt from registration requirements under various SEC regulations.

The transaction exemptions are the most important because they are very broad and can enable an issuer to avoid the high cost and complicated procedures associated with registration. Because the exemptions overlap somewhat, an offering may qualify for more than one. Hence, many sales of securities occur without registration. Even when a transaction is exempt from the registration requirements, the offering is still subject to the antifraud provisions of the 1933 act (as well as those of the 1934 act discussed later in this chapter).

BE AWARE   The issuer of an exempt security does not have to disclose the same information that other issuers do.

REGULATION A OFFERINGS   Securities issued by an issuer that has offered less than $5 million in securities during any twelve-month period are exempt from registration.[13] Under Regulation A,[14] the issuer must file with the SEC a notice of the issue and an offering circular, which must also be provided to investors before the sale. This is a much simpler and less expensive process than the procedures associated with full registration.

Testing the Waters.   Companies are allowed to "test the waters" for potential interest before preparing the offering circular. To *test the waters* means to determine potential interest without actually selling any securities or requiring any commitment on the part of those who express interest. Small-business issuers (companies with annual revenues of less than $25 million) can also use an integrated registration and reporting system that uses simpler forms than the full registration system.

Using the Internet.   Some companies have sold their securities via the Internet using Regulation A. **EXAMPLE 20.2**   The Spring Street Brewing Company became the first company to sell securities via an online initial public offering (IPO). Spring Street raised about $1.6 million—without having to pay any commissions to brokers or underwriters. ● Such online IPOs are particularly attractive to small companies

---

12. 15 U.S.C. Section 77c.
13. 15 U.S.C. Section 77c(b).
14. 17 C.F.R. Sections 230.251–230.263.

● *Exhibit* 20–1 **Exemptions for Securities Offerings under the 1933 Securities Act**

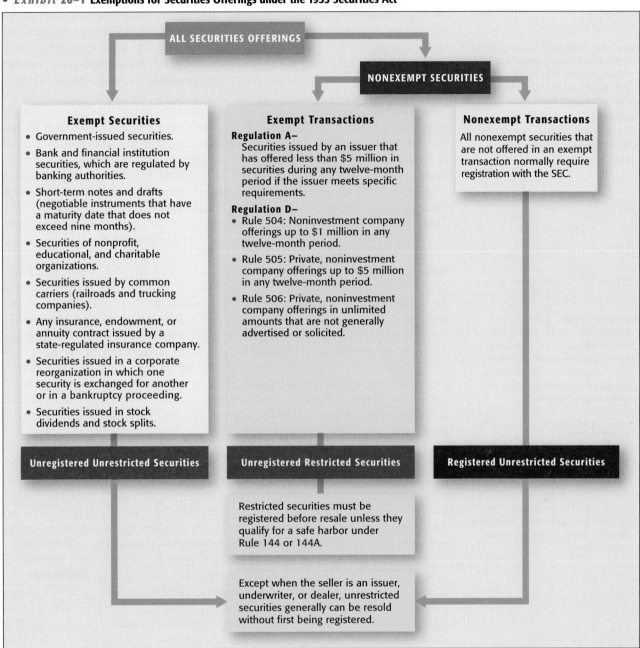

and start-up ventures that may find it difficult to raise capital from institutional investors or through underwriters. By making the offering online under Regulation A, the company can avoid both commissions and the costly and time-consuming filings required for a traditional IPO under federal and state law.

SMALL OFFERINGS—REGULATION D The SEC's Regulation D contains several exemptions from registration requirements (Rules 504, 505, and 506) for offers that involve a small dollar amount or are made in a limited manner.

Investment Company A company that acts on the behalf of many smaller shareholders and owners by buying a large portfolio of securities and professionally managing that portfolio.

Mutual Fund A specific type of investment company that continually buys or sells to investors shares of ownership in a portfolio.

Rule 504. Rule 504 is the exemption used by most small businesses. It provides that noninvestment company offerings up to $1 million in any twelve-month period are exempt. Noninvestment companies are firms that are not engaged primarily in the business of investing or trading in securities. (In contrast, an **investment company** is a firm that buys a large portfolio of securities and professionally manages it on behalf of many smaller shareholders/owners. A **mutual fund** is a type of investment company.)

EXAMPLE 20.3 Zeta Enterprises is a limited partnership that develops commercial property. Zeta intends to offer $600,000 of its limited partnership interests for sale between June 1 and next May 31. Because an interest in a limited partnership is a security, as discussed earlier, its sale would be subject to the registration and prospectus requirements of the Securities Act of 1933. Under Rule 504, however, the sales of Zeta's interests are exempt from these requirements because Zeta is a noninvestment company making an offering of less than $1 million in a twelve-month period. Therefore, Zeta can sell its limited partnership interests without filing a registration statement with the SEC or issuing a prospectus to any investor. •

Accredited Investor In the context of securities offerings, a "sophisticated" investor, such as a bank, an insurance company, an investment company, the issuer's executive officers and directors, and any person whose income or net worth exceeds certain limits.

Rule 505. Another exemption is available under Rule 505 for private, noninvestment company offerings up to $5 million in any twelve-month period. The offer may be made to an unlimited number of *accredited investors* and up to thirty-five unaccredited investors. **Accredited investors** include banks, insurance companies, investment companies, employee benefit plans, the issuer's executive officers and directors, and persons whose income or net worth exceeds a certain threshold.

The SEC must be notified of the sales, and precautions must be taken because these restricted securities may be resold only by registration or in an exempt transaction. No general solicitation or advertising is allowed. The issuer must provide any unaccredited investors with disclosure documents that generally are the same as those used in registered offerings.

KEEP IN MIND An investor can be "sophisticated" by virtue of his or her education and experience or by investing through a knowledgeable, experienced representative.

Rule 506. Private, noninvestment company offerings in unlimited amounts that are not generally solicited or advertised are exempt under Rule 506. This exemption is often referred to as the *private placement* exemption because it exempts "transactions not involving any public offering."[15] To qualify for the exemption, the issuer must believe that each unaccredited investor has sufficient knowledge or experience in financial matters to be capable of evaluating the investment's merits and risks.[16]

The private placement exemption is perhaps most important to firms that want to raise funds through the sale of securities without registering them. **EXAMPLE 20.4** To raise capital to expand its operations, Citco Corporation decides to make a private $10 million offering of its common stock directly to two hundred accredited investors and thirty highly sophisticated, but unaccredited, investors. Citco provides all of these investors with a prospectus and material information about the firm, including its most recent financial statements.

As long as Citco notifies the SEC of the sale, this offering will likely qualify for the private placement exemption. The offering is nonpublic and not generally advertised. There are fewer than thirty-five unaccredited investors, and each of them possesses sufficient knowledge and experience to evaluate the risks involved. The issuer has provided all purchasers with the material information. Thus, Citco will *not* be required to comply with the registration requirements of the Securities Act of 1933. •

---

15. 15 U.S.C. Section 77d(2).
16. 7 C.F.R. Section 230.506.

RESALES AND SAFE HARBOR RULES   Most securities can be resold without registration. The Securities Act of 1933 provides exemptions for resales by most persons other than issuers or underwriters. The average investor who sells shares of stock does not have to file a registration statement with the SEC.

Resales of restricted securities, however, trigger the registration requirements unless the party selling them complies with Rule 144 or Rule 144A. These rules are sometimes referred to as "safe harbors."

Rule 144.   Rule 144 exempts restricted securities from registration on resale if all of the following conditions are met:

1. There is adequate current public information about the issuer. ("Adequate current public information" refers to the reports that certain companies are required to file under the Securities Exchange Act of 1934.)
2. The person selling the securities has owned them for at least six months if the issuer is subject to the reporting requirements of the 1934 act.[17] If the issuer is not subject to the 1934 act's reporting requirements, the seller must have owned the securities for at least one year.
3. The securities are sold in certain limited amounts in unsolicited brokers' transactions.
4. The SEC is notified of the resale.[18]

Rule 144A.   Securities that at the time of issue are not of the same class as securities listed on a national securities exchange or quoted in a U.S. automated interdealer quotation system may be resold under Rule 144A.[19] They may be sold only to a qualified institutional buyer (an institution, such as an insurance company or a bank that owns and invests at least $100 million in securities). The seller must take reasonable steps to ensure that the buyer knows that the seller is relying on the exemption under Rule 144A.

CONTRAST   Securities do not have to be held for a specific period (six months or one year) to be exempt from registration on a resale under Rule 144A, as they do under Rule 144.

Violations of the 1933 Act

It is a violation of the Securities Act of 1933 to intentionally defraud investors by misrepresenting or omitting facts in a registration statement or prospectus. Liability is also imposed on those who are negligent for not discovering the fraud. Selling securities before the effective date of the registration statement or under an exemption for which the securities do not qualify results in liability.

REMEDIES   Criminal violations are prosecuted by the U.S. Department of Justice. Violators may be fined up to $10,000, imprisoned for up to five years, or both. The SEC is authorized to seek civil sanctions against those who willfully violate the 1933 act. It can request an injunction to prevent further sales of the securities involved or ask the court to grant other relief, such as an order to a violator to refund profits. Parties who purchase securities and suffer harm as a result of false or omitted statements may also bring suits in a federal court to recover their losses and other damages.

17. Before 2008, when amendments to Rule 144 became effective, the holding period was one year if the issuer was subject to the reporting requirements of the 1934 act. See the revised SEC Rules and Regulations at 72 Federal Rules 71546-01, 2007 WL 4368599, Release No. 33-8869. This reduced holding period allows nonpublic issuers to raise capital electronically from private and overseas sources more quickly.
18. 17 C.F.R. Section 230.144.
19. 17 C.F.R. Section 230.144A.

510 UNIT FIVE | *The Regulatory Environment*

DEFENSES There are three basic defenses to charges of violations under the 1933 act. A defendant can avoid liability by proving that (1) the statement or omission was not material, (2) the plaintiff knew about the misrepresentation at the time of purchasing the securities, or (3) the defendant exercised *due diligence* in preparing the registration and reasonably believed at the time that the statements were true and that there were no omissions of material facts.

The due diligence defense is the most important because it can be asserted by any defendant, except the issuer of the stock. The defendant must prove that she or he reasonably believed, at the time the registration statement became effective, that the statements in it were true and there were no omissions of material facts.

The following case involved allegations of omissions of material information from an issuing company's registration statement. The defendants contended that the omissions were not material.

Case 20.1 **Litwin v. Blackstone Group, LP**

United States Court of Appeals, Second Circuit, 634 F.3d 706 (2011).

BACKGROUND AND FACTS Blackstone Group, LP, manages investments. Its corporate private equity division accounts for nearly 40 percent of the assets under the company's management. In preparation for an initial public offering (IPO), Blackstone filed a registration statement with the Securities and Exchange Commission (SEC). At the time, corporate private equity's investments included FGIC Corporation and Freescale Semiconductor, Inc. FGIC insured investments in subprime mortgages. Before the IPO, FGIC's customers began to suffer large losses. By the time of the IPO, this situation was generating substantial losses for FGIC and, in turn, for Blackstone.

Meanwhile, Freescale had recently lost an exclusive contract to make wireless 3G chipsets for Motorola, Inc. (its largest customer). Blackstone's registration statement did not mention the impact on its revenue of the investments in FGIC and Freescale. Martin Litwin and others who invested in the IPO filed a suit in a federal district court against Blackstone and its officers, alleging material omissions from the statement. Blackstone filed a motion to dismiss, which the court granted. The plaintiffs appealed.

IN THE WORDS OF THE COURT . . .
STRAUB, Circuit Judge:
* * * *

Materiality is an inherently fact-specific finding that is satisfied when a plaintiff alleges a statement or omission that a reasonable investor would have considered significant in making investment decisions. * * * However, it is not necessary to assert that the investor would have acted differently if an accurate disclosure was made. Rather, when a district court is presented with a motion [to dismiss] a complaint may not properly be dismissed on the ground that the alleged misstatements or omissions are not material unless they are so obviously unimportant to a reasonable investor that reasonable minds could not differ on the question of their importance. [Emphasis added.]
* * * *

In this case, the key information that plaintiffs assert should have been disclosed is whether, and to what extent, the particular known trend, event, or uncertainty might have been reasonably expected to materially affect Blackstone's investments. * * * Plaintiffs are not seeking the disclosure of the mere fact of Blackstone's investment in FGIC, of the downward trend in the real estate market, or of Freescale's loss of its exclusive contract with Motorola. Rather, plaintiffs claim that Blackstone was required to disclose the manner in which those then-known trends, events, or uncertainties might reasonably be expected to materially impact Blackstone's future revenues.

* * * The question, of course, is not whether a loss in a particular investment's value will merely affect revenues, because * * * it will almost certainly have some effect. *The relevant question is whether Blackstone reasonably expects the impact to be material.* [Emphasis added.]

* * * Because Blackstone's Corporate Private Equity segment plays such an important role in Blackstone's business and provides value to all of its other asset management and financial advisory services, a reasonable investor would almost certainly want to know information related to that segment that Blackstone reasonably expects will have a material adverse effect on its future revenues. Therefore, the alleged * * * omissions relating to FGIC and Freescale were plausibly material.

DECISION AND REMEDY The U.S. Court of Appeals for the Second Circuit vacated the lower court's dismissal and remanded the case. The plaintiffs had provided sufficient allegations that Blackstone had omitted material information that it was required to disclose under the securities laws for the case to go to trial.

THE LEGAL ENVIRONMENT DIMENSION *Litwin alleged that Blackstone had negligently omitted material information from the registration statement. What will he and the others have to show to prove their case?*

The Securities Exchange Act of 1934

The Securities Exchange Act of 1934 provides for the regulation and registration of securities exchanges, brokers, dealers, and national securities associations, such as the National Association of Securities Dealers (NASD). Unlike the 1933 act, which is a one-time disclosure law, the 1934 act provides for continuous periodic disclosures by publicly held corporations to enable the SEC to regulate subsequent trading.

The Securities Exchange Act of 1934 applies to companies that have assets in excess of $10 million and five hundred or more shareholders. These corporations are referred to as Section 12 companies because they are required to register their securities under Section 12 of the 1934 act. Section 12 companies are required to file reports with the SEC annually and quarterly, and sometimes even monthly if specified events occur (such as a merger). Other provisions in the 1934 act require all securities brokers and dealers to be registered, keep detailed records of their activities, and file annual reports with the SEC. The act also authorizes the SEC to engage in market surveillance to deter undesirable market practices such as fraud, market manipulation (attempts at illegally influencing stock prices), and misrepresentation.

Section 10(b), SEC Rule 10b-5, and Insider Trading

Section 10(b) is one of the more important sections of the Securities Exchange Act of 1934. This section prohibits the use of any manipulative or deceptive mechanism in violation of SEC rules and regulations. Among the rules that the SEC has promulgated pursuant to the 1934 act is **SEC Rule 10b-5,** which prohibits the commission of fraud in connection with the purchase or sale of any security.

SEC Rule 10b-5 A rule of the Securities and Exchange Commission that makes it unlawful, in connection with the purchase or sale of any security, to make any untrue statement of a material fact or to omit a material fact if such omission causes the statement to be misleading.

APPLICABILITY OF SEC RULE 10B-5 SEC Rule 10b-5 applies to almost all trading of securities, whether on organized exchanges, in over-the-counter markets, or in private transactions. Generally, the rule covers just about any form of security. The securities need not be registered under the 1933 act for the 1934 act to apply.

Private parties can sue for securities fraud under the 1934 act and SEC Rule 10b-5. The basic elements of a securities fraud action are as follows:

1. A *material misrepresentation* (or omission) in connection with the purchase or sale of securities.
2. *Scienter* (a wrongful state of mind).
3. *Reliance* by the plaintiff on the material misrepresentation.
4. *An economic loss.*
5. *Causation,* meaning that there is a causal connection between the misrepresentation and the loss.

LEARNING OBJECTIVE 3 **What is insider trading? Why is it prohibited?**

Insider Trading The purchase or sale of securities on the basis of inside information—that is, information that has not been made available to the public.

INSIDER TRADING One of the major goals of Section 10(b) and SEC Rule 10b-5 is to prevent so-called **insider trading,** which occurs when persons buy or sell securities on the basis of *inside information* (information that is not available to the public). Corporate directors, officers, and others such as majority shareholders, for instance, often have advance inside information that can affect the future market value of the corporate stock. Obviously, if they act on this information, their positions give them a trading advantage over the general public and other shareholders.

The 1934 Securities Exchange Act defines inside information and extends liability to those who take advantage of such information in their personal transactions when they know that the information is unavailable to those with whom they are dealing. Section 10(b) of the 1934 act and SEC Rule 10b-5 apply to anyone who has access to or receives information of a nonpublic nature on which trading is based—not just to corporate "insiders."

DISCLOSURE UNDER SEC RULE 10B-5　　Any material omission or misrepresentation of material facts in connection with the purchase or sale of a security may violate not only the Securities Act of 1933 but also the antifraud provisions of Section 10(b) of the 1934 act and SEC Rule 10b-5. The key to liability (which can be civil or criminal) under Section 10(b) and SEC Rule 10b-5 is whether the insider's information is *material*.

The following are some examples of material facts calling for disclosure under SEC Rule 10b-5:

1. Fraudulent trading in the company stock by a broker-dealer.
2. A dividend change (whether up or down).
3. A contract for the sale of corporate assets.
4. A new discovery, a new process, or a new product.
5. A significant change in the firm's financial condition.
6. Potential litigation against the company.

Note that any one of these facts, by itself, is not *automatically* considered a material fact. Rather, it will be regarded as a material fact if it is significant enough that it would likely affect an investor's decision as to whether to purchase or sell the company's securities.

The following is one of the *Classic Cases* interpreting materiality under SEC Rule 10b-5.

Classic Case 20.2　　**Securities and Exchange Commission v. Texas Gulf Sulphur Co.**

United States Court of Appeals, Second Circuit, 401 F.2d 833 (1968).

BACKGROUND AND FACTS　　In 1963, the Texas Gulf Sulphur Company (TGS) drilled a hole that appeared to yield a core with an exceedingly high mineral content, although further drilling would be necessary to establish whether there was enough ore to be mined commercially. TGS kept secret the results of the core sample. After learning of the ore discovery, officers and employees of the company made substantial purchases of TGS's stock or accepted stock options (rights to purchase stock). On April 11, 1964, an unauthorized report of the mineral find appeared in the newspapers. On the following day, April 12, TGS issued a press release that played down the discovery and stated that it was too early to tell whether the ore find would be significant. Later on, TGS announced a strike of at least 25 million tons of ore. The news led to a substantial increase in the price of TGS stock.

The Securities and Exchange Commission (SEC) brought a suit in a federal district court against the officers and employees of TGS for violating the insider-trading prohibition of SEC Rule 10b-5. The officers and employees argued that the prohibition did not apply. They reasoned that the information on which they had traded was not material, as the find had not been commercially proved. The trial court held that most of the defendants had not violated SEC Rule 10b-5, and the SEC appealed.

IN THE WORDS OF THE COURT . . .
WATERMAN, Circuit Judge.
　　* * * *
　　* * * Whether facts are material within Rule 10b-5 when the facts relate to a particular event and are undisclosed by those persons who are knowledgeable thereof *will depend at any given time upon a balancing of both the indicated probability that the event will occur and the anticipated magnitude of the event in light of the totality of the company activity.* Here, * * * knowledge of the possibility, which surely was more than marginal, of the existence of a mine of the vast magnitude indicated by the remarkably rich drill core located rather close to the surface (suggesting mineability by the less expensive openpit method) within the confines of a large anomaly (suggesting an extensive region of mineralization) might well have affected the price of TGS stock and would certainly have been an important fact to a reasonable, if speculative, investor in deciding whether he should buy, sell, or hold. [Emphasis added.]
　　* * * *
　　* * * A major factor in determining whether the * * * discovery was a material fact is the importance attached to the drilling results by

Classic Case 20.2–Continued

those who knew about it. * * * The timing by those who knew of it of their stock purchases * * * –purchases in some cases by individuals who had never before purchased * * * TGS stock–virtually compels the inference that the insiders were influenced by the drilling results.

DECISION AND REMEDY   The appellate court ruled in favor of the SEC. All of the trading by insiders who knew of the mineral find before its true extent had been publicly announced had violated SEC Rule 10b-5.

WHAT IF THE FACTS WERE DIFFERENT?   *Suppose that further drilling revealed that this site did not contain enough ore*

for it to be mined commercially. Would the defendants still have been liable for violating SEC Rule 10b-5? Why or why not?

IMPACT OF THIS CASE ON TODAY'S LEGAL ENVIRONMENT   *This classic case affirmed the principle that the test of whether information is "material," for SEC Rule 10b-5 purposes, is whether it would affect the judgment of reasonable investors. The corporate insiders' purchases of stock and stock options indicated that they were influenced by the results and that the information about the results was material. The courts continue to cite this case when applying SEC Rule 10b-5 to other cases of alleged insider trading.*

THE PRIVATE SECURITIES LITIGATION REFORM ACT   One of the unintended effects of SEC Rule 10b-5 was to deter the disclosure of forward-looking information. To understand why, consider an example.

   EXAMPLE 20.5   QT Company announces that its projected earnings in a future time period will be a certain amount, but the forecast turns out to be wrong. The earnings are in fact much lower, and the price of QT's stock is affected—negatively. The shareholders then file a lawsuit against the company, alleging that the directors violated SEC Rule 10b-5 by disclosing misleading financial information. •

Safe Harbor Provisions.   In an attempt to rectify this problem and promote disclosure, Congress passed the Private Securities Litigation Reform Act of 1995. The act provides a "safe harbor" for publicly held companies that make forward-looking statements, such as financial forecasts. Those who make such statements are protected against liability for securities fraud as long as the statements are accompanied by "meaningful cautionary statements identifying important factors that could cause actual results to differ materially from those in the forward-looking statement."[20]

Limitations on Class-Action Suits.   After the act was passed, a number of securities class-action suits were filed in state courts to skirt its requirements. In response, Congress passed the Securities Litigation Uniform Standards Act of 1998 (SLUSA).[21]

   The act placed stringent limits on the ability of plaintiffs to bring class-action suits in state courts against firms whose securities are traded on national stock exchanges. SLUSA not only prevents the purchasers and sellers of securities from bringing class-action fraud claims under state securities laws, but also applies to investors who are fraudulently induced to hold on to their securities.[22]

OUTSIDERS AND SEC RULE 10B-5   The traditional insider-trading case involves true insiders—corporate officers, directors, and majority shareholders who have access to (and trade on) inside information. Increasingly, however, liability under Section 10(b) of the 1934 act and SEC Rule 10b-5 has been extended to certain "outsiders"—those persons who trade on inside information acquired indirectly.

---

20. 15 U.S.C. Sections 77z-2, 78u-5.

21. Pub. L. No. 105-353. This act amended many sections of Title 15 of the *United States Code.*

22. *Merrill Lynch, Pierce, Fenner & Smith, Inc. v. Dabit,* 547 U.S. 71, 126 S.Ct. 1503, 164 L.Ed.2d 179 (2006).

Two theories have been developed under which outsiders may be held liable for insider trading: the *tipper/tippee theory* and the *misappropriation theory.*

Tipper/Tippee Theory. Anyone who acquires inside information as a result of a corporate insider's breach of his or her fiduciary duty can be liable under SEC Rule 10b-5. This liability extends to **tippees** (those who receive "tips" from insiders) and even remote tippees (tippees of tippees).

The key to liability under this theory is that the inside information must be obtained as a result of someone's breach of a fiduciary duty to the corporation whose shares are involved in the trading. The tippee is liable under this theory only if the following occur:

Tippee A person who receives inside information.

1. There is a breach of a duty not to disclose inside information.
2. The disclosure is in exchange for personal benefit.
3. The tippee knows (or should know) of this breach and benefits from it.

Misappropriation Theory. Liability for insider trading may also be established under the misappropriation theory. This theory holds that an individual who wrongfully obtains (misappropriates) inside information and trades on it for her or his personal gain should be held liable because, in essence, she or he stole information rightfully belonging to another.

The misappropriation theory has been controversial because it significantly extends the reach of SEC Rule 10b-5 to outsiders who ordinarily would *not* be deemed fiduciaries of the corporations in whose stock they trade. The United States Supreme Court, however, has held that liability under SEC Rule 10b-5 can be based on the misappropriation theory. It is not always wrong to disclose material, nonpublic information about a company to another person. Nevertheless, a person who obtains the information and trades securities on it can be liable.

INSIDER REPORTING AND TRADING—SECTION 16(B) Section 16(b) of the 1934 act provides for the recapture by the corporation of all profits realized by an insider on any purchase and sale or sale and purchase of the corporation's stock within any six-month period.[23] It is irrelevant whether the insider actually uses inside information. *All such* **short-swing profits** *must be returned to the corporation.* In this context, *insiders* means officers, directors, and large stockholders of Section 12 corporations (those owning at least 10 percent of the class of equity securities registered under Section 12 of the 1934 act). To discourage such insiders from using nonpublic information about their companies for their personal benefit in the stock market, they must file reports with the SEC concerning their ownership and trading of the corporation's securities.

Short-Swing Profits Profits earned by a purchase and sale, or sale and purchase, of the same security within a six-month period. Under Section 16(b), these profits must be returned to the corporation if earned by company insiders from transactions in the company's stock.

Section 16(b) applies not only to stock but also to warrants, options, and securities convertible into stock. In addition, the courts have fashioned complex rules for determining profits. Note that the SEC exempts a number of transactions under Rule 16b-3.[24] For all of these reasons, corporate insiders are wise to seek specialized counsel before trading in the corporation's stock. Exhibit 20–2 on the facing page compares the effects of SEC Rule 10b-5 and Section 16(b).

---

23. A person who expects the price of a particular stock to decline can realize profits by "selling short"— selling at a high price and repurchasing later at a lower price to cover the "short sale."
24. 17 C.F.R. Section 240.16b-3.

• *Exhibit* **20–2** **Comparison of SEC Rule 10b-5 and Section 16(b)**

AREA OF COMPARISON	SEC RULE 10b-5	SECTION 16(b)
What is the subject matter of the transaction?	Any security (does not have to be registered).	Any security (does not have to be registered).
What transactions are covered?	Purchase or sale.	Short-swing purchase and sale or short-swing sale and purchase.
Who is subject to liability?	Almost anyone with inside information under a duty to disclose—including officers, directors, controlling shareholders, and tippees.	Officers, directors, and certain shareholders who own 10 percent or more.
Is omission or misrepresentation necessary for liability?	Yes.	No.
Are there any exempt transactions?	No.	Yes, there are a number of exemptions.
Who may bring an action?	A person transacting with an insider, the SEC, or a purchaser or seller damaged by a wrongful act.	A corporation or a shareholder by derivative action.

Regulation of Proxy Statements

Section 14(a) of the Securities Exchange Act of 1934 regulates the solicitation of proxies (see Chapter 10) from shareholders of Section 12 companies. The SEC regulates the content of proxy statements. Whoever solicits a proxy must fully and accurately disclose in the proxy statement all of the facts that are pertinent to the matter on which the shareholders are to vote. SEC Rule 14a-9 is similar to the antifraud provisions of SEC Rule 10b-5. Remedies for violations are extensive, ranging from injunctions to prevent a vote from being taken to monetary damages.

Violations of the 1934 Act

As mentioned earlier, violations of Section 10(b) of the Securities Exchange Act of 1934 and SEC Rule 10b-5, including insider trading, may be subject to criminal or civil liability. For either criminal or civil sanctions to be imposed, however, *scienter* must exist—that is, the violator must have had an intent to defraud or knowledge of her or his misconduct (see page 293 in Chapter 12). *Scienter* can be proved by showing that the defendant made false statements or wrongfully failed to disclose material facts.

Violations of Section 16(b) include the sale by insiders of stock acquired less than six months before the sale (or less than six months after the sale if selling short). These violations are subject to civil sanctions. Liability under Section 16(b) is strict liability. Neither *scienter* nor negligence is required.

In the following case, the defendants were accused of securities fraud in violation of Section 10(b) and SEC Rule 10b-5. At issue was whether they had acted with *scienter*.

Case 20.3   Gebhart v. Securities and Exchange Commission

United States Court of Appeals, Ninth Circuit, 595 F.3d 1034 (2010).

BACKGROUND AND FACTS   Alvin Gebhart worked at Mutual of New York (MONY), where he sold annuities and mutual funds. Jack Archer, a fellow MONY salesperson, told Gebhart about Community Service Group (CSG)—a business venture that purchased mobile home parks, converted them to resident ownership, and assisted residents in purchasing them. MHP Conversions, LLC, which was created to facilitate the conversion process, issued promissory notes that were sold to individual investors to raise funds for CSG's purchase of the parks. Each note stated that it would "ultimately be secured by a deed of trust" on the particular park to be purchased with the funds.

In 1996, Gebhart moved from MONY to Mutual Service Corporation (MSC), a broker-dealer and member of the National Association of Securities Dealers (NASD). His wife, Donna Gebhart, joined him at MSC. Over the next several years, the Gebharts, on Archer's recommendation, sold nearly $2.4 million in MHP promissory notes to forty-five of their clients, who bought the notes based on the Gebharts' positive statements about the investment. It became obvious later that these statements were false. The Gebharts had failed to disclose that their statements were based on information provided by Archer rather than their own investigation. At the time of MHP's collapse, the Gebharts' clients had more than $1.5 million invested in outstanding MHP notes.

The Gebharts were fired, and in 2002, the NASD filed a complaint against them for securities fraud. A NASD hearing panel found that the Gebharts had acted in good faith and rejected the fraud charges. The NASD National Adjudicatory Council (NAC) reversed. The NAC found that the Gebharts had committed fraud. The Securities and Exchange Commission (SEC) upheld the NAC's ruling, and the Gebharts petitioned a federal appellate court to review the SEC's decision.

IN THE WORDS OF THE COURT . . .
FISHER, Circuit Judge.
* * * *

To establish a violation of Section 10(b) and Rule 10b-5, the SEC is required to "show that there has been a misstatement or omission of material fact, made with *scienter*." "The plaintiffs may establish scienter by proving either actual knowledge or recklessness."
* * * *

Scienter * * * *is a subjective inquiry. It turns on the defendant's actual state of mind. Thus, although we may consider the objective unreasonableness of the defendant's conduct to raise an inference of scienter, the ultimate question is whether the defendant knew his or her statements were false, or was consciously reckless as to their truth or falsity.* [Emphasis added.]
* * * *

The Gebharts contend that the SEC applied an erroneous *scienter* standard in this case by focusing exclusively on * * * objective inquiry and disregarding evidence of subjective good faith. We disagree. The SEC considered all of the evidence bearing on the Gebharts' actual state of mind, including the Gebharts' extreme departure from ordinary standards of care, and found that the Gebharts were consciously aware of the risk that their statements were false. There was no error.

The SEC certainly considered the objective unreasonableness of the Gebharts' actions as *part* of its analysis. The SEC found that the Gebharts failed to perform any meaningful investigation into the MHP promissory notes—an extreme departure from ordinary standards of care that "created the substantial [and obvious] risk * * * that their representations were not true." The SEC found that the Gebharts "made no effort to investigate or understand why their clients were being sold second (and not first) deeds of trust; no effort to identify the first trust deed holders or the amounts of those outstanding trust deeds; and no effort to ensure their clients' investments were actually being secured by recorded trust deeds." The Gebharts made "no effort" to corroborate Archer's representations that the parks were not overly encumbered.

The SEC properly considered the objective unreasonableness of the Gebharts' actions as some evidence supporting the inference that the Gebharts acted with *scienter,* but did not treat it as dispositive [a deciding factor]. The * * * [SEC] evaluated "the evidence the Gebharts put forward to demonstrate their good faith beliefs" as "part of the complete mix of facts bearing on an evaluation of their [actual] state of mind" and concluded that the "evidence from the Gebharts about their subjective belief was not sufficient to overcome" the inference of *scienter* created by the evidence as a whole. The Gebharts' assertions of good faith were "not plausible" and lacked "credibility." Based on the evidence as a whole, the SEC determined that the Gebharts "knew they had no direct knowledge of the truth or falsity" of their statements, and made their statements "despite not knowing whether they were true or false." The SEC correctly applied the appropriate *scienter* standard.

DECISION AND REMEDY   The U.S. Court of Appeals for the Ninth Circuit upheld the SEC's decision. The Gebharts had acted with *scienter* and had thus committed securities fraud in violation of Section 10(b) and Rule 10b-5.

THE LEGAL ENVIRONMENT DIMENSION   *At one point in the opinion, the court noted that "there is no evidence in the record that the Gebharts ever intended to defraud anyone." Why, then, did the court conclude that the Gebharts had acted with scienter?*

CRIMINAL PENALTIES   For violations of Section 10(b) and Rule 10b-5, an individual may be fined up to $5 million, imprisoned for up to twenty years, or both. A partnership or a corporation may be fined up to $25 million. Under Section 807 of the Sarbanes-Oxley Act of 2002, for a *willful* violation of the 1934 act the violator may be imprisoned for up to twenty-five years in addition to being subject to a fine.

For a defendant to be convicted in a criminal prosecution under the securities laws, there can be no reasonable doubt that the defendant knew he or she was acting wrongfully—a jury is not allowed merely to speculate that the defendant may have acted willfully.

CASE EXAMPLE 20.6   Martha Stewart, founder of a well-known media and homemaking empire, was charged with intentionally deceiving investors based on public statements she had made. In 2001, Stewart's stockbroker allegedly had informed Stewart that the head of ImClone Systems, Inc., was selling his shares in that company. Stewart then sold her ImClone shares. The next day, ImClone announced that the U.S. Food and Drug Administration had not approved Erbitux, the company's greatly anticipated medication.

After the government began investigating Stewart's ImClone trades, she publicly stated that she had previously instructed her stockbroker to sell her ImClone stock if the price fell to $60 per share. The government prosecutor claimed that Stewart's statement showed she had the intent to deceive investors. The court, however, acquitted Stewart on this charge because "to find the essential element of criminal intent beyond a reasonable doubt, a rational juror would have to speculate."[25] ●

CIVIL SANCTIONS   The SEC can also bring suit in a federal district court against anyone violating or aiding in a violation of the 1934 act or SEC rules by purchasing or selling a security while in the possession of material nonpublic information.[26] The violation must occur on or through the facilities of a national securities exchange or from or through a broker or dealer. The court may assess a penalty for as much as triple the profits gained or the loss avoided by the guilty party. The Insider Trading and Securities Fraud Enforcement Act of 1988 enlarged the class of persons who may be subject to civil liability for insider trading and gave the SEC authority to give monetary rewards to informants.[27]

As mentioned earlier, private parties may also sue violators of Section 10(b) and Rule 10b-5. A private party may obtain rescission (cancellation) of a contract to buy securities or damages to the extent of the violator's illegal profits. Those found liable have a right to seek contribution from those who share responsibility for the violations, including accountants, attorneys, and corporations. For violations of Section 16(b), a corporation can bring an action to recover the short-swing profits.

▶ State Securities Laws

BE AWARE   Federal securities laws do not take priority over state securities laws.

Today, every state has its own corporate securities laws, or blue sky laws, that regulate the offer and sale of securities within its borders. The phrase *blue sky laws* dates to a 1917 decision by the United States Supreme Court in which the Court declared that the purpose of such laws was to prevent "speculative schemes which have no more basis than so many feet of 'blue sky.'"[28] Article 8 of the Uniform Commercial

---

25. *United States v. Stewart*, 305 F.Supp.2d 368 (S.D.N.Y. 2004).
26. The Insider Trading Sanctions Act of 1984, 15 U.S.C. Sections 78u(d)(2)(A), (C).
27. 15 U.S.C. Section 78u-1.
28. *Hall v. Geiger-Jones Co.*, 242 U.S. 539, 37 S.Ct. 217, 61 L.Ed. 480 (1917).

Code, which has been adopted by all of the states, also imposes various requirements relating to the purchase and sale of securities.

Requirements under State Securities Laws

LEARNING OBJECTIVE 4 What are some of the features of state securities laws?

Typically, state laws have disclosure requirements and antifraud provisions, many of which are patterned after Section 10(b) of the Securities Exchange Act of 1934 and SEC Rule 10b-5. State laws also provide for the registration of securities offered or issued for sale within the state and impose disclosure requirements. Methods of registration, required disclosures, and exemptions from registration vary among states. Unless an exemption from registration is applicable, issuers must register or qualify their stock with the appropriate state official, often called a *corporations commissioner.* Additionally, most state securities laws regulate securities brokers and dealers.

Concurrent Regulation

State securities laws apply mainly to intrastate transactions. Since the adoption of the 1933 and 1934 federal securities acts, the state and federal governments have regulated securities concurrently. Issuers must comply with both federal and state securities laws, and exemptions from federal law are not exemptions from state laws.

The dual federal and state system has not always worked well, particularly during the early 1990s, when the securities markets underwent considerable expansion. In response, Congress passed the National Securities Markets Improvement Act of 1996, which eliminated some of the duplicate regulations and gave the SEC exclusive power to regulate most national securities activities. The National Conference of Commissioners on Uniform State Laws then substantially revised the Uniform Securities Act to coordinate state and federal securities regulation and enforcement efforts. The new version was offered to the states for adoption in 2002. Seventeen states have adopted the Uniform Securities Act, and other states are considering its adoption.[29]

 Corporate Governance

Corporate Governance A set of policies or procedures affecting the way a corporation is directed or controlled.

Corporate governance can be narrowly defined as the relationship between a corporation and its shareholders. Some argue for a broader definition—that corporate governance specifies the rights and responsibilities among different participants in the corporation, such as the board of directors, managers, shareholders, and other stakeholders, and spells out the rules and procedures for making decisions on corporate affairs. Regardless of the way it is defined, effective corporate governance requires more than just compliance with laws and regulations. (For a discussion of corporate governance in other nations, see this chapter's *Beyond Our Borders* feature below.)

Beyond Our Borders   **Corporate Governance in Other Nations**

Corporate governance has become an issue of concern not only for U.S. corporations, but also for corporate entities around the world. With the globalization of business, a corporation's bad acts (or lack of control systems) can have far-reaching consequences. Different models of corporate governance exist, often depending on the degree of capitalism in the particular nation. In the

---

29. At the time this book went to press, the Uniform Securities Act had been adopted in Georgia, Hawaii, Idaho, Indiana, Iowa, Kansas, Maine, Michigan, Minnesota, Mississippi, Missouri, New Mexico, Oklahoma, South Carolina, South Dakota, Vermont, and Wisconsin, as well as in the U.S. Virgin Islands. You can find current information on state adoptions at www.nccusl.com.

United States, corporate governance tends to give priority to shareholders' interests. This approach encourages significant innovation and cost and quality competition.

In contrast, the coordinated model of governance that prevails in continental Europe and Japan considers the interests of so-called stakeholders—employees, managers, suppliers, customers, and the community—to be a priority. The coordinated model still encourages innovation and cost and quality competition, but not to the same extent as the U.S. model.

• **For Critical Analysis**
Why does the presence of a capitalist system affect a nation's perspective on corporate governance?

Effective corporate governance is essential in large corporations because corporate ownership (by shareholders) is separated from corporate control (by officers and managers). Under these circumstances, officers and managers may attempt to advance their own interests at the expense of the shareholders. The well-publicized corporate scandals in the early 2000s clearly illustrate the reasons for concern about managerial opportunism.

Attempts at Aligning the Interests of Officers with Those of Shareholders

Some corporations have sought to align the financial interests of their officers with those of the company's shareholders by providing the officers with *stock options,* which enable them to purchase shares of the corporation's stock at a set price. When the market price rises above that level, the officers can sell their shares for a profit. Because a stock's market price generally increases as the corporation prospers, the options give the officers a financial stake in the corporation's well-being and supposedly encourage them to work hard for the benefit of the shareholders.

Options have turned out to be an imperfect device for providing effective governance, however. Executives in some companies have been tempted to "cook" the company's books in order to keep share prices higher so that they could sell their stock for a profit. Executives in other corporations have experienced no losses when share prices dropped. Instead, their options were "repriced" so that they did not suffer from the share price decline and could still profit from future increases above the lowered share price. Thus, although stock options theoretically can motivate officers to protect shareholder interests, stock option plans have often become a way for officers to take advantage of shareholders.

With stock options generally failing to work as planned and numerous headline-making scandals occurring within major corporations, there has been an outcry for more "outside" directors (those with no formal employment affiliation with the company). The theory is that independent directors will more closely monitor the actions of corporate officers. Hence, today we see more boards with outside directors. Note, though, that outside directors may not be truly independent of corporate officers— they may be friends or business associates of the leading officers.

 Ethical Issue

Should shareholders have more control over corporate officers' compensation? Over the last several years, executive compensation has become a hotly debated issue. Many critics argue that the chief executive officers (CEOs) of public companies are paid too much, especially in comparison with the wages earned by the average worker. The Dodd-Frank Wall Street Reform and Consumer Protection Act (see page 501) included a "say-on-pay" provision that gave shareholders the right to vote on executive compensation for senior executives at every public U.S. company. In 2009, shareholders defeated a pay package for a U.S. CEO for the first time, voting against proposed compensation of more than $50 million for Ray Irani, the head of Occidental Petroleum. Two years later, shareholders voted to reject executive pay arrangements at thirty-five U.S. firms.

These votes on executive pay are nonbinding, however—the board of directors does not have to abide by them. Furthermore, more than 90 percent of shareholder votes on executive pay have been in favor of the proposed compensation plans. Despite "say on pay," the average compensation for a U.S. CEO in 2011 was almost $10 million—up 6 percent from the previous year. The average U.S. employee would have to work almost 250 years to match that salary.

The Goal Is to Promote Accountability

Effective corporate governance standards are designed to address problems (such as those briefly discussed above) and to motivate officers to make decisions that promote the financial interests of the company's shareholders. Generally, corporate governance entails corporate decision-making structures that monitor employees (particularly officers) to ensure that they are acting for the benefit of the shareholders. Thus, corporate governance involves, at a minimum:

1. The audited reporting of financial progress at the corporation, so managers can be evaluated.
2. Legal protections for shareholders, so violators of the law, who attempt to take advantage of shareholders, can be punished for misbehavior and victims may recover damages for any associated losses.

Effective corporate governance can have considerable practical significance because corporate decision makers necessarily become more accountable for their actions to shareholders. Firms that are more accountable to shareholders typically report higher profits, higher sales growth, higher firm value, and other economic advantages. Thus, a corporation with better corporate governance and greater accountability to investors may also have a higher valuation than a corporation that is less concerned about governance.

Corporate Governance and Corporate Law

State corporation statutes set up the legal framework for corporate governance. Under the corporate law of Delaware, where most major companies incorporate, all corporations must have certain structures of corporate governance in place. The most important structure, of course, is the board of directors because the board makes the major decisions about the future of the corporation.

Some argue that shareholder democracy is the key to improving corporate governance. If shareholders could have more say on major corporate decisions, they presumably could have more control over the corporation. Essential to shareholder democracy is the election of the board of directors, usually at the corporation's annual meeting.

Although shareholders vote for directors, they often find it difficult to elect their nominees because organizing enough shareholders to sway an election can be very costly. In 2010, the SEC announced that it would work to modernize shareholder voting and proxy rules to reduce these costs and give shareholders direct access to other shareholders through the company's facilities for communicating with shareholders. The SEC's goal is to make the contest more even between the shareholders' candidates and the company's nominees.

"Honesty is the single most important factor having a direct bearing on the final success of an individual, a corporation, or a product."
Ed McMahon, 1923–2009
(American entertainer)

THE BOARD OF DIRECTORS   Under corporate law, a corporation must have a board of directors elected by the shareholders. Almost anyone can become a director, though some organizations, such as the New York Stock Exchange, require certain standards of service for directors of their listed corporations.

Directors are responsible for ensuring that the corporation's officers are operating wisely and in the exclusive interest of shareholders. The directors receive reports from the officers and give them managerial directions. In reality, though, corporate directors devote a relatively small amount of time to monitoring officers.

Ideally, shareholders would monitor the directors' supervision of the officers. In practice, however, it can be difficult for shareholders to monitor directors and hold them responsible for corporate failings. Although the directors can be sued for failing to do their jobs effectively, directors are rarely held personally liable.

THE AUDIT COMMITTEE   A crucial committee of the board of directors is the *audit committee,* which oversees the corporation's accounting and financial reporting processes, including both internal and outside auditors. Unless the committee members have sufficient expertise and are willing to spend the time to carefully examine the corporation's accounts, however, the audit committee may be ineffective.

The audit committee also oversees the corporation's "internal controls," which are the measures taken to ensure that reported results are accurate. They are carried out largely by the company's internal auditing staff. As an example, these controls help to determine whether debts owed to a corporation are collectible. If the debts are not collectible, it is up to the audit committee to make sure that the corporation's financial officers do not simply pretend that payment will eventually be made. (This chapter's *Linking the Law to Taxation* feature on page 526 discusses how corporations, at least during the next few years, might benefit from *deleveraging,* or repurchasing, their debts.)

THE COMPENSATION COMMITTEE   Another important committee of the board of directors is the *compensation committee.* This committee monitors and determines the compensation the company's officers are paid. As part of this process, the committee is responsible for assessing the officers' performance and for designing a compensation system that will better align the officers' interests with those of shareholders.

The Sarbanes-Oxley Act

In 2002 following a series of corporate scandals, Congress passed the Sarbanes-Oxley Act.[30] The act separately addresses certain issues relating to corporate governance. Generally, the act attempts to increase corporate accountability by imposing strict disclosure requirements and harsh penalties for violations of securities laws. Among other things, the act requires chief corporate executives to take responsibility for the accuracy of financial statements and reports that are filed with the SEC.

LEARNING OBJECTIVE 5 **What certification requirements does the Sarbanes-Oxley Act impose on corporate executives?**

Additionally, the act requires that certain financial and stock-transaction reports be filed with the SEC earlier than was required under the previous rules. The act also created a new entity, called the Public Company Accounting Oversight Board, which regulates and oversees public accounting firms. Other provisions of the act establish private civil actions and expand the SEC's remedies in administrative and civil actions.

We highlight some of the act's key provisions relating to corporate accountability in Exhibit 20–3 on the following page.

---

30. 15 U.S.C. Sections 7201 *et seq.*

• *Exhibit* 20-3 **Some Key Provisions of the Sarbanes-Oxley Act Relating to Corporate Accountability**

Certification Requirements—Under Section 906 of the Sarbanes-Oxley Act, the chief executive officers (CEOs) and chief financial officers (CFOs) of most major companies listed on public stock exchanges must certify financial statements that are filed with the SEC. CEOs and CFOs have to certify that filed financial reports "fully comply" with SEC requirements and that all of the information reported "fairly represents in all material respects, the financial conditions and results of operations of the issuer."

Under Section 302 of the act, CEOs and CFOs of reporting companies are required to certify that a signing officer reviewed each quarterly and annual filing with the SEC and that it contains no untrue statements of material fact. Also, the signing officer or officers must certify that they have established an internal control system to identify all material information and that any deficiencies in the system were disclosed to the auditors.

Effectiveness of Internal Controls on Financial Reporting—Under Section 404(a), all public companies are required to assess the effectiveness of their internal control over financial reporting. Section 404(b) requires independent auditors to report on management's assessment of internal controls, but companies with a public float of less than $75 million are exempted from this requirement.

Loans to Directors and Officers—Section 402 prohibits any reporting company, as well as any private company that is filing an initial public offering, from making personal loans to directors and executive officers (with a few limited exceptions, such as for certain consumer and housing loans).

Protection for Whistleblowers—Section 806 protects "whistleblowers"—employees who report ("blow the whistle" on) securities violations by their employers—from being fired or in any way discriminated against by their employers.

Blackout Periods—Section 306 prohibits certain types of securities transactions during "blackout periods"—periods during which the issuer's ability to purchase, sell, or otherwise transfer funds in individual account plans (such as pension funds) is suspended.

Enhanced Penalties for—

• *Violations of Section 906 Certification Requirements*—A CEO or CFO who certifies a financial report or statement filed with the SEC knowing that the report or statement does not fulfill all of the requirements of Section 906 will be subject to criminal penalties of up to $1 million in fines, ten years in prison, or both. *Willful* violators of the certification requirements may be subject to $5 million in fines, twenty years in prison, or both.

• *Violations of the Securities Exchange Act of 1934*—Penalties for securities fraud under the 1934 act were also increased (as discussed earlier in this chapter). Individual violators may be fined up to $5 million, imprisoned for up to twenty years, or both. *Willful* violators may be imprisoned for up to twenty-five years in addition to being fined.

• *Destruction or Alteration of Documents*—Anyone who alters, destroys, or conceals documents or otherwise obstructs any official proceeding will be subject to fines, imprisonment for up to twenty years, or both.

• *Other Forms of White-Collar Crime*—The act stiffened the penalties for certain criminal violations, such as federal mail and wire fraud, and ordered the U.S. Sentencing Commission to revise the sentencing guidelines for white-collar crimes (see Chapter 7).

Statute of Limitations for Securities Fraud—Section 804 provides that a private right of action for securities fraud may be brought no later than two years after the discovery of the violation or five years after the violation, whichever is earlier.

MORE INTERNAL CONTROLS AND ACCOUNTABILITY   The Sarbanes-Oxley Act includes some traditional securities law provisions but also introduces direct *federal* corporate governance requirements for public companies (companies whose shares are traded in the public securities markets). The law addresses many of the corporate governance procedures just discussed and creates new requirements in an attempt to make the system work more effectively. The requirements deal with independent monitoring of company officers by both the board of directors and auditors.

Sections 302 and 404 of Sarbanes-Oxley require high-level managers (the most senior officers) to establish and maintain an effective system of internal controls. Moreover, senior management must reassess the system's effectiveness annually. Some companies already had strong and effective internal control systems in place before the passage of the act, but others had to take expensive steps to bring their internal controls up to the new federal standard. These include "disclosure controls and procedures" to ensure that company financial reports are accurate and timely. Assessment must include the documenting of financial results and accounting policies before reporting the results. After the act was passed, hundreds of companies reported that they had identified and corrected shortcomings in their internal control systems.

The Sarbanes-Oxley Act initially required all public companies to have an independent auditor file a report with the SEC on management's assessment of internal controls. Congress, however, enacted an exemption for smaller companies in 2010 in an effort to reduce compliance costs. Public companies with a market capitalization, or public float, of less than $75 million no longer need to have an auditor report on management's assessment of internal controls.

CERTIFICATION AND MONITORING REQUIREMENTS   Section 906 requires that chief executive officers and chief financial officers certify that the information in the corporate financial statements "fairly represents in all material respects, the financial conditions and results of operations of the issuer." These corporate officers are subject to both civil and criminal penalties for violation of this section. This requirement makes officers directly accountable for the accuracy of their financial reporting and avoids any "ignorance defense" if shortcomings are later discovered.

Sarbanes-Oxley also includes requirements to improve directors' monitoring of officers' activities. All members of the corporate audit committee for public companies must be outside directors. The New York Stock Exchange (NYSE) has a similar rule that also extends to the board's compensation committee. The audit committee must have a written charter that sets out its duties and provides for performance appraisal. At least one "financial expert" must serve on the audit committee, which must hold executive meetings without company officers being present. The audit committee must establish procedures to encourage "whistleblowers" to report violations. In addition to reviewing the internal controls, the committee also monitors the actions of the outside auditor.

"Make money your God and it will plague you like the devil."
Henry Fielding, 1707–1754
(English author)

▶ Online Securities Fraud and Ponzi Schemes

A major problem facing the SEC today is how to enforce the antifraud provisions of the securities laws in the online environment. In 1999, in the first cases involving illegal online securities offerings, the SEC filed lawsuits against three individuals for illegally offering securities on an Internet auction site. In essence, all three indicated that their companies would go public soon and attempted to sell unregistered securities via the Web auction site.

All of these actions were in violation of Sections 5, 17(a)(1), and 17(a)(3) of the 1933 Securities Act. Since then, the SEC has brought a variety of Internet-related fraud cases and regularly issues interpretive releases to explain how securities laws apply in the online environment.

Online Investment Scams

An ongoing problem is how to curb online investment scams. As discussed in Chapter 7, the Internet has created a new vehicle for criminals to use to commit fraud and has provided them with new ways of targeting innocent investors. The criminally inclined can use spam, online newsletters and bulletin boards, chat rooms, blogs, and tweets to spread false information and perpetrate fraud. For a relatively small cost, criminals can even build sophisticated Web pages to facilitate their investment scams.

FRAUDULENT E-MAILS   There are countless variations of online investment scams, most of which promise spectacular returns for small investments. A person might receive spam e-mail, for example, that falsely claims a home business can "turn $5 into $60,000 in just three to six weeks." Another popular investment scam claims "your stimulus package has arrived" and promises you can make $100,000 a year using your home computer. Although most people today are dubious of the bogus claims made in spam messages, such offers can be more attractive during times of economic recession. Often, investment scams are simply the electronic version of pyramid schemes in which the participants attempt to profit solely by recruiting new participants.

ONLINE INVESTMENT NEWSLETTERS AND FORUMS   Hundreds of online investment newsletters provide free information on stocks. Legitimate online newsletters can help investors gather valuable information, but some of these newsletters are used for fraud. The law allows companies to pay people who write these newsletters to tout their securities, but the newsletters are required to disclose who paid for the advertising. Many fraudsters either fail to disclose or lie about who paid them. Thus, an investor reading an online newsletter may believe that the information is unbiased, when in fact the fraudsters will directly profit by convincing investors to buy or sell particular stocks.

The same deceptive tactics can be used on online bulletin boards (such as newsgroups and usenet groups), blogs, and social networking sites, including Twitter. While hiding their true identity, fraudsters may falsely pump up a company or reveal some "inside" information about a new product or lucrative contract to convince people to invest. By using multiple aliases on an online forum, a single person can easily create the illusion of widespread interest in a small stock.

Hacking into Online Stock Accounts

Millions of people now buy and sell investments online through online brokerage companies such as E*Trade and TD Ameritrade. Sophisticated hackers have learned to use online investing to their advantage. By installing keystroke-monitoring software on computer terminals in public places, such as hotels, libraries, and airports, hackers can gain access to online account information. All they have to do is wait for a person to access an online trading account and then monitor the next several dozen keystrokes to determine the customer's account number and password. Once they have the log-in information, they can access the customer's account and liquidate her or his existing stock holdings.

The hackers then use the customer's funds to purchase thinly traded, micro-cap securities, also known as penny stocks. The goal is to boost the price of a stock that the hacker has already purchased at a lower price. Then, when the stock price goes up, the hacker sells all the stock and wires the funds to either an offshore account or a dummy corporation, making it difficult for the SEC to trace the transactions and prosecute the offender.

EXAMPLE 20.7   Aleksey Kamardin, a twenty-one-year-old Florida college student, purchased 55,000 shares of stock in Fuego Entertainment using an E*Trade account in his own name. Kamardin then hacked into other customers' accounts at E*Trade and other brokerage companies, and used their funds to purchase a total of 458,000 shares of Fuego stock. When the stock price rose from $0.88 per share to $1.28 per share, Kamardin sold all of his shares, making a profit of $9,164 in about three hours. Kamardin did this with other thinly traded stocks as well, allegedly making $82,960 in about five weeks. The SEC filed charges against him, and he was later ordered to return the profits, plus interest. ●

Ponzi Schemes

In recent years, the SEC has filed an increasing number of enforcement actions against perpetrators of *Ponzi schemes* (an illegal pyramid scheme). In these scams, the fraudster promises high returns to investors and then uses their funds to pay previous investors. In 2009, Bernie Madoff was convicted of bilking investors out of more than $65 billion in the largest Ponzi scheme to date (see page 61 in Chapter 3).

OFFSHORE FRAUD Ponzi schemes sometimes target U.S. residents and convince them to invest in offshore companies or banks. **CASE EXAMPLE 20.8** In 2012, Texas billionaire R. Allen Stanford, of the Stanford Financial Group, was convicted for orchestrating a $7 billion scheme to defraud more than five thousand investors. Stanford had advised clients to buy certificates of deposit with improbably high interest rates from his Antigua-based Stanford International Bank. Although some early investors were paid returns from the funds provided by later investors, Stanford used $1.6 billion of the funds for personal expenditures. He also falsified financial statements that were filed with the SEC and reportedly paid more than $100,000 in bribes to an Antigua official to ensure that the bank would not be audited.[31] ●

"RISK-FREE" FRAUD Another type of fraud scheme offers risk-free or low-risk investments to lure investors. **EXAMPLE 20.9** For several years, Debi Mitchom used her firm to fraudulently obtain at least $10 million from dozens of investors by selling securities in her Best Buy Fund. Mitchom told investors that she had a proven track record of successful securities trading and showed them falsified financial documents. In reality, Mitchom was not a registered investment adviser and had suffered substantial investment losses. Mitchom promised investors returns averaging 20 percent with minimal risk to their principal and claimed to be using an investment strategy based on short-term price trends. She used less than half of the funds entrusted to her for trading purposes and personally spent at least $3 million. ●

---

31. *United States v. Stanford*, 2012 WL 1699459 (2012).

▶ Reviewing . . . Investor Protection and Corporate Governance

Dale Emerson served as the chief financial officer for Reliant Electric Company, a distributor of electricity serving portions of Montana and North Dakota. Reliant was in the final stages of planning a takeover of Dakota Gasworks, Inc., a natural gas distributor that operated solely within North Dakota. Emerson went on a weekend fishing trip with his uncle, Ernest Wallace. Emerson mentioned to Wallace that he had been putting in a lot of extra hours at the office planning a takeover of Dakota Gasworks. When he returned from the fishing trip, Wallace purchased $20,000 worth of Reliant stock. Three weeks later, Reliant made a tender offer to Dakota Gasworks stockholders and purchased 57 percent of Dakota Gasworks stock. Over the next two weeks, the price of Reliant stock rose 72 percent before leveling out. Wallace then sold his Reliant stock for a gross profit of $14,400. Using the information presented in the chapter, answer the following questions.

1. Would registration with the SEC be required for Dakota Gasworks securities? Why or why not?
2. Did Emerson violate Section 10(b) of the Securities Exchange Act of 1934 and SEC Rule 10b-5? Why or why not?
3. What theory or theories might a court use to hold Wallace liable for insider trading?
4. Under the Sarbanes-Oxley Act of 2002, who would be required to certify the accuracy of financial statements filed with the SEC?

▶ Debate This

Inside trading should be legalized.

Linking the Law *to Taxation*

The Tax Consequences of Deleveraging during an Economic Crisis

Part of corporate governance involves making sure that the corporation effectively examines trade-offs involved in any future action. When corporate boards or upper management makes decisions, those decisions affect employees, customers, and shareholders. In a time of economic crisis, *deleveraging,* or repurchasing debt, is one possible action that a corporation may take to reduce its debt.

Why Companies Leverage

Corporations engage in leveraging—borrowing on a large scale in order to make additional investments—particularly in boom times. Leverage in capital structure is neither good nor bad. Companies in volatile industries avoid taking on too much debt, but other companies have found that debt is an important part of their capital structure. In any event, corporations have to be flexible in their ratio of debt to equity as market conditions change.

Recessions, such as the one that began in 2008, create uncertainty. Uncertainty is the enemy of capital markets. Formerly routine credit transactions become unavailable, even to solvent firms, and companies that have leveraged—have large debt loads—may find that credit has disappeared altogether. Suppliers may refuse to ship goods to such corporations unless they agree to pay cash on delivery. This pessimism ripples through the economy. Today, not only have auto manufacturers suffered, but so too have community hospitals, restaurants, hotels, and a host of firms in other industries.

The Downside of Deleveraging

Many corporations' publicly traded debt instruments have been selling at very deep discounts. One way for a company to improve its balance sheet and to reassure suppliers that it will be able to pay its bills is to retire that debt (at deep discounts). Some corporations could do this by issuing additional shares of stock to obtain the financing for such debt retirement. Moreover, repurchasing corporate debt may be a beneficial use of cash for corporations

when consumer demand slows and alternative capital investments do not offer immediate returns.

Until 2009, however, corporate finance officers faced a daunting cost for such debt retirement plans. Under tax code and regulatory changes made in the 1980s, the difference between the original issue price of debt and the lower price for which it was repurchased was treated as taxable income. Finance managers call this a tax liability on "phantom income" (calculated as the difference between the issued price and the repurchase price of corporate debt). Such tax liabilities have prevented many corporations from necessary capital restructuring. Additionally, the tax liability on phantom income helped to create a perverse preference for bankruptcy. To avoid the tax liability, a heavily leveraged firm might choose bankruptcy over debt retirement even though bankruptcy destroys asset values, customer relations, and, most of all, jobs.

A New Tax Incentive for Finance Managers to Consider

In 2009, as part of the economic stimulus bill, the Obama administration created a new tax break that applies to the retirement of heavily discounted debt instruments by corporations. Under this provision, tax liabilities on phantom income will not trigger corporate income taxes until 2014. At that time, corporations that have retired discounted debt will be able to spread out their tax liabilities over a five-year period.

Soon after the provision was enacted, homebuilder Hovnanian Enterprises paid $105 million to repurchase $315 million of its unsecured debt. That $210 million of phantom income will not be taxable until 2014. At about the same time, GE Capital, a unit of General Electric, offered to buy back $1.46 billion of its bonds.

FOR CRITICAL ANALYSIS

If you were a finance manager in a large corporation, under what circumstances might you argue that the corporation should deleverage?

Key Terms

▶ Chapter Summary: Investor Protection and Corporate Governance

The Securities Act of 1933 (See pages 503–510.)	Prohibits fraud and stabilizes the securities industry by requiring disclosure of all essential information relating to the issuance of securities to the investing public.

1. *Prospectus*—The issuer must provide investors with a *prospectus* that describes the security being sold, the issuing corporation, and the risk attaching to the security.
2. *Registration requirements*—Securities, unless exempt, must be registered with the SEC before being offered to the public. The *registration statement* must include detailed financial information about the issuing corporation; the intended use of the proceeds of the securities being issued; and certain disclosures, such as interests of directors or officers and pending lawsuits.
3. *Exemptions*—The SEC has exempted certain offerings from the requirements of the Securities Act of 1933. Exemptions may be based on the size of the issue, whether the offering is private or public, and whether advertising is involved. Exemptions are summarized in Exhibit 20–1 on page 507.
4. *Violations*—Intentionally defrauding investors by misrepresenting or omitting facts in the registration statement or prospectus is a violation of the 1933 act.

The Securities Exchange Act of 1934 (See pages 511–517.)	Provides for the regulation and registration of securities exchanges, brokers, dealers, and national securities associations (such as the NASD). Maintains a continuous disclosure system for all corporations with securities on the securities exchanges and for those companies that have assets in excess of $10 million and five hundred or more shareholders (Section 12 companies).

1. *SEC Rule 10b-5 [under Section 10(b) of the 1934 act]*—
   a. Applies to almost all trading of securities—a firm's securities do not have to be registered under the 1933 act for the 1934 act to apply.
   b. Applies to insider trading by corporate officers, directors, majority shareholders, and any persons receiving inside information (information not available to the public) who base their trading on this information.
   c. Liability for violations can be civil or criminal.
   d. May be violated by failing to disclose "material facts" that must be disclosed under this rule.
   e. Liability may be based on the tipper/tippee or the misappropriation theory.
2. *Insider trading [under Section 16(b) of the 1934 act]*—To prevent corporate insiders from taking advantage of inside information, the 1934 act requires officers, directors, and shareholders owning 10 percent or more of the issued stock of a corporation to turn over to the corporation all short-term profits (called *short-swing profits*) realized from the purchase and sale or sale and purchase of corporate stock within any six-month period.
3. *Regulation of proxies*—The SEC regulates the content of proxy statements sent to shareholders of Section 12 companies. Section 14(a) is essentially a disclosure law, with provisions similar to the antifraud provisions of SEC Rule 10b-5.
4. *Violations*—Violations of the 1934 act may be subject to criminal or civil liability.

State Securities Laws (See pages 517–518.)	All states have corporate securities laws *(blue sky laws)* that regulate the offer and sale of securities within state borders. These laws are designed to prevent "speculative schemes which have no more basis than so many feet of 'blue sky.'" States regulate securities concurrently with the federal government. The Uniform Securities Act of 2002, which has been adopted by seventeen states and is being considered by several others, is designed to promote coordination and reduce duplication between state and federal securities regulation.

Corporate Governance (See pages 518–523.)	1. *Definition*—Corporate governance is the system by which business corporations are governed, including policies and procedures for making decisions on corporate affairs. 2. *The need for corporate governance*—Corporate governance is necessary in large corporations because corporate ownership (by the shareholders) is separated from corporate control (by officers and managers). This separation of corporate ownership and control can often result in conflicting interests. Corporate governance standards address such issues. 3. *Sarbanes-Oxley Act of 2002*—This act attempts to increase corporate accountability by imposing strict disclosure requirements and harsh penalties for violations of securities laws.

(Continued)

Chapter Summary: Investor Protection and Corporate Governance, Continued

Online Securities Fraud and Ponzi Schemes (See pages 523–525.)	A major problem facing the SEC today is how to enforce the antifraud provisions of the securities laws in the online environment. Internet-related forms of securities fraud include numerous types of investment scams and hacking into online trading accounts. Ponzi schemes also pose a significant problem for the SEC.

ExamPrep

ISSUE SPOTTERS

—Check your answers to these questions against the answers provided in Appendix D at the end of the text.

1. When a corporation wishes to issue certain securities, it must provide sufficient information to enable an unsophisticated investor to evaluate the financial risk involved. Specifically, the law imposes liability for making a false statement or omission that is "material." What sort of information would an investor consider material? **(See pages 505–510.)**

2. Lee is an officer of Magma Oil, Inc. Lee knows that a Magma geologist has just discovered a new deposit of oil. Can Lee take advantage of this information to buy and sell Magma stock? Why or why not? **(See pages 511–513.)**

BEFORE THE TEST

Go to **www.cengagebrain.com**, enter the ISBN 9781133586548, and click on "Find" to locate this textbook's Web site. Then click on "Access Now" under "Study Tools," and select Chapter 20 at the top. There, you will find a Practice Quiz that you can take to assess your mastery of the concepts in this chapter. Additionally, you will find Flashcards and a Glossary of important terms, as well as Video Questions (when assigned).

For Review

Answers for the even-numbered questions in this For Review *section can be found in Appendix E at the end of this text.*

1. What is meant by the term *securities*?
2. What are the two major statutes regulating the securities industry?
3. What is insider trading? Why is it prohibited?
4. What are some of the features of state securities laws?
5. What certification requirements does the Sarbanes-Oxley Act impose on corporate executives?

Questions and Case Problems

20–1. Registration Requirements. Langley Brothers, Inc., a corporation incorporated and doing business in Kansas, decides to sell common stock worth $1 million to the public. The stock will be sold only within the state of Kansas. Joseph Langley, the chairman of the board, says the offering need not be registered with the Securities and Exchange Commission. His brother, Harry, disagrees. Who is right? Explain. **(See pages 506–508.)**

20–2. **Question with Sample Answer: Insider Trading.** David Gain was chief executive officer (CEO) of Forest Media Corp., which became interested in acquiring RS Communications, Inc., in 2013. To initiate negotiations, Gain met with RS's CEO, Gill Raz, on Friday, July 12. Two days later, Gain phoned his brother Mark, who, on Monday, bought 3,800 shares of RS stock. Mark discussed the deal with their father, Jordan, who bought 20,000 RS shares on Thursday. On July 25, the day before the RS bid was due, Gain phoned his parents' home, and Mark bought another 3,200 RS shares. The same routine was followed over the next few days, with Gain periodically phoning Mark or

Jordan, both of whom continued to buy RS shares. Forest's bid was refused, but on August 5, RS announced its merger with another company. The price of RS stock rose 30 percent, increasing the value of Mark and Jordan's shares by $664,024 and $412,875, respectively. Did Gain engage in insider trading? What is required to impose sanctions for this offense? Could a court hold Gain liable? Why or why not? **(See pages 511–513.)**

—For a sample answer to Question 20–2, go to Appendix F at the end of this text.

20–3. Securities Violations. In 1997, WTS Transnational, Inc., required financing to develop a prototype of an unpatented fingerprint-verification system. At the time, WTS had no revenue, $655,000 in liabilities, and only $10,000 in assets. Thomas Cavanagh and Frank Nicolois, who operated an investment banking company called U.S. Milestone (USM), arranged the financing using Curbstone Acquisition Corp. Curbstone had no assets but had registered approximately 3.5 million shares of stock with the Securities and Exchange Commission (SEC). Under the terms of the deal, Curbstone acquired WTS, and the resulting entity was named Electro-Optical Systems Corp. (EOSC). New EOSC shares were issued to all of the WTS shareholders. Only Cavanagh and others affiliated with USM could sell EOSC stock to the public, however. Over the next few months, these individuals issued false press releases, made small deceptive purchases of EOSC shares at high prices, distributed hundreds of thousands of shares to friends and relatives, and sold their own shares at inflated prices through third party companies they owned. When the SEC began to investigate, the share price fell to its actual value, and innocent investors lost more than $15 million. Were any securities laws violated in this case? If so, what might be an appropriate remedy? [*SEC v. Cavanagh*, 445 F.3d 105 (2d Cir. 2006)] **(See pages 511–517.)**

20–4. Case Problem with Sample Answer. Duty to Disclose. Orphan Medical, Inc., was a pharmaceutical company that focused on central nervous system disorders. Its major product was the drug Xyrem. In June 2004, Orphan merged with Jazz, and Orphan shareholders received $10.75 per share for their stock. Before the merger was final, Orphan completed a phase of testing of Xyrem that indicated that the U.S. Food and Drug Administration (FDA) would allow the drug to go to the next stage of testing, which was necessary for the drug to be widely marketed. If that happened, the value of the drug and Orphan would go up, and the stock would have been worth more than $10.75. Little Gem Life Sciences, LLC, was an Orphan shareholder that received $10.75 a share. It sued, claiming violations of federal securities laws because shareholders were not told, during the merger process, that the current stage of FDA tests had been successful. Little Gem claimed that if the information had been public, the stock price would have been higher. The district court dismissed the suit, holding that it did not

meet the standards required by the Private Securities Litigation Reform Act. Little Gem appealed. Did Orphan's directors have a duty to reveal all relevant drug-testing information to shareholders? Why or why not? [*Little Gem Life Sciences, LLC v. Orphan Medical, Inc.*, 537 F.3d 913 (8th Cir. 2008)] **(See pages 511–514.)**

—For a sample answer to Case Problem 20–4, go to Appendix G at the end of this text.

20–5. Violations of the 1934 Act. To comply with accounting principles, a company that engages in software development must either "expense" the cost (record it immediately on the company's financial statement) or "capitalize" it (record it as a cost incurred in increments over time). If the project is in the pre- or post-development stage, the cost must be expensed. Otherwise it may be capitalized. Capitalizing a cost makes a company look more profitable in the short term. Digimarc Corp., which provides secure personal identification documents such as drivers' licenses using digital watermark technology, announced that it had improperly capitalized software development costs over at least the previous eighteen months. The errors resulted in $2.7 million in overstated earnings, requiring a restatement of prior financial statements. Zucco Partners, LLC, which had bought Digimarc stock within the relevant period, filed a suit in a federal district court against the firm. Zucco claimed that it could show that there had been disagreements within Digimarc over its accounting. Is this sufficient to establish a violation of SEC Rule 10b-5? Why or why not? [*Zucco Partners, LLC v. Digimarc Corp.*, 552 F.3d 981 (9th Cir. 2009)] **(See pages 511–517.)**

20–6. Insider Trading. Jabil Circuit, Inc., is a publicly traded electronics and technology company headquartered in St. Petersburg, Florida. In 2008, a group of shareholders who owned Jabil stock from 2001 to 2007 sued the company and its auditors, directors, and officers for insider trading. Stock options were a part of Jabil's compensation for executives. In some situations, stock options were backdated to a point in time when the stock price was lower, so that the options were worth more to certain company executives. Backdating is not illegal so long as it is reported, but Jabil did not report the fact that backdating had occurred. Thus, expenses were underreported, and net income was overstated by millions of dollars. The shareholders claimed that by rigging the stock price by backdating, the executives had engaged in insider trading and could pick favorable purchase prices and that there was a general practice of selling stock before unfavorable news about the company was reported to the public. The shareholders, however, had no specific information about these stock trades or when (or even if) a particular executive was aware of any accounting errors during the time of any backdating purchases. Were the shareholders' allegations sufficient to assert that insider trading had occurred under Rule 10b-5? Why or why not? [*Edward J. Goodman Life Income Trust v. Jabil Circuit, Inc.*, 594 F.3d 783 (11th Cir. 2010)] **(See pages 511–512.)**

20–7. Violations of the 1934 Act. Matrixx Initiatives, Inc., makes and sells over-the-counter pharmaceutical products. Its core brand is Zicam, which accounts for 70 percent of its sales. Matrixx received reports that some consumers had lost their sense of smell (a condition called *anosmia*) after using Zicam Cold Remedy. Four product liability suits were filed against Matrixx, seeking damages for anosmia. In public statements relating to revenues and product safety, however, Matrixx did not reveal this information. James Siracusano and other Matrixx investors filed a suit in a federal district court against the company and its executives under Section 10(b) of the Securities Exchange Act of 1934 and SEC Rule 10b-5, claiming that the statements were misleading because they did not disclose the information regarding the product liability suits. Matrixx argued that to be material, information must consist of a statistically significant number of adverse events that require disclosure. Because Siracusano's claim did not allege that Matrixx knew of a statistically significant number of adverse events, the company contended that the claim should be dismissed. What is the standard for materiality in this context? Should Siracusano's claim be dismissed? Explain. [*Matrixx Initiatives, Inc. v. Siracusano*, ___ U.S. ___, 131 S.Ct. 1309, 179 L.Ed.2d 398 (2011)] **(See pages 511–517.)**

20–8. Disclosure under SEC Rule 10b-5. Dodona I, LLC, invested $4 million in two securities offerings from Goldman, Sachs & Co. The investments were in collateralized debt obligations (CDOs). Their value depended on residential mortgage-backed securities (RMBS), whose value in turn depended on the performance of subprime residential mortgages. Before marketing the CDOs, Goldman had noticed several "red flags" relating to investments in the subprime market, in which it had invested heavily. To limit its risk, Goldman began betting against subprime mortgages, RMBS, and CDOs, including the CDOs it sold to Dodona. In an internal e-mail, one Goldman official commented that the company had managed to "make some lemonade from some big old lemons." Nevertheless, Goldman's marketing materials provided only boilerplate statements about the risks of investing in the securities. The CDOs were later downgraded to junk status, and Dodona suffered a major loss while Goldman profited. Assuming that Goldman did not affirmatively misrepresent any facts about the CDOs, can Dodona still recover under SEC Rule 10b-5? If so, how? [*Dodona I, LLC v. Goldman, Sachs & Co.*, 2012 WL935815 (S.D.N.Y. 2012)] **(See pages 511–514.)**

20–9. **A Question of Ethics: Violations of the 1934 Act.** *Melvin Lyttle told John Montana and Paul Knight about a "Trading Program" that purportedly would buy and sell securities in deals that were fully insured, as well as monitored and controlled by the Federal Reserve Board. Without checking the details or even verifying whether the Program existed, Montana and Knight, with Lyttle's help, began to sell interests in the Program to investors. For a minimum investment of $1 million, the investors were promised extraordinary rates of return—from 10 percent to as much as 100 percent per week—without risk. They were told, among other things, that the Program would "utilize banks that can ensure full bank integrity of The Transaction whose undertaking[s] are in complete harmony with international banking rules and protocol and who [sic] guarantee maximum security of a Funder's Capital Placement Amount." Nothing was required but the investors' funds and their silence—the Program was to be kept secret. Over a four-month period in 1999, Montana raised approximately $23 million from twenty-two investors. The promised gains did not accrue, however. Instead, Montana, Lyttle, and Knight depleted the investors' funds in high-risk trades or spent the funds on themselves. [SEC v. Montana, 464 F.Supp.2d 772 (S.D.Ind. 2006)] **(See pages 511–517.)**

1. The Securities and Exchange Commission (SEC) filed a suit in a federal district court against Montana and the others, seeking an injunction, civil penalties, and disgorgement (giving up) of profits with interest. The SEC alleged, among other things, violations of Section 10(b) of the Securities Exchange Act of 1934 and SEC Rule 10b-5. What is required to establish a violation of these laws? Explain how and why the facts in this case meet, or fail to meet, these requirements.

2. It is often remarked, "There's a sucker born every minute!" Does that phrase describe the Program's investors? Ultimately, about half of the investors recouped the amount they invested. Should the others be considered at least partly responsible for their own losses? Why or why not?

How to Brief Cases and Analyze Case Problems

How to Brief Cases

To fully understand the law with respect to business, you need to be able to read and understand court decisions. To make this task easier, you can use a method of case analysis that is called *briefing*. There is a fairly standard procedure that you can follow when you "brief" any court case. You must first read the case opinion carefully. When you feel you understand the case, you can prepare a brief of it.

Although the format of the brief may vary, typically it will present the essentials of the case under headings such as the following:

1. **Citation.** Give the full citation for the case, including the name of the case, the date it was decided, and the court that decided it.
2. **Facts.** Briefly indicate (a) the reasons for the lawsuit; (b) the identity and arguments of the plaintiff(s) and defendant(s), respectively; and (c) the lower court's decision—if appropriate.
3. **Issue.** Concisely phrase, in the form of a question, the essential issue before the court. (If more than one issue is involved, you may have two—or even more—questions here.)
4. **Decision.** Indicate here—with a "yes" or "no," if possible—the court's answer to the question (or questions) in the *Issue* section above.
5. **Reason.** Summarize as briefly as possible the reasons given by the court for its decision (or decisions) and the case or statutory law relied on by the court in arriving at its decision.

An Example of a Briefed Sample Court Case

As an example of the format used in briefing cases, we present here a briefed version of the sample court case that was presented in the Appendix to Chapter 1 in Exhibit 1A–3 on pages 27–29.

UNITED STATES v. JONES
Supreme Court of the United States,
__ U.S. __, 132 S.Ct. 945, 181 L.Ed.2d 911 (2012).

FACTS Antoine Jones owned and operated a nightclub in the District of Columbia and was suspected of drug trafficking. As part of an investigation, the government installed a Global Positioning System (GPS) tracking device underneath a vehicle belonging to Jones's wife. Although it did not have a valid warrant, the government tracked the vehicle for four weeks, ultimately gathering enough evidence of drug trafficking to obtain an indictment. Before the trial, Jones filed a motion to suppress the evidence obtained with the device, arguing that the government had violated his Fourth Amendment rights by subjecting him to an unlawful "search." The district court held that most of the evidence was admissible, and Jones was convicted and sentenced to life in prison. A federal appellate court reversed the conviction, and the government appealed to the United States Supreme Court.

ISSUE Did the government engage in a "search" within the meaning of the Fourth Amendment by installing the GPS tracking device and then monitoring the vehicle's movements?

DECISION Yes. The United States Supreme Court affirmed the judgment of the federal appellate court. The government engaged in a Fourth Amendment "search" by installing and using the tracking device.

REASON The Fourth Amendment prohibits "unreasonable searches and seizures" based on "the right of the people to be secure in their persons, houses, papers, and effects." A vehicle is an "effect," and the government's installation and use of the tracking device constituted a "search." Traditionally, the Supreme Court recognized the Fourth Amendment's close connection to property rights and found a "search" only if the government's conduct would have amounted to trespass under English common law. In 1967, however, the Supreme Court ruled that the Fourth Amendment also protects a person's "reasonable expectation of privacy."

Whether or not Jones had a reasonable expectation of privacy in either the vehicle's undercarriage or its movements on public streets was irrelevant in this situation. The Court reasoned that its precedent on privacy did not eliminate the traditional rule that a common law trespass may also establish a search. In this case, the government engaged in trespass, and therefore a search, by installing the tracking device without consent.

Review of Sample Court Case

Next, we provide a review of the briefed version to indicate the kind of information that is contained in each section.

CITATION The name of the case is *United States v. Jones*. The U.S. government is the plaintiff, and Antoine Jones is the defendant. The United States Supreme Court decided this case in 2012. The case citation includes a citation to the *Supreme Court Reporter,* which contains only decisions of the United States Supreme Court. The case can be found in Volume 132 of the *Supreme Court Reporter,* beginning on page 945.

FACTS The *Facts* section identifies the parties, summarizes the relevant facts, and explains the procedural history leading up to the decision being summarized.

ISSUE The *Issue* section presents the central issue(s) that the court must decide. In this case, for example, the United States Supreme Court must determine whether the government's conduct constituted a "search" for purposes of the Fourth Amendment. Most cases address more than one issue, but this textbook's author has edited many cases to focus on just one issue.

DECISION The *Decision* section summarizes the court's decision about an issue. The decision reflects the opinion of the judge or, if a panel heard the case, the majority's opinion. For an appellate court case, the *Decision* section will frequently explain whether the appellate court "affirmed" or "reversed" a lower court's ruling. In either situation, the appellate court may remand the case, meaning it sends the case back for further proceedings consistent with its decision.

REASON The *Reason* section explains how the court arrived at its decision, summarizing the key legal principles and authorities. In the *Jones* case, for example, the Supreme Court held that the government performed a Fourth Amendment search by installing and using a GPS tracking device. The Court found that a search may occur if the government violates either a reasonable expectation of privacy or a person's property rights.

Analyzing Case Problems

In addition to learning how to brief cases, students of business law and the legal environment also find it helpful to know how to analyze case problems. Part of the study of business law and the legal environment usually involves analyzing case problems, such as those included in selected chapters of this text.

For each case problem in this book, we provide the relevant background and facts of the lawsuit and the issue before the court. When you are assigned one of these problems, your job will be to determine how the court should decide the issue, and why. In other words, you will need to engage in legal analysis and reasoning. Here, we offer some suggestions on how to make this task less daunting. We begin by presenting a sample problem:

> While Janet Lawson, a famous pianist, was shopping in Quality Market, she slipped and fell on a wet floor in one of the aisles. The floor had recently been mopped by one of the store's employees, but there were no signs warning customers that the floor in that area was wet. As a result of the fall, Lawson injured her right arm and was unable to perform piano concerts for the next six months. Had she been able to perform the scheduled concerts, she would have earned approximately $60,000 over that period of time. Lawson sued Quality Market for this amount, plus another $10,000 in medical expenses. She claimed that the store's failure to warn customers of the wet floor constituted negligence and therefore the market was liable for her injuries. Will the court agree with Lawson? Discuss.

Understand the Facts

This may sound obvious, but before you can analyze or apply the relevant law to a specific set of facts, you must have a clear understanding of those facts. In other words, you should read through the case problem carefully—more than once, if necessary—to make sure you understand the identity of the plaintiff(s) and defendant(s) and the progression of events that led to the lawsuit.

In the sample case problem just given, the identity of the parties is fairly obvious. Janet Lawson is the one bringing the suit—therefore, she is the plaintiff. She is bringing the suit against Quality Market, so it is the defendant. Some of the case problems you may work on have multiple plaintiffs or defendants. Often, it is helpful to use abbreviations for the parties. A plaintiff, for example, may be denoted by a *pi* symbol (π), and a defendant by a *delta* (Δ) or triangle.

The events leading to the lawsuit are also fairly straightforward. Lawson slipped and fell on a wet floor, and she contends that Quality Market should be liable for her injuries because it was negligent in not posting a sign warning customers of the wet floor.

When you are working on case problems, realize that the facts should be accepted as they are given. For example, in our sample problem, it should be accepted that the floor was wet and that there was no sign. In other words, avoid making conjectures, such as "Maybe the floor wasn't too wet," or "Maybe an employee was getting a sign to put up," or "Maybe someone stole the sign." Questioning the facts as they are presented will only create confusion in your analysis.

Legal Analysis and Reasoning

Once you understand the facts given in the case problem, you can begin to analyze the case. The IRAC method is a helpful tool to use in the legal analysis and reasoning process. IRAC is an acronym for Issue, Rule, Application, Conclusion. Applying this method to our sample problem would involve the following steps:

1. First, you need to decide what legal **issue** is involved in the case. In our sample case, the basic issue is whether Quality Market's failure to warn customers of the wet floor constituted negligence. As discussed in Chapter 6, negligence is a *tort*—a civil wrong. In a tort lawsuit, the plaintiff seeks to be compensated for another's wrongful act. A defendant will be deemed negligent if he or she breached a duty of care owed to the plaintiff and the breach of that duty caused the plaintiff to suffer harm.

2. Once you have identified the issue, the next step is to determine what **rule of law** applies to the issue. To make this determination, carefully review the text of the chapter in which the relevant rule of law for the problem appears. Our sample case problem involves the tort of negligence, which is covered in Chapter 6. The applicable rule of law is the tort law principle that business owners owe a duty to exercise reasonable care to protect their customers ("business invitees").

   Reasonable care, in this context, includes either removing—or warning customers of—*foreseeable* risks about which the owner *knew* or *should have known*. Business owners need not warn customers of "open and obvious" risks, however. If a business owner breaches this duty of care (fails to exercise the appropriate degree of care toward customers), and the breach of duty causes a customer to be injured, the business owner will be liable to the customer for the customer's injuries.

3. The next—and usually the most difficult—step in analyzing case problems is the **application** of the relevant rule of law to the specific facts of the case you are studying. In our sample problem, applying the tort law principle just discussed presents few difficulties. An employee of the store had mopped the floor in the aisle where Lawson slipped and fell, but no sign was present indicating that the floor was wet. That a customer might fall on a wet floor is clearly a foreseeable risk. Therefore, the failure to warn customers about the wet floor was a breach of the duty of care owed by the business owner to the store's customers.

4. Once you have completed Step 3 in the IRAC method, you should be ready to draw your **conclusion.** In our sample problem, Quality Market is liable to Lawson for her injuries because the market's breach of its duty of care caused Lawson's injuries.

The fact patterns in the case problems presented in this text are not always as simple as those in our sample problem. Often, for example, a case has more than one plaintiff or defendant. A case may also involve more than one issue and have more than one applicable rule of law. Furthermore, in some case problems the facts may indicate that the general rule of law should not apply.

For example, suppose that a store employee advised Lawson not to walk on the floor in the aisle because it was wet, but Lawson decided to walk on it anyway. This fact could alter the outcome of the case because the store could then raise the defense of assumption of risk (see Chapter 6).

Nonetheless, a careful review of the chapter should always provide you with the knowledge you need to analyze the problem thoroughly and arrive at accurate conclusions.

The Constitution of the United States

We the People of the United States, in Order to form a more perfect Union, establish Justice, insure domestic Tranquility, provide for the common defence, promote the general Welfare, and secure the Blessings of Liberty to ourselves and our Posterity, do ordain and establish this Constitution for the United States of America.

ARTICLE I

Section 1. All legislative Powers herein granted shall be vested in a Congress of the United States, which shall consist of a Senate and House of Representatives.

Section 2. The House of Representatives shall be composed of Members chosen every second Year by the People of the several States, and the Electors in each State shall have the Qualifications requisite for Electors of the most numerous Branch of the State Legislature.

No Person shall be a Representative who shall not have attained to the Age of twenty five Years, and been seven Years a Citizen of the United States, and who shall not, when elected, be an Inhabitant of that State in which he shall be chosen.

Representatives and direct Taxes shall be apportioned among the several States which may be included within this Union, according to their respective Numbers, which shall be determined by adding to the whole Number of free Persons, including those bound to Service for a Term of Years, and excluding Indians not taxed, three fifths of all other Persons. The actual Enumeration shall be made within three Years after the first Meeting of the Congress of the United States, and within every subsequent Term of ten Years, in such Manner as they shall by Law direct. The Number of Representatives shall not exceed one for every thirty Thousand, but each State shall have at Least one Representative; and until such enumeration shall be made, the State of New Hampshire shall be entitled to chuse three, Massachusetts eight, Rhode Island and Providence Plantations one, Connecticut five, New York six, New Jersey four, Pennsylvania eight, Delaware one, Maryland six, Virginia ten, North Carolina five, South Carolina five, and Georgia three.

When vacancies happen in the Representation from any State, the Executive Authority thereof shall issue Writs of Election to fill such Vacancies.

The House of Representatives shall chuse their Speaker and other Officers; and shall have the sole Power of Impeachment.

Section 3. The Senate of the United States shall be composed of two Senators from each State, chosen by the Legislature thereof, for six Years; and each Senator shall have one Vote.

Immediately after they shall be assembled in Consequence of the first Election, they shall be divided as equally as may be into three Classes. The Seats of the Senators of the first Class shall be vacated at the Expiration of the second Year, of the second Class at the Expiration of the fourth Year, and of the third Class at the Expiration of the sixth Year, so that one third may be chosen every second Year; and if Vacancies happen by Resignation, or otherwise, during the Recess of the Legislature of any State, the Executive thereof may make temporary Appointments until the next Meeting of the Legislature, which shall then fill such Vacancies.

No Person shall be a Senator who shall not have attained to the Age of thirty Years, and been nine Years a Citizen of the United States, and who shall not, when elected, be an Inhabitant of that State for which he shall be chosen.

The Vice President of the United States shall be President of the Senate, but shall have no Vote, unless they be equally divided.

The Senate shall chuse their other Officers, and also a President pro tempore, in the Absence of the Vice President, or when he shall exercise the Office of President of the United States.

The Senate shall have the sole Power to try all Impeachments. When sitting for that Purpose, they shall be on Oath or Affirmation. When the President of the United States is tried, the Chief Justice shall preside: And no Person shall be convicted without the Concurrence of two thirds of the Members present.

Judgment in Cases of Impeachment shall not extend further than to removal from Office, and disqualification to hold and enjoy any Office of honor, Trust, or Profit under the United States: but the Party convicted shall nevertheless be liable and subject to Indictment, Trial, Judgment, and Punishment, according to Law.

Section 4. The Times, Places and Manner of holding Elections for Senators and Representatives, shall be prescribed in each State by the Legislature thereof; but the Congress may at any time by Law make or alter such Regulations, except as to the Places of chusing Senators.

The Congress shall assemble at least once in every Year, and such Meeting shall be on the first Monday in December, unless they shall by Law appoint a different Day.

Section 5. Each House shall be the Judge of the Elections, Returns, and Qualifications of its own Members, and a Majority of each shall constitute a Quorum to do Business; but a smaller Number may adjourn from day to day, and may be authorized to compel the Attendance of absent Members, in such Manner, and under such Penalties as each House may provide.

Each House may determine the Rules of its Proceedings, punish its Members for disorderly Behavior, and, with the Concurrence of two thirds, expel a Member.

Each House shall keep a Journal of its Proceedings, and from time to time publish the same, excepting such Parts as may in their Judgment require Secrecy; and the Yeas and Nays of the Members of either House on any question shall, at the Desire of one fifth of those Present, be entered on the Journal.

Neither House, during the Session of Congress, shall, without the Consent of the other, adjourn for more than three days, nor to any other Place than that in which the two Houses shall be sitting.

Section 6. The Senators and Representatives shall receive a Compensation for their Services, to be ascertained by Law, and paid out of the Treasury of the United States. They shall in all Cases, except Treason, Felony and Breach of the Peace, be privileged from Arrest during their Attendance at the Session of their respective Houses, and in going to and returning from the same; and for any Speech or Debate in either House, they shall not be questioned in any other Place.

No Senator or Representative shall, during the Time for which he was elected, be appointed to any civil Office under the Authority of the United States, which shall have been created, or the Emoluments whereof shall have been increased during such time; and no Person holding any Office under the United States, shall be a Member of either House during his Continuance in Office.

Section 7. All Bills for raising Revenue shall originate in the House of Representatives; but the Senate may propose or concur with Amendments as on other Bills.

Every Bill which shall have passed the House of Representatives and the Senate, shall, before it become a Law, be presented to the President of the United States; If he approve he shall sign it, but if not he shall return it, with his Objections to the House in which it shall have originated, who shall enter the Objections at large on their Journal, and proceed to reconsider it. If after such Reconsideration two thirds of that House shall agree to pass the Bill, it shall be sent together with the Objections, to the other House, by which it shall likewise be reconsidered, and if approved by two thirds of that House, it shall become a Law. But in all such Cases the Votes of both Houses shall be determined by Yeas and Nays, and the Names of the Persons voting for and against the Bill shall be entered on the Journal of each House respectively. If any Bill shall not be returned by the President within ten Days (Sundays excepted) after it shall have been presented to him, the Same shall be a Law, in like Manner as if he had signed it, unless the Congress by their Adjournment prevent its Return in which Case it shall not be a Law.

Every Order, Resolution, or Vote, to which the Concurrence of the Senate and House of Representatives may be necessary (except on a question of Adjournment) shall be presented to the President of the United States; and before the Same shall take Effect, shall be approved by him, or being disapproved by him, shall be repassed by two thirds of the Senate and House of Representatives, according to the Rules and Limitations prescribed in the Case of a Bill.

Section 8. The Congress shall have Power To lay and collect Taxes, Duties, Imposts and Excises, to pay the Debts and provide for the common Defence and general Welfare of the United States; but all Duties, Imposts and Excises shall be uniform throughout the United States;

To borrow Money on the credit of the United States;

To regulate Commerce with foreign Nations, and among the several States, and with the Indian Tribes;

To establish an uniform Rule of Naturalization, and uniform Laws on the subject of Bankruptcies throughout the United States;

To coin Money, regulate the Value thereof, and of foreign Coin, and fix the Standard of Weights and Measures;

To provide for the Punishment of counterfeiting the Securities and current Coin of the United States;

To establish Post Offices and post Roads;

To promote the Progress of Science and useful Arts, by securing for limited Times to Authors and Inventors the exclusive Right to their respective Writings and Discoveries;

To constitute Tribunals inferior to the supreme Court;

To define and punish Piracies and Felonies committed on the high Seas, and Offenses against the Law of Nations;

To declare War, grant Letters of Marque and Reprisal, and make Rules concerning Captures on Land and Water;

To raise and support Armies, but no Appropriation of Money to that Use shall be for a longer Term than two Years;

To provide and maintain a Navy;

To make Rules for the Government and Regulation of the land and naval Forces;

To provide for calling forth the Militia to execute the Laws of the Union, suppress Insurrections and repel Invasions;

To provide for organizing, arming, and disciplining, the Militia, and for governing such Part of them as may be employed in the Service of the United States, reserving to the States respectively, the Appointment of the Officers, and the Authority of training the Militia according to the discipline prescribed by Congress;

To exercise exclusive Legislation in all Cases whatsoever, over such District (not exceeding ten Miles square) as may, by Cession of particular States, and the Acceptance of Congress, become the Seat of the Government of the United States, and to exercise like Authority over all Places purchased by the Consent of the Legislature of the State in which the Same shall be, for the Erection of Forts, Magazines, Arsenals, dock-Yards, and other needful Buildings;—And

To make all Laws which shall be necessary and proper for carrying into Execution the foregoing Powers, and all other Powers vested by this Constitution in the Government of the United States, or in any Department or Officer thereof.

Section 9. The Migration or Importation of such Persons as any of the States now existing shall think proper to admit, shall not be prohibited by the Congress prior to the Year one thousand eight hundred and eight, but a Tax or duty may be imposed on such Importation, not exceeding ten dollars for each Person.

The privilege of the Writ of Habeas Corpus shall not be suspended, unless when in Cases of Rebellion or Invasion the public Safety may require it.

No Bill of Attainder or ex post facto Law shall be passed.

No Capitation, or other direct, Tax shall be laid, unless in Proportion to the Census or Enumeration herein before directed to be taken.

No Tax or Duty shall be laid on Articles exported from any State.

No Preference shall be given by any Regulation of Commerce or Revenue to the Ports of one State over those of another: nor shall Vessels bound to, or from, one State be obliged to enter, clear, or pay Duties in another.

No Money shall be drawn from the Treasury, but in Consequence of Appropriations made by Law; and a regular Statement and Account of the Receipts and Expenditures of all public Money shall be published from time to time.

No Title of Nobility shall be granted by the United States: And no Person holding any Office of Profit or Trust under them, shall, without the Consent of the Congress, accept of any present, Emolument, Office, or Title, of any kind whatever, from any King, Prince, or foreign State.

Section 10. No State shall enter into any Treaty, Alliance, or Confederation; grant Letters of Marque and Reprisal; coin Money; emit Bills of Credit; make any Thing but gold and silver Coin a Tender in Payment of Debts; pass any Bill of Attainder, ex post facto Law, or Law impairing the Obligation of Contracts, or grant any Title of Nobility.

No State shall, without the Consent of the Congress, lay any Imposts or Duties on Imports or Exports, except what may be absolutely necessary for executing its inspection Laws: and the net Produce of all Duties and Imposts, laid by any State on Imports or Exports, shall be for the Use of the Treasury of the United States; and all such Laws shall be subject to the Revision and Controul of the Congress.

No State shall, without the Consent of Congress, lay any Duty of Tonnage, keep Troops, or Ships of War in time of Peace, enter into any Agreement or Compact with another State, or with a foreign Power, or engage in War, unless actually invaded, or in such imminent Danger as will not admit of delay.

ARTICLE II

Section 1. The executive Power shall be vested in a President of the United States of America. He shall hold his Office during the Term of four Years, and, together with the Vice President, chosen for the same Term, be elected, as follows:

Each State shall appoint, in such Manner as the Legislature thereof may direct, a Number of Electors, equal to the whole Number of Senators and Representatives to which the State may be entitled in the Congress; but no Senator or Representative, or Person holding an Office of Trust or Profit under the United States, shall be appointed an Elector.

The Electors shall meet in their respective States, and vote by Ballot for two Persons, of whom one at least shall not be an Inhabitant of the same State with themselves. And they shall make a List of all the Persons voted for, and of the Number of Votes for each; which List they shall sign and certify, and transmit sealed to the Seat of the Government of the United States, directed to the President of the Senate. The President of the Senate shall, in the Presence of the Senate and House of Representatives, open all the Certificates, and the Votes shall then be counted. The Person having the greatest Number of Votes shall be the President, if such Number be a Majority of the whole Number of Electors appointed; and if there be more than one who have such Majority, and have an equal Number of Votes, then the House of Representatives shall immediately chuse by Ballot one of them for President; and if no Person have a Majority, then from the five highest on the List the said House shall in like Manner chuse the President. But in chusing the President, the Votes shall be taken by States, the Representation from each State having one Vote; A quorum for this Purpose shall consist of a Member or Members from two thirds of the States, and a Majority of all the States shall be necessary to a Choice. In every Case, after the Choice of the President, the Person having the greater Number of Votes of the Electors shall be the Vice President. But if there should remain two or more who have equal Votes, the Senate shall chuse from them by Ballot the Vice President.

The Congress may determine the Time of chusing the Electors, and the Day on which they shall give their Votes; which Day shall be the same throughout the United States.

No person except a natural born Citizen, or a Citizen of the United States, at the time of the Adoption of this Constitution, shall be eligible to the Office of President; neither shall any Person be eligible to that Office who shall not have attained to the Age of thirty five Years, and been fourteen Years a Resident within the United States.

In Case of the Removal of the President from Office, or of his Death, Resignation or Inability to discharge the Powers and Duties of the said Office, the same shall devolve on the Vice President, and the Congress may by Law provide for the Case of Removal, Death, Resignation or Inability, both of the President and Vice President, declaring what Officer shall then act as President, and such Officer shall act accordingly, until the Disability be removed, or a President shall be elected.

The President shall, at stated Times, receive for his Services, a Compensation, which shall neither be increased nor diminished during the Period for which he shall have been elected, and he shall not receive within that Period any other Emolument from the United States, or any of them.

Before he enter on the Execution of his Office, he shall take the following Oath or Affirmation: "I do solemnly swear (or affirm) that I will faithfully execute the Office of President of the United States, and will to the best of my Ability, preserve, protect and defend the Constitution of the United States."

Section 2. The President shall be Commander in Chief of the Army and Navy of the United States, and of the Militia of the several States, when called into the actual Service of the United States; he may require the Opinion, in writing, of the principal Officer in each of the executive Departments, upon any Subject relating to the Duties of their respective Offices, and he shall have Power to grant Reprieves and Pardons for Offenses against the United States, except in Cases of Impeachment.

He shall have Power, by and with the Advice and Consent of the Senate to make Treaties, provided two thirds of the Senators present concur; and he shall nominate, and by and with the Advice and Consent of the Senate, shall appoint Ambassadors, other public Ministers and Consuls, Judges of the supreme Court, and all other Officers of the United States, whose Appointments are not herein otherwise provided for, and which shall be established by Law; but the Congress may by Law vest the Appointment of such inferior Officers, as they think proper, in the President alone, in the Courts of Law, or in the Heads of Departments.

The President shall have Power to fill up all Vacancies that may happen during the Recess of the Senate, by granting Commissions which shall expire at the End of their next Session.

Section 3. He shall from time to time give to the Congress Information of the State of the Union, and recommend to their Consideration such Measures as he shall judge necessary and expedient; he may, on extraordinary Occasions, convene both Houses, or either of them, and in Case of Disagreement between them, with Respect to the Time of Adjournment, he may adjourn them to such Time as he shall think proper; he shall receive Ambassadors and other public Ministers; he shall take Care that the Laws be faithfully executed, and shall Commission all the Officers of the United States.

Section 4. The President, Vice President and all civil Officers of the United States, shall be removed from Office on Impeachment for, and Conviction of, Treason, Bribery, or other high Crimes and Misdemeanors.

ARTICLE III

Section 1. The judicial Power of the United States, shall be vested in one supreme Court, and in such inferior Courts as the Congress may from time to time ordain and establish. The Judges, both of the supreme and inferior Courts, shall hold their Offices during good Behaviour, and shall, at stated Times, receive for their Services a Compensation, which shall not be diminished during their Continuance in Office.

Section 2. The judicial Power shall extend to all Cases, in Law and Equity, arising under this Constitution, the Laws of the

United States, and Treaties made, or which shall be made, under their Authority;—to all Cases affecting Ambassadors, other public Ministers and Consuls;—to all Cases of admiralty and maritime Jurisdiction;—to Controversies to which the United States shall be a Party;—to Controversies between two or more States;—between a State and Citizens of another State;—between Citizens of different States;—between Citizens of the same State claiming Lands under Grants of different States, and between a State, or the Citizens thereof, and foreign States, Citizens or Subjects.

In all Cases affecting Ambassadors, other public Ministers and Consuls, and those in which a State shall be a Party, the supreme Court shall have original Jurisdiction. In all the other Cases before mentioned, the supreme Court shall have appellate Jurisdiction, both as to Law and Fact, with such Exceptions, and under such Regulations as the Congress shall make.

The Trial of all Crimes, except in Cases of Impeachment, shall be by Jury; and such Trial shall be held in the State where the said Crimes shall have been committed; but when not committed within any State, the Trial shall be at such Place or Places as the Congress may by Law have directed.

Section 3. Treason against the United States, shall consist only in levying War against them, or, in adhering to their Enemies, giving them Aid and Comfort. No Person shall be convicted of Treason unless on the Testimony of two Witnesses to the same overt Act, or on Confession in open Court.

The Congress shall have Power to declare the Punishment of Treason, but no Attainder of Treason shall work Corruption of Blood, or Forfeiture except during the Life of the Person attainted.

ARTICLE IV

Section 1. Full Faith and Credit shall be given in each State to the public Acts, Records, and judicial Proceedings of every other State. And the Congress may by general Laws prescribe the Manner in which such Acts, Records and Proceedings shall be proved, and the Effect thereof.

Section 2. The Citizens of each State shall be entitled to all Privileges and Immunities of Citizens in the several States.

A Person charged in any State with Treason, Felony, or other Crime, who shall flee from Justice, and be found in another State, shall on Demand of the executive Authority of the State from which he fled, be delivered up, to be removed to the State having Jurisdiction of the Crime.

No Person held to Service or Labour in one State, under the Laws thereof, escaping into another, shall, in Consequence of any Law or Regulation therein, be discharged from such Service or Labour, but shall be delivered up on Claim of the Party to whom such Service or Labour may be due.

Section 3. New States may be admitted by the Congress into this Union; but no new State shall be formed or erected within the Jurisdiction of any other State; nor any State be formed by the Junction of two or more States, or Parts of States, without the Consent of the Legislatures of the States concerned as well as of the Congress.

The Congress shall have Power to dispose of and make all needful Rules and Regulations respecting the Territory or other Property belonging to the United States; and nothing in this Constitution shall be so construed as to Prejudice any Claims of the United States, or of any particular State.

Section 4. The United States shall guarantee to every State in this Union a Republican Form of Government, and shall protect each of them against Invasion; and on Application of the Legislature, or of the Executive (when the Legislature cannot be convened) against domestic Violence.

ARTICLE V

The Congress, whenever two thirds of both Houses shall deem it necessary, shall propose Amendments to this Constitution, or, on the Application of the Legislatures of two thirds of the several States, shall call a Convention for proposing Amendments, which, in either Case, shall be valid to all Intents and Purposes, as part of this Constitution, when ratified by the Legislatures of three fourths of the several States, or by Conventions in three fourths thereof, as the one or the other Mode of Ratification may be proposed by the Congress; Provided that no Amendment which may be made prior to the Year One thousand eight hundred and eight shall in any Manner affect the first and fourth Clauses in the Ninth Section of the first Article; and that no State, without its Consent, shall be deprived of its equal Suffrage in the Senate.

ARTICLE VI

All Debts contracted and Engagements entered into, before the Adoption of this Constitution shall be as valid against the United States under this Constitution, as under the Confederation.

This Constitution, and the Laws of the United States which shall be made in Pursuance thereof; and all Treaties made, or which shall be made, under the Authority of the United States, shall be the supreme Law of the Land; and the Judges in every State shall be bound thereby, any Thing in the Constitution or Laws of any State to the Contrary notwithstanding.

The Senators and Representatives before mentioned, and the Members of the several State Legislatures, and all executive and judicial Officers, both of the United States and of the several States, shall be bound by Oath or Affirmation, to support this Constitution; but no religious Test shall ever be required as a Qualification to any Office or public Trust under the United States.

ARTICLE VII

The Ratification of the Conventions of nine States shall be sufficient for the Establishment of this Constitution between the States so ratifying the Same.

AMENDMENT I [1791]

Congress shall make no law respecting an establishment of religion, or prohibiting the free exercise thereof; or abridging the freedom of speech, or of the press; or the right of the people peaceably to assembly, and to petition the Government for a redress of grievances.

AMENDMENT II [1791]

A well regulated Militia, being necessary to the security of a free State, the right of the people to keep and bear Arms, shall not be infringed.

AMENDMENT III [1791]

No Soldier shall, in time of peace be quartered in any house, without the consent of the Owner, nor in time of war, but in a manner to be prescribed by law.

AMENDMENT IV [1791]

The right of the people to be secure in their persons, houses, papers, and effects, against unreasonable searches and seizures, shall not be violated, and no Warrants shall issue, but upon probable cause, supported by Oath or affirmation, and particularly describing the place to be searched, and the persons or things to be seized.

AMENDMENT V [1791]

No person shall be held to answer for a capital, or otherwise infamous crime, unless on a presentment or indictment of a Grand Jury, except in cases arising in the land or naval forces, or in the Militia, when in actual service in time of War or public danger; nor shall any person be subject for the same offence to be twice put in jeopardy of life or limb; nor shall be compelled in any criminal case to be a witness against himself, nor be deprived of life, liberty, or property, without due process of law; nor shall private property be taken for public use, without just compensation.

AMENDMENT VI [1791]

In all criminal prosecutions, the accused shall enjoy the right to a speedy and public trial, by an impartial jury of the State and district wherein the crime shall have been committed, which district shall have been previously ascertained by law, and to be informed of the nature and cause of the accusation; to be confronted with the witnesses against him; to have compulsory process for obtaining witnesses in his favor, and to have the Assistance of Counsel for his defence.

AMENDMENT VII [1791]

In Suits at common law, where the value in controversy shall exceed twenty dollars, the right of trial by jury shall be preserved, and no fact tried by jury, shall be otherwise re-examined in any Court of the United States, than according to the rules of the common law.

AMENDMENT VIII [1791]

Excessive bail shall not be required, nor excessive fines imposed, nor cruel and unusual punishments inflicted.

AMENDMENT IX [1791]

The enumeration in the Constitution, of certain rights, shall not be construed to deny or disparage others retained by the people.

AMENDMENT X [1791]

The powers not delegated to the United States by the Constitution, nor prohibited by it to the States, are reserved to the States respectively, or to the people.

AMENDMENT XI [1798]

The Judicial power of the United States shall not be construed to extend to any suit in law or equity, commenced or prosecuted against one of the United States by Citizens of another State, or by Citizens or Subjects of any Foreign State.

AMENDMENT XII [1804]

The Electors shall meet in their respective states, and vote by ballot for President and Vice-President, one of whom, at least, shall not be an inhabitant of the same state with themselves; they shall name in their ballots the person voted for as President, and in distinct ballots the person voted for as Vice-President, and they shall make distinct lists of all persons voted for as President, and of all persons voted for as Vice-President, and of the number of votes for each, which lists they shall sign and certify, and transmit sealed to the seat of the government of the United States, directed to the President of the Senate;—The President of the Senate shall, in the presence of the Senate and House of Representatives, open all the certificates and the votes shall then be counted;—The person having the greatest number of votes for President, shall be the President, if such number be a majority of the whole number of Electors appointed; and if no person have such majority, then from the persons having the highest numbers not exceeding three on the list of those voted for as President, the House of Representatives shall choose immediately, by ballot, the President. But in choosing the President, the votes shall be taken by states, the representation from each state having one vote; a quorum for this purpose shall consist of a member or members from two-thirds of the states, and a majority of all states shall be necessary to a choice. And if the House of Representatives shall not choose a President whenever the right of choice shall devolve upon them, before the fourth day of March next following, then the Vice-President shall act as President, as in the case of the death or other constitutional disability of the President.—The person having the greatest number of votes as Vice-President, shall be the Vice-President, if such number be a majority of the whole number of Electors appointed, and if no person have a majority, then from the two highest numbers on the list, the Senate shall choose the Vice-President; a quorum for the purpose shall consist of two-thirds of the whole number of Senators, and a majority of the whole number shall be necessary to a choice. But no person constitutionally ineligible to the office of President shall be eligible to that of Vice-President of the United States.

AMENDMENT XIII [1865]

Section 1. Neither slavery nor involuntary servitude, except as a punishment for crime whereof the party shall have been duly convicted, shall exist within the United States, or any place subject to their jurisdiction.

Section 2. Congress shall have power to enforce this article by appropriate legislation.

AMENDMENT XIV [1868]

Section 1. All persons born or naturalized in the United States, and subject to the jurisdiction thereof, are citizens of the United States and of the State wherein they reside. No State shall make or enforce any law which shall abridge the privileges or immunities of citizens of the United States; nor shall any State deprive any person of life, liberty, or property, without due process of law; nor deny to any person within its jurisdiction the equal protection of the laws.

Section 2. Representatives shall be apportioned among the several States according to their respective numbers, counting the whole number of persons in each State, excluding Indians not taxed. But when the right to vote at any election for the choice of electors for President and Vice President of the United States, Representatives in Congress, the Executive and Judicial officers of a State, or the members of the Legislature thereof, is denied to any of the male inhabitants of such State, being twenty-one years of age, and citizens of the United States, or in any way abridged, except for participation in rebellion, or other crime, the basis of representation therein shall be reduced in the proportion which the number of such male citizens shall bear to the whole number of male citizens twenty-one years of age in such State.

Section 3. No person shall be a Senator or Representative in Congress, or elector of President and Vice President, or hold any office, civil or military, under the United States, or under any State, who having previously taken an oath, as a member of Congress, or as an officer of the United States, or as a member of any State legislature, or as an executive or judicial officer of any State, to support the Constitution of the United States, shall have engaged in insurrection or rebellion against the same, or given aid or comfort to the enemies thereof. But Congress may by a vote of two-thirds of each House, remove such disability.

Section 4. The validity of the public debt of the United States, authorized by law, including debts incurred for payment of pensions and bounties for services in suppressing insurrection or rebellion, shall not be questioned. But neither the United States nor any State shall assume or pay any debt or obligation incurred in aid of insurrection or rebellion against the United States, or any claim for the loss or emancipation of any slave; but all such debts, obligations and claims shall be held illegal and void.

Section 5. The Congress shall have power to enforce, by appropriate legislation, the provisions of this article.

Amendment XV [1870]

Section 1. The right of citizens of the United States to vote shall not be denied or abridged by the United States or by any State on account of race, color, or previous condition of servitude.

Section 2. The Congress shall have power to enforce this article by appropriate legislation.

Amendment XVI [1913]

The Congress shall have power to lay and collect taxes on incomes, from whatever source derived, without apportionment among the several States, and without regard to any census or enumeration.

Amendment XVII [1913]

Section 1. The Senate of the United States shall be composed of two Senators from each State, elected by the people thereof, for six years; and each Senator shall have one vote. The electors in each State shall have the qualifications requisite for electors of the most numerous branch of the State legislatures.

Section 2. When vacancies happen in the representation of any State in the Senate, the executive authority of such State shall issue writs of election to fill such vacancies: Provided, That the legislature of any State may empower the executive thereof to make temporary appointments until the people fill the vacancies by election as the legislature may direct.

Section 3. This amendment shall not be so construed as to affect the election or term of any Senator chosen before it becomes valid as part of the Constitution.

Amendment XVIII [1919]

Section 1. After one year from the ratification of this article the manufacture, sale, or transportation of intoxicating liquors within, the importation thereof into, or the exportation thereof from the United States and all territory subject to the jurisdiction thereof for beverage purposes is hereby prohibited.

Section 2. The Congress and the several States shall have concurrent power to enforce this article by appropriate legislation.

Section 3. This article shall be inoperative unless it shall have been ratified as an amendment to the Constitution by the legislatures of the several States, as provided in the Constitution, within seven years from the date of the submission hereof to the States by the Congress.

Amendment XIX [1920]

Section 1. The right of citizens of the United States to vote shall not be denied or abridged by the United States or by any State on account of sex.

Section 2. Congress shall have power to enforce this article by appropriate legislation.

Amendment XX [1933]

Section 1. The terms of the President and Vice President shall end at noon on the 20th day of January, and the terms of Senators and Representatives at noon on the 3d day of January, of the years in which such terms would have ended if this article had not been ratified; and the terms of their successors shall then begin.

Section 2. The Congress shall assemble at least once in every year, and such meeting shall begin at noon on the 3d day of January, unless they shall by law appoint a different day.

Section 3. If, at the time fixed for the beginning of the term of the President, the President elect shall have died, the Vice President elect shall become President. If the President shall not have been chosen before the time fixed for the beginning of his term, or if the President elect shall have failed to qualify, then the Vice President elect shall act as President until a President shall have qualified; and the Congress may by law provide for the case wherein neither a President elect nor a Vice President elect shall have qualified, declaring who shall then act as President, or the manner in which one who is to act shall be selected, and such person shall act accordingly until a President or Vice President shall have qualified.

Section 4. The Congress may by law provide for the case of the death of any of the persons from whom the House of Representatives may choose a President whenever the right of choice shall have devolved upon them, and for the case of the death of any of the persons from whom the Senate may choose a Vice President whenever the right of choice shall have devolved upon them.

Section 5. Sections 1 and 2 shall take effect on the 15th day of October following the ratification of this article.

Section 6. This article shall be inoperative unless it shall have been ratified as an amendment to the Constitution by the legislatures of three-fourths of the several States within seven years from the date of its submission.

Amendment XXI [1933]

Section 1. The eighteenth article of amendment to the Constitution of the United States is hereby repealed.

Section 2. The transportation or importation into any State, Territory, or possession of the United States for delivery or use therein of intoxicating liquors, in violation of the laws thereof, is hereby prohibited.

Section 3. This article shall be inoperative unless it shall have been ratified as an amendment to the Constitution by conventions in the several States, as provided in the Constitution, within seven years from the date of the submission hereof to the States by the Congress.

Amendment XXII [1951]

Section 1. No person shall be elected to the office of the President more than twice, and no person who has held the office of President, or acted as President, for more than two years of a term to which some other person was elected President shall be elected to the office of President more than once. But this Article shall not apply to any person holding the office of President when this Article was proposed by the Congress, and shall not prevent any person who may be holding the office of President, or acting as President, during the term within which this Article becomes operative from holding the office of President or acting as President during the remainder of such term.

Section 2. This article shall be inoperative unless it shall have been ratified as an amendment to the Constitution by the legislatures of three-fourths of the several States within seven years from the date of its submission to the States by the Congress.

AMENDMENT XXIII [1961]

Section 1. The District constituting the seat of Government of the United States shall appoint in such manner as the Congress may direct:

A number of electors of President and Vice President equal to the whole number of Senators and Representatives in Congress to which the District would be entitled if it were a State, but in no event more than the least populous state; they shall be in addition to those appointed by the states, but they shall be considered, for the purposes of the election of President and Vice President, to be electors appointed by a state; and they shall meet in the District and perform such duties as provided by the twelfth article of amendment.

Section 2. The Congress shall have power to enforce this article by appropriate legislation.

AMENDMENT XXIV [1964]

Section 1. The right of citizens of the United States to vote in any primary or other election for President or Vice President, for electors for President or Vice President, or for Senator or Representative in Congress, shall not be denied or abridged by the United States, or any State by reason of failure to pay any poll tax or other tax.

Section 2. The Congress shall have power to enforce this article by appropriate legislation.

AMENDMENT XXV [1967]

Section 1. In case of the removal of the President from office or of his death or resignation, the Vice President shall become President.

Section 2. Whenever there is a vacancy in the office of the Vice President, the President shall nominate a Vice President who shall take office upon confirmation by a majority vote of both Houses of Congress.

Section 3. Whenever the President transmits to the President pro tempore of the Senate and the Speaker of the House of Representatives his written declaration that he is unable to discharge the powers and duties of his office, and until he transmits to them a written declaration to the contrary, such powers and duties shall be discharged by the Vice President as Acting President.

Section 4. Whenever the Vice President and a majority of either the principal officers of the executive departments or of such other body as Congress may by law provide, transmit to the President pro tempore of the Senate and the Speaker of the House of Representatives their written declaration that the President is unable to discharge the powers and duties of his office, the Vice President shall immediately assume the powers and duties of the office as Acting President.

Thereafter, when the President transmits to the President pro tempore of the Senate and the Speaker of the House of Representatives his written declaration that no inability exists, he shall resume the powers and duties of his office unless the Vice President and a majority of either the principal officers of the executive department or of such other body as Congress may by law provide, transmit within four days to the President pro tempore of the Senate and the Speaker of the House of Representatives their written declaration that the President is unable to discharge the powers and duties of his office. Thereupon Congress shall decide the issue, assembling within forty-eight hours for that purpose if not in session. If the Congress, within twenty-one days after receipt of the latter written declaration, or, if Congress is not in session, within twenty-one days after Congress is required to assemble, determines by two-thirds vote of both Houses that the President is unable to discharge the powers and duties of his office, the Vice President shall continue to discharge the same as Acting President; otherwise, the President shall resume the powers and duties of his office.

AMENDMENT XXVI [1971]

Section 1. The right of citizens of the United States, who are eighteen years of age or older, to vote shall not be denied or abridged by the United States or by any State on account of age.

Section 2. The Congress shall have power to enforce this article by appropriate legislation.

AMENDMENT XXVII [1992]

No law, varying the compensation for the services of the Senators and Representatives, shall take effect, until an election of Representatives shall have intervened.

URLs for Selected Statutes Referenced in the Text

Administrative Procedure Act of 1946
5 U.S.C. Sections 551–706.

www.law.cornell.edu/uscode/5/ch5.html

The text of the Administrative Procedure Act of 1946 can be accessed on the Web site maintained by the Legal Information Institute, which is part of Cornell Law School.

Americans with Disabilities Act of 1990
42 U.S.C. Sections 12101–12213.

www.eeoc.gov/policy/ada.html

You can find Titles I and V of the Americans with Disabilities Act of 1990 on the Equal Employment Opportunity Commission's Web site.

Article 2 of the Uniform Commercial Code
UCC 2–101 through 2–725.

www.law.cornell.edu/ucc/2/overview.html

The Legal Information Institute at Cornell University offers this hypertext publication of Article 2 of the Uniform Commercial Code (UCC). You can access the UCC by parts (Part 1 through Part 7) or scroll down the page to find specific UCC sections (such as 2–201). You can also perform a "Full Text Search" of the entire UCC. To locate an individual state's version of the UCC, click on the link that appears after the clause "For Article 2 as enacted by a particular state and any proposed revisions" and follow the links to the desired state.

Clayton Act of 1914
15 U.S.C. Sections 13–26.

www.stolaf.edu/people/becker/antitrust/statutes/clayton.html

The text of the Clayton Act of 1914 can be accessed on the Web site maintained by St. Olaf College in Northfield, Minnesota.

Digital Millennium Copyright Act of 1998
17 U.S.C. Sections 1201–1205, 1301–1332.

www.copyright.gov/title17/92appb.html

This page within the United States Copyright Office's Web site features every section of the final version of the Digital Millennium Copyright Act.

Electronic Signatures in Global and National Commerce Act of 2000
15 U.S.C. Sections 7001–7006.

www.findlaw.com/casecode/uscodes

This is a page within the FindLaw Web site. In the "Title" box, type "15," and in the "Section" box, type a relevant section number (such as "7001"). Click on "Search." The text of the statute will appear on the resulting page. At the bottom of the page, you will find links to "Notes" on each code section and "Next," which will take you to the next section in the statute.

Federal Arbitration Act of 1925
9 U.S.C. Sections 1–15.

www.law.cornell.edu/uscode/text/9/chapter-1

This URL takes you to a Web page that features the Federal Arbitration Act of 1925, as amended. Scroll through the table of contents and click on the specific chapter to access the text of the statute. Cornell University maintains this Web site.

Federal Trade Commission Act of 1914
15 U.S.C. Sections 41–58.

www.fda.gov/RegulatoryInformation/Legislation/ucm148712.htm

The U.S. Food and Drug Administration posts the full text of the Federal Trade Commission Act at this Web site.

Foreign Corrupt Practices Act of 1977
15 U.S.C. Sections 78dd-1 through 78dd-3.

www.justice.gov/criminal/fraud/fcpa

Click on "Statute" to access the text of the act. The U.S. Department of Justice maintains this Web site, which also provides information on the statute's legislative history, amendments, and related regulations.

ICANN's Uniform Domain Name Dispute Resolution Policy
UDRP Paragraphs 1–9.

www.icann.org/dndr/udrp/policy.htm

This is a page within the Web site of the Internet Corporation for Assigned Names and Numbers (ICANN).

Racketeer Influenced and Corrupt Organizations Act of 1970
18 U.S.C. Sections 1961–1968.

uscode.house.gov/search/criteria.shtml

In the "Title" box, type "18," and in the "Section" box, type a relevant section number (for example, "1961"). In the list of "documents found," click on the citation to access the text of the statute.

Securities Act of 1933
15 U.S.C. Sections 77a–77aa.

www.sec.gov/about/laws/sa33.pdf

The Securities and Exchange Commission (SEC) provides a version of the Securities Act of 1933 on a pdf.

Securities Exchange Act of 1934
15 U.S.C. Sections 78a–78mm.

www.sec.gov/about/laws/sea34.pdf

The Securities and Exchange Commission (SEC) provides a version of the Securities Exchange Act of 1934 on a pdf.

Sherman Act of 1890
15 U.S.C. Sections 1–7.

uscode.house.gov/search/criteria.shtml

In the "Title" box, type "15," and in the "Section" box, type a relevant section number (for example, "15"). Click on "Search." In the list of "documents found," scroll to the citation with the appropriate title (such as, "Sec. 15. Suits by persons injured"). Click on the citation to access the text of the statute.

Title VII of the Civil Rights Act of 1964
42 U.S.C. Section 2000e.

www.eeoc.gov/policy/vii.html

The Equal Employment Opportunity Commission's Web site features the full text of the Civil Rights Act of 1964.

Uniform Electronic Transactions Act (UETA)
UETA 1–21.

www.law.upenn.edu/library/archives/ulc/fnact99/1990s/ueta99.htm

This is a page within the Web site of the University of Pennsylvania Law School, which provides drafts of uniform and model acts in association with the National Conference of Commissioners on Uniform State Laws.

Uniform Limited Liability Company Act (ULLCA)
www.law.upenn.edu/library/archives/ulc/fnact99/1990s/ullca96.htm

You can find the complete text of the ULLCA at the University of Pennsylvania's Web site.

Uniform Limited Partnership Act (ULPA)
www.law.upenn.edu/library/archives/ulc/ulpa/final2001.htm

The University of Pennsylvania Law School maintains a full text of the ULPA on its Web site.

United Nations Convention on Contracts for the International Sale of Goods (CISG)
CISG Articles 1–101.

cisgw3.law.pace.edu/cisg/text/cisg-toc.html

To access the text of this treaty, select the article number that you wish to view from the list on this Web page. Pace University School of Law maintains this Web site.

Answers to *Issue Spotters*

Chapter 1

1A. No. The U.S. Constitution is the supreme law of the land and applies to all jurisdictions. A law in violation of the Constitution (in this question, the First Amendment to the Constitution) will be declared unconstitutional.

2A. Case law includes courts' interpretations of statutes, as well as constitutional provisions and administrative rules. Statutes often codify common law rules. For these reasons, a judge might rely on the common law as a guide to the intent and purpose of a statute.

Chapter 2

1A. Yes. Submission of the dispute to mediation or nonbinding arbitration is mandatory, but compliance with a decision of the mediator or arbitrator is voluntary.

2A. Tom could file a motion for a directed verdict. This motion asks the judge to direct a verdict for Tom on the ground that Sue presented no evidence that would justify granting relief. The judge grants the motion if there is insufficient evidence to raise an issue of fact.

Chapter 3

1A. Maybe. On the one hand, it is not the company's "fault" when a product is misused. Also, keeping the product on the market is not a violation of the law, and stopping sales would hurt profits. On the other hand, suspending sales could reduce suffering and could stop potential negative publicity if sales continued.

2A. When a corporation decides to respond to what it sees as a moral obligation to correct for past discrimination by adjusting pay differences among its employees, an ethical conflict is raised between the firm and its employees and between the firm and its shareholders. This dilemma arises directly out of the effect such a decision has on the firm's profits. If satisfying this obligation increases profitability, then the dilemma is easily resolved in favor of "doing the right thing."

Chapter 4

1A. No. Even if commercial speech is not related to illegal activities nor misleading, it may be restricted if a state has a substantial interest that cannot be achieved by less restrictive means. In this case, the interest in energy conservation is substantial, but it could be achieved by less restrictive means. That would be the utilities' defense against the enforcement of this state law.

2A. Yes. The tax would limit the liberty of some persons, such as out-of-state businesses, so it is subject to a review under the equal protection clause. Protecting local businesses from out-of-state competition is not a legitimate government objective. Thus, such a tax would violate the equal protection clause.

Chapter 5

1A. Under the Administrative Procedure Act (APA), the ALJ must be separate from the agency's investigative and prosecutorial staff. *Ex parte* communications between the ALJ and a party to a proceeding are prohibited. Under the APA, an ALJ is exempt from agency discipline except on a showing of good cause.

2A. Yes. Administrative rulemaking starts with the publication of a notice of the rulemaking in the *Federal Register*. Among other details, this notice states where and when the proceedings, such as a public hearing, will be held. Proponents and opponents can offer their comments and concerns regarding the pending rule. After the agency reviews all the comments from the proceedings, it considers what was presented and drafts the final rule.

Chapter 6

1A. Probably. To recover on the basis of negligence, the injured party as a plaintiff must show that the truck's owner owed the plaintiff a duty of care, that the owner breached that duty, that the plaintiff was injured, and that the breach caused the injury. In this problem, the owner's actions breached the duty of reasonable care. The billboard falling on the plaintiff was the direct cause of the injury, not the plaintiff's own negligence. Thus, liability turns on whether the plaintiff can connect the breach of duty to the injury. This involves the test of proximate cause—the question of foreseeability. The consequences to the injured party must have been a foreseeable result of the owner's carelessness.

2A. Yes. Under the doctrine of strict liability, persons may be liable for the results of their acts regardless of their intentions or their exercise of reasonable care (that is, regardless of fault).

Chapter 7

1A. Yes. With respect to the gas station, she has obtained goods by false pretenses. She might also be charged with larceny and forgery, and most states have special statutes covering illegal use of credit cards.

2A. Yes. The Counterfeit Access Device and Computer Fraud and Abuse Act of 1984 provides that a person who accesses a computer online, without permission, to obtain classified data (such as consumer credit files in a credit agency's database) is subject to criminal prosecution. The crime has two elements: accessing the computer without permission and taking data. It is a felony if done for private financial gain. Penalties include fines and imprisonment for up to twenty years.

Chapter 8

1A. Yes, this is patent infringement. A software maker in this situation might best protect its product, save litigation costs, and profit from its patent by the use of a license. In the context of this problem, a license would grant permission to sell a patented item. (A license can be limited to certain purposes and to the licensee only.)

2A. Yes. This may be an instance of trademark dilution. Dilution occurs when a trademark is used, without permission, in a way that diminishes the distinctive quality of the mark. Dilution does not require proof that consumers are likely to be confused by a connection between the unauthorized use and the mark. The products involved do not have to be similar. Dilution does require, however, that a mark be famous when the dilution occurs.

Chapter 9

1A. Under the principle of comity, a U.S court would defer and give effect to foreign laws and judicial decrees that are consistent with U.S. law and public policy.

2A. The practice described in this problem is known as dumping. Seen as an unfair international trade practice, dumping is the sale of imported goods at "less than fair value." Based on the price of those goods in the exporting country, an extra tariff can be imposed on the imports. This is known as an antidumping duty.

Chapter 10

1A. Under the partners' fiduciary duty, a partner must account to the partnership for any personal profits or benefits derived without the consent of all the partners in connection with the use of any partnership property. Thus, in this problem, the partner may not keep the funds.

2A. Yes. Yvon, as a shareholder, can bring a shareholder's derivative suit against the corporation. A shareholder's derivative suit helps to correct a wrong suffered by the corporation because of the actions of its corporate officers and directors. Since corporate officers and directors are most likely not to take against themselves, it is important that shareholders have this right to do so when a wrong has occurred. When Yvon brings a derivative suit, she is not pursuing rights or benefits for herself, but is acting as a guardian for the corporation. Any damages recovered from such a suit would go to the corporation, and not to Yvon.

Chapter 11

1A. Yes. Under the doctrine of promissory estoppel (or detrimental reliance), Maria (the promisee) is entitled to payment of the promised amount when she graduates. There was a promise, she relied on it, and her reliance was substantial and definite. She went to college for nearly four years, incurring considerable expenses. It would only be fair to enforce the promise.

2A. First, it might be noted that the Uniform Electronic Transactions Act (UETA) does not apply unless the parties to a contract agree to use e-commerce in their transaction. In this deal, of course, the parties used e-commerce. The UETA removes barriers to e-commerce by giving the same legal effect to e-records and e-signatures as to paper documents and signatures. The UETA does not include rules for those transactions, however.

Chapter 12

1A. No. When parties base their contract on a common assumption about a material fact that proves false, the transaction may be avoided if, because of the mistake, a different exchange of values occurs from the exchange of values that the parties contemplated. In other words, what the buyer actually found on the property was not part of the bargain between the buyer and the seller.

2A. Contracts that are executory on both sides—contracts on which neither party has performed—can be rescinded solely by agreement.

Contracts that are executed on one side—contracts on which one party has performed—can be rescinded only if the party who has performed receives consideration for the promise to call off the deal.

Chapter 13

1A. A shipment of nonconforming goods constitutes an acceptance and a breach, unless the seller seasonably notifies the buyer that the nonconforming shipment does not constitute an acceptance and is offered only as an accommodation. Without the notification, the shipment is an acceptance and a breach. Thus, here, the shipment was both an acceptance and a breach.

2A. Yes. In a case of anticipatory repudiation, as in this problem, a buyer can resort to any remedy for breach even though the buyer told the seller—the repudiating party in this problem—that the buyer would wait for the seller's performance.

Chapter 14

1A. Each of the parties can place a mechanic's lien on the debtor's property. If the debtor does not pay what is owed, the property can be sold to satisfy the debt.

2A. Yes. A debtor's payment to a creditor made for a preexisting debt, within ninety days of a bankruptcy filing, can be recovered if it gives a creditor more than he or she would have received in the bankruptcy proceedings. A trustee can recover this preference using his or her specific avoidance powers.

Chapter 15

1A. The major terms that must be disclosed under the Truth-in-Lending Act include the loan principal, the interest rate at which the loan is made, the annual percentage rate or APR (the actual cost of the loan on a yearly basis), and all fees and costs associated with the loan. These disclosures must be made on standardized forms and based on uniform calculation formulas. Certain types of loans have special disclosure requirements.

2A. Foreclosure is the process that allows a lender to repossess and auction off property that is securing a loan. The two most common types of foreclosure are judicial foreclosure and power of sale foreclosure. In the former—available in all states—a court supervises the process. This is the more common method of foreclosure. In the latter—available in only a few states—a lender forecloses on and sells the property without court supervision.

If the sale proceeds cover the mortgage debt and foreclosure costs, the debtor receives any surplus. If the proceeds do not cover the debt and costs, the mortgagee can seek to recover the difference through a deficiency judgment, which is obtained in a separate action. A deficiency judgment entitles the creditor to recover this difference from a sale of the debtor's other nonexempt property. Before a foreclosure sale, a mortgagor can redeem the property by paying the debt, plus any interest and costs. This is called the equitable right of redemption.

Chapter 16

1A. Workers' compensation laws establish a procedure for compensating workers who are injured on the job. Instead of suing to collect benefits, an injured worker notifies the employer of an injury and files a claim with the appropriate state agency. The right to recover is normally determined without regard to negligence or fault, but intentionally inflicted injuries are not covered. Unlike the potential for recovery in a lawsuit based on negligence or fault, recovery under a workers' compensation statute is limited to the specific amount designated in the statute for the employee's injury.

2A. No. A closed shop—a company that requires union membership as a condition of employment—is illegal. A union shop—a company that does not require union membership as a condition of employment but requires workers to join the union after a certain time on the job—is illegal in a state with a right-to-work law. A right-to-work law makes it illegal to require union membership for continued employment.

Chapter 17

1A. Yes. One type of sexual harassment occurs when a request for sexual favors is a condition of employment, and the person making the request is a supervisor or acts with the authority of the employer. A tangible employment action, such as continued employment, may also lead to the employer's liability for the supervisor's conduct. That the injured employee is a male and the supervisor a female, instead of the other way around, would not affect the outcome. Same-gender harassment is also actionable.

2A. Yes, if she can show that she was not hired solely because of her disability. The other elements for a discrimination suit based on a disability are that the plaintiff (1) has a disability and (2) is otherwise qualified for the job. Both of these elements appear to be satisfied in this problem.

Chapter 18

1A. The Comprehensive Environmental Response, Compensation, and Liability Act (CERCLA) regulates the clean-up of hazardous waste disposal sites. Any potentially responsible party can be charged with the entire cost to clean up a hazardous waste–disposal site.

Potentially responsible parties include the person who generated the waste (ChemCorp), the person who transported the waste to the site (Disposal), the person who owned or operated the site at the time of the disposal (Eliminators), and the current owner or operator of the site (Fluid). A party held responsible for the entire cost may be able to recoup some of it in a lawsuit against other potentially responsible parties.

2A. Yes. On the ground that the hardships to be imposed on the polluter and on the community are greater than the hardships suffered by the residents, the court might deny an injunction—if the plant is the core of a local economy, for instance, the residents may be awarded only damages.

Chapter 19

1A. Size alone does not determine whether a firm is a monopoly—size in relation to the market is what matters. A small store in a small, isolated town is a monopolist if it is the only store serving that market. Monopoly involves the power to affect prices and output. If a firm has sufficient market power to control prices and exclude competition, that firm has monopoly power. Monopoly power in itself is not a violation of Section 2 of the Sherman Act. The offense also requires an intent to acquire or maintain that power through anticompetitive means.

2A. This agreement is a tying arrangement. The legality of a tying arrangement depends on the purpose of the agreement, the agreement's likely effect on competition in the relevant markets (the market for the tying product and the market for the tied product), and other factors. Tying arrangements for commodities are subject to Section 3 of the Clayton Act. Tying arrangements for services can be agreements in restraint of trade in violation of Section 1 of the Sherman Act.

Chapter 20

1A. The average investor is not concerned with minor inaccuracies but with facts that if disclosed would tend to deter him or her from buying the securities. This would include facts that have an important bearing on the condition of the issuer and its business—liabilities, loans to officers and directors, customer delinquencies, and pending lawsuits.

2A. No. The Securities Exchange Act of 1934 extends liability to officers and directors for taking advantage of inside information in their personal transactions when they know it is unavailable to the persons with whom they are dealing.

Answers to Even-Numbered *For Review* Questions

Chapter 1

2. *What is the common law tradition?*

Because of our colonial heritage, much of American law is based on the English legal system. In that system, after the Norman Conquest, the king's courts sought to establish a uniform set of rules for the entire country. What evolved in these courts was the common law—a body of general legal principles that applied throughout the entire English realm. Courts developed the common law rules from the principles underlying judges' decisions in actual legal controversies.

4. *What is the difference between remedies at law and remedies in equity?*

An award of compensation in either money or property, including land, is a remedy at law. Remedies in equity include a decree for *specific performance* (an order to perform what was promised), an *injunction* (an order directing a party to do or refrain from doing a particular act), and *rescission* (cancellation) of a contract (and a return of the parties to the positions that they held before the contract's formation). As a rule, courts will grant an equitable remedy only when the remedy at law (money damages) is inadequate. Remedies in equity on the whole are more flexible than remedies at law.

Chapter 2

2. *Before a court can hear a case, it must have jurisdiction. Over what must it have jurisdiction? How are the courts applying traditional jurisdictional concepts to cases involving Internet transactions?*

To hear a case, a court must have jurisdiction over the person against whom the suit is brought or over the property involved in the suit. The court must also have jurisdiction over the subject matter. Generally, courts apply a "sliding-scale" standard to determine when it is proper to exercise jurisdiction over a defendant whose only connection with the jurisdiction is the Internet.

4. *What is discovery, and how does electronic discovery differ from traditional discovery?*

Discovery is the process of obtaining information and evidence about a case from the other party or third parties. Discovery entails gaining access to witnesses, documents, records, and other types of evidence. Electronic discovery differs in its subject (e-media rather than traditional sources of information).

Chapter 3

2. *How can business leaders encourage their companies to act ethically?*

Ethical leadership is important to create and maintain an ethical workplace. Managers can set standards and apply those standards to themselves and their firm's employees.

4. *What are six guidelines that an employee can use to evaluate whether his or her actions are ethical?*

Guidelines for evaluating whether behavior is ethical can be found in the law, business rules and procedures, social values, an individual's conscience, an individual's promises and obligations to others, and personal or societal heroes. An action is most likely ethical if it is consistent with the law, or at least the "spirit" of the law, as well as company policies, and if it can survive the scrutiny of one's conscience and the regard of one's heroes without betraying one's commitments to others.

Chapter 4

2. *What constitutional clause gives the federal government the power to regulate commercial activities among the various states?*

To prevent states from establishing laws and regulations that would interfere with trade and commerce among the states, the Constitution expressly delegated to the national government the power to regulate interstate commerce. The commerce clause—Article I, Section 8, of the U.S. Constitution—expressly permits Congress "[t]o regulate Commerce with foreign Nations, and among the several States, and with the Indian Tribes."

4. *What is the Bill of Rights? What freedoms does the First Amendment guarantee?*

The Bill of Rights consists of the first ten amendments to the U.S. Constitution. Adopted in 1791, the Bill of Rights embodies protections for individuals against interference by the federal government. Some of the protections also apply to business entities. The First Amendment guarantees the freedoms of religion, speech, and the press, and the rights to assemble peaceably and to petition the government.

Chapter 5

2. *How do the three branches of government limit the power of administrative agencies?*

The judicial branch of the government exercises control over agency powers through the courts' review of agency actions. The executive branch exercises control over agencies both through the president's powers to appoint federal officers and through the president's veto powers. The legislative branch has the power to create and fund agencies, and the authority to investigate the implementation of the laws and the agencies that it has created. Individual legislators may also affect agency policy through their "casework" activities. Congress has the power to "freeze" the enforcement of most federal regulations before the regulations take effect. Other legislative checks on agency actions include the Administrative Procedure Act, the Freedom of Information Act, and other laws.

4. *What sequence of events must normally occur before an agency rule becomes law?*

The most common rulemaking procedure, called notice-and-comment rulemaking, involves three basic steps: public notice of the proposed rulemaking, a period for public comment (including the agency's response to significant comments), and issuance of the final rule.

Chapter 6

2. *What are the four elements of negligence?*

The four elements of negligence are (1) a duty of care owed by the defendant to the plaintiff, (2) the defendant's breach of that duty, (3) the plaintiff's suffering a legally recognizable injury, and (4) the in-fact and proximate cause of that injury by the defendant's breach.

4. *What are the elements of a cause of action in strict product liability?*

Under Section 402A of the *Restatement (Third) of Torts,* the elements of an action for strict product liability are as follows:

1. The product must be in defective condition when the defendant sells it.
2. The defendant must normally be engaged in the business of selling (or distributing) that product.
3. The product must be unreasonably dangerous to the user or consumer because of its defective condition (in most states).
4. The plaintiff must incur physical harm to self or property by use or consumption of the product.
5. The defective condition must be the proximate cause of the injury or damage.
6. The goods must not have been substantially changed from the time the product was sold to the time the injury was sustained.

Chapter 7

2. *What are five broad categories of crimes?*

Traditionally, crimes have been grouped into the following categories: violent crime (crimes against persons), property crime, public order crime, white-collar crime, and organized crime. White-collar crime is an illegal act or series of acts committed by an individual or business entity using some nonviolent means, usually in the course of a legitimate occupation.

4. *What constitutional safeguards exist to protect persons accused of crimes?*

Under the Fourth Amendment, before searching or seizing private property, law enforcement officers must obtain a search warrant, which requires probable cause. Under the Fifth Amendment, no one can be deprived of "life, liberty, or property without due process of law." The Fifth Amendment also protects persons against double jeopardy and self-incrimination. The Sixth Amendment guarantees the right to a speedy trial, the right to a jury trial, the right to a public trial, the right to confront witnesses, and the right to counsel. All evidence obtained in violation of the Fourth, Fifth, and Sixth Amendments must be excluded from the trial, as well as all evidence derived from the illegally obtained evidence. Individuals who are arrested must be informed of certain constitutional rights, including their Fifth Amendment right to remain silent and their Sixth Amendment right to counsel. The Eighth Amendment prohibits excessive bail and fines, and cruel and unusual punishment.

Chapter 8

2. *Why is the protection of trademarks important?*

As stated in Article I, Section 8, of the Constitution, Congress is authorized "[t]o promote the Progress of Science and useful Arts, by securing for limited Times to Authors and Inventors the exclusive Right to their respective Writings and Discoveries." Laws protecting patents and trademarks, as well copyrights, are designed to protect and reward inventive and artistic creativity.

4. *What laws protect authors' rights in the works they generate?*

Copyright law protects the rights of the authors of certain literary or artistic productions. Currently, the Copyright Act of 1976, as amended, covers these rights.

Chapter 9

2. *What is the act of state doctrine? In what circumstances is this doctrine applied?*

The act of state doctrine is a judicially created doctrine that provides that the judicial branch of one country will not examine the validity of public acts committed by a recognized foreign government within its own territory. This doctrine is often employed in cases involving expropriation or confiscation.

4. *What are three clauses commonly included in international business contracts?*

Choice-of-language, forum-selection, and choice-of-law clauses are commonly used in international business contracts.

Chapter 10

2. *What is meant by joint and several liability? Why is this often considered to be a disadvantage of doing business as a general partnership?*

Joint and several liability means that a third party may sue any one or more of the partners without suing all of them or the partnership itself. This might be considered a disadvantage because it makes it easier for a third party to sue the firm and its partners.

4. *What is cumulative voting?*

Cumulative voting is a method of voting designed to allow minority shareholders representation on the board of directors.

The number of board members to be elected is multiplied by the number of voting shares a shareholder owns.

Chapter 11

2. *What elements are necessary for an effective acceptance?*

An acceptance is a voluntary act on the part of the offeree that shows consent, or agreement, to the terms of an offer. The acceptance must be unequivocal and must be timely communicated to the offeror.

4. *What is a covenant not to compete? When will such a covenant be enforceable?*

A covenant not to compete is a contractual promise to refrain from conducting business similar to that of another party for a certain period of time and within a specified geographic area. If such a covenant is ancillary to an agreement to sell an ongoing business or is contained in an employment contract, and is reasonable in terms of time and geographic area, it will be enforceable.

Chapter 12

2. *What are the elements of fraudulent misrepresentation?*

Fraudulent misrepresentation has three elements: (1) misrepresentation of a material fact must occur, (2) there must be an intent to deceive, and (3) the innocent party must justifiably rely on the misrepresentation. Also, to collect damages, a party must have been injured as a result of the misrepresentation.

4. *What is the standard measure of compensatory damages when a contract is breached?*

In a contract for the sale of goods, the usual measure of compensatory damages is an amount equal to the difference between the contract price and the market price. When the buyer breaches and the seller has not yet produced the goods, compensatory damages normally equal the lost profits on the sale rather than the difference between the contract price and the market price. On the breach of a contract for a sale of land, when specific performance is not available, the measure of damages is also the difference between the contract and the market price. The measure on the breach of a construction contract depends on who breaches, and when. Recovery for an innocent contractor is generally based on funds expended or expected profit, or both; and for a nonbreaching owner, the cost to complete the project.

Chapter 13

2. *Under the UCC, if an offeree includes additional or different terms in an acceptance, will a contract result? If so, what happens to these terms?*

Under the UCC, a contract can be formed even if the acceptance includes an offeree's additional or different terms. If one of the parties is a nonmerchant, the contract does not include the additional terms. If both parties are merchants, the additional terms automatically become part of the contract unless (1) the original offer expressly limits acceptance to the terms of the offer, (2) the new or changed terms *materially* alter the

contract, or (3) the offeror objects to the new or changed terms within a reasonable period of time. (If the additional terms expressly require the offeror's assent, the offeree's expression is not an acceptance, but a counteroffer.) Under some circumstances, a court might strike the additional terms.

4. *What remedies are available to a buyer or lessee if the seller or lessor breaches the contract?*

Depending on the circumstances at the time of the seller's or lessor's breach, the buyer or lessee may have the right to cancel the contract, recover the goods, obtain specific performance, obtain cover, replevy the goods, recover damages, reject the goods, withhold delivery, resell or dispose of the goods, stop delivery, or revoke acceptance.

Chapter 14

2. *In a bankruptcy proceeding, what constitutes the debtor's estate in property? What property is exempt from the estate under federal bankruptcy law?*

In a bankruptcy proceeding, a debtor's estate in property consists of all the debtor's legal and equitable interests in property currently held, wherever located, together with certain jointly owned property, property transferred in transactions voidable by the trustee, proceeds and profits from the property of the estate, and certain after-acquired property. Federal law exempts the following:

1. Up to $21,625 in equity in the debtor's residence and burial plot (the homestead exemption).
2. Interest in a motor vehicle up to $3,450.
3. Interest, up to $550 for a particular item, in household goods and furnishings, wearing apparel, appliances, books, animals, crops, and musical instruments (the aggregate total of all items is limited to $11,525).
4. Interest in jewelry up to $1,450.
5. Interest in any other property up to $1,150, plus any unused part of the $21,625 homestead exemption up to $10,825.
6. Interest in any tools of the debtor's trade up to $2,175.
7. A life insurance contract owned by the debtor (other than a credit life insurance contract).
8. Certain interests in accrued dividends and interest under life insurance contracts owned by the debtor, not to exceed $11,525.
9. Professionally prescribed health aids.
10. The right to receive Social Security and certain welfare benefits, alimony and support, certain retirement funds and pensions, and education savings accounts held for specific periods of time.
11. The right to receive certain personal-injury and other awards up to $21,625.

4. *In a Chapter 11 reorganization, what is the role of the debtor in possession?*

Under Chapter 11, a debtor in possession (DIP) is allowed to continue to operate his or her business while the bankruptcy proceeds. The DIP's role is similar to that of a trustee in a liquidation, or Chapter 7, proceeding.

Chapter 15

2. When is private mortgage insurance required? Which party does it protect?

A creditor may require private mortgage insurance if a mortgagor does not make a down payment of at least 20 percent of the purchase price for residential real property. The creditor is protected if the borrower defaults because in that event the insurer reimburses the creditor for a portion of the loan.

4. What is a short sale, and what advantages over mortgage foreclosure might it offer borrowers?

A short sale is a sale of real property for an amount that is less than the balance owed on the mortgage loan. Unlike a mortgage foreclosure, both the lender and the borrower must consent to a short sale. Following a short sale, and after the sale proceeds are applied, the borrower still owes the balance of the mortgage debt to the lender unless the lender agrees to forgive the remaining debt.

Chapter 16

2. What federal statute governs working hours and wages?

The Fair Labor Standards Act is the most significant federal statute governing working hours and wages.

4. What are the two most important federal statutes governing immigration and employment today?

The key federal statutes governing immigration and the employment of noncitizens are the Immigration Reform and Control Act (IRCA) of 1986 and the Immigration Act of 1990.

Chapter 17

2. What is the difference between disparate-treatment discrimination and disparate-impact discrimination?

Intentional discrimination by an employer against an employee is known as disparate-treatment discrimination. Disparate-impact discrimination occurs when, as a result of educational or other job requirements or hiring procedures, an employer's workforce does not reflect the percentage of nonwhites, women, or members of other protected classes that characterizes qualified individuals in the local labor market. Disparate-impact discrimination does not require evidence of intent.

4. What are three defenses to claims of employment discrimination?

Among other defenses, employers can justify discrimination on the ground that it was a result of a business necessity, a bona fide occupational qualification, or a seniority system.

Chapter 18

2. What does the Environmental Protection Agency do?

The Environmental Protection Agency coordinates federal environmental responsibilities.

4. What major federal statutes regulate air and water pollution?

Air pollution is regulated at the federal statutory level by the Clean Air Act and its many amendments. Water pollution is covered at the same level by the Federal Water Pollution Control Act (the Clean Water Act) and its amendments. These amendments include the Water Quality Act, the Safe Drinking Water Act, the Marine Protection, Research, and Sanctuaries Act (the Ocean Dumping Act), and the Oil Pollution Act.

Chapter 19

2. What type of activity is prohibited by Section 2 of the Sherman Act?

Section 2 prohibits the misuse, and attempted misuse, of monopoly power in the marketplace.

4. What agencies of the federal government enforce the federal antitrust laws?

The federal agencies charged with enforcing the federal antitrust laws are the U.S. Department of Justice and the Federal Trade Commission.

Chapter 20

2. What are the two major statures regulating the securities industry?

The primary statutes regulating the securities industry are the Securities Act of 1933 and the Securities Exchange Act of 1934, which created the Securities and Exchange Commission.

4. What are some of the features of state securities laws?

Typically, state laws have disclosure requirements and antifraud provisions patterned after Section 10(b) of the Securities Exchange Act of 1934 and SEC Rule 10b-5. State laws provide for the registration or qualification of securities offered or issued for sale within the state. Also, most state securities laws regulate securities brokers and dealers.

Appendix F

Sample Answers for Questions with Sample Answer

1–3A. QUESTION WITH SAMPLE ANSWER

1. The U.S. Constitution—The U.S. Constitution is the supreme law of the land. A law in violation of the Constitution, no matter what its source, will be declared unconstitutional and will not be enforced.

2. The federal statute—Under the U.S. Constitution, when there is a conflict between federal law and state law, federal law prevails.

3. The state statute—State statutes are enacted by state legislatures. Areas not covered by state statutory law are governed by state case law.

4. The U.S. Constitution—State constitutions are supreme within their respective borders unless they conflict with the U.S. Constitution, which is the supreme law of the land.

5. The federal administrative regulation—Under the U.S. Constitution, when there is a conflict between federal law and state law, federal law prevails.

2–2A. QUESTION WITH SAMPLE ANSWER

Marya can bring suit in all three courts. The trucking firm did business in Florida, and the accident occurred there. Thus, the state of Florida would have jurisdiction over the defendant. Because the firm was headquartered in Georgia and had its principal place of business in that state, Marya could also sue in a Georgia court. Finally, because the amount in controversy exceeds $75,000, the suit could be brought in federal court on the basis of diversity of citizenship.

3–2A. QUESTION WITH SAMPLE ANSWER

Factors for the firm to consider in making its decision include the appropriate ethical standard. Under the utilitarian standard, an action is correct, or "right," when, among the people it affects, it produces the greatest amount of good for the greatest number. When an action affects the majority adversely, it is morally wrong. Applying the utilitarian standard requires the following:

1. A determination of which individuals will be affected by the action in question.

2. An assessment, or cost-benefit analysis, of the negative and positive effects of alternative actions on these individuals.

3. The choice of the alternative that will produce maximum societal utility.

Ethical standards may also be based on a concept of duty, which postulates that the end can never justify the means and that human beings should not be treated as mere means to an end. But ethical decision making in a business context is not always simple, particularly when an action will have different effects on different groups of people: shareholders, employees, society, and other stakeholders, such as the local community. Thus, another factor to consider is to whom the firm believes it owes a duty.

4–2A. QUESTION WITH SAMPLE ANSWER

As the text points out, Thomas has a constitutionally protected right to his religion and the free exercise of it. In denying his unemployment benefits, the state violated these rights. Employers are obligated to make reasonable accommodations for their employees' beliefs, right or wrong, that are openly and sincerely held. Thomas's beliefs were openly and sincerely held. By placing him in a department that made military goods, his employer effectively put him in a position of having to choose between his job and his religious principles. This unilateral decision on the part of the employer was the reason Thomas left his job and why the company was required to compensate Thomas for his resulting unemployment.

5–2A. QUESTION WITH SAMPLE ANSWER

The court will consider first whether the agency (the Food and Drug Administration) followed the procedures prescribed in the Administrative Procedure Act (APA). Ordinarily, courts will not require agencies to use procedures beyond those of the APA. Courts will, however, compel agencies to follow their own rules. If an agency has adopted a rule granting extra procedures, the agency must provide those extra procedures, at least until the rule is formally rescinded. Ultimately, in this case, the court will most likely rule for the food producers.

6–2A. QUESTION WITH SAMPLE ANSWER

To answer this question, you must first decide if there is a legal theory under which Harley may be able to recover. You may recall reading about the intentional tort of "wrongful interference with a contractual relationship." To recover damages under this theory, Harley would need to show:

1. That he and Martha had a valid contract,

2. That Lothar knew of this contractual relationship between Martha and Harley, and

3. That Lothar intentionally convinced Martha to break her contract with Harley.

Even though Lothar hoped that his advertisements would persuade Martha to break her contract with Harley, the question states that Martha's decision to change bakers was based solely on the advertising and not on anything else that Lothar did. Lothar's advertisements did not constitute a tort. Note, though, that while Harley cannot collect from Lothar for Martha's actions, he does have a cause of action against Martha for her breach of their contract.

7-2A. QUESTION WITH SAMPLE ANSWER

This is fraud committed in e-mail sent via the Internet. The elements of the tort of fraud are as follows:

1. The misrepresentation of material facts or conditions made with knowledge that they are false or with reckless disregard for the truth.
2. The intent to induce another to rely on the misrepresentation.
3. Justifiable reliance on the misrepresentation by the deceived party.
4. Damages suffered as a result of the reliance.
5. A causal connection between the misrepresentation and the injury.

If any of this e-mailer's recipients reply to her false plea with funds, it is likely that all of the requirements for fraud will have been met. The sort of fraud described in this problem is similar to the "Nigerian letter fraud scam." In this type of scam, an individual sends an e-mail promising its recipient a percentage of funds held in a bank account or payable from a government agency or other source if he or she will send funds to help a fictitious official transfer the amount in the account to another bank. The details of the scam are often adjusted to current events, with perpetrators referring to news-making conflicts, tax refunds or payments, and other occurrences.

8-2A. QUESTION WITH SAMPLE ANSWER

Professor Littrell will prevail, as he has not violated federal copyright law. Under Section 107 of the Copyright Act, the reproduction of copyrighted works for teaching purposes (including multiple copies for classroom use) falls under the "fair use" doctrine and is not an infringement of copyright.

9-2A. QUESTION WITH SAMPLE ANSWER

Yes, it is a reasonable approach to rely on the producers' financial records. The records reflect the producers' costs reasonably well because the producers have used the same allocation methodologies for a number of years. Historically, such records are relied on to present important financial information to shareholders, lenders, tax authorities, auditors, and other third parties. Provided that the producers' records and books comply with generally accepted accounting principles and were verified by independent auditors, it is reasonable to use them to determine the production costs and fair market value of canned pineapple in the United States.

10-2A. QUESTION WITH SAMPLE ANSWER

The court would likely consider the terms of any contracts between the parties and whether or not the parties were acting in good faith. One way to avoid conflicts such as those described in the problem is to institute a Web site in conjunction with a franchisor's franchisees. When a Web site directs interested parties to a franchisee, for example, all parties would seem to benefit. Because territorial conflicts can occur not only between a franchisor and its franchisees but also between competing franchisees, some companies have instituted specific "no compete" pledges.

11-3A. QUESTION WITH SAMPLE ANSWER

Tuan's claim that no contract existed because Lewis had given no consideration for Tuan's promise is supported by the preexisting duty rule. Lewis was already obligated to Ben to do his best to win the race, and the same consideration (attempting to win the race) could not be used in a second contract with Tuan. Because Lewis had a preexisting duty to try to win the race, a majority of courts would likely hold that Tuan was correct in arguing that no contract existed because Lewis gave no consideration.

12-3A. QUESTION WITH SAMPLE ANSWER

Yes. When the subject matter of a contract is destroyed, the contract becomes objectively impossible to perform. Millie was objectively incapable of delivering the full 1,000 bushels of corn to Frank because her farm had not produced 1,000 bushels. Because of the objective impossibility of performing the contract, Millie's duties to Frank were discharged. She could not be held to have breached the contract.

13-3A. QUESTION WITH SAMPLE ANSWER

Yes. Under UCC 2–205, a merchant offeror, who in a signed writing gives assurance that an offer will remain open, creates an irrevocable offer (without payment of consideration) for the time period stated in the assurance up to a three-month period. Jennings, as a merchant, was obliged to hold the offer (which had been made in a signed writing—the letter) open until October 9. Wheeler's acceptance of the offer before October 9 created a valid contract, which Jennings breached when he sold the Thunderbird to a third party.

14-2A. QUESTION WITH SAMPLE ANSWER

1. Any person, including a rancher or farmer, can voluntarily petition himself or herself into bankruptcy. The person has only to be a debtor. This includes partnership and corporations that are liable on a claim held by a creditor, as well as individuals. The debtor does not have to be insolvent to file a petition. Under the Code, a debtor is presumed to be insolvent when his or her debts exceed the fair market value of nonexempt assets. Thus, even though Burke owns a $500,000 ranch and has debts of only $70,000, she can voluntarily petition herself into bankruptcy.
2. Neither Oman nor Sneed—nor any combination of Burke's creditors—can involuntarily petition Burke into bankruptcy. The Code provides that involuntary bankruptcy proceedings cannot be commenced against a farmer. The definition of a farmer includes persons who receive 50 percent of their gross income from farming operations such as tilling the soil, ranching, or the production or raising of crops or livestock. Because Burke obviously fits the definition of a farmer, no creditor can force her into bankruptcy.

15-2A. QUESTION WITH SAMPLE ANSWER

The answer is likely no. A court would most likely find that this issue was novel and permit the plaintiff to survive a motion to dismiss. Courts have held, however, that splitting a loan without the consumer's consent violates the TILA's mandate to group all disclosures for a single transaction into one writing. Even if the plaintiff acquiesced to splitting the loan, the practice appears to circumvent the purpose of HOEPA through an artificial restructuring of the loan transaction. If loan splitting were allowed to circumvent consumer protections, lenders would have a strong incentive to divide loans as necessary to keep individual loan costs as low as possible.

16-2A. QUESTION WITH SAMPLE ANSWER

An agent owes fiduciary duties to the principal. Two such duties are the duty of obedience and the duty to account. Since the agent is acting on behalf of the principal, it is only fitting that a duty be imposed on the agent to follow all lawful, clearly stated instructions of the principal. Whenever an agent deviates from these instructions, the agent is usually in breach of the fiduciary duty owed. In addition, the agent has a duty to account to the principal for all property or funds received by the agent on behalf of the principal.

This duty also requires the agent (unless otherwise agreed) to maintain separate accounts for the principal's funds and the agent's personal funds. No intermingling is allowed. Any funds received by the agent by virtue of the agency belong to the principal. It is a breach of an agent's fiduciary duty to account to secretly retain benefits or profits that by right belong to the principal. Funds so retained by the agent are held in constructive trust on behalf of the principal. Thus, Giberson can recover these funds from Iliana. Also, since Iliana breached her duty of obedience, Giberson has grounds for termination of the agency relationship.

17–2A. QUESTION WITH SAMPLE ANSWER

Under Title VII of the Civil Rights Act, an employer must offer a reasonable accommodation to resolve a conflict between an employee's sincere religious belief and a condition of employment. Reasonable accommodation is required unless such an accommodation would create an undue hardship for the employer's business. In this hypothetical scenario, the only accommodation that Caldwell considered reasonable was a complete exemption from the no-facial-jewelry policy. This could be construed to impose an undue hardship on Costco. The company's dress code could be based on the belief that employees reflect on their employers, especially employees who regularly interact with customers, as Caldwell did in her cashier position. Caldwell's facial jewelry could have affected Costco's public image. Under this reasoning and in such a situation, an employer has no obligation to offer an accommodation before taking other action. Thus, Caldwell is not likely to succeed in a lawsuit against Costco for religious discrimination.

18–2A. QUESTION WITH SAMPLE ANSWER

Fruitade has violated a number of federal environmental laws if such actions are being taken without a permit. First, because the dumping is in a navigable waterway, the River and Harbor Act of 1886, as amended, has been violated. Second, the Clean Water Act of 1972, as amended, has been violated. This act is designed to make the waters safe for swimming, to protect fish and wildlife, and to eliminate discharge of pollutants into the water. Both the crushed glass and the acid violate this act. Third, the Toxic Substances Control Act of 1976 was passed to regulate chemicals that are known to be toxic and could have an effect on human health and the environment. The acid in the cleaning fluid or compound could come under this act.

19–3A. QUESTION WITH SAMPLE ANSWER

This is a classic case of an anticompetitive group boycott in violation of the Sherman Act, Section 1. No-Glow Department Store and the manufacturers have reached an agreement whereby the manufacturers boycotted (refused to deal with) Jorge's Appliance Corp. This boycott was intended to eliminate Jorge's as a competitive force in Sunrise City. This is definitely a *per se* Sherman Act violation, and No-Glow and the manufacturers cannot argue that their actions are permitted as long as Jorge's elimination as a competitor does not substantially affect the relevant market.

20–2A. QUESTION WITH SAMPLE ANSWER

There is likely enough evidence in the facts of this problem to find that David violated the law because there was a clear pattern: every time David called his brother or father, Mark or Jordan bought more RS stock. To establish liability under Section 10(b) and SEC Rule 10b-5, there must be proof of an intent to defraud or knowledge of misconduct with respect to (in this case) a failure to disclose material facts used at the time of a trade. People generally buy when they believe the price of a stock is going up and sell when they believe it is going down. Insider trading can be established when it can be inferred that the most likely source of that belief was an insider. For example, the proximity in time of a stock purchase or sale with a phone conversation between a trader and someone with inside information provides a reasonable basis for inferring an exchange of that information. Thus, in this problem, on this basis, a court could hold David liable for insider trading.

Sample Answers for *Case Problems with Sample Answer*

2–5A. CASE PROBLEM WITH SAMPLE ANSWER

The purpose behind most venue statutes is to ensure that a defendant is not "haled into a remote district, having no real relationship to the dispute." The events in dispute have no connection to Minnesota. The Court stated: "Looked at through the lens of practicality—which is, after all, what [the venue statute] is all about— Nestlé's motion can really be distilled to a simple question: does it make sense to compel litigation in Minnesota when this state bears no relationship to the parties or the underlying events?" The court answered no to this simple question. The plaintiff resides in South Carolina, her daughter's injuries occurred there, and all of her medical treatment was provided (and continues to be provided) in that state. South Carolina is the appropriate venue for this litigation against Nestlé to proceed.

3–4A. CASE PROBLEM WITH SAMPLE ANSWER

The law does not codify all ethical requirements. A firm may have acted unethically but still not be legally accountable unless the party that was wronged can establish some basis for liability. Rules of law are designed to require plaintiffs to prove certain elements that establish a defendant's liability in order to recover for injuries or loss. Ethical codes and internal guidelines may have significance in evaluating a company's conduct, but they are not rules of law—a violation of a company policy is not a basis for liability.

In this case, Havensure had the burden of proving liability. Prudential's violation of its own company guideline was clearly wrongful—and might be a matter of concern for insurance regulators—but this misconduct did not create an obligation to Havensure. Havensure cannot establish a cause of action against Prudential for violating its own policy.

In the actual case on which this problem is based, the court ruled in Prudential's favor.

4–6A. CASE PROBLEM WITH SAMPLE ANSWER

The establishment clause prohibits the government from passing laws or taking actions that promote religion or show a preference for one religion over another. In assessing a government action, the courts look at the predominant purpose for the action and ask whether the action has the effect of endorsing religion.

Although here DeWeese claimed to have a nonreligious purpose for displaying the poster of the Ten Commandments in a courtroom, his own statements showed a religious purpose. These statements reflected his views about "warring" legal philosophies and his belief that "our legal system is based on moral absolutes from divine law handed down by God through the Ten Commandments." This plainly constitutes a religious purpose that violates the establishment clause because it has the effect of endorsing Judaism or Christianity over other religions.

In the case on which this problem is based, the district court ruled in favor of the ACLU. DeWeese appealed to the U.S. Court of Appeals for the Sixth Circuit, which affirmed the district court's ruling.

5–6A. CASE PROBLEM WITH SAMPLE ANSWER

The United States Supreme Court held that greenhouse gases fit within the Clean Air Act's (CAA's) definition of "air pollutant." Thus, the Environmental Protection Agency (EPA) has the authority under that statute to regulate the emission of such gases from new motor vehicles. According to the Court, the definition, which includes "any" air pollutant, embraces all airborne compounds "of whatever stripe." The EPA's focus on Congress's 1990 amendments (or their lack) indicates nothing about the original intent behind the statute (and its amendments before 1990). Nothing in the statute suggests that Congress meant to curtail the agency's power to treat greenhouse gases as air pollutants. In other words, the agency has a preexisting mandate to regulate "any air pollutant" that may endanger the public welfare.

The EPA also argued that, even if it had the authority to regulate greenhouse gases, the agency would not exercise that authority because any regulation would conflict with other administration priorities. The Court acknowledged that the CAA conditions EPA action on the agency's formation of a "judgment," but explained that judgment must relate to whether a pollutant "cause[s], or contribute[s] to, air pollution which may reasonably be anticipated to endanger public health or welfare." Thus, the EPA can avoid issuing regulations only if the agency determines that greenhouse gases do not contribute to climate change (or if the agency reasonably explains why it cannot or will not determine whether they do). The EPA's refusal to regulate was thus "arbitrary, capricious, or otherwise not in accordance with law." The Court remanded the case for the EPA to "ground its reasons for action or inaction in the statute."

6–8A. CASE PROBLEM WITH SAMPLE ANSWER

No, Dobrovolny's claim is not likely to succeed. The majority of states recognize strict product liability. The purpose of strict product liability is to ensure that the costs of injuries resulting from defective products are borne by the manufacturers rather than by the injured persons. The law imposes this liability as a matter of public policy. Some state courts limit the application of the tort theory of strict product liability to situations involving personal injuries rather than property damage.

In this problem, Nebraska recognizes strict product liability, but the state's courts limit its application. The issue is whether these limits apply when a product self-destructs without causing damage to persons or other property. When a product injures only itself, the reasons for imposing liability in tort lose their significance. The consumer has not been injured, and the loss concerns the consumer's benefit of the bargain from the contract with the seller of the product. But a consumer with only a damaged product who may not recover in tort is not without other remedies. Recovery can be sought on a contract theory for breach of warranty. Product value and quality are the purposes of warranties.

Thus, the court here is likely to deny Dobrovolny's claim in tort on a strict product liability theory. But he might then seek to recover for breach of warranty on contract principles for the loss of his truck. If there were no express warranties that the truck would not spontaneously combust, relief may be possible for breach of the implied warranty of merchantability or fitness for a particular purpose.

In the actual case on which this problem is based, the court issued a decision in Ford's favor.

7–5A. CASE PROBLEM WITH SAMPLE ANSWER

Under the Fourth Amendment, a police officer must obtain a search warrant to search private property. In the case of a traffic stop, it seems unreasonable to require an officer to obtain a warrant to search one of the vehicle's occupants. But it seems reasonable to apply some standard to prevent police misconduct.

An officer might be held to a standard of probable cause, which consists of reasonable grounds to believe that a person should be searched. In some situations, however, an officer may have a reasonable suspicion short of probable cause to believe that a person poses a risk of violence. In a traffic-stop setting, for example, this risk would not stem from the normal reaction of a person stopped for a driving infraction, but from the possibility that evidence of a more serious crime might be discovered. A criminal's motivation to use violence to prevent the discovery could be great. And because the vehicle is already stopped, the additional intrusion is minimal. Under these circumstances, a limited search of the person for weapons would protect the officer, the individual, and the public. Thus, an officer who conducts a routine traffic stop could perform a pat-down search of a passenger on a reasonable suspicion that the person may be armed and dangerous.

In the case on which this problem is based, a jury convicted Johnson of the charge, but a state appellate court reversed the conviction. The United States Supreme Court reversed the appellate court's judgment and remanded the case.

8–6A. CASE PROBLEM WITH SAMPLE ANSWER

Whenever the form or expression of an idea is copied, an infringement of copyright occurs. An exception to liability is made under the "fair use" doctrine. A person can reproduce copyrighted material for purposes such as criticism, comment, reporting, teaching, scholarship, or research. Also, once a copyright owner sells or gives away a copy of a work, the copyright owner no longer has the right to control the distribution of that copy.

Here, UMG gave free, unsolicited, promotional CDs to music critics and others. There was no indication that the recipients agreed to a license, so none was created. Having given away these copies, UMG conveyed title of the promotional CDs to the recipients and could no longer control their distribution. The recipients, including Augusto, could sell, or otherwise dispose of, them. There was no copyright infringement.

In the actual case on which this problem is based, the court issued a judgment in Augusto's favor.

9–4A. CASE PROBLEM WITH SAMPLE ANSWER

The key international legal principles at play here are comity and sovereign immunity. Comity requires one nation to give effect to the laws and judicial decrees of another. Sovereign immunity prevents the U.S. courts from exercising jurisdiction over foreign nations unless certain conditions are met. In this case, the United States Supreme Court reversed and remanded the Ninth Circuit's decision. The Court found that lower courts gave insufficient weight to the sovereign status of the Republic of the Philippines and its Commission in considering whether the interests of those parties would be prejudiced if the case proceeded. Giving full effect to sovereign immunity promotes the comity and dignity interest that contributed to the development of the immunity doctrine.

The claims here arise from historically and politically significant events for the Republic and its people. They have a unique interest in resolving matters related to Arelma's assets. A foreign state has a comity interest in using its courts for a dispute if it has a right to do so. Other nations should not bypass the courts of the Philippines without good cause. To seize assets of the Philippines would be a specific affront. The lower courts erred in ruling on the merits of the case. The Pimentel class has interests, but the courts did not accord proper weight to the compelling sovereign immunity claim.

10–6A. CASE PROBLEM WITH SAMPLE ANSWER

In a member-managed limited liability company (LLC), all of the members participate in management, and decisions are made by majority vote. The managers of an LLC—whether member or manager managed—owe fiduciary duties to the company and its members. These duties include the duty of loyalty and the duty of care. An LLC's operating agreement can include provisions governing decision-making procedures. For example, the agreement can set forth procedures for choosing or removing members or managers.

Here, Bluewater is member managed. Under the applicable state law, every member of a member-managed LLC is entitled to participate in managing the business. The Bluewater operating agreements provide for a "super majority" vote to remove and buy out a member—if the "member has either committed a felony or under any other circumstances that would jeopardize the company status" as a contractor. Without giving a reason, however, three of the four members of Bluewater "fired" the fourth member.

Under these facts and principles, Smith, Mosser, and Floyd breached their fiduciary duties, the Bluewater operating agreements, and the state LLC statute. The Bluewater members breached their fiduciary duties by their treatment of Williford. The defendants also breached the Bluewater operating agreements. A super majority ouster was allowed only when the member to be ousted had committed a felony or had jeopardized the company's status as an approved contractor—the defendants' ouster notice alleged neither. By attempting to oust Williford, the defendants violated Mississippi's LLC statute, which provides that every member of a member-managed LLC is entitled to participate in managing the business. As a member of both Bluewater LLCs, Williford was entitled to participate in the management of both, and he could not be "fired."

In the actual case on which this problem is based, the court issued a judgment in Williford's favor with a damages award of nearly $350,000. A state intermediate appellate court reversed the judgment, but the Mississippi Supreme Court reversed the appellate court's ruling and affirmed the trial court's judgment, based in part on the reasoning stated above.

11–8A. CASE PROBLEM WITH SAMPLE ANSWER

The court in this case could impose a quasi contract to avoid the unjust enrichment of Kim at Kris's expense. There are three elements to recover on this basis:

1. One party must confer a benefit on another party.

2. The other party must appreciate or know of the benefit.

3. The other party must retain the benefit under circumstances that would make it inequitable to do this without paying for it.

Here, Kris asserted that she "loaned" Kim the funds that her sister asked for. The loan conferred a benefit on Kim, who clearly knew of it. Kris's use of the word *loan* implied that she gave her sister the funds with the expectation of being repaid. These circumstances met the test for an award to Kris of recovery in *quantum meruit*.

In the actual case on which this problem is based, the trial court stated, "All equities lie with the plaintiff and whether or not there is a written contract to support the amount is not necessarily required. It's whether or not someone gives something over, pays something for somebody and it's inequitable for that person to retain the benefit of that without returning the money." The court granted a judgment in Kris's favor for the repayment of the loans. On appeal, a state intermediate appellate court affirmed.

12–6A. CASE PROBLEM WITH SAMPLE ANSWER

Yes. When an assignment is made, the assignee should notify the obligor of the assignment. Notice is not necessary to establish the validity of the assignment—the assignment is effective immediately, whether or not notice is given. But until the obligor has notice of the assignment, the obligor can discharge his or her obligations to the assignor by performance. This performance constitutes a discharge to the assignee. Once the obligor receives proper notice, only performance to the assignee can discharge the obligor's obligations.

In this problem, Wilkinson (the obligor) was not notified that Arnold (the assignor) had assigned his interest in the property to Sam (the assignee). Sam should have provided the notice. His failure to do so caused him to lose the right to receive the rent and the notice of renewal from Wilkinson. Thus, although the assignment was valid, the lack of notice meant that Wilkinson could discharge his obligations under the lease to Arnold. And this is what Wilkinson did—he paid the rent to Arnold and renewed the lease by notice to Arnold. If Sam had given Wilkinson proper notice of the assignment, Wilkinson's payment of rent and notice to Arnold would not have discharged the duties, and Sam could have successfully claimed that the lease was void.

On this reasoning, in the actual case on which this problem is based, the court determined that Wilkinson's renewal of the lease by notice to Arnold was sufficient.

13–7A. CASE PROBLEM WITH SAMPLE ANSWER

Under the UCC, a buyer who has accepted nonconforming goods may keep the goods and recover for any loss "resulting in the ordinary course of events" according to "any manner which is reasonable." But the buyer must notify the seller of the breach within a reasonable time after the defect is discovered. A failure to give notice of the defect to the seller bars the buyer from pursuing any remedy. When the goods delivered are not as promised, the measure of damages equals the difference between the value of the goods as accepted and their value if they had been delivered as warranted, unless special circumstances indicate damages of a different amount. The buyer may also be entitled to incidental and consequential damages under the UCC.

In this problem, Woodridge bought eighty-seven trailers from STM through McCarty, an independent sales agent. McCarty showed Woodridge title documents that Woodridge later claimed were defective, presumably because the documents did not indicate Woodridge was the buyer. Instead of notifying STM that Woodridge considered the purported defects to be a breach of their contract, however, Woodridge told McCarty to keep the documents and sell the trailers for Woodridge. Woodridge did not tender the trailers or the documents to STM to give the seller the opportunity to cure the alleged breach. By undertaking to sell the trailers, Woodridge acted inconsistently with STM's ownership. This meant that Woodridge accepted the trailers. Much later, after the trailers had been resold and their proceeds were unaccounted for, Woodridge demanded that STM refund the contract price. But Woodridge did not notify STM about the alleged defect in the title documents until the suit was filed three months later. This is not a reasonable time under the circumstances. Thus, Woodridge did not have a right to recover damages for accepted goods.

In the case on which this problem is based, the court issued a judgment in favor of STM. On Woodridge's appeal, the U.S. Court of Appeals for the Eleventh Circuit affirmed the judgment, according to the reasoning set out here.

14–7A. CASE PROBLEM WITH SAMPLE ANSWER

Gholston can recover damages because EZ Auto willfully violated the automatic stay. EZ Auto repossessed the car even though it received notice of the automatic stay from the bankruptcy court. Moreover, EZ Auto retained the car even after it was reminded of the stay by Gholston's attorney. Thus, EZ Auto knew about the automatic stay and violated it intentionally. Because Gholston suffered direct damages as a result, she can recover from EZ Auto.

15–7A. CASE PROBLEM WITH SAMPLE ANSWER

Ordinarily, a deficiency judgment will be for the difference between the borrower's outstanding debt and the final sales price at the foreclosure sale. Courts will not apply the sales price, however, if the property sells for far less than its fair market value. That was the case here, so Beach Community Bank is entitled to the difference between First Brownsville's outstanding debt and the property's fair market value at the time of the foreclosure sale. Based on the court's foreclosure judgment and the expert testimony at the deficiency judgment hearing, First Brownsville owes Beach Community Bank $454,475.

16–6A. CASE PROBLEM WITH SAMPLE ANSWER

The facts support a conclusion that Jonathan was an independent contractor and not an employee. In deciding whether a worker is categorized as an employee or an independent contractor, the courts consider the amount of control that the employer exercises over the details of the work. For instance, is the work done under the employer's direction or by a specialist without supervision? Control indicates employee status.

In this problem, Jonathan could argue that he was under William's direction and control. It was his first day on the new job. There was no way for him to know what to do without William's direction. He might assert that William told him to load certain tires on a trailer, substantiating Jonathan's claim of employee status. But this instruction was minimal. The relationship between the parties before the accident was independent contractor and employer. For a decade, Jonathan operated his own business. His accumulated skill, experience, and judgment in the business established that he controlled his work without oversight.

In the actual case on which this problem is based, the court held that Jonathan was an independent contractor.

17–6A. CASE PROBLEM WITH SAMPLE ANSWER

Yes. Dawson established a claim for retaliatory discharge, according to the U.S. Court of Appeals for the Ninth Circuit. Under Oregon law, it is an unlawful employment practice for an employer to discriminate against an individual based on sexual orientation. It is also unlawful for an employer to discharge an individual because that person has filed a complaint. To establish a *prima facie* case of retaliatory discharge, a plaintiff must prove that:

1. The defendant intentionally retaliated against the employee because he or she filed a discrimination complaint.
2. The defendant did so with the intent of forcing the employee to leave the employment.
3. The employee left the employment as a result of the retaliation.

Dawson engaged in a protected activity when he went to the human resources department and filed a complaint. "The protected activity occurred at most two days before the discharge and the treatment of Dawson was a topic during both the protected activity and the discharge." Therefore, Dawson has offered enough evidence that "a reasonable trier of fact could find in favor of Dawson on his retaliation claim." The federal appellate court held that the district court had erred in granting a summary judgment for the employer. The court reversed the decision and remanded the case for trial.

18–5A. CASE PROBLEM WITH SAMPLE ANSWER

The appeals court found that the plaintiffs failed to establish that the National Park Service (NPS) acted in an arbitrary and capricious manner when it adopted the plan. When an agency acts in an arbitrary and capricious manner, the court has grounds for intervention. Otherwise, it defers to the expertise of the agency, as revealed in the record. Here, the court found that the environmental impact statement was comprehensive and that the NPS had credible reason to believe that the use of rafts on the river did not damage the wilderness status of portions of the park. Since the NPS acted within its statutory guidelines and followed proper procedure in its decision making, the court would not intervene in the agency's decision.

19–6A. CASE PROBLEM WITH SAMPLE ANSWER

No. DVRC's action does not represent an attempt to monopolize in violation of the Sherman Act. DVRC merely returned to a position that it had a right to from the beginning. In their contract, DVRC had expressly informed Christy that their relationship could change at any time. Thus Christy knew from the beginning that its ski rental business could operate only with DVRC's permission, subject to DVRC's business judgment. If DVRC had terminated a profitable relationship without any economic justification, it might have shown a willingness to forgo short-term profits to achieve an anticompetitive end. But there is no indication that DVRC terminated a profitable business relationship or that DVRC was motivated by anything other than a desire to make more profits. Rather than forgoing short-term profits, DVRC can expect to increase its short-term profits by operating its own ski rental facility. The court in the case on which this problem is based dismissed Christy's suit, and the U.S. Court of Appeals for the Tenth Circuit affirmed that decision.

20–4A. CASE PROBLEM WITH SAMPLE ANSWER

No. The appeals court affirmed that there was no negligence by the officers of Orphan Medical, Inc. There was no duty to disclose early drug trial data nor was there a duty to give shareholders access to such data. There was no evidence of an intent to mislead investors in Orphan. Federal drug procedure is technical and lengthy. The fact that one stage of testing was successful was no guarantee that further testing would be successful or that the U.S. Food and Drug Administration would allow the drug to be widely marketed. Hence, officers had good reason to be careful not to set off speculation by releasing good news that might, in the long run, turn out not to be favorable.

Glossary

A

Acceleration Clause • A clause that makes the entire loan balance become due if the borrower misses or is late making the monthly payments.

Acceptance • A voluntary act by the offeree that shows consent, or agreement, to the terms of an offer.

Accord and Satisfaction • An agreement and payment (or other performance) between two parties, one of whom has a right of action against the other.

Accredited Investor • In the context of securities offerings, a "sophisticated" investor, such as a bank, an insurance company, an investment company, the issuer's executive officers and directors, and any person whose income or net worth exceeds certain limits.

Actionable • Capable of serving as the basis of a lawsuit.

Act of State Doctrine • A doctrine providing that the judicial branch of one country will not examine the validity of public acts committed by a recognized foreign government within its own territory.

Actual Malice • The deliberate intent to cause harm, which exists when a person makes a statement either knowing that it is false or showing a reckless disregard for whether it is true.

Actus Reus • A guilty (prohibited) act. The commission of a prohibited act is one of the two essential elements required for criminal liability.

Adhesion Contract • A standard-form contract in which the stronger party dictates the terms.

Adjudication • The proceeding in which an administrative law judge hears and decides issues that arise when an administrative agency charges a person or a firm with an agency violation.

Adjustable-Rate Mortgage (ARM) • A mortgage in which the rate of interest paid by the borrower changes periodically.

Administrative Agency • A federal or state government agency established to perform a specific function.

Administrative Law • The body of law created by administrative agencies in order to carry out their duties and responsibilities.

Administrative Law Judge (ALJ) • One who presides over an administrative agency hearing and has the power to administer oaths, take testimony, rule on questions of evidence, and make determinations of fact.

Administrative Process • The procedure used by administrative agencies in the administration of law.

Affidavit • A statement of facts confirmed by the oath or affirmation of the party making it and made before a person having the authority to administer the oath or affirmation.

Affirmative Action • Job-hiring policies that give special consideration to members of protected classes in an effort to overcome present effects of past discrimination.

Agency • A relationship between two parties in which one party (the agent) agrees to represent or act for the other (the principal).

Agent • A person authorized by another to act for or in place of him or her.

Agreement • A meeting of two or more minds in regard to the terms of a contract, usually broken down into two events: an offer and an acceptance.

Alien Corporation • A designation in the United States for a corporation formed in another country but doing business in the United States.

Alternative Dispute Resolution (ADR) • The resolution of disputes in ways other than those involved in the traditional judicial process, such as negotiation, mediation, and arbitration.

Annual Percentage Rate (APR) • The cost of credit on a yearly basis, typically expressed as an annual percentage.

Answer • Procedurally, a defendant's response to a complaint.

Anticipatory Repudiation • An assertion or action by a party indicating that he or she will not perform an obligation that the party is contractually obligated to perform at a future time.

Antitrust Law • Laws protecting commerce from unlawful restraints.

Appraiser • An individual who specializes in determining the value of specified real or personal property.

Appropriation • In tort law, the use by one person of another person's name, likeness, or other identifying characteristic without permission and for the benefit of the user.

Arbitration • The settling of a dispute by submitting it to a disinterested third party who renders a decision that is often legally binding.

Arbitration Clause • A clause in a contract that provides that, in the event of a dispute, the parties will submit the dispute to arbitration rather than litigate the dispute in court.

Arson • The intentional burning of another's building.

Articles of Incorporation • The document filed with the appropriate governmental agency, usually the secretary of state, when a business is incorporated.

Articles of Organization • The document filed with a designated state official by which a limited liability company is formed.

Articles of Partnership • A written agreement that sets forth each partner's rights in, and obligations to, the partnership.

Artisan's Lien • A possessory lien on personal property of another person to ensure payment to a person who has made improvements on and added value to that property.

Assault • Any word or action intended to make another person fearful of immediate physical harm.

Assignment • The act of transferring to another all or part of one's rights arising under a contract.

Assumption of Risk • A doctrine under which a plaintiff may not recover for injuries or damage suffered from risks he or she knows of and has voluntarily assumed.

Attachment • The legal process of seizing another's property under a court order to secure satisfaction of a judgment yet to be rendered.

Attempted Monopolization • Any action by a firm to eliminate competition and gain monopoly power.

Authorization Card • A card signed by an employee that gives a union permission to act on his or her behalf in negotiations with management.

Automatic Stay • A suspension of all judicial proceedings on the occurrence of an independent event.

Award • The monetary compensation given to a party at the end of a trial or other proceeding.

B

Bankruptcy Court • A federal court of limited jurisdiction that handles only bankruptcy proceedings.

Battery • The unexcused, harmful or offensive, intentional touching of another.

Beyond a Reasonable Doubt • A standard of proof under which if there is any reasonable doubt that a criminal defendant committed the crime with which she or he has been charged, then the verdict must be "not guilty."

Bilateral Contract • A type of contract that arises when a promise is given in exchange for a return promise.

Bilateral Mistake • A mistake that occurs when both parties to a contract are mistaken about the same material fact.

Bill of Rights • The first ten amendments to the U.S. Constitution.

Binding Authority • Any source of law that a court must follow when deciding a case.

Bona Fide Occupational Qualification (BFOQ) • An identifiable characteristic reasonably necessary to the normal operation of a particular business.

Breach • The failure to perform a legal obligation.

Breach of Contract • The failure, without legal excuse, of a promisor to perform the obligations of a contract.

Brief • A written summary or statement prepared by one side in a lawsuit to explain its case to the judge.

Bureaucracy • The organizational structure, consisting of government bureaus and agencies, through which the government implements and enforces the laws.

Burglary • The unlawful entry or breaking into a building with the intent to commit a felony.

Business Ethics • A consensus as to what constitutes right or wrong behavior in the world of business and how moral principles are applied by businesspersons.

Business Invitee • A person, such as a customer or a client, who is invited onto business premises by the owner of those premises.

Business Judgment Rule • A rule that immunizes corporate management from liability for actions that are undertaken in good faith and are within both the power of the corporation and the authority of management to make.

Business Necessity • An employment practice that discriminates against members of a protected class but is necessary for job performance.

Business Tort • Wrongful interference with another's business rights.

Bylaws • A set of governing rules adopted by a corporation or other association.

C

Case Law • The rules of law announced in court decisions.

Categorical Imperative • An ethical guideline according to which an action is evaluated in terms of what would happen if everyone else in the same situation (category) acted the same way.

Causation in Fact • An act or omission without which an event would not have occurred.

Certification Mark • A mark used by one or more persons, other than the owner, to certify the region, materials, mode of manufacture, quality, or other characteristic of specific goods or services.

Checks and Balances • The system by which each of the three branches of the national government exercises a check on the actions of the others.

Choice-of-Language Clause • A clause in a contract designating the official language by which the contract will be interpreted in the event of a future disagreement over the contract's terms.

Choice-of-Law Clause • A clause in a contract designating the law (such as the law of a particular state or nation) that will govern the contract.

Citation • A reference to a publication in which a legal authority—such as a statute or a court decision—or other source can be found.

Civil Law • The branch of law dealing with the definition and enforcement of all private or public rights, as opposed to criminal matters.

Civil Law System • A system of law derived from the Roman Empire and based on a code rather than case law. Most European nations have this system.

Click-on Agreement • An agreement that arises when a buyer, engaging in a transaction on a computer, indicates assent to be bound by the terms of an offer by clicking on a button that says, for example, "I agree."

Close Corporation • A corporation whose shareholders are limited to a small group of persons.

Closed Shop • A firm that requires union membership by its workers as a condition of employment. The closed shop was made illegal by the Labor-Management Relations Act of 1947.

Cloud Computing • A subscription-based or pay-per-use service that, in real time over the Internet, extends a computer's software or storage capabilities.

Collective Bargaining • The process by which labor and management negotiate the terms and conditions of employment.

Collective Mark • A mark used by members of a cooperative, association, labor union, or other organization to certify the region, materials, mode of manufacture, quality, or other characteristic of specific goods or services.

Comity • The principle by which one nation defers to and gives effect to the laws and judicial decrees of another nation. This recognition is based primarily on respect.

Commerce Clause • The provision in Article I, Section 8, of the U.S. Constitution that gives Congress the power to regulate interstate commerce.

Commercial Impracticability • A doctrine under which a court may excuse the parties from performing a contract when the performance becomes much more difficult or costly due to an event that the parties did not foresee or anticipate at the time the contract was made.

Commingle • To put funds or goods together into one mass so that the funds or goods no longer have separate identities.

Common Law • The body of law developed from custom or judicial decisions in English and U.S. courts.

Comparative Negligence • A rule in tort law that reduces the plaintiff's recovery in proportion to the plaintiff's degree of fault, rather than barring recovery completely.

Compelling Government Interest • A test of constitutionality that requires the government to have convincing reasons for passing any law that restricts fundamental rights, such as free speech, or distinguishes between people based on a suspect trait.

Compensatory Damages • A monetary award equivalent to the actual value of injuries or damage sustained by the aggrieved party.

Complaint • The pleading made by a plaintiff or a charge made by the state alleging wrongdoing on the part of the defendant.

Concentrated Industry • An industry in which a large percentage of market sales is controlled by either a single firm or a small number of firms.

Concurrent Jurisdiction • Jurisdiction that exists when two different courts have the power to hear a case.

Condition • A qualification, provision, or clause in a contractual agreement. The occurrence or nonoccurrence of the condition creates, suspends, or terminates the obligations of the contracting parties.

Condition Precedent • In a contractual agreement, a condition that must be met before a party's promise becomes absolute.

Confiscation • A government's taking of a privately owned business or personal property without a proper public purpose or an award of just compensation.

Conforming Goods • Goods that conform to contract specifications.

Consequential Damages • Special damages that compensate for a loss that is not direct or immediate.

Consideration • The value given in return for a promise or a performance in a contractual agreement.

Constitutional Law • The body of law derived from the U.S. Constitution and the constitutions of the various states.

Constructive Discharge • A termination of employment brought about by making the employee's working conditions so intolerable that the employee reasonably feels compelled to leave.

Consumer-Debtor • One whose debts result primarily from the purchases of goods for personal, family, or household use.

Contract • An agreement that can be enforced in court; formed by two or more competent parties who agree, for consideration, to perform or to refrain from performing some legal act now or in the future.

Contractual Capacity • The capacity required by the law for a party who enters into a contract to be bound by that contract.

Contributory Negligence • A rule in tort law that completely bars the plaintiff from recovering any damages if the damage suffered is partly the plaintiff's own fault.

Conversion • Wrongfully taking or retaining possession of an individual's personal property and placing it in the service of another.

Copyright • The exclusive right of an author to publish, print, or sell an intellectual production for a statutory period of time.

Corporate Governance • A set of policies or procedures affecting the way a corporation is directed or controlled.

Corporate Social Responsibility • The idea that corporations can and should act ethically and be accountable to society for their actions.

Corporation • A legal business form that complies with statutory requirements.

Correspondent Bank • A bank in which another bank has an account (and vice versa) for the purpose of facilitating fund transfers.

Cost-Benefit Analysis • A decision-making technique that involves weighing the costs of a given action against the benefits of that action.

Co-Surety • One who assumes liability jointly with another surety for the payment of an obligation.

Counterclaim • A claim made by a defendant in a civil lawsuit against the plaintiff.

Counteroffer • An offeree's response to an offer in which the offeree rejects the original offer and at the same time makes a new offer.

Covenant Not to Compete • A contractual promise of one party to refrain from competing with another party for a certain period of time and within a certain geographic area.

Cover • A remedy that allows the buyer or lessee, on the seller's or lessor's breach, to purchase or lease the goods from another seller or lessor and substitute them for the goods due under the contract.

Cram-Down Provision • A provision of the Bankruptcy Code that allows a court to confirm a debtor's Chapter 11 reorganization plan even though only one class of creditors has accepted it.

Creditors' Composition Agreement • An agreement formed between a debtor and his or her creditors in which the creditors agree to accept a lesser sum than that owed by the debtor in full satisfaction of the debt.

Crime • A wrong against society proclaimed in a statute and punishable by society through fines, imprisonment, or death.

Criminal Law • Law that has to do with wrongful actions committed against society for which society demands redress.

Cure • The right of a party who tenders nonconforming performance to correct that performance within the contract period.

Cyber Crime • A crime that occurs online, in the virtual community of the Internet, as opposed to the physical world.

Cyber Fraud • Any misrepresentation knowingly made over the Internet with the intention of deceiving another and on which a reasonable person would and does rely to his or her detriment.

Cyberlaw • An informal term used to refer to all laws governing online communications and transactions.

Cyber Mark • A trademark in cyberspace.

Cybersquatting • The act of registering a domain name that is the same as, or confusingly similar to, the trademark of another and then offering to sell that domain name back to the trademark owner.

Cyberterrorist • A hacker whose purpose is to exploit a target computer to create a serious impact, such as sabotage.

Cyber Tort • A tort committed in cyberspace.

D

Damages • Money sought as a remedy for a breach of contract or a tortious action.

Debtor in Possession (DIP) • In Chapter 11 bankruptcy proceedings, a debtor who is allowed to continue in possession of the estate in property (the business) and to continue business operations.

Deed in Lieu of Foreclosure • An alternative to foreclosure in which the mortgagor voluntarily conveys the property to the lender in satisfaction of the mortgage.

Defamation • Anything published or publicly spoken that causes injury to another's good name, reputation, or character.

Default Judgment • A judgment entered by a court against a defendant who has failed to appear in court to answer or defend against the plaintiff's claim.

Defendant • One against whom a lawsuit is brought.

Delegation • The transfer of a contractual duty to a third party.

Delegation Doctrine • A doctrine based on the U.S. Constitution, which has been construed to allow Congress to delegate some of its power to administrative agencies to make and implement laws.

Deposition • The testimony of a party to a lawsuit or a witness taken under oath before a trial.

Discharge • The termination of a debtor's obligation, or the termination of one's obligation under a contract.

Disclosed Principal • A principal whose identity is known to a third party at the time the agent makes a contract with the third party.

Discovery • A method by which the opposing parties obtain information from each other to prepare for trial.

Disparagement of Property • An economically injurious falsehood made about another's product or property.

Disparate-Impact Discrimination • Discrimination that results from certain employer practices or procedures that, although not discriminatory on their face, have a discriminatory effect.

Disparate-Treatment Discrimination • Intentional discrimination against individuals on the basis of color, gender, national origin, race, or religion.

Dissociation • The severance of the relationship between a partner and a partnership.

Distributed Network • A network that can be used by persons located (distributed) around the country or the globe to share computer files.

Distribution Agreement • A contract between a seller and a distributor of the seller's products setting out the terms and conditions of the distributorship.

Diversity of Citizenship • A basis for federal court jurisdiction over a lawsuit between citizens of different states.

Divestiture • The act of selling one or more of a company's divisions or parts, such as a subsidiary or plant.

Dividend • A distribution to corporate shareholders of corporate profits or income, disbursed in proportion to the number of shares held.

Docket • The list of cases entered on a court's calendar and thus scheduled to be heard by the court.

Domain Name • An Internet address consisting of a series of letters and symbols used to identify site operators on the Web.

Domestic Corporation • A corporation that does business in, and is organized under the law of, a given state.

Double Jeopardy • A situation occurring when a person is tried twice for the same criminal offense.

Dram Shop Act • A state statute that imposes liability on the owners of bars and taverns for injuries resulting from accidents caused by intoxicated persons when they contributed to the intoxication.

Due Process Clause • The provisions in the Fifth and Fourteenth Amendments that guarantee that no person shall be deprived of life, liberty, or property without due process of law.

Dumping • The selling of goods in a foreign country at a price below the price charged for the same goods in the domestic market.

Duress • Unlawful pressure brought to bear on a person, causing the person to perform an act that she or he would not otherwise have performed.

Duty of Care • The duty of all persons, as established by tort law, to exercise a reasonable amount of care in their dealings with others.

E

E-Contract • A contract that is formed electronically.

E-Evidence • A type of evidence that consists of all computer-generated or electronically recorded information.

E-Signature • An electronic sound, symbol, or process attached to or logically associated with a record and executed or adopted by a person with the intent to sign the record.

Embezzlement • The fraudulent appropriation of funds or other property by a person to whom the funds or property has been entrusted.

Employment at Will • A common law doctrine under which either party may terminate an employment relationship at any time for any reason.

Employment Discrimination • Treating employees or job applicants unequally on the basis of race, color, national origin, religion, gender, age, or disability.

Enabling Legislation • A statute enacted by Congress that authorizes the creation of an administrative agency and specifies the name, composition, and powers of the agency being created.

Entrapment • A defense in which the defendant claims that he or she was induced by a public official—usually undercover—to commit a crime that he or she would not otherwise have committed.

Environmental Impact Statement (EIS) • A statement required by the National Environmental Policy Act for any major federal action that will significantly affect the quality of the environment.

Equal Protection Clause • The provision in the Fourteenth Amendment that guarantees that a state may not "deny to any person within its jurisdiction the equal protection of the laws."

Equitable Principles and Maxims • General propositions or principles of law that have to do with fairness (equity).

Equitable Right of Redemption • The right of a mortgagor who is in default to redeem or purchase the property before foreclosure proceedings by paying the full amount of the debt, plus any interest and costs.

Establishment Clause • The provision in the First Amendment that prohibits the government from establishing any state-sponsored religion or enacting any law that promotes religion or favors one religion over another.

Estate in Property • All of the property owned by a person, including real estate and personal property.

Estop • Bar, impede, or preclude.

Ethical Reasoning • A reasoning process in which an individual links his or her moral convictions or ethical standards to the particular situation at hand.

Ethics • Moral principles and values applied to social behavior.

Exclusionary Rule • In criminal procedure, a rule under which any evidence that is obtained in violation of the accused's rights guaranteed by the Fourth, Fifth, and Sixth Amendments to the U.S. Constitution, as well as any evidence derived from illegally obtained evidence, will not be admissible in court.

Exclusive-Dealing Contract • An agreement under which a seller forbids a buyer to purchase products from the seller's competitors.

Exclusive Jurisdiction • Jurisdiction that exists when a case can be heard only in a particular court or type of court.

Executed Contract • A contract that has been completely performed by both parties.

Executory Contract • A contract that has not yet been fully performed.

Export • The sale of goods and services by domestic firms to buyers located in other countries.

Express Contract • A contract in which the terms of the agreement are stated in words, oral or written.

Express Warranty • A seller's or lessor's oral or written promise, ancillary to an underlying sales or lease agreement, as to the quality, description, or performance of the goods being sold or leased.

Expropriation • The seizure by a government of a privately owned business or personal property for a proper public purpose and with just compensation.

F

Federal Form of Government • A system of government in which the states form a union and the sovereign power is divided between the central government and the member states.

Federal Question • A question that pertains to the U.S. Constitution, acts of Congress, or treaties. A federal question provides a basis for federal jurisdiction.

Fiduciary Relationship • A relationship founded on trust and confidence.

Filtering Software • A computer program that is designed to block access to certain Web sites based on their content.

Final Order • The final decision of an administrative agency on an issue.

Firm Offer • An offer (by a merchant) that is irrevocable without the necessity of consideration for a stated period of time (not to exceed three months). A firm offer by a merchant must be in writing and must be signed by the offeror.

Fixed-Rate Mortgage • A standard mortgage with a fixed, or unchanging, rate of interest.

Forbearance • An agreement between a lender and a borrower in which the lender agrees to temporarily cease requiring mortgage payments, to delay foreclosure, or to accept smaller payments than previously scheduled.

Force Majeure Clause • A provision in a contract stipulating that certain unforeseen events—such as war, political upheavals, or acts of God—will excuse a party from liability for nonperformance of contractual obligations.

Foreclosure • A proceeding in which a creditor either takes title to, or forces the sale of, the debtor's property in satisfaction of a debt.

Foreign Corporation • In a given state, a corporation that does business in the state without being incorporated therein.

Foreign Exchange Market • A worldwide system in which foreign currencies are bought and sold.

Forgery • The fraudulent making or altering of any writing in a way that changes the legal rights and liabilities of another.

Formal Contract • A contract that by law requires a specific form for its validity.

Forum-Selection Clause • A provision in a contract designating the court, jurisdiction, or tribunal that will decide any disputes arising under the contract.

Franchise • Any arrangement in which the owner of a trademark, trade name, or copyright licenses another to use that trademark, trade name, or copyright in the selling of goods or services.

Franchisee • One receiving a license to use another's (the franchisor's) trademark, trade name, or copyright in the sale of goods and services.

Franchisor • One licensing another (the franchisee) to use the owner's trademark, trade name, or copyright in the selling of goods or services.

Fraudulent Misrepresentation • Any misrepresentation, either by misstatement or by omission of a material fact, knowingly made with the intention of deceiving another and on which a reasonable person would and does rely to his or her detriment.

Free Exercise Clause • The provision in the First Amendment that prohibits the government from interfering with people's religious practices or forms of worship.

Free-Writing Prospectus • Any type of written, electronic, or graphic offer that describes the issuing corporation or its securities and includes a legend indicating that the investor may obtain the prospectus at the Securities and Exchange Commission's Web site.

G

Garnishment • A legal process whereby a creditor appropriates a debtor's property or wages that are in the hands of a third party.

General Partner • A partner who assumes responsibility for the management of the partnership and liability for its debts.

Good Samaritan Statute • A state statute stipulating that persons who provide emergency services to someone in peril cannot be sued for negligence.

Grand Jury • A group of citizens called to decide, after hearing the state's evidence, whether a reasonable basis exists for believing that a crime has been committed and that a trial ought to be held.

Group Boycott • The refusal of a group of competitors to deal with a particular person or firm.

Guarantor • A person who agrees to satisfy the debt of another (the debtor) only if and when the debtor fails to pay the debt.

H

Hacker • A person who uses one computer to break into another.

Historical School • A school of legal thought that emphasizes the evolutionary process of law and looks to the past to discover what the principles of contemporary law should be.

Home Equity Loan • A loan for which the borrower's home equity—the portion of the home's value that is paid off—is the collateral.

Homestead Exemption • A law allowing an owner to designate his or her house (and adjoining land) as a homestead and thus exempt it from liability for his or her debt.

Horizontal Merger • A merger between two firms that are competing in the same marketplace.

Horizontal Restraint • Any agreement that in some way restrains competition between rival firms competing in the same market.

I

I-9 Verification • The process of verifying the employment eligibility and identity of a new worker.

I-551 Alien Registration Receipt • A document, commonly known as a "green card," that shows that a foreign-born individual has been lawfully admitted for permanent residency in the United States.

Identity Theft • The theft of personal information, such as a person's name, driver's license number, or Social Security number, to access the victim's financial resources.

Implied Contract • A contract formed in whole or in part from the conduct of the parties (as opposed to an express contract).

Implied Warranty • A warranty that the law derives from either the situation of the parties or the nature of the transaction.

Implied Warranty of Fitness for a Particular Purpose • A warranty that arises when a seller knows the particular purpose for which a buyer will use the goods and knows that the buyer is relying on his or her skill and judgment to select suitable goods.

Implied Warranty of Merchantability • A warranty by a merchant seller or lessor of goods that the goods are reasonably fit for the general purpose for which they are sold or leased.

Impossibility of Performance • A doctrine under which a party to a contract is relieved of his or her duty to perform when performance becomes objectively impossible or totally impracticable (through no fault of either party).

Incidental Beneficiary • A third party who incidentally benefits from a contract but whose benefit was not the reason the contract was formed.

Independent Contractor • One who works for, and receives payment from, an employer but whose working conditions and methods are not controlled by the employer. An independent contractor is *not* an employee but may be an agent.

Indictment • A charge by a grand jury that a named person has committed a crime.

Informal Contract • A contract that does not require a specified form or formality to be valid.

Information • A formal accusation or complaint (without an indictment) issued in certain types of actions (usually criminal actions involving lesser crimes) by a government prosecutor.

Initial Order • An agency's disposition in a matter other than a rulemaking. An administrative law judge's initial order becomes final unless it is appealed.

Injunction • A court decree ordering a person to do or refrain from doing a certain act.

Insider Trading • The purchase or sale of securities on the basis of inside information—that is, information that has not been made available to the public.

Installment Contract • A contract in which payments due are made periodically.

Intellectual Property • Property resulting from intellectual, creative processes.

Intended Beneficiary • A third party for whose benefit a contract is formed and who can sue the promisor if the contract is breached.

Intentional Tort • A wrongful act that is knowingly committed.

Interest-Only (IO) Mortgage A mortgage that allows the borrower to pay only the interest portion of the monthly payment for a specified period of time.

International Law • The law that governs relations among nations.

Interpretive Rule • An administrative agency rule that is simply a statement or opinion issued by the agency explaining how it interprets and intends to apply the statutes it enforces.

Interrogatory • A series of written questions for which written answers are prepared and then signed under oath by the plaintiff or the defendant.

Investment Company • A company that acts on the behalf of many smaller shareholders and owners by buying a large portfolio of securities and professionally managing that portfolio.

Investment Contract • In securities law, a transaction in which a person invests in a common enterprise reasonably expecting profits that are derived primarily from the efforts of others.

J

Joint and Several Liability • A doctrine under which a plaintiff may sue, and collect a judgment from, any of several jointly liable defendants.

Judicial Foreclosure • A court-supervised foreclosure proceeding in which the court determines the validity of the debt and, if the borrower is in default, issues a judgment for the lender.

Judicial Review • The process by which a court decides on the constitutionality of legislative enactments and actions of the executive branch.

Jurisdiction • The authority of a court to hear and decide a specific case.

Jurisprudence • The science or philosophy of law.

Justiciable Controversy • A controversy that is not hypothetical or academic but real and substantial.

L

Larceny • The wrongful taking and carrying away of another person's personal property with the intent to permanently deprive the owner of the property.

Law • A body of enforceable rules governing relationships among individuals and between individuals and their society.

Lease • Under Article 2A of the UCC, a transfer of the right to possess and use goods for a period of time in exchange for payment.

Legal Positivism • A school of legal thought centered on the assumption that there is no law higher than the laws created by a national government.

Legal Realism • A school of legal thought that generally advocates a less abstract and more realistic approach to the law, an approach that takes into account customary practices and the circumstances in which transactions take place.

Legislative Rule • An administrative agency rule that carries the same weight as a congressionally enacted statute.

Lessee • A person who acquires the right to the possession and use of another's goods in exchange for rental payments.

Lessor • A person who transfers the right to the possession and use of goods to another in exchange for rental payments.

Letter of Credit • A written instrument, usually issued by a bank on behalf of a customer or other person, in which the issuer promises to honor drafts or other demands for payment by third parties in accordance with the terms of the instrument.

Libel • Defamation in writing or other form having the quality of permanence (such as a digital recording).

License • In the context of intellectual property law, an agreement permitting the use of a trademark, copyright, patent, or trade secret for certain limited purposes.

Lien • A claim against specific property to satisfy a debt.

Limited Liability Company (LLC) • A hybrid form of business enterprise that offers the limited liability of a corporation but the tax advantages of a partnership.

Limited Liability Partnership (LLP) • A form of partnership that allows professionals to enjoy tax benefits of a partnership while limiting their personal liability for the malpractice of other partners.

Limited Partner • A partner who contributes capital to the partnership but has no right to participate in the management or operation of the business and assumes no liability for partnership debts beyond the capital contributed.

Limited Partnership (LP) • A partnership consisting of one or more general partners and one or more limited partners.

Liquidated Damages • An amount, stipulated in a contract, that the parties to the contract believe to be a reasonable estimate of the damages that will occur in the event of a breach.

Liquidation • The sale of the assets of a business or an individual for cash and the distribution of the cash received to creditors, with the balance going to the owner(s).

Litigation • The process of resolving a dispute through the court system.

Lockout • An employer's act of shutting down the business to prevent employees from working.

Long Arm Statute • A state statute that permits a state to obtain personal jurisdiction over nonresident defendants.

M

Mailbox Rule • A rule providing that an acceptance of an offer becomes effective on dispatch.

Malpractice • Professional misconduct or the lack of the requisite degree of skill as a professional.

Market Concentration • The degree to which a small number of firms control a large percentage share of a relevant market; determined by calculating the percentages held by the largest firms in that market.

Market Power • The power of a firm to control the market price of its product. A monopoly has the greatest degree of market power.

Market-Share Liability • A theory under which liability is shared among all firms that manufactured and distributed a particular product during a certain period of time.

Mechanic's Lien • A statutory lien on the real property of another created to ensure priority of payment for work performed.

Mediation • A method of settling disputes outside the courts by using a neutral third party who acts as a communicating agent between the parties and assists them in negotiating a settlement.

Member • A person who has an ownership interest in a limited liability company.

Mens Rea • Mental state, or intent. Normally, a wrongful mental state is as necessary as a wrongful act to establish criminal liability.

Merchant • A person who is engaged in the purchase and sale of goods.

Meta Tag • A key word in a document that can serve as an index reference to the document.

Minimum Wage • The lowest hourly wage that an employer may pay a worker.

Mirror Image Rule • A common law rule that requires that the terms of the offeree's acceptance adhere exactly to the terms of the offeror's offer for a valid contract to be formed.

Mitigation of Damages • A rule requiring a plaintiff to do whatever is reasonable to minimize the damages caused by the defendant.

Money Laundering • Engaging in financial transactions to conceal the identity, source, or destination of illegally gained funds.

Monopolization • The possession of monopoly power in the relevant market and the willful acquisition or maintenance of that power, as distinguished from growth or development as a consequence of a superior product, business acumen, or historic accident.

Monopoly • A term generally used to describe a market in which there is a single seller or a very limited number of sellers.

Monopoly Power • The ability of a monopoly to dictate what takes place in a given market.

Moral Minimum • The minimum degree of ethical behavior expected of a business firm.

Mortgage • A written document that gives a creditor (the mortgagee) an interest in, or lien on, the debtor's (mortgagor's) real property as security for a debt.

Motion for a Directed Verdict • A motion for the judge to direct a verdict for the party who filed the motion on the ground that the other party has not produced sufficient evidence to support her or his claim.

Motion for a New Trial • A motion asserting that the trial was so fundamentally flawed that a new trial is necessary to prevent a miscarriage of justice.

Motion for Judgment *n.o.v.* • A motion requesting the court to grant judgment in favor of the party making the motion on the ground that the jury's verdict against him or her was unreasonable and erroneous.

Motion for Judgment on the Pleadings • A motion requesting the court to decide the issue solely on the pleadings without proceeding to trial.

Motion for Summary Judgment • A motion requesting the court to enter a judgment without proceeding to trial. The motion can be based on evidence outside the pleadings and will be granted only if no facts are in dispute.

Motion to Dismiss • A pleading in which a defendant admits the facts as alleged by the plaintiff but asserts that the plaintiff's claim has no basis in law.

Mutual Fund • A specific type of investment company that continually buys or sells to investors shares of ownership in a portfolio.

Mutual Rescission • An agreement between the parties to cancel their contract, releasing the parties from further obligations under the contract.

N

National Law • Law that pertains to a particular nation.

Natural Law • The belief that government and the legal system should reflect universal moral and ethical principles that are inherent in human nature.

Negative Amortization • The condition when the payment made by the borrower is less than the interest due on the loan and the difference is added to the principal, thereby increasing the balance owed on the loan over time.

Negligence • The failure to exercise the standard of care that a reasonable person would exercise in similar circumstances.

Negligence *Per Se* • An action or failure to act in violation of a statutory requirement.

Negotiation A process in which parties attempt to settle their dispute informally, with or without attorneys to represent them.

Normal Trade Relations (NTR) Status • A status granted by each member country of the World Trade Organization to other member countries.

Notice-and-Comment Rulemaking • A procedure in agency rulemaking that requires notice, opportunity for comment, and a published draft of the final rule.

Notice of Default • A formal notice to a borrower who is behind in making mortgage payments that the borrower is in default and may face foreclosure.

Notice of Sale • A formal notice to a borrower who is in default on a mortgage that the mortgaged property will be sold in a foreclosure proceeding.

Novation • The substitution, by agreement, of a new contract for an old one, with the rights under the old one being terminated.

Nuisance • A common law doctrine under which persons may be held liable for using their property in a manner that unreasonably interferes with others' rights to use or enjoy their own property.

O

Offer • A promise or commitment to do or refrain from doing some specified act in the future.

Offeree • A person to whom an offer is made.

Offeror • A person who makes an offer.

Online Dispute Resolution (ODR) • The resolution of disputes with the assistance of organizations that offer dispute-resolution services via the Internet.

Operating Agreement • In a limited liability company, an agreement in which the members set forth the details of how the business will be managed and operated.

Order for Relief • A court's grant of assistance to a complainant. In bankruptcy proceedings. The order relieves the debtor of the immediate obligation to pay the debts listed in the bankruptcy petition.

Ordinance • A regulation enacted by a city or county legislative body that becomes part of that state's statutory law.

P

Partially Disclosed Principal • A principal whose identity is unknown by a third party, but the third party knows that the agent is or may be acting for a principal at the time the agent and the third party form a contract.

Partnering Agreement • An agreement between a seller and a buyer who frequently do business with each other concerning the terms and conditions that will apply to all subsequently formed electronic contracts.

Partnership • An agreement by two or more persons to carry on, as co-owners, a business for profit.

Patent • A government grant that gives an inventor the exclusive right or privilege to make, use, or sell his or her invention for a limited time period.

Peer-to-Peer (P2P) Networking • The sharing of resources (such as files, hard drives, and processing styles) among multiple computers without the need for a central network server.

Penalty • A sum named in a contract as punishment for a default.

Perfect Tender Rule • A rule under which a seller or lessor is required to deliver goods that conform perfectly to the requirements of the contract.

Performance • The fulfillment of one's duties arising under a contract.

***Per Se* Violation** • A type of anticompetitive agreement that is considered to be so injurious to the public that there is no need to determine whether it actually injures market competition.

Persuasive Authority • Any legal authority or source of law that a court may look to for guidance but on which it need not rely in making its decision.

Petition in Bankruptcy • The document that is filed with a bankruptcy court to initiate bankruptcy proceedings.

Phishing • The attempt to acquire financial or other personal information from consumers by sending e-mail messages that purport to be from a legitimate business.

Pierce the Corporate Veil • To disregard the corporate entity and hold the shareholders personally liable for a corporate obligation.

Plaintiff • One who initiates a lawsuit.

Plea Bargaining • The process by which a defendant and the prosecutor in a criminal case work out a mutually satisfactory disposition, subject to court approval.

Pleadings • Statements made by the plaintiff and the defendant in a lawsuit that detail the facts, charges, and defenses of a case.

Police Powers • Powers possessed by states as part of their inherent sovereignty.

Potentially Responsible Party (PRP) • A party liable for the costs of cleaning up a hazardous waste–disposal site. Any person who generated the hazardous waste, transported it, owned or operated the waste site at the time of disposal, or owns or operates the site at the present time may be responsible for some or all of the clean-up costs.

Power of Sale Foreclosure • A foreclosure procedure that is not court supervised and is available only in some states.

Precedent • A court decision that furnishes an example or authority for deciding subsequent cases involving identical or similar facts.

Predatory Lending • Loan terms or lending procedures that are excessive, deceptive, or not properly disclosed.

Predatory Pricing • The pricing of a product below cost with the intent to drive competitors out of the market.

Preemption • A doctrine under which certain federal laws preempt, or take precedence over, conflicting state or local laws.

Preemptive Rights • Rights held by shareholders that entitle them to purchase newly issued shares of a corporation's stock, equal in percentage to shares already held, before the stock is offered to any outside buyers.

Preference • In bankruptcy proceedings, a property transfer or payment made by the debtor that favors one creditor over others.

Preferred Creditor • A creditor who has received a preferential transfer from a debtor.

Prepayment Penalty Clause • A clause in a mortgage loan contract that requires the borrower to pay a penalty if the mortgage is repaid in full within a certain period.

Price Discrimination • Setting prices in such a way that two competing buyers pay two different prices for an identical product or service.

Price-Fixing Agreement • An agreement between competitors to fix the prices of products or services at a certain level.

Prima Facie Case • A case in which the plaintiff has produced sufficient evidence to prove his or her conclusion if the defendant produces no evidence to rebut it.

Primary Source of Law • A document that establishes the law on a particular issue, such as a constitution, a statute, an administrative rule, or a court decision.

Principal • A person who, by agreement or otherwise, authorizes an agent to act on his or her behalf in such a way that the acts of the agent become binding on the principal.

Principle of Rights • The principle that human beings have certain fundamental rights. A key factor in determining whether a business decision is ethical is how it affects others' rights.

Privilege • A legal right, exemption, or immunity granted to a person or a class of persons.

Probable Cause • Reasonable grounds for believing that a person should be arrested or searched.

Probate Court • A state court of limited jurisdiction that conducts proceedings relating to the settlement of a deceased person's estate.

Procedural Law • Law that establishes the methods of enforcing the rights established by substantive law.

Product Liability • The liability of manufacturers, sellers, and lessors of goods to consumers, users, and bystanders for injuries or damages that are caused by the goods.

Promise • An assertion that something either will or will not happen in the future.

Promissory Estoppel • A doctrine that can be used to enforce a promise when the promisee has justifiably relied on it, and justice will be better served by enforcing it.

Prospectus • A written document, required by securities laws, that describes the security being sold, the financial operations of the issuing corporation, and the investment or risk attaching to the security.

Protected Class • A group of persons with defining characteristics—such as race, color, religion, national origin, gender, age, and disability—who historically have been discriminated against.

Proximate Cause • Legal cause, which exists when the connection between an act and an injury is strong enough to justify imposing liability.

Proxy • A written agreement between a stockholder and another under which the stockholder authorizes the other to vote his or her shares in a certain manner.

Puffery • A salesperson's often exaggerated claims concerning the quality of property offered for sale.

Punitive Damages Monetary damages that may be awarded to a plaintiff to punish the defendant and deter similar conduct in the future.

Q

Quasi Contract • A fictional contract imposed on parties by a court in the interests of fairness and justice.

Question of Fact • In a lawsuit, an issue that involves only disputed facts and not what the law is on a given point.

Question of Law • In a lawsuit, an issue involving the application or interpretation of a law.

Quorum • The number of members of a decision-making body that must be present before business may be transacted.

Quota • A set limit on the amount of goods that can be imported.

R

Ratification • The act of accepting and giving legal force to an obligation that previously was not enforceable.

Reaffirmation Agreement • An agreement between a debtor and a creditor in which the debtor voluntarily agrees to pay a debt dischargeable in bankruptcy.

Reamortize • Change the way mortgage payments are configured, extending the term over which payments will be made.

Reasonable Person Standard • The standard of behavior expected of a hypothetical "reasonable person."

Reformation • A court-ordered correction of a written contract so that it reflects the true intentions of the parties.

Remedy • The relief given to an innocent party to enforce a right or compensate for the violation of a right.

Reorganization • A plan for the readjustment of a corporation and its debts, the submission of the plan to a bankruptcy court, and the court's approval or rejection of the plan.

Reply • Procedurally, a plaintiff's response to a defendant's answer.

Resale Price Maintenance Agreement • An agreement between a manufacturer and a retailer in which the manufacturer specifies what the retail prices of its products must be.

Res Ipsa Loquitur • A doctrine under which negligence may be inferred simply because an event occurred, if it is the type of event that would not occur in the absence of negligence.

Respondeat Superior • A principle of law whereby a principal or an employer is held liable for the wrongful acts committed by agents or employees acting within the scope of their agency or employment.

Restitution • An equitable remedy under which a person is restored to his or her original position before formation of a contract.

Retained Earnings • The portion of a corporation's profits that has not been paid out as dividends to shareholders.

Revocation • In contract law, the withdrawal of an offer by the offeror. Unless the offer is irrevocable, it can be revoked at any time prior to acceptance without liability.

Right of Contribution • The right of a co-surety who pays more than her or his proportionate share on a debtor's default to recover the excess paid from other co-sureties.

Right of Reimbursement • The legal right of a person to be repaid or indemnified for costs, expenses, or losses incurred or expended on behalf of another.

Right of Subrogation • The right of a person to stand in the place of (be substituted for) another, giving the substituted party the same legal rights against the debtor that the creditor had.

Right-to-Work Law • A state law providing that employees may not be required to join a union as a condition of retaining employment.

Robbery • The act of forcefully and unlawfully taking personal property of any value from another.

Rulemaking • The actions of administrative agencies when formally adopting new regulations or amending old ones.

Rule of Four • A rule of the United States Supreme Court under which the Court will not issue a writ of *certiorari* unless at least four justices approve.

Rule of Reason • A test by which a court balances the positive effects (such as economic efficiency) of an agreement against its potentially anticompetitive effects.

S

S Corporation • A business corporation that qualifies for special income tax treatment.

Sale • The passing of title to property from the seller to the buyer for a price.

Sales Contract • A contract for the sale of goods under which the ownership of goods is transferred from a seller to a buyer for a price.

Scienter • Knowledge by the misrepresenting party that material facts have been falsely represented or omitted with an intent to deceive.

Search Warrant • An order granted by a public authority, such as a judge, that authorizes law enforcement personnel to search particular premises or property.

Seasonably • Within a specified time period or, if no period is specified, within a reasonable time.

Secondary Source of Law • A publication that summarizes or interprets the law, such as a legal encyclopedia, a legal treatise, or an article in a law review.

SEC Rule 10b-5 • A rule of the Securities and Exchange Commission that makes it unlawful, in connection with the purchase or sale of any security, to make any untrue statement of a material fact or to omit a material fact if such omission causes the statement to be misleading.

Secured Creditor • A lender or seller who has a security interest in collateral that secures a debt.

Security • Generally, a stock certificate, bond, note, or other document or record evidencing an ownership interest in a corporation or a promise of repayment of debt by a corporation.

Self-Defense • The legally recognized privilege to protect oneself or one's property against injury by another.

Self-Incrimination • The giving of testimony that may subject the testifier to criminal prosecution.

Seniority System • A system in which those who have worked longest for the employer are first in line for promotions, salary increases, and other benefits.

Service Mark • A mark used in the sale or advertising of services to distinguish the services of one person from those of others.

Sexual Harassment • The demanding of sexual favors in return for job promotions or other benefits, or language or conduct that is so sexually offensive that it creates a hostile working environment.

Shareholder's Derivative Suit • A suit brought by a shareholder to enforce a corporate cause of action against a third person.

Short Sale • A sale of real property for an amount that is less than the balance owed on the mortgage loan.

Short-Swing Profits • Profits earned by a purchase and sale, or sale and purchase, of the same security within a six-month period. Under Section 16(b), these profits must be returned to the corporation if earned by company insiders from transactions in the company's stock.

Shrink-Wrap Agreement • An agreement whose terms are expressed in a document located inside a box in which goods (usually software) are packaged.

Slander • Defamation in oral form.

Slander of Quality (Trade Libel) • The publication of false information about another's product, alleging that it is not what its seller claims.

Slander of Title • The publication of a statement that denies or casts doubt on another's legal ownership of any property, causing financial loss to that property's owner.

Small Claims Court • A special court in which parties may litigate small claims (such as $5,000 or less) without an attorney.

Sole Proprietorship • The simplest form of business organization, in which the owner is the business.

Sovereign Immunity • A doctrine that immunizes foreign nations from the jurisdiction of U.S. courts when certain conditions are satisfied.

Spam • Bulk e-mails sent in large quantities without the consent of the recipients.

Specific Performance • An equitable remedy requiring exactly the performance that was specified in a contract. Usually, it is granted only when money damages would be an inadequate remedy and the subject matter of the contract is unique (for example, real property).

Standing to Sue • The requirement that an individual must have a sufficient stake in a controversy before he or she can bring a lawsuit.

Stare Decisis • A common law doctrine under which judges are obligated to follow the precedents established in prior decisions.

Statute of Frauds • A state statute under which certain types of contracts must be in writing to be enforceable.

Statute of Limitations • A federal or state statute setting the maximum time period during which a certain action can be brought or certain rights enforced.

Statutory Law • The body of law enacted by legislative bodies.

Statutory Right of Redemption • A right provided by statute in some states under which mortgagors can buy back their property after a judicial foreclosure for a limited period of time.

Stock Buyback • A company's purchase of shares of its own stock on the open market.

Stock Certificate • A certificate issued by a corporation evidencing the ownership of a specified number of shares in the corporation.

Stock Option • A right to buy a given number of shares of stock at a set price, usually within a specified time period.

Strict Liability • Liability regardless of fault.

Strike • An action undertaken by unionized workers when collective bargaining fails. The workers leave their jobs, refuse to work, and (typically) picket the employer's workplace.

Subprime Mortgage • A high-risk loan made to a borrower who does not qualify for a standard mortgage because of a poor credit rating or high debt-to-income ratio.

Substantive Law • Law that defines, describes, regulates, and creates legal rights and obligations.

Summons • A document informing a defendant that a legal action has been commenced against her or him and that the defendant must appear in court on a certain date to answer the plaintiff's complaint.

Supremacy Clause • The requirement in Article VI of the U.S. Constitution that provides that the Constitution, laws, and treaties of the United States are "the supreme Law of the Land."

Surety • A third party who agrees to be primarily responsible for the debt of another.

Suretyship • An express contract in which a third party (the surety) promises to be primarily responsible for a debtor's obligation to a creditor.

Symbolic Speech • Nonverbal expressions of beliefs.

T

Tangible Employment Action • A significant change in employment status, such as a change brought about by firing or failing to promote an employee.

Tangible Property • Property that has physical existence and can be distinguished by the senses of touch and sight.

Tariff • A tax on imported goods.

Tender • A timely offer or expression of willingness to pay a debt or perform an obligation.

Tender of Delivery • A seller's or lessor's act of placing conforming goods at the disposal of the buyer or lessee and giving the buyer or lessee whatever notification is reasonably necessary to enable the buyer or lessee to take delivery.

Third Party Beneficiary • One for whose benefit a promise is made in a contract but who is not a party to the contract.

Tippee • A person who receives inside information.

Tort • A civil wrong not arising from a breach of contract.

Tortfeasor • One who commits a tort.

Toxic Tort • A civil wrong arising from exposure to a toxic substance, such as asbestos, radiation, or hazardous waste.

Trade Dress • The image and overall appearance of a product.

Trademark • A word, symbol, sound, or design that has become sufficiently associated with a good or has been registered with a government agency.

Trade Name • A name used in commercial activity to designate a particular business.

Trade Secret • Information or a process that gives a business an advantage over competitors that do not know the information or process.

Treaty • A formal written agreement negotiated between two or more nations.

Treble Damages • Damages that, by statute, are three times the amount that the fact finder determines is owed.

Trespass to Land • The entry onto, above, or below the surface of land owned by another without the owner's permission.

Trespass to Personal Property • The unlawful taking or harming of another's personal property or the interference with another's right to the exclusive possession of his or her personal property.

Tying Arrangement • An agreement between a buyer and a seller in which the buyer of a specific product or service becomes obligated to purchase additional products or services from the seller.

U

Unconscionable Contract or Clause • A contract or clause that is void on the basis of public policy because one party is forced to accept terms that are unfairly burdensome and that unfairly benefit the other party.

Undisclosed Principal • A principal whose identity is unknown by a third person, and the third person has no knowledge that the agent is acting for a principal at the time the agent and the third person form a contract.

Uniform Law • A model law created by the National Conference of Commissioners on Uniform State Laws and/or the American Law Institute for the states to consider adopting.

Unilateral Contract • A contract that results when an offer can be accepted only by the offeree's performance.

Unilateral Mistake • A mistake that occurs when one party to a contract is mistaken as to a material fact.

Union Shop • A firm that requires all workers, once employed, to become union members within a specified period of time as a condition of their continued employment.

Unreasonably Dangerous Product • A product that is defective to the point of threatening a consumer's health and safety.

Unsecured Creditor • A creditor whose debt is not backed by any collateral.

U.S. Trustee • A government official who performs certain administrative tasks that a bankruptcy judge would otherwise have to perform.

Utilitarianism • An approach to ethical reasoning in which an action is evaluated in terms of its consequences for those whom it will affect. A "good" action is one that results in the greatest good for the greatest number of people.

V

Venue • The geographic district in which a legal action is tried and from which the jury is selected.

Vertically Integrated Firm • A firm that carries out two or more functional phases (manufacture, distribution, and retailing, for example) of the chain of production.

Vertical Merger • The acquisition by a company at one level in a marketing chain of a company at a higher or lower level in the chain (such as a company merging with one of its suppliers or retailers).

Vertical Restraint • Any restraint of trade created by agreements between firms at different levels in the manufacturing and distribution process.

Vesting • The creation of an absolute or unconditional right or power.

Vicarious Liability • Legal responsibility placed on one person for the acts of another.

Vishing • A variation of phishing that involves some form of voice communication.

Voir Dire • The process in which the attorneys question prospective jurors to learn about their personal characteristics that may affect their ability to serve as impartial jurors.

Voluntary Consent • Knowledge of, and genuine assent to, the terms of a contract.

W

Watered Stock • Shares of stock issued by a corporation for which the corporation receives, as payment, less than the stated value of the shares.

Wetlands • Water-saturated areas of land that are designated by a government agency as protected areas that support wildlife and therefore cannot be filled in or dredged by private contractors or parties without a permit.

White-Collar Crime • Nonviolent crime committed by individuals or corporations to obtain a personal or business advantage.

Workers' Compensation Laws • State statutes establishing an administrative procedure for compensating workers for injuries that arise out of—or in the course of—their employment, regardless of fault.

Workout Agreement • A formal contract between a debtor and his or her creditors in which the parties agree to negotiate a payment plan for the amount due on the loan instead of proceeding to foreclosure.

Workout • An out-of-court agreement between a debtor and creditors that establishes a payment plan for discharging the debtor's debts.

Writ of Attachment • A writ used to enforce obedience to an order or judgment of the court.

Writ of Certiorari • A writ from a higher court asking a lower court for the record of a case.

Writ of Execution • A writ that puts in force a court's decree or judgment.

Table of Cases

Index

A

Articles of partnership, 235
Artisan's lien, 352
Assault, 128, 163
Assignees, 296
Assignments, 296–298
Assignors, 296
Assumption of risk, 140, 151
Assurance, 333
Attachment, 353
Attempted monopolization, 487–488
Attorney, accused person's right to, 174, 175
Attractive nuisance doctrine, 135
Audit committees, 521, 523
Auditing, 523
Authority, in agency relationship, 407–408
Authorization cards, 426
Authorized acts, 408–409
Authors, identification of, 144
Auto emissions, 463–464
Automatic stay, filing of bankruptcy operating as, 363
Average prime offer rate, 388
Avoidance powers, of bankruptcy trustees, 365
Awards, jury's, 48

B

Background checks, 421
BACT (best available control technology), 468
Balloon payments, 387
Bank of America, 381
Bankruptcy, 350–380
    automatic stay provision, 363
    consumer impact, 376
    contract discharges in, 304
    court decisions, 21, 358–359
    creditors' rights, 350–357
    debtor protections, 357–358
    federal law governing, 358–359, 376. *See also*
            Bankruptcy Code
    increase in filings, 376
    lender impact, 376
Bankruptcy Abuse Prevention and Consumer Protection
  Act (2005), 359, 376
Bankruptcy Code
    Chapter 7-Liquidation, 359, 360–369
    Chapter 11-Reorganization, 359, 369–371
    Chapter 12-Family Farmers and Fisherman, 359,
        372
    Chapter 13-Individuals' Repayment Plan, 359,
        372–375

defined, 358
    overview of, 359
Bankruptcy courts
    defined, 33
    role of, 358
    social media use, 357
Bankruptcy Reform Act (1978), 358
Bankruptcy Reporter (Bankr. or B.R.), 21
Bankruptcy trustees, 364–366, 370, 373
Banks
    export trading company investments, 215
    failures, 385
    international transfers of funds, 220
    letters of credit, 220–221
    mortgage loans. *See* Mortgages
Bargained-for exchange, 272
Basis of the bargain, 341
Battery, 128, 163
Benchmarking, 153
Beneficiaries, 298–299
Bentham, Jeremy, 69
Berne Convention, 201–202
Bernhart, Michelle, 70
Best available control technology (BACT), 468
Best practical control technology (BPCT), 468
Beyond a reasonable doubt, 159–160, 176
BFOQs (bona fide occupational qualifications), 452
Bilateral contracts, 262–263
Bilateral mistakes, 291
Bill of Rights, 84–93. *See also specific amendments*
    corporations considered person under, 241–242
    defined, 84
    limits on federal and state governmental actions, 85
    summary of protections, 84–85
Binding authorities, 9
Blue sky laws, 517–518
Boards of directors, 249–253
    audit committees, 521
    compensation committee, 521
    compensation of, 250
    criminal liability, 162
    election of, 243, 250
    fiduciary duties, 251–253
    independence of, 519
    interlocking directorates, 491–492
    meetings, 251
    monitoring of officers' activities, 523
    rights of, 251
    role of, 241
    structure of, 251, 520–521

Real property, 134, 358. *See also* Land
Reamortization, 390
Reasonable accommodation, 439, 450–452
Reasonable decisions and supervision, 251
Reasonable duty of care, 135
Reasonable person standard, 138, 301
Receivers, 370
Recession (2008-), 381
Recording mortgages, 384
Redemption rights, 391, 394
Reformation, 277, 312–313
Regional reporters, 19–20
Registration of trademark, 189
Registration statements, 504–506
Regulation. *See* Government regulation
Regulation A offerings, 506–507
Regulation D, 507–508
Regulatory Flexibility Act, 119
Reimbursement
    principal's duty of, 406–407
    surety's right of, 357
Rejection, buyer's or lessee's right of, 337, 338–339
Relevant market, 486
Reliance, 294, 511
Religion
    discrimination based on, 439–440
    ethical standards, 68
    freedom of, 91–93
Remedies
    for breach of contract, 289, 306–314, 335–340
    in civil vs. criminal cases, 159
    damages. *See* Damages
    defined, 10, 289
    equitable remedies, 10–11, 311–313
    for infringement, 198, 202
    at law, 10–11
    for mortgage violations under HOEPA, 387
    under Securities Act, 509
    under Title VII, 446
Reorganization, under Chapter 11 bankruptcy, 359, 369–371
Repayment plans (Chapter 13 bankruptcy), 372–375
Replies, 44
Reports or reporters, 19–20
Republic of Korea-United States Free Trade Agreement (KORUS FTA), 216
Repudiation, 302, 333, 335
Requests for information, 45–46
Res ipsa loquitur, 142
Resale price maintenance agreements, 484

Resales of securities, 509
Rescission
    contracts, 302–303, 311, 517
    mortgages, 386
    remedies in equity, 10
Resolutions, 244
Resource Conservation and Recovery Act (1976), 8, 462, 472
Respondeat superior, 409–410
Respondents, 25
Responsible corporate officer doctrine, 162
Restatement (Third) of Agency, 401, 408
Restatement (Second) of Contracts, 279, 304, 305
Restatement of Torts, 201
Restatement (Second) of Torts, 147–148
Restatement (Third) of Torts, 148–149
Restaurants and bars, dram shop acts, 143
Restitution, 311
Restraint of trade, 276–277, 481–484, 490–491, 496
Retained earnings, 241, 246
Retaliation, by employers, 443
Retirement plans, 417
Reverse discrimination, 438–439
Revised Model Business Corporation Act, 241
Revocation, 268, 339
RICO (Racketeer Influenced and Corrupt Organizations) Act (1970), 168–169
Right to Financial Privacy Act (1978), 96
Right(s)
    of buyers/lessees, 337–338
    to confront witnesses, 174
    of contribution, 357
    of corporate directors, 250
    to counsel, 174, 175
    creditors', 350–357
    human rights, 11–12, 222
    indemnification rights, 250, 407
    of inspections, 246, 250, 334
    to jury trial, 174
    to privacy. *See* Privacy rights
    to public trial, 174
    of redemption, 391, 394
    of reimbursement, 357
    of sellers/lessors, 335–336
    of shareholders, 245–247
    of subrogation, 357
    of sureties and guarantors, 357
    voidable rights, 365
Rights theory, 68–69
Right-to-work laws, 426

international protections, 203–204
laws protecting, 189
licensing, 195
marketing issues, 204–205
other intellectual property forms vs., 202
registration, 189
types of, 191
Trading with the Enemy Act (1917), 215
Transfers of property, under Chapter 7 bankruptcy, 366
Transfers of shares, 246–247
Transportation, U.S. Department of, 106
Transportation Security Administration (TSA), 97–98
Treasury, U.S. Department of, 106
Treaties, 210
Treble damages, 493
Trespass, 134–135, 136
Trial courts
case titles, 23–24
jurisdiction, 34
role of, 19
state trial courts, 39
U.S. district courts, 21, 41, 42
Trials
criminal trials, 176
process, 46–48
right to jury, 46–48
TRIPS agreement, 203–204
Trustees, bankruptcy, 364–366, 370, 373
Truth-in-Lending Act (TILA) (1968), 385–386
TV programmers and distributors, Sherman Act
violations, 480–481
Twitter, 201
Tying arrangements, 490–491

U

UCC. *See* Uniform Commercial Code (UCC)
Unanimous opinions, 25
Unauthorized acts, 409
Unconscionability, 44
Unconscionable contracts or clauses, 277
Undisclosed principals, 408–409
Undue hardship, 439–440, 451
Undue influence, 294
Unemployed workers, discrimination against, 438
Unemployment compensation, 417
Unenforceable contracts, 265
Unequivocal acceptance, 270
Unfair labor practices, 429

Uniform Commercial Code (UCC)
adoption of, 6–7, 322
Article 2 (Sales), 322–324
Article 2a (Leases), 324
choice-of-law clauses, 217
e-documents, 281
franchising, 232
online acceptances, 279
Uniform Electronic Transactions Act (UETA), 271, 281, 282–283
Uniform laws, defined, 6
Uniform Limited Liability Company Act (ULLCA), 239, 240
Uniform Partnership Act (UPA), 237
Uniform resource locators (URLs), 24
Uniform Securities Act, 518
Uniform Trade Secrets Act, 201
Unilateral contracts, 262–263
Unilateral mistakes, 290–291
Unilateral refusals to deal, 487
Unintentional discrimination, 437–438
Unintentional torts, 128, 137–143. *See also* Negligence
Union shop, 426
Unions, 425–428, 494
United Nations
Convention on Contracts for the International Sale of Goods, 217
Convention on the Recognition and Enforcement of Foreign Arbitral Awards, 218
United States Citizenship and Immigration Services, 422, 423
United States Code (U.S.C.), 18
United States Code Annotated (U.S.C.A.), 18
United States Constitution
affirmative action, 453
amendments to. *See* Bill of Rights; *individual amendments*
brevity of, 79
checks and balances, 80–81, 108
commerce clause, 81–83
corporations, 241–242
criminal protections, 171–175
delegation doctrine, 108
due process clause, 93–94
equal protection clause, 94–95
establishment clause, 91
exports, 215
federal question, 34
free exercise clause, 91–92